Sociology

This book is offered to teachers of sociology in the hope that it will help our students understand their place in today's society and, more broadly, in tomorrow's world.

John J. Macionis

ANNOTATED INSTRUCTOR'S EDITION

Sociology

fifth edition

John J. Macionis

Kenyon College

Prentice Hall, Englewood Cliffs, New Jersey 07632

Acquisitions Editor: Nancy Roberts
Development Editors: Susanna Lesan, Ann Hofstra Grogg
Production Editor: Barbara Reilly
Editor-in-Chief: Charlyce Jones Owen
Marketing Manager: Kris Kleinsmith
Art Director: Anne Bonanno Nieglos
Interior Designer: Lorraine Mullaney
Cover Designer: Anthony Gemmellaro
Buyer: Mary Ann Gloriande
Photo Editor: Lorinda Morris Nantz
Photo Researchers: Barbara Salz, Joelle Burrows
Associate Editor: Sharon Chambliss
Copy Editor: Diana Drew
Editorial Assistant: Pat Naturale
Cover photo: David Levine, *Sporting Crowd,* 1971. Watercolor. 14 x 21 1/2 inches. Collection
　　　　of the Samuel L. Millbank Family. Courtesy Forum Gallery, New York.
　　　　© David Levine. Photo by Adam Reich.

Printed in the United States of America
10 9 8 7 6 5 4 3 2 1

STUDENT ISBN 0-13-101155-3
AIE ISBN 0-13-118480-6

Prentice-Hall International (UK) Limited, *London*
Prentice-Hall of Australia Pty. Limited, *Sydney*
Prentice-Hall Canada Inc., *Toronto*
Prentice-Hall Hispanoamericana, S.A., *Mexico*
Prentice-Hall of India Private Limited, *New Delhi*
Prentice-Hall of Japan, Inc., *Tokyo*
Simon & Schuster Asia Pte. Ltd., *Singapore*
Editora Prentice-Hall do Brasil, Ltda., *Rio de Janeiro*

Printed on Recycled Paper

Brief Contents

v

Contents

**PART III
SOCIAL INEQUALITY**

**PART V
SOCIAL CHANGE**

Global Maps: Windows on the World

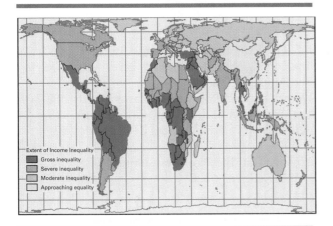

National Maps: Seeing Ourselves

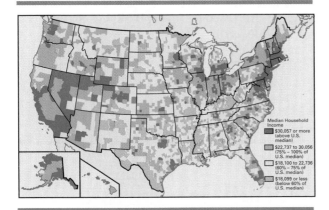

Boxes

Preface

Across the United States, the number of students studying sociology is increasing rapidly: Almost 1 million men and women each year enroll in the introductory course alone. Why this groundswell of interest in sociology? History provides a clue: Just as the rapid changes linked to industrialization stimulated the development of sociology a century ago, the transformations wrought by the emerging postindustrial society are generating new currents of sociological thinking as this century draws to a close.

At home, the development of new information technology (coupled with the marked decline of traditional industries) is reshaping the workplace—changing the location and even our conception of work. And, around the world, a single global economy now connects nations the way the burgeoning national economy linked cities a century ago. Change brought on by this process of globalization is rippling through the world's political systems, challenging educators everywhere to rethink their curricula, and setting off waves of migration, especially to the United States. Even the stunning cultural diversity that has long fascinated and frustrated humankind may now be eroding as communications technology—from satellite transmissions to facsimile machines—draws members of thousands of world societies into a global conversation.

Against this backdrop of ongoing change, we are proud to offer the fifth edition of *Sociology*. As in the past, this new edition of *Sociology* is authoritative, comprehensive, thought-provoking, and, as daily electronic mail messages from students around the country testify, plain fun to read.

But much is new to *Sociology*, fifth edition, the most substantial revision yet to this book. Our goal has been ambitious—to achieve a still higher standard of excellence for sociology's most popular text while giving today's students a good grasp of both their diverse society and the changing world.

THE ORGANIZATION OF THIS TEXT

Part I introduces the foundations of sociology. Underlying the discipline is the *sociological perspective*—the focus of Chapter 1, which explains how this invigorating point of view brings the world to life in a new and instructive way. Chapter 2 spotlights *sociological investigation*, or the "doing of sociology," and explains how to use the logic of science to study human society. We demonstrate major research strategies in action through well-known examples of sociological work. By learning how sociologists see the world and carry out research, passive readers become active, critical participants in the issues, debates, and controversies that frame our discipline.

Part II targets the foundations of social life. Chapter 3 focuses on the central concept of *culture*, emphasizing the cultural diversity that makes up our society and our world. Chapter 4 links culture to the concept of *society*, presenting four time-honored models for understanding the structure and dynamics of social organization. Assigned in sequence, this unique chapter provides students with the background to comprehend more deeply the ideas of important thinkers—including Emile Durkheim, Karl Marx, Max Weber, and Gerhard and Jean Lenski—that appear in subsequent chapters. Alternatively, instructors may assign any of the chapter's four parts at some later point in the course. Chapter 5 delves into *socialization*, explaining how our humanity blossoms as we learn to participate in society. Chapter 6 provides a micro-level look at the patterns of *social interaction* that make up our everyday lives. Chapter 7 gives full-chapter coverage of *groups and organizations*, two additional and vital elements of social structure. Chapter 8 completes the unit by investigating how the operation of society generates both *deviance* and *conformity*.

Part III offers an unparalleled treatment of social inequality, beginning with three chapters devoted to *social stratification*. Chapter 9 casts the spotlight on inequality, introducing major concepts and presenting theoretical explanations for the persistence of social stratification. This chapter is rich with illustrations of how stratification has changed historically, and how it varies around the world today. Chapter 10 investigates *social inequality in the United States*, exploring our perceptions of inequality and assessing how well they square with research findings. Chapter 11 extends the analysis by taking *a global view of social stratification* and revealing the extent of differences in wealth and power between rich and poor societies. Both Chapters 10 and 11 point up how social stratification in the United States reflects trends in the rest of the world, just as they probe our society's role in sustaining global stratification. *Race and ethnicity,* specific dimensions of social inequality both in North America and the rest of the world, are detailed in Chapter 12. *Sex and gender,* which is the focus of Chapter 13, establishes the biological foundation of sex and sexuality, and then goes on to trace how societies crystallize the distinction of sex into systems of gender stratification. *Aging and the elderly,* a topic of increasing concern to "graying" societies such as ours, is addressed in Chapter 14.

Part IV dedicates a full chapter to each key social institution. In a change from previous editions, this part opens with *the economy and work,* Chapter 15, because most sociologists recognize that the economy has the greatest impact on all other institutions. This chapter highlights the processes of industrialization and postindustrialization, explains the emergence of a global economy, and suggests what such transformations mean for the U.S. labor force. Chapter 16, *politics and government,* investigates the roots of social power both in the United States and around the world. In addition, this chapter elucidates a number of key issues involving the U.S. military, war, and peace. Chapter 17, *the family,* reports on the central importance of families to social organization, and underscores the diversity of family life both here and in other societies. Chapter 18, *religion,* addresses the timeless human search for ultimate purpose and meaning, surveys world religions, and notes how religious beliefs are linked to other dimensions of social life. Chapter 19, *education,* chronicles the expansion of schooling in industrial societies. Here, again, educational patterns in the United States are contrasted with those of many other societies to add depth and global context. Chapter 20, *health and medicine,* explains why health is a social issue just as much as it is a matter of biological processes. Paralleling the discussions of other institutions, this chapter traces the historical emergence of scientific medicine, analyzes current medical issues (including the ongoing battle over health care reform) from various points of view, and compares health care in the United States to the pursuit of health and well-being in other societies.

Part V examines important dimensions of global social change. Chapter 21 focuses on the powerful impact of *population growth and urbanization* in the United States and throughout the world. Chapter 22—new chapter to this edition—highlights the connections between how we live and *the natural environment.* Chapter 23 probes how people seek or resist social change through various forms of *collective behavior and social movements.* Chapter 24 concludes the text with an overview of *social change* that highlights *traditional, modern, and postmodern* societies. This chapter rounds out the text by explaining how and why world societies change, and critically analyzing the benefits and liabilities of traditional, modern, and postmodern ways of life.

CONTINUITY: ESTABLISHED FEATURES OF *SOCIOLOGY*

Although introductory sociology texts have much in common, they are not all the same. The extraordinary success of *Sociology* stems from a combination of a dozen distinctive features.

Unsurpassed writing style. Most important, this text offers a lively writing style widely praised by students and faculty alike as elegant and inviting. *Sociology* is an enjoyable text that gives students incentive to read—even beyond their assignments.

Engaging and instructive chapter openings. Engaging chapter-opening vignettes, which spark readers' interest as they introduce important themes, are one of the most popular features of *Sociology.* In a snappy, compelling style, readers discover, for example, how the Titanic tragedy illustrates the life and death consequences of social inequality, how the success of McDonald's exemplifies the proliferation of bureaucracy, and how the wrenching conflict that has torn apart the former Yugoslavia reflects the power of ethnicity. This revision retains the best chapter-opening vignettes from earlier editions and offers eleven new ones as well.

A celebration of social diversity. *Sociology* invites students from all social backgrounds to discover a fresh and exciting way to see their world and understand themselves. Readers will navigate the diverse currents of U.S. society, coming face to face with people of African, Asian, European, and Latino ancestry, as well as women and men of various class positions and at all points in the life course. Just as important, without flinching from the problems that people on society's margins confront, this text does not view these individuals as social problems but rather takes note of their achievements.

Inclusive focus on women and men. Beyond devoting a full chapter to the important concepts of sex and gender, *Sociology* "mainstreams" gender into *every* chapter, showing how the topic at hand affects women and men differently, and citing how gender operates as a basic dimension of social organization.

Instructive and varied examples. Sociologist George Herbert Mead once described an effective teacher as a person who can transform simple information into real knowledge. Mead's insight applies to books as well as teachers; on virtually every page of *Sociology*, therefore, illuminating examples bring concepts to life and demonstrate to students the value of applying sociology to our everyday world.

A global perspective. *Sociology* has taken a leading role in expanding the horizons of our discipline beyond the United States. Each chapter of this text encompasses comparative material that explores the social diversity of the entire world. Just as important, this text explains that social trends in the United States—from musical tastes, to the price of wheat, to the growing disparity between rich and poor—are influenced by what happens elsewhere. Conversely, students will see how social patterns and policies in the United States and other rich societies affect poor societies around the world. In short, more than ever before, to understand our own society we must comprehend this nation's place in the larger world.

Theoretically clear and balanced. *Sociology* puts theory within easy reach. The discipline's major theoretical approaches are introduced in Chapter 1 and then are systematically reapplied in later chapters. Woven throughout the text are threads of the social-conflict, structural-functional, and symbolic-interaction paradigms. Individual chapters also incorporate key concepts of social-exchange analysis, ethnomethodology, cultural ecology, and sociobiology.

Chapter 4—unique to this text—gives students an easy-to-grasp introduction to important social theorists *before* they encounter their work in later chapters. The ideas of Gerhard and Jean Lenski, Max Weber, Karl Marx, and Emile Durkheim appear in distinct sections that instructors may assign together or separately at different points in the course.

Emphasis on critical thinking. Critical-thinking skills include the ability to challenge widely held assumptions, formulate probing questions, identify and weigh relevant evidence, and reach reasoned conclusions. This text encourages students to gain new sociological insights, to seek out contradictions as well as to formulate consistent arguments, and to make connections among the various dimensions of social life.

Recent sociological research. *Sociology* blends classic sociological tenets with the latest research, as reported in the leading publications in the field. Several hundred new studies inform this revision and the vast majority of research cited in the text has been published since 1980. In addition, the statistical data found throughout are the most recent available.

Learning aids. This text incorporates several specific features to help students learn. In each chapter, **key concepts,** identified by boldface type, are followed by *precise, italicized definitions.* An alphabetical listing of key concepts, together with their definitions, appears at the end of each chapter; a complete **Glossary** is found at the end of the book.

Each chapter also contains a numbered **Summary** and four **Critical-Thinking Questions** that help students to review material and assess their understanding. Chapters end with lists of **Suggested Readings,** which identify classic texts of enduring value, note examples of topical contemporary U.S. research, and point up global studies that allow for international comparisons.

Outstanding images: photography and fine art. The author has developed the finest program of photography and artwork available in any sociology textbook. This edition of *Sociology* has more than one hundred examples of fine art as well as hundreds more color photographs. Each of these captioned images complements the text in a visually appealing way. Moreover, dovetailing with *Sociology's* emphasis on diversity, the images are the creation of artists of various social backgrounds and historical periods. In addition to art by Europeans such as Vincent Van Gogh and U.S. artists like George Tooker, this edition showcases paintings by African-American artists Jacob Lawrence and Henry Ossawa Tanner, Latino artists Frank Romero and Diego Rivera, folk artists including Grandma Moses, and the Australian painter and feminist Sally Swain.

Thought-provoking theme boxes. Although boxes highlight most introductory texts, *Sociology* provides a wealth of uncommonly good ones—generally three per chapter. Boxes fall into six types that amplify central themes of the text: *Social Policy* boxes, new to this edition, apply sociological theory and research to today's political debates. *Social Diversity* boxes focus on

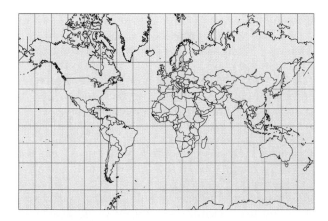 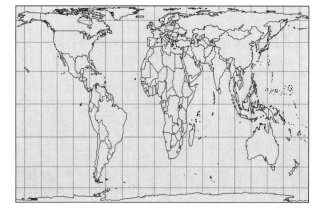

All maps distort reality, since they portray a three-dimensional world in two dimensions. Most of us are familiar with the Mercator projection (devised by the Flemish mapmaker Gerhardus Mercator, 1512-1594), which accurately presents the shape of countries (a vital concern to early seafaring navigators). But Mercator maps like the one at left distort the size of land masses (more so the farther they lie from the equator), thereby exaggerating the dimensions of Europe and North America. The Peters projection, at right, is used in this text because it accurately displays the size of all nations.

multicultural issues and enhance the voices of people of color and women. *Global Sociology* boxes prompt readers to think about their own way of life by examining the fascinating cultural diversity found in our world. *Critical Thinking* boxes teach students to ask sociological questions about their surroundings, and help them to evaluate important, controversial issues. *Sociology of Everyday Life* boxes examine sociological insights in light of familiar, everyday experiences. Finally, *Profile* boxes introduce many of the men and women who have shaped the discipline of sociology.

Sociology, fifth edition, contains seventy-one boxes in all, most of which have been updated or are entirely new to this edition. A complete listing of this text's boxes appears after the Table of Contents.

"Windows on the World" global maps. Another popular feature of *Sociology* is **Windows on the World** maps. This series of twenty-five global maps— many updated for this edition—are truly sociological maps that present, in global perspective, important patterns such as income disparity, favored languages and religions, the extent of prostitution, permitted marriage forms, the degree of political freedom, the incidence of HIV infection, the extent of the world's rain forests, and a host of other issues. **Windows on the World** use a new, non-Eurocentric projection, devised by cartographer Arno Peters, that accurately portrays the relative size of all the continents. A complete listing of **Windows on the World** maps follows the Table of Contents.

INNOVATION: CHANGES IN THE FIFTH EDITION

Each new edition of *Sociology* has broken new ground, one reason that more than 1 million students have learned from this sociological bestseller. A revision raises high expectations, but, after two years of work guided by the generous suggestions of faculty and students, we are confident that no one will be disappointed. Here is a summary of the innovations that define *Sociology*, fifth edition.

"Seeing Ourselves" national maps. We follow the introduction of global maps in the last edition with a series of twenty-three U.S. maps in this revision. These maps graphically present data for the roughly 3,100 counties in the United States, highlighting suicide rates, median household income, labor force participation, college attendance, divorce rates, most widespread religious affiliation, availability of doctors, air quality, and, as a measure of popular culture, where most of the Elvis fans live.

Each **Seeing Ourselves** map includes an explanatory caption plus several questions to awaken students' understanding of social forces. A complete listing of the new **Seeing Ourselves** maps follows the Table of Contents.

A new chapter: "The Natural Environment." The last two decades have witnessed a steadily building interest in the state of the natural environment. As sociologists have long recognized, environmental quality has much to do with how we organize social life. Therefore, *Sociology,* fifth edition, offers the first full chapter on the natural environment to be found in an introductory textbook.

Chapter 22 ("The Natural Environment") takes a decidedly sociological look at environmental issues, delving into how changing technology, population increase, and popular notions about the desirability of "growth" affect humanity's consumption of resources and generate problems of pollution. While highlighting issues of special concern in the United States, this new chapter also shows how and why environmental patterns are necessarily global in scope.

A new ordering of institutional chapters. While sociologists appreciate the importance of all the social institutions, most of today's practitioners hold that the economy has particular importance for shaping other dimensions of social life. Therefore, this revision places "The Economy and Work" (Chapter 15) first, and then proceeds to investigate "Politics and Government" (Chapter 16), "Family" (Chapter 17), "Religion" (Chapter 18), "Education" (Chapter 19), and "Health and Medicine" (Chapter 20).

The reordering of chapters in this new edition traces how the Industrial Revolution, launched two centuries ago, reshaped all aspects of social organization. This sequence also underscores how today's Information Revolution (and the emergence of a postindustrial economy) is once again recasting all facets of social life.

New topics. The fifth edition of *Sociology* also offers dozens of new or expanded discussions. Here is a partial listing, by chapter: *Chapter 1:* How and why suicide rates vary across the United States; *Chapter 2:* The emergence of feminist research methods, and recent research on the experience of racism by affluent African Americans; *Chapter 3:* A clarification of the subtle differences between culture, nation, and society, and contrasts between "high culture" and "popular culture"; *Chapter 4:* A major new section on postindustrial societies; *Chapter 5:* An examination of developmental research by Carol Gilligan; *Chapter 6:* New material on gender and interpersonal communication; *Chapter 7:* What is the "McDonaldization of society"? *Chapter 8:* A probing look at hate crimes; *Chapter 9:* South Africa's bold steps toward black majority rule; *Chapter 10:* New data on the distribution of U.S. income and wealth; new coverage of the problem of child poverty; *Chapter 11:* The most recent data on and analysis of global income distribution;

Chapter 12: An expanded discussion of Asian Americans that highlights people of Korean and Filipino descent; *Chapter 13:* New material on bisexuality; *Chapter 14:* What is the "aging mystique"?; *Chapter 15:* New sections spotlighting the trend toward employing temporary workers in the United States and the emerging global economy; *Chapter 16:* New assessment of the possibilities of a global political system plus coverage of Singapore's "soft authoritarianism," war crimes in the former Yugoslavia, and recent developments in the debate surrounding gays in the military; *Chapter 17:* A new look at child care, grandparenting, and gay parenting; *Chapter 18:* New research probing the true extent of religiosity in the United States; *Chapter 19:* An expanded examination of school choice and adult education; *Chapter 20:* New sections on eating disorders, genetic medicine, and the Clinton health care reforms; *Chapter 21:* Expanded analysis of demographic transition theory and investigation of where today's baby boomers live; *Chapter 22:* An entirely new chapter on the natural environment; *Chapter 23:* New material on gender and social movements; *Chapter 24:* New sections on the alleged cultural decline of the United States and postmodernity.

The latest statistical data. No text has more current statistical data than this one. The author, in collaboration with Carol Singer, a professional government documents librarian employed by the District of Columbia Reference Center, has ensured that each chapter of *Sociology,* fifth edition, has the most up-to-date statistics available—in many cases, for 1992 and even 1993. In addition, this revision is filled with hundreds of new research findings.

A WORD ABOUT LANGUAGE

This text's commitment to presenting the social diversity of the United States and the world carries with it the responsibility to use language thoughtfully. In most cases, we prefer the terms *African American* and *person of color* to the word *black.* We use the terms *Hispanic* or *Latino* to refer to people of Spanish descent. Most tables and figures refer to "Hispanics" because the Census Bureau employs this term in collecting statistical data about our population.

Students should realize, however, that many individuals do not describe themselves in these terms. Although the term "Hispanic" is commonly used in the eastern part of the United States, and "Latino" and the feminine form "Latina" are widely heard in the West, across the United States, people of Spanish descent generally identify with a particular ancestral nation, whether it be Argentina, Mexico, some other Latin American country, or Spain or Portugal in Europe.

The same holds true for Asian Americans. Although *Asian American* is a useful shorthand in sociological analysis, most people of Asian descent think of themselves in terms of a specific country of origin (say, Japan, the Philippines, Taiwan, or Vietnam).

In this text, the term "Native American" refers to all people who trace their ancestry to the inhabitants of the Americas (including the Hawaiian Islands) prior to contact with Europeans. Here again, however, most people in this broad category identify with their historical society (for example, Cherokee, Hopi, or Zuni). The term "American Indian" designates only those Native Americans who live in the continental United States, not including Native peoples living in Alaska or Hawaii.

Learning to think globally also leads us to use more language more carefully. This text avoids the word "American"—which literally designates two continents—to refer to just the United States. Thus, for example, the "American economy" is more correctly called the "U.S. economy." This convention may seem a small point, but it implies the significant recognition that we in this country represent only one society (albeit a very important one) in the Americas.

SUPPLEMENTS

Sociology, fifth edition, is the heart of an unparalleled learning package that includes a wide range of proven instructional aids as well as several new ones. As the author of the text, I maintain a keen interest in all the supplements to ensure their quality and integration with the text. The supplements for this revision have been thoroughly updated, improved, and expanded.

The Annotated Instructor's Edition. Faculty can request *Sociology* in an annotated instructor's edition (AIE). The AIE is a complete student text annotated by the author on every page. Annotations have won praise from instructors because of how well they enrich class presentations. Margin notes include summaries of research findings, statistics from the United States or other nations, insightful quotations, information illustrating patterns of social diversity in the United States, and high-quality survey data from the National Opinion Research Center's (NORC) General Social Survey.

Data File. This is the "instructor's manual" that is of interest even to those who have never used one before. The *Data File* provides far more than detailed chapter outlines and discussion questions; it contains statistical profiles of the United States and other nations, summaries of important developments and significant research, and supplemental lecture material for every chapter of the text. The *Data File* has been prepared by Stephen W. Beach (Kentucky Wesleyan College) with the assistance of John J. Macionis, and is also available in DOS formats.

Test Item File. A revised test item file for this edition has been prepared by Edward Kick, University of Utah. This file is available in both printed and computerized forms. The file contains 2400 items—100 per chapter—in multiple choice, true-false, and essay formats. Questions are identified as more simple "recall" items or more complex "inferential" issues; the answers to all questions are page-referenced to the text. *Prentice Hall TestManager 2.0* is a test generator and classroom management system designed to provide maximum flexibility in producing and grading tests and quizzes. It is available in both DOS and Macintosh formats. Prentice Hall also provides a test preparation service to users of this text that is as easy as one call to our toll-free 800 number.

Core Test Item File. This general test item file consists of over 350 additional test questions appropriate for introductory sociology courses. All of the questions have been class tested, and an item analysis is available for every question.

Social Survey Software. This is the supplement that is changing the way instructors teach and students learn. STUDENT CHIP *Social Survey Software* is an easy yet powerful program that allows users to investigate U.S. society and other nations of the world by calling on the best source of survey data available, the General Social Survey. John J. Macionis and Jere Bruner (Oberlin College) have transformed 260 GSS items into CHIP data sets and linked them to the chapters of *Sociology*, fifth edition. Jere W. Bruner and Karen Lynch Frederick (Saint Anselm College) have written a helpful *Instructor's Manual* as well as an easy-to-understand *Social Survey Software Student Manual* that leads students through multivariate analysis of attitudes and reported behavior by sex, race, occupation, level of income and education, and a host of other variables. *Social Survey Software*, which investigators can now manipulate either by keyboard or mouse, also has a new graphing feature. The STUDENT CHIP microcomputer program was developed by James A. Davis (Harvard University) and is available in both IBM and MacIntosh formats.

The New York Times Supplement

Themes of the Times. The New York Times and Prentice Hall are sponsoring *Themes of the Times*, a program designed to enhance student access to current information relevant to the classroom.

Through this program, the core subject matter provided in the text is supplemented by a collection of timely articles from one of the world's most distinguished newspapers, *The New York Times.* These articles demonstrate the vital, ongoing connection between what is learned in the classroom and what is happening in the world around us.

To enjoy the wealth of information of *The New York Times* daily, a reduced subscription rate is available. For information, call toll-free: 1-800-631-1222.

Prentice Hall and *The New York Times* are proud to co-sponsor *Themes of the Times.* We hope it will make the reading of both textbooks and newspapers a more dynamic, involving process.

Seeing Ourselves: Classic, Contemporary, and Cross-Cultural Readings in Sociology, 3/E. Create a powerful teaching package by combining this text with the new, third edition of the best-selling anthology, *Seeing Ourselves,* edited by John J. Macionis and Nijole V. Benokraitis (University of Baltimore). Better than ever, *Seeing Ourselves,* third edition, now has seventy-five selections, thirty-one new to this edition. Instructors relish this reader's unique format: Clusters of readings—from classic works to well-rounded looks at contemporary issues and cross-cultural comparisons—correspond to each chapter in *Sociology,* fifth edition. The **classics** (twenty-nine in all) now include selections by Emile Durkheim, Karl Marx, George Herbert Mead, Max Weber, Georg Simmel, Ferdinand Toennies, Margaret Mead, C. Wright Mills, W. E. B. DuBois, Mirra Komarovsky, Jessie Bernard and others.

The **contemporary** readings (twenty-four) range from Shulamit Reinharz on feminist research and Dianne Herman pointing out the cultural roots of sexual violence to William Bennett's contention that the United States is entering a period of cultural decline, Deborah Tannen's insights on why the two sexes often talk past each other, Sally Helgeson on the competitive edge women bring to the corporate world, Robert Reich's investigation of the domestic consequences of the global economy, William Julius Wilson's account of the ghetto underclass, William O'Hare's profile of affluent Latinos, Naomi Wolf on the "beauty myth," Betty Friedan's views on aging, James Woods on homosexuality in the workplace, Catharine MacKinnon's analysis of pornography as a power issue, Lester Brown's survey of the state of the world's environment, and Robert Bellah's thoughts on the difficulty of finding a sense of meaningful participation in modern society.

Cross-cultural selections (twenty-two) include well-known works such as "The Nacirema" by Horace Miner, "India's Sacred Cow" by Marvin Harris, and "The Amish: A Small Society" by John Hostetler. Other cross-cultural articles explore particular issues and problems: how race and class affect socialization, ways in which advertising depicts people of various backgrounds, differences between Japanese corporations and their U.S. counterparts, global patterns of crime, the staggering burden of African poverty, varying cultural attitudes toward homosexuality, traditional arranged marriage in India, Islam's view of women, academic achievement among Southeast Asian immigrants, how the AIDS epidemic is ravaging other continents, and the plight of indigenous peoples worldwide. *Seeing Ourselves* is a low-cost resource that provides exceptional quality and flexibility for instructors seeking to supplement reading assignments in the text with primary sources.

Media Supplements

ABC News/Prentice Hall Video Library for Sociology Series I, II, III (Issues in Sociology), IV (Global Culturalism) and V (Issues in Diversity). Video is the most dynamic supplement you can use to enhance a class. But the quality of the video material and how well it relates to your course still makes all the difference. Prentice Hall and ABC News are now working together to bring you the best and most comprehensive video ancillaries available in the college market.

Through its wide variety of award-winning programs—*Nightline, Business World, On Business, This Week with David Brinkley, World New Tonight,* and *The Health Show*—ABC offers a resource for feature and documentary-style videos related to the chapters in *Sociology,* 5/e. The programs have extremely high production quality, present substantial content, and are hosted by well-versed, well-known anchors.

Prentice Hall and its authors and editors provide the benefit of having selected videos and topics that will work well with this course and text and include notes on how to use them in the classroom. An excellent video guide in the *Data File* carefully and completely integrates the videos into your lecture. The guide has a synopsis of each video showing its relation to the chapter and discussion questions to help students focus on how concepts and theories apply to real-life situations.

Prentice Hall Images in Sociology: Laser Videodisc, Series II Using the latest technology, *Images in Sociology* presents illustrations both from within the text and from outside sources in an integrated framework appropriate for classroom use. These images include maps, graphs, diagrams, and other illustrations, as well as video segments taken from the *ABC News/Prentice Hall Video Library for Sociology*. See your local Prentice Hall representative for details on how to preview this videodisc.

Multimedia Presentation Manager: MM Presentation Manager is an Authorware application for instructors who wish to use multimedia but who do not yet wish to develop their own applications. The program provides an extremely friendly environment in which an instructor can control a variety of content types (video, laserdisc, text, audio, graphic, animation, and programs) to create multimedia lectures and presentations. Please see your Prentice Hall representative for more details.

PowerPoint Presentation Manager for Introductory Sociology. This easy to use Windows-based program provides 23 units of material that coincide with a typical introductory sociology table of contents. Within each unit, the instructor will have two 40-minute self-contained lectures suitable for classroom presentation. Please see your Prentice Hall representative for more details.

Other supplements available to aid in classroom teaching are:

Prentice Hall Color Transparencies: Sociology Series III

Instructor's Guide to *Prentice Hall Color Transparencies: Sociology Series III*

Film/Video Guide: *Prentice Hall Introductory Sociology,* Revised Edition

Study Guide

Prentice Hall StudyManager

Critical Thinking Audiocassette Tape

IN APPRECIATION

The conventional practice of designating a single author obscures the efforts of dozens of women and men that have resulted in *Sociology,* fifth edition. Nancy Roberts, editor-in-chief at Prentice Hall and valued friend, has contributed enthusiasm, support, and sound advice throughout the revision process. Susanna Lesan, developmental editor-in-chief at Prentice Hall, has played a vital role in the development of this text since its first edition, with day-to-day responsibility for coordinating and supervising the editorial process. I also have a large debt to the members of the Prentice Hall sales staff, the men and women who have given this text such remarkable support over the years. Thanks, especially, to Carol Carter and Kris Kleinsmith, who direct our marketing campaign. I also offer heartfelt thanks to Pat Naturale, Bill Webber, Charlyce Jones Owen, Will Ethridge, and Phil Miller for all that they have done to make this text what it is today. The author extends a special note of respect and gratitude to Ed Stanford, whose career at Prentice Hall—from sales rep to sociology editor to president—represents the very best in college publishing.

The production of *Sociology,* fifth edition, was supervised by Barbara Reilly, who appreciates the fact that a book is nothing more than a million details. Keeping track of each and every one has consumed her time and energy over the past year, and she has done an extraordinary job. The interior design of the book is the creative work of Lorraine Mullaney. Final page layout was the responsibility of Learning Design Associates, of Columbus, Ohio, in collaboration with Barbara Reilly and the author. Copy editing of the manuscript was provided by Ann Hofstra-Grogg, Diana Drew, and Amy Macionis. Barbara Salz did a wonderful job of researching photographs, as did Joelle Burrows with the fine art, both under the supervision of Lorinda Morris-Nantz, head of Prentice Hall Photo Archives. The high quality and timeliness of the supplements to this text reflect the efforts of Sharon Chambliss, associate editor of sociology. Skillful research by Carol Singer, librarian at the National Agricultural Library in Washington, D.C., is responsible for keeping the statistical data in this text up-to-date.

It goes without saying that every colleague knows more about some topics covered in this book than the author does. For that reason, I am grateful to the hundreds of faculty and students who have written to me to offer comments and suggestions. More formally, I am grateful to the following people who have reviewed some or all of this manuscript:

Jon P. Alston, Texas A&M University
Cathy Blair, Worthington Community College
Janet Carlisle Bogdan, LeMoyne College
Robert Bolin, New Mexico State University
Valeria Brown, Cuyahoga Community College
Brent T. Bruton, Iowa State University
Thomas E. Carroll, University of Missouri
Larry D. Crawford, Morehouse College
Lovberta Cross, Shelby State Community College
William M. Cross, Illinois College
Lynn England, Brigham Young University
Al Gedicks, University of Wisconsin—La Crosse
Ronald Hardert, Arizona State University
Charles Harper, Creighton University
Harry L. Humphries, Pittsburg State University
Rachel Kahn-Hut, San Francisco State University
Eric Lichten, Long Island University
Larry Lyon, Baylor University
Duane A. Matcha, Siena College
James A. Mathisen, Wheaton College
Lester Milbrath, State University of New York—
    Buffalo
Anne R. Peterson, Columbus State Community
    College
Robert Pinder, Texas Tech University
Rebecca Riehm, Jefferson Community College
Ellen Rosengarten, Sinclair Community College
Paul Sharp, Auburn University
Lawrence Sneden, California State University—
    Northridge
William E. Snizek, Virginia Polytechnic Institute
    and State University
Carol Stix, Pace University
William Tolone, Illinois State University
Theodore C. Wagenaar, Miami University
Gregory L. Weiss, Roanoke College
J. Allen Williams, Jr., University of Nebraska—
    Lincoln

I also wish to thank the following colleagues for
sharing their wisdom in ways that have improved this
book: Doug Adams (The Ohio State University), Kip
Armstrong (Bloomsburg University), Rose Arnault
(Fort Hays State University), Philip Berg (University of
Wisconsin, La Crosse), Bill Brindle (Monroe Commun-
ity College), John R. Brouillette (Colorado State
University), Karen Campbell (Vanderbilt University),
Gerry Cox (Fort Hays State University), James A. Davis
(Harvard University), Keith Doubt (Northeast Missouri
State University), Helen Rose Fuchs Ebaugh (Univer-
sity of Houston), Heather Fitz Gibbon (The College of
Wooster), Kevin Fitzpatrick (University of Alabama-
Birmingham), Dona C. Fletcher (Sinclair Community
College), Charles Frazier (University of Florida), Karen
Lynch Frederick (Saint Anselm College), Charlotte
Gotwald (York College of Pennsylvania), Steven
Goldberg (City College, City University of New York),
Jeffrey Hahn (Mount Union College), Dean Haledjian
(Northern Virginia Community College), Peter
Hruschka (Ohio Northern University), Glenna Huls
(Camden County College), Jeanne Humble (Lexington
Community College), Harry Humphries (Pittsburg
State University), Cynthia Imanaka (Seattle Central
Community College), Jarvis Gamble (Owens Technical
College), Patricia Johnson (Houston Community
College), Ed Kain (Southwestern University), Irwin
Kantor (Middlesex County College), Thomas Korllos
(Kent State University), Rita Krasnow (Virginia
Western Community College), Michael Levine
(Kenyon College), George Lowe (Texas Tech
University), Don Luidens (Hope College), Larry Lyon
(Baylor University), Li-Chen Ma (Lamar University),
Errol Magidson (Richard J. Daley College), Alan Mazur
(Syracuse University), Meredith McGuire (Trinity
College), Dan McMurry (Middle-Tennessee State
University), Jack Melhorn (Emporia State University),
Ken Miller (Drake University), Richard Miller (Navarro
College), Alfred Montalvo (Emporia State University),
Joe Morolla (Virginia Commonwealth University),
Craig Nauman (Madison Area Technical College),
Daniel Quinn (Adrian College), Toby Parcel (The Ohio
State University), Anne Peterson (Columbus State
Community College), Nevel Razak (Fort Hays State
College), Virginia Reynolds (Indiana University of
Pennsylvania), Laurel Richardson (The Ohio State
University), Ellen Rosengarten (Sinclair Community
College), Howard Schneiderman (Lafayette College),
Ray Scupin (Linderwood College), Harry Sherer (Irvine
Valley College), Walt Shirley (Sinclair Community
College), Glen Sims (Glendale Community College),
Verta Taylor (The Ohio State University), Len
Tompos (Lorain County Community College),
Christopher Vanderpool (Michigan State University),
Marilyn Wilmeth (Iowa University), Stuart Wright
(Lamar University), Dan Yutze (Taylor University),
Wayne Zapatek (Tarrant County Community
College), and Frank Zulke (Harold Washington
College).

Thank you one and all.

About the Author

John J. Macionis (pronounced ma-SHOW-nis) grew up in Philadelphia, Pennsylvania. He received his bachelor's degree from Cornell University and his doctorate in sociology from the University of Pennsylvania. His publications are wide-ranging, focusing on community life in the United States, interpersonal intimacy in families, effective teaching, humor, and the importance of global education. He is coauthor of *The Sociology of Cities* and he has coedited the third edition of the companion volume to this text, *Seeing Ourselves: Classic, Contemporary, and Cross-Cultural Readings in Sociology*. Macionis also has written a brief version of this book, *Society: The Basics.*

John Macionis is professor of sociology at Kenyon College in Gambier, Ohio. He has served as chair of the Anthropology-Sociology Department, director of Kenyon's multidisciplinary program in humane studies, and chair of the college's faculty.

Professor Macionis teaches a wide range of upper-level courses but his favorite course is Introduction to Sociology, which he teaches every semester. He enjoys extensive contact with students, making an occasional appearance on campus with his guitar and each term inviting his students to enjoy a home-cooked meal. Macionis is a frequent visitor to other campuses as well and participates regularly in teaching programs abroad. In the fall of 1994, he directed the global education course for the University of Pittsburgh's Semester at Sea program, teaching four hundred students on a floating campus that visits twelve countries as it circles the globe.

Professor Macionis lives on a farm in rural Ohio with his wife Amy and children McLean and Whitney. Their home serves as a popular bed and breakfast where they enjoy visiting with old friends and making new ones.

The author welcomes (and responds to) comments and suggestions about his book from faculty and students. Write to Palme House, Kenyon College, Gambier, Ohio 43022. His internet address is MACIONIS@ KENYON.EDU

xxvii

Every page of the Annotated Instructor's Edition of Sociology 5/e contains information and data that will enhance the usefulness of the text. The annotations, as well as the separately bound Data File, offer substantial material directly related to the topic at hand. Annotations are of eight types:

GLOBAL: Facts or observations placing the topic at hand in a global context.

DATA FILE: A cross-reference to material in the *Data File*, which includes detailed chapter outlines, discussion topics, and additional lecture material.

SOCIAL SURVEY: Data from the National Opinion Research Center's *General Social Survey*. Entries are identified as taken from the *Chippendale Social Survey Software* package available with this text or from the *GSS Codebook*.

Jacob Lawrence, *Nigerian Series: Street to Mbari,* 1964. Gouache on paper, 20 1/4 x 30 3/8 inches. Courtesy of Terry Dintenfass Gallery, New York.

DIVERSITY: Data or insights analyzing the issue in terms of race, ethnicity, or gender.

THE MAP: Comments about the global maps ("Windows on the World") or the "interactive" national maps ("Seeing Ourselves") that are new to this edition of the text.

Q: A noteworthy quotation by a sociologist, a historical figure, or one of today's newsmakers.

NOTE: A worthwhile comment on theory or method, information on the text's artwork or photography, or the etymology of an important term.

RESOURCE: An article or book useful for further reading or to support a class discussion.

Q: "For the most part we do not first see then define; we define and then see." U.S. social critic Walter Lippman

The Sociological Perspective

More than 5.5 billion people live on the planet we call Earth, in cities and across the countryside of 190 nations. But imagine for a moment this vast world reduced to a microcosm—a single village of 1,000 people. If we were to pay a visit to this "global village," we could quickly learn a great deal about our own, much larger world. A survey of the village population would reveal more than half (575) of the inhabitants to be Asians, including 200 people from the People's Republic of China. Next, in terms of numbers, we would find 130 Africans, 125 Europeans, and about 100 Latin Americans. North Americans— including people from the United States, Canada, and Mexico—would account for a scant 65 village residents.

A longer stay in this village might afford the opportunity for careful study of its way of life and yield some startling conclusions: The village is very

productive, generating a seemingly endless array of goods and services for sale. Yet most of the inhabitants can do no more than look at such treasures, since half of the village's total income is earned by just 120 individuals.

Food is the village's greatest concern. Every year, village workers produce far more food than is necessary to feed everyone; even so, 500 of the people in the village—including most of the children—are poorly nourished and typically fall asleep hungry. For the worst-off 200 residents, a lack of food and safe drinking water renders them unable to work and vulnerable to life-threatening diseases.

The village contains many examples of splendid housing. But while the richest 60 families live in luxurious surroundings with every convenience, about 600 of their neighbors live in shanty housing that offers neither comfort nor safety.

DATA FILE: The *Data File* material for this chapter includes a detailed outline and a comparative view of the development of sociology in China.

Q: "O wad some Pow'r the giftie gie us; To see ourselves as others see us! It wad frae mony a blunder free us; And foolish notion." Scottish poet Robert Burns

NOTE: The word "discipline" is Latin for "to instruct," making one who is instructed a "disciple."

NOTE: It is not sociology's empirical territory, as Peter Berger (1992) suggests, that we can call our own; it is our perspective. Even so, this distinctive point of view has become absorbed into many other disciplines—history comes to mind—as well as everyday consciousness.

Villagers can boast of their community's many schools, including numerous colleges and universities. About 75 of the village inhabitants have completed a college degree and a few even have doctorates. At the same time, about half the village's school-aged children have never been inside a classroom. Overall, 700 of the village's people can neither read nor write.[1]

Finally, over its history, the people of this village have attained notable achievements in the arts and in science. They have imaginatively solved one after another of the problems that confront them, taming nature and (for those who can afford to) gaining the capacity to travel farther and more quickly with each passing generation. But the people of the village have also learned that their growing ability to affect their surroundings comes at a high price: More than ever before, the deterioration of the physical environment threatens their future well-being.

And, perhaps most important, the village population remains fractured by many proud divisions based on nationality, religion, language, and skin color. At virtually any time, fighting disrupts the peace of the community. For all their accomplishments, people have yet to devise a means by which to control conflict before it explodes into war.

As this chapter explains, there are many ways to think about human beings and the world we have created. Since the beginning of time, poets and philosophers have done so; more recently, a wide range of disciplines—from anthropology to zoology—has arrived on the scene, each offering particular insights into the human drama. But probably the most fascinating perspective of all is that of *sociology*, because it explains and ties together so many dimensions of human life. As we shall see, sociology provides rich opportunities to explore not just our own society but the broader world as well.

---

[1]These data are based on research by the World Development Forum (April 15, 1990) and calculations by the author.

THE SOCIOLOGICAL PERSPECTIVE

The discipline of **sociology** is defined as *the scientific study of human society*. At the heart of sociology is a distinctive point of view that we shall describe throughout this chapter.

Seeing the General in the Particular

Peter Berger (1963) describes the sociological perspective as *seeing the general in the particular*. This means that sociologists see general patterns in the behavior of particular individuals. While acknowledging that each individual is unique, in other words, we also recognize that social forces shape us into various *kinds* of people who think and act in distinctive ways. Every society places individuals into numerous categories on the basis of age (say, as children or adults), sex (as women or men), class (as rich or poor), as well as on the basis of color and cultural background. We begin to think sociologically as we start to realize how our particular life experiences are shaped by the general categories into which we happen to fall.

Every chapter of this text provides many illustrations of how the general structures of society affect our particular feelings, thoughts, and actions. We all know that children differ from adults. But, as Chapter 5 ("Socialization") explains, much of this difference arises from the fact that our society assigns meaning to age, creating what we experience as distinct stages of life. As we see it, children are "dependent," while adults should behave "responsibly." Furthermore, our society considers old age to be a time of diminishing standing and disengagement from earlier routines. One reason we know that society (and not simply biology) is at work here is that people in various times and places have defined the stages of life in quite different ways. The Hopi, for example, expect their children to behave independently, and the Abkhasians accord their highest esteem to their oldest members.

Seeing the world sociologically also makes us aware of the importance of gender. As Chapter 13 ("Sex and Gender") describes, every society attaches certain meanings to each sex; our society accords women and men different kinds of work and family responsibilities. Individuals experience this process in terms of the range of advantages and opportunities they face; in the United States, men's work typically carries with it more power and greater income. As Chapter 6 ("Social Interaction in Everyday Life") explains, society intrudes into even in the most intimate conversations between

DIVERSITY: Other examples of the "general in the particular": Proportion of U.S. adults (age 25 or over) completing four years or more of college: 21.4%; whites: 22.2%; African Americans: 11.5%; Hispanics: 9.7%; Mexican Americans: 6.2%; Cuban Americans: 18.5%; Puerto Ricans: 10.1%; Asians and Pacific Islanders: 39.1%. Other examples include the fluctuating divorce rate over the course of this century (look ahead to Figure 17–4) and educational achievement by income (Figure 19–1) or by race and ethnicity (Figure 19–2).

RESOURCE: Contemporary research utilizing the sociological perspective to reveal how gender affects verbal and nonverbal communication is included in the Macionis and Benokraitis companion reader, *Seeing Ourselves: Classic, Contemporary, and Cross-Cultural Readings in Sociology*, 3/e. The reader also offers Horace Miner's selection "Body Ritual Among the Nacerima."

We can easily grasp the power of society over the individual by imagining how different our lives would be had we been born in place of any of these children from, respectively, Bolivia, India, Guatemala, Botswana, the People's Republic of China, and South Africa.

men and women. Gender expectations affect the manner in which women and men express themselves, a difference that often makes talking to one other difficult and frustrating.

A sociological look around us reveals the power of class position as well. Chapter 9 ("Social Stratification") and Chapter 10 ("Social Class in the United States") provide ample evidence that how we live—and, sometimes, whether we live at all—has a great deal to do with the ranking we receive at birth through our parents. More broadly, as Chapter 11 ("Global Stratification") argues, our lives reflect not only our position in our "home" society but also our country's standing in the hierarchy of nations that characterizes the world as a whole.

Seeing the Strange in the Familiar

Especially at the beginning, the sociological perspective amounts to *seeing the strange in the familiar*. This does not mean that sociologists focus on the bizarre elements of society. Rather, looking sociologically requires us to give up the familiar idea that human behavior is simply a matter of what people *decide* to do in favor of the initially strange notion that society guides our thoughts and deeds.

For individualistic North Americans, learning to "see" how society affects us may take a bit of practice. Asked why you came to be a student at your particular college, you might offer any of the following personal reasons:

SOCIAL SURVEY: "How do you feel about opportunities for young people to go to college? Should opportunities be . . ." (GSS 1985, N = 677; Codebook, 1993:526)

"Increased" 42.5%   "Reduced a little" 2.6%
"Increased a little" 25.6%   "Reduced a lot" 0.5%
"Kept the same as now" 25.6%   DK/NR 3.0%

SOCIAL SURVEY: "Does everybody have the opportunity to obtain an education corresponding to his or her abilities and talents?" (GSS 1985, N = 1,473; Codebook, 1993:129)

"Yes" 69.8%   "No" 27.9%   DK/NR 2.3%

Q: "The world belongs to me because I understand it." Honoré de Balzac

Traveling abroad, people have a heightened awareness of social patterns that "natives" take for granted. For the same reason, foreign students and other visitors who come to the United States are often keen observers of our social scene. Without leaving the country, however, we can become more aware of ourselves and our surroundings by learning to use the sociological perspective.

I wanted to stay close to home.

This college has the best women's basketball team.

A journalism degree from this university ensures a good job.

My girlfriend goes to school here.

I wasn't accepted at the school I really wanted to attend.

Such responses are certainly real to the people expressing them. But do they tell the complete story? The sociological perspective provides additional insights that may not be readily apparent.

Thinking sociologically about college attendance, we might first realize that, had we lived a century or two ago, our "choice" to go to college probably never would have existed at all. Similarly, for young people throughout most of the world, even primary schooling is a sought-after prize. But even limiting our attention to today's United States, we see that whether one attends college or not has much to do with general social patterns. A look around the classroom suggests that some categories of people are more likely than others to become students. More often than not, students are relatively young—generally between eighteen and twenty-four years of age. Why? Because our society traditionally has linked college attendance to this period of life. But more than age is involved, since

most college-age members of our society do not matriculate on any campus: In 1991, only one-third of eighteen- to twenty-four-year-olds were enrolled in college.

Social background also plays a big part by shaping an individual's range of opportunities. Traditionally, college students come from families with above-average incomes. As Chapter 19 ("Education") explains, young people lucky enough to live in families earning more than $75,000 are twice as likely to go to college as their counterparts in families with annual earnings below $20,000. As Chapter 12 ("Race and Ethnicity") points out, our society links both race and ethnicity to income. The net result is that more young whites (34 percent) are in college than African Americans (24 percent) and Hispanics[2] (18 percent) (Kominski & Adams, 1993).

Although initially it may seem strange to explain personal choices in terms of social forces, the sociological perspective empowers us to understand how our own experiences—including the opportunities and barriers we face—are linked to our standing in the larger society around us. The box illustrates further how social forces affect a seemingly personal matter: the choice of names.

Individuality in Social Context

Sociological insights often challenge common sense by revealing how human behavior is not as individualistic as we may think. For most of us, daily living carries a heavy load of personal responsibility, so that we pat ourselves on the back when we enjoy success and kick ourselves when things go wrong. Proud of our individuality, even in painful times, we resist the idea that we act in socially patterned ways.

Perhaps the most compelling demonstration of how social forces affect human behavior is the study of suicide. Why? Because nothing could be more personal than taking one's own life. This is why Emile Durkheim (1858–1917), a pioneer of sociology writing a century ago, chose suicide as a topic of research. He was able to reveal social forces at work even in the apparent isolation of the ultimate self-destructive act.

Durkheim examined records of suicide in and around his native France. The statistics clearly showed

---

[2]These data represent men and women aged twenty and twenty-one. Hispanics or Latinos may be of any race; about 85 percent state their race as white. Here we are comparing Hispanics with non-Hispanic whites. (See "A Word About Language" in the Preface.)

SOCIAL DIVERSITY

What's in a Name? How Social Forces Affect Personal Choices

On the fourth of July in 1918, twins were born to Abe and Becky Friedman in Sioux City, Iowa. The first to arrive was called Esther Pauline Friedman; her sister was named Pauline Esther Friedman. Today, these women are known to almost everyone in the United States, but by the new names they later adopted: Ann Landers and Abigail ("Dear Abby") Van Buren.

These two women are among tens of thousands of people in our society who changed their names to advance their careers. At first glance, changing one's name may seem to be little more than a matter of particular preferences. But take a closer look, from a sociological point of view, at the following list. How many of these well-known people can you identify from the names that they were given at birth?

1. Frank Casteluccio
2. Cherilyn Sarkisian
3. Cheryl Stoppelmoor
4. Robert Allen Zimmerman
5. Larry Zeigler
6. Nathan Birnbaum
7. Paul Rubenfeld
8. George Kyriakou Panayiotou
9. Annie Mae Bullock
10. Patricia Andrejewski
11. Malden Sekulovich
12. Jerome Silberman
13. Bernadette Lazzara
14. Karen Ziegler
15. Ramon Estevez
16. Henry John Deutschendorf, Jr.
17. Allen Stewart Konigsberg
18. Patsy McClenny
19. Jacob Cohen
20. William Claude Dukenfield
21. Lee Yuen Kam
22. Raquel Tejada
23. Frederick Austerlitz
24. Sophia Scicoloni

Can you see the pattern in these changes? Historically, women and men of various national backgrounds have adopted *English-sounding* names. Why? Because our society has long accorded high social prestige to those of Anglo-Saxon background. Once again, in other words, personal choice turns out to be guided by social forces.

1. Frankie Valli, 2. Cher, 3. Cheryl Ladd, 4. Bob Dylan, 5. Larry King, 6. George Burns, 7. Pee Wee Herman, 8. George Michael, 9. Tina Turner, 10. Pat Benatar, 11. Karl Malden, 12. Gene Wilder, 13. Bernadette Peters, 14. Karen Black, 15. Martin Sheen, 16. John Denver, 17. Woody Allen, 18. Morgan Fairchild, 19. Rodney Dangerfield, 20. W. C. Fields, 21. Bruce Lee, 22. Raquel Welch, 23. Fred Astaire, 24. Sophia Loren

that some categories of people were more likely than others to choose to take their own lives. Specifically, Durkheim found, men, Protestants, wealthy people, and the unmarried each had significantly higher suicide rates than did women, Catholics and Jews, the poor, and married people. Durkheim explained these differences by reasoning that suicide varied according to people's *social integration*. Low suicide rates, in other words, characterized categories of people who have strong ties to others. By contrast, high suicide rates were found among types of people who are typically more individualistic.

In the male-dominated societies studied by Durkheim, men certainly had more autonomy than women. Whatever its advantages, reasoned Durkheim, this freedom also meant lower social integration, contributing to a higher suicide rate among men. Likewise,

Catholic and Jewish rituals foster stronger social ties, and thus lower rates of suicide, than do individualistic Protestant beliefs. The wealthy clearly have much more freedom than the poor, but with a predictably higher suicide rate. Finally, with weaker social bonds than married people, single people, too, are at greater risk of suicide.

A century later, statistical evidence still supports Durkheim's analysis. Figure 1-1 shows suicide rates for four categories of the U.S. population. Whites had 13.3 recorded suicides for every 100,000 people in 1991, almost twice the rate of African Americans (6.7). Also, for both races, suicide is more common among men than among women. White men (21.7) are four times more likely than white women (5.2) to take their own lives. Among African Americans, the rate for men (12.1) is six times that for women (1.9). Following

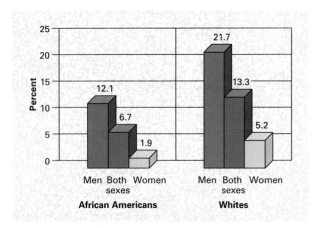

FIGURE 1–1 Rate of Death by Suicide, by Race and Sex, for the United States

Rates indicate the number of deaths by suicide for every 100,000 people in each category for 1991.

(U.S. National Center for Health Statistics, 1992)

Durkheim's argument, we conclude that the higher suicide rate among whites and men (and especially white men) is due to their greater affluence and autonomy. By contrast, the lower rate among women and people of color follows from their limited social choices. In sum, suicide rates (and rates of all kinds) reveal general social patterns in the actions of particular individuals.

THE IMPORTANCE OF GLOBAL PERSPECTIVE

In recent years, many academic disciplines including sociology have incorporated a **global perspective,** *the study of the larger world and our society's place in it.* What is the importance of a global perspective for sociology?

First, global awareness is a logical extension of the sociological perspective. Sociology's basic insight is that where we are placed in our society profoundly affects our individual experiences. It stands to reason, then, that the position of our society in the larger world system also affects everyone in the United States. As the opening paragraphs of this chapter suggest, the members of the "global village" are not equal—far from it, in fact, since some nations (including the United States) are dozens of times richer than others in terms of material production.

Global Map 1–1 illustrates the relative economic development of the world. The world's **most-developed countries** are *industrialized societies that are relatively rich.*[3] These affluent nations include the United States and Canada, most of Western Europe, and also Japan and Australia. Taken together, these forty societies produce the lion's share of the world's goods and services and control most of the world's wealth. Average individuals in these countries enjoy a high material standard of living, not because they are particularly bright or exceptionally hardworking, but because they had the good fortune to be born in an affluent region of the world.

A second category of societies are the world's **less-developed countries,** which are *societies characterized by limited industrialization and moderate-to-low personal income.* Individuals living in any of these roughly ninety nations—which include the countries of Eastern Europe and (farther down the income scale) most of Latin America—are more likely to have settled in rural areas than cities, to peddle bicycles or ride animals rather than to drive automobiles, and to receive only a few years of schooling. Most less-developed countries also have especially pronounced social inequality, so that a significant share of the population lacks safe housing and adequate nutrition.

Finally, almost half of the world's people live in the sixty **least-developed countries,** which are *societies with little industrialization in which severe poverty is the rule.* As Global Map 1–1 shows, most of the poorest societies in the world are in Africa and Asia. While a small number of people in each of these nations is rich, the majority confront the burden of surviving each day with poor housing, unsafe water, too little food, little or no sanitation, and, perhaps most seriously of all, little opportunity to improve their lives. Again, these people live on the edge of survival not because of any personal shortcoming, but because of the way their societies and the larger world are organized.

Chapter 11 ("Global Stratification") explores the many causes and consequences of global wealth and poverty in detail. But every chapter of this text highlights life in the world beyond our own borders. Why? Here are three reasons that global thinking is an important component of the sociological perspective.

---

[3]This edition of the text no longer employs the terms "First World," "Second World," and "Third World." Chapter 11 ("Global Stratification") provides the reasons for this change, along with a full discussion of world social stratification.

Q: "To blandly subsume, say, Ethiopia, India, and Brazil under the one banner of Third Worldhood is as absurd and denigrating as the old assertion that all Chinese look alike." Trinidad-born novelist Shiva Naipaul

Q: "The world is a book and those who study just their own society read only a single page." Old saying

GLOBAL: At the beginning of 1994, the community of nations numbered 190; only 10 percent of them are ethnically homogeneous.

GLOBAL: Any of the text's global maps serve to illustrate the power of society to affect the lives of individuals.

THE MAP: Chapter 11 ("Global Stratification") provides various explanations for the income differences shown in Global Map 1–1.

Window on the World

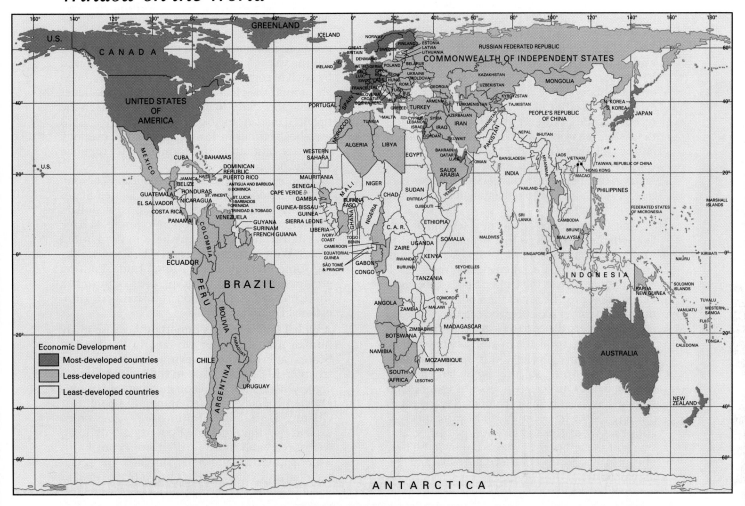

GLOBAL MAP 1–1 Economic Development in Global Perspective*

Most-developed countries—including the United States, Canada, most of the nations of Western Europe, Australia, and Japan—employ industrial technology to provide their people, on average, with material plenty. Less-developed countries—found throughout Latin America and including the nations of Eastern Europe—have limited industrial capacity and offer their people a standard of living that, while about average for the world as a whole, is far below that familiar to people in the United States. These societies also contain a significant share of poor people with minimal housing and inadequate diet. The least-developed countries of the world are those in which poverty is most severe and extensive. In these poorest nations, although small numbers of elites live very well, the majority of people struggle to survive on a small fraction of the income common in the United States.

*Note: Data for this map are provided by the World Bank and the United Nations. Most-developed countries had 1991 per capita gross domestic product (GDP) of at least $8,000. Many are far richer than this, however; the figure for the United States stands at $21,500. Less-developed countries had a per capita GDP ranging from $2,500 to $8,000. The least-developed countries of the world had a per capita GDP below $2,500. Figures used here reflect the new United Nations "purchasing power parities" system. This calculation avoids distortion caused by exchange rates when transforming all currencies to U.S. dollars. Instead, the data reflect the local purchasing power of each domestic currency.

Prepared by the author using data from the *World Development Report* (World Bank, 1993). Map projection from *Peters Atlas of the World* (1990).

GLOBAL: The number of telephone calls made from the United States to another country: 1970, 23.4 million; 1980, 200.0 million; 1990, 1.00 trillion (FCC data).

Q: "One can be an excellent physicist without ever stepping outside of one's society; I know this is not so for a sociologist." Peter Berger (1992)

GLOBAL: Evidence of ties linking the United States and the rest of the world: Michael Jackson sells more records abroad than he does in the United States; conversely, salsa has replaced ketchup as this nation's favorite condiment.

Q: "The Negro is a sort of seventh son...gifted with second sight . . . the sense of always looking at oneself through the eyes of others . . ." W. E. B. Du Bois

1. **Societies all over the world are increasingly interconnected, making traditional distinctions between "us" and "them" less and less valid.** For most of our history as a nation, we in the United States have been remarkably indifferent to the world around us. Separated from Europe and Asia by vast oceans, we have taken only passing note of our neighbors to the north (Canada) and south (Mexico and other Latin American nations). In recent decades, however, the United States and the rest of the world have become linked as never before. Jet aircraft—some traveling faster than sound—allow people to traverse continents in hours, while new electronic devices transmit pictures, sounds, and written documents around the globe in seconds.

One consequence of this new technology, as later chapters explain, is that people all over the world now share many tastes in music, clothing, and food. With their economic clout, most-developed nations such as the United States now cast a long shadow over the rest of the world, influencing members of other societies who eagerly gobble up our hamburgers, dance to rock-and-roll music, and, more and more, speak the English language.

But if we have projected our way of life onto much of the world, so, also, is the larger world coming to us. Our society now receives more immigrants in a year than the combined yearly totals during most of this century, and we are quick to adopt many of the sights, sounds, tastes, and smells of the rest of the world as our own. All this, of course, has greatly enhanced the racial and cultural diversity of this country.

Just as important as sharing patterns of living is the emergence of a global economy. The world no longer contains hundreds of independent economic systems. On the contrary, many large corporations manufacture and market goods throughout the world, just as financial markets are linked by satellite communication so that they now operate around the clock. As a result, no stock trader in New York dares to ignore what happens in the financial markets in Tokyo and Hong Kong, just as no wheat farmer in Iowa can afford to overlook the price of grain in the former Soviet republic of Georgia.

In short, economic activity has leaped beyond political borders. Businesses in the United States have invested hundreds of billions of dollars abroad, while foreign economic interests have invested trillions of dollars here in the United States. With eight out of ten new U.S. jobs involving some kind of international trade, gaining greater global understanding goes right to the "bottom line" (Council on International Educational Exchange, 1988).

2. **A global perspective is important because many human problems that we face in the United States are far more serious elsewhere.** As Chapter 10 ("Social Class in the United States") argues, more than 30 million members of our society are officially counted among the poor. But Chapter 11 ("Global Stratification") goes on to explain that the problem of poverty is both more widespread and more severe throughout Latin America, Africa, and Asia. Similarly, the social standing of women (which is below that of men in

One important reason to gain a global understanding is that familiar problems such as poverty are far more serious in many societies of the world than they are in the United States. So poor is the east African nation of Somalia, that this child has less than a fifty-fifty chance to grow to adulthood.

SOCIAL SURVEY: "It's hardly fair to bring a child into the world the way things look for the future." (*CHIP1 Social Survey Software*, ANOMIA51; GSS 1973–89, N = 14,399). The data suggest minorities experience greater social marginality than whites do.

	"Agree"	"Disagree"
Whites	35.9%	64.1%
Afri Amer	53.8%	46.2%
Hispanics	55.5%	44.5%

NOTE: An interesting query to pose to white students (have them respond confidentially in writing) is whether they would agree to become black for a specific amount of cash. If so, for how much?
Q: ". . . [I]t has historically been the case with white people, in their regard for black people, that even though we might be *with* them, we weren't considered *of* them." Malcolm X

the United States) is especially low in poorer societies of the world.

Then, too, many of the toughest problems we are grappling with at home are global in their causes and consequences. Environmental pollution is one example: As Chapter 22 ("The Natural Environment") demonstrates, the world is a single ecosystem in which the action (or inaction) of each nation has implications for all others.

3. **Thinking globally is important because studying other societies is an excellent means to learn more about ourselves.** We can hardly consider the life of a young woman growing up in Saudi Arabia or a man living in the African nation of Botswana without thinking about what it means to live in the United States. Making these comparisons often leads to unexpected lessons. Chapter 11 ("Global Stratification") takes us on a visit to a squatter settlement in Madras, India, for example. There we find that, despite their desperate lack of basic material comforts, people thrive in the love and support of family members. Such patterns prompt us to think about why poverty in the United States so often involves isolation and anger. Moreover, we might also wonder if material things—so crucial to our sense of a "rich" life—are the best way to gauge human well-being.

The question is not whether we should study ourselves or people who live elsewhere. In a world increasingly linked with each passing year, we can understand our society only to the extent that we comprehend our nation's place in the larger world (Macionis, 1993).

THE SOCIOLOGICAL PERSPECTIVE IN EVERYDAY LIFE

Thinking globally—about how life in other societies differs from our familiar routines—inevitably stimulates the sociological perspective. But even in our own home towns, some kinds of situations prompt us to see our surroundings sociologically, even before we take a first course in sociology.

Sociology and Social Diversity

Recognizing cultural diversity sparks the sociological perspective. Whenever we encounter people who behave in ways that initially seem strange, we are reminded of the power of social forces to shape how we act. As we recognize and experience the extent of

social diversity in this society, then, we find ourselves easing into the role of sociologist. The experience of social diversity awaits us virtually everywhere; we need only open our eyes and our minds to the varied social rhythms that are found in communities across the United States.

Sociology and Social Marginality

Sociological thinking is especially common among people we tend to label as "different." **Social marginality**, that is, *being excluded from social activity as an "outsider,"* is something we all experience from time to time. For some categories of people, however, being an outsider is part of daily living. The more acute people's social marginality, the more likely they are to embrace the sociological perspective.

No African American, for example, lives for long in the United States without learning how much race affects personal experiences. But because whites are the dominant majority, they think about race only occasionally and often imagine that race affects only people of color rather than themselves as well.

Much the same is true of women, gay people, people with disabilities, and the very old. All those relegated to the outskirts of social life are likely to recognize social patterns others take for granted. They have stepped back from society (or perhaps, more correctly, society has stepped back from them), and therefore they take a more sociological view of their surroundings.

Sociology and Social Crisis

U.S. sociologist C. Wright Mills (1959) suggested that social disruption also sparks sociological thinking. For example, the Great Depression of the 1930s threw one-fourth of the labor force out of work. In this catastrophic situation, unemployed workers could not help but see general social forces at work in their particular lives. Rather than claiming, "Something is wrong with me; I can't find a job," they were likely to say, "The economy has collapsed; there are no jobs to be found!"

The decade of the 1960s also enhanced sociological awareness in the United States. The civil rights, women's liberation, and antiwar movements all challenged accepted social patterns, highlighting ways in which people's lives are shaped by the political, economic, military, and technological elements of "the system." Although people debated the merits of these movements, each certainly called attention to the power of social forces.

PROFILE

C. Wright Mills: The Sociological Imagination

Charles Wright Mills (1916–1962) managed to cause a stir with most everything he did. Even arriving for a class at New York's Columbia Uni-versity—astride his motorcycle, and clad in a sweatshirt and boots—he was likely to turn some heads. Dur-ing the conservative 1950s, Mills not only dressed a bit out of the main-stream; he critically challenged most of the beliefs the majority of us take for granted. In the process, he won both followers and adversaries.

Mills's most enduring contri-bution was his insistence that a sociological imagination is no dry enterprise detached from life, but a vital perspective by which people could forge a more gentle and just way of life.

In the following excerpt* Mills argues that the key to bringing about change is learning to under-stand the social forces that have shaped our individual lives.

When a society becomes industri-alized, a peasant becomes a worker; a feudal lord is liquidated or be-comes a businessman. When classes rise or fall, a man is employed or un-employed; when the rate of in-vestment goes up or down, a man takes new heart or goes broke. When wars happen, an insurance salesman becomes a rocket launcher; a store clerk, a radar man; a wife lives alone; a child grows up without a father. Neither the life of an individual nor the history of a society can be under-stood without understanding both.

Yet men do not usually define the troubles they endure in terms of historical change. . . . The well-being they enjoy, they do not usu-ally impute to the big ups and downs of the society in which they live. Seldom aware of the intricate connection between the patterns of their own lives and the course of world history, ordinary men do not usually know what this connection means for the kind of men they are becoming and for the kinds of history-making in which they might take part. They do not possess the quality of mind essential to grasp the interplay of men and society, of biography and history, of self and world. . . .

It is this quality . . . that . . . may be called the sociological imagi-nation.

---

*In this excerpt, Mills uses male pronouns to apply to all people. It is interesting, and even ironic, that an out-spoken critic of society such as Mills reflected the con-ventional writing practices of his time as far as gender was concerned.

SOURCE: Mills (1959): 3–5.

Worth noting, too, is that the converse is often true: Sociological thinking often fosters social change. The more we learn about the operation of "the system," the more we may wish to change it in some way. As women and men have confronted the power of gender, for example, many have actively tried to reduce the traditional differences that set men apart from women.

In short, an introduction to sociology is an invita-tion to learn a new way of looking at familiar patterns of social life. At this point, we might well consider whether this invitation is worth accepting. In other words, what are the benefits of learning to use the sociological perspective?

Benefits of the Sociological Perspective

As we learn to use the sociological perspective, we can readily apply it to our daily lives. Doing so provides four general benefits.

1. **The sociological perspective challenges familiar understandings of ourselves and of others, so that we can critically assess the validity of com-monly held assumptions.** Thinking sociologically, in other words, we start to realize that certain ideas we have taken for granted are not entirely true.

   As we have already seen, a good example of a widespread but misleading "truth" is that women

RESOURCE: Excerpts of Peter Berger's *Invitation to Sociology* and C. Wright Mills's *The Sociological Imagination* are found in the Macionis and Benokraitis reader, *Seeing Ourselves: Classic, Contemporary, and Cross-Cultural Readings in Sociology,* 3/e, Prentice Hall, 1995.

DATA FILE: Included among this chapter's material is a comparative profile of sociology and the other social sciences.

DIVERSITY: Ask members of the class if anyone in the United States can *really* be president. Of 42 presidents: men = 42; whites = 42; Jews = 0; Catholics = 1 (JFK); Divorced = 1 (Ronald Reagan); Born in a log cabin = 1 (Millard Fillmore). Note, however, that only 15 were clearly in the upper class of their day.

and men in the United States are "autonomous individuals" who are personally responsible for their lives. By thinking this way, we are sometimes too quick to praise particularly successful people as being personally superior to those who have not fared as well. On the other side of the coin, people who do not measure up may be unfairly condemned as personally deficient. A sociological approach encourages us to ask whether these beliefs are actually true and, to the extent that they are not, why they are so widely held.

2. **The sociological perspective allows us to recognize both the opportunities and the constraints that characterize our lives.** To think sociologically is to realize that, for better or worse, our society operates in a particular and deliberate way. This recognition is important because no one is able to live with complete disregard for society's rules. In the game of life, we may decide how to play our cards, but it is society that deals us the hand. The more we understand about how the game works, the more effective players we will be, since knowledge of this kind is power. Sociology helps us to understand what we are likely and unlikely to accomplish for ourselves and how the goals we adopt can be realized more effectively.

3. **The sociological perspective, therefore, empowers us to be active participants in our society.** Without an awareness of how society operates, we are likely to accept the status quo. The greater our understanding of the operation of society, however, the more we can take an active part in shaping social life. For some, this may mean embracing society as it is; others, however, may attempt nothing less than trying to change the entire world in some way. The discipline of sociology advocates no one particular political orientation, and sociologists themselves weigh in at all points across the political spectrum. But evaluating any aspect of social life—whatever one's eventual goal—depends on the ability to identify social forces and to assess their consequences.

Some thirty years ago, U.S. sociologist C. Wright Mills pointed out how what he called the "sociological imagination" helps people to actively engage the world around them. This important sociologist is highlighted in the Profile box. Other sociologists will be featured in boxes throughout this book.

4. **The sociological perspective helps us to recognize human diversity and to confront the challenges of living in a diverse world.** Sociological thinking highlights our world's remarkable variety of human social patterns. North Americans represent a scant 5 percent of the world's population, and, as the remaining chapters of this book explain, many of our fellow human beings live in ways that differ dramatically from our own. Like people everywhere, we tend to define our own way of life as proper and "natural." But the more we think sociologically, the more we appreciate that today's world presents us with countless competing versions of correct behavior.

THE ORIGINS OF SOCIOLOGY

Like the "choices" made by individuals, major historical events rarely just happen. They are typically products of powerful social forces that are always complex and only partly predictable. So it was with the emergence of sociology itself. Having described the discipline's distinctive perspective and its benefits, we can now consider how and why sociology emerged in the first place.

Although human beings have mused about society since the beginning of our history, sociology is of relatively recent origin. It is one of the youngest academic disciplines—far younger than history, physics, or economics, for example. Only in 1838 did the French social thinker Auguste Comte, introduced in the box on page 12, coin the term *sociology* to describe a new way of looking at the world.

Science and Sociology

The nature of society held the attention of virtually all the brilliant thinkers of the ancient world, including the Chinese philosopher K'ung Fu-tzu or Confucius (551–479 B.C.E.) and the Greek philosophers Plato (c. 427–347 B.C.E.) and Aristotle (384–322 B.C.E.).[4] Similarly, the Roman emperor Marcus Aurelius (121–180 C.E.), the medieval thinkers St. Thomas Aquinas (c. 1225–1274) and Christine de Pizan (c. 1363–1431), and the great English playwright William Shakespeare (1564–1616) all reflected on the state of human society. Yet, as Emile Durkheim noted almost a century ago, none of these social thinkers approached society from a sociological point of view.

---

[4]Throughout this text, the abbreviation B.C.E. designates "before the common era." We use this terminology in place of the traditional B.C. ("before Christ") in recognition of the religious plurality of our society. Similarly, in place of the traditional A.D. (*anno Domini*, or "in the year of our Lord"), we employ the abbreviation C.E. ("common era").

PROFILE

Auguste Comte: Weathering a Storm of Change

What sort of person would invent *sociology*? Certainly someone living in times of momentous change.

Comte (1798–1857) grew up in the shadow of the French Revolution, which brought a sweeping transformation to his country. And if that wasn't sufficient, another revolution was going on at the same time as factories were sprouting up across continental Europe, recasting the lives of the entire population. Just as people enduring a storm cannot help but think of the weather, so those living during Comte's turbulent era became keenly aware of the state of society.

Drawn from a small town by the bustle and activity of Paris, Comte was soon deeply involved in the exciting events of his time. He sought to understand the human drama that was all around him. Once equipped with knowledge of how society operates, Comte believed, people would be able to build a better future for themselves. He divided his new discipline into two parts: how society is held together (which he called *social statics*), and how society changes (*social dynamics*). From the Greek and Latin words meaning "the study of society," Comte came to describe his work as *sociology*.

Looking back in history . . . we find that no philosophers ever viewed matters [from a sociological perspective] until quite recently. . . . It seemed to them sufficient to ascertain what the human will should strive for and what it should avoid in established societies. . . . Their aim was not to offer us as valid a description of nature as possible, but to present us with the idea of a perfect society, a model to be imitated. (1972:57; orig. 1918)

What sets sociology apart from earlier social thought? Prior to the birth of sociology, philosophers and theologians mostly were concerned with imagining the ideal society. None attempted an analysis of society as it really was. Pioneers of the discipline such as Auguste Comte and Emile Durkheim reversed these priorities. Although they were certainly concerned with how human society could be improved, their major goal was to understand how society actually operates.

The key to achieving this goal, according to Comte, was the development of a scientific approach to studying society. Looking back in time, Comte sorted human efforts to comprehend society into three distinct stages (1975; orig. 1851–54). The earliest era, extending through the medieval period in Europe, he termed the *theological stage*. At this point, thoughts about the world were guided by religion.

More specifically, people regarded society as an expression of God's will—at least insofar as humans were capable of fulfilling a divine plan.

With the Renaissance, this theological approach to society gave way to what Comte called the *metaphysical stage*. During this period, people gradually came to understand society as a natural, rather than supernatural, phenomenon. Human nature figured heavily in metaphysical visions of society; the English philosopher Thomas Hobbes (1588–1679), for example, suggested that society reflected not the perfection of God as much as the failings of a rather selfish human nature.

What Comte heralded as the final, *scientific stage* in the long quest to understand society was encouraged by scientists such as the Polish astronomer Copernicus (1473–1543), the Italian astronomer and physicist Galileo[5] (1564–1642), and the English physicist and mathematician Isaac Newton (1642–1727).

---

[5]Illustrating Comte's stages, the ancient Greeks and Romans viewed the planets as gods; Renaissance thinkers saw them as astral influences (giving rise to astrology); by the time of Galileo, scientists understood planets as natural objects behaving in orderly ways.

NOTE: The artwork below, of unknown origin, characterizes the awakening of human reason and curiosity that marked the Renaissance.
NOTE: Leonardo da Vinci sketched a flying machine in the fifteenth century; however, despite his great genius (both as a painter and a scientist), the technology of his times simply would not support such a device.

Q: "O, when degree is shak'd,
Which is the ladder of all high designs,
The enterprise is sick! . . .
Take but degree away, untune that string,
And hark what discord follows!"
Shakespeare (*Troilus and Cressida*) reflecting on the erosion of the traditional feudal hierarchy.

This medieval drawing conveys the mix of apprehension and excitement with which early scientists began to question conventional understandings of the universe. Early sociologists, too, challenged many ideas that people had long taken for granted, explaining that society is neither fixed by God's will nor by human nature. On the contrary, Comte and other sociological pioneers claimed, society is a system that we can study scientifically and, based on what we learn, act deliberately to improve.

Comte's contribution came in applying this scientific approach—first used to study the physical world—to the study of society.

Comte was thus a proponent of **positivism,** defined as *a means to understand the world based on science.* As a positivist, Comte believed that society conforms to invariable laws, much like the physical world operates according to gravity and other laws of nature.

Sociology emerged as an academic discipline in the United States at the beginning of this century, with early sociologists such as Lester Ward (1841–1913) pursuing Comte's vision of a scientific sociology. Even today, most sociologists agree that science is a crucial part of sociology, but, as Chapter 2 ("Sociological Investigation") explains, we now realize that human behavior is often far more complex than events in the natural world. Put another way, human beings are more than physical objects. We are creatures with considerable imagination and spontaneity, so that our behavior can never be fully explained by any rigid "laws of society."

Social Change and Sociology

Striking transformations in eighteenth- and nineteenth-century Europe drove the development of sociology. As the social ground trembled under their feet, people understandably focused their attention on society.

First came technological discoveries that produced a factory-based industrial economy. Second, factories drew millions of people from the countryside, causing an explosive growth of cities. Third, people in these expanding industrial cities soon entertained new ideas about democracy and political rights. We shall briefly describe each of these three changes.

A New Industrial Economy

During the Middle Ages, most people in Europe tilled fields near their homes or engaged in small-scale *manufacturing* (a word derived from Latin words meaning "to make by hand"). But by the end of the eighteenth century, factories appeared as inventors applied new sources of energy—first water power and then steam power—to the operation of large machines. Now, instead of laboring at home, or in tightly knit groups, workers became part of a large and anonymous industrial work force, toiling away from home for strangers who owned the factories. This change in the system of production prompted a rapid breakdown of traditions that had guided members of small communities for centuries.

The Growth of Cities

Factories sprouting across England and elsewhere in Europe became magnets attracting people in need of work. This "pull" was accentuated by an additional "push" from the villages. As the English textile industry expanded, landowners fenced off more and more farmland to raise sheep—the source of wool. This so-called "enclosure movement" pushed countless tenant farmers from the countryside toward cities in search of work in the new factories.

Some villages were abandoned; other factory towns grew rapidly into large cities. Medieval towns had been small, self-contained worlds within defensive walls. As late as 1700—the dawning of the industrial era—London was Europe's largest city with only 500,000 people. Within two centuries, that city's population had increased by *thirteen times* to 6.5 million (Chandler & Fox, 1974).

Urban growth on this scale dramatically changed people's lives. Cities churned with strangers, in numbers that overwhelmed available housing. Widespread social problems—including poverty, disease, pollution, crime, and homelessness—were the order of the day. Such social crises further stimulated development of the sociological perspective.

Political Change

During the Middle Ages, as Comte noted, most people thought of society as an expression of divine will. Royalty claimed to rule by "divine right," as if the entire social order were simply God's plan for humanity. This belief is evident in lines from the old Anglican hymn "All Things Bright and Beautiful":

> The rich man in his castle,
> The poor man at his gate,
> He made them high and lowly
> And ordered their estate.

With economic development and the rapid growth of cities, changes in political thought were inevitable. Starting in the seventeenth century, every kind of tradition came under spirited attack. In the writings of Thomas Hobbes, John Locke (1632–1704), and Adam Smith (1723–1790), we see a shift in focus from the moral obligations of people to remain loyal to their rulers to the idea that society is the product of individual self-interest. The key phrases in the new political climate, therefore, were *individual liberty* and *individual rights*. Echoing the thoughts of Locke, our own Declaration of Independence is a clear statement of these new political ideas. Here we read that each individual has "certain unalienable rights," including "life, liberty, and the pursuit of happiness."

The political revolution in France that began soon afterward, in 1789, was an even more dramatic break with political and social traditions. As he surveyed his society after the French Revolution, the French social analyst Alexis de Tocqueville (1805–1859) exaggerated only slightly when he exclaimed that the changes we have described amounted to "nothing short of the regeneration of the whole human race" (1955:13; orig. 1856). In this context, it is easy to see why Auguste

The birth of sociology came at a time of rapid social change. The discipline developed in those regions of Europe where the Industrial Revolution most disrupted traditional ways of life, drawing people from isolated villages to rapidly growing industrial cities.

NOTE: Sociology courses were prompted by change driven by the Industrial Revolution in the United States. Williams College offered a course in social ethics in 1865; Johns Hopkins taught social science in its opening year, 1876, which was also the year William Graham Sumner taught his first sociology course at Yale; Cornell introduced a social science course in 1884; the University of Chicago founded the first formal sociology department in 1892.

Q: "[Functional] theory aims at the explanation of anthropological facts at all levels of development by their function, by the part which they play within the integral system of culture, by the manner in which they are related to each other within the system . . ." Bronislaw Malinowski

Comte and other pioneers soon developed the new discipline of sociology. Sociology flowered in precisely those societies—France, Germany, and England— where change was greatest.

Individual sociologists reacted differently to the new social order then, just as they respond differently to society today. Some found the emerging modern world to be deeply disturbing. Auguste Comte, for example, feared that people would be overpowered by change and uprooted from long-established local communities. Comte took a conservative turn, seeking a rebirth of traditional family, community, and morality.

A different view of these massive changes characterized the German social critic Karl Marx (1818–1883), whose ideas Chapter 4 ("Society") presents at length. Marx worried little about the loss of traditional social patterns, which he detested. But neither could he condone the way industrial technology concentrated its new wealth in the hands of a small elite, while the masses faced only hunger and misery.

Clearly, Comte and Marx advanced radically different views on the problems of modernity. Yet they shared the conviction that we must understand society as more than individual choice. The sociological perspective animates the work of each, revealing that people's individual lives are framed by the broader society in which they live. This lesson, of course, is as true today as it was a century ago.

The major issues that concern sociologists are featured in subsequent chapters of this book. These important social forces include culture, social class, race, ethnicity, gender, the economy, and the family. They all involve ways in which individuals are guided, united, and divided in the larger arena of society.

SOCIOLOGICAL THEORY

The task of weaving isolated observations into understanding brings us to another dimension of sociology: theory. A **theory** is *a statement of how and why specific facts are related.* Recall that Emile Durkheim observed that some categories of people (men, Protestants, the wealthy, and the unmarried) have higher suicide rates than others (women, Catholics and Jews, the poor, and the married). He explained these observations by creating a theory: A high risk of suicide results from a low level of social integration.

Of course, as Durkheim pondered the issue of suicide, he considered any number of possible theories. But merely linking facts together is no guarantee that a theory is correct. To evaluate a theory,

sociologists employ methods of scientific research, described in the next chapter, to gather evidence. Scientific facts allow sociologists to confirm some theories while rejecting or modifying others. As a scientist, Durkheim was not content merely to imagine what the cause of suicide might be; he set about collecting data to show precisely which categories of people committed suicide with the highest frequency. By poring over his data, Durkheim was able to settle on a theory that was consistent with all available evidence. Because of ongoing research, sociological theories are not set in stone; on the contrary, we refine theory as new evidence becomes available, just as other types of scientists do. National Map 1–1 on page 16, which displays the suicide rate for each of the fifty states, provides a chance to do some theorizing.

In attempting to develop theories about human society, sociologists face a wide range of choices. What issues should they study? How should they link facts together to form theories? In making sense of society, sociologists are guided by one or more general frameworks or theoretical paradigms (Kuhn, 1970). A **theoretical paradigm** is *a set of assumptions that guides thinking and research.*

We suggested earlier that two of sociology's founders—Auguste Comte and Karl Marx—made sense of the emerging modern society in different ways. Such differences persist today as some sociologists highlight how societies stay the same, while others focus on patterns of change. Similarly, some direct attention to what joins people together, while others investigate how society divides people according to gender, race, or social class. Some sociologists seek to understand the operation of society as it is, while others encourage what they view as desirable social change.

In short, sociologists often disagree about what the most interesting questions are; even when they agree about the questions, they may still differ over the answers. Nonetheless, sociological theory is far from chaotic, because sociologists utilize three major theoretical paradigms that allow them to analyze effectively virtually any dimension of society.

The Structural-Functional Paradigm

The **structural-functional paradigm** is *a framework for building theory based on the assumption that society is a complex system whose parts work together to promote stability.* As its name suggests, this paradigm leads us, first, to see society as composed of **social structure**, meaning *a relatively stable pattern of social behavior.* Social structure is what gives shape to family life,

THE MAP: The highest suicide rate for any state is Nevada (24.5 per 100,000 people), with Montana in second place (20.9). The District of Columbia is lowest (6.1). Interestingly, this pattern is almost precisely the opposite of state-by-state homicide rates.

Q: "Societies, like living bodies, begin as germs—originate from masses which are extremely minute in relation to the masses some of them eventually reach." Herbert Spencer

SOCIAL SURVEY: One indicator of contemporary attitudes on issues central to Spencer's sociology is the following GSS item: "Government should (position 1) or should not (position 7) do something to reduce income differences between rich and poor": 1, 17.4%; 2, 11.5%; 3, 19.0%; 4, 17.7%; 5, 12.3%; 6, 7.7%; 7, 12.3%; DK/NR, 2.0%. (GSS 1993, N = 1,057; Codebook, 1993:130).

Seeing Ourselves

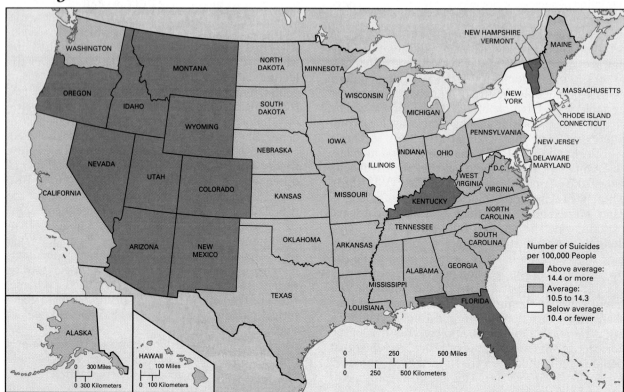

NATIONAL MAP 1–1 Suicide Rates Across the United States

This map identifies states in which suicide rates are particularly high, average, or unusually low. Look for patterns in the map. High suicide rates are common to the mountain states in which population is low and people live spread apart from one another. Low suicide rates, by contrast, characterize states that are more densely populated. Do these data support or contradict Durkheim's theory of suicide?

Prepared by the author using data from the 1990 decennial census.

behavior in the workplace, or the dynamics of a college classroom. Second, this paradigm leads us to identify each structure's **social functions**, or *consequences of the social pattern for the operation of society*. All social patterns—whether we consider family life or just a simple handshake—function to perpetuate society, at least in its present form.

The structural-functional paradigm owes much to the ideas of Auguste Comte, who sought to promote social integration during a time of dramatic change. A second architect of this theoretical approach, English sociologist Herbert Spencer (1820–1903), is introduced in the box on page 18. One of the most influential thinkers of his time, Spencer was a student of both the

human body and society. He came to see that the two have much in common. The structural parts of the human body include the skeleton, muscles, and various internal organs. All these elements are interdependent, each contributing to the survival of the entire human organism. In the same way, reasoned Spencer, various social structures are interdependent, working to keep society operating. The structural-functional approach, then, leads sociologists to identify various structures of society, investigating the function of each.

Several decades after Comte's death, Emile Durkheim continued the development of sociology in France. Like Spencer, his English counterpart, Durkheim investigated ways in which modern societies

Q: "May we not by frequent aid to the worthy render them unworthy; and are we not almost certain by helping those who are already unworthy to make them more unworthy still?" Herbert Spencer, *The Principles of Ethics* (1904)

NOTE: A positive function is also termed a *eufunction* (*eu* is the Greek prefix "good"), which contrasts to dysfunction (*dys* means "ill" or "bad").

NOTE: Another dysfunction of American auto-mania: 45,000 auto-related deaths annually.

NOTE: While Comte thought we should study laws of society in order to be more effective in our interventions, Spencer contended that once we understood society we would conclude such intervention to be pointless and typically destructive.

remain integrated. Because of the importance of his ideas to many later chapters, Durkheim's structural-functional analysis is detailed in Chapter 4 ("Society").

As sociology developed in the United States, the approach of Herbert Spencer and Emile Durkheim was carried forward by Talcott Parsons (1902–1979). The major proponent of the structural-functional paradigm in U.S. sociology, Parsons treated society as a system, seeking to identify the major tasks any and all societies have to perform to survive and ways they accomplish them.

A contemporary U.S. sociologist whose work falls within the structural-functional approach, Robert K. Merton has shown that social patterns have differing consequences for various members of a society. For example, conventional families may accomplish important tasks such as childbearing, but they also limit the opportunities of women.

Merton (1968) also notes that some functions of any social pattern are more obvious than others. The **manifest functions** of any social structure are *the recognized and intended consequences of any social pattern.* By contrast, **latent functions** are *consequences that are largely unrecognized and unintended.* To illustrate, consider the rapid increase of motor vehicles during this century. One manifest function of this new technology is to expand the economy by allowing more efficient transportation of goods from one place to another. Another manifest function of cars is to serve as *status symbols*, since we sometimes judge people's social standing by the things they own. But the rise of automobile transportation also has significant latent functions. Because they allow people to travel about in relative isolation, cars reinforce our national emphasis on personal autonomy. This reinforcement is one reason that private automobiles have long been favored by most people over public transit systems.

Merton makes a further point: It is unlikely that *all* the effects of a single social structure will be useful. Merton used the term **social dysfunctions** to designate *undesirable consequences of any social pattern for the operation of society.* One of the dysfunctions of our society's reliance on some 200 million motor vehicles, highlighted in Chapter 22 ("The Natural Environment"), is the effect on air quality, which is especially poor in large cities. No doubt, too, easy travel made possible by cars has undermined the strength of traditional families and local neighborhoods, changes lamented by many people in the United States.

Critical evaluation. The positivist roots of the structural-functional paradigm are evident in this approach's tendency to see the social world as stable and orderly.

The spirit of the structural-functional paradigm is conveyed by the painting I and the Village, *completed in 1911 by Russian-American artist Marc Chagall (1881–1985). Here, recalling the tightly integrated Russian villages of his youth, Chagall conveys the essential unity of human beings who share a social setting; he also suggests that human society is bound up with the natural world.*

Marc Chagall, *I and the Village,* 1911. Oil on canvas, 63 5/8 x 59 5/8 inches. The Museum of Modern Art, New York. Mrs. Simon Guggenheim Fund.

The job of sociologists, from this point of view, is to employ scientific research to learn how society works.

Despite its strong influence on the discipline of sociology, however, recent decades have revealed limitations of the structural-functional paradigm. By assuming that society operates more or less "naturally," critics point out, structural-functionalism tends to overlook how social patterns vary from place to place and change over time. Thus, the notion that any particular arrangement is natural seems hazardous at best. Further, by emphasizing social integration, structural-functionalism tends to pay less attention to divisions based on social class, race, ethnicity, and gender and to downplay how such divisions often generate tension and conflict. This focus on social

NOTE: Herbert Spencer was influenced by Thomas Robert Malthus (whose thesis on population is discussed in Chapter 21). He was a friend of industrialist Andrew Carnegie. Spencer wrote the first textbook in sociology, *Principles of Sociology*, in 1879 as part of a larger philosophical treatise.

Q: "...the money-strong represent, in some sense, the survival of the fittest—not necessarily the best. That is, their success, certainly no guarantee of righteousness, does prove a certain adaptation to conditions. . . . They are not necessarily the ablest in other regards, since only certain kinds of ability count in making money; other kinds . . . being even a hindrance. Men of genius will seldom shine in this way, because as a rule, only a somewhat commonplace mind will give itself whole-heartedly to the commercial trade." Charles Horton Cooley

PROFILE

Herbert Spencer: The Survival of the Fittest

The most memorable idea of the English philosopher Herbert Spencer (1820–1903) was his assertion that the passing of time witnesses "the survival of the fittest." Many people associate this immortal phrase with the theory of species evolution developed by the natural scientist Charles Darwin (1809–1882). The idea was actually Spencer's, however, and when he expressed it, he was referring to society, not to living creatures. But this confusion over Spencer's remark suggests how deeply early sociological thought was influenced by comparisons between the social and natural worlds.

Spencer's view of society, which came to be known as *social Darwinism*, was built on the following principle: Success would come to the most intelligent, ambitious, and productive people, while those less able would fall behind. This "survival of the fittest," claimed Spencer, would steadily improve society by favoring its best members.

Positive social evolution, from Spencer's point of view, would take place naturally, that is, providing people did not meddle with a free-market economy. For this opinion, nineteenth-century industrialists widely applauded Spencer. Indeed, John D. Rockefeller, who gobbled up companies to gain control of much of the U.S. oil industry, often recited Spencer's words to young children in Sunday school, teaching them to think of the growth of giant businesses as merely the "survival of the fittest."

But others objected to the idea that society was nothing more than a selfish jungle. Critics of Spencer clamored for social welfare programs that would assist the new industrial poor. But Spencer responded that welfare damaged society by favoring its least worthy members.

Gradually, Spencer's doctrine of social Darwinism fell out of favor among social scientists, although it remains influential among many people in this country. From a sociological point of view, Spencer's thinking represents only a partial explanation of personal success, and favoring the rich and powerful does not necessarily benefit society as a whole. In addition, Spencer's ideas seem to many people to be a view of society with little room for human compassion.

stability at the expense of conflict and change gives the structural-functional paradigm a conservative character. As a critical response to this approach, sociologists have developed another theoretical orientation: the social-conflict paradigm.

The Social-Conflict Paradigm

The **social-conflict paradigm** is *a framework for building theory based on the assumption that society is characterized by inequality and conflict that generate change.* This approach complements the structural-functional paradigm by highlighting not integration but division based on social inequality. Guided by this paradigm, sociologists investigate how factors such as social class, race, ethnicity, sex, and age are linked to unequal distribution of money, power, education, and social prestige. Therefore, rather than identifying how social structure promotes the operation of society as a whole, this approach focuses on how these patterns benefit some people while being harmful to others. One of the pioneering U.S. sociologists, whose work was framed by a concern for racial conflict, is introduced in the box on page 20.

The social-conflict paradigm leads sociologists to view society as an arena in which people's incompatible interests fuel conflict. Not surprisingly, dominant categories—the rich in relation to the poor,

GLOBAL: Herbert Spencer's writings were translated into Chinese in 1895; the first sociology course in the People's Republic of China was offered in 1906 (see Dai Kejing, 1993).

NOTE: Two sources for the history of American sociology: Albion Small, "Fifty Years of Sociology in the United States," *American Journal of Sociology* 21, 6 (May 1916):721–864; Robert E. L. Faris, *Chicago Sociology 1920–1932*, University of Chicago Press, 1967.

Q: "The most valid procedure with a historical thinker of this kind is not to try to have sport with his marginal failings but to rescue whatever is viable by cutting out what has proved wrong, tempering what is overstated, tightening what is loosely put, and setting the whole in its proper place among usable perspectives." Richard Hofstadter (referring to Herbert Spencer, but the comment could be applied to Marx or many other thinkers)

whites in relation to people of color, and men in relation to women—typically try to protect their privileges by supporting the status quo. Those with fewer privileges commonly counter these efforts by attempting to increase their share of social resources.

To illustrate, Chapter 19 ("Education") explains how secondary schools in the United States prepare some students for college and emphasize vocational training for others. A structural-functional analysis might lead us to consider how society as a whole benefits from "tracking" students according to their academic abilities. The social-conflict paradigm supports the contrasting argument that "tracking" confers privileges on some that it denies to others, so that schools operate to perpetuate social inequality.

Research guided by the social-conflict paradigm has shown that schools place students in college-preparatory tracks not just because of their intelligence but based on the privileged background of their families. Once ensured of becoming part of the educational elite with a college degree, most go on to occupations that confer both prestige and high income. By contrast, schools generally fill vocational tracks with students of modest backgrounds, sometimes with little regard for their actual potential. There they receive no preparation for college, and, thus, like their parents before them, they typically enter low-paying jobs. In both cases, the social standing of one generation is passed on to another, with schools justifying the practice in terms of alleged individual merit (Bowles & Gintis, 1976; Oakes, 1982, 1985).

Social conflict in the United States is not, of course, limited to schools. Our history contains many episodes of strife between labor and management, movements for change facing off against counter-movements, and the struggle for equality on the part of people of color, women, and others whom society has disadvantaged. In each such case, the social-conflict paradigm points up how social structure fosters not stability but conflict between the forces of change and those seeking to maintain the status quo.

Finally, many sociologists who embrace the social-conflict paradigm attempt not only to understand society but to reduce social inequality. This was the goal of W. E. B. Du Bois, and also Karl Marx, the social thinker who has had a singularly important influence upon the development of the social-conflict paradigm. Marx had little patience with those who sought merely to understand how society works. In a well-known declaration (inscribed on his monument in London's Highgate Cemetery), Marx asserted: "The philosophers have only interpreted the world, in various ways; the point, however, is to change it."

Critical evaluation. The social-conflict paradigm has developed rapidly in recent decades. Yet, like other approaches, it has come in for its share of criticism. Because this paradigm highlights power struggles, it gives little attention to people's unity based on interdependence and shared values. In addition, say critics, insofar as the social-conflict approach advocates explicitly political goals, it gives up any claim to

There are various types of social-conflict theories, all of which illuminate ways in which society is organized to benefit some categories of people at the expense of others. In the painting Our Gang *(1886), we see Joseph Decker's keen awareness that skin color places some people in positions of dominance while transforming others into marginal members of society. Notice how the artist has placed the African-American boy with his back against a wall, which is, in turn, covered with posters that seem to point at him like fingers of accusation. (In fact, Decker originally named this painting* The Accused, *as if to say that color alone can stand as a social crime.)*

PROFILE

W. E. B. Du Bois: Sociology as Problem Solving

One of sociology's pioneers, who has not received the attention he deserves, is William Edward Burghardt Du Bois (1868–1963). Born to a poor Massachusetts family, Du Bois showed extraordinary aptitude as a student. After graduating from high school, he went to college, one of only a handful of the young people of his town (and the only person of African descent) to do so. After graduating from Fisk University in Nashville, Tennessee, Du Bois realized a childhood ambition by enrolling at Harvard, where he earned the first doctorate awarded by that university to a person of color.

Du Bois believed sociologists should direct their efforts to contemporary problems, and for him the vexing issue of race was the paramount concern. Although he was accepted in the intellectual circles of his day, Du Bois believed that African Americans and whites lived in separate social worlds. This contention led Du Bois to help found the National Association for the Advancement of Colored People (NAACP). As a sociologist, Du Bois maintained that research—although scientifically rigorous and fair-minded—should attempt to answer questions that would improve society.

After taking a position at the University of Pennsylvania in Philadelphia, Du Bois produced a sociological classic, *The Philadelphia Negro: A Social Study* (1899). In this systematic investigation of Philadelphia's African-American community at the turn of the century, Du Bois rejected the widespread notion of black inferiority, attributing the problems of blacks in the United States largely to white prejudice. He was critical not only of whites but also of successful people of color, whom he scolded for being so eager to win white acceptance that they abandoned all ties with those still in need. "The first impulse of the best, the wisest and the richest," he lamented, "is to segregate themselves from the mass" (1899:317).

At the time he wrote *The Philadelphia Negro*, Du Bois was optimistic about overcoming racial division in the United States. By the end of his life, however, he had grown bitter that so little had changed. At the age of ninety-three, Du Bois emigrated to Africa, and he died in Ghana two years later.

Although his research was not widely read at the time of his death, today Du Bois's books are receiving the attention of a new generation of scholars. A model of sound sociology, his work addresses many of the problems that continue to beset our society.

SOURCES: Based, in part, on Baltzell (1967) and Du Bois (1967; orig. 1899).

scientific objectivity. As Chapter 2 ("Sociological Investigation") explains in detail, advocates of this approach respond that *all* social approaches have political consequences, albeit different ones.

An additional criticism, which applies equally to both the structural-functional and social-conflict paradigms, is that they paint society with broad strokes, describing our lives as a composite of "family," "social class," and so on. A third theoretical paradigm views society less in terms of abstract generalizations and more in terms of everyday, face-to-face interaction.

The Symbolic-Interaction Paradigm

Both the structural-functional and social-conflict paradigms share a **macro-level orientation,** meaning *a focus on broad social structures that characterize society as a whole.* They take in the big picture, rather like observing a city from high above in a helicopter, taking note of how highways carry traffic from place to place, and of the striking contrasts between rich and poor neighborhoods. The symbolic-interaction paradigm differs by providing a **micro-level orientation,**

NOTE: Herbert Blumer first used the term "symbolic interaction-ism" in 1937.

NOTE: Harriet Martineau's lifelong activism was guided by a Comptean view of the world as comprehensible and changeable. Her achievements are all the more impressive in light of her almost total deafness from the age of about twelve.

Q: "Theories should be as simple as possible, but not more so." Albert Einstein

Q: "Serious differences among social scientists occur not between those who would observe without thinking and those who would think without observing; the differences have rather to do with what kinds of thinking, what kinds of observing, and what kinds of links, if any, there are between the two." C. Wright Mills

Many women contributed to the emergence of sociology, although their achievements have long been unrecognized. Harriet Martineau (1802–1876) (left), born to a rich English family, translated the writings of Auguste Comte from French in 1853. Soon afterward, she established her own reputation as a sociologist with studies of slavery, factory laws, and women's rights. In the United States, Jane Addams (1860–1935) (right) was a social worker known for her public activism on behalf of poor immigrants to this country. In 1889, Addams founded Hull House, a Chicago settlement house, in a poor, inner-city neighborhood. There, she engaged with intellectuals and immigrants alike in discussions of the pressing problems of her day. Her contribution to the welfare of others earned Addams a Nobel Peace Prize in 1931.

meaning *a focus on patterns of social interaction in specific situations.* Exploring urban life in this way occurs at street level, and might involve observing how friends interact in public parks or how pedestrians respond to homeless people. The **symbolic-interaction paradigm,** then, is *a theoretical framework based on the assumption that society is the product of the everyday interactions of individuals.*

How do millions of people weave their lives together into the drama of society? One answer, detailed in Chapter 6 ("Social Interaction in Everyday Life"), is that we become linked to one another through the reality we construct in countless social situations. Occasionally, humans respond to others in direct, physical terms, as when someone ducks to avoid a punch. But mostly we respond to each other in terms of the meaning we attach to objects and events. Through this process of constructing meaning, we define our identities, rights, and obligations toward others.

Notice, too, that the process of reality construction is highly variable. For example, one person may define a homeless man on a city street as "just a bum looking for a handout" and ignore him. Another, however, might define him as a "fellow human being in need" and offer assistance. In the same way, one pedestrian may respond to a police officer walking nearby with a sense of security, while another may be overcome with a feeling of nervous anxiety. Sociologists guided by the symbolic-interaction approach view society as a mosaic of subjective meanings and responses.

The symbolic-interaction paradigm rests, in part, on the thinking of Max Weber (1864–1920), a German sociologist who emphasized the need to understand a setting from the point of view of the people

in it. Weber's approach is presented at length in Chapter 4 ("Society").

On this foundation, others have devised a number of specific approaches to learning about social life. Chapter 5 ("Socialization") discusses the ideas of U.S. sociologist George Herbert Mead (1863–1931), who traces the roots of human personality to social experience. Chapter 6 ("Social Interaction in Everyday Life") presents the work of Erving Goffman (1922–1982), whose *dramaturgical analysis* emphasizes how we resemble actors on a stage as we play out our various roles before others. Other contemporary sociologists, including George Homans and Peter Blau, have developed *social-exchange analysis.* In their view, social interaction is guided by what each individual stands to gain and lose from others. Chapter 17 ("Family") applies this approach to the process of courtship, explaining that people typically seek mates who offer at least as much—in terms of physical attractiveness, intelligence, and social background—as they provide in return.

Critical evaluation. The social-interaction paradigm helps to overcome a limitation typical of macro-level approaches to understanding society. Without denying the reality of social structures such as "the family" and "social class," we must remember that society basically amounts to *people interacting.* Put another way, this micro-approach helps convey more of how individuals actually experience society.

For just this reason, however, the symbolic-interaction paradigm sometimes leads to the error of ignoring larger social structure. Highlighting what is unique in each social scene risks overlooking the widespread effects of our culture as well as factors such as class, gender, and race.

SOCIAL SURVEY: The importance of a person's race "to getting ahead in life" (GSS 1987, N = 1,564; *Codebook*, 1993:585):

"Essential" 1.9%   "Not very important" 33.7%
"Very important" 12.0%   "Not important at all" 22.3%
"Fairly important" 23.9% DK/NR 6.2%

SOCIAL SURVEY: "How do people get ahead?" (*CHIP1 Social Survey Software*, GETAHEAD1; GSS 1973–89, N = 14,633)

	Hard work	Luck/Help	Both
Whites	65.1%	11.7%	23.2%
Hispanics	63.7%	15.6%	20.7%
Afri Amer	57.4%	15.7%	26.9%

The essential insight of the symbolic-interaction paradigm is that, as people engage one another, they build social reality. In her portrayals of Latin-American women, including Hat Dance, '91, *Canadian artist Irene Klar suggests that we all derive our identity, not from within, but from others with whom we interact.*

Table 1–1 summarizes the important characteristics of the structural-functional paradigm, the social-conflict paradigm, and the symbolic-interaction paradigm. As we have explained, certain kinds of questions suggest the use of one or another particular paradigm. By and large, however, the greatest benefits come from linking the sociological perspective to all three, as we shall now illustrate with an analysis of sports in the United States.

Sports: Three Theoretical Paradigms in Action

To North Americans, sports seem indispensable. Almost everyone has engaged in some type of sport, from gym classes throughout the school years to recreational sports by young adults to fitness programs for elderly people. In the United States, men and women regularly flock to sporting events, and the sale of sporting goods is a multibillion-dollar industry. Television carries sports into millions of living rooms as part of newscasts as well as regular programming that averages more than three hours a day (Coakley, 1990).

What insights can the sociological perspective provide about this familiar element of our way of life? Each of the three major theoretical paradigms in sociology contributes part of the answer.

The Functions of Sports

A structural-functional approach directs attention to ways in which sports help society to operate. The manifest functions of sports include providing recreation, physical conditioning, and a relatively harmless way to "let off steam." Sports have important latent functions as well, from fostering social relationships to generating tens of thousands of jobs. Perhaps most important, sports encourage specific attitudes and behavior that are central to our way of life.

Learning to be a team player and to play by the rules are social skills developed through playing or even watching sports. Sports also capture the personal effort and discipline essential to success in other areas of life. Moreover, sports generate the keen sense of competition that members of our individualistic society value so much in celebrating a "winner" (Spates, 1976a; Coakley, 1990). When he said, "Winning is not everything, but making the effort to win is," coach Vince Lombardi was speaking not only about football; he was also defending our culture.

Sports also have dysfunctional consequences, of course. For example, colleges and universities intent on fielding winning teams may recruit students for their athletic ability rather than for their academic aptitude. This emphasis can adversely affect the academic standards of the school and leave the athletes themselves little time to learn anything but their sport. Len Bias, a University of Maryland basketball star who died tragically from a cocaine overdose in 1986, earned no academic credits during his last semester—a situation far from rare among athletes who must practice from four to five hours a day (Bingham, 1987). The tragedy of Len Bias takes on added significance since he was part of the 1 percent of male college players who earn a professional sports contract. For too many others, the long-term benefits of attending college turn out to be minimal.

In sum, the structural-functional paradigm suggests that sports contribute in a variety of ways to the

NOTE: In global perspective, societies that place little emphasis on personal competition (People's Republic of China) engage in few of the aggressive sports popular in North America. Anthropologists have also found that aggressive sports are favored by warlike peoples more than by those who are more peaceful (Sipes, 1973).

NOTE: The odds of a high school athlete joining a professional sports team is roughly 10,000:1.

DATA FILE: Information on the field of sports sociology is found in the *Data File*.

DIVERSITY: In 1993, fifteen head coaches or managers in the major professional sports were African American or Latino. The percent of minority head coaches or managers by sport is: National Basketball Association, 26 percent; Major League Baseball, 21 percent; National Football League, 11 percent.

operation of our society. Most important, perhaps, sports serve to symbolize our competitive and success-oriented way of life.

Sports and Conflict

A social-conflict analysis of sports begins by pointing out that sports are closely related to patterns of social inequality. Some sports—including tennis, swimming, golf, and skiing—are expensive, which limits participation to more affluent people. By contrast, the sports with mass appeal—football, baseball, and basketball—are those accessible to people at all income levels. In short, the games people play are not simply a matter of choice; they reflect patterns of economic inequality.

In the United States, sports are also oriented toward males. Our society has long limited the opportunities of females in most sports, even when they have the talent, interest, and economic means to participate. The first modern Olympic Games held in 1896, for example, excluded women from competition entirely (Mangan & Park, 1987). Until quite recently, Little League teams in most parts of the country also barred girls. Such exclusion has been defended by ungrounded notions that girls and women lack the ability to engage in sports or risk losing their femininity if they do so. Joan Benoit, a gold medalist marathon runner in the 1984 Olympic Games, conceded that becoming a serious athlete seemed somehow "wrong" for a woman: "When I first started running I was so embarrassed I'd walk when cars passed me. I'd pretend I was looking at the flowers" (quoted in Coakley, 1986:115).

Thus our society encourages males to be athletes while expecting females to be attentive observers and cheerleaders. About twice the share of male high school seniors claim to be active in sports (57 percent) compared to senior females (31 percent) (U.S. Congress, 1989). But the fitness movement and political efforts by women are reducing this inequity. The number of high school women in sports programs shot up from 300,000 in 1970 to more than 2 million today. In addition, more women than ever before now play professionally, and women's sports enjoy growing spectator interest. Still, women continue to take a back seat to men in professional sports—particularly in those that provide the most earnings and social prestige.

Although our society traditionally excluded people of color as well from "big league" sports, the opportunity to earn a high income in athletics has expanded greatly in recent decades. Professional baseball was the first major U.S. sport to admit African-American players, when Jackie Robinson broke the "color line" in 1947. By 1993, African Americans (12 percent of the U.S. population) accounted for 17 percent of Major League Baseball players, 68 percent of National Football League (NFL) players, and 77 percent of

TABLE 1–1 The Three Major Theoretical Paradigms: A Summary

Theoretical Paradigm	Orientation	Image of Society	Illustrative Questions
Structural-functional	Macro-level	A system of interrelated parts that is relatively stable based on widespread consensus as to what is morally desirable; each part has functional consequences for the operation of society as a whole	How is society integrated? What are the major parts of society? How are these parts interrelated? What are the consequences of each for the operation of society?
Social-conflict	Macro-level	A system characterized by social inequality; each part of society benefits some categories of people more than others; conflict-based social inequality promotes social change	How is society divided? What are major patterns of social inequality? How do some categories of people attempt to protect their privileges? How do other categories of people challenge the status quo?
Symbolic-interaction	Micro-level	An ongoing process of social interaction in specific settings based on symbolic communications; individual perceptions of reality are variable and changing	How is society experienced? How do human beings interact to create, sustain, and change social patterns? How do individuals attempt to shape the reality perceived by others? How does individual behavior change from one situation to another?

NOTE: Average salaries for players in the major sports have risen rapidly in recent decades. Basketball players were the highest-paid players in 1970 (averaging $180,000); by 1993, this figure had risen to about $800,000. Average earnings for baseball players has soared from $29,000 in 1970 to more than $1 million today; football earnings from $23,000 in 1970 to about $400,000.

DIVERSITY: Average salary in Major League Baseball by race/ethnicity: African Americans, $1,051,696; Latins (born out of U.S.), $873,581; whites, $867,476; Hispanic Americans, $552,887 (Center for Study of Sport in Society, 1991). Sommers (1990) concludes pay differentials reflect performance differences and not categorical discrimination.

The painting Strike, *by contemporary African-American artist Jacob Lawrence, suggests that baseball is more than mere diversion and entertainment. Like all sports, baseball provides valuable lessons about how members of our society expect one another to think and to behave.*

Jacob Lawrence, *Strike*, 1949. Tempera on masonite, 20 x 24 inches. The Howard University Gallery of Art (Permanent Collection), Washington, D.C.

National Basketball Association (NBA) players (Center for the Study of Sport in Society, 1993).

The increasing proportion of people of African descent in professional sports is largely due to the fact that individual athletic performances can be measured precisely. For this reason, white prejudice cannot easily diminish the achievement of minority athletes. It is also true that many people of color make a particular effort to excel in athletics, where they recognize greater opportunity than in other kinds of careers (Steele, 1990). In recent years, in fact, African-American athletes have earned higher salaries than white players. Nonetheless, racial discrimination still taints professional sports in the United States almost fifty years after Jackie Robinson's achievement. In 1992, for example, racial slurs by Cincinnati Reds owner Marge Schott prompted a national debate over the continued presence of racism in professional sports. And, just as important, while people of color are now common as players, most managers, head coaches, and owners of sports teams are still white.

Taking a wider view, who gains the greatest benefits from professional sports? Although millions of fans follow the teams, the vast earnings they generate are controlled by the small number of people (predominantly white men) for whom teams are income-generating property. In the last decade or so, professional athletes have gained a larger share of what their teams earn. By the early 1990s, for example, Major League

Baseball players' salaries accounted for more than half of all baseball revenues, and the average annual player's salary had climbed to $1 million, some thirty times higher than the average in 1970, and far above the salaries of baseball's past greats like Babe Ruth. Even so, team owners (all but 4 of 195 owners in the three major sports are white) oversee a huge business operation that controls a vast national audience (Leifer, 1990; Center for the Study of Sport in Society, 1993).

In sum, the social-conflict paradigm analyzes professional sports in terms of differences of wealth and power. As noted earlier, sports may reflect the importance of competition and achievement in our society, but they are also bound up with extensive social inequality.

Sports as Interaction

At the macro-level, a sporting event appears to be a formal system; at the micro-level, however, it is a complex drama of face-to-face interaction. In part, participants' behavior reflects their assigned positions, and, of course, everyone takes account of the rules of the game. Players are also spontaneous, however, so that we can never predict the precise outcome of a contest. Informed by the symbolic-interaction paradigm, then, we see sports less as a system than as an ongoing process.

From this point of view, too, we expect each player to understand the game a little differently.

NOTE: In Major League Baseball, player salaries (which average more than $1 million annually) now consume more than half of all revenues. The fact that both attendance and viewership have been flat markets in recent years has pinched owners, and half of the 26 teams have reported losing money at least one year since 1991.

DIVERSITY: As the percentage of African Americans in professional sports grows, some whites experience racial prejudice in the form of a "white men can't jump" syndrome. Says Matt Godlewski of Ft. Lauderdale's Boyd Anderson High: "'For a white guy, you're a pretty good runner.' These words are spoken to me nearly every day by people of all races."

NOTE: Los Angeles County produces more major league players than all states outside of California combined. Apparently this is due to the region's mild climate and athletic culture.

Some players, for example, thrive in a setting of stiff competition, playing the game simply for the thrill of winning. For others, however, love[6] of the game may be greater than the need for victory. Such people may actually perform less well under pressure. Still others use sports as a means to build personal friendships; they may avoid competition for fear that it will alienate people from one another (Coakley, 1986).

Beyond different attitudes toward competition, team members will also shape their particular realities according to the various prejudices, jealousies, and ambitions they bring to the field. Then, too, the behavior of any single player is likely to change over time. A rookie in professional baseball often feels quite self-conscious during the first few games in the big leagues. Eventually, however, a comfortable sense of fitting in with the team usually emerges. Coming to feel at home on the field was slow and painful for Jackie Robinson, who was initially only too aware that many white players, and millions of white fans, resented his presence in Major League Baseball (Tygiel, 1983). In time, however, his outstanding performance and his confident and cooperative manner off the field won him the respect of the entire nation.

In spite of varied motives and perceptions, we expect each player to display team spirit and other elements of good sportsmanship. Most of us also think athletes should stand for the ideals of honesty, hard work, and, above all, the will to win. In reality, of course, many fall quite short of these ideals. During the last decade, scandals have linked professional athletes with illegal drugs, prompting programs of mandatory drug testing. The ideal image of the athlete was also shaken in 1989 by the withdrawal from baseball of Cincinnati Reds manager Pete Rose. A model athlete who earned the nickname "Charlie Hustle," Rose engaged for years in gambling, in violation of the rules of Major League Baseball.

The three theoretical paradigms certainly offer different insights, but none is more correct than the others. Applied to any issue, each paradigm generates its own interpretations so that, to fully appreciate the sociological perspective, you should become familiar with all three. Together, they stimulate fascinating debates and controversies, many of which are covered in the chapters that follow.

---

[6]The ancient Romans recognized this fact, evident in our word "amateur," literally "lover," which designates one who engages in some activity for the sheer love of it.

SUMMARY

1. The sociological perspective shows that our individual lives are shaped by society. This point of view may be described as "seeing the general in the particular."

2. Because people in the United States see events in terms of individual choice, the impact of society on our lives often goes unrecognized. Therefore, looking sociologically at our lives initially seems like "seeing the strange in the familiar."

3. Emile Durkheim's research demonstrating that suicide rates are higher among some categories of people than others shows that society affects even the most personal of our actions.

4. Global awareness is an important dimension of the sociological perspective. Thinking globally is important, first, because societies of the world increasingly are interconnected; second, because many social problems are most serious beyond the borders of the United States; and, third, because thinking globally helps us learn more about ourselves.

5. The sociological perspective sometimes arises naturally, as when we enter an unfamiliar setting. Similarly, socially marginal people are more likely than others to perceive the effects of society. For everyone, periods of social crisis foster sociological thinking.

6. There are four general benefits to using the sociological perspective. First, it challenges our familiar understandings of the world, helping us to separate fact from fiction; second, it helps us to appreciate the opportunities and constraints that frame our lives; third, it encourages more active participation in society; fourth, it increases our awareness of social diversity in the United States and in the world as a whole.

NOTE: The number of bachelor's degrees in sociology peaked at 35,996 in 1973; it dropped to 14,939 in 1989 and has been rising slowly since then.
Q: "The social elements of human behavior are present any time that two or more people encounter one another." Pitirim Sorokin

Q: "I cannot see that lectures can do so much good as reading the books from which the lectures are taken." English social critic Samuel Johnson

7. Auguste Comte gave sociology its name in 1838. Whereas previous social thought focused on what society ought to be, Comte's new discipline of sociology employed scientific methods to understand society as it is.

8. Sociology emerged as a reaction to the rapid transformation of Europe during the eighteenth and nineteenth centuries. Three dimensions of change—the rise of an industrial economy, the explosive growth of cities, and the emergence of new political ideas—together directed attention to the operation of society.

9. Theory involves linking insights to explain social life. Various theoretical paradigms guide sociologists as they construct theories.

10. The structural-functional paradigm is a framework for exploring how social structures promote the stability and integration of society. This approach minimizes the importance of social inequality, conflict, and change.

11. The social-conflict paradigm highlights social inequality, which often generates conflict and change. At the same time, this approach minimizes the extent of society's integration and stability.

12. In contrast to these broad, macro-level approaches, the symbolic-interaction paradigm is a micro-level framework that focuses on face-to-face interaction in specific settings.

13. Each of the three major theoretical paradigms provides important insights about the character of sports. The structural-functional paradigm emphasizes that sports reinforce the individualism and competition central to our way of life. The social-conflict paradigm links sports to patterns of social inequality. The symbolic-interaction paradigm portrays sports as the interplay of individuals who find various purpose and meaning in their actions.

14. Because each paradigm highlights different dimensions of any social issue, the richest sociological understanding is derived from applying all three.

KEY CONCEPTS

global perspective the study of the larger world and our society's place in it

latent functions consequences of any social pattern that are unrecognized and unintended

least-developed countries societies with little industrialization in which severe poverty is the rule

less-developed countries societies characterized by limited industrialization and moderate-to-low personal income

macro-level orientation a focus on broad social structures that characterize society as a whole

manifest functions the recognized and intended consequences of any social pattern

micro-level orientation a focus on patterns of social interaction in specific situations

most-developed countries relatively rich, industrialized societies

positivism understanding the world based on science

social-conflict paradigm a framework for building theory based on the assumption that society is characterized by inequality and conflict that generate change

social dysfunction the undesirable consequences of any social pattern for the operation of society

social function the consequences of any social pattern for the operation of society

social marginality the state of being excluded from social activity as an "outsider"

social structure a relatively stable pattern of social behavior

sociology the scientific study of human society

structural-functional paradigm a framework for building theory based on the assumption that society is a complex system whose parts work together to promote stability

symbolic-interaction paradigm a theoretical framework based on the assumption that society is the product of the countless everyday interactions of individuals

theoretical paradigm a set of assumptions that guides thinking and research

theory a statement of how and why specific facts are related

CRITICAL-THINKING QUESTIONS

1. In what ways does using the sociological perspective make us seem less in control of our lives? In what ways does it give us greater power over our surroundings?

2. What changes does sociological thinking produce in how you understand your own biography?

3. Provide a sociological explanation of why sociology developed where and when it did.

4. Guided by the discipline's three major theoretical paradigms, what kinds of questions might a sociologist ask about (a) gender, (b) war, (c) humor, and (d) the mass media?

SUGGESTED READINGS

Classic Sources

C. Wright Mills. *The Sociological Imagination*. New York: Oxford University Press, 1959.
   This classic elaborates on the benefits of learning to think sociologically and links this perspective to the possibilities for social activism.

Peter Berger. *An Invitation to Sociology*. Garden City, N.Y.: Anchor Books, 1963.
   Berger's readable classic account of the sociological perspective highlights its value for enhancing human freedom.

W. E. B. Du Bois. *The Philadelphia Negro: A Social Study*. New York: Schocken Books, 1967.
   Worth reading is W. E. B. Du Bois's classic study of the African-American community in Philadelphia.

Contemporary Sources

John J. Macionis and Nijole V. Benokraitis, eds. *Seeing Ourselves: Classic, Contemporary, and Cross-Cultural Readings in Sociology*. 3d ed. Englewood Cliffs, N.J.: Prentice Hall, 1995.
   The new edition of the companion reader to this text is enlarged, providing seventy-five edited readings that follow the chapter flow of this book. For each topic, find classic essays by sociology's "greats," articles on contemporary issues and research, and cross-cultural perspectives.

Robert C. Bannister. *Jessie Bernard: The Making of A Feminist*. New Brunswick, N.J.: Rutgers University Press, 1991.
   This account of one of sociology's leaders in this century explores the link between society and biography and also highlights the development of feminism in sociology.

Ellen Fitzpatrick. *Endless Crusade: Women Social Scientists and Progressive Reform*. New York: Oxford University Press, 1990.
   This account of the origins of social science in the United States traces the careers of four women whose fascination with society was coupled to a passion for reform.

John Henrik Clarke, ed. *Marcus Garvey and the Vision of Africa*. New York: Vintage, 1990.
   This collection of essays by and about Marcus Garvey explains the life and times of this leader of the African-American community.

Jay J. Coakley. *Sport in Society: Issues and Controversies*. 5th ed. St. Louis: Times Mirror/Mosby College Publishing, 1994.
   A comprehensive sociological analysis of sports is found in this paperback.

Careers in Sociology. Washington, D.C.: American Sociological Association.

Bettina J. Huber. *Career Possibilities for Sociology Graduates*. Washington, D.C.: American Sociological Association.
   These two publications describing career possibilities in sociology are available free from the American Sociological Association, 1722 N Street NW, Washington, D.C. 20036.

Global Sources

Mike Featherstone. *Global Culture: Nationalism, Globalization and Modernity*. Newbury Park, Calif.: Sage, 1991.

Roland Robertson. *Globalization: Social Theory and Global Culture*. Newbury Park, Calif.: Sage, 1992.
   These two books provide a sophisticated overview of the process of globalization. The first, a collection of two dozen essays, explains the importance of global thinking to members of our society. The second offers one analyst's reflections on the meanings of globalization for our society as well as for sociology.

Donald M. Snow. *Distant Thunder: Third-World Conflict and the New International Order*. New York: St. Martin's Press, 1992.
   This author claims that the poverty of least-developed nations now represents the key source of international instability and the greatest threat to the peace of our world.

Jack Levine, *On the Block*, 1986–1992. Oil on canvas, 72 x 63 inches. Midtown Payson Galleries, New York.

DATA FILE: An annotated outline of Chapter 2 and other teaching material is in the *Data File*.

Q: "Information is difference that makes a difference." Gregory Bateson

Q: "It is the essence of the human mind to take apart what experience presents as a whole." Peter Berger

Q: "Philosophers know very little about what is very important; scientists know a great deal about what is far less worth knowing." E. Digby Baltzell

Q: "From my earliest years, I have accepted many false opinions as true." René Descartes

Q: "It is the pursuit of truth that gives us life, and it is to that pursuit that our loyalty is due." William Graham Sumner

Sociological Investigation

While on a visit to Atlanta during the holiday season at the close of 1984, sociologist Lois Benjamin (1991) paid a call to the mother of an old friend from college. Benjamin was anxious to learn what had become of her friend, a woman she refers to simply as Sheba. In college, both women had shared a dream of earning a graduate degree, finding a teaching position, and writing books. Benjamin was proud that her dream of living in the world of ideas had come true. But as she soon found out, such was not the case for Sheba.

There had been early signs of trouble. Benjamin recalled that Sheba's world had gradually unraveled after finishing college. Enrolling in a graduate program in Canada, Sheba became increasingly critical of the world around her and cut herself off from others. In letters to Benjamin, Sheba had explained that as an African-American woman, she felt

she was the target of racial hostility. Before long, her bitterness overwhelmed her and she flunked out of school, blaming her white professors for her failure. At this point, she left North America, finally earning a Ph.D. in England and settling in Nigeria. Since then, there had been no word.

When she reached Sheba's home, Benjamin was initially delighted to find that her old friend had returned to the United States. But as she finally looked upon the woman, she was shocked by Sheba's collapsing health. Her friend had suffered a mental breakdown, which left her almost entirely unresponsive to others.

Many months later, Sheba's emotional collapse still troubled Benjamin. She knew that many factors combine to cause such a personal tragedy. But, having experienced the sting of racism in her own career, Benjamin was convinced that this form of hatred played a major role in Sheba's story. Partly as a tribute to her friend, Benjamin set out to explore the effects of race in the lives of bright and well-educated people of color in the United States.

Doing so, Benjamin was aware, challenged conventional wisdom in several respects. Other researchers had concluded that race was now less of a barrier to African Americans than it had been in previous generations (Wilson, 1978). Benjamin knew, too, that many of her colleagues in sociology think that racism affects poor black people far more than those with prestigious jobs and high incomes. But her own experiences, and those of her friend Sheba, seemed to contradict such thinking. If so, then racism continues to shape the lives of people of color at all levels of the social ladder.

To investigate her contention, Benjamin spent the next two years traveling from city to city throughout North America, interviewing one hundred successful African Americans. She asked them how race affected their personal lives and influenced their work. In the words of these men and women—an array of distinguished people Benjamin calls the "Talented One Hundred"[1]—she found evidence that, even among African Americans of privilege, racism remains a heavy burden.

We will return to Lois Benjamin's research later in this chapter to learn more about her conclusions and how she conducted her research. For the moment, notice that the sociological perspective helped this woman to see broad social patterns operating in the lives of individuals. Just as important, Benjamin's work demonstrates the *doing* of sociology, the process of *sociological investigation*.

Many people think that scientists work only in laboratories, carefully taking measurements using complex equipment. But, as this chapter will explain, sociologists also conduct scientific research in the familiar terrain of neighborhood streets, offices, the workplace, and even prisons, to unfamiliar locales throughout the world—in short, wherever people can be found.

This chapter highlights the methods that sociologists use to conduct research. Along the way, we shall see that research involves not just procedures for gathering information but controversies about whether research should strive to be objective or to offer a bold prescription for change. Certainly, for example, Lois Benjamin did not undertake her exploration of racism simply to document its existence; she sought to make the world better. We shall begin tackling questions of values after addressing the basics of sociological investigation.

THE BASICS OF SOCIOLOGICAL INVESTIGATION

Sociological investigation begins with just two simple requirements. The first was the focus of Chapter 1: *Look at the world using the sociological perspective.* Suddenly, from this point of view, we see all around us curious patterns of behavior that call out for further study.

Lois Benjamin suspected a pattern when she tried to understand the tragedy of her friend's life. Her sociological imagination prompted her to wonder how race affects the lives of talented African Americans. This brings us to the second requirement for sociological investigation: *Be curious and ask questions.* Benjamin sought to learn more about how racial identity remains strong even for people who have significant personal achievements. She asked questions: What effect does being part of a racial minority have on a person's self-identity? Do black people and white people understand racial dynamics in the same way? Are racial tensions easing or becoming more pronounced?

These two requirements—seeing the world sociologically and asking questions—are fundamental to sociological investigation. Yet they are only the beginning. They draw us into the social world, stimulating our curiosity. But then we face the challenging task of finding answers to our questions. To understand the kind of insights sociology offers, we need to realize that there are various kinds of "truth."

Science as One Form of "Truth"

When we say we "know" something, we can mean any number of things. Most members of our society, for instance, claim to believe in the existence of God. Few would assert that they have direct contact with God,

---

[1]Benjamin derived her concept from the term "Talented Tenth" used by W. E. B. Du Bois (1899) to describe African-American leaders in his day.

NOTE: *Empiricism* (the Greek root means "experience") refers to the philosophical doctrine that only the senses support claims of truth. The closely linked concept of *positivism* defines truth as "positive" facts based on sense experience, while dismissing as speculation metaphysical or theological claims about ultimate causes of events.

NOTE: Science and religion do not conflict but complement one another. Scientific truths involve proximate causes of events; religious truths highlight ultimate causes. See Chapter 18 ("Religion"), especially the Critical Thinking box, "The Creation Debate."

SOCIAL SURVEY: Members of our "scientific" society still cling to metaphysical truth: 99% of GSS respondents knew their astrological sign. (GSS 1993, N = 1,606; *Codebook*, 1993:70).

but they are believers all the same. This kind of knowing is often called "belief" or "faith." A second kind of truth rests on the pronouncement of some recognized expert. Parents with questions about raising their children, for example, often consult child psychologists or other experts about which practices are "right." In still other cases, ordinary people define truth through simple agreement. We come to "know" that, say, sexual intercourse among young children is wrong because virtually everyone says it is. Of course, people in other times and places may recognize a different "truth." Ask the Melanesians of New Guinea about sexual intercourse among children too young to reproduce, and they shrug it off as harmless.

In a world of different "truths," we may encounter people whose ways of knowing are different from our own. Imagine being a Peace Corps volunteer who has just arrived in a small, traditional society in Latin America to help the local people to grow more food. Taking to the fields, you observe farmers carefully placing a dead fish directly on top of the ground where they have planted a seed. Curious, you ask about this practice, and they reply that the fish is a gift to the god of the harvest. A local elder adds sternly that the harvest was poor one year when no fish were offered as gifts.

From that society's point of view, using fish as gifts to the harvest god makes sense. The people believe in it, their experts endorse it, and everyone seems to agree that the system works. But, with scientific training in agriculture, you have to shake your head and wonder. The scientific "truth" in this situation is something entirely different: The decomposing fish fertilize the ground, producing a better crop.

Science, then, is yet another way of knowing. **Science** is *a logical system that bases knowledge on direct, systematic observation.* Standing apart from faith, the wisdom of "experts," and general agreement, scientific knowledge is based on **empirical evidence**, meaning *information we are able to verify with our senses.*

Our Peace Corps example does not mean, of course, that people in traditional societies ignore what their senses tell them, or that members of technologically advanced societies reject all ways of knowing except science. A medical researcher using science to seek an effective treatment for cancer, for example, may still practice her religion as a matter of faith; she may turn to experts when making financial decisions; and she may derive political opinions from family and friends. In short, we all embrace various kinds of truths at the same time.

There are many kinds of truth. The Emergence of Clowns *by U.S. artist Roxanne Swentzell presents the story of creation according to the Santa Clara Pueblo. Life began, they believe, when four clowns emerged onto the earth's surface, each facing a different direction. All of the world's people have creation beliefs of some kind (including the Biblical accounts in Genesis). As members of a scientific society, we sometimes dismiss such stories as "myth" (from Greek, meaning "story"). Whether or not they are entirely factual, they do convey basic truths about the way in which each society searches for human origins and struggles to find meaning in the universe. It is science, not "myth," that is powerless to address such questions of meaning.*

Roxanne Swentzell, *The Emergence of the Clowns*, 1988. Coiled and scraped clay: 48 x 48 x 23 inches. The Collection of the Heard Museum, Phoenix, Arizona.

Common Sense Versus Scientific Evidence

Scientific evidence sometimes challenges our common sense. Here are six statements that many North Americans assume are "true," although each is at least partly contradicted by scientific research.

1. **Poor people are far more likely than rich people to break the law.** Chapter 8 ("Deviance") explains that official arrest statistics bear out this statement. But research also reveals that the criminal justice system is more likely to prosecute wrongdoing by poor people while treating offenses by the well-to-do more leniently. Further, many

RESOURCE: A counterpoint arguing that people have more sociological common sense than instructors (and their textbooks) is James A. Mathisen, "A Further Look at 'Common Sense' in Introductory Sociology," *Teaching Sociology* 17, 3 (July 1989): 307–15.
NOTE: Other examples of misleading common sense: The fecundity of "welfare mothers" is actually below that of other women; remarriages are more prone to divorce than first marriages.

Q: Mark Twain described the credibility hierarchy, in descending order, as: "Lies, damn lies, and statistics."
Q: "Science is meaningless because it gives no answer to the question, the only question of importance for us: 'What shall we do and how shall we live?'" Leo Tolstoy

researchers argue that our society creates laws in such a way as to reduce the risk that affluent people will be criminalized.

2. **The United States is a middle-class society in which most people are more or less equal.** Data presented in Chapter 10 ("Social Class in the United States") show that the richest 5 percent of our people control half our country's total wealth. If people are equal, then, some are much "more equal" than others.

3. **Most poor people ignore opportunities to work.** Research included in Chapter 10 indicates that this statement is true of some but not most poor people. In fact, about half of poor individuals in the United States are children and elderly people whom no one would expect to work.

4. **Differences in the social behavior of females and males are "human nature."** Much of what we call "human nature" is created by the society in which we are raised, as Chapter 3 ("Culture") details. Further, as Chapter 13 ("Sex and Gender") argues, some societies define "feminine" and "masculine" very differently from the way we do.

5. **People change as they grow old, losing many former interests while becoming focused on their health.** Chapter 14 ("Aging and the Elderly") reports that aging actually changes our personalities very little. Problems of health increase in old age, but, by and large, elderly individuals retain their distinctive personalities.

6. **Most people marry because they are in love.** To members of our society, few statements are so self-evident. But as surprising as it may seem, global research shows that, in most societies, marriage has little to do with love. Chapter 17 ("Family") explains why this is the case.

These examples confirm the old saying that "It's not what we don't know that gets us into trouble as much as things we *do* know that just aren't so." We have all been brought up believing conventional truths, being bombarded by expert advice, and pressured to accept the opinions of friends. As adults, we must learn to evaluate critically what we see, read, and hear in order to separate what is true from what is not. As a scientific discipline, sociology can help us to do that. Like any way of knowing, science has limitations, as we shall see. But scientific sociology is a useful way to assess many kinds of information.

THE ELEMENTS OF SCIENCE

Sociologists apply science to the study of society in much the same way that natural scientists investigate the physical world. The work of social scientists lies in discovering how various dimensions of social life are interrelated. Thus a sociologist might ask questions such as:

What segments of the population are most likely to vote in national elections? Why?
Are abused children at risk of becoming child abusers themselves?
Are city dwellers less neighborly than people living in rural areas?

To answer these questions, sociologists use the elements of science to gather empirical evidence. The following sections of this chapter introduce many important components of scientific investigation.

Concepts, Variables, and Measurement

A crucial element of science is the **concept**, *a mental construct that represents some part of the world, inevitably in a simplified form.* "Society" is itself a concept, as are the structural parts of societies, including "religion" and "the economy." Sociologists also use concepts to describe individuals, as when we speak of their "sex," "race," or "social class."

A **variable** is *a concept whose value changes from case to case.* The familiar variable "price," for example, changes from item to item in a supermarket. Similarly, people use the concept "social class" to evaluate people as "upper class," "middle class," "working class," or "lower class."

The use of variables depends on **measurement**, *the process of determining the value of a variable in a specific case.* Some variables are easy to measure, as when we add up our income at tax time. But measuring most sociological variables can be far more difficult. For example, how would you measure a person's "social class"? You might be tempted to look at dress, listen to patterns of speech, or note a home address. You could be more precise, investigating income, occupation, and education.

But researchers know that almost any variable can be measured in more than one way. Having a very high income may suggest that a person is "upper class." But what if the income comes from selling automobiles, an occupation most people think of as "middle class"? And if the individual has only an eighth-grade

NOTE: Awards in medical malpractice suits illustrate statistical measures. Modal settlement is zero (the most common award); median award is $18,000, since most awards are small; mean award approaches $100,000 because the average is skewed upwards by a few high awards.

NOTE: The mode is a nominal level of measurement, the median is ordinal, and the mean is an interval/ratio measure.

GLOBAL: The misleading character of averages is illustrated by the $16,000 per capita gross national product of oil-rich United Arab Emirates, which is close to the U.S. figure of $20,000. Yet U.A.E. has triple the U.S. infant mortality and adult illiteracy rates, suggesting that most people have a low standard of living. That nation's considerable wealth, in short, is highly concentrated among a small elite.

SOCIOLOGY OF EVERYDAY LIFE

Three Useful (and Simple) Statistical Measures

We all talk about "averages": the average age of the U.S. population, the average price of a gallon of gasoline, or Barry Bonds's batting average. Sociologists, too, are interested in averages, and they use three different statistical measures to describe what is typical.

Assume that we wish to describe the salaries paid to seven members of a sociology department at a local college:

$24,300 $35,000 $31,700 $33,000
$35,000 $75,000 $28,500

The simplest statistical measure is the **mode**, defined as *the value that occurs most often in a series of numbers*. In this example, the mode is $35,000, since that value occurs

twice, while each of the others occurs only once. If all the values were to occur only once, there would be no mode; if two values occurred twice, there would be two modes. Although easy to identify, sociologists rarely use a mode in their research because this measure provides information about only some, rather than all, of the values.

A more common statistical measure, the **mean**, refers to *the arithmetic average of a series of numbers* and is calculated by adding all the values together and dividing by the number of cases. The sum of the seven incomes is $262,500; dividing by seven yields a mean income of $37,500. But notice that the mean is actually higher than the income of six of the seven

sociologists. Because the mean is "pulled" by any especially high or low value (in this case, the $75,000 paid to one sociologist who also serves as a dean), it has the drawback of giving a distorted picture of any distribution with extreme scores.

The **median** is *the value that occurs midway in a series of numbers arranged in order of magnitude or, simply, the middle case*. Here the median income for the seven people is $33,000, since three incomes are higher and three are lower. (With an even number of cases, the median is halfway between the two middle cases.) Since a median is unaffected by an extreme score, it generally gives a better picture of what is "average" than the mean does.

---

education, then you might conclude that the person is "lower class." To resolve such a dilemma, sociologists sensibly (if somewhat arbitrarily) combine these three measures—income, occupation, and education—into a single composite assessment of social class described in Chapter 9 ("Social Stratification") and Chapter 10 ("Social Class in the United States").

Another challenge is describing a number of people, say, residents of a city or individuals with the same occupation, with respect to a variable such as income. Reporting a long stream of numbers is cumbersome and conveys nothing about the people as a whole. Thus sociologists use various *statistical measures* to describe people collectively. The box explains how this is done.

In conducting research, the value of any variable depends, in part, on how the sociologist defines it. **Operationalizing a variable** means *specifying exactly what one is to measure in assigning a value to a variable.* If we were measuring people's social class, for example,

we would have to decide if we were going to measure income, occupational prestige, education, or something else and, if we measure more than one of these, how to combine the scores. When reporting the results of research, sociologists should specify how they operationalized each variable so that readers understand the conclusions.

Reliability and Validity of Measurement

Useful measurement involves two further considerations. **Reliability** is *the quality of consistent measurement*. For a measure to be reliable, in other words, repeated measurements must produce the same result. An unreliable technique for measuring social class is of little value to sociologists, just as a scale giving inconsistent readings of weight would be useless to a physicist.

Even consistency is no guarantee of validity, however. **Validity** means *the quality of measuring precisely*

Q: "We shall discover the laws of social forms only by collecting such societary phenomena of the most diverse contents, and by ascertaining what is common to them in spite of their diversity." Georg Simmel

NOTE: David Hume (1711–1776) argued that science can empirically determine (1) correlation and (2) temporal ordering of variables but not (3) the actual causal connection, which defies observation.

Perhaps with Hume's thought in mind, the National Cancer Institute acknowledged higher cancer rates among people living near nuclear power plants but argued that research "can neither confirm nor deny a link...because statistical studies, by their very nature, cannot prove cause and effect."

Q: "We cannot work without hoping that others will advance further than we have." Max Weber

Men who drink coffee are more likely than tea drinkers to die from a heart attack. But does this mean that coffee causes heart disease? No—the link between those two variables is spurious. Both coffee drinking and heart disease are caused by a third variable, high levels of stress.

what one intends to measure. Say you want to investigate how religious people are, so you ask how often they attend religious services. Notice that, in trying to gauge *religiosity*, what you are actually measuring is *attendance at services*, which may or may not amount to the same thing. Generally, religious people do attend services more frequently, but people also participate in religious rituals for social reasons, out of habit, or because of a sense of duty to someone else. Moreover, many devout believers avoid organized religion altogether. Thus, even when a measurement yields consistent results (making it reliable), it can still miss the real, intended target (and lack validity). In sum, sociological research is no better than the quality of measurement that it employs.

Relationships Among Variables

The real payoff in sociological investigation comes from determining the relationships among variables. Ideally, scientists relate variables in terms of **cause and effect**, *a relationship in which change in one variable causes change in another.* A familiar cause-and-effect relationship occurs when a girl teases her brother until he becomes angry. *The variable that causes the change* (in this case, the teasing) is called the **independent variable.** *The variable that changes* (the behavior of the brother) is called the **dependent variable.** The value of one variable, in other words, is dependent on the value of another. Why is linking variables in terms of cause and effect important? Because doing so allows researchers to *predict*, that is, to use what they do know to speculate about what they don't know.

Because science puts a premium on prediction, people may be tempted to think that a cause-and-effect relationship is present any time variables change together. Consider, for instance, that the marriage rate in the United States falls to its lowest point in January, exactly the same month as our national death rate peaks. This hardly means that people die because they fail to marry (or that they don't marry because they die). In fact, it is the dreary weather in much of the nation during January (and perhaps also the postholiday blahs) that causes both a low marriage rate and a high death rate. On the other end of the stick, the warmer and sunnier summer months have the highest marriage rate as well as the lowest death rate. Thus researchers often have to untangle cause and effect relationships that are not readily apparent.

To take a second case, sociologists have long recognized that juvenile delinquency is more common among young people who live in crowded housing. Say we operationalize the variable "juvenile delinquency" by measuring the number of arrests of persons under the age of eighteen, and operationalize "crowded housing" by evaluating the amount of square feet of living space per person in a home. We would find that delinquency rates are, indeed, high in areas that are densely populated. But should we conclude that crowding in the home is the independent variable that causes delinquency, the dependent variable?

Not necessarily. *When two (or more) variables are related in some way* (that is, when they change together), they demonstrate **correlation.** We know there is some relationship between these two variables because they change together, as shown in Part (a) of Figure 2–1. This relationship *may* mean that crowding causes delinquency, but there are other possibilities as well. Think sociologically for a minute about what general category of people lives in crowded housing. The answer: people with less money, power, and choice—the poor. Police are also more likely to respond to the mischief of poor children by making an arrest. In short, crowded housing and juvenile delinquency are found together because *both* are caused by a third factor—poverty—as shown in Part (b) of Figure 2–1. Put otherwise, the apparent relationship between crowding and delinquency is "explained away" by a third variable—low income—that causes them both to change. The term **spurious correlation** means *an apparent, although false, association between two (or more) variables caused by some other variable.*

Unmasking a correlation as spurious requires using scientific **control**, meaning *the ability to neutralize the effect of one or more variables in order to assess the relationships among other variables.* In the example above, we would ask whether the relationship between housing density and delinquency persists if we limit our investigation to persons of a single income level. If, doing this, a correlation between density and delinquency remains (that is, if young people living in more crowded housing continue to show higher rates of delinquency than young people with the same family income in less crowded housing), we gain confidence that crowding does in fact cause delinquency. But if the relationship disappears when we control for income, as shown in Part (c) of the figure, we conclude that we have been dealing with a spurious correlation. Research has, in fact, shown that virtually all correlation between crowding and delinquency disappears if the effects of income are controlled (Fischer, 1984). So we have now sorted out the relationship among the three variables, as illustrated in Part (d) of the figure. Housing density and juvenile delinquency have a spurious correlation; evidence shows that both variables rise or fall according to people's income.

To sum up, correlation means only that two (or more) variables change together. Cause and effect implies not only correlation but also that change in one variable actually causes change in another. A researcher should conclude that two variables are linked by cause and effect only after demonstrating (1) the two variables are correlated; (2) the independent (or causal) variable precedes the dependent variable in time; and (3) there is no evidence that a third variable is responsible for a spurious correlation between the two.

Natural scientists identify cause-and-effect relationships more easily than social scientists because the laboratories used for study of the physical world allow control of many variables at one time. The sociologist, carrying out research in a workplace or on the streets, faces a considerably more difficult task. Often sociologists must be satisfied with demonstrating only correlation. Furthermore, human behavior is highly complex, involving dozens of causal variables at any one time.

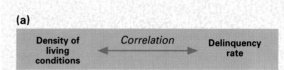

If two variables vary together, they are said to be correlated. In this example, density of living conditions and juvenile delinquency increase and decrease together.

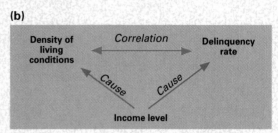

Here we consider the effect of a third variable: income level. Low income level may cause *both* high-density living conditions *and* a high delinquency rate. In other words, as income level decreases, both density of living conditions and the delinquency rate increase.

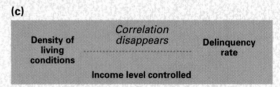

If we control income level — that is, examine only cases with the same income level — do those with higher-density living conditions still have a higher delinquency rate? The answer is *no*. There is no longer a correlation between these two variables.

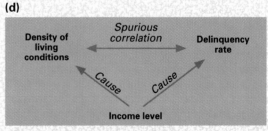

This finding leads us to conclude that income level is a cause of both density of living conditions and the delinquency rate. The original two variables (density of living conditions and delinquency rate) are thus correlated, but neither one causes the other. Their correlation is therefore *spurious*.

FIGURE 2–1 Correlation and Cause: An Example

Q: "At least in science, we show the greatest respect for an author by leaving him behind." Peter Berger
DATA FILE: W. S. Slater's "The Proper Study," an amusing poem about sociological research, is found in the *Data File*.
Q: "Truth is what serves the German people." Joseph Goebbels, Ph.D.

Q: "The direction of our scientific exertions...is conditioned by the society in which we live, and most directly by the political climate. ...[S]tudents turn to research on issues that have obtained political importance." Gunnar Myrdal
NOTE: Anthony Jones (1989) describes sociology as having "weak boundaries," a trait that allows easy incorporation of political events and values into research.

CRITICAL THINKING

The Samoa Controversy: The Interplay of Science and Politics

Margaret Mead (1901–1978) remains the most prominent anthropologist* in history. Several years after her death, however, replication of one of her most well-known studies raised questions of objectivity and, more generally, about the interplay of science and politics.

The research in question, conducted early in Mead's career, was an investigation of growing up in Samoa, a beautiful South Pacific island. To the surprise of Westerners, who tend to view adolescence as a stormy time due to rapid biological changes, Mead reported little difficulty as young Samoans came of age. Thus, she concluded, the experience of growing up is not biologically programmed but varies significantly from one society to

_____
*Closely related to sociology, anthropology studies human culture, often with a focus on preindustrial rather than industrial societies.

As a pioneer of social research, Margaret Mead studied other societies to help us think more critically about our own. Her career also alerts us to the fact that researchers—especially when they investigate controversial issues—do not easily separate their work from their personal values.

another. Her results immediately became ammunition for those who argued that environment, rather than biology, is the greater influence on human behavior.

Early in this century, the upper hand in this "nature-nurture" debate was held by scientists who viewed biology as more influential. Advocates of a biological foundation for human behavior also claimed that categories of people differed in fundamental ways. This kind of thinking had more than academic importance: It was used by opponents of immigration to pressure the government to restrict the entrance of various "foreigners" into the United States on the grounds that they were biologically inferior.

Mead's research provided the foundation for a counterattack. As she saw it, people everywhere are essentially alike, differing only

The Ideal of Objectivity

Assume that ten people who work for a magazine in Milwaukee, Wisconsin, are collaborating on a story about that city's best restaurants. With their editor picking up the tab, they head out on the town for a week of fine dining. Later, they get together to compare notes. Do you think one restaurant would be everyone's clear favorite? That hardly seems likely.

In scientific terms, each of the ten probably operationalizes the concept "best restaurant" differently. For one, it might be a place that serves delicious steaks at reasonable prices; for another, the choice might turn on a rooftop view of Lake Michigan; for yet another, stunning decor and attentive service might be the deciding factors. Like so many other

things in life, the best restaurant turns out to be mostly a matter of individual taste.

Personal values are fine when it comes to restaurants, but they pose a challenge to scientific research. On the one hand, sociologists and other scientists have personal opinions about whatever they study. On the other, science strives for **objectivity**, *a state of personal neutrality in conducting research*. Objectivity in scientific research depends on carefully adhering to scientific procedures in order not to bias the results. Scientific objectivity is an ideal rather than a reality, of course, since complete impartiality is virtually impossible for any researcher to achieve. Even the subject a researcher selects to study and the framing of the questions are likely to grow out of personal experience, as the research on race by Lois Benjamin attests.

Q: "People kill each other for prophetic certainties, hardly for falsifiable hypotheses." Peter Berger

RESOURCE: Max Weber's statement on value-free research is among the classics in the Macionis and Benokraitis reader *Seeing Ourselves: Classic, Contemporary, and Cross-Cultural Readings in Sociology,* 3/e.

Q: James D. Wright (1989) suggests that good science makes for bad politics, and vice versa.

Q: "Theories and concepts emerge in sociology like popcorn, puffed up by their own steam." Joseph Gusfield, explaining why no "social scientific Newton" is likely to emerge from sociology

Q: "Unfettered thought is the essence of research methods." Stanislav Andreski

because of their dissimilar environments. Her position reflected the ideas of her graduate school mentor, Franz Boas, himself a famous anthropologist. Both Boas and Mead were outspoken opponents of what they viewed as false biological doctrine being used to discriminate against some categories of people. They maintained that no category of human beings is inherently different—and certainly none is "better"—than any other.

Mead's research went a long way toward discrediting biological views of human behavior. Yet shortly after her death, Derek Freeman, who also conducted research in Samoa, challenged Mead's conclusions and pointed once again to the possible importance of biology to human behavior. As Freeman saw it, Mead had selectively represented Samoan society according to her personal politics. Freeman's

observations support the conclusion that biology plays a greater role in human behavior than Mead was willing to recognize.

Social science scholars still debate this issue. Siding with Freeman, some paint Mead as a young (twenty-four years old when she arrived in Samoa in 1925) and unseasoned researcher, prompted by her teacher to produce evidence supporting an environmental doctrine of human behavior. Her conclusions are too "neat," critics claim, suggesting that she saw only what she was looking for. In short, they assert, Margaret Mead's work is really more "politically correct" than it is scientifically factual.

To Mead's defenders, however, Freeman stands as the villain in the controversy. They argue that, especially given the limited development of research skills in the social sciences at that time, Mead's

conclusions are basically sound. It is Freeman, they charge, who is playing politics by advocating a view of human behavior that is largely determined by biology. To those in Mead's camp, Freeman has sought to advance his own politics and career by unjustly attacking the work of a great social scientist.

No doubt, some truth can be found on both sides of this complex controversy. One point, however, seems quite clear: Human beings are passionate and political creatures who inevitably fall short of the scientific goal of complete objectivity in research.

SOURCES: Based on Mead (1961; orig. 1928), Freeman (1983), Holmes (1983), and Weiner (1983).

But scientists cultivate detachment and follow specific methods to lessen the chance that even unconscious biases will distort their work. As an additional safeguard, researchers should try to identify their personal leanings to help readers evaluate their conclusions in the proper context.

The influential German sociologist Max Weber wrestled with the problem of personal values distorting scientific study. Weber accepted the idea that personal beliefs would play a part in a sociologist's selection of a research topic. Why, after all, would one person study world hunger, another investigate the effects of racism, and still another examine religious cults? While acknowledging the *value-relevant* nature of research, Weber (1958; orig. 1918) admonished researchers to be *value-free* in their pursuit of conclusions. Only by being

dispassionate, he claimed, can researchers study the world *as it is* rather than telling others how they think *it should be.* This detachment, for Weber, is a defining feature of science that sets it apart from the world of politics. Politicians, in other words, are committed to a particular outcome; scientists try to maintain an openminded readiness to accept the results of their investigations, whatever they may be.

By and large, sociologists accept Weber's argument, although most realize that we can never be completely aware of our own biases. Moreover, sociologists are not "average" people: Most are white men who are highly educated and more politically liberal than the population as a whole (Wilson, 1979). Sociologists need to remember that they, too, are affected by their own social backgrounds.

Chapter 2 Sociological Investigation **37**

DATA FILE: Supplementary material for this chapter includes an account of how recently celebrated research by James Coleman was condemned initially as "politically incorrect."

Q: "...every social theory is a tacit theory of politics [and] also a personal theory inevitably representing...the personal experience of the individuals who author it." Alvin Gouldner (1970b)

Q: "As in all sciences, in sociology interpretation is all. A science may be loaded down with too many facts, its vision blurred by peering too intently at the machinery for collecting them. The collected facts can be brought to life, as the statisticians themselves agree, only by a compelling vision of their meaning. Untouched by the magic of a sufficiently powerful and trained imagination, data play dead." Philip Rieff

Belgian artist René Magritte (1898–1967) painted L'Appel des Cimes *to explore how human beings construct reality. Do the results of scientific research precisely mirror objective reality? Or do scientific investigators subjectively construct what they think they see? Magritte prods us to think critically about the relationship between any object and our understanding of it.*

Some Limitations of Scientific Sociology

People first employed science to probe the operation of the natural world. Now we also use science to study the social world; doing so, however, has several important limitations.

1. **Human behavior is too complex to allow sociologists to predict precisely any individual's actions.** Astronomers calculate the movement of planets with remarkable precision, announcing years in advance when a comet will next pass near the Earth. But planets and comets are just objects; humans, by contrast, have minds of their own. Because no two people react in exactly the same way to any event, the best sociologists can do is to show that categories of people tend to act in some distinctive way. This is no failing of sociology; it is simply consistent with the nature of our mission: studying creative, spontaneous people.

2. **Because humans respond to their surroundings, the mere presence of a researcher may affect the behavior being studied.** An astronomer gazing at the moon has no effect whatever on that celestial body. But people often react to being observed. Some may become anxious or defensive; others may try to "help" by providing the answers or actions they think researchers expect of them.

3. **Social patterns change constantly; what is true in one time or place may not hold true in another.** Atoms and molecules do not consciously shape their environment, but human beings do, in remarkably variable ways. The study of society, therefore, must take account of diversity and change.

4. **Because sociologists are part of the social world they study, objectivity in social research is especially difficult.** Barring health hazards, chemists are not personally affected by what goes on in test tubes. But sociologists live in the society they study. Therefore, social scientists face a greater challenge in controlling—or even recognizing—personal values that may distort their work.

The Importance of Subjective Interpretation

The logic of science does not eliminate subjectivity from research. Nor would that be desirable, since creative thinking is vital to sociological investigation in three key ways.

One strategy for limiting distortion caused by personal values is **replication**, *repetition of research by others in order to assess its accuracy.* If other researchers repeat a study using the same procedures and obtain the same results, everyone gains confidence that the original research (as well as the replication) was conducted objectively. The need for replication in scientific investigation is probably the reason that the search for knowledge is called *re*search in the first place. But only a small proportion of social science research is actually subjected to replication (far less than is the case in the natural sciences). If a replication does not square with the results of an original study, the difference may spark conflict, as in the case detailed in the box on pages 36–37.

First, science is basically a series of steps that guides research, rather like a recipe directs the efforts of a cook. But just as more than a recipe is required to make a great chef, so scientific procedure will never, by itself, produce a great sociologist. Also needed is an inspired human imagination. Robert Nisbet (1970) points out that insight comes not from science itself but from the lively thinking of creative human beings. The genius of physicist Albert Einstein, anthropologist Margaret Mead, and sociologist Max Weber lay not only in their use of the scientific method but also in their curiosity and imagination.

Second, science cannot embrace the vast and complex range of human motivations and feelings, including greed, love, pride, and despair. Science helps us gather facts about how people act, but it can never fully explain how people make sense of what they do (Berger & Kellner, 1981).

Third, scientific data never speak for themselves. Sociologists and other scientists always face the ultimate task of *interpretation* as they create meaning from a collection of observations. For this reason, sociology (like other disciplines) is an art as well as a science.

Politics and Research

As Max Weber observed long ago, a fine line separates politics from science. Most sociologists endorse Weber's goal of value-free research. But a growing number of researchers are challenging the notion that politics and science can—or should—be distinct.

Alvin Gouldner (1970a, 1970b) was among the first to claim that the notion of "value-free" research paints a "storybook picture" of sociology. All aspects of social life, he argues, have political implications since all social arrangements are likely to benefit some people more than others. In short, Gouldner concluded, what is *social* is inevitably *political*. This connection also holds true for research, which almost always has political consequences.

If sociologists have no choice about their work being political, Gouldner continues, they do have a choice about *which* positions are worthy of support. Moreover, as he sees it, sociologists are obligated to endorse political objectives that will improve society. Although this viewpoint is not limited to sociologists of any one political orientation, it is common among those with left-leaning politics, especially those influenced by the ideas of Karl Marx. His ringing assertion, noted in Chapter 1 ("The Sociological Perspective"),

was that while it is important to understand the world, the crucial task is to change it (1972:109; orig. 1845).

In recent years, many colleges and universities have become embroiled in a debate over what has been called "political correctness." In simple terms, this controversy pits advocates of Weberian value-free teaching and research against proponents of Marx's view that since all knowledge is political, sociologists have an obligation to promote positive societal change.

Gender and Research

One political dimension of research involves gender—the relative social standing of females and males. Sociologists are becoming increasingly aware that gender-related issues can play a major part in their work. Margrit Eichler (1988) identifies five dangers to sound research that relate to gender.

1. **Androcentricity.** Androcentricity (*andro* is the Greek word for "male"; *centricity* means "being centered on") refers to approaching an issue from a male perspective. Sometimes researchers approach a setting as if only the activities of men are important, while ignoring what women do. For years, research in the area of occupations focused on the paid work of men while overlooking the housework and child care traditionally performed by women (Counts, 1925; Hodge, Treiman, & Rossi, 1966). Similarly, until recently, studies of status attainment were based on fathers and sons (Blau & Duncan, 1967; Sewell, Haller, & Ohlendorf, 1970). Clearly, research that seeks to understand human behavior cannot ignore half of humanity.

   Eichler notes that the parallel situation of *gynocentricity*—seeing the world from a female perspective—is equally limiting to sociological investigation. However, in our male-dominated society, this problem arises much less frequently.

2. **Overgeneralizing.** This problem occurs when researchers use data drawn from only people of one sex to support conclusions about both sexes. Historically, sociologists have studied men and then made sweeping claims about "humanity" or "society." Gathering information about a community from public officials or other prominent persons (who are likely to be men), and then drawing conclusions about the community as a whole, illustrates the problem of overgeneralizing.

   Here, again, the bias can occur in reverse. For example, in an investigation of childrearing practices, collecting data only from women would

<u>Q</u>: "There is no position from which sociological research is not biased in one way or another." Howard S. Becker

RESOURCE: An excerpt from Shulamit Reinharz's book *Feminist Methods in Social Research* is included in the Macionis and Benokraitis reader.

<u>Q</u>: "Advocacy research often justifies playing fast and loose with the facts in service to a noble cause." Neil Gilbert

<u>Q</u>: "As all truth is someone's truth, let's have mine." Harvey Mansfield, Jr.

<u>Q</u>: "Researchers must examine their assumptions about gender . . . Of all the beliefs that anthropologists bring to the field, [these] may be the most difficult to put aside, [operating] on an unconscious level." Maureen Giovannini (1992)

Feminist research is not concerned simply with studying the social standing of women. It also transforms scientific research so that an investigator assumes a posture of social parity with others, working cooperatively toward solving their common problems.

allow researchers to draw conclusions about "motherhood" but not about the more general issue of "parenthood."

3. **Gender insensitivity**. This refers to the failure of a researcher to consider the variable of gender at all. As is evident throughout this book, many social forces affect men and women quite differently. A study of growing old in the United States that overlooked the fact that most elderly men live with spouses while elderly women typically live alone would be weakened by its gender insensitivity.

4. **Double standards**. Researchers must be careful not to distort what they study by evaluating women and men using different standards. If, for example, a researcher investigating families describes a couple as "man and wife," the biased language may suggest a biased approach as well, especially if the researcher defines the man as the "head of household" and treats him accordingly, while assuming that the woman simply engages in family "support work."

5. **Interference**. Beyond affecting researchers, gender often shapes the attitudes of subjects, which can also distort a study. Interference occurs if a subject reacts to the sex of the researcher rather than to the research itself. For instance, while studying a small community in Sicily, Maureen Giovannini

(1992) reported that many men responded to her as a woman to the point that she was unable to work effectively as a researcher. Gender dynamics precluded her from certain activities, such as private conversations with men, that were deemed inappropriate for single women. In addition, local residents denied Giovannini access to places considered off limits to members of her sex.

Of course researchers can choose to focus their work on one sex or the other. But all sociologists, as well as people who read their work, should think critically about how gender affects the process of sociological investigation.

Feminist Research

Pervasive attention to men at the expense of women in the past has encouraged some researchers to make special efforts to investigate the lives of women. Feminist research is a new and evolving approach. At this point, however, virtually all its advocates hold, first, that its focus should be the condition of women in society and, second, that women generally experience subordination. Thus feminist research rejects Weber's value-free orientation in favor of being overtly political—doing research *about* and *for* women.

Some proponents of feminist research advocate employing any and all conventional scientific techniques, including all those described in this chapter. Others maintain that feminist research involves transforming the essence of sociological investigation, which they see as a masculine pursuit of knowledge. Whereas scientific investigation has traditionally demanded detachment, feminists deliberately foster a sympathetic understanding between investigator and subject. Moreover, conventional scientists take charge of the research agenda by organizing in advance what issues will be raised and how they will be discussed. Feminist researchers, by contrast, favor a less structured approach to gathering information so that participants in research can offer their own ideas on their own terms (Stanley & Wise, 1983; Nielsen, 1990; Stanley, 1990; Reinharz, 1992).

Alterations in research premises and methods provoke more conventional sociologists to charge that feminist research is less science than simple political activism. Feminists respond that research and politics should not—indeed cannot—be distinct. They point to the growing feminist literature that has helped to advance the movement to secure for women social standing equal to that of men. The broader point is

Q: "We can no longer view the world as Descartes and Laplace would have us do, as 'rational onlookers,' from outside. Our place is within the same world that we are studying, and whatever scientific understanding we achieve must be a kind of understanding that is available to participants within the process of nature, i.e., from inside." Stephen Toulmin

Q: "Social science is *part* of the social world as well as a *conception* of it . . . . Utilitarian culture . . . fostered acute sentiments of detachment. Positivism transformed this detachment into an ideology and morality." Alvin Gouldner
NOTE: The word "experiment" contains the Latin root *per*, "to try out." This is also the root of the word "peril"—a link demonstrated by the Zimbardo research.

that traditional ideas contrasting politics and science have now been joined by some new thinking that merges these two dimensions.

Research Ethics

Like all investigators, sociologists must be mindful that research can be harmful as well as helpful to subjects or communities. For this reason, the American Sociological Association—the major professional association of sociologists in North America—has established formal guidelines for the conduct of research (1984).

The primary ethical guideline is that sociologists strive to be both technically competent and fair-minded in conducting their research. Sociologists must disclose research findings in full, without omitting significant data. Further, they must point out all possible interpretations of data, and they are ethically bound to make their results available to other qualified sociologists, some of whom may wish to replicate the study.

Researchers must strive to protect the rights, privacy, and safety of anyone involved in a research project. Sociologists are obligated to terminate any research, however promising it may seem, if they become aware of any potential danger to participants. If research is likely to cause subjects even discomfort or inconvenience, sociologists must ensure in advance that all participants understand and accept any risks.

Subjects who agree to take part in research are entitled to full anonymity if they wish it, and sociologists must protect this trust even if they come under legal pressure to release confidential information. Clearly, researchers should never offer anonymity to subjects unless they are willing and able to carry through on their commitment.

Sociologists are ethically bound to inform subjects of the true purpose of their work. Researchers must also disclose to subjects, in advance of the research, any political organization or business that they represent, and they must include this information, along with any sources of funding, in published reports of their findings. No sociologist should accept funding from any organization that seeks to influence the research process for its own purposes.

There are also global dimensions to research ethics. Before beginning research in other countries, investigators must become familiar enough with that society to understand what people *there* are likely to perceive as a violation of privacy or a source of personal danger. In a multicultural society such as our own, moreover, the same rule applies to studying people whose cultural background is different from that of the investigator. The box on pages 42–43 offers several tips about how outsiders can effectively and sensitively study Hispanic communities.

THE METHODS OF SOCIOLOGICAL RESEARCH

A **research method** is *a strategy for systematically conducting research.* Four commonly used methods of sociological investigation are introduced here. None is inherently better or worse than any other; but in the same way that a carpenter selects a particular tool for a particular task, researchers find one or another method suitable for certain kinds of research.

Experiments

The logic of science is most clearly expressed in the **experiment,** *a research method for investigating cause and effect under highly controlled conditions.* Experimental research is *explanatory,* meaning that it investigates not just what happens but why. Typically, researchers turn to an experiment to test a specific **hypothesis,** *an unverified statement of a relationship between variables.*

Ideally, experimental research allows us to evaluate a hypothesis in three steps. First, the experimenter measures the dependent variable (or effect); second, the investigator exposes the dependent variable to the independent variable (the cause or "treatment"); and third, the researcher measures the dependent variable again to see if the predicted change has taken place. If the expected change has occurred, the experiment lends support to the hypothesis; if not, the hypothesis is discounted.

Successful experiments require that researchers carefully control all extraneous factors that might intrude into the experiment and affect what is being measured. This control is most easily accomplished in a laboratory, an artificial setting specially constructed for research purposes. Another means for neutralizing any outside influences is the strategy of dividing subjects between an *experimental group* and a *control group.* At the outset, the researcher measures the dependent variable for subjects in both groups but exposes only the experimental group to the independent variable or treatment. Then the investigator measures the subjects in both groups again. A host of factors (such as some news event) occurring during the course of the research might influence attitudes or

SOCIAL DIVERSITY

Conducting Research with Hispanics

In a society as racially, ethnically, and religiously diverse as our own, the work of sociological investigators will inevitably involve confronting people who differ in myriad ways from themselves. Learning—in advance—some of the distinctive traits of any category of people being studied can both facilitate the research process and ensure that no hard feelings are left when the work is completed.

Gerardo Marín and Barbara VanOss Marín have compiled a number of useful tips for sociological investigators who plan to conduct research with people of Spanish descent.

1. **Be careful with terms.** The Maríns point out that the term "Hispanic" is a label of convenience used by the Census Bureau. Few people of Spanish descent think of themselves as either "Hispanic" or "Latino"; most identify with a particular country (generally, with a

Researchers must always remain respectful of subjects and mindful of their well-being. In part, this means investigators must become familiar— well ahead of time—with the cultural patterns of those they wish to study.

nation of Latin America such as Cuba or Argentina, or with Spain).

2. **Realize that cultural values may differ.** By and large, the United States is a nation of individualistic, competitive people. Many Hispanics, by contrast, have a more collective orientation. An outsider may judge the behavior of a particular Hispanic man or woman as too conformist or overtrusting when, in fact, the person is simply acting in normative ways.

The Maríns add that Hispanics tend to favor harmonious relations with others. Some subjects, therefore, may appear to agree with a researcher's statement out of politeness more than belief in the validity of the assertion.

behavior of members of the experimental group, but we expect such factors to affect individuals in the control group as well. Thus the use of a control group "washes out" many extraneous factors: Comparing the before-and-after measurements of the two groups, a researcher is able to assess how much of the observed change is due only to the independent variable.

Worth remembering is the fact that subjects may alter their behavior simply in response to a researcher's attention, as one classic experiment revealed. In the late 1930s, the Western Electric Company hired researchers to investigate worker productivity in its Hawthorne factory near Chicago (Roethlisberger & Dickson, 1939). One experiment tested the hypothesis that increasing the available lighting would raise worker output. To test this idea, researchers measured initial productivity (the dependent variable); then they

increased the lighting (the independent variable); finally, they measured productivity a second time. Productivity increased, supporting the hypothesis. But when the research team subsequently *reduced* the lighting, productivity again increased, contradicting the initial hypothesis. In time, the researchers realized that the employees were working harder (even if they could not see as well) simply because people were paying attention to them. From this research, social scientists coined the term **Hawthorne effect** to refer to *a change in a subject's behavior caused by the awareness of being studied.*

An Illustration: The Stanford County Prison

Social life behind prison walls is an important topic of study, although social scientists cannot easily perform

Q: "In science as in love, a concentration on technique is likely to lead to impotence." Peter Berger (1963)

Q: "To know is nothing at all. To imagine is everything." Anatole France

Q: "It's not the things we don't know that get us into trouble. It's the things we know that just ain't so." Artemus Ward

3. **Family dynamics may differ.** Generally speaking, Hispanic cultures have strong family loyalties. Asking subjects to reveal information about another family member may make them uncomfortable, and some respondents may even refuse to do so. The Maríns add that, in the home, a researcher's request to speak privately with a Hispanic woman may provoke suspicion or outright disapproval from her husband or father.

4. **Attitudes toward time and efficiency may differ.** Spanish cultures, the Maríns explain, tend to be more concerned with the quality of relationships than with simply getting a job done. Say a non-Hispanic researcher is trying to rush through an interview with a Hispanic family (perhaps with the intention of not delaying the family's dinner). What the investigator perceives as a polite course of action may be perceived as rude by others who wish to proceed at a more relaxed pace.

5. **Attitudes toward space may differ.** Finally, the Maríns explain, people of Spanish descent typically maintain closer physical contact with others than many non-Hispanics do. Researchers, therefore, can seem "standoffish" to others, who wonder why they have seated themselves across the room. Conversely, researchers may inaccurately label Hispanics "pushy" when they move closer than the non-Hispanic researcher may find comfortable.

Of course, Hispanics differ among themselves just as people in every other category do, and these generalizations apply to some more than to others. But researchers should be aware of such cultural perceptions when carrying out their work. The challenge of conducting social research in the United States is great, indeed, since differences of the kind noted here apply to each of the dozens of distinctive categories of people that make up this large and multicultural society.

SOURCE: Marín and Marín (1991).

this kind of research "in the field." Concerned about prison violence, Philip Zimbardo devised an artificial "laboratory" in which to investigate this issue (Zimbardo, 1972; Haney, Banks, & Zimbardo, 1973).

Zimbardo started with the hypothesis that prison violence is caused not so much by antisocial prisoners or guards as by the nature of prison itself. In other words, Zimbardo suspected that, once inside a prison, even healthy and emotionally stable people become prone to violent behavior. Thus Zimbardo treated the prison setting as the independent variable capable of causing change in the dependent variable, people's behavior.

To test this hypothesis, Zimbardo's research team placed an ad in a Palo Alto, California, newspaper, offering young men $15 a day to help with a two-week research project. Each of the seventy who responded was given a series of physical and psychological tests. The researchers selected the healthiest twenty-four for their experiment. Then they randomly assigned the men to one of two groups; half were designated "prisoners" and half were to perform as "guards." The plan called for the guards and prisoners to spend the next two weeks in the "Stanford County Prison," a mock prison specially constructed in the basement of the psychology building on the Stanford University campus.

The "prisoners" began their part of the experiment when the Palo Alto police "arrested" them at their homes soon afterward. After searching and handcuffing the men, the police took them to the local police station to be fingerprinted. Then they transported their captives to the "prison" on the Stanford campus, where the "guards" assisted in securing the prisoners

RESOURCE: This three-volume set describes the history of polling in the United States: *George H. Gallup: The Gallup Poll— Public Opinion 1935–1971.* New York: Random House, 1972.
SOCIAL SURVEY: *Social Survey Software,* using the new Student Chip program, accompanies this text. It provides 1972 through 1991 NORC General Social Survey data and now has graphing and statistical capability. Each GSS involves about 1,500 subjects, selected

from a multistage survey in which researchers first randomly select geographical areas and then randomly select adults over age eighteen from each area. Excluded are individuals who are in any way "institutionalized" (including college students).
NOTE: "Pop" research, although widely read, is often based on poor surveys. For example, the last "Hite survey" of male-female relationships involved a survey return rate of only 4.5 percent.

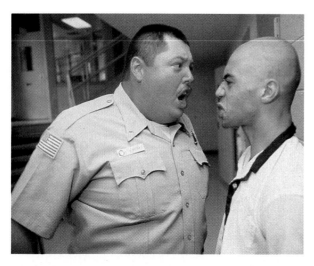

Philip Zimbardo's research helps to explain why violence is a common element in our society's prisons. At the same time, his work demonstrates the dangers that sociological investigation poses for subjects and the need for investigators to observe ethical standards that protect the welfare of people who participate in research.

behind bars. Zimbardo and his associates sat back with a video camera to see what would happen next.

The experiment soon turned into more than anyone had bargained for. The researchers observed both guards and prisoners falling into stereotypical behavior, becoming embittered toward one another and gradually losing their sense of basic human decency. Guards insulted the prisoners and humiliated them by assigning them tasks such as cleaning out toilets with their bare hands. The prisoners, for their part, displayed increasing hostility toward the guards. Within four days, the researchers removed five prisoners from the study "because of extreme emotional depression, crying, rage and acute anxiety" (1973:81). Before the end of the first week, the situation had deteriorated so badly that the researchers canceled the experiment. Zimbardo explains (1972:4): "The ugliest, most base, pathological side of human nature surfaced. We were horrified because we saw some boys (guards) treat others as if they were despicable animals, taking pleasure in cruelty, while other boys (prisoners) became servile, dehumanized robots who thought only of escape, of their own individual survival and of their mounting hatred for the guards."

What unfolded in the "Stanford County Prison" supported Zimbardo's hypothesis that prison violence

is rooted in the social character of prisons themselves, rather than the personalities of guards and prisoners. This finding also raises questions about the way our society operates prisons, suggesting the need for basic prison reform. But also note how this experiment reveals the dangers of research to the physical and mental well-being of subjects. Such threats are not always as obvious as they were in this case. Therefore researchers must consider carefully the potential harm to subjects at all stages of their work and end any study, as Zimbardo responsibly did, if subjects may suffer harm of any kind.

Survey Research

A **survey** is *a research method in which subjects respond to a series of items in a questionnaire or an interview.* The most widely used of all research methods, surveys are particularly well suited to studying what investigators cannot observe directly, such as political attitudes, religious beliefs, or the subjective effects of racism. Although researchers sometimes employ surveys to study the relationship among variables, they most often turn to surveys in *descriptive* research, in which subjects' responses paint a picture of some issue of interest.

Population and Sample

In survey research, a **population** refers to *the people who are the focus of research.* Lois Benjamin, whose research we introduced at the beginning of this chapter, wanted to learn about the effects of racism on talented African Americans. All such men and women, therefore, are the population of her study. To offer another example, political analysts try to predict voting patterns that involve every adult in the country as the survey population.

However, contacting such vast numbers of people generally requires far more time and money than researchers have available. Fortunately there is an alternative that is far easier and yields results that are, by and large, just as accurate. This is the technique of using a **sample**, meaning *a part of a population researchers select to represent the whole.* The precise size of a sample varies. The box describes the evolution of national political surveys, which now accurately assess the entire electorate using a carefully selected sample of some fifteen hundred people.

Although we may not be familiar with the term, we use the logic of sampling all the time. If you look around the room and notice five or six students

NOTE: *Literary Digest* began political polling in 1916; in 1932, it correctly predicted Franklin Delano Roosevelt's victory over Herbert Hoover. Three months before the 1936 election, however, George Gallup warned that the *Digest* poll would incorrectly foretell Alf Landon's victory. The *Digest* predicted the Landon margin at 57%, although he actually received only 37% of the vote. The *Digest* sent out 20 million postcards based on telephone listings and automobile registrations, of which only 3 million came back. Gallup's prophecy made him the national pollster, although he subsequently erred on occasion, as when he wrongly predicted the victory of Thomas Dewey over Harry Truman in the presidential race of 1948. Richard Reeves (1983)

SOCIOLOGY OF EVERYDAY LIFE

National Political Surveys

One hundred million men and women voted in the presidential election of 1992. Like most political campaigns in the United States, however, this one ended with little suspense, because, before the first vote was cast, surveys had predicted Bill Clinton the winner.

Surveys, or *polls*, form an integral part of our nation's political life. But how can information drawn from about fifteen hundred subjects predict what 100 million people will do? The key to accurate prediction is selecting a sample that represents the population as a whole.

Strategies for producing accurate surveys evolved slowly. In 1936, a survey by the *Literary Digest* predicted that Republican Alfred E. Landon would handily defeat Democrat Franklin Delano Roosevelt. It could hardly have been more wrong, as Landon lost to Roosevelt in a historic landslide. The reason for such an error was simply that

the magazine's sample did not represent the voting population. The *Digest* mailed survey ballots to 20 million people (far more than would be included in a poll today), drawing names from telephone listings and automobile registrations. These sources introduced the bias, since, especially then, people who owned

a telephone or car were more affluent and, therefore, more likely to be Republicans.

This embarrassing prediction did nothing for the prestige of the *Literary Digest*, which soon went out of business. But that same year a young researcher named George Gallup (1902–1984) not only correctly called the election but predicted that the *Literary Digest* would be off the mark. Gallup went on to become one of the best-known national survey researchers in the United States. Today, the Gallup organization carries out surveys around the world, routinely providing the public not only with accurate predictions about election returns but also with information on a host of other issues as well.

SOURCE: Adapted, in part, from Babbie (1992).

nodding off, you might conclude that the class finds the teacher to be dull. Such a conclusion involves making an inference about *all* the people (the "population") after observing *some* of the people (the "sample"). But how can we know if a sample actually represents the entire population?

A common technique is *random sampling,* which requires that each element in the population have the same chance of being included in the sample. If this is the case, mathematical laws of probability dictate that a representative sample is likely, at least within known limits. Seasoned researchers use computers to generate random samples. Novice researchers, however,

sometimes assume that "randomly" walking up to people on the street produces a random sample. Unfortunately, this is unlikely for two reasons. First, any part of a city—whether a rich neighborhood or a "college town"—is likely to contain more of some kinds of people than others. Second, any researcher is apt to find some people more approachable than others, again introducing a bias.

Although good sampling is no simple task, it offers a considerable savings in time and expense. We are spared the tedious work of contacting everyone in a population, while obtaining essentially the same results.

NOTE: Surveys taken during political campaigns do not always predict election outcomes very well. The problem is not survey error as much as changing political opinions. Primary election surveys, especially, reveal that opinions often change dramatically over a short time.

NOTE: The Census Bureau reports that 63% of people returned the 1990 census forms.

DIVERSITY: The 1990 census showed an unexpected rise from 49 million to 58 million in the number of people of German ancestry. The reason turned out to be that "German" was listed first on the 1990 survey and fourth back in 1980. Similarly, the 1990 form used "French Canadian" as an example in the ancestry section, apparently causing the number of people claiming such ancestry to triple from 780,000 in 1980 to 2.2 million in 1990.

Questionnaires and Interviews

Selecting subjects is only the first step in carrying out a survey. Also needed is a plan for asking questions and recording answers. Surveys employ two general techniques: questionnaires and interviews.

A **questionnaire** is *a series of written questions a researcher prepares for subjects to answer.* As they read the questionnaire, subjects select a response from several provided by the researcher (similar to multiple-choice examination questions). This strategy, which limits the subjects' responses, is called a *closed-ended format*; its advantage is to make the researcher's task of analyzing the results relatively easy. In some cases, however, a researcher may want subjects to respond freely. An *open-ended format* allows subjects to express various shades of opinion. Of course, the researcher later has to make sense out of what can be a bewildering array of answers.

How to present questions to subjects forms another part of the research strategy. Most often, researchers employ a *self-administered survey*, in which they mail questionnaires to respondents with a request to complete the items and mail it back. Since no researcher is present when subjects read the questionnaire, it must be both inviting and clearly written. *Pretesting* a self-administered questionnaire with a small number of people before sending it to the entire sample can avoid the costly problem of finding out—too late—that instructions or questions were confusing.

Using the mail has the advantage of involving a large number of people over a wide geographical area at relatively small expense. But some people treat such questionnaires as "junk mail"; typically, fewer than half are completed and returned. Researchers often employ follow-up mailings to coax reluctant subjects.

Finally, keep in mind that many people are not capable of completing a questionnaire on their own. Young children obviously cannot, nor can many hospital patients, as well as a surprising number of adults who simply lack the reading and writing skills needed to wade through a comprehensive questionnaire.

An **interview** is *a series of questions administered personally by a researcher to respondents.* Open-ended interviews allow the researcher to ask follow-up questions that probe and clarify the subject's responses. In the ensuing conversation, however, the researcher must guard against influencing a subject, a problem that can arise if the researcher so much as raises an eyebrow when the person begins to answer. In comparing the interview with the questionnaire, experienced investigators know that a subject is more likely to complete a survey if contacted personally by the researcher. However, a disadvantage of interviews is that tracking people down and personally interrogating them is costly and time consuming, especially if all subjects do not live in the same area.

Telephone interviews are clearly easier to accomplish, especially if subjects reside over a wide geographical area. The impersonality of "cold calls" by telephone, however, is likely to result in a low completion rate.

In both questionnaires and interviews, the wording of questions has a significant effect on answers (Fowler, Jr., & Mangione, 1989). When asked if they object to homosexuals serving in the military, for example, most adults in the United States say "yes." Yet, asked if homosexuals should be exempt from military service, most say "no" (NORC, 1991). Emotionally loaded language almost always sways subjects. For instance, the term "welfare mothers" rather than "women who receive public assistance" injects an emotional element into a survey that encourages respondents to answer more negatively. In still other cases, the wording of questions may suggest what other people think, thereby steering the respondent. People are more likely to respond positively to the question "Do you *agree* that the police force is doing a good job?" than to the question "Do you *think* that the police force is doing a good job?" Questions opening with the phrase "Do you agree" bias a subject's answers because they suggest that others endorse the statement.

Researchers should also avoid double questions like "Do you think that the government should cut spending and raise taxes to reduce the deficit?" The problem here is that a subject could very well agree with one part of the question but reject the other, so that saying yes or no distorts the actual opinion the researcher is seeking.

An Illustration: Studying the African-American Elite

We opened this chapter with a brief account of Lois Benjamin's investigation of the effects of racism on talented African-American men and women. Contrary to some published research, she was convinced that personal achievement did not lift minorities above the ordeal of hostility based on color. Her own experiences as the only black professor in the history of the University of Tampa seemed to confirm this view. But was

SOCIAL SURVEY: "In general, do you feel that surveys usually serve a good purpose, or do you feel that they are usually a waste of time and money?" (GSS 1982, N = 1,506; *Codebook*, 1993:310)

   "Good purpose" 70.6%   "Waste of time/money" 14.2%

   "Depends" 8.4%   DK/NR 6.8%

NOTE: Although widely used in survey research, "snowball sampling" is really a crude approach unlikely to represent a population accurately.

NOTE: Survey organizations have found that enclosing a small amount of money with a questionnaire (say, a dollar bill) greatly improves the response rate. Even with follow-up mailings, however, response rates rarely exceed 75 percent.

she the exception or the rule? To answer this question, Benjamin set out to discover what others like herself had to say.

Clearly, Benjamin wanted to employ some sort of a survey. But should she use a questionnaire or conduct interviews? She chose the latter approach because, first, she wanted to be able to enter into a conversation with her subjects, to ask follow-up questions, and to be able to pursue topics that she could not have anticipated in advance. A second reason to favor interviews over questionnaires is that racism is a sensitive topic. Subjects are unlikely to offer responses to what they may find to be painful questions in the absence of a supportive relationship with the investigator.

The choice to conduct interviews carried with it the requirement to keep the number of people in the study fairly small. Benjamin settled for one hundred men and women. But, given the time needed to complete interviews, she remained busy for more than two years scheduling meetings, traveling to meet informants, and taping conversations. Another two years was needed to transcribe her tapes, sort out what the hours and hours of talk told her about the issue of race, and write up her results.

Once a researcher selects a survey technique, the next order of business is building a sample. Here Benjamin faced a difficult problem. She considered using all individuals listed in *Who's Who in Black America* as her population; beginning here, she might have drawn a random sample from this source. But while she consulted this source, she decided to rely upon personal contacts to generate her sample. In simple terms, she began her work with people she knew and asked respondents to suggest others to include in the research. Sociologists refer to this technique as *snowball sampling* because the number of individuals identified in this way grows rapidly over time. The advantage of snowball sampling is that it is fairly easy to do; people we already know can provide easy introductions to their friends and colleagues. A drawback, however, is that snowball sampling rarely produces a sample that is representative of the larger population. In this case, the social networks into which Benjamin entered probably contain many like-minded individuals; moreover, her sample certainly was biased toward people willing to talk openly about race.

Although not rigorous in a scientific sense (as Benjamin knew), snowball sampling is fairly common in sociological research. At the very least, an investigator must remain mindful of the need to engage a diverse range of people. Benjamin defends her sample

Learning about most sensitive topics (such as the wounds of racism) demands that researchers establish a comfortable rapport with their subjects. Using her personal skills as well as her training in sociological investigation, Lois Benjamin made one hundred men and women feel sufficiently at ease that they were willing to share their sometimes painful life histories. In the process, Benjamin gained an understanding of how even the most successful people of color in the United States have confronted barriers based on race.

as varied, at least in terms of sex, age, and region of the country. Table 2–1 provides a profile of the individuals who participated in her investigation.

Benjamin's interviews were guided by a series of questions asked of everyone, but the conversations were open-ended so that either her subjects or she could pursue issues as they wished. Like many interviewers, Benjamin gathered information in a wide range of settings. Some meetings took place in offices (hers or theirs), some in hotel rooms, some in cars. Benjamin tape-recorded each interview—which lasted from two-and-one-half to three hours—so that she would not be distracted from the conversation by the need to take notes. At the end of her interviews, however, she faced the arduous task of transcribing some three hundred hours of tape-recorded conversations.

As is ethically required, Benjamin offered full anonymity to any individual who wanted it. Even so, many of her respondents—including such notables as Vernon E. Jordan, Jr. (former president of the National

NOTE: Conducting interviews, as Lois Benjamin did, is something like traveling abroad. We have some idea of our direction and destination, but the unexpected always arises along the way. Imaginative improvisation is needed to make the most of an interview opportunity and sometimes even to "save a situation."

NOTE: Lois Benjamin did not clearly operationalize "talented African Americans," so that the population her sample represents remains only vaguely defined.

TABLE 2–1 The Talented One Hundred: Lois Benjamin's African-American Elite

Sex	Age	Childhood Racial Setting	Childhood Region	Highest Educational Degree	Occupational Sector	Income	Political Orientation
Male 63%	35 or younger 6%	Mostly Black 71%	West 6%	Doctorate 32%	College/ University 35%	More than $50,000 64%	Radical 13%
Female 37%	36 to 54 68%	Mostly White 15%	North/ Central 32%	Medical/ Law 17%	Private, Profit 17%	$35,000 to $50,000 18%	Liberal 38%
	55 or older 26%	Racially Mixed 14%	South 38%	Master's 27%	Private, Nonprofit 9%	$20,000 to $34,999 12%	Moderate 28%
			Northeast 12%	Bachelor's 13%	Government 22%	Less than $20,000 6%	Conservative 5%
			Other 12%	Less 11%	Self-Employed 14%		Depends on Issue 14%
					Retired 3%		Unknown 2%
100%	100%	100%	100%	100%	100%	100%	100%

SOURCE: Adapted from Lois Benjamin, *The Black Elite: Facing the Color Line in the Twilight of the Twentieth Century* (Chicago: Nelson-Hall, 1991), p. 276.

Urban League) and Yvonne Walker-Taylor (first woman president of Wilberforce University)—were accustomed to being in the public eye and permitted Benjamin to use their names.

What surprised this researcher, however, was the eagerness with which many informants responded to her request for an interview. Many normally very busy men and women appeared to go out of their way to contribute to this project. Furthermore, once the interviews were under way, many displayed a high degree of emotion. Benjamin reports that, at some point in their conversations, about forty of her one hundred subjects shed tears. For many, the research was therapeutic—an opportunity to release feelings and share experiences that they had never shared before. How did Benjamin, herself, respond to such sentiments? She reports that, as her subjects laughed, reflected, or cried, she laughed, reflected, or cried with them. Interesting questions, in light of this close rapport, are whether a formal and aloof researcher could have completed this research, and whether or not a white investigator could have done so.

Benjamin's research helps us to understand the continuing importance of race in shaping the daily lives of individuals in the United States. As we noted at the beginning of this chapter, other researchers have documented important gains in social standing among African Americans in recent decades. But Benjamin's interviews reveal that many members of the Talented One Hundred are not confident in their achievements. On the contrary, they are anxious that their racial identity may at some time undermine their success. Benjamin reports, too, many are concerned that a race-based "glass ceiling" stands between them and the highest positions in our society. Summing up her respondents' thoughts and feelings, Benjamin states that, despite the improving social standing of people of color, they continue to feel the sting of racial hostility in the United States. And, contradicting conventional wisdom, rising into this nation's social elite based on personal achievement is no protection from racism. Benjamin concludes that color remains a basic factor guiding how members of our society subjectively perceive themselves and others.

Given that Benjamin finds that a "color line" continues to exist in this country, she ends her study urging a greater commitment to change. Following the lead of W. E. B. Du Bois, Benjamin sees research not merely as a source of knowledge but as a strategy for assisting the people she is studying.

Q: "The possibility of drawing inferences from what has been observed and described in London, as to what we might expect in New York or Chicago, rests on the assumption that the same forces create everywhere essentially the same conditions." Robert Park

Q: "[Community studies are] the poor sociologist's substitute for the novel." Ruth Glass

RESOURCE: Ivy Goduka's article, "Applying U.S. Ethics to Research in South Africa," explains the dangers of doing research in politically volatile societies; it is one of the cross-cultural selections in the Macionis and Benokraitis reader *Seeing Ourselves*, 3/e.

CRITICAL THINKING

Table Reading: An Important Skill

A table provides a great deal of information in a small amount of space, so learning to read tables can increase your reading efficiency. When you spot a table, look first at the title to see what information it contains. In Table 2–1, the title indicates that the table provides a profile of the one hundred subjects participating in Lois Benjamin's research. Across the top of the table, you will see eight dimensions that define these women and men. Reading vertically under each dimension, various categories are presented, each with a percentage, and all the percentages add up to one hundred, as indicated at the bottom of the columns.

Starting at the top left, we see that Benjamin's sample was predominantly men (63 percent), with fewer (37 percent) women included. In terms of age, most of the respondents (68 percent) were in the middle stage of life, and a majority grew up in the south or north/central regions of the United States. The majority of these people of color also grew up in a predominantly black environment.

These individuals are, indeed, a professional elite. Notice that half have earned either a doctorate (32 percent) or a medical or law degree (17 percent), and only a small number (11 percent) have less than a bachelor's degree. Given the extensive education of these men and women (and Benjamin's own position as a professor), we should not be surprised that the largest share (35 percent) work in academic institutions. In terms of income, these are affluent individuals, with most (64 percent) earning more than $50,000 annually (an income received by only one-fifth of all workers).

Finally, we see that these one hundred individuals are generally left-of-center in their political orientations. In part, this probably reflects their extensive schooling (which fosters political liberalism); in addition, academics are generally more liberal in their views than our society as a whole.

Participant Observation

Participant observation is *a method in which researchers systematically observe people while joining in their routine activities.* Researchers choose this method in order to gain an inside look at social life in settings ranging from night clubs to religious seminaries. Cultural anthropologists commonly employ participant observation (which they often call *fieldwork*) to study communities in other societies. They term their descriptions of unfamiliar cultures *ethnographies*; sociologists prefer to describe their accounts of people in particular settings as *case studies*.

Undertaking a case study, social scientists will probably have only a vague understanding of the patterns they wish to investigate. Thus, participant observation is *descriptive* and often *exploratory*. Researchers are likely to begin with few, if any, specific hypotheses to test, since they may not even know what the important questions will turn out to be. Compared to experiments and survey research, then, participant observation has fewer hard-and-fast rules. But it is precisely this flexibility that allows investigators to explore the unknown and to adapt to the unexpected.

As its name suggests, participant observation has two sides. On the one hand, gaining an "insider's" look depends on becoming a participant in the setting—"hanging out" with others, attempting to act, think, and even feel the way they do. Unlike other research methods, participant observation requires a researcher to become immersed in a social setting, not for a week or two but for months or even years. On the other hand, for the duration of the study, the researcher must also maintain the role of "observer," mentally stepping back from the action to apply the sociological perspective to events that others take for granted. The twin roles of "insider" participant and "outsider" observer often come down to a series of careful compromises. Researchers are likely to record such tensions in their *field notes*, a daily record of how

NOTE: According to 1990 census data, the most representative places in the United States are Tulsa, Oklahoma, and Charleston, West Virginia.

RESOURCE: A good example of a researcher assessing how his own values influenced his work is the methodological appendix to William Foote Whyte's *Street Corner Society* (1981; orig. 1943).

John Sloan's urban scene, The Lafayette, *piques our imagination. Like Sloan, we have all seen people enter and leave particular places that we know nothing about. Provided, of course, that they can gain access, investigators employ participant observation to gain an insider's understanding of such settings.*

John Sloan (1871–1951). Oil on canvas. 30 1/2 x 36 1/8 inches. Signed (lower left): John Sloan. Painted in 1928. The Metropolitan Museum of Art, Gift of Friends of John Sloan, 1928. (28.18)

the investigation proceeds. These notes form the basis for the final research report and should convey not only the researcher's conclusions but something of the research experience itself.

Sociologists often work alone in this kind of study, so they must remain mindful that results depend on the interpretations of a single individual. Participant observation is typically **qualitative research,** meaning *inquiry based on subjective impressions.* Unlike experiments or surveys, participant observation usually involves little **quantitative research,** *investigation based on the analysis of numerical data.* Some scientists disparage a method that relies so heavily on personal impressions as lacking in scientific rigor. Yet its personal approach is also a strength; while a highly visible team of sociologists attempting to administer formal surveys would disrupt many social settings, a sensitive participant-observer can often gain considerable insight into people's natural behavior.

An Illustration: Street Corner Society

In the late 1930s, a young sociologist named William Foote Whyte carried out what has become a classic illustration of participant observation. A graduate student at Harvard University, Whyte was fascinated by the lively street life of a nearby, rather rundown section of Boston. He embarked on a four-year study of this

neighborhood, which he renamed "Cornerville" to protect the privacy of its inhabitants.

Cornerville was home to first- and second-generation Italian immigrants. Many were poor and lived quite unlike the more affluent Bostonians familiar to Whyte. A common notion in Boston held that Cornerville was a place to avoid: a poor, chaotic slum inhabited by racketeers. Unwilling to accept easy stereotypes, Whyte set out to discover for himself exactly what kind of life went on inside this community. His celebrated book, *Street Corner Society* (1981; orig. 1943), describes Cornerville as a highly organized community with its own code of values, complex social patterns, and distinctive social conflicts.

Whyte's research points up the advantages of participant-observation as well as some of its pitfalls. He could have taken his clipboard and questionnaire to one of Cornerville's community centers and asked local people to talk about their lives. Or he could have asked members of the community to come to his Harvard office for interviews. Many Cornerville residents would probably have refused to talk to him at all under those circumstances, and, in any case, their behavior would not have been very natural. Whyte realized that he had to downplay the role of observer if people were to be comfortable in his presence. Therefore, he tried to fit into Cornerville's everyday social patterns.

50 Chapter 2 Sociological Investigation

GLOBAL: Culture shock can create significant barriers to research conducted in unfamiliar settings. These include language problems, which may result in a researcher spending twice the usual time to complete interviews as well as errors of understanding. In another culture, a researcher may also unintentionally "steer" a subject, per-haps even coercing agreement to participate in the study in the first place. Researchers are likely to find negotiating with officials to be frustrating, because formal regulations as well as informal social patterns vary from those in the United States.

One night early in his study, Whyte joined a group of Cornerville people who frequented a gambling establishment. After listening to one fellow explain how gambling was organized, Whyte asked naively, "I suppose the cops were all paid off?" The man's reaction taught Whyte something about the tension between being a participant and being an observer:

The gambler's jaw dropped. He glared at me. Then he denied vehemently that any policeman had been paid off and immediately switched the conversation to another subject. For the rest of that evening I felt very uncomfortable.

The next day [a local acquaintance] explained the lesson of the previous evening. "Go easy on that 'who,' 'what,' 'why,' 'when,' 'where' stuff, Bill. You ask those questions and people will clam up on you. If people accept you, you can just hang around, and you'll learn the answers in the long run without even having to ask the questions." (1981:303)

Gaining entry to the community—that is, becoming a participant—was the crucial first step in Whyte's research. But how could an upper-middle-class Anglo-Saxon graduate student from Harvard become part of the life of a poor Italian immigrant community like Cornerville? The answer involves patience, ingenuity, and sometimes simple luck. Initial efforts to "break in" to a strange social environment may be embarrassing, and sometimes even dangerous, as Whyte soon found out. On another evening, Whyte dropped in at a local bar, hoping to buy a woman a drink and encourage her to talk about Cornerville. He looked around the room but could find no woman alone. Presently, he noticed a fellow talking with two women, which he took to be an opportunity:

I approached the group and opened with something like this:

"Pardon me. Would you mind if I joined you?" There was a moment of silence while the man stared at me. Then he offered to throw me down the stairs. I assured him that this would not be necessary, and demonstrated as much by walking right out of there without any assistance. (1981:289)

This experience taught Whyte another important lesson: Imposing on people is not only impolite, it can be downright hazardous. Fortunately, however, his luck soon took a turn for the better when he met a young man named "Doc" in the local social service agency. Doc listened sympathetically to the problem and took Whyte under his wing, introducing his new friend to others in the neighborhood. With Doc's help, Whyte soon became a "regular" among the people of Cornerville.

Whyte's friendship with Doc illustrates the importance of a *key informant* in field research. Key informants introduce a researcher to a community and often suggest how to gather specific information. But using a key informant also has its dangers. Because any key informant is familiar with only part of a community, such help may introduce bias into research. Moreover, in the eyes of others the reputation of the key informant—for better or worse—may rub off on the investigator. In sum, while the help of a key informant is invaluable at the outset, a participant-observer should soon seek a broader range of contacts.

During several years of living in Cornerville, Whyte learned that it was hardly the disorganized slum some thought it to be. Many immigrants were working hard to become established and successful, and many were proud to have sent children to college. Whyte studied various social divisions in Cornerville, and he even found a few criminals. Yet he was able to see that this distinctive Boston neighborhood was composed mostly of people who, though poor, were working hard to build a future for themselves.

In sum, participant observation is a method of tensions and contrasts. Its flexibility helps a researcher respond to an unfamiliar setting but makes replication quite difficult for others. Sympathetic understanding requires involvement, while scientific observation demands detachment. A single researcher with little funding can tell the story of an entire community, but the time required to do so makes this a demanding type of research. Perhaps for all these reasons, participant-observation research is used less often than other methods described in this chapter. Yet the depth of understanding gained through research of this kind has greatly enriched our knowledge of many types of human communities.

Secondary and Historical Analysis

Not all research requires investigators to collect their own data personally. In many cases, sociologists engage in **secondary analysis,** *a research method in which a researcher utilizes data collected by others.*

The most widely used statistics are gathered by government agencies. The Bureau of the Census continuously publishes information about the U.S. population, much of which draws the interest of sociologists. Similar material is available from Statistics Canada, a branch of the Canadian government. Global investigations benefit from various publications of the United Nations and the World Bank. In short, a wide range of data is as close as the college library.

The obvious advantage of using available data—whether government statistics or the findings of individual researchers—is a savings in time and money. This strategy enables sociologists with low budgets to undertake research that might otherwise be impossible. Just as important, the quality of government data is generally better than what even well-funded researchers could hope to obtain on their own.

Still, secondary analysis has inherent problems. For one thing, available data may not have been gathered in a systematic and unbiased way. Using second-hand data is sometimes a bit like buying a used car: Bargains are plentiful, but you have to shop carefully to avoid ending up with a "lemon."

Emile Durkheim's nineteenth-century study of suicide, described in Chapter 1 ("The Sociological Perspective"), is one of the best-known sociological investigations of existing records. But Durkheim's research also illustrates some of the dangers of this approach. He found that official death records yielded information on the suicide rates of various types of people, but he had no way to assess how many accidents were incorrectly classified as suicides or what number of suicides were recorded as accidents or deaths due to some other cause.

Moreover, the way in which original researchers phrased questions or selected respondents may or may not work well for subsequent investigators. Sociologists who utilize data collected by others, then, must be ever vigilant for error and bias.

National Map 2–1 makes use of Census Bureau data to show where in the United States affluent minorities reside. This map illustrates both the strengths and weaknesses of secondary data.

An Illustration: A Tale of Two Cities

Since we are all trapped in the present, secondary analysis provides a key to investigating the past. The award-winning study *Puritan Boston and Quaker Philadelphia*, carried out by E. Digby Baltzell (1979), exemplifies historical sociology's use of existing data. Upon a chance visit to Bowdoin College in Maine, Baltzell was startled to learn that this small school had graduated more famous individuals than his own, much bigger University of Pennsylvania. This discovery sparked his sociological imagination, leading him to investigate historical patterns of achievement in New England and Pennsylvania.

Baltzell first wanted to find out if, indeed, New England had produced far more than its share of national leaders in diverse fields such as politics, law, and the arts; further, his hunch was that his native Pennsylvania had produced few such luminaries. As a source of data, Baltzell turned to the *Dictionary of American Biography*, twenty volumes of biographical information on more than thirteen thousand men and women. Baltzell knew that by using this source he could consider only those people deemed worthy by the editors of the *Dictionary*. He proceeded, accepting some inevitable bias, because he knew of no better place to find the information he needed.

Baltzell's next problem was how to measure the magnitude of personal achievement. He decided to base his ranking on the stated policy of the *Dictionary* to reflect stature in the length of each individual's biography. Such ratings are open to argument, of course, but Baltzell could hardly have done better entirely on his own.

By the time Baltzell had identified the seventy-five individuals with the longest biographies, a striking pattern had emerged. Massachusetts had the most top achievers, claiming twenty-one of the seventy-five. All the New England states, together, had thirty-one of the entries. By contrast, Pennsylvania had only two, and the entire Middle Atlantic region, just twelve. Closing in on the explanation, Baltzell soon discovered that most of the great achievers from New England had their roots in and around the city of Boston. Again, in stark contrast, there turned out to be far less personal accomplishment in the history of his own Philadelphia, a city with both more people and more money than Boston.

What could explain the disparity? Baltzell drew inspiration from the German sociologist Max Weber (1958; orig. 1904–5), whose research linking achievement to religion is detailed in Chapter 4 ("Society"). Baltzell began contrasting the religious environments that have historically dominated Boston and Philadelphia. Here lay the key to this historical puzzle: The Puritan founders of Boston were determined in their pursuit of public achievement, just as their Quaker counterparts in Philadelphia were fervent in their avoidance of it.

Both cities were founded by refugees fleeing religious persecution in England. But the groups viewed the world quite differently. Convinced of humanity's innate sinfulness, Boston Puritans built a rigid society in which family, church, and school regulated people's behavior. Hard work was the means to glorify God, and public prominence the most

THE MAP: Generally speaking, African Americans, Asian Americans, and Latinos are concentrated in different regions of the country (see National Map 12-2). The largest urban regions (surrounding New York and Los Angeles) are home to affluent minorities of all kinds (although often in distinctive neighborhoods). In most cases, however, a single county contains a disproportionate share of affluent people of only one minority category. The general pattern is that, at all income levels, people of various racial and ethnic categories live in different regions of the country as well as in different communities.

Seeing Ourselves

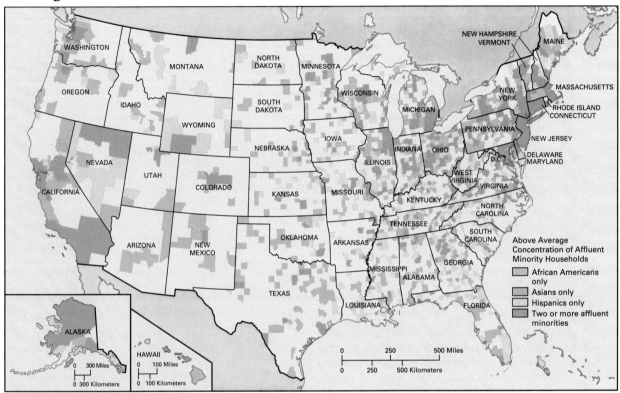

NATIONAL MAP 2–1 Affluent Minorities: Residential Patterns

Based on 1990 census data, this map identifies the counties of the United States that contain an above-average share of affluent minority households—those earning at least $50,000 annually. (For the entire country, 13.2 percent of African Americans, 16.1 percent of Hispanics, and 35.0 percent of Asians fall into this favored category.) The strengths of Census Bureau data are that they are readily available and also of high quality. At the same time, however, we have to accept the Census Bureau's definition of affluent, as well as the mapmaker's idea of what constitutes "above average."

Where in the United States do affluent members of each minority category live? Based on these data, would you conclude that affluent minorities tend to integrate among themselves or reside in separate communities?

Adapted from *American Demographics* magazine, Dec. 1992, pp. 34–35. Reprinted with permission. ©1992, *American Demographics* magazine, Ithaca, New York. Data from the 1990 decennial census.

reassuring sign that one had received God's blessing. Puritanism fostered a hierarchical and disciplined life in which people vigorously sought and respected achievement.

Philadelphia's Quakers, by contrast, built their way of life on the notion that human beings are inherently good. They saw little need for strong social institutions to "save" individuals from sinfulness. Although many Quakers pursued wealth, they remained convinced that all people are equal. Even their most successful

members celebrated personal modesty and discouraged each other from standing apart by seeking fame or pursuing public office.

In Baltzell's sociological imagination, Boston and Philadelphia took the form of two social "test tubes": Puritanism was poured into one, Quakerism into the other. From our vantage point centuries later, we can see that different "chemical reactions" occurred in each case. Without claiming that one religion is in any sense "better" than the other, Baltzell convincingly

Interesting, although anecdotal, ways to describe the difference between the two cities: Puritan Boston named streets after great families, Quaker Philadelphia named streets after trees; a Boston accent often leads people to overestimate someone, a Philadelphia accent lends little prestige to a speaker. Boston's lead- ing university (Harvard) was founded within a decade of the city's settlement and is at the top of the Ivy League; the founders of Philadelphia did not establish their university (University of Pennsylvania) for 60 years, and it remains the least well-known Ivy.

TABLE 2–2 Four Research Methods: A Summary

Method	Application	Advantages	Limitations
Experiment	For explanatory research that specifies relationships among variables; generates quantitative data	Provides greatest ability to specify cause-and-effect relationships; replication of research is relatively easy	Laboratory settings have artificial quality; unless research environment is carefully controlled, results may be biased
Survey	For gathering information about issues that cannot be directly observed, such as attitudes and values; useful for descriptive and explanatory research; generates quantitative or qualitative data	Sampling allows surveys of large populations using questionnaires; interviews provide in-depth responses	Questionnaires must be carefully prepared and may produce low return rate; interviews are expensive and time consuming
Participant observation	For exploratory and descriptive study of people in a "natural" setting; generates qualitative data	Allows study of "natural" behavior; usually inexpensive	Time consuming; replication of research is difficult; researcher must balance roles of participant and observer
Secondary analysis	For exploratory, descriptive, or explanatory research whenever suitable data are available	Saves time and expense of data collection; makes historical research possible	Researcher has no control over possible bias in data; data may not be suitable for current research needs

argues that the two belief systems set in motion different orientations toward personal achievement, which shaped the history of each region and may shape the accomplishments of people who live there even today. For example, the Kennedy family (despite being Catholic) still exemplifies the Puritan pursuit of fame and leadership. There has never been a comparable family in the entire history of Philadelphia.

As in all research, Baltzell's historical data do not *prove* his conclusions in any absolute sense. The best we can say is that his theory seems consistent with the data, and, as always, future research may support or challenge his contentions. Especially when dealing with events far removed from the present, researchers must make considerable use of their interpretive skills. Baltzell's research reminds us that, in the end, sociological investigation encompasses a complex weave of scientific skills, personal values, and a lively and practiced imagination.

Table 2–2 summarizes the four major methods of sociological investigation. We now turn to our final consideration: how we can relate the specific facts obtained through sociological investigation to theory.

The Interplay of Theory and Method

Methods of sociological investigation guide the discovery of facts about our social world. Facts, however, are not the final goal of research. As suggested in Chapter 1 ("The Sociological Perspective"), what sociologists really strive for is the development of theory —combining facts into cogent patterns of meaning.

As they reflect on their work, sociological investigators move between facts and theory in two directions. **Deductive logical thought** is *reasoning that transforms general ideas into specific hypotheses suitable for scientific testing.* From a general understanding of some issue, in other words, the researcher *deduces* a hypothesis and selects a method by which to test it. Of course, the data collected may or may not support the hypothesis. Data supporting the hypothesis suggest that the general theory is on the right track. Data refuting the hypothesis alert the researcher that the theory should be revised or perhaps rejected entirely. The deductive logical model, then, proceeds from the general (theory) to the specific (facts used for evaluation).

Philip Zimbardo's Stanford County Prison experiment illustrates how this model operates. Zimbardo began with the general idea that prisons themselves alter human behavior. He then fashioned a specific hypothesis: Placed in a prison setting, even emotionally well-balanced young men would exhibit violent behavior. The fact that violence erupted soon after Zimbardo's experiment began certainly supports this hypothesis. Had his experiment produced amicable behavior between "prisoners" and "guards," his original theory would clearly have required reformulation.

NOTE: Sherlock Holmes, celebrated for his great powers of deduction, actually engaged in *inductive reasoning*. While investigating a particular crime scene, for example, Holmes was speaking with the woman of the house when he suddenly noticed the housekeeper searching for the cord to close the drapes. "Why did you dismiss your previous servant?" he asked. "How did you know?" came her startled reply. "Elementary," he explained, "your present servant is obviously new to her duties."

A second type of logical thought works in the other direction. Through **inductive logical thought**, or *reasoning that builds specific observations into general theory*, a researcher organizes specific observations into a more general theory about human behavior.

E. Digby Baltzell's research illustrates the inductive logical model. He began by noting that one New England college had produced a surprising number of high achievers. Speculating that this fact might involve a regional pattern, he collected additional facts until he discerned the importance of religious values to achievement.

Just as researchers commonly employ several methods over the course of one study, they also make use of *both* types of logical thought. Figure 2–2 illustrates how sociological investigation often begins with general ideas that lead (deductively) to hypotheses, which, in turn, are evaluated on the basis of specific observations. These observations then (inductively) guide the modification of the original theory.

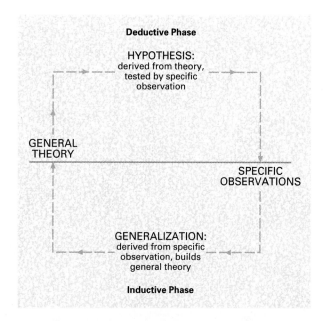

FIGURE 2–2 Deductive and Inductive Logical Thought

PUTTING IT ALL TOGETHER: TEN STEPS IN SOCIOLOGICAL INVESTIGATION

Any research project in sociology should include each of the following ten steps.

1. **Define the topic of investigation.** We can find ideas for social research anywhere and everywhere. Remain curious and observe the world using the sociological perspective. As Max Weber suggested and the research noted in this chapter illustrates, the issue you choose for study is likely to have some personal significance.

2. **Find out what has already been learned about the topic.** You are probably not the first person to develop an interest in a particular issue. Spend time in the library to see what theories and methods researchers have applied to your topic. Theory guides the kinds of questions you ask, and research methods indicate strategies for discovering answers. In reviewing existing research, note problems that may have come up before.

3. **Assess the requirements for carrying out research on the topic.** What resources are necessary to support your research? How much time will you need? Can you do the work yourself? What expenses will you have along the way? What sources of funding might be available to support your research? You must answer all these questions before you actually begin to design the research project.

4. **Specify the questions you are going to ask.** Are you seeking to explore an unfamiliar social setting? To describe some category of people? Or to investigate cause and effect among variables? If your study is exploratory, identify general questions that will guide the work. If it is descriptive, specify the population and the characteristics of interest. If it is explanatory, state the hypothesis to be tested and carefully operationalize each variable.

5. **Consider the ethical issues involved in the research.** Not all research raises serious ethical issues, but you should be sensitive to this matter throughout your investigation. Will you promise anonymity to the subjects? If so, how will you ensure that anonymity will be maintained? Can the research harm anyone? How might you design the study to minimize the chances for injury?

6. **Devise a research strategy.** Consider all major research strategies—as well as innovative combinations of approaches—before deciding how to proceed. Keep in mind that the appropriate method depends on the kind of questions you are asking as well as the resources available to support your research.

What we "see" in our surroundings, or in the research data we derive from them, depends on us as well as on what we study. To illustrate, examine Target With Four Faces, *constructed of plaster, paper, cloth, and canvas by artist Jasper Johns. The assemblage is provocative—demanding that we make sense of it—because it places human faces in menacing combination with a target. But why are the faces the same? Why are the eyes hidden from view? The riddle of this artwork is made even more vexing by the artist's denial that it has any meaning at all. In the end, our response to all art depends on our own sensibilities. We might highlight the pleasing textures and colors that are used, the disturbing statement the work seems to make, or perhaps ponder the inconsistency between these two levels of meaning. Developing such skills of interpretation is as important to scientific research as it is to appreciating fine art.*

Jasper Johns, *Target with Four Faces*, 1955. Assemblage: encaustic and collage on canvas with objects, 26 x 26", surmounted by four tinted plaster faces in wood box with hinged front. Box, closed, 3 3/4 x 26 x 3 1/2". Overall dimensions with box open, 33 5/8 x 26 x 3". The Museum of Modern Art, NY. Gift of Mr. & Mrs. Robert C. Scull.

7. **Using the method, gather your data.** The chosen research method provides the system for data collection. Be sure to record accurately all information in a way that will make sense later (it may be some time before you actually write up the results of your work). Remain vigilant for any bias that may creep into the research.

8. **Interpret the findings.** Scrutinize the data in terms of the initial questions and decide what answers they suggest. If your study involves a specific hypothesis, you should be able to confirm, reject, or modify the hypothesis based on the data. Keep in mind that there may be several ways to interpret the results of your study, consistent with different theoretical paradigms, and you should consider them all. Ask other people to review your work and suggest alternative interpretations. Try to assess how personal values or your expectations of results may affect how you make sense of the data.

9. **Based on the findings, state your conclusions.** Prepare a final report explaining what you have learned from the research. Consider the contributions of your work both to sociological theory and to improving sociological methods of research. What is the value of your research to people outside of sociology? Finally, evaluate your own work. What problems arose during the research process? What questions are left unanswered? Note ways in which your own biases may have affected your conclusions.

10. **Publish your research!** There are many ways to present your work, including journals and public presentations on campus and at professional meetings. The important point is to share what you have learned with others and to let others respond to your work. Doing this, you gain a place among countless women and men who, through their research, have expanded our understanding of human behavior.

SUMMARY

1. Sociologists use the logic of science to investigate the social world. Science provides the logical foundation of all sociological research and, more broadly, helps us to critically evaluate information we encounter every day.

2. Two basic requirements for sociological investigation are (1) using the sociological perspective to view the surrounding world and (2) being curious and asking questions about society.

3. Measurement is the process of determining the value of a variable in any specific case. Sound measurement is both reliable and valid.

4. A goal of science is specifying the relationship among variables. Correlation means that two or more variables change value together. More useful are relationships of cause and effect in which a researcher can use an independent variable to predict change in a dependent variable.

5. The scientific ideal is objectivity. Although investigators select topics of study according to their personal interests, value-free research depends on suspending personal biases as much as possible.

6. Issues involving gender often generate bias in research. Investigators should avoid examining issues from the point of view of only one sex or basing generalizations about humanity on data collected from only men or women.

7. Social scientists must recognize that studying unique and responsive people poses challenges that are not found in the natural sciences.

8. Human curiosity and imagination remain vital to any research project. Similarly, researchers must always bring their data to life through interpretation.

9. Rejecting conventional ideas about scientific objectivity, some sociologists argue that research inevitably involves political values. Thus researchers should use their work to promote what they see as desirable social change.

10. Because sociological research has the potential to cause discomfort or even harm to subjects, sociological investigators are bound by ethical guidelines.

11. Experiments, which must be performed under controlled conditions, attempt to specify the relationship between two (or more) variables.

12. The survey, which may involve questionnaires or interviews, is a strategy for gathering people's responses to statements or questions.

13. Participant observation involves direct observation of a social setting for an extended period of time. Using this method, the investigator functions both as a participant in the setting and as a careful observer of it.

14. Secondary analysis, or making use of available data, is often preferable to collecting one's own data; it is also essential in the study of historical issues.

15. Theory and research are linked through two kinds of thinking. Deductive thought transforms general ideas into specific hypotheses suitable for testing. Inductive thought organizes specific observations into general ideas.

KEY CONCEPTS

cause and effect a relationship between two variables in which change in one (the independent variable) causes change in another (the dependent variable)

concept a mental construct that represents some part of the world, inevitably in a simplified form

control the ability to neutralize the effect of one or more variables in order to assess the relationships among other variables

correlation a relationship between two (or more) variables

deductive logical thought reasoning that transforms general ideas into specific hypotheses suitable for scientific testing

dependent variable a variable that is changed by another (independent) variable

empirical evidence information we are able to verify with our senses

experiment a research method for investigating cause and effect under highly controlled conditions

Hawthorne effect a change in a subject's behavior caused by the awareness of being studied

hypothesis an unverified statement of a relationship between variables

independent variable a variable that causes change in another (dependent) variable

inductive logical thought reasoning that builds specific observations into general theory

interview a series of questions administered personally by a researcher to respondents

mean the arithmetic average of a series of numbers

measurement the process of determining the value of a variable in a specific case

median the value that occurs midway in a series of numbers arranged in order of magnitude or, simply, the middle case

mode the value that occurs most often in a series of numbers

objectivity a state of personal neutrality in conducting research

operationalizing a variable specifying exactly what one is to measure in assigning a value to a variable

participant observation a research method in which researchers systematically observe people while joining in their routine activities

population the people who are the focus of research

qualitative research inquiry based on subjective impressions

quantitative research inquiry based on the analysis of numerical data

questionnaire a series of written questions a researcher prepares for subjects to answer

reliability the quality of consistent measurement

replication repetition of research by others in order to assess its accuracy

research method a strategy for systematically conducting research

sample a part of a population researchers select to represent the whole

science a logical system that bases knowledge on direct, systematic observation

secondary analysis a research method in which a researcher utilizes data collected by others

spurious correlation an apparent, although false, relationship between two (or more) variables caused by some other variable

survey a research method in which subjects respond to a series of questions in a questionnaire or an interview

validity the quality of measuring precisely what one intends to measure

variable a concept whose value changes from case to case

CRITICAL THINKING QUESTIONS

1. What does it mean to state that there are various kinds of truth? What is the basic rationale for employing science as a way of knowing?

2. What sorts of things do scientists do as they strive for objectivity? Why do some sociologists see objectivity as an undesirable goal?

3. Identify several ways in which sociological research is similar to—and different from—research in natural science.

4. What considerations might lead a sociologist to decide to use one method of research over another?

SUGGESTED READINGS

Classic Sources

Alvin Gouldner. *The Coming Crisis in Western Sociology.* New York: Avon Books, 1970.

Gouldner provides one of the best efforts to evaluate the place of values and politics in sociological research.

Robert K. Merton, Marjorie Fiske, and Patricia L. Kendall. *The Focused Interview: A Manual of Problems and Procedures.* 2d ed. New York: The Free Press, 1990.

This book is a new edition of a classic account of how and why social scientists conduct interviews.

Delbert C. Miller. *Handbook of Research Design and Social Measurement.* 5th ed. Newbury Park, Calif.: Sage, 1991.

Here is a well-respected guide to research strategies, including how to utilize the library to advantage.

Contemporary Sources

Chava Frankfort-Nachmias and David Nachmias. *Research Methods in the Social Sciences.* 5th ed. New York: St. Martin's Press, 1995.

This book introduces the process of sociological investigation in terms that are easy for beginning students to understand.

Edward Erwin, Sidney Gendin, and Lowell Kleiman, eds. *Ethical Issues in Scientific Research: An Anthology.* Hamden, Conn.: Garland, 1993.

This collection of essays ranges from the role of values in research to issues of deception and fraud to experimentation on animals and humans.

Dorothy Ross. *The Origins of American Social Science.* New York: Cambridge University Press, 1991.

This book reviews the development of sociology, political science, economics, and history in the United States, highlighting how they differ from the natural sciences.

Floyd J. Fowler, Jr. *Survey Research Methods.* Newbury Park, Calif.: Sage, 1993.

This book provides plenty of technical detail about implementing sociology's most widely used method of investigation.

Danny L. Jorgensen. *Participant Observation: A Methodology for Human Studies.* Newbury Park, Calif.: Sage, 1989.

This book analyzes one of sociology's basic research strategies.

Margrit Eichler. *Nonsexist Research Methods: A Practical Guide.* Winchester, Mass.: Unwin Hyman, 1988.

Shulamit Reinharz. *Feminist Methods in Social Research.* New York: Oxford University Press, 1992.

The first of these books explores how gender and sexism can affect the research process. The second provides details about how feminism has transformed various research strategies.

James A. Davis and Tom W. Smith. *The NORC General Social Survey: A User's Guide.* Newbury Park, Calif.: Sage, 1992.

This book details the methodology that produces the General Social Survey, the best single annual survey of attitudes and behaviors in the United States.

Davis W. Stewart and Prem N. Shamdasani. *Focus Groups: Theory and Practice.* Newbury Park, Calif.: Sage, 1990.

"Focus groups"—small groups that interact intensively in an attempt to answer some basic questions—are widely used in industry. This book details the operation of focus groups, including how to recruit members, how to conduct group discussions, and how to analyze data.

Sociology Writing Group. *A Guide to Writing Sociology Papers.* New York: St. Martin's Press, 1986.

Howard S. Becker, with a chapter by Pamela Richards. *Writing for Social Scientists: How To Start and Finish Your Thesis, Book, or Article.* Chicago: University of Chicago Press, 1986.

All researchers need to develop skills for communicating their findings to others in a clear and interesting way. These two books (the second aimed at more advanced writers) can help you to do just that.

David M. Oshinsky, Richard P. McCormick, and Daniel Horn. *The Case of the Nazi Professor.* New Brunswick, N.J.: Rutgers University Press, 1989.

In the world of academia, politics, scholarship, and teaching are often deeply intertwined. This account of a university looking back fifty years to reconsider the record of a member of its faculty probes these interconnections.

Elijah Anderson. *Street Wise.* Chicago: University of Chicago Press, 1990.

Here is a readable and enlightening case study of an African-American community in Philadelphia.

James S. Jackson. *Life in Black America.* Newbury Park, Calif.: Sage, 1991.

Based on the National Survey of Black Americans, this source discusses not only research findings but also methodological issues raised in research involving African Americans.

Global Sources

Gerardo Marín and Barbara VanOss Marín. *Research with Hispanic Populations.* Newbury Park, Calif.: Sage, 1991.

This book explores the meaning of Hispanic ethnicity and its implications for sociological research.

Melvin L. Kohn. *Cross-National Research in Sociology.* Newbury Park, Calif.: Sage, 1989.

Global research offers valuable insights into other societies as well our own way of life. This paperback includes seventeen essays on global research.

James Ensor, *L'Intrique,* 1890

DATA FILE: Chapter 3 includes a detailed chapter outline, supplementary lecture material, and discussion questions.
DATA FILE: Details about the experience of culture shock, along with an update on the Yąnomamö, are found in the *Data File*.
Q: "Man has no nature; what he has is history . . ." José Ortega y Gassett

NOTE: The chapter opening art is *L'Intrigue* by James Ensor.
Q: "Natives who beat drums to drive off evil spirits are objects of scorn to smart Americans who blow horns to break up traffic jams." Mary Ellen Kelly
Q: "The child that is born into any society finds that most of the problems . . . confronted in the course of . . . life have already been met and solved by those who have lived before." Ralph Linton

3 Culture

A small aluminum motorboat chugged steadily along the muddy Orinoco River, deep within South America's vast tropical rain forest. Anthropologist Napoleon Chagnon was nearing the end of a three-day journey to the home territory of the Yąnomamö, one of the most technologically primitive societies remaining on earth.

Some twelve thousand Yąnomamö live in villages scattered along the border of Venezuela and Brazil. Their way of life could hardly be more different from our own. The Yąnomamö wear little cloth-

ing and live without electricity, automobiles, or other conveniences that most people in the United States take for granted. Their traditional weapons, used for both hunting and warfare, are the bow and arrow. Many of the Yąnomamö have experienced little contact with the outside world.

Thus Chagnon would be as strange to them as they would be to him.

By 2:00 in the afternoon, Chagnon had almost reached his destination. The hot sun made the humid air almost unbearable. The anthropologist's clothes were soaked with perspiration, and his face and hands swelled from the bites of innumerable gnats swarming around him. But he scarcely noticed, so preoccupied was he with the fact that in just a few moments he would be face to face with people unlike any he had ever known.

Chagnon's heart pounded rapidly as the boat glided onto the riverbank near a Yąnomamö village. Sounds of activity came from nearby. Chagnon and his guide climbed from the boat and walked toward the village, stooping as they pushed their way through the dense undergrowth. Chagnon describes what happened next.

I looked up and gasped when I saw a dozen burly, naked, sweaty, hideous men staring at us down the shafts of their drawn arrows! Immense wads of green tobacco were stuck between their lower teeth and lips making them look even more hideous, and strands of dark green slime dripped or hung from their nostrils—strands so long that they clung to their [chests] or drizzled down their chins.

My next discovery was that there were a dozen or so vicious, underfed dogs snapping at my legs, circling me as if I were to be their next meal. I just stood there holding my notebook, helpless and pathetic. Then the stench of the decaying vegetation and filth hit me and I almost got sick. I was horrified. What kind of welcome was this for the person who came here to live with you and learn your way of life, to become friends with you? (1983:10)

Fortunately for Chagnon, the Yąnomamö villagers recognized his guide and lowered their weapons. Reassured that he would survive at least the afternoon, Chagnon was still shaken by his inability to make any sense of the people surrounding him. And this was to be his home for a year and a half! He wondered why he had forsaken physics to study human culture in the first place.

The 5.5 billion people living on the earth are members of a single biological species: *Homo sapiens.* Even so, the differences among people the world over can easily overwhelm us. Entering the world of the Yąnomamö, Chagnon experienced a severe case of **culture shock,** *personal disorientation that accompanies exposure to an unfamiliar way of life.* Like most of us, Chagnon had been raised to keep his clothes on, even in hot weather, and to use a handkerchief when his nose was running—especially in front of others. The Yąnomamö clearly had other ideas about how to live. The nudity that embarrassed Chagnon was customary to them. They recognized the green slime hanging from their nostrils as the result of inhaling a hallucinogenic drug, a practice common among friends. The "stench" that made Chagnon recoil in disgust no doubt smelled like "Home Sweet Home" to the inhabitants of that Yąnomamö village.

In short, despite being the same creatures biologically, human beings have very different ideas about what is pleasant and repulsive, polite and rude, beautiful and ugly, right and wrong. This capacity for startling difference is a wonder of our species: the expression of human culture.

WHAT IS CULTURE?

Sociologists define **culture** as *the beliefs, values, behavior, and material objects that define a people's way of life.* Culture includes what we think, how we act, and what we own. But culture is also a bridge linking the past, the present, and the future. In short, culture is nothing less than an ongoing social heritage (Soyinka, 1991).

To begin to understand all that culture entails, it is helpful to distinguish between ideas and objects. What sociologists call **nonmaterial culture** is *the intangible creations of human society,* including ideas ranging from altruism to zen. **Material culture,** on the other hand, is *the tangible products of human society,* involving objects ranging from armaments to zippers.

Taken together, cultural patterns form a broad plan for living: The way we dress, when and what we eat, where we work, and how we spend our free time are all grounded in culture. Chemists tell us that only ninety-two elements occur naturally on the earth, but sociologists know that the world is home to countless variations of human culture. Our own culture leads us to sleep in houses of wood or brick, but people of other cultures live in huts fashioned from brush, igloos of ice, or tepees made of animal skins. Culture also provides us with standards of success, beauty, and goodness, as well as reverence for a superhuman power, be it a deity, the forces of nature, or long-dead ancestors.

Culture also shapes our personalities—what we commonly (yet inaccurately) describe as "human nature." The warlike Yąnomamö look on aggression as natural in their children, just as the Semai of Malaysia expect their young to be peaceful and cooperative. The cultures of the United States and Japan both stress achievement and hard work, but members of our society value individualism more than do the Japanese, who embrace tradition more strongly.

No cultural trait is inherently "natural" to humanity, although most people around the world view their own way of life that way. What is natural to our species is the capacity to create culture, and we realize this potential as members of a particular society. Every other form of life—from ants to zebras—behaves in uniform, species-specific ways. To a world traveler, the

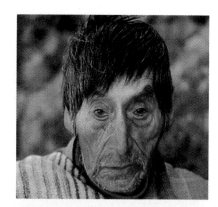

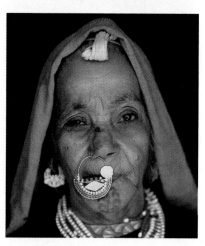

Human beings around the globe create diverse ways of life. Such differences begin with outward appearance: Contrast the women shown here from Iran, Kenya, New Guinea, and Egypt, and the men from Taiwan (Republic of China), Peru, India, and New Guinea. Less obvious, but of even greater importance, are internal differences, since culture also shapes our goals in life, our sense of justice, and even our innermost personal feelings.

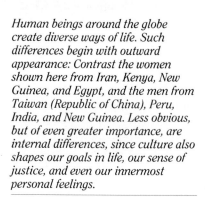

Chapter 3 Culture   **63**

NOTE: Light from the nearest galaxy (Andromeda) takes 2 million years to reach the earth; this light left those stars before there were humans on the planet.

Q: "What we have loved,
        Others will love,
        And we will teach them how."
        William Wordsworth

Q: "[Human beings] are the only animals that blush. Or need to."
Mark Twain

Q: "There can obviously be no culture without a society [and] no cultureless human society is known; it would even be hard to imagine. But it does not hold on the subhuman level . . . ants and bees do have genuine societies without culture . . ." A. L. Kroeber

enormous diversity of human life stands out in contrast to the behavior of, say, cats, which is much the same everywhere. This uniformity follows from the fact that most living creatures are guided by *instincts*, biological programming over which animals have no control. A few animals—notably chimpanzees and related primates—have the capacity for basic elements of culture, as researchers have noted by observing them use tools and teach simple skills to their offspring. But the creative power of humans far exceeds that of any other form of life; *only humans rely on culture rather than instinct to ensure the survival of their kind* (Harris, 1987).

To understand how this came to be, we must briefly review the history of our species on the earth.

Culture and Human Intelligence

In a universe perhaps 15 billion years old, our planet is a relatively young 4.5 billion years of age, and the human species is a wide-eyed infant of only 250,000. Not for a billion years after the earth was formed did life appear on our planet. Far later—some 65 million years ago—our history took a crucial turn with the appearance of the mammals we call primates.

What sets primates apart is their intelligence, based on the largest brains (relative to body size) of all living creatures. As primates evolved, the human line diverged from that of our closest relatives, the great apes, about 12 million years ago. But our common lineage shows through in the traits humans share with today's chimpanzees, gorillas, and orangutans: great sociability, affectionate and long-lasting bonds for child rearing and mutual protection, the ability to walk upright (normal in humans, less common among other primates), and hands that manipulate objects with great precision.

Studying fossil records, scientists conclude that, about 2 million years ago, our distant ancestors grasped cultural fundamentals such as the use of fire, tools, and weapons, created simple shelters, and fashioned basic clothing. Although these Stone Age achievements may seem modest, they mark the point at which our ancestors embarked on a distinct evolutionary course, making culture the primary strategy for human survival.

To comprehend what newcomers to the earth humans are, Carl Sagan (1977) suggests superimposing the 15-billion-year history of our universe on a single calendar year. The life-giving atmosphere of the earth did not develop until the autumn, and the earliest humanlike beings did not appear until December 31— the last day of the year—at 10:30 at night! Yet not until

250,000 years ago, which is mere minutes before the end of Sagan's "year," did our own species finally emerge. These *Homo sapiens* (derived from Latin meaning "thinking person") have continued to evolve so that, about 40,000 years ago, humans who looked more or less like ourselves roamed the earth. With larger brains, these "modern" *Homo sapiens* produced culture at a rapid pace, as the wide range of tools and cave art from this period suggests. Still, what we call "civilization," based on permanent settlements and specialized occupations, began in the Middle East (especially in what is today Iraq and Egypt) only about 12,000 years ago (Hamblin, 1973; Wenke, 1980). In terms of Sagan's "year," this cultural flowering occurred during the final *seconds* before midnight on New Year's Eve. And what of our modern, industrial way of life? Begun only 300 years ago, it amounts to a mere millisecond flash in Sagan's scheme.

Human culture, then, was a long time in the making. As culture became a strategy for survival, our ancestors descended from the trees into the tall grasses of central Africa. There, walking upright and hunting in groups had clear advantages. From this point on, the human capacity to create a way of life—as opposed to simply acting out biological imperatives— steadily increased along with the size of the human brain. Gradually, culture pushed aside the biological forces we call instincts so that humans gained the mental power *to fashion the natural environment for our benefit*. Ever since, people have made and remade their worlds in countless ways, which explains today's fascinating (and, as Napoleon Chagnon's experiences show, sometimes disturbing) cultural diversity.

Culture, Nation, and Society

At this point, clarification of the proper use of several terms will be helpful. We often use the concepts "culture," "nation," and "society" interchangeably. But, to sociologists, each word has a precise meaning. *Culture* refers to a shared way of life. A *nation* is a political entity, that is, a place within designated borders such as the United States, Canada, or Zimbabwe. *Society*, the topic of the next chapter, is the organized interaction of people in a nation or within some other boundary.

We correctly describe the United States, then, as both a nation and as a society. But many societies— including the United States—are *multicultural*, meaning that they include various ways of life that blend (and sometimes collide) in our everyday lives.

In the world as a whole, how many cultures are there? The number of cultures contained in the human record is a matter of speculation. Based on the number of human languages that are known, we can estimate that between five and six thousand distinctive cultures have existed on earth (Durning, 1993). As Chapter 22 ("The Natural Environment") and Chapter 24 ("Social Change and Modernity") explain, the cultural diversity of the world recently has been decreasing. Even so, at least one thousand different cultures continue to flourish, and hundreds of them, some with greater presence than others, are found in the United States.

The tally of world nations has risen and fallen throughout history as a result of political events. The dissolution of the former Soviet Union added fourteen nations to the count; the ongoing strife in the former Yugoslavia will add several more. At present, there are 190 politically independent nations in the world.

THE COMPONENTS OF CULTURE

Although the cultures found in all the world's nations differ in many ways, they all are built on five major components: symbols, language, values, norms, and material objects. We begin with the most important: symbols.

Symbols

Reality for human beings is not objects or action but *meaning*. In other words, we are human to the extent that we create an environment that is *symbolic*. A **symbol**, then, is *anything that carries a particular meaning recognized by people who share culture*. A whistle, a wall of graffiti, a flashing red light, and a fist raised in the air all serve as symbols. We can see the human capacity to create and manipulate symbols reflected in the very different meanings associated with the simple act of winking the eye. In some settings this action conveys interest; in others, understanding; in still others, insult.

We are so dependent on our culture's symbols that we take them for granted. Occasionally, however, we become keenly aware of a symbol when someone uses it in an unconventional way, as when a person in a political demonstration burns a U.S. flag. Entering an unfamiliar society also reminds us of the power of symbols; culture shock is really the inability to "read" meaning in one's surroundings. Like Napoleon Chagnon confronting the Yąnomamö, we feel lost, unsure of how to act, and sometimes frightened—a consequence of being outside the symbolic web of culture that joins individuals in meaningful social life.

Because cultures vary, an action or object with a specific meaning in one time or place may have a very different significance in another. To people in North America, a baseball bat symbolizes sport and recreation, but the Yąnomamö would probably view this well-carved club as an implement of hunting or war. A dog is a beloved household pet to people in North America but a prized wintertime meal to residents of northern China. Likewise, cows revered as sacred by India's Hindus are routinely consumed as "quarter-pounders" by hungry people in the United States. Thus symbols both bind together individuals of one society and separate people living in different societies of the world.

In global perspective, we need to remember that behavior that seems normal to us may offend people elsewhere. Women serving in the 1991 Gulf War discovered that simply wearing shorts in an Islamic society like Saudi Arabia was widely condemned as inappropriate. The box on pages 66–67 explains how an innocent gesture for members of one society may provoke an angry response from people in another who "read" according to a different symbolic system.

Then, too, symbolic meanings vary even within a single society. A fur coat, prized by one person as a symbol of success, may represent to another the inhumane treatment of animals. Similarly, a Confederate flag that for one individual embodies regional pride may symbolize to someone else racial oppression.

Cultural symbols also change over time. Blue jeans were created more than a century ago as sturdy and inexpensive clothing for people engaged in physical labor. In the liberal political climate of the 1960s, this working-class aura made jeans popular among affluent students—many of whom wore them to look "different" or sometimes to identify with working people. A decade later, "designer jeans" emerged as fashionable "status symbols," signifying big clothing budgets, the opposite of their working-class roots. In recent years, everyday jeans remain as popular as ever, simply as comfortable apparel.

In sum, symbols allow people to make sense of their lives, and without them human existence would be meaningless. Manipulating symbols correctly allows us to operate and be understood by others within our own culture. In a world of cultural diversity, however, the use of symbols may cause embarrassment and even conflict.

Language

Helen Keller (1880–1968) became a national celebrity because she overcame a daunting disability: being

RESOURCE: Leslie White's article "Symbol: The Basic Element of Culture" and Robert Merton's "Manifest and Latent Functions" are two classics on culture found in the Macionis and Benokraitis reader *Seeing Ourselves*, 3/e.
GLOBAL: Sanskrit is the oldest living language.

GLOBAL: Not all written languages utilize alphabets. Some, including ancient Egyptian, Mayan, and Chinese, use ideograms.
DATA FILE: An excerpt from Helen Keller's *The Story of My Life* appears in the *Data File*.

GLOBAL SOCIOLOGY

Travelers Beware! The Meaning of Gestures in Other Societies

A young man from Wisconsin is enjoying a summer trip in the African nation of Nigeria. He stands by the side of a country road, trying to "thumb a ride" to the next town. A truckload of locals approaches him. They take one look and come to a screeching halt. But they are not about to offer a ride to our hapless visitor; instead, they pile out of the truck, angrily denounce him, rough him up, and leave him sitting sore and confused on the ground.

What has happened here? Are Nigerians hostile to foreigners? No, except that, like people everywhere, they don't take kindly to insults. What the young man from the United States meant as a request for a ride, Nigerians see as a crude and offensive gesture.

Since so much of human communication involves gestures and body language rather than spoken words—especially when we encounter people whose language differs

from our own—we need to be mindful that the careless use of even a simple hand movement may provoke an angry response. Here are six bodily gestures that seem innocent enough to members of our society but that may bring a stern response from people elsewhere.

Figures (a) and (b) each would offend members of Islamic societies. Since Muslims typically perform bathroom hygiene with the left hand, they find the sight of a

(a)

(b)

(c)

blind and deaf from infancy. As a young girl, she was cut off from the symbolic world around her. Only when her teacher, Anne Mansfield Sullivan, broke through Keller's isolation with the concept of language did Helen Keller begin to realize her human potential. This remarkable woman, who later became a renowned educator herself, recalls the moment she acquired language.

> We walked down the path to the well-house, attracted by the smell of honeysuckle with which it was covered.

Someone was drawing water, and my teacher placed my hand under the spout. As the cool stream gushed over one hand, she spelled into the other the word water, first slowly, then rapidly. I stood still, my whole attention fixed upon the motions of her fingers. Suddenly I felt a misty consciousness as of something forgotten—a thrill of returning thought; and somehow the mystery of language was revealed to me. I knew then that "w-a-t-e-r" meant the wonderful cool something that was flowing over my hand. That living word awakened my soul; gave it light, hope, joy, set it free! (1903:21–24)

GLOBAL: For a deeper examination of comparative research on human expressiveness, look ahead to the box "Human Emotions in Global Perspective" in Chapter 6 ("Social Interaction in Everyday Life").

NOTE: Because cultures involve different realities, humor rarely travels well, as discussed in Chapter 6 ("Social Interaction in Everyday Life").

GLOBAL: The low level of interest shown by people in the United States for other cultures is suggested by the fact that there are more *teachers* of English in the former Soviet Union than there are *students* of Russian in the United States.

Q: "Social sciences show that values do not fly on their own wings; they must be embodied in our rituals." Amitai Etzioni

person eating with that hand, illustrated in Figure (a), to be revolting. Islam also holds that the sole of a shoe is unclean; therefore, to display the bottom of the foot, as in Figure (b), is insulting. Figure (c) displays the common "A-OK" gesture by which people in North America express approval and pleasure. In France, however, this symbol conveys the insult "You're worth zero," while Germans take this gesture as a crude word for "rectum." Figure

(d) shows the simple curling of a finger, meaning "come here." Malaysians attach the same meaning to this gesture as we do, but they use it exclusively for calling animals; thus, they would take no pleasure in being beckoned in this way. Figure (e) shows the familiar "thumbs up" gesture widely employed in North America to mean "Good job!" or "All right!" In Nigeria (as the hapless hitchhiker noted above learned), and also in Australia, flashing this

gesture (especially with a slight upward motion) transmits the insulting message "Up yours!" Finally, Figure (f) shows a gesture that members of our society read as "Stop!" or "No, thanks." But display this gesture to a motorist or street vendor anywhere in West Africa and you will probably have a fight on your hands. There it means "You have five fathers" or, more simply, "You bastard!"

SOURCES: Examples are drawn from Ekman et al. (1984) and Axtell (1991).

(d)

(e)

(f)

Language, the key to the world of culture, is *a system of symbols that allows members of a society to communicate with one another*. All cultures have a spoken language, although some, including the Yąnomamö, have no system of writing. Written symbols themselves are culturally variable, and various alphabets are used around the world. Moreover, members of societies in the Western world write from left to right, people in North Africa and West Asia write right to left, and people in East Asia write from top to bottom.

Global Map 3–1 shows regional use of the world's three most widely spoken languages. Chinese is the official language of one-fifth of humanity (more than 1 billion people). English is the mother tongue of about 10 percent (500 million) of the world's people, with Spanish the official language of 6 percent (300 million). Notice, too, that English is close to becoming a global language, since it is given preference as a second language in most of the world.

For people everywhere, cultural heritage is rooted in language. Language is, in fact, the major means of

Window on the World

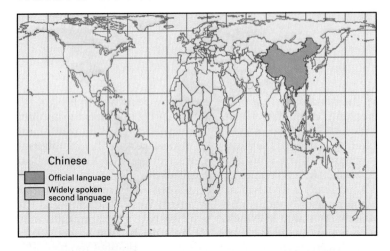

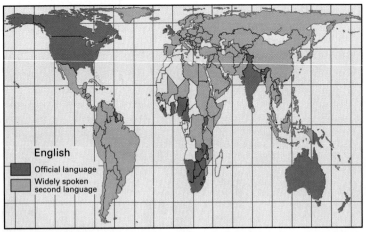

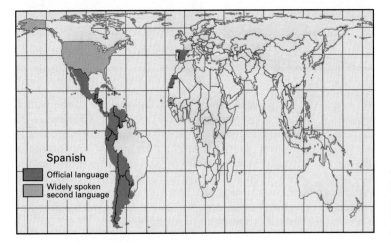

GLOBAL MAP 3–1
Language in Global Perspective

Chinese (including Mandarin, Cantonese, and dozens of other dialects) is the native tongue of one-fifth of the world's people, almost all of whom live in Asia. More precisely, although all Chinese people read and write with the same characters, they employ any of several dozen dialects. The "official" dialect, taught in schools throughout the People's Republic of China and the Republic of Taiwan, is Mandarin (the dialect of Beijing, China's historic capital city). Cantonese (the language of Canton, which differs in sound from Mandarin roughly the way French does from Spanish) is the second most common Chinese dialect.

English is the native tongue or official language in several world regions and has become the preferred second language in most of the world.

The largest concentration of Spanish speakers is in Latin America and, of course, in Spain. Spanish is also the preferred second language of the United States.

From *Peters Atlas of the World* (1990).

NOTE: In societies with an oral tradition, people display what we would consider amazing powers of memorization. Ancient Romans recited Virgil's *Aeneid*, the mythic tale of the founding of Rome, from memory, although it is some 400 pages in length.

NOTE: Although humans have been able to teach chimps to use symbols, there is little evidence to support the position that chimps are capable of teaching other chimps to do so.

cultural transmission, *the process by which one generation passes culture to the next.* Just as our bodies contain the genes of our ancestors, so we think and act every day using the symbolic system of those who came before us. The power of language lies in gaining access to centuries of accumulated wisdom.

For most of human history, people have transmitted culture through speech, which sociologists term the *oral cultural tradition.* Not until five thousand years ago did humans devise writing, and, even then, only a relatively few people ever learned to read and write. When the United States was founded just over two centuries ago, only a small elite was literate. Today, perhaps 25 million adults (about one in seven) in this country cannot read and write—an almost insurmountable barrier to opportunity in a society that increasingly demands symbolic skills. In the poorest societies of the world, moreover, four out of five people cannot use written language.

Language skills not only put us in touch with the past, they also free the human imagination. Connecting symbols in new ways, we can conceive of life other than as it is. Language—both spoken and written—distinguishes human beings as the only creatures who are self-conscious, mindful of our limitations and aware of our ultimate mortality. Yet our symbolic power also enables us to dream and hope for a future better than the present.

Is Language Uniquely Human?

Creatures great and small direct sounds and other physical cues to one another, and these are certainly forms of communication. Although in most cases, such signals are instinctive, research has shown that some animals have at least a rudimentary ability to use symbols to communicate with one another and with humans.

Perhaps the most significant achievement of this kind is the capacity of a twelve-year-old pygmy chimp named Kanzi. Chimpanzees lack the physical ability to speak words as humans do. But researcher E. Sue Savage-Rumbaugh noticed that Kanzi was able to learn language the same way a human child does—by listening and observing adults. Savage-Rumbaugh has raised Kanzi to have a vocabulary of several hundred words, which he "speaks" by pointing to pictures or pushing keys on a special keyboard. Kanzi's learning is more than simple rote; he spontaneously replies to spoken English he has not heard before. For example, Kanzi has correctly responded to requests like "Will you get a diaper for your sister?" or "Put the melon in the potty." In short, Kanzi has the language ability of a

All animals are expressive. Only humans, however, find symbolic meaning in facial gestures.

human child of two-and-one-half years (Eckholm, 1985; Linden, 1993).

By human standards, the language skills of chimps such as Kanzi (as well as dolphins and a few other animals) are limited. Further, research confirms that even specially trained animals cannot, on their own, pass on language skills to others of their kind. But animals' demonstrated language warns us against assuming that humans alone can lay claim to culture.

Does Language Shape Reality?

Because the Yanomamö have many different words for warfare and fighting, do they actually experience the world differently from people whose language lacks these symbols? The answer is yes, since language provides the building-blocks of reality.

Edward Sapir (1929, 1949) and Benjamin Whorf (1956), two anthropologists who specialized in linguistic studies, argued that languages are not just different sets of labels for the same reality. Rather, symbolic systems differ in various ways, since every language has words or expressions with no precise counterparts in other tongues. Further, each language fuses symbols with distinctive emotions. Thus, as multilingual people can attest, a single idea often "feels" different if spoken in, say, Spanish rather than in English or Chinese (Falk, 1987).

Formally, then, what we now call the **Sapir-Whorf hypothesis** states that *people perceive the world through the cultural lens of language.* Using different symbolic systems, a Turk, a Brazilian, and a Filipino actually experience "distinct worlds, not merely the

SOCIAL SURVEY: "Does everyone in this country have the opportunity to obtain an education corresponding to their abilities and talents?" (GSS 1985, N = 1,473; *Codebook*, 1993:129). These data illustrate the cultural value of equal opportunity.

"Yes" 69.8%   "No" 27.9%   DK/NR 2.3%

SOCIAL SURVEY: "Some people think that the best way for blacks to improve their position is through civil rights groups (posi-

tion 1). Other people think that the best way . . . is for each individual black to become better trained and more qualified (position 7). Where would you place yourself on this scale?" 1, 6.8%; 2, 3.5%; 3, 3.1%; 4, 25.7%; 5, 13.2%; 6, 7.5%; 7, 38.4%; DK/NR, 1.6%. (GSS 1987, African Americans only, N = 544; *Codebook*, 1993:393). Here is evidence of our cultural emphasis on personal merit shaping people's views on civil rights.

same world with different labels attached" (Sapir, 1949:162).

Of course, with the capacity to manipulate and create language, humans everywhere can shape for themselves how they experience the world. Consider how an invention like the computer has introduced new symbols including "bytes," "interface," and "E-mail" to our language. In addition, people deliberately change language. The pursuit of social equality in a predominantly white society led African Americans to replace the word "Negro" first with the term "black" and then with "African American" or "person of color." A generation later, such symbolic changes have helped improve white people's perceptions of African Americans. Similarly, although adult males in English-speaking societies have long been called "men," adult females often have been condescendingly referred to as "girls." The recent emphasis on calling women "women" is both cause and effect of a heightened awareness of sexual equality. In short, a system of language guides how we understand the world but does not limit how we do so.

Values and Beliefs

What accounts for the popularity of film characters such as James Bond, Dirty Harry, Rambo, and Thelma and Louise? The answer tells us as much about ourselves as about them. Each is ruggedly individualistic, suspicious of "the system," and relies primarily on personal skill and effort. The fact that we applaud such people suggests that we celebrate sturdy individualism, traditionally for men but increasingly for women, too.

Sociologists call such patterns **values**, *culturally defined standards by which people judge desirability, goodness, and beauty, and which serve as broad guidelines for social living.* Values are judgments, from the standpoint of a culture, of what ought to be.

Values are broad principles that support **beliefs**, *specific statements that people who share culture hold to be true.* While values are abstract standards, in other words, beliefs are particular matters that individuals consider to be valid.

Cultural values and beliefs shape our personalities and affect how we perceive our surroundings. We learn from families, schools, and religious organizations to think and act according to approved principles, to pursue worthy goals, and to believe a host of cultural truths while rejecting alternatives as false.

In a nation as large and diverse as the United States, of course, few cultural values and beliefs are shared by everyone. Over the centuries, people from around the world have entered this country, producing a cultural mosaic. Relatively speaking, then, our society is more culturally diverse than a historically isolated nation such as Japan. Even so, there is a broad shape to our national life that most people recognize and that persists over time.

Key Values of U.S. Culture

According to sociologist Robin Williams (1970), the following ten values are among the most central to our way of life.

1. **Equal opportunity**. Our sense of fairness dictates that everyone should have the opportunity to get ahead, although, due to varying talents and efforts, we expect that some people will end up being more successful than others. In other words, while people in the United States do not endorse equality of *condition*, we do believe in equal *opportunity*, that everyone should have a chance to obtain the good things in life.

2. **Achievement and success**. Our way of life encourages competition. In principle, we believe, each individual's rewards should reflect personal merit. Moreover, the greater success one garners, the more he or she is seen as a worthy person—a "winner."

3. **Material comfort**. Success, in the United States, generally means making money and enjoying what it will buy. People in the United States may quip that "money won't buy happiness," but most diligently pursue wealth all the same.

4. **Activity and work**. U.S. heroes, from Olympic figure skating star Kristi Yamaguchi to film's famed archeologist Indiana Jones, are "doers," people who get the job done. Members of our society prefer *action* to *reflection*; through hard work, we try to control events rather than passively accepting our fate. For this reason, many of us take a dim view of cultures that appear more easygoing or philosophical.

5. **Practicality and efficiency**. Just as people in the United States value activity (especially that which earns money), so we praise the ability to solve problems with minimal effort. "Building a better mousetrap" is a cultural goal, especially when it's done in the most cost-effective way.

6. **Progress**. Despite occasional waves of nostalgia, members of our society historically have believed

that the present is better than the past. Compared to the Japanese, moreover, we are far more optimistic about the future. This embrace of progress is evident in widespread advertising that what is the "very latest" is necessarily the "very best."

7. **Science**. We often turn to scientists to solve problems, convinced that the work of scientific experts will improve our lives. We believe we are rational people, which probably explains our cultural tendency (especially among men) to devalue emotions and intuition as sources of knowledge.

8. **Democracy and free enterprise**. Members of our society recognize numerous individual rights that cannot be overridden by government. Our political system has come to be based on the ideal of free elections in which all adults freely select their own leaders. In the same way, we believe that the U.S. economy responds to the needs and choices of selective, individual consumers.

9. **Freedom**. Our cultural value of freedom means that we favor individual initiative over collective conformity. Although we acknowledge that everyone has responsibilities to others, we believe that individuals should be free to pursue personal goals without unreasonable interference from anyone else.

10. **Racism and group superiority**. Despite our ideas about equality and freedom, most people in the United States evaluate individuals according to their sex, race, ethnicity, and social class. Our society values males over females, whites over people of color, people with northwestern European backgrounds over those whose ancestors came from other lands, and more privileged people over those who are disadvantaged. Although we like to describe ourselves as a nation of equals, there is little doubt that some of us are "more equal" than others.

Values: Inconsistency and Conflict

As the listing above suggests, cultural values can be inconsistent and even outright contradictory (Lynd, 1967; Bellah et al., 1985). Living in the United States, we sometimes find ourselves torn between the "me first" attitude of an individualistic, success-at-all-costs way of life and the opposing need to belong to some larger community. Similarly, we affirm our belief in equality of opportunity only to turn around and promote or degrade others because of their race or sex.

Australian feminist Sally Swain alters a famous artist's painting to make fun of our culture's tendency to ignore the everyday lives of women. The spoof is entitled Mrs. Chagall Feeds the Baby.

Some value inconsistency is the product of change. New trends sometimes are at odds with older cultural orientations. For example, what some observers have tagged a new "culture of victimization" now challenges our society's longtime belief in individual responsibility. The box on pages 72–73 takes a closer look.

Value inconsistency also occurs because cultural patterns vary according to people's age, sex, ethnicity, religion, race, and social class. Individuals who are favored in one sense while disadvantaged in another—a situation sociologists term *status inconsistency*—are especially prone to contradictory values. Clarence Thomas, an African American appointed to the Supreme Court in 1991, began his climb to prominence in a poor Georgia family. His changing fortunes

GLOBAL: Finns tend to be the most shy and melancholy people in the world; people in Finland typically avoid looking others in the eye, and few ever say I love you (even between lovers). Finns also have a high rate of alcoholism and suicide. Longtime speculation traces this cultural posture to the fact that much of the country is dark for half the year.

NOTE: Children's stories and games often reflect a culture's values. Consider the significance of "The Little Train That Could," tales of Davy Crockett and Daniel Boone, and popular board games "Chutes and Ladders," "Monopoly," and "Risk."

SOCIOLOGY OF EVERYDAY LIFE

Don't Blame Me! The New "Culture of Victimization"

A New York man recently survived his leap in front of a subway train; he then successfully sued the city for $650,000, claiming the train failed to stop in time to prevent his serious injuries. In Washington, D.C., after realizing that he had been videotaped smoking crack cocaine in a hotel room, the city's mayor blamed his woman companion for "setting him up" and suggested that his arrest by police was racially motivated. After ten women accused Oregon Senator Bob Packwood of sexual harassment, he tried to defuse the scandal by checking into an alcohol treatment center. In the most celebrated case of its kind, Dan White gunned down the mayor of San Francisco and a city council member only to tell the jury that eating "junk food" (the so-called Twinkie defense) had driven him temporarily insane.

Each of these cases involves a claim of victimization. Rather than taking the blame for our mishaps and misdeeds, in other words, more

Reinforcing "victimization" as an emerging culture, many popular "tell all" television programs feature people who deny personal responsibility for various calamities that have befallen them.

and more members of our society are pointing the finger elsewhere and painting themselves as victims. Sociologist Irving Horowitz claims we are developing a new "culture of victimization" in which "everyone is a victim" and "no one accepts responsibility for anything."

One indication of this cultural trend is the proliferation of "addictions," a term that once was associated exclusively with the uncontrollable use of drugs. We now hear about gambling addicts, compulsive overeaters, sex addicts, and even people who excuse mounting credit-card debts as a shopping addiction. Bookstores overflow with manuals to help people come to terms with numerous new medical or psychological conditions ranging from the "Cinderella Complex" to the "Casanova Complex" and even "Soap Opera Syndrome." And the U.S.

left him with both an appreciation for the plight of poor minorities and a strong belief in the ability of each individual to rise above circumstance.

In sum, value inconsistency and conflict lead to strained and awkward balancing acts in how we view the world. Sometimes we may pursue one value at the expense of another, believing in the idea of equal opportunity, say, while opposing the acceptance of gays by the U.S. military. At other times, we try to ignore such contradictions. National surveys, for example, show that while most U.S. adults acknowledge that some people are born to great fortunes while others confront abject poverty, they also maintain that the United States offers equal opportunity for all (NORC, 1993). Clearly, both views cannot be completely true. But we seem to have learned to live with significant cultural contradictions.

Values in Action: The Games People Play

Cultural values affect every aspect of our lives. Children's games, for example, may seem like lighthearted fun, but they are also an important way we teach young people what our culture deems important.

Using the sociological perspective, James Spates (1976a) sees in the familiar game King of the Mountain our cultural emphasis on achievement and success.[1]

> In this game, the King (winner) is the one who scrambles to the top of some designated area and holds it against all challengers (losers). This is a very gratifying

---

[1] The excerpt presented here has been slightly modified on the basis of unpublished versions of the study, with the permission of the author.

SOCIAL SURVEY: These response sets suggest value inconsistency. Half of people in the U.S. believe a wealthy background is of little importance to getting ahead (a); yet, at least half suspect that inequality exists to benefit the rich and powerful (b).

(a) "For getting ahead in life . . . how important is coming from a wealthy family?" (GSS 1987, N = 1,564; *Codebook*, 1993:583)
"Essential" 3.9   "Not very important" 29.8%

"Very important" 18.5%   "Not important at all" 16.9%
"Fairly important" 27.6%   DK/NR 3.2%

(b) "Inequality continues to exist because it benefits the rich and powerful." (GSS 1987, N = 1,564; *Codebook*, 1993:588)
"Strongly agree" 13.9%   "Disagree" 16.5%
"Agree" 32.7%   "Strongly disagree" 3.8%
"Neither agree nor disagree" 24.2% DK/NR 8.9%

courts are ever more clogged by lawsuits driven by the need to blame someone—and often to collect big money—for the kind of misfortune that we used to accept as part of life.

What's going on here? Is U.S. culture changing? Historically, our way of life has been based on a cultural ideal of "rugged individualism," the notion that—for better or worse—people are responsible for whatever triumph or tragedy befalls them. But this value has been eroded by a number of factors. First, we have become more aware (partly through the work of sociologists) of how society shapes our lives. This knowledge has expanded the categories of people claiming to be victims well beyond those who have suffered historical disadvantages (such as African Americans and women) to include even well-off

people. In a 1991 issue, for example, *Newsweek* touted the emerging movement among affluent white men seeking help in overcoming the alleged pressures of privilege.

Second, there has been a small revolution in the legal system by which many lawyers—especially since gaining the right to advertise their services in 1977—now encourage a sense of injustice among clients they hope to shepherd into court. The number of million-dollar lawsuit awards has risen more than twenty-five-fold in the last twenty-five years.

Third, there has been a proliferation of "rights groups" that promote what Amitai Etzioni calls "rights inflation." Beyond the traditional constitutional liberties are many newly claimed rights, including those of hunters (as well as those of animals), the rights of smokers

(and nonsmokers), the right of women to control their bodies (and the rights of the unborn), the right to own a gun (and the right to be safe from violence). Expanding and competing claims for unmet rights, then, generate victims on all sides.

Does this shift signal a fundamental realignment in our culture? Perhaps, but the new popularity of being a victim also springs from some established cultural forces. For example, the claim to victimization depends on a long-standing belief that everyone has the right to life, liberty, and the pursuit of happiness. What is new, however, is that the explosion of "rights" now does more than alert us to clear cases of injustice; it threatens to erode our sense of responsibility as members of a larger society.

SOURCES: Based on Etzioni (1991) and Taylor (1991).

game from the winner's point of view, for one learns what it is like (however brief is the tenure at the top before being thrown off) to be an unequivocal success, to be unquestionably better than the entire competition. (1976a:286)

Each player endeavors to become number one at the expense of all other players. But success has its price, and King of the Mountain teaches that as well.

The King can never relax in such a pressurized position and constant vigilance is very difficult to endure, psychologically, for long. Additionally, the sole victor is likely to feel a certain alienation from others: Whom can he trust? Truly, "it is lonely at the top." (1976a:286)

Just as King of the Mountain conveys our cultural emphasis on winning, Tag, Keep Away, and Monkey in

the Middle teach the lessons of being a loser. Spates observes that the loser in Tag, designated as "It," is singled out as unworthy of joining the group. This experience of being excluded can be so difficult to bear that other players may allow themselves to be tagged just to end "It's" ordeal. All players thus learn the importance of competing successfully, as well as the trials of not fitting in. Drawing on these sociological observations, we can appreciate better the prominence of competitive team sports in U.S. culture and why star athletes are often celebrated as cultural heroes.

Norms

For most of our history, women and men in the United States held to the idea that sexual intercourse should occur only within the bounds of marriage. By the late

NOTE: "Norm" is derived from Latin *norm(a)*, meaning "a carpenter square, a rule, or a pattern." The root of "moral" is *mor* or *mos*, meaning "custom."

NOTE: Not all norms are neatly characterized as mores or folkways; these concepts are best used as endpoints of a continuum.

Q: "Yes, I am a hard worker. You know, when I am working on anything I keep at it night and day, sleeping a few hours with my clothes on. I sleep from 1:00 to 6:00 in the morning, and then I jump up and go to work again as fresh as a bird. But I tell you we have lots of fun in the laboratory. Some time ago, I had forty-two men working with me on the incandescent lamp in a big building. I hired a German to play an organ for us all night, and we worked by the music. Oh, we enjoy this kind of life." Thomas A. Edison, on hard work in America, July 1889

1960s, however, beliefs had changed so that sexual activity became widely viewed as a form of recreation, sometimes involving people who hardly knew each other. By the mid-1980s, the rules changed again. Amid growing fears of sexually transmitted diseases, especially the deadly acquired immune deficiency syndrome (AIDS), people began rethinking the wisdom of the "sexual revolution," and more men and women were limiting their sexual activity to a single partner (McKusick et al., 1985; Smilgas, 1987).

Such patterns illustrate the operation of **norms**, *rules and expectations by which a society guides the behavior of its members.* Norms may be *proscriptive,* mandating what we should *not* do, as when health officials warn us to avoid casual sex. *Prescriptive* norms, on the other hand, state what we *should* do. Following practices of "safe sex," for example, has become such a norm in recent years.

Some norms apply virtually anywhere and at any time. For example, parents expect obedience from children regardless of the setting. Other norms, however, are situation-specific. We expect an audience to applaud at the completion of a musical performance; applause at the end of a classroom lecture is acceptable (if rare); applause at the completion of a sermon by a priest or rabbi, however, would be considered rude.

Mores and Folkways

Norms have varying importance. William Graham Sumner (1959; orig. 1906), an early U.S. sociologist, used the term **mores** (pronounced MORE-ays; the rarely used singular form is *mos*) to refer to *norms that have great moral significance.* Proscriptive mores, often called *taboos,* include our society's prohibition against adults having sexual relations with children. Prescriptive mores include "standards of decency" that require people in public places to wear a certain minimal amount of clothing.

Because they are deemed vital to social life, mores usually apply to everyone, everywhere, all the time. For the same reason, violation of mores typically brings a swift and strong reaction from others. From early childhood, for example, we learn that stealing is a serious wrong that provokes a stern response.

Sumner used the term **folkways** to designate *norms that have less moral significance than mores.* Folkways include countless norms that guide our everyday lives, including how we dress and interact with others. In short, while mores distinguish between right and wrong, folkways draw a line between right and rude. Because they are less important than mores, societies afford individuals more personal discretion in matters involving folkways and punish infractions leniently. For example, a man who does not wear a tie to a formal dinner party is violating a part of folkways we call "etiquette." Although perhaps the subject of derisive comment, his action is likely to be tolerated. But imagine if the man were to arrive at the dinner party wearing *only* a tie. Violating cultural mores, he would be inviting more serious sanctions.

Cultural norms, then, steer behavior by defining what is right and wrong, proper and improper. Although we sometimes bristle when others pressure us to conform, we generally embrace norms as part of the symbolic road map of culture because they make our encounters with others predictable and trustworthy.

Social Control

Generally, students remain quiet in class, listening attentively to the teacher while occasionally taking notes. The enthusiastic student who looks for every chance to speak up is therefore courting criticism as a "nerd."

As members of cultural systems, we respond to each other with *sanctions,* which take the form of either reward or punishment. Sanctions can be powerful even when they are informal, as when a student who talks too much provokes groans of irritation from others. Some sanctions are formal, ranging from grades in school to prosecution by the criminal justice system. Taken together, all kinds of sanctions form the heart of a culture's system of **social control**, *various means by which members of society encourage conformity to norms.*

As we learn cultural norms, we develop the capacity to respond critically to our own behavior. Doing wrong—for instance, stealing from another—provokes us to experience *guilt,* the discomfort of judging our actions as wrong. Both guilt and *shame*—the painful acknowledgment of the disapproval of others—stem from internalizing cultural norms, that is, building them into our own personalities. Only cultural creatures can experience guilt and shame: This is probably what Mark Twain had in mind when he quipped that human beings "are the only animals that blush . . . or need to."

"Ideal" and "Real" Culture

Societies employ values and norms as moral guidelines for their members. As such, these cultural elements do not capture actual behavior as much as they state how

NOTE: Ideal culture often is revealed in legends; "legend" is derived from Latin meaning "things to be read." Thus the Greeks celebrated Homer; the Romans, Virgil; the Christian saints, Joan of Arc; medieval nobles, King Arthur; and moderns, a list of rugged individualists, from Davy Crockett to James Bond, Rambo, and Thelma and Louise.

Q: "Myths and taboos are not meant only to reflect reality, but to create it." Richard Farson

NOTE: A detailed discussion of how technology has historically shaped human society is found in the first section of Chapter 4 ("Society").

we *should* behave. We must remember, then, that **ideal culture**, *social patterns mandated by cultural values and norms*, is not the same as **real culture**, *actual social patterns that only approximate cultural expectations.*

To illustrate, most women and men acknowledge the importance of sexual fidelity in marriage. Even so, at least one-third of married people are sexually unfaithful to their spouses at some point in the marriage. Such discrepancies are common to all societies, since no one lives up to ideal standards all the time. But a culture's moral prodding is crucial to shaping the lives of individuals all the same, calling to mind the old saying "Do as I say, not as I do."

Material Culture and Technology

In addition to intangible elements such as values and norms, every culture encompasses a wide range of tangible (from Latin meaning "touchable") human creations that sociologists term *artifacts.* The Yanomamö gather forest materials to construct huts and hammocks. They craft bows and arrows to hunt and defend themselves, fashion tools for farming, and beautify their bodies with colored paints. An unfamiliar people's material culture may seem as strange to us as their language, values, and norms.

Although distinct, material and nonmaterial elements of culture are related. The material creations of a particular society typically express its cultural values. The fact that the Yanomamö spend much of their time making weapons, for instance, reflects the importance they place on warfare and militaristic skills. A Yanomamö male's poison-tipped arrows, for example, are among his most prized possessions.

Artifacts also provide clues to our own cultural values. Surely, our cherished values of individuality and independence have driven us to have a high regard for privately owned automobiles (and just as much scorn for mass transportation). We have constructed some 4 million miles of freeways in the United States, and our nation's people own 150 million cars, about one car for every licensed driver!

In addition to reflecting values, material culture also reveals a society's **technology**, *knowledge that a society applies to the task of living in a physical environment.* In short, technology ties the world of nature to the world of culture. With their relatively simple technology, the Yanomamö interfere little with the natural environment. They are forced to remain keenly aware of the cycles of rainfall and the movement of animals they hunt for food. By contrast, technologically complex societies (such as those of North America) have an

Standards of beauty—including how color should be used in everyday surroundings—vary significantly from one culture to another. Members of the Ndebele in South Africa lavishly paint their homes. Members of the societies of Europe and North America, by contrast, make far less use of color so that their surroundings seem subdued by comparison.

enormous impact on the natural world, reshaping the environment (for better or ill) according to their own interests and priorities.

Because we give science such great importance and praise the sophisticated technology it has produced, members of our society tend to judge cultures with simpler technology as less advanced. Some facts would support such an assessment. Life expectancy is one good measure of a society's level of well-being. Females born in the United States in 1990 can expect to live almost to the age of eighty, males to about seventy-two. Napoleon Chagnon estimated the life expectancy of the Yanomamö at only about forty years.

However, we must be careful not to make self-serving judgments about cultures that differ from our own. Although many Yanomamö are eager to gain modern technology (such as steel tools and shotguns), it may surprise you to learn that they are generally well fed by world standards and most are quite satisfied with their lives (Chagnon, 1992). Remember, too, that while our powerful and complex technology has produced work-reducing devices and seemingly miraculous forms of

NOTE: More complex technology empowers humanity to manipulate the natural world; members of industrial societies, therefore, risk losing sensitivity to the natural environment and the requirements of living in an ecological system. Look ahead to Chapter 22 ("The Natural Environment").

DIVERSITY: Subcultural communities such as the Amish are often seen by outsiders as internally homogeneous. John Hostetler

(1980; see especially his Chapter 13) makes clear that the Amish are in many respects internally diverse.

Q: "[The Amish have] polarized over the shape or color of a garment, the style of a house, carriage, or harness, the use of labor-saving farm machinery or the pace of singing. The list is mind-boggling." John A. Hostetler

Cultural patterns are not equally accessible to all members of a society. Formal training in technique, color, and composition, for example, is usually necessary in order to gain standing in the "high culture" pursuit of fine art. We reserve the term "folk art" for the work of people—generally of lower social position—who are drawn by their love of art to paint, even though they have no formal training at all. Anna Mary Robertson (Grandma) Moses, the most popular folk artist of this century, began painting while in her seventies. During the next two decades she produced numerous paintings, yarn pictures, and decorative tiles. Her idyllic landscapes, including Joyride, *and interiors celebrate U.S. rural traditions and country life.*

Grandma Moses: *Joy Ride.* Copyright © 1991, Grandma Moses Properties Co., New York.

medical treatment, it has also contributed to unhealthy levels of stress, eroded the quality of the natural environment, and created weapons capable of destroying in a flash everything that humankind has managed to achieve throughout history.

Finally, technology is another cultural element that varies substantially within the United States. Although many of us cannot imagine life without CD players, televisions, and microwave ovens, some members of our society cannot afford such items, and others reject them on principle. The Amish, for example, live in small farming communities across Pennsylvania, Ohio, and Indiana. They shun most modern conveniences as a matter of religious conviction. With their traditional black garb and horse-drawn buggies, the Amish may seem like a curious relic of the past. Yet their communities thrive, grounded in strong families and individuals who enjoy a sense of identity and purpose. And many of the thousands of outsiders who observe them each year come away with the suspicion that Amish communities may be "islands of sanity in a culture gripped by commercialism and technology run wild" (Hostetler, 1980:4).

High Culture and Popular Culture

In everyday conversation, we usually reserve the term "culture" for sophisticated art forms such as classical literature, music, dance, and painting. We praise college professors, film directors, or dance choreographers as "cultured," because they presumably appreciate the "finer things in life." The term "culture" itself has the same Latin root as the word "cultivate," suggesting that the "cultured" individual has cultivated or refined tastes.

By contrast, we speak less generously of ordinary people, assuming that they are less cultivated and their cultural patterns are somehow less worthy. In more concrete terms, we are tempted to judge the music of Mozart as "more cultured" than Motown, fine cuisine as better than fish sticks, and polo as more polished than ping pong.

When we make such judgments, we are recognizing that all cultural patterns are not equally accessible to all members of a society (Hall & Neitz, 1993). Sociologists use the shorthand term **high culture**[2] to refer to *cultural patterns that distinguish a society's elite;* **popular culture,** then, designates *cultural patterns that are widespread among a society's population.*

Common sense may suggest that high culture is superior to popular culture. It is the lives of elites, after

---

[2]The term "high culture" is derived from the more popular term "highbrow." Influenced by phrenology, the bogus nineteenth-century theory that personality was affected by the shape of the human skull, people a century ago contrasted the praiseworthy tastes of those they termed "highbrows" with the contemptible appetites of others they derided as "lowbrows."

FIGURE 3–1

Recorded Immigration to the United States, by Region of Birth, 1880–1890 and 1980–1990

(U.S. Immigration and Naturalization Service, 1991)

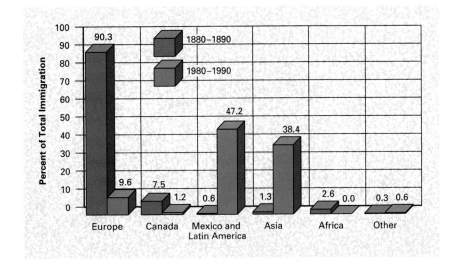

all, and not those of ordinary women and men, that make up most of documented history. But sociologists are uneasy with such a sweeping evaluation (Gans, 1974). When sociologists use the term "culture," they refer to *all* elements of a society's way of life, even while recognizing that cultural patterns vary throughout a population.

One reason to resist quick judgments about the merits of high culture versus popular culture is, first, that neither elites nor ordinary people have uniform tastes and interests; people in both categories differ in numerous ways. Second, do we praise high culture because it is inherently better than popular culture, or simply because its supporters have more prestige and power to begin with? For example, there is no difference between a violin and a fiddle; however, we name the instrument one way when it is used to produce a type of music typically enjoyed by a person of higher position, and the other way when producing music appreciated by an individual with lower social standing.

One additional point. Given their technological know-how, modern, industrial societies like our own create and disperse many cultural elements on an unprecedented scale. In other words, as John Hall and Mary Jo Neitz (1993:6) point out, culture in the United States is now a process of mass production, mass distribution, and mass consumption. This mass scale means that the production of material things (clothing, for example) as well as the shaping of public attitudes (say, about fashion) are under the control of large organizations that utilize vast marketing systems and the mass media. Again, the popularity of such cultural patterns does not mean that they are good or bad, but it does imply that industrial societies are very efficient in generating many, changing cultural elements.

CULTURAL DIVERSITY: MANY WAYS OF LIFE IN ONE WORLD

The United States has never been characterized by a single way of life, a fact that follows from this nation's history of immigration. Between 1820 (when the government began keeping track of immigration) and 1990, more than 55 million people came to these shores from other countries. A century ago, as shown in Figure 3–1, most immigrants hailed from Europe. By the 1980s, however, a large majority of newcomers were arriving from Latin America and Asia. This massive immigration has made the United States—far more than most nations of the world—a land of cultural diversity.

Cultural variety has always been with us, evident in the distinctive accents of, say, New Englanders or southerners. Ours has also been a nation of religious pluralism, a land of many ethnic traditions, and a home to countless people who try to be like no one else.

Given this diversity, what sociologists sometimes describe as our "cloth of culture" might more accurately be called a "patchwork quilt." To understand the reality of life in the United States, then, we must move beyond widespread cultural patterns, such as the key values identified by Robin Williams (1970), to consider cultural diversity.

DATA FILE: A brief account of Cajuns as a U.S. subculture is found in the *Data File*.

Q: "The urban community turns out, upon closer scrutiny, to be a mosaic of minor communities, many of them strikingly different from one another . . ." Robert Park

DIVERSITY: Recall the "What's in a Name?" box in Chapter 1 ("The Sociological Perspective"); the so-called "melting pot" in the

United States actually involved Anglicizing the cultural patterns of other ethnic categories.

Q: "As long as black people are viewed as 'them,' the burden falls on blacks to do all the cultural and moral work necessary for healthy race relations. The implication is that only certain Americans can define what it means to be an American—and the rest must simply 'fit in'." Cornel West

Subculture

The term **subculture** refers to *cultural patterns that distinguish some segment of a society's population*. Inner-city teens, elderly Polish Americans, "Yankee" New Englanders, homeless people, and very rich families all display subcultural patterns. Occupations, too, foster distinctive subcultures, involving unusual ways of acting, speaking, and dressing, as anyone who has ever spent time with surfers, cowboys, race-car drivers, jazz musicians, or even sociologists can attest. Rural people sometimes poke fun at the ways of "city slickers," who, in turn, jeer back at their "country cousins." Sexual orientation generates yet another subculture in our society, especially in cities like San Francisco, Los Angeles, and New York, where large numbers of gay men and women live.

Although categories of people may differ among themselves in some respects, we should be careful not to assume that any particular individuals are defined by one or another subculture. We all participate simultaneously in numerous subcultures without necessarily becoming very committed to any of them.

In some cases, however, important cultural traits such as ethnicity or religion do set off people from one another—sometimes with tragic results. Consider the former nation of Yugoslavia in southeastern Europe. The recent turmoil there has been fueled by astounding cultural diversity. This *one* small country (which before its breakup was no bigger than the state of Wyoming, with a population of 25 million) made use of *two* alphabets, *three* religions, and *four* languages; it was home to *five* major nationalities, was divided into *six* separate republics, and absorbed the cultural influences of *seven* other nations with which it shared borders. The cultural conflict that threw this nation into civil war shows that subcultures are a source not only of pleasing variety but also of tensions and outright violence.

We in the United States have historically taught our children to view this country as a "melting pot" in which many nationalities blend into a single "American" culture. But, given the extent of our cultural diversity, we might well question the truth of this notion. As Chapter 12 ("Race and Ethnicity") explains, people of different ways of life have mixed and melded to some extent in the United States, but cultural divisions in our society remain powerful and persistent.

The problem here is that cultural diversity involves not just *variety* but also *hierarchy*. Too often, what we view as "dominant" cultural patterns characterize powerful segments of the U.S. population, while those

we term "subcultures" are traits of disadvantaged people. This dilemma has led some researchers to focus on the less powerful members of our society in a new approach called multiculturalism.

Multiculturalism

In recent years, the United States has been facing up to the challenge of **multiculturalism**, *an educational program recognizing past and present cultural diversity in U.S. society and promoting the equality of all cultural traditions*. This movement represents a sharp turn from the past, when our society downplayed cultural diversity and defined itself primarily in terms familiar to European (and especially English) immigrants. At this point, a spirited debate continues over whether we should stress the common elements in our national experience, or highlight the diversity that characterizes a nation of immigrants.

E Pluribus Unum, the familiar Latin words that appear on each U.S. coin, means "out of many, one." This motto symbolizes not only our national political confederation, but it also describes the cultural goal of forging a new and distinctive way of life from the varied experiences of immigrants from around the world. The notion of the United States as a cultural "melting pot" is as old as the nation itself. George Washington, the first U.S. president, confidently predicted that future immigrants would learn the new nation's ways to become "one people" (Gray, 1991).

But, from the outset, reality differed from this ideal. Instead of melting together into a single heritage, cultures in the United States hardened into a hierarchy. Dominating the public life of this nation were English social patterns and institutions (including language, economy, legal system, and religion). Members of the non-English minority were advised to model themselves after "their betters." "Melting," in effect, turned out to be a process of Anglicization. As multiculturalists see it, early in our history, this society set up the English way of life as an ideal to which all should aspire and by which all should be judged.

For more than two centuries, historians in the United States have highlighted the role of descendants of the English and other Europeans and described events from their point of view, in the process pushing to the side the perspectives and accomplishments of Native Americans, people of African descent, and immigrants from Asia. Multiculturalists condemn this singular pattern as **Eurocentrism**, *the dominance of European (particularly English) cultural patterns*. Molefi

THE MAP: The regions of the United States with culturally diverse children are those with the greatest number of immigrants.
DIVERSITY: Chapter 12 ("Race and Ethnicity") contains the box "The Coming Minority-Majority?" which outlines the increasing cultural diversity of the next century. See also National Maps 12–1 and 12–2.

DATA FILE: The state-by-state standing of laws regarding English as an official language is found in the *Data File*.
GLOBAL: The diffusion of the English language and U.S. culture is evident in the rising percentage of box office receipts abroad from U.S. films: France, 59%; Great Britain, 89%; Italy, 85%. English has become the universal language of entertainment—dominating television and popular music as well as film.

Seeing Ourselves

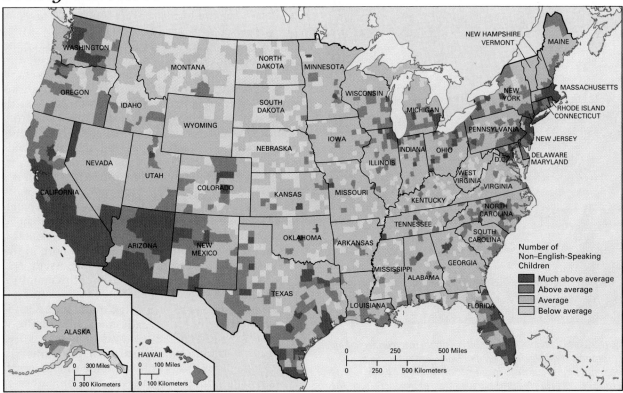

NATIONAL MAP 3–1 Language Diversity Across the United States

According to the 1990 Census, 6.3 million children (14 percent of all children aged five through seventeen) speak a language other than English at home. Most of these children are of Hispanic ancestry. These boys and girls are not spread equally throughout the country, however. Children in California, for example, speak more than one hundred languages at home and at school. How would you describe the geographical distribution of these children? What do you think accounts for this pattern?

Adapted from *American Demographics* magazine, April 1993, p. 40. Reprinted with permission. © 1993, *American Demographics* magazine, Ithaca, New York. Data from the 1990 decennial census.

Kete Asante, a leading advocate of multiculturalism, suggests that like "the fifteenth-century Europeans who could not cease believing that the earth was the center of the universe, many today find it difficult to cease viewing European culture as the center of the social universe" (1988:7).

Few deny that our culture has wide-ranging roots. But multiculturalism is controversial at the very least because it asks us to rethink the norms and values at the core of our society. Not surprisingly, battles over how to describe our nation's culture are now raging on many fronts.

A first contested issue centers on language. For a decade, Congress has debated a proposal to designate English as the official language of the United States. It has yet to decide the matter, although, by 1991, legislatures in sixteen states had enacted such a directive. To some, "official English" may seem unnecessary, since for centuries this language has been central to U.S. culture. Yet, by 1990, some 30 million men and women—at least one in ten—spoke a language other than English in their homes. And their ranks will swell to an estimated 40 million by the beginning of the next century. Spanish is our

As the world's people become increasingly interconnected by communications technology and trade, every society is becoming multicultural. Residents of Mexico City, for example, eagerly consume a wide range of products from the United States. The most popular piñata, in fact, is currently a rendering of television bad-boy Bart Simpson. On the other side of the equation, people in the United States welcome many elements of Mexican culture. To cite one example, members of our society now consume more salsa than ketchup.

Christopher Columbus and other European explorers by recognizing, first, that the so-called "New World" had been inhabited for tens of thousands of years before Europeans arrived here and, second, by assessing the tragic impact of the European conquest on the native peoples of this hemisphere. As detailed in Chapter 12 ("Race and Ethnicity"), from the point of view of Native Americans, contact with Europeans unleashed five centuries of domination and death from war and disease. In short, a multicultural approach would recover the history and achievements of many women and men whose cultural backgrounds up to now have kept them on the sidelines of history.

Second, proponents claim, multiculturalism is a means to come to terms with our country's even more diverse *present*. During the 1980s, the Hispanic population of the United States increased by more than 50 percent, and the number of Asian Americans doubled. According to some projections, children born in the 1990s will live to see people of African, Asian, and Hispanic ancestry become a *majority* of this country's population.

Third, proponents assert that multiculturalism is a way to strengthen the academic achievement of African-American children and others who may feel left out of traditional educational programs. To counter pervasive Eurocentrism, some multicultural-ists are calling for **Afrocentrism**, *the dominance of African cultural patterns in people's lives*, which they see as a corrective for centuries of minimizing or alto-gether ignoring the cultural achievements of African societies and African Americans.

Fourth and finally, proponents see multicultural-ism as worthwhile preparation for all people in the United States to live in a world that is increasingly interdependent. As various chapters of this book explain, social patterns in this country are becoming more closely linked to issues and events elsewhere in the world. Multiculturalism undermines nationalistic prejudices by pointing out global connectedness.

Although multiculturalism has found widespread favor in the last several years, it has provoked its share of criticism as well. What most troubles opponents of mul-ticulturalism is that it encourages divisiveness rather than unity by urging individuals to identify with their own category rather than with the nation as a whole.

A second criticism is that multiculturalism erodes any claim to common truth by maintaining that we should evaluate all ideas according to the race (and sex) of those who present them. Is there no common hu-manity, critics ask, but only an "African experience," a "European experience," and so on?

second national language, and other U.S. tongues include Italian, German, French, Filipino, Japanese, Korean, Vietnamese and a host of Native-American languages—several hundred languages in all. National Map 3–1, on page 79, takes a look at where in the United States there are large numbers of children whose first language is not English.

A second controversy involves how our nation's schools—from the early grades through college—should teach about culture. It is among educators that the clash over multiculturalism has been most intense. Two basic positions have emerged from this discussion.

Proponents defend multiculturalism, first, as a strategy to present a more accurate picture of our country's *past*. Proposed educational reforms seek, for example, to temper the simplistic praise directed at

GLOBAL: Kenneth Jackson points out that there is scarcely a 24-hour restaurant or grocery in Paris; France historically imposed its way of life on colonies and today even has a common vacation period for its people. In this context, the United States appears to be a more culturally diverse society.

Q: "A cultural lag occurs when one of two parts of culture which are correlated changes before or in greater degree than the other part does, thereby causing less adjustment between the two parts than existed previously." William F. Ogburn

Q: "The atomic bomb was produced in two and one-half years...a decade later we have [not controlled] atomic energy [nor] banned the atomic bomb." William F. Ogburn

A third problem, say the critics, is that multiculturalism may not end up helping minorities as proponents say it does. Critics argue that multiculturalist initiatives (from African-American studies to all-black dorms) seem to demand precisely the kind of racial segregation that our nation has struggled for decades to end. Then, too, an Afrocentric curriculum may well deny children a wide range of important knowledge and skills by forcing them to study only certain topics from a single point of view. Historian Arthur Schlesinger, Jr. (1991:21) puts the matter bluntly: "If a Kleagle of the Ku Klux Klan wanted to use the schools to handicap black Americans, he could hardly come up with anything more effective than the 'Afrocentric' curriculum."

Is there any common ground in this debate? Although sharp differences exist, the answer is yes. Virtually everyone agrees that we all need to gain greater appreciation of our cultural diversity. Further, because racial and ethnic minorities may constitute a majority of the U.S. population during the next century, efforts in this direction are needed now. But precisely where the balance is to be struck—between the *pluribus* and the *unum*—will likely remain a divisive issue for some time to come.

Counterculture

Cultural diversity sometimes takes the form of active rejection of some widely shared ideas or objects. **Counterculture** refers to *cultural patterns that strongly oppose those widely accepted within a society.* People who embrace a counterculture may well challenge widely held notions about morality, perhaps provoking efforts by others to repress them.

In many societies, countercultures spring from adolescence (Spates, 1976b, 1983; Spates & Perkins, 1982). Most of us are familiar with the youth-oriented counterculture of the 1960s that attracted considerable media coverage. Hippies criticized the cultural mainstream as overly competitive, self-centered, and materialistic. Instead, they favored a cooperative lifestyle in which "being" took precedence over "doing" and the capacity for personal growth—or "expanded consciousness"—was prized over material possessions like homes and cars. Such differences led many hippies at that time to "drop out" of the larger society. Note, however, the growing popularity of the idea of personal growth over the last several decades. This trend reminds us that what is countercultural at one point in time may become much more popular later on.

Counterculture may involve not only distinctive values, but unconventional behavior (including dress and forms of greeting) as well as music. Many members of the 1960s counterculture, for instance, drew personal identity from long hair, headbands, and blue jeans, from displaying a peace sign rather than offering a handshake, and from enjoying ever-present rock and roll music, a musical form that had far less of the mainstream respectability it enjoys today.

Countercultures still exist, of course. In the United States, the Ku Klux Klan and other white supremacist groups promote violence and racial hatred in order to protect what they see as "real American values." In Europe, young "punks" express contempt for others by their shaved heads or multicolored hairstyles, black leather, and chains—all intended to offend more conventional members of their societies.

Cultural Change

All societies throughout history have recognized the basic human truth that "All things shall pass." Even the dinosaurs, who thrived on this planet for some 160 million years, remain only as fossils. And what of the human species, which, at 250,000 years of age, is far too young to have left fossils? Whether humanity will survive for millions of years to come is a hotly debated question. All we can say with certainty is that, given our reliance on culture, for as long as we survive our record will be one of rapid and dramatic change.

Cultural change is continuous, even though we may perceive it only over a period of years. Consider, for example, recent trends in family life. As more women have joined the labor force, many have delayed marriage and having children, or remained single and had children all the same. With both women and men now enjoying greater financial independence, the divorce rate has risen to twice what it was fifty years ago. And over one generation, the number of single-parent households more than doubled, so that a majority of our nation's children now live with only one parent before they reach the age of eighteen.

Table 3–1 presents another dimension of change, comparing the attitudes of first-year college students in 1968 with those of men and women matriculating in 1992. Some things have changed only slightly: About the same proportion of students look forward to raising a family. But the students of the 1990s are much more interested in being well off financially, while their counterparts in the late 1960s were concerned with developing a philosophy of life. (Worth noting is an emerging countertrend during the last five years, suggesting young people are moving away from the materialism of the 1980s.) Note, too, that changes

SOCIAL SURVEY: Data sets in the *STUDENT CHIP Social Survey* program allow students to analyze cultural changes by comparing attitudes among various age cohorts. One example is ABNOMOTM, which reveals steadily increasing support for the availability of legal abortion to married women. (*CHIP1 Social Survey Software*, ABNOMOTM; GSS 1972-91, N = 23,243)

Birth year	"Yes"	"No"
Before 1910	33.7%	66.3%
1910–19	39.1%	60.9%
1920–29	41.0%	59.0%
1930–39	43.8%	56.2%
1940–49	49.4%	50.6%
1950–59	49.0%	51.0%
1960–71	42.8%	57.2%

TABLE 3–1 Attitudes Among Students Entering U.S. Colleges, 1968 and 1992

		1968	1992	Change
Life Objectives (Essential or Very Important)				
Develop a philosophy of life	Male	79	44	–35
	Female	87	47	–40
Keep up with political affairs	Male	52	41	–11
	Female	52	37	–15
Help others in difficulty	Male	50	52	+ 2
	Female	71	72	+ 1
Raise a family	Male	64	69	+ 5
	Female	72	72	0
Be successful in my own business	Male	55	48	– 7
	Female	32	37	+ 5
Be well off financially	Male	51	76	+ 25
	Female	27	71	+ 44

Note: To allow comparisons, data from the early 1970s rather than 1968 are used for some items.

SOURCES: Richard G. Braungart and Margaret M. Braungart, "From Yippies to Yuppies: Twenty Years of Freshmen Attitudes," *Public Opinion*, vol. 11, no. 3 (September–October 1988): 53–56; Eric L. Dey, Alexander W. Astin, William S. Korn, and Ellyne R. Riggs, *The American Freshman: National Norms for Fall 1992* (Los Angeles: UCLA Higher Education Research Institute, 1992).

in attitude have generally been greater among women than among men. This differential, no doubt, reflects the fact that the women's movement, concerned with social equality for the two sexes, intensified after 1968.

Change in one dimension of a culture usually sparks other transformations as well. As noted earlier, for instance, women's rising participation in the labor force involves changing patterns of marriage. Such connections illustrate the principle of **cultural integration**, *the close relationship among various elements of a cultural system.* Some elements of a cultural system, however, typically change more rapidly than others. William Ogburn (1964) observed that technology moves quickly, generating new elements of material culture (like "test-tube babies") faster than nonmaterial culture (such as ideas about parenthood) can keep up with them. Ogburn called this inconsistency **cultural lag**, *the fact that cultural elements change at different rates, which may disrupt a cultural system.* In a culture with the technical ability to allow one woman to give birth to a child by using another woman's egg, which has been fertilized in a laboratory with the sperm of a total stranger, how are we to apply the traditional notions of motherhood and fatherhood?

Cultural changes are set in motion in three ways. The first is *invention*, the process of creating new cultural elements. Invention has given us the telephone (1876), the airplane (1903), and the aerosol spray can (1941), all of which have had a tremendous impact on our way of life. The process of invention goes on constantly, as indicated by the thousands of applications submitted annually to the United States Patent Office.

Discovery, a second cause of cultural change, involves recognizing and understanding something not fully understood before—from a distant star, to the foods of another culture, to the muscle power of U.S. women. Discovery often results from scientific research; many medical breakthroughs occur this way. Yet discovery can also happen quite by accident, as when Marie Curie left a rock on a piece of photographic paper in 1898 and thus discovered radium.

The third cause of cultural change is *diffusion*, the spread of cultural traits from one society to another. Missionaries and anthropologists like Napoleon Chagnon have introduced new cultural elements to many Yanomamö villages. Cultural traits have likewise spread from the United States throughout the world: jazz music, with its roots deep in the culture of African Americans; computers, first constructed in the mid-1940s in a Philadelphia laboratory; and even the United States Constitution, used by several other countries to construct their own political systems.

Diffusion works the other way as well, so that much of what we assume is inherently "American" actually comes from other cultures. Ralph Linton (1937) explained that many commonplace elements of our way of life—most clothing and furniture, clocks, newspapers, money, and even the English language—are all derived from other cultures. As the technology of travel and communication makes the world smaller, the rate of cultural diffusion increases as well.

Ethnocentrism and Cultural Relativity

A question in the well-known game Trivial Pursuit asks which beverage is most popular in the United States. Milk? Soft drinks? Coffee? The answer is soft drinks, but all of the beverages mentioned are favored by members of our society. But if members of the Masai of eastern Africa were to join the game, their answer might well be "Goat blood." To most of us, of course, the idea of drinking blood is downright unnatural, if not revolting. But we should keep in mind that drinking cow's milk (which we all "know" is healthier than soft drinks or coffee) is intolerable to billions of people in the world, including most Chinese (Harris, 1985).

NOTE: Regarding Table 3–1, Dey, Astin, Korn, & Riggs (1992) offer an indicator of likely increase in student activism. In 1991, 40.5% of first-year students in their sample claimed to have participated in a political demonstration. This is a rising proportion and higher than the figure (15.5%) found in 1966.

NOTE: The term "ethnocentrism" was introduced by William Graham Sumner in *Folkways* (1906):13.

Q: "Ethnocentrism is the technical name for this view of things in which one's own group is the center of everything, and all others are scaled and rated with reference to it." William Graham Sumner (1906:13)

People everywhere consider their own values, norms, and beliefs to be natural and right. For example, the tradition in Japan is to name intersections, rather than streets; to North Americans, whose practice is to do the opposite, this cultural pattern is irritating, at best. Most North Americans are particular about keeping several feet of "personal space" between them and others; most Arabs, who routinely stand much closer to one another while engaged in conversation, thus view North Americans as rude and stand-offish (Hall, 1966).

Favoring what is familiar in this way, we often respond with suspicion or hostility to others who offend our own ideas of what is proper. Even Napoleon Chagnon, trained as an anthropologist to have an open mind, recoiled with disgust at the "naked, sweaty, and hideous" Yąnomamö. Later, Chagnon encountered several cultural practices that, from his point of view, seemed outrageous. For example, Yąnomamö men offer to share their wives sexually with younger brothers or friends. From the men's point of view, this practice symbolizes friendship and generosity. By our cultural standards, however, this behavior smacks of moral perversity and gross unfairness to women. Would we be right in condemning the Yąnomamö for their actions?

At first glance, the answer would seem to be yes. After all, our culture provides us with standards to judge right and wrong. People everywhere exhibit **ethnocentrism**, *the practice of judging another culture by the standards of one's own culture.* Although some amount of ethnocentrism is universal, it is also troubling. Why should we expect others to endorse our ethical principles rather than their own? Should we assume our norms are in some sense superior to those of others?

Ethnocentrism is deeper in our way of life than we may initially think. Take the seemingly trivial matter of people in North America referring to the region of the world dominated by China as the "Far East." Such a term, which has little meaning to the Chinese, is an ethnocentric expression for an area that is far east *of us.* For their part, the Chinese use a character to designate their nation that is translated as "Middle Kingdom," suggesting that they, too, see their society as the center of the world.

Ethnocentrism functions to enhance morale and solidarity among members of a society. But it can be dysfunctional as well, since judging the practices of others as an outsider yields not only a self-serving but a distorted view of our culturally diverse world. Note how odd Figure 3–2, on page 84, appears to us, since we are accustomed to placing the United States at the top and center of a map of the Western Hemisphere.

In outdoor markets throughout the southern region of the People's Republic of China, dogs are a prized food. To a North American observer, selecting a puppy for dinner may seem cruel and abnormal. From the Chinese point of view, however, our common practice of drinking milk provokes disgust. Truly what is "natural" behavior for human beings is living according to the guidelines of one's own culture.

An alternative to ethnocentrism is to try to imagine unfamiliar cultural traits from the point of view of others rather than ourselves. The casual observer who puzzles at an Amish farmer tilling hundreds of acres with a team of horses rather than a tractor might initially dismiss such a farming strategy as hopelessly backward and inefficient. But, from the Amish point of view, hard work is a foundation of religious discipline. The Amish are well aware of farm tractors; they simply realize that using such machinery would be their undoing.

This alternative approach is **cultural relativism**, *the practice of judging a culture by its own standards.* Cultural relativism is a difficult attitude to assume because it requires not only understanding the values and norms of another society but also suspending cultural standards we have known all our lives. But, as people of the world come into increasing contact with one another, the need to more fully understand other cultures grows steadily.

In the ever-expanding global economy, for example, U.S. business is learning that success depends on cultural sophistication and sensitivity. Consider the troubles several corporations had when they carelessly translated their advertising slogans into Spanish. General Motors soon learned that sales of its Nova were hampered by a product name that in Spanish means "Doesn't Go." The phrase "Turn It Loose," used

GLOBAL: In general, Eastern (say, Indian) and Western (U.S.) cultures differ in the following orientations: spiritual versus material; feminine versus masculine; consensus versus control; community versus individualism; connectedness versus separateness.

Q: "What Western man needs to learn is how to be content in an empty room." Blaise Pascal

Q: "What the U.S. does best is understand itself. What it does worst is understand others." Carlos Fuentes, Mexican writer

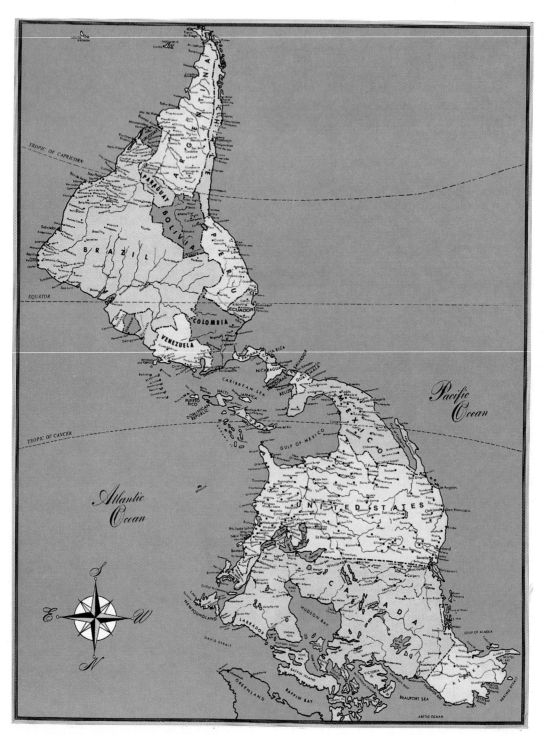

FIGURE 3–2 The View from "Down Under"

North America should be "up" and South America "down," or so we think. But, because we live on a globe, such notions are conventions rather than absolutes. The reason that this map of the Western Hemisphere looks wrong to us is not that it is geographically inaccurate; it simply violates our ethnocentric assumption that the United States should be "above" the rest of the Americas.

Q: "What is truth on one side of the Pyrenees is error on the other." Blaise Pascal (17th-century philosopher and mathematician)
DATA FILE: The excerpt from Ralph Linton's "One Hundred Percent American," found in the *Data File*, supports a discussion of ethnocentrism.

RESOURCE: Another source for a discussion of ethnocentrism and cultural relativity is Horace Miner's "Body Ritual Among the Nacirema" (*American Anthropologist* 58, 3[1956]:503–7). The article is included in the Macionis and Benokraitis reader *Seeing Ourselves*, 3/e.

in a promotion of Coors beer, startled customers who read words meaning "Suffer from Diarrhea." Braniff airlines turned "Fly in Leather" into clumsy Spanish reading "Fly Naked." Eastern Airlines transformed its slogan "We Earn Our Wings Daily" into words customers read as "We Fly Daily to Heaven." And even Frank Perdue fell victim to poor marketing when his pitch "It Takes a Tough Man to Make a Tender Chicken" ended up as Spanish for "It Takes a Sexually Excited Man to Make a Chicken Affectionate" (Helin, 1992).

Cultural understanding is the key to successful business ventures. It may also turn out to be crucial to a peaceful world as well. But cultural relativity has problems of its own. One can find virtually any kind of behavior somewhere in the world; does that mean that anything and everything has equal claim to being morally right? What about Yąnomamö men who routinely offer their wives to others or violently punish a woman who displeases them? Even in the unlikely event that Yąnomamö women accept this sort of treatment, should we pronounce such practices morally right simply because the Yąnomamö themselves accept them?

Since we all are members of a single species, we might assume there must be universal standards of conduct for everyone. But what are they? In trying to discern what is truly good, how can we avoid imposing our own standards of fair play on everyone else? There are no simple answers. But here are several general guidelines to keep in mind when encountering other cultures.

First, realize that, while cultural differences may be fascinating, they can also be deeply disturbing; be prepared for an emotional dimension in encountering them. Second, try to observe unfamiliar cultural surroundings with an open mind. At best, resist making quick judgments of others. Third, try to imagine what you see from *their* point of view rather than *yours*. Fourth, after careful and critical thought, try to evaluate what you find in another culture. After all, there is no moral virtue in passively accepting everything one encounters. But, in reaching that judgment, bear in mind that—despite sensitivity and imagination— you can never really experience the world as others do. Fifth, and finally, turn the argument around and try to evaluate your own way of life as others might see it. After all, in studying others, ultimately we learn about ourselves.

A Global Culture?

Today, more than ever before, we can observe many of the same cultural patterns the world over. Walking

the streets of Seoul (South Korea), Kuala Lumpur (Malaysia), Madras (India), Cairo (Egypt), and Casablanca (Morocco), we find familiar forms of dress, hear well-known pop music, and see advertising for many of the same products we use at home. Just as important, as suggested earlier by Global Map 3–1, English is rapidly emerging as the preferred second language of most of the world. Are we witnessing the birth of a global culture?

The world is still broken up into about 190 nation-states and thousands of different societies based on common language, cultural heritage, and kinship ties. Further, as the recent violence in Germany, the former Yugoslavia, the Middle East, India, and elsewhere attests, many people are intolerant of others who differ culturally from themselves. Yet, on a broader level, the societies of the world now have more contact with one another, and enjoy more cooperation, than ever before. Global connections involve the flow of goods, information, and people.

1. **The global economy: the flow of goods.** Throughout history, societies have traded with each other. The extent of international trade, however, has never been greater. Since products are an important dimension of culture, the emerging global economy has introduced many of the same consumer goods (from T-shirts to rock music to automobiles) the world over.

2. **Global communications: the flow of information.** Satellite-based communications now enable people throughout the world to experience— often as they happen—the sights and sounds of events taking place thousands of miles away. Even a century ago, communication links in most of the world were based on written messages delivered by boat, train, horse and wagon, or occasionally by telegraph wire. Today, there are few regions where a person cannot locate a telephone, radio, television, computer and modem, or a facsimile (fax) machine that transmit information almost instantly.

3. **Global migration: the flow of people.** As people learn more about the rest of the world, they are increasingly likely to relocate to a place where they imagine life will be better. War and other strife also force people to move. Whatever the reason, new transportation technology—especially air travel—now makes relocating easier than ever before. As a result, most societies contain significant numbers of people born in another country (22 million people, about 9 percent of the U.S. population, were born abroad).

NOTE: The word "chauvinism" is derived from Chauvin, a soldier in Napoleon's army remembered for his spirited patriotism.
Q: ". . . we have failed to understand the relativity of cultural habits, and we remain debarred from much profit and enjoyment in our human relations with people of different cultural standards, and untrustworthy in our dealings with them." Ruth Benedict

DIVERSITY: In the United States, the need for multicultural skills is greatest among the young. Compare the age-based diversity (in 1990) among people ages 70 to 74 (8% African American, 4% Latino, 2% Asian and Pacific Islander) with the percentages among preschoolers (15% African American, 13% Latino, 3% Asian and Pacific Islander).

The flow of immigrants around the world is generally from poor societies to rich nations. Despite vigorous efforts by U.S. authorities to control the border between Mexico and the United States, hundreds of people make their way into this country every day. Here a group of people aspiring to a better life look toward the border, waiting for dark before continuing their journey northward.

These global links have made the cultures of the world more similar in at least superficial respects. But there are three important limitations to the global culture thesis. First, the flow of goods, information, and people has been uneven throughout the world. Generally speaking, urban areas (that are centers of commerce, communication, and people) are more closely linked to one another, while rural villages remain isolated. Chagnon (1992) reports, for example, that there are still a few Yąnomamö settlements in Venezuela that have had little or no contact with outsiders. Then, too, the greater economic and military power of North America and Western Europe means that nations in these regions influence the rest of the world more than the other way around.

A second problem with the global culture thesis is that it assumes that people everywhere want and are able to *afford* various goods and services. As Chapter 11 ("Global Stratification") explains, the grinding poverty in much of the world deprives people of even the basic necessities of a safe and secure life.

Third, although any number of cultural traits are now found throughout much of the world, we should not conclude that people everywhere attach the same meanings to them. When we in the United States eagerly embrace, say, a "new" form of African music, we do so on our own terms with little understanding

of the music's meaning to its creators. Similarly, when people in other parts of the world begin playing basketball or reading the U.S. press, they will always view these things through their own cultural "lenses" (Featherstone, 1990; Hall & Neitz, 1993).

THEORETICAL ANALYSIS OF CULTURE

Culture provides us with the means to understand ourselves and the surrounding world. Sociologists and anthropologists, however, have the special task of comprehending culture. Analyzing such a complex concept requires employing several theoretical approaches.

Structural-Functional Analysis

Recall from Chapter 1 ("The Sociological Perspective") that structural-functional analysis presents society as a relatively stable system of integrated parts functioning to meet human needs. From this point of view, then, various cultural traits each work to maintain the overall operation of society.

The reason for the stability of a cultural system, as functionalists see it, is that core values, like the U.S. values noted earlier, anchor its way of life (Parsons, 1964; Williams, 1970). This assertion that ideas (rather than, say, the system of material production) are the basis of human reality aligns structural-functionalism with the philosophical doctrine of *idealism*. Core values are evident in most everyday activities, serving both to direct and bind together members of a society. New arrivals, of course, will not necessarily share a society's core values. But, according to the functionalist melting-pot idea, immigrants gradually embrace such values over time.

The structural-functional approach helps make sense of an unfamiliar cultural setting. Recall, for example, the Amish farmer plowing hundreds of acres with a team of horses. Within the Amish cultural system, relying on horses while rejecting tractors and automobiles makes sense because it ensures that there is plenty of hard work. Continuous labor—usually outside the home for men and inside for women—functions to maintain the Amish value of discipline, which shapes Amish religious life. Long days of teamwork, along with family meals and recreation at home, not only make the Amish self-sufficient but unify families and local communities (Hostetler, 1980).

Of course, Amish practices have dysfunctions as well. Their trait of "shunning," by which a community

Q: "The function of any recurrent activity, such as the punishment of a crime, or a funeral ceremony, is the part it plays in the social life as a whole and therefore the contribution it makes to the maintenance of the structural continuity." A. R. Radcliffe-Brown, *American Anthropologist* 37 (1935):395–96

NOTE: An interesting way to launch a functional analysis of culture is to analyze cultural heroes. What makes an act heroic?

NOTE: Ralph Linton (1937) first used the term "cultural universals" to refer to cultural traits found throughout a *single* society. The term has come to be used to designate a surprising number of cultural traits existing in *all* societies.

NOTE: Anthropology traditionally has had special interest in traits common to all cultures and traits that are unique to one.

ends social contact with anyone judged to have violated Amish mores, may ensure conformity but at the cost of generating tensions and, from time to time, lasting divisions in a community.

Because cultures are strategies to meet human needs, we would expect that cultures the world over would have some elements in common. The term **cultural universals** refers to *traits that are part of every known culture.* Comparing hundreds of cultures, George Murdock (1945) found dozens of traits common to them all. One cultural universal is the family, which functions everywhere to control sexual reproduction and to care for children. Funeral rites, too, are found everywhere, because all human communities cope with the reality of death. Jokes are also a cultural universal, acting as a relatively safe means of releasing social tensions.

Critical evaluation. A strength of the structural-functional paradigm is showing how culture operates as an integrated system for meeting human needs. One limitation of this approach, however, is its tendency to paint cultural values as embraced by everyone in a society. As we have explained, the cultural patterns favored by powerful people often dominate a society, while the ways of life of others are pushed to the margins. Put another way, societies typically have more culture-based conflict than structural-functional analysis suggests. Similarly, by emphasizing cultural stability, this paradigm downplays the extent of change.

Social-Conflict Analysis

The social-conflict paradigm presents culture in a very different light. To conflict theorists, social inequality transforms a cultural system into a dynamic arena of controversy. Conflict analysis draws attention to the ways in which any particular aspect of culture benefits some members of society at the expense of others.

Social-conflict analysis critically questions why certain values dominate in a society. What forces generate one set of values rather than another? Who benefits from these social arrangements? Sociologists using this paradigm, especially those influenced by Karl Marx, argue that values are shaped by a society's system of economic production. "It is not the consciousness of men that determines their existence," Marx proclaimed. "It is their social existence that determines their consciousness" (1977:4; orig. 1859). Social-conflict theory, then, is rooted in the philosophical doctrine of *materialism,* the assertion that how people fashion their material world (for example, the capitalist economy in the United States) has a

We tend to think of funerals as an expression of respect for the deceased. The social function of funerals, however, has much more to do with the living. For survivors, funerals reaffirm their sense of unity and continuity in the face of separation and disruption.

powerful effect on other dimensions of their culture. Such a materialist approach contrasts with the idealist leanings of structural-functionalism.

Social-conflict analysis suggests that the competitive and individualistic values of U.S. society reflect our capitalist economy and thus serve the interests of people who own factories and other businesses. The culture of capitalism further teaches us to believe that the rich and powerful have more talent and discipline than others and therefore deserve their wealth and privileges. Viewing capitalism as somehow "natural," then, leads people to distrust efforts to decrease the economic disparity found in the United States.

Eventually, however, the strains fostered by social inequality push a society toward transformation. The civil rights movement and the women's movement exemplify the drive for change supported by disadvantaged segments of the U.S. population. Both, too, have encountered opposition from defenders of the status quo.

NOTE: More detail concerning social-conflict analysis of society is found in the section of Chapter 4 ("Society") dealing with the work of Karl Marx.

RESOURCE: Dianne Herman's gender conflict article "The Rape Culture" is included in the culture selections in the Macionis and Benokraitis reader, *Seeing Ourselves*, 3/e.

Q: "We don't expect dreamers to explain their dreams; no more would we expect lifestyle participants to explain their lifestyles." Marvin Harris

RESOURCE: Marvin Harris's article "India's Sacred Cow" is included in the Macionis and Benokraitis reader *Seeing Ourselves*, 3/e.

Critical evaluation. The strength of the social-conflict paradigm lies in showing that, if cultural systems address human needs, they do so unequally. Put otherwise, this orientation holds that a key function of cultural elements is to maintain the dominance of some people over others. This inequity, in turn, generates pressure toward change. A limitation of the social-conflict paradigm is that, stressing the divisiveness of culture, it understates the ways in which cultural patterns integrate members of society. Thus we should consider both social-conflict and structural-functional insights to gain a fuller understanding of culture.

Cultural Ecology

A third theoretical paradigm is derived from ecology, the natural science that explores the relationship between a living organism and its environment. **Cultural ecology**, then, is *a theoretical paradigm that explores the relationship between human culture and the physical environment*. This paradigm leads us to ask, for instance, how climate or the availability of natural resources shape cultural patterns.

Consider the case of India, a nation that contends with widespread hunger and malnutrition, yet has cultural norms that prohibit the killing of cows. According to Hindu belief, cows are sacred animals. To North Americans who enjoy so much beef, this is puzzling. Why should Indians not consume beef to supplement their diet?

Investigating rural India's ecology, Marvin Harris (1975) concluded that the Hindu veneration of the cow makes sense because the importance of these animals extends well beyond their value as a food source. Harris points out that cows cost little to raise, since they consume grasses of no interest to humans. And cows produce two valuable resources: oxen (their neutered offspring) and manure. Unable to afford expensive farm machinery, Indian farmers rely on oxen to power their plows. For Indians, killing cows would be as clever as farmers in the United States destroying factories that build tractors. Furthermore, each year millions of tons of cow manure are processed into building material and burned as fuel (India has little oil, coal, or wood). To kill cows, then, would deprive Indians of homes and a major source of heat. In sum, there are sound ecological reasons for Indian culture to protect the cow.

Critical evaluation. Cultural ecology expands our understanding of culture by highlighting its interplay with the environment. This approach reveals how societies devise cultural patterns in response to particular natural conditions. However, this paradigm has two limitations. First, only rarely can we draw simple or direct connections between the environment and culture because cultural and physical forces interact in complex ways. Second, it is easier to discern the effect of environment on culture in technologically simple settings like rural India. A far more difficult task is investigating cases of technologically sophisticated societies that extensively manipulate the natural world.

Sociobiology

Sociology has maintained a rather uneasy relationship with biology. In part, this uneasiness stems from a rivalry between two disciplines that study human life. But it also runs deeper because early biological assertions about human behavior—for example, that some categories of people are inherently "better" than others—were expressions of historical racism and ethnocentrism rather than legitimate science. Early sociologists provided evidence to refute such thinking.

By the middle of this century, sociologists had demonstrated that culture rather than biology is the major force shaping human behavior. But this does not mean that biology has nothing to do with how we live. Exploring the connections between our biological existence and the culture we create is the task of **sociobiology**, *a theoretical paradigm that explores ways in which biological forces affect human culture*.

Sociobiology rests upon the logic of evolution. In *On the Origin of Species*, Charles Darwin (1859) asserted that living organisms change over long periods of time as a result of *natural selection*, a matter of four simple principles. First, all living things live and reproduce within a natural setting. Second, genes—the basic units of life that carry traits of one generation into the next—vary randomly in each species. Genetic variation allows any species to "try out" new life patterns in a particular environment. Third, due to this variation, some organisms are more likely to survive than others and to pass on their advantageous genes to their offspring. Fourth and finally, over thousands of generations, genetic patterns that promote survival and reproduction become dominant. In this way, as biologists say, a species *adapts* to its environment, and dominant traits represent the "nature" of the organism.

Sociobiologists suggest that the large number of cultural universals reflects the fact that we are all members of a single biological species. One example of special interest to sociobiologists is the universal pattern we commonly call the "double standard" by which men engage in sexual activity more freely than

Q: "Between God and ourselves stands nature." Pope Pius XII
NOTE: From the point of view of sociobiology, genes use bodies (and societies) to create more genes. Thus, the chicken and egg dilemma is solved in the following way: Eggs come first; eggs use chickens to create more eggs.

NOTE: Scientists discovered 50 years ago that DNA (deoxyribonucleic acid) is analogous to the body's 3-billion-bit-long computer program, shaped like a double helix, that generates protein and transmits human heredity. Scientists expect to have "mapped" human DNA early in the next century. As this work is completed, we will know much more about the role of genetics in affecting human culture.

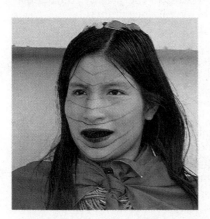  

We claim that beauty is in the eye of the beholder, which suggests the importance of culture in setting standards of attractiveness. All of the people pictured here—from Turkey, South Africa, Nigeria, Ecuador, Japan, and Myanmar (Burma)—are beautiful to members of their own society. At the same time, sociobiologists point out that, in every society on earth, people are attracted to youthfulness. The reason is that, as sociobiologists see it, attractiveness underlies our choices about reproduction, which is most readily accomplished in early adulthood.

women do. As sex researcher Alfred Kinsey put it, "Among all people everywhere in the world, the male is more likely than the female to desire sex with a variety of partners" (quoted in Barash, 1981:49).

We all know that children result from joining a woman's egg with a man's sperm. But the biological significance of a single sperm and a single egg are dramatically different. For healthy men, sperm represents a "renewable resource" produced by the testes throughout most of life. A man releases hundreds of millions of sperm in a single ejaculation—technically, enough to fertilize every woman in North America (Barash, 1981:47). A newborn female's ovaries, however, contain her entire lifetime allotment of follicles or immature eggs. A woman commonly releases a single mature egg

cell from her ovaries each month. So, while a man is biologically capable of fathering thousands of offspring, a woman is able to bear only a relatively small number of children.

Given this difference, each sex is well served by a distinctive reproductive strategy. Biologically, a man reproduces his genes most efficiently through a strategy of sexual promiscuity. This scheme, however, opposes the reproductive interests of a woman. Each of her relatively few pregnancies demands that she carry the child for nine months, give birth, and provide care for some time afterward. Thus, efficient reproduction on the part of the woman depends on carefully selecting a mate whose qualities will contribute to their child's survival and successful reproduction (Remoff, 1984).

RESOURCE: David Barash's *The Whisperings Within* (Harper & Row, 1981) provides a good discussion of the politics of sociobiology (see Chapter 8).
Q: "Although the genes have given away most of their sovereignty, they maintain a certain amount of influence in at least the behavioral qualities that underlie the variations between cultures." Edward O. Wilson

NOTE: The final section of Chapter 5 ("Socialization") provides further discussion of the "constraint versus freedom" controversy.
Q: "Society is indeed a contract between those who are living, those who are dead, and those who are yet to be born." Edmund Burke

The "double standard" certainly involves more than biology; it is also a product of the historical domination of women by men (Barry, 1983). But sociobiology suggests that this cultural pattern, like many others, has an underlying bio-logic. Simply put, it has developed around the world because women and men everywhere tend toward distinctive reproductive strategies.

Critical evaluation. Sociobiology has succeeded in generating insights about the biological roots of some cultural patterns, especially those that are universal. But sociobiology remains controversial for several reasons.

First, some critics fear that sociobiology may revive older biological arguments that supported the oppression of one race or sex. Defenders respond, however, that sociobiology has no connection to any past pseudoscience of racial superiority. On the contrary, sociobiology serves to unite rather than divide humanity by asserting that we all share a single evolutionary history. The notion that men are inherently superior to women is also inconsistent with sociobiological thinking. Sociobiology does rest on the assumption that men and women differ biologically in some ways that culture will not overcome—if, in fact, any society intended to. But, far from asserting that males are somehow more important than females, sociobiology emphasizes how both sexes are vital to human reproduction.

Second, say the critics, sociobiologists have as yet amassed little evidence to support their theories. Edward O. Wilson (1975, 1978), generally credited as the founder of this field, optimistically claimed that sociobiology would reveal the biological roots of human culture. But a generation of work shows that biological forces do not shape human behavior in any rigid sense. Rather, abundant evidence supports the conclusion that human behavior is *learned* within a cultural system. The contribution of sociobiology, then, lies in its explanation of why some cultural patterns are more common than others.

CULTURE AND HUMAN FREEDOM

We have introduced the elements of human culture, examined cultural diversity and change, and drawn insights about culture from various theoretical paradigms. Our final question is how culture affects us as individuals. Does it bind us to the past, constraining our human imagination? Or does it enhance our capacity to think critically and to make choices?

Culture as Constraint

Over the long course of human evolution, culture became our strategy for survival. But though we cannot live without it, culture does have some negative consequences. Cultural beings experience the world through symbols and meaning; just as we are the only species that names itself, so we are the only animal that can experience alienation. Further, with its roots deep in the past, culture becomes mostly a matter of habit, limiting our choices and perhaps driving us to repeat troubling patterns. Racial prejudice, for example, manages to find its way into the lives of each new generation. Similarly, women of all colors have often felt powerless in the face of cultural patterns that reflect the dominance of men.

No cultural pattern is entirely positive. Our society's insistence on competitive achievement urges us toward excellence, yet this same pattern also isolates us from one another. Material comforts improve our lives in many ways, yet our preoccupation with objects diverts us from the security and satisfaction of close relationships or strong religious faith. Our emphasis on personal freedom affords us privacy and autonomy, yet our culture often denies us the support of a human community in which to share life's problems (Slater, 1976; Bellah et al., 1985). In short, culture is as vital to humans as biological instinct is to other forms of life. But, all the same, it poses special problems for us.

Culture as Freedom

Human beings may appear to be prisoners of culture, just as other animals are prisoners of biology. But careful thought about the ideas presented in this chapter suggests a crucial difference. Over millions of years of human evolution, the unfolding of culture gradually took our species from a world shaped largely by biology to a world we highly intelligent creatures shape for ourselves.

Therefore, although culture seems at times to circumscribe our lives, it embodies the human capacity for hope and creative choice. The evidence that supports this conclusion lies all around us. Fascinating cultural diversity exists in our own society, and even greater variety is found around the world. Furthermore, far from being static, culture is ever-changing, and it presents us with a continuous source of human opportunity. The more we discover about the operation of our culture, the greater our ability to use the freedom it offers us.

SUMMARY

1. Culture refers to a way of life shared by members of a society. Several species have limited forms of culture, but only human beings rely on culture for survival.

2. As the brain grew larger over the long course of human evolution, culture steadily replaced biological instincts. The first elements of culture appeared some 2 million years ago; the complex culture that we call civilization emerged during the last 10,000 years.

3. The term "culture" refers to a way of life; the concept "nation" means a political entity; the term "society" designates the organized interaction of people in a nation or within some other boundary.

4. Culture is built on symbols, which come into being as we attach meaning to objects and actions. Language is the symbolic system by which we transmit culture from generation to generation.

5. Values represent general orientations to the world around us; beliefs are statements people who share a culture hold to be true.

6. Cultural norms guide human behavior. Mores consist of norms of great moral significance; folkways, norms that guide everyday life, permit greater individual discretion.

7. Values and norms are expressions of ideal culture; in practice, real culture varies considerably from these standards.

8. Material creations reflect cultural values as well as a society's technology.

9. High culture refers to patterns that distinguish a society's elites; popular culture includes patterns widespread in a society.

10. All societies contain some cultural diversity; our own contains a great deal. Subculture refers to distinctive cultural forms that characterize a segment of society; counterculture means patterns strongly at odds with a widely accepted way of life. Multiculturalism represents efforts to enhance awareness and appreciation of cultural diversity.

11. Culture is never static: Invention, discovery, and diffusion all generate cultural change. Not all parts of a cultural system change at the same rate, however; this differential produces cultural lag.

12. Having learned the standards of one culture, we often evaluate other cultures ethnocentrically. One alternative to ethnocentrism, called cultural relativism, means judging different cultures according to their own standards.

13. The structural-functional paradigm views culture as a relatively stable system built on core values. Specific cultural traits function to help maintain the overall social system.

14. The social-conflict paradigm envisions cultural systems as dynamic arenas of inequality and conflict. Cultural patterns typically benefit some categories of people more than others.

15. The cultural-ecology paradigm explores ways in which human culture is shaped by the natural environment.

16. Sociobiology studies the influence of humanity's evolutionary past on present patterns of culture.

17. Culture can constrain human needs and ambitions; yet as cultural creatures we have the capacity to shape and reshape the world to meet our needs and pursue our dreams.

KEY CONCEPTS

Afrocentrism the dominance of African cultural patterns in people's lives

beliefs specific statements that people who share culture hold to be true

counterculture cultural patterns that strongly oppose those widely accepted within a society

cultural ecology a theoretical paradigm that explores the relationship between human culture and the physical environment

cultural integration the close relationship among various elements of a cultural system

cultural lag the fact that cultural elements change at different rates, which may disrupt a cultural system

cultural relativism the practice of judging a culture by its own standards

cultural transmission the process by which one generation passes culture to the next

cultural universals traits that are part of every known culture

culture the beliefs, values, behavior, and material objects that define a people's way of life

culture shock personal disorientation that accompanies exposure to an unfamiliar way of life

ethnocentrism the practice of judging another culture by the standards of one's own culture

Eurocentrism the dominance of European (especially English) cultural patterns

folkways norms that have less moral significance than mores

high culture cultural patterns that distinguish a society's elite

ideal culture as opposed to real culture, the social patterns mandated by cultural values and norms

language a system of symbols that allows members of a society to communicate with one another

material culture tangible products of human society, such as clothing and cities

mores norms that have great moral significance

multiculturalism an educational program recognizing past and present cultural diversity in U.S. society and promoting the equality of all cultural traditions

nonmaterial culture intangible creations of human society, such as values and norms

norms rules and expectations by which a society guides the behavior of its members

popular culture cultural patterns that are widespread among a society's population

real culture as opposed to ideal culture, the actual social patterns that only approximate cultural expectations

Sapir-Whorf hypothesis a hypothesis stating that people perceive the world through the cultural lens of language

social control various means by which members of a society encourage conformity to norms

sociobiology a theoretical paradigm that explores ways in which biological forces affect human culture

subculture cultural patterns that distinguish some segment of a society's population

symbol anything that carries a particular meaning recognized by people who share culture

technology knowledge that a society applies to the task of living in a physical environment

values culturally defined standards by which people judge desirability, goodness, and beauty, and which serve as broad guidelines for social living

CRITICAL-THINKING QUESTIONS

1. Discuss the validity of the statement "Culture is human nature."

2. How does a schoolroom activity such as a "spelling bee" express U.S. cultural values? Identify other common activities that express various cultural values.

3. Why do members of every society tend to be ethnocentric? Point out at least one positive and negative function of ethnocentrism. Can you do the same with cultural relativism?

4. In what ways does culture constrain us? In what ways does it liberate us?

SUGGESTED READINGS

Classic Sources

Napoleon A. Chagnon. *Yąnomamö: The Fierce People.* 4th ed. New York: Holt, Rinehart and Winston, 1992.

> Napoleon Chagnon's updated account of the Yąnomamö offers fascinating insights into a culture very different from our own. It is also a compelling tale of carrying out fieldwork in an unfamiliar world.

Marvin Harris. *Good to Eat: Riddles of Food and Culture.* New York: Simon and Schuster, 1985.

> Cultural ecologist Marvin Harris explains many puzzling cultural practices.

Margaret Mead. *Coming of Age in Samoa: A Psychological Study of Primitive Youth for Western Civilization.* New York: Wm. Morrow, 1928.

> Margaret Mead, perhaps the best-known student of culture, conducted this study of the Samoan Islands demonstrating the variability of cultural systems.

Contemporary Sources

Roger E. Axtell. *Gestures: The DO's and TABOOs of Body Language Around the World.* New York: Wiley, 1991.

> This amusing book examines how the use of gestures can get travelers into trouble.

John Henrik Clarke, ed. *Marcus Garvey and the Vision of Africa.* New York: Vintage, 1990.

> This collection of essays by and about Marcus Garvey explains the life and times of this leader of the African-American community.

Molefi Kete Asante. *The Afrocentric Idea.* Philadelphia: Temple University Press, 1987.

_____. *Afrocentricity.* Trenton, N.J.: Africa World Press, 1988.

> These two books provide a good introduction to the concept of Afrocentrism and its challenge to conventional views of U.S. culture.

Peggy Reeves Sanday. *Divine Hunger: Cannibalism as a Cultural System.* Cambridge, UK: Cambridge University Press, 1986.

> Cannibalism is a practice almost impossible for Westerners to comprehend. Yet, as this book explains, this consuming passion is quite acceptable to some cultures.

John A. Hostetler, ed. *Amish Roots: A Treasury of History, Wisdom, and Lore.* Baltimore: Johns Hopkins Press, 1989.

> The Amish are a fascinating North American counterculture. This book is a collection of articles that surveys Amish history and contemporary life organized by a long-respected scholar of Amish background.

James Davison Hunter. *Culture Wars: The Struggle to Define America.* New York: Basic Books, 1991.

Frances Moore Lappé. *Rediscovering America's Values.* New York: Ballantine Books, 1989.

Faye Ginsburg and Anna Lowenhaupt, eds. *Uncertain Terms: Negotiating Gender in American Culture.* Boston: Beacon Press, 1990.

> These three books comment on our national way of life. The first highlights our country's contemporary debate between supporters of traditional "family values" and progressive change. The second argues that core values like freedom and democracy are betrayed by our social institutions. The third examines how variables such as gender, race, and class affect the experience of membership in our society.

Robert N. Bellah, Richard Madsen, William M. Sullivan, Ann Swidler, and Steven M. Tipton. *The Good Society.* New York: Alfred Knopf, 1991.

> In this sequel to their well-known *Habits of the Heart,* this team of sociologists explores the need for a collective, institutional life in an individualistic society.

Global Sources

Mike Featherstone, ed. *Global Culture: Nationalism, Globalization, and Modernity.* London: Sage, 1990.

> These two dozen essays explore various ways in which a global culture is emerging.

Joana McIntyre Varawa. *Changes in Latitude: An Uncommon Anthropology.* New York: Harper & Row, 1990.

> This fascinating book describes how a woman from Hawaii past midlife traveled to Fiji on vacation only to find a new home, a new husband, and a host of new challenges.

Craig Storti. *The Art of Crossing Cultures.* Yarmouth, MN: Intercultural Press, 1990.

> This brief book explores the excitement as well as the difficulties of cross-cultural experience.

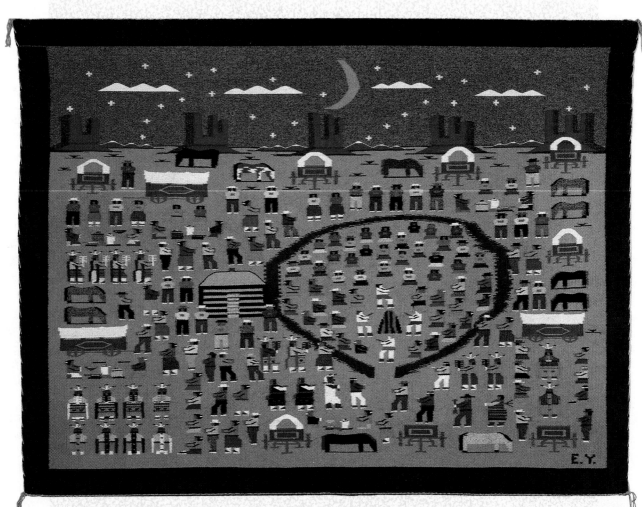

Jerry Jacka Photography

NOTE: The chapter-opening art is a Navajo rug by Ellen Yazzie.
DATA FILE: The *Data File* provides an outline of Chapter 4 along with discussion questions and supplementary lecture material.
Q: "Our lives are connected by a thousand different threads." Herman Melville
NOTE: Instructors may use this chapter in a variety of ways. Assign all of it to provide students with a detailed introduction to important historical and theoretical material encountered in later chapters. Alternatively, assign its sections separately along with later chapters (perhaps linking Weber with the discussion of bureaucracy in Chapter 7; Durkheim with the account of deviance found in Chapter 8; Marx with the discussion of social inequality in Chapter 9). The chapter can be omitted entirely without breaking the flow of the text.
Q: "Society is no comfort to one not sociable." William Shakespeare

Society

4

"*I* *thought at first it was a doll's head," said Helmut Simon, a German tourist who, in 1991, made one of the scientific finds of the century. Simon was hiking across a huge glacier in southwest Austria near the Italian border when he stumbled upon a familiar shape protruding from the melting ice. He soon realized that it was not a doll but a human body: the so-call Iceman, who lived some 5,300 years ago, making him the oldest member of our species to be discovered preserved and intact.*

Experts from around the world soon were buzzing with excitement. At the time of his death, they estimate the Iceman was about thirty years of age, with a height of five feet two inches, and weighing about 110 pounds. He was a shepherd, tending his flock high in the Alps in early fall, when, scientists speculate, he was over-taken by a cold storm that forced him to take refuge in a narrow ridge in the mountain. Tired from his ordeal, he lay down and fell asleep, and, as the temperature continued to fall, he silently froze to death. Deep snows and a wall of ice soon entombed his body in a massive glacier. There, at a flesh-preserving temperature of twenty-one degrees Fahrenheit, he remained for fifty-three centuries. Only an unusual melt of the glacier—and the luck of a hiker with a sharp eye—led to the Iceman's discovery.*

From examining the Iceman's garments, scientists are astonished that this "cave man's" society

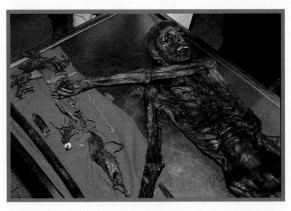

was so advanced. The Iceman's hair was neatly trimmed, and his body displayed numerous tattoos that probably symbolized his standing in his home community. He wore a skillfully stitched leather coat over which a woven grass cape provided greater protection from the elements. His shoes, also made

Q: "The first thing an ecological-evolutionary perspective requires is that we establish the relationship of our societies to the rest of the world. . . *Societies are part of the natural order.*" Gerhard and Jean Lenski
Q: "Political activity is shadow play . . . technology is the underlying reality." David Warsh

Q: "Had there been no technological innovations during the last 10,000 years, all societies would be small, nomadic populations of hunters and gatherers living much the way our Stone Age ancestors did." Gerhard and Jean Lenski
Q: "The most pressing problems of humanity . . . involve . . . systems [that] must be studied as a whole in all of the complexity of their interactions." René Dubois

of leather, were stuffed with grass for comfort and warmth. He carried with him an ax, a wood-handled knife, and a bow that shot feathered arrows with flint points. A primitive backpack held additional tools and personal items, including plants with medicinal qualities.

The value of this discovery lies in challenging conventional thinking that, at the dawning of civilization, our ancestors were little more than unorganized bands of people clad only in bits of animal skins and with few skills. In fact, the members of early human societies seem to have been surprisingly concerned with their personal appearance and possessed a wide range of abilities (Rademaekers & Schoenthal, 1992).

This chapter takes a broad look at human societies, traces their historical development, and suggests future trends. The central concept of **society** refers to *people who interact in a defined territory and share culture.* We shall examine this deceptively simple term using four approaches, all of which have great importance to sociologists and are used in most later chapters. **Gerhard Lenski** and **Jean Lenski** describe the changing character of human society over the last ten thousand years. Focusing on how *technology* shapes social life, their analysis shows that a technological breakthrough often has revolutionary consequences for society as a whole. The remainder of the chapter presents classic visions of society developed by three of sociology's founders. Like the Lenskis, **Karl Marx** also understood human history as a long and complex process of social change. For Marx, however, the story of society spins around *social conflict*, which results from inequality rooted in how people produce material goods. **Max Weber** recognized the importance of productive forces as well, but he sought to demonstrate the power of *human ideas* to shape society. Weber believed that modern society is based on human rationality, an approach to the world that encourages change. Finally, **Emile Durkheim** investigated patterns of *social solidarity*—how societies are held together. Identifying two key sources of solidarity, Durkheim contrasted traditional and modern societies.

All four visions of society answer important questions: How do societies of the past and present differ from one another? How and why do societies change? What forces divide a society? What forces hold a society together? In what respects are societies improving the human condition? Making it worse? The theorists included in this chapter all investigated these questions, although they disagree on the answers. We shall highlight the similarities and differences in their views as we proceed.

GERHARD LENSKI AND JEAN LENSKI: SOCIETY AND TECHNOLOGY

The Iceman, introduced at the opening of this chapter, was a member of a very early human society. He had already died before people in Egypt began to build the Great Pyramids, before the flowering of culture in ancient Greece, and before Europeans could boast of a single city.

As members of a modern, industrialized society who take for granted rapid transportation and global communication, we must regard this ancestor from our distant past with curiosity. But sociologists who study the past (in cooperation with archeologists and anthropologists) can explain quite a bit about our human heritage. Gerhard Lenski and Jean Lenski, introduced in the box, have chronicled the great differences among societies that have flourished and declined throughout human history. Just as important, the work of these researchers helps us better understand how we live today.

The Lenskis call the focus of their research **sociocultural evolution,** *the process of change that results from a society's gaining new information, particularly technology* (Lenski, Lenski, & Nolan 1991:65). This approach employs the biological process of evolution to examine how societies, like living organisms, change over time as they gain greater ability to manipulate their physical environments. The Lenskis see technology as the key factor shaping other cultural patterns. Societies with rudimentary technology can support only a small number of people who live a simple way of life. Technologically complex societies—while not necessarily "better" in many respects—develop large populations engaged in highly diverse activities.

The Lenskis also explain that the amount of technological information a society has in its grasp affects the rate at which it changes. In general, the more simple a society's technology, the slower it changes. In fact, some of the clothing worn by the Austrian Iceman differs only slightly from garments used by shepherds in the same area early in this century. In

Q: "Technology does not determine all a society's characteristics, of course. It does, however, determine two fundamental things. First it determines the *range of what is possible.* . . . Second, its technology determines *the relative costs of its options.*" Gerhard and Jean Lenski

NOTE: Until about 150 years ago, the fastest a person traveled

(short of falling out of a tall tree) was about 35 mph, the speed of a fast horse.

NOTE: Hunting and gathering people mused over the stars, and we still imagine the constellations in terms that were relevant to them— mostly animals and hunters. If we were beginning the process from scratch, what meaning would we impose on the stars today?

PROFILE

Gerhard Lenski and Jean Lenski: The Evolution of Technology

Gerhard Lenski is a contemporary U.S. sociologist who is well known for his research on religion, social inequality, and history. Jean Lenski, a writer and poet, has frequently collaborated with her husband in sociological research. Together, they

have brought to the attention of their sociological colleagues a wide range of research on the role of technology in human societies.

The Lenskis' approach to understanding society has much in common with that of Marvin Harris, the cultural ecologist described in Chapter 3 ("Culture"). Recall that cultural ecology focuses on the specific cultural strategies that societies use to survive in a particular natural environment. The Lenskis highlight the role of technology in circumscribing a society's capacity to produce and process material resources from its natural surroundings.

Cultural ecology and sociocultural evolution are different, however, in an important respect. While both emphasize that the natural environment shapes cultural patterns, the Lenskis' analysis explains

why this is true of some societies more than others. With little ability to manipulate nature, technologically simple societies are influenced the most by their surroundings. Technologically sophisticated societies, by contrast, have greater power to contend with the physical world, even recasting nature according to human designs. Therefore, technologically simple societies tend to resemble one another, with minor variations that reflect different natural environments. More technologically complex societies, on the other hand, reveal the striking cultural diversity described in Chapter 3.

striking contrast, highly industrialized societies, with access to much more technological information, change so quickly that people witness dramatic transformations during their lifetimes. Consider some familiar elements of North American culture that would probably puzzle—or even alarm—people who lived just a few generations ago: laser surgery, test-tube babies, genetic engineering, the threat of nuclear holocaust, computer-based virtual reality, smart bombs, fiber optics, transsexualism, space shuttles, and artificial hearts (Lenski & Lenski, 1982).

As a society extends its technological reach, the effects of its growing power ripple through the cultural system, causing many more changes. In other words, a single innovation (say, harnessing the power of the wind) can be applied to many existing cultural elements (to produce windmills, kites, sailing ships, and, eventually, airplanes). Consider, as more recent

examples, the many ways modern life has been changed by the computer or the unleashing of the power of the atom.

Drawing on the Lenskis' work, we will describe five general types of societies distinguished by their technology: hunting and gathering societies, horticultural and pastoral societies, agrarian societies, industrial societies, and postindustrial societies.

Hunting and Gathering Societies

Hunting and gathering refers to *simple technology for hunting animals and gathering vegetation.* From the emergence of our species until about ten thousand years ago, all humans were hunters and gatherers. Although hunting and gathering societies remained common several centuries ago, only a few persist today, including the Aka and Pygmies of Central

In technologically simple societies, successful hunting wins men great praise. However, the gathering of vegetation by women is a more dependable and easily available source of nutrition.

Africa, the Bushmen of southwestern Africa, the Aborigines of Australia, the Kaska Indians of northwest Canada, and the Batek and Semai of Malaysia (Endicott, 1992; Hewlett, 1992).

With scarcely any technology to make food production efficient, most members of these societies must search continually for game and edible plants. Only in areas where food is plentiful do hunters and gatherers enjoy any leisure. Foraging for food demands a large amount of land, so hunting and gathering societies remain at some distance from one another and are limited in population to several dozen people. Most small groups are also nomadic, moving on as they deplete vegetation in one area or in pursuit of migratory animals. Although periodically returning to favored sites, they rarely form permanent settlements.

Hunting and gathering societies are based on kinship. The family obtains and distributes food, teaches necessary skills to children, and protects its members. While most activities are common to everyone and center on seeking their next meal, some specialization occurs by age and sex. The very young and the very old contribute only what they can, while healthy adults secure most of the food. The gathering of vegetation—the more reliable food source—is typically the work of women, while men do the less certain work of hunting. Therefore, although the two sexes have somewhat different responsibilities, most hunters and gatherers probably saw men and women as having comparable social importance (Leacock, 1978).

Hunting and gathering societies have few formal leaders. Most recognize a *shaman*, or spiritual leader, who enjoys high prestige but receives no greater material rewards. Limited technology mandates that hunters and gatherers expect even their shaman to help procure food. Men who hunt with exceptional skills are admired, as are women who are unusually productive in gathering vegetation. But, overall, the social organization of hunters and gatherers is relatively simple and egalitarian.

Hunting and gathering societies rarely use their handcrafted weapons—the spear, the bow and arrow, and stone knife—to wage war. Nonetheless they are often ravaged by the forces of nature. Storms and droughts can easily destroy their food supply, and their simple skills leave them vulnerable to accident and disease. Continual risks encourage cooperative activities and sharing of food, strategies that increase everyone's odds of survival. Nonetheless, many die in childhood, and perhaps half perish before the age of twenty (Lenski, Lenski, & Nolan 1991:91).

During this century, technologically complex societies have slowly closed in on the few remaining hunters and gatherers, reducing their landholdings and depleting game and vegetation. The Lenskis predict that the 1990s may well witness the tragic end of hunting and gathering societies on Earth. Fortunately, study of this way of life has already produced valuable information about human history and our fundamental ties to the natural world.

Horticultural and Pastoral Societies

Ten to twelve thousand years ago, a new technology began to change many hunting and gathering societies. **Horticulture** is *a technology based on using hand tools to cultivate plants*. The most important tools of horticulturalists are the hoe to work the soil and the digging stick to punch holes in the ground for seeds. Humans first used these tools in fertile regions of the Middle East and Southeast Asia. From these regions, knowledge of these devices spread by cultural diffusion as far as Western Europe and China by about six thousand years ago. In Central and South America, the cultivation of plants emerged independently about nine thousand years ago, although horticulture was less efficient there because of the rocky soil and mountainous terrain.

Not all societies were quick to abandon hunting and gathering in favor of horticulture. Hunters and

DATA FILE: Supplementary lecture material on the cultural traits of pastoral societies is found in the *Data File*.
NOTE: Warfare is more common among horticulturalists while being rare among hunting and gathering people. The reason: increasing population density that limits both available land and hunting.

NOTE: Chapter 9 ("Social Stratification") examines the relative degree of social inequality in the types of societies described by the Lenskis. See, especially, Figure 9–1, the Kuznets Curve.
NOTE: While private ownership of land is very rarely found among hunting and gathering peoples, it is usually (although not exclusively) the case among horticulturalists.

Pastoralism historically has flourished in regions of the world where arid soil does not support crops. Pastoral people still thrive in northern Africa, living today much as they did a thousand years ago.

gatherers living amid plentiful vegetation and game probably had little reason to embrace the new technology (Fisher, 1979). The Yąnomamö, described in Chapter 3 ("Culture"), illustrate the common practice of combining horticulture with more traditional hunting and gathering (Chagnon, 1992). Then, too, in particularly arid regions (such as the Middle East) or mountainous areas (such as in the Alps where the "Iceman" lived), horticulture was of relatively little value. People in such places developed **pastoralism**, *technology that supports the domestication of animals.* Some societies combined horticulture and pastoralism to produce more varied foods. Today, many horticultural-pastoral societies thrive in South America, Africa, and throughout Asia.

The domestication of plants and animals greatly increased food production, enabling societies to support many hundreds of people. Societies that emphasized pastoralism remained nomadic, leading their herds to fresh grazing lands. Those that emphasized horticulture formed settlements, relocating only when they depleted the soil. These settlements, joined by trade, comprised multicentered societies with overall populations often exceeding five thousand.

Domesticating plants and animals increased efficiency to the point of generating a *material surplus*, more resources than necessary to sustain day-to-day living. At this point, not everyone had to produce food, so some people could create crafts, engage in trade, cut hair, apply tattoos, or serve as priests. In comparison to hunting and gathering societies, horticultural and pastoral societies display far more specialized and complex social arrangements.

Hunters and gatherers recognize numerous spirits inhabiting the world. Horticulturalists, however, are characterized by the practice of ancestor worship and are likely to have a conception of God as Creator. Pastoral societies carry this belief further, viewing God as directly involved in the well-being of the entire world. This view of God ("The Lord is my shepherd . . . ," Psalm 23) is widespread among members of our own society because Christianity, Islam, and Judaism were originally pastoral religions.

Expanding productive technology also intensifies social inequality. As some families produce more food than others, they assume positions of relative privilege and power. Forging alliances with other privileged families ensures that such social advantages endure over generations. From the power of such elites, rudimentary government emerges. However, technology also places limits on this power. Without the ability to communicate or to travel quickly, a ruler can control only a small number of people. Furthermore, the exercise of power often breeds opposition, and there is evidence of frequent revolts and other forms of political conflict in these societies.

The domestication of plants and animals enabled societies to become much more productive than was possible relying on hunting and gathering. But advancing technology is never entirely beneficial. The Lenskis point out that, throughout history, increased production has generally paralleled a rise in social inequality. Horticulturalists and pastoralists also stand out as more warlike, just as they may engage in slavery and, in some cases, cannibalism.

RESOURCE: The companion reader *Seeing Ourselves*, 3/e, includes Marvin Harris's article "India's Sacred Cow," which explains the Hindu veneration of the cow in terms of India's ecology and technology.
NOTE: Peter Berger (1986:99) points out that today's average people live better in many respects than the elites of agrarian societies. For example, as late as World War I, Schoenbrunn, the fabulous summer palace of the Hapsburgs (monarchs of Austria), did not have an indoor toilet.
GLOBAL: For most of our history, our species has lived in hunting and gathering societies; during the last 2,000 years, however, agrarian societies have predominated, and they still contain about 70% of the world's people.

Of Egypt's 130 pyramids, the Great Pyramids at Giza are the largest. Each of the three major structures stands more than forty stories high and is composed of 3 million massive stone blocks. Some 4,500 years ago, tens of thousands of people labored to construct these pyramids so that one man, the pharaoh, might have a god-like monument for his tomb. Clearly social inequality in this agrarian society was striking.

Agrarian Societies

About five thousand years ago—around the time the Iceman was alive—another technological revolution was beginning to transform much of the world. This was the discovery of **agriculture**, *the technology of large-scale farming using plows harnessed to animals or more powerful sources of energy.* Agrarian technology first appeared in the Middle East and gradually diffused throughout the world. The Lenskis state that the social significance of the animal-drawn plow, along with other technological innovations of the period—including irrigation, the wheel, writing, numbers, and the expanding use of metals—clearly qualifies this era as "the dawn of civilization" (1991:160).

Farmers with animal-drawn plows cultivated fields vastly larger than the garden-sized plots worked by horticulturalists. Plows have the additional advantage of turning, and thereby aerating, the soil to increase fertility. Agrarian societies can thus farm the same land for decades, encouraging permanent settlements. Large food surpluses, transported on animal-powered wagons, allowed agrarian societies to expand to unprecedented size in both population and land area. As an extreme case, the Roman Empire at its height (about 100 C.E.) boasted a population of 70 million spread over some 2 million square miles (Stavrianos, 1983; Lenski, Lenski, & Nolan, 1991).

As always, greater surplus meant more specialization. Tasks once performed by everyone, such as clearing land, building, and processing food, became distinct occupations. Money replaced the old barter system about this time. While barter depends on people trading goods directly with one another, money is a universal standard of value that indirectly ties all goods and services together into an expanding economy. The appearance of money further enhanced trade, sparking the growth of cities. Ancient Rome reached 1 million people, and cities in modern agrarian societies such as India and Egypt are now many times that size. Settlements steadily became larger and more commercial, quite unlike the small, personal villages of an earlier era.

Agrarian societies exhibit dramatic social inequality. In many cases—including the United States early in its history—a segment of the population is slaves or peasants who labor for elites. Freed from the need to work, elites engage in the study of philosophy, art, and literature. This explains the historical link between "high culture," as discussed in Chapter 3 ("Culture"), and social privilege.

In hunting and gathering and also in horticultural societies, women gain prestige from producing much of the food. Agricultural technology, however, appears to have propelled men into a position of clear social dominance (Boulding, 1976; Fisher, 1979). The box looks more closely at the declining position of women at this point in the course of sociocultural evolution.

Religion plays an important role in reinforcing the power of agricultural elites. Religious doctrine typically propounds the idea that people are morally obligated to perform whatever tasks correspond to their place in the social order. Many of the "Wonders of the Ancient

GLOBAL: The Lenskis report the following typical densities in persons per square mile: hunting and gathering societies, less than one; horticultural societies, in the range of 10 to 40; agrarian societies, over 100. Industrial societies have densities that range from about 70 (U.S.) to many hundreds (most European nations), nearing 1,000 in a few cases (such as Japan and the Netherlands).

NOTE: Chapter 15 ("The Economy and Work") details the facets of the Industrial Revolution: (1) new forms of energy, (2) factories, (3) mass production, (4) productive specialization, and (5) wage labor.
NOTE: The Lenskis point out that the term "Industrial Revolution" did not enter common usage until the final decades of the 19th century; at that point, it already described events that had begun almost two centuries before.

SOCIAL DIVERSITY

Technology and the Changing Status of Women

In technologically simple societies of the past, women produced more food than men did. Hunters and gatherers highly valued meat, but men's hunting was not a dependable source of nourishment. Thus vegetation gathered by women was the primary means of ensuring survival. Similarly, tools and seeds used in horticulture developed under the control of women, who already had primary responsibility for providing and preparing food. With cultivation under the control of women, men typically engaged in trade and tended herds of animals. Only at harvest time did everyone work together.

About five thousand years ago, societies discovered how to mold metals. This technology spread by cultural diffusion, primarily along trade networks composed of men. Thus it was men who devised the metal plow and, since they already managed animals, soon thought to hitch the implement to cattle.

This innovation initiated the transition from horticulture to agriculture and thrust men for the first time into a dominant position in the production of food. Elise Boulding explains that this technological breakthrough thus undermined the social standing of women:

The shift of the status of the woman farmer may have happened quite rapidly, once there were two male specializations relating to agriculture: plowing and the care of cattle. This situation left women with all the subsidiary tasks, including weeding and carrying water to the fields. The new fields were larger, so women had to work just as many hours as they did before, but now they worked at more secondary tasks. . . . This would contribute further to the erosion of the status of women.

SOURCES: Based on Boulding (1976) and Fisher (1979).

World," such as the Great Wall of China and the Great Pyramids of Egypt, were possible only because emperors and pharaohs had virtually absolute power to mobilize their people and demand a lifetime of labor without pay.

In agrarian societies, then, elites gain unparalleled power. To maintain control of large empires, leaders require the services of a wide range of administrators. Along with the growing economy, the political system becomes established as a distinct element of society.

In relation to societies described so far, the Lenskis conclude, agrarian societies have greater internal diversity and social inequality. And, unlike horticultural and pastoral societies, agrarian societies are more distinct from one another because advancing technology provides increasing control over the natural world.

Industrial Societies

Industrialism, as found in the United States, Canada, and much of the Northern Hemisphere, is *technology that powers sophisticated machinery with advanced sources of energy.* Before the industrial era, the major source of energy was the muscle power of humans and other animals. At the dawning of the Industrial Revolution, about 1750, mills and factories relied on flowing water and then steam to power ever-larger and, more efficient machinery.

Once this technology was at hand, societies began to change faster, as shown in Figure 4–1 on page 102. Industrial societies transformed themselves more in a century than they had in thousands of years before. As explained in Chapter 1 ("The Sociological Perspective"), this stunning change stimulated the birth of sociology itself. During the nineteenth century, railroads and steamships revolutionized transportation, and steel-framed skyscrapers recast the urban landscape, dwarfing the cathedrals that symbolized an age gone by.

Early in the twentieth century, automobiles further reshaped Western societies, and electricity was fast becoming the basis for countless "modern conveniences." Electronic communication, including the telephone, radio, and television, were mass producing cultural patterns and gradually making a large world seem smaller and smaller. More recently, transportation technology has given humanity the capacity to

GLOBAL: Marvin Harris (1983) describes the power of expanding technology, estimating that hunters and gatherers had to expend 1 calorie of human energy to produce 3 calories of food value. For horticultural societies, the ratio is 1:15; for agrarian societies, 1:50; and for industrial societies, 1:5000.

NOTE: The long-run consequences of the Industrial Revolution may be the emergence of a global culture, as suggested by modernization theory (Chapter 11, "Global Stratification"), and also discussed in Chapter 24 ("Social Change and Modernity").

In the 1936 film Modern Times, *a young Charlie Chaplin gave one of his finest performances—in effect, a warning that modern, industrial technology might enslave people as easily as it could liberate them.*

fly faster than sound and even to break entirely the bonds of Earth. Nuclear power, used for destruction ten years before it generated electricity, has also forever changed the world. During the last generation, computers have ushered in the *Information Revolution*, dramatically increasing humanity's capacity to process words and numbers.

In agrarian societies, most men and women work in the home. Industrial machinery, however, led to the creation of factories, a far less personal setting for work. Lost in the process were close working relationships, strong kinship ties, and also many of the traditional values, beliefs, and customs that had guided agrarian life for centuries.

Industrialism engendered societies of unparalleled prosperity. Although health in industrial cities was initially poor, a rising standard of living and advancing health-related technology gradually controlled diseases that had for centuries killed both children and adults.

Consequently, life expectancy increased, fueling rapid population growth. Industrialization also pulled people from the countryside to the cities where the factories were built. Although perhaps one in ten members of agrarian societies live in cities, three of four people in industrial societies are now urbanites.

Occupational specialization, which expanded over the long course of sociocultural evolution, has become more pronounced than ever. Industrial people often size up one another in terms of their jobs rather than (as agrarian people do) according to their kinship ties. Rapid change and movement from place to place also generate cultural diversity, leading to the emergence of numerous subcultures and countercultures, as described in Chapter 3 ("Culture").

The family, too, has been changed by industrial technology, with far less of its traditional significance as the center of social life. No longer does the family serve as the primary setting for economic production, learning, and religious worship. And, as Chapter 17

**FIGURE 4–1 The Increasing Number
of Technological Innovations**

This figure illustrates the number of technological innovations in Western Europe after the beginning of the Industrial Revolution in the mid-eighteenth century. Technological innovation occurs at an accelerating rate because each innovation combines with existing cultural elements to produce many further innovations.

(Lenski, Lenski, & Nolan, 1991:57)

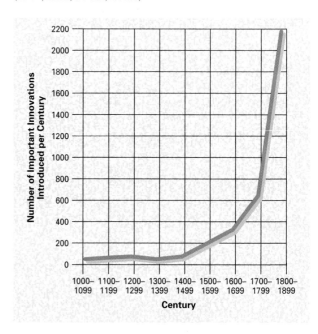

NOTE: Further discussion of postindustrial society is found in Chapter 15 ("The Economy and Work").
NOTE: Marion Levy suggests the ratio of inanimate to animate sources of energy as a good index of modernization.

GLOBAL: James Williams Gibson (*The Perfect War: Technowar in Vietnam*, Boston: Atlantic Monthly, 1986) argues that the American defeat in Vietnam was caused by an ethnocentric view that military power involves only technology.

("Family") explains in detail, technological change has also played a part in replacing many so-called traditional families with single people, divorced people, single-parent families, and step-families.

The Lenskis suggest that early industrialization concentrated the benefits of advancing technology on a small segment of the population, with the majority living in poverty. In time, however, the material benefits of industrial productivity spread more widely. Poverty remains a serious problem in industrial societies, but compared to the situation a century ago, the standard of living has risen about fivefold, and economic, social, and political inequality has diminished. Some social leveling, detailed in Chapter 9 ("Social Stratification"), occurs because industrial societies demand a literate and skilled labor force. While most people in agrarian societies are illiterate and have no political rights, industrial societies provide state-funded schooling and numerous political rights to virtually everyone. Industrialization, in fact, intensifies demands for political participation, as seen most recently in South Korea, Taiwan, the People's Republic of China, the former Soviet Union, and the societies of Eastern Europe.

Postindustrial Societies

Many industrial societies, including the United States, now appear to be entering yet another phase of technological development, and we can briefly extend the Lenskis' analysis to take account of recent trends. A generation ago sociologist Daniel Bell (1973) coined the term **postindustrialism** to refer to *technology that supports an information-based economy*. While the primary form of production in industrial societies involves factories and machinery generating material goods, postindustrial production centers on the creation, processing, storage, and application of information. At the individual level, members of industrial societies recognize the need to learn mechanical skills; people in postindustrial societies, however, realize that more and more jobs demand information-based skills using computers, satellites, facsimile machines, and other forms of communication technology.

As this transformation of key skills suggests, the emergence of postindustrialism brings dramatic change to a society's occupational structure. Chapter 15 ("The Economy and Work") looks at this process in detail, explaining that a postindustrial society utilizes less and less of its labor force for industrial production. At the same time, the ranks of clerical workers, managers, and other people who process information (in

A century ago, the Industrial Revolution drew the labor force together into factories where large machinery and needed energy sources were situated. Today, a countertrend is underway as the Information Revolution now permits people to develop ideas and to process information virtually anywhere.

fields ranging from academia and advertising to marketing and public relations) swell rapidly.

The technological breakthrough that sparked the emergence of the postindustrial society was the development of the computer. Computer technology sits at the core of the Information Revolution; in the same way that the factory-based Industrial Revolution recast agrarian societies two centuries ago, the computer and products derived from it are transforming industrial societies today.

The Information Revolution is most evident in industrial societies, yet the reach of this new technology is so great that it is affecting the entire world. As explained in Chapter 3 ("Culture"), the unprecedented, worldwide flow of information centered in rich nations such as our own has the predictable effect of tying societies together and fostering more common patterns of global culture.

Another key idea from Chapter 3 has an important application to postindustrialism. This is the concept of cultural lag, by which some elements of

GLOBAL: Six nations—the United States, United Kingdom, Japan, the former Soviet Union, France, and Germany—generate half of the world's scientific output.

NOTE: Roughly 15 to 20% of all people who have ever lived are alive now. However, about 90% of all *scientists* who have ever lived are living today.

Q: "We have too many men of science, too few of God. We have grasped the mystery of the atom and rejected the Sermon on the Mount. . . . Ours is a world of nuclear giants and ethical infants. We know more about war than we do about peace, more about killing than about living." General Omar N. Bradley, 1948

TABLE 4–1 Sociocultural Evolution: A Summary

Type of Society	Historical Period	Productive Technology	Population Size
Hunting and Gathering Societies	Only type of society until about 10,000 years ago; still common several centuries ago; the few examples remaining today are threatened by extinction	Primitive weapons	25–40 people
Horticultural and Pastoral Societies	From about 10,000 years ago, with decreasing numbers after about 3000 B.C.E.	Horticultural societies use hand tools for cultivating plants; pastoral societies are based on the domestication of animals	Settlements of several hundred people, interconnected through trading ties to form societies of several thousand people
Agrarian Societies	From about 5,000 years ago, with large but decreasing numbers today	Animal-drawn plow	Millions of people
Industrial Societies	From about 1750 to the present	Advanced sources of energy; mechanized production	Millions of people
Postindustrial Societies	Emerging in recent decades	Computers that support an information-based economy	Millions of people

societies (especially technology) change faster than others (such as values and norms). Despite the fact that information is fast replacing objects as the center of our economy, our legal notions about property are still based on tangible things.

Consider, for example, our national practice by which government officials monitor the flow of property in and out of this country. Customs officers require travelers to declare all the property that they wish to carry with them when they arrive, and baggage is subject to physical search. Curiously, while people are lining up to discuss purchases of liquor, antiques, or oriental rugs, an individual in possession of valuable ideas, computer programs, or various kinds of encoded information can easily and legally walk past customs officials announcing "Nothing to declare!" since our legal system has yet to fully recognize the importance of nontangible property. In short, while recent decades have witnessed rapid technological change, many of our ways of thinking remain rooted in an earlier era.

Table 4–1 presents a summary of how technology shapes societies at different stages of sociocultural evolution.

The Limits of Technology

Technology has shown itself able to remedy many human problems, raising productivity, eliminating disease, and sometimes simply relieving boredom. An important limitation of technology, however, is that it provides no "quick fix" for many social problems. Poverty remains the plight of millions of women and men in this country (detailed in Chapter 10, "Social Class in the United States") and of 1 billion people worldwide (see Chapter 11, "Global Stratification"). Moreover, with the capacity to reshape the world, technology has created new problems that our ancestors could hardly have imagined. Industrial societies provide more personal freedom, often at the cost of the sense of community that characterized agrarian

Q: "The bourgeoisie, during its rule of scarcely one hundred years, has created more massive and more colossal productive forces than have all preceding generations together." Karl Marx and Friedrich Engels

Q: "Marxist social scientists typically ask questions about matters on which they already believe to have the answers, at least in broad outline. This is a useful methodology for prophets; it decisively flaws the work of social scientists." Peter Berger (1986:5)

TABLE 4–1 (continued)

Type of Society	Settlement Pattern	Social Organization	Examples
Hunting and Gathering Societies	Nomadic	Family centered; specialization limited to age and sex; little social inequality	Pygmies of central Africa Bushmen of southwestern Africa Aborigines of Australia Semai of Malaysia Kaska Indians of Canada
Horticultural and Pastoral Societies	Horticulturalists form relatively small permanent settlements; pastoralists are nomadic	Family centered; religious system begins to develop; moderate specialization; increased social inequality	Middle Eastern societies about 5000 B.C.E. Various societies today in New Guinea and other Pacific islands Yąnomamö today in South America
Agrarian Societies	Cities become common, though they generally contain only a small proportion of the population	Family loses significance as distinctive religious, political, and economic systems emerge; extensive specialization; increased social inequality	Egypt during construction of the Great Pyramids Medieval Europe Numerous nonindustrial societies of the world today
Industrial Societies	Cities contain most of the population	Distinct religious, political, economic, educational, and family systems; highly specialized; marked social inequality persists, diminishing somewhat over time	Most societies today in Europe and North America, Australia, and Japan generate most of the world's industrial production
Postindustrial Societies	Population remains concentrated in cities	Similar to industrial societies with information processing and other service work gradually replacing industrial production	Industrial societies noted above are now entering postindustrial stage

life. Further, although the most powerful societies of today's world engage in all-out warfare infrequently, international conflict now poses unimaginable horrors. Should nations ever unleash even a fraction of their present stockpiles of nuclear weapons, human society would almost certainly regress to a technologically primitive state if, indeed, we survive at all.

Another problem involves humanity's relation to the natural environment. Each stage in sociocultural evolution has introduced more powerful sources of energy and stimulated our appetite for greater measures of the earth's natural resources. Advanced technology has a profound effect on our planet's environment. While the postindustrial society of the United States seems "cleaner" in some respects, industrial production and pollution have simply moved to other nations, and, in global perspective, demand for energy and material goods continues to increase even faster than the earth's population. An issue of vital concern—one that is the focus of

Chapter 22 ("The Natural Environment")—is whether humanity can continue to pursue material prosperity without subjecting the planet to damage and strains from which it will never recover.

In some respects, then, technological advances have improved life and brought the world's people closer within a "global village." What remains, however, are daunting problems of establishing peace, justice, and a safe and sustainable environment—problems that technology alone can never solve.

KARL MARX: SOCIETY AND CONFLICT

The first of our classic visions of society comes from Karl Marx (1818–1883). Few observed the industrial transformation of Europe as keenly as he did. Marx spent most of his adult life in London, then the capital of the vast British Empire. He was awed by the productive power of industry; not only were European

RESOURCE: The *Manifesto of the Communist Party* is included in the Macionis and Benokraitis reader, *Seeing Ourselves: Classic, Contemporary, and Cross-Cultural Readings in Sociology*.

Q: "The truth is that we are all caught in a great economic system which is heartless." Woodrow Wilson

NOTE: The following quotations suggest that the Roman Catholic Church has taken differing positions on the morality of capitalism.

Q: "Every man has by nature the right to possess property as his own." Pope Leo XIII

Q: "It is impossible to reduce society to one level." Pope Leo XIII

Q: "The needs of the poor must take priority over the desires of the rich; and the rights of workers over the maximization of profits." Pope John Paul II

PROFILE

Karl Marx: An Agenda for Change

Few names evoke as strong a response as Karl Marx. Some consider him a genius and a prophet, while others see only evil in his ideas. Everyone agrees that Marx stands among the social thinkers with the greatest impact on the world's people. Today, more than one-fifth of all humanity live in societies that consider themselves Marxist.

Nor was Marx a stranger to controversy during his lifetime. Born in the German city of Trier, he earned a doctorate in 1841 and began working as a newspaper editor. But his relentless social criticism drew him into conflict with government authorities, who managed to drive Marx from Germany to Paris. Soon controversy forced him to flee from France as well, and Marx spent the rest of his life in London.

Along with Max Weber and Emile Durkheim, Marx was a major figure in the development of sociology, as we saw in Chapter 1 ("The Sociological Perspective"). However, sociologists in the United States paid relatively little attention to his ideas until the 1960s. Why? The answer lies in Marx's explicit criticism of industrial-capitalist society. Early U.S. sociologists dismissed his ideas as mere "politics" rather than serious scholarship. For Marx, scholarship *was* politics. While most sociologists heeded Max Weber's call for value-free research by attempting to minimize or conceal their own values (see Chapter 2, "Sociological Investigation"), Marx's work was explicitly value-laden. Marx did not merely observe society; he offered a rousing prescription for profound social change. As we have come to recognize the extent to which values shape all ideas, Marx's social analysis has finally received the attention it deserves as an important part of sociology.

SOURCE: Based, in part, on Ritzer (1983).

societies producing more goods than ever before, but a global system of commerce was funneling resources from around the world through British factories at a dizzying rate.

Beyond the new technology, Marx was stunned by the concentration of industry's riches in the hands of a few. A walk almost anywhere in London revealed dramatic extremes of splendid affluence and wretched squalor. A handful of aristocrats and industrialists lived in fabulous mansions well staffed by servants, where they enjoyed luxury and privileges barely imaginable by the majority of their fellow Londoners. Most people labored long hours for low wages, living in slums or even sleeping in the streets, where many eventually succumbed to poor nutrition and disease.

Marx was both saddened and angered by the social inequities he saw around him. The technological miracles of industrialization had finally made possible human society without want. Instead, however, industry had done little to improve the lives of most people. To Marx, industrialization introduced a fundamental contradiction: In a society so rich, how could so many be so poor? Just as important, Marx asked, how can this situation be changed? Many people, no doubt, think of Karl Marx as a man determined to tear societies apart. But he was motivated by compassion for humanity and sought to help a society already badly divided forge a new and just social order.

The key to Marx's thinking is the idea of **social conflict**, *struggle between segments of society over valued resources*. Social conflict can, of course, take many forms: Individuals may quarrel, some colleges have long-standing rivalries, and nations sometimes go to war. For Marx, however, the most significant form of social conflict involved classes that arise from the way a society produces material goods.

NOTE: "Capitalism" is derived from the Latin word *caput*, meaning "head." The term was first used in 12th-century Europe at a time of expanding commerce. "Conflict" is derived from the Latin meaning "a striking together."

Q: "[I] wish that Karl would accumulate capital instead of just writing about it." Comment attributed to Marx's mother, who lamented how her son could barely pay his debts for most of his life

Q: "I am not a Marxist." Karl Marx

SOCIAL SURVEY: "Do you tend to feel or not that the rich get richer and the poor get poorer?" (GSS 1978, N = 1,532; *Codebook*, 1993:199)

"Yes, do feel"	54.6%
"No, do not feel"	38.8%
DK/NR	6.6%

Society and Production

Living in the nineteenth century, Marx observed the early stage of industrial capitalism in Europe. This economic system, Marx noted, transformed a small part of the population into **capitalists**, *people who own factories and other productive enterprises.* A capitalist's goal is profit, which results from selling a product for more than it costs to produce. Capitalism casts most of the population as industrial workers, whom Marx termed the **proletariat**, *people who provide labor necessary to operate factories and other productive enterprises.* Workers sell their labor for the wages they need to live. To Marx, an inevitable conflict between capitalists and workers has its roots in the productive process itself. To maximize profits, capitalists must minimize wages, generally their single greatest expense. Workers, however, want wages to be as high as possible. Since profits and wages come from the same pool of funds, ongoing conflict occurs. Marx argued that this conflict would end only by fundamentally changing the capitalist system. This revolutionary upheaval, he believed, would eventually come to pass.

Marx's analysis of society draws on the philosophical approach called *materialism*, which asserts that how humans produce material goods shapes the rest of society. Marx did not think that an economic system determines cultural values, politics, and family patterns in any total or rigid sense. But just as the Lenskis argue the fundamental importance of technology, so Marx argued that the "economic structure of society" is "the real foundation . . . The mode of production in material life determines the general character of the social, political, and spiritual processes of life" (1959:43; orig. 1859).

Marx therefore viewed the economic system as the social *infrastructure* (*infra* is Latin meaning "below"). Other social institutions, including the family, the political system, and religion, which are built on this foundation, form society's *superstructure*. These institutions extend economic principles into other areas of life, as illustrated in Figure 4–2. In practical terms, social institutions reinforce the domination of the capitalists, by legally protecting their wealth, for example, and transmitting property from one generation to the next through the family.

Generally speaking, members of industrial-capitalist societies do not view their legal or family systems as hotbeds of social conflict. On the contrary, individuals come to see their rights to private property as "natural." To illustrate, people in the United

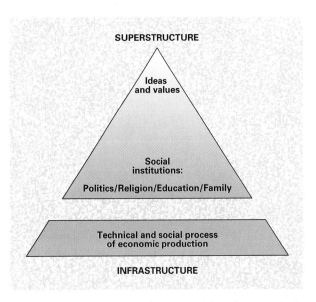

FIGURE 4–2 Karl Marx's Model of Society

This diagram illustrates Marx's materialist view that the process of economic production shapes the entire society. Economic production involves both technology (industry, in the case of capitalism) and social relationships (for capitalism, the relationship between the capitalists, who control the process, and the workers, who are simply a source of labor). Upon this infrastructure, or economic foundation, are built the major social institutions as well as core cultural values and ideas. Taken together, these additional social elements represent the society's superstructure. Marx maintained that all the other parts of the society are likely to operate in a manner consistent with the economic system.

States find it easy to think that affluent people have earned their wealth, while those who are poor or out of work lack skills or motivation. Marx challenged this kind of reasoning, asserting that it stemmed from a social system—preoccupied with the "bottom line"—that treats human well-being as a market commodity. Poverty and unemployment are not inevitable; as Marx saw it, grand wealth clashing with grinding poverty represents merely one set of human possibilities generated by capitalism (Cuff & Payne, 1979).

Marx rejected capitalist common sense as **false consciousness**, *explanations of social problems in terms of the shortcomings of individuals rather than the flaws of society.* Marx was saying, in effect, that industrial capitalism itself is responsible for many of the social problems he saw all around him. False consciousness, he maintained, helps victimize people by obscuring the real cause of their problems.

All societies use art to convey political ideas. This fact is most evident in socialist countries where, following Marx's thinking, governments expect people to apply the lessons of economic revolution to all dimensions of social life. This billboard in the Chinese city of Xi'an urges people to support the political and economic system as a path toward a more prosperous future.

Conflict in History

Marx believed that the potential of ideas is realized in action. He studied how societies have changed throughout history, noting that they often evolve gradually, although they sometimes change in rapid, revolutionary fashion. Marx observed (as do the Lenskis) that change is partly prompted by technological advance. But he steadfastly held that conflict underlies all transformations of society.

To recast the Lenskis' analysis in Marxist terms, early hunters and gatherers formed primitive communist societies. The word *communism* means simply that the production of food and other material goods is a common effort shared more or less equally by all members of society. Because the resources of nature were available to all hunters and gatherers (rather than privately owned), and because everyone performed similar work (rather than dividing work into highly specialized tasks), there was little possibility for social conflict.

Horticulture, Marx noted, introduced significant social inequality. Among horticultural, pastoral, and early agrarian societies—which Marx lumped together as the "ancient world"—the victors in frequent warfare forced military captives into slavery. A small elite (the "masters") and their slaves were thus locked into an irreconcilable pattern of social conflict (Zeitlin, 1981).

Agriculture brought still more wealth to members of the elite, fueling further social conflict. Agrarian serfs, occupying the lowest reaches of European feudalism from about the twelfth to the eighteenth centuries, were only slightly better off than slaves. In Marx's view, the power of both the church and the state defended feudal inequality by declaring that the existing social order embodied God's will. Thus, to Marx, feudalism amounted to little more than "exploitation, veiled by religious and political illusions" (Marx & Engels, 1972:337; orig. 1848).

Gradually, new productive forces undermined the feudal order. Commerce grew steadily throughout the Middle Ages as trade networks expanded and the power of guilds increased. Merchants and skilled craftsworkers in the cities formed a new social category, the *bourgeoisie* (a French word meaning "of the town"). Profits earned in the expanding trade brought the bourgeoisie increasing wealth. After the mid-eighteenth century, with factories at their command, the bourgeoisie became true capitalists with power that soon rivaled that of the ancient, landed nobility. While the nobility regarded this upstart "commercial" class with disdain, the capitalists steadily gained control of the developing industrial-capitalist societies in Europe. To Marx's way of thinking, then, technological breakthroughs explain only part of the Industrial Revolution. This momentous event was also a class revolution by which the agrarian elite was overthrown by capitalists who presided over the new industrial economy.

Industrialization also fostered the development of the proletariat. English landowners converted fields once tilled by serfs into grazing land for sheep to secure wool for the prospering textile mills. Forced from the land, serfs migrated to cities to work in

Sir Luke Fildes's painting Awaiting Admission to the Casual Ward *shows the numbing poverty common among immigrants drawn to cities as the Industrial Revolution began. Marx saw in such suffering a fundamental contradiction of modern society: Industrial technology promised material plenty for all, yet capitalism concentrated wealth in the hands of a few.*

factories, where they joined the burgeoning industrial proletariat. Marx envisioned these workers one day joining hands across national boundaries to form a unified class, setting the stage for historic confrontation, this time between capitalists and the exploited workers.

Much of Marx's analysis centers on destructive aspects of industrial capitalism—especially ways it promotes class conflict and alienation. In examining his views on these topics, we will come to see why he advocated the overthrow of capitalist societies.

Capitalism and Class Conflict

"The history of all hitherto existing society is the history of class struggles." With this declaration, Marx and his collaborator Friedrich Engels began their best-known statement, the *Manifesto of the Communist Party* (1972:335; orig. 1848). The idea of social class is at the heart of Marx's critique of capitalist society. Industrial capitalism, like earlier types of society, contains two major social classes—the dominant and the oppressed—reflecting position in the productive system. Capitalists and proletarians are the historical descendants of masters and slaves in the ancient world and nobles and serfs in feudal systems. In each case, one class controls the other as productive property. Marx used the term **class conflict** (and sometimes *class struggle*) to refer to *antagonism between entire classes over the distribution of wealth and power in society*.

Class conflict, then, dates back to civilizations long dead. What distinguishes the conflict in capitalist systems is how out in the open it has become. Agrarian nobles and serfs, for all their differences, were bound together by long-standing tradition and a host of mutual obligations. Industrial capitalism dissolved those ties, so that people confronted each other in "naked self-interest," motivated not by pride or honor but the pursuit of cash. With no personal ties to their oppressors, Marx concluded, the proletariat had little reason to tolerate their oppression.

Chapter 4 Society **109**

SOCIOLOGY OF EVERYDAY LIFE

Alienation and Industrial Capitalism

These excerpts from the book *Working* by Studs Terkel illustrate how men and women may experience the effects of alienation created by the dull, repetitive nature of their jobs.

Phil Stallings is a twenty-seven-year-old auto worker in a Ford assembly plant in Chicago.

I start the automobile, the first welds. From there it goes to another line, where the floor's put on, the roof, the trunk, the hood, the doors. Then it's put on a frame. There is hundreds of lines. . . . I stand in one spot, about two- or three-feet area, all night. The only time a person stops is when the line stops. We do about thirty-two jobs per car, per unit. Forty-eight units an hour, eight hours a day. Thirty-two times forty-eight times eight. Figure it out. That's how many times I push that button.

The noise, oh it's tremendous. You open your mouth and you're liable to get a mouthful of sparks. [Shows his arms.] That's a burn, these are burns. You don't compete against the noise. You go to yell and at the same time you're straining to maneuver the gun to where you have to weld.

You got some guys that are uptight, and they're not sociable. It's too rough. You pretty much stay to yourself. You get involved with yourself. You dream, you think of things you've done. I drift back continuously to when I was a kid and what me and my brothers did. The things you love most are what you drift back into.

It don't stop. It just goes and goes and goes. I bet there's men who have lived and died out there, never seen the end of the line. And they never will—because it's endless. It's like a serpent. It's just all body, no tail. It can do things to you. . . .

Twenty-four-year-old Sharon Atkins is a college graduate working as a telephone receptionist for a large midwestern business.

I don't have much contact with people. You can't see them. You don't know if they're laughing, if they're being satirical or being kind. So your conversations become very abrupt. I notice that in talking to people. My conversation would be very short and clipped, in short sentences, the way I talk to people all day on the telephone. . . .

You try to fill up your time with trying to think about other things: what you're going to do on the weekend or about your family. You have to use your imagination. If you don't have a very good one and you bore easily, you're in trouble. Just to fill in time, I write real bad poetry or letters to myself and to other people and never mail them. The letters are fantasies, sort of rambling, how I feel, how depressed I am.

. . . I never answer the phone at home.

SOURCE: Terkel (1974).

Even though industrial capitalism had brought class conflict out in the open, Marx realized that fundamental social change would not come easily. First, he claimed, workers must *become aware* of their shared oppression and see capitalism as its true cause. Second, they must *organize and act* to address their problems. This means workers must replace false consciousness with **class consciousness,** *the recognition by workers of their unity as a class in opposition to capitalists and, ultimately, to capitalism itself.* Because the inhumanity of early capitalism seemed so obvious to him, Marx concluded that industrial workers would inevitably rise up en masse to destroy industrial capitalism. In doing so, they would cease to be merely a social class *in* themselves and become a social class acting *for* themselves.

And what of the workers' adversaries, the capitalists? The formidable wealth and power of capitalists, protected by the institutions of society, might seem invulnerable. But Marx saw a weakness in the capitalist armor. Motivated by a desire for personal gain, capitalists fear the competition of other capitalists. Thus Marx thought that capitalists would be reluctant to band together, even though they, too, share common interests. Furthermore, he reasoned, capitalists keep employees' wages low in their drive to maximize profits. This strategy, in turn, bolsters the resolve of workers to forge an alliance against them. In the long run, Marx claimed, capitalists could only contribute to their own undoing by striving to advance their narrow self-interest.

SOCIAL SURVEY: "On the whole, how satisfied are you with the work you do—would you say you are very satisfied, moderately satisfied, a little dissatisfied, or very dissatisfied?" (GSS 1993, N = 1,277; *Codebook*, 1993:237). In GSS survey items, workers do not express strong dissatisfaction with their work.

"Very satisfied"   41.7%   "A little dissatisfied"   10.4%
"Moderately satisfied"   39.6%   "Very dissatisfied"   4.5%

DK/NR   3.8%

RESOURCE: The novels of Charles Dickens provide moving accounts of life during the early decades of industrial capitalism. His most critical statement is *Hard Times*, in which he argues—reminiscent of Marx—that elites will some day have to account for the suffering of the masses: "Reality will take a wolfish turn, and make an end of you!" (Norton, 1966:125; orig. 1854)

Capitalism and Alienation

Marx also condemned capitalism for producing widespread **alienation,** *the experience of isolation resulting from powerlessness.* Dominated by capitalists and dehumanized by their jobs (especially monotonous and repetitive factory work), proletarians find little satisfaction and feel individually powerless to improve their situation. Capitalist society itself gives rise to a major contradiction, observed Marx: As human beings have used technology to gain power over the world, the productive process has increasingly assumed power over human beings.

Workers view themselves merely as a commodity, a source of labor, bought by capitalists and discarded when no longer needed. Marx cited four ways in which capitalism alienates workers.

1. **Alienation from the act of working**. Ideally, people work both to meet their immediate needs and to develop their long-range potential. Capitalism, however, denies workers a say in what is produced or how production is carried out. Further, work is often tedious, involving countless repetitions of routine tasks. The modern-day replacement of human labor by machines would hardly have surprised Marx; as far as he was concerned, capitalism had turned human beings into machines long ago.

2. **Alienation from the products of work**. The product of work belongs not to workers but to capitalists, who dispose of it to gain profits. Thus, Marx reasoned, the more workers invest of themselves into their work, the more they lose.

3. **Alienation from other workers**. Marx saw work as the productive affirmation of human community. Industrial capitalism, however, renders work competitive rather than cooperative. As the box on page 110 illustrates, factory work often provides little chance for human companionship.

4. **Alienation from human potential**. Industrial capitalism alienates workers from their own human potential. Marx argued that a worker "does not fulfill himself in his work but denies himself, has a feeling of misery rather than well-being, does not freely develop his physical and mental energies, but is physically exhausted and mentally debased. The worker, therefore, feels himself to be at home only during his leisure time, whereas at work he feels homeless" (1964a:124–25; orig. 1844). In short, industrial capitalism distorts an activity that should express

Marxism, one of the world's most influential social movements, has shaped the economic and political life of one-fifth of the world's people. For years, the conventional wisdom in the United States was that, once established, socialism stifled its opposition, rendering government immune to overthrow. But that notion collapsed along with the socialist regimes of Eastern Europe and the former Soviet Union. The political transformation of this world region is symbolized by the removal of statues of Vladimir Lenin (1870–1924), architect of Soviet Marxism, in city after city during the last few years.

the best qualities in human beings into a dull and dehumanizing experience.

Marx viewed alienation, in its various forms, as a barrier to social change. But he hoped that industrial workers would overcome their alienation by uniting into a true social class, aware of the cause of their problems and galvanized to transform society.

Revolution

The only way out of the trap of capitalism, contended Marx, was deliberately to refashion society. He

SOCIAL SURVEY: "How important is hard work for getting ahead?" (*CHIP1 Social Survey Software*, OPABLE1; GSS 1987, N = 1,472). Other GSS items support the idea that U.S. society is closer to a meritocracy.

RACE/ETH	"Very important"	All other responses
Afri Amer	74.2%	25.8%
Hispanics	80.4%	19.6%
Whites	57.7%	42.3%

SES	"Very important"	All other responses
High	49.9%	50.1%
Middle	60.2%	39.8%
Low	74.7%	25.3%

NOTE: One illustration of Marxist false consciousness is the last Social Survey item, in which the lowest SES category (presumably

PROFILE

Max Weber: Expanding the Boundaries of Sociology

To be called merely a "sociologist" would probably have offended Max Weber. Not that he disliked the study of society; in fact, he spent most of his life doing just that. But Weber's contribution to understanding humanity is so broad and rich that no single discipline can properly claim him.

Born to a prosperous German family, Weber completed law school and set off on a legal career. But he soon felt confined by the work of a lawyer. Continuing his studies, he became a college professor. With his curiosity racing across the entire human condition, he compiled an amazing legacy of scholarship.

The influence of Weber's parents stands out in his work. His mother's devout Calvinism probably encouraged Weber's study of world religions and his classic study of Calvinism and its impact on industrial capitalism, which is discussed shortly. From his father, a notable politician, Weber clearly gained insights into the workings of bureaucracy and political life.

Weber flirted with politics, and his wife Marianne was a leading feminist of her time. But Weber found politics to be incompatible with scholarly work. Politics, he claimed, demands action and personal conviction, while scholarship requires impartiality and patient reflection. Weber tried to resolve this personal dilemma by urging his colleagues to become involved in politics outside of the classroom while striving for scientific neutrality in their professional work.

For many reasons, Weber's life was far from happy. He did not get on well with his father, and soon after his father's death Weber began to suffer from psychological problems. Illness sharply limited his ability to work during the remainder of his life. Even so, the exceptional number of major studies he produced has led many to regard him as the most brilliant sociologist in history.

envisioned a more humane and egalitarian productive system, one that would enhance rather than undermine social ties. This system he termed *socialism*. Marx knew well the obstacles to a socialist revolution; even so, he was disappointed that workers in England did not overthrow industrial capitalism during his lifetime. Still, convinced of the basic immorality of capitalist society, he was sure that, in time, the working majority would realize they held the key to a better future in their own hands. This transformation would certainly be revolutionary, and perhaps even violent. The end product, however, would be a cooperative socialist society that would meet the needs of all.

The discussion of social stratification in Chapter 9 reveals more about changes in industrial-capitalist societies since Marx's time and why the revolution he longed for has not taken place. Later chapters also suggest why people in the societies of Eastern Europe recently revolted against established socialist governments. But, in his own time, Marx looked toward the future with hope (1972:362; orig. 1848): "The proletarians have nothing to lose but their chains. They have a world to win."

MAX WEBER: THE RATIONALIZATION OF SOCIETY

With a broad understanding of law, economics, religion, and history, Max Weber (1864–1920) produced what many regard as the greatest individual contribution to sociology. This scholar, introduced in the box, generated ideas so wide ranging that, here, we can deal only with his vision of how modern society differs from earlier types of social organization.

Weber's sociology reflects the philosophical approach called *idealism*, which emphasizes how human ideas shape society. Weber understood the power of technology, and he shared many of Marx's ideas about social conflict. But he departed from Marx's materialist analysis, arguing that societies differ primarily in terms of the ways in which their members think about the world. For Weber, ideas—especially beliefs and values—have transforming power. Thus he saw modern society as the result of not just new technology and productive systems but new ways of thinking. This emphasis on ideas contrasts with Marx's focus on production, leading scholars to describe Weber's work as "a debate with the ghost of Karl Marx" (Cuff & Payne, 1979:73–74).

Weber conducted his research comparatively, contrasting social patterns in different times and places. To sharpen comparisons, he constructed **ideal types**, *abstract statements of the essential characteristics of any social phenomenon*. He explored religion by contrasting the ideal "Protestant" with the ideal "Jew," "Hindu," and "Buddhist," knowing that these models precisely described no actual individuals. We have already used this technique, of course, in comparing "hunting and gathering societies" and "industrial societies."

An ideal type has much in common with the more familiar idea of stereotype, in that both are abstract conceptualizations. Unlike a stereotype, however, an ideal type is essentially factual and judgmentally neutral rather than being infused with positive or negative connotations (Theodorson & Theodorson, 1969). Thus, Weber's use of the word *ideal* does not mean that something is "good" or "the best"; we could analyze "criminals" as well as "priests" as ideal types.

Tradition and Rationality

Rather than categorizing societies in terms of technology or productive systems, Max Weber highlighted differences in the ways people view the world. In simple terms, Weber concluded that members of preindustrial societies embrace *tradition*, while people in industrial-capitalist societies endorse *rationality*.

By **tradition**, Weber meant *sentiments and beliefs passed from generation to generation*. Thus social patterns in traditional societies are guided by the past. Traditional people evaluate particular actions as right and proper precisely because they have been accepted for so long.

Modern society takes a different view of the world, argued Weber, because it encourages **rationality**, *deliberate, matter-of-fact calculation of the most efficient means to accomplish a particular goal*. Sentiment has no place in a rational world view, which treats tradition simply as one kind of information. Ideally speaking, modern people choose to think and act on the basis of present and future consequences, evaluating jobs, schooling, and even relationships in terms of what we put into them and what we expect to receive in return.

Weber viewed both the Industrial Revolution and capitalism as evidence of a historical surge of rationality. He used the phrase **rationalization of society** to denote *the historical change from tradition to rationality as the dominant mode of human thought*. Modern society, therefore, has been "disenchanted," as scientific thinking and technology have swept away sentimental ties to the past.

The importance of science, then, is one good indicator of how rationalized a society is. To suggest the global pattern of rationalization, Global Map 4–1, on page 114, shows expenditures on the sciences for the world's nations. The Commonwealth of Independent States and the United States spend a great deal on scientific projects. Many of the more traditional societies in Latin America, Africa, and Asia devote far less of their resources to scientific pursuits.

Weber's comparative perspective—and the data found in the map—suggest that various societies place different values on technological advance. What one society might herald as a breakthrough, another might deem unimportant, and a third might strongly oppose as a threat to tradition. Elites in ancient Greece, for instance, devised many surprisingly elaborate mechanical devices to perform household tasks. But since they were well served by slaves, they viewed such inventions as mere entertainment. In the United States today, the Amish are guided by their traditions to staunchly oppose modern technology.

In Weber's view, then, technological innovation is promoted or hindered by the way people understand their world. He concluded that people in many societies of the world discovered keys to technological change; however, only in the rational cultural climate of Western Europe did people exploit these discoveries to spark the Industrial Revolution (1958; orig. 1904–5).

Rationality, Calvinism, and Industrial Capitalism

Is industrial capitalism a rational economic system? Here, again, Weber and Marx come down on opposite

NOTE: Rationalization is for Weber the eclipse of tradition and sentiment; this loss of deep human passions, for Weber, is one of the costs of modern living. Knowing that many people would struggle to find ultimate meaning in life, Weber concluded his analysis of rationalization pointing out that "the arms of the old churches are open widely and compassionately . . ."

NOTE: An illustration of disenchantment is found in the practice of

early Calvinists of keeping an accounting of their moral deeds in the form of a daily ledger. Today, "accounting" refers merely to profit and loss and "accountants" focus on money rather than morality.

GLOBAL: Socialist societies are more centralized and rationalized than capitalist societies; the People's Republic of China, for example, has but a single time zone, although it spans roughly the same longitude as the United States, which has four time zones.

Window on the World

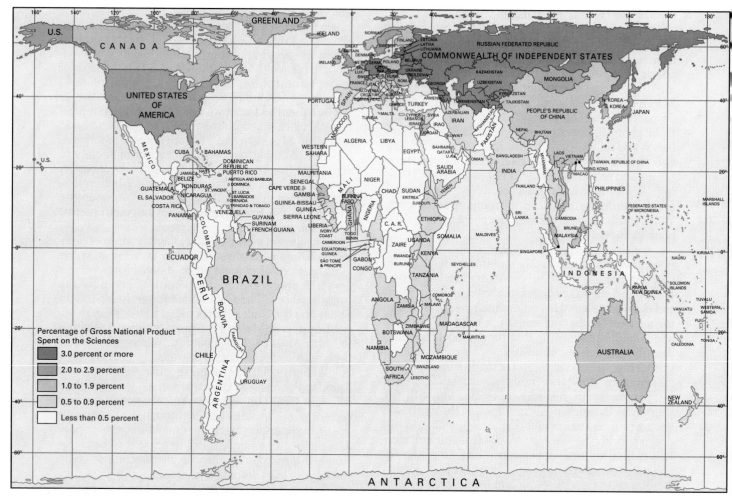

GLOBAL MAP 4–1 Spending on Science in Global Perspective

In general, industrial societies spend relatively more of their gross national product (the value of all goods and services produced annually) on scientific pursuits than less industrialized societies do. From Weber's point of view, such expenditures are an indicator of a society's world view: Less industrialized societies embrace tradition, while more industrialized nations espouse rationality as a source of meaning.

From *Peters Atlas of the World* (1990).

sides. Weber considered industrial capitalism as the essence of rationality, since capitalists pursue profit in eminently rational ways. Marx, however, dismissed capitalism as the antithesis of rationality, claiming that it failed to meet the basic needs of most of the people (Gerth & Mills, 1946:49).

But, to look more closely at Weber's position, how did industrial capitalism emerge as a rational system

of thought? Weber's answer is that industrial capitalism is the legacy of Calvinism—a Christian religious movement spawned by the Protestant Reformation. Weber knew that Calvinists approached life in a highly disciplined and rational way. But how did a religion spark the development of a new economy?

Central to the doctrine of John Calvin (1509–1564) is *predestination,* the idea that an all-knowing and all-powerful God has preordained some people for salvation and others for eternal damnation. With everyone's fate set before birth, Calvinists taught that people could do nothing to alter their destiny. Nor could they even know what their future would be. The only certainty was what hung in the balance: heavenly glory or hellfire for all of eternity.

The lives of Calvinists, then, were framed by hopeful visions of salvation and anxious fears of damnation. For such people, not knowing one's fate was intolerable. Calvinists gradually came to a resolution of sorts. Those chosen for glory in the next world, they concluded, should see signs of divine favor in *this* world as well. This conclusion prompted Calvinists to interpret worldly prosperity as a sign of God's grace. Anxious to acquire this reassurance, Calvinists threw themselves into a quest for success, applying rationality, discipline, and hard work to their tasks. This pursuit of riches was not for its own sake, however, since self-indulgently spending money was clearly sinful. Calvinists also were little moved to share their wealth with the poor, since they saw poverty as a sign of God's rejection. Their ever-present purpose was to carry forward what they held to be their personal *calling* from God.

All the same, as they reinvested their profits for greater success, Calvinists built the foundation of capitalism. They piously used wealth to generate more wealth, practiced personal thrift, and eagerly embraced whatever technological advances would aid their efforts.

These traits, Weber explained, distinguished Calvinism from other world religions. Catholicism, the traditional religion in most of Europe, gave rise to a passive, "otherworldly" view of life with hope of greater reward in the life to come. For Catholics, material wealth had none of the spiritual significance that so motivated Calvinists. And so it was, Weber concluded, that industrial capitalism became established primarily in areas of Europe where Calvinism was strong.

Weber's study of Calvinism provides striking evidence of the power of ideas to shape society (versus Marx's view of ideas as merely reflecting the process of economic production). But always skeptical of simple explanations, Weber knew that something as complex as industrial capitalism has many causes. His thesis is partly an effort to counter Marx's narrow explanation of modern society in economic terms. In fact, Weber (1961; orig. 1920) stressed that the development of industrial capitalism involved a host of factors—economic and legal forces among them—in addition to a distinctive world view (Collins, 1986).

But Weber never wavered in his contention that the defining characteristic of the modern world was rationality. As religious fervor weakened among later generations of Calvinists, he noted, success-seeking personal discipline remained. A *religious* ethic became simply a "*work* ethic," in pursuit of profit rather than the glory of God. From this point of view, industrial capitalism appears as "disenchanted" religion, with wealth now valued for its own sake. It is revealing that "accounting," which to early Calvinists meant a daily record of moral deeds, now refers simply to keeping track of money.

Rational Social Organization

Weber contended that, by giving momentum to the Industrial Revolution and sparking the development of capitalism, rationality had defined the character of modern society. Rational social organization confers the following seven traits on today's social life.

1. **Distinctive social institutions.** Rationality promotes the emergence of distinctive **social institutions,** defined as *the major spheres of social life organized to meet basic human needs.* Among hunters and gatherers, the family was the center of virtually all activities. Gradually, however, other social institutions, including religious, political, and economic systems, separated from family life. In modern societies, institutions of education and health care have also appeared. The separation of social institutions—each detailed in a later chapter—is a rational strategy to address human needs more efficiently.

2. **Specialized tasks.** Distinctive social institutions encourage specialized activities. Recall that members of traditional societies carry out mostly the same tasks. Individuals in modern, rational societies, however, pursue more narrow activities like studying biology, welding, or driving a taxi.

3. **Personal discipline.** Modern society puts a premium on a deliberate, disciplined approach to life. For early Calvinists, of course, discipline was rooted in religious belief. Although now distanced from its religious origin, discipline is still encouraged by cultural values such as achievement, success, and efficiency.

4. **Awareness of time.** A rational world view depends on an awareness of time. In modern societies, the traditional rhythm of sun and seasons gives way to scheduling events precisely according to hour and minute. Interestingly, clocks began appearing in

Max Weber agreed with Karl Marx that modern society is alienating to the individual, but the two thinkers identified different causes of this estrangement. For Marx, economic inequality is the culprit; for Weber, the issue is pervasive and dehumanizing bureaucracy. George Tooker's painting Landscape *echoes Weber's sentiments.*

European cities some five hundred years ago as commerce began to expand; soon, people began to think (to borrow Benjamin Franklin's phrase) that "time is money."

5. **Technical competence.** Members of traditional societies evaluate one another largely on the basis of *who* they are—how they are joined to others in the web of kinship. Modern rationality, by contrast, prompts us to judge people according to *what* they are—that is, with an eye toward their skills and abilities.

6. **Impersonality.** Because technical competence takes priority over close relationships in a rational society, the world becomes impersonal. Modern society increasingly amounts to the interplay of specialists concerned with particular tasks, rather than people sensitive to human feelings. Weber explained that we tend to devalue personal feelings and emotions as "irrational" because they sometimes run counter to rational principles.

7. **Large-scale organizations.** Finally, modern rationality is exemplified by the expansion of large-scale organizations. As early as the horticultural era, organizations deliberately administered activities like religious celebrations, public works, and

warfare. As societies became larger and more complex, so did their organizations. In medieval Europe, the Catholic Church grew into an enormous organization with thousands of officials; the employees of today's federal government, however, number in the millions.

Rationality and Bureaucracy

The medieval church was not entirely rational, Weber argued, because its purpose was largely to preserve tradition. Truly rational organizations, celebrating efficiency rather than tradition, appeared only in the last few centuries. The organizational type Weber termed *bureaucracy* became pronounced along with capitalism as an expression of rationality.

Bureaucracy, the organizing principle of modern businesses, government agencies, labor unions, and universities, is explored in depth in Chapter 7 ("Groups and Organizations"). For now, it is important to stress that Weber considered bureaucracy to be the clearest expression of a rational world view because its organizational elements—offices, duties, and policies—are created to achieve specific goals as efficiently as possible. By contrast, traditional social organization places little emphasis on efficiency and is typically hostile to change. Weber asserted that bureaucracy had done for society as a whole what industrialization had done for the production of material goods.

> The decisive reason for the advance of bureaucratic organization has always been its purely technical superiority over any other form of organization. The fully developed bureaucratic apparatus compares with other organizations exactly as does the machine with the nonmechanical modes of production. (1978:973; orig. 1921)

Rational bureaucracy, Weber continued, also has a natural affinity to capitalism.

> Today, it is primarily the capitalist market economy which demands that the official business of public administration be discharged precisely, unambiguously, continuously, and with as much speed as possible. Normally, the very large capitalist enterprises are themselves unequalled models of strict bureaucratic organization. (1978:974; orig. 1921)

Rationality and Alienation

So far, we have emphasized the unparalleled efficiency of modern society. Worth remembering, however, is that Karl Marx reached much the same conclusion, at

Q: "When I fulfill my obligations as a brother, husband, or citizen, when I execute contracts, I perform duties that are defined externally to myself . . . Even if I conform in my own sentiments and feel their reality subjectively, such reality is still objective, for I did not create them; I merely inherited them." Emile Durkheim

Q: "The only question that a man can ask is not whether he can live outside society, but in what society he wishes to live." Emile Durkheim

PROFILE

Emile Durkheim: Showing the Power of Society

Why would wanting to be a sociology professor be controversial? Because there *weren't* any, at least

not in France until Emile Durkheim became the first in 1887. Up to this time, the study of human behavior was left up to biologists and psychologists. But Durkheim made the assertion—widely disputed at the time—that one can comprehend humanity, not by looking at the individual, but only by examining human society.

Durkheim's investigation of suicide, detailed in Chapter 1 ("The Sociological Perspective"), offers persuasive evidence of society's power to shape people's lives. In this classic study, Durkheim showed that *where* people are embedded within society—as women or men,

rich or poor, or as members of various religions—affects even this most personal act.

Durkheim's work, like that of Marx and Weber, appears in many later chapters. His contributions to the understanding of crime figure prominently in Chapter 8 ("Deviance"). Durkheim also spent much of his life investigating religion, which he held to be a foundation of social integration (see Chapter 18, "Religion"). Just as important, Durkheim is also one of the major architects of the structural-functional paradigm, which is used in almost every chapter that follows.

---

least as far as the productive efficiency of capitalism was concerned. But Marx ultimately rejected this type of society because it led to alienation, economic inequality, and other destructive consequences.

Weber, too, criticized modern industrial capitalism, but for different reasons. For him, the primary problem was not the economic inequality that so troubled Marx, but alienation and dehumanization. The price of rational efficiency, concluded Weber, was stifling impersonality and regulation.

Large-scale organizations, Weber observed, tend to treat people as a series of cases rather than as unique individuals. In addition, much of modern society's highly specialized work involves tedious repetition. Most important, Weber feared that rational formality was extinguishing the human spirit. In the end, Weber envisioned modern society as a vast and growing system of rules seeking to regulate virtually every human endeavor. Caught up in the system, he concluded, human beings are becoming alienated from their own spontaneity and creativity.

An irony found in the work of Marx appears once again in Weber's thinking: Rather than serving

humanity, modern society turns on its creators and enslaves them. In language reminiscent of Marx's description of the human toll of industrial capitalism, Weber portrayed the modern individual as "only a small cog in a ceaselessly moving mechanism that prescribes to him an endlessly fixed routine of march" (1978:988; orig. 1921). Thus, even knowing the advantages of modern society, Weber ended his life deeply pessimistic. He feared that the logical conclusion of the rationalization of society would be the reduction of people to robots.

EMILE DURKHEIM: SOCIETY AND FUNCTION

"To love society is to love something beyond us and something in ourselves." These are the words of Emile Durkheim (1858–1917), another architect of sociology, introduced in the box. In this curious phrase (1974:55; orig. 1924) we find one more influential vision of human society.

DATA FILE: A discussion of crime rates, which illustrates Durkheim's conception of social fact, is included in the *Data File*.
NOTE: Durkheim claimed that society must be studied as an entity, *sui generis*, Latin meaning "of its own kind, a thing unto itself."

Q: "By 'social facts,' [Durkheim] should be understood to mean social phenomena, or factors, or forces, and by the rule that they should be studied as things he meant that they are to be seen as 'realities external to the individual' and independent of the observer's conceptual apparatus." Steven Lukes
DATA FILE: The *Data File* highlights the distinction between Marx's concept of alienation and Durkheim's notion of anomie.

Social Fact: Society Beyond Ourselves

The starting point for understanding the work of Emile Durkheim is his recognition of the **social fact**, *any pattern that is rooted in society rather than the experience of individuals*. To assert the existence of social facts, then, is to say that society has an objective existence beyond our own subjective perceptions of the world. As examples of social facts, Durkheim had in mind cultural norms, values, religious beliefs, and long-standing rituals.

Durkheim's use of this concept becomes clearer with three additional observations. First, he explained, society has *structure* because social patterns exist in orderly relationship to one another. Second, society has *power*, because the social world surrounds us, shaping our thoughts and actions. Third, society has an *objective existence* because it operates apart from any individual's subjective experience of it.

For Durkheim, then, individuals standing alone can never capture the essence of society; in this sense, society is more than the sum of its parts. Society is a complex organism that springs from our collective life, gaining an existence and momentum of its own. Once created by people, society turns and confronts its creators, demanding a measure of obedience. For our part, we experience the reality of society as we feel the tug of morality. A classroom of first graders, a family sharing a meal, and people milling about a country auction are all examples of the countless situations that have an organization apart from any particular individual who has ever participated in them. If this is so, reasoned Durkheim, society truly exists beyond us, preceding us, making claims on us while we are here, and remaining after we are gone.

Function: Society in Action

The next step in understanding Durkheim's vision of society is the concept of *function*. Durkheim explained that the significance of any social fact lies, not in the experience of individuals, but in its contribution to the general life of society.

As obvious as the power of society was to him, Durkheim knew that most people miss the crucial role of society in their lives. We think of crime, for example, as harmful acts that offenders inflict on victims. For Durkheim, though, the function of crime has little to do with particular people and everything to do with society as a system. As Chapter 8 ("Deviance") explains, the process of identifying and responding to acts as criminal is what vitalizes society as a moral system. For this reason, Durkheim rejected the common view of crime as "pathological." On the contrary, he concluded, crime is quite "normal" for the most basic of reasons: No society could exist without it (1964a, orig. 1895; 1964b, orig. 1893).

The Individual: Society in Ourselves

Durkheim contended that society is not only "beyond us"; it is also "something in ourselves." Individuals, in other words, build personality by internalizing social facts. Through the social patterns we learn growing up, we nurture our humanity. Society provides a moral education that regulates what Durkheim saw as the natural insatiability of human beings. We are in danger of being overpowered by our own desires, Durkheim asserted, because "the more one has, the more one wants, since satisfactions received only stimulate instead of filling needs" (1966:248; orig. 1897). Society, then, must instill restraints in each of us.

The need for societal regulation is illustrated by Durkheim's study of suicide (1966; orig. 1897), detailed in Chapter 1 ("The Sociological Perspective"). In nineteenth-century France, as well as in the United States today, it is precisely the *least* regulated categories of people that suffer the *highest* rates of suicide. The greater autonomy afforded to men, for example, yields a suicide rate four times higher than that among women.

Compared to traditional societies, however, modern societies impose fewer restrictions on individuals. Durkheim knew the advantages of human freedom, but he also warned of a rise in **anomie**, *a condition of society in which individuals receive little moral guidance*. The familiar image of people leaping from office buildings during a stock-market crash is an extreme example of anomic suicide. Here, a radical collapse of the social environment disrupts society's support and regulation of the individual, sometimes with fatal results. Interestingly, sudden affluence does much the same thing, tearing individuals out of established social patterns and overwhelming them with unregulated free choice. The high frequency of suicide and accidental death among rock performers of recent decades who experienced sudden stardom clearly suggests the dangers of extreme individualism. Durkheim instructs us, therefore, that the needs of the individual must be balanced by the claims and guidance of society—a balance that has become precarious in the modern world.

RESOURCE: An example of a small society that approximates Durkheim's concept of mechanical solidarity is the Amish, described in John Hostetler's article in the Macionis and Benokraitis reader, *Seeing Ourselves*, 3/e.

Q: "In a word, we must discover the rational substitutes for those religious notions that for a long time have served as the vehicle for the most essential moral ideas." Emile Durkheim, *Moral Education*, 1961:9. (This is the idea behind the concept of "civil religion"; see Chapter 18, "Religion.")

Historically, most members of human societies engaged in a narrow range of activities: searching out food and building shelters. Modern societies, explained Durkheim, display a rapidly expanding division of labor. Increasing specialization is evident on the streets of societies beginning to industrialize: Providing people with their weight is the livelihood of this man in Istanbul, Turkey; on a Bombay street in India, another earns a small fee for cleaning ears.

Evolving Societies: The Division of Labor

Like Marx and Weber, Durkheim experienced firsthand the rapid social changes transforming Europe during the nineteenth century. In these changes Durkheim saw evolving forms of social organization.

Research led Durkheim to conclude that, in societies with simple technology, strong tradition operates as a powerful moral system demanding unbending conformity. The *collective conscience* of traditional societies is so strong that the community moves quickly to punish any person who dares to step very far beyond accepted ways of life. Durkheim called this intense moral consensus **mechanical solidarity**, meaning *social bonds, based on shared moral sentiments, that unite members of preindustrial societies.* In horticultural and agrarian societies, for example, social solidarity springs from *likeness*, insofar as everyone acts and thinks in the same ways. Durkheim called such solidarity "mechanical" because people feel a more or less automatic sense of belonging.

The decline of mechanical solidarity marked the emergence of modern society. But, continued Durkheim, a new type of solidarity emerged to fill some of the void left by discarded traditions. This new social integration Durkheim termed **organic solidarity**, defined as *social bonds, based on specialization,*

that unite members of industrial societies. In this case, social solidarity flows from *differences* among people who, although conforming less in moral terms, find that specialization makes them rely on one another.

Therefore, Durkheim saw societies evolving as they gained a greater **division of labor,** or *specialized economic activity.* As we have already seen in Max Weber's analysis, modern societies rationally promote efficiency through specialization. From Durkheim's point of view, the result is a complex web of functional interdependence by which each person counts on the efforts of tens of thousands of others—most complete strangers—who help produce the products and provide the services we use every day.

All societies require some degree of social solidarity by which to motivate their members to join with others to carry out everyday tasks. The mechanical solidarity found in traditional societies is basically a system of morality; organic solidarity, operating in modern, industrial societies, owes its force to practicality. Put otherwise, members of modern societies depend more and more on people we trust less and less. Why, then, should we put our faith in people we hardly know and whose beliefs probably differ from our own? Durkheim's answer is, "Because we can't live without them."

SOCIAL SURVEY: "Do you think that most people would try to take advantage of you if they got a chance, or would they try to be fair?" (GSS 1993, N = 1,057; Codebook, 1993:202). This item is one possible index of anomie.

"Would take advantage of you"	36.3%	"Depends"	7.0%
		DK/NR	1.0%
"Would try to be fair"	55.7%		

But Durkheim knew that trust comes hard in a world in which morality sometimes seems like so much shifting sand. This recognition prompts what we might call "Durkheim's dilemma": We enjoy the technological advance and greater personal freedom of modern society, only at the cost of receding morality and the ever-present danger of anomie.

Like Marx and Weber, Durkheim had misgivings about the direction society was taking. But, of the three, Durkheim was the most optimistic. Confidence in the future sprang from his hope that we could enjoy more privacy and greater freedom while creating for ourselves the moral regulation that had once been forced on us by tradition.

CRITICAL EVALUATION: FOUR VISIONS OF SOCIETY

This chapter opened with several important queries about human societies. We will conclude by summarizing how each of the four visions of society answers these questions.

How Have Societies Changed?

According to the Lenskis' model of sociocultural evolution, societies over the course of history differ primarily in terms of their technology. Modern society is distinctive mostly because of its industrial productivity. Karl Marx, who also stressed historical differences in the productive system, was more concerned with demonstrating that all societies (except perhaps for simple hunters and gatherers) contend with social conflict. For Marx, modern society stands out only in that conflict has become more obvious. In contrast to Marx, Max Weber distinguished societies in terms of characteristic ways of thinking. Preindustrial societies, he claimed, are traditional, while modern societies embrace a rational world view. Finally, for Emile Durkheim, traditional societies are characterized by mechanical solidarity based on likeness. In industrial societies, mechanical solidarity gives way to organic solidarity based on difference.

Why Do Societies Change?

As the Lenskis see it, social change is first and foremost a matter of technological innovation that, over time, can transform an entire society. Marx's materialist approach pointed to the struggle between classes as the "engine of history" pushing societies toward revolutionary reorganization. Weber's idealist approach argues that modes of thought also contribute to social change. He demonstrated how rational Calvinism bolstered the Industrial Revolution, which, in turn, reshaped much of modern society. Finally, Durkheim maintained that an expanding division of labor was the key dimension of social change.

What Holds Societies Together?

The Lenskis claim that societies are united by shared culture, although cultural patterns vary according to a society's level of technological development. But they add that inequality intensifies as technology becomes more complex, diminishing somewhat with the onset of industrialization. Marx spotlighted social division, explaining how class conflict has been the mark of human societies throughout history. From his point of view, social unity could occur only if production became a truly cooperative endeavor. Acknowledging the importance of economic divisions, Weber added that members of a society share a distinctive world view. Just as tradition fused people together in the past, so modern societies have created rational, large-scale organizations that link people's lives. Finally, Durkheim contrasted the morality-based mechanical solidarity of preindustrial societies with modern society's more practical organic solidarity, a change reflecting an increasing division of labor.

Are Societies Improving?

The four visions differ, finally, on the issue of human progress. From their survey of history, the Lenskis conclude that industrial societies provide important advantages, such as a higher standard of living and a longer life span. But the potential threat to our planet posed by advancing technology—through war or environmental pollution—means that we cannot pronounce modern industrial societies better than others in any absolute sense.

Marx applauded the power of advancing technology, but he concluded that only a radical reorganization of society would make those benefits available to everyone. He looked to the future for the ending of historic class conflict as socialism placed production under the control of all people.

Weber found little comfort in Marx's vision, fearing that socialist revolution would only intensify the power of large-scale organizations to dominate people's lives. Thus Weber's view of the human future is probably the most pessimistic of all.

NOTE: Various assessments of social change—corresponding to the ideas of Marx, Weber, and Durkheim—are found in Chapter 24 ("Social Change and Modernity").

Q: "The nail that stands up gets hit down." Japanese proverb that might describe social control in a traditional society
Q: "Man will never fly. Not in a thousand years." Wilbur Wright

Durkheim, by contrast, is the most optimistic. He saw in the twilight of tradition the possibility for more freedom than individuals had ever known. Individualism has dangers, however, as Durkheim's concern with anomie suggests. Despite this reservation, Durkheim comes closest to applauding the history of human societies as a march of genuine "progress."

The significant differences among these four approaches do not mean that any one of them is, in an absolute sense, right or wrong. Society is exceedingly complex, and we benefit from using various points of view. We shall turn to each these visions in later chapters.

SUMMARY

Gerhard and Jean Lenski

1. Sociocultural evolution explores the societal consequences of technological advance.

2. The earliest hunting and gathering societies were composed of a small number of family-centered nomads. Such societies have all but vanished from today's world.

3. Horticulture began some ten thousand years ago as people devised hand tools for cultivation. Pastoral societies domesticate animals and engage in extensive trade.

4. Agriculture, some five thousand years old, is large-scale cultivation using animal-drawn plows. This technology allows societies to expand into vast empires, characterized by more productivity, greater specialization, and increasing inequality.

5. Industrialization began 250 years ago in Europe, as people harnessed advanced energy sources to power sophisticated machinery. In industrial societies, most people live in cities and pursue highly specialized work away from home.

Karl Marx

6. Marx's materialist analysis pointed up conflict between social classes.

7. Conflict in "ancient" societies involved masters and slaves; in agrarian societies, it places nobles and serfs in opposition; in industrial-capitalist societies, capitalists confront the proletariat.

8. Industrial capitalism alienates workers in four ways: from the act of working, from the products of work, from other workers, and from human potential.

9. Marx believed that, once workers had overcome their own false consciousness, they could overthrow capitalists and the industrial-capitalist system.

Max Weber

10. The idealist approach of Weber reveals that ways of thinking, especially beliefs and values, have a powerful effect on society.

11. Weber contrasted the tradition of preindustrial societies to the rationality of modern, industrial societies.

12. Weber feared that rationality, embodied in efficiency-conscious bureaucratic organizations, would stifle human creativity.

Emile Durkheim

13. Durkheim explained that society has an objective existence apart from individuals.

14. His approach relates social elements to the larger society through their functions.

15. Societies require solidarity; mechanical solidarity is based on traditional likeness, while organic solidarity is based on the division of labor or specialization.

KEY CONCEPTS

agriculture the technology of large-scale farming using plows harnessed to animals or more powerful sources of energy

alienation the experience of isolation resulting from powerlessness

anomie Durkheim's designation of a condition of society in which individuals receive little moral guidance

capitalists people who own factories and other productive enterprises

class conflict antagonism between entire classes over the distribution of wealth and power in society

class consciousness the recognition by workers of their unity as a social class in opposition to capitalists and to capitalism itself

division of labor specialized economic activity

false consciousness Marx's term for explanations of social problems in terms of the shortcomings of individuals rather than the flaws of society

horticulture technology based on using hand tools to cultivate plants

hunting and gathering simple technology for hunting animals and gathering vegetation

ideal type an abstract statement of the essential characteristics of any social phenomenon

industrialism technology that powers sophisticated machinery with advanced sources of energy

mechanical solidarity Durkheim's term for social bonds, based on shared moral sentiments, that unite members of preindustrial societies

organic solidarity Durkheim's term for social bonds, based on specialization, that unite members of industrial societies

pastoralism technology that supports the domestication of animals

postindustrialism technology that supports an information-based economy

proletariat people who provide labor necessary for the operation of factories and other productive enterprises

rationality deliberate, matter-of-fact calculation of the most efficient means to accomplish a particular goal

rationalization of society Weber's term for the historical change from tradition to rationality as the dominant mode of human thought

social conflict struggle between segments of society over valued resources

social fact any pattern that is rooted in society rather than the experiences of individuals

social institution a major sphere of social life organized to meet a basic human need

society people who interact in a defined territory and share culture

sociocultural evolution the Lenskis' term for the process of change that results from a society's gaining new cultural information, particularly technology

tradition sentiments and beliefs passed from generation to generation

CRITICAL-THINKING QUESTIONS

1. In terms of sociocultural evolution, why has the world's environment become increasingly threatened by humanity?

2. As general approaches to understanding society, contrast Marx's concept of materialism with Weber's idealism.

3. Does Marx's concept of alienation differ from Durkheim's concept of anomie? How?

4. Do you see implications of these visions of society for the changing standing of women? What issues might be raised by a feminist critique of these theories?

SUGGESTED READINGS

Classic Sources

Robert C. Tucker, ed. *The Marx-Engels Reader.* 2d ed. New York: W. W. Norton, 1978.

This is an excellent source of essays by Karl Marx and Friedrich Engels.

Max Weber. *The Protestant Ethic and the Spirit of Capitalism.* New York: Charles Scribner's Sons, 1958; orig. 1904–5.

Perhaps Max Weber's best-known study is his analysis of Protestantism and capitalism.

Emile Durkheim. *The Division of Labor in Society.* New York: The Free Press, 1964; orig. 1895.

This is Durkheim's major contribution to our understanding of modern societies.

Contemporary Sources

Gerhard Lenski, Jean Lenski, and Patrick Nolan. *Human Society: An Introduction to Macrosociology.* 6th ed. New York: McGraw-Hill, 1991.

A comprehensive account of Gerhard Lenski and Jean Lenski's analysis of human societies is found in this textbook.

Bernard Barber. *Constructing the Social System.* New Brunswick, N.J.: Transaction, 1993.

A noted sociologist draws on various sources in his efforts to develop a broad theory of society.

Shirley Ardener, ed. *Defining Females: The Nature of Women in Society.* New York: Berg, 1991.

This book highlights the distinctive ways in which women are defined, with particular attention to virginity, motherhood, and other expressions of sexuality.

Robert A. Nisbet. *The Sociological Tradition.* New Brunswick, N.J.: Transaction, 1993.

Originally published in 1966, this volume sets out the common questions and themes that define the work of all major sociological thinkers.

Steven Lukes. *Emile Durkheim, His Life and Work: A Historical and Critical Study.* New York: Harper & Row, 1972.

This is one of the most thorough studies to date of Emile Durkheim and his pioneering studies of society and the individual.

Ruth A. Wallace, ed. *Feminism and Sociological Theory.* Newbury Park, Calif.: Sage Publications, 1989.

Sociological theory has yet to respond adequately to the large number of women who entered the field of sociology in recent decades. This book takes a significant step in that direction.

Global Sources

Uta Gerhardt, ed. *Talcott Parsons on National Socialism.* Hawthorne, N.Y.: Aldine de Gruyter, 1993.

This account of the life of U.S. sociologist Talcott Parsons examines how he applied his research to the World War II effort and to the shaping of a democratic future for Germany.

Max Weber. *The Religion of China.* New York: The Free Press, 1951; orig. 1900–20.

Weber, perhaps more than any other sociologist, derived his ideas from cultural and historic comparisons. In this account of Chinese society, Weber contrasts Taoism and Confucianism with Calvinism and the spirit of Western capitalism.

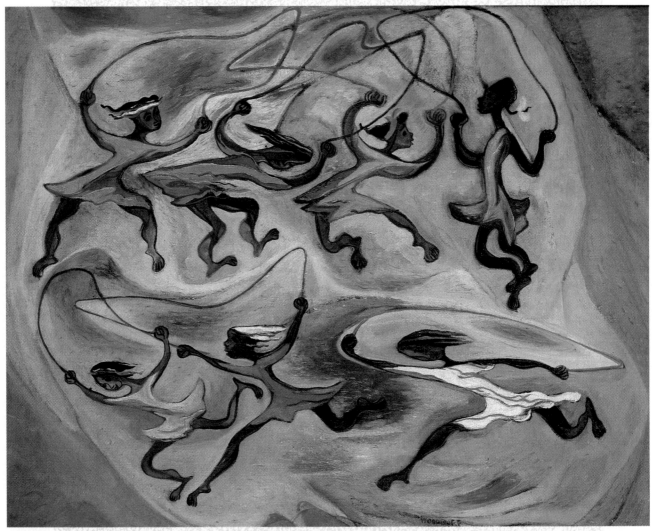

Hale Woodruff, *Girls Skipping*, 1949. Oil on canvas, 24 x 32 inches. Courtesy of Michael Rosenfeld Gallery, New York.

DATA FILE: An outline of Chapter 5, along with supplementary lecture material and discussion questions, is found in the *Data File*.
NOTE: The chapter-opening art is Hale Woodruff's *Girls Skipping*.
Q: "Asking how people grew up may make all men equal yet."
Clarence Darrow

Q: "Anna walks about aimlessly . . . She regards her hands as if she had seen them for the first time. It was impossible to hold her attention for more than a few seconds . . . she gazes vacantly about the room. Speech is entirely lacking . . . The prognosis is not favorable . . ." Notes by the director of the home to which Anna was taken, November 6, 1939 (Davis, 1947:433)

Socialization

On a cold winter day in 1938, a social worker walked anxiously to the door of a rural Pennsylvania farmhouse. Investigating possible child abuse, the social worker soon discovered a five-year-old girl hidden in a second-floor storage room. The child, whose name was Anna, was wedged into an old chair with her arms tied above her head so that she could not move. She was dressed in filthy garments, and her arms and legs—looking like matchsticks—were so frail that she could not use them.

Anna's situation can only be described as tragic. She was born in 1932 to an unmarried and mentally impaired woman of twenty-six who lived with her father. Enraged by his daughter's "illegitimate" motherhood, the grandfather did not even want the child in his house. Anna therefore spent her first six months in various institutions.

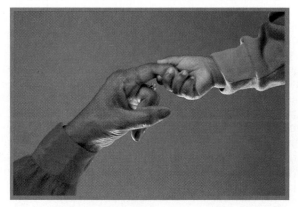

Finally, because her mother was unable to pay for such care, Anna returned to the hostile home of her grandfather.

At this point, her ordeal intensified. To lessen the grandfather's anger, Anna's mother moved the child to the attic room, where she received little attention and just enough milk to keep her alive. There she stayed—day after day, month after month, with essentially no human contact—for five long years.

Upon learning of the discovery of Anna, sociologist Kingsley Davis (1940) traveled immediately to see the child. He found her at a county home, where local authorities had taken her. Davis was appalled by Anna's condition. She was emaciated and feeble. Unable to laugh, smile, speak, or even show anger, she was completely unresponsive, as if the world around her did not even exist.

NOTE: The term *tabula rasa* (Latin, meaning "clean slate") was introduced by English philosopher John Locke (1632–1704). An empiricist, Locke believed that human personalities were "written on" by experience.

NOTE: "Nature" has the Latin root *nat(us)*, meaning "born"; "nurture" has the Latin root *nutrit(us)*, meaning "nourished."

NOTE: We sometimes take highly correlated IQ scores among family members (who share genes) as evidence that intelligence has a genetic component. No doubt, this is so, but the correlation of IQ scores for unrelated individuals reared together is twice as high as that of identical twins reared apart. Thus, "nurture" appears to be the more important in determining "intelligence." (Cf. Thomas J. Bouchard, Jr., and Matthew McGue, "Familial Studies of Intelligence: A Review," *Science* 212, 1981:1055–59.)

THE IMPORTANCE OF SOCIAL EXPERIENCE

Here is a deplorable but instructive case of a human being deprived of virtually all social contact. Although physically alive, Anna hardly seemed human. Her plight reveals that, isolated from others, an individual develops little or no capacity for thought, emotion, and meaningful behavior. In short, in the absence of social experience, an individual is more an *object* than a *person*.

This chapter explores what Anna was deprived of—the means by which we become fully human. This process is **socialization**, *the lifelong social experience by which individuals develop human potential and learn the patterns of their culture.* Unlike other living species whose behavior is biologically set, human beings rely on social experience to learn the nuances of their culture in order to survive.

Social experience is also the foundation of **personality**, which refers to *a person's fairly consistent patterns of thinking, feeling, and acting.* We build a personality by internalizing the sense we make of our social surroundings. As personality develops, we share a culture while remaining, in some respects, distinct individuals. But in the absence of social experience, as the case of Anna shows, personality does not emerge at all.

Social experience is vital for society just as it is for individuals. Societies live beyond the life span of any one person. As explained in earlier chapters, then, every society must teach something of its past way of life to its new members. The lifelong process of socialization is the way in which society transmits culture from one generation to the next (Elkin & Handel, 1984).

Human Development: Nature and Nurture

Virtually helpless at birth, the human infant needs others to provide for its care and nourishment. A child also relies on others to teach patterns of culture. Although Anna's short life makes these facts very clear, a century ago most people mistakenly believed that human behavior was the product of biology.

Charles Darwin, whose groundbreaking ideas are described in Chapter 3 ("Culture"), held that a species evolves over thousands of generations as genetic variations enhance survival and reproduction. As Darwin's influence grew, others applied his model to human behavior. By the end of the nineteenth century, most people spoke of human behavior as if it were the instinctive "nature" of our species.

Such notions are still with us. People sometimes claim, for example, that our economic system is a reflection of "instinctive human competitiveness," that some people are "born criminals," or that women are more emotional while men are more rational (Witkin-Lanoil, 1984). The term *human nature* is often applied to familiar personality traits as if people were born with them, just as we are born with five senses. More accurately, however, human nature involves creating and learning cultural traits, as we shall see.

People trying to explain cultural diversity also misconstrued Darwin's thinking. After centuries of world exploration and empire building, Western Europeans knew well that people in much of the world behaved quite differently from the way they did. They attributed such contrasts to biology rather than to culture. It was an easy—although terribly damaging—step to conclude that members of technologically simple societies were biologically less evolved and, therefore, less human. Such a self-serving and ethnocentric view helped them justify their colonial practices, including land seizures and slavery, since it is easier to exploit others if you are convinced that they are not truly human in the same sense you are.

In the twentieth century, naturalistic explanations of human behavior came under fire. Psychologist John B. Watson (1878–1958) devised a theory called *behaviorism*, which held that specific patterns of behavior are not instinctive but learned. All the world's cultures are the creation of a single biological species, Watson continued, so that no humans are more or less "evolved" than others. Such a position means that Watson saw one human species, but many variants of human behavior. Any individual, he maintained, can be shaped in countless ways by a cultural environment:

> Give me a dozen healthy infants . . . and my own specified world to bring them up in, and I will guarantee to take any one at random and train him to become any type of specialist that I might select—doctor, lawyer, artist, merchant-chief, and yes, even beggar-man and thief—regardless of his talents, penchants, tendencies, abilities, vocations, and race of his ancestors. (1930:104)

In short, Watson was convinced that learning—or *nurture*—was far more influential than biology—or *nature*—to human behavior.

Anthropologists added support to Watson's theory by showing how variable culture can be, even comparing societies with similar technology. An outspoken proponent of the "nurture" view, anthropologist Margaret Mead summed up the evidence: "The

RESOURCE: Elijah Anderson's *Growing Up on the Streets,* included in the companion reader, *Seeing Ourselves,* demonstrates the effect of environment (especially class and race) on the process of socialization.

NOTE: Genetic transmission of intelligence does not imply any aggregate IQ differences among races. Richard Lewontin offers this analogy: Imagine planting seeds in two gardens—one of poor soil, and one of rich soil. In both gardens the growing plants will reach different heights; such within-group variation represents genetic differences. The average difference between the two gardens, however, is environmental. (Cf. Richard C. Lewontin, "Race and Intelligence," in N. J. Block and Gerald Dworkin, eds., *The IQ Controversy: Critical Readings,* Pantheon, 1976:78–92.)

 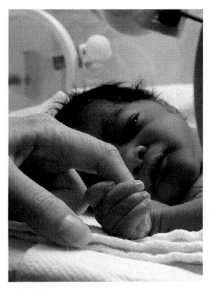 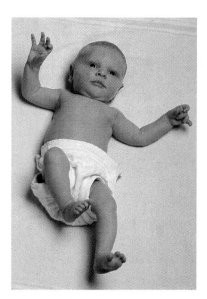

Human infants display various reflexes—biologically based behavior patterns that enhance survival. The sucking reflex, which actually begins before birth, enables the infant to obtain nourishment. The grasping reflex, triggered by placing a finger on the infant's palm causing the hand to close, helps the infant to maintain contact with a parent and, later on, to grasp objects. The Moro reflex, activated by startling the infant, has the infant swinging both arms outward and then bringing them together across the chest. This action, which disappears after several months of life, probably developed among our evolutionary ancestors so that a falling infant could grasp the body hair of a parent.

differences between individuals who are members of different cultures, like the differences between individuals within a culture, are almost entirely to be laid to differences in conditioning, especially during early childhood, and this conditioning is culturally determined" (1963:280; orig. 1935).

Today, social scientists are cautious about describing any type of behavior as instinctive. Even sociobiology, discussed in Chapter 3 ("Culture"), does not challenge the conclusion that human behavior is primarily guided by the surrounding culture. This does not mean that biology plays *no* part in human behavior. Human life, after all, depends on the functioning of the human body. We also know that children share some biological traits with their parents, especially physical characteristics such as height, weight, hair and eye color, and facial features. Intelligence and many personality characteristics (for example, how one reacts to stimulation or frustration) probably have some genetic component, as does the potential to excel in such activities as art and music (Herrnstein, 1973). But whether a person develops an inherited potential depends on the opportunities associated with social position (Plomin & Foch, 1980; Goldsmith, 1983).

In sum, clear evidence supports the conclusion that nurture is far more important than nature in shaping human behavior. We should not think of nature as opposing nurture, though, since we express our human nature by creating, learning, and modifying culture. For humans, then, nature and nurture stand as inseparable.

Social Isolation

For obvious ethical reasons, researchers cannot subject human beings to experimental isolation. Consequently, much of what we know about this issue comes from rare cases of abused children like Anna. Researchers have, however, studied the effects of social isolation on animals.

Effects of Social Isolation on Nonhuman Primates

Psychologists Harry Harlow and Margaret Harlow (1962) conducted a classic investigation of the effects of social isolation on nonhuman primates. They placed rhesus monkeys—whose behavior is in some ways

NOTE: It may not be a coincidence that all the isolated children of record are females.

DIVERSITY: Children of deaf parents sometimes learn sign language first and spoken/written language later when they reach school. Such children often have difficulty learning language then because, as researchers now recognize, language acquisition requires learning certain skills in a particular time frame.

NOTE: Susan Curtiss explains that the family of Genie was violent due to a father who wanted no children; the first child in the family died from exposure at 2.5 months; the second child died at 2 years; the third child survived, but only after the paternal grandmother took him into her own home; Genie was the family's fourth child.

The personalities we develop depend largely on the environment in which we live. When a child's world is shredded by violence, the damage can be profound and lasting. This drawing was made by a young boy living in a low-income neighborhood in south-central Los Angeles, where rioting exploded in 1992. What are the likely effects of such an environment on a child's self-confidence and capacity to form trusting ties to others?

surprisingly similar to that of humans—in various conditions of isolation to observe the consequences.

The Harlows found that complete social isolation for a period of even six months (with adequate nutrition) seriously disturbed the monkeys' development. When isolated monkeys subsequently encountered others of their kind, they were fearful and unable to defend themselves against aggression.

Modifying their experiment, the Harlows isolated infant rhesus monkeys with an artificial "mother" of wire mesh with a wooden head and the nipple of a feeding tube where the breast would be. These monkeys survived physically, but they, too, were subsequently unable to interact with other monkeys.

A further variation of the research, however, showed that a covering of soft terry cloth encouraged the infant monkeys to cling to the artificial mother, and they apparently derived emotional benefit from the closeness. Subsequently, these monkeys displayed less emotional distress. The Harlows thus concluded that normal emotional development requires affectionate cradling as part of parent-infant interaction.

The Harlows made two other discoveries. First, so long as they were surrounded by other infants, monkeys were not adversely affected by the absence of a mother. This finding suggests that deprivation of

social experience, rather than the specific absence of a parent, has devastating effects. Second, the Harlows found that, after social isolation for only about three months, infant monkeys eventually regained normal emotional patterns. The damage of short-term isolation, then, can be overcome; longer-term isolation, however, appears to inflict on monkeys irreversible emotional and behavioral damage.

Effects of Social Isolation on Children

The case of Anna, described at the beginning of this chapter, is the best-known instance of the long-term social isolation of a human infant. After her discovery, however, Anna benefited from extensive social contact and soon showed some improvement. When Kingsley Davis (1940) visited her in the county home after ten days, he noted that she was more alert, showed some human expression, and even smiled with obvious pleasure. During the next year, Anna made slow but steady progress, as she experienced the humanizing effects of socialization, showing greater interest in other people and gradually learning to walk. After a year and a half, she could feed herself, walk alone for short distances, and play with toys.

Consistent with the observations of the Harlows, however, it was becoming apparent that Anna's five years of social isolation had left her permanently damaged. At the age of eight her mental and social development was still less than that of a two-year-old. Not until she was almost ten did she show the first signs of using language. Complicating the problem is the fact that Anna's mother was mentally retarded, so that Anna may have been similarly disadvantaged. The puzzle was never untangled, because Anna died at age ten from a blood disorder, possibly related to her long years of abuse (Davis, 1940, 1947).

A second, quite similar case involves another girl, found at about the same time as Anna and under strikingly similar circumstances. After more than six years of virtual isolation, this girl—known as Isabelle—displayed the same lack of human responsiveness as Anna (Davis, 1947). Unlike Anna, though, Isabelle benefited from special efforts by psychologists to aid her development. Within a week, Isabelle was attempting to speak, and a year and a half later, her vocabulary was nearly two thousand words. The psychologists concluded that Isabelle had progressed through what is normally about six years of development with two years of intensive effort. By the time she was fourteen, Isabelle was attending sixth-grade classes in school, apparently well on her way to at least an approximately normal life.

Q: "Anatomy is destiny." Sigmund Freud
Q: "My life has been aimed at one goal only: to infer or to guess how the mental apparatus is constructed and what forces interplay and counteract it." Sigmund Freud

Q: "The principal task of civilization, its actual *raison d'etre*, is to defend us against nature." Sigmund Freud
NOTE: Champions of psychoanalysis included Franz Boas, Margaret Mead, and Ruth Benedict, all of whom interpreted this approach as favoring nurture over nature.

A final case of childhood isolation involves a thirteen-year-old girl in California isolated in a small room from the age of about two (Curtiss, 1977; Pines, 1981). For years Genie's parents victimized her in a host of ways, including locking her in a garage. Upon discovery, Genie's condition was similar to that of the two children we have described. Genie was emaciated (weighing only fifty-nine pounds) and had the mental development of a one-year-old. She was given intensive treatment by specialists and is alive today. Yet even after years of care, her ability to use language remains that of a young child.

All the evidence points to the crucial role of social experience in personality development. Human beings are resilient creatures, sometimes able to recover from even the crushing experience of abuse and isolation. But there is a point—precisely when is unclear from the limited number of cases—at which social isolation in infancy results in irreparable developmental damage.

UNDERSTANDING THE SOCIALIZATION PROCESS

Socialization is a highly complex process, and no one researcher has fully explained how we gain our humanity. The following sections highlight the work of five pioneers in the field of human development who made important contributions to our understanding of socialization.

Sigmund Freud: The Elements of Personality

Sigmund Freud (1856–1939) lived in Vienna at a time when most Europeans thought human behavior was biologically fixed. Trained in the natural sciences to be a physician, Freud turned to the analysis of personality and developed a celebrated theory of psychoanalysis. Many aspects of this work bear directly on understanding socialization.

Basic Human Needs

Freud contended that biology plays an important part in personality development, although not in terms of simple instincts as is common to most other species. For Freud, what is instinctive is two general human needs or drives. First, he claimed, humans have a basic need for bonding, which he described as the life instinct, or *eros* (from the Greek god of love). Second, opposing this need, he asserted that people also have an aggressive drive, which he called the death instinct,

Sigmund Freud stands among the pioneers who charted the human personality. His daughter, Anna Freud, also shown here in a 1913 family photograph, further developed her father's theory of psychoanalysis.

or *thanatos* (from the Greek meaning "death"). Freud postulated that these opposing forces generate tension in the personality. It is this interplay of forces—much of which is unconscious—that forms the foundation of the human drama.

Freud's Model of Personality

Freud incorporated both basic drives and the influence of society into a broader model of personality with three parts: id, ego, and superego. The **id** represents *the human being's basic drives*, which are unconscious and demand immediate satisfaction. (The word *id* is simply Latin for "it," suggesting the tentative way in which Freud explored the unconscious mind.) Rooted in our biology, the id is present at birth, making a newborn a bundle of needs that demands attention, touching, and food. But society opposes such a self-centered orientation, so the id's desires inevitably encounter resistance. This cultural opposition suggests why one of the first words a child learns is "no."

To avoid frustration, the child learns to approach the world realistically. This accomplishment forms the second component of the personality, the **ego** (Latin

RESOURCE: Probably the most sociological of Freud's twenty-four books is *Civilization and Its Discontents*. The sociological implications of Freud's work are explored in Philip Rieff's *Freud: The Mind of the Moralist* (Doubleday, 1961).
NOTE: Freud's influence on popular culture is evident in the characterization of anything unintended as "Freudian."

NOTE: Piaget's stages of development are *maturational*; in this, he is distinguished from George Herbert Mead, for whom biology played virtually no role in social development.

for "I"), which is *a person's conscious efforts to balance innate pleasure-seeking drives with the demands of society.* The ego arises as we gain awareness of our distinct existence; it develops as we face up to the fact that we cannot have everything we want.

Finally, the human personality develops the **superego** (Latin meaning "above" or "beyond" the ego), which is *the presence of culture within the individual.* In this overlay of personality, we can see *why* we cannot have everything we want. The superego consists of the internalized values and norms of our culture and takes the form of conscience. First expressed as the recognition of parental control, the superego eventually matures as the child learns that parental control is itself a reflection of something broader: the moral demands of the larger culture.

A child first encounters the world as a bewildering array of physical sensations and need satisfactions. With gradual development of the superego, however, the child's comprehension extends beyond pleasure and pain to the moral concepts of right and wrong. In other words, initially a child can feel good only in the physical sense. Later a child feels good for behaving in culturally appropriate ways and feels bad (the experience of guilt) for failing to do so.

In a well-adjusted personality, the ego successfully manages the opposing forces of the id and the superego. If conflicts are not successfully resolved, personality disorders result. Freud held childhood to be the critical period in the formation of an individual's personality because conflicts initiated during this early stage of life are an unconscious source of later personality problems.

Freud termed society's efforts to control human drives *repression*. In his view, some repression is inevitable, since people must be coerced into looking beyond themselves. Often the competing demands are resolved through compromise, so that basic needs are redirected into socially approved forms. This process, which Freud named *sublimation*, transforms fundamentally selfish drives into socially acceptable activities. Sexual urges, for example, may lead to marriage, and aggression can be released through sports.

Critical evaluation. Freud's work sparked controversy in his own lifetime, and some of that controversy still smolders today. The world he knew vigorously repressed human sexuality, and few of his contemporaries were prepared to concede that sex is a basic human need. Recently, Freud has drawn fire for his depictions of humanity in allegedly male terms, thereby devaluing the lives of women (Donovan & Littenberg, 1982). But Freud provided a foundation that influenced virtually everyone who later studied the human personality. Of special importance to sociology is his notion that we internalize social norms and that childhood experiences have lasting importance to socialization.

Jean Piaget: Cognitive Development

Jean Piaget (1896–1980) is also among the foremost psychologists of the century. Much of his work centered on human *cognition*—how people think and understand. Early in his career, Piaget was fascinated by the behavior of his three children, wondering not only what they knew but *how* they comprehended the world. Systematic observations led him to conclude that children's conceptions of their surroundings change as they grow older. Piaget identified four stages of cognitive development, each a product of biological maturation and increasing social experience.

The Sensorimotor Stage

Piaget noted that the first step in human development is the **sensorimotor stage**, *the level of human development in which individuals experience the world only through sensory contact.* In this stage, which corresponds roughly to the first two years of life, the infant explores the world by touching, looking, sucking, and listening.

Children gain skills at imitating the actions or sounds of others during the sensorimotor stage, but they have no comprehension of symbols. Very young children reason only in the limited sense of direct physical experience.

The Preoperational Stage

The second plateau in Piaget's account of development is the **preoperational stage**, *the level of human development in which individuals first use language and other symbols.* At about age two, children begin to engage the world mentally, thinking about things they cannot sense directly. As they begin to attach meaning to the world, they learn to distinguish between ideas and objective reality. At this age, children realize that their dreams are not real, and they appreciate the element of fantasy in fairy tales (Kohlberg & Gilligan, 1971; Skolnick, 1986). Unlike adults, however, they attach names and meanings only to specific things. A child at this stage who takes pleasure in describing a favorite toy, for example, is not yet able to describe the qualities of toys in general.

Without abstract concepts, a child cannot judge size, weight, or volume. In one of his best-known experiments, Piaget placed two identical glasses containing equal volumes of water on a table. He asked several children aged five and six if the amount in each glass was the same. They nodded that it was. The children then watched Piaget take one of the glasses and pour its contents into a taller, narrower glass, raising the level of the water. He asked again if each glass held the same amount. The typical five- and six-year-old now insisted that the taller glass held more water. But children over the age of seven, who are able to think more abstractly, could usually comprehend that the amount of water remained the same.

During the preoperational stage, children still have a very egocentric view of the world (Damon, 1983). For example, we have all seen young children place their hands in front of their faces and exclaim, "You can't see me!" They assume that if they cannot see you, then you are unable to see them. They perceive the world only from their own vantage point and have yet to learn that a situation may appear different to another person.

The Concrete Operational Stage

Next, in Piaget's model, is the **concrete operational stage**, *the level of development at which individuals first perceive causal connections in their surroundings.* At this point, typically between seven and eleven, children begin to understand how and why things happen, which yields far greater ability to manipulate their environment.

In addition, girls and boys at this level can attach more than one symbol to a particular event or object. For instance, if you say to a girl of five, "Today is Wednesday," she might respond, "No, it's my birthday!" indicating an inability to use more than one symbol at a time. Within a few years, however, she would be able to respond, "Yes, this Wednesday is my birthday!"

A final development during the concrete operational stage is transcending earlier egocentrism so that children can imagine themselves in the position of another person. As we shall explain shortly, perceiving a situation from another's point of view is the foundation of complex social activities, such as games.

During the concrete operational stage, however, the thinking of children remains tied to concrete objects and events. They may understand that hitting a brother without provocation will bring punishment, but children still cannot conceive of situations in which hitting a brother would be fair nor can they comprehend why parents punish.

In a well-known experiment, Jean Piaget demonstrated that children over the age of seven had entered the concrete operational stage of development because they could recognize that the quantity of liquid remained the same when poured from a wide beaker into a tall one.

The Formal Operational Stage

The fourth level in Piaget's model is the **formal operational stage**, *the level of human development at which individuals use highly abstract thought to imagine alternatives to reality.* By about the age of twelve, children begin to reason using abstract qualities rather than thinking only of concrete situations. If, for example, you were to ask a child of seven or eight, "What would you like to be when you grow up?" you might prompt a concrete response such as, "A teacher." Once the final stage of cognitive development is attained, however, the child is capable of responding abstractly, "I would like a job that is exciting." At this point, the child has gained the marvelous human quality of imagination, which frees us from the immediate bounds of our lives. Children capable of formal operations often display a keen interest in imaginative literature like science fiction (Skolnick, 1986). They also are able to comprehend metaphors. Hearing the phrase "A penny for your thoughts" might lead a younger child to think of money, but the older child will recognize a gentle invitation to intimacy.

Critical evaluation. If Freud envisioned humanity torn by the opposing forces of biology and society, Piaget believed the human mind to be active and creative, so that children soon learn to shape their social world. Piaget's contribution to understanding socialization is showing that this capacity unfolds gradually as the result of biological maturation and the gaining of social experience.

In global perspective, there is some question as to whether people in every culture progress through Piaget's stages and do so in the same time frame. For instance, living in a society that changes very slowly is likely to inhibit the ability to imagine alternatives to reality. Finally, even in our own society, as many as 30 percent of thirty-year-olds apparently do not reach the formal operational stage at all (Kohlberg & Gilligan, 1971:1065). This finding again underscores the importance of social experience in the development of personality. Regardless of biological maturity, people who are not exposed to highly creative and imaginative thinking are less likely to develop this capacity in themselves.

Lawrence Kohlberg: Moral Development

More recently, Lawrence Kohlberg (1981) has extended Piaget's work to the issue of moral reasoning, that is, the ways in which individuals come to judge situations as right or wrong. Following Piaget's lead, Kohlberg argues that moral development occurs in stages.

Young children who experience the world in terms of pain and pleasure (Piaget's sensorimotor stage) are at the *preconventional* level of moral development. At this early stage, in other words, "rightness" amounts to "what serves my needs" or "what feels good to me."

The *conventional* level of moral development, Kohlberg's second stage, begins to appear among teenagers (corresponding to Piaget's last, formal operational stage). At this point, young people are less self-centered in their moral reasoning, defining right and wrong in terms of what pleases parents and what is consistent with broader cultural norms. Individuals at this stage also try to assess intention as well as simply observing what others do in reaching moral judgments.

A final stage of moral development, the *postconventional* level, moves individuals beyond the specific norms of their society to ponder more abstract ethical principles. At this level, people can philosophically reflect on the meaning of liberty, freedom, or justice. Put otherwise, individuals are now capable of actively criticizing their own society and of arguing, for instance, that what is traditional or legal still may not be right.

Critical evaluation. Like the work of Piaget, Kohlberg's model explains that moral development occurs in more or less identifiable stages. Some of the same criticisms made about Piaget's ideas also apply to Kohlberg's work. Whether this model applies to people

in all societies, for example, remains unconfirmed. Then, too, many people in the United States apparently do not reach the postconventional level of moral reasoning, although exactly why is also, at present, an open question.

The greatest problem with Kohlberg's research, however, is that his subjects were only boys. Kohlberg commits the research error, described in Chapter 2 ("Sociological Investigation") of generalizing the results of his male subjects to all of humanity. This problem provoked his colleague Carol Gilligan to investigate further how gender affects moral reasoning.

Carol Gilligan: The Gender Factor

Carol Gilligan, who is introduced in the box, was disturbed that Kohlberg's research had involved only boys. This narrow focus, as she sees it, is typical of much social science, which uses the behavior of males as the norm for how everyone should act.

Therefore Gilligan (1982, 1990) set out systematically to compare the moral development of females and males. Simply put, her conclusion is that females and males tend to have a different process of moral reasoning. Males, she contends, have a *justice perspective*, relying on formal rules or appealing to abstract principles to reach judgments about right and wrong. Boys playing soccer, say, are quick to condemn one of their number for touching the ball with his hands or ignoring a boundary line on the field. Girls, on the other hand, have a *care and responsibility perspective*, which leads them to judge a situation with an eye toward personal relationships and loyalties. Girls playing soccer may be quick to reassure a player who has accidentally touched the ball with her hands. In other situations, breaking a rule may not be perceived as wrong if it is done to help someone else who is in need.

Worth noting is the fact that rule-based male reasoning, according to Kohlberg's analysis, is morally superior to person-based female thinking. Gilligan's point is that we must be careful not to set up male standards as the norms by which we evaluate everyone. She reminds us that the impersonal application of rules has long dominated men's lives in the workplace. Concern for attachments, by contrast, has been more relevant to women's lives as wives, mothers, and caregivers. But should we assume that the first approach to moral reasoning is somehow better than the second?

Critical evaluation. The strength of Gilligan's work is that it both sharpens our understanding of human

RESOURCE: In her *Seeing Ourselves* article, "Cognitive Development: Children's Understanding of Homelessness," Mary E. Walsh applies a developmental perspective to an important contemporary social problem.
DATA FILE: An overview of Mead's ideas about teaching is provided in the *Data File*.

NOTE: George Herbert Mead also wrote about teaching; see "The Psychology of Social Consciousness Implied in Instruction" (*Science* XXXI, 1910:688–93) and "The Teaching of Science in College" (*Science* XXIV, 1906:390–97).
RESOURCE: Mead's statement "The Self" is among the classics included in the *Seeing Ourselves* reader.

PROFILE

Carol Gilligan: Socialization and Girls' Self-Esteem

Carol Gilligan, an educational psychologist at Harvard University, has focused her research on the personality development of young girls. Initially, she attempted to correct a research bias by which other investigators used data drawn from the study of boys to describe everyone. Girls and boys, she subsequently found, utilize distinctive frameworks for assessing fairness.

Gilligan's later research has targeted the issue of self-esteem. Her research team followed more than two thousand girls, ranging from six to eighteen years in age, for five years. As the interviews were completed, the researchers reported a clear pattern: Young girls start out with considerable confidence and self-esteem, only to find these vital resources slipping away as they pass through adolescence.

Why? Gilligan claims that the answer lies in culture. Our way of life, she argues, still defines the ideal woman as eager to please, as calm, controlled, and cooperative. Then, too, as girls move from the elementary grades to secondary school, they encounter fewer women teachers and find that most authority figures are men. The overall result is that women struggle in early adulthood to regain much of the personal strength they had a decade before.

Illustrating this trend, Gilligan and her colleagues returned to a girls' school—one site of their research—to present their findings. The younger girls who had been interviewed were eager that their names appear in the forthcoming book; the older girls, by contrast, were much less confident: Many were fearful that they would be talked about.

SOURCES: Gilligan (1990) and Winkler (1990).

development and points up the problems of overgeneralizing and gender insensitivity in conducting and evaluating research.

One question about Gilligan's work is the source of the differences she documents between females and males. Is it nature or nurture? Some researchers have argued that these patterns reflect cultural conditioning. Thus, according to this view, as the lives of men and women gradually become more alike—as women enter the workplace and men take responsibility for child rearing—the moral reasoning of the two sexes will also show greater similarity.

George Herbert Mead: The Social Self

Perhaps no single individual captured in his work so many facets of socialization as did George Herbert Mead (1863–1931), who is introduced in the box on page 134. Mead's approach (1962; orig. 1934), called *social behaviorism*, is akin to that of psychologist John

B. Watson, described earlier. Both recognized the power of the environment to shape human behavior. But behaviorists like Watson focused on behavior itself, thereby ignoring *thinking*, which Mead held was the key to our humanity.

The Self

Mead's central concept is the **self**, *a dimension of personality composed of an individual's self-awareness and self-image.* Mead's genius lay in seeing that self is inseparable from society, a connection explained in a series of steps.

First, Mead asserted, *self emerges from social experience.* The self is not part of the body, and it does not exist at birth. Mead rejected the position that personality is guided by biological drives (as asserted by Freud) or biological maturation (as Piaget claimed). For Mead, self develops *only* through social experience. In the absence of interaction, as we see from

Q: "The self . . . has a development; it is not initially there, at birth, but arises in the process of social experience . . ." George Herbert Mead

RESOURCE: Italian playwright Luigi Pirandello (1867–1936) made use of the sociological perspective in his work. Many of his plays reveal ideas strikingly similar to those of George Herbert Mead (and also Erving Goffman). See, especially, "The Pleasure of Honesty."

NOTE: Believing in the plasticity of human personality, George Herbert Mead also believed in people's ability to reform society. For a discussion of his views on social reform, see Dmitri N. Shalin, *American Journal of Sociology* 93, 4 (January 1988):913–51.

NOTE: Piaget argued that social behavior is shaped by maturational stages; in contrast, Mead argued that stages of life are defined and structured by society.

PROFILE

George Herbert Mead: The Self Is Society

Few people were surprised that George Herbert Mead became a college professor. He was born to a Massachusetts family with a strong intellectual tradition, and both his parents were academics. His mother served for ten years as president of Mount Holyoke College, and his father was both a preacher and teacher at a number of colleges.

But Mead also had a hand in shaping his own life, first rebelling against the strongly religious atmosphere of his home and community. After completing college, he restlessly traveled about the Pacific Northwest, surveying for the railroad and reading as much as he could. He gradually settled on the idea of studying philosophy, which he did at Harvard and in Europe.

Mead took a teaching position at the new University of Chicago. But his outlook still veered from the conventional. For one thing, he rarely published, an activity expected of many academics. Mead's fame spread only after his death, when colleagues and former students collected and published his lecture notes. For another, Mead drew together a wide range of ideas to help launch the new field of social psychology.

Finally, never content with life as it was, Mead was an active social reformer. To him, the course of an entire society is as ongoing and changeable as the life of any individual. This insight follows from his basic contention: Society may have the power to shape individuals, but people also have the capacity to act back on their society.

SOURCES: Based, in part, on Coser (1977) and Schellenberg (1978).

the cases of isolated children, the body may grow but no self will emerge.

Second, Mead explained, *social experience is the exchange of symbols*. Using words, a wave of the hand, or a smile, people create meaning, which is a distinctively human experience. We can use reward and punishment to train a dog, after all; but the dog attaches no meaning to actions. Human beings, by contrast, search for meanings as we infer intention in what people do. In short, a dog responds to *what you do*; a human responds to *what you have in mind* as you do it.

Return to our friendly dog for a moment. You can train a dog to walk to the porch and return with an umbrella. But the dog grasps no meaning in the act, no intention behind the command. Thus, if the dog cannot find the umbrella, it is incapable of the *human* response: to look for a raincoat instead, based on understanding actions in terms of meanings.

Third, says Mead, *to understand someone's intention, you must imagine the situation from that person's point of view*. Using symbols, we can imaginatively place ourselves in another person's shoes and thus see ourselves as that person does. This capacity allows us to anticipate how others will respond to us even before we act. The simplest act of tossing a ball toward someone requires stepping outside ourselves to imagine how another will respond to our throw. Social interaction, then, involves seeing ourselves as others see us—a process that Mead termed *taking the role of the other*.

The Looking-Glass Self

Thinking about ourselves amounts to imagining ourselves through the eyes of others. Charles Horton Cooley (1864–1929), one of Mead's colleagues, suggested that others represent a mirror or looking glass

Q: "Each to each a looking glass,
    Reflects the other that doth pass."
    Charles Horton Cooley (1964:184; orig. 1902)
NOTE: Playing "peek-a-boo" reveals the inability of young children to take the role of the other. Tots assume that, since they cannot see you, you cannot see them.

Q: "Thought makes the whole dignity of man." Blaise Pascal, French mathematician and philosopher (1623–1662)
NOTE: Sometimes young children are hurt by adults who seem not to appreciate primitive "homemade" gifts such as artwork from school. This feeling reflects children's limited capacity to "take the role of the other." They cannot comprehend that the adult does not see the same value in the gift as they do.

George Herbert Mead wrote: "No hard-and-fast line can be drawn between our own selves and the selves of others." The painting Les Réfugiés *by Fateh Al-Moudarres conveys this important idea. Although we tend to think of ourselves as unique individuals, each person's characteristics develop in an ongoing process of interaction with others.*

in which we perceive ourselves. Cooley (1964; orig. 1902) used the phrase **looking-glass self** to capture *the idea that self-image is based on how others respond to us.* Whether we think of ourselves as clever or clumsy, worthy or worthless, depends in large measure on what we think others think of us. This insight goes a long way to explaining Carol Gilligan's finding that young women lose self-confidence as they come of age in a society that discourages women from being too assertive.

The I and the Me

The fact that we are able to see ourselves through others indicates that the self has two components. First, *the self is subject* in that it can initiate social action. Mead claimed humans are innately active and spontaneous, and he dubbed this subjective element of the self the *I* (the subjective form of the personal pronoun).

Second, *the self is object* because, taking the role of another, we form impressions of ourselves. Mead called this objective element of the self the *me* (the objective form of the personal pronoun). All social experience begins with someone initiating action (the I-phase of self) and then guiding the action (the me-phase of self) through reflectively taking the role of the other. Social experience is thus the interplay of the I and the me: Our actions are spontaneous yet guided by how others respond to us.

Mead stressed that even thinking is social experience. Our thoughts are partly creative (representing the I), but in thought we also become objects to ourselves (representing the me) as we imagine how others will respond to our ideas.

Development of the Self

According to Mead, gaining a self amounts to learning to take the role of the other. Like Freud and Piaget, Mead regarded early childhood as the crucial time for this task, but he did not link the development of self to biological maturation. Mead maintained that the self emerges over time with increasing social experience.

Infants respond to others only in terms of *imitation*. They mimic behavior without understanding underlying intentions. Unable to use symbols, Mead concluded, infants have no self.

Children learn to use language and other symbols in the form of *play* and, especially, role playing. At first they model themselves on key people in their lives—such as parents—we call *significant others*. Playing "mommy and daddy," for example, helps children imagine the world from their parents' point of view.

Gradually, children learn to take the roles of several others at once. In other words, the maturing self is able to orient actions in response to various others. This skill is the key to moving from simple play involving one role to complex *games* involving many roles. A three- or four-year-old can play "catch" (requiring taking the role of one partner). But not until age seven or eight can a child engage in team sports, since games demand simultaneously taking the role of numerous others.

DATA FILE: The *Data File* offers a cross-cultural look at Taiwanese parenting styles.

NOTE: The significance of the family is shown in the fact that four of the five most powerful "social readjustment" experiences involve family members: death of spouse (100), divorce (73), marital separation (65), death of close family member (63), and jail term (63). (Holmes & Rahe, 1967)

Q: "For most [children of divorce], divorce was the most important cause of enduring pain and anomie in their lives." Judith S. Wallerstein and Sandra Blakeslee (1989)

Q: "Middle-class parents seem to regard child rearing as more problematic than do working-class parents." Melvin Kohn (1977:6)

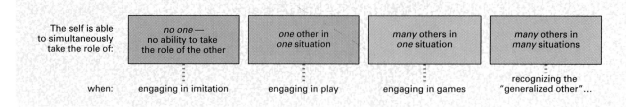

FIGURE 5–1 Building on Social Experience
George Herbert Mead described the development of self as the process of gaining social experience. This is largely a matter of taking the role of the other with increasing sophistication.

Figure 5–1 shows the logical progression from imitation to play to games. But a final stage in the development of self remains. A game involves taking the role of others in just one situation. But members of a society also need to see themselves as others in general might. In other words, we recognize that people in any situation throughout society share cultural norms and values, and we begin to incorporate these general patterns into the self. Mead used the term **generalized other** to refer to *widespread cultural norms and values we use as references in evaluating ourselves.*

Of course, the emergence of self is not the end of socialization. Quite the contrary: Mead claimed that socialization continues as long as we have social experience, so that changing circumstances can reshape who we are. The self may change, for example, with divorce, disability, or unexpected wealth. Mead also maintained that we direct our own lives, acting back on society and thereby playing a large part in our own socialization.

Critical evaluation. The strength of Mead's work lies in exploring social experience itself. He succeeded in explaining how symbolic interaction is the foundation of both self and society.

Some critics disparage Mead's view as radically social, acknowledging no biological element in the emergence of self. In this position, he stands apart from Freud (who identified general drives within the organism) and Piaget (whose stages of development are tied to biological maturity).

Mead's concepts of the I and the me are often confused with Freud's concepts of the id and the superego. One difference is that Freud rooted the id in the biological organism, while Mead rejected any link between the self and biology (although he never specified the origin of the I). Freud's concept of the superego and Mead's concept of the me both reflect the power of society to shape personality. But for Freud,

superego and id are locked in continual combat. Mead, however, understood the I and the me as working closely and cooperatively together (Meltzer, 1978).

AGENTS OF SOCIALIZATION

We are affected in at least some small way by every social experience we have. In modern industrial societies, however, several social contexts are agents of socialization with special importance.

The Family

The family is the most important agent of socialization. As we have seen, infants are almost entirely dependent on others to meet their needs, and this responsibility almost always falls on parents and other family members. Typically, the family stands as a child's entire social world, at least until the onset of schooling, and it remains central to social experiences throughout the life course (Riley, Foner, & Waring, 1988). The family is also crucial for transmitting culture from one generation to the next. Within countless family activities, parents teach their children various values, attitudes, and prejudices about themselves and others.

Family-based socialization is not all intentional. Children learn continuously from the kind of environment that adults create. Whether children learn to think of themselves as strong or weak, smart or stupid, loved or simply tolerated and whether they believe the world to be trustworthy or dangerous largely stem from this early environment.

Parenting styles vary from home to home, but research points to the importance of *attention* in the social development of children. Physical contact, verbal stimulation, and responsiveness from others have all been shown to foster intellectual growth (Belsky, Lerner, & Spanier, 1984).

Q: "Home is the place that, if you have to go there, they have to take you in." Robert Frost
SOCIAL SURVEY: The Student Chip software allows students to analyze the effect of class on a family's perception of the ideal child.

SOCIAL SURVEY: "How important is it that a child obey its parents well?" (*CHIP1 Social Survey Software*, OBEYS1; GSS 1973–83, N = 7,253)

SES	"Very important"	Other
High	17.1%	82.9%
Middle	30.6%	69.4%
Low	41.1%	58.9%

Another crucial function of the family is providing children with a social position. In other words, parents not only bring children into the physical world, they also place them in society in terms of class, religion, race, and ethnicity. In time, all these elements of identity become part of a child's self-concept. Of course, some aspects of social position may change over time, and in some societies more than others, but social standing at birth affects us throughout our lives.

Investigating the importance of social class to socialization, Melvin Kohn (1977) interviewed working-class and middle-class parents in the United States. He found that working-class parents stress behavioral conformity, while middle-class parents typically tolerate a wider range of behavior and show greater concern for the intentions and motivations that underlie their children's actions.

Kohn explained this difference in terms of the education and occupations common to parents in each category. Working-class parents usually have limited education and often hold jobs in which others closely supervise them. They therefore expect similar obedience and conformity in their children. By contrast, with more schooling, middle-class parents typically have jobs that provide more autonomy and encourage the use of imagination. These parents are therefore likely to inspire the same qualities in their children.

Class differences in socialization have long-term effects on children's ambition, partly explaining why middle-class children are more likely than working-class children to go to college themselves and are generally more confident of success in later careers (Wilson, 1959; Ballantine, 1989). In many ways, then, parents teach children to follow in their footsteps, and to adapt to the constraints or privileges of their inherited social positions.

Sociological research indicates that affluent parents tend to encourage creativity in their children while poor parents tend to foster conformity. While this general difference may be valid, parents at all class levels can and do provide loving support and guidance by simply involving themselves in their children's lives. Henry Ossawa Tanner's painting The Banjo Lesson *stands as a lasting testament to this process.*

Schooling

Schooling enlarges children's social world to include people with social backgrounds that differ from their own. As children experience social diversity, they learn the significance society attaches to people's race and sex and often act accordingly: Studies document the tendency of children to cluster together in play groups composed of one race and gender (Lever, 1978; Finkelstein & Haskins, 1983).

Formally, schooling teaches children a wide range of knowledge and skills. Beyond formal instruction, what sociologists call the *hidden curriculum* indirectly teaches children important cultural values. Activities such as spelling bees and sports encourage children to be competitive and to strive for success. Children also receive countless formal and informal messages that their society's way of life is morally good.

Family life is based on personal relationships. Thus school presents a new experience for children, with evaluations of skills like reading based on impersonal, standardized tests. Here, the emphasis shifts from *who they are* to *how they perform*. As such evaluations define personal abilities, they greatly affect how children view themselves. At the same time, the confidence or anxiety that children develop at home can have a significant effect on how well they perform in school (Belsky, Lerner, & Spanier, 1984).

Q: "I am always ready to learn, although I do not always like being taught." Winston Churchill

NOTE: Schooling emerged only with the declining economic value of children. "School" is derived from the Greek word *schole*, meaning "leisure employed in learning."

NOTE: The word "peer" is derived from the Latin *par*, meaning "equal."

NOTE: Television viewing has increased steadily, from 5 hours a day in 1960 to 6 hours daily in 1970; the average household now switches on a television for 7 hours a day. The mean daily viewing time for individuals is 4.3 hours. Women watch more than men do, people over 55 more than those under 25, and African Americans more than whites.

Q: "The medium is the message." Marshall McLuhan

School is probably children's first experience with rigid formality. The school day is organized as a strict time schedule, subjecting children to impersonal regimentation and fostering traits, such as punctuality, that will be expected by the large organizations that may employ them later in life.

Finally, schools further socialize children into culturally approved gender roles. As Raphaela Best (1983) points out, instructional activities for boys and girls often differ, so that boys engage in more physical activities and spend more time outdoors, while girls tend to be more sedentary, sometimes even helping the teacher with various housekeeping chores. Such gender distinctions continue through the college years. College women encounter pressure to select majors in the arts or humanities, while men are steered toward the physical sciences. Further, the informal campus culture often provides more support for the academic achievement of men, while making romantic life a central concern of women (Holland & Eisenhart, 1990).

Peer Groups

By the start of schooling, children have discovered another setting for activity in the **peer group**, *a social group whose members have interests, social position, and age in common*. A young child's peer group is generally neighborhood playmates; later, peer groups are composed of friends from school or other activities.

The peer group differs from the family and the school because it affords an escape from the direct supervision of adults. Of course, this freedom constitutes much of the attraction of peer groups to their members in the first place. With considerable independence, peer groups offer individuals valuable experience in forging social relationships on their own and developing a sense of themselves apart from their families. Peer groups also provide the opportunity to discuss interests that may not be shared by adults (such as styles of dress and popular music) as well as topics young people may wish to avoid in the presence of parents and teachers (such as drugs and sex).

The ever-present possibility of activity not condoned by adults is, no doubt, the reason parents have long expressed concern about who their children's friends are. In a rapidly changing society, peer groups often rival parents in influence, and the attitudes of parents and children may be separated by a "generation gap." The importance of peer groups typically peaks during adolescence, as young people begin to break away from their families and think of themselves as responsible adults. It is during this stage of life that young people often display anxious conformity to peers because this new identity and sense of belonging eases some of the apprehension provoked by breaking away from the family.

The conflict between parents and peers may be more apparent than real, however, for even during adolescence children remain strongly influenced by their families. Peers may guide short-term concerns such as style of dress and musical taste, but parents retain more sway over the long-term aspirations of their children. One study, for example, found that parents had more influence than even best friends on young people's educational aspirations (Davies & Kandel, 1981).

Finally, any neighborhood or school operates as a social mosaic composed of numerous peer groups. As we will see in Chapter 7 ("Groups and Organizations"), members tend to perceive their own peer group in positive terms while discrediting others. In fact, individuals are often influenced by opposing peer groups, and by peer groups they would like to join, as much as by those to which they belong. Such action represents what sociologists call **anticipatory socialization**, *the process of social learning directed toward gaining a desired position*. Later on, jobs are likely to provoke further anticipatory socialization. For instance, a young lawyer who hopes to eventually become a partner in her law firm may conform to the attitudes and behavior of other partners to promote her inclusion into this select group.

The Mass Media

The **mass media** are *impersonal communications directed to a vast audience*. The term "media" is derived from Latin meaning "middle," suggesting that media function to connect people. The development of *mass media* occurs as communications technology (first newspapers and, more recently, radio and television) spread information on a mass scale.

In the United States today, the mass media have an enormous effect on our attitudes and behavior. For this reason, they are an important component of the socialization process. Television, introduced in 1939, has rapidly become the dominant medium in the United States. In 1950, according to the Census Bureau, only 9 percent of U.S. households had one or more television sets. By 1992, this proportion had soared to 98 percent (while only 94 percent had telephones). Videocassette recorders (VCRs) have recently become the fastest growing appliance in history and are found in three-fourths of homes (up from 1 percent in 1980). One-fourth of all households also have video game equipment.

THE MAP: Generally, older, poorer, less educated, and unemployed people are the most avid television watchers; our society's primary newspaper readers include older people, but also those more affluent and better educated.

GLOBAL: Some 250,000 television sets are built each day, roughly equal to the number of people added to the earth's population. In global perspective, the mass media (especially television) are most widespread in industrial societies that change quickly; however, the media have the greatest effect when introduced to traditional societies—see the Chapter 24 opening about Brazil's Kaiapo Indians.

Q: "Today the television set, standard equipment in the American home, so blurs the distinction between the public environment and the privacy of the family that it is ever-present even as the tiniest babies are ushered into the social system." Rose K. Goldsen

Seeing Ourselves

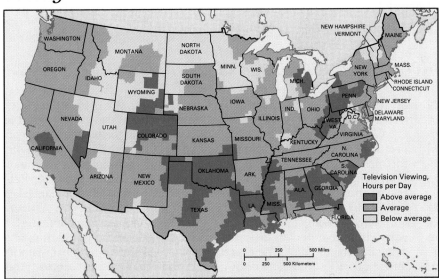

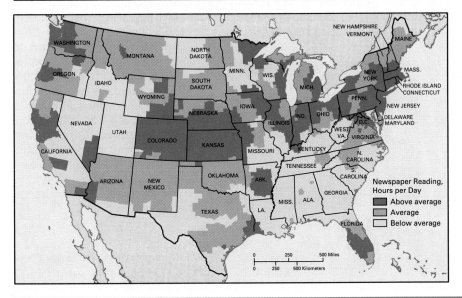

NATIONAL MAP 5–1
Television Viewing and Newspaper Reading Across the United States

The map on the left identifies U.S. counties in which television watching is above average, average, and below average. The map below provides comparable information for time devoted to reading newspapers. What do you think accounts for the high level of television viewing across much of the South and in rural West Virginia? Does your theory also account for patterns of newspaper reading?

From *American Demographics* magazine, August 1993, p. 64. Reprinted with permission. © 1993, *American Demographics* magazine, Ithaca, New York. Data from Young and Rubicam, San Francisco.

The latest statistics show that the average household turns on a television for seven hours each day (U.S. Bureau of the Census, 1993). Before most children learn to read, watching television has become a regular routine, and young girls and boys spend almost as many hours in front of a television as they do in school. Indeed, television consumes as much of children's time as interacting with parents (Singer & Singer, 1983; APA, 1993).

The United States contains one television set for every person, indicating our national fascination with "the tube." But television viewing is not spread equally throughout the country. National Map 5–1 identifies the areas in which television use is greatest, and compares this with regions where people spend the most time reading newspapers.

Comedian Fred Allen once quipped that we call television a "medium" because it is rarely well done.

SOCIAL SURVEY: "How many hours a day do you watch TV?"
(*STUDENT CHIP Social Survey Software*, TVHRS1; GSS 1975–91,
N = 14,034)

SES	0–1	2–3	4+
High	36.4%	49.5%	14.1%
Middle	22.7%	47.2%	30.0%
Low	15.9%	41.9%	42.2%

All	24.5%	46.6%	29.0%

High SES only, N = 3,295

RAC/ETH	0–1	2–3	4+
Afri Amer	18.3%	53.0%	28.7%
Latino	28.6%	55.4%	16.1%
Wh Anglo	37.5%	49.2%	13.3%

SOCIAL DIVERSITY

When Advertising Offends: Another Look at Aunt Jemima

Commercial advertisers want to sell products. However, some old ad campaigns are becoming counter-productive because they offend their audience by portraying categories of people in inaccurate and unfair ways.

A century ago, the vast majority of consumers in the United States were white people, and many were uneasy with growing racial and cultural diversity. Businesses commonly exploited this discomfort, depicting various categories of people in ways that were clearly condescending. In 1889, for example, a pancake mix first appeared featuring a servant mammy named "Aunt Jemima." Although somewhat modernized, this logo is widely used in the mass media, and the product continues to hold a commanding share of its market. Likewise, the hot cereal "Cream of Wheat" is still symbolized by the African-American chef Rastus, and "Uncle Ben" is familiar to millions of households as a brand name for rice. But to many people, use of such caricatures—which, after all, originally depicted the black slaves or servants of white people—is racially insensitive at best.

Changes in advertising have occurred in recent decades in all the mass media. The stereotypical Frito Bandito, long familiar to older television viewers, was abandoned in 1971 by Frito-Lay (a company, ironically, whose first product was a corn chip invented by a Latino living in San Antonio). The characterization of Latinos as bandits or outlaws, embodied in the bumbling cartoon figure of Frito Bandito, discredited an entire segment of the

population. A host of other such images have also disappeared as businesses in the United States confront a new reality: the growing voice and financial power of minorities, who represent a market worth one-half trillion dollars a year. Taken together, Americans of African, Latino, and Asian descent represent 20 percent of the population and may constitute a national majority by the end of the next century. And, just as important, the share of the minority population that is affluent is steadily increasing.

Businesses are responding to the growing financial power of minorities. In the last ten years businesses have doubled their spending on advertising aimed at African Americans to about $1 billion annually. The results of this policy shift have been encouraging for the businesses involved—far higher sales— and pleasing to people who have historically found little to like in commercial advertising.

SOURCES: Based on Westerman (1989) and Simpson (1992).

For a variety of reasons, television (as well as all the media) have provoked plenty of criticism. One issue involves various alleged biases in television programming. Liberal critics maintain that television shows are conservative since they rarely challenge the status quo (Gans, 1980; Parenti, 1986). For example, television has traditionally portrayed men and women according to cultural stereotypes, showing men in positions of power and women as mothers or subordinates (Cantor & Pingree, 1983; Ang, 1985; Brown, 1990). Similarly, television shows have long favorably portrayed affluent people, while casting less affluent people (Archie Bunker is the classic example) as ignorant and wrong-headed. In addition, although racial and ethnic minorities tend to watch more television than others, until recently they have been all but absent from programming. The successful 1950s comedy "I Love Lucy," for example, was turned down by major television producers because it featured Desi Arnaz—a Cuban—in a starring role. Even today, television often portrays

DIVERSITY: Rothman, Powers, & Rothman (1993) surveyed 146 top-grossing films since 1946 and found that, prior to the 1960s, Hollywood portrayed the two sexes in conventional gender terms. Since then, however, popular films have shown women in ways supportive of the women's movement, while casting men in more negative roles.
DIVERSITY: Concern about portrayal of African Americans in the

mass media began with "Amos 'n' Andy" in the 1950s, as critics compared this show to old minstrel shows of the 19th century. During the 1970s, J. J. on "Good Times" continued this portrayal with his memorable exclamation "dy-no-myte"; today, "Martin" isn't much better, showing African Americans as libido-driven. Generally, say critics, black people appear in too many sitcoms and display too much bafoonery. (Cf. Hammer, 1992)

FIGURE 5–2
The Politics
of the Hollywood Elite

A recent survey of 104 television writers and producers shows that, on four social issues, the Hollywood elite is far more liberal than U.S. adults taken as a whole. This discrepancy suggests why, in the eyes of critics, Hollywood does not support what conservatives consider "American family values."

SOURCE: The Center for Media and Public Affairs and National Opinion Research Center (1992).

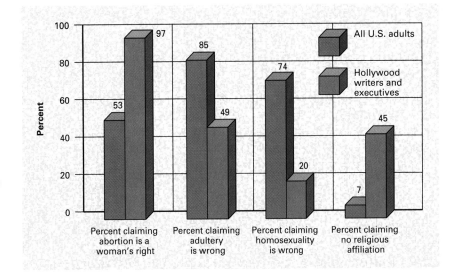

minorities in ways attractive to white middle-class people (as in the affluent African-American family on "The Cosby Show").

The number of people of African and Latino descent making appearances in all the mass media has increased mainly because advertisers recognize the marketing advantages of appealing to these large segments of U.S. society (Wilson & Gutiérrez, 1985). The box on page 140 offers a critical look at the problem of media advertising portraying minorities in terms of negative stereotypes.

Another dimension of television in which significant change is taking place is news reporting. Recognition of social diversity is far greater than even a decade ago, due, in large measure, to personnel policies. One-third of all television reporters are now women, almost double the proportion found a generation ago, and 8 percent are African Americans, an increase from less than 1 percent in 1970 (Hess, 1991). The effect of greater inclusiveness is that television now presents a broader view of our society.

On the other side of the debate, conservative critics argue that the television and film industries offer a biased picture of the world because they are dominated by a "cultural elite" who are far more liberal than the population as a whole (Rothman, Powers, & Rothman, 1993). Figure 5–2 provides the results of one survey of top television writers and producers that appears to support this contention (Woodward, 1992).

In sum, television and the other mass media have enriched our lives in many ways, contributing to socialization by bringing us a wide range of entertaining and educational programming. Furthermore, television and films increase our understanding of diverse cultures and provoke discussion of current issues. At the same time, the power of the media—especially television—to shape how we think will ensure that the mass media remain controversial.

Beyond the agents of socialization we have described, other spheres of life play a part in social learning. For most people in the United States, these include religious organizations, the workplace, the military, and social clubs. As a result, socialization inevitably involves inconsistencies as we absorb different information from various sources. In the end, socialization is not a simple learning process; it is a complex balancing act in which we encounter a wide range of ideas as we try to form our own distinctive personalities and world views.

SOCIALIZATION
AND THE LIFE COURSE

Although childhood learning has particular importance to human development, socialization continues throughout our lives. A long view over the life course reveals that social experience is organized according to age. This perspective results in the distinctive stages people in industrial societies commonly understand as childhood, adolescence, adulthood, and, as a final phase of adulthood, old age.

Q: "Television is chewing gum for the eyes." Frank Lloyd Wright
NOTE: The first U.S. president seen on a television broadcast was Harry Truman.
DIVERSITY: Clairol Corporation reports that television shows twice as many blonde women as there are in real life—and infinitely more good-looking people. . . .

Q: "One cannot love lumps of flesh, and little infants are nothing more." Samuel Johnson
Q: "In medieval society, the idea of childhood did not exist. As soon as the child could live without the constant solicitude of the mother, his nanny, or his cradle-rocker, he belonged to adult society." Philippe Ariès

Childhood

Charles Dickens's classic novel *Oliver Twist* is set in London early in the nineteenth century, when the Industrial Revolution was bringing sweeping changes to English society. Oliver's mother died in childbirth, and, barely surviving himself, he began life as an indigent orphan, "buffeted through the world—despised by all, and pitied by none" (Dickens, 1886:36; orig. 1837–39). Knowing little pleasure in his early years, Oliver Twist began a life of toil and drudgery in a workhouse, laboring long hours to pay for filthy shelter and meager food.

We think of *childhood*—roughly the first twelve years of life—as a time of freedom from the burdens of the adult world. But until roughly a century ago, as *Oliver Twist* testifies, children in Europe and North America carried most of the burdens of adults and were far more vulnerable. Historian Philippe Ariès (1965) explains that, once they were able to survive without constant care, medieval Europeans expected children to take their place in the world as working adults. Although "child labor" is now scorned in the United States, this pattern persists in poor societies, especially in Africa and Asia. Global Map 5–1 shows that work is commonplace for children in poor societies of the world.

The notion of young children working long hours may be startling because our common sense suggests that youngsters are very different from adults—inexperienced in the ways of the world and biologically immature. But much of this difference is rooted in culture. Because technologically complex societies are more affluent, they do not require everyone to work. In addition, such societies extend childhood to allow time for learning many complex skills required for adult activities. These facts prompt us to define children and adults in contrasting ways, with "irresponsible" children looked after by "responsible" adults (Benedict, 1938). In global perspective, however, this pattern is far from an inevitable consequence of biological maturation. Much the same variability holds true regarding sexuality: The childhood sexuality our society finds disturbing poses little problem for the Melanesian cultures of southwest New Guinea.

Recently, sociologists and psychologists have found evidence that our conception of childhood is changing yet again. Especially among affluent families, childhood is contracting as children contend with mounting pressures to dress, speak, and act like adults (Elkind, 1981; Winn, 1983). Evidence of what is called the "hurried child" pattern includes ten-year-old boys in designer jeans and girls of the same age adorned with jewelry, makeup, and perfume. The mass media and rock and roll music now interject into a child's world sexuality, violence, and a host of other issues that were considered only a generation ago to be strictly the realm of adults. Pressure to grow up quickly is also exerted in the home because greater numbers of mothers work, requiring children to fend more for themselves. Furthermore, many of today's parents are delighted if their children can read, spell, or discuss world events before their peers can do these things, believing that these abilities indicate greater intelligence. Schools also encourage rapid maturation by emphasizing achievement, which reflects positively on both parents and teachers. In the view of child psychologist David Elkind (1981), the "hurried child" pattern is a detrimental change in U.S. society's conception of childhood because children are confronting issues that they lack the experience to understand, let alone successfully resolve.

Adolescence

As industrialization gradually thrust childhood forward as a distinct stage of life, adolescence emerged as a buffer stage between childhood and adulthood. Corresponding roughly to the teenage years, this is the stage of life for learning various specialized skills required for adult life.

We generally associate adolescence with emotional and social turmoil; young people experience conflict with their parents and struggle to develop their own, separate identities. Since adolescence commonly occurs at the onset of puberty, we may be tempted simply to attribute the social turmoil of this stage of life to physiological changes. However, thinking sociologically, the instability of adolescence also reflects inconsistencies in socialization. For example, adults expect adolescents to be increasingly self-reliant and responsible for themselves, yet adults view teenagers as unequipped for the occupations that would give them financial independence.

The adult world also gives adolescents mixed messages about sexuality. The mass media often encourage sexual activity, while parents urge restraint; for their part, schools provide instruction in "safe sex" even as they hand out condoms to students (Gibbs, 1993). Consider, also, that an eighteen-year-old may face the adult responsibility of going to war, while simultaneously being denied the right to drink alcohol.

DATA FILE: The entangled interactions of the two sexes in the socialization process are explored by R. D. Laing in the *Data File*.

Q: "Youth, to some extent, lacks experience." Spiro T. Agnew

Q: "Youth is wholly experimental." Robert Louis Stevenson

Q: "Only a moment, a moment of strength, of romance, of glamour . . . a flick of sunshine upon a strange shore." Joseph Conrad

DATA FILE: The *Data File* provides a summary of comparative research by Ruth Benedict on adolescence.

Q: "When I was fourteen my father was so ignorant I could hardly stand to have the old man around. But when I got to be twenty-one, I was astonished at how much he had learned in seven years." Mark Twain

Window on the World

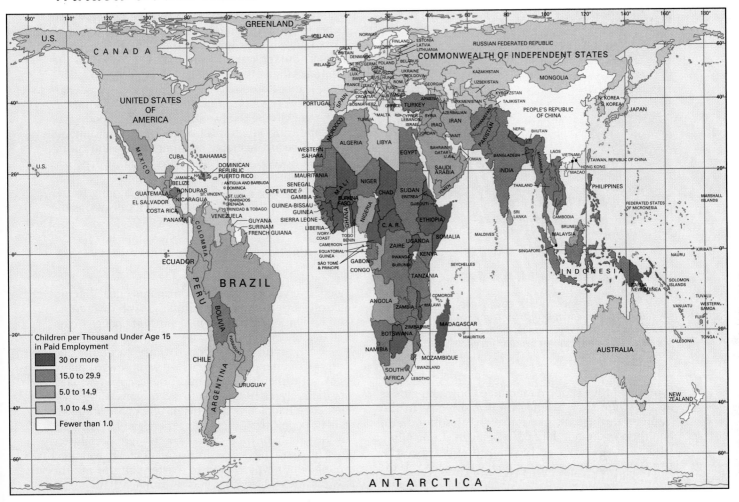

GLOBAL MAP 5–1 Child Labor in Global Perspective

Industrialization has the effect of prolonging childhood and discouraging children from engaging in work and other activities deemed suitable only for adults. Thus child labor is relatively uncommon in the United States and other industrial societies. In less industrialized nations of the world, however, children form a vital economic asset, and they typically begin working as soon as they are able.

From *Peters Atlas of the World* (1990).

As is true of all stages of life, the experience of adolescence varies according to social background. Young people from working-class families often move directly from high school into the adult world of work and parenthood. Wealthier families, however, provide the resources for their children to attend college and perhaps graduate school, which may extend adolescence into the late twenties and even the thirties. For different reasons, of course, poverty also can extend adolescence. Especially in the inner cities, many young minorities cannot attain full adult standing because jobs are not available or accessible.

Further evidence that adolescence is not simply a matter of biological maturation is provided by cross-cultural research. When anthropologist Margaret Mead studied the Samoan Islanders in the 1920s, she

Q: "The powerful play goes on and you may contribute a verse."
Walt Whitman

Q: "Let me be myself and then I am satisfied. I know that I am a woman with inward strength and plenty of courage." Anne Frank

NOTE: "Adult" is derived from the Latin word *adultus*, meaning "grown."

Q: "From birth to age 18, a girl needs good parents; from 18 to 35, she needs good looks; from 35 to 55, she needs a good personality; from 55 on she needs cash." Sophie Tucker

Adolescence is a time of mixed messages about the world. On the one hand, parents may instruct teens about the need for sexual restraint; the mass media, on the other hand, extol sex as a means to promote countless products.

found that they simply pronounced boys and girls as adults when they reached their mid-teens. In the Samoan culture, unlike our own, childhood and adulthood were not defined as being in strong opposition to each other, so the transition between the two stages of life was not dramatic (M. Mead, 1961; orig. 1928).

Adulthood

At the age of thirty-five, Eleanor Roosevelt, one of the most widely admired women in the United States, wrote in her diary: "I do not think I have ever felt so strangely as in the past year . . . all my self confidence is gone and I am on the edge, though I never was better physically I feel sure" (quoted in Sheehy, 1976:260). Perhaps Eleanor Roosevelt was troubled by the attention her husband was paying to another, younger woman; perhaps as she looked into the future, she could not see what challenges or accomplishments might bring further satisfaction to her life. But as she struggled with what today we might call a "midlife crisis," there was much that she could not foresee. Her husband, Franklin Delano Roosevelt,

was shortly to become disabled by poliomyelitis, although his rising political career would ultimately lead to the White House. And Eleanor herself would become one of the most active and influential of all First Ladies. After her husband's death, she would remain outspoken and serve as a delegate to the United Nations.

Eleanor Roosevelt's life illustrates two major characteristics of *adulthood*, which our culture defines as beginning during the twenties. First, adulthood is the period during which most of life's accomplishments typically occur, including pursuing careers and raising families. Second, especially in later adulthood, people reflect upon what they have been able to accomplish, perhaps feeling great satisfaction or coming to the sobering realization that many of the idealistic dreams of their youth will never come true.

Early Adulthood

Personalities are largely formed by the start of adulthood. Even so, a marked shift in an individual's life situation—brought on by unemployment, divorce, or serious illness—can result in significant change to the self (Dannefer, 1984).

Early adulthood—from twenty to about age forty—is generally a time of working toward many goals set earlier in life. Young adults learn to manage for themselves a host of day-to-day responsibilities that had been handled by parents or others. Beginning a family, people draw on the experience of having lived in the family of their parents, although as children they may have perceived little of adult life. In addition, young adults typically try to master patterns of intimate living with another person who may have just as much to learn.

Early adulthood is also a period of juggling conflicting priorities: parents, partner, children, and work (Levinson et al., 1978). Women, especially, face up to the difficulty of "doing it all," since our culture still confers on them primary responsibility for child rearing and household chores, even if they have demanding occupations outside the home (Hochschild, 1989).

Middle Adulthood

Young adults usually cope optimistically with such tensions. But in middle adulthood—roughly age forty to sixty—people begin to sense that marked improvements in life circumstances are less likely. The distinctive quality of middle adulthood is greater reflection as people assess their achievements in light of earlier

DATA FILE: A look at the baby-boom generation turning 40 is highlighted in the *Data File*.

NOTE: Figure 14–1 provides data about the rapidly increasing proportion of people in the United States over the age of sixty-five.

GLOBAL: The social standing of the elderly in industrial societies is lower than in agrarian societies, a pattern explained by more rapid change. Hoyt Alverson reports that, for the Tswana in southern Africa, the word "aging" means "seeing with one's own eyes." Similarly, "knowledge" is defined as "remembering things past," so that elders are the wisest of all for the Tswana.

expectations. They become more aware of the fragility of health, which the young typically take for granted. Some women who have already spent many years raising a family find middle adulthood especially trying. Children grow up and require less attention, husbands become absorbed in their careers, leaving these women with spaces in their lives that they find difficult to fill. Women who divorce during middle adulthood may experience serious financial problems (Weitzman, 1985). For all these reasons, an increasing number of women mark middle adulthood by returning to school. Doing so is not always easy, especially for those who have spent several decades working primarily in the home. Even so, the trend is for more women entering midlife to enroll in school and, subsequently, enter the labor force (U.S. Bureau of the Census, 1993).

Growing older means that both men and women face the reality of physical decline, but our society's traditional socialization has made this prospect more painful for women. Because good looks are defined as more important for women, wrinkles, weight gain, and loss of hair are more traumatic for them. Men, of course, have their own particular difficulties. Some confront limited achievement knowing that their careers are unlikely to change for the better. Others, realizing that the price of career success has been neglect of family or personal health, harbor uncertainties about their self-worth even as they bask in the praise of others (Farrell & Rosenberg, 1981). Women, too, who devote themselves single-mindedly to careers in early adulthood, may experience regrets about what they have given up in pursuit of occupational success.

Eleanor Roosevelt's midlife crisis may well have involved some of the personal transitions we have described. But her story also illustrates the fact that some people passing midlife have yet to experience their greatest productivity and personal satisfaction. Socialization in our youth-oriented culture has convinced many people (especially the young) that life ends at forty. As the average life expectancy in the United States has increased, however, such limiting notions about growing older have begun to change. Major transformations may become less likely, but the potential for learning and new beginnings continues all the same.

Old Age

Old age comprises the later years of adulthood and the final stage of life itself, beginning about the mid-sixties. Here again, societies attach different meanings to a time of life. Among preindustrial people, advancing age typically affords great influence and respect. As explained in Chapter 14 ("Aging and the Elderly"), this privilege is linked to the fact that, in traditional societies, elderly people control most of the land and other wealth; moreover, since their societies change slowly, older people amass a lifetime of wisdom (Sheehan, 1976; Hareven, 1982).

In industrial societies, however, younger people typically work apart from the family, becoming more independent of their elders. Rapid change and our society's youth orientation promote a definition of what is older as unimportant or even obsolete. To younger people, then, the elderly appear unaware of new trends and fashions, and their knowledge and experience often seem irrelevant.

No doubt, however, this anti-elderly bias will diminish as the proportion of older people steadily increases. The share of our population over sixty-five has almost tripled since the beginning of this century, so that today more men and women are elderly than in their teens. Moreover, life expectancy is still increasing, so more and more individuals will live well past the age of sixty-five. Looking to the next century, the Census Bureau (1992) predicts that the fastest-growing segment of our population will be those over eighty-five, whose numbers will soar sixfold.

At present, the final phase of socialization differs in an important way from learning earlier in life. For the young, advancing age typically means entering new roles and assuming new responsibilities. Old age, however, involves the opposite process: leaving roles that have long provided us with both satisfaction and social identity. Retirement is one example. Although retirement sometimes fits the common image of being a period of restful activity, it often means the loss of familiar routines and sometimes outright boredom. Like any life transition, retirement demands that a person learn new and different ways of living while simultaneously *un*learning patterns and routines that guided earlier stages in life. A nearly equal transition is required of the nonworking wife or husband who must change routines to accommodate a partner now spending more time in the home.

Dying

Historically, death was caused by disease and accident during any stage of life, because living standards were lower and medical technology was primitive. Today, however, almost 85 percent of people in the United States die after the age of fifty-five (U.S. Bureau of the

Q: "Just as I choose a ship to sail in or a house to live in, so I choose a death for my passage from life." Seneca, Roman philosopher (4 B.C.E.–65 C.E.)
RESOURCE: A discussion of cultural variation with regard to death is E. Bendann's *Death Customs: An Analysis of Burial Rites* (New York: Knopf, 1930).

Q: "All my possessions for a moment of time." The last words of Queen Elizabeth I
Q: "Beware ye as ye pass by,
    As ye be now so once was I.
    As I be now, so must ye be.
    Prepare for death and follow me."
Eighteenth-century New England epitaph

continue. The fourth stage, *resignation*, is often accompanied by psychological depression. Finally, adjustment to death is completed in the fifth stage, *acceptance*. At this point, rather than being paralyzed by fear and anxiety, the person whose life is coming to an end sets out to use constructively whatever time remains.

As the proportion of women and men in old age increases, we can expect our culture to become more comfortable with the idea of death. Today, people in the United States and elsewhere discuss death more widely than they did decades ago, and many individuals view death as preferable to months or even years of suffering and social isolation in hospitals and rest homes. In addition, married couples are more likely to anticipate their own deaths in discussion and estate planning. This openness may ease somewhat the disorientation that usually accompanies the death of a spouse—a greater problem for women, who usually outlive their husbands.

The Life Course: An Overview

This brief examination of the life course leads to two general conclusions. First and more important, although the essential traits of each stage of life are linked to the biological process of aging, they are mostly socially constructed. For this reason, people in other societies may experience a stage of life quite differently (or not at all). Second, each stage of the life course presents characteristic problems and transitions that involve learning something new and, in many cases, unlearning what has become familiar.

Two additional points are worth noting. Just because societies organize human experience according to age in no way negates the effects of other forces, such as class, race, ethnicity, and gender. Thus, the general patterns we have described are all subject to further modification as they apply to various categories of people. Finally, people's life experiences also vary depending on when, in the history of the society, they were born. A **cohort** is *a category of people with a common characteristic, usually their age.* Age-cohorts are likely to have been influenced by the same major events and thus display similar reactions to particular issues (Riley, Foner, & Waring, 1988). Women and men born early in this century, for example, were shaped by two world wars and economic depression unknown to many of their children. In this sense, too, general patterns pertaining to the life course will vary.

The infancy of photography in the 1840s was also a time of deadly epidemics in the United States, with between one-third and one-half of children dying before the age of ten. Many grieving parents rushed to capture their dead children on film. The post-mortem photograph, in most cases the only picture ever taken of someone, suggests a far greater acceptance of death during the nineteenth century than is found today. In this century, death has become rare among the young so that dying has been separated from life as a grim reality that people do their best to deny.

Census, 1993). Therefore, members of our society reaching old age can look forward to decades of life. But the reality is also that socialization in old age cannot be separated from eventual physical decline and the recognition of impending death.

After observing many dying people, Elisabeth Kübler-Ross (1969) concluded that death is an orderly transition involving five distinct stages. Because our culture tends to ignore the reality of death, a person's first reaction to the prospect of death is usually *denial*. The second stage is *anger*; here a person begins to accept the idea of dying but views it as a gross injustice. In the third stage, anger gives way to *negotiation*, the attitude that death may not be inevitable and that one might strike a bargain with God allowing life to

GLOBAL: Death practices display remarkable cultural variety. Societies burn, bury, leave out in the weather, embalm, smoke, and even pickle their dead members. Similarly funerals are times for laughter, tears, revelry, solemnity, fighting, or even sex—depending on the culture.

RESOURCE: Global death patterns are described by Sergei Kan, *Symbolic Immortality: The Tlingit Potlatch of the Nineteenth Century*, Washington, DC: Smithsonian, 1989; and Peter Metcalf and Richard Huntington, *Celebrations of Death: The Anthropology of Mortuary Ritual*, Cambridge University Press, 1991.

The demand by guards that new prisoners publicly disrobe is more than a matter of issuing new clothing; such a degrading ritual is also the first stage in the process by which the staff in a total institution attempts to break down an individual's established social identity.

RESOCIALIZATION: TOTAL INSTITUTIONS

A final type of socialization, experienced by more than 1 million people in our society at any one time, involves being confined—often against their will—in prisons or mental hospitals. This is the special world of the **total institution**, *a setting in which people are isolated from the rest of society and manipulated by an administrative staff.*

According to Erving Goffman (1961), total institutions have three distinctive characteristics. First, staff members supervise all spheres of daily life, including where residents (often called "inmates") eat, sleep, and work. Second, a rigid routine subjects inmates to standardized food, sleeping quarters, and activities. Third, formal rules govern how inmates behave in every setting, from how they dress to when and where they may smoke.

Total institutions impose such regimented routines with the goal of **resocialization**, *radically altering an inmate's personality through deliberate control of the environment.* The power of a total institution to achieve resocialization lies in forcibly segregating people from other sources of social experience. An inmate's isolation is achieved through physical barriers such as walls and fences topped with barbed wire and guard towers, barred windows, and locked doors. (This is, no doubt, why we commonly say that someone is *at* college but *in* prison.) Cut off in this way, the inmate's entire world can be manipulated by the administrative staff to produce lasting change—or at least immediate compliance—in the inmate.

Resocialization is a two-part process. First, the staff tries to erode the new inmate's established identity through what Goffman describes as "abasements, degradations, humiliations, and profanations of self" (1961:14). For example, the staff requires inmates to surrender personal possessions, including clothing and grooming articles normally used to maintain a person's distinctive appearance. In their place, the staff gives inmates standard-issue items that make everyone look alike. In addition, inmates all have standard haircuts, so that, once again, what was personalized becomes uniform. The staff also processes new inmates by searching, weighing, fingerprinting, and photographing them and by assigning them a serial number. Once inside the walls, individuals surrender the right to privacy; guards may demand that inmates undress publicly as part of the admission procedure and routinely monitor their living quarters. Such "mortifications of self" undermine the identity and autonomy that the inmate brings to the total institution from the outside world.

The second part of the resocialization process includes efforts to systematically build a different self. The staff manipulates inmate behavior through a system of rewards and punishments. The privilege of keeping a book or making a telephone call may seem trivial to outsiders, but, in the rigid environment of the total institution, they can be powerful motivations toward conformity. Noncompliance carries the threat that privileges will be withdrawn or, in more serious cases, that the inmate will suffer physical pain or further isolation from other inmates. The duration of confinement in a prison or mental hospital also depends on an inmate's display of cooperation with the rules and regulations of the institution. Goffman emphasizes that conformity involves inward motivation as well as outward behavior: That is, the staff may still punish a person who lives by the rules, in other words, for having "an attitude problem."

Resocialization can cause considerable change in an inmate. The rebuilding of the self is extremely complex, however, and no two people will respond to any resocialization program in precisely the same way (Irwin, 1980). Some inmates may experience "rehabilitation" or "recovery" (meaning change that is officially approved), while others may gradually sink into an embittered state because of the perceived injustice of their incarceration. Furthermore, over a considerable period of time, the rigidly controlled environment of a total institution may render people completely *institutionalized,* incapable of the independence required for living in the outside world.

SOCIALIZATION AND HUMAN FREEDOM

Through socialization, society shapes how we think, feel, and act. If society has this power over us, in what sense are we free? This chapter ends with a closer look at this important question.

Children and adults throughout North America delight in watching the Muppets, stars of television and film. Observing the expressive antics of Kermit the Frog, Miss Piggy, and the rest of the troupe, one almost believes that these puppets are real rather than mere objects animated by movement that originates backstage. The sociological perspective suggests that human beings are like puppets in that we, too, respond to the backstage guidance of society—indeed, more so, in that society affects not just our outward behavior but our innermost feelings.

But our analysis of socialization also reveals where the puppet analogy breaks down. Viewing human beings as the puppets of society leads into the trap that Dennis Wrong (1961) has called an "oversocialized" conception of the human being. In part, Wrong wishes to remind us that we are biological as well as social creatures, a point emphasized by Sigmund Freud, who identified inherent human drives. To the extent that we are imbued with drives or a particular temperament, we can never be entirely the puppets of society.

The fact that human beings may be subject to *both* biological and social influences, however, hardly advances the banner of human freedom. Here is where the ideas of George Herbert Mead are of crucial importance. Mead recognized the power of society to act on human beings, but he argued that human spontaneity and creativity (conceptualized in the I) empower us to continually *act back* on society. Thus the process of socialization affirms the human capacity for choice as we reflect, evaluate, and act. Therefore, although we may initially seem like puppets, Peter Berger points out that unlike puppets, "we have the possibility of stopping in our movements, looking up and perceiving the machinery by which we have been moved" (1963:176). Doing this, we can act to change our own behavior by, so to speak, jerking down on the strings. If our pull is powerful enough, we can even change society itself. As Berger adds, the more we utilize the sociological perspective to study how the machinery of our society works, the freer we become.

SUMMARY

1. Socialization is the process through which social experience confers human qualities on an individual. For society as a whole, socialization is the means by which one generation transmits culture to the next.

2. A century ago, people thought most human behavior was guided by biological instinct. Today, we understand human behavior to be primarily a product of nurture rather than nature. So-called human nature is actually the capacity to create variable cultural patterns.

3. The permanently damaging effects of social isolation reveal the importance of social experience to human development.

4. Sigmund Freud envisioned the human personality as composed of three parts. The id represents general human drives (the life and death instincts), which Freud claimed were innate. The superego embodies cultural values and norms internalized by individuals. Competition between the needs of the id and the restraints of the superego are mediated by the ego.

5. Jean Piaget believed that human development reflects both biological maturation and increasing social experience. He asserted that socialization involves four major stages of development: sensorimotor, preoperational, concrete operational, and formal operational.

6. Lawrence Kohlberg applies Piaget's approach to the issue of moral development. Individuals, he claims, first judge rightness in preconventional terms, according to their individual needs. Next, conventional moral reasoning takes account of the attitudes of parents and the norms of the larger society. Finally, postconventional moral reasoning provides for a philosophical critique of society itself.

7. Beginning with a critique of Kohlberg's reliance on male subjects, Carol Gilligan discovered that gender affects moral reasoning. Females, she claims, look to the effect of decisions on relationships, while males rely more on abstract standards of rightness.

8. To George Herbert Mead, socialization is based on the emergence of the self, which he viewed as partly autonomous (the I) and partly guided by society (the me). Mead claimed that, beginning with imitation, self develops through play and games and eventually recognizes the "generalized other."

9. Charles Horton Cooley used the term "looking-glass self" to underscore that self is influenced by how we think others respond to us.

10. Commonly the first setting of socialization, the family has the greatest influence on a child's attitudes and behavior.

11. School exposes children to greater social diversity and introduces the experience of impersonal evaluation. In addition to formal lessons, schools informally teach a wide range of cultural ideas, including attitudes about competitiveness and achievement.

12. Members of youthful peer groups are subject to adult supervision less than in the family or in school. Peer groups take on great significance among adolescents.

13. The mass media, especially television, have a considerable impact on the socialization process. The average U.S. child now spends as much time watching television as attending school.

14. As is true of each phase of the life course, the characteristics of childhood are socially constructed. Medieval Europeans scarcely recognized childhood as a stage of life. In industrial societies such as the United States, people define childhood as being much different from adulthood.

15. Members of our society consider adolescence, the transition between childhood and adulthood, to be a difficult period. This is not the case in all societies, however.

16. During early adulthood, socialization involves settling into careers and raising families. Later adulthood is marked by considerable reflection about initial goals in light of actual achievements.

17. In old age, people make many transitions, including retirement. While the elderly typically enjoy high prestige in preindustrial societies, industrial societies are more youth oriented.

18. Members of industrial societies typically fend off death until old age. Adjustment to the death of a spouse (an experience more common to women) and acceptance of one's own death are part of socialization for the elderly.

19. Total institutions such as prisons and mental hospitals have the goal of resocialization—radically changing the inmate's personality.

20. Socialization demonstrates the power of society to shape our thoughts, feelings, and actions. Yet, as free humans, we also have the capacity to act back on society and, in so doing, shape ourselves and our world.

KEY CONCEPTS

anticipatory socialization the process of social learning directed toward gaining a desired position

cohort a category of people with a common characteristic, usually their age

concrete operational stage Piaget's term for the level of human development at which individuals first perceive causal connections in their surroundings

ego Freud's designation of a person's conscious attempt to balance pleasure-seeking drives and the demands of society

formal operational stage Piaget's term for the level of human development at which individuals use highly abstract thought to imagine alternatives to reality

generalized other George Herbert Mead's term for widespread cultural norms and values we use as references in evaluating ourselves

id Freud's designation of the human being's basic drives

looking-glass self Cooley's assertion that self is based on how others respond to us

mass media impersonal communications directed toward a vast audience

peer group a social group whose members have interests, social position, and age in common

personality a person's fairly consistent patterns of thinking, feeling, and acting

preoperational stage Piaget's term for the level of human development in which individuals first use language and other symbols

resocialization deliberate control of an environment intended to radically alter an inmate's personality

self George Herbert Mead's term for a dimension of personality composed of an individual's self-awareness and self-conception

sensorimotor stage Piaget's term for the level of human development in which individuals experience the world only through sensory contact

socialization the lifelong social experience by which individuals develop human potential and learn patterns of their culture

superego Freud's designation of the presence of culture within the individual in the form of internalized values and norms

total institution a setting in which people are isolated from the rest of society and manipulated by an administrative staff

CRITICAL-THINKING QUESTIONS

1. What do cases of social isolation teach us about the importance of social experience to human development?

2. Describe the two sides of the nature-nurture debate. In what sense are human nature and nurture not opposed to one another?

3. In what ways does a comparison of the theories of Freud, Piaget, Kohlberg, Gilligan, and Mead suggest that research findings build on one another? In what ways do they seem incompatible?

4. Consider how humans are, and are not, free in the midst of organized society.

SUGGESTED READINGS

Classic Sources

George Herbert Mead. *Mind, Self, and Society from the Standpoint of a Social Behaviorist*. Charles W. Morris, ed. Chicago: University of Chicago Press, 1962; orig. 1934.
> Compiled after Mead's death by his students, this paperback presents Mead's analysis of the development of self.

Philippe Ariès. *Centuries of Childhood: A Social History of Family Life*. New York: Vintage Books, 1965.
> This book is a classic study of the history of the family, exploring changing conceptions of childhood.

Contempory Sources

Judith Rich Harris and Robert Liebert. *Infancy and the Child*. Englewood Cliffs, N.J.: Prentice Hall, 1992.

Grace Craig. *Human Development*. 7th ed. Englewood Cliffs, N.J.: Prentice Hall, 1995.
> Many dimensions of socialization are discussed in these two books. The first focuses on infancy; the second surveys the entire life course.

George Gilder. *Life After Television*. New York: W.W. Norton, 1990.
> This critique casts the mass media, and especially television, as politically antidemocratic and culturally vulgar.

George H. Hill, Lorraine Raglin, and Charles Floyd Johnson. *Black Women and Television*. New York: Garland, 1990.
> This celebration of the television accomplishments of African-American women notes interesting "firsts."

Lisa A. Lewis. *Gender Politics and MTV: Voicing the Difference*. Philadelphia: Temple University Press, 1990.
> This analysis of MTV spotlights women entertainers and argues that women have gained considerable power in the world of rock music and videos.

Carl N. Degler. *In Search of Human Nature: The Decline and Revival of Darwinism in American Social Thought*. New York: Oxford University Press, 1991.
> The nature-nurture debate has a long history among intellectuals in the United States. This book provides a fascinating look at the changing fortunes of the concept of human nature.

Mary Ellen Colton and Susan Gore, eds. *Adolescent Stress: Causes and Consequences*. Hawthorne, N.Y.: Aldine de Gruyter, 1991.
> These fourteen essays provide an overview of what is known about adolescent stress; they include information about successful intervention programs.

Harriette Pipes McAdoo and John Lewis McAdoo, eds. *Black Children: Social, Educational, and Parental Environments*. Beverly Hills, Calif.: Sage Publications, 1985.
> This collection of essays explores the distinctive elements of socialization among African-American children.

Joseph P. Goodwin. *More Man than You'll Ever Be: Gay Folklore and Acculturation in Middle America*. Bloomington: Indiana University Press, 1989.
> Gay people are deprived of many of the social supports that heterosexuals take for granted. As a result, a gay folklore has emerged that is influential in the social development of millions of people.

Mary Ellen Brown, ed., *Television and Women's Culture: The Politics of the Popular*. Newbury Park, Calif.: Sage Publications, 1990.
> This collection of thirteen essays examines various dimensions of how television involves women, both as actors and as audience.

Dorothy C. Holland and Margaret A. Eisenhart. *Educated in Romance: Women, Achievement, and College Culture*. Chicago: University of Chicago Press, 1990.
> This book examines the role of gender in socialization on the college campus.

Carol Gilligan. *In a Different Voice: Psychological Theory and Women's Development*. Cambridge, Mass.: Harvard University Press, 1982.
> This influential book points out that the social development of women and men differs in important respects.

Global Sources

Margaret Mead. *Coming of Age in Samoa*. New York: Dell, 1961; orig. 1928.
> While still in her early twenties, Margaret Mead completed what is probably the best-known book in anthropology, in which she argues that the problems of adolescence are socially created rather than rooted in biology.

Derek Freeman. *Margaret Mead and Samoa: The Making and Unmaking of an Anthropological Myth*. Cambridge, Mass.: Harvard University Press, 1983.
> As a counterpoint to Mead's work, Derek Freeman suggests that human development is not free from biological influence.

David I. Kertzer and K. Warner Schaie, eds. *Age Structuring in Comparative Perspective*. Hillsdale, N.J.: Lawrence Erlbaum, 1989.
> This book contains fourteen essays that investigate how people organize their lives by age in various societies. It offers historical and cross-cultural material on the links between age, power, and retirement.

M. E. J. Wadsworth. *The Imprint of Time: Childhood, History, and Adult Life*. New York: Clarendon Press, 1991.
> Long-term studies of cohorts are difficult and, therefore, rare in social science. This book reports on an ongoing study of more than five thousand men and women living across Britain, all born in 1946, and interviewed periodically since then.

Pierre Auguste Renoir, *Le Moulin de la Galette*, 1876. Paris, Musée d'Orsay. Art Resource, New York.

DATA FILE: An outline of Chapter 6, as well as supplemental lecture material and topics for class discussion, appear in the *Data File*.

NOTE: The chapter-opening art is Auguste Renoir's *Dancing at the Moulin de la Galette*.

Q: "When I use a word, it means just what I choose it to mean—nothing more nor less." Humpty Dumpty

Q: "All the world's a stage,
And all the men and women merely players.
They have their exits and their entrances,
And one man in his time plays many parts."
William Shakespeare (*As You Like It*, V)

Social Interaction in Everyday Life

*H*arold and Sybil are on their way to another couple's home in an unfamiliar section of the city (Tannen, 1990:62). They are now late and, for the last twenty minutes, they have traveled in circles looking for a street they cannot seem to find. Harold, who is driving, is getting angrier and angrier the longer he keeps looking for Beechwood Terrace. Sybil, sitting next to him, is also annoyed. Both realize that the evening is off to a bad start.

Here we have a simple case of two individuals sharing the experience of getting lost on the way to visit some friends. But there is more here than we initially realize. Harold and Sybil are lost in more ways than one, being unable to understand why they are growing more and more enraged at their situation and at each other.

Consider the predicament, first, from Harold's point of view. Like most

men, Harold cannot tolerate becoming lost. The longer he drives around, as Harold sees it, the more he feels incompetent in handling what should be a simple situation. Sybil is seething, too, but for a different reason. She cannot figure out why Harold does not simply pull over and ask someone where Beechwood Terrace is. If she were driving, she fumes to herself, they already would have arrived and would now be comfortably settled with drink in hand.

Why don't men like to ask for directions? Because men value their independence, they are uncomfortable asking for help (and also reluctant to accept it). To ask someone for assistance is an admission of inadequacy, and, to make matters worse, it is an acknowledgement that others know something they don't. If it takes Harold a few more minutes to find Beechwood Terrace on his own—and secure

Q: "A status, as distinct from the individual who may occupy it, is simply a collection of rights and duties." Ralph Linton (1937:113)

Q: "It is crucial that responsibilities, resources, and rights be assigned to statuses, not to particular individuals. For only by doing so can societies establish general and uniform rules or norms that will apply to many and diverse individuals who are to occupy the statuses . . ." Melvin Tumin (1985:21)

his self-respect in the process—he thinks the bargain is a good one.

If men pursue self-sufficiency and are sensitive to hierarchy, women are more attuned to others and strive for connectedness. Asking for help is right to Sybil because, from her point of view, sharing information reinforces social bonds. Requesting directions seems as natural to Sybil as continuing to search on his own appears to Harold. But the two people are unlikely to resolve their situation since neither one understands the other's different point of view.

Analyzing such examples of everyday life is the focus of this chapter. We begin by presenting many of the building blocks of common experience and continue by exploring the almost magical way in which face-to-face interaction generates reality. Throughout, the discussion highlights the importance of gender to our everyday experiences.

The central concept is **social interaction**, *the process by which people act and react in relation to others.* Social interaction is the key to creating the reality we perceive. And we interact according to particular social guidelines.

SOCIAL STRUCTURE: A GUIDE TO EVERYDAY LIVING

Earlier chapters have described the organization of social life. Chapter 3 ("Culture") examined the symbolic web that unites members of a society into one or more cultures, based on shared norms and values. Chapter 4 ("Society") explained that the social world is shaped by its technological development, its economic system, and its particular world view and moral beliefs. Chapter 5 ("Socialization") showed how individuals gain humanity only as they engage others in society.

Despite this evidence of society's power over us, our way of life celebrates individual autonomy, so that we resist the idea that we are part of any kind of system. Instead, we emphasize personal responsibility for behavior and highlight the unique elements of our personalities. But behaving in patterned ways does not threaten our individuality. On the contrary, social structure in everyday life actually promotes our individuality in two key ways.

First, and more basic, in the absence of the surrounding society, we would never become fully human at all, as Chapter 5 ("Socialization") explained. This development occurs as we blend our unique qualities with the values and norms of the larger culture to produce distinct personalities.

Second, as members of an ongoing society, we rely on social structure to make sense out of any social situation. The world can be disorienting, even frightening, when behavioral guidelines are unclear. Entering an unfamiliar setting generally inhibits us from freely expressing ourselves. Stepping onto the campus for the first time, for example, we feel understandable anxiety at not knowing quite what to expect. We look to others, therefore, for clues about what sort of behavior is appropriate. Only after we understand the rules that apply to the situation are we likely to feel comfortable enough to "act like ourselves."

This is not to deny that social structure places some constraints on everyday life. Established social patterns inevitably discourage the unconventional. Traditional values and norms in North America, for example, still reflect the expectation that males will be dominant and assertive and that females will adopt a subordinate and supportive stance. By pressuring each of us to fit neatly into "masculine" or "feminine" categories, social structure gives us identity at the cost of narrowing our range of thought and action.

Keep in mind, however, that social structure *guides* but never *rigidly determines* human behavior. A saxophone is designed to make only certain kinds of sounds, just as "fatherhood" is a design that encourages a certain kind of behavior. Like musical instruments, however, any social arrangement can be "played" creatively in a wide range of ways.

STATUS

One of the basic building blocks of social interaction is **status**, which refers to *a recognized social position that an individual occupies.* The sociological meaning of the term "status" differs markedly from its everyday meaning of "prestige." In common usage, a bank president has more "status" than a bank teller. Sociologically, however, both "bank president" and "bank teller" are statuses because they represent socially defined positions, even though one does confer more power and prestige than the other.

Every status involves various rights, duties, and expectations. The statuses people occupy thus guide the way they act in any setting. In the college classroom, for example, professors and students have distinctive, well-defined responsibilities. Similarly, family interaction turns on the interplay of mother, father, daughters, sons, and others. In all these situations,

Q: "*Ascribed* statuses are those which are assigned to individuals without reference to their innate differences or abilities. They can be predicted and trained for from the moment of birth. The *achieved* statuses are . . . those requiring special qualities [and] are left open to be filled through competition and individual effort." Ralph Linton (1937:115)

NOTE: As applied to everyday life, ascribed status and achieved status are actually two endpoints on a continuum.
NOTE: The issue of status consistency—the degree of consistency in social ranking—is discussed in Chapter 10 ("Social Class in the United States").

statuses define connections among people, which is why, in the case of families, we commonly call others "relations." A status, then, defines who and what we are *in relation to* others.

Status is also a key component of social identity. Occupational status, for example, is a major part of most people's self-concept and is quickly offered as part of a social introduction. The importance of such a status is also evident in the way people continue to identify themselves in terms of their life's work long after retirement.

Status Set

We all occupy many statuses simultaneously. The term **status set** refers to *all the statuses a person holds at a given time.* A girl may be a *daughter* to her parents, a *sister* to her siblings, a *friend* to members of her social circle, and a *goalie* to others on her hockey team. Just as status sets branch out in different directions, they also change over the life course. A child grows into an adult, a student becomes a lawyer, and people marry to become husbands and wives, sometimes becoming single again as a result of divorce or death. Joining an organization or finding a job enlarges our status set; withdrawing from activities diminishes it. Individuals gain and lose dozens of statuses over a lifetime.

Ascribed and Achieved Status

Sociologists analyze statuses in terms of how people obtain them. An **ascribed status** is *a social position that someone receives at birth or involuntarily assumes later in life.* Examples of ascribed statuses include being a daughter, a Latino, a teenager, or a widower. Ascribed statuses are matters about which people have little or no choice.

By contrast, an **achieved status** refers to *a social position that someone assumes voluntarily and that reflects personal ability and effort.* Among achieved statuses in the United States are being an honors student, an Olympic athlete, a wife, a computer programmer, a member of Phi Beta Kappa, or a thief. In each case, the individual has a definite choice in the matter.

Most statuses actually involve a combination of ascription and achievement. That is, people's ascribed statuses influence the statuses they are likely to achieve. Children cannot be lawyers until they become adults. Moreover, the adults who achieve a law degree are likely to have an ascribed trait in common: being born into relatively privileged families. More generally, any person of a privileged sex, race, ethnicity, or age has far more opportunity to realize desirable achieved

In any rigidly ranked setting, no interaction can proceed until people assess each other's social standing. In traditional, rural villages throughout India, caste position is a master status; therefore, individuals alert others to their social identity by wearing caste marks on their foreheads.

statuses than does someone without such advantages. By contrast, many less desirable statuses, such as criminal, welfare recipient, or drug addict are more easily "achieved" by people disadvantaged by ascription.

Master Status

Some statuses are more significant than others. A **master status** is *a status that has exceptional importance for social identity, often shaping a person's entire life.* In our society, a person's occupation is often a master status since it suggests something about our social background, education, and income. Similarly, being "a Rockefeller" or "a Kennedy" is enough by itself to push an individual into the limelight.

NOTE: The case of Dr. Charles Drew, used in past editions to illustrate race as a master status, was incorrect. Drew was readily treated by a hospital after his injury in a 1950 auto accident. Drew's sister reports: "That story is not true. They did everything they could to save him. We have tried to get this matter corrected for years." (*New York Times*, October 6, 1991)

NOTE: "Status" has two Latin roots: *sta* is derived from *stare*, meaning "to stand"; *tus* means "the use of." Thus, status is literally "the use of standing." The term "role" appears to be derived from the French word *rôle*, meaning a roll (of paper) that contains an actor's part.

SOCIAL DIVERSITY

Physical Disability as Master Status

The experiences of the following two women help to explain how a physical disability can become a master status, defining an individual. The first is twenty-nine-year-old Donna Finch, who holds a master's degree in social work and lives with her husband and son in Muskogee, Oklahoma. She is also blind.

Most people don't expect handicapped people to grow up, they are always supposed to be children. . . . You aren't supposed to date, you aren't supposed to have a job, somehow you're just supposed to disappear. I'm not saying this is true of anyone else, but in my own case I think I was more intellectually mature than most children, and more emotionally immature. I'd say that not until the last four or five years have I felt really whole.

Rose Helman is an elderly woman living near New York City. She suffers from spinal meningitis and is also blind.

You ask me if people are really different today than in the '20s and '30s. Not too much. They are still fearful of the handicapped. I don't know if fearful is the right word, but uncomfortable at least. But I can understand it somewhat; it happened to me. I once asked a man to tell me which staircase to use to get from the subway out to the street. He started giving me directions that were confusing, and I said, "Do you mind taking me?" He said, "Not at all." He grabbed me on the side with my dog on it, so I asked him to take my other arm. And he said, "I'm sorry, I have no other arm." And I said, "That's all right, I'll hold onto the jacket." It felt funny hanging onto the sleeve without the arm in it.

SOURCE: Orlansky and Heward (1981).

In a negative sense, serious disease can also operate as a master status. Sometimes even lifelong friends avoid cancer patients or people with acquired immune deficiency syndrome (AIDS) simply because of their illness. Most societies of the world also limit the opportunities of women, whatever their abilities, making gender, too, a master status.

Finally, we sometimes dehumanize people with physical disabilities by perceiving them only in terms of their impairments. In the box, two people with physical disabilities describe this problem.

ROLE

Besides status, a second major component of social interaction is **role**, *behavior expected of someone who holds a particular status.* Ralph Linton (1937) described a role as the dynamic expression of a status: Individuals *hold* a status and *perform* a role. In other words, various obligations and privileges attached to a status call out a particular role. The student role, for example, involves obligations of attending classes and completing assignments, and the privilege of being able to devote much of one's time to personal enrichment through academic study.

Cultural norms involve *role expectations*, suggesting how a person holding a particular status ought to act. As noted in Chapter 3 ("Culture"), however, real culture only approximates ideal culture, so that actual role performance varies according to an individual's unique personality. In addition, cultural diversity in a society ensures that people will perform comparable roles differently.

Like a status, a role is relational, organizing our behavior toward other people. The parent's role, for example, centers on responsibilities toward a child. Correspondingly, the role of daughter or son consists

NOTE: Barbara Laslett (1978) points out that role conflict and role strain were probably more pronounced in the Middle Ages than they are today, because families not only raised children but were productive, educational, and religious units.

NOTE: The Families and Work Institute found that 25% of respondents (employees of Fortune 1000 companies) had refused overtime for family reasons; 24% refused travel for the same reason; 19% refused relocations; 10% refused promotions. (The *Wall Street Journal*, July 22, 1991:B1)

largely of obligations toward a parent. Other examples of such role pairs include wives and husbands, baseball pitchers and catchers, physicians and patients, and performers and members of an audience.

Role Set

Because individuals occupy many statuses simultaneously—a status set—they perform multiple roles. The total number of roles usually exceeds the number of statuses because each status can require an individual to carry out several roles in relation to various other people.

Robert Merton (1968) introduced the term **role set** to identify *a number of roles attached to a single status.* Figure 6–1 illustrates the status set and corresponding role sets of one individual. Four statuses are presented, each linked to a different role set. First, this woman occupies the status of "wife," with corresponding roles toward her husband ("conjugal roles" such as confidante and sexual partner), with whom she would share a "domestic role" toward the household. Second, she also holds the status of "mother," with routine responsibilities toward her children (the "maternal role") and activities in various organizations such as the PTA (the "civic role"). Third, as a professor, she interacts with students (the "teaching role") as well as with other academics (the "colleague role"). Fourth, her work as a researcher (the "laboratory role") provides the data she uses in her publications (the "author role"). Of course, Figure 6–1 lists only some of this person's status and role sets, since an individual generally occupies several dozen statuses at one time, each linked to a role set. This woman might be, additionally, a daughter caring for aging parents and a coach of a girl's soccer team.

Role Conflict and Role Strain

The personal performances required by an array of role sets often make heavy demands on an individual's time and energy. This holds especially true for members of industrial societies, who routinely assume many statuses and an even greater number of roles. As mothers working outside the home can testify, carrying out the role of parent as well as the role of breadwinner taxes both physical and emotional strength. Sociologists thus recognize **role conflict** as *incompatibility among roles corresponding to two or more different statuses.*

We experience role conflict when we find ourselves pulled in various directions while trying to respond to the many statuses we hold. Some aspiring politicians, for example, may decide not to run for

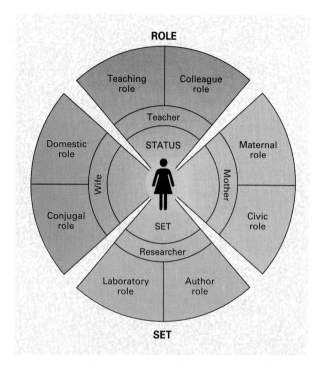

FIGURE 6–1 Status Set and Role Set

national office because the demands of such a campaign would impoverish family life; in other cases, ambitious people may defer having children or choose to remain childless in order to build their careers as quickly as possible.

Even the many roles linked to a single status may make competing demands on us. The concept of **role strain** refers to *incompatibility among roles corresponding to a single status.* A plant supervisor may enjoy being friendly with other workers. At the same time, however, the supervisor's responsibility for everyone's performance requires maintaining some measure of personal distance from each employee. In short, performing the roles attached to even one status may involve a "balancing act" of trying to fulfill various duties and obligations.

One strategy for minimizing role conflict is "insulating" roles from one another (Merton, 1968). Instead of downplaying a particular role, people "compartmentalize" their lives so that they perform roles linked to one status at one time and place and carry out roles corresponding to another status elsewhere at some other time. A familiar example of compartmentalizing is leaving the job "at work." Many individuals are successful in closing the door on their occupations

Q: "Status and role serve to reduce the ideal patterns for social life to individual terms." Ralph Linton (1937:114)

DATA FILE: William J. Goode's strategies for reducing role strain are included in the *Data File*.

RESOURCE: Luigi Pirandello's writing is wonderfully sociological, as the excerpt on this page suggests.

Q: "For some types of role exit, society has coined a term to denote exiters: divorcée, retiree, recovered alcoholic, widow, alumnus. This is usually the case for exits that are common and have been occurring for a long time. . . . In addition to these institutionalized exits, however, there are numerous exits that are simply referred to with the prefix "ex": ex-doctor, ex-executive, ex-nun, ex-convict . . ." Helen Rose Fuchs Ebaugh (1988:1)

We learn from what we see. Thus each one of us selects others as role models, *people whose behavior we wish to emulate. The National Civil Rights Museum in Memphis, Tennessee, contains this sculpture of Rosa Parks, a woman of color and a seamstress, who boarded a public bus on December 1, 1955, in Montgomery, Alabama. Although she took her place in the section reserved for African Americans, the driver ordered her to give up her seat to a white man. When she courageously refused, police arrested her. The episode led to the Montgomery Bus Boycott, which lasted for a year and finally brought an end to racial segregation on that city's buses.*

when they go home to assume the responsibilities of spouse or parent.

Another strategy for reducing role conflict is to define some roles as more important than others. A new mother, for instance, might devote most of her efforts to parenting and put her career on hold, at least for the present. Resolving role conflict in this way, however, depends on being able to afford not to work—an option not always available.

Setting priorities also reduces the strain among roles linked to a single status. Adopting this approach, a person concentrates on one particular role (from among the many tied to the status), while downplaying another with which it conflicts. A father, for example, may decide that maintaining a close and trusting relationship with his child is more important than enforcing cultural norms as a disciplinarian.

Role Exit

Recent research has focused on *role exit*, the process by which people disengage from social roles that have been central to their lives. Helen Rose Fuchs Ebaugh

(1988) began to study this issue after she herself left the life of a Catholic nun to become a university sociologist. Studying a range of "exes," including ex-nuns, ex-doctors, ex-husbands, and ex-alcoholics, Ebaugh identified elements common to the process of "becoming an ex."

According to Ebaugh, people initiate the process of role exit by reflecting critically on their existing lives and raising doubts about their ability or willingness to persist in a certain role. As they imagine alternative roles, they ultimately reach a turning point when they decide to pursue a new life. In adopting an "ex role," we see how a past role can continue to influence our lives even after the role has been formally abandoned. But "exes" face the challenge of building a new sense of self, which emerges in changes in outward appearance and behavior (an ex-nun, for example, begins to wear stylish clothing and makeup).

"Exes" must also grapple with changing responses from those who may have known them in their earlier role as well as those who do not realize how new and unfamiliar their present role may be. Forming new relationships is especially challenging for an "ex," who must learn many new social skills. Ebaugh reports, for example, that nuns who begin dating after decades in the church are often startled to learn that sexual norms are now vastly different from those they knew as teenagers.

In modern society, fewer and fewer people expect to live within one job or one marriage. The study of role exit, therefore, seems likely to gain importance.

THE SOCIAL CONSTRUCTION OF REALITY

More than fifty years ago, the Italian playwright Luigi Pirandello skillfully applied the sociological perspective to social interaction. In *The Pleasure of Honesty*, Angelo Baldovino—a brilliant man with a checkered past—enters the fashionable home of the Renni family and introduces himself in a most peculiar way:

> Inevitably we construct ourselves. Let me explain. I enter this house and immediately I become what I have to become, what I can become: I construct myself. That is, I present myself to you in a form suitable to the relationship I wish to achieve with you. And, of course, you do the same with me. (1962:157–58)

This curious introduction suggests that, while social interaction is guided by status and role, each human being has considerable ability to shape what

RESOURCE: Deborah Tannen's article on gender and communication is included among the contemporary selections in the companion reader, *Seeing Ourselves*.

Q: "There is always a rivalry between the spontaneous definitions of the situation made by the member of the organized society and the definitions that society has provided for him." W.I. Thomas (1923:42)

NOTE: Arlene Kaplan Daniels recalls that a strategy of women's organizations in the early 1970s was to jot a personal note on a letter to a member of Congress. The staff thus thought the official knew the writer and passed the letter along for personal attention. Often, she explained, the official did not realize she or he didn't know the writer and sometimes even answered the letter.

happens moment to moment. "Reality," then, is not as fixed as we may think. The social world does have an objective existence, of course; it has existed long before we were born, affects us throughout our lives, and continues after we die. But, in everyday terms, society is nothing more than the behavior of countless people. If society affects individuals, then individuals creatively shape society (Berger & Luckmann, 1967).

The phrase **social construction of reality** identifies *the process by which people creatively shape reality through social interaction*. This idea stands at the foundation of the symbolic-interaction paradigm in sociology, as described in earlier chapters. In this context, Angelo Baldovino's remark suggests that, especially in an unfamiliar situation, quite a bit of "reality" remains unclear in everyone's mind. Pirandello's character will simply use his ability to "present himself" in terms that he thinks suit his purposes. As others do the same, a complex reality emerges, although few people are so "up front" about their deliberate efforts to foster an impression.

Social interaction, then, amounts to a process of negotiating reality. Usually, interaction results in at least some agreement about how to define a situation. But participants rarely share precisely the same perception of events. Subjective realities vary because social interaction brings together people with different interests and intentions, each of whom is seeking a somewhat different situational outcome.

Steering reality in this way is sometimes referred to as "street smarts." In his biography *Down These Mean Streets*, Piri Thomas recalls moving to a new apartment in New York City's Spanish Harlem, which placed him squarely on the turf of the local street gang. Returning home one evening, young Piri found himself cut off by Waneko, the gang's leader, who was flanked by a dozen others.

> "Whatta ya say, Mr. Johnny Gringo," drawled Waneko.
>
> *Think man,* I told myself, *think your way out of a stomping. Make it good.* "I hear you 104th street coolies are supposed to have heart," I said. "I don't know this for sure. You know there's a lot of streets where a whole 'click' is made out of punks who can't fight one guy unless they all jump him for the stomp." I hoped this would push Waneko into giving me a fair one. His expression didn't change.
>
> "Maybe we don't look at it that way."
>
> *Crazy, man. I cheer inwardly, the* cabron *is falling into my setup....* "I wasn't talking to you," I said. "Where I come from, the pres is president 'cause he got heart when it comes to dealing."

> Waneko was starting to look uneasy. He had bit on my worm and felt like a sucker fish. His boys were now light on me. They were no longer so much interested in stomping me as seeing the outcome between Waneko and me. "Yeah," was his reply....
>
> I knew I'd won. Sure, I'd have to fight; but one guy, not ten or fifteen. If I lost, I might still get stomped, and if I won I might get stomped. I took care of this with my next sentence. "I don't know you or your boys," I said, "but they look cool to me. They don't feature as punks."
>
> I had left him out purposely when I said "they." Now his boys were in a separate class. I had cut him off. He would have to fight me on his own, to prove his heart to himself, to his boys, and most important, to his turf. He got away from the stoop and asked, "Fair one, Gringo?" (1967:56–57)

This situation reveals the drama—sometimes subtle, sometimes savage—by which human beings creatively build reality. There are limits, of course, to what even the most skillful and persuasive personality can achieve. Should a police officer have come upon the fight that ensued between Piri and Waneko, both young men might well have ended up in jail. Not everyone enters a negotiation with equal standing; the police officer would probably have the last word simply because of a status that holds greater power than that of the other two players (Molotch & Boden, 1985).

The Thomas Theorem

By displaying his wits and boxing with Waneko until they both tired, Piri Thomas won acceptance that evening and became one of the group. U.S. sociologist W. I. Thomas (1966:301; orig. 1931) succinctly expressed this insight in what has come to be known as the **Thomas theorem**: *Situations we define as real become real in their consequences.*

Applied to social interaction, Thomas's insight means that although reality is initially "soft" as it is fashioned, it can become "hard" in its effects. In the case of Piri Thomas, having succeeded in defining himself as worthy, this young man *became* worthy in the eyes of his new comrades.

Ethnomethodology

We have explained that, as symbolic-interactionists see it, reality is not something "out there"; rather, reality is created by people engaging one another. But how, exactly, do we define reality for ourselves? Answering this question is the objective of *ethnomethodology*, a specialized approach within the symbolic-interaction paradigm.

Cultures frame reality in different ways. This man lay on the street in Bombay, India, for several hours and then quietly died. In the United States, such an event would probably have provoked someone to call the rescue squad. In a poor society in which death on the streets is a fact of everyday life, however, many Indians responded not with alarm but with simple decency by stopping to place incense on his body before continuing on their way.

The term itself has two parts: the Greek *ethno* refers to people and how they understand their surroundings; "methodology" designates a set of methods or principles. Combining them makes **ethnomethodology,** *the study of the way people make sense of their everyday lives.*

Ethnomethodology was devised in the 1950s by Harold Garfinkel, a sociologist dissatisfied with the then widespread view of society as a broad "system" with a life of its own (recall the approach of Emile Durkheim, described in Chapter 4, "Society"). Garfinkel wanted to explore how we build understandings of countless social situations (Heritage, 1984). The task of understanding everyday life is extremely complex, however; we can do it only by taking for granted many ideas about how the world operates.

Think, for a moment, about what we assume about human behavior when driving onto a freeway. We expect that traffic on our side of the road will flow in a particular direction, at a predictable and steady speed, and that other drivers will display at least some basic caution and courtesy. Although we may not be

consciously aware of these conventions, they are extremely important to us. To see how significant they are, imagine the disruption caused by any driver who violates them.

Garfinkel recognized that a useful technique for exposing the unacknowledged patterns of everyday life is to *break the rules.* We can, he suggested, tease out how people build a reality by deliberately ignoring conventional rules and observing how people respond. Although he never advocated doing this on the highway, Garfinkel (1967) and his students did refuse to "play the game" in less threatening situations. Some students entered stores and insisted on bargaining for items, a strategy that brought to the surface assumptions about how shopping is carried out. Others recruited people into simple games (like tic-tac-toe), only to intentionally flout the rules, an action that made clear our assumptions about fair play. Still others initiated conversations while slowly moving closer and closer to the other person. The discomfort that ensued revealed that we generally conform to unspoken rules about the use of space.

One measure of the importance of the rules of everyday behavior is how disturbed people become when the rules are broken. Garfinkel's students were met with bewilderment and often anger by their "victims," as shown in the following simple exchange (1967:44):

Acquaintance:	"How are you?"
Student:	"How am I in regard to what? My health, my finances, my school work, my peace of mind, my . . ."
Acquaintance:	[now red in the face and suddenly out of control] "Look! I was just trying to be polite. Frankly, I don't give a damn how you are."

The provocative character of ethnomethodology, coupled with its focus on commonplace experiences, has led some sociologists to view it as less-than-serious research. Even so, ethnomethodology has succeeded in heightening awareness of many unnoticed patterns of everyday life.

Reality Building in Global Perspective

Taking a broader view of reality construction, people do not build everyday experience "out of thin air." In part, what we see in our surroundings depends on our interests: Lovers discover romance in the night sky,

THE MAP: The data in this map did not result from a national survey. Rather, a profile of people joining Elvis fan clubs was compared to a demographic profile of each of roughly 3,000 U.S. counties to generate the data shown here. Communities in which Elvis remains a cultural icon are very much like the one in which Elvis, himself, grew up: small towns with a main street for shopping and surrounding farms or mills.

Seeing Ourselves

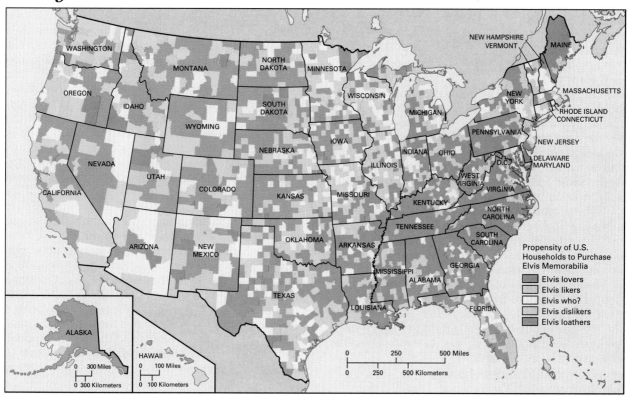

NATIONAL MAP 6–1 Where Are the Elvis Fans?

Elvis Presley died in 1977. But millions of people across the United States are members of fan clubs that celebrate the career of the first rock and roll superstar. This map identifies counties across the country in which Elvis fans are most likely—and least likely—to live. Examining the map, what can you say about the counties that are home to Elvis fans? In which regions of the nation does "the King" live on? Is his following stronger in urban areas or rural counties?

From *American Demographics* magazine, August 1993, p. 64. Reprinted with permission. © 1993 *American Demographics* magazine, Ithaca, New York. Data from DICI, Bellaire, Tex.

while scientists perceive the same stars as hydrogen atoms fusing into helium. Social background also directs our perceptions, since we build reality using elements in the surrounding culture. For this reason, residents of, say, Spanish Harlem encounter the world somewhat differently from the way people living on the affluent East Side of Manhattan experience it.

To offer another example, we would not expect people across the United States to embrace the same heroes or to share the same tastes in music. Take the case of Elvis Presley fans: National Map 6–1 shows that people who purchase Elvis memorabilia live in certain types of communities.

In global perspective, reality varies even more, so that social experiences common to, say, women in Saudi Arabia would seem bizarre to many women in the United States. Similarly, social reality changes over time. People living in Japan a century ago forged social worlds very different from those typical of that nation today.

Because reality is grounded in the surrounding culture, how we interpret any object or action depends on time and place. The meanings people attach to the two sexes, to stages of the life course, or even to the days of the week vary from culture to culture. Supporting this conclusion, Wendy Griswold (1987) asked people from different societies—the West Indies, Great Britain, and the United States—to interpret several novels. She found that the messages her respondents drew from what they read depended on the basic "blueprint" of their culture.

Similarly, JoEllen Shively (1992) screened "western" films to an audience composed of both white men of European descent and Native-American men. Both categories claimed to enjoy the films but saw different meanings in them. The white men interpreted the films as praising rugged individuals for striking out toward the West with the intention of imposing their will on nature. Native-American men, by contrast, saw in the same films a celebration of land and nature apart from any human ambitions.

The general conclusion is that what people see in a book, a film—or anything else—is guided by their distinctive social world. This fact poses a significant challenge to people everywhere as societies engage one another in more and more ways.

Finally, in light of global cultural diversity, do people everywhere respond to their surroundings with the same feelings? Researchers who have conducted cross-cultural investigation of human emotions conclude that the answer is yes—and no—as the box on pages 164–65 explains.

DRAMATURGICAL ANALYSIS: "THE PRESENTATION OF SELF"

Erving Goffman (1922–1982) developed a fascinating and enduring approach to studying everyday life. He observed that people socially constructing reality behave very much like actors performing on a stage. If we imagine ourselves in the role of a director scrutinizing the action in some situational "theater," we can engage in **dramaturgical analysis**, *the investigation of social interaction in terms of theatrical performance.*

Dramaturgical analysis offers a fresh look at two now-familiar concepts. In this theoretical scheme, a status mirrors a part in a play, and a role serves as a script, supplying dialogue and action for each of the characters. In any setting, then, each of us is both an actor and part of the audience. Goffman called the intricate interaction that makes up everyday life the **presentation of self**, *the effort of an individual to create specific impressions in the minds of others.* This process, sometimes termed *impression management*, contains several distinctive elements (Goffman, 1959, 1967).

Performances

As we present ourselves in everyday situations, we convey information—consciously and unconsciously—to others. In theatrical terms, then, we engage in a *performance*. A performance includes an individual's dress (costume), any objects carried along (props), and a tone of voice and gestures (manner). In addition, people key their performances to a specific setting (stage). We may joke loudly on a sidewalk, for example, but assume a more reverent manner upon entering a church. To turn the argument around, individuals commonly design settings, such as a home or office, to assist a performance by invoking the desired reactions in others.

Consider, for example, how a physician's office guides social interaction and conveys appropriate information to an audience of patients. Physicians enjoy considerable prestige and power in the United States, which is evident to patients immediately upon entering the doctor's office. First, the physician is nowhere to be seen. Instead, in what Goffman describes as the "front region" of the setting, the patient encounters a receptionist who functions as a gatekeeper, deciding if and when the patient can meet the physician. A simple survey of the doctor's waiting room, with patients (often impatiently) waiting to gain entry to the inner sanctum, leaves little doubt that the medical team controls events.

The physician's private office and examination room constitute the "back region" of the setting. Here the patient confronts a wide range of props, such as medical books and framed degrees, that reinforce the impression that the physician, and not the patient, has the specialized knowledge necessary to guide their interaction. In the office, the physician usually remains seated behind a desk—the larger and grander the desk, the greater the statement of power—while the patient is provided with only a chair.

The physician's appearance and manner convey still more information. The usual costume of white lab coat may have the practical function of keeping clothes from becoming soiled, but its social function is to let others know at a glance the physician's status. A stethoscope around the neck or a black medical bag in hand has the same purpose. A doctor's highly technical terminology—occasionally necessary but frequently mystifying—also emphasizes the hierarchy in the situation. The use of the title "Doctor" by patients who, in turn, are frequently addressed only by their first names also underscores the physician's dominant position. The overall message of a doctor's performance is clear: "I will help you only if you allow me to take charge."

NOTE: Encountering others, interaction usually proceeds with "small talk," meaning that little is at stake. Only when sufficient information has been exchanged to guide more substantial discussion does "big talk" begin.

Q: "Words and images are like shells, no less integral parts of nature than the substances they cover, but better addressed to the eye and more open to observation." George Santayana, 1922

Nonverbal Communication

Novelist William Sansom describes a fictional Mr. Preedy—an English vacationer on a beach in Spain:

> He took care to avoid catching anyone's eye. First, he had to make it clear to those potential companions of his holiday that they were of no concern to him whatsoever. He stared through them, round them, over them—eyes lost in space. The beach might have been empty. If by chance a ball was thrown his way, he looked surprised; then let a smile of amusement light his face (Kindly Preedy), looked around dazed to see that there were people on the beach, tossed it back with a smile to himself and not a smile *at* the people. . . .
>
> . . . [He] then gathered together his beach-wrap and bag into a neat sand-resistant pile (Methodical and Sensible Preedy), rose slowly to stretch his huge frame (Big-Cat Preedy), and tossed aside his sandals (Carefree Preedy, after all). (1956; quoted in Goffman, 1959:4–5)

Through his conduct, Mr. Preedy offers a great deal of information about himself to anyone caring to observe him. Notice that he does so without uttering a single word. This illustrates the process of **nonverbal communication**, *communication using body movements, gestures, and facial expressions rather than speech.*

We use our bodies to convey information to others, as suggested by the common phrase *body language*. Facial expressions form the most significant element of nonverbal communication. As noted earlier, smiling and other facial gestures form an almost universal language to express basic emotions like pleasure, surprise, and anger. Further, people express particular shades of meaning with their faces according to the demands of the situation. We distinguish, for example, between the deliberate smile of Kindly Preedy on the beach, a spontaneous smile of joy at seeing a friend, a pained smile of embarrassment, and a full, unrestrained smile of self-satisfaction we often associate with the "cat who ate the canary."

Eye contact is another important element of nonverbal communication. Generally, we use eye contact to initiate social interaction. Someone across the room "catches our eye," for example, sparking a conversation. Avoiding the eyes of another, by contrast, discourages communication. Hands, too, speak for us. Common hand gestures in our culture convey, among other things, an insult, a request for a ride, an invitation for someone to join us, or a demand that others stop in their tracks. Gestures also supplement spoken words. Pointing in a menacing way at someone, for example, intensifies a word of warning, as shrugging

African-American artist Jacob Lawrence captured the element of drama in everyday experiences in his painting Vaudeville. *The fact that the words "person" and "mask" are derived from the same Latin root (the word* persona*) raises the intriguing question of whether our public behaviors are authentic or contrived. In most cases, no doubt, they are a little of each.*

Jacob Lawrence, Theatre Series, No. 8: *Vaudeville,* 1951. Hirshorn Museum and Sculpture Garden, Smithsonian Institute, Gift of Joseph H. Hirshorn, 1966.

the shoulders adds an air of indifference to the phrase "I don't know," and rapidly waving the arms lends urgency to the single word "Hurry!"

Most nonverbal communication is culture specific. Hand gestures and body movements have different meanings from place to place, so that many gestures significant to North Americans mean nothing— or something very different—to members of other societies. As described in the box, "Travelers Beware!

Q: "Emotions are shown primarily in the face, not in the body . . . there are facial patterns specific to each emotion." Paul Ekman

NOTE: Michael G. Flaherty (1988:25) described the structural and emergent qualities of everyday life as situational "elasticity."

GLOBAL SOCIOLOGY

Human Emotions in Global Perspective

On a New York sidewalk, a woman reacts angrily to the skateboarder who hurtles past her. Apart from a few choice words, her facial expression broadcasts a strong emotion that most North Americans easily recognize. But would an observer from New Guinea be able to interpret her emotion? In other words, do all people share similar emotions, and do they express them in the same way?

Paul Ekman (1980) and his colleagues studied emotions around the world and even among members of a small society in New Guinea. Their conclusion is that people everywhere do experience the same basic emotions—including anger, fear, disgust, happiness, surprise, and sadness. Moreover, people around the world recognize these feelings in the same distinctive facial gestures. To Ekman, this commonality suggests that much of our emotional life is universal— rather than culturally variable— because the display of emotion is biologically programmed in our facial features, muscles, and central nervous system.

But while the reality of emotions is rooted in our biology, Ekman and others note three ways in which emotional life differs significantly in global perspective.

First, *what triggers an emotion varies from one society to another.* Whether people define a particular situation as an insult (causing anger), a loss (calling forth sadness), or a mystical event (provoking surprise and awe) depends on the cultural surroundings of the individual.

Second, *people display emotions according to the norms of their culture.* Every society has rules about when, where, and to whom an individual may exhibit certain emotions. People in the United States typically approve of emotional expression in the home among family members but consider such behavior out of place at work. Similarly, we expect children to express emotions to parents, although parents are taught to guard their emotions in front of children.

Third, *societies differ in terms of how people cope with emotions.* Some societies encourage the expression of feelings, while others belittle emotions and demand that their members suppress them. Societies also display significant gender differences in this regard. In the United States, most people regard emotional expression as feminine, expected of women but a sign of weakness among men. In other societies, however, this sex typing of emotions is less pronounced or even reversed.

In sum, emotional life in global perspective has both common and variable dimensions. People around the world experience many of the same human feelings. But what sparks a particular emotion, how a person expresses feelings, and what people think about emotions in general are variable products of social learning.

SOURCES: Ekman (1980a; 1980b), Lutz and White (1986), and Lutz (1988).

The Meaning of Gestures in Other Societies," in Chapter 3 ("Culture"), what many of us call the "A-Okay" gesture with thumb touching forefinger means "You're a zero" to the French, and conveys a crude word for "rectum" to many Germans and Italians (Ekman, Friesen, & Bear, 1984).

Performances sometimes convey mixed messages. A common case in point is when an unconscious element of nonverbal communication contradicts our intentional behavior. A teenage boy provides an explanation for returning home at a late hour, for example, but his mother begins to doubt his words because he avoids looking her in the eye. The movie star on a television talk show claims that her recent flop at the box office is "no big deal," but the nervous swing of her leg suggests otherwise. In practical terms, carefully observing nonverbal communication (which most of us cannot easily control) provides clues to deception, in much the same way that a lie detector records telltale changes in breathing, pulse rate, perspiration, and blood pressure.

Detecting lies is a difficult task, because no bodily gesture directly indicates deceit as, for example, a smile indicates pleasure. Even so, because each performance

Q: "We are, I fear, getting to know one another. Reticence, secrecy, concealment of self have been transformed into social problems; once they were aspects of civility . . ." Philip Rieff

Q: "If we never tried to seem a little better than we are, how could we improve or 'train ourselves from the outside inward'?" Charles Horton Cooley (1964:352; orig., 1902)

To most people in the United States, these expressions convey anger, fear, disgust, happiness, surprise, and sadness. But do people elsewhere in the world define them in the same way? Research suggests that all human beings experience the same basic emotions and display them to others in the same basic ways. But culture plays a part by specifying the situations that trigger one emotion or another.

involves so many expressions, few people can confidently lie without allowing some piece of contradictory information to arouse the suspicions of a careful observer. The key, therefore, to identifying deceit is to scan a complete performance with an eye for any discrepancies in the information that is conveyed.

Specifically, Paul Ekman (1985) suggests scrutinizing four types of information provided by a performer —words, voice, body language, and facial expression.

1. **Words.** Language is the major channel of communication, but a liar can manipulate words with

relative ease by mentally rehearsing what will be said. One clue to deceit, however, is a simple slip of the tongue—something the performer did not mean to say in quite that way. For example, a young man who is deceiving his parents by claiming that his roommate is a male friend rather than a female lover might inadvertently use the word "she" rather than "he" in a conversation. The more complicated the deception, the more likely a performer is to make a revealing mistake.

2. **Voice.** This refers to the qualities of speech other than words. Tone and patterns of speech contain

Q: "Male nonverbal communication has certain elements and effects that distinguish it from its female counterpart." Henley, Hamilton, and Thorne (1992:10)

NOTE: The examples in this section are illustrative of a very broad social pattern. Are there social situations or concepts that are *not* "gendered"?

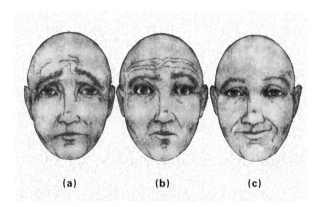

(a)   **(b)**   **(c)**

FIGURE 6–2 Which Is An "Honest Face"?

Telling lies is no easy task because most people lack the ability to manipulate all their facial muscles. Looking at the three faces above, the expression of grief in sketch (a) is probably genuine, since few people can deliberately lift the upper eyelids and inner corners of the eyebrows in this way. Likewise, the apprehension displayed in (b) also appears authentic, since intentionally raising the eyebrows and pulling them together is nearly impossible. People who fake emotions usually do a poor job of it, as illustrated by the phony expression of pleasure shown in (c). Genuine delight, for most people, would produce a balanced smile.

clues to deception because they are hard to control. A person trying to hide a powerful emotion, for example, cannot easily prevent the voice from trembling or breaking. Similarly, the individual may speak quickly (suggesting anger) or slowly (indicating sadness). Nervous laughter, inappropriate pauses between words, or nonwords, such as "ah" and "ummm," also hint at discomfort.

3. **Body language.** A "leak" of *body language* that a performer is unable to conceal may tip off an observer to deception as well. Subtle body movements, for example, give the impression of nervousness, as does sudden swallowing or rapid breathing. These are especially good clues to deception because few people can control them. Sometimes, *not* using the body in the expected way to enhance words—as when a person tries to fake excitement—also suggests deception.

4. **Facial expressions.** Because facial expressions are hard to control, they may give away a phony performance (see Figure 6–2). A sad person feigning happiness, for example, generally "flashes" momentary frowns through a crooked smile. In this case, the concealed emotion "leaks" through the deliberate facade. A signal of fear or worry is raising and drawing together the eyebrows, a movement virtually impossible for most people to make voluntarily. Crossing the face of a person who is supposedly at ease, this expression sounds the alarm of deception.

In sum, lies are detectable, but the ability to notice relevant clues usually requires training. Knowing the other person well makes detecting deception easier; parents, for example, can usually spot deception in their children. Clues to deception are also more evident if a person is trying to contain strong emotions. Even so, some people are skilled at managing their verbal and nonverbal performances. There are, in short, both good and bad liars.

Gender and Personal Performances

Because women are socialized to be less assertive than males, they tend to be especially sensitive to nonverbal communication. In fact, gender is a central element in personal performances. Based on the work of Nancy Henley, Mykol Hamilton, and Barrie Thorne (1992), we can extend the present discussion of personal performances to spotlight the importance of gender.

Demeanor

Goffman (1967) links *demeanor*—general conduct or deportment—to social power. Simply put, people in positions of power have far greater personal discretion in how they act; subordinates act more formally and self-consciously. Off-color remarks, swearing, or casual acts like removing shoes or putting feet up on the desk may be acceptable for the boss, but rarely for employees (Henley, Hamilton, & Thorne, 1992). Similarly, people in positions of dominance can interrupt the performances of others with impunity, while those subject to their power are expected to display deference by becoming silent (Smith-Lovin & Brody, 1989).

For women, who generally occupy positions of lesser power, demeanor is a matter of particular concern. As Chapter 13 ("Sex and Gender") explains, about half of all working women in the United States hold clerical or service jobs that place them under the control of supervisors, who are usually men. Women, then, must craft their personal performances more carefully than men and display a greater degree of deference in everyday interaction.

Q: "Both field and laboratory studies have found that people tend to approach females more closely than males, to seat themselves closer to females and otherwise intrude on their territory. . . . In the larger aspect of space, women are also less likely to have their own room or other private space in the home." Henley, Hamilton, and Thorne (1991:13)

Q: "A woman's sex is treated as the most salient characteristic of her being; this is not the case for males." Henley, Hamilton, and Thorne

Use of Space

How much space does a personal performance require? Here again, power plays a key role, since using more space conveys a nonverbal message of personal importance. According to Henley, Hamilton, and Thorne (1992), men use significantly more space than women do. Typically, men command more space when they pace back and forth before an audience making a formal presentation or even when they lounge casually about the beach on vacation. Why? Because our society traditionally has measured femininity by how little space women occupy (the standard of "daintiness"), while men enhance their masculinity by controlling as much territory as possible (the standard of "turf").

The concept of **personal space** refers to *the surrounding area in which an individual makes some claim to privacy*. In the United States, individuals typically remain at least several feet apart, maintaining more personal space than people in societies of the Middle East or Japan. But gender further modifies these patterns. In daily life, men readily intrude on the personal space of women. A woman's intrusion into a man's personal space, however, is likely to be construed as a sexual overture. Here again, women have less power in everyday interaction than men do.

Staring, Smiling, and Touching

Eye contact encourages interaction. Women more than men actively keep conversations going by sustaining eye contact longer. Men, on the other hand, engage in more *staring*. By making women the targets of stares, men reveal both their social dominance in the United States and their tendency to define women as sexual objects.

Although frequently conveying pleasure, *smiling* can also project various meanings. In a male-dominated world, women often smile to indicate appeasement or acceptance of submission. For this reason, Henley, Hamilton, and Thorne maintain, women smile more than men; in extreme cases, smiling may reach the level of nervous habit.

Finally, *touching* constitutes an intriguing social pattern. Mutual touching generally conveys intimacy and caring. Apart from close relationships, however, touching is generally something men do to women (although rarely, in our culture, to other men). A male physician touches the shoulder of his female nurse as they examine a report, a young man who has just begun dating touches the back of his woman friend as he guides her across the street, or a male skiing instructor excessively touches his female students. In these examples—as well as many others—the touching may evoke little response, so common is it in everyday life. But it amounts to a subtle ritual by which men express their dominant position in an assumed hierarchy that subordinates women.

Idealization

Complex motives underlie human behavior. Even so, Goffman suggests, in our performances we tend to *idealize* our intentions. We try to convince others that what we do reflects ideal cultural standards rather than less virtuous motives.

Idealization is easily illustrated by returning to the world of physicians and patients. In a hospital, physicians engage in a performance commonly described as "making rounds." Entering the room of a patient, the physician often stops at the foot of the bed and silently examines the patient's chart. Afterward, physician and patient briefly converse. In ideal terms, this routine involves a physician making a personal visit to inquire about a patient's condition.

In reality, something less exemplary is usually going on. A physician who sees perhaps thirty-five patients a day may remember little about most of them. Reading the chart gives the physician the opportunity to rediscover the patient's identity and medical problems. Openly revealing the actual impersonality of much medical care would undermine the culturally ideal perception of the physician as deeply concerned about the welfare of others.

Idealization is woven into the fabric of everyday life in countless ways. Physicians and other professionals typically idealize their motives for entering their chosen careers. They describe their work as "making a contribution to science," perhaps "answering a calling from God," or "serving the community." Rarely do such people concede the less honorable, although common, motives of seeking the high income, power, and prestige these occupations confer. More generally, civility involves idealization, since we all smile and make polite remarks to people we do not like. Such small hypocrisies ease our way through social interactions. Even when we suspect that others are putting on an act, we are unlikely to openly challenge their performance, for reasons that we shall explain next.

Embarrassment and Tact

The eminent professor consistently mispronounces the dean's name; the visiting dignitary rises from the table to speak, unaware of the napkin that still hangs from her neck; the president becomes ill at a state

NOTE: "Embarrass" is derived from words meaning "to block or obstruct." "Tact" is derived from the Latin *tact(us)* meaning "sense of touch."
DATA FILE: A summary of a classic study of embarrassment is included in the *Data File*.

GLOBAL: Worth noting is the fact that English does not follow the pattern of romance languages of designating all nouns as either female or male.
NOTE: Boys, but not girls, are designated as Jr., II, or III.

 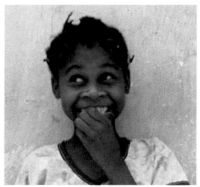 

Hand gestures vary widely from one culture to another. Yet people everywhere define a chuckle, grin, or smirk in response to someone's performance as an indication that one does not take another person seriously. Therefore, the world over, people who cannot restrain their mirth tactfully cover their faces.

dinner. As carefully as individuals may craft their performances, slipups of this kind frequently occur. The result is *embarrassment*, which in a dramaturgical analysis means the discomfort that follows a spoiled performance. Goffman describes embarrassment simply as "losing face."

Embarrassment looms as an ever-present danger because, first, idealized performances typically contain some deception. Second, most performances involve a complex array of elements, any one of which, if badly done, can shatter the intended impression.

A curious fact is that an audience usually overlooks flaws in a performance, thereby allowing an actor to avoid embarrassment. We discretely inform a man that his zipper is open (creating limited embarrassment) in order to help him avoid an even greater loss of face. In Hans Christian Andersen's classic fable "The Emperor's New Clothes," the child who blurts out that the emperor is parading about naked tells the truth but is scolded for being rude.

Members of an audience not only ignore flaws in a performance, Goffman explains; they often help the performer recover from them. *Tact* is an effort to help another person "save face." After hearing a supposed expert make an embarrassingly inaccurate remark, for example, people may tactfully ignore the comment as if it was never spoken at all. Alternatively, mild laughter may indicate they wish to dismiss what they have heard as a joke. Or a listener may simply respond, "I'm sure you didn't mean that," suggesting that the statement will not be allowed to destroy the actor's overall performance.

Why is tact such a common response? Merely because embarrassment provokes discomfort not simply for one person but for *everyone*. Just as everyone

in a theater feels uneasy when an actor forgets a line, people who observe awkward behavior are reminded of how fragile their own performances often are. Socially constructed reality thus functions like a dam holding back a sea of chaotic possibility. Should one person's performance spring a leak, others tactfully assist in making repairs. Everyone, after all, jointly engages in building reality, and no one wants it to be suddenly swept away.

In sum, Goffman's research shows that our behavior may be spontaneous in some respects, but we employ many familiar social patterns in our interaction with others. Almost four hundred years ago, William Shakespeare wrote:

> All the world's a stage,
> And all the men and women merely players:
> They have their exits and their entrances;
> And one man in his time plays many parts.
> (*As You Like It*, II)

Human behavior does not, of course, consist simply of stage and script. But, in a lifetime, each individual does play many parts in ways that combine social structure with expressions of a unique personality. Therefore, Shakespeare's observation still contains a good measure of truth.

INTERACTION IN EVERYDAY LIFE: TWO ILLUSTRATIONS

We have now examined a number of dimensions of social interaction. The final sections of this chapter illustrate these lessons by focusing on two important, yet quite different, elements of everyday life.

NOTE: "Androcentrism" is a masculine bias—in this case, of language. (*Andro* is Greek, meaning "male.")
NOTE: The value function of language is also evident in terms, such as "lady doctor," which suggest an exceptional case.

GLOBAL: In Japan, says Ellen Rudolph (1991), women display their greater subservience to men by speaking more quietly, looking down, and employing more deferential language.
DIVERSITY: "Widower" is the derivative term (from widow) reflecting the fact that marital standing is not a master status for men.

Language: The Gender Issue

As Chapter 3 ("Culture") explains, language is the thread that joins members of a society into the symbolic web we call culture. In everyday life, language conveys meaning on more than one level. Besides the *manifest* content, or what is explicitly stated, the *latent* content conveys various additional assumptions about reality. One latent message involves gender. Language defines men and women differently in at least three ways, involving control, value, and attention (Henley, Hamilton, & Thorne, 1992).[1]

The Control Function of Language

A young man drives into the gas station, eager to display his new motorcycle, and proudly asks, "Isn't she a beauty?" On the surface, the question has little to do with gender. Yet, it is curious that a common linguistic pattern confers the female "she," and never the male "he," on a man's prized possession.

As we suggested at the beginning of this chapter, the language men use often reveals their concern with competence and control. In this case, a man attaches a female pronoun to a motorcycle (car, yacht, or other object) because it reflects *ownership*.

A more obvious control function of language relates to people's names. Traditionally in the United States, and in many other parts of the world, a woman takes the family name of the man she marries. While few people consider this an explicit statement of a man's ownership of a woman, many believe that it reflects male dominance. For this reason, an increasing proportion of married women have retained their own name (more precisely, the family name obtained from their father) or merged two family names.

The Value Function of Language

Language usually attaches greater value, force, or significance to what is defined as masculine. Although we may not think much about it, this pattern is deeply rooted in the English language. For instance, the positive adjective "virtuous," meaning "morally worthy" or "excellent," is derived from the Latin word *vir* meaning "man." By contrast, the disparaging adjective "hysterical" is derived from the Greek word *hyster*, meaning "uterus."

In numerous, more familiar ways, language also confers different value on the two sexes. Traditional masculine terms such as "king" or "lord" have retained their positive meaning, while comparable terms, such as "queen," "madam," or "dame" have acquired negative connotations in contemporary usage. Language thus both mirrors social attitudes and helps to perpetuate them.

Similarly, use of the suffixes "ette" and "ess" to denote femininity generally devalues the words to which they are added. For example, a "major" has higher standing than a "majorette," as does a "host" in relation to a "hostess." And, certainly, men's groups with names such as the Los Angeles Rams carry more stature than women's groups with names like the Radio City Music Hall Rockettes.

The Attention Function of Language

Language also shapes reality by directing greater attention to masculine endeavors. The most obvious example is our use of personal pronouns. In the English language, the plural pronoun "they" is neutral as it refers to both sexes. But the corresponding singular pronouns "he" and "she" convey gender. According to traditional grammatical practice, we use "he" along with the possessive "his" and objective "him" to refer to *all people*. Thus, we assume that the masculine pronoun in the bit of wisdom "He who hesitates is lost" refers to women as well as to men. But this practice also reflects the traditional cultural pattern of neglecting the lives of women. Some research suggests that people continue to respond to allegedly inclusive male pronouns as if only males were involved (MacKay, 1983).

The English language has no gender-neutral, third-person singular personal pronoun. In recent years, however, the plural pronoun "they" increasingly has gained currency as a singular pronoun ("*Everyone* should do as *they* please"). This usage remains controversial because it violates grammatical rules. Yet, in an age of growing concern over gender-linked bias, English and other languages spoken in the United States may eventually evolve to accept such gender-neutral constructions.

Even as our languages evolve, gender is likely to remain a source of miscommunication between women and men. In the box on page 171, Harold and Sybil—whose misadventures finding a friend's home opened this chapter—return to illustrate how the two sexes often seem to be speaking different languages.

---

[1]The following sections draw primarily upon Henley, Hamilton, & Thorne (1992). Additional material is drawn from Thorne, Kramarae, & Henley (1983), MacKay (1983), and others as noted.

Q: "There are very few jokes about sociologists." Peter Berger (1963:1)

NOTE: Humor's origin in incongruity is evident in Woody Allen's line: "More than any time in history, mankind faces a crossroads. One path leads to despair and utter hopelessness, the other to total extinction. Let us pray that we have the wisdom to choose correctly."

NOTE: Laughter also accompanies tickling. This is a disruption of what is conventional in a physical sense; tickling is also an ambiguous situation in which one does not know if the other's motives are loving or aggressive.

Humor: Playing with Reality

Humor plays a vital part in our everyday lives. Comedians are among our favorite entertainers, most newspapers contain cartoon pages, and even professors and the clergy include humor in their performances. Like many aspects of everyday life, humor is largely taken for granted. While everyone laughs at a joke, few people think about what makes something funny or why humor is found among humans everywhere in the world. Many of the ideas developed in this chapter provide insights into the character of humor, as we shall now see.[2]

The Foundation of Humor

Humor stems from the contrast between two incongruous realities. Generally, one socially constructed reality is more *conventional* because it corresponds to what people expect in a specific situation. The other reality is dubbed *unconventional*, representing a significant violation of cultural patterns. Humor, therefore, arises from contradiction, ambiguity, and "double meanings" generated by two differing definitions of the same situation. Note how this principle works in this simple piece of humor.

> The husband quips: "My wife and I have no secrets from each other . . . At least none she knows about."

In this example, the first thought represents a conventional reality. A man claims he and his wife are close. The second sentence, however, provides an unconventional meaning that collides with what we are led to expect.

The same simple pattern is evident in the humor of virtually all comedians.

> Groucho Marx, trying to sound manly: "This morning, I shot a lion in my pajamas." (Turning to the camera): "What the lion was doing in my pajamas I'll never know . . ."

> On the television show "M*A*S*H," Frank Burns asks "Why do people take such an instant dislike to me?" Trapper responds, "Because it saves time."

Here, again, each of these jokes contains two major elements, a conventional assertion followed by an unconventional one.

Of course, a joke can be built the other way around, so that the audience is led to *expect* an unconventional answer and gets a very ordinary one. When a reporter asked the famous desperado Willy Sutton why he robbed banks, for example, he replied dryly: "Because that's where the money is." However a joke is constructed, the greater the opposition or incongruity between the two definitions of reality, the greater the potential for humor.

When telling jokes, the comedian can strengthen this opposition in various ways. One technique, often used by Groucho Marx, George Burns, Gracie Allen, and other comics of the screen, is to present the first, or conventional, remark in conversation with another actor, then to turn toward the audience (or the camera) when delivering the second, or unconventional, line. This "shift of channel" underscores the incongruity of the two parts. Many stand-up comics also "reset" the audience back to conventional expectations by saying "But, seriously, folks . . ." after one joke is finished and before the next one is begun.

To construct the strongest contrast in meaning, comedians pay careful attention to their performances—the precise words they use, as well as the timing of each part of the delivery. A joke is "well told" if the comic creates the sharpest possible opposition between the realities, just as humor falls flat in a careless performance. Since the key to humor lies in the opposition of realities, it is not surprising that the climax of a joke is termed the "*punch* line."

The Dynamics of Humor: "Getting It"

Someone who does not understand both the conventional and unconventional realities embedded in a joke offers the typical complaint: "I don't get it." To "get" humor, members of an audience must understand the two realities involved well enough to perceive their incongruity.

But getting a joke can be more challenging still, because some of the information listeners must grasp is usually left unstated. Listeners, therefore, must pay attention to the stated elements of the joke and then inferentially complete the joke in their own minds. As a simple case, consider the observation of movie producer Hal Roach upon reaching his one hundredth birthday:

> If I had known I would live to be one hundred, I would have taken better care of myself!

Here, "getting" the joke depends on realizing that Roach *must* have taken pretty good care of himself since he lived to be one hundred in the first place.

---

[2]The ideas contained in this discussion are those of the author (1987), except as otherwise noted. The general approach draws on work presented earlier in this chapter, especially on the ideas of Erving Goffman.

NOTE: Examples for eliciting the pleasure of "getting jokes": What campus departments or offices would use these call letters for their radio station? WIXL (honors program); WSOS (security office); WURU (counseling service); WYMI (philosophy department); WYYY (religion department); WYRU (sociology department). (Barry Glassner and John Western)

NOTE: Humor can also be generated by leading an audience to expect two incongruous realities, one of which fails to materialize. Groucho Marx once quipped: "I worked myself up from nothing to a state of extreme poverty . . ."

NOTE: Laughing at one's own joke is rather rude or odd, because there is no punch at all.

Q: "You can pretend to be serious, but you cannot pretend to be witty." Sacha Guitry

SOCIOLOGY OF EVERYDAY LIFE

Gender and Language: "You Just Don't Understand!"

Countless dimensions of everyday life reflect the power of gender. In the story that opened this chapter, a couple faces a situation that rings all too true to many people: When they are lost men do not like to ask for directions, while women can't seem to understand why not.

Deborah Tannen, who has conducted extensive research on the linguistic differences that separate the sexes, explains. Men, she claims, see everyday encounters as competitive situations; thus, asking for help amounts to a man letting someone else "one up" him. Men go to great lengths to avoid such subordination. By contrast, because women in the United States hold a generally subordinate position, they are socialized to ask for help. Sometimes, Tannen points out, women will ask for assistance even when they don't need it.

A similar gender-linked problem common to couples involves (what men call) "nagging." Consider the following exchange (Adler, 1990:74):

Sybil: "What's wrong, honey?"
Harold: "Nothing . . ."
Sybil: "Something is bothering you; I can tell."
Harold: "I told you nothing is bothering me. Leave me alone."

Sybil: "But I can see that something is wrong."
Harold: "OK. Just why do you think something is bothering me?"
Sybil: "Well, for one thing, you're bleeding all over your shirt."
Harold: [now irritated] "It doesn't bother me."
Sybil: [losing patience] "WELL, IT SURE IS BOTHERING ME!"
Harold: "I'll go change my shirt."

The problem couples face in communicating is that what one partner *intends* by a comment is not always what the other *hears* in the words. To Sybil, her opening question is an effort at cooperative problem solving. She can see that

something is wrong with Harold (who has carelessly cut himself while doing yard work) and wants to help solve the problem. But Harold interprets her pointing out his problem as belittling, and tries to close off the discussion. Sybil, confident that Harold would be more positive toward her if he just understood that she only wants to be helpful, repeats herself. This reaction sets in motion a vicious circle in which Harold, thinking Sybil is trying to manipulate him and make him feel incapable of looking after himself, responds by digging in his heels. His response, in turn, makes Sybil all the more sure that there is a problem that requires attention. And round it goes until somebody loses patience.

In the end, Harold gives in only to the extent that he agrees to change his shirt. But notice he still refuses to discuss the original problem. Misunderstanding his wife's motives, Harold just wants Sybil to leave him alone. For her part, Sybil fails to understand her husband's view of the situation and walks away thinking that he has been insensitive to her for no good reason.

SOURCES: Adler (1990) and Tannen (1990).

A more complex joke is the following, written on the wall of a college rest room:

Dyslexics of the World, Untie!

This joke demands more of the audience. One must know, first, that dyslexia is a condition in which people routinely reverse letters; second, one must identify the line as an adaptation of Karl Marx's call to the world's workers to unite; third, one must recognize "untie" as an anagram of "unite," as one might imagine a disgruntled dyslexic person would write it.

Why would an audience be required to make this sort of effort in order to understand a joke? Simply because our enjoyment of a joke is heightened

Because humor involves challenging established social conventions, "outsiders"—particularly ethnic and racial minorities—have always been disproportionately represented among our society's comedians. In her comedy career, Whoopi Goldberg (shown here in the movie, Sister Act*) has poked fun at virtually every kind of formality and pretense.*

by the pleasure of having completed the puzzle necessary to "get it." In addition to feeling clever at having understood a complex joke, "getting it" also confers a favored status as an "insider" in the larger audience. These insights also explain the frustration that accompanies not getting a joke: the fear of mental inadequacy coupled with a sense of being socially excluded from a pleasure shared by others. Not surprisingly, "outsiders" in such a situation may fake "getting" the joke; sometimes, too, others may tactfully explain a joke to them to end their sense of being left out.

But, as the old saying goes, if a joke has to be explained, it won't be very funny. Besides taking the edge off the language and timing on which the *punch* depends, an explanation completely relieves the audience of any mental involvement, substantially reducing their pleasure.

The Topics of Humor

People throughout the world smile and laugh, providing ample evidence that humor is a universal human trait. But since people around the world live in diverse cultures, they differ in what they find funny. Musicians frequently travel to perform for receptive audiences across the globe, suggesting that music may be the "common language" of humanity. Comedians rarely do this, demonstrating that humor does not travel well.

What is humorous to the Chinese, then, may be lost on Iraqis or people in the United States. To some degree, too, the social diversity of U.S. society means that people will find humor in different situations. New Englanders, southerners, and westerners have their own brands of humor, as do Latinos and Anglos, fifteen- and forty-year-olds, bankers and construction workers.

For everyone, however, humor deals with topics that lend themselves to double meanings or *controversy*. For example, the first jokes many of us learned as children concerned what our culture defines as a childhood taboo: sex. The mere mention of "unmentionable acts" or even certain parts of the body can dissolve young faces in laughter.

The controversy inherent in humor often walks a fine line between what is funny and what is considered "sick." During the Middle Ages, the word *humors* (derived from the Latin *humidus*, meaning "moist") referred to a balance of bodily fluids that determined a person's degree of health. Most societies value the ability to take conventional definitions of reality lightly (in other words, to have a "sense of humor"). In fact, empirical evidence supports the old saying "Laughter is the best medicine," because maintaining a sense of humor does contribute to a person's physical health by decreasing stress (Robinson, 1983; Haig, 1988). At the extreme, however, people who always take conventional reality lightly risk being defined as deviant or even mentally ill (mental hospitals have long been dubbed "funny farms").

Every social group considers some topics too sensitive for humorous treatment. A violation may result in the comedian being admonished for telling a "sick" joke, one that pokes fun at a situation that is expected to be handled with reverence. Some topics, in other words, are "off limits," because people expect them to be understood in only one way. People's religious beliefs, tragic accidents, or appalling crimes are the stuff of "sick" jokes.

The Functions of Humor

As a widespread means of communication, humor has survival value for any society and for the entire human species. A structural-functional analysis suggests that humor has a valuable function as a social "safety valve," allowing people to release potentially disruptive sentiments safely. Put another way, jokes express ideas that might be dangerous if taken seriously, as in the case of racial and ethnic jokes. Called to account for a remark that could be defined as offensive, a speaker may defuse the situation by simply stating, "I didn't mean anything by what I said; it was just a joke!" Likewise, rather than taking offense at another's behavior, a person might use humor as a form of tact, smiling, as if to say, "I could be angry at this, but I'll assume you were only kidding."

Like theater and art, humor also allows a society to challenge orthodox ideas and to explore alternatives to the status quo. Sometimes, in fact, humor may actually promote social change by loosening the hold of convention.

Humor and Conflict

If humor holds the potential to liberate those who laugh, it can also be used to oppress others. Men who tell jokes about feminists, for example, typically are voicing some measure of hostility to the interests of women (Benokraitis & Feagin, 1986; Powell & Paton, 1988). Similarly, jokes at the expense of gay people reveal the tensions surrounding sexual orientation in the United States. Generally, humor is often a sign of real conflict in situations where one or both parties do not wish to bring the conflict out into the open (Primeggia & Varacalli, 1990).

"Put down" jokes, which make one category of people feel good at the expense of another, are common around the globe. After collecting and analyzing jokes from many societies, Christie Davies (1990) concluded that conflict among ethnic groups is a driving force behind humor virtually everywhere. Typically, jokes label some disadvantaged category of

people as stupid or ridiculous, thereby imputing greater wisdom and skills to those who are better off. In the United States, Poles have long been the "butt" of jokes, as have Newfoundlanders ("Newfies") in eastern Canada, the Irish in Scotland, Sikhs in India, Turks in Germany, Hausas in Nigeria, Tasmanians in Australia, and Kurds in Iraq.

Disadvantaged people, of course, also make fun of the powerful. Women in the United States have long joked about men, just as African Americans portray white people in humorous ways, and poor people poke fun at the rich. Throughout the world, people target their leaders with humor, and officials in some countries take such jokes seriously enough to vigorously repress them.

The significance of humor is therefore much greater than first impressions suggest. Michael Flaherty (1984, 1990) points out that humor amounts to a means of mental escape from the conventional world that may not be entirely to our liking. As long as we maintain a sense of humor, then, we assert our freedom and are never prisoners of society. And, in doing so, we change the world and ourselves just a little.

Although quite different, the power of gender in our language and the way humor plays with reality are both important dimensions of everyday life. Each demonstrates our power to socially construct a world of meaning and then to react to what we have made. Each also demonstrates the value of the sociological perspective for understanding—and more actively participating in—this process.

SUMMARY

1. By guiding behavior within culturally approved bounds, social structure renders everyday life understandable and predictable.

2. A major component of social structure is status. Within an entire status set, a master status has particular significance.

3. Ascribed statuses are essentially involuntary, while achieved statuses are largely earned. In practice, however, most statuses incorporate elements of both ascription and achievement.

4. Role is the dynamic expression of a status. Like statuses, roles are relational, guiding people as they interact.

5. When roles corresponding to two or more statuses are incompatible, role conflict results. Likewise, incompatibility among various roles linked to a single status can generate role strain.

6. The phrase "social construction of reality" conveys the important idea that people build the social world through their interaction.

7. The Thomas theorem states, "Situations defined as real become real in their consequences."

8. People build social reality using elements of their culture and according to their available social resources.

9. Ethnomethodology explores how people generate understandings of everyday social situations. This approach sometimes utilizes norm-violation to help identify social conventions that people take for granted.

10. Dramaturgical analysis studies how people construct personal performances. This approach casts everyday life in terms of theatrical performances.

11. People speak, use body language, and fashion physical settings to assist their performances. Often performers attempt to idealize their intentions.

12. To the extent that they have less social power, women craft their situational behavior differently than men.

13. Social behavior carries the ever-present danger of embarrassment. Tact is a common response to a "loss of face" by others.

14. Language is vital to the process of socially constructing reality. In various ways, language defines females and males differently, generally to the advantage of males.

15. Humor stems from the contrast between conventional and unconventional definitions of a situation. Because comedy is framed by a specific culture, people throughout the world find humor in very different situations.

KEY CONCEPTS

achieved status a social position that someone assumes voluntarily and that reflects personal ability and effort

ascribed status a social position that someone receives at birth or involuntarily assumes later in life

dramaturgical analysis Erving Goffman's term for the investigation of social interaction in terms of theatrical performance

ethnomethodology Harold Garfinkel's term for the study of the way people make sense of their everyday lives

master status a status that has exceptional importance for social identity, often shaping a person's entire life

nonverbal communication communication using body movements, gestures, and facial expressions rather than speech

personal space the surrounding area in which an individual makes some claim to privacy

presentation of self the effort of an individual to create specific impressions in the minds of others

role behavior expected of someone who holds a particular status

role conflict incompatibility among the roles corresponding to two or more different statuses

role set a number of roles attached to a single status

role strain incompatibility among roles corresponding to a single status

social construction of reality the process by which people creatively shape reality through social interaction

social interaction the process by which people act and react in relation to others

status a recognized social position that an individual occupies

status set all the statuses a person holds at a given time

Thomas theorem W. I. Thomas's assertion that situations we define as real become real in their consequences

CRITICAL-THINKING QUESTIONS

1. Why do sociologists suggest that most statuses reflect elements of both ascription and achievement?

2. Consider ways in which a physical disability can serve as a master status. How do people commonly characterize, say, a person with the physical disability cerebral palsy with regard to mental ability? With regard to sexuality?

3. Drawing on personal experiences, assess the validity of the Thomas theorem.

4. Paralleling the dramaturgical analysis of a doctor's office found in this chapter, develop a similar analysis of a college classroom. What about a professor's office?

SUGGESTED READINGS

Classic Sources

Erving Goffman. *The Presentation of Self in Everyday Life.* Garden City, N.Y.: Doubleday Anchor Books, 1959.
   Erving Goffman's first book is his best-known work.

Peter L. Berger and Thomas Luckmann. *The Social Construction of Reality: A Treatise in the Sociology of Knowledge.* Garden City, N.Y.: Doubleday Anchor Books, 1967.
   This book elaborates on the argument that individuals generate meaning through their social interaction.

Contemporary Sources

Fred Davis. *Fashion, Culture, and Identity.* Chicago: University of Chicago Press, 1992.
   How do people choose their clothes, and what do clothes say about them?

David A. Karp and William C. Yoels. *Sociology and Everyday Life.* 2d ed. Itasca, Ill.: Peacock, 1993.
   This paperback provides many examples of rich insights about everyday life that the sociological perspective offers.

Dennis Brissett and Charles Edgley. *Life as Theater: A Dramaturgical Sourcebook.* 2d ed. Hawthorne, N.Y.: Aldine de Gruyter, 1990.
   This survey of social psychology is based on the dramaturgical point of view.

Mary Ellen Brown, ed. *Television and Women's Culture: The Politics of the Popular.* Newbury Park, Calif.: Sage, 1990.
   Television has assumed a central place in U.S. society. This book brings together thirteen essays that explore television and women from a feminist perspective.

Michele Fine and Adrian Ash. *Women with Disabilities.* Philadelphia: Temple University Press, 1990.

How do people define others with physical disabilities? How do these individuals construct their own identity? This book provides some answers.

Norman K. Denzin. *Studies in Symbolic Interaction: A Research Annual.* Vol. 12. Greenwich, Conn.: JAI Press, 1991.
   This review of recent developments in symbolic interaction highlights postmodern and feminist views of society.

Kathleen Kelley Reardon. *Persuasion in Practice.* Newbury Park, Calif.: Sage, 1991.
   A crucial aspect of personal performances is their believability. This book explores persuasiveness in face-to-face interaction, in the mass media, and in large organizations.

Melvin Patrick Ely. *The Adventures of Amos 'n' Andy: A Social History of an American Phenomenon.* New York: The Free Press, 1991.
   An account of one of the most popular radio and television programs in the history of the United States provides keen insights into race relations.

Global Sources

Catherine A. Lutz. *Unnatural Emotions: Everyday Sentiments on a Micronesian Atoll and Their Challenge to Western Theory.* Chicago: University of Chicago Press, 1988.
   This report of research on a Pacific island suggests ways in which emotions, and how people think about them, are culturally variable.

Christie Davies. *Ethnic Humor Around the World: A Comparative Analysis.* Bloomington: Indiana University Press, 1990.
   Relatively little attention has been paid to the sociological analysis of humor. This book applies a global perspective to the issue.

Paul Gauguin, *The Market*, 1892. Kunstmuseum, Basle.

DATA FILE: An outline and supplementary lecture material for Chapter 7 are included in the *Data File*.
DATA FILE: Does the United States have too many lawyers? The *Data File* investigates this question.

Q: "No man is an island, entire of itself; every man is a piece of the continent, a part of the main . . . any man's death diminishes me, because I am involved in mankind. And therefore never send to know for whom the bell tolls; it tolls for thee."
John Donne

Groups and Organizations

*B*ack in 1937, the opening of a new restaurant in Pasadena, California, attracted little attention from the local community and went unnoticed by the nation as a whole. Yet this seemingly insignificant small business, owned and operated by Mac and Dick McDonald, was eventually to revolutionize the restaurant industry, introducing the concept of "fast-food" to our vocabulary and providing an organizational model that would be copied by countless other businesses and even schools and churches.

The basic formula of the McDonald brothers was serving food quickly, to large numbers of people, at an attractive price. Employees were trained to perform highly-specialized jobs, so that one person grilled hamburgers, while others "dressed" them, made french fries, mixed milkshakes, and presented the food to the customesr in assembly-line fashion.

As the years went by, the single McDonald's restaurant moved from Pasadena to San Bernadino, where it became increasingly popular, providing locals with a tasty meal and the McDonald brothers with a good living. But, in 1954, events took an unexpected turn when Ray Kroc, a traveling blender and mixer merchant, happened to pay a visit to the McDonalds.

Kroc was fascinated by the brothers' efficient system, and, almost immediately, he saw the potential for a greatly expanded system of fast-food restaurants. Initially, Kroc launched his plans in partnership with the McDonald brothers. Soon, however, he bought out their interests and set out on his own to become one of the greatest success stories of all time. Today, people in the United States and dozens of countries around the world enjoy food and drinks at almost fifteen thousand McDonald's restaurants.

SOCIAL SURVEY: "How many close friends do you have?" (*CHIP1 Social Survey Software*, FRINUM1; GSS 1986, N = 1,360)

AGE	0–4	5 or more
18–34	51.5%	48.5%
35–64	49.6%	50.4%
65&up	36.9%	63.1%

RESOURCE: An excerpt of Cooley's analysis of primary groups

appears in the companion reader, *Seeing Ourselves: Classic, Contemporary, and Cross-Cultural Readings in Sociology, 3/e.*

Q: "By primary groups I mean those characterized by intimate face-to-face association and cooperation. They are primary in several senses, but chiefly in that they are fundamental in forming the social nature and ideals of individuals." Charles Horton Cooley (1962:23; orig. 1909)

Around the world, families are the most important primary group. In industrial societies, however, numerous friendship groups stand alongside families, joining individuals on the basis of shared interests rather than kinship.

From a sociological point of view, the success of McDonald's reveals much more than the popularity of hamburgers. As sociologist George Ritzer (1993) explains, the larger importance of this story lies in the extent to which the principles that guide the operation of McDonald's are coming to dominate social life in the United States as well as the rest of the world.

This chapter will explain how this is so. We begin with an examination of *social groups*, the clusters of people in which we carry out much of our daily lives. As we shall describe, the scope of group life has expanded greatly during this century. From a world built on the family, the local neighborhood, and the small business, the structure of our society now turns on the operation of vast businesses and other bureaucracies that sociologists describe as *formal organizations*. Providing the reasons for this expanding scale of life, as well as explaining what it means for us as individuals, are the chapter's key objectives.

SOCIAL GROUPS

Virtually everyone moves through life with a sense of belonging; that is the experience of group life. A **social group** refers to *two or more people who identify and interact with one another.* Human beings continually come together to form couples, families, circles of friends, neighborhoods, churches, businesses, clubs, and numerous large organizations. Whatever the form,

groups encompass people with shared experiences, loyalties, and interests. In short, while maintaining their individuality, the members of social groups also think of themselves as a special "we."

Groups Versus Other Collectivities

People often use the term "group" imprecisely. Below, we distinguish the group from three other collectivities: category, aggregate, and crowd.

Category

A *category* refers to people who have some status in common. Women, single fathers, military recruits, homeowners, and Roman Catholics are all examples of categories of interest to sociologists.

Why are categories not considered groups? Simply because, while the individuals involved are aware that they are not the only ones to hold that particular status, most of them are strangers to one another.

Aggregate

An *aggregate* is a number of people who are in the same place at the same time—riders on a city subway train, for example. Unlike a category, then, people in an aggregate share space. Still, such people cannot be correctly termed a group, since the individuals present in the situation interact little, if at all, and have no sense of belonging together.

Crowd

A *crowd* refers to a large number of people in proximity to one another who do interact to a greater or lesser extent. In cases of little interaction (say, people enjoying the beach on a hot summer day), crowds are simply large aggregates. In cases of greater common identity and some interaction (for example, students sitting together in a lecture hall), a crowd can qualify as a loosely formed group. In general, then, crowds span the range from anonymous aggregates to interacting groups.

Finally, people in any of these collectivities are likely, under certain circumstances, to transform themselves into a group. For instance, although women are a category of people, those who start to identify with one another based on their gender can become a group. Similarly, people riding in a subway train that crashes under the city streets generally become keenly aware of their common plight and begin to help each other.

NOTE: "Primary" is derived from the Latin word *prime*, meaning "first"; the root of "secondary" is the Latin word *secund(us)*, meaning "following."

NOTE: Cooley did his first research for the U.S. Census collecting statistics on street railways, becoming a full-time sociologist at the age of 28.

NOTE: Primary groups involve bonds of affection, but not neces-

sarily bonds of intimacy. Parents generally strive to treat children in an evenhanded and equal—if therefore impersonal—fashion. The adjective form of "family"—*familiar*—also implies something less than intimacy.

NOTE: Edward Shils and Morris Janowitz (1948) concluded that strong primary group ties among soldiers gave German forces an advantage over Allied forces in World War II.

PROFILE

Charles Horton Cooley: The Primary Group Is Morally Good

Many men and women fear that the world is becoming so fast paced and impersonal that people are losing touch with one another. This is nothing new: Charles Horton Cooley shared this concern a century ago as he grew up in a small town and witnessed rapid change across the United States.

Cooley's home was in Ann Arbor, Michigan, where he spent his childhood and returned to teach, serving on the faculty of the University of Michigan from 1892 until his death. His major contribution to sociology was exploring the character of the primary group.

Cooley noted a disturbing trend: As the United States became more urban and industrialized, people seemed to become ever more individualistic and competitive, displaying less concern for the traditional family and local neighborhood. This transformation made Cooley uneasy because he was convinced of the crucial importance of small, cooperative groups to social life. Primary groups are a moral good, he declared, because they engender in people a feeling of belonging as well as a sense of fairness and compassion.

Cooley hoped that calling attention to the importance of primary groups would shore up traditional values and a socially cohesive way of life. Certainly, the United States has continued to change since Cooley's lifetime, and not entirely in ways he would have wished. But Charles Horton Cooley might take heart in the fact that many of his social concerns are with us still.

SOURCES: Rieff (1962) and Coser (1977).

Primary and Secondary Groups

Acquaintances commonly greet one another with a smile and the simple phrase "Hi! How are you?" The response is usually a well-scripted "Just fine, thanks. How about you?" This answer, of course, is often more formal than truthful. In most cases, providing a detailed account of how you are *really* doing would prompt the other person to make a hasty and awkward exit.

Sociologists classify social groups by measuring them against two ideal types based on whether members display genuine personal concern toward each other or maintain social distance. This variation is the key to distinguishing *primary* from *secondary* groups.

According to Charles Horton Cooley (1864–1929), who is introduced in the box, a **primary group** is *a small social group in which relationships are both personal and enduring*. Bound together by strong and lasting loyalties that Cooley termed *primary relationships*, the members of a primary group spend a great deal of time together, share many activities, and feel that they know one another well. As a result, they typically display sincere concern for each another's welfare. The family is any society's most important primary group.

Cooley called personal and tightly integrated groups *primary* because they are among the first groups we experience in life. In addition, the family and early play groups also hold primary importance in the socialization process, shaping personal attitudes and behavior. We look to members of our primary groups in forming our social identity as well, evident in the fact that members of primary groups almost always think of themselves as "we."

The strength of primary relationships gives many individuals considerable comfort and security. In the familiar social circles of family or friends, people feel they can "be themselves" without constantly worrying about the impressions they are making.

NOTE: Cooley used only the term *primary group*; others introduced the term *secondary group* into sociological terminology, inferring the concept from Cooley's writings.
Q: "In our own life the intimacy of the neighborhood has been broken up by the growth of an intricate mesh of wider contacts which leaves us strangers to people who live in the same house." Charles Horton Cooley (1962:26; orig. 1909)

SOCIAL SURVEY: "How often do you spend an evening with relatives?" (*STUDENT CHIP Social Survey Software*, SOCREL1; GSS 1974–91, N = 14,061)

SES	Weekly	Less often
High	26.3%	73.7%
Middle	36.4%	63.6%
Low	42.5%	57.5%

Members of primary groups generally provide one another with personal, financial, and emotional support. Even so, people generally think of a primary group as an end in itself rather than as a means to other ends. For example, we readily call on family members or close friends to help us move into a new apartment, without expecting to pay for their services. And we would do the same for them. A friend who never returns a favor, however, is likely to leave us feeling "used" and questioning the depth of the friendship.

Members of a primary group view one another as unique rather than interchangeable. We usually do not care who cashes our check at the bank or fills our tank at the corner gas station. Yet in primary groups—especially the family—we are bound to others by emotion and loyalty. Although brothers and sisters experience periodic conflict, they always remain siblings.

In contrast to the primary group, the **secondary group** is *a large and impersonal social group devoted to some specific interest or activity*. Secondary groups are typically larger than primary groups. For example, people who work together in an office, enroll in the same college course, live in the same city neighborhood, or belong to a particular political organization form secondary groups.

In most respects, secondary groups have precisely the opposite characteristics of primary groups. *Secondary relationships* usually involve weak emotional ties and little personal knowledge of one another. Secondary groups vary in duration, but they are frequently short term, beginning and ending without particular

significance. Students in a college course, for instance, who may not see one another after the semester ends, exemplify the secondary group.

Members of secondary groups have little chance to develop a deep concern for one another's overall welfare because they share only a single interest or activity. Sometimes the passing of time will transform a group from secondary to primary, as with co-workers who share an office for many years. Generally, however, people in a secondary group only occasionally think of themselves as "we," and the boundary distinguishing members from nonmembers is usually far less clear than it is in primary groups.

The emotional life of secondary relationships is not intense because people depend on such ties to achieve only limited ends. That is, while primary relationships have a *personal orientation*, secondary relationships have a *goal orientation*. Secondary ties need not be aloof or cold, however. On the contrary, social interactions among students, co-workers, and business associates can be enjoyable even if they are rather impersonal.

In primary groups, members define each other according to *who* they are, that is, in terms of kinship or unique, personal qualities. Members of secondary groups, by contrast, look to one another for *what* they are or what they can do for each other. In secondary groups, in other words, we are always mindful of what we offer others and what we receive in return. This "scorekeeping" comes through most clearly in business relationships. Likewise, the people next door typically expect that a neighborly favor will be reciprocated.

The goal orientation of secondary groups encourages members to carefully craft their behavior. In these roles, then, we remain characteristically impersonal and polite. The secondary relationship, therefore, is one in which the question "How are you?" may be asked without really expecting a truthful answer.

The characteristics of primary and secondary groups are summarized in Table 7–1. As the table suggests, we have described these two types of social groups in ideal terms that do not precisely fit any actual groups in our lives. But placing these concepts as ends of a continuum provides a helpful shorthand for describing and analyzing group life.

By spotlighting the balance of primary and secondary ties, we can track changes in society itself. In general, primary relationships dominate preindustrial societies as people live and work within families and local villages. Strangers stand out in the social landscape. By contrast, secondary ties take precedence in modern, industrial societies, in which people assume

TABLE 7–1 Primary Groups and Secondary Groups: A Summary

	Primary Group ⟷	Secondary Group
Quality of relationships	Personal orientation	Goal orientation
Duration of relationships	Usually long term	Variable; often short term
Breadth of relationships	Broad; usually involving many activities	Narrow; usually involving few activities
Subjective perception of relationships	As an end in itself	As a means to an end
Typical examples	Families; circles of friends	Co-workers; political organizations

NOTE: Some categories of groups—peer groups, for example—cut across the primary-secondary continuum.
NOTE: The basically secondary character of neighborhood is suggested by the old saying "Good fences make good neighbors."
THE MAP: Generally speaking, New England is a high litigation region, while the Midwest and Rocky Mountain states have lower

scores. Significant correlates are degree of urban population, affluence, and levels of migration (see National Map 24-1). The litigation index reflects percent of auto accidents that end up in court, extent of malpractice litigation, number of trial lawyers, extent of municipal litigation, and campaign spending by state's chief justice.

Seeing Ourselves

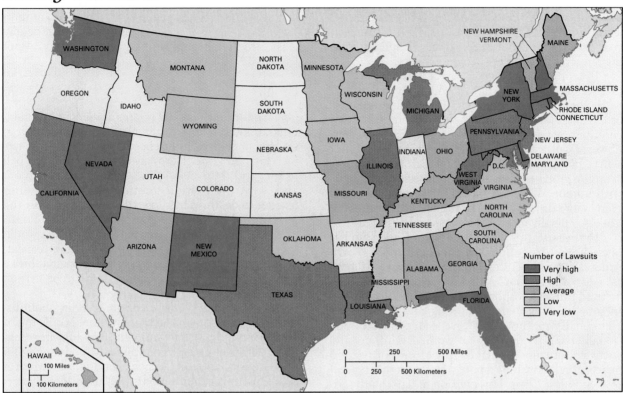

NATIONAL MAP 7–1 The Quality of Relationships: Lawsuits Across the United States
Social conflicts are found everywhere, but whether people tend to resolve them informally or resort to legal action varies from state to state. It stands to reason that, in regions of the country where litigation is least common, people's social ties are typically more primary in character. By contrast, where people are most likely to turn to lawyers, social ties would seem to be more secondary. Looking at the map, what do the states with high levels of litigation have in common? What traits mark the states in which people are reluctant to sue each other?

Prepared by the author using data from Frum & Wolfe (1994).

highly specialized social roles. In today's world, we all routinely engage in impersonal, secondary contacts with virtual strangers—people about whom we know very little and may never meet again (Wirth, 1938).

Not all regions of the United States are equally primary or secondary, however. National Map 7–1 looks at people's tendency to sue each other as one indicator of the quality of our social relationships.

Group Leadership

Social groups vary in the extent to which members recognize *leaders*—people charged with responsibility

for directing the group's activities. Some friendship groups grant one member the clear status of leader; others do not. Within families, parents have leadership roles, although husband and wife may disagree about who is really in charge. In secondary groups like corporations, leadership is likely to involve a formal chain of command with a hierarchy of clearly defined duties.

Two Leadership Roles

Groups generally benefit from two kinds of leadership (Bales, 1953; Bales & Slater, 1955). **Instrumental leadership** refers to *group leadership that emphasizes the* *completion of tasks*. Members look to instrumental leaders to "get things done." **Expressive leadership**, by contrast, *focuses on collective well-being*. Expressive leaders take less of an interest in the performance goals of a group than with group morale and minimizing tension and conflict among members.

Because they concentrate on performance, instrumental leaders usually have secondary relationships with other group members. Instrumental leaders give orders and reward or punish people according to their contribution to the group's efforts. Expressive leaders, however, cultivate primary relationships. They offer sympathy to a member having a tough time, work to keep the group united, and lighten serious moments with humor. While successful instrumental leaders enjoy more distant *respect* from members, expressive leaders generally receive more personal *affection*.

In the past, this differentiation of leadership has been linked to gender. In the traditional North American family, cultural norms bestow instrumental leadership on men. As fathers and husbands, they assume primary responsibility for providing family income, making major decisions, and disciplining children. By contrast, expressive leadership has traditionally been the purview of women. Mothers and wives historically have encouraged supportive and peaceful relationships among family members (Parsons & Bales, 1955). This division of labor partly explains why many children have greater respect for their fathers but closer personal ties with their mothers (Macionis, 1978). Changes in family gender roles have blurred the gender-linked distinction between instrumental and expressive leadership. In other group settings, women and men are both assuming leadership roles.

Three Leadership Styles

Sociologists also describe group leadership using three general orientations to power. *Authoritarian leadership* focuses on instrumental concerns, taking personal charge of decision making and demanding strict compliance from subordinates. Although this leadership style wins little affection from group members, an authoritarian leader may earn praise in a crisis situation requiring immediate decisions.

Democratic leadership has a more expressive focus, with concern for including everyone in the decision-making process. Although less successful during crises, when there is little time for discussion, democratic leaders can otherwise draw on the ideas of all members to forge reflective and imaginative responses to the tasks at hand.

Laissez-faire leadership (from the French phrase meaning, roughly, "to leave alone") downplays position and power. Because these leaders allow the group to function more or less on its own, they are generally least effective in promoting group goals (White & Lippitt, 1953; Ridgeway, 1983).

Group Conformity

Okiki, a thirteen-year-old honors student at a Lorain, Ohio, middle school, sat in class, her arms and legs shaking nervously. In her book bag she had a twelve-inch kitchen knife. Her plan was to wait for the bell to ring and then rush to the front of the classroom and, with the help of another student, stab her teacher to death. Why? To settle a grudge against the teacher and to show her classmates (at least a dozen of whom placed bets as to whether or not she would "chicken out") that she was worthy of their respect. Hearing about the plot, an assistant principal broke up the plan only minutes before it was to be carried out (Gregory, 1993).

The fact that young teens are anxious about fitting in surprises no one, although many people might be amazed at the lengths some will go to gain acceptance. Sociologists have confirmed the power of group pressure to shape human behavior and found that it remains strong in adulthood as well as in adolescence.

Asch's Research

Solomon Asch (1952) conducted a classic investigation that revealed the power of group conformity. He recruited student subjects for an alleged study of visual perception. Before the actual experiment, he obtained the cooperation of all subjects but one in each small group to impose a condition of group pressure on the remaining subject. After the subjects sat down around a table, Asch asked each one, in turn, to look at a "standard" line, as shown on Card 1 in Figure 7–1, and match it to one of three lines on Card 2.

Anyone with normal vision could easily see that the line marked "A" on Card 2 is the correct choice. Initially, as planned, everyone gave the correct answer. Then Asch's secret accomplices began answering incorrectly, causing the naive subject (who was seated to answer last) to become bewildered and uncomfortable.

What happened? Asch found that more than one-third of all subjects placed in this situation chose to conform to the others by answering incorrectly. His investigation suggests that many of us are willing

NOTE: The stress experienced by subjects in this conformity research raises ethical issues, as discussed in Chapter 2.

NOTE: "Whistle-blowing" can be a dangerous practice, according to one CBS News survey. Interviewing people who had subsequently lost their jobs as a result, one in six had endured severe financial hardship or divorce; one in ten had attempted suicide.

to compromise our own judgment to avoid the discomfort of being different from others, even from people we do not know.

Milgram's Research

Stanley Milgram—a former student of Solomon Asch—conducted controversial conformity experiments of his own. In Milgram's initial study (1963, 1965; Miller, 1986), a researcher explained to pairs of recruits that they were about to engage in a study of memory. One was assigned the role of "teacher" and the other—the insider to the study—became the "learner."

The learner sat in an ominous contraption resembling an electric chair with an electrode attached to one arm. The researcher then instructed the teacher to read aloud pairs of words. Then the teacher repeated the first word of each pair and asked the learner to recall the corresponding second word.

As mistakes occurred, the researcher instructed the teacher to shock the learner using a "shock generator," a bogus but forbidding piece of equipment with a shock switch and a dial marked to regulate electric current from 15 volts (labeled "mild shock") to 300 volts (marked "intense shock") to 450 volts (marked "Danger: Severe Shock" and "XXX").

Beginning at the lowest level, the researcher instructed the teacher to increase the shock by 15 volts every time the learner made a mistake. The researcher explained to the teacher that the shocks would become "extremely painful" but cause "no permanent tissue damage."

The results provided striking evidence of the ability of authority figures to obtain compliance. None of forty subjects assigned in the role of teacher during the initial research even questioned the procedure before 300 volts had been applied, and twenty-six of the subjects—almost two-thirds—went all the way to 450 volts.

Just as troubling, Milgram's teachers "shocked" learners who had been instructed to object verbally and to protest that they had heart conditions. Many teachers turned up the voltage even as learners screamed and pretended to fall unconscious. Understandably, many subjects found the experiment extremely stressful, and it violated a key ethical guideline noted in Chapter 2 ("Sociological Investigation"). But many followed orders all the same.

Milgram (1964) then modified his research to see if Solomon Asch had found a high degree of group conformity only because the task of matching lines seemed trivial. What if groups pressured people to administer electrical shocks?

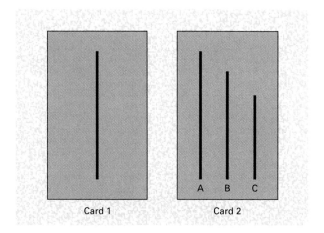

FIGURE 7–1 Cards Used in Asch's Experiment in Group Conformity

(Asch, 1952:452–53)

To investigate, he varied the experiment so that a group of three teachers, two of whom were his accomplices, made decisions jointly. Milgram's rule was that each of the three teachers would suggest a shock level when the learner made an error and they would then administer the *lowest* of the three suggestions. This arrangement gave the naive subject the power to lessen the shock level regardless of what the other two teachers suggested.

The accomplices recommended increasing the shock level with each error, placing group pressure on the third member to do the same. Responding to this group pressure, subjects applied voltages three to four times higher than in experiments when they were acting alone. Thus Milgram's research suggests that people are surprisingly likely to follow the directions of not only "legitimate authority figures," but also of groups of ordinary individuals.

Janis's Research

Even the experts succumb to group pressure, according to Irving L. Janis (1972, 1989). Janis contends that a number of U.S. foreign policy errors, including the failure to foresee the Japanese attack on Pearl Harbor in World War II, the disastrous U.S. invasion of Cuba in 1961, and our ill-fated involvement in the Vietnam War, may have been the result of group conformity among our highest-ranking political leaders.

We often think that "brainstorming" will improve decision making. Janis argues, however, that group-based decision making sometimes backfires. First, rather than examining a problem from many points of

Q: ". . . Some similarities in status attributes between the individual and the reference group must be perceived or imagined, in order for the comparison to occur at all." Robert K. Merton (1968:296)
DATA FILE: Supplementary material for this chapter includes an account of using small groups to combat racism.

Q: "With higher levels of aspiration than the less educated, the better educated man had more to lose in his own eyes and in the eyes of his friends by failure to achieve some sort of status in the Army. Hence, frustration was greater for him than for others if a goal he sought was not attained." Samuel A. Stouffer (1949:153)
NOTE: Consider the line "It's harder to have made money and lost it than to never have had it at all" in terms of relative deprivation.

In many traditional societies, children of the same age forge strong loyalties, generally with members of their own sex. Among the Masai in Kenya, for example, boys born during the same four-year period undergo ritual circumcision together and maintain a group bond throughout their lives.

view, group members may seek consensus, thereby *narrowing* the range of options. Second, groups may develop a distinctive set of terms that favor a single interpretation of events. Third, having settled on a position, members of the group may come to see anyone with another view as the "opposition." Janis called this process **groupthink,** *the tendency of group members to conform by adopting a narrow view of some issue.*

Janis claims that groupthink led the Kennedy administration to invade Cuba—a plan that failed and provoked international criticism of the United States. Arthur Schlesinger, Jr., former adviser to President John Kennedy, confessed guilt "for having kept so quiet during those crucial discussions in the Cabinet Room," but added that the group discouraged anyone from challenging what, in hindsight, he views as "nonsense" (quoted in Janis, 1972:30, 40).

Reference Groups

How do we know if a particular attitude or decision is good? Frequently, we evaluate our views by using others as a **reference group,** *a social group that serves as a point of reference in making evaluations or decisions.*

A young man who imagines his family's response to a woman he is dating is using his family as a reference group. Similarly, a banker who assesses her colleagues' reactions to a new loan policy is using her co-workers as a standard of reference. As these examples suggest, reference groups can be primary or secondary. In either case, the motivation to conform to a group

means that the attitudes of members can greatly affect our personal evaluations.

We also use groups that we do *not* belong to for reference. People preparing for job interviews typically consider how those in the company dress and act, and then adjust their personal performances accordingly. The use of groups by nonmembers illustrates the process of *anticipatory socialization,* described in Chapter 5 ("Socialization"). By conforming, then, individuals hope to win acceptance to the group.

Stouffer's Research

Samuel A. Stouffer (1949) and his associates conducted a classic study of reference group dynamics during World War II. In a survey, researchers asked soldiers to evaluate the chances of promotion for a competent soldier in their branch of the service. Common sense suggests that soldiers serving in outfits with a relatively high promotion rate would be optimistic about their future advancement. Yet survey results revealed just the opposite: Soldiers in branches of the service with low promotion rates were actually more optimistic about their own chances to move ahead.

The key to this paradox lies in sorting out the groups against which the soldiers measured their progress. Those in branches with lower promotion rates looked around them and saw people like themselves. They had not been promoted, in other words, but neither had many others. Thus they did not feel deprived and expressed favorable attitudes about their chances for promotion.

Soldiers in a service branch with a higher promotion rate, however, could easily think of people who had been promoted sooner or more often than they had. Using these people as a reference group, even soldiers who *had* been promoted were likely to feel they had come up short. These were the soldiers who voiced more negative attitudes in their evaluations.

Stouffer's research demonstrates that we do not make judgments about ourselves in isolation, nor do we compare ourselves with just anyone. Instead, we use specific social groups as standards in developing individual attitudes. Regardless of our situation in *absolute* terms, then, we perceive well-being subjectively, *relative* to some specific reference group (Merton, 1968; Mirowsky, 1987).

Ingroups and Outgroups

Everyone favors some groups over others, whether due to political outlook, social prestige, or simply manner of dress. Across the United States, for example,

NOTE: A *Times-Mirror* poll found that a growing share of older people in the United States express dissatisfaction with their financial situation, while young people are more positive. Actual earning data, however, show the opposite, with the incomes of the elderly rising through the 1980s, while incomes of people in their twenties actually fell. How do reference groups explain this pattern?

Q: "Nothing is great or little otherwise than by comparison." Jonathan Swift, *Gulliver's Travels*
NOTE: Ethnocentrism is one expression of valuing one's own ingroup while undervaluing those who differ as an outgroup.
DATA FILE: The controversy over efforts by the Boy Scouts to restrict their membership on the basis of specific principals is highlighted in the *Data File*.

students wear high school jackets and place school decals on car windows to indicate that, to them, school serves as an important social group. Students attending another school may become the targets of derision just because they belong to a rival group.

Such allegiance illustrates an important process of group dynamics: the opposition of ingroups and outgroups. An **ingroup** is *a social group commanding a member's esteem and loyalty.* An ingroup exists in relation to an **outgroup**, *a social group toward which one feels competition or opposition.*

Social life is the interplay of both kinds of groups. A campus football team, for example, is both an ingroup to its members and an outgroup for students uninterested in sports. A town's Democrats generally think of themselves as an ingroup in relation to the local Republicans. All ingroups and outgroups work on the principle that "we" have valued characteristics that "they" lack.

Tensions among groups often help to sharpen their boundaries and give people a clearer social identity. However, this form of group dynamics also promotes self-serving distortions of reality. Research has shown that the members of ingroups hold overly positive views of themselves and unfairly negative views of various outgroups (Tajfel, 1982).

Power also plays a role in group relations. If they have the power to do so, members of an ingroup may socially injure people they view as an outgroup. For example, whites have historically viewed people of color in negative terms and subjected them to social, political, and economic disadvantages. Internalizing these negative attitudes, people of African, Latino, Asian, and Native American descent often struggle to overcome negative self-images based on widely held stereotypes. In short, ingroups and outgroups both foster loyalty and generate tension and conflict.

Group Size

If you are the first person to arrive at a party, you are in a position to observe some fascinating group dynamics. Until about six people enter the room, everyone generally shares a single conversation. But as more people arrive, the group divides into two or more smaller clusters. It is apparent that size plays a crucial role in how group members interact.

To understand why, consider the mathematical connection between the number of people in a social group and the number of relationships among them. As Figure 7–2 on page 186 shows, two people form a single relationship; adding a third person generates three relationships; a fourth person yields six. Adding

One way in which young people learn approved norms is by emulating role models. Members of our competitive society celebrate athletics; thus, athletes serve as role models that foster conformity in children.

people one at a time increases the number of relationships much more rapidly since every new individual can interact with everyone already there. Thus, ten relationships connect five people. And, by the time six people join one conversation, fifteen different relationships connect them, leaving too many people unable to speak. So the group usually divides at this point.

The Dyad

German sociologist Georg Simmel (1858–1918) explored the social dynamics in the smallest social groups. Simmel (1950; orig. 1902) used the term **dyad** to designate *a social group with two members.* In North America and most of the world, love affairs, marriages, and the closest friendships are dyadic.

What makes the dyad a special relationship? First, explained Simmel, like a stool with only two legs, the dyad is typically less stable than groups with three or more members. Both members of a dyad must actively participate in the relationship; if either withdraws, the group collapses. Because the stability of marriages is important to society, the marital dyad is supported with legal and often religious ties. In contrast, a large group is inherently more stable. A volunteer fire company, for example, does not dissolve even if a few members drop out.

Second, social interaction in a dyad is typically more intense than in other groups. In such a one-to-one relationship, neither member shares the other's

SOCIAL SURVEY: "How many of your friends know each other?"
(*CHIP1 Social Survey Software*, FRNDKNO1; GSS 1985, N = 1,423)

SES	All/most	Few/none
High	55.6%	44.4%
Middle	61.4%	38.6%
Low	64.1%	35.9%

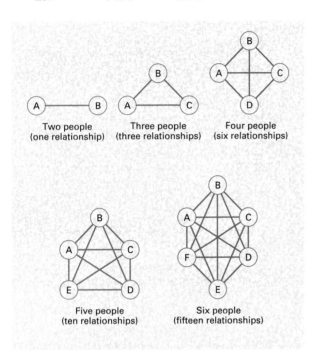

Two people
(one relationship)

Three people
(three relationships)

Four people
(six relationships)

Five people
(ten relationships)

Six people
(fifteen relationships)

FIGURE 7–2 Group Size and Relationships

attention with anyone else. For this reason, dyads also have the potential to be the most meaningful social bonds we ever experience. Marriage in our culture is dyadic; ideally, we expect powerful emotional ties to unite husbands and wives. As we shall see in Chapter 17 ("Family"), however, marriage in other societies can involve more than two people. In that case, the household usually is more stable, although some of the marital relationships may be less strong.

The Triad

Simmel also probed the **triad**, *a social group with three members.* A triad encompasses three relationships, each uniting two of the three people. A triad is more stable than a dyad because, should the relationship between any two members become strained, the third can act as a mediator to restore the group's vitality. This process also helps explain why members of a dyad (say, a married couple) often seek out a third person (a trusted friend or counselor) to air tensions between them.

Nonetheless, two of the three can form a coalition to press their views on the third, or two may intensify their relationship, leaving the other feeling like a "third wheel." For example, two members of a

Q: "A dyad . . . depends on each of its two elements alone—in its death, though not in its life: For its life, it needs both, but for its death, only one." Georg Simmel (1950:124)

Q: "Among three elements [of a triad], each one operates as an intermediary between the other two, exhibiting the twofold function of such an organ, which is to unite and to separate." Georg Simmel (1950:135)

triad who develop a romantic interest in each other are likely to understand the old saying "Two's company, three's a crowd."

As groups grow beyond three members, they become progressively more stable because the loss of even several members does not threaten the group's existence. At the same time, increases in group size typically reduce the intense personal interaction possible only in the smallest groups. Larger groups are thus based less on personal attachments and more on formal rules and regulations. Such formality helps a large group persist over time, though the group is not immune to change. After all, their numerous members give large groups more contact with the outside world, opening the door to new attitudes and behavior (Carley, 1991).

Does a social group have an ideal size? The answer depends on the group's purpose. A dyad offers unsurpassed emotional intensity, while a group of several dozen people is likely to be more stable, capable of accomplishing larger, more complex tasks, and better able to assimilate new members or ideas. People typically find more *pleasure* in smaller groups, while deriving greater *satisfaction* from accomplishing tasks in larger organizations (Slater, 1958; Ridgeway, 1983; Carley, 1991).

Social Diversity

Social diversity affects group dynamics, especially the likelihood that members will interact with someone of another group. Peter Blau (1977, 1982; South & Messner, 1986) points out four ways in which the composition of social groups affects intergroup association.

1. **Large groups turn inward.** Extending Simmel's analysis of group size, Blau claims that the larger a group, the more likely members are to maintain relationships exclusively among themselves. The smaller the group, by contrast, the greater the odds that members will reach beyond their immediate social circle.

   To illustrate, consider the efforts of many colleges to enhance social diversity. Increasing the number of, say, international students may add a dimension of difference to a campus, but, as their numbers rise, these students eventually are able to maintain their own distinctive social group. Thus intentional efforts to promote social diversity may well have the unintended effect of promoting separatism.

NOTE: Because of Simmel's focus on the intricate details of situational social life, Everett Hughes dubbed him "the Freud of sociology."

DIVERSITY: Members of small racial and ethnic communities are more likely to marry out of their category than are members of larger categories (Gurak & Fitzpatrick, 1982).

NOTE: Networks are a characteristic feature of modern societies in which social ties are not built around kinship and neighborhood but a wide range of individual experiences and interests.

RESOURCE: Elizabeth Bott's classic *Family and Social Network* (The Free Press, 1957 and 1971) relates networks to other aspects of social structure.

DATA FILE: Supplementary material on networking women is included in the *Data File*.

2. **Heterogeneous groups turn outward.** The more internally heterogeneous a group is, the more likely its members are to interact with members of other groups. We would expect, for example, that campus groups that recruit members of both sexes and people of various ethnic and geographic backgrounds would promote more intergroup contact than those that choose members of one social type.

3. **Social parity promotes contact.** An environment in which all groups have roughly equal standing encourages people of all social backgrounds to mingle and form social ties. Thus, whether groups insulate their members or not depends on whether the groups themselves form a social hierarchy.

4. **Physical boundaries promote social boundaries.** Blau contends that physical space affects the chances of contacts among groups. To the extent that a social group is physically segregated from others (by having its own dorm or dining area, for example), its members are less apt to engage other people.

Networks

Formally, a **network** is *a web of social ties that links people who may have little common identity and interaction.* In other words, a network is a "fuzzy" group that brings people into occasional contact without a group's sense of boundaries and belonging. Computer networks, or other high-technology links, now routinely connect people living all over the world. If we think of a group as a "circle of friends," then, we might describe a network as a "social web" expanding outward, often reaching great distances and including large numbers of people.

Some network contacts are regular, as among college friends who years later stay in touch by mail and telephone. More commonly, however, a network includes people we *know of*—or who *know of us*—but with whom we interact infrequently, if at all. As one woman with a widespread reputation as a community organizer explains, "I get calls at home, someone says, 'Are you Roseann Navarro? Somebody told me to call you. I have this problem . . .'" (quoted in Kaminer, 1984:94). For this reason, peoples' social networks have been characterized as "clusters of weak ties" (Granovetter, 1973).

Network ties may be weak, but they serve as a significant resource. For example, many people rely on their networks to find jobs. Even the scientific genius

A distinctive characteristic of a triad is that the social bond that joins two members can intensify, to the exclusion of the third.

Albert Einstein needed a hand in landing his first job. After a year of unsuccessful interviewing, he obtained employment only when the father of one of his classmates put him in touch with an office manager who hired him (Clark, 1971; cited in Fischer, 1977:19). This use of networks to advantage suggests that, as the saying goes, *who you know* is often just as important as *what you know.*

A survey by Nan Lin (1981) confirmed the importance of networks, determining that almost 60 percent of 399 men in a U.S. city had found a job through networks. Lin concluded that networks were the greatest single occupational resource, but he also found that networks do not provide equal advantages to everyone. His results showed that the sons of men with important occupational positions gained the greatest advantages from their networks. This finding supports the notion that networks link people of similar social background.

Peter Marsden (1987) discovered that the most extensive social networks are maintained by people who are young, well educated, and living in urban areas. The networks of men and women tend to be the same size, although women include more relatives in their networks, while those of men include more coworkers. Women's networks, therefore, may not carry quite the same clout that the "old-boy" networks do. Even so, research suggests that, as gender inequality lessens in the United States, this difference is diminishing over time (Moore, 1991, 1992).

GLOBAL: Communications technology (including electronic mail using computers) is now generating rapidly expanding global networks. Internet links 25 million people in 90 countries.
DATA FILE: Supplementary material on how race, gender, and class affect voluntary association memberships is included in the *Data File.*

Q: "A formal, rationally organized social structure involves clearly defined patterns of activity in which, ideally, every series of actions is functionally related to the purposes of the organization." Robert K. Merton (1968:249)
NOTE: The number of voluntary associations in the United States continues to rise; 70% of adults belong to at least one (Caplow et. al., 1991).

FORMAL ORGANIZATIONS

A century ago, social life was centered in small groups of family members, neighbors, and co-workers. Today our lives revolve far more around **formal organizations,** *large, secondary groups that are organized to achieve their goals efficiently.* Formal organizations, such as corporations or branches of government, differ from small family or friendship groups in more than simply the size of their membership. Their greater size renders social relationships less personal and fosters a planned or formal atmosphere. People design formal organizations to accomplish specific tasks rather than to meet personal needs.

When you think about it, organizing a society with more than 250 million members is a remarkable feat. Countless tasks are involved, from collecting taxes to delivering the mail. Most of these responsibilities are carried out by large, formal organizations. The United States government, the nation's largest formal organization, employs more than 5 million people in various agencies and the armed forces. Each government division includes an array of smaller organizations with specific goals. Such large groups develop lives and cultures of their own, so that as members come and go, the statuses they fill and the roles they perform remain unchanged over the years.

Types of Formal Organizations

Amitai Etzioni (1975) has identified three types of formal organizations, distinguished by why people participate. These types are normative organizations, coercive organizations, and utilitarian organizations.

Normative Organizations

People join *normative organizations* to pursue goals they consider morally worthwhile, deriving personal satisfaction, and perhaps social prestige, but no monetary reward for their efforts. Sometimes called *voluntary associations,* these include community service groups (such as the PTA, the Lions Club, the League of Women Voters, Red Cross, and Kiwanis), political parties, religious organizations, and numerous other confederations concerned with specific social issues. In global perspective, people in the United States are especially likely to be members of voluntary associations (Curtis, Grabb, & Baer, 1992). Moreover, because affluent women historically have not participated in the paid labor force, they have traditionally played a central role in civic and charitable organizations.

Coercive Organizations

In Etzioni's typology, *coercive organizations* are distinguished by involuntary membership. That is, people are forced to join the organization as a form of punishment (prisons) or treatment (psychiatric hospitals). Coercive organizations have extraordinary physical features, such as locked doors, barred windows, and security personnel (Goffman, 1961). These are settings that segregate people as "inmates" or "patients" for a period of time and sometimes radically alter their attitudes and behavior. Recall from Chapter 5 ("Socialization") the power of *total institutions* to transform a human being's overall sense of self.

Utilitarian Organizations

According to Etzioni, people join *utilitarian organizations* in pursuit of material rewards. Large business enterprises, for example, generate profits for their owners and income in the form of salaries and wages for their employees. Joining utilitarian organizations is usually a matter of individual choice, although, obviously, most people must join one utilitarian organization or another to make a living.

From differing vantage points, any particular organization may fall into *all* these categories. A psychiatric hospital, for example, serves as a coercive organization for a patient, a utilitarian organization for a psychiatrist, and a normative organization to a part-time hospital volunteer.

Origins of Bureaucracy

Formal organizations date back thousands of years. Religious and political administration extended the power of elites over millions of people living in vast areas. Formal organization also allowed rulers to collect taxes, undertake military campaigns, and construct monumental structures, from the Great Wall of China to the pyramids of Egypt.

The power of these early organizations was limited, however, not because elites lacked grandiose ambition, but by the traditional character of preindustrial societies. Long-established cultural patterns placed greater importance on preserving the past or carrying out "God's will" than on organizational efficiency. Only in the last few centuries did there emerge what Max Weber called a "rational world view," as described in Chapter 4 ("Society"). In the wake of the Industrial Revolution, the organizational structure called *bureaucracy* became commonplace in Europe and North America.

Although formal organization is vital to modern, industrial societies, it is far from new. Twenty-five centuries ago, the Chinese philosopher and teacher K'ung Fu-Tzu (known to Westerners as Confucius) endorsed the idea that government offices should be filled by the most talented young men. This led to what was probably the world's first system of civil service examinations. Here, would-be bureaucrats compose essays to demonstrate their knowledge of Confucian texts.

Characteristics of Bureaucracy

Bureaucracy is *an organizational model rationally designed to perform complex tasks efficiently*. In a bureaucratic business or government agency, officials deliberately enact and revise policy to make the organization as efficient as possible. To appreciate the power and scope of bureaucratic organization, consider the telephone system in the United States. Using any one of more than 160 million phones, you can be connected within seconds to any other phone—in homes, businesses, and automobiles. Such communication is beyond the imagination of those who lived in the ancient world.

Of course, the telephone system depends on technological developments such as electricity and computers. But neither could the system exist without the organizational capacity to keep track of every telephone call—noting which phone called which other phone, when, and for how long—and presenting all this information to tens of millions of telephone users in the form of monthly bills.

In global context, the availability of telephones and other forms of electronic communications is a good indicator of the extent of bureaucratic organization. As shown in Global Map 7–1, facsimile (fax) machines are most common throughout the United States and Canada, Western Europe, Japan, and Australia and

NOTE: Photocopier machines, now essential to bureaucratic organizations, first appeared in the 1950s. Many people were skeptical that they would catch on.

NOTE: "Paperwork" is closely related to the negative connotation of bureaucracy. Some indicators of the sheer volume of paperwork in the United States: We mail more than 160 billion items per year, and the consumption of writing and printing paper has risen faster than the gross national product. (Edward Tenner)

Window on the World

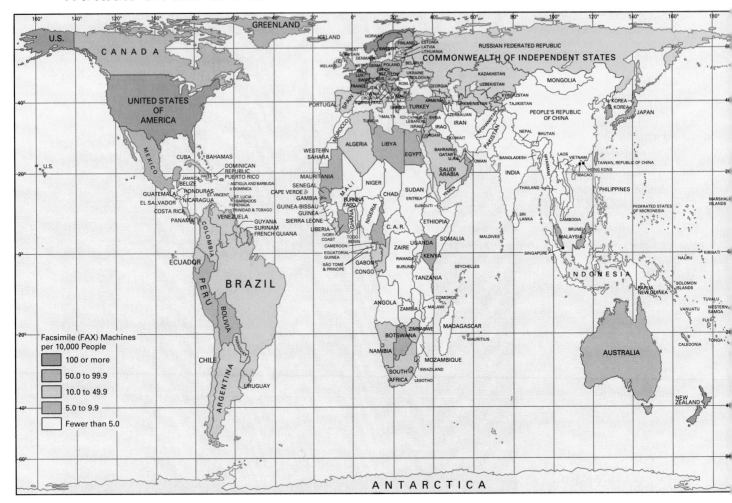

GLOBAL MAP 7–1 Data Transmission in Global Perspective

The expansion of formal organization depends partly on available technology. Facsimile (fax) machines and other devices for transmitting data are widespread in economically developed regions of the world, including the United States, Canada, Western Europe, Japan, and Australia. In poor societies, such devices are all but unknown to most people. Note, too, that the wealthy elite in small nations like Kuwait make extensive use of advanced technology to support their global business operations.

From *Peters Atlas of the World* (1990).

New Zealand. In most nations of the world, however, such devices are limited to government agencies and large businesses. Thus the proliferation of bureaucracy is closely tied to economic development.

What specific traits promote organizational efficiency? Max Weber (1978; orig. 1921) identified six key elements of the ideal bureaucratic organization.

1. **Specialization.** Through most of human history, people's lives centered on securing food and shelter. Bureaucracy embodies a far wider set of imperatives and assigns to individuals highly specialized duties.

2. **Hierarchy of offices.** Bureaucracies arrange personnel in a vertical hierarchy of offices. Each

NOTE: The section in Chapter 4, "Max Weber: The Rationalization of Society," provides general background for this discussion of bureaucracy. It introduces Weber's thesis of increasing rationalization; this section focuses more narrowly on bureaucracy as a major manifestation of that process.

NOTE: Beyond the 5 million regular employees of the U.S. government, millions of "contractors" also perform various official duties.

Q: "In small groups, members typically have a chance to interact directly with one another; once the group exceeds a relatively limited size, such interaction must be mediated through formal arrangements. . . . Thus no large group can function without the creation of offices, the differentiation of status positions, and the delegation of tasks and responsibilities." Lewis A. Coser (1971:188)

person is thus supervised by "higher-ups" in the organization while, in turn, supervising others in lower positions.

3. **Rules and regulations.** Cultural tradition holds scant sway in bureaucracy. Instead, operations are guided by rationally enacted rules and regulations. These rules guide not only the organization's own functioning but, as much as possible, its larger environment. Ideally, a bureaucracy seeks to operate in a completely predictable fashion.

4. **Technical competence.** A bureaucratic organization expects officials to have the technical competence to carry out their official duties. Bureaucracies regularly monitor the performance of staff members. Such impersonal evaluation based on performance contrasts sharply with the custom, followed through most of human history, of favoring relatives—whatever their talents—over strangers.

5. **Impersonality.** In bureaucratic organizations, rules take precedence over personal feelings. This impersonality encourages uniform treatment for each client as well as other workers. From this detached approach stems the notion of the "faceless bureaucrat."

6. **Formal, written communications.** An old adage states that the heart of bureaucracy is not people but paperwork. Rather than casual, verbal communication, bureaucracy relies on formal, written memos and reports. Over time, this correspondence accumulates into vast *files*. The files guide the subsequent operation of an organization in roughly the same way that social background shapes the life of an individual.

These traits represent a clear contrast to the more personal character of small groups. Bureaucratic organization promotes efficiency by carefully recruiting personnel and limiting the unpredictable effects of personal tastes and opinions. In smaller, informal groups, members allow one another considerable discretion in their behavior; they respond to each other personally and consider everyone more or less equal in rank. Table 7–2 summarizes the differences between small social groups and large formal organizations.

The Informal Side of Bureaucracy

Weber's ideal bureaucracy deliberately regulates every activity. In actual organizations, however, human beings have the creativity (or the stubbornness) to

TABLE 7–2 Small Groups and Formal Organizations: A Comparison

	Small Groups	Formal Organizations
Activities	Members typically engage in many of the same activities	Members typically engage in distinct, highly specialized activities
Hierarchy	Often informal or nonexistent	Clearly defined, corresponding to offices
Norms	Informal application of general norms	Clearly defined rules and regulations
Criteria for membership	Variable, often based on personal affection or kinship	Technical competence to carry out assigned tasks
Relationships	Variable; typically primary	Typically secondary, with selective primary ties
Communications	Typically casual and face to face	Typically formal and in writing
Focus	Person oriented	Task oriented

resist conforming to bureaucratic blueprints. Sometimes informality helps to meet a legitimate need overlooked by formal regulations. In other situations informality may amount to simply cutting corners in one's job (Scott, 1981).

Formally, power resides in offices, not with the people who occupy them. Nonetheless, personality greatly affects patterns of organizational leadership. Studies of U.S. corporations reveal that the qualities and quirks of individuals, including their charisma or skill in interpersonal relations, have a tremendous impact on organizational outcomes (Halberstam, 1986).

Authoritarian, democratic, and laissez-faire types of leadership—described earlier in this chapter—also reflect individual personality as much as any organizational plan. Then, too, decision making within an organization does not always conform to the defined hierarchy and the official regulations. As the recent U.S. savings and loan scandal reveals, officials

According to Max Weber, bureaucracy is an organizational strategy that promotes efficiency. Impersonality, however, also fosters alienation among employees, who may become indifferent to the formal goals of the organization. The behavior of this municipal employee in Bombay, India, is understandable to members of formal organizations almost anywhere in the world.

A classic study of the Western Electric factory in Chicago revealed that few employees reported fellow workers who violated rules, as the company required (Roethlisberger & Dickson, 1939). On the contrary, workers socially isolated those who *did,* labeling them "squealers" who could not be trusted. Although the company formally set productivity standards, workers informally created their own definition of a fair day's work, criticizing those who exceeded it as "rate-busters" and those who fell short as "chiselers."

Such informal social structures suggest that people often strive to personalize rigidly defined social situations. This leads us to take a closer look at some of the problems of bureaucracy.

Problems of Bureaucracy

Despite our reliance on bureaucracy to manage countless dimensions of everyday life, many members of our society are ambivalent about this organizational form. The following sections review several of the problems associated with bureaucracy, ranging from its capacity to dehumanize and alienate individuals to the dangers it poses to personal privacy and political democracy.

Bureaucratic Alienation

Max Weber touted bureaucracy as a model of productivity. Nonetheless, Weber was keenly aware of bureaucracy's potential to *dehumanize* those it purports to serve. The impersonality that fosters efficiency, in other words, simultaneously denies officials and clients the ability to recognize each other's unique, personal needs. On the contrary, officials must treat each client impersonally as a standard "case."

The impersonal bureaucratic environment, then, is a source of *alienation*. As noted in Chapter 4 ("Society"), Weber contended that formal organizations can reduce a human being to "a small cog in a ceaselessly moving mechanism" (1978:988; orig. 1921). In a world of more and more formal organizations, therefore, Weber was deeply pessimistic about the future of humankind. Although formal organizations are intended to serve humanity, he feared that humanity may well end up serving formal organizations.

Bureaucratic Ritualism

Then there is the familiar problem of inefficiency, often encountered when formal organizations attempt to respond to special needs or circumstances. Anyone who has ever tried to replace a lost driver's license,

and their friends may personally benefit through abuse of organizational power. In the "real world" of organizational life, officials who attempt to operate strictly by the book may even find themselves denied the promotions and power that flow from informal alliances. In some organizations, too, people in leadership positions rely on subordinates to handle much of their own work. Many secretaries, for example, have far more authority and responsibility than their official job titles and salaries suggest.

Communication offers another example of how informality creeps into large organizations. Formally, memos and other written communications disseminate information through the hierarchy. Typically, however, individuals cultivate informal networks or "grapevines" that spread information much faster, if not always accurately. Grapevines are particularly important to subordinates because high officials often attempt to conceal important information from them.

Sometimes employees modify or ignore rigid bureaucratic structures to advance their own interests.

Q: "[Through bureaucracy,] the performance of each individual worker is mathematically measured, each man becomes a little cog in the machine and, aware of this, his one preoccupation is whether he can become a bigger cog." Max Weber (cited in Coser, 1971:231)

NOTE: Pedantry, slavish attention to rules, has the Latin root *ped*, meaning "foot," implying a servile follower.

NOTE: Following Weber's analysis, the most effective way to destroy a bureaucratic organization would be to eliminate not its officers, but its files.

Q: "The bureaucratic structure exerts a constant pressure upon the official to be methodical, prudent, disciplined . . . This may be exaggerated to the point where primary concern with conformity to the rules interferes with the achievement of the purposes of the organization." Robert K. Merton (1968:252–53)

George Tooker's painting Government Bureau *is a powerful statement about the human costs of bureaucracy. The artist depicts members of the public in monotonous similitude—reduced from human beings to mere "cases" to be disposed of as quickly as possible. Set apart from others by their positions, officials are "faceless bureaucrats" concerned more with numbers than with providing genuine assistance (notice that the artist places the fingers of the officials on calculators).*

George Tooker, *Government Bureau*, 1956. Egg tempera on gesso panel, 19 5/8 x 29 5/8 inches. The Metropolitan Museum of Art, George A. Hearn Fund, 1956 (56.78).

return defective merchandise to a discount store, or change an address on a magazine subscription knows that bureaucracies sometimes can be maddeningly unresponsive.

The problem of inefficiency is captured in the concept of *red tape*, a phrase describing a tedious preoccupation with organizational routines and procedures that comes from the red tape used by eighteenth-century English administrators to wrap official parcels and records (Shipley, 1985). Sociologist Robert Merton (1968) points out that red tape amounts to a new twist in the already familiar concept of group conformity. He coined the term **bureaucratic ritualism** to designate *a preoccupation with organizational rules and regulations to the point of thwarting an organization's goals.*

Ritualism impedes individual and organizational performance as it stifles creativity and imagination (Whyte, 1957; Merton, 1968). Thus bureaucratic ritualism stands as another expression of the alienation that Weber feared would arise from bureaucratic rigidity.

Bureaucratic Inertia

If bureaucrats are preoccupied with following the rules, they also can jealously preserve their organization even when its purpose has been fulfilled. Weber noted that "once fully established, bureaucracy is among the social structures which are hardest to destroy" (1978:987; orig. 1921).

Bureaucratic inertia refers to *the tendency of bureaucratic organizations to perpetuate themselves.*

Formal organizations, in other words, tend to take on a life of their own beyond their formal objectives. Occasionally, a formal organization that meets its goals will simply disband—as the anti-British Sons of Liberty did after the American Revolution. More commonly, an organization stays in business by redefining its goals so it can continue to provide a livelihood for its members.

For example, consider the history of the National Association for Infantile Paralysis, the sponsor of the well-known March of Dimes (Sills, 1969). This organization came into being as part of the drive to find a cure for polio. Researchers accomplished this goal with the development of the Salk vaccine in the early 1950s. Subsequently, however, the organization did not dissolve, redirecting its efforts even today toward other medical problems such as birth defects.

Bureaucracy and Privacy

A more recent problem surrounding the growth of formal organizations is the erosion of personal privacy (Long, 1967; Smith, 1979). This issue springs from a large organization's long-standing tendency to treat people impersonally and to collect and store information about individuals. In recent decades, however, the danger to privacy has increased as organizations have become armed with powerful computer technology.

In the United States, more people now have more information about each and every citizen than ever before in our history. Bureaucracy may be essential to

Q: "It is organization which gives birth to the dominion of the elected over the electors, of the mandataries over the mandators, of the delegates over the delegators. Who says organization says oligarchy." Robert Michels

GLOBAL: As an example of successful opposition to entrenched leaders, Brazilian President Fernando Collor de Mello was impeached in 1993 on corruption charges.

SOCIAL SURVEY: "How concerned are you about the amount of information collected by:" (Yankelovich Clancy Shulman poll for *Time*, October 1991)

	Not very	Very/somewhat
Federal govt.	21%	78%
Credit organs.	21%	78%
For marketing	29%	69%

a vast and complex society, but the result is ever-larger banks of personal information. As they issue driver's licenses, for example, government agencies gather information that they can dispatch to police or other officials at the touch of a button. Similarly, the Internal Revenue Service, the Social Security Administration, and programs that benefit veterans, students, the poor, and unemployed people all collect extensive information.

The explosive growth of credit in the U.S. economy has also fueled the drive for information. Today, members of our society carry almost 1 billion credit cards (an average of almost six per adult), enabling them to receive credit from total strangers. But, here again, one result of this convenience is proliferating data banks that contain an extensive financial history of the individual involved.

How do we experience the erosion of privacy? One way is through the escalating amount of junk mail—now half of all documents the post office delivers. Mailing lists for this material grow exponentially as one organization sells its list to others. Had a baby recently? If so, you probably have found yourself on the mailing lists of companies that market all kinds of infant products. Have you ever rented an X-rated video? Many video stores keep records of the movie preferences of customers and pass them along to other organizations willing to pay for the list.

In response to this trend, many states have enacted laws giving citizens the right to examine records about themselves kept by employers, banks, and credit bureaus. The U.S. Privacy Act of 1974 also limits the exchange of personal information among government agencies and permits citizens to examine and correct most government files.

The United States is virtually alone in this concern for limiting the collection of personal information by organizations. In fact, in many other nations of the world, governments are developing new and complex systems for gathering, storing, and disseminating information about their people. The box provides a brief look at this pattern.

Oligarchy

Early in this century, Robert Michels (1876–1936) pointed out the link between bureaucracy and political **oligarchy**, *the rule of the many by the few* (1949; orig. 1911). According to what Michels called "the iron law of oligarchy," the pyramidlike structure of bureaucracy places a few leaders in charge of vast and powerful government organizations.

The earliest human societies did not possess the organizational means for even the most power-hungry ruler to control everyone. But the power of elites increased with the steady expansion of formal organizations over the centuries.

Max Weber credited bureaucracy's strict hierarchy of responsibility with increasing organizational efficiency. By applying Weber's thesis to the organization of government, Michels reveals that this hierarchical structure discourages democracy. While the public expects organizational officials to subordinate personal interests to organizational goals, people who occupy powerful positions can—and often do—use their access to information and the media and numerous other advantages to promote their personal interests. Oligarchy, then, thrives in the hierarchical structure of bureaucracy and undermines people's control over their elected leaders.

Political competition and checks and balances in this nation's system of government prevent the flagrant oligarchy found in some societies. In 1974, for example, Richard Nixon was forced to resign as president of the United States, and three presidents since then have been defeated in their bids for reelection. Even so, among national officeholders, the 1992 elections—in a year the public was determined to "throw the bums out"—resulted in only 19 of 349 congressional incumbents being defeated by their challengers. Incumbents clearly enjoy enormous advantages of power and funding over challengers.

Oligarchy remains well entrenched in many regions of the world. Most nations on the African continent, for example, remain under the control of one-party political systems. Yet, as Chapter 16 ("Politics and Government") explains, there has been a recent trend toward political democracy. Over the course of the last few years, popular uprisings have toppled communist regimes in Eastern Europe, and many longtime officials were sent packing by the people of the former Soviet Union. And in Brazil, a public outcry over corruption in 1992 forced President Fernando Collor de Mello from office.

Parkinson's Law and the Peter Principle

Finally, and on a lighter note, we acknowledge two additional insights concerning the limitations of bureaucratic organizations. The concerns of C. Northcote Parkinson and Laurence J. Peter are familiar to all who have ever been a part of a formal organization.

C. Northcote Parkinson (1957) summed up his understanding of bureaucratic inefficiency with the

SOCIAL SURVEY: "How concerned are you about threats to your personal privacy in America today?" (GSS 1982, N = 1,506; *Codebook*, 1993:309)

"Very concerned" 44.6% "Not concerned at all" 10.9%
"Somewhat concerned" 28.6% DK/NR 1.5%
"Only a little concerned" 14.4%

SOCIAL SURVEY: "Should employers be allowed or not allowed to:" (*Time* poll)
"listen in on employee telephone conversations" (Yes, 6%; No, 93%)
"scan the work area with video cameras" (Yes, 38%; No, 56%)
"require employees to take drug tests" (Yes, 76%; No, 19%)

GLOBAL SOCIOLOGY

Government and Personal Privacy: A Report from Thailand

Adults in Thailand will soon be required by law to carry a government identification card that bears a photograph and a string of computer language. But, unlike most identification cards, this one, when inserted in a computer terminal, calls up a complete social profile of the individual, including physical description, fingerprints, home address, names of parents and children, marital status, education, job, income, religion, and police record.

Is such technology merely a lawful way to assist various government officials, as the Thai government claims? Or, as critics warn, a giant step toward giving "big brother" unprecedented information about citizens?

Expanding government bureaucracies coupled with sophisticated computer technology (much of which comes from U.S. corporations) represent a growing threat to personal freedom in many nations of the world. Several countries—including Indonesia and the Philippines—are closely monitoring the

Thai program as they consider similar systems of their own.

In other regions of the world, government agencies utilizing computer technology are also subjecting people to unprecedented scrutiny. Israel, for example, has long used such a system to monitor Palestinians living in occupied lands. And, until recently, South Africa has maintained technological surveillance over its black majority.

A global trend, then, is declining privacy as bureaucracy expands and applies new forms of technology to the task of managing the lives of citizens. And the danger of government manipulation is especially great in Thailand and other societies that contain categories of people who have few political rights to begin with.

SOURCES: Smith (1979), Dunn (1991), and Miller (1991).

assertion: "*Work expands to fill the time available for its completion.*" Enough truth underlies this tongue-in-cheek assertion that it is known today as Parkinson's Law. To illustrate, assume that a bureaucrat working at the Division of Motor Vehicles processes fifty driver's license applications in an average day. If one day this worker had only twenty-five applications to examine, how much time would the task require? The logical answer is half a day. But Parkinson's Law suggests that if a full day is available to complete the work, a full day is how long it will take.

Because organizational employees have little personal involvement in their jobs, few are likely to seek extra work to fill their spare time. Bureaucrats do strive

to *appear* busy, however, and their activity often prompts organizations to take on more employees. The added time and expense required to hire, train, supervise, and evaluate a larger staff make everyone busier still, setting in motion a vicious cycle that results in *bureaucratic bloat*. Ironically, the larger organization may accomplish no more real work than it did before.

In the same spirit as Parkinson, Laurence J. Peter (Peter & Hull, 1969) devised the Peter Principle: "*Bureaucrats are promoted to their level of incompetence.*" The logic here is simple: Employees competent at one level of the organizational hierarchy are likely to earn promotion to higher positions. Eventually, however, they will reach a position where they are in over their

NOTE: "Peter's Corollary" is that, eventually, all positions in a large organization will be filled with incompetents.

NOTE: Evidence of bureaucracy's expansion: In 1950, 10 million farmers were served by 84,373 employees in Department of Agriculture (ratio of 118:1); by 1990, the numbers were 2.9 million farmers but 129,000 D.O.A. employees (22:1). Based on rates of growth and decline, by 2060 there will be more bureaucrats than farmers. Put otherwise, between 1950 and 1990, the number of farms fell 60%, the number of farmers dropped 70%, but the number of farm bureaucrats rose 53% (Littmann, 1992).

RESOURCE: An excerpt from Sally Helgesen's "The Female Advantage" is among the contemporary selections found in the Macionis and Benokraitis reader, *Seeing Ourselves*.

PROFILE

Rosabeth Moss Kanter: People are the Greatest Resource

How did a woman who began her career in the 1960s studying communes and other utopian settlements end up shaping the real-world decisions of the most successful U.S. corporations? Part of the answer is that many ideas about organizations first raised in the 1960s have now found a receptive audience in corporate boardrooms across the country.

Rosabeth Moss Kanter, a professor of business administration at Harvard University, has helped businesses learn to reorganize toward greater success and higher profits. For her work, Kanter has been honored with numerous honorary doctoral degrees and feature stories in national publications. Her achievements rank her among the most influential women in our society.

Kanter divides her career between academic duties and Goodmeasure, Inc., a corporate consulting firm she and her husband founded. She is the author of several widely read books that apply sociological insights to the task of making corporations more effective.

What lessons does Kanter offer corporate executives that warrant fees as high as $15,000 for a single appearance? She challenges conventional organizational wisdom by demonstrating that *people*—not technology or machinery—are a corporation's most important resource. In the long run, she maintains, an organizational environment that develops human potential will ensure success. Reflecting on her career, Kanter explains:

I remember when participation was what was being talked about on college campuses by Vietnam war protesters or people looking for student power. Now it's a respectable concept in corporate America, and now very large companies are figuring out how to divide themselves into small units. Many ideas and values of the '60s have been translated into the workplace. Take, for example, the right of workers to free expression, the desirability of participation and teamwork, the idea that authority should not be obeyed unquestioningly, the idea that smaller can be better because it can create ownership and family feeling. All of these are now mainstream ideas.

SOURCES: Murray (1984) and McHenry (1985).

heads; there, they perform poorly and are thus no longer eligible for promotions.

Reaching their level of incompetence dooms officials to a future of inefficiency. Adding to the problem, after years in the office they have almost certainly learned how to avoid demotion by hiding behind rules and regulations and taking credit for work actually performed by their more competent subordinates.

Gender and Race in Organizations

Rosabeth Moss Kanter, introduced in the box, has analyzed how ascribed statuses such as gender and race figure in the power structure of bureaucratic hierarchies. To the extent that an organization has a dominant social composition, the gender- or race-based ingroup enjoys greater social acceptance, respect, credibility, and access to informal social networks.

As Figure 7–3 on page 197 shows, white men in the United States represent about 40 percent of the U.S. population between the ages of twenty and sixty-four but hold two-thirds of management jobs. White women, a category of comparable size, trail with about 23 percent of managerial positions. The members of various minorities lag further behind, even taking account of their smaller populations.

DIVERSITY: A growing number of women are trying to resolve role conflicts by leaving organizational jobs ("cashing out") and starting their own small businesses; 400,000 women did so in 1990.

NOTE: An interesting question is whether women need to learn about organizations or organizations need to learn about women.

NOTE: During the 1980s, major corporations that initiated work-teams included Boeing, Caterpillar, Digital Equipment, Ford, and General Motors. A few, including Procter & Gamble, have used them since the 1960s.

Q: "It's not all wonderful stuff. But we've found that when you treat people like adults, 95 percent act like adults." Roger Gasaway, plant manager in G.E.'s Salisbury plant

Q: "Bureaucratic organization has usually come into power on the basis of a leveling of economic and social differences." Max Weber

FIGURE 7–3

U.S. Managers by Race, Sex, and Ethnicity, 1992

(U.S. Equal Opportunity Commission and Census Bureau)

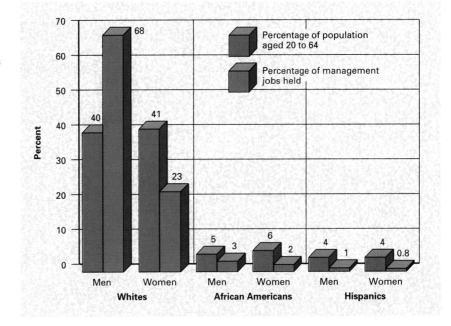

A smaller representation in the workplace, argues Kanter, can leave women, people of color, and those from economically disadvantaged backgrounds feeling like socially isolated outgroups. They are often uncomfortably visible, taken less seriously, and given fewer chances for promotion than others. Understandably, minorities themselves often end up thinking that they must work twice as hard as those in dominant categories to maintain their present position, let alone advance to a higher position (Kanter, 1977; Kanter & Stein, 1979:137).

Kanter (1977) finds that providing a structure of unequal opportunities has important consequences for everyone's on-the-job performance. According to Kanter, a company that has many "dead-end" jobs only encourages workers to become "zombies" with little aspiration, poor self-concept, and little loyalty to the organization. Widespread opportunity, by contrast, typically motivates employees, turning them into "fast-trackers" with higher aspirations, more self-esteem, and stronger commitment to the organization.

Kanter claims that broadening opportunity also encourages leaders to value the input of subordinates and to be concerned with their morale and well-being. It is officials with no real power, she maintains, who jealously guard what privileges they do have and rigidly supervise subordinates.

Table 7–3 summarizes Kanter's findings. In her view, organizations that become more open and flexible—that is, those that "humanize" their structure—bring out the best in their employees and improve the "bottom line."

Humanizing Bureaucracy

Humanizing bureaucracy means *fostering an organizational atmosphere that recognizes and encourages the contributions of everyone.* Research by Kanter (1977, 1983, 1989; Kanter & Stein, 1980) and others (Peters & Waterman, Jr., 1982) shows that "humanizing" bureaucracy produces both happier employees and healthier profits. Based on the discussion so far, we can identify three paths to a more humane organizational structure.

1. **Social inclusiveness.** The social composition of the organization should, ideally, make no one feel "out of place" because of gender, race, or ethnicity. The performance of all employees will improve to the extent that no one is subject to social exclusion.

2. **Sharing of responsibilities.** Humanizing bureaucracy means reducing rigid, oligarchical structures by spreading power and responsibility more widely. Managers cannot benefit from the ideas of employees who have no channels for expressing their opinions. Knowing that superiors are open to suggestions encourages all employees to think creatively, increasing organizational effectiveness.

NOTE: Management policies can encourage the involvement of employees. At Honda's plant at Marysville, Ohio—the U.S.'s most productive—assembly line workers (referred to as "associates") have considerable opportunity to shape the production process. All employees—from the president to the maintenance staff—wear similar uniforms in the plant to encourage exchange of ideas.

NOTE: Illustrating the effects of an organization's environment, Theodore Caplow (1992) argues that an organizational trend is toward bigger human resources divisions, which is a response to the increasing number of government regulations that affect business operations.

3. **Expanding opportunities for advancement.** Expanding opportunity reduces the number of employees stuck in routine, dead-end jobs with little motivation to perform well. The organization should encourage employees at all levels to share ideas and to try new approaches, and define everyone's job as the start of an upward career path.

Critical evaluation. Kanter's work takes a fresh look at the concept of bureaucracy and its application to business organizations. Perhaps rigid formality may have made sense in the past, when organizations hired unschooled workers primarily to perform physical labor. But today's educated work force can contribute a wealth of ideas to bolster organizational efficiency—if the organization encourages and rewards innovation.

Kanter's suggested changes may encounter resistance, however, since they mandate a redistribution of power. Interestingly, some research suggests that women leaders are particularly likely to embrace the kinds of changes Kanter advocates. If so, we can expect organizations to evolve as women gradually fill more executive positions traditionally held by men (Helgesen, 1990).

But whether leaders are women or men, Kanter maintains, loosening up rigid organizational constraints is the key to improved performance. In this way, profitable companies treat employees as a resource to be developed rather than as a group to be controlled. In short, while the basic bureaucratic model may still promote efficiency, effectiveness is enhanced by flexible management styles coupled with efforts to spread power and opportunity throughout the organization (Kanter, 1985).

Organizational Environment

How any organization performs depends on not just its internal structure but also its **organizational environment**, *a range of factors external to an organization that affect its operation.* Such factors include technology, politics, the economy, and population patterns, as well as other organizations.

Technology is especially important in the modern organizational environment. We have already suggested that today's organizations could hardly exist without the capacity to communicate provided by telephone systems and facsimile (fax) machines and the ability to process and store information afforded by copiers and computers.

Technological changes currently under way are likely to have two somewhat contradictory consequences for organizational structure. On the one hand, the proliferation of personal computers and facsimile machines provides individuals throughout an organization with an unprecedented amount of information. This increased access may produce some leveling in the traditional hierarchy by which information and decision making have been concentrated at the top of an organizational pyramid. On the other hand, as suggested earlier in this chapter, computer technology also enables organizational leaders to monitor the activities of workers more closely than ever before (Markoff, 1991).

TABLE 7–3 Kanter's Research: A Summary

	Advantaged Employees	Disadvantaged Employees
Social composition	Being represented in high proportions helps employees to fit in more easily and to enjoy greater credibility; they experience less stress and are usually candidates for promotion	Being represented in low proportions puts employees visibly "on display" and results in their not being taken seriously; they tend to fear making mistakes and losing ground rather than optimistically looking toward advancement
Power	In powerful positions, managers contribute to high morale and support subordinates; such employees tend to have a democratic leadership style	In positions of low power, managers tend to foster low morale and restrict opportunities for subordinates to advance; such employees tend to have an authoritarian leadership style
Opportunity	High opportunity encourages optimism and high aspirations, loyalty to the organization, use of "higher-ups" as reference groups, and constructive responses to problems	Low opportunity promotes pessimism and low aspirations, weak attachment to the job, use of peers as reference groups, and ineffective griping in response to problems

SOURCE: Based on Rosabeth Moss Kanter, *Men and Women of the Corporation* (New York: Basic Books, 1977), pp. 246–49.

DATA FILE: The *Data File* explains how the McDonaldization of society extends even to McFunerals. Service Corporation International currently operates 662 funeral homes in 39 states and is aggressively buying operations overseas. S.C.I. now handles about 10% of all U.S. funerals (Myerson, 1993).

Q: "Specialists without spirit, sensualists without heart; this nullity imagines that it has attained a level of civilization never before achieved." Max Weber on the modern organizational type (1958:182; orig. 1904–1905)

A second dimension of the organizational environment is *politics*. Changes in law often have dramatic consequences for the operation of an organization, as many industries have learned in the face of new environmental standards imposed by the state. In global perspective, a dramatic change like the reorganization of the Soviet government in 1991 rippled throughout virtually every organization in that country.

Third, the state of the *economy* has obvious importance for an organization's well-being. Businesses in the United States expand or contract along with cycles in the overall economy. Even people's ability to get an organization off the ground depends on the availability of funds, which varies according to economic trends and banking policies (Pennings, 1982).

Fourth, *population patterns*—such as the size and composition of the surrounding populace—also affect organizations. The average age, typical education, and social diversity of a local community obviously shapes both the available work force and the market for an organization's products or services.

Fifth, *other organizations* also form part of the organizational environment. The people who operate a hospital, for example, must be responsive to organizations of doctors, nurses' associations, and unions of other hospital workers. Similarly, to remain competitive, a hospital must remain keenly aware of the kinds of equipment and procedures available at other facilities. And what happens in hospitals everywhere reflects policies set by the insurance industry (Fennell, 1980).

In sum, no organization operates in a social vacuum. But, just as formal organizations are shaped by their environment, so they act to color the entire society, as we shall now explain.

The McDonaldization of Society

At the beginning of this chapter, we noted the extraordinary success of the McDonald corporation.[1] From its take-off in the mid-1950s, there are now almost 15,000 McDonald's restaurants in the United States and throughout much of the world. There are more than 850 pairs of golden arches in Japan, for example, and the world's largest McDonald's recently opened for business in China's capital city of Beijing.

But the effect of McDonald's extends far beyond the sale of billions of hamburgers. McDonald's has

The "McDonaldization" of the United States has not only changed the way companies do business, it is also sparking new collaborative efforts among diverse business sectors. In Westchester, Illinois, Burger King and Amoco opened the nation's first fast-food gas station, where customers can gas up as they fill their own tank.

become part of our culture, a conclusion supported by one poll in which 98 percent of schoolchildren could identify Ronald McDonald. This level of recognition places him just about in a dead heat with Santa Claus.

But most important, as we suggested at the outset of this chapter, the organizational principles that underlie McDonald's are steadily coming to dominate our society. Our way of life is becoming "McDonaldized"—an awkward way of saying that many other aspects of life are organized in ways that resemble the famous restaurant chain. Parents buy toys at worldwide chain stores like Toys 'Я' Us; we drive to Jiffy Lube for a ten-minute oil change; communication is sliding more and more toward voice mail over the telephone, E-mail via computer, and junk mail in the box; more vacations take the form of packaged resorts and tours; television presents news in the form of ten-second sound bites; college admission officers size up students they have never met by glancing over their GPA and SAT scores; and professors assign ghost-written textbooks[2] and evaluate students with tests mass-produced for them by publishing companies. The list goes on and on.

---

[1]The material in this entire section is based on George Ritzer's (1993) book of the same name.

[2]Half a dozen popular sociology texts were not authored by the person or persons whose names appear on the cover. This book is not one of them.

GLOBAL: Two global maps from other chapters may be of interest here. One, in Chapter 4 ("Society"), shows world scientific expenditures, a good measure of the relative rationalization of society. The other, in Chapter 13 ("Sex and Gender"), illustrates the sharing of housework; in many less economically developed societies, women's lives remain bounded by the home despite the increase in formal organization.

NOTE: A partial explanation of the character of Japanese organizations is that the Japanese have transferred traditional solidarities involving family and locality to the corporation.
NOTE: Another contrast: Japan trains 10 engineers for each lawyer; the United States trains 10 lawyers for each engineer.
DATA FILE: The Data File includes supplementary material on how U.S. corporations can meet the Japanese challenge.

McDonaldization: Four Principles

What do all these developments have in common? According to George Ritzer, the "McDonaldization of society" involves four basic organizational principles.

1. **Efficiency.** Ray Kroc, the marketing genius behind the expansion of McDonald's, set out with the goal of serving a hamburger, french fries, and a milkshake to a customer in fifty seconds. Today, one of the company's most popular items is the Egg McMuffin, an entire breakfast in a single sandwich. In the restaurant, customers bus their own trays or, better still, drive away from the pickup window taking the packaging and whatever mess they make with them.

    Efficiency is now a value almost without critics in our society. We are likely to conclude that anything that can be done quickly is, for that reason alone, good.

2. **Calculability.** The first McDonald's operating manual declared the weight of a regular raw hamburger to be 1.6 ounces, its size to be 3.875 inches across, and its fat content to be 19 percent. A slice of cheese weighs exactly half an ounce. Fries are cut precisely 9/32 inches thick.

    Think about how many objects around the home, the workplace, or the campus are designed and mass produced uniformly according to a rational plan. Not just our environment but our life experiences—from traveling the nation's interstates to sitting at home viewing television—are now more deliberately planned than ever before.

3. **Predictability.** An individual can walk into a McDonald's restaurant anywhere and receive the same sandwiches, drinks, and desserts prepared in precisely the same way. Predictability, of course, is the result of a highly rational system that specifies every course of action and leaves nothing to chance.

4. **Control through automation.** The most unreliable element in the McDonald's system is human beings. People, after all, have good and bad days, sometimes let their minds wander, or simply decide to try something a different way. To eliminate, as much as possible, the unpredictable human element, McDonald's has automated its equipment to cook food at fixed temperatures for set lengths of time. Even the cash register at a McDonald's is little more than pictures of the items so as to minimize the responsibility of the human being taking the customer's order.

The scope of McDonaldization is expanding in the United States. Highly automated bakeries now produce bread with scarcely any human intervention, just as chickens emerge from automated hatcheries. In supermarkets, laser scanners are replacing (less reliable) human checkers. Most of this country's shopping now occurs in malls, in which everything from temperature and humidity to the kinds of stores and products are subject to continuous control and supervision.

Can Rationality Be Irrational?

There can be no argument about the popularity or the efficiency of McDonald's and similar organizations. But there is another side to the story.

Max Weber observed the increasing rationalization of the world with alarm, fearing that formal organizations could crush the human spirit. As he saw it, rational systems exact a terrible price for their efficiency—*dehumanization*. Each of the four principles noted above depends on reining in human creativity, discretion, and autonomy. Moreover, as George Ritzer contends, there is considerable evidence that McDonald's food is not particularly good for people or the natural environment (see Chapter 22, "The Natural Environment"). More generally, Ritzer echoes Weber in asserting that "the ultimate irrationality of McDonaldization is that people could lose control over the system and it would come to control us" (1993:145).

Formal Organizations in Japan

Not all types of formal organization are as impersonal as those in the United States. Those found in Japan, a small nation that has had remarkable economic success, have a distinctive organizational environment—a culture rooted in strong collective identity and solidarity. While most members of our society prize rugged individualism, the Japanese maintain traditions of cooperation.

Because of Japan's social cohesiveness, formal organizations in that society approximate very large primary groups. William Ouchi (1981) highlights five distinctions between formal organizations in Japan and their counterparts in industrial societies of the West. In each case, the Japanese organization reflects that society's more collective orientation. The box considers the prospects of applying these five key principles of Japanese organizations in the United States.

1. **Hiring and advancement.** Organizations in the United States hold out promotions and raises in

RESOURCE: Boye De Mente's excerpt "Japanese Etiquette and Ethics in Business" is one of the cross-cultural selections included in the reader, *Seeing Ourselves*.

NOTE: As noted in Chapter 4, worker alienation has been linked to rigid bureaucracy (Weber) and rigid class structure (Marx). Japan has a favorable position in both respects. Japanese workers enjoy greater involvement in a more personalized organizational environment.

Additionally, the compensation ratio (management/workers) in Japan is roughly half that in the United States.

GLOBAL: William Ouchi argues that their respective organizational contexts mean that business leaders in the United States can make quick decisions but often struggle to achieve implementation. In contrast, Japanese leaders (who involve many others early on) are slow to make decisions, but implementation is subsequently rapid.

GLOBAL SOCIOLOGY

The Japanese Model: Will It Work in the United States?

What the company wants is for us to work like the Japanese. Everybody go out and do jumping jacks in the morning and kiss each other when they go home at night. You work as a team, rat on each other, and lose control of your destiny. That's not going to work in this country.

John Brodie
President, United Paperworkers
Local 448
Chester, Pennsylvania

Who can argue with the economic success of the Japanese? Economic competition from Asia (and, increasingly, from Europe) is forcing U.S. companies to reconsider longtime notions about how corporate organizations should operate.

Among the most interesting examples of new organizations are Japanese manufacturing plants built here in the United States. By and large, these "transplant-organizations" have been quite successful in terms of productivity, demonstrating the ability of organizations to both adapt to and modify a new environment. Yet some voices in this country—workers, union leaders, and managers—speak as bitterly about transplanting Japanese organizational techniques as they do about importing Japanese cars.

Manufacturing plants operated in the United States by Honda, Nissan, and Toyota employ more than 250,000 people and have achieved the same high level of efficiency and quality that have won these companies praise in Japan.

However, traditional Japanese practices such as worker participation are not readily embraced in this country. Our corporate culture, with its rigid hierarchy, its heritage of individualism, and its history of labor-management conflict, renders proposals to enhance worker participation controversial.

Some employees in the United States perceive worker participation as increasing their workload. While still responsible for building cars, for instance, workers would also have to worry about quality control, unit costs, and overall efficiency—concerns usually shouldered by management. Moreover, some employees see the broad

To a large extent, organizational life reflects the surrounding culture. But, stirred by the economic power of Japanese corporations, more and more workers in the United States are employing some of Japan's organizational techniques, such as quality control groups. However, few experts think that organizational patterns can be easily transplanted from one society to another.

training favored by the Japanese as a demanding routine of moving from job to job, always having to learn new skills. Many union leaders also are suspicious of new plans formulated by management, fearing that any alliance of workers and managers may undermine union strength. Some managers, too, have looked cautiously on worker participation programs. Sharing with employees the power to procure supplies, direct production, and even schedule vacations does not come easily in light of past practices. Finally, U.S. corporations have a short-term outlook on profits, which discourages investing time and money in organizational restructuring.

Nonetheless, worker participation programs are changing the U.S. workplace. A recent government survey found that 70 percent of large businesses had initiated at least some programs of this kind. The advantages go right to the bottom line: Productivity and profits are usually higher when workers have a say in decision making. And most employees in worker participation programs—even those who may not want to sign up for morning jumping jacks—seem happier about their jobs. Workers who have long used only their bodies are now enjoying the opportunity to use their minds as well.

SOURCES: Hoerr (1989) and Florida & Kenney (1991).

GLOBAL: Boye De Mente argues that a crucial difference between Japanese and U.S. companies is that, in principle, the Japanese emphasize the worker more than the job; in the United States, we do the converse.

GLOBAL: A final difference between the two countries is that most U.S. executives have a secretary; relatively few Japanese business people do. In part, this difference reflects the more directly personal style of doing business in Japan.

salary as prizes won through individual competition. In Japanese organizations, however, companies hire new school graduates together, and all employees of a particular age cohort receive the same salary and responsibilities. Only after several years is anyone likely to be singled out for special advancement.

2. **Lifetime security.** Employees in the United States expect to move from one company to another to advance their careers. U.S. companies are also quick to lay off employees when economic setbacks strike. By contrast, Japanese companies typically hire employees for life, fostering strong, mutual loyalties among members of an organization. Japanese companies avoid layoffs by providing expendable workers with retraining and other jobs in the organization.

3. **Holistic involvement.** In the United States, the home and the workplace are usually distinct spheres. Japanese organizations differ by playing a broad role in their employees' lives, often providing home mortgages, sponsoring recreational activities, and scheduling social events. This interaction beyond the workplace strengthens collective identity and offers the respectful Japanese worker an opportunity informally to voice suggestions and criticisms.

4. **Nonspecialized training.** Bureaucratic organization in the United States is based on specialization; many people spend an entire career at a single task. From the outset, a Japanese organization trains employees in all phases of its operation, again with the idea that employees will remain with the organization for life.

5. **Collective decision making.** In the United States, key executives are responsible for most organizational decisions. Although Japanese leaders also take responsibility for their organization's performance, they involve workers in "quality circles" that discuss any decision that affects them. A closer working relationship is also encouraged by greater economic equality between management and workers. The salary differential between executives and the lower-ranking employees is about half that found in the United States.

These characteristics give the Japanese a strong sense of organizational loyalty. The cultural emphasis on *individual* achievement in our society finds its parallel in Japanese *groupism*. By tying their personal interests to those of their company, workers realize their ambitions through the organization.

GROUPS AND ORGANIZATIONS IN GLOBAL PERSPECTIVE

As this chapter has explained, formal organizations and their surrounding society interact, each influencing the other. In global perspective, we can see that bureaucracy does not take a consistent organizational form; formal organizations in the United States and Japan, for example, differ in a number of ways.

Organizations have also changed over time. Several centuries ago, most businesses in Europe and the United States were small, family enterprises. But as Western societies responded to the Industrial Revolution, the rational world view described by Max Weber came to the fore. Primary relationships came to be defined as a barrier to organizational efficiency. Thus, the organizational tradition in the West is to scorn *nepotism* (favoritism shown to a family member) or other forms of personal bias. Weber's model of bureaucracy maintains that the key to efficiency is impersonal, secondary relationships based on technical specialization and impartiality.

The development of formal organizations in Japan followed a different route. Historically, that society was even more socially cohesive, organized according to family-based loyalties. As Japan rapidly industrialized, people there did not discard primary relationships as inefficient, as Westerners did. On the contrary, the Japanese modeled their large businesses on the family, in effect transferring traditional family loyalties to corporations.

From our point of view, then, Japan seems to be simultaneously modern and traditional, promoting organizational efficiency by cultivating personal ties. Perhaps Japanese workers are now becoming more individualistic. Yet the Japanese model still demonstrates that organizational life need not be so dehumanizing.

Economically challenged as never before, U.S. businesses are taking a closer look at organizational patterns elsewhere, especially in Japan. In fact, many efforts to "humanize" bureaucracy in the United States are clear attempts to mimic the Japanese way of doing things.

Beyond the benefits for U.S. business organizations, there is another reason to study the Japanese approach carefully. Our society is less socially cohesive now than the more family-based society Weber knew. A rigidly bureaucratic form of organization only atomizes society further. Perhaps by following the lead of the Japanese, our own formal organizations can promote—rather than diminish—a sense of collective identity and responsibility.

Q: Akio Morita, a founder of SONY corporation, claims that Japanese corporations look ahead ten years in their business ventures, while corporations in the United States look ahead about ten minutes.

GLOBAL: Terry Besser (1993) argues that lower rates of absenteeism and turnover among Japanese workers does not necessarily indicate higher organizational commitment. Self-reported levels of commitment to organizations for workers in the United States and Japan are, in fact, similar.

In the future, Japan's organizational structures will not be the only ones attracting interest. Everywhere, as nations modernize, organizations are taking on particular forms based on distinctive cultures. Businesses in Poland are gaining vitality as that country establishes a convertible currency and opens to global trade. European nations as a whole are engaged in a new and promising formation of a multinational economic system. Organizations throughout the People's Republic of China have come under renewed control by that nation's Communist party. In the former Soviet Union, associations of all kinds are coming out from under rigid political control for the first time in three-quarters of a century. Each of these developments is likely to have some effect on organizational patterns in the United States.

As some analysts point out, U.S. organizations are still the envy of the world for their productive efficiency; after all, there are few places on earth where the mail arrives as quickly and dependably as in the United States (Wilson, 1991). But the extent of global diversity and change demands that we be cautious about asserting any "absolute truths" about formal organizations and, just as important, that we be curious about the possibilities for reorganizing our future.

SUMMARY

1. Social groups are important building blocks of societies that foster common identity and distinctive patterns of interaction.

2. Primary groups tend to be small and person oriented; secondary groups are typically large and goal oriented.

3. There are two kinds of leadership. Instrumental leaders are concerned with realizing a group's goals; expressive leaders focus on the collective well-being of members.

4. The process of group conformity is well documented by researchers. Because members often seek consensus, groups do not necessarily generate a wider range of ideas than do individuals working alone.

5. Individuals use reference groups—both ingroups and outgroups—to form attitudes and make decisions.

6. Georg Simmel argued that dyads have a distinctive intensity but lack stability because of the effort necessary to maintain them. A triad can easily dissolve into a dyad by excluding one member.

7. Peter Blau has demonstrated that the structural characteristics of groups—including size, internal homogeneity, relative social parity, and physical segregation—all affect the behavior of group members.

8. Social networks are relational webs that link people who typically have little common identity and limited interaction.

9. Formal organizations are large, secondary groups that seek to perform complex tasks efficiently. According to their members' reasons for joining, formal organizations are classified as normative, coercive, or utilitarian.

10. Bureaucratic organization expands in modern societies to perform many complex tasks efficiently. Bureaucracy is based on specialization, hierarchy, rules and regulations, technical competence, impersonal interaction, and formal, written communications.

11. Ideal bureaucracy may promote efficiency, but bureaucracy also generates alienation and inefficiency, tends to perpetuate itself beyond the achievement of its goals, and contributes to the contemporary erosion of privacy.

12. Formal organizations often mirror oligarchies. Rosabeth Moss Kanter's research has shown that the concentration of power and opportunity in U.S. corporations can compromise organizational effectiveness.

13. Humanizing bureaucracy means recognizing people as an organization's greatest resource. To develop human resources, organizations should spread responsibility and opportunity widely.

14. Technology, politics, the economy, population patterns, and other organizations combine to form the environment in which a particular organization must operate.

15. Reflecting the collective spirit of Japanese culture, formal organizations in Japan are based on more personal ties than are their counterparts in the United States.

CRITICAL-THINKING QUESTIONS

1. What are the key differences between primary and secondary groups? Identify examples of each in the daily round of life.

2. What are some of the positive functions of group conformity (for example, fostering team spirit)? Note several dysfunctions.

3. According to Max Weber, what are the six characteristic traits of bureaucracy? How do Japanese organizations differ from those common to the United States?

4. What does the "McDonaldization of society" mean? Cite familiar examples of this trend beyond those discussed in this chapter

KEY CONCEPTS

bureaucracy an organizational model rationally designed to perform complex tasks efficiently

bureaucratic inertia the tendency of bureaucratic organizations to perpetuate themselves

bureaucratic ritualism a preoccupation with organizational rules and regulations to the point of thwarting an organization's goals

dyad a social group with two members

expressive leadership group leadership that emphasizes collective well-being

formal organization a large secondary group organized to achieve its goals efficiently

groupthink the tendency of group members to conform by adopting a narrow view of some issue

humanizing bureaucracy fostering an organizational atmosphere that recognizes and encourages the contributions of everyone

ingroup a social group commanding a member's esteem and loyalty

instrumental leadership group leadership that emphasizes the completion of tasks

network a web of social ties that links people who may have little common identity and interaction

oligarchy the rule of the many by the few

organizational environment a range of factors external to an organization that affects its operation

outgroup a social group toward which one feels competition or opposition

primary group a small social group in which relationships are both personal and enduring

reference group a social group that serves as a point of reference in making evaluations or decisions

secondary group a large and impersonal social group devoted to some specific interest or activity

social group two or more people who identify and interact with one another

triad a social group with three members

SUGGESTED READINGS

Classic Sources

George C. Homans. *The Human Group.* New Brunswick, N.J.: Transaction, 1992 (orig. 1950).

This is an early and enduring sociological investigation of the group, the setting for much of our lives.

A. Paul Hare, Edgar F. Borgatta, and Robert F. Bales. *Small Groups: Studies in Social Interaction.* Rev. ed. New York: Alfred A. Knopf, 1965.

This collection of classic contributions to the study of small groups contains important essays by Emile Durkheim, Charles Cooley, Georg Simmel, Solomon Asch, and other notable men and women.

Contemporary Sources

Richard H. Hall. *Organizations: Structures, Processes, and Outcomes.* Englewood Cliffs, N.J.: Prentice Hall, 1991.

Hall provides an overview of the sociological study of formal organizations.

Cecilia L. Ridgeway. *The Dynamics of Small Groups.* New York: St. Martin's Press, 1983.

This is a good resource for most of the issues about group life raised in this chapter.

Barbara Czarniawska-Joerges. *Exploring Complex Organizations: A Cultural Perspective.* Newbury Park, Calif.: Sage, 1992.

The author applies an anthropological fieldwork approach to the study of large organizations, trying to show organizational behavior from the point of view of the actors themselves.

Arthur G. Miller. *The Obedience Experiments: A Case Study of Controversy in Social Science.* New York: Praeger, 1986.

Controversy has followed the obedience experiments of Stanley Milgram for more than thirty years. This book reviews Milgram's work and related studies and tackles broad ethical questions such research raises.

John Scott. *Social Network Analysis: A Handbook.* Newbury Park, Calif.: Sage, 1992.

A comprehensive sourcebook, this volume explains procedures for conducting research on social networks.

Irving L. Janis. *Crucial Decisions: Leadership in Policymaking and Crisis Management.* New York: The Free Press, 1989.

This book by the originator of the term "groupthink" examines organizational leadership.

Sally Helgesen. *The Female Advantage: Women's Ways of Leadership.* New York: Doubleday/Currency, 1990.

This intriguing book argues that women typically have a more humanized leadership style that works to the advantage of corporations.

Rosabeth Moss Kanter. *When Giants Learn to Dance: Mastering the Challenges of Strategy, Management, and Careers in the 1990s.* New York: Simon & Schuster, 1989.

Kanter, one of the best-known sociologists in the field of formal organizations, examines the future of corporations in the United States.

Nicole Woolsey Biggart. *Charismatic Capitalism: Direct Selling Organizations in America.* Chicago: University of Chicago Press, 1989.

Opposing conventional wisdom, some organizations deliberately foster emotional intensity among their members. This study of businesses highlights companies such as Mary Kay cosmetics and Amway products that have used emotional, motivational techniques successfully.

Global Sources

Patricia Caplan. *Class and Gender in India: Women and Their Organizations in a South Indian City.* New York: Tavistock, 1985.

This author analyzes women's associations in the context of national politics in India.

Boye De Mente. *Japanese Etiquette and Ethics in Business.* 5th ed. Lincolnwood, Ill.: NTC Business Books, 1987.

This is one of the best books contrasting formal organizations in the United States with those in Japan.

Cynthia Cockburn. *In the Way of Women: Men's Resistance to Sex Equality in Organizations.* Ithaca, N.Y.: ILR Press, 1991.

Great Britain is the setting for this study of gender inequality in four organizations

Leon Golub, *Mercenaries V*, 1984.

DATA FILE: An outline of Chapter 8 and supplementary lecture material are found in the *Data File*.

Q: "Morality is simply the attitude that we adopt towards people whom we personally dislike." Oscar Wilde

Q: "To be good is noble. To tell people how to be good is even nobler, and much less trouble." Mark Twain

NOTE: In 1994, Rodney King's civil lawsuit against the city of Los Angeles was settled. King received several million dollars.

Q: "The nail that sticks up gets hit down." Japanese proverb

Q: "I can resist everything except temptation." Oscar Wilde

Q: "Let us be thankful for the fools; but for them the rest of us could not succeed." Mark Twain

Q: "I try to avoid temptation, unless I can't resist it." Mae West

Deviance

Sirens sliced through the night as police cruisers joined in angry pursuit of the 1988 Hyundai speeding through a suburban neighborhood in Los Angeles. As the black-and-white cars closed in on their quarry, a helicopter chattered overhead, its powerful floodlight bathing the sudden eruption in a shimmering brilliance.

Twenty-five-year-old Rodney Glen King, the lone occupant of the Hyundai, brought his car to a halt, opened his door, and scrambled into the street. In an instant, police swarmed around him, and a sergeant lunged forward, staggering King with the discharge of a fifty-thousand-volt Taser stun gun. Unarmed, King fell to the pavement and tried to get back on his feet. As a group of eleven police looked on, three officers took turns kicking King and striking him with their clubs. By the time the beating ended, King had sustained

a crushed cheekbone, a broken ankle, damage to his skull, a burn on his chest, and internal injuries.

The beating of an unemployed construction worker by the police might have attracted little notice except for the resident of a nearby apartment building who had observed the event—through the eyepiece of his video camera. In a matter of hours, what appeared to be a flagrant abuse of power was being replayed on television screens across the United States (Lacayo, 1991; Morrow, 1991).

The King beating touched off a firestorm of debate. To some critics, the incident is all too familiar: a black man being brutalized by white police for little or no reason. Sociologist and law professor Jerome Skolnick explained the need for caution in asserting that the case was racially motivated. But he concluded that "racist police are more likely to be brutal and brutal police are more likely to be racist."

NOTE: To illustrate changing conceptions of deviance, consider the falling rate of campus offenses concerned with traditional moral decorum and honesty and the rising rate of political offenses concerned with sexual or racial harassment or other "insensitivity."

DIVERSITY: Juveniles are subject to various standards—including truancy laws and labeling as incorrigible—that do not apply to adults.

GLOBAL: Although tattoos are widely viewed as deviant in our society, Polynesians regard such skin decoration as a symbol of high social standing. Similarly, even the incest taboo (although universal) has variable kinship application.

RESOURCE: Nathaniel Hawthorne's *The Scarlet Letter* (Norton, 1978) is a wonderfully sociological tale of deviance and social control, and of the human spirit courageously emerging from a cloak of conformity.

The officers involved in the King controversy were charged with assault with a deadly weapon and use of excessive force. In a first trial, the jury acquitted the four, sparking several days of rioting in Los Angeles in which fifty-three people died. Subsequently, a federal prosecution for violating King's civil rights brought convictions for two of the officers.

Even as the furor over the Rodney King incident subsided, many people maintain that poor people, and especially minorities, find little justice in our legal system. Others wonder if we ask the impossible of police who try to hold back a rising tide of crime and drug abuse in cities wracked by poverty. Routinely risking personal harm for low pay, police officers often see themselves embroiled in a literal war on crime, in which atrocities are committed by people on both sides.

Every society struggles to establish some notion of justice, to reward people who play by the rules, and to punish those who do not conform. But, as the Rodney King incident so vividly demonstrated, the line that separates good and evil is no simple matter of black and white. This chapter investigates many of the questions that underlie this case: How do societies create a moral code in the first place? To what extent can societies control crime? Why are some people more likely than others to be charged with offenses? And what are the legitimate purposes of the criminal justice system? We shall begin by defining several basic concepts.

WHAT IS DEVIANCE?

Deviance is *the recognized violation of cultural norms.* Norms guide virtually all human activities, and so the concept of deviance covers a correspondingly broad spectrum. One distinctive category of deviance is **crime**, *the violation of norms a society formally enacts into criminal law.* Even criminal deviance is extensive, ranging from minor traffic violations to serious offenses such as rape and murder. A subcategory of crime, **juvenile delinquency**, refers to *the violation of legal standards by the young.*

Some instances of deviance barely raise eyebrows; other cases command a swift and severe response. Members of our society pay little notice to mild nonconformity like left-handedness or boastfulness; we take a dimmer view of dropping out of school, and we dispatch the police in response to a violent crime like rape.

Not all deviance involves action or even choice. For some categories of individuals, just *existing* may be sufficient to provoke condemnation from others. To whites who are in the majority, the mere presence of people of color may cause some discomfort. Similarly, many people of all races consider the poor disreputable to the extent that they do not measure up to conventional middle-class standards. Gay men and lesbians also confront derision and even hostility from those who are intolerant of their sexual orientation.

Examples of nonconformity that come readily to mind—stealing from a convenience store, neglecting a pet, driving while intoxicated—involve overtly breaking some rule. But since we all have shortcomings, we sometimes define especially righteous people—those who never raise their voices or are enthusiastic about paying their taxes—as deviant, even if we accord them a measure of respect (Huls, 1987). Deviant actions or attitudes, then, can be negative or positive. In either case, deviance involves *difference* that causes us to react to another person as an "outsider" (Becker, 1966).

Social Control

All societies target their members with efforts at social control. Like norms, social control takes many forms. Socialization, discussed in Chapter 5, is a complex process by which family, peer groups, and the mass media influence people's attitudes and behavior. Conforming to approved patterns earns people praise from parents, friends, and teachers; deviance, generally speaking, provokes criticism and scorn.

Many instances of deviance prompt only informal responses, such as a scowl or a bit of "friendly advice." Charges of more serious deviance, however, may propel an individual into the **criminal justice system,** *a formal reaction to alleged violations of law on the part of police, courts, and prison officials.*

In sum, deviance is much more than a matter of individual choice or personal failing. *How* a society defines deviance, *whom* individuals target as deviant, and *what* people decide to do about nonconformity are all issues of social organization. Only gradually, however, have people recognized this essential truth, as we shall now explain.

The Biological Context

Chapter 5 ("Socialization") noted that people a century ago understood—or, more correctly, misunderstood—human behavior as an expression of biological instincts. Understandably, early interest in criminality emphasized biological causes.

NOTE: "Glueck" rhymes with "book."

NOTE: Phrenology, the nineteenth-century pseudo-science, contended that personality traits and behavioral dispositions could be determined by the shape of a person's skull.

DIVERSITY: Look ahead to Chapter 23 to the five photos showing changing hair styles in the United States over recent decades;

fashion is a matter of changing conceptions of conformity and deviance.

GLOBAL: In 17th-century England, not attending church was a crime; in the United States today, doing so is a matter of individual choice; in Albania, however, any religious expression is illegal (even "crossing oneself" can result in a prison sentence).

Early Research

In 1876 Caesare Lombroso (1835–1909), an Italian physician who worked in prisons, suggested that criminals had distinctive physical features—low foreheads, prominent jaws and cheekbones, protruding ears, hairiness, and unusually long arms that made them resemble the apelike ancestors of human beings.

Although he later acknowledged the importance of social forces in criminality, Lombroso's early theory that some people were literally born criminals was extremely popular, especially among powerful people who dismissed the idea that flaws in social arrangements might account, in part, for criminal deviance (Jones, 1986).

But the defect in Lombroso's research was that the physical features he attributed to prisoners actually existed throughout the entire population. We now know that there are no physical attributes, of the kind described by Lombroso, distinguishing criminals and noncriminals (Goring, 1972; orig. 1913).

Delinquency and Body Structure

Although Lombroso's theory had been discredited, William Sheldon (1949) suggested that body structure might be related to criminality. He categorized hundreds of young men in terms of body type and, checking for any criminal history, concluded that delinquency was most likely among boys with muscular, athletic builds.

Sheldon Glueck and Eleanor Glueck (1950) confirmed Sheldon's conclusion. They cautioned, however, that a powerful build is not necessarily a *cause* of criminality. Parents, they suggested, treat powerfully built males with greater emotional distance so that they, in turn, grow up to display less sensitivity toward others. Moreover, if people expect muscular, athletic boys to act like bullies, they may treat them accordingly, thereby prompting aggressive behavior in a self-fulfilling prophesy.

Genetic Research

To date, there exists no conclusive evidence that criminality is the product of any specific genetic flaw. What is likely, however, is that people's overall genetic composition, in combination with social influences, accounts for some variation in criminality. In other words, biological factors probably have a real, if modest, effect on whether or not individuals engage in criminal activity (Rowe, 1983; Rowe & Osgood, 1984; Wilson & Herrnstein, 1985; Jencks, 1987).

The kind of deviance people create reflects the moral values they embrace. The Berkeley campus of the University of California has long celebrated its open-minded tolerance of sexual diversity. Thus, in 1992, when Andrew Martinez decided to attend classes wearing virtually nothing, people were reluctant to accuse "The Naked Guy" of immoral conduct. However, in Berkeley's politically correct atmosphere, it was not long before school officials banned Martinez from campus—charging that his nudity constituted a form of sexual harassment.

Sociobiologists continue to investigate possible connections between genetics and crime. They note, for example, that men commit far more violence than women and that parents are more likely to abuse disabled or foster children than healthy or natural children (Daly & Wilson, 1988).

Critical evaluation. Biological theories that try to explain crime in terms of rare physical traits of individuals can, at best, explain only a small proportion of all crimes. Recent sociobiological research is promising, but, at this point, we know too little about the links between genes and human behavior to draw firm conclusions.

In any case, an individualistic biological approach cannot address the issue of how some kinds

NOTE: Psychology's more individualistic orientation is evident in that approach's tendency to speak of *personal disorders* rather than *social deviance*.

Q: "The assumption is that there is a containing external social structure which holds individuals in line and that there is also an internal buffer which protects people against deviation of the social and legal norms." Walter C. Reckless

RESOURCE: The implications of art and the role of the artist for culture and deviance are explored in Philip Rieff's introductory essay "The Impossible Culture: Wilde as a Modern Prophet" in Oscar Wilde, *The Soul of Man Under Socialism and Other Essays* (New York: Harper & Row, 1970).

Q: "It is always a good idea to tell the truth unless, of course, you are an exceptionally good liar." J. K. Jerome

of behaviors come to be defined as deviant in the first place. Therefore, although there is much to be learned about how human biology may affect behavior, research currently places far greater emphasis on social influences (Gibbons & Krohn, 1986; Liska, 1991).

Personality Factors

Like biological theories, psychological explanations of deviance focus on cases of individual abnormality, this time involving personality. Some personality traits are hereditary, but psychologists think that temperament is mostly a product of social experiences. Therefore, they explain the outbreak of deviance as the result of "unsuccessful" socialization.

The work of Walter Reckless and Simon Dinitz (1967) illustrates a psychological approach to explaining juvenile delinquency. These researchers began by asking teachers to identify boys about age twelve who seemed likely and unlikely to engage in delinquent acts. Interviews with both categories of boys and their mothers provided information on each boy's self-concept—how he viewed himself and how he related to others. The "good boys" displayed a strong conscience (or *superego*, in Sigmund Freud's terminology), coped well with frustration, and identified positively with cultural norms and values. The "bad boys," by contrast, had a weaker conscience, displayed little tolerance for frustration, and identified less with conventional culture.

Over a four-year period, the researchers found that the "good boys" did have fewer contacts with the police than the "bad boys." Since all the boys studied lived in areas where delinquency was widespread, the investigators attributed staying out of trouble to a personality that reined in impulses toward deviance. Based on this conclusion, Reckless and Dinitz call their analysis *containment theory*.

Critical evaluation. Psychological research has demonstrated that personality patterns have some connection to delinquency and other types of deviance. Nevertheless, the value of this approach is limited by a key fact: The vast majority of serious crimes are committed by people whose psychological profiles are *normal*.

In sum, both biological and psychological approaches view deviance as an individual attribute without exploring how conceptions of right and wrong initially arise, why people define some rule breakers but not others as deviant, and the role of social power in shaping a society's system of social control. We now turn to these issues by delving into sociological explanations of deviance.

The Social Foundations of Deviance

Although we tend to view deviance in terms of the free choice or personal failings of individuals, all behavior—deviance as well as conformity—is shaped by society. Three *social* foundations of deviance, identified below, are detailed in later sections of the chapter.

1. **Deviance varies according to cultural norms.** No thought or action is inherently deviant; it becomes deviant only in relation to particular norms. The life patterns of rural Vermonters, small-town Texans, and urban Californians differ in significant ways; for this reason, what people in each category prize or scorn varies also. Laws, too, differ from place to place. Texans, for example, can legally consume alcohol in a car, a practice that draws the attention of police in most other states. Casinos are a focal point in Atlantic City, New Jersey, Las Vegas, Nevada, and on a few Indian reservations elsewhere; such gambling is illegal everywhere else in the United States. Further, most cities and towns have at least one unique statute: Only in Seattle, for example, is a person suffering from the flu subject to arrest simply for appearing in public.

   In global context, deviance is even more diverse. Albania outlaws any public display of religious faith, such as "crossing" oneself; Cuba can prosecute its citizens for "consorting with foreigners"; police can arrest people in Singapore for selling chewing gum; U.S. citizens risk arrest by their own government for traveling to Libya or Iraq.

2. **People become deviant as others define them that way.** Each of us violates cultural norms, perhaps even to the extent of breaking the law. For example, most of us have at some time walked around talking to ourselves or "borrowed" supplies, such as pens and paper, from the workplace. Whether such activities are sufficient to define us as mentally ill or criminal depends on how others perceive, define, and respond to any given situation.

3. **Both rule making and rule breaking involve social power.** Karl Marx viewed norms, and especially law, to be a strategy by which powerful people protect their interests. For example, the owners of an unprofitable factory have a legal right to close their business, even if doing so puts thousands of people out of work. If workers commit an act of vandalism that closes the same factory for a single day, however, they are subject

Q: "Crime is normal because a society exempt from it is utterly impossible." Emile Durkheim (1964:67)

Q: "Crime, then, is necessary; it is bound up with the fundamental conditions of all social life and by that very fact it is useful, because these conditions of which it is a part are themselves indispensable to the normal evolution of morality and law." Emile Durkheim (1964:70)

RESOURCE: A classic selection from Durkheim on crime is included in the third edition of the Macionis and Benokraitis reader, *Seeing Ourselves*.

NOTE: Andres Serrano, who created "Piss Christ," a photograph of a crucifix submerged in his own urine, maintains that art reaches its greatest power when it is most provocative. Is his work art or obscenity?

to criminal prosecution. Similarly, a homeless person who stands on a street corner denouncing the city government risks arrest for disturbing the peace; a mayoral candidate during an election campaign does exactly the same thing while receiving extensive police protection. In short, norms and their application are linked to social inequality.

STRUCTURAL-FUNCTIONAL ANALYSIS

We now turn to exactly how deviance is inherent in the operation of society. The structural-functional paradigm examines how deviance makes important contributions to a social system.

Emile Durkheim: The Functions of Deviance

Emile Durkheim's (1964a, orig. 1895; 1964b, orig. 1893) pioneering study of deviance began by noting that there is nothing abnormal about deviance since it performs four functions essential to society.

1. **Deviance affirms cultural values and norms.** Culture involves moral choices: People must prefer some attitudes and behaviors to others. Conceptions of what is morally right exist only in opposition to notions of what is wrong. Just as there can be no righteousness without evil, there can be no justice without crime. Deviance, in short, is indispensable to the process of generating and sustaining morality.

2. **Responding to deviance clarifies moral boundaries.** By defining people as deviant, a society sets the boundary between right and wrong. For example, a college marks the line between academic honesty and cheating by imposing disciplinary procedures on those who commit plagiarism.

3. **Responding to deviance promotes social unity.** People typically react to serious deviance with collective outrage. In doing so, Durkheim explained, they reaffirm the moral ties that bind them. For example, most members of our society joined together in condemning a rash of shootings of foreign tourists in Miami during 1993.

4. **Deviance encourages social change.** Deviant people, Durkheim claimed, patrol a society's moral boundaries, suggesting alternatives to the status quo and encouraging change. Today's deviance, he declared, may well become tomorrow's morality (1964a:71). In the 1950s, for example, many people

Artists have an important function in any society: to explore alternatives to conventional notions about how to live. For this reason, while we celebrate artists' creativity, we also accord them a mildly deviant identity. Governments display this same ambivalence toward the artistic community, encouraging work that promotes patriotism but suppressing work that challenges conventional morality. When city officials in Cincinnati moved to block the display of photographs by the controversial photographer Robert Mapplethorpe, artists marched in outspoken defense of their freedom of expression.

denounced rock and roll music as a threat to the morals of youth and an affront to traditional musical tastes. Since then, however, rock and roll has been swept up in the musical mainstream and become a multibillion dollar industry perhaps more "all-American" than apple pie.

An Illustration: The Puritans of Massachusetts Bay

Durkheim's functional analysis of deviance is supported by Kai Erikson's (1966) historical investigation of the early Puritans of Massachusetts Bay. This highly religious "society of saints," Erikson discovered, created deviance to clarify various moral boundaries. Durkheim explained this process using words that apply well to the Puritans.

Imagine a society of saints, a perfect cloister of exemplary individuals. Crimes, properly so called, will there be unknown; but faults which appear [insignificant] to the layman will create there the same scandal that the

Q: "Puritanism is the lurking fear that someone, somewhere, may be happy." H. L. Mencken

Q: "Contrary to current ideas, the criminal no longer seems a totally unsociable being, a sort of parasitic element, a strange and inassimilable body, introduced into the midst of society. On the contrary, he plays a definite role in social life." Emile Durkheim (1964:72)

Q: "It is the conflict between culturally accepted values and the socially structured difficulties of living up to these values which exerts pressure toward deviant behavior and disruption of the normative system." Robert K. Merton (1968:245)

Q: ". . . differential pressures for deviant behavior will continue to be exerted upon certain groups and strata as long as the structure of opportunity and the cultural goals remain substantially unchanged." Robert K. Merton (1968:246)

society's changing moral boundaries. By constantly defining a small number of people as deviant, in sum, Puritan society ensured that the social functions of deviance were carried out.

Merton's Strain Theory

While some deviance is inevitable in all societies, Robert Merton (1938, 1968) argues that excessive deviance arises from particular social arrangements. Merton's theory is concerned with cultural *goals* (such as financial success) and the *means* (such as schooling and hard work) available to achieve them. The essence of conformity, then, is pursuing conventional goals by approved means.

But not everyone who desires conventional success has the opportunity to achieve it. Young people raised in poor inner-city neighborhoods, for example, may see little hope of becoming successful if they "play by the rules." As a result, they may seek wealth through one or another kind of crime—say, by dealing cocaine. Merton called this type of deviance *innovation*—the attempt to achieve a culturally approved goal (wealth) using unconventional means (drug sales). Figure 8–1 shows that innovation involves accepting the goal of success while rejecting the conventional means of becoming rich.

This kind of deviance, according to Merton, results from "strain" between our society's emphasis on material success and the limited opportunity it provides to become successful. The poor, especially, may respond to this dilemma by engaging in what we conventionally define as theft, selling illegal drugs, or other forms of street hustling. The box on page 214 highlights the life of mobster Al Capone to explain why, historically, Merton's "innovation" has been attractive to people at the margins of our society.

The inability to become successful by normative means may also prompt another type of deviance that Merton calls *ritualism* (see Figure 8–1). Ritualists resolve the strain of limited success by abandoning cultural goals in favor of almost compulsive efforts to live "respectably." In essence, they embrace the rules to the point that they lose sight of goals entirely. Lower-level bureaucrats, Merton suggests, often succumb to ritualism as a way of gaining respectability.

A third response to the inability to succeed is *retreatism*—the rejection of cultural goals and means as a form of dropping out. Retreatists include some alcoholics and drug addicts, and some of the street people common to U.S. cities. The deviance of retreatists lies in unconventional living and, perhaps more seriously, accepting this situation.

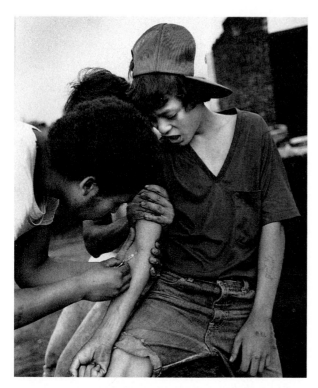

No social class stands apart from others as being either criminal or free from criminality. According to various sociologists, however, people with less stake in society and their own future typically exhibit less resistance to some kinds of deviance. Photographer Stephen Shames captured this scene on a Bronx, New York, rooftop in 1983.

ordinary offense does in ordinary consciousness. . . . For the same reason, the perfect and upright man judges his smallest failings with a severity that the majority reserve for acts more truly in the nature of an offense. (1964a:68–69)

Deviance, in short, is inevitable in society, however righteous individuals may be.

The kind of deviance the Puritans created changed over time, depending on the moral issues they confronted. How much dissent to allow, how to respond to outsiders, what their religious goals should be—they resolved all these questions in the process of celebrating some of their members while condemning others as deviant.

Finally, Erikson discovered, although the reasons for deviance changed, the Puritans declared a steady proportion of their number as deviant over time. Erikson saw this stability as support for Durkheim's idea that deviants served as moral markers, outlining a

Q: "In this life one frequently finds greater rewards for vice than for virtue." René Descartes (1641)
RESOURCE: Useful insights about violent subcultures are found in the *American Journal of Sociology* 95, 1 (July 1989):174–87; also see the early study by Frederick Thrasher, *The Gang* (University of Chicago Press, 1927).

Q: "The inescapable conclusion is that society secretly wants crime and needs crime . . ." Karl Menninger, *The Crime of Punishment*
NOTE: Good illustrations of the functional consequences of crime, in terms of reaffirming norms and increasing social unity, are found in Truman Capote's *In Cold Blood* (Signet, 1965); see especially pages 279–280.

The fourth response to failure is *rebellion*. Like retreatists, rebels reject both the cultural definition of success and the normative means of achieving it. Rebels, however, go one step further by advocating radical alternatives to the existing social order. They may promote unconventional values and norms using political or religious language and withdraw from society, forming a counterculture.

Deviant Subcultures

Richard Cloward and Lloyd Ohlin (1966) extended Merton's theory in their investigation of delinquent youth. They maintain that criminal deviance results not simply from limited legitimate opportunity but also from available illegitimate opportunity. In short, deviance or conformity follow from the *relative opportunity structure* that young people face in their lives.

The life of Al Capone shows how ambitious individuals denied legitimate opportunity could take advantage of organized crime to forge a successful career. Where illegal opportunities predominate, Cloward and Ohlin predict the development of *criminal subcultures* that offer the knowledge, skills, and other resources people need to succeed in unconventional ways.

But, especially in poor and highly transient neighborhoods, even illegal opportunity may be lacking. Here, delinquency is likely to surface in the form of *conflict subcultures* where violence is ignited by frustration and a desire for fame or respect. Alternatively, those who fail to achieve success, even using criminal means, may embrace *retreatist subcultures* that advocate dropping out through abuse of alcohol or other drugs.

Albert Cohen (1971) suggests that delinquency is most pronounced among lower-class youths because society offers them little opportunity to achieve success in conventional ways. Because conventional definitions of success call for achieving wealth and all its trappings, they find little basis for self-respect in their impoverished condition. In response, they may create a delinquent subculture that "defines as meritorious the characteristics [these youths] *do* possess, the kinds of conduct of which they *are* capable" (1971:66). For example, because the dominant culture values the calculated pursuit of wealth, a delinquent subculture may extol stealing "for the hell of it."

Walter Miller (1970) agrees that delinquent subcultures typically develop among lower-class youths who contend with the least legitimate opportunity. He describes six focal concerns of delinquent subcultures: (1) *trouble*, arising from frequent conflict with teachers and police; (2) *toughness*, the value placed on physical

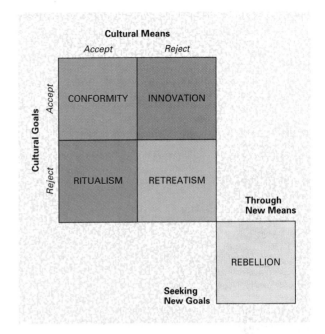

FIGURE 8–1 Merton's Strain Theory of Deviance

(Based on Merton, 1968:230–46)

size, strength, and athletic skills, especially among males; (3) *smartness*, the ability to succeed on the streets, to outthink or "con" others, and to avoid being similarly taken advantage of; (4) *excitement*, the search for thrills, risk, or danger to gain needed release from a daily routine that is predictable and unsatisfying; (5) a concern with *fate*, derived from the lack of control these youths feel over their own lives; and (6) *autonomy*, a desire for freedom often expressed as resentment toward figures of authority.

Hirschi's Control Theory

A final argument that builds on Durkheim's analysis of deviance is Travis Hirschi's (1969) *control theory*. Hirschi assumes that everyone finds at least some deviance tempting; what requires explanation is not deviance, but *conformity*. He suggests that conformity arises from four types of social controls.

1. **Attachment.** Strong social attachments to others encourage conformity; weak relationships in the family, peer group, and school leave people freer to engage in deviance.

2. **Commitment.** The higher one's commitment to legitimate opportunity, the greater the advantages of conformity. A young person bound for college,

SOCIAL DIVERSITY

Al Capone: Crime and Social Marginality

At the onset of Prohibition, which outlawed alcoholic beverages in the United States between 1920 and 1933, Al Capone seized the opportunity to build a vast criminal empire. For someone willing to take the risk, there was an enormous amount of money to be made in bootlegging.

Capone rose to power and gained great wealth during an era when U.S. cities bustled with millions of European immigrants, most poor but eager to share in the American Dream of success. Condemned by their backgrounds, their languages, and their religions to second-class citizenship, immigrants collided time and again with barriers of prejudice and discrimination. The vast majority nonetheless patiently remained "conformists," in Merton's terminology, hoping that their lives would improve with the passing of time.

But some saw in organized crime a means to achieve their goals. So it was that Alphonse Capone—a brilliant and ambitious man, yet socially handicapped by having grown up in an Italian slum

in New York City—came to dominate one of the largest criminal empires of our history.

Capone's life exemplifies Merton's "innovator," an individual who pursues the culturally approved goal of success according to unconventional means. For people like Al Capone, this type of deviance is a product of ambition coupled to a lack of legitimate opportunity. In the words of one analyst of the criminal underworld:

> The typical criminal of the Capone era was a boy who had . . . seen what was rated as success in the society he had been thrust into— the Cadillac, the big bankroll, the elegant apartment. How could he acquire that kind of recognizable status? He was almost always a boy of outstanding initiative, imagination, and ability; he was the kind of boy who, under different conditions, would have been a captain of industry or a key political figure of his time. But he hadn't the opportunity of going to Yale and becoming a banker or broker; there was no passage for him to a law degree from Harvard. There was, however, a relatively easy way of acquiring these goods that he was incessantly told were available to him as an American citizen, and without which he had begun to feel he could not properly count himself as an American citizen. He could become a gangster. (Allsop, 1961:236)

But even those gangsters who managed to garner wealth and power lacked the prestige accorded to members of more "respectable"

families. Thus many distanced themselves from their ethnic origins by, for example, changing their names. Capone's first employer was a fellow immigrant and reputed Mafia boss who called himself Mr. Frankie Yale and ran a speakeasy on Coney Island that he named the Harvard Inn. Similarly, as the leader of the Chicago rackets, Capone demanded that others address him as Anthony Brown and surrounded himself with men who displayed none of the ethnic traits he sought to leave behind.

Capone even engaged in the public generosity favored by many upper-class people when, during the Depression, he provided food to Chicago's poor. Later he enrolled his son Anthony at prestigious Yale University, and subsequently he celebrated the young man's wedding to a well-to-do woman from Nashville.

Surely one of the most notorious U.S. criminals of this century, "Scarface" Al Capone modeled his life on achieving the American Dream. His deviance—like that of thousands of young people dealing drugs in today's cities—was motivated by hunger for success amid limited opportunity.

SOURCES: Allsop (1961) and Baltzell (1964).

Q: "We are moral beings to the extent that we are social beings." Emile Durkheim

Q: ". . . control theory assumes the existence of a common value system within the society or group whose norms are being violated." Travis Hirschi

Q: "Anyone who does what is forbidden, that is, who violates a

taboo, becomes taboo himself." Sigmund Freud, *Totem and Taboo* (1950:32)

Q: "From this point of view, deviance is not a quality of the act a person commits, but rather a consequence of the application by others of rules and sanctions to an 'offender.' The deviant is one to whom the label has successfully been applied; deviant behavior is behavior that people so label." Howard S. Becker (1966:9)

with good career prospects, has a high stake in conformity. In contrast, someone with little confidence in future success is more likely to drift toward deviance.

3. **Involvement.** Extensive involvement in legitimate activities—such as holding a job, going to school and completing homework, or pursuing hobbies—inhibits deviance. People with little legitimate involvement—who simply "hang out" waiting for something to happen—have time and energy for deviant activity.

4. **Belief.** Strong beliefs in conventional morality and respect for authority figures also restrain tendencies toward deviance; people with weak beliefs are more vulnerable to temptations toward deviance.

Hirschi's analysis explains many kinds of deviant behavior, and it has gained support from subsequent research. Here, again, a person's location in society as well as strength of moral convictions are crucial in generating a stake in conformity or allowing everyday temptations to cross the line into actual deviance (Wiatrowski, Griswold, & Roberts, 1981; Sampson & Laub, 1990; Free, 1992).

Critical evaluation. Durkheim's pioneering work in the functions of deviance remains central to sociological thinking. Even so, recent critics point out that a community does not always come together in reaction to crime; sometimes fear of crime drives people to withdraw from public life (Liska & Warner, 1991).

Derived from Durkheim's analysis, Merton's strain theory has also come under criticism for explaining some kinds of deviance (theft, for example) far better than others (such as crimes of passion or mental illness). In addition, not everyone seeks success in conventional terms of wealth, as strain theory implies. As explained in Chapter 3 ("Culture"), members of our society embrace many different cultural values and are motivated by various notions of personal success.

The general argument of Cloward and Ohlin, Cohen, Miller, and Hirschi—that deviance reflects the opportunity structure of society—has been confirmed by subsequent research (Allan & Steffensmeier, 1989). However, these theories, too, fall short in assuming that everyone shares the same cultural standards for judging right and wrong. Moreover, we must be careful not to define deviance in ways that unfairly focus attention on poor people. If crime is defined to include stock fraud as well as street theft, criminals are more likely to include affluent individuals. Finally, all structural-functional theories imply that everyone who

We create special settings that permit behavior that would otherwise be viewed as deviant. In this Los Angeles disco for young people, boisterous dancing, screaming, and body painting are the norm.

violates conventional cultural standards will be defined as deviant. Becoming deviant, however, is actually a highly complex process, as the next section explains.

SYMBOLIC-INTERACTION ANALYSIS

The symbolic-interaction paradigm directs attention to how people construct reality in countless everyday settings. Applied to deviance, this theoretical orientation reveals that definitions of deviance and conformity are surprisingly flexible.

Labeling Theory

The central contribution of symbolic-interaction analysis is **labeling theory**, *the assertion that deviance and conformity result, not so much from what people do, but from how others respond to those actions.* Labeling theory stresses the relativity of deviance, meaning the same behavior may be defined in any number of ways. Howard S. Becker claims that deviance is, therefore, nothing more than "behavior that people so label" (1966:9).

Consider these situations: A woman takes an article of clothing from a roommate; a married man at a convention in a distant city has sex with a prostitute; a member of Congress drives home intoxicated after a party. The reality of each situation depends on the response of others. We might define the first situation as borrowing or as theft. The consequences of the second case depend largely on whether the news of the

The world is full of people who are unusual in one way or another. This Indian man grew the fingernails on one hand for more than thirty years just to do something that no one else had ever done. Should we define such behavior as harmless eccentricity or as evidence of mental illness?

man's behavior follows him back home. In the third situation, is the official an active socialite or a dangerous drunk? The social creation of reality, then, is a highly variable process of detection, definition, and response.

People sometimes contend with deviant labels for involvement in situations completely beyond their control. For example, victims of violent rape are sometimes subjected to labeling as deviants because of the misguided assumption that they must have encouraged the offender. Similarly, individuals with acquired immune deficiency syndrome (AIDS) sometimes find that they are shunned by employers, friends, and even family members.

Primary and Secondary Deviance

Edwin Lemert (1951, 1972) notes that many episodes of norm violation are insignificant and transitory, provoking little reaction from others and with little effect on a person's self-concept. Lemert calls such passing episodes *primary deviance*.

But what happens if other people take notice of someone's deviance and make something of it? If, for example, people begin to think of a boisterous friend as an unsuitable social companion, that person, feeling left out, might become angry, escalating criticism from others. Such a response is *secondary deviance*, which may take the form of defending deviant actions, lying about them, or getting used to them. In other words, in response to people's reaction to some earlier violation, an individual adopts secondary deviance as a role with far greater consequences for social identity and self-definition. Initial labeling, then, can encourage individuals to develop deviant identities, thereby fulfilling the expectations of others.

Stigma

The onset of secondary deviance marks the emergence of what Erving Goffman (1963) called a *deviant career*. Typically, this occurs as a consequence of acquiring a **stigma**, *a powerfully negative social label that radically changes a person's self-concept and social identity*.

Stigma operates as a master status (see Chapter 6, "Social Interaction in Everyday Life"), overpowering other dimensions of social identity so that an individual is diminished and discounted in the minds of others and, consequently, socially isolated. Sometimes an entire community formally stigmatizes individuals through what Harold Garfinkel (1956) calls a *degradation ceremony*. A criminal prosecution is one example, operating much like a high school graduation except that people stand before the community to be labeled in a negative rather than a positive way.

Retrospective Labeling

Once people have stigmatized a person, they may engage in **retrospective labeling**, *the interpretation of someone's past consistent with present deviance* (Scheff, 1984). For example, after discovering that a priest who has worked for years with children has sexually molested a child, others rethink his past, perhaps musing, "He always did want to be around young children." Obviously, retrospective labeling involves a highly selective and prejudicial view of a person's biography, guided more by the present stigma than by any attempt to be fair. But this process may nonetheless deepen a person's deviant identity.

Labeling and Mental Illness

Labeling theory is especially applicable to mental illness, since a person's mental condition is difficult to

SOCIAL SURVEY: "What about sexual relations between two adults of the same sex? Do you think that it is always wrong, almost always wrong, wrong only sometimes, or not wrong at all?" (GSS 1993, N = 1,075; *Codebook*, 1993:265)

"Always wrong"	62.4%	"Not wrong at all"	20.7%
"Almost always wrong"	4.1%	DK/NR	5.9%
"Wrong only sometimes"	6.9%		

define. Psychiatrists often assume that mental disorders have a concrete reality similar to diseases of the body. There is truth to this, insofar as heredity, diet, stress, and chemical imbalances in the body do account, in part, for mental disturbances. However, what we call "mental illness" is also a matter of social definitions people sometimes make with the intention of forcing others to conform to conventional standards (Thoits, 1985).

Is a woman who believes that Jesus rides the bus to work with her every day seriously deluded or merely expressing her religious faith in a highly graphic way? If a man refuses to bathe, much to the dismay of his family, is he insane or simply unconventional? Is a homeless woman who refuses to allow police to take her to a city shelter on a cold night mentally ill or simply trying to live independently?

Psychiatrist Thomas Szasz charges that the label of insanity is widely applied to what is actually only "difference"; therefore, he claims, the notion of mental illness should be abandoned (1961, 1970; Vatz & Weinberg, 1983). Illness, Szasz argues, afflicts only the body, making mental illness a myth. Being "different" in thought or action may irritate others, but it is no grounds on which to define someone as sick. To do so, Szasz claims, simply enforces conformity to the standards of people powerful enough to get their way.

Szasz's views have provoked controversy; many of his colleagues reject the notion that all mental illness is a fiction. Others have hailed his work, however, for pointing out the danger of abusing medical practice in the interest of promoting conformity. Most of us, after all, have experienced periods of extreme stress or other mental disability at some time in our lives. Such episodes, although upsetting, are usually of passing importance. If, however, they form the basis of a social stigma, they may lead to further deviance as a self-fulfilling prophecy (Scheff, 1984).

The Medicalization of Deviance

Labeling theory, particularly the ideas of Szasz and Goffman, helps to explain an important shift in the way we understand deviance. Over the last fifty years, the growing influence of psychiatry and medicine in the United States has encouraged the **medicalization of deviance**, *the transformation of moral and legal issues into medical matters.*

In essence, medicalization amounts to a change in labels. Conventional moral judgment involves calling people or their behavior "bad" or "good." However, the scientific objectivity of modern medicine passes

no moral judgment, instead utilizing clinical diagnoses such as "sick" and "well."

To illustrate, until the middle of this century, people generally viewed alcoholics as weak and morally deficient people easily tempted by the pleasure of drink. Gradually, however, medical specialists redefined alcoholism so that most people now consider alcoholism a disease, rendering individuals "sick" rather than "bad." Similarly, obesity, drug addiction, child abuse, promiscuity, and other behaviors that used to be a matter of morality are today widely defined as illnesses for which those afflicted need help rather than punishment.

The Complex Case of Homosexuality

Some forms of behavior have been defined and redefined over time. For centuries, most women and men in the United States considered homosexuality a moral issue, a straightforward example of being "bad" against a heterosexual standard of "good." But the American Psychiatric Association (APA) in 1952 officially declared being gay or lesbian a "sociopathic personality disturbance." In the wake of this pronouncement by medical authorities, by 1970 two-thirds of adults agreed that homosexuality was a "sickness that could be cured."

More recently, however, homosexual and bisexual people have asserted that they may be *different* without being *deviant* at all. Supporters of this view note the lack of success in "curing" homosexuality and the growing evidence that sexual orientation is a matter of biology rather than personal choice. In 1974, the APA switched again, redefining homosexuality as simply a "form of sexual behavior" (Conrad & Schneider, 1980:193–209).

Furthermore, people who oppose all deviant labels for gays have countered traditional prejudices by defining hostility toward homosexuals as "homophobia." This strategy suggests that deviance may lie in "conventional" people and not those they victimize.

The Significance of Labels

Whether we define deviance as a moral or medical issue has three profound consequences. First, it affects *who responds* to deviance. An offense against common morality typically provokes a reaction by citizens or police. Applying medical labels, however, places the situation under the control of clinical specialists, including counselors, psychiatrists, and physicians.

A second difference is *how people respond* to a deviant. A moral approach defines the deviant as an "offender" subject to punishment. Medically, however,

Q: "A person becomes delinquent because of an excess of definitions favorable to violation of law over definitions unfavorable to violations of law. This is the principle of differential association."
Edwin Sutherland

Q: Summing up his key points, Edwin Sutherland asserts that "Criminal behavior is learned . . . in interaction with other persons . . . [mainly] in intimate personal groups . . . [and] includes techniques of committing the crime . . . [and] motives, drives, rationalizations, and attitudes."

GLOBAL: Socialist societies also have organized crime; perhaps 200 criminal organizations now exist in Russia and the number is growing as a market system develops and political freedoms expand.

"patients" need treatment (for their own good, of course). Therefore, while punishment is designed to fit the crime, treatment programs are tailored to the patient and may involve virtually any therapy that a specialist thinks will prevent future deviance (von Hirsh, 1986).

Third, and most important, the two labels differ on the issue of *the personal competence of the deviant person*. Morally, people take responsibility for their own behavior; we all do wrong, in other words, but at least we understand what we are doing and must face the consequences. Medically speaking, however, if we are sick we are no longer responsible for what we do. Defined as personally incompetent and unaware of what is in our own best interest, we become vulnerable to more intense, often involuntary, treatment. For this reason alone, attempts to define deviance in medical terms should be made only with extreme caution.

Sutherland's Differential Association Theory

Related to the issue of how we view others' behavior is how we come to define our own. Edwin Sutherland (1940) suggested that we learn social patterns, including deviance, through association with others, especially in primary groups.

We all encounter forces promoting criminality as well as those supporting conformity. The likelihood that a person will engage in criminal activity depends upon the frequency of association with those who encourage norm violation compared with those who encourage conformity. This is Sutherland's theory of *differential association.*

Sutherland's theory is illustrated by a study of drug and alcohol use among young adults in the United States (Akers et al., 1979). Analyzing responses to a questionnaire completed by junior and senior high school students, researchers discovered a close link between the extent of alcohol and drug use and the degree to which peer groups encouraged such activity. The investigators concluded that young people embrace delinquent patterns as they receive praise and other rewards for defining deviance rather than conformity in positive terms.

Critical evaluation. Labeling theory links deviance not to *action* but to the *reaction* of others. Thus some people are defined as deviant while others who think or behave in the same way are not. The concepts of stigma, secondary deviance, and deviant career demonstrate how people sometimes incorporate the label of deviance into a lasting self-concept.

Yet labeling theory has several limitations. First, because this theory takes a highly relative view of deviance, it glosses over how some kinds of behavior, such as murder, are condemned virtually everywhere (Wellford, 1980). Labeling theory is thus most usefully applied to less serious deviance, such as sexual behavior and mental illness.

Second, the consequences of deviant labeling are unclear: Research is inconclusive as to whether deviant labeling produces subsequent deviance or discourages further violations (Smith & Gartin, 1989; Shermin & Smith, 1992).

Third, not everyone resists the label of deviance; some people may actually want to be defined as deviant (Vold & Bernard, 1986). For example, individuals may engage in civil disobedience leading to arrest to call attention to social injustice.

While Sutherland's differential association theory has had considerable influence in sociology, it provides little insight into why society's norms and laws define certain kinds of activities as deviant in the first place. This important question is addressed by social-conflict analysis, described in the next section.

SOCIAL-CONFLICT ANALYSIS

The social-conflict paradigm links deviance to social inequality. This approach suggests that who or what is labeled as deviant depends on the relative power of categories of people.

Deviance and Power

Alexander Liazos (1972) points out that the term "deviance" brings to mind "nuts, sluts, and 'preverts'" who share the trait of powerlessness. Bag ladies (not tax evaders) and unemployed men on street corners (not those who profit from wars) carry the stigma of deviance.

Social-conflict theory explains this pattern in three ways. First, the norms—including laws—of any society generally reflect the interests of the rich and powerful. People who threaten the wealthy, either by taking their property or by advocating a more egalitarian society, may be readily defined as "common thieves" or "political radicals." As noted in Chapter 4 ("Society"), Karl Marx argued that all social institutions tend to support the capitalist economic system and protect the interests of the rich, capitalist class. Echoing Marx, Richard Quinney makes the point succinctly: "Capitalist justice is by the capitalist class, for the capitalist class, and against the working class" (1977:3).

Q: "In this century, America's only permanent growth industry has been organized crime." Selwyn Raab

NOTE: Power affects how labels are applied. An audience may discredit a privileged person for acting foolishly; observing a less privileged person (say, women or people of color) acting foolishly, they are more likely to discredit the individual's entire category.

Q: "When a rule is enforced, the person who is supposed to have broken it may be seen as a special kind of person, one who cannot be trusted to live by the rules agreed on by the group. He is regarded as an *outsider*. But the person . . . may have a different view of the matter . . . not accept[ing] the rule by which he is being judged . . . Hence, a second meaning of the term emerges: the rule-breaker may feel that his judges are *outsiders*." Howard S. Becker, *Outsiders* (1963)

Artist Frank Romero painted The Closing of Whittier Boulevard *based on a recollection of his youth in East Los Angeles. To many young Latinos, identified here by their distinctive "low-rider" cars, police represent a hostile Anglo culture likely to use heavy-handed tactics to discourage them from venturing out of their neighborhood.*

Second, even if their behavior is called into question, the powerful have the resources to resist deviant labels. Corporate executives who might order the dumping of hazardous wastes are rarely held personally accountable for these acts. While such actions pose dangers for all of society, they are not necessarily viewed as criminal.

Third, the widespread belief that norms and laws are natural and good masks their political character. For this reason, we may condemn the *unequal application* of the law but give little thought to whether the *laws themselves* are inherently fair (Quinney, 1977).

Deviance and Capitalism

Steven Spitzer (1980) argues that deviant labels are applied to people who impede the operation of capitalism. First, because capitalism is based on private control of property, people who threaten the property of others—especially the poor who steal from the rich—are prime candidates for labeling as deviants. Conversely, the rich who exploit the poor are unlikely to be defined as deviant. Landlords, for example, who charge poor tenants high rents and evict those who cannot pay are not considered a threat to society; they are simply "doing business."

Second, because capitalism depends on productive labor, those who cannot or will not work risk deviant labeling. Many members of our society think of people who are out of work—even if through no fault of their own—as deviant.

Third, capitalism depends on respect for figures of authority, so people who resist authority are generally labeled as deviant. Examples are children who skip school or talk back to parents and teachers; adults who do not cooperate with employers or police; and anyone who opposes "the system."

Fourth, capitalism rests on the widespread acceptance of the status quo; those who undermine or challenge the capitalist system are subject to deviant labeling. In this category fall antiwar activists, environmentalists, labor organizers, and anyone who endorses an alternative economic system.

To turn the argument around, people label positively whatever enhances the operation of capitalism. Winning athletes, for example, have celebrity status because they express the values of individual achievement and competition vital to capitalism. Additionally, Spitzer notes, we define using drugs of escape (marijuana, psychedelics, heroin, and crack) as deviant, while embracing drugs that promote adjustment to the status quo (such as alcohol and caffeine).

People who are a "costly yet relatively harmless burden" on society, says Spitzer, include Robert Merton's retreatists (for example, those addicted to alcohol or other drugs), the elderly, and people with physical disabilities, mental retardation, and mental illness. These people are subject to control by social welfare agencies. But those who directly threaten the capitalist system, including the inner-city "underclass" and revolutionaries—Merton's innovators and rebels—come under the purview of the criminal justice system and, in times of crisis, military forces such as the National Guard.

Note that both the social welfare and criminal justice systems apply labels that place responsibility for social problems on individuals rather than the social system. Welfare recipients are deemed unworthy freeloaders; poor people who vent their rage at their plight

Over the course of three decades, as many as 2 million U.S. women have requested silicone breast implants, in many cases after disfiguring breast surgery. Recently, hundreds of women have become ill with symptoms caused by leaking of the silicone gel in the body. Perhaps most troubling of all, Dow Corning, a major manufacturer of the implants, apparently continued to dispense them even after reviewing mounting evidence that they represented a threat to health. Although a civil suit is in progress, it is unlikely that any corporate officials will ever face criminal charges.

are labeled rioters; anyone who actively challenges the government is branded a radical or a communist; and those who attempt to gain illegally what they cannot otherwise acquire are called common thieves.

White-Collar Crime

Until 1989, few people other than Wall Street stockbrokers had ever heard of Michael Milken. Yet Milken had accomplished a stunning feat, becoming the highest paid U.S. worker in half a century. With salary and bonuses in 1987 totaling $550 million—*about $1.5 million a day*—Milken ranks behind only Al Capone, whose earnings in 1927 reportedly reached $600 million in current dollars (Swartz, 1989). Milken has something else in common with Capone: The government

accused him of criminality, in this case, breaching securities and exchange laws.

Milken's activities exemplify **white-collar crime**, defined by Edwin Sutherland in 1940 as *crimes committed by persons of high social position in the course of their occupations* (Sutherland & Cressey, 1978). As the Milken case suggests, white-collar crime rarely involves uniformed police converging on a scene with drawn guns and does not refer to crimes such as murder, assault, or rape that are committed by people of high social position. Instead, white-collar crimes are acts by powerful people making use of their occupational positions to enrich themselves or others illegally, often causing significant public harm in the process (Hagan & Parker, 1985; Vold & Bernard, 1986). For this reason, sociologists sometimes call white-collar offenses that occur in government offices and corporate board rooms *crime in the suites* as opposed to *crime in the streets*.

The most common white-collar crimes are bank embezzlement, tax fraud, credit fraud, bribery, and antitrust violations. Most cases of white-collar crime, like most street crimes, involve relatively little money and cause limited harm to individuals. But the occasional major crime—like the savings and loan scandal a few years ago—attracts a great deal of attention and causes substantial losses to many people (Weisburd et al., 1991). The government program to bail out the savings and loan industry will end up costing U.S. taxpayers $600 billion dollars—$2,500 for every adult and child in the country.

Sutherland (1940) argued that most white-collar offenses provoke little reaction from others. When they do, however, they are more likely to end up in a civil hearing rather than in a criminal courtroom. *Civil law* regulates economic affairs between private parties, while *criminal law* encompasses specific laws that define every individual's moral responsibility to society. In civil settlements, a loser pays for damage or injury, but no party is labeled a criminal. Further, since corporations have the legal standing of persons, white-collar offenses commonly involve the organization as a whole rather than particular individuals.

And when white-collar criminals are charged and convicted, the odds are they will not go to jail. One accounting shows that fewer than three in ten embezzlers convicted in the U.S. District Court system spent a single day in prison; most were placed on probation (U.S. Bureau of Justice Statistics, 1992). Similarly, just ninety people were jailed for all federal environmental crimes between 1986 and 1991 (Gold, 1991).

The main reason for such leniency is that, as Sutherland noted years ago, the public voices less

Q: "No doubt alcohol, tobacco, and so forth, are things that a saint must avoid, but sainthood is also a thing that human beings must avoid." George Orwell
DIVERSITY: Edwin Schur argues that sociological analysis has long stressed the positive functions of deviance by women (cf. Kingsley Davis's 1937 analysis of prostitution) with little attention to the structural position of women in relation to men in U.S. society.

Q: ". . . in our society being treated as deviant has been a standard feature of life as a female." Edwin M. Schur
NOTE: Allegations of sexual harassment leveled at Clarence Thomas and the William Kennedy Smith rape trial provoked public discussion of where moral boundaries are to be placed. No doubt, both involve issues in which boundaries are shifting.

concern about white-collar crime than about street crime. Corporate crime, in effect, victimizes everyone—and no one. White-collar criminals don't stick a gun in anyone's ribs, and the economic costs are usually spread throughout the population.

Critical evaluation. According to social-conflict theory, the inequality in wealth and power that pervades our way of life also guides the creation and application of laws and other norms. This approach suggests that the criminal justice and social welfare systems act as political agents, controlling categories of people who threaten the capitalist system.

Like other approaches to deviance, however, social-conflict theory has its critics. First, this approach assumes that laws and other cultural norms are created directly by the rich and powerful. This assumption is, at least, an oversimplification, since many segments of our society influence, and benefit from, the political process. Laws also protect workers, consumers, and the environment, sometimes in opposition to the interests of capitalists.

Second, social-conflict analysis implies that criminality springs up only to the extent that a society treats its members unequally. However, according to Durkheim, all societies generate deviance, whatever their economic or political system.

We have presented various sociological explanations for crime and other types of deviance. Table 8–1 summarizes the contributions of each approach.

DEVIANCE AND SOCIAL DIVERSITY

The shape of deviance in a society has much to do with the relative power and privilege of different categories of people. The following sections examine two examples: how gender is linked to deviance, and how racial and ethnic hostility motivates hate crimes.

Deviance and Gender

Virtually every society in the world applies more stringent normative controls to women than to men. Historically, our society has limited the roles of women largely to the home. Even today, in the United States and many other societies, opportunities in the workplace, in politics, and in the military are limited for women. Elsewhere in the world, the normative constraints placed on women are even more glaring. In Saudi Arabia, women cannot legally operate motor vehicles; in Iran, women who dare to expose their hair or wear makeup in public can be whipped.

TABLE 8–1 Sociological Explanations of Deviance: A Summary

Theoretical Paradigm	Major Contributions
Structural-functional analysis	While what is deviant may vary, deviance itself is found in all societies; deviance and the social response it provokes serve to maintain the moral foundation of society; deviance can also direct social change.
Symbolic-interaction analysis	Nothing is inherently deviant but may become defined as such through the response of others; the reactions of others are highly variable; the label of deviance can lead to the emergence of secondary deviance and deviant careers.
Social-conflict analysis	Laws and other norms reflect the interests of powerful members of society; those who threaten the status quo are likely to be defined as deviant; social injury caused by powerful people is less likely to be defined as criminal than social injury caused by people who have little social power.

Given the importance of gender to the social construction of deviance, we need to pause a moment to see how gender figures in to some of the theories we have already discussed. Robert Merton's strain theory, for example, defines cultural goals in terms of financial success. Traditionally, however, this preoccupation with material things has dominated the thinking of men, while women have been socialized to define success in terms of relationships, particularly marriage and motherhood (Leonard, 1982). Only recently have women and men come to recognize the "strain" caused by the cultural ideals of equality clashing with the reality of gender-based inequality.

Labeling theory, the major approach in symbolic-interaction analysis, offers some insights into ways in which gender influences how we define deviance. To the extent that we judge the behavior of females and males by different standards, the very process of labeling involves sex-linked biases. Further, because society generally places men in positions of power over women, men often escape direct responsibility for actions that victimize women. In the past, at least, men engaging in sexual harassment or other assaults against women have been tagged with only mildly deviant labels; sometimes, they have suffered no adverse consequences and even have won societal approval.

DATA FILE: Material about domestic violence against women is included in the *Data File*.

Q: "I am as pure as the driven slush." Tallulah Bankhead

NOTE: In 1992, college authorities reported fourteen campus murders to police.

NOTE: Changes in our view of violence are suggested by how common violence among officials was two centuries ago. For example, Vice President Aaron Burr shot and killed Alexander Hamilton (first U.S. Secretary of the Treasury) in a duel in 1804 in Weehawken, New Jersey.

SOCIAL POLICY

Date Rape: Exposing Dangerous Myths

Completing a day of work during a business trip to the courthouse in Tampa, Florida, thirty-two-year-old Sandra Abbott* pondered how she would return to her hotel. An attorney with whom she had been working—a pleasant enough man—made the kind offer of a lift. As his car threaded its way through the late afternoon traffic, their conversation was animated. "He was saying all the right things," Abbott recalled, "so I started to trust him."

He wondered if she would join him for dinner; she happily accepted. After lingering over an enjoyable meal, they walked together to the door of her hotel room. The new acquaintance angled for an invitation to come in, but Abbott hesitated, sensing that he might have something more on his mind. She explained that she was old-fashioned about relationships but would allow him to come in for a little while with the understanding that talk was *all* they would do.

Sitting on the couch in the room, soon Abbott was overcome with drowsiness. Feeling comfortable in the presence of her new

*A pseudonym; the facts of this case are from Gibbs (1991a).

friend, she let her head fall gently onto his shoulder, and, before she knew it, she fell asleep. That's when the attack began. Abbott was startled back to consciousness as the man thrust himself upon her sexually. She shouted "No!" but he paid no heed. Abbott describes what happened next:

> I didn't scream or run. All I could think of was my business contacts

The 1992 rape conviction of heavyweight boxing champion Mike Tyson suggests that our society is taking the problem of sexual violence against women more seriously.

and what if they saw me run out of my room screaming rape. I thought it was my fault. I felt so filthy, I washed myself over and over in hot water. Did he rape me?, I kept asking myself. I didn't consent. But who's gonna believe me? I had a man in my hotel room after midnight. (Gibbs, 1991a:50)

Abbott knew that she had said "No!" and thus had been raped. She notified the police, who conducted an investigation and turned their findings over to the state attorney's office. But the authorities backed away from Abbott. In the absence of evidence like bruises, a medical examination, and torn clothes, they responded, there was little point in prosecuting.

The case of Sandra Abbott is all too typical. Even today, in most incidences of sexual attack, a victim makes no report to police, and no offender is arrested. The reason for such inaction is that many people have a misguided understanding of rape. Three inaccurate notions about rape are so common in the United States that they might be called "rape myths."

A first myth is that rape usually involves strangers. A sexual attack brings to mind young men who

By contrast, women who are victimized may have to convince an unsympathetic audience that they are not to blame for what happened. Research confirms an important truth: Whether people define a situation as deviance—and, if so, whose deviance it is—depends on the sex of both the audience and the actors (King & Clayson, 1988). The box takes a closer look at the issue of date rape, in which many women and men are

standing up for an end to a double standard that has long threatened the well-being of women.

Finally, a notable irony is that social-conflict analysis—despite its focus on social inequality—has long neglected the importance of gender. If, as conflict theory suggests, economic disadvantage is a primary cause of crime, why do women (whose economic position is much worse than that of men) commit far

DIVERSITY: According to the U.S. Bureau of Justice Statistics, three-fourths of rapes are intraracial; about 36 percent occur at the victim's home; most multi-offender ("gang") rapes are committed by men under twenty-one years of age (62 percent); police rearrest 52 percent of convicted rapists within three years.
NOTE: In 1992, the American Medical Association and the Surgeon General declared violent men to be a major threat to

women's health. According to the National League of Cities, about one-fourth of visits to emergency rooms by women are for injuries caused by domestic violence.
NOTE: With thirty on the record for 1992, "hate-crime" homicides account for only a tiny fraction of the 20,000 killings annually in the United States.

lurk in the shadows and suddenly spring on their unsuspecting victims. But this pattern is the exception rather than the rule: Experts report that only one in five rapes involves strangers. For this reason, people have begun to speak more realistically about *acquaintance rape* or, more simply, *date rape*. A rape—legally speaking, the carnal knowledge of a female forcibly and against her will—is typically committed by a man who is known to, and even trusted by, his victim. But common sense dictates that being a "friend" (or even a husband) does not prevent a man from committing murder, assault, or rape.

A second myth about rape is that women provoke their attackers. Surely, many people think, a woman claiming to have been raped must have done *something* to encourage the man, to lead him on, to make him think that she really wanted to have sex.

In the case described above, didn't Sandra Abbott agree to have dinner with the man? Didn't she invite him into her room? Such self-doubt often paralyzes victims. But having dinner with a man—or even inviting him into her hotel room—is hardly a woman's state-

ment of consent to have sex with him any more than she has agreed to have him beat her with a club.

A third myth is the notion that rape is simply sex. If there is no knife held to a woman's throat, or if she is not bound and gagged, then how can sex be a crime? The answer is simply that *forcing a woman to have sex without her consent is rape*.

To accept the idea that rape is sex one would also have to see no difference between brutal combat and playful wrestling. In the absence of consent, as Susan Brownmiller (1975) explains, rape is not sex but violence. "Having sex" implies intimacy, caring, communication, and, most important of all, consent—none of which is present in cases of rape. Beyond the brutality of being physically violated, date rape also undermines a victim's sense of trust.

The more people believe these myths about rape—that offenders are strangers, that victims provoke their attackers, and that rape is just spirited sex—the more women will fall victim to sexual violence. The ancient Babylonians stoned married women who became victims of rape, claiming that the women

had committed adultery. To a startling extent, ideas about rape have not changed over thousands of years, which helps to explain why, even today, perhaps one in twenty rapes results in an offender being sent to jail.

Nowhere has the issue of date rape been more widely discussed than at colleges and universities. On the campus, students have easy access to one another, the collegiate setting encourages trust, and young people often have much to learn about relationships and about themselves. While this open environment encourages communication, it also permits sexual violence.

To counter the problem of sexual violence, we must begin by exposing the myths about rape. In addition, some critics have raised questions about the large role of alcohol in campus social life and the effect of cultural patterns that define sex as a sport. To address the crisis of date rape, everyone needs to understand two simple truths: Forcing sex without a woman's consent is rape, and when a woman says "no," she means just that.

SOURCES: Gibbs (1991a, 1991b) and Gilbert (1992).

fewer crimes than men do? The crime discussion, beginning on page 224, which examines crime rates in the United States, will provide an answer to this question.

Hate Crimes

More than a decade ago the concept of **hate crime** came into our language to designate *a criminal act*

carried out against a person or that individual's property by an offender motivated by racial or other bias. In addition to racial bias, a hate crime may express hostility based on religion, ancestry, sexual orientation, or physical disability.

Although hate crimes are nothing new, the federal government has only tracked them since 1990. While still a small share of all crime, their numbers

THE MAP: The states that have enacted hate-crime legislation are almost exactly those that voted for Democrat Bill Clinton in the 1992 presidential election (look ahead to National Map 16–1 for election results).
SOCIAL SURVEY: "Do you think the use of marijuana should be made legal or not?" (GSS 1993, N = 1,057; *Codebook*, 1993:142)
   "Should" 22.1%   "Should not" 72.9%   DK/NR 5.0%

NOTE: Drug abuse is closely linked to serious crime. In 1988, the Justice Department tested men arrested in New York, Washington, D.C., San Diego, and nine other cities and found that 75% tested positive for drug use. "If we're going to do something about the crime rate, we are going to have to confront the drug problem," stated study director James Stewart.

Seeing Ourselves

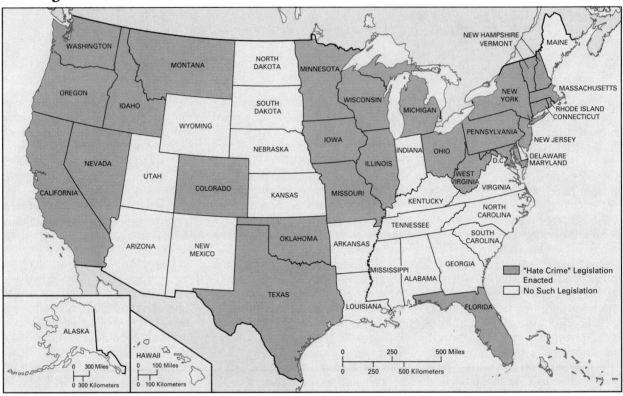

NATIONAL MAP 8–1 Hate Crime Legislation Across the United States

The states shown in purple have legally mandated harsher penalties for crimes motivated by racial, ethnic, or other bias. Generally, laws of this kind are favored by political liberals. Can you see a pattern in the map?
Hint: Most of the states that have enacted hate-crime laws supported Democrat Bill Clinton in the 1992 presidential election (as shown in National Map 16–1).

From "Punishing Hate Crimes," *The New York Times*, June 12, 1993. Copyright ©1993 by *The New York Times* Company. Reprinted by permission.

are rising. A survey conducted by the National Gay and Lesbian Task Force (cited in Berrill, 1992:19–20) in eight U.S. cities found that one in five lesbians and gay men had been physically assaulted because of their sexual orientation; more than 90 percent claimed to have been at least verbally abused for this reason. Research indicates that hate-motivated violence is especially likely to target people who contend with multiple stigmas, such as gay men of color.

It is not the race or ancestry of the victim that qualifies an offense as a hate crime, it is the fact that such considerations *motivate* the offender. Such a crime, then, is an expression of hatred directed at some category of people. The box describes a recent

case—the basis for a Supreme Court ruling upholding stiffer sentences for crimes motivated by hate.

National Map 8–1 shows that, as of mid-1993, twenty-seven states had enacted hate-crime legislation. Based on current trends, it is likely that many more states will do so in the next few years.

CRIME

All societies have a formal means for dealing with perceived violations of law, generally through statutes of criminal law enacted by local, state, or national government. Because various jurisdictions employ different

NOTE: Technically, the *corpus delecti* ("body of a crime") is composed of (1) *actus reus* ("guilty act"), which is the physical act (or omission) in violation of criminal law; (2) *mens rea* ("guilty mind") or mental resolve to commit the crime; (3) causal order, by which the criminal intent proceeds and is related to the criminal act; (4) all legal elements, the factors attached to the specific crime in a particular jurisdiction according to the wording of the criminal statute.

NOTE: The *State Survey of Prison Inmates, 1991* reported a drop in marijuana use and a rise in cocaine use by prison inmates; half of all inmates claim to have used cocaine in some form (compared to about one-fourth in 1986). About 14 percent of inmates report committing their offense while under the influence of cocaine or crack.

Q: "The fundamental sociological problem is not crime but the law . . ." Peter Berger (1963:37)

SOCIAL POLICY

Hate Crimes: Punishing Actions or Attitudes?

On an October evening in 1989, Todd Mitchell, an African-American teenager, and a group of friends were milling about the front of their apartment complex in Kenosha, Wisconsin. They had just watched the film *Mississippi Burning* and were fuming over a scene in which a white man beats a young black boy kneeling in prayer.

"Do you feel hyped up to move on some white people?" asked Mitchell. Minutes later, a young white boy walked toward the group on the other side of the street. Mitchell commanded: "There goes a white boy; go get him!" The group surrounded the white boy, beating him to the ground and leaving him bloody and in a coma. They took his tennis shoes as a trophy of their conquest.

The black boys were identified and charged with the beating. At the trial of Todd Mitchell, who acted as the ringleader, the jury took the unusual step of finding the young man guilty of aggravated battery *motivated by racial hatred*. Instead of the typical two-year prison sentence, the jury committed Mitchell to jail for four years.

The enhancement of sentences for crimes motivated by bias is quickly becoming the law of the land. Supporters of hate-crime legislation make three arguments in favor of this trend. First, an offender's intentions have always been part of criminal deliberations, so this case represents nothing new. Second, crimes motivated by racial

Hostility has fueled attacks on Turks and other immigrants in Germany in recent years. In 1993, an angry mob burned this house causing loss of life and revealing the viciousness of racial and ethnic hatred.

or other bias inflame the public mood more than those carried out for more common reasons like monetary gain. Third, supporters continue, such crimes are typically more harmful to the victims than those that involve other motives.

Critics, however, see in hate-crime laws a threat to free speech and expression. Under such a law, offenders are sentenced not for their actions, but for their underlying attitudes. As Harvard law professor Alan Dershowitz cautions, "As much as I hate bigotry, I fear much more the Court attempting to control the minds of its citizens." In short, according to the critics, hate-crime statutes open the door to punishing beliefs rather than behavior.

In 1993, the Supreme Court upheld the sentence handed down to Todd Mitchell. In a unanimous decision, the justices rejected the idea of punishing an individual's beliefs. At the same time, they reasoned, an abstract belief is no longer protected when it becomes the motive for a crime.

SOURCES: Greenhouse (1993) and Terry (1993).

legal standards, however, behavior that provokes a swift response in one time and place may merit barely a raised eyebrow in another.

In centuries past, for example, a Chinese commoner who simply looked at the Chinese emperor in public committed a serious crime. Today, a citizen of the People's Republic of China who expressed support for the nation's historic monarchy would likely face criminal charges. Closer to home, the U.S. judicial

system has also undergone sweeping changes, supporting slavery for two centuries, for example, then condemning racial discrimination.

The Components of Crime

Technically, our society conceives of crime as having two distinct parts: the *act* itself (or, in some cases, the failure to do what the law requires) and *criminal intent*

SOCIAL SURVEY: "Is there a place near here where you would be afraid to walk at night?" (*Student Chip Social Survey Software*, FEARNAUT; GSS 1974–91, N = 5,698)

SEX	"Yes"	"No"
Men	20.5%	79.5%
Women	59.6%	40.4%

RACE/ETHNICITY

Afri Amer	54.4%	45.6%
Latino	45.0%	55.0%
White Anglo	40.8%	59.2%

DIVERSITY: As a backdrop to delinquency patterns: 20 percent of U.S. children are living in poverty; for whites, the figure is 15 percent; for Hispanics, 40 percent; for African Americans, 45 percent.

(in legal terminology, *mens rea*, or "guilty mind"). Intent is a matter of degree, ranging from a deliberate action to negligence in which a person acts (or fails to act) in a manner that may reasonably be expected to cause harm. Juries weigh the degree of intent in determining the seriousness of a crime and may find one person who kills another guilty of first-degree murder, second-degree murder, or negligent manslaughter. Alternatively, they may rule a killing justifiable.

Types of Crime

In the United States, the Federal Bureau of Investigation gathers information on criminal offenses and regularly reports the results in a publication called *Crime in the United States*. Two major types of offenses contribute to the FBI "crime index."

Crimes against the person constitute *crimes against people that involve violence or the threat of violence.* Such "violent crimes" include murder and manslaughter (legally defined as "the willful killing of one human being by another"), aggravated assault ("an unlawful attack by one person upon another for the purpose of inflicting severe or aggravated bodily injury"), forcible rape ("the carnal knowledge of a female forcibly and against her will"), and robbery ("taking or attempting to take anything of value from the care, custody, or control of a person or persons by force or threat of force or violence and/or putting the victim in fear").

Crimes against property encompass *crimes that involve theft of property belonging to others.* "Property crimes" range from burglary ("the unlawful entry of a structure to commit a [serious crime] or a theft") to larceny-theft ("the unlawful taking, carrying, leading, or riding away of property from the possession of another"), auto theft ("the theft or attempted theft of a motor vehicle"), and arson ("any willful or malicious burning or attempt to burn the personal property of another").

A third category of offenses, not incorporated into major crime indexes, is **victimless crimes**, *violations of law in which there are no readily apparent victims.* So-called crimes without complaint include illegal drug use, prostitution, and gambling. "Victimless crime" is often a misnomer, however. How victimless is a crime when young people abusing drugs may have to steal to support a drug habit? How victimless is a crime if a young pregnant woman smoking crack causes the death or permanent injury of her baby? How victimless is a crime when a young runaway lives a desperate life of prostitution on the streets? And how victimless is a crime when a gambler falls so deeply into debt that he can no longer afford mortgage payments? In truth, the people who commit such crimes are themselves both offenders and victims.

Because public opinion about such activities varies considerably, the laws regulating victimless crimes differ from place to place. In the United States, gambling is legal only in a few locations, including Nevada and part of New Jersey; prostitution is legal only in part of Nevada; homosexual (and some heterosexual) behavior among consenting adults is still legally restricted in about half of the states. Where such laws do exist, enforcement is generally uneven.

Criminal Statistics

Statistics gathered by the Federal Bureau of Investigation show that crime rates have generally risen in recent decades, despite increases in government spending on anticrime programs. During the 1980s, the police recorded some 8 million serious crimes annually, documenting a 23 percent jump in violent crime across the decade. Property crime, however, showed a modest trend in the other direction, falling by 3 percent (U.S. Federal Bureau of Investigation, 1991). Figure 8–2 illustrates the relative frequency and the trend for various serious crimes.

Always read crime statistics with caution, however, since they include only crimes known to the police. The police learn about almost all homicides, but assaults—especially among acquaintances—are far less likely to be reported. The police record even a smaller proportion of property crimes, especially those involving items of little value. Some victims may not realize that a crime has occurred, or they may assume they have little chance of recovering their property even if they notify the police.

As already noted, women do not report most cases of rape to the police. However, rising public support for rape victims has prompted more women to come forward, a trend reflected in a 25 percent increase in the number of forcible rapes reported to police during the 1980s (Harlow, 1991).

One way to evaluate official crime statistics is through a *victimization survey*, in which a researcher asks a representative sample of people about being victimized. These surveys indicate that actual criminality occurs at a rate three times higher than what official reports suggest.

The "Street" Criminal: A Profile

Government statistics paint a broad-brush picture of people arrested for violent and property crimes. We

NOTE: Violence is also linked to urbanization. Gerhard Falk (1990) calculates that New York state has a murder rate of 12.5 per 100,000 inhabitants; without New York City (which has 48% of the state's people but 87% of its murders) the state rate would be 3.1 per 100,000. This pattern is more or less true across the country.

DIVERSITY: Many criminals are uneducated: One study of New York prison inmates found that, on average, white inmates read at about the tenth grade level, African-American inmates at the eighth grade level, and Latinos at the sixth grade level.

Q: "I call [juvenile delinquents] drifters . . . Drift is motion gently guided by underlying influences . . . a gradual process [that is] unperceived by the actor, in which the first stage may be accidental . . ." David Matza (1964:29)

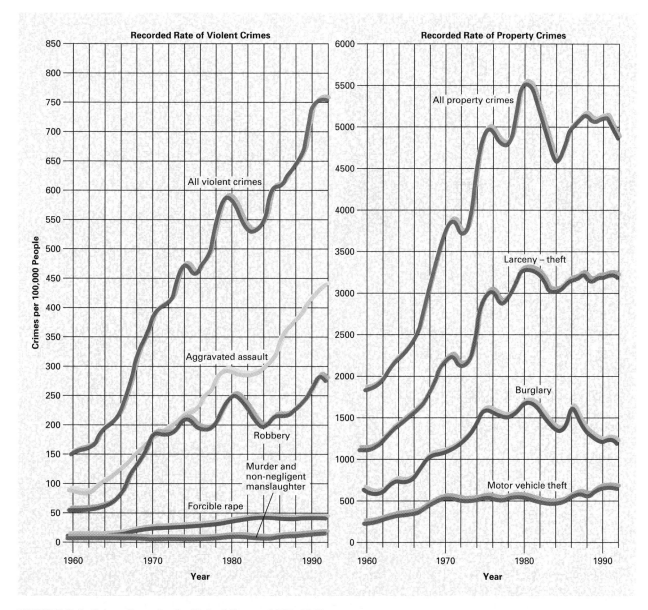

FIGURE 8–2 Crime Rates in the United States, 1960–1992

(U.S. Federal Bureau of Investigation, 1993)

now examine the breakdown of these arrest statistics by age, gender, social class, race, and ethnicity.

Age

Official crime rates rise sharply during adolescence and peak at about age nineteen, falling thereafter. Although people between the ages of fifteen and twenty-four represent only 14 percent of the U.S. population, they accounted for 42.1 percent of all arrests for violent crimes in 1992 and 44.7 percent for property crimes (U.S. Federal Bureau of Investigation, 1993).

A notable—and disturbing—trend is that young offenders are committing crimes that are more serious. The number of adults arrested for murder, for

The creators of this photograph, part of the United Colors of Benetton advertising campaign, intended to make the statement that people are linked together regardless of color. But so strong are our notions about crime and race that many individuals mistakenly interpreted the photograph as a white police officer escorting a black suspect. What can sociology contribute toward a more accurate understanding of the connection between crime and color?

Social Class

Criminality is more widespread among people of lower social position; however, the matter is more complicated than it appears on the surface (Wolfgang, Figlio, & Sellin, 1972; Clinard & Abbott, 1973; Braithwaite, 1981; Thornberry & Farnsworth, 1982; Wolfgang, Thornberry, & Figlio, 1987).

In part, this pattern reflects the historical tendency to view poor people as less worthy than those whose wealth and power confer "respectability" (Tittle & Villemez, 1977; Tittle, Villemez, & Smith, 1978; Elias, 1986). But it is a mistake to assume that being socially disadvantaged means being criminal. While crime—especially violence—is a serious problem in the poorest inner-city neighborhoods, most people who live in these communities have no criminal records, and most crimes there are committed by a relatively few hard-core offenders (Wolfgang, Figlio, & Sellin, 1972; Elliott & Ageton, 1980; Harries, 1990).

Moreover, as John Braithwaite reminds us, the connection between social standing and criminality depends on what kind of crime one is talking about (1981:47). If we expand our definition of crime beyond street offenses to include white-collar crime, the "common criminal" has much higher social position.

Race and Ethnicity

Both race and ethnicity have a strong influence on crime rates, although the reasons are many and complex. Official statistics indicate that 67.6 percent of arrests for index crimes in 1992 involved whites. However, arrests of African Americans were higher than for whites in proportion to their numbers; black people represent about 12 percent of the population and 31.8 percent of arrests for property crimes (versus 65.8 percent for whites) and 44.8 percent of arrests for violent crimes (53.6 percent for whites) (U.S. Federal Bureau of Investigation, 1993).

What accounts for African Americans experiencing a disproportionate level of arrests? Several factors are important. First, keep in mind that arrest records do not qualify as statements of proven guilt. To the degree that prejudice related to color or class prompts white police to arrest blacks more readily, and leads citizens more willingly to report black people to police as potential offenders, African Americans are overly criminalized (Liska & Tausig, 1979; Unnever, Frazier, & Henretta, 1980; Smith & Visher, 1981).

Second, race in the United States closely relates to social standing, which, as we have already explained,

example, has been dropping in recent years. At the same time, however, the number of teenagers charged with homicide has risen sharply.

Gender

Official statistics suggest that the vast majority of crime is committed by males. Although each sex constitutes roughly half of the population, police collared males in 74.5 percent of all property crime arrests in 1992. This means that men are arrested three times as often as women for these crimes. In the case of violent crimes, the disparity is even greater: 87.5 percent of arrests involved males and just 12.5 percent were of females (a seven-to-one ratio).

Some of this gender difference stems from the reluctance of law enforcement officials to define women as criminals. Even so, the arrest rate for women has been moving closer to that of men, which is probably one indication of increasing sexual equality in our society. Between 1983 and 1992, the *increase* in arrests of women was greater (37.5 percent) than that for men (16.9 percent) (U.S. Federal Bureau of Investigation, 1993). In global perspective, this pattern holds, with the greatest gender difference in crime rates marking societies that most limit the social opportunities of women.

SOCIAL SURVEY: "What do you think about U.S. spending on halting the rising crime rate?" (*STUDENT CHIP Social Survey Software*, NATCRIM1; GSS 1973–91, N = 16,140)

	"Too little"	"About right"	"Too much"
Afri Amer	75.7%	18.3%	6.0%
Latino	71.3%	22.7%	6.0%
White Anglo	69.6%	25.0%	5.5%

SOCIAL SURVEY: "Do you happen to have in your home (house or garage) any guns or revolvers?" (GSS 1993, N = 1,075; *Codebook*, 1993:277)

"Yes" 42.1%   "No" 57.1%   DK/NR 0.8%

DIVERSITY: States with the highest proportion of homes with guns are Florida and Texas, where about 60 percent of households have at least one firearm.

There are almost enough guns in the United States to arm every woman, man, and child; about half of all households contain one or more such weapons. The "death clock" in New York City's Times Square tallies both the number of guns and the annual death toll from firearms. Guns are not the only key to our country's high crime rate, since unarmed criminality in the United States is also high by world standards. But the ready availability of guns does contribute to accidental shootings—especially by children—and it also raises the odds that interpersonal violence will become deadly.

affects the likelihood of engaging in street crimes. Judith Blau and Peter Blau (1982) suggest that criminality is promoted by the sting of being poor in the midst of affluence as poor people come to perceive society as unjust. Because unemployment among African-American adults is double the rate among whites, and because almost half of black children grow up in poverty (in contrast to about one in six white children), no one should be surprised at proportionately higher crime rates for African Americans (Sampson, 1987).

Third, remember that the official crime index excludes arrests for crimes ranging from drunk driving to white-collar offenses. Clearly, this omission contributes to the view of the typical criminal as a person of color. If we broaden our definition of crime to include driving while intoxicated, insider stock trading, embezzlement, and cheating on income tax returns, the proportion of white criminals rises dramatically.

Finally, some categories of the population have unusually low rates of arrest. People of Asian descent, who account for about 3 percent of the population, figure in only 1 percent of all arrests. As Chapter 12 ("Race and Ethnicity") documents, Asian Americans enjoy higher than average incomes and have a particularly successful record of educational achievement, which enhances job opportunities. Moreover, the cultural patterns that characterize Asian-American communities emphasize family solidarity and discipline, both of which serve to inhibit criminality.

Crime in Global Perspective

By world standards, the United States has a lot of crime. The New York metropolitan area recorded 2,401 murders in 1992. Rarely does a day pass with no murder in New York; typically more New Yorkers are hit with stray bullets than are gunned down deliberately in cities elsewhere in the world.

The homicide rate in the United States stands at about five times that of Europe, the rape rate seven times higher, and the rate of property crime is twice as high. The contrast is even greater between our society and the nations of Asia, including India and Japan, where rates of violent and property crime are among the lowest in the world.

Elliott Currie (1985) suggests that crime stems from our culture's emphasis on individual economic success, frequently at the expense of family and community cohesion. The United States also has extraordinary cultural diversity, the legacy of centuries of immigration. Moreover, economic inequality is higher in this country than in most other industrial societies. Taken together, our society has a relatively weak social fabric, which, combined with considerable frustration among this country's have-nots, generates widespread criminal behavior.

Another contributing factor to violence in the United States is extensive private ownership of guns. Of 22,540 murder victims in the United States in 1992, 68.2 percent died from shootings. By the early 1990s, Texas and several other southern states reported that deaths from gunshots exceeded automobile-related

Q: "In the severity of its crime rates, the United States more closely resembles the most volatile countries of the Third World than other developed Western societies . . ." Elliott Currie

RESOURCE: Elliott Currie's global analysis of crime is included in the Macionis and Benokraitis reader, *Seeing Ourselves.*

Q: "If a man is a minority of one, we lock him up." Oliver Wendell Holmes

Q: "The entire [criminal justice] system . . . is charged with enforcing the law and maintaining order. What is distinctive about the responsibility of the police is that they are charged with performing these functions where all eyes are upon them and where the going is roughest, on the street." The President's Commission on Law Enforcement and the Administration of Justice, 1966

fatalities. Rising public demand for gun control led Congress in 1993 to pass the so-called Brady Bill, named for President Ronald Reagan's press secretary who was shot along with the president a decade before. The law requires a seven-day waiting period for the purchase of handguns, with the purpose of discouraging impulsive buying and allowing police time to perform background checks on purchasers.

But there are already as many guns in the hands of private individuals as there are people in the United States. Further, guns represent only one piece in this nation's crime puzzle. As Elliott Currie notes, the number of Californians killed each year by knives alone exceeds the number of Canadians killed by weapons of all kinds. Most experts do think, however, that gun control will help curb the level of violence.

It is true that crime rates are soaring in some of the largest cities of the world like São Paulo, Brazil, which have rapid population growth and millions of desperately poor people. By and large, however, the traditional character of less economically developed societies and their strong family structure allow local communities to control crime informally (Clinard & Abbott, 1973; *Der Spiegel,* 1989).

One exception to this pattern is crimes against women. Rape is a rapidly growing problem throughout the world, especially in poor societies. Traditional social patterns that curb the economic opportunities available to women also promote prostitution. Global Map 8–1 shows the extent of prostitution in various world regions.

Finally, as noted in earlier chapters, a process of "globalization" is at hand by which various societies of the world are becoming more closely linked. This trend holds for crime as well. Some types of crime have always been multinational, including terrorism, espionage, and arms dealing (Martin & Romano, 1992).

A more recent case in point is the illegal drug trade. In part, the problem of illegal drugs in the United States is a "demand" issue, since there is a very profitable market for cocaine and other drugs in this country, as well as legions of young people willing to risk arrest or even violent death by engaging in the lucrative drug trade. But the "supply" side of the issue is just as important. In the South American nation of Colombia, 20 percent of the people depend on cocaine production for their livelihood, and the rate is higher in the poorest regions of the country. Furthermore, not only is cocaine Colombia's most profitable export, but the drug outsells all other exports combined (including coffee). Clearly, then, understanding crimes such as drug dealing requires analyzing social conditions both in this country and elsewhere.

THE CRIMINAL JUSTICE SYSTEM

The criminal justice system is a society's formal response to crime. We shall briefly introduce the key elements of this scheme: police, the courts, and the punishment of convicted offenders.

Police

The police generally serve as the point of contact between the population and the criminal justice system. In principle, the police maintain public order by uniformly enforcing the law. In reality, 550,000 full-time police officers in the United States (in 1992) cannot effectively monitor the activities of 250 million people. As a result, the police exercise considerable discretion about which situations warrant their attention and how to handle them. Although police work demands some degree of discretion, the ability of police to pursue a situation as they see fit also fosters unequal treatment of some categories of people, as suggested by the Rodney King incident in Los Angeles, described at the beginning of this chapter.

How, then, do police carry out their duties? In a study of police behavior in five cities, Douglas Smith and Christy Visher (1981; Smith, 1987) concluded that, because they must act quickly, police rely on external cues to guide their actions. First, the more serious they perceive the situation to be, the more likely they are to make an arrest. Second, police assess the victim's preference as to how the matter should be handled. In general, if a victim demands that police make an arrest, they are likely to do so. Third, police more often arrest suspects who appear uncooperative. Fourth, they are more likely to arrest suspects whom they have arrested before, presumably because this suggests guilt. Fifth, the presence of bystanders increases the likelihood of arrest. According to Smith and Visher, the presence of observers prompts police to appear in control of the situation and also to use an arrest to move the interaction from the street (the suspect's turf) to the police department (where law officers have the edge). Sixth, all else being equal, police are more likely to arrest people of color than whites. Smith and Visher concluded that police generally consider people of African or Hispanic descent as either more dangerous or more likely to be guilty. In the researchers' view,

Q: "There is no distinctly American criminal class except for Congress." Mark Twain

Q: "If . . . only one person were of a contrary opinion, mankind would be no more justified in silencing that one person than he, if he had the power, would be justified in silencing mankind." John Stuart Mill, *On Liberty*

GLOBAL: The People's Republic of China is much more efficient than the United States in disposing of prisoners. In the final days before the Chinese New Year in 1993, courts closed their books on fifty-five people convicted of crimes ranging from fraud to murder; all were quickly sentenced and shot in the back of the head with no delay and little fanfare.

Q: "Don't call a man honest just because he never had a chance to steal." Yiddish proverb

Window on the World

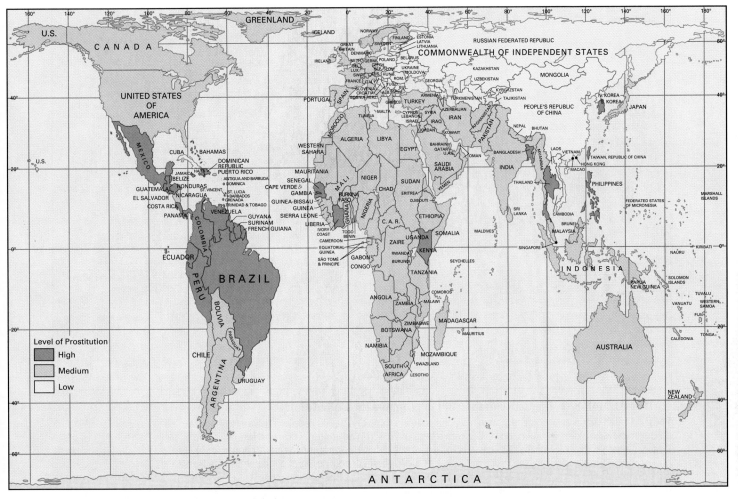

GLOBAL MAP 8–1 Prostitution in Global Perspective

Generally speaking, prostitution is widespread in societies of the world where women have low standing in relation to men. Officially, at least, the now-defunct socialist regimes in Eastern Europe and the former Soviet Union, as well as the People's Republic of China, boasted of gender equality, including the elimination of "vice" such as prostitution. By contrast, in much of Latin America, a region of pronounced patriarchy, prostitution is commonplace. In many Islamic societies patriarchy is also strong but religious forces restrain this practice. Western, industrial societies display a moderate amount of prostitution.

From *Peters Atlas of the World* (1990).

this perception contributes to the disproportionately high arrest rates among these categories of people.

Finally, the concentration of police relative to population varies throughout the United States. Typically, the hand of law enforcement is heaviest in cities with high concentrations of nonwhites and with large income disparities between rich and poor (Jacobs, 1979). Looking nationally, as shown in National Map 8–2, on page 232, the concentration of police is several times higher in some states than in others.

THE MAP: The U.S. average is 23 police employees per 10,000 people; by state, the top three are Washington D.C., 92.1; New Jersey, 41.0; New York, 36.9; the three lowest are Minnesota, 20.1; Kentucky, 20.1; and West Virginia, 16.2. Washington, D.C., with the highest police ratio, also has the highest homicide rate, suggesting that police cannot, by themselves, effectively control crime.

DIVERSITY: Although varying by jurisdiction, women make up about 12% of U.S. police officers; African Americans (men and women) represent about 15%, and Latinos about 6%.

GLOBAL: Japanese nationals are five times more likely to be victims of homicide while in the United States than while in Japan according to the Foreign Ministry of Japan.

Seeing Ourselves

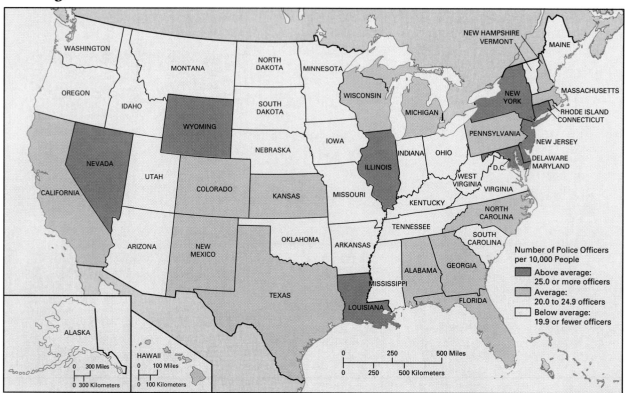

NATIONAL MAP 8–2 The Concentration of Police Across the United States

For the United States as a whole, there are 23 police officers for every 10,000 people. The range of police strength shows striking variation, however, from a high of 75.1 in Washington, D.C., to a low of 15.4 in South Dakota. What do states that have high concentrations of police have in common? What accounts for lower police power? Finally, Washington, D.C., not only has the highest concentration of police, it also leads the nation in homicide rates. What does this suggest about the ability of police to curb crime?

Prepared by the author using data from The U.S. Federal Bureau of Investigation.

Courts

After arrest, a court determines a suspect's guilt or innocence. In principle, our courts rely on an adversarial process involving attorneys—who represent the defendant on the one side and the state on the other—in the presence of a judge who monitors adherence to legal procedures.

In practice, however, about 90 percent of criminal cases are resolved prior to court appearance through **plea bargaining,** *a legal negotiation in which the prosecution reduces a defendant's charge in exchange for a guilty plea.* For example, a defendant charged with

burglary may agree to plead guilty to the lesser charge of possession of burglary tools; another charged with selling cocaine may go along with pleading guilty to mere possession.

Plea bargaining is widespread because it spares the system the time and expense of court trials. A trial is usually unnecessary if there is little disagreement as to the facts of the case. By selectively trying only a small proportion of the cases, the courts can also channel their resources into those they deem most important (Reid, 1991).

But this process pressures defendants (who are presumed innocent) to plead guilty. A person can exercise

SOCIAL SURVEY: "Do you favor or oppose the death penalty for persons convicted of murder?" (GSS 1993, N = 1,606; *Codebook* 1993:137)

	"Favor"	
"Favor"	71.7%	
"Oppose"	21.0%	
DK/NR	7.3%	

(*CHIP1 Social Survey Software*, CAPPUN1,2; GSS 1974–89,

N = 18,863)		
SEX	"Favor"	"Oppose"
Men	78.8%	21.2%
Women	70.0%	30.0%
RACE/ETHNICITY		
Afri Amer	47.7%	52.3%
Hisp Amer	69.7%	30.3%
Whites	77.5%	22.5%

the right to a trial, but only at the risk of receiving a more severe sentence if found guilty. In essence, say critics, plea bargaining undercuts the rights of defendants as it circumvents the adversarial process.

Punishment

On January 5, 1993, a bound and hooded Westley Allan Dodd dropped through the trap door on a scaffold in Walla Walla, Washington, to his death. Few could feel compassion for a man who admitted raping, torturing, and then killing three young boys. But any such event causes people to reconsider the wisdom of legal execution and, more broadly, to ponder the purpose of punishment.

Scholars, too, reflect on the purposes of punishment. They commonly advance four justifications.

Retribution

The celebrated justice of the Supreme Court, Oliver Wendell Holmes, stated "The first requirement of a sound body of law is that it should correspond with the actual feelings and demands of the community." Because people react to crime with a passion for revenge, Holmes continued, "the law has no choice but to satisfy [that] craving" (quoted in Carlson, 1976).

From this point of view, punishing satisfies a society's need for **retribution**, *an act of moral vengeance by which society subjects an offender to suffering comparable to that caused by the offense.* Retribution is based on a view of society as a system of moral balance. When criminality upsets this balance, punishment exacted in comparable measure restores the moral order, as suggested in the biblical dictum "An eye for an eye."

Retribution stands as the oldest justification for punishment. During the Middle Ages, most people viewed crime as sin—an offense against God as well as society—that warranted harsh punishment. Although sometimes criticized today because it offers little to reform the offender, retribution remains a strong justification for punishment.

Deterrence

A second justification for punishment, **deterrence**, amounts to *the attempt to discourage criminality through punishment.* Deterrence is based on the Enlightenment notion that humans are calculating and rational creatures. From this point of view, self-interested people will forgo deviance if they perceive that the pains of punishment outweigh the pleasure of mischief.

Initially, deterrence represented reform of the system of harsh punishments based on retribution.

Dutch painter Vincent Van Gogh (1853-1890) strongly identified with suffering people that he found around him. Perhaps this is why he included his own likeness in this portrait of the dungeon-like prisons of the nineteenth century. Since then, the stark isolation and numbing depersonalization of prison life has changed little. Prisons are still custodial institutions in which officials make few efforts at rehabilitation.
Vincent Van Gogh, *Prisoner's Round.* Dutch. Pushkin State Museum, Moscow.

Why put someone to death for stealing, critics asked, if that crime could be discouraged with a prison sentence? As the concept of deterrence became better accepted, execution and physical mutilation of criminals were replaced by milder forms of punishment such as incarceration.

Punishment may deter in two ways. *Specific deterrence* demonstrates to an individual offender that crime does not pay. Through *general deterrence*, the punishment of one person serves as an example to others.

Rehabilitation

The third justification for punishment is **rehabilitation**, *a program for reforming the offender to preclude*

Societal Protection

A final justification for punishment is **societal protection**, *a means by which society renders an offender incapable of further offenses temporarily through incarceration or permanently by execution.* Like deterrence, social protection is a rational approach to punishment and seeks to protect society from crime.

Table 8–2 summarizes these four justifications of punishment.

Critical evaluation. We have identified four purposes of punishment. Assessing the actual consequences of punishment, however, is no simple task.

The value of retribution reminds us of Durkheim's theory of the functions of deviance, presented earlier in this chapter. Durkheim believed that punishing the deviant person increases people's moral awareness. To accomplish this objective, punishment was traditionally a public event. Public executions occurred in England until 1868; the last public execution in the United States took place in Kentucky in 1937. Even today, the mass media ensure public awareness of executions carried out inside prison walls (Kittrie, 1971).

Nonetheless, it is difficult to prove scientifically that punishment upholds social morality. Often it advances one conception of social morality at the expense of another, as when our government imprisons people who refuse to perform military service.

To some degree, punishment serves as a specific deterrent. Yet our society also has a high rate of **criminal recidivism**, *subsequent offenses by people previously convicted of crimes.* One 1991 study of state prison inmates found that 62 percent had been incarcerated before, and 45 percent had been sentenced three or more times (U.S. Bureau of Justice Statistics, 1991). Put in other terms, once released from jail, half of former inmates are returned to prison within several years. Such a high rate of recidivism raises questions about the extent to which punishment actually deters crime. Then, too, only about one-third of all crimes are known to police, and of these, only about one in five results in an arrest. The old adage that "crime doesn't pay" rings rather hollow when we consider that such a small proportion of offenses ever result in punishment.

General deterrence is even more difficult to investigate scientifically, since we have no way of knowing how people might act if they were unaware of punishments meted out to others. In the debate over capital punishment, permitted in thirty-six states, critics of the practice point to research suggesting that the death penalty has limited value as a general deterrent in the United States, which is the only Western, industrial

TABLE 8–2 Four Justifications of Punishment: A Summary

Retribution	The oldest justification of punishment that remains important today. Punishment is atonement for a moral wrong by an individual; in principle, punishment should be comparable in severity to the deviance itself.
Deterrence	An early modern approach. Deviance is viewed as social disruption, which society acts to control. People are viewed as rational and self-interested, so that deterrence requires that the pains of punishment outweigh the pleasures of deviance.
Rehabilitation	A modern approach linked to the development of social sciences. Deviance is viewed as the product of social problems (such as poverty) or personal problems (such as mental illness). Social conditions are improved and offenders subjected to intervention appropriate to their condition.
Societal protection	A modern approach easier to implement than rehabilitation. If society is unable or unwilling to improve offenders or reform social conditions, protection from further deviance is afforded by incarceration or execution.

subsequent offenses. Rehabilitation paralleled the development of the social sciences in the nineteenth century. According to early sociologists, crime and other deviance sprang from an unfavorable environment marked by poverty or a lack of parental supervision, for example. Proponents of rehabilitation argued that, just as offenders learned to be deviant, they learn to obey the rules if placed in the right setting. *Reformatories* or *houses of correction*, therefore, afforded offenders a controlled environment that might help them learn proper behavior (recall the description of total institutions in Chapter 5, "Socialization").

Rehabilitation resembles deterrence in that both motivate the offender toward conformity. But rehabilitation emphasizes constructive improvement, while deterrence and retribution simply make the offender suffer. In addition, while retribution demands that the punishment fit the crime, rehabilitation focuses on the distinctive problems of each offender. Thus identical offenses might prompt similar acts of retribution but different programs of rehabilitation.

NOTE: The minimum age at which an offender can be put to death is now effectively sixteen based on the Supreme Court's decision in *Thompson* v. *Oklahoma* (June 1988). The essential issue is how old does a person have to be to be consciously evil and to act accordingly?

Q: "Eighty-six percent of incarcerated juveniles owned at least one firearm at some time in their lives; 83 percent owned a gun at the time they were incarcerated. Of those who had ever owned a gun, two-thirds acquired their first firearm by the age of fourteen. A large majority (73 percent) had owned three or more types of guns; nearly two-thirds (65 percent) owned at least three firearms just before being jailed. In short, the tendency is for these young inmates to have owned guns in both quantity and variety." James D. Wright, Joseph F. Sheley, and M. Dwayne Smith (1993).

society that routinely executes serious offenders (Sellin, 1980; van den Haag & Conrad, 1983; Archer & Gartner, 1987; Lester, 1987; Bailey & Peterson, 1989; Bailey, 1990; Bohm, 1991).

Efforts at rehabilitation spark controversy as well. Prisons accomplish short-term societal protection by keeping offenders off the streets, but they do very little to reshape attitudes or behavior in the long term (Carlson, 1976). Perhaps this result is to be expected, since according to Sutherland's theory of differential association, placing a person among criminals for a long period of time should simply strengthen criminal attitudes and skills. And because incarceration severs whatever social ties inmates may have in the outside world, individuals may be prone to further crime upon their release, consistent with Hirschi's control theory.

Finally, inmates returning to the surrounding world contend with the stigma of being ex-convicts, often an obstacle to successful integration. One study of young offenders in Philadelphia found that boys who were sentenced to long prison terms—those likely to acquire a criminal stigma—later committed both more crimes and more serious ones (Wolfgang, Figlio, & Sellin, 1972).

Ultimately, we should never assume that the criminal justice system—the police, courts, and prisons—can eliminate crime. The reason, echoed throughout this chapter, is simple: Crime—in fact, all kinds of deviance—is more than simply the acts of "bad people"; it is inextricably bound up in the operation of society itself.

SUMMARY

1. Deviance refers to violations that span a wide range, from mild breaches of etiquette to serious violence.

2. Biological explanations of crime, from Caesare Lombroso's research in the nineteenth century to developing research in human genetics, has yet to produce much insight into the causes of crime.

3. Psychological explanations of deviance focus on abnormalities in the individual personality, which arise from either biological causes or the social environment. Psychological theories help to explain some kinds of deviance.

4. Social forces produce nonconformity because deviance (1) exists in relation to cultural norms, (2) results from a process of social definition, and (3) is shaped by the distribution of social power.

5. Sociology links deviance to the operation of society rather than the deficiencies of individuals. Using the structural-functional paradigm, Durkheim claimed that responding to deviance affirms values and norms, clarifies moral boundaries, promotes social unity, and encourages social change.

6. The symbolic-interaction paradigm is the basis of labeling theory, which holds that deviance arises in the reaction of others to a person's behavior.

Labeling theory focuses on secondary deviance and deviant careers, which result from acquiring the stigma of deviance.

7. Following the approach of Karl Marx, social-conflict theory holds that laws and other norms reflect the interests of the most powerful people in society. Social-conflict theory also spotlights white-collar crimes that cause extensive social harm, although the offenders are rarely defined as criminals.

8. Official statistics indicate that arrest rates peak in adolescence, then drop steadily with advancing age. Three-fourths of property crime arrests are of males, as are almost nine of ten arrests for violent crimes.

9. People of lower social position commit more street crime than those with greater social privilege. When white-collar crimes are included among criminal offenses, however, this disparity in overall criminal activity diminishes.

10. More whites than African Americans are arrested for street crimes. However, African Americans are arrested more often than whites in proportion to their respective populations. Asian Americans show lower than average rates of arrest.

11. The police exercise considerable discretion in their work. Research suggests that factors such as the seriousness of the offense, the presence of bystanders, and the accused being African American make arrest more likely.

12. Although ideally an adversarial system, U.S. courts predominantly resolve cases through plea bargaining. An efficient method of handling cases where the facts are not in dispute, plea bargaining nevertheless places less powerful people at a disadvantage.

13. Justifications of punishment include retribution, deterrence, rehabilitation, and societal protection. Because its consequences are difficult to evaluate scientifically, punishment—like deviance itself— sparks controversy among sociologists and the public as a whole.

KEY CONCEPTS

crime the violation of norms a society formally enacts into criminal law

crimes against the person (violent crimes) crimes against people that involve violence or the threat of violence

crimes against property (property crimes) crimes that involve theft of property belonging to others

criminal justice system a formal reaction to alleged violations of the law on the part of police, courts, and prison officials

criminal recidivism subsequent offenses by people previously convicted of crimes

deterrence the attempt to discourage criminality through punishment

deviance the recognized violation of cultural norms

hate crime a criminal act carried out against a person or that individual's property by an offender motivated by racial or other bias

juvenile delinquency the violation of legal standards by the young

labeling theory the assertion that deviance and conformity result, not so much from what people do, as from how others respond

medicalization of deviance the transformation of moral and legal issues into medical matters

plea bargaining a legal negotiation in which the prosecution reduces a defendant's charge in exchange for a guilty plea

rehabilitation a program for reforming the offender to preclude subsequent offenses

retribution an act of moral vengeance by which society subjects an offender to suffering comparable to that caused by the offense

retrospective labeling the interpretation of someone's past consistent with present deviance

societal protection a means by which society renders an offender incapable of further offenses temporarily through incarceration or permanently by execution

stigma a powerfully negative social label that radically changes a person's self-concept and social identity

victimless crimes violations of law in which there are no readily apparent victims

white-collar crime crimes committed by people of high social position in the course of their occupations

CRITICAL-THINKING QUESTIONS

1. How does a sociological view of deviance differ from the common sense notion that bad people do bad things?

2. Identify Durkheim's functions of deviance. From his point of view, would a society free from deviance be possible?

3. In general, how does social power affect deviant labeling? Suggest the importance of gender, race, and class in this process.

4. What do official crime statistics teach us about this form of deviance?

SUGGESTED READINGS

Classic Sources

Kai Erikson. *Wayward Puritans: A Study in the Sociology of Deviance.* New York: Wiley, 1966.

> This historical account of the Puritans of Massachusetts Bay finds strong support for Durkheim's functional theory of deviance.

Thomas Szasz. *The Myth of Mental Illness: Foundations of a Theory of Personal Conduct.* New York: Harper & Row, 1961.

> This influential and controversial treatise condemns the concept of mental illness as a fiction utilized to impose conformity on those who simply differ.

Contemporary Sources

Allen E. Liska. *Perspectives in Deviance.* 4th ed. Englewood Cliffs, N.J.: Prentice Hall, 1995.

> This resource includes most of the issues raised in this chapter.

Gregory M. Herek and Kevin T. Berrill. *Hate Crimes: Confronting Violence Against Lesbians and Gay Men.* Newbury Park, Calif.: Sage, 1992.

> This collection of essays analyzes the legal, psychological, and social issues surrounding bias crimes against homosexual men and women.

Sally Engle Merry. *Getting Justice and Getting Even: Legal Consciousness Among Working-Class Americans.* Chicago: University of Chicago Press, 1990.

> Does our society live up to its stated ideal of "equal justice under the law"?

Edwin M. Schur. *Labeling Women Deviant: Gender, Stigma, and Social Control.* Philadelphia: Temple University Press, 1984.

> Why have women been virtually ignored in much analysis of deviance? This book offers an answer and tries to remedy the problem.

Robert Johnson. *Death Work: A Study of the Modern Execution Process.* Pacific Grove, Calif.: Brooks/Cole, 1990.

> This gripping account of a researcher's personal investigation of the ultimate punishment makes a strong case for its abolition.

Anne Campbell. *The Girls in the Gang.* 2d ed. Cambridge, Mass.: Basil Blackwell, 1991.

> Most research about youth gangs in the United States is about and by men. Anne Campbell provides a rare and insightful account of young women in New York street gangs.

Donna Gaines. *Teenage Wasteland: Suburbia's Dead End Kids.* New York: HarperCollins, 1992.

> Beginning as an exploration of a suicide pact among four New Jersey teenagers, this study probes the aspirations and fascination with deviance among troubled youth.

M. David Ermann and Richard J. Lundman, eds. *Corporate and Governmental Deviance: Problems of Organizational Behavior in Contemporary Society.* 4th ed. New York: Oxford University Press, 1992.

> This collection of eleven essays investigates patterns of deviance by governmental and corporate elites.

Thomas Szasz. *A Lexicon of Lunacy: Metaphoric Malady, Moral Responsibility, and Psychiatry.* New Brunswick, N.J.: Transaction, 1993.

> In his latest book, a controversial medical activist argues that scientific diagnosis typically reflects cultural definitions.

Freda Adler and William S. Laufer, eds. *The Legacy of Anomie: Advances in Criminological Theory.* Vol. 6. New Brunswick, N.J.: Transaction Books, 1994.

> This collection of essays describes the continuing utility of anomie theory, with its roots in the thinking of Emile Durkheim and further developed by Robert Merton, for understanding deviant behavior.

Global Sources

Ikuyo Sato. *Kamikaze Biker: Parody and Anomy in Affluent Japan.* Chicago: University of Chicago Press, 1991.

> In the tradition of Emile Durkheim, this account of juvenile delinquency in Japan highlights the breakdown of traditional social controls that often accompanies material affluence.

John M. Martin and Anne T. Romano. *Multinational Crime: Terrorism, Espionage, Drug and Arms Trafficking.* Newbury Park, Calif.: Sage, 1992.

> The "globalization" trend is affecting even patterns of crime, as this book explains.

Robert Y. Thornton with Katsuya Endo. *Preventing Crime in America and Japan.* Armonk, N.Y.: M. E. Sharpe, 1992.

> Based on comparative research in two cities, this report provides insights into the different strategies for controlling crime in Japan and the United States.

Hans-Gunther Heiland, Louise I. Shelley, and Hisao Katoh, eds. *Crime and Control in Comparative Perspectives.* Hawthorne, N.Y.: Aldine de Gruyter, 1991.

> This broad comparison of global crime patterns includes both more- and less-developed nations as well as those with capitalist and socialist economies.

Diego Riviera, *The Dinner of the Capitalist.* Secretaria de Educacion Publica, Mexico City.

DATA FILE: The *Data File* contains a detailed outline of Chapter 9, along with supplementary lecture material and additional discussion topics.

Q: "All the animals are equal, but some are more equal than others." George Orwell, *Animal Farm*

Q: "I have no respect for the passion for equality, which seems to me to be merely idealizing envy." Oliver Wendell Holmes

NOTE: Eighty percent of the Titanic casualties were men, but times may have changed. A 1992 survey by the Pittsburgh *Post-Gazette* found that 65 percent of men today claim they would not give up their lifeboat seat for a woman or child; 67 percent said they would but only for their own spouse; 54 percent said they would for their own mother.

Social Stratification

*O*n April 10, 1912, the ocean liner Titanic slipped away from the docks of Southampton, England, on its maiden voyage across the North Atlantic to New York. A proud symbol of the new industrial age, the towering ship carried twenty-three hundred passengers, some enjoying more luxury than most travelers today could imagine. Poor immigrants crowded the lower decks, however, journeying to what they hoped would be a better life in the United States.

Two days out, the crew received radio warnings of icebergs in the area but paid little notice. Then, near midnight, as the ship steamed swiftly and silently westward, a lookout was stunned to see a massive shape rising out of the dark ocean directly ahead. Moments later, the Titanic collided with a huge iceberg, almost as tall as the ship itself, which split open

its starboard side as if the grand vessel were just a giant tin can.

Seawater exploded into the ship's lower levels, and within twenty-five minutes people were rushing for the lifeboats. By 2:00 in the morning the bow of the Titanic was submerged and the stern reared high above the water. Clinging to the deck, quietly observed by those in the lifeboats, hundreds of helpless passengers solemnly passed their final minutes before the ship disappeared into the frigid Atlantic (Lord, 1976).

The tragic loss of more than sixteen hundred lives made news around the world. Looking back dispassionately at this terrible accident with a sociological eye, however, we see that some categories of passengers had much better odds of survival than others. In an age of conventional gallantry, women and children boarded the boats first, so that 80 percent of the casualties were men. Class, too, was at work. Of people holding first-class tickets, more than 60 percent were saved, primarily because they were on the upper decks, where warnings were sounded first and lifeboats were accessible. Only 36 percent of the second-class passengers survived, and of the third-class passengers on the lower decks, only 24 percent escaped drowning. On board the Titanic, *class turned out to mean much more than the quality of accommodations: It was truly a matter of life or death.*

The fate of the *Titanic* dramatically illustrates the consequences of social inequality for the ways people live—and sometimes whether they live at all. This chapter explores the important concept of social stratification. Chapter 10 continues the story by highlighting social inequality in the United States, and Chapter 11 examines how our society fits into a global system of wealth and poverty.

WHAT IS SOCIAL STRATIFICATION?

For tens of thousands of years, humans the world over lived in small hunting and gathering societies. Although members of these bands might single out one person as being swifter, stronger, or more skillful in collecting food, everyone had more or less the same social standing. As societies became more complex—a process detailed in Chapter 4 ("Society")—a monumental change came about. The social system elevated entire *categories* of people above others, providing them with more money, power, and schooling.

Sociologists use the concept social stratification to refer to *a system by which a society ranks categories of people in a hierarchy*. Social stratification is a matter of four basic principles.

1. **Social stratification is a characteristic of society, not simply a function of individual differences.** Social inequality stands as a basic dimension of how a society is organized. Sociologists set out to identify the ways in which members of a society are unequal and to measure how unequal they are. Further, basic patterns of inequality—for instance, whether societies are divided into landlords and peasants, stockholders and wage laborers—differ according to time and place. The extent to which people attribute their standing to birth or to personal achievement also varies from society to society.

A focus on achievement is commonplace in industrial societies such as the United States, although people typically exaggerate its importance. Did a higher percentage of the first-class passengers on the *Titanic* survive because they were smarter or better swimmers than second- and third-class passengers? Hardly. They fared better because of their privileged position on the ship. Similarly, children born into wealthy families are more likely than those born into poverty to enjoy health, achieve academically, succeed in their life's work, and live well into old age. Neither rich nor poor people are responsible for creating social stratification, yet this system shapes the lives of them all.

2. **Social stratification persists over generations.** To understand that stratification stems from society rather than simply growing out of individual differences, note how such systems persist over time. Social position is closely linked to the family, so that children assume the standing of their parents. In agrarian societies, the vast majority of people spend their entire lives at one social level, as their children do after them. In industrial societies, too, social position is initially ascribed, although it may change over time as a result of personal efforts or, occasionally, by sheer chance.

The concept of **social mobility** refers to *change in people's position in a system of social stratification*. Social mobility may be *upward* or *downward*. Our society celebrates the achievements of a Nancy Kerrigan or a Bill Cosby, both of whom rose to prominence from modest beginnings. People may also move downward socially as a result of business setbacks, unemployment, or illness.

Nevertheless, as explained in Chapter 10 ("Social Class in the United States"), for most people social standing remains much the same over a lifetime. Somewhat more common is *horizontal* social mobility by which people move from one occupation to another that is comparable.

3. **Social stratification is universal but variable.** Social stratification is found everywhere. At the same time, its character and extent vary widely from one society to another. Among the members of technologically simple societies, social differentiation is minimal and based mostly on age and sex. As societies develop sophisticated technology for growing food, they also forge complex

DIVERSITY: Regarding Point 4 below, Joan Huber Rytina, William H. Form, and John Pease found that people of higher social position saw the United States as a more "open" society. Moreover, they found that whites perceived more opportunity than blacks did. [See *American Journal of Sociology* 75, 4 (January 1970):703–16.]

GLOBAL: In the Hindu *varna* system, *Brahmins* were traditionally priests, *Kshatriyas* were military and political leaders, *Vaishyas* farmers and merchants, *Shudras* the peasants and menial laborers, and *Dasyus* the untouchables outside the *varna* system. *Jati* is a more recent development (500 C.E.) including some 3,000 specialized occupational groups.

and more rigid systems for distributing what they produce. Industrialization has the effect of increasing social mobility and of reducing at least some kinds of social inequality.

4. **Social stratification involves not just inequality but beliefs.** Any system of inequality not only gives some people more resources than others but defines these arrangements as fair. Just as *what* is unequal differs from society to society, then, so does the justification for inequality—the explanation of *why* people should be unequal. Virtually everywhere, however, people with the greatest social privileges express the strongest support for their society's system of social stratification, while those with fewer social resources are more likely to seek change.

CASTE AND CLASS SYSTEMS

In describing social stratification in particular societies, sociologists often use two opposing standards: "closed" systems that allow little change in social position and "open" systems that permit considerable social mobility (Tumin, 1985).

The Caste System

A **caste system** amounts to *social stratification based on ascription*. A pure caste system, in other words, is "closed" so that birth alone determines one's social destiny with no opportunity for social mobility based on individual efforts. Caste systems are thus rankings of *categories* of people, so that knowing your social category is sufficient to indicate your social ranking.

Two Illustrations: India and South Africa

A number of the world's societies—most of them agrarian—approximate caste systems, including traditional villages in India. The Indian system of castes (or *varna*, a Sanskrit word that means "color") is composed of four major rankings (Brahmin, Kshatriya, Vaishya, and Shudra), although the social identification that guides everyday life is based on membership in one of several thousand subcaste groups found in local communities.

One case of an eroding caste system in an industrial society is racial apartheid in South Africa. Of a total population exceeding 40 million, about one South African in eight (about 5 million people) is of European ancestry, approximately the same proportion as people of African descent in the United States. Yet this white

The personal experience of poverty is captured in Sebastiao Salgado's haunting photograph, which stands as a universal portrait of human suffering. The essential sociological insight is that, however strongly individuals feel its effects, our social standing is largely a consequence of the way in which a society (or a world of societies) structures opportunity and reward. To the core of our being, then, we are all the products of social stratification.

minority commands an overwhelming share of wealth and power. Representing three-fourths of South Africans, 30 million blacks have far fewer rights and privileges. In a middle position are another 3 million South Africans, known as "coloreds," who are of mixed race, along with about 1 million Asians. The box on pages 242–43 describes the current state of South African apartheid.

In a caste system, birth determines the fundamental shape of people's lives in four crucial respects. First, traditional caste groups are linked to occupation, so that generations of a family perform the same type of work. In rural India, although some occupations (such as farming) are open to all, castes are socially identified with the work their members do (as priests, barbers, leather workers, sweepers, and so on). In South Africa, whites hold almost all the desirable jobs, while the black majority is consigned primarily to manual labor and other work in service to whites.

Second, a rigid system of social stratification would break down quickly if people married outside their own castes. In such cases, what rank would their children hold? To shore up the hierarchy, then, caste systems mandate that people marry others of the same social ranking. Sociologists call this pattern *endogamous* marriage (*endo* stems from Greek, meaning "within").

GLOBAL SOCIOLOGY

Race as Caste: A Report from South Africa

At the southern tip of the African continent lies South Africa, a territory about the size of Alaska, with a population of more than 40 million. Long inhabited by people of African descent, Dutch traders and farmers settled the region in the mid-seventeenth century. Early in the nineteenth century, a new wave of British colonists pushed the descendants of these settlers from the Netherlands inland. By the beginning of this century, the British had gained control of the country, calling it the Union of South Africa. In 1961 the Republic of South Africa formally severed ties with the United Kingdom and became politically independent.

But freedom was a reality only for the white minority. To ensure their political control, the whites developed the policy of *apartheid*, or separation of the races. A common practice for many years, apartheid was enshrined in a 1948 law denying the black majority South African citizenship, ownership of land, and any formal voice in the government.

Under this policy, blacks became a subordinate caste, receiving only the education needed to perform the low-paying jobs deemed inappropriate for whites. In this racial caste system, even white people of limited means became accustomed to having a black household servant. Under such conditions, blacks earned, on average, only one-fourth what whites received.

Nelson Mandela, leader of the African National Congress (ANC), who was imprisoned by the white apartheid government for twenty-seven years, celebrates his election victory as South Africa's first black president.

A final plank in the platform of apartheid was the forcible resettlement of millions of blacks to so-called homelands, poor districts set aside by whites to confine and control blacks. The overall effect was that, in a land rich with natural resources, most blacks lived close to abject poverty.

The prosperous white minority traditionally has defended apartheid by defining blacks as a threat to their cultural traditions or, more fundamentally, as inferior beings. As resistance to apartheid increased, however, whites were forced to rely on a system of brutal military repression to maintain their power. Under this system, police could arrest and detain any black person simply for appearing to oppose white rule.

But even severe repression has not kept blacks—and a growing number of sympathetic whites—from challenging apartheid. Violent confrontations have been frequent, especially among younger blacks impatient for a political voice and economic opportunity. Through the 1980s, some two hundred U.S. corporations also severed direct economic ties with South Africa.

Tradition in India directs parents to select their children's marriage partners, often before the children reach their teens. In South Africa, sexual relationships and marriage between the races were banned by law until 1985, and interracial marriage remains infrequent since racial categories continue to live in separate areas and have little social contact.

Third, powerful cultural beliefs underlie caste systems. Caste in India is built on Hindu traditions that

mandate accepting one's social position as a moral duty; therefore, people must carry out their life's work, whatever it may be. South African society has long divided work into "white jobs" and "black jobs," and these notions, too, have had great moral force, at least in some circles.

Fourth, caste systems constrain the social contact members have with each other. Hindu thought defines higher caste groups in India as ritually "pure," while

GLOBAL: The average black South African consumes about 10 percent of what the typical white person does; life expectancy for blacks is 58 years, compared to 70 years for whites.

RESOURCE: Daphne Topouzis's article, "Women's Poverty in Africa," is included in the new edition of the Macionis and Benokraitis reader, *Seeing Ourselves*.

NOTE: The Latin root of caste, *cast(us)*, means "chaste" or "pure"; its later use (for example, the Portuguese word *casta*) means "race" or "blood."

GLOBAL: In 1990, the Dutch Reformed Church reversed its earlier position and declared apartheid to be in error.

This foreign divestiture staggered the South African economy, hurting both blacks and whites in the process. But it accomplished its primary objective: to pressure the Pretoria regime to make significant reforms toward the dismantling of apartheid.

Beginning in 1984, the government granted all South Africans the right to form labor unions, to enter various occupations once restricted to whites, and to own property. Additionally, officials have abolished a host of "petty apartheid" regulations that segregated the races in public places, including beaches and hospitals.

In 1990, the legalization of the antiapartheid African National Congress (ANC) and the release from prison of its leader, Nelson Mandela, opened the political system and raised the hope for more basic change. In 1992, a majority of white voters endorsed, in principle, bringing apartheid to an end. Subsequently, negotiations between the government and the ANC led to scheduling national elections in 1994 in which all adults—regardless of race—voted for the first time. The election of Nelson Mandela

as South Africa's new president marked the end of white minority rule.

Such dramatic reform has enraged traditionalists, who charge the government is selling out white interests. But despite formal legal changes, South African social stratification actually has hardly changed at all. The legal right to own property means little to millions of black people who are dirt poor; opening hospitals to South Africans of every race is an empty gesture for those who cannot afford to pay for medical care; ending racial barriers to the professions offers little real opportunity to men and women without much schooling. The harsh reality is that more than one-third of all black adults cannot find any work at all, and, by the government's own estimate, half of all black people live in desperate conditions.

The worst off are those termed *ukuhleleleka* in the Xhosa language, which means the marginal people. Some 7 million black South Africans fall into this category, living on the edge of society and on the edge of life itself. In Soweto-by-the-Sea, an idyllic-sounding community, thousands of people live crammed

into shacks built of packing cases, corrugated metal, cardboard, and other discarded materials. There is no electricity for lights or refrigeration. Without plumbing, people use buckets to haul sewage; women line up awaiting their turn at a single tap that provides water for more than one thousand people. Jobs are hard to come by, partly because Ford and General Motors closed their factories in nearby Port Elizabeth and partly because people keep migrating to the town from regions where life is even worse. Those who can find work are lucky to earn $200 a month.

With the end of white minority rule, South Africa has made real progress toward breaking down apartheid, and many analysts now offer the opinion that there is no longer any turning back. Yet even when the traditional notions about race are finally overcome, this still-divided society will face an equal challenge in resolving the underlying problem of intense and persistent poverty among most of its people.

SOURCES: Fredrickson (1981), Price (1991), Wren (1991), Contreras (1992), and various news reports.

lower caste groups are deemed "polluted." Because a member of a higher caste is defiled by contact with a member of a lower caste, the two keep their distance in all routine activities. Apartheid in South Africa has promoted a similar social segregation, here based on race.

Caste systems are typical of agrarian societies, because such arrangements foster the habits of diligence and discipline that agriculture demands. Most Indians still live in rural villages, which helps to explain

the persistence of caste there. But the Hindu caste system now has little significance for urban areas, where most people exercise greater choice about their marriage partners as well as their work (Bahl, 1991). By the same token, the fact that industrialization and urbanization promote political ideas favoring individual choice and rights helps explain why caste systems seem invariably to break down as societies industrialize, as South Africa has done.

A desire to better one's social position fuels immigration the world over, with the flow of humanity generally from poorer nations to richer ones. In 1991, these Albanians sailed across the Adriatic Sea to Italy, hoping to find greater economic opportunity. The Italian authorities, however, turned their ship away.

In our own society, examples of caste survive insofar as we treat people categorically on the basis of their race or sex. However, as later chapters explain, such traditional attitudes, now cast as "isms" such as racism and sexism, are increasingly denounced as unjust. Yet this change in attitude does not signal the end of social stratification. On the contrary, it simply marks a change in its character, as the next sections explain.

The Class System

A caste system bolsters stable, agrarian life; industrial societies, by contrast, depend on individual initiative and specialized talents. Industrialization thus propels social hierarchy toward a **class system**, *social stratification based on individual achievement.*

Social "classes" are not as rigidly defined as castes. A class system is more "open" so that as people gain schooling and develop their individual talents, they may experience some social mobility in relation to their parents and siblings, blurring class distinctions. Social categories also break down as people immigrate from abroad or move from rural regions to industrial cities, lured by better jobs and greater opportunity for education (Lipset & Bendix, 1967; Cutright, 1968; Treiman, 1970). Movement of this kind further stimulates social mobility as newcomers take low-paying jobs, typically pushing others up the social ladder (Tyree, Semyonov, & Hodge, 1979). Another characteristic of industrial societies is the extension of political rights (Glass, 1954; Blau & Duncan, 1967). With all these factors operating, class systems typically abandon the caste practice of according distinctive rights and duties to different categories of people in favor of granting everyone—in principle, at least—equal standing before the law.

Class systems, in other words, stand on a new conception of fairness: Talent and effort, rather than birth, should be the major factors influencing social position. Careers become matters of individual choice and achievement, not a duty passed from generation to generation. Greater individuality also translates into more freedom in the selection of marriage partners, with parents and cultural traditions playing a diminished role.

Status Consistency

Status consistency refers to *the degree of consistency of a person's social standing across various dimensions of social inequality.* By linking social ranking to birth, caste systems generate high status consistency, meaning that an individual tends to have the same relative standing with regard to wealth, prestige, power, ritual purity, and so on. Because class systems permit greater social mobility, however, they offer characteristically low status consistency. Therefore, an individual is likely to have higher ranking on one dimension of difference (say, income) than on another (such as social prestige). In the United States, for example, a college professor might earn a moderate income of about $30,000 annually while, at the same time, enjoying high prestige from this occupation. Its characteristic pattern of low status consistency is one important reason that social classes (compared to castes) are not well defined.

RESOURCE: Social stratification in preindustrial England is portrayed by Peter Laslett in *The World We Have Lost*, 3rd ed. (New York: Scribner's, 1984); see especially Chapter 2.

NOTE: The leisure of the nobility allowed them to pursue what we think of as "high culture."

NOTE: The word "aristocracy" is derived from the Greek word *aristoi*, meaning "the best people." Elite Greeks took this meaning rather literally, as did most of the hereditary nobility of medieval Europe.

NOTE: Ferdinand Lundberg (*America's 60 Families*, 1937) estimates Queen Victoria's estate at $45 million upon her death in 1901, some of it in the form of slum housing in London.

NOTE: Fifty-eight U.S. citizens have been knighted by a British monarch; the last was Ronald Reagan.

Caste and Class Together: The United Kingdom

There are no pure caste or class systems; in every society, social stratification involves some combination of these two forms. This mix of caste and class is most evident in societies in which centuries of agriculture have given way to industrialization. A case in point is Great Britain, a nation whose social system weaves together traditional caste distinctions and modern class differences.

The Estate System

In the Middle Ages, social stratification in England (which, together with Wales, Scotland, and Northern Ireland constitutes today's United Kingdom of Great Britain and Northern Ireland) took the form of a castelike system of three *estates*. A hereditary nobility, or *first estate*, accounted for only 5 percent of the population. These nobles maintained wealth and power through the ownership of land (Laslett, 1984). Typically, they had no occupation at all, for to be "engaged in trade" or any other type of work for income was deemed "beneath" them. Well tended by servants, many nobles used their extensive leisure time to cultivate refined tastes in art, music, and literature.

Vast landholdings were preserved from generation to generation by the practice of *primogeniture* (from Latin meaning "first born"). This law mandated that property pass only to a family's eldest son rather than being divided among all children. While this system maintained great estates over the generations, it forced younger sons to find other ways to support themselves. One strategy for such men was to enter the clergy— the *second estate*—where spiritual power was supplemented by the church's extensive landholdings. Others became military officers, lawyers, or took up work that has come down to us today as "honorable" callings for "gentlemen." In an age when few women could expect to earn a living on their own, the daughter of a noble family depended for her security on marrying well.

Below the nobility and the clergy, the vast majority of men and women formed the *third estate*, or "commoners." With little property, most commoners were serfs who worked plots of land belonging to nobles. The phrase "one's *lot* in life" literally describes the daily focus of commoners during the Middle Ages. Unlike the nobility and the clergy, most commoners had little access to schooling, so most remained illiterate.

As the Industrial Revolution steadily enlarged England's economy, some commoners, especially those living in cities, gained wealth and power that rivaled and sometimes surpassed that of the nobility. This economic expansion, along with the extension of schooling and legal rights to more people, combined to blur social rankings even further as a class system emerged. In a pointed illustration of how far the pendulum has swung, a descendant of nobility, now making a living as a writer, was asked in a recent interview if Britain's castelike estates had finally broken down. Playfully she retorted, "Of course they have, or *I* wouldn't be here talking to someone like *you!*" (*New Haven Journal-Courier*, November 27, 1986).

The United Kingdom Today

Social stratification in the United Kingdom still retains the mark of a long, feudal past. Some people in that country continue to enjoy considerable inherited wealth, which ensures the highest prestige, admission to expensive, elite schools, and political influence. A traditional monarch remains as the United Kingdom's head of state, and Parliament's House of Lords is composed of "peers" of noble birth. A sign of the times, however, is the fact that actual control of government resides in the House of Commons, where the prime minister and other commoners are more likely to have achieved their position through individual effort than through ascription. In the same way, most of the highest-paid people throughout British society are individuals of extraordinary achievement rather than noble birth.

Below the upper class, roughly one-fourth of the British population falls into the middle class. Some are moderately wealthy, with high incomes from professions and business. These richer "commoners," along with members of the upper class, make up the 10 percent of Britons with significant financial holdings in the form of stocks and bonds (Sherrid, 1986). Most members of the British middle class, however, earn too little to accumulate substantial wealth.

Below the middle class, across a boundary that cannot be precisely defined, lie roughly half of all Britons known as the working class. As in the United States, members of the working class earn modest incomes, generally performing manual labor. Although the British economy expanded during the 1980s, traditional industries such as coal mining and steel production declined, subjecting many working-class families to unemployment. Some slipped into poverty, joining the remaining one-fourth of Britons who are socially and economically deprived. Lower-class people—or, more simply, the poor—are heavily concentrated in northern and western regions of the United Kingdom plagued by economic decay.

people from one another over long periods. In Great Britain, families of long-standing affluence and those living in chronic poverty speak so differently that they seem to be, as the saying goes, a single people divided by a common language.

Another Example: Japan

Social stratification in Japan also mixes the traditional and the contemporary. Japan is at once the world's oldest, continuously operating monarchy and a modern society in which wealth follows individual achievement.

Feudal Japan

For centuries, Japan was an agrarian society with a rigid caste system composed of nobles and commoners. This system dates back to the fifth century C.E., with the ascent of the "imperial family," which claims a divine right to rule. At a time of limited government organization, however, the emperor depended on the assistance of a network of regional nobles or *shoguns*. Most of these nobles were men recognized for their excellence in military combat.

Below the nobility stood the *samurai*, or warrior caste. The word *samurai* means "to serve," indicating that this second rank of Japanese society comprised soldiers who cultivated elaborate martial skills and pledged their loyalty to the nobility. To set themselves off from the rest of the commoners, the *samurai* dressed and behaved in distinctive ways, according to their traditional code of honor.

As in Great Britain, the majority of people in Japan at this time in history were commoners who labored to eke out a bare subsistence. Feudal society in Japan afforded commoners no political voice, just as European serfs had little political power. Unlike their European counterparts, however, Japanese commoners were not lowest in rank. The *burakumin*, or "outcasts," stood further down on that country's hierarchy and were shunned even by commoners as unworthy. Much like the lowest caste groups in India, "outcasts" lived apart from others, engaged in the most distasteful occupations, and, like everyone else, had no opportunity to change their standing.

Japan Today

Important changes in nineteenth-century Japan—industrialization, the growth of cities, and the opening of Japanese society to outside influences—combined to weaken the traditional caste structure. In 1871 the Japanese legally banned the social category

In 1993, Japan's Crown Prince Naruhito wed Masako Owada, a commoner. The marriage symbolized today's Japan, with one individual representing ancient Japanese traditions and the other the new rise of a highly educated business class. Notice how this official photograph reveals that the princess is actually taller than the prince, perhaps suggesting that Japan is gradually loosening its rigid system by which wives lived in the shadows of their husbands.

Today the United Kingdom is a typical class system with unequally distributed wealth, power, and prestige but affording opportunity for people to move upward or downward. One legacy of the estate system, however, is that social mobility occurs less frequently in the United Kingdom than in the United States (Kerckhoff, Campbell, & Winfield-Laird, 1985). Compared with members of our society, therefore, Britons are relatively more resigned to remaining in the social position to which they were born (Snowman, 1977).

The greater rigidity of British stratification is exemplified in the importance of accent as a mark of social position. Distinctive patterns of speech develop in a society as stratification segregates categories of

GLOBAL: The average income in Japan is below that in the U.S. (see Table 11–1); to the observer, however, Japan appears as a more "middle-class" society. There is little of the striking urban poverty found in the United States; even so, the recent emergence of homelessness has challenged the positive view many Japanese have of their society.

GLOBAL: The status/honor element of Japanese society is still evi-

dent in young people aspiring to join *ichi-ryu* (meaning "first-class") corporations even if their income would be greater elsewhere (De Mente, 1992).

GLOBAL: Soichiro Honda died in 1991, a symbol of Japan's postwar success. The son of a blacksmith, he began his empire by purchasing secondhand army engines and bicycles that he fused into motorbikes.

of "outcast," although even today people look down on women and men who trace their lineage to this rank. After Japan's defeat in World War II, the nobility, too, lost legal standing, and, as the years have passed, fewer and fewer Japanese accept the notion that their emperor rules by divine right.

Thus social stratification in Japan is a far cry from the rigid caste system in force centuries ago. Today, analysts describe the Japanese population in terms of social gradations, including "upper," "upper-middle," "lower-middle," and "lower." But since classes have no firm boundaries, they disagree about what proportion of the population falls in each.

But the Japanese class system still reveals this nation's fascinating ability to retain tradition in modernity. Because many Japanese people revere past practices, family background is never far from the surface in assessing someone's social standing. Therefore, despite legal reforms that grant all people equal standing before the law and a modern culture that stresses individual achievement, the Japanese continue to perceive each other through the centuries-old lens of caste.

This dynamic mix echoes from the campus to the corporate board rooms. The most prestigious universities—now gateways to success in the industrial world—admit students with outstanding scores on rigorous entrance examinations, a process detailed in Chapter 19 ("Education"). Still, the highest achievers and business leaders in Japan are products of privilege, with *samurai* or noble background. At the other extreme, "outcasts" continue to live in isolated communities cut off from opportunity to better themselves (Hiroshi, 1974; Norbeck, 1983).

Finally, traditional ideas about gender continue to shape Japanese society. Despite legal reforms that confer formal equality on the sexes, women are clearly subordinate to men in many important respects. Japanese parents are more likely to push sons than daughters toward college, and the nation thus retains a significant "gender gap" in education (Brinton, 1988). As a consequence, women predominate in lower-level support positions in the corporate world, only rarely assuming leadership roles. In this sense, too, individual achievement in Japan's modern class system operates in the shadow of centuries of traditional privileges.

The Former Soviet Union

During the last decade, the former Union of Soviet Socialist Republics (U.S.S.R.) underwent changes so dramatic that some observers have heralded a second Russian revolution. The history of this military superpower has been a grand experiment, first, to eliminate

Eva Nagy, standing in front of her fashionable clothing store, represents the "new rich" class emerging in Hungary in the wake of that country's economic reforms. There seems to be little doubt that, in time, Eastern Europe's move toward a market economy will raise productivity and boost living standards. And it also seems likely that, in the process, economic inequality will increase as well.

class differences and, more recently, to reintroduce some aspects of a Western market economy that will further transform social stratification in the world's largest country.

A Classless Society?

The Soviet Union was born out of a revolution in 1917 that brought an end to a feudal estate system ruled by a hereditary nobility. The Russian Revolution transferred most farms, factories, and other productive property from private ownership to state control. This transformation was guided by the ideas of Karl Marx, who asserted that private ownership of productive property is the basis of social classes (see Chapter 4, "Society"). As the state gained control of the economy, the Soviet Union boasted of approaching a milestone in human history: becoming a classless society.

Analysts outside of the Soviet Union were always skeptical of this claim, pointing out that Soviet society remained clearly stratified (Lane, 1984). The occupations of the people in the former Soviet Union were clustered into four major categories, listed here in descending order of income, prestige, and power: (1) high government officials, also known as *apparatchiks*;

GLOBAL: Social hierarchy in the former Soviet Union was based more on power than on wealth. For example, Eduard A. Shevardnadze, Soviet Foreign Minister between 1985 and 1991, claimed an annual salary of $25,000. James Baker, his U.S. counterpart, earned $99,500 and is a millionaire several times over.
NOTE: Estimates place the fortune of the Soviet Communist party, dissolved in August 1991, at roughly $175 billion.

Q: "The alliance of the working class, the rural peasantry, and the intelligentsia . . . has been strengthened. The social, political, and ideological unity of Soviet society, with the working class its leading force, has formed . . . The supreme goal of the Soviet state is the building of a classless communist society . . ." The U.S.S.R. Constitution (1977)

(2) the Soviet intelligentsia, including lower government officials and professional workers such as engineers, scientists, college professors, and physicians; (3) manual workers in state-controlled industries; and (4) the rural peasantry.

The fact that these categories enjoyed very different living standards indicates that the former Soviet Union was never classless in the sense of having no social inequality. At the same time, however, it is reasonable to say, more modestly, that placing factories, farms, colleges, and hospitals under state control did reduce economic inequality (although not necessarily differences of power) to less than what is found in capitalist societies such as the United States.

The Second Soviet Revolution

Economic reforms accelerated in the mid-1980s when Mikhail Gorbachev came on the scene. His economic program, popularly known as *perestroika*, meaning "restructuring," was an effort to solve a dire economic problem: While the Soviet system had succeeded in minimizing economic inequality, everyone was relatively poor, and living standards lagged far behind those of other industrial nations. Gorbachev's program was an effort to stimulate economic expansion by reducing inefficient centralized control of the economy.

Gorbachev's reforms soon escalated into one of the most dramatic social movements in history as popular uprisings toppled one socialist government after another throughout Eastern Europe and, ultimately, in the Soviet system itself. In essence, people blamed their economic plight as well as their lack of basic freedoms on a repressive ruling class of Communist party officials.

From the founding of the Soviet Union in 1917 until its demise in 1991, the Communist party retained a monopoly of power, often brutally repressing any opposition. Near the end, some 18 million party members (about 6 percent of the Soviet people) not only made all the decisions about Soviet life but also enjoyed privileges such as vacation homes, chauffeured automobiles, and access to prized consumer goods and elite education for their children (Zaslavsky, 1982; Shipler, 1984; Theen, 1984). The second Soviet revolution, then, mirrors the first in an important respect: The goal was nothing less than the overthrow of the ruling class.

Because of the magnitude of this change, this new confederation of nations called the Commonwealth of Independent States remains in flux, and no one is confidently predicting its future. But it seems likely that the enormous political power once held by a handful of party officials has come to an end.

The case of the Soviet Union demonstrates that social inequality involves more than economic resources. While Soviet society lacked the extremes of wealth and poverty found in Great Britain, Japan, and the United States, elite standing in that nation was based on *power* rather than wealth. Thus, despite their awesome power, neither Mikhail Gorbachev nor his successor Boris Yeltsin earned nearly as much as U.S. president Bill Clinton.

And what about social mobility in the Soviet Union? Evidence suggests that during this century there was more upward social mobility in the Soviet Union than in Great Britain, Japan, or even the United States. One reason was that Soviet society lacked the concentrated wealth that families pass from one generation to the next in other societies. Even more important, rapid industrialization and bureaucratization during this century pushed a large proportion of the working class and rural peasantry upward to occupations in industry and government. In the last few decades, however, the Soviet people experienced decreasing social mobility. Most analysts conclude that the country's earlier high rate of upward movement resulted more from industrial development than from socialism (Dobson, 1977; Lane, 1984; Shipler, 1984).

The fact that broad societal changes affect people's social standing exemplifies what sociologists call **structural social mobility**, *a shift in the social position of large numbers of people due more to changes in society itself than to individual efforts.* Half a century ago, industrialization created a vast number of new factory jobs that drew rural people to cities. Similarly, the growth of bureaucracy propelled countless Soviet citizens from plowing to paperwork. Now, with new laws sanctioning individual ownership of private property and business, further structural social mobility is likely, perhaps introducing greater economic inequality. But, equal or not, everyone hopes to enjoy a higher standard of living.

Ideology: Stratification's "Staying Power"

Looking around the world at the extent of social inequality, we might wonder how societies persist without distributing their resources more equally. Caste-like systems in Great Britain and Japan lasted for centuries, placing most wealth and power in the hands of several hundred families. Even more striking, for two thousand years most people in India accepted the idea that their lives should be privileged or poor because of the accident of birth.

A key reason for the remarkable persistence of social hierarchies is that they are built on **ideology**,

NOTE: Max Weber's concern with power and bureaucracy would have led him to disagree with Marx's economic analysis of socialism as "classless."

Q: "But is there anyone thus intended by nature to be a slave, and for whom such a condition is expedient and right, or rather is all slavery a violation of nature? There is no difficulty in answering this question, on grounds of both reason and of fact. For that some should rule and others be ruled is a thing not only necessary, but expedient; from the hour of their birth, some are marked out for subjection, others for rule." Aristotle, *Politics*

NOTE: Since every society has some kind of social stratification, ideology may be described as the assertion that specific kinds of *inequality* should not be defined as *injustice*.

cultural beliefs that, directly or indirectly, justify social stratification. Any beliefs—for example, the assertion that rich people are intelligent or poor people are lazy—are ideological to the extent that they favor the interests of certain categories of people.

Plato and Marx on Ideology

The ancient Greek philosopher Plato (427–347 B.C.E.) claimed that justice was primarily a matter of agreement about who should have what. As he saw it, societies generally teach their members to view stratification systems as basically "fair."

Karl Marx, too, understood this fact, although he was far more skeptical about claims of fairness than Plato was. Examining capitalist societies, Marx saw that the economy channels wealth and power in the hands of a few, all the while defining the practice as simply "the laws of the marketplace." The legal system, Marx continued, defines a basic right to own property and, tied to kinship, funnels money and privileges from one generation to the next. In short, Marx concluded, ideas as well as resources come under the control of a society's elite, which helps to explain why established hierarchies are so difficult to change.

Both these thinkers realized that ideology is rarely a simple matter of privileged people conspiring together to generate self-serving ideas about social inequality. By contrast, ideology usually takes the form of cultural patterns that evolve over a long period of time. As people learn to embrace their society's conception of fairness, they may question the rightness of their own position but are unlikely to challenge the system itself.

Historical Patterns of Ideology

The ideas that shore up social stratification change along with a society's economy and technology. Early agrarian societies depended on slaves to perform burdensome manual labor. In ancient Greece, for example, the practice of slavery was justified by the widespread notion that people differed greatly in their intellectual capacities. Aristotle (384–322 B.C.E.) spoke for his times when he stated that some people deserve nothing more than slavery, which places them under the control of their natural "betters."

Agrarian societies in Europe during the Middle Ages also required the routine labor of most people in the fields in order to support the small aristocracy. In this context, noble and serf alike were taught that occupation was rightfully determined by birth and

In medieval Europe, people accepted rigid social differences, which divided them from birth until death, as part of a divine order for the world. This fifteenth-century painting by the Limbourg brothers—used to illustrate a book for the brother of the king—portrays life as orderly and cyclical. In this example, showing indoor life during January, the Duke of Berry is seated near the fireplace surrounded by a host of attendants that cater to his every whim. The firescreen behind him appears to give him a halo, surely intended by the artists to suggest the common notion of the time that nobles enjoyed their privileges by grace of God.
Limbourg Brothers, *Le Duc de Berry à table, Tres Riches Heures du Duc de Berry,* January, folio iv, Chantilly, Musée Conde.

each person's work was a matter of moral responsibility. In short, caste systems always rest on the assertion that social ranking is the product of a "natural" order.

With the rise of industrial capitalism, a new idea came to the fore: that wealth and power were prizes

NOTE: The word "snob" was first used in the eighteenth century to mean a cobbler or shoemaker; its meaning gradually broadened to include anyone of common standing. By the mid-nineteenth century, "snob" meant someone of common background who aspired to be included among the ranks of the well-bred.

Q: "Where there is voluntary agreement, there . . . is justice." Plato

DIVERSITY: Justifications for inequality are embedded in gender. Among men, inequality is viewed more in terms of (class-like) individual merit; the subordination of women has been defended on the basis of (caste-like) duty and natural order.

Q: "The true snob never rests; there is always a higher goal to obtain, and there are, by the same token, always more and more people to look down upon." Russell Lynes

CRITICAL THINKING

Ideology: When Is Inequality Unjust?

Inequality is not the same as injustice; a society typically defines some inequality as just and other kinds as unjust. As a cultural issue, justifications for social stratification vary across history and from place to place.

A millennium ago, the feudal estate system was taking root in Europe. This rigidly stratified social order drew strength from the teachings of the church, which claimed social arrangements on earth reflected the will of God.

The divine plan, religious beliefs maintained, was for most people to assume the station of serfs, driving the feudal economy with their muscles. By and large, of course, people born to such a life knew nothing else, but anyone who imagined an alternative challenged not only the nobility but the church and, ultimately, God. Although their lives were framed with far more comforts, the nobility was part of the same plan, and nobles, too, performed their various duties of defending their realm and maintaining law

and order with a sense of divine purpose.

The religious justification that cloaked the entire medieval estate system and helped to sustain this form of inequality for centuries is clearly expressed in the following stanza from "All Things Bright and Beautiful," a hymn sung in parish churches throughout England.

The rich man in his castle,
The poor man at his gate,
He made them high and lowly
And ordered their estate.

During the Industrial Revolution, newly rich industrialists gradually toppled the feudal nobility, advancing a new ideology in the process. Capitalists scorned the centuries-old notion that social hierarchy should rest on the accident of birth. The natural order of things, the new thinking went, was for the most talented and hard-working individuals to dominate society.

John D. Rockefeller (1839–1937), who made a vast fortune in oil, was fond of defending the wealth and power of early industrialists as the

product of extraordinary effort and initiative. Such a scheme, he continued, was consistent with the laws of nature. The poor, once the object of charity (since, after all, the medieval world defined being poor as part of God's plan rather than any person's fault), were redefined as lacking ambition and ability and, consequently, became the object of scorn.

The ideological shift from birth to individual achievement as the basis of social inequality was evident to the early nineteenth-century German writer Johann Wolfgang von Goethe, who quipped:

Really to own
What you inherit,
You first must earn it
With your merit.

Clearly, medieval and modern justifications of inequality differ dramatically: What an earlier era defined as fair, a later one rejected as wrongheaded. Yet both cases illustrate the role of ideology: cultural beliefs that define a particular kind of hierarchy as fair and natural.

fairly won by those who display the greatest individual merit. Class systems celebrate individualism and achievement, defining wealth as virtually synonymous with intelligence and hard work. Poverty, the object of charity under feudalism, was transformed into a scorned state of personal inadequacy. The box takes a closer look at the transition from the medieval notion of divinely sanctioned inequality to the modern idea that stratification reflects unequal effort and ability.

Throughout human history, most people probably have regarded social stratification as unshakable. However, challenges to the status quo do arise and

sometimes succeed. Especially as traditions weaken, people begin to question cultural "truths" and unmask their political foundations and consequences.

For example, historic notions of a "woman's place" today seem far from natural and are losing their power to deprive women of opportunities. For the present, however, the contemporary class system still subjects women to caste-like expectations that they perform traditional tasks out of altruism and duty while men are financially rewarded for their efforts. To illustrate, far more power, prestige, and financial rewards are accorded to a chef (typically a man) than to a family

DIVERSITY: Socialism has done relatively little for incorporating women into positions of power; the ruling elites of both the former Soviet Union and the People's Republic of China, for instance, historically have been almost entirely male.

Q: "Whether we like to admit it or not, a society which encourages the full flowering of individual liberty is, and can only be, a stratified society." Andrew Hacker

NOTE: Davis and Moore's thesis suggests that agrarian societies, with little productive specialization, do not have to provide differential rewards to the mass of "commoners." Such societies, however, demand persistence; thus, faithfully performing one's duty carries the reward of honor.

RESOURCE: Davis and Moore's analysis is one of the classics in the companion reader, *Seeing Ourselves*.

cook (usually a woman), although they perform much the same work.

Yet, while gender differences persist in the United States, there is little doubt that women and men are steadily becoming more equal in important respects. The continuing struggle for racial equality in South Africa also exemplifies widespread rejection of apartheid, which for decades shaped economic, political, and educational life in that nation. Apartheid has never been widely accepted by blacks, and it is losing support as a "natural" system among whites who reject ideological racism (Friedrich, 1987; Contreras, 1992).

THE FUNCTIONS OF SOCIAL STRATIFICATION

Why are societies stratified at all? One answer, consistent with the structural-functional paradigm, is that social inequality has vital social consequences for the operation of society. This argument was set forward some fifty years ago by Kingsley Davis and Wilbert Moore (1945).

The Davis-Moore Thesis

In 1945 Kingsley Davis and Wilbert Moore proposed a theory of social stratification that remains influential—and controversial—to this day. The **Davis-Moore thesis** is *the assertion that social stratification is a universal pattern because it has beneficial consequences for the operation of a society.*

Davis and Moore begin their analysis by pointing out that some degree of social stratification has existed in every known society. This is the case, they reason, because social inequality has important functions for social organization. But what are they? Davis and Moore answer this question by noting that society is a complex system of many occupational positions, each of which has a particular importance. Some jobs—say, changing spark plugs in a car—are easy to do (with a little instruction) and can be performed by virtually anyone. Other jobs—such as performing a human organ transplant—are far more challenging and can be accomplished only by people with scarce talents who have received a long and expensive education. Functionally speaking, it is these positions of high day-to-day responsibility that are the most important.

In general, Davis and Moore explain, the greater the functional importance of a position, the more rewards a society will attach to it. Doing so makes sense, since rewarding important work with income, prestige, power, and leisure time encourages people to do these things. In effect, by distributing resources unequally, a society encourages the discovery and development of human resources by motivating each person to aspire to doing the most significant work possible. The overall effect of a system of unequal rewards—which is what social stratification amounts to—is that a society becomes much more productive.

In practice, if a society recognizes that the work of a surgeon requires greater or rarer skills and more extensive training than that of an auto mechanic, it will bestow rewards accordingly. At all levels of society, as well, greater rewards flow to those who work better, harder, or longer than others do. Social stratification, then, functions to enhance the performance of productive social roles.

The Davis-Moore thesis does not deny that a society could be egalitarian, but a system of equal rewards can exist only to the extent that a society's members are prepared to allow *any* person to perform *any* job. Equality would also demand that someone who carries out a job poorly be rewarded just as much as another who performs well. Logic dictates that a system of equal rewards would not motivate people toward their best efforts and would thereby reduce a society's productive efficiency.

The Davis-Moore thesis is an explanation of the fact that *some* form of stratification exists everywhere; it does not defend any *particular* system of inequality. Nor do Davis and Moore specify what reward should be attached to any occupational position. They merely point out that positions deemed crucial by a society must yield sufficient reward to draw talent away from less important positions.

Meritocracy

The Davis-Moore thesis implies that the most productive societies embrace **meritocracy**, *a system of social stratification based on personal merit.* In such a system, societies endeavor to develop the abilities and talents of each individual. Individuals, in turn, maximize their rewards by striving to be "all that they can be," as the army recruiters say. To become more meritocratic, a society must promote equality of opportunity for everyone. But equality of opportunity is not the same as equality of condition; meritocracies recognize and reward differences in individual ability and effort. In addition, the more a society approaches a meritocracy, the more social mobility it will have, blurring social categories as individuals move up or down in the system depending on their performance.

CRITICAL THINKING

Big Bucks: Are the Rich Worth What They Earn?

For an hour of work, a Los Angeles priest earns about $5, a bus driver in San Francisco makes about $15, and a Detroit auto worker earns roughly $20. These wages shrink in comparison to the $5,000 actor Burt Reynolds makes for every hour he spends making movies, the $25,000 per hour pulled down by singer Dolly Parton for her Las Vegas nightclub act, the $40,000 per hour that Barry Bonds earns for playing baseball with the San Francisco Giants, the $100,000 Bill Cosby commands for an hour on the stage, or the $200,000 paid to Oprah Winfrey for each hour she chats with guests before the television cameras.

According to the Davis-Moore thesis, rewards reflect an occupation's value to society. But are the antics of Bill Cosby worth as much

to our society as the work of all one hundred United States senators? In short, do earnings really reflect the social importance of work?

Salaries in industrial-capitalist societies such as the United States are a product of the market forces of supply and demand. In simple terms, if you can do something better than others, and people value it, you will be well rewarded. According to this view, movie stars, top athletes, skilled professionals, and many business executives have rare talents that are much in demand; thus they may earn many times more than the typical worker in the United States.

But critics claim that the market is really a poor evaluator of occupational importance. First, they claim, the U.S. economy is dominated by a small proportion of people who manipulate the system for their own benefit. Corporate executives, for example, pay themselves high salaries and fat bonuses even in years that their companies flounder.

In this light, class systems are more meritocratic than caste systems. To the extent that members of caste societies speak of "merit" (from Latin, meaning "worthy of praise"), they mean the dutiful persistence in low-skill labor necessary to the operation of their agrarian society. Caste systems, in short, confer honor on those who remain "in their place."

For this reason, caste systems inevitably waste human potential. But then why do modern industrial societies retain many caste-like class qualities? No society, in fact, has ever distributed rewards solely on the basis of individual talent and achievement. The reason may be that, left unchecked, meritocracy erodes the social fabric of kinship and community. No one, for example, evaluates family members solely on the basis of performance. In short, class systems in industrial societies retain some caste elements to promote social cohesion and stability.

Critical evaluation. In its investigation of the functions of social stratification, the Davis-Moore thesis has made a lasting contribution to sociological analysis. Even so, critics claim it is flawed in several respects. Melvin Tumin (1953) argues, first, that one cannot easily measure the functional importance of occupations. As he sees it, the widely held respect for the work of physicians is, at least in part, the result of a deliberate effort by medical schools to restrict admissions so that the supply of physicians is low and the demand for their services is high.

Further, actual rewards—especially income—may have little to do with an individual's functional importance to society. With an income that has exceeded $50 million per year, television personality Oprah Winfrey earns more in two days than President Bill Clinton earns all year. Would anyone argue that hosting a talk show measures up in societal significance to

DATA FILE: Supplementary material on how people in the United States understand social inequality—based on General Social Survey data—is found in the *Data File*.

NOTE: Denouncing a high executive salary, an AFL-CIO official pointed out that the $40 million in question exceeds what a minimum-wage worker would have earned, toiling since the birth of Christ.

SOCIAL SURVEY: "How important for getting ahead is natural ability?" (*CHIP1 Social Survey Software*, OPABLE2; GSS 1987, N = 1,486)

INCOME	"Very important"	"Less important"
Above average	53.0%	47.0%
Average	61.3%	38.7%
Below average	63.6%	36.4%

In 1990, for example, Steven J. Ross was the highest paid corporate leader in the United States, receiving $39 million in salary, bonuses, and one-time stock options, despite the fact that his company—Time Warner—actually fared poorly compared to other large corporations. Looking across the board, chief executive officers of all the biggest U.S. companies boosted their own pay about 10 percent in 1990 (to an average of $2.5 million annually) even though the average price of their company stocks *dropped* by the same amount (Crystal, 1991). In global perspective, Japanese executives earn far less than their counterparts in this country, despite the fact that most Japanese corporations have handily outperformed their rivals in the United States.

A second problem with the idea that the market measures people's contributions to society is that many people who make clear and significant contributions receive surprisingly little money. Hundreds of thousands of teachers, counselors, and health-care workers contribute every day to the welfare of others for little salary, partly because many of these people do not think of income as the best measure of the value of their work.

In 1987, according to Wall Street analysts, the notorious "junk-bond" king Michael Milken earned $550 million dealing on Wall Street, in the process benefiting a small number of investors other than himself while weakening the nation's economy. During the same year, Rachel Stuart counseled thirty-five poor women in rural Louisiana who were preparing to give birth. Her work helped them to deliver healthy babies. Since the cost of neonatal care for a single premature baby runs as high as $200,000, Stuart probably saved the public millions; yet she is paid $4,000 a year for her work (Werman, 1989).

Using income to measure social worth, then, is a hazardous venture. Some people say that market forces represent the most accurate measure of occupational worth; what, they ask, would be better? But others contend that what is lucrative may or may not be socially valuable. From this standpoint, the market system amounts to a closed game in which only a handful of people have the money to play.

the responsibilities of the presidency? The box takes a critical look at the link between pay and societal importance.

A second charge made by Tumin is that the Davis-Moore thesis misrepresents the consequences of social stratification for the development of individual talents. Our society does reward individual achievement, but families also display the caste-like pattern of transferring wealth and power from generation to generation, without regard to talent. Additionally, for women, people of color, and others with limited opportunities, social hierarchy stands as a barrier to personal accomplishment. In practice, Tumin concludes, social stratification in the United States functions to develop some people's abilities to the fullest while ensuring that others *never* reach their potential.

Third, by suggesting that social stratification benefits all of society, the Davis-Moore thesis ignores how social inequality promotes conflict and even outright revolution. This assertion leads us to the social-conflict paradigm, which provides a very different explanation for the persistence of social hierarchy.

STRATIFICATION AND CONFLICT

Social-conflict analysis argues that, rather than benefiting society as a whole, social stratification is a system by which some people command advantages at the expense of others. This analysis draws heavily on the ideas of Karl Marx; additional contributions were made by Max Weber.

Karl Marx: Class and Conflict

Karl Marx, whose approach to understanding social inequality is detailed in Chapter 4 ("Society"), argued

SOCIAL SURVEY: "How important for getting ahead in life is ambition?" (GSS 1987, N = 1,285, *Codebook*, 1993:584)

"Essential"	41.6%	"Not very important"	0.7%
"Very important"	44.9%	"Not important at all"	0.2%
"Fairly important"	10.4%	DK/NR	2.2%

Q: "The ruling ideas of each age have ever been the ideas of its ruling class." Karl Marx, *The Communist Manifesto*

Q: "The difference of natural talents in different men is, in reality, much less than we are aware of . . . The difference between . . . a philosopher and a street porter, for example, arises not so much from nature, as from habit, custom, and education." Adam Smith

John George Brown made a fortune a century ago as a painter who portrayed the world as most people wanted to see it (left). Photographer Jacob Riis, among others, found far less fame during his own lifetime by capturing something closer to the truth. This is Riis's well-known image of New York's "street arabs" (right), who survived as best they could on the mean streets of this growing industrial city.

that two major social classes correspond to the two basic relationships people have to the means of production: Individuals can own productive property or they can labor for others. In medieval Europe, the nobility and the church owned the productive land on which peasants toiled. Similarly, in industrial class systems, the *capitalists* (or the bourgeoisie) control factories, which utilize the labor of *workers* (proletariat). So great are the disparities in wealth and power that arise from this productive system, Marx contended, that conflict between these two classes is inevitable. In time, he believed, oppression and misery would drive the working majority to organize and ultimately to overthrow capitalism once and for all.

Marx's analysis drew on his observations of capitalism in the early nineteenth century, a time at which society seemed irrevocably divided into contending classes. Indeed, his analysis seemed borne out in the era of the great captains of industry that followed. Andrew Carnegie, J. P. Morgan, and John Jacob Astor (one of the few very rich passengers to perish on the *Titanic*) lived in fabulous mansions filled with priceless art and staffed by dozens of servants. Their fortunes were staggering: Estimates place the wealth of John Jacob Astor at $25 million; Andrew

Carnegie reportedly earned more than $20 million a year as this century began (worth close to $100 million in today's dollars)—all at a time when the wages paid to the average worker totaled roughly $500 a year (Baltzell, 1964; Pessen, 1990).

Throughout the course of capitalist development, Marx claimed, the economy has primary importance as the social institution with the greatest influence on the rest of society. Other institutions serve, in general, to support the operation of the economy. This means, for example, that the family enables wealthy people to pass their property from generation to generation, and the legal system defends this process through inheritance law. Similarly, exclusive schools bring children of the elite together, training them in the ways of their class and encouraging the informal social ties that will benefit them throughout their lives. Overall, from Marx's point of view, the operation of capitalist society contributes to the *reproduction of the class structure*, meaning that society operates to perpetuate class divisions over time.

Critical evaluation. By exploring how the capitalist economic system generates conflict between classes, Marx's analysis of social stratification has had an

This cartoon, titled "Capital and Labour," appeared in the English press in 1843, when the ideas of Karl Marx were first gaining attention. It links the plight of that country's coal miners to the privileges enjoyed by those who owned coal-fired factories.

CAPITAL AND LABOUR.

enormous influence on sociological thinking in recent decades. Because it is revolutionary—calling for the overthrow of capitalist society—Marxism is also highly controversial.

One of the strongest criticisms of the Marxist approach is that it denies one of the central tenets of the Davis-Moore thesis: that motivating people to perform various social roles requires some system of unequal rewards. Marx separated reward from performance, endorsing an egalitarian system based on the principle of "from each according to ability; to each according to need" (1972:388). Critics argue that severing rewards from performance is precisely the flaw that explains the low productivity characteristic of the former Soviet Union and other socialist economies around the world.

Defenders of Marx rebut this line of attack by pointing to considerable evidence supporting Marx's general view of humanity as inherently social rather than unflinchingly selfish (Clark, 1991; Fiske, 1991). They counter that we should not assume that individual rewards (much less *monetary* compensation alone) are the only way to motivate people to perform their social roles.

A second problem is that, although few doubt that capitalist society does perpetuate poverty and privilege as Marx suggested, the revolutionary developments he considered inevitable have failed to materialize. The next section explores why the socialist revolution Marx predicted and promoted has not occurred, at least in advanced capitalist societies.

Why No Marxist Revolution?

Despite Marx's prediction, capitalism is still thriving. Even so, as we shall see, Western capitalism has evolved in some of the ways Marx anticipated. But why have workers in the United States not overthrown capitalism? Ralf Dahrendorf (1959) suggested four reasons.

1. **The fragmentation of the capitalist class.** First, in the century since Marx's death, the capitalist class in the United States has fragmented. Nineteenth-century companies were typically owned by single *families*; today they are owned by numerous *stockholders*. A further development is the emergence of a large *managerial class*, whose members may or may not own a significant share of the companies they manage. In addition, a growing share of business owners control small companies, which make them, at best, petty capitalists (Wright, 1985; Wright, Levine, & Sober, 1992).

2. **New kinds of jobs and a rising standard of living.** Marx's industrial proletariat has also been transformed by the so-called white-collar revolution. As Chapter 15 ("The Economy and Work") details, a century ago the vast majority of workers in the United States were farmers or filled the ranks of **blue-collar occupations,** *lower-prestige work involving mostly manual labor.* Today, most of the labor force holds **white-collar occupations,** *higher-prestige work involving mostly mental activity.*

Q: "Repetitive labor—the doing of things over and over again, and always in the same way—is a terrifying prospect to a certain kind of mind. It is terrifying to me. I could not possibly do the same thing day in and day out. But to other minds, perhaps I might say to the majority of minds, repetitive operations hold no terrors." Henry Ford
Q: "The small tradespeople, shopkeepers, and retired tradespeople generally, the handicraftsmen and peasants—all these sink gradually into the proletariat." Karl Marx and Friedrich Engels
NOTE: Peter Berger (1986) suggests a flaw of Marxism is the empirical failure of the polarization thesis. Berger suggests that neo-Marxists have attempted to resolve this problem through global dependency theory (discussed in Chapter 11). Polarization, in short, has not occurred *within* industrial societies as much as it has among the world's nations as a whole.

These jobs include positions in sales, management, and other service work, frequently in large, bureaucratic organizations.

While many of today's white-collar workers perform repetitive tasks like the industrial workers described by Marx, evidence suggests that most do not think of themselves in those terms. Apparently, as the white-collar revolution has progressed, many people have come to perceive their social positions as higher than those held by their parents and grandparents. One important reason for thinking this way is that workers' overall standard of living in the United States rose fourfold over the course of the century in dollars controlled for inflation, even as the work week decreased. As a result of a rising tide of social mobility, our society seems less sharply divided between rich and poor than it did to people during Marx's lifetime (Edwards, 1979; Gagliani, 1981; Wright & Martin, 1987).

3. **More extensive worker organization.** Workers have organizational strengths they lacked a century ago. Workers have won the right to organize into labor unions that can make demands of management backed by threats of work slowdowns and strikes. Although the recent trend in union membership is downward, research suggests that well-established unions continue to enhance the economic standing of the workers they represent (Rubin, 1986). Further, labor and management now regularly engage in contract negotiations. If not always peaceful, worker-management disputes are now institutionalized.

4. **More extensive legal protections.** During this century, the government has extended laws to protect workers' rights and give them greater access to the courts for redressing grievances. Government programs such as unemployment insurance, disability protection, and Social Security also provide workers with substantially greater financial resources than the capitalists of the last century were willing to grant them.

Taken together, these four developments suggest that, despite persistent and marked stratification, our society has smoothed many of capitalism's rough edges. Consequently, social conflict today is less intense than it was a century ago.

A Counterpoint

Many sociologists continue to find value in Marx's analysis, often in modified form (Miliband, 1969; Edwards, 1979; Giddens, 1982; Domhoff, 1983; Stephens, 1986). Advocates of social-conflict analysis respond with their own set of four key points, defending Marx's analysis of capitalism.

1. **Wealth remains highly concentrated.** As Marx contended, wealth remains in the hands of the few. In the United States, about half of all privately controlled corporate stock is owned by just 1 percent of individuals, who persist as a capitalist class.

2. **White-collar jobs offer little to workers.** As defenders of Marx's thinking see it, the jobs generated by the white-collar revolution offer no more income or security (and often less) than did factory jobs a century ago. In addition, much white-collar work is as monotonous and routine as factory work, especially the low-level clerical jobs commonly held by women.

3. **Progress requires struggle.** Labor organizations may have advanced the interests of the workers over the last half century, but regular negotiation between workers and management hardly signals the end of social conflict. In fact, many of the concessions workers have won came about precisely through the class conflict Marx described. Workers still struggle to gain concessions from capitalists and, in the 1990s, to hold on to the advances already achieved. Even today, for instance, half of all workers in the United States have no pension program.

4. **The law still favors the rich.** Workers have gained some legal protections over the course of this century. Even so, the law still defends the overall distribution of wealth in the United States. Just as important, "average" people cannot use the legal system to the same advantage as the rich do.

In sum, according to social-conflict theory, the fact that no socialist revolution has taken place in the United States hardly invalidates Marx's analysis of capitalism. As we shall see in Chapter 10 ("Social Class in the United States"), pronounced social inequality persists, as does social conflict—albeit less overtly and violently than in the nineteenth century.

Finally, some defenders of capitalism point to the collapse of communist regimes in Eastern Europe and the former Soviet Union as proving the superiority of capitalism to socialism. Most analysts agree that socialism failed to meet the needs of the people it purported to serve, either in terms of raising living standards or ensuring personal freedoms. But, to be fair, socialism's failings do not excuse flaws in capitalism.

NOTE: The shrinking stature of the U.S. rich is suggested by this comparison: When William Henry Vanderbilt died in 1885, his obituary covered the entire front page of *The New York Times*. When Sam Walton died in 1992, his death was reported on 1/20th of a page.
Q: "Status is the shadow of wealth." C. Wright Mills

Q: "There is probably less economic injustice and class conflict now than at any time since the Industrial Revolution began." E. Digby Baltzell (1964)
NOTE: "Mainstream" U.S. sociology has followed Weber in focusing on *stratification* as hierarchal differences in income and consumption. The "political-economy" approach derived from Marx, however, spotlights *class*, that is, differences in productive wealth.

Many critics maintain that capitalism in the United States has yet to demonstrate its ability to address problems of public education and desperate poverty, especially among the urban underclass (Uchitelle, 1991). Table 9–1 summarizes the contributions of the two contrasting sociological approaches to understanding social stratification.

Max Weber: Class, Status, and Power

Max Weber, whose approach to social analysis is described in Chapter 4 ("Society"), agreed with Karl Marx that social stratification sparks social conflict, but he differed with Marx in several important respects.

Weber considered Marx's model of two social classes simplistic. Instead, he viewed social stratification as the interplay of three distinct dimensions. First is economic inequality—the issue so vital to Marx—which Weber termed *class* position. Weber's use of "class" refers not to crude categories but to a continuum on which anyone can be ranked from high to low. Second is *status*, meaning amount of social prestige, which forms an additional continuum. Third, Weber noted the importance of *power*, which is yet another dimension of social hierarchy.

The Socioeconomic Status Hierarchy

Marx believed that social prestige and power were generally derived from economic position; thus he saw no reason to treat them as distinct dimensions of social inequality. Weber disagreed, recognizing that stratification in industrial societies has characteristically low status consistency. Thus, continued Weber, a person might have high standing on one dimension of inequality but a lower position on another. For example, bureaucratic officials might wield considerable power yet have little wealth or social prestige. So while Marx viewed inequality in terms of two clearly defined classes, Weber saw something more subtle at work in the stratification of industrial societies. Weber's key contribution in this area, then, lies in identifying the multidimensional nature of social rankings. Sociologists often use the term **socioeconomic status** (SES) to refer to *a composite ranking based on various dimensions of social inequality*.

A population that varies widely in class, status, and power—Weber's three dimensions of difference—creates a virtually infinite array of social categories, all of which pursue their own interests. Thus, unlike Marx, who saw focused conflict between two classes, Weber considered social conflict as highly variable and complex.

Inequality in History

Weber suggested that each of his three dimensions of social inequality stands out at different points in the history of human societies. Agrarian societies, he maintained, emphasize status or social prestige, typically in the form of honor or symbolic purity. Members of these societies gain such status by conforming to cultural norms corresponding to their rank.

Industrialization and the development of capitalism level traditional rankings based on birth but generate striking financial differences in the population. Thus, Weber argued, the crucial difference among such people lies in the economic dimension of class.

With time, industrial societies witness a surging growth of the bureaucratic state. This expansion of

TABLE 9–1 Two Explanations of Social Stratification: A Summary

Structural-Functional Paradigm	Social-Conflict Paradigm
Social stratification keeps society operating. The linkage of greater rewards to more important social positions benefits society as a whole.	Social stratification is the result of social conflict. Differences in social resources serve the interests of some and harm the interests of others.
Social stratification encourages a matching of talents and abilities to appropriate positions.	Social stratification ensures that much talent and ability within society will not be utilized at all.
Social stratification is both useful and inevitable.	Social stratification is useful to only some people; it is not inevitable.
The values and beliefs that legitimize social inequality are widely shared throughout society.	Values and beliefs tend to be ideological; they reflect the interests of the more powerful members of society.
Because systems of social stratification are useful to society and are supported by cultural values and beliefs, they are usually stable over time.	Because systems of social stratification reflect the interests of only part of society, they are unlikely to remain stable over time.

SOURCE: Adapted in part from Arthur L. Stinchcombe, "Some Empirical Consequences of the Davis-Moore Theory of Stratification," *American Sociological Review*, Vol. 28, No. 5 (October 1963):808.

Q: "There is no more possibility of defeating the operation of [economic] laws than there is of thwarting the laws of nature that determine the humidity of the atmosphere or the revolution of the earth upon its axis." Andrew Carnegie

NOTE: The Lenskis's analysis of historical changes in human societies—including the types noted here—is found in the first section of Chapter 4, "Society."
Q: "Nothing is more customary in man than to recognize superior wisdom in the person of his oppressor." Alexis de Tocqueville, *Democracy in America*

government, coupled with the proliferation of other types of formal organizations, means that power gains importance in the stratification system. Power is also crucial to the organization of socialist societies, evident in their extensive government regulation of many aspects of life. The elite members of such societies are likely to be high-ranking officials rather than rich people.

This historical analysis provides the key to a final disagreement between Weber and Marx. Looking to the future, Marx believed that social stratification could be largely eliminated by abolishing private ownership of productive property. Weber doubted that overthrowing capitalism would significantly diminish social stratification in modern societies. While doing so might lessen economic disparity, Weber reasoned, the significance of power based on organizational position would only increase. In fact, Weber imagined that a socialist revolution might actually increase social inequality by expanding government and concentrating power in the hands of a political elite. Recent popular uprisings against entrenched bureaucracies in Eastern Europe and the former Soviet Union lend support to Weber's position.

Critical evaluation. Weber's multidimensional analysis of social stratification retains enormous influence among sociologists, especially in the United States. Some analysts (particularly those influenced by Marx's ideas) argue that while social class boundaries have blurred, striking patterns of social inequality persist in the United States as elsewhere in the industrial world.

As we shall see in Chapter 10 ("Social Class in the United States"), the enormous wealth of the most privileged members of our society contrasts sharply with the grinding poverty of millions who barely meet their day-to-day needs. Moreover, the upward social mobility that historically fueled optimism in this country all but ceased in the 1970s, and, during the 1980s, economic inequality actually increased. Against this backdrop of economic polarization, the 1990s already has seen a renewed emphasis on "classes" in conflict rather than on the subtle shadings of a "multidimensional hierarchy."

STRATIFICATION AND TECHNOLOGY IN GLOBAL PERSPECTIVE

We can weave together a number of observations made in this chapter by considering the relationship between a society's technology and its type of social stratification. Gerhard Lenski and Jean Lenski's model

of sociocultural evolution, which Chapter 4 ("Society") details, puts social stratification in historical perspective and also helps us to understand the varying degrees of inequality found around the world today (Lenski, 1966; Lenski, Lenski, & Nolan, 1991).

Hunting and Gathering Societies

Simple technology limits the production of hunting and gathering societies to only what is necessary for day-to-day living. No doubt some individuals are more successful hunters or gatherers than others, but the group's survival depends on all sharing what they have. With little or no surplus, therefore, no categories of people emerge as better off than others. Thus social stratification among hunters and gatherers, based on age and sex, is less complex than among societies with more advanced technology.

Horticultural, Pastoral, and Agrarian Societies

Technological advances generate surplus production, while intensifying social inequality. In horticultural and pastoral societies, a small elite controls most of the surplus. Agrarian technology based on large-scale farming generates even greater abundance; but marked inequality leads various categories of people to lead strikingly different lives. The social distance between the favored strata—hereditary nobility—and the serfs who work the land looms as large as at any time in human history. In most cases, lords wield god-like power over the masses.

Industrial Societies

Industrialization decreases social inequality to some degree. The eclipse of tradition and the need to develop individual talents gradually erode caste rankings in favor of greater individual opportunity. The increasing productivity of industrial technology steadily raises the living standards of the historically poor majority. Specialized, technical work also demands the expansion of schooling, sharply reducing illiteracy. A literate population, in turn, tends to press for a greater voice in political decision making, further diminishing social inequality.

As already noted, continuing technological advances transform much blue-collar labor into higher-prestige white-collar work. All these transformations help to explain why Marxist revolutions occurred in agrarian societies—such as the former Soviet Union (1917), Cuba (1959), and Nicaragua (1979)—in which social inequality is most pronounced, rather than in

Q: "Equality of condition is incompatible with civilization." James Fenimore Cooper
Q: "All animals are equal. But some animals are more equal than others." George Orwell, *Animal Farm*
Q: "All wealth and power are like clouds passing by." Chinese Poet Li Bi (Bye)

industrial societies, as Marx predicted more than a century ago.

Initially, industrialization appears to increase the concentration of wealth—the pattern so troubling to Marx. With time, however, the share of all property in the hands of the very rich declines somewhat. Estimates suggest the proportion of all wealth controlled by the richest 1 percent of U.S. families peaked at about 36 percent just before the stock market crash in 1929; even during the entrepreneurial 1980s, this economic elite owned less than one-third of all wealth (Williamson & Lindert, 1980; Beeghley, 1989; *1991 Green Book*).

Finally, industrialization diminishes the domination of women by men, a pattern that is generally strongest in agrarian societies. The movement toward social parity for the sexes derives from the industrial economy's need to cultivate individual talent as well as a growing belief in basic human equality.

The Kuznets Curve

The general pattern described above amounts to the following: *In human history, technological progress first increases but then moderates the intensity of social stratification.* This pattern would suggest that, if greater inequality is functional for agrarian societies, then industrial societies benefit from a more egalitarian climate. This historical trend, recognized by Nobel prize-winning economist Simon Kuznets (1955, 1966), is illustrated by the Kuznets curve, shown in Figure 9–1.[1]

Current patterns of social inequality around the world generally square with the Kuznets curve. As shown in Global Map 9–1 on page 260, industrial societies have somewhat less income inequality—one important measure of social stratification—than nations that remain predominantly agrarian. Specifically, mature industrial societies such as the United States and the nations of Western Europe exhibit less income inequality than many of the less industrialized societies of Latin America, Africa, and Asia.

The pattern, however, is not perfectly consistent; income disparity reflects a host of factors beyond technology, especially political and economic priorities. World societies that have had socialist economic systems (including the People's Republic of China, the Soviet Union, and the nations of Eastern Europe) display relatively little income inequality.

---

[1]This section reflects the ideas of Simon Kuznets and the discussion of his work by Peter Berger (1986:43-46).

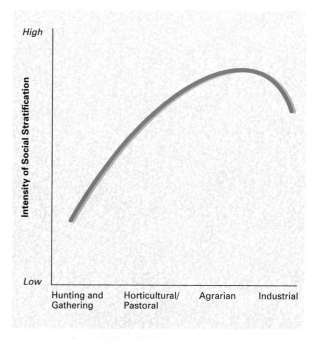

FIGURE 9–1 Social Stratification and Technological Development: The Kuznets Curve

The Kuznets curve suggests that greater technological sophistication is generally accompanied by more pronounced social stratification. The trend reverses itself, however, as industrial societies gradually become more egalitarian. Rigid caste-like distinctions are relaxed in favor of greater opportunity and equality under the law. Political rights are more widely extended, and there is even some leveling of economic differences. The Kuznets curve may also be usefully applied to the relative social standing of the two sexes.

Keep in mind, however, that an egalitarian society like the People's Republic of China has an average income level that is quite low by world standards; further, on noneconomic dimensions such as political power, China's society displays pronounced inequality.

And what of the future? Even if the general global patterns suggested by Kuznets appear valid, his analysis does not necessarily mean that industrial societies will gradually become less and less stratified. In the abstract, members of our society endorse the principle of equal opportunity for all; even so, this goal has not—and may never—become a reality. The objective of social equality, like all concepts related to social stratification, is controversial, as the final section of this chapter explains.

SOCIAL SURVEY: "Is it government's responsibility to reduce income differences between the rich and the poor?" (*CHIP1 Social Survey Software*, REDISTR; ISSP 1985)

	"Yes"	"No"
U.S.	34.6%	65.4%
Australia	52.6%	47.4%
Germany	66.9%	33.1%
U.K.	71.5%	28.5%
Austria	77.4%	22.6%

Window on the World

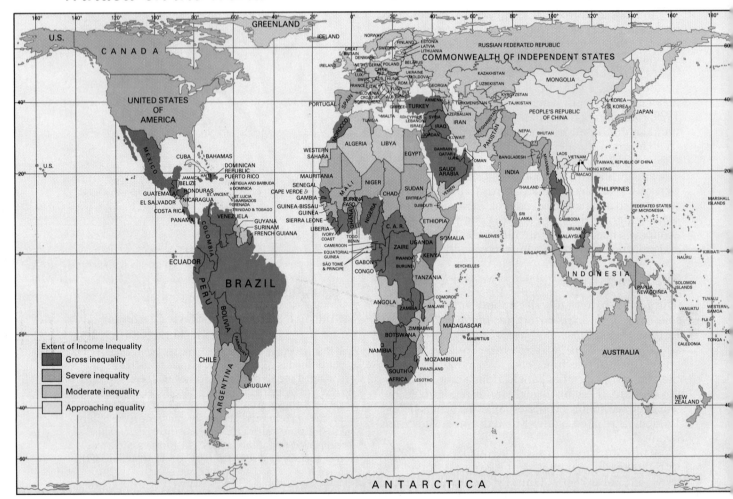

GLOBAL MAP 9–1 Income Disparity in Global Perspective

Societies throughout the world differ in the rigidity and intensity of social stratification as well as in overall standard of living. This map highlights income inequality. Generally speaking, countries that have had centralized, socialist economies (including the People's Republic of China, the former Soviet Union, and Cuba) display the least income inequality, although their standard of living has been relatively low. Industrial societies with predominantly capitalist economies, including the United States and most of Western Europe, have higher overall living standards, accompanied by severe income disparity. The less-industrialized societies in Latin America and Africa (including Mexico, Brazil, and Zaire) exhibit the most pronounced inequality of income.

From *Peters Atlas of the World* (1990).

NOTE: Figure 11–1 shows the distribution of the world's income by fifths of humanity:

Richest 20%:   70% of income
Second 20%:   20% of income
Middle 20%:   5% of income
Fourth 20%:   3% of income
Poorest 20%:   2% of income

SOCIAL STRATIFICATION: FACTS AND VALUES

The year was 2081 and everybody was finally equal. They weren't only equal before God and the law. They were equal every which way. Nobody was smarter than anybody else. Nobody was better looking than anybody else. Nobody was stronger or quicker than anybody else. All this equality was due to the 211th, 212th, and 213th Amendments to the Constitution and the unceasing vigilance of agents of the Handicapper General.

With these words, novelist Kurt Vonnegut, Jr. (1961) begins the story of "Harrison Bergeron," an imaginary account of a future United States in which social inequality has been totally abolished. Although the ideal of equality might be appealing in principle, Vonnegut is not celebrating this achievement in practice. Far from it: He describes a nightmare of social engineering in which every individual talent that makes one person different from another has been systematically neutralized by agents of the government.

The state mandates that the most physically attractive people wear masks that render them average looking, that intelligent people don earphones that every few seconds send distracting shrieks of noise, and that the legs of the best dancers be precisely fitted with weights to make their movements just as cumbersome as everyone else's. In short, although we may imagine that social equality would liberate people to make the most of their talents, Vonnegut suggests that

an egalitarian society can exist only by reducing everyone to a lowest common denominator.

All accounts of hierarchy and equality involve such value judgments. The Davis-Moore thesis casts social stratification as necessary to social life because some occupational roles have greater importance than others. Social inequality, from this point of view, reflects both variation in human abilities and the variable tasks of society. Equality ends up being a danger since, in a society of diverse people, it could exist only as the product of the relentless and stifling efforts of officials like Vonnegut's fictitious "Handicapper General."

Social-conflict analysis, advocated by Karl Marx, also mixes facts and values. Marx rejected the argument that stratification serves human societies, condemning social hierarchy as a product of greed. Guided by egalitarian values, he advocated social arrangements that enable everyone to share equally all important resources. Rather than undermining the quality of life, Marx maintained that equality would enhance humanity.

The next chapter ("Social Class in the United States") takes a close look at inequality in our own society. But we shall find that, here again, even people who agree on the basic facts often interpret them quite differently. This lesson is repeated in Chapter 11 ("Global Inequality"), which examines inequality among the world's nations and explains why it exists. At all levels, then, the study of social stratification involves a complex, ongoing debate likely to produce no single truth.

SUMMARY

1. Social stratification refers to categories of people ranked in a hierarchy. Stratification is: (1) a characteristic of society, not something that merely arises from individual differences; (2) persistent over many generations; (3) universal, yet variable in form; and (4) supported by cultural beliefs.

2. Caste systems, common in agrarian societies, are based on ascription and permit little or no social mobility. Caste hierarchy, which is supported by strong moral beliefs, shapes a person's entire life, including occupation and marriage.

3. Class systems, typical of industrial societies, reflect a greater measure of individual achievement. The

emphasis on achievement allows for social mobility, and, consequently, classes are less clearly defined than castes.

4. Historically socialist societies have claimed to be classless, based on their public ownership of productive property. While such societies may exhibit far less economic inequality than their capitalist counterparts, they are notably stratified with regard to power.

5. Social stratification persists due to support from various social institutions and the power of ideology to define inequality as just, natural, or the expression of divine will.

6. The Davis-Moore thesis states that social stratification is universal because it contributes to the operation of society. In class systems, unequal rewards motivate the most able people to perform the occupational roles most important to the functioning of society.

7. Critics of the Davis-Moore thesis note that (1) it is difficult to determine objectively the functional importance of any occupational position; (2) stratification prevents many people from developing their abilities; and (3) social stratification often generates social conflict.

8. Karl Marx, a key architect of social-conflict analysis, recognized two major social classes in industrial societies. The capitalists, or bourgeoisie, own the means of production in pursuit of profits; the proletariat, by contrast, offer their labor in exchange for wages.

9. The socialist revolution that Marx predicted has not occurred in industrial societies such as the United States. While some sociologists see this fact as evidence that Marx's analysis was flawed, others point out that our society is still marked by pronounced social inequality and substantial class conflict.

10. Max Weber identified three distinct dimensions of social inequality: economic class, social status or prestige, and power. Taken together, these three dimensions form a complex hierarchy of socioeconomic standing.

11. Gerhard Lenski and Jean Lenski observe that, historically, technological advances have been associated with more pronounced social stratification. A limited reversal of this trend occurs in advanced, industrial societies, as represented by the Kuznets curve.

12. Social stratification is a complex and controversial area of research because it deals not only with facts but with various values that suggest how society should be organized.

KEY CONCEPTS

blue-collar occupations lower-prestige work involving mostly manual labor

caste system a system of social stratification based on ascription

class system a system of social stratification based on individual achievement

Davis-Moore thesis the assertion that social stratification is a universal pattern because it has beneficial consequences for the operation of a society

ideology cultural beliefs that, directly or indirectly, justify social stratification

meritocracy a system of social stratification based on personal merit

social mobility change in people's position in a system of social stratification

social stratification a system by which society ranks categories of people in a hierarchy

socioeconomic status (SES) a composite ranking based on various dimensions of social inequality

status consistency the degree of consistency of a person's social standing across various dimensions of social inequality

structural social mobility a shift in the social position of large numbers of people due more to changes in society itself than to individual efforts

white-collar occupations higher-prestige work involving mostly mental activity

CRITICAL-THINKING QUESTIONS

1. How is social stratification a product of society rather than simply an expression of individual differences?

2. Identify and give examples of several dimensions of difference that distinguish caste and class systems.

3. Explain the Davis-Moore thesis. Can you apply this thesis to caste systems or just to class systems?

4. What developments over the course of this century have lessened the likelihood of a Marxist class revolution in the United States? What trends render Marxism still relevant?

SUGGESTED READINGS

Classic Sources

Max Weber. *The Protestant Ethic and the Spirit of Capitalism.* New York: Charles Scribner's Sons, 1958 (orig. 1904-5).

This account of the development of European capitalism highlights the importance of cultural factors in paving the way for economic development.

C. Wright Mills. *The Power Elite.* New York: Oxford University Press, 1956.

In this treatise, written in the Marxist tradition, Mills argues that U.S. society is dominated by a small, well-integrated group that controls the economy, the government, and the military.

Contemporary Sources

Charles E. Hurst. *Social Inequality: Forms, Causes, and Consequences.* Needham Heights, Mass.: Allyn & Bacon, 1992.

This source provides great detail about many of the issues raised in this chapter.

David B. Grusky, ed. *Social Stratification: Class, Race, and Gender in Sociological Perspective.* Boulder, Colo.: Westview Press, 1992.

This recent collection of essays brings together a number of influential statements about social diversity and hierarchy.

Susan Tucker. *Telling Memories Among Southern Women: Domestic Workers and Their Employers in the Segregated South.* New York: Schocken, 1991.

Based on interviews with twenty-one African-American domestics and the white women who employed them, this book provides powerful insights into the barriers and bridges between two racial categories in the Deep South.

Rosalind Miles. *The Woman's History of the World.* Topfield, Mass.: Salem House, 1989.

Gender is a key dimension of social inequality. This book explains how male domination has shaped human history and celebrates the achievements of women of the past.

Edward Pessen. *Riches, Class, and Power: America Before the Civil War.* New Brunswick, N.J.: Transaction, 1990.

This historical study of social stratification takes exception to the widespread notion that, prior to the Civil War, the United States was a more or less egalitarian society.

Erik Ohlin Wright. *Classes.* London: Verso, 1985.

The author attempts to adapt a Marxist approach to the realities of social stratification in the late twentieth century.

Global Sources

James Curtis and Lorne Tepperman, eds. *Haves and Have Nots: An International Reader on Social Inequality.* Englewood Cliffs, N.J.: Prentice Hall, 1994.

This collection of essays offers a global survey of social stratification.

Sven E. Olsson. *Social Policy and the Welfare State in Sweden.* Lund: Arkiv, 1990.

This analysis of social stratification in Sweden highlights the role of culture and national politics in the creation of this nation's extensive welfare system.

Allan Carlson. *The Swedish Experiment in Family Politics: The Myrdals and the Interwar Population Crisis.* New Brunswick, N.J.: Rutgers University Press, 1989.

Another analysis of Swedish society, this book examines how values penetrate research dealing with social stratification.

Sidney Verba with Steven Kelman, Gary R. Orren, Ichiro Miyake, Joji Watanuki, Ikuo Kabashima, and G. Donald Ferree, Jr. *Elites and the Idea of Equality: A Comparison of Japan, Sweden, and the United States.* Cambridge, Mass.: Harvard University Press, 1987.

This book provides a comparative study of social equality in three distinctive societies.

Deborah Posel. *The Making of Apartheid: Conflict and Compromise.* Oxford, U.K.: Clarendon Press, 1991.

This is a historical account of the rise of a modern caste system.

Robert Gwathmey, *Sharecropper*, c. 1945.

DATA FILE: An outline of Chapter 10, along with supplementary lecture material and discussion topics, is found in the *Data File*.

Q: "the blind musician
  extending an old tin cup
  collects a snowflake"
  Nick Virgilio, Camden, N.J.

Q: "In our society, it is murder, psychologically, to deprive a man of a job or an income. You are in effect saying to that man that he has no right to exist." Martin Luther King, Jr.

NOTE: Camden's infant mortality rate is 20 per 1,000 live births, twice the U.S. average and comparable to many less economically developed countries.

Social Class in the United States

Nigeria Collins died one month and one day after she was born. She lies today in a corner of Evergreen Cemetery in Camden, New Jersey, a small city across the river from Philadelphia. She is not the only infant buried in this patch of scrub grass littered with trash and broken glass. Hundreds of other babies lie here in a place that should guard the remains of people who grew up, grew old, and eventually died.

A half-century ago, Camden was one of the busiest industrial cities in the United States. Its shipyard built battleships, its factories turned out record players and other consumer goods, and its processing plants canned soup and other foods.

But today Camden is perhaps the most down-and-out city in the country. The slide started in the 1950s, as people with the initiative and the cash were lured to the leafy green of the surrounding

suburbs, leaving behind the poor, especially the minority poor. Today, two-thirds of the city's households live in poverty, and block upon block of housing is falling down, burned out, or boarded up. Camden also bears other familiar marks of cities in crisis: some two hundred liquor stores but not a single movie theater, a flourishing drug trade but no safe park, and street violence that erupts everywhere, often, and without warning.

The tragedy of Camden is all the more wrenching because this is a city of children: About half of its people (now numbering barely 100,000) are under the age of twenty-one. These youngsters cope in a world twisted by poverty, one that claims many infants like Nigeria Collins before they are even old enough to know what did them in. To the lucky survivors who reach their teens, the streets of Camden offer little hope, and many succumb to the

265

DIVERSITY: Government estimates of before-tax mean income, 1992, for households and families:

Highest 5 percent:	$145,244	$156,290
Highest fifth:	$91,494	$99,252
Second fifth:	$47,235	$53,365
Middle fifth:	$30,794	$36,777
Fourth fifth:	$18,281	$23,337
Lowest fifth:	$7,328	$9,708

Q: "What I want to see above all else is that this country remain a country where someone can always get rich." Ronald Reagan, 1983

Q: "No citizen should ever be wealthy enough to buy another, and none poor enough to be forced to sell himself." Jean Jacques Rousseau, *The Social Contract* (II, 46)

turbulent life of drug dealing or prostitution (Fedarko, 1992).

The story of Camden is also stark evidence of the pervasive power of social stratification to shape the lives of people throughout the United States. Whether individuals achieve great success or collapse with broken spirits is not simply a matter of their individual talents and ambitions. Our fate also reflects the distribution of wealth, power, and opportunity in our society.

DIMENSIONS OF SOCIAL INEQUALITY

The United States stands apart from Japan and most of Europe in never having had a titled aristocracy. With the significant exception of our racial history, this nation has never known a caste system that rigidly ranks categories of people.

Even so, U.S. society is highly stratified. The rich not only control most of the money, but they also benefit from the most schooling, they enjoy the best health, and they consume the greatest share of almost all goods and services. Such privilege contrasts sharply with the poverty of millions of women and men who struggle from day to day simply to survive. This chapter will explain that the popular portrayal of the United States as a "middle-class society" does not square with many important facts.

For several reasons, we generally underestimate the extent of stratification in our society.

1. **We embrace the legal principle of equality.** Founded in the wake of the Enlightenment, the United States has steadily pursued the ideal of equal standing under the law for all people. This principle encourages us to view everyone as equal even though our society historically has denied people of color and women full participation.

2. **Our culture celebrates individual autonomy and achievement.** Our belief is that people are the authors of their own social positions. We tend to play up the effect of individual effort on social standing and to play down how birth confers on some people advantages and opportunities that others can barely imagine.

3. **We tend to interact with people like ourselves.** Throughout the United States, primary groups—including family, neighbors, and friends—typically are composed of people with similar social standing. While we may speak of "how the other half lives," generally we have only brief and impersonal encounters with people very different from ourselves.

4. **The United States is an affluent society.** As noted back in Chapter 1 ("The Sociological Perspective"), the overall standard of living in the United States is extremely high in global perspective. This affluence leads us to imagine that everyone in our society is relatively well off.

When people do acknowledge their differences, they often speak of a "ladder of social class" as if inequality were a matter of a single factor such as money. More accurately, however, social class in the United States has several dimensions. *Socioeconomic status* (SES), discussed in Chapter 9 ("Social Stratification"), amounts to a composite measure of social position that encompasses not just money but power, occupational prestige, and schooling.

Income

One important dimension of inequality involves **income,** *occupational wages or salaries and earnings from investments.* The Bureau of the Census reports that the median U.S. family income in 1992 was $36,812. The first part of Figure 10–1 illustrates the distribution of income among all families[1] in the country. The 20 percent of families with the highest earnings (at least $64,300 annually, with mean earnings of about $100,000) received 44.6 percent of all income, while the bottom 20 percent (earning less than $17,000, with a mean of about $9,700) received only about 4.4 percent.

At the top of the income pyramid, the highest paid 5 percent of U.S. families (earning at least $107,000 per year, with a median of about $156,000) secured 17.6 percent of all income, more than the earnings of the lowest-paid 40 percent. In short, the bulk of the nation's income is earned by a small proportion of families, while the rest of the population makes do with far less.

As detailed later in this chapter, income disparity in the United States increased during the 1980s as a result of changes in the economy, new tax policies, and cuts in social programs that assist low-income

---

[1] Reported for households rather than families, median income is somewhat lower: $30,786 in 1992. The Census Bureau defines a household as one or more persons sharing a living unit; a family, by contrast, is two or more persons related by blood, marriage, or adoption. Most of the income difference between families and households is due to size: 1992 families contained, on average, 3.16 people compared to 2.63 people for households.

NOTE: Income disparity ratios (top 20% as a multiple of the bottom 20%) vary by state. The greatest income disparities are found in Louisiana (14.5:1) and Mississippi (11.1:1). Generally speaking, the South is the most unequal region with the greatest concentration of poor people and agricultural jobs.

GLOBAL: The earnings ratio (rich incomes as a multiple of poor incomes) is almost ten times greater in the U.S. than in Japan.

GLOBAL: The salaries of the three CEOs of the "Big Three" auto makers for 1990, a year of poor corporate performance, totaled $7.3 million. (GM's Robert Stempel, $1.6 M; Ford's Harold Poling, $1.2 M; Chrysler's Lee Iacocca, $4.5 M). By contrast, the heads of Japan's "Big Three" received a total of $1.8 million (Toyota's Shoichiro Toyoda, $690,000; Nissan's Yutaka Kume, $550,000; Honda's Nobuhiko Kawamoto, $550,000). (McCarroll, 1992)

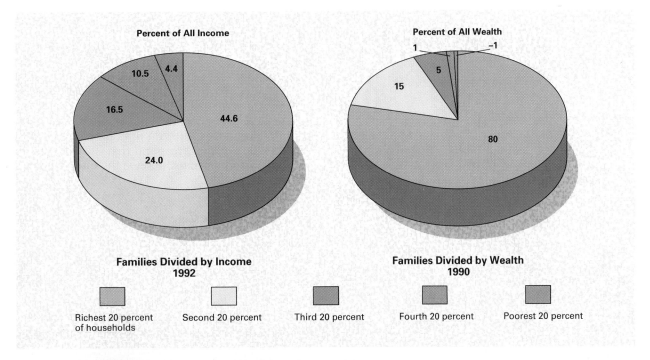

FIGURE 10–1 Distribution of Income and Wealth in the United States

(Income data from U. S. Bureau of the Census, 1993; wealth data are author estimates based on the Joint Economic Committee, 1986, and Kennickell & Shack-Marquez, 1992)

people (Levy, 1987; Reich, 1989; Cutler & Katz, 1992). Since 1990, however, income disparity has eased downward, a trend accelerated by the 1993 income tax hikes proposed by the Clinton administration and enacted by Congress, which place most of the increase on the shoulders of the top-earning 5 percent.

Chapter 9 ("Social Stratification") explained that, generally speaking, income disparity declines as industrialization proceeds (according to the Kuznets curve). Figure 10–2 on page 268 confirms this trend, showing that disparities in standard of living are more pronounced in societies that are less developed economically. Looking only at industrial societies, however, we see that the United States is characterized by greater economic disparity than is found almost anywhere else.

Wealth

Income is but one component of the broader economic factor of **wealth**, *the total amount of money and valuable goods that a person or family controls*. Wealth—in the form of stocks, bonds, real estate, and other privately owned property—is distributed even less equally than is income.

The second part of Figure 10–1 shows the approximate distribution of wealth in the United States in 1990. The richest 20 percent of U.S. households own approximately 80 percent of the country's entire wealth. High up in this privileged category are the wealthiest 5 percent of households—the "super-rich"—who control more than half the nation's property. Richer still—with wealth into the tens of millions of dollars—1 percent of U.S. families possess about 30 percent of our nation's privately held resources. And at the very top of the wealth pyramid, the *three* richest U.S. families have a combined wealth in excess of $40 billion, which equals the total property of more than half a million average families, representing enough people to fill the cities of Boston, Milwaukee, and New Orleans (Joint Economic Committee, 1986; Millman et al., 1993; Rogers, 1993).

The wealth of the typical U.S. family—the median case—is about $40,000, roughly the same as median annual family income (*1991 Green Book*). Lesser wealth is also different in *kind*: The richest people have most of their property in the form of stocks and other income-producing investments. The wealth of average people resides primarily in property that generates no income, such as a home.

GLOBAL: In global perspective, economic inequality in the United States is slightly greater than in most other industrial societies. Share of income (%) received by top and bottom 20 percent, by country (for 1985): Switzerland, 45: 5; U.S., 42: 5; Australia, 42: 4; Sweden, 37: 8; Canada, 40: 6; UK, 40: 6; Spain, 40: 7; Japan, 38: 9. (The World Bank, 1993)
NOTE: If wealth were in the form of bricks, the richest individuals in the United States would have a pile as high as the Eiffel Tower (1,056 feet), while most people would have a stack only a few feet from the ground. Still others would be "in the hole."
DIVERSITY: Median 1990 household wealth by age: under 35, $6,000; 35–44, $33,200; 45–54, $57,500; 55–64, $80,000; 65–69, $83,500; 70–74, $82,100; 75 and older, $61,500 (Longina & Crown, 1991)

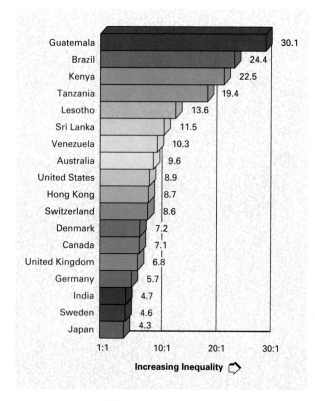

FIGURE 10–2 Extent of Income Inequality in Global Perspective

Ratios represent the standard of living, based on all consumption, for the most affluent 20 percent of the population as a multiple of the standard of living of the poorest 20 percent.

(The World Bank, 1993)

When financial liabilities are balanced against assets, the least affluent 40 percent of U.S. families have little or no wealth. The negative percentage shown in Figure 10–1 for the wealth of the poorest 20 percent of the population means that people in this bottom fifth actually live in debt.

Power

In the United States, as elsewhere, wealth stands as an important source of power. People who own substantial shares of corporations, for example, make decisions that create jobs for ordinary people or scale back operations, putting men and women out of work.

More broadly, the small proportion of families who own most of the property in the United States also have a great deal of say about the national political agenda. Thomas Jefferson (1953; orig. 1785), the third U.S. president and a wealthy man himself, cautioned that the vitality of a democratic system depends on "subdividing property" so that the many, not just the few, have a strong voice in political affairs.

Chapter 16 ("Politics and Government") presents the debate surrounding wealth and power in detail. Some analysts maintain that, while the rich have certain advantages, they do not dominate the political process. Others respond that, in general, the political system operates to serve the interests of the "super-rich."

Occupational Prestige

Occupation, too, is an important dimension of social standing, since one's job affects all the factors discussed thus far: income, wealth, and power. In addition, occupation is an important source of social prestige since we commonly evaluate each other according to the kind of work we do, envying and respecting some, shunning and looking down on others.

For more than half a century, sociologists have measured the relative social prestige of various occupations (Counts, 1925; Hodge, Treiman, & Rossi, 1966; NORC, 1993). Table 10–1 presents the results of a recent survey involving a random sample of adults in the United States. In general, people accord high prestige to occupations—such as physicians, lawyers, and engineers—that also generate high income.

High prestige reflects more than just high pay, however, since these occupations also typically require considerable ability and demand extensive education and training. By contrast, less prestigious work—as a waitress or janitor, for example—not only pays less but usually requires less ability and schooling. In global perspective, occupational prestige rankings are much the same in all industrial societies (Ma, 1987; Lin & Xie, 1988).

White-collar work that involves mental activity free from extensive supervision confers greater prestige than blue-collar occupations that require supervised, manual labor. There are exceptions to this pattern, however. As the table shows, for example, a blue-collar police officer enjoys greater social prestige than a white-collar bank teller.

In any society, privileged categories of people tend to hold the occupations providing the greatest prestige. Reading down from the beginning of Table 10–1, one passes a dozen occupations before reaching "registered nurse," an occupation in which *most* workers are women. As Chapter 13 ("Sex and Gender") discusses,

NOTE: The Joint Economic Committee of Congress provided this profile of the U.S. rich in 1983:
The super rich: .5% of the population, or 420,000 households with wealth over $2.5 million (median = $8.8M)
The very rich: .5% or 420,000 households with wealth between $1.5 and $2.5 million (median = $1.7M)

The rich: about 9%, or 7.5 million households with wealth between $200,000 and $1.5 million (median = $420,000)
The rest of us: 90%, or some 76 million households with wealth under $200,000 (median $40,000)

TABLE 10–1 The Relative Social Prestige of Selected Occupations in the United States

White-collar Occupations	Prestige Score	Blue-collar Occupations	White-collar Occupations	Prestige Score	Blue-collar Occupations
Physician	86		Bookkeeper	47	
Lawyer	75			47	Machinist
College/university professor	74			47	Mail carrier
Architect	73		Musician/composer	47	
Chemist	73			46	Secretary
Physicist/astronomer	73		Photographer	45	
Aerospace engineer	72		Bank teller	43	
Dentist	72			42	Tailor
Clergy	69			42	Welder
Psychologist	69			41	Apprentice electrician
Pharmacist	68			40	Farmer
Optometrist	67			40	Telephone operator
Registered nurse	66			39	Carpenter
Secondary-school teacher	66			38	TV repairperson
Accountant	65			37	Security guard
Athlete	65			36	Brick/stone mason
Electrical engineer	64			36	Child care worker
Elementary-school teacher	64		File clerk	36	
Economist	63			36	Hairdresser
Veterinarian	62			35	Baker
Airplane pilot	61			34	Bulldozer operator
Computer programmer	61			34	Meter reader
Sociologist	61			32	Bus driver
Editor/reporter	60			31	Auto body repairperson
	60	Police officer	Retail apparel salesperson	30	
Actor	58			30	Truck driver
Radiologic technician	58		Cashier	29	
Dietician	56			28	Elevator operator
Radio/TV announcer	55			28	Garbage collector
Librarian	54			28	Taxi driver
	53	Aircraft mechanic		28	Waiter/waitress
	53	Firefighter		27	Bellhop
Dental hygienist	52			25	Bartender
Painter/sculptor	52			23	Farm laborer
Social worker	52			23	Household laborer
	51	Electrician		23	Midwife
Computer operator	50			22	Door-to-door salesperson
Funeral director	49			22	Janitor
Realtor	49			09	Shoe shiner

SOURCE: Adapted from *General Social Surveys 1972–1993: Cumulative Codebook* (Chicago: National Opinion Research Center, 1993), pp. 937–45.

women are highly concentrated in so-called pink-collar occupations—the service work and clerical positions (including secretaries, waitresses, and beauticians) that provide little income and fall near the bottom of the prestige hierarchy.

Similarly, reading the table in reverse order shows how many jobs that provide the least amount of prestige and income are commonly performed by people of color. The important point here is that social stratification typically involves various dimensions of inequality (based on income and work as well as sex and race) *that are superimposed on each other*, forming a complex, and often steep, hierarchy.

Schooling

Industrial societies generally define schooling as necessary for all and offer primary, secondary, and some college education at public expense. Like other dimensions of inequality, however, schooling is a resource enjoyed in abundance by some and very little by others.

Table 10–2 indicates how much formal education U.S. men and women aged twenty-five and over had acquired in 1991. According to the table, more than three-fourths had completed high school, although just over 20 percent were college graduates.

TABLE 10–2 Schooling of U.S. Adults, 1991 (aged 25 and over)

	Women	Men
Not a high-school graduate	21.7%	21.4%
8 years or less	10.3	11.0
9–11 years	11.4	10.4
High-school graduate	78.4	78.5
High school only	41.0	36.0
1–3 years college	18.6	18.2
College graduate or more	18.8	24.3

SOURCE: U.S. Bureau of the Census, 1992.

Here, again, we see that dimensions of inequality are linked. Schooling affects both occupation and income, since most (but not all) of the better paying, white-collar jobs shown in Table 10–1 require a college degree or other advanced study. Similarly, most of the blue-collar occupations that offer less income and social prestige demand less schooling.

ASCRIPTION AND SOCIAL STRATIFICATION

To some degree, the class system in the United States rewards individual talent and effort. But, as explained in Chapter 9 ("Social Stratification"), class systems retain elements of caste. Ascription—who we are at birth—greatly influences what we become later in life.

Ancestry

Nothing affects social standing in the United States as much as our birth into a particular family, an event over which we have no control. Ancestry, or what we commonly call *social background*, determines our point of entry into the system of social inequality. Some families in the United States, including duPonts, Rockefellers, Roosevelts, and Kennedys, are known around the world. On a more modest scale, certain families in practically every community in the United States have amassed wealth and power over several generations.

Being born to privilege or poverty sets the stage for our future schooling, occupation, and income. Research suggests that about half of the richest individuals—those with hundreds of millions of dollars in wealth—derived their fortunes primarily from inheritance (Thurow, 1987; Queenan, 1989). By the same token, the "inheritance" of poverty and the lack of opportunity that goes with it just as surely shape the future for those in need. The operation of the family, which transmits property, power, and possibilities from one generation to the next, accounts, more than any other single factor, for the persistence of social stratification.

Race and Ethnicity

Race has a strong connection to social position in the United States. Overall, whites have higher occupational standing than African Americans and also receive more schooling, especially at the college level and beyond. These differences are evident in median income: for African Americans, families earned $21,161 in 1992, which was about 54 percent of the $38,909 earned by white families (U.S. Bureau of the Census, 1993).

Another reason for this disparity involves family patterns: African-American families with children are three times more likely than their white counterparts to have only one parent in the home. Single-parenthood, in turn, is a strong predictor of low income. If we compare only families that include married couples, the racial disparity is far smaller, with African-American families earning 84 percent of what white families earn.

Over time, any income differential builds into a considerable "wealth gap." Thus, calculated for 1988, the median wealth of African-American adults was about $4,100, which is just 10 percent of the $43,300 found among whites (O'Hare, 1989; *1991 Green Book*).

Finally, the effects of race are significant even among affluent families. The box takes a closer look.

As in the case of race, ethnic background relates to social stratification in the United States. Throughout our nation's history, people of English ancestry have acquired the most wealth and greatest power. The rapidly growing Latino population in the United States, by contrast, has long been relatively disadvantaged. In 1990, median family income among all Hispanics was approximately $23,901, about 61 percent of the comparable figure for all white families. A detailed examination of how race and ethnicity affect social standing is presented in Chapter 12 ("Race and Ethnicity").

Gender

Societies also place men and women in different social positions. Of course, people of both sexes are born into families at every social level. Yet, on average, women have lower social standing than men because they earn less income, accumulate less wealth, enjoy less occupational prestige, and place lower in some aspects of educational achievement than men do (Bernard, 1981; Lengermann & Wallace, 1985).

SOCIAL DIVERSITY

Two Colors of Affluence: Do Black People and White People Differ?

The typical African-American family has only about 54 percent of the income of the average white family. This fact underlies the greater risk of poverty among people of color. But there is another side to black America—an affluent side—that expanded dramatically during the 1980s.

The number of affluent African-American families—those with annual incomes over $50,000—is increasing. In 1990, more than 1 million African-American families were financially privileged; adjusted for inflation, this represents a fivefold increase over two decades before. Today, almost 15 percent of African-American families—more than 2 million adults and their children—are affluent. About 15 percent of Latino families rank as affluent, too, while 30 percent of non-Hispanic white families and 35 percent of Asian families have that much income.

Black and white affluence differs in several key respects. First, well-off people of African descent are not *as rich* as their white counterparts. Almost 40 percent of affluent white families (14 percent of all white families) earn more than $75,000 a year; only 26 percent of affluent African-American families (3 percent of all black families) reach this level of income.

Second, African Americans are more likely than white people to achieve affluence through more than one income. Such multiple earners may be two employed

spouses or employed parents with working children.

Third, affluent African Americans are more likely to derive their income from salaries rather than from investments. Three-fourths of affluent white families have investment income, compared to only half of affluent African-American families.

Beyond differences in income, affluent people of color contend with social barriers that do not affect whites. Even African Americans with the money to purchase a home, for example, may find they are unwelcome as neighbors. For this reason, a smaller proportion of affluent African-American families (40 percent) live in the suburbs (the richest areas of the country) than do affluent white families (61 percent).

Affluent Americans come in all colors. Yet race has a powerful effect on the lives of affluent people, just as it does on the lives of all of us.

SOURCES: O'Hare (1989) and U.S. Bureau of the Census (1991).

Perhaps the most dramatic difference, explained presently, is that households headed by women are ten times more likely to be poor than those headed by men. A full picture of the connection between gender and social stratification is found in Chapter 13 ("Sex and Gender").

Religion

Religion, too, has a bearing on social standing in the United States. Among Protestant denominations, with which almost two-thirds of individuals identify, Episcopalians and Presbyterians have significantly higher social standing, on average, than Lutherans and Baptists. Jews, too, have high social standing, while Roman Catholics hold a more modest position (Roof, 1979).

Even John Fitzgerald Kennedy—a member of one of this country's wealthiest and most powerful families—was elected our first Catholic president in 1960 only by overcoming opposition directed against him because of his religion. Understandably, then, throughout our history many upwardly mobile people have converted to a higher-ranking religion (Baltzell, 1979). Chapter 18 ("Religion") offers a closer look at the role of religion in the U.S. class system.

SOCIAL SURVEY: "Differences in income in America are too large." (GSS 1987, N = 1,285; *Codebook*, 1993:597)

"Strongly agree"	14.2%	"Disagree"	15.6%
"Agree"	41.2%	"Strongly disagree"	3.2%
"Neither agree nor disagree"	21.5%	DK/NR	4.3%

NOTE: C. Wright Mills (1956:101) claimed that the term "millionaire" was coined in 1843 upon the death of Pierre Lorillard to indicate his great wealth; only after the Industrial Revolution were great
fortunes common.

DIVERSITY: The social dominance of White Anglo Saxon
Protestants (the acronym WASP was first used by E. Digby
Baltzell, 1964) is evident in the widespread perception that these
people *lack* racial, ethnic, or religious identity.

SOCIAL CLASSES IN THE UNITED STATES

As Chapter 9 ("Social Stratification") explained, people living in rigid caste systems are keenly aware of everyone's social ranking. Defining the social categories in a more fluid class system, however, poses a number of challenges.

Consider the joke about the fellow who orders a pizza, asking that it be cut into six slices because he isn't hungry enough to eat eight. While all sociologists acknowledge extensive social inequality in the United States, they have long debated precisely how to divide up this social hierarchy. Some who follow Karl Marx's thinking about classes contend that there are two major categories; other sociologists suggest that there are as many as six classes (Warner & Lunt, 1941) or even seven (Coleman & Rainwater, 1978). Still others endorse Max Weber's contention that there are no clear classes at all; from this point of view, people have different positions on various dimensions of social inequality so that the United States exhibits not clear-cut classes but a complex status hierarchy.

The reason for this difficulty in defining classes is the relatively low level of status consistency characteristic of U.S. society. Especially toward the middle of the class system, an individual's social standing on one dimension often contradicts his or her position on another (Gilbert & Kahl, 1993). A government official, for example, may have the power to administer a multimillion dollar budget yet earn a modest personal income for doing so. Similarly, members of the clergy typically enjoy ample prestige while possessing only moderate power and earning low incomes. Or consider a lucky professional gambler who accumulates considerable wealth yet has little power or prestige.

Finally, the social mobility typical of class systems—again, most pronounced near the middle—means that social position may well change during one's lifetime. Mobility further blurs the lines between social classes.

Having noted the necessary reservations, we will identify four general social classes in the United States: the upper class, the middle class, the working class, and the lower class. As we shall explain, however, further distinctions exist, and some of these categories are more clear-cut than others.

The Upper Class

The upper class contains 3 or 4 percent of the U.S. population. The yearly income of upper-class families is at least $100,000 and can exceed ten times that much. As a general rule, the stronger a family's claim to being upper class, the more of its income is derived from inherited wealth in the form of stocks and bonds, real estate, and other investments.

In 1993, *Forbes* magazine profiled the richest four hundred people in the United States, estimating their combined wealth at $328 billion. These richest individuals had a *minimum* net worth of $300 million and included seventy-nine billionaires. The upper class thus comprises Karl Marx's "capitalists"—those who own much of the nation's productive property.

Besides their immense wealth, many members of the upper class work as top executives in large corporations and as senior government officials, further enhancing their power to shape events in the nation and, increasingly, the entire world. Members of the upper class also attain extensive education, typically in the most expensive and highly regarded schools and colleges. Historically, though less so today, the upper class has been composed of white Anglo-Saxon Protestants (WASPs) (Baltzell, 1964, 1976, 1988).

Upper-Uppers

Sociologists make a useful distinction between the "upper-upper class" and the "lower-upper class." The *upper-upper class*, often described as "society" or "bluebloods," includes just 1 percent of the U.S. population (Warner & Lunt, 1941; Coleman & Neugarten, 1971; Rossides, 1990). Membership is almost always the result of ascription or birth, as suggested by the old quip that the easiest way to become an "upper-upper" is to be born one. These families possess enormous wealth, primarily inherited rather than earned. For this reason, we sometimes say that members of the upper-upper class have *old money*. Noting the favor accorded to this segment of U.S. society, C. Wright Mills commented that "prestige is the shadow of money and power" (1956:83).

Set apart by their wealth, members of the upper-upper class live in a world of exclusive affiliations. They inhabit elite neighborhoods, such as Beacon Hill in Boston, Rittenhouse Square or the Main Line in Philadelphia, the Gold Coast of Chicago, and Nob Hill in San Francisco. Schools and colleges extend this privileged environment. Their children typically attend private secondary schools with others of similar background, completing their formal education at high-prestige colleges and universities. In the historical pattern of European aristocrats, they study liberal arts rather than vocationally directed subjects.

NOTE: The "Forbes Four Hundred"—a listing of the richest 400 people in the United States—contains interesting facts and patterns about U.S. wealth. This special issue of *Forbes* appears in late October each year. To make the 1993 list, wealth of at least $300 million was needed, with average (mean) wealth more than twice that figure. In 1980, the list began with individuals worth $230 million. Fewer than half of the people listed in 1993 were there a decade before. Such listings are skewed toward the new-rich corporate elite, whose wealth is mostly in the form of stocks (rather than, say, art) and whose compensation is a matter of public record.

Q: "None of my children has the slightest interest in making money. Not the slightest." Joseph Kennedy, speaking proudly of his sons, John, Robert, and Ted (Baltzell, 1964:302). In fact, the Kennedy fortune has been shrinking with time.

A popular distinction in the United States and elsewhere sets off the "new rich" from people with "old money." Men and women who suddenly begin to earn high incomes tend toward public extravagance because they enjoy the new thrill of high-roller living and they want others to know of their success. Those who grow up surrounded by wealth, by contrast, are more accustomed to their privileges and more quiet about them. In short, the "conspicuous consumption" of the lower-upper class (left) differs from the more private pursuits and characteristic understatement of the upper-upper class (right).

Women of the upper-upper class often maintain a full schedule of volunteer work for charitable organizations. Main Line women, for example, were primarily responsible for establishing the Philadelphia Museum of Art, and that city's old-money families continue to support the organization with donations of time, artworks, and money. While helping the larger community, as Susan Ostrander (1980, 1984) explains, such charitable activities also help families to forge networks that establish them as members of the city's elite.

Lower-Uppers

The remaining 2 or 3 percent of the people in the upper class fall into the *lower-upper class*. From the point of view of most of us, such people seem every bit as privileged as the upper-upper class. The major difference, however, is that lower-uppers depend on earnings rather than wealth as the primary source of their income; few people in this category inherit more than a modest amount of money from their parents.

Especially in the eyes of members of "society," the lower-upper class constitute the "new rich," people who can never savor the highest levels of prestige enjoyed by those with rich and famous grandparents. Thus, while the new rich typically live in expensive homes, they often find themselves excluded from the clubs and associations maintained by old-money families.

Historically, the American Dream has not aimed at becoming a member of the upper-upper class (difficult to do except, perhaps, through marriage) but at joining the ranks of the lower-upper class through exceptional accomplishment. The young author whose novel is made into a popular Hollywood movie; the athlete who accepts a million-dollar contract to play in the big leagues; the clever computer whiz who designs a new program that sets a standard for the industry—these are the lucky and talented achievers who reach the level of the lower-upper class. Their success stories fascinate most of us because this kind of upward social mobility has long stood as a cultural goal. Perhaps this is why most members of our society display little interest in the upper-upper class, who move in rarified circles far from most people's everyday reality, while at the same time aspiring to the "lifestyles of the rich and famous." The box examines the distinctions between "society" and the people we see on television shows like *Dallas* and *Dynasty*—those who seem like the rest of us except that they have made a lot of money.

The Middle Class

The middle class includes 40 to 45 percent of the U.S. population. Because it is so large and represents the

CRITICAL THINKING

Caste and Class: The Social Register *and* Who's Who

The upper-upper class is small and exclusive; this level of the U.S. class structure comes closest of all to being a social group. There is even a listing of these privileged members of our society: the *Social Register*, first published in 1887 as industrial fortunes were being made. Regional versions of the *Social Register* exist for various urban areas across the country, noting those who have (or at least used to have) "old money."

Because membership in the upper-upper class is typically based on birth, this level of our society operates much like a caste: You are either "in" or "out." With tradition as a guide, blueblood parents urge their children to seek out one of their own kind as a partner, thus perpetuating the class into another generation. Family is thus crucial to the upper-upper class, as it is to all caste groups. In the *Social Register*, listings are by family rather than by individual.

The listing for David Rockefeller, a member of one of the most socially prominent families in the United States, indicates (1) the family's address and home telephone number; (2) Mrs. Rockefeller's maiden name; (3) the names of the Rockefeller children, noting the boarding schools and colleges they are attending; and (4) exclusive social clubs to which the family belongs. Echoing the practice of aristocrats of a past age, listings in the *Social Register* make no mention of occupation or place of business; nor do they cite any mark of individual achievement.

The lower-upper class, by contrast, is an elite built on achievement. This larger category of "new rich" individuals has no clear boundaries, and its members do not engage in formal rituals (like debutante balls) the way old-money families often do.

There is a listing—roughly speaking—of people at this class

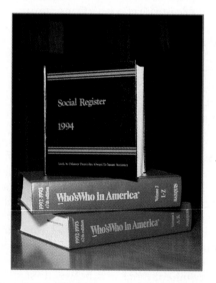

level: the national edition of *Who's Who in America*. Here, instead of "established" families, we find individuals distinguished for high achievement in various pursuits: outstanding athletes, the most successful business people, college presidents, Nobel prize winners, and famous entertainers.

Who's Who also contains a few people, including David Rockefeller, who are also listed in a *Social Register*, but the information provided is quite different. David Rockefeller's entry in *Who's Who* includes a brief biography (date of birth, schooling, and honorary degrees), a list of accomplishments (military decorations, government service, books authored), and—most important—his position as board chair of Chase Manhattan Bank. The address provided in *Who's Who* is his place of business.

Comparing the two listings suggests that there are two kinds of elites in the United States. The caste-like *Social Register* lists high-prestige families according to *who they are.* The more class-like *Who's Who* lists individuals on the basis of *what they have done.* But, as the dual listings of David Rockefeller suggest, social privilege and personal achievement frequently overlap.

aspirations of many more people, the middle class exerts tremendous influence on our cultural patterns. Television and other mass media usually depict middle-class people, and most commercial advertising is directed toward these "average" consumers. The middle class encompasses far more racial and ethnic diversity than the upper class. While many upper-class people (especially upper-uppers) know each other personally, such exclusiveness and familiarity do not characterize the middle class.

Q: "The prosperity of the middle and lower classes depends on the good fortune of and light taxes on the rich." Andrew Mellon

DIVERSITY: Typically, suburbs are high-income areas: The suburban county with the highest median income, according to the 1990 Census, is Fairfax, Va., where median income stood at $59,284.

Q: "When some learn that the American Dream does not fit all that is true about the realities of our life, they denounce the Dream and deny the truth of any of it. Fortunately, most of us are wiser and better adjusted to social reality; we recognize that, though it is called a Dream and some of it is false, by virtue of our firm belief in it we have made some of it true." W. Lloyd Warner, *Social Class in America*

For more than a century, the Campbell's Soup Company was one of Camden, New Jersey's, major employers. Today, this company is a multinational with production facilities in various locations in the United States and abroad. Recently, the company's owners decided to demolish the antiquated Camden factory, saving only the trademark soup-can water tower, which will be restored as a landmark. For the working people of Camden, the departure of Campbell's is one in a long chain of economic setbacks that has left this city among the poorest in the United States.

Upper-Middles

The top half of this category is often termed the *upper-middle class*, based on above-average income in the range of $50,000 to $100,000 a year. Family income may be even greater if both wife and husband work. High income allows upper-middle-class families gradually to accumulate considerable property—a comfortable house in a fairly expensive area, several automobiles, and investments. Two-thirds of upper-middle-class children receive college educations, and postgraduate degrees are common. Many are in high-prestige white-collar occupations (physicians, engineers, lawyers, accountants, or business executives). Lacking the power of the upper class to influence national or international events, the upper-middle class often plays an important role in local political affairs.

Middle-Middles

The rest of the middle class falls close to the center of the U.S. class structure. People in the *middle-middle-class* typically work in less prestigious white-collar occupations (bank tellers, middle managers, or sales clerks) or in highly skilled blue-collar jobs (including electrical work and carpentry). Commonly, household income is between $35,000 and $50,000 a year, which roughly equals the median household income for the United States as a whole ($36,812 in 1992).

Income at this level provides a secure, if modest, standard of living. Middle-class people generally accumulate a small amount of wealth over the course of their working lives, and most eventually own a house. Middle-class men and women are likely to be high school graduates, but only about four in ten young people at this class level attend college, usually at less expensive state-supported schools.

The Working Class

Including about one-third of the population, the working class refers to people who have lower incomes than those in the middle class and little or no accumulated wealth. In Marxist terms, the working class forms the core of the industrial proletariat. The blue-collar occupations of the working class generally yield a household income of between $15,000 and $35,000 a year, somewhat below the national average. Working-class families thus find themselves vulnerable to financial problems brought on by unemployment or illness.

Besides generating less income than the occupations of the middle class, working-class jobs typically provide less personal satisfaction. Tasks tend to be routine, requiring discipline but rarely imagination, and workers are usually subject to continual supervision. Such jobs also provide fewer benefits, like medical insurance and pension programs. About half of working-class families own their homes, usually in lower-cost neighborhoods. College is a goal that only about one-third of working-class children will realize.

As these facts suggest, working-class people lack the power to shape events, and many express a sense of fatalism about their lives. Families live in modest neighborhoods because they cannot afford better housing. Many want their children to attend college but lack the money to send them. They find little satisfaction in their jobs, but they have little opportunity for upward mobility. Still, many working-class families express a great deal of pride in what they do have, especially in comparison to those who are not working at all.

The Lower Class

The remaining 20 percent of our population make up the lower class. A lack of work and income renders their lives unstable and insecure. In 1992, the federal government classified some 37 million Americans (14.5 percent of the population) as poor. Millions more—the so-called working poor—are only marginally better off. Most lower-class people in the United States are white; however, people of African or Hispanic descent and other minorities are disproportionately represented at the low end of the socioeconomic scale.

About half of the heads of officially poor households do not work at all, in many cases because they are women with children who cannot secure affordable child care. The remainder of the poor and the near poor have low-prestige jobs that provide minimal income and little intrinsic satisfaction. Barely half manage to complete high school, and only one in four enrolls in college. Given limited schooling, many lower-class men and women are functionally illiterate.

Society segregates the lower class—and especially poor people of color—into particular neighborhoods and schools. Overall, just 45 percent of the lower-class families own their own home, typically in the least desirable neighborhoods. Poor districts generally are found in inner cities, but lower-class families also live in all rural counties, especially in the South.

Wherever they live, lower-class children learn early on the harsh reality that many people consider them only marginal members of society. Observing the struggles of their parents and other lower-class adults, they may conclude that their own future holds little hope for breaking the cycle of poverty. Cut off from the resources of an affluent society, lower-class life often generates self-defeating resignation (Jacob, 1986).

Some may simply give up or decide to get by on public assistance. Others, however, work desperately— some at two or three jobs—to make ends meet. In a study conducted in a northern city, Carol Stack (1975) observed a poor community whose members, far from lacking initiative and responsibility, devised ingenious means to survive. They did so, she concluded, because they simply had no choice.

THE DIFFERENCE CLASS MAKES

Social stratification affects nearly every dimension of social life. We will briefly examine some of the ways social standing is linked to our health, values, politics, and family life.

Class and Health

Health is one of the most important correlates of social standing. As the desperate story of Camden, New Jersey, presented at the beginning of this chapter, suggests, children born into poor families are several times more likely to die—from disease, neglect, accidents, or violence—during their first year of life than children born into more privileged families (Gortmaker, 1979; Children's Defense Fund, 1991).

Among adults, people with above-average incomes are twice as likely to describe their health as excellent as are low-income people. Conversely, only 4 percent of better-paid people complain that their health is merely fair or poor, although this assessment is made by 23 percent of low-income individuals (Adams & Benson, 1990). This general pattern holds in Great Britain and in virtually every other industrial society (Doyal, 1981).

Adequate income buys many things that support a long life. Nutritious foods, a safe environment, and regular medical care all promote well-being for those who can afford them. Medical costs have risen sharply in recent years to an average exceeding $2,900 annually per person in the United States. Without government assistance, expenses at this level are simply out of reach for a family of four with an annual income of, say, $15,000. Thus categories of people who suffer greater poverty also do not live as long as others. African-American children, who are three times more likely to be poor than white children, can expect to live, on average, 6.5 fewer years than whites (U.S. Bureau of the Census, 1993).

Compared to more privileged people, men and women in the lower social classes also live and work in more dangerous environments. Factories, mines, and construction sites contain greater threats to health than office buildings, just as the neighborhoods of the poor are all too often plagued by drug use and crime. As a consequence of greater stress, people with fewer

SOCIAL SURVEY: "Would you say that people can be trusted or that you can't be too careful in dealing with people?" (*STUDENT CHIP Social Survey Software*, TRUST1; GSS 1972-91, N = 15,382)

SES	"Trust"	"Can't"
High	63.8%	36.2%
Middle	44.9%	55.1%
Low	26.6%	73.4%

NOTE: During the 1980s, the U.S. spent four times the money on the Strategic Defense Initiative (dubbed "Star Wars") technology than it did on Head Start. (Schwarz & Volgy, 1992)

Q: "Nobody talks more about free enterprise and competition and of the best man winning than the man who inherited his father's store or farm." C. Wright Mills

privileges suffer from more problems of mental health (Link, Dohrenwend, & Skodol, 1986; Mirowsky & Ross, 1989). Moreover, when problems do arise, low-income people are hard pressed to afford the professional help they need.

Class and Values

Cultural values also vary somewhat from class to class. Women and men with the highest social standing have an unusually strong sense of family history since their social position is based on wealth and social prestige passed down from generation to generation (Baltzell, 1979). Many people of more modest backgrounds, by contrast, do not know the full names of even their four grandparents. With their birthright privileges, the "old rich" also tend to be understated in their manners and tastes, as if to say, "I know who I am and I don't have to prove anything to anyone else."

Below the upper class, consumption takes on greater importance to social standing as class boundaries start to blur. This pattern, termed *conspicuous consumption* by the early U.S. sociologist Thorstein Veblen (1857–1929), means that people buy expensive clothes, cars, or even sunglasses not just for their everyday utility but to serve as *status symbols* that "make a statement" about their owners. Perhaps this is why designer clothing—avoided by members of "society"—is nonetheless prized by those directly below them in class.

Because of their greater personal and financial security, this country's people in the middle-class express greater tolerance than their working-class counterparts toward controversial behavior such as homosexuality (Humphries, 1984). As Chapter 5 ("Socialization") explained, working-class people grow up in an atmosphere of greater supervision and discipline that prefigures their experience on the job as adults. In raising their children, then, they encourage conformity to conventional beliefs and practices (Kohn, 1977).

Even the way we think about time varies according to social class. Generations of wealth give upper-class families a keen awareness of the past. Middle-class people, especially those who are upwardly mobile, muse optimistically about the future. The drive for daily survival focuses the attention of lower-class people more on the present, and this present-time orientation is often a realistic assessment of the limited opportunities for advancement available to people in the lower class (Liebow, 1967; Lamar, Jr., 1985; Jacob, 1986).

Life expectancy is closely related to social-class position. Poor people—especially young males—who struggle to get by in cities around the world, have a strikingly high rate of death and injury from illness, accident, and violence. Some individuals caught up in poverty engage in perilous behavior because they have little reason to think the future will be brighter than the present. The boy shown here, from a poor neighborhood in Rio de Janiero, died shortly after this photograph was taken in a "train surfing" accident.

Class and Politics

Political attitudes tend to follow class lines. More privileged people in the United States support the Republican party, while those with fewer advantages favor the Democrats.

Looking more closely, their desire to protect wealth prompts well-off people to take a more conservative approach to economic issues, favoring less government regulation of the economy. But on social issues, such as abortion rights and other feminist concerns, affluent people are more liberal.

People of lower social standing show the opposite pattern. They favor liberal policies on economic issues while endorsing a more conservative social agenda (Nunn, Crockett, & Williams, 1978; Erikson, Luttbeg, & Tedin, 1980; Syzmanski, 1983; Humphries, 1984).

Another clear pattern is that individuals with higher incomes, more schooling, and high-prestige white-collar jobs are more likely to vote and to support various political organizations than are those in the lower class (Hyman & Wright, 1971; Wolfinger & Rosenstone, 1980). As an explanation, or perhaps as a result, privileged people are better served by the political system.

RESOURCE: Lillian Rubin's *Worlds of Pain* (Basic, 1976) shows the influence of class on the family life of women. While middle-class women seek in a spouse personal qualities such as sensitivity and sharing, working-class women have greater concern for basic traits such as holding a steady job and refraining from excessive drinking and domestic violence. In short, until economic standing is secure, we have little ability to consider other relational issues.

NOTE: Erik Olin Wright (1993) has argued that classes are discrete categories because (1) they correspond to different mechanisms for generating income, and (2) they are useful for explaining class conflict. An interesting debate on this issue is found in *American Sociological Review*, Vol. 58, No. 1, February 1993.

In the United States, women typically earn lower incomes than men do. Therefore, as the proportion of families headed by women has increased, so has the share of this country's families living in poverty.

Class, Family, and Gender

Finally, family life is closely related to social class. Because women and men typically marry someone of comparable social position, distinctive family patterns emerge at each class level. Family size is one case in point. In general, lower-class parents have more children than middle-class parents do; they marry earlier in life and make less use of birth control. Upper-class families, too, have more children, partly because they can afford the added child-rearing expenses.

Child-rearing practices also display the effect of social position. Working-class parents encourage children to conform to conventional norms and remain obedient and respectful to authority figures. In contrast, parents of higher social standing motivate children to express their individuality and to use their imagination more freely. This difference reflects parents' expectations about their children's future: The odds are that less privileged children will take jobs demanding close adherence to specified rules, while more advantaged children will probably enter fields that demand more creativity (Kohn, 1977).

And it stands to reason that the more social resources a family has, the more parents can develop their children's talents and abilities. According to one recent calculation, an affluent family with annual income of $100,000 will spend almost $300,000 raising a child born in 1990 to the age of eighteen. Middle-class people with income in the $40,000 a year range will spend about $200,000, while families with annual income under $30,000 will spend about $150,000 (Exter, 1991). To be sure, children involve substantial financial expenditure for all parents, but privilege tends to beget privilege. In this way, family life reproduces a society's class structure from generation to generation.

Class also extends into the lives of spouses. Elizabeth Bott (1971) documented that working-class couples maintain a more rigid division of responsibilities even to the point that many husbands and wives spend little time together. Middle-class marriages, she found, are more egalitarian, offering greater sharing and marked by more interpersonal intimacy. This insight helps to explain the fact that divorce is more common among disadvantaged couples, whose limited communication skills can be overwhelmed by stress brought on by low-income living (Kitson & Raschke, 1981; Fergusson, Horwood, & Shannon, 1984).

Finally, as Chapter 17 ("Family") explains, the number of families headed by women increased dramatically during the 1980s. This fact looms large because women raising children without the support of husbands are very vulnerable to poverty. This risk is most pronounced among African Americans, although more women in all categories are grappling with the economic burdens of single parenthood.

SOCIAL MOBILITY

Ours is a dynamic society marked by a significant measure of social mobility. As we noted in the last chapter, social mobility involves individuals moving upward or downward in the stratification system. Earning a college degree, securing a higher-paying job, or becoming a member of a two-career household contributes to *upward social mobility*, while dropping out of school, losing a job, or starting to live in a female-headed household may signal *downward social mobility*.

Social mobility is not just a matter of the changing fortunes of individuals. Changes in society itself account for most social mobility, at least over long periods. During the first half of this century, for example, industrialization expanded the economy, dramatically raising living standards for millions of people in the United States. Even without being very good swimmers, so to speak, people were able to "ride a rising tide of prosperity." As explained presently, *structural social mobility* in a downward direction has more recently dealt many people economic setbacks.

NOTE: An additional distinction is often made between vertical social mobility—a change of ranking—and horizontal social mobility—a change in social position (often a job change) within a given level.

Q: "The more a ruling class is able to assimilate the most prominent men of the dominated classes, the more stable and dangerous its rule." Karl Marx

Q: "There is no permanent class of hired laborers amongst us. Twenty-five years ago, I was a hired laborer. The hired laborer of yesterday labors on his own account today, and will hire the labor of others tomorrow." Abraham Lincoln

In studying social mobility, sociologists distinguish between changes within a single generation and shifts between generations of a family. **Intragenerational social mobility** refers to *a change in social position occurring during a person's lifetime.* Sociologists pay even greater attention to **intergenerational social mobility**, *upward or downward social mobility of children in relation to their parents.* The importance of social mobility across generations is that it reflects changes in society that affect virtually everyone.

Social Mobility: Myth and Reality

In few societies do people dwell on social mobility as much as in the United States. Historically, moving up has been central to the American Dream. But is there as much social mobility as we like to think?

Studies of intergenerational mobility (that, unfortunately, have focused almost exclusively on men) show that almost 40 percent of the sons of blue-collar workers attain white-collar jobs and almost 30 percent of sons born into white-collar families end up doing blue-collar work. Horizontal mobility—a change of occupation at one class level—is even more common so that about 80 percent of sons show at least some type of social mobility in relation to their fathers (Blau & Duncan, 1967; Featherman & Hauser, 1978).

Available research points to four general conclusions about social mobility in the United States.

1. **Social mobility, at least among men, has been fairly high.** The widespread notion that the United States has considerable social mobility is basically true. Mobility is what we would expect in an industrial class system.

2. **The long-term trend in social mobility has been upward.** Again, this widely held assumption squares with the facts. Industrialization, the expansion of the U.S. economy, and the growth of white-collar work over the course of this century have greatly boosted average incomes and living standards.

3. **Within a single generation, social mobility is usually incremental, not dramatic.** Only a very few move "from rags to riches." While sharp rises or falls in individual fortunes may command public attention, most instances of social mobility involve subtle shadings *within* one class level rather than striking changes *between* classes.

4. **The short-term trend has been stagnation, with some income polarization.** As we shall explain presently, the rising real income (that is, adjusted

The "fear of falling" economically attends not only working-class people. In recent years, white-collar workers as well have been losing job security. Here, in Washington, D.C., professional men and women who are out of work line up in front of a federal employment office in hopes of landing a new job with the government.

for inflation) that carried through most of this century hit a plateau in the early 1970s. Real income for the U.S. population as a whole also changed little during the 1980s, rising slowly in the early 1990s (Veum, 1992).

Mobility by Income Level

Different categories of people often experience different patterns of mobility, which national figures can mask. Figure 10–3, on page 280, shows how families in the United States fared during the 1980s according to their income level. Well-to-do families (the highest 20 percent) saw their incomes jump from $64,600 in 1980 to $82,350 in 1990, a 27 percent increase. People in the second 20 percent also made gains, albeit more modest. The middle fifth of the population, however, saw a slight decrease in income, a trend that carried through the fourth and fifth quintiles. These changes underlie the fact, noted earlier, that income disparity has grown in recent years.

Mobility by Race, Ethnicity, and Gender

Patterns of mobility have also varied according to race, ethnicity, and gender. White people, generally in a more privileged position to begin with, have been more likely to experience upward mobility in recent years, while the social standing of African Americans is more likely to have slipped (Featherman & Hauser, 1978;

NOTE: To some extent, getting ahead economically today depends on limiting or entirely avoiding the expenses of child rearing. YUP-PIES (young upwardly mobile professionals) are often DINKS (double-income-no-kids).

NOTE: Our society's belief in opportunity—and even the personal obligation to be upwardly mobile—is suggested by admonitions such as "pull yourself up by your own bootstraps," which, curiously, is a physical impossibility.

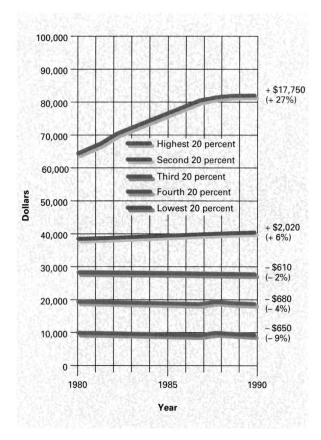

FIGURE 10–3 Median After-Tax Income, U.S. Families, 1980–1990 (in estimated 1992 dollars, adjusted for inflation)

(Congressional Budget Office)

Pomer, 1986). Even through the economic expansion of the 1980s, African Americans made virtually no improvement, thus falling further behind white people in terms of income. Statistically, African-American families earned 65 percent of what white families did in 1980, sliding to about 54 percent of white income by 1992 (Jacob, 1986; DeParle, 1991b).

Latino families also suffered an economic setback during this period. In 1980, these men and women earned 73 percent as much as (non-Hispanic) whites but by 1992, garnered 61 percent as much. For Americans of African and Hispanic descent, falling wage rates were the structural cause of downward mobility; they reflect the problem of persistent discrimination as well.

Historically, women have had less opportunity for upward mobility than men. As we shall see in Chapter

13 ("Sex and Gender"), the majority of working women hold clerical jobs (such as secretary) and service positions (like waitress). Such work offers little chance for advancement, creating barriers to upward movement. Another experience common to women (and less often to men) who divorce is downward social mobility, since they may lose not only income but a host of benefits including health care and insurance coverage.

But the broader picture is that, in recent years, the earnings gap between women and men is closing. Women working full time earned 60 percent as much as men working full time in 1980, with the proportion rising to an all-time high of 71 percent in 1992. However, much of this change was due to a *drop* in men's earnings through the 1980s, while the income of women remained about the same (U.S. Bureau of the Census, 1993).

The United States has long been termed a "land of opportunity." In truth, it has been that for many people, although some continue to fare far better than others. Looking globally, however, we find that rates of social mobility in the United States during this century have not exceeded those of other industrial societies. And as the economies of the world become more interrelated, we can expect that the structural shifts—both upward and downward—that occur in Europe and Japan will also affect us here in the United States (Lipset & Bendix, 1967; McRoberts & Selbee, 1981; Kaelble, 1986; Erikson & Goldthorpe, 1992).

The "Middle-Class Slide"

The expectation of upward social mobility is deeply rooted in our national culture. Through much of our history, in fact, economic expansion fulfilled the promise of prosperity by raising the overall standard of living. But, as we already noted, beginning in the early 1970s stagnation and—for some categories of people—actual decline in living standards began to shake our national confidence (Pampel, Land, & Felson, 1977; Blumberg, 1981; Levy, 1987). A number of recent trends suggest this reversal in fortunes.

1. **For many workers, earnings have stalled.** The annual income of a fifty-year-old man working full time climbed by 50 percent between 1958 and 1973 (from $21,000 to $32,000 in 1990 dollars adjusted for inflation). Between 1973 and 1990, however, this worker's income stayed the same, even as the cost of necessities like housing, education, and medical care rose rapidly (DeParle, 1991a).

THE MAP: Generally speaking, lower-income counties are those in which pessimism about the future is widespread. One interesting exception is counties containing large college campuses where many people, although fairly affluent, are doomsayers.

DIVERSITY: The number of earners per family has increased in recent decades, meaning people work harder to stay where they are. Labor department figures show that, in 1950, 66% of families had one earner; by 1990, this had dropped to 35%. During this period, two- (or more) earner families increased from 26% to 65%.

Seeing Ourselves

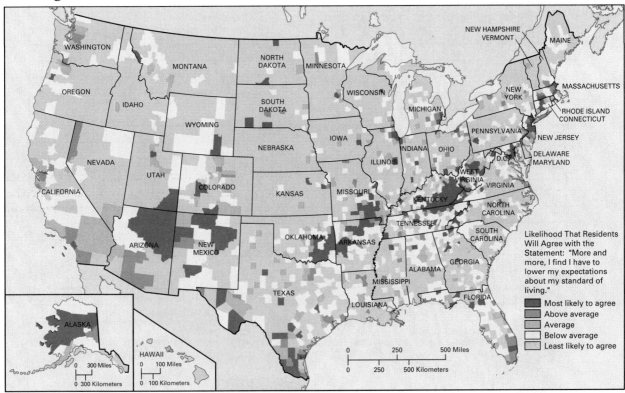

NATIONAL MAP 10–1 "Fear of Falling" Across the United States

This map shows, for all U.S. counties, how likely people are to agree with the statement "More and more, I find I have to lower my expectations about my standard of living." What can you say about regions (including the Appalachians in Kentucky and West Virginia) where pessimism is commonplace? But pessimism is pronounced not only in poor rural areas. Rich cities, including New York, Chicago, and Los Angeles, also contain people fearful of losing their jobs.

From *American Demographics* magazine, February 1994, p. 60. Reprinted with permission. ©1994 *American Demographics* magazine, Ithaca, New York. Data from Yankelovich *Monitor* and Clarita's *Prizm* system.

2. **Multiple job-holding is up.** According to the Census Bureau, 4.7 percent of the U.S. labor force worked at two or more jobs in 1975; by 1991, the proportion had risen to 6.2 percent.

3. **More jobs offer little income.** In 1979, the Census Bureau classified 12 percent of full-time workers as "low-income earners" because they earned less than $6,905; by 1992, this segment had swelled to 18 percent, who earned less than the comparable figure that year of $13,091.

4. **Young people are remaining at home.** Fully 60 percent of young people, aged twenty to twenty-four, are now living with their parents. And the average age at marriage has moved upward three years since 1975 (to 24.5 years for women and 26.5 years for men).

Taken together, these facts paint a disturbing picture. Rather than looking optimistically toward the future, more people in the United States now feel the economic security long associated with middle-class living slipping away. National Map 10–1 reveals where in the United States pessimism about the future is most widespread.

Dubbed the *middle-class slide*, this downward structural mobility is rooted in economic transformation.

DIVERSITY: During the last decade, some economic polarization has occurred in the United States (gini coefficients rose from .366 in 1980 to .430 in 1990). "Middle-class slide" accounts for about two-thirds of this change. Another one-third improved their economic standing, participating in what could be termed a "middle-class rise."

DIVERSITY: The rural poverty rate paralleled the trend shown in Figure 10–4, rising from 16.6% in 1973 to 22.9% in 1990.

NOTE: The number of weeks a typical U.S. worker needs to work to buy the average-priced new car rose from 23 in 1980 to 30 in 1991.

RESOURCE: Secretary of Labor Robert Reich's analysis of the effects of the global economy on inequality in the United States is included in the Macionis and Benokraitis companion reader, *Seeing Ourselves.*

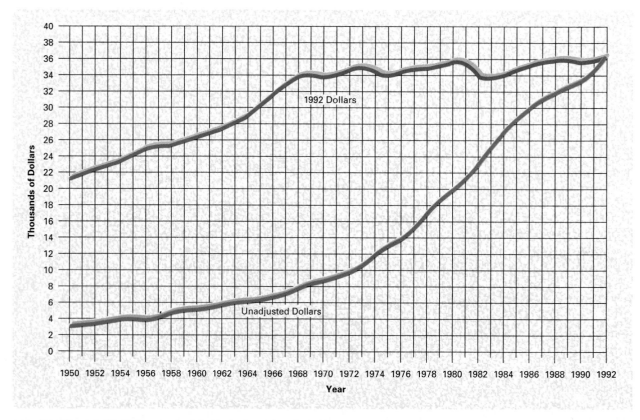

FIGURE 10–4 Median Income, U.S. Families, 1950–1992

(U.S. Bureau of the Census, 1993)

The brisk pace of economic expansion, long taken for granted, has now slowed for a generation. Figure 10–4 shows median U.S. family income between 1950 and 1992 in constant 1992 dollars. Between 1950 and 1973, median family income swelled by 65 percent; however, it has remained roughly stable since then (U.S. Bureau of the Census, 1993).

Earlier in this century, the rapid surge in white-collar positions drew millions of workers from blue-collar and farming jobs, encouraging optimistic predictions that the United States was becoming an affluent, middle-class society (Kerckhoff, Campbell, & Winfield-Laird, 1985). Since 1980, however, new jobs in the U.S. economy have typically paid *less* than in the past, prompting downward social mobility.

The U.S. Class Structure in Global Perspective

Underlying the middle-class slide is a global economic transformation. Much of the industrial production that offered U.S. workers high-paying jobs a generation ago has been transferred overseas (Blumberg, 1981; Rosen, 1987; Thurow, 1987). The United States is now a vast market for industrial goods such as cars, and popular items like stereos and cameras, produced in Japan, Korea, and elsewhere.

High-paying jobs in manufacturing, which accounted for 26 percent of the U.S. labor force in 1960, support less than 15 percent of workers today. In their place, the economy now offers jobs in various types of "service work," which typically pay far less. Indicative of the shift is that USX (formerly United States Steel) now employs fewer people than McDonald's, which is enjoying a rapid expansion, and fast-food clerks make far less per hour than steel workers do. Not surprisingly, then, one study predicts the fastest-growing jobs throughout the 1990s will be cashiers, nurses, janitors, waiters, and truck drivers (Howe & Strauss, 1991).

The global reorganization of work is not bad news for everyone. On the contrary, this trend is the engine

Q: "The difference of natural talents in different men is, in reality, much less than we are aware of. . . . The difference between . . . a philosopher and a street porter, for example, arises not so much from nature, as from habit, custom, and education." Adam Smith *The Wealth of Nations*. Bk. 1 sec. 2, 15

NOTE: A 1988 media story began by describing Lyndon Johnson standing on Tom Fletcher's porch in Inez, Kentucky, two decades before to launch the War on Poverty (*U.S. News and World Report*, January 11, 1988:18–24). Tom Fletcher lived in the same house a generation later, and his life is about the same as it was then. Perhaps Ronald Reagan was right when he quipped, "We had a war on poverty, and poverty won."

driving the upward social mobility for the small number of rich men and women who manage and invest in multinational companies. But this process has hurt many individuals of moderate income whose factory jobs have been "exported" overseas (Reich, 1989, 1991). Moreover, during the recession that opened the 1990s, the process of "scaling back" also undercut the security of many white-collar workers. Trend watchers announced that the "Yuppies" (young, upwardly mobile professionals) of the 1980s are being transformed into the "Dumpies" (downwardly mobile professionals) of the 1990s.

Just as industrialization spawned prosperity a century ago, today's deindustrialization has hurt the standard of living and shaken the confidence of many people. Compared to a previous generation, far fewer now expect to improve their social position, and a growing number worry about being able to maintain the way of life they knew as children in their parents' home. The standard of living in the United States has stopped rising even though women and men are working harder than ever: Half of today's families have two or more people in the labor force, double the proportion in 1950.

POVERTY IN THE UNITED STATES

Social stratification simultaneously creates "haves" and "have-nots." Poverty is therefore an inevitable product of all systems of social inequality. Sociologists employ the concept of poverty in two different ways, however. **Relative poverty** refers to *the deprivation of some people in relation to those who have more*. Relative poverty is universal and inevitable; even a rich society has some members who live in relative poverty. Much more serious is **absolute poverty**, or *a deprivation of resources that is life threatening*. Defined in this way, poverty is a pressing, but solvable, human problem.

As the next chapter ("Global Stratification") explains, the global dimensions of absolute poverty place the lives of perhaps 800 million people—one in seven of the earth's entire population—at risk. Even in the affluent United States, however, the wrenching reality of poverty results in hunger, inadequate housing, and poor health.

The Extent of U.S. Poverty

As part of President Lyndon Johnson's "war on poverty," the United States government began counting the poor in 1964. Officials established a *poverty threshold*, an annual income level below which a person or family was defined as poor and, therefore, entitled to certain benefits.

In creating the poverty threshold, the government's intention was to gauge the number of people living close to absolute poverty. Mollie Orshansky (1969:38), one of its original architects, explains that the poverty threshold reflects the income needed "to purchase a nutritionally adequate diet on the assumption that no more than a third of the family income is used for food." In simple terms, then, the poverty threshold is three times what the government estimates people must spend to eat. The government keys the exact dollar amount to family size and adjusts it annually to reflect the changing cost of living.

Figure 10–5, on page 284, shows the official poverty rate as calculated annually since 1960. The long-term trend is downward, although the poverty rate rose early in the 1980s and jumped again after 1989. In 1992, a total of 36.9 million men, women, and children—14.5 percent of the U.S. population—were officially living in poverty. Another 12.3 million people—the *marginally poor*—were supported by incomes above this level but within 25 percent of the poverty threshold.

For two adults and two children living in an urban area in 1992, the poverty threshold was $14,335. The income of the typical poor family, however, is about $5,751 *below* the poverty threshold. The *poorest of the poor* struggle to get by earning no more than half the poverty threshold figure. Estimates suggest that almost 40 percent of the poor—and four in ten poor children as well—fall within this most disadvantaged category (Littman, 1989; Children's Defense Fund, 1991).

Those who have never known poverty do not easily imagine its consequences. For some children, like Nigeria Collins, whose early death was noted at the beginning of this chapter, poverty means never even having a chance at life. For most, it means the insecurity of living from day to day, which people experience as stress as well as hunger. Estimates place the number of people in the United States who endure daily hunger as high as 20 million (Schwartz-Nobel, 1981; Physicians' Task Force on Hunger in America, 1987).

Who Are the Poor?

Although no single description covers all poor people, poverty is pronounced among certain categories of our population. Children, people of color, women, and residents of rural areas all shoulder higher risks of being poor. Where these categories overlap, the problem of poverty is especially serious.

Q: "No one need go hungry in this country, so long as he is willing and able to negotiate the corridors of the welfare system." *Up From Dependency*, Reagan administration report on poverty

NOTE: Since 1959, poverty rates have declined; then, 18 percent of whites and 55 percent of African Americans were poor.

DIVERSITY: The importance of family patterns to poverty is indicated by the fact that, among two-parent families with children, the poverty rate is just 7.8%. Among all female heads of households, it was 44.5% in 1991. Put otherwise, in 1990, 54% of children on welfare had never-married parents; 33% had separated or divorced parents. (From House Ways and Means Committee data quoted in Michael Marriott, "Fathers Find that Child Support Means Owing More than Money." *The New York Times*, July 20, 1992:A1, A13).

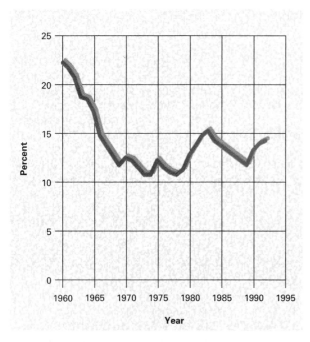

FIGURE 10–5 The Poverty Rate in the United States, 1960–1992

(U.S. Bureau of the Census, 1993)

Age

A generation ago, the elderly were at greatest risk for poverty. But this is no longer the case. From 30 percent in 1967, the poverty rate for seniors over the age of sixty-five fell to 12.9 percent in 1992, yielding just over 4 million elderly poor. This rate is below the overall poverty rate of 14.5 percent. This dramatic decline was due to expanding financial support from government and private employers. Even so, with the number of older people increasing, 10.8 percent of the poor are still elderly people.

Today, the burden of poverty falls most heavily on children. In 1992, 21.9 percent of people under age eighteen (14.6 million children) were officially classified as poor. Tallied another way, four in ten of the U.S. poor are children under the age of eighteen. The box offers a closer look at the current problem of child poverty in the United States.

Race and Ethnicity

In absolute numbers, two-thirds of all poor people are white (Latino and non-Latino); about 30 percent are African Americans. But in relation to their overall numbers, African Americans are about three times as likely as white people to be poor. In 1992, 33.3 percent of African Americans (almost 10.6 million people) lived in poverty, compared to about 29.3 percent of Latinos (6.7 million), 12.5 percent of Asians and Pacific Islanders (.9 million), and 11.6 percent of non-Latino white people (18.6 million). Since 1980, the "poverty gap" among the races has increased (U.S. Bureau of the Census, 1993).

Since both children and people of color are disproportionately poor, minority children are especially likely to live in poverty. In 1992, 21.9 percent of boys and girls under the age of eighteen were poor; this included 16.9 percent of white children, 39.9 percent of young Latinos, and 46.6 percent of African-American youth.

Gender and Family Patterns

Of the U.S. poor over age eighteen, 62.5 percent are women and 37.5 percent are men. This disparity reflects the fact that women who head households bear the brunt of poverty. Of all poor families, 52.4 percent are headed by women with no husband present, while just 5.9 percent of poor families are headed by single men.

Most women heading poor households with children do not work. The problem is not just that child care is expensive; most of the jobs for which poor women are qualified pay poorly. In the absence of opportunity for work that will support a household, two-thirds of women in this situation turn to government assistance.

The link between single-parent families and poverty also means that divorce threatens even middle-class women and their children with poverty. Andrew Cherlin (1990) concludes that the income of single-parent families typically plummets by more than one-third within several months of divorce or separation.

The term **feminization of poverty** describes *the trend by which women represent an increasing proportion of the poor.* In 1960, 25 percent of all poor households were headed by women; the majority of poor families had both wives and husbands in the home. By 1992, however, the proportion of poor households headed by a single woman had doubled to more than 50 percent.

The feminization of poverty is thus part of a larger trend: the rapidly increasing number of households—at all class levels—headed by women. But since households headed by women are at high risk of poverty, women (and their children) represent an increasing share of the U.S. poor.

NOTE: In 1904, Robert Hunter (*Poverty*) estimated the U.S. poverty rate at 13% (defining poverty as annual income under $460 in the North and $300 in the South). Living standards rose sharply thereafter; but, in 1963, Michael Harrington (*The Other America*) claimed that at least 20% of the U.S. population was poor. Poverty definitions are thus keyed to the expectations of a particular historical era. (See Gilbert, 1994)

Q: *Interviewer's question*, "How do you break the cycle of poverty? You can't just hand out money."
Toni Morrison: "Why not? Everybody gets everything handed to them. The rich get it handed—they inherit it. I don't mean just inheritance of money. I mean what people take for granted among the middle and upper classes, which is nepotism, the old-boy network. There's shared bounty of class." *Time*, May 22, 1989:122

SOCIAL DIVERSITY

U.S. Children: Bearing the Burden of Poverty

We cringe at the sight of starving children in countries such as Somalia, the war-torn African society in which the average person tries to live on less than $200 per year. But the existence of child poverty in the United States may be an even greater tragedy, since ours is such a rich nation with per capita income one hundred times higher than that of Somalia.

One in five children under the age of eighteen (almost 15 million boys and girls) in the United States today is poor. This represents about the same number as when the government's "war on poverty" began thirty years ago. In the interim, U.S. society has become almost twice as productive. A national commitment to assist the elderly has cut poverty among senior citizens by more than half. Child poverty, however, remains as serious as ever.

Perhaps the best general measure of how well a society cares for its children is the child mortality rate, the number of children who die during the first year of life for every one thousand live births. The figure shows that, ranked twentieth in the world, the United States falls behind most other industrial societies. For the country as a whole, the 1990 infant mortality rate was 11. Among African Americans, who have triple the white risk of poverty, the rate was 19. In some of the most economically depressed areas of the country (like Camden, New Jersey, described in the chapter opening), the infant mortality rate exceeds 20.

Poor children constitute a diverse category: 61 percent are white, 34 percent African American, and 5 percent are Asian; of these, 21 percent are also culturally Hispanic. What they have in common is living in households with low income—47 percent of poor boys and girls live in households with incomes at less than half the poverty threshold (that is, less than $7,168 in 1992). Researchers have found a strong link between rising rates of child poverty and the increasing share of single-parent households (Eggebeen & Lichter, 1991). Today, about eight in ten poor children live in a household with a single mother, and in the same proportion of cases this household contains no full-time worker.

The reasons for poverty, discussed presently, are complex and controversial, involving changing family patterns and economic trends. But everyone agrees that the blame does not lie with the children. Tragically, however, the burden of poverty does. From a moral point of view, analysts argue, we should not tolerate the suffering this situation brings. From a practical point of view, the cost of social intervention that eliminates the deforming experience of poverty in the lives of children is certain to be much cheaper than dealing with the problems of unemployment, drug use, crime, and violence that will come later on.

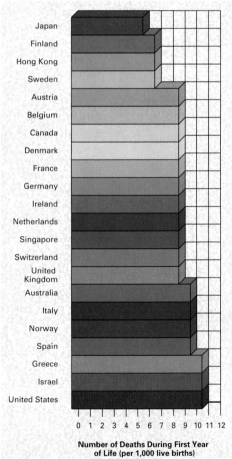

Infant Mortality Rates in Global Perspective, 1990

(United Nations Development Programme, 1993)

SOURCES: Adapted from the Children's Defense Fund (1992); also Marriott (1992).

NOTE: Because women and children tend to suffer together from poverty, the feminization of poverty might also be termed the "juvenilization of poverty." Children are now the poorest of the U.S. poor

Q: "No man suffers from poverty unless it be more than his fault—unless it be his *sin*." Preacher/Social Darwinist Henry Ward Beecher.

SOCIAL SURVEY: "Is it government's responsibility to reduce income differences between the rich and the poor?" (*CHIP1 Social Survey Software*; ISSP, 1985)

	"Yes"	"No"		"Yes"	"No"
U.S.	34.6%	65.4%	U.K.	71.5%	28.5%
Australia	52.6%	47.4%	Austria	77.4%	22.6%
Germany	66.9%	33.1%			

A widespread stereotype links poverty to people of color in the inner cities of the United States. Although minorities are more likely to be disadvantaged, most of the U.S. poor are white people. Furthermore, although inner cities have the greatest concentration of poverty, rural residents are at higher risk of poverty than their urban counterparts.

Area of Residence

The highest poverty rate is found among people who live in central cities: 20.5 percent in 1992. For urban areas taken as a whole, however, the poverty rate was 13.9 percent—actually lower than the 16.8 percent found in rural areas. Suburbs, too, have destitute people, but being the richest region of all, their poverty rate is just 9.7 percent.

Generally speaking, cities offer higher living standards than the countryside because jobs and social services are concentrated there. National Map 10–2 provides a visual picture of income levels across the United States, indicating the counties in which poverty is most pronounced.

Explaining Poverty

For one of the richest nations on earth to contain tens of millions of poor people raises serious social and moral concerns. It may well be true, as some analysts remind us, that many of the people counted among the officially poor in the United States are better off than the poor in other countries—40 percent of U.S. poor families own their home, for example, and 60 percent own a car (Jenkins, 1992). But it is also true, as noted earlier, that malnutrition and outright hunger are widespread in this country, along with violence, illness, and a host of other problems that accompany economic deprivation.

Figure 10–6, on page 288, provides responses from a representative sample of adults in the United States as to whether the government or poor people themselves should take the lead in combating poverty. The results suggest that the public is of two minds about the causes of poverty and how to remedy the problem. One-fourth of this survey's respondents thought the government should do more, and another one in four countered that people should take responsibility for themselves. Note, further, that the remaining half of all respondents agreed with both contentions.

We now examine more closely the arguments underlying each of these two approaches to the problem of low income. Together, they frame a lively and pressing political debate.

One View: Blame the Poor

One side of the issue is based on the following view: *The poor are primarily responsible for their own poverty.* Throughout our history, people in the United States have been a self-reliant lot, embracing the notion that social standing is mostly a matter of talent and individual effort. From this point of view, our society affords considerable opportunity for anyone able and willing to take advantage of it. The poor, then, are those who cannot or will not work, men and women with fewer skills, less schooling, or simply lower motivation. This line of reasoning leads us to conclude that, whatever the specific reasons for poverty, the poor are somehow undeserving. This view is inherent, to various degrees, in responses placed on the right side of the continuum in Figure 10–6 on page 288.

One well-known researcher who held this view was anthropologist Oscar Lewis (1961), who investigated the poor barrios of Latin American cities. Lewis

Seeing Ourselves

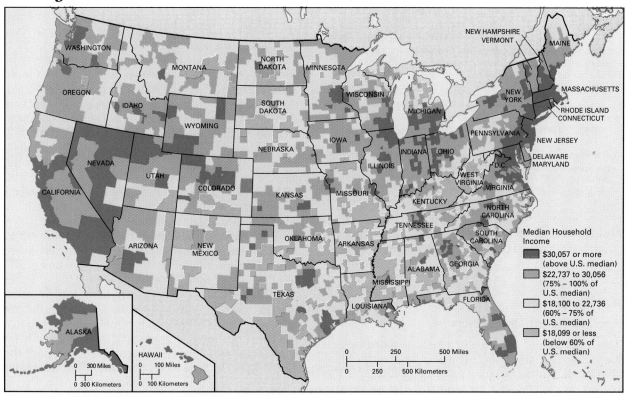

NATIONAL MAP 10–2 Median Household Income Across the United States

This map shows median household income for all 3,014 counties in the United States as recorded by the 1990 census. Surprisingly, just 15 percent of all counties can boast of a median household income greater than the median for the entire country. What do these counties (shown in dark green) have in common? Low-income counties (shown in red) with high rates of poverty also are not randomly spread throughout the nation. What do low-income counties have in common? Do the patterns found here square with our assertion linking affluence to urban areas and poverty to rural places?

From *American Demographics* magazine, Oct. 1992, p. 9. Reprinted with permission. ©1992 *American Demographics* magazine, Ithaca, New York. Data from the 1990 decennial census.

doubted that most poor people could do much about their plight, and he did not blame them individually for their poverty. Rather, Lewis contended that a *culture of poverty* holds down the poor, fostering resignation to poverty as a matter of fate. Socialized in this environment, children come to believe that there is little point to aspiring to a better life. The result is a self-perpetuating cycle of poverty, as one generation transmits its way of life to the next.

In his research in the United States, Edward Banfield (1974) came to much the same conclusion.

Banfield maintains that, especially in areas of intense poverty such as the inner cities, a lower-class subculture has taken hold, eroding personal ambition and achievement. One element of this subculture, as he sees it, is a present-time orientation that encourages living for the moment. While most better-off people are guided by a future orientation to study, plan, save, and work hard, in short, Banfield saw poor people as living largely for the moment. In doing this, he concluded, they end up perpetuating their own poverty and, therefore, reaping more or less what they deserve.

NOTE: The 1992 median income for families headed by a married couple was $42,064; for male heads of household with no wife present, $27,821; for female heads of household with no husband present, $17,221.

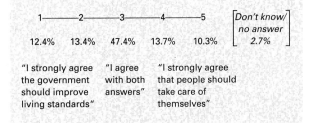

Question: "Some people think that the government in Washington should do everything possible to improve the living standards of all poor Americans [they are at point 1 below]. Other people think it is not the government's responsibility, and that each person should take care of himself [they are at point 5 below]. Where would you place yourself on this scale, or haven't you made up your mind on this?"

1———2———3———4———5   Don't know/ no answer

12.4% 13.4% 47.4% 13.7% 10.3%   2.7%

"I strongly agree the government should improve living standards"   "I agree with both answers"   "I strongly agree that people should take care of themselves"

FIGURE 10–6 Government or People: Who Is Responsible for Poverty?

(*General Social Surveys, 1972–1993: Cumulative Codebook.* Chicago: National Opinion Research Center, 1993:332)

Another View: Blame Society

The other side of the issue can be articulated as follows: *Society is primarily responsible for poverty.* This alternative position, argued by William Ryan (1976), holds that society—not people themselves—distributes the resources and, therefore, is responsible for poverty. Looking at societies around the world, from this point of view, we see that those that distribute wealth very unequally (including the United States) face significant relative poverty; societies that strive for more economic equality (such as Sweden and Japan) lack such extremes in income.

Poverty, Ryan insists, is not inevitable; this problem is caused simply by low income, not personal deficiency. Ryan interprets any lack of ambition on the part of poor people as a *consequence* rather than a *cause* of their lack of opportunity. He therefore dismisses Lewis's and Banfield's analysis as little more than "blaming the victims" for their own suffering.

In Ryan's view, social policies that empower the poor would give them real economic opportunity and yield more economic equality. In Figure 10–6, the responses on the left side of the continuum express support for action by the government to reduce poverty.

Weighing the Evidence

Each of these explanations of poverty has won its share of public support, and each has advocates among

government policy makers. As Banfield sees it, society should strive to encourage equality of opportunity, especially for the young, but should otherwise leave people alone to fend for themselves according to their talents and interests.

Ryan holds that society should reduce poverty by government action to redistribute income in a more equal manner. Programs like a comprehensive child-care package, for example, could help poor mothers gain job skills, or a tax-funded guaranteed minimum income could be established for every U.S. family.

Certainly both of these approaches are possible, and our society periodically leans toward one or the other. The Reagan and Bush administrations were sympathetic toward the first; the Clinton administration is more in tune with the second. But, based on research, what can sociologists contribute to the debate?

The existing data about the poor are subject to various interpretations and lend support to both sides. One fact that advances the position of Lewis and Banfield is that most poor adults in the United States do not hold full-time jobs. Government statistics show that 41.1 percent of the heads of poor families did not work at all during 1992. In fact, only 15.3 percent of the heads of families in poverty worked steadily (at least fifty weeks) during that year (U.S. Bureau of the Census, 1993). So we can conclude that one major cause of poverty is *not holding a job.*

But the *reasons* that people do not work seem more consistent with Ryan's position. Middle-class women combine working and child rearing, but doing so is much harder for poor women who cannot afford child care. Few U.S. employers provide child-care programs for their employees, and most low-paid workers cannot afford to obtain child care on their own. For their part, low-income men claim that there are no jobs to be found, that illness or disability has sidelined them, or, in the case of the elderly, that they have retired. Rightly or wrongly, most poor adults in the United States feel they have few options and alternatives (Popkin, 1990).

The Working Poor

But not all poor people are jobless, and the *working poor* command the sympathy and support of people on both sides of the poverty debate. In 1992, 15.3 percent of poor heads of households (1.2 million people) labored full time for the entire year and yet could not escape poverty. Another 25.8 percent of these heads of families (1.5 million people) remained poor despite their part-time employment.

From another angle, 5.2 percent of full-time workers earn so little they remain poor. This figure represents twice the comparable rate in 1980, suggesting, once again, that the 1980s was a difficult decade for low-income people (U.S. Bureau of the Census, 1993).

"Working poverty" places people in a bind. Jobs provide low wages that barely make ends meet but consume the time and energy needed to get training or schooling that might open new doors. Most people are reluctant to risk the job they do have in the hope of finding something better. At the 1994 minimum wage level of $4.25 per hour, a full-time worker could not support a family above the official poverty line (Levitan & Shapiro, 1987; Schwartz & Volgy, 1992).

Summing up, individual ability and personal initiative do play a part in shaping everyone's social position. On balance, though, evidence points toward society—not individual character traits—as the primary source of poverty. Some poor people do lack ambition. Overall, however, the poor are *categories* of people—women heads of families, people of color, people isolated from the larger society in inner-city areas—without the same opportunities as others.

Homelessness

Many low-income people in the United States lack the resources to support even basic housing. In light of the enormous wealth of the United States and its commitment to providing opportunity for everyone, homelessness may be fairly described as a scar on our society that demands an effective response (Schutt, 1989).

Counting the Homeless

There is no precise count of homeless people. Fanning out across the cities of the United States on the night of March 20, 1991, Census Bureau officials tallied 178,828 people at shelters and 49,793 on the streets in neighborhoods where homeless people are known to live. Officials stressed that this count was not intended as an enumeration of homeless people; it merely helped the Census Bureau more accurately estimate the entire population of the United States (U.S. Bureau of the Census, 1991).

One problem with this research is that homeless people live not just in cities but also in rural counties, which are the poorest of all. One study estimated 20,000 homeless people in rural Ohio alone (Toomey, First, & Rife, 1990). Therefore, if the numbers were all added up, experts suggest, we would find that about 500,000 people are homeless *on any given night* and three times this number—1.5 million people—are

An increase in homelessness since 1980 has intensified the controversy over poverty in the United States. Some homeless people—including individuals released from mental hospitals as part of the "deinstitutionalization movement"—have personal problems that render them unable to cope with a demanding world. But an increasing share of homeless people in the United States are families such as this one, who are victims of their economic situation. The predicament of homelessness caused by poverty, captured here, by photographer Mary Ellen Mark, remains a hotly contested issue. What is clear is that major causes of rising homelessness include economic stagnation, a declining stock of low-income housing, and cutbacks in social service programs.

homeless *for some time during the course of any year* (Kozol, 1988; Wright, 1989).

Causes of Homelessness

The familiar stereotypes of homeless people—men sleeping in doorways and women carrying everything they own in a shopping bag—have recently been undermined by the reality of the "new homeless": those thrown out of work because of plant closings, people forced out of apartments by rising rents or condominium conversions, and others unable to meet mortgage or rent payments because they must work for low wages. Today, no stereotype of the homeless paints a complete picture of this varied category of men, women, and children. But virtually all homeless people have one status in common: *poverty*. For that reason, the explanations of poverty already offered also apply to homelessness.

One side of the debate places responsibility on *personal* traits of the homeless themselves. One-third

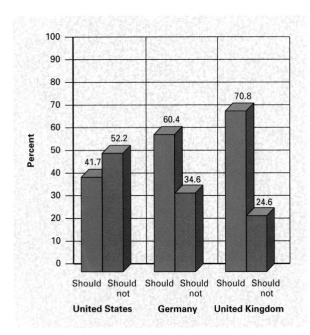

FIGURE 10–7 Attitudes Toward Government Action to Reduce Income Differences, 1990

Question: "On the whole, do you think it should or should not be the government's responsibility to reduce income differences between the rich and poor?"

Note: Adding undecided and non-responding individuals yields 100 percent.
(General Social Survey; International Social Survey Program)

of homeless people are substance abusers, and one-fourth of homeless adults are mentally ill. Perhaps it should not be surprising that a fraction of 1 percent of our population, for one reason or another, is unable to cope with our complex and highly competitive society (Bassuk, 1984; Whitman, 1989).

On the other side of the debate, advocates assert that homelessness results from *societal* factors, including a small and declining stock of low-income housing in the United States, high unemployment, and the economic transition toward low-paying jobs described earlier (Kozol, 1988; Schutt, 1989; Bohannan, 1991). Supporters of this position claim that one-third of all homeless people are entire families, and children are the fastest growing category of the homeless. A minister living in a Pennsylvania town that has lost hundreds of industrial jobs due to plant closings describes the real-life effects of economic recession:

> Yes, there are new jobs. There's a new McDonald's and a Burger King. You can take home $450 in a month from jobs like that. That might barely pay the rent.

What do you do if someone gets sick? What do you do for food and clothes? These may be good jobs for a teenager. Can you ask a thirty-year-old man who's worked for GM since he was eighteen to keep his wife and kids alive on jobs like that? There are jobs cleaning rooms in the hotel. . . . Can you expect a single mother with three kids to hold her life together with that kind of work? (Kozol, 1988:6)

No one disputes that a large proportion of homeless people are personally impaired, although how much is cause and how much is effect are often difficult to untangle. But structural changes in the U.S. economy, sliding incomes during the 1980s, and government policies that reduced support for lower-income people have all contributed to homelessness.

A comprehensive response to homelessness must consider both personal and societal dimensions of the problem. Increasing the supply of low-income housing (other than shelters) is one important step. Additionally, low-income people must have the opportunity to earn the income necessary to pay for housing. But homelessness is more than a housing problem; it is also a *human* problem. People who endure months or years of insecure living come to need various types of social services. Solving the problem of homelessness, therefore, also demands coming to terms with the social damage caused by poverty.

Class and Welfare, Politics and Values

This chapter has presented a great many facts about social class in the United States. In the end, however, our understanding of what it means to be wealthy and privileged or poor and perhaps homeless also turns on politics and values. For one thing, class itself shapes how we think about social stratification: Richer people play up the role of personal merit and defend differences in social standing; poorer people are more likely to point to the role of society in creating inequality and support distributing wealth and other resources more equally (Rytina, Form, & Pease, 1970; NORC, 1991).

But, compared to most people in the world, members of our society place great weight on individual factors in explaining social inequality. When asked, "How important is hard work for getting ahead in life?" almost 90 percent of respondents said it was "essential" or "very important" (NORC, 1991:549). Such cultural values encourage us to see successful people as personally meritorious and the poor as personally deficient. These attitudes go a long way in explaining why our society spends much more than other industrial nations on education (to promote opportunity) but much less on public assistance programs (which directly support the poor).

Our cultural emphasis on individualism is also a key reason that our society tolerates a higher level of poverty than most other industrial societies do. Figure 10–7 provides comparative survey data about government's role in reducing income disparities. A slight majority of U.S. adults oppose government action to reduce income differences, while commanding majorities in Germany and the United Kingdom support government programs aimed at greater economic equality.

The fact that members of our society support a relatively high level of income disparity translates into a harsh view of the poor, which Richard Sennett and Jonathan Cobb (1973) term the *hidden injury of class*. In other words, while affluent people display privilege as a personal "badge of ability," poverty erodes the self-image of disadvantaged people. And, to the extent that we view poor people as undeserving, we perceive public assistance programs as, at best, a waste of money and, at worst, a threat to personal initiative. Ironically, the poor themselves share this thinking, which discourages half the people eligible for support from ever seeking it (Waxman, 1983; Handler & Hasenfeld, 1991; U.S. Bureau of the Census, 1993).

Curiously, this same value system paints a more positive picture of government benefits provided to allegedly "deserving" well-to-do men and women. Current tax law, to take just one example, allows homeowners to deduct from their income interest paid on home mortgages and also real estate tax payments. The tax savings realized from this policy—which goes to people affluent enough to own their own homes and mostly benefits the top 20 percent of the income pyramid—amounts to more than $40 billion annually, more than *five times* the amount of government funds being set aside to provide housing for the poor. Our cultural tendency to equate privilege with personal merit leads us to nod approvingly at "wealthfare" while angrily denouncing welfare for the poor.

Finally, the drama of social stratification extends far beyond the borders of the United States. The most striking social disparities are found not by looking inside one country but by comparing living standards in various parts of the world. In Chapter 11, we broaden our investigation of social stratification, focusing on global inequality.

SUMMARY

1. Social inequality in the United States involves disparities in a host of variables, including income, wealth, and power.

2. White-collar occupations generally confer higher incomes and more prestige than blue-collar work. The pink-collar occupations typically held by women offer little social prestige or income.

3. Schooling is also a resource that is distributed unequally. About three-fourths of people over age twenty-five complete high school, but only one-fifth are college graduates.

4. Ascription exerts a powerful effect on stratification in the United States; ancestry, race and ethnicity, gender, and religion are all related to social position.

5. The upper class, which is small (about 4 percent), includes the richest and most powerful families. Members of the upper-upper class, or the old rich, derive their wealth through inheritance over several generations; those in the lower-upper class, or the new rich, depend on earned income as their primary source of wealth.

6. The middle class includes 40 to 45 percent of the population. The upper-middle class may be distinguished from the lower-middle class on the basis of higher income, higher-prestige occupations, and more schooling.

7. The working class includes about one-third of our population. With below-average income, working-class families have less financial security than those in the middle class. Only one-third of working-class children reach college, and most eventually work in blue-collar or lower-prestige white-collar jobs.

8. About one-fifth of the U.S. population belongs to the lower class, which is defined as those living at or below the official poverty threshold. People of African and Hispanic descent, as well as all women, are disproportionately represented in the lower class.

9. Social class affects nearly all aspects of life, beginning with health and survival in infancy and encompassing a wide range of attitudes and patterns of family living.

10. Social mobility is common in the United States as it is in other industrial societies; typically, however, there are only small changes from one generation to the next.

11. Since the early 1970s, changes in the U.S. economy have reduced the standard of living for low- and moderate-income families. One important trend is a decline in manufacturing industries in the United States, paralleling growth in low-paying, service-sector jobs.

12. Some 37 million people in the United States are officially classified as poor. About 40 percent of the poor are children under the age of eighteen. Two-thirds of the poor are white, but African Americans and Hispanic Americans are disproportionately represented among low-income people. The "feminization of poverty" refers to the rising share of poor families headed by women.

13. Oscar Lewis and Edward Banfield advanced the *culture of poverty* thesis, suggesting how poverty can be perpetuated by the social patterns of the poor themselves. Opposing this view, William Ryan argues that poverty is caused by a society's unequal distribution of wealth.

KEY CONCEPTS

absolute poverty a deprivation of resources that is life threatening

feminization of poverty the trend by which women represent an increasing proportion of the poor

income occupational wages or salaries and earnings from investments

intergenerational social mobility upward or downward social mobility of children in relation to their parents

intragenerational social mobility a change in social position occurring during a person's lifetime

relative poverty the deprivation of some people in relation to those who have more

wealth the total amount of money and valuable goods that a person or family controls

CRITICAL-THINKING QUESTIONS

1. Distinguish income from wealth. How is each distributed in the United States? Describe inequality with regard to occupational prestige and schooling.

2. Identify some of the effects of U.S. social stratification on health, values, politics, and family patterns.

3. What economic changes underlie the so-called middle-class slide?

4. What categories of people are at high risk of poverty in the United States? What evidence supports the assertion that the poor are responsible for their low social position? that society is primarily responsible for poverty?

SUGGESTED READINGS

Classic Sources

Robert S. Lynd and Helen Merrell Lynd. *Middletown in Transition: A Study in Cultural Conflicts.* New York: Harcourt, Brace & World, 1937.

In their second sociological study of Muncie, Indiana, a team of researchers led by the Lynds offers a comprehensive look at life with a particular eye to the effect of social class.

E. Franklin Frazier. *Black Bourgeoisie: The Rise of a New Middle Class.* New York: The Free Press, 1957.

This midcentury account of the rising affluence of some African Americans examines the interplay of class and race in the experience of upward social mobility.

Michael Young. *The Rise of the Meritocracy: 1870–2033.* New Brunswick, N.J.: Transaction, 1993 (orig. 1958).

This fanciful and futuristic account of the rise of a merit-based class system in Great Britain still offers valuable insights about modern systems of social inequality.

Contemporary Sources

Dennis Gilbert and Joseph A. Kahl. *The American Class Structure: A New Synthesis.* 4th ed. Belmont, Calif.: Wadsworth, 1993.

This book provides greater detail about many of the issues raised in this chapter.

Katherine S. Newman. *Declining Fortunes: The Withering of the American Dream.* New York: Basic Books, 1993.

The baby boomers, explains the author, are the first generation that, on average, will not live as well as their parents. But these men and women—a diverse lot—make different sense of this decline.

Paul Fussell. *Class: A Guide Through the American Status System.* New York: Summit Books, 1983.

In this book, the author takes a probing—and often amusing—look at social differences in the United States.

David Riesman. *Abundance for What?* New Brunswick, N.J.: Transaction Books, 1993.

A noted sociologist discusses the social consequences of this country's overall affluence.

Howard G. Schneiderman, ed. *The Protestant Establishment Revisited.* New Brunswick, N.J.: Transaction Books, 1992.

Howard G. Schneiderman, ed. *Judgment and Sensibility: Religion and Stratification.* New Brunswick, N.J.: Transaction Books, 1994.

These books represent a collection of essays by one distinguished sociologist, himself born to membership in our society's upper class. They probe the difficulty of establishing authoritative leadership in a society at once quite unequal and yet built on a cultural ideal of equality.

Cynthia M. Duncan, ed. *Rural Poverty in America.* New York: Praeger, 1992.

This collection of essays describes the plight of almost 10 million rural people who are poor in the United States, with special attention to minorities.

Jeffrey A. Will. *The Deserving Poor.* Hamden, Conn.: Garland, 1993.

Using General Social Survey data, this book studies public attitudes toward the poor, exploring how public opinion divides the poor into "deserving" and "undeserving" categories.

Lois Benjamin. *The Black Elite: Facing the Color Line in the Twilight of the Twentieth Century.* Chicago: Nelson-Hall, 1991.

Based on interviews with one hundred African-American achievers, this book describes the effects of race even among privileged people.

Barbara Ehrenreich. *Fear of Falling: The Inner Life of the Middle Class.* New York: HarperCollins, 1990.

Loren Baritz. *The Good Life: The Meaning of Success for the American Middle Class.* New York: HarperCollins, 1988.

The first of these books, by a well-known political analyst of the left, is a readable and insightful investigation of average people who experienced economic decline during the 1980s. The second explores the aspirations of typical people and what these expectations suggest about our culture.

Theodore R. Marmor, Jerry L. Mashaw, and Philip L. Harvey. *America's Misunderstood Welfare State: Persistent Myths, Enduring Realities.* New York: Basic Books, 1990.

Dorothy C. Miller. *Women and Social Welfare: A Feminist Analysis.* New York: Praeger, 1990.

The first of these books argues that few people understand how the welfare system operates—and that this gap in communication is one of the system's most serious defects. The second analyzes public assistance programs from a feminist point of view.

The State of America's Children, 1992. Washington, D.C.: Children's Defense Fund, 1992.

This recent report by the nation's foremost children's advocacy organization outlines the extent of child poverty and offers an agenda for change.

Stephanie Golden. *The Women Outside: Meaning and Myths of Homelessness.* Berkeley: University of California Press, 1992.

Elliot Liebow. *Tell Them Who I Am: The Lives of Homeless Women.* New York: The Free Press, 1993.

These two books highlight the problem of homelessness among women.

David A. Snow and Leon Anderson. *Down on Their Luck: A Study of Homeless Street People.* Berkeley: University of California Press, 1993.

Based on observations and interviews carried out on the streets, this book highlights the commonalities (rather than the differences) between homeless people and the rest of us.

Global Sources

Louise Lamphere, ed. *Structuring Diversity: Ethnographic Perspectives on the New Immigration.* Chicago: University of Chicago Press, 1992.

Based on studies of immigrants in six U.S. cities, various researchers explore how newcomers experience our society's social stratification.

Robert Erikson and John H. Goldthorpe. *The Constant Flux: A Study of Class Mobility in Industrial Societies.* Oxford, U.K.: Clarendon Press, 1992.

This report of a massive research effort explains why rates of social mobility are basically the same in all industrial societies.

David Alfaro Siqueiros, *Echo of a Scream*, 1937.

DATA FILE: The *Data File* contains a detailed outline of Chapter 11, along with discussion topics and supplementary lecture material.

Q: "We now live in a global village . . ." Marshall McLuhan, 1967

NOTE: The chapter opening art is *Echo of a Scream* (1937) by David Alfaro Siqueiros.

Q: "Why is it that, according to the United Nations, almost 800 million people located in the so-called 'Third World' will be starving by the end of the century?" Andrew Webster

Global Stratification

*H*alf an hour from the center of Cairo, Egypt's capital city, the bus bumped along a dirt road and jerked to a stop. It was not quite dawn, and the Mo'edhdhins would soon climb the minarets of Cairo's many mosques to call the Islamic faithful to morning prayers. The driver turned, genuinely bewildered, to the busload of students from the United States and their instructor. "Why," he said, mixing English with some Arabic, "do you want to be here? And in the middle of the night?"

Why, indeed? No sooner had we left the bus than smoke and stench, the likes of which we had never before encountered, swirled around us. Eyes squinting, handkerchiefs pressed against noses and mouths, we moved slowly uphill along a path ascending mountains of trash and garbage that extended for miles. We had reached the Cairo dump,

where the refuse generated by 15 million people in one of the world's largest cities ends up.[1] We walked hunched over and with great care, since only a scattering of light came from small fires smoldering around us.

Suddenly, from the shadows, spectral shapes appeared. After a moment, we identified them as dogs peering curiously through the curtain of haze. As startled as we were, they quickly bolted, vanishing into the thick air. Ahead of us, we could see blazing piles of trash encircled by people seeking warmth and enjoying companionship.

Human beings actually inhabit this inhuman place, creating a surreal scene, like the aftermath of the next global war. As we

[1]This portrayal is based on the author's visit to the Cairo dump with more than one hundred students in 1988. It also draws on the discussion found in Spates & Macionis (1987) and conversations with James L. Spates, who has also traveled to the Cairo dump.

NOTE: A useful illustration here is to refer back to the "global village" vignette that opens Chapter 1 ("The Sociological Perspective").
GLOBAL: Refugees are on the rise, predominantly in the poorest regions of the world. Some 20 million people are displaced across international borders with another 25 million displaced within their own countries. As the numbers rise, rich countries are becoming more restrictive about admitting refugees.

Q: "While we may want to keep the term 'Third World' to describe a number of societies that are relatively poor, it would be wrong to see this poverty as being unconnected with the relative wealth of the 'First World.' In short, we need a global perspective if we are to make sense of the pattern of affluence and disadvantage in the world." Andrew Webster (1984:6)

approached, the fires cast an eerie light on their faces. We stopped some distance from them, separated by a vast chasm of culture and circumstances. But smiles eased the tension, and soon we were sharing the comfort of their fire. At that moment, the melodious call to prayer sounded across the city.

The people of the Cairo dump, called the Zebaleen, belong to a religious minority—Coptic Christians—in a predominantly Muslim society. Barred by religious discrimination from many jobs, the Zebaleen use donkey carts and small trucks to pick up refuse throughout the city and haul it here. The nightlong routine reaches a climax at dawn when the hundreds of Zebaleen gather at the dump, swarming over the new piles in search of anything of value.

That morning, we watched men, women, and children accumulate bits of metal and ribbon, examine scraps of discarded food, and slowly fill their baskets with odds and ends that would get them through another day. Every now and then, someone gleefully displayed a "precious" find that would bring the equivalent of a few dollars in the city. Watching in silence, we became keenly aware of our sturdy shoes and warm clothing and self-conscious that our watches and cameras represented more money than most of the Zebaleen earn in a year.

Although they are unfamiliar to most members of our society, the Zebaleen of the Cairo dump are hardly unique. Their counterparts live in almost every country of the world. In poor societies around the globe, as we shall see, poverty is not only more widespread than in the United States but also far more severe.

GLOBAL ECONOMIC DEVELOPMENT

Chapter 10 ("Social Class in the United States") explained that significant inequality characterizes the population of this country. In global perspective, however, social stratification is even more pronounced. The value of all the goods and services produced on earth each year (roughly $20 to $25 trillion) serves as the entire world's "income." Figure 11–1 divides this

figure by fifths of the population, providing a distribution similar to that found in Figure 10–1 for the United States. Recall that the richest 20 percent of the U.S. population earns about 45 percent of the national income; the richest 20 percent of humanity, however, receives 70 percent of global income. At the other end of the social pyramid, the poorest 20 percent of the U.S. population earns 4.4 percent of our national income; the poorest fifth of the world's people, by contrast, struggles to survive on just 2 percent of the global income.

In short, income is distributed much less equally in the world as a whole than it is in the United States. For this reason, the average member of our society lives very well by world standards. In fact, most of the people living below our government's poverty threshold enjoy a standard of living far higher than that of the majority of the earth's people.

The Problem of Terminology

How we understand any issue depends a great deal on how we define our terms. In their efforts to understand the unequal distribution of global income, social scientists have long placed the societies of the world into several broad classifications.

A familiar scheme that emerged after World War II called the rich, industrialized countries the "First World," the somewhat less industrialized, socialist countries the "Second World," and the largely nonindustrialized, poor countries the "Third World." In recent years, however, this "Three Worlds" model has lost some of its validity. For one thing, it was a product of cold war politics by which the capitalist West (the First World) faced off against the socialist East (the Second World), while the rest of the world (the Third World) remained more or less on the sidelines. The sweeping transformation of Eastern Europe and the former Soviet Union means that there no longer exists a distinctive Second World; just as important, the superpower opposition that defined the cold war has markedly declined.

A second problem with the "Three Worlds" model is that it lumped together as the Third World more than one hundred countries at significantly different levels of development. Some relatively better off nations of the Third World (such as Chile in South America) have ten times the per-person productivity seen in the poorest countries of the world (including Ethiopia in Eastern Africa). Such a difference has significant consequences for people's chances simply to survive childhood. For those lucky enough to reach adulthood, relative economic development strongly affects whether people get enough to eat, have the opportunity to go to school, and have the strength to engage in meaningful work.

The changes and social differences that mark today's world call for a modestly revised system of classification. As the following sections explain, the *most-developed countries* of the world are those with the most-developed economies and the highest overall standard of living for their people. Next, the world's *less-developed countries* are those in which economic development, far below that of rich societies like the United States, is more or less typical for world nations taken as a whole. Finally, our planet's *least-developed countries* are those marked by the lowest productivity and the most severe and extensive poverty.

Compared to the older "Three Worlds" system, this new form of classification has two main advantages. First, it focuses on perhaps the single most important dimension that underlies social life—economic development—while ignoring the earlier issue of whether societies are capitalist or socialist. Second, this revision provides a more precise picture of the relative economic development of the world's countries because it does not lump together all less-industrialized countries into a single Third World.

Nonetheless, to sort out the 190 nations on earth into any three categories (or, even more crudely, to divide humanity into the "rich North" and the "poor South") ignores striking differences in their ways of life. The societies we place in each of the three levels of economic development have rich and varied histories, speak hundreds of languages, and encompass diverse peoples who are proud of their cultural distinctiveness.

Keep in mind, too, that just as the world's nations form a social hierarchy that ranges from very rich to very poor, so every country on earth is also internally stratified. This means that the extent of global inequality is actually greater than national comparisons suggest, since the most well-off people in rich societies live worlds apart from the poorest people in countries with the least-developed economies.

The Most-Developed Countries

Chapter 1 ("The Sociological Perspective") defined the world's *most-developed countries* as relatively rich, industrialized nations. These nations are rich because the Industrial Revolution first took hold there more than two centuries ago, increasing their productive capacity one hundred-fold. To offer an idea of how this development enriched our own region of the world, consider

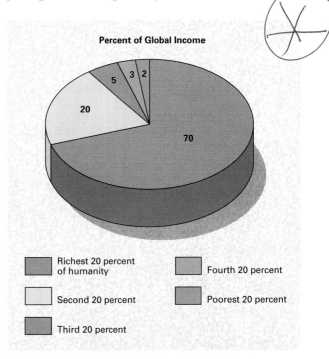

Percent of Global Income

Richest 20 percent of humanity

Second 20 percent

Third 20 percent

Fourth 20 percent

Poorest 20 percent

FIGURE 11–1 Distribution of World Income

(Based on Sivard, 1988, and The World Bank, 1993)

that today people in the United States spend more money just caring for household pets than Europeans did attending to all their needs during the Middle Ages.

A look back at Global Map 1–1 on page 7 identifies the roughly thirty-five high-income countries of the world. They include most of the nations of Western Europe, including England, where industrialization first took hold about 1750. Canada and the United States are also rich nations; in North America, the Industrial Revolution was well under way by 1850. In Asia, one of the world's leading economic powers is Japan; recent economic growth also places Hong Kong and Singapore in this favored category. Finally, to the south of Asia in the global region known as Oceania, Australia and New Zealand are also prosperous, industrial nations.

Taken together, countries with the most-developed economies cover roughly 25 percent of the earth's land area—including parts of five continents—while lying mostly in the northern hemisphere. In mid-1994, the population of these nations was almost 850 million, representing about 15 percent of the earth's people. By global standards, rich nations are not densely populated; even so, some countries (such as Japan) are

GLOBAL: One indicator of economic development is the rate (per 1000 people of all ages) of passenger car ownership (world average, 78). Most economically developed countries: U.S., 537; Australia, 500; Germany (FRG), 438; Canada, 427; UK, 292; Less-developed nations: Germany (GDR), 199; Czechoslovakia, 171; Bulgaria, 115; Poland, 98; Soviet Union, 40; Least-developed nations: El Salvador, 28; Cuba, 20; Senegal, 14; South Korea, 13; North Korea, 1; P.R.

China, 0.1. (*The World in Figures*, 1988)

GLOBAL: The World Bank calculates that one hundred million people in the Commonwealth of Independent States and the nations of Eastern Europe were poor (roughly 25%) prior to the recent reforms. They calculate that roughly the same number (representing about 15%) of the people are poor in rich societies including the U.S., Canada, and the nations of Western Europe.

Japan represents the world's high-income countries, in which industrial technology and economic expansion have produced material prosperity. The presence of market forces is evident in this view of downtown Tokyo (top left). The Commonwealth of Independent States represents the middle-income countries of the world. Industrial development has been slower in the former Soviet Union, as socialist economies have performed sluggishly. Residents of Moscow, for example, chafe at having to wait in long lines for their daily needs (above). The hope is that the introduction of a market system will raise living standards, although it probably will also increase economic disparity. Bangladesh (left) represents the low-income countries of the world. As the photograph suggests, these nations have limited economic development and rapidly increasing populations. The result is widespread poverty.

crowded while others (like Canada) are sparsely settled. Inside their borders, however, about three-fourths of the people in high-income countries crowd together in or near cities.

Most-developed countries reveal significant cultural differences—the nations of Europe, for example, have more than thirty official languages. But these societies share an industrial capacity that generates, on average, a rich material life for their people. Per capita income in these societies ranges from about $8,000 annually (in Portugal and Cyprus) to more than $20,000 annually (in the United States and Switzerland).[2] This prosperity is so great that members of most-developed countries enjoy more than half the world's total income.

Finally, just as people in a single society perform specialized work, so do various global regions form a division of labor. Generally speaking, high-income countries dominate global scientific efforts and employ the most complex and productive technology. Production in rich societies is capital-intensive, meaning that production depends on extensive investment in factories and related machinery. The most-developed countries also stand at the forefront of new information technology; the majority of the largest corporations that design and market computers, for instance, are centered in rich societies. With the lion's share of wealth, high-income countries also control the world's financial markets; daily events in the financial exchanges of New York, London, and Tokyo affect people throughout the world.

The Less-Developed Countries

The *less-developed countries* of the world are those with per capita income of about $5,000, which is close

---

[2]These data reflect the United Nations' (1993) recently introduced concept of "purchasing power parities," which avoid distortion caused by exchange rates when converting all currencies to U.S. dollars. Instead, the data reflect the local purchasing power of each nation's currency.

When natural disasters strike rich societies, as in the 1993 floods in the midwest region of the United States, property loss is great but the loss of life is low. In poor societies, the converse is true, evident in the aftermath of this cyclone that devastated coastal Bangladesh, killing tens of thousands of poor people who lived on land prone to flooding.

to the median for the world's *nations* (but above that for the world's *people* since most people live in the poorest countries). These societies have experienced only limited industrialization, which is evident primarily in cities. But about half of their people still live in rural areas and engage in agricultural production. Especially in the countryside, adequate housing, schooling, and medical care are hard to come by and far below what members of high-income countries take for granted.

Typical incomes in these nations are significantly less than those in the rich societies described above. At the high end, Greece (Europe) and Barbados (Latin America) provide people with about $8,000 in annual income. Panama (Central America), Albania (Europe), Algeria (Africa), and the Philippines (Asia) mark the lower end of this category with roughly $3,000 annually in per capita income. Looking back at Global Map 1–1 (page 7) shows that about ninety of the world's nations fall into this classification, and they are a very diverse lot.

One group of middle-income countries includes the former Soviet Union and the nations of Eastern Europe (in the past, also known as the Second World). The former Soviet Union's military strength rivaled that of the United States, giving it "superpower" status. Its satellites in Eastern Europe, including Poland, the German Democratic Republic (East Germany), Czechoslovakia, Hungary, Romania, and Bulgaria, had predominantly socialist economies until popular revolts between 1989 and 1991 swept aside their governments. Since then, these nations have begun to introduce market systems. This process, detailed in Chapter 15 ("The Economy and Work"), has yet to solve serious economic woes; on the contrary, in the short term, at least, nations of the former Eastern Bloc are battling high inflation and some people enjoy fewer consumer goods than ever.

A second category of less-developed countries are most of the oil-producing nations of the Middle East (or, less ethnocentrically, western Asia). These nations, including Saudi Arabia, Oman, and Iran, are very rich, but their wealth is so concentrated that most people receive little benefit and remain poor.

The third, and largest, category of less-developed countries are found in Latin America and northern and western Africa. These nations (which might be termed the better-off countries of the Third World) include Argentina and Brazil in South America as well as Algeria and Botswana in Africa. Although South Africa's white minority lives as well as people in the United States, this country, too, must be considered less developed because its majority black population lives with far less income.

Taken together, less-developed countries span roughly 40 percent of the earth's land area. Roughly 2 billion people or more than one-third of humanity live in these nations. Compared to high-income countries,

Q: "Not very long ago, the earth numbered two thousand million inhabitants: five hundred million men, and one thousand five hundred million natives. The former had the World; the others had use of it . . . In the colonies the truth stood naked, but the citizens of the mother country preferred it with clothes on . . ." Frantz Fanon, *The Wretched of the Earth*, 1963

DATA FILE: Excerpts from the Papal Encyclical concerning global inequality are found in the *Data File*.
NOTE: India is about ten times as densely populated as the United States.
GLOBAL: Asia has the largest *absolute number* of poor (some 750 million people, between 20 and 25%); Africa has the higher *proportion* of poor people (30%), rising to 40% by 2000.

By and large, rich nations such as the United States wrestle with the problem of relative poverty, meaning that poor people get by with less than we think they should have. In poor countries such as Somalia, absolute poverty means that people lack what they need to survive. Here people gather near the Juba River to bury in a common grave family members who died from starvation.

therefore, these societies are more densely populated although, again, some nations (such as El Salvador) are far more crowded than others (like Russia).

The Least-Developed Countries

The *least-developed countries* of the world are primarily agrarian societies with little industry and in which most people are very poor. These fifty nations, identified in Global Map 1–1 on page 7, are found primarily in central and eastern Africa as well as Asia. Low-income countries (or the poorest nations within the so-called Third World) represent about 35 percent of the planet's land area but are home to half its people. Combining these facts, the population density for poor countries is generally high, although it is much higher in Asian countries (such as India and the People's Republic of China) than in more sparsely settled central African nations (like Chad or Zaire).

In poor countries, barely 25 percent of the people live in cities; most inhabit villages and engage in farming as their families have done for centuries. In fact, about half of the entire world's population are peasants, and most of them live in the least-developed countries. By and large, peasants are staunchly traditional, following the folkways of their ancestors. Especially in villages, industrial technology is all but absent, so that people endure poverty on a massive scale. Constant hunger, unsafe housing, and high rates of disease plague members of the world's poorest societies.

This broad overview of global economic development is the foundation for understanding the problem of global inequality. For people living in affluent nations such as the United States and Canada, the scope of human want in much of the world is difficult to grasp. From time to time, televised scenes of famine in the poorest countries of the world including Ethiopia and Bangladesh give people in the United States a shocking glimpse of the absolute poverty that makes every day a life-and-death struggle. Behind these images lie cultural, historical, and economic forces that we shall explore in the remainder of this chapter.

GLOBAL POVERTY

Poverty always means suffering. People in the world's poorest countries, however, typically contend with more severe hardship than the poor in our society (see Chapter 10, "Social Class in the United States"). This does not mean, of course, that deprivation here at home constitutes only a minor issue. Especially in a rich society, the lack of food, housing, and health care for tens of millions of people—many of them children—amounts to a national tragedy. Yet, poverty in poor counties is far *more severe* and much *more extensive* than in the United States.

The Severity of Poverty

Poverty in poor countries is more severe than it is in rich nations such as the United States. The data in Table 11–1

Q: "In China, we waste nothing but time; in America, you waste everything but time." Comment made to the author by a student in the People's Republic of China

RESOURCE: Daphne Topouzis's article "Women's Poverty in Africa" is in the Macionis and Benokraitis reader.

NOTE: Global production statistics exclude the value of housework.

✱GLOBAL: Newspaper circulation (per 1000 people) is another indicator of development (world average, 100). First World: Japan, 567; UK, 348; Germany (FRG), 411; U.S., 267; Canada, 220; Israel, 170; Second World: Germany (GDR), 552; Soviet Union, 422; Bulgaria, 256; Hungary, 254; Poland, 214; Romania, 160; Third World: Cuba, 144; Argentina, 93; El Salvador, 62; Brazil, 46; Ghana, 31; Haiti, 7.5. (*The World in Figures*, 1988)

suggest why. The first column of figures shows, for countries at each level of economic development, the gross domestic product (GDP).[3] Industrial societies typically have a high economic output due mainly to their industrial technology. A large, industrial nation like the United States had a 1991 GDP of about $5.6 trillion; Japan's GDP stood at about $3.4 trillion. Comparing GDP figures shows that the world's richest nations are thousands of times more productive than the poorest countries on earth.

The second column of figures in Table 11–1 indicates per capita GDP in terms of what the United Nations (1993) calls "purchasing power parities," so that we get a better idea of people's income in terms of what it can buy in a local economy. The resulting figures for rich countries like the United States, Switzerland, and Canada are very high—in the range of $20,000. Per capita GDP for less-developed countries, including Lithuania and Brazil, are much lower—in the $5,000 range. And in the world's least-developed countries, per capita annual income is down to just a few hundred dollars. In Zaire or Ethiopia, for example, a typical person labors all year to make what the average worker in the United States earns in several days.

The third column of Table 11–1 provides a measure of the quality of life in the various nations. Income is obviously one important component of well-being, although certainly not the only one. The index used here, calculated by the United Nations (1993), reflects not just income but education (rates of adult literacy and the average number of years of schooling) and longevity (how long people typically live). Index values are decimals that fall between hypothetical extremes of 1 (highest) and zero (lowest). By this calculation, Japan enjoys the highest quality of life (.983), and the African nation of Guinea has the lowest (.045). With a quality of life index of .976, the United States ranks fifth in the world.

---

[3]Gross domestic product (GDP) refers to all the goods and services on record as produced by a country's economy in a given year. Income earned outside the country by individuals or corporations is excluded from this measure; this is the key difference between GDP and gross national product (GNP), which includes foreign earnings. For countries that invest heavily abroad (Kuwait, for example), GDP is considerably less than GNP; for countries in which other nations invest heavily (Hong Kong), GDP is considerably higher than GNP. For countries that both invest heavily abroad and have considerable foreign investment at home (including the United States), the two measures are roughly the same. For the present purpose, simply notice the striking differences in the productivity of the various world economies.

TABLE 11–1 Wealth and Well-Being In Global Perspective, 1991

Country	Gross Domestic Product ($ billion)	GDP Per Capita (PPP$)*	Quality of Life Index
Most-Developed Countries			
Japan	3,362	17,616	.983
Canada	511	19,232	.982
Switzerland	232	20,874	.978
Sweden	206	17,014	.977
United States	5,610	21,449	.976
Australia	300	16,051	.972
United Kingdom	877	15,804	.964
Germany	1,574	18,213	.957
Less-Developed Countries			
Eastern Europe			
Hungary	60	6,116	.887
Lithuania	20	4,913	.881
Russia and CIS	1,200	7,968	.862
Poland	160	4,237	.831
Latin America			
Argentina	114	4,295	.832
Mexico	283	5,918	.805
Brazil	414	4,718	.730
Asia			
Korea, Republic of	283	6,733	.872
Thailand	93	3,986	.715
Middle East			
Saudi Arabia	108	10,989	.688
Iran, Islamic Republic of	100	3,253	.557
Africa			
Botswana	4	3,419	.552
Algeria	3	3,011	.528
Least-Developed Countries			
Latin America			
Honduras	3	1,470	.472
Haiti	3	933	.275
Asia			
China, People's Republic of	370	1,990	.566
India	222	1,072	.309
Africa			
Zaire	1	367	.262
Ethiopia	6	369	.172
Guinea	3	501	.045

* These data are the United Nations' new "purchasing power parity" calculations that avoid currency rate distortion by showing the local purchasing power of each domestic currency. Figures are for 1990.

SOURCES: United Nations Development Programme, *Human Development Report, 1993* (New York: Oxford University Press, 1993); The World Bank, *World Development Report, 1993: Investing in Health* (New York: Oxford University Press, 1993).

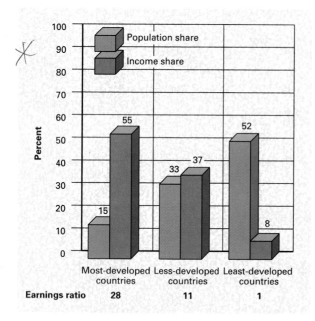

FIGURE 11–2 The Relative Share of Income and Population by Level of Economic Development

One key reason that quality of life differs so much among the societies of the world is that economic productivity is lowest in precisely the regions of the globe where population growth is highest. Figure 11–2 shows the division of global population and global income for countries at each level of economic development. The most-developed societies are by far the most advantaged: Although they include only 15 percent of the world's people, they receive 55 percent of the planet's income. Less-developed countries contain about 33 percent of the global population; these people earn about 37 percent of the world's income. This leaves half of the planet's population with just 8 percent of global income. Factoring together income and population, for every dollar received by individuals in the least-developed countries, their counterparts in the most-developed nations enjoy 28 dollars.

As noted earlier, the population of each society is also subject to *internal* stratification. As a result, the most affluent people in high-income countries like the United States live far better than the poorest people in low-income nations such as Egypt. With this striking contrast in mind, one can better imagine the experience of visiting Cairo's Zebaleen dump-dwellers, described at the beginning of this chapter.

Relative Versus Absolute Poverty

A distinction made in the last chapter has an important application to global inequality. The members of rich societies typically focus on the *relative poverty* of some of their members, highlighting how those people lack resources that are taken for granted by others. Relative poverty, by definition, cuts across every society, even those with overall high income.

But especially important in a global context is the concept of *absolute poverty*, a lack of resources that is life threatening. Commonly, human beings in absolute poverty lack the nutrition necessary for health and long-term survival.

In a rich society like the United States, most people we consider poor are deprived in the relative sense. That is, women, men, and children fall short of the standard of living that we like to think is the birthright of everyone in our society. To be sure, some absolute poverty exists in the United States. Inadequate nutrition that leaves children or elderly people vulnerable to illness and even outright starvation is a reality in this nation. But such immediately life-threatening poverty strikes only a small proportion of the U.S. population; in the least-developed countries of the world, one-third or more of the people are in desperate need.

Since absolute poverty is a deadly threat, a revealing indicator of the extent of this problem around the world is examining a country's median age at death. In other words, what is the age below which half of all people born in a society will die? Global Map 11–1 shows that death in high-income countries, on average, occurs among the elderly who have passed the age of seventy-five. Death occurs somewhat earlier in middle-income nations, reflecting a lower standard of living. But in many low-income countries of Africa and western Asia, the greater extent of absolute poverty is brought home by the fact that half of all deaths occur among children under the age of ten.

The Extent of Poverty

Poverty in poor countries is more extensive than it is in rich nations such as the United States. Chapter 10 ("Social Class in the United States") indicated that the government officially classifies 14.5 percent of the U.S. population as poor. In less-developed countries, however, most people live no better than the poor in our country; in the world's least-developed countries most people are living close to the edge of survival. As the high death rates among children suggest, the extent of

Window on the World

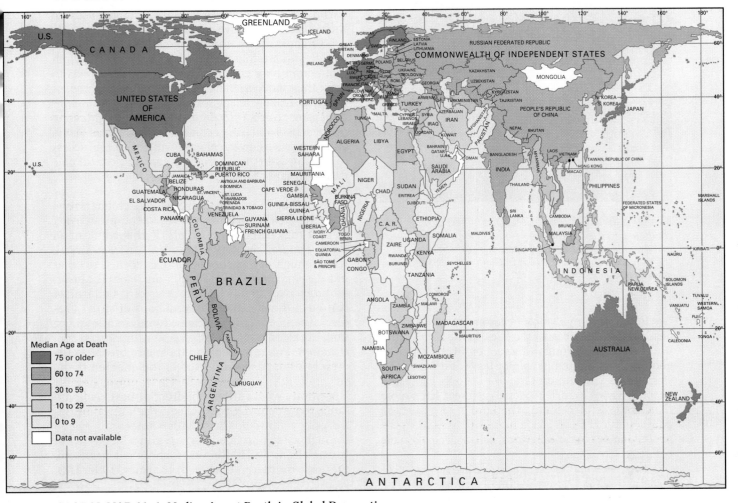

GLOBAL MAP 11–1 Median Age at Death in Global Perspective

This map identifies the age below which half of all deaths occur in any year. In the high-income countries of the world, including the United States, it is the elderly who face death—that is, people age seventy-five or older. In middle-income countries, including most of Latin America, most people die years or even decades sooner. In low-income countries, especially in Africa and parts of Asia, it is children who die, with half of all lives ending before individuals reach ten years of age.

Adapted from *World Development Report* (The World Bank, 1993). Map projection from *Peters Atlas of the World* (1990).

absolute poverty is greatest in Africa, where half the population is ill nourished. In the world as a whole, at any given time, 20 percent of the people (about 1 billion) lack the nutrition they need to work regularly. Of these, at least 800 million are at risk for their lives (Sivard, 1988; Helmuth, 1989; United Nations Development Programme, 1993).

Members of rich societies, such as the United States, tend to be *overnourished*. On average, a member of a high-income society consumes about 3,500 calories daily, an excess that contributes to obesity and related health problems. Most people in the poorest countries do not consume enough food or, more commonly, enough of the right kinds of food.

All around the world, poverty weighs most heavily on children. Faced with little opportunity to improve their lives, many young people fall into despair and cushion their suffering with drugs. These boys in Guatemala sniff glue almost every day.

In simple terms, lack of necessary nutrition makes death a way of life in poor societies. In the ten minutes it takes to read through this section of the chapter, about three hundred people in the world will die of starvation. This amounts to about forty thousand people a day, or 15 million people each year. Even more than in the United States, the burden of poverty in poor countries falls on children. As we have seen, in the poorest nations of central Africa, half of all children die before they reach age ten.

Two further comparisons reveal the human toll of global poverty. First, at the end of World War II, the United States obliterated the Japanese city of Hiroshima with an atomic bomb. The worldwide loss of life from starvation reaches the Hiroshima death toll *every three days*. Second, the loss of life from hunger every five years surpasses the number of deaths from war, revolution, and murders during the last 150 years (Burch, 1983). Given the magnitude of this problem, easing world hunger is one of the most serious responsibilities facing humanity today.

Poverty and Children

As the last chapter explained, poverty in the United States hits children hardest. The same is true worldwide, and the extent and severity of child poverty are greatest in low-income countries. As we have already explained, death often comes early in poor societies, where families lack adequate food, safe water, secure housing, and access to medical care. In many cases, too, children in poor countries leave their families because their chances to survive are better on the streets.

Organizations combating child poverty in the world estimate that poverty forces some 75 million children in poor countries to work on the streets to assist their families. In many cases, such "work" means begging, stealing, selling sex, or serving as a courier for drug gangs. Such a life almost always means dropping out of school and places children at high risk of illness and violence. Many street girls, with little or no access to medical assistance, become pregnant: a case of children who cannot support themselves having still more children.

Another 25 million of the world's children have deserted their families altogether, sleeping and living as best they can on the streets. Perhaps half of all street children are found in Latin America. Brazil, where much of the population has flocked to cities in a desperate search for a better life, faces the greatest problem of street children. According to a United Nations estimate, Brazil has millions of street children, teenagers and younger, living in alleyways, under bridges, or in makeshift huts of their own construction. Public response to the plight of street children is often anger—directed at the children themselves. Public opinion in Rio de Janeiro, Brazil's largest city, views street children, at best, as a nuisance to be controlled by police. When this unrealistic policy fails, death squads sometimes sweep through a neighborhood, engaging in a bloody act of "urban cleansing." In Rio, several hundred street children are murdered each year (Larmer, 1992, U.S. House of Representatives, 1992).

Poverty and Women

Women in Sikandernagar, one of India's countless rural villages, begin work at 4:00 in the morning, lighting the fires, milking the buffalo, sweeping floors, and traveling to the well for water. Then they begin the chores of caring for their families. By 8:00, when many people in the United States are just beginning their day, these women move on to their "second shift," working under the hot sun in the fields until 5:00 in the afternoon. Returning home, the women gather wood for their fires, all the time searching for whatever plants they can find to enrich the evening meal. The buffalo, too, are ready for a meal, and the women tend to them. It is well past dark before their eighteen-hour day is through (Jacobson, 1993:61).

NOTE: Of every 100 ministerial-level positions worldwide, four are held by women. By global region: Africa, 2.5; Asia and Pacific Islands, 1.6; Latin America, 4.0; Socialist nations, 4.6; Industrialized nations, 8.9. (Dr. Nafis Sadik, "Success in Developing Nations Depends on Women," *Popline*, Vol. 13, March–April, 1991, p. 4)

RESOURCE: Robert B. Reich's analysis of the consequences of the emerging global economy for workers in the United States, and also David Berreby's article "The Global Population Crisis," are included in the Macionis and Benokraitis reader, *Seeing Ourselves*.

NOTE: Points 1–3 below are incorporated into modernization theory; points 4–6 are elements of dependency theory. Both theories are discussed later in this chapter.

In rich societies, as Chapter 13 ("Sex and Gender") explains, the work women do is typically unrecognized, undervalued, and underpaid; women receive less income for their efforts than men do. In poor societies, all these things are true to an even greater degree. Women do most of the work in poor societies, and families depend on women's work to provide whatever meager income is available. At the same time, tradition also accords women primary responsibility for child rearing and maintaining the household, while rarely receiving much schooling. In poor societies, the United Nations estimates that men own 90 percent of the land, a far greater hold than men enjoy in industrial nations. While wives and mothers have considerable say about property that formally belongs to husbands and sons, strong traditions reinforced by law give men ultimate control of this chief source of wealth in agrarian societies. Clearly, multi-layered systems of tradition and law subordinate women in poor societies. Caught in a spiral of circumstance that promises little hope for change, women are disproportionately the poorest of the poor. More than 500 million of the world's 800 million people living in absolute poverty are women.

Gender bias is strongest in low-income societies, especially in Asia where cultural traditions favor males the most. As the box on pages 306–7 explains, this pattern is evident in virtually every dimension of life, even in a mother's decision whether or not to bear a child in the first place.

Correlates of Global Poverty

What accounts for severe and extensive poverty in low-income countries? The rest of this chapter weaves together explanations from the following facts about poor societies.

1. **Technology.** Poor societies are largely agrarian, lacking the productive power of industrial technology (glance ahead to Global Maps 15–1 and 15–2 on page 410). Energy from human muscles or beasts of burden falls far short of the force unleashed by steam, oil, or nuclear fuels; this technological disparity limits the use of complex machinery. Moreover, the focus in agrarian societies on farming, rather than on specialized production, inhibits development of human skills and abilities.

2. **Population growth.** As Chapter 21 ("Population and Urbanization") explains in detail, countries with the least-developed economies have the highest birth rates in the world. Despite high death rates from poverty, the populations of poor societies in Africa, for example, double every twenty-five years. In such countries, more than half the people are just entering their childbearing years, so future population growth looms large. Even an expanding economy cannot support such surges in population. During 1993, for example, the population of Kenya swelled by 4 percent; as a result, even with some economic development, living standards did not improve at all.

3. **Cultural patterns.** Societies yet to industrialize are typically very traditional. Kinship groups pass down folkways and mores from generation to generation. Adhering to long-established ways of life, such people resist innovations—even those that promise a richer material life.

   The members of poor societies often accept their fate, although it may be bleak, in order to maintain family vitality and cultural heritage. Such attitudes bolster social bonds, but at the cost of discouraging development. The box on page 308 explains why traditional people in India respond to their poverty differently from the way that poor people in the United States commonly do.

4. **Social stratification.** Low-income societies distribute their wealth very unequally. Chapter 9 ("Social Stratification") explained that social inequality is more pronounced in agrarian societies, where land is a vital resource, than in industrial societies. In the farming regions of Bangladesh, for example, 10 percent of the landowners own more than half the land, while almost half of farming families have little or no land of their own (Hartmann & Boyce, 1982). According to another estimate, the richest 10 percent of Central Americans control more than three-fourths of that region's land (Barry, 1983). Such concentrations of land and wealth have prompted widespread demands for land reform in many agrarian societies.

5. **Gender inequality.** As we have already explained, poor societies subordinate women even more than industrial societies do. Moreover, such women tend to have many children, which, in turn, holds down living standards. For this reason, an increasing number of analysts conclude that economic development in much of the world is closely linked to improving the social standing of women.

6. **Global power relationships.** A final cause of global poverty lies in the relationships among the nations of the world. Historically, wealth flowed from poor societies to rich nations due to

GLOBAL SOCIOLOGY

Infanticide and Sexual Slavery: Gender Bias in Poor Societies

Rani, a young woman living in a remote Indian village, returned home from the hospital after delivering a baby girl. There was no joy in the family. On the contrary, upon learning of the birth, the men somberly filed out of the mud house. Rani and her mother-in-law then set about the gruesome task of mashing oleander seeds into several drops of oil to make a poisonous paste, which they pushed down the baby's throat. The day came to an end as Rani returned from a nearby field where she had buried the child.

As she walked home, Rani felt not sadness at losing her daughter but bitterness at not having had a son. Members of her village, like people living in poor societies across Asia and other world regions, favor boys while defining girls as a

A global pattern is that poverty forces women into sexual slavery as prostitutes. These four Vietnamese women working in a brothel in Cambodia will never escape their poverty and may well fall victim to AIDS, which is spreading rapidly across Southeast Asia.

economic liability. Why? The basic reason is that, in male-dominated societies, most power and wealth falls into the hands of men. Parents recognize that boys are a better investment of their meager resources, since males have a better chance of surviving later as adults and go on to earn more for their families. Then, too, custom dictates that parents of a girl offer a dowry to the family of her prospective husband. In short, given the existing social structure, families are better off with boys and without girls.

One consequence of this double standard is high rates of sex-selective abortion throughout rural India, China, and other Asian nations. In India, a curious fact is that even villages that lack running water typically have a doctor who

colonialism, *the process by which some nations enrich themselves through political and economic control of other countries.* Some analysts claim that this global exploitation spurred some nations to *develop* economically while others simultaneously were *underdeveloped.* The societies of Western Europe colonized much of Latin America for more than three hundred years and also controlled parts of Asia, notably India, for long periods. Africa, too, endured up to a century of colonization, most of which ended in the 1960s.

During this century, about 130 former colonies gained their independence, leaving only a small number of countries as colonies today (Strang, 1990). As we shall see, however, a continuing pattern of domination has emerged. **Neocolonialism** (*neo* comes from Greek, meaning "new") amounts to *a new form of global power relationships that involves not direct political control but economic*

exploitation by multinational corporations. **Multinational corporations,** in turn, are *large corporations that operate in many different countries.* As Chapter 15 ("The Economy and Work") explains, multinational corporations historically developed through rapid corporate growth and mergers. These corporations now wield such tremendous economic power that corporate decision makers have some of the same power over poor countries that the leaders of colonial powers did in the past.

GLOBAL INEQUALITY: THEORETICAL ANALYSIS

There are two major explanations for the unequal distribution of the world's wealth and power—*modernization theory* and *dependency theory*. Each suggests not only why so many of the world's people are poor

Q: "We [multinational corporations] are not without cunning. We will not make Britain's mistake. Too wise to govern the world, we shall simply own it." Ludwell Denny (cited in Vaughan, 1978:20)

NOTE: Modernization theory draws on the ideas of Ferdinand Toennies, Emile Durkheim, and Max Weber. Among the architects of this approach in the United States was Talcott Parsons.

GLOBAL: Assuming (1) about one-fifth of people who have ever lived are living now, (2) virtually all of the people who lived in human history were poor by contemporary standards, and (3) at least one-third of today's global population is poor, then only one-seventh of humanity has ever known any degree of affluence. According to modernization theory, such affluence (and not poverty) is what social scientists must explain.

employs either amniocentesis or ultrasound to determine the sex of a fetus. The woman's typical response, upon hearing the results of the test, is either elation at carrying a boy or resolve to terminate the pregnancy quickly so that she may "try again." Although there are no precise counts of abortion and female infanticide, analysts point out that, in some rural regions of Asia, men outnumber women by as many as ten to one.

For girls who manage to survive infancy, the pattern of gender bias persists. Generally speaking, parents provide girls with less food, schooling, and medical care than they give to boys. In times of drought or other crisis, families may leave girls to die while they channel what little resources they have toward the survival of a son.

Another dimension of gender bias is the exploding growth of sexual slavery involving young women. Thailand, especially its capital, Bangkok, is emerging as the sex-tourism capital of the world, although similar red-light districts can be found in other large cities throughout the region (and, increasingly, in Eastern Europe as well). In some cases, parents sell female infants to agents who pay others to raise them, then "harvest their crop" when the girls approach their teenage years and are old enough to work in a brothel. In other cases, girls who see little future in a rural village make their own way to the city, only to fall into the hands of pimps who soon have them working in brothels, soliciting in bars, or performing in sex shows. Pimps provide girls with clothes and housing, but at a price that exceeds the girls' salaries. The result is a system of debt bondage that keeps women virtual prisoners of their unscrupulous employers. Those who run away are pursued by agents and forced to return.

The numbers involved are rapidly mounting: Thailand alone now has 2 million prostitutes (8 percent of the country's female population); as many as half of these are children. The future for these girls and women is bleak. Most suffer from a host of diseases brought on by abuse and neglect, and 40 percent are now infected with the virus that causes AIDS.

SOURCES: Anderson & Moore (1993) and Reaves (1993).

but why we in the United States enjoy such comparative advantages.

The two explanations overlap to some extent. Both acknowledge enormous inequality on our planet, and they agree that changes are needed to guarantee the future security of humanity, rich and poor alike. Yet, emphasizing different causes of global poverty, they reach differing conclusions about what to do about this pressing problem.

Modernization Theory

Modernization theory is *a model of economic and social change that explains global inequality in terms of differing levels of technological development among societies.* Modernization theory emerged in the 1950s, a period of fascination with technology in the United States and a time of hostility toward the United States in many poor societies. Socialist countries—especially the Soviet Union—were gaining influence among low-income nations by asserting that poor societies simply could not make economic progress under the sway of rich, capitalist countries. In response, U.S. policy makers framed a broad defense of rich nations' free-market economies that has shaped official foreign policy toward poor nations ever since.[4]

Historical Perspective

Modernization theorists point out that the *entire world* was poor as recently as several centuries ago. Because poverty has been the norm throughout human history, *affluence*—not deprivation—demands an explanation.

Affluence came within reach of a small segment of humanity during the twilight of the Middle Ages as

[4] The following discussion of modernization theory draws primarily on Rostow (1960, 1978), Bauer (1981), and Berger (1986).

Q: "In India," observers say, "a child is always in someone's arms."

Q: "One billion more people are being fed today than in the early 1970s, but the number of hungry people continues to increase." John W. Helmuth

Q: "For hunger is a curious thing: at first it is with you all the time, waking and sleeping and in your dreams, and your belly cries out incessantly, and there is a gnawing and a pain . . . Then the pain is no longer sharp but dull, and this too is with you always so that you think of food many times a day . . . Then that too is gone, all pain, all desire, only a great emptiness is left, like the sky, like a well in drought, and it is now that the strength drains from your limbs . . ."
Kamala Markandaya, *Nectar in a Sieve*

GLOBAL SOCIOLOGY

A Different Kind of Poverty: A Report from India

India

Most North Americans know that India is one of the poorest societies of the world: Per capita earnings in this low-income Asian nation are only $1,000 a year (see Table 11–1). Deprivation pervades this vast society, where one-third of all the world's hungry people reside.

But few members of our society fully comprehend the reality of poverty in India. Most of the country's 900 million people live in conditions far worse than those our society labels as "poor." A traveler's first experience of Indian life is sobering and sometimes shocking; in time, the outsider also learns that, in India, people understand poverty differently from the way we do.

Arriving in Madras, one of India's largest cities with 6.5 million inhabitants, a visitor immediately recoils from the smell of human sewage that hangs over the city like a malodorous cloud. Untreated sewage also renders much of the region's water unsafe to drink. The sights and sounds of Madras are strange and intense—streets are choked by motorbikes, trucks, carts pulled by oxen, and waves of people. Along the roads, vendors sitting on burlap cloth hawk fruits, vegetables, and cooked meals. Seemingly oblivious to the urban chaos all around them, people work, talk, bathe, and sleep in the streets. Tens of millions of homeless people fill the cities of India.

Madras is also dotted by more than a thousand shanty settlements, containing about half a million people, many of whom have converged on the city from traditional rural villages in search of a better life. Shantytowns are clusters of huts constructed of branches, leaves, and discarded material. These dwellings offer little privacy and no refrigeration, running water, or bathrooms. The visitor from the United States understandably feels uneasy entering such a community, since the poorest sections of our inner cities seethe with frustration and, oftentimes, explode with violence.

Less-developed societies may be poor, but strong traditions and vital families place most people in a network of social support. Thus people endure poverty with the help of their kin, which contrasts to the often isolating poverty in the United States.

But here, too, India offers a sharp contrast. No angry young people hang out at the corner, no drugs pervade the area, and there is surprisingly little danger. Instead, the social units of shantytowns are strong families—children, parents, and sometimes elderly grandparents—who extend a smile and a welcome. In traditional societies like India, ways of life change slowly over many generations. To most Indians, life is shaped by *dharma*—the Hindu concept of duty and destiny—that encourages them to accept their fate, whatever it may be. Mother Teresa, who has won praise for her work among the poorest of India's people, goes to the heart of the cultural differences: "Americans have angry poverty," she explains. "In India, there is worse poverty, but it is a happy poverty."

No one who clings to the edge of survival should be called truly "happy." But the deadly horror of poverty in India is eased by the strength of families and traditional communities, a sense that life has a purpose, and a world view that encourages each person to accept whatever society offers. As a result, the visitor comes away from a first encounter with Indian poverty in confusion: "How can people be so poor, and yet apparently content, vibrant, and so *alive*?"

SOURCE: Based on the author's research in Madras, India, November 1988.

Q: "Capitalism has become one of the most dynamic forces in human history, transforming one society after another, and today it has become established as an international system determining the economic fate of most of mankind and, at least indirectly, its social, political, and cultural fate as well." Peter Berger (1986:115)

RESOURCE: The cultural value placed on achievement is regarded by some sociologists as the crucial factor in advancing or inhibiting development. See, for example, Daniel Lerner, *The Passing of Traditional Society: Modernizing the Middle East* (The Free Press, 1958).

economic activity expanded in Western Europe. Initially, this economic growth was limited to trade in and among cities. By the beginning of the sixteenth century, exploration of other parts of the world revealed vast commercial potential.

Then an even greater economic force was unleashed as the Industrial Revolution began to transform Western Europe by the close of the eighteenth century and, soon after, reshaped the United States as well. Industrial technology and the innovations of countless entrepreneurs created new wealth on a grand scale. At the outset, modernization theorists concede, this new wealth benefited only a few. Yet industrial technology was so productive that gradually the standard of living of even the poorest people began to rise. The specter of absolute poverty, which had cast a menacing shadow over humanity for its entire history, was finally being routed.

During this century, the standard of living in high-income societies—where the Industrial Revolution began—has jumped at least fourfold. Many middle-income societies in Asia and Latin America are now industrializing, and they, too, are gaining greater wealth. But without industrial technology, low-income countries contend with the same meager productivity they have endured throughout history.

The Importance of Culture

Why didn't people the world over share in the Industrial Revolution so that they, too, could enjoy material plenty? Modernization theory holds that not everyone is eager to seek out and utilize new technology. Whether a society does so or not depends on whether its *cultural environment* emphasizes tradition or the benefits of innovation and greater productivity.

In a word, then, the greatest barrier to economic development is *traditionalism*. In societies that celebrate strong family systems and revere the past, ancient ways offer powerful guides to understanding the present and shaping the future. Predictably, traditionalism creates a form of "cultural inertia" that discourages the adaptation of technological advances that would improve the standard of living. For example, Western innovations and technological advances have encountered fierce resistance in Iran because they threaten traditional Islamic family relationships, customs, and religious beliefs.

Max Weber (1958; orig. 1904–5) explained that, at the end of the Middle Ages, Western Europe stood out as having a distinctive cultural environment that favored change. As detailed in Chapter 4 ("Society"),

Two centuries ago, children in European societies routinely performed exhausting and dangerous work. Today, boys and girls do precisely the same in low-income societies around the world. Poor societies rely on the labor of everyone, so that childhood as we know it simply does not exist.

the Protestant Reformation reshaped traditional Catholicism to generate a progress-oriented culture. Material affluence—regarded with suspicion by the Catholic church—became a personal virtue, and individualism steadily eroded the established emphasis on kinship and community. Taken together, these changing cultural patterns nurtured the Industrial Revolution, which allowed one segment of humanity to prosper.

Rostow's Stages of Modernization

Modernization theory maintains that low-income countries need not have a future as wretched as their past. As technological advances diffuse around the world, all societies are gradually converging on one general form: the industrial model. According to W. W. Rostow (1960, 1978), the process of modernization follows four overarching stages.

NOTE: Daniel Lerner (1958) points out that, when survey research is conducted in our own society, only a small proportion of respondents reply "I don't know." In traditional societies, he found, such responses are common, suggesting the difficulty traditional people have imagining the world being different from what it is. For instance, when Lerner asked a peasant in Turkey what he would do if he were President, he responded, "My God, How can you ask such a thing? How can I . . . I cannot . . . president of Turkey . . . master of the whole world?" (1958:3)

NOTE: The subtitle of Walt Whitman Rostow's (1960) work, "A Non-Communist Manifesto," suggests its opposition to Marx's thinking.

Q: "Wealth doesn't create poverty; wealth creates prosperity." George Gilder

1. **Traditional stage.** Initially, cultural traditions are strong, so poor societies resist technological innovation. Socialized to venerate the past, people in traditional societies cannot easily imagine how life can be different. They build their lives around their families and local communities, granting little individual freedom to one another, and so, inhibiting change. Life in such communities is often spiritually rich but lacking in material abundance.

   A century ago, much of the world was in this initial stage of economic development. And, because Bangladesh and Somalia are still at the traditional stage, they remain impoverished to this day.

2. **Take-off stage.** As a society experiences a weakening of tradition, the economy begins to grow. A limited market emerges as people produce goods not just for their own consumption but in order to trade with others for profit. Paralleling these developments, greater individualism and a stronger achievement orientation take hold, often at the expense of family ties and long-standing norms and values.

   Great Britain reached take-off by about 1800, the United States around 1820. Thailand, a middle-income country in eastern Asia, has now entered this stage.

   Rostow stresses that economic take-off in poor societies depends on progressive influences—including foreign aid, the availability of advanced technology and investment capital, and schooling abroad—that only rich nations can provide.

3. **Drive to technological maturity.** By this time, a society is in full pursuit of a higher standard of living. An active, diversified economy drives a population eager to enjoy the benefits of industrial technology. At the same time, however, people begin to realize (and sometimes lament) that industrialization is eroding traditional life in families and local communities. Great Britain reached this point by about 1840, the United States by 1860. Today, Mexico, the U.S. territory of Puerto Rico, and the Republic of Korea are among the nations driving to technological maturity.

   By this stage of economic development, absolute poverty has greatly declined. Cities swell with people drawn from the rural hinterland in search of economic opportunity, occupational specialization renders relationships less personal, and heightened individualism often sparks movements pressing for expanded political rights. Societies approaching technological maturity also provide basic schooling to all their people, with advanced training for some. As people discredit tradition as "backward," they open the door to further change. The social position of women steadily becomes more equal to that of men. But, at least in the short term, the process of development may subject women to new and unanticipated problems, as the box explains.

4. **High mass consumption.** Economic development driven by industrial technology steadily raises living standards. This rise occurs, Rostow explains, as mass production stimulates mass consumption. More simply put, people soon learn to "need" the expanding array of goods that their society produces.

   The United States reached the mass consumption stage by 1900. Other high-income societies were not far behind. Japan, for example, was sufficiently industrialized to become a military power early in this century. After recovering from the destruction of World War II, the Japanese entered an era of high mass consumption, and Japan now has the world's second largest economy (behind only the United States). Closing in on this level of economic development are two of the most prosperous small societies of East Asia, Hong Kong and Singapore.

The Role of Rich Nations

Modernization theory claims that high-income countries play a crucial role in global economic development. More specifically, rich societies are the key to *solving* global inequality in the following ways:

1. **Assisting in population control.** As we have already noted, population growth is greatest in the poorest societies of the world. Rising population easily overtakes economic advances, lowering the standard of living. Curbing global population, therefore, is crucial to combating poverty. Rich nations can help control population growth by exporting birth control technology and helping to promote its use. Part of this process is also encouraging programs that advance the social standing of women. Once economic development is under way and women earn more income, their lives will be less centered on child rearing, so birth rates should decline as they have in industrialized societies.

Q: ". . . the plight of women [in modernizing Bangladesh] is all too obvious in the streams of unattached mothers and children who pour into towns to beg, in the growth of prostitution, in the desperation with which rural women have left the seclusion of their homes to seek work . . ." Sultana Alam

Q: "Women-headed households are of fairly recent origin in the Third World." Sultana Alam

Q: "There is widespread agreement today, from Chile to China, that an economy allowing market forces the fullest feasible sway will perform better than one in which all decisions are centrally administered." Peter Berger (1986:130)

GLOBAL SOCIOLOGY

Modernization and Women: A Report from Rural Bangladesh

Bangladesh

In global perspective, gender inequality is greatest where people are poorest. Economic development, then, weakens traditional male domination and gives women opportunities to work outside the home. Birth control emancipates women from a continual routine of childbearing, allowing them to benefit from schooling and to earn more in the paid work force.

Even as living standards rise, however, economic development has drawbacks for women. Investigating a poor, rural district of Bangladesh, Sultana Alam (1985) reports that women confront several new problems as a result of modernization.

First, economic opportunity draws men from rural areas to cities in search of work, leaving women and children to fend for themselves. Men sometimes sell their land and simply abandon their wives, who are left with nothing but their children.

Second, the eroding strength of the family and neighborhood leaves women who are deserted in this way with few sources of assistance. The same holds true for women who become single through divorce or

the death of a spouse. In the past, Alam reports, kin or neighbors readily took in a Bangladeshi woman who found herself alone. Today, as

One consequence of modernization in developing societies might be termed "the sexualization of women." Rather than being defined in terms of traditional kinship roles, women are increasingly valued for their sexual attractiveness. It is noteworthy that many of the growing number of prostitutes in the cities of low-income countries have discarded traditional dress for Western styles of clothing.

Bangladesh struggles to advance economically, the number of poor households headed by women is increasing. Rather than enhancing women's autonomy, Alam argues, this spirit of individualism has actually reduced the social standing of women.

Third, economic development—as well the growing influence of Western movies and mass media—undermine women's traditional roles as wives, sisters, and mothers while redefining women as objects of men's sexual attention. The cultural emphasis on sexuality that is familiar to us now encourages men in poor societies to desert aging spouses for women who are younger and more physically attractive. The same emphasis contributes to the world's rising tide of prostitution noted earlier in this chapter.

Modernization, then, does not affect men and women in the same ways. In the long run, the evidence suggests, modernization does give the sexes more equal standing. In the short run, however, the economic position of many women actually declines, and women are also forced to contend with new problems that were virtually unknown in traditional societies.

SOURCES: Based on Alam (1985) and Mink (1989).

2. **Increasing food production.** Modernization theory asserts that "high-tech" farming methods, exported from rich societies to poor nations, will raise agricultural yields. Such techniques, collectively referred to as the *Green Revolution*, involve the use of new hybrid seeds, modern irrigation methods, chemical fertilizers, and pesticides for insect control.

3. **Introducing industrial technology.** Technological transfers should involve industry as well as

agriculture. Rich nations can accelerate economic growth in poor societies by introducing machinery and information technology. Such cultural diffusion helps to shift the economies of low-income countries from a focus on agriculture to industrial and service work that improves productivity.

4. **Instituting programs of foreign aid.** Investment capital from rich nations can boost the prospects of poor societies striving to reach the take-off stage. Developing countries can spend this money to purchase high technology—fertilizers and irrigation projects to raise agricultural productivity and power plants and factories to improve industrial output.

Critical evaluation. Modernization theory, which explains how industrialization transforms virtually all of social life, has influential supporters among social scientists (Parsons, 1966; W. Moore, 1977, 1979; Bauer, 1981; Berger, 1986) and has shaped the foreign policy of the United States and other rich nations for decades. Proponents maintain that the economic development of Western societies is not a unique historical event; in fact, Asia provides a second case of poor societies that have made impressive strides with the assistance of rich countries. South Korea, Taiwan, the former British colony of Singapore, and the current British colony of Hong Kong each received extensive foreign aid, and each has a striking record of economic development.

From the outset, however, modernization theory has come under fire from socialist countries (and sympathetic analysts in the West) as a thinly veiled defense of capitalism. Its most serious flaw, according to critics, is that modernization simply has not occurred in many of the world's poor societies. Between 1980 and 1990, in fact, fifty low- and middle-income countries actually saw their living standards fall.

A second criticism lodged against modernization theory concerns its assessment of the role of rich nations. Modernization theorists contend that the presence of high-income countries in the world today makes development *easier* than ever before since these rich nations can offer assistance to poor ones. But, critics counter, rich nations have little interest in giving up their hold on the world's wealth. As they see it, this self-interest stands as a barrier to development that almost ensures the perpetuation of global poverty. Put otherwise, critics claim that high-income countries industrialized from a position of global *strength*; we should not expect low-income countries today to modernize from a position of global *weakness.*

Third, critics charge that modernization theory treats rich and poor societies as worlds unto themselves, failing to see how international relations historically has affected the standing of all nations. It was colonization, they maintain, that boosted the fortunes of Europe to begin with; further, this economic windfall came at the expense of countries in Latin America and Asia that are still reeling from the consequences.

Fourth, critics contend that modernization theory holds up the world's most-developed countries as the standard by which the rest of humanity should be judged, thus betraying an ethnocentric bias. As Chapter 22 ("The Natural Environment") explains, our Western conception of "progress" has contributed to the degradation of the physical environment throughout the world. Moreover, not every culture buys into our notions about competitive, materialistic living.

Fifth, and finally, modernization theory draws criticism for suggesting that the causes of global poverty lie almost entirely in the poor societies themselves. Critics see this analysis as little more than "blaming the victims" for their own plight. Instead, they argue, an analysis of global inequality should focus as much attention on the behavior of *rich* nations as that of poor nations (Wiarda, 1987).

From all these concerns has emerged a second major approach to understanding global inequality. This is dependency theory.

Dependency Theory

Dependency theory is *a model of economic and social development that explains global inequality in terms of the historical exploitation of poor societies by rich societies.* Dependency theory offers an analysis of global inequality dramatically different from modernization theory, for it places primary responsibility for global poverty on rich nations. Dependency theory holds that high-income countries have systematically impoverished low-income countries, making poor societies *dependent* on rich ones. This destructive process, which dependency theorists claim continues today, extends back for centuries.

Historical Perspective

Everyone agrees that, before the Industrial Revolution, people knew little of the affluence present in some of the world today. Dependency theory asserts, however,

One side of the "Christopher Columbus controversy" is illustrated by artist Diego Rivera in his mural Colonial Domination. *As this painting expresses in graphic detail, the arrival of Europeans to this hemisphere initiated considerable conflict and violence, placing the Americas under the political control of European nations for more than three hundred years.*

that many people living in poor countries were actually better off economically in the past than their descendants are now. André Gunder Frank (1975), a noted proponent of this approach, argues that the *development* of rich societies resulted from the same colonial ties that *underdeveloped* poor societies.

Dependency theory hinges on the assertion that the economic positions of the rich and poor nations of the world are linked and cannot be understood correctly in isolation from one another. This analysis maintains that poor nations are not simply lagging behind rich ones on a single "path of progress." Rather, the increasing prosperity of the most-developed countries came largely at the expense of less-developed societies. In short, then, some nations became rich *only because other nations became poor.* Both are products of the onset of global commerce that began half a millennium ago.

The Importance of Colonialism

Late in the fifteenth century, Europeans began the exploration of North America to the west, the massive continent of Africa to the south, and the vast expanse of Asia to the east. Across the United States, 1992 marked the quincentennial of the first voyage of Christopher Columbus, who sailed westward from Spain believing that he could reach the Orient. The unintended outcome of Columbus's quest—what Europeans termed "the discovery of the New World"—has long been celebrated as a stunning achievement. In recent decades, however, historians have provided a more complete understanding of this fateful collision of two worlds (Sale, 1990; Gray, 1991).

What Europeans dubbed "the age of exploration" more accurately amounted to an era of conquest. Colonial efforts by adventurers following Christopher Columbus brought vast wealth to European nations. In the nineteenth century, most of the world was under the control of European governments. Spain and Portugal colonized nearly all of Latin America from the sixteenth until the mid-nineteenth centuries. By the beginning of the twentieth century, Great Britain boasted, "The sun never sets on the British Empire." The United States, itself originally thirteen small British colonies on the eastern seaboard, pushed across the continent, purchased Alaska, gained control of Haiti, Puerto Rico, and part of Cuba as well as Guam, the Philippines, and the Hawaiian Islands.

On the African continent, Europeans in collaboration with Africans initiated a brutal form of human exploitation—the slave trade, which persisted from about 1500 until 1850. But soon after worldwide

Q: "The struggle between the capitalist class and the proletariat could then be reinterpreted as a struggle between colonizers and colonized, with the working classes of the imperialist countries being co-opted by their respective bourgeoisies. Thus the immiseration thesis, so central to the Marxian drama of revolutionary redemption, is saved by being globalized. And . . . the new theory of imperialism helped to assuage the disappointment that, again contrary to Marx's prediction, the working classes of Western Europe and North America became not more, but less revolutionary . . ." Peter Berger (1986:121)

NOTE: The United States was a British colony from 1607 to 1776, more than one-third of our history.

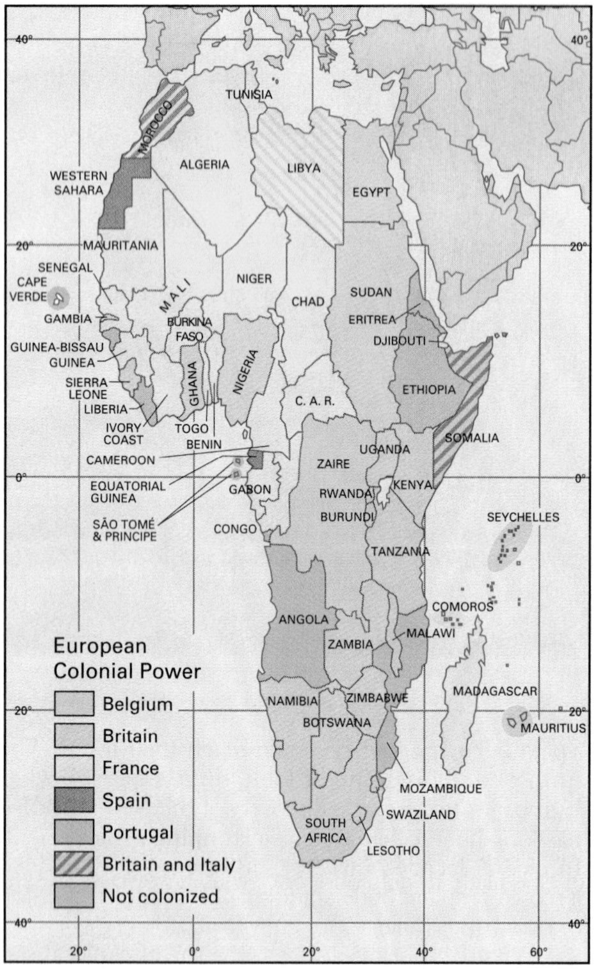

FIGURE 11–3 Africa's Colonial History

suppression of slavery, Europeans rapidly spread their influence across Africa, as Figure 11–3 shows, and held these nations for more than a century until most of Africa achieved independence in the early 1960s.

Overt colonialism has largely disappeared from the world. However, according to dependency theory, *political* liberation has not translated into *economic* autonomy. Far from it, since poor societies maintain economic relationships with rich nations that reproduce the colonial pattern. This neocolonialism is fueled by a capitalist world economy.

Wallerstein's Capitalist World Economy

Immanuel Wallerstein (1974, 1979, 1983, 1984) explains the origins of contemporary global inequality using a model of the "capitalist world economy."[5] Wallerstein's term *world economy* suggests that the productivity of all nations depends on the operation of a global economic network. He traces the roots of this global system to the economic expansion that began five hundred years ago as rich nations turned their eyes to the wealth of the rest of the world. Centered in the most-developed countries, then, the dominant character of the world economy is capitalist.

Wallerstein terms rich nations the *core* of the world economy. Colonialism enriched this core by funneling raw materials from around the globe to Western Europe. A longer-term benefit of this wealth was helping to ignite the Industrial Revolution. Formal colonialism may have ended, but multinational corporations operate profitably around the globe, still drawing wealth to North America, Western Europe, and Japan.

Low-income countries represent the *periphery* of the world economy. Originally drawn into this system by colonial exploitation, poor nations continue to support rich ones by providing inexpensive labor and vast markets for industrial products. A remaining category of countries are those on the *semiperiphery* of the world economy, including middle-income countries like Portugal and the Republic of Korea that have closer ties to the global economic core.

According to Wallerstein, the world economy benefits rich societies (by generating profits) and harms the rest of the world (by perpetuating poverty). The world economy thus imposes a state of dependency upon poor nations, which remain under the control of rich ones. This dependency involves the following three factors:

1. **Narrow, export-oriented economies.** Unlike the diversified economies of core nations, production in poor countries centers on a few raw materials or agricultural products that colonial powers forced laborers to extract or farmers to grow for export. Coffee and fruits from Latin American nations, oil from Nigeria, hardwoods from the Philippines, and palm oil from Malaysia are some of the products central to the economies of these poor societies.

   Multinational corporations maintain this pattern today by purchasing raw materials cheaply in poor societies and transporting them to core societies where factories process them for profitable

---

[5]While based on Wallerstein's ideas, this section also is informed by the work of Frank (1980, 1981), Delacroix & Ragin (1981), and Bergesen (1983).

Q: "The hopes for development, at that time so lively, today appear very far from being realized." Pope John Paul II, *The Social Concerns of the Church*

GLOBAL: Inflation is a stunning problem in many poor societies, making the problem of simply maintaining one's standard of living difficult. In Argentina,.for example, annual inflation has at times soared to 80,000 percent.

NOTE: Some analysts distinguish between multinational and global corporations. MNCs consume only raw material and labor from a poor nation. Global corporations also locate research and development in the local country, which stimulates greater economic development. One global corporation is Hewlett Packard, which has a major research and development center in Guadalajara, Mexico.

sale. Corporations thus discourage production of food or goods needed by local people in poor societies. These corporations also own a great deal of land and have turned traditional farmers into low-paid farm laborers. Overall, then, rich nations effectively prevent poor societies from developing industries of their own.

2. **Lack of industrial capacity.** Without an industrial base, poor societies face a double bind. Not only do they count on rich nations to buy their inexpensive raw materials but they also depend on rich nations to sell them whatever expensive manufactured goods they can afford.

In a classic example of this double dependency, British colonialists allowed the people of India to raise cotton, shipping Indian cotton to the textile mills of Birmingham and Manchester back in England. There, English factories wove it into cloth, and traders shipped the finished goods back for profitable sale in India.

Dependency theorists also blast the Green Revolution, widely praised by modernization theorists. To promote agricultural productivity, poor countries end up buying expensive fertilizers, pesticides, and mechanical equipment from core nations. Typically, rich countries profit more from "high-tech" farming than poor societies do.

3. **Foreign debt.** Such unequal trade patterns have plunged poor countries into deeper and deeper debt to industrialized societies. Collectively, the poor nations of the world owe rich countries more than $1 trillion, including hundreds of billions of dollars owed to the United States (The World Bank, 1993). This staggering debt is a financial burden few poor societies can bear. Excessive debt, which drains the resources of any society, can destabilize a poor country's economy, making matters worse for nations already reeling from high unemployment and rampant inflation (Walton & Ragin, 1990).

Moreover, the debt crisis requires continuous transfers of wealth from poor to rich societies—roughly $50 billion annually (United Nations Development Programme, 1993)—further impoverishing peripheral societies and increasing their dependency on rich nations. This debt crisis, say the dependency theorists, plays into the vicious circle that makes rich nations richer and poor nations poorer.

Seeing no way out of the "debt trap," some low-income countries have simply stopped making payments. Cuba, for example, refused to make further payments on its $7 billion foreign debt a decade ago. Because failure to repay loans threatens their economic growth, the United States and other rich nations strongly oppose such actions and have proposed various programs to refinance these debts.

The Role of Rich Nations

Nowhere is the difference between modernization theory and dependency theory sharper than in the role they assign to rich nations. Modernization theory highlights the *production of wealth* in determining whether a nation is rich or poor. From this point of view, rich societies create new wealth through technological innovation. Their success in this regard does not impoverish other nations. According to modernization theory, as poor nations modernize by adopting more productive technology and embracing pro-growth attitudes, they will prosper.

By contrast, dependency theory casts global inequality in terms of the *distribution of wealth*. This approach contends that rich societies have unjustly seized the wealth of the world for their own purposes. That is, the *over*development of some of the globe is directly tied to the *under*development of the rest of it.

Dependency theorists dismiss the idea that any program of population control, agricultural and industrial technology, or foreign aid proposed by rich societies is likely to help poor countries. They contend, to the contrary, that rich nations act simply in pursuit of profit. Selling technology makes money, and foreign aid typically goes to ruling elites (rather than the poor majority) who will maintain a favorable "business climate" for multinational corporations (Lappé, Collins, & Kinley, 1981).

Hunger activists Frances Moore Lappé and Joseph Collins (1986) claim that the capitalist culture of the United States encourages people to think of absolute poverty as somehow inevitable. Following this line of reasoning, poverty results from "natural" processes including having too many children and from disasters such as droughts. But they challenge this kind of thinking, pointing out that the world produces enough grain so every man, woman, and child could consume 3,600 calories a day, sufficient to make everyone on the planet overweight! Even most of the poorest societies grow enough to feed their people. The problem, therefore, is not production but poverty: too many people cannot afford to buy available food. This approach explains why, at the same time that millions in India suffer from malnutrition, this Asian

NOTE: A U.S. Presidential Commission, *Overcoming World Hunger, the Challenge Ahead*, sketched the following dimensions of inequality between rich and poor societies: per capita GNP, $5500 vs. $500; deaths per 1000 live births, 20 vs. 120; daily grams of protein per person, 97 vs. 54; number of people per doctor, 680 vs. 3500.

Q: "Current leftist journals are full of tortured attempts to interpret the developments of the last few years in Europe and elsewhere, most of them attempts to deny the obvious. I have every expectation that sociologists will be whole-hearted participants in this enterprise, bravely led by the old cohorts of dependency theory." Peter Berger (1992)

After decades of war and communist rule, Vietnam is now attracting foreign investment, evident in this commercial display outside a Hanoi government building. Whether this inflow of capital will raise living standards, as modernization theory contends, or block development, as dependency theory maintains, remains to be seen.

nation *exports* beef, wheat, and rice. Similarly, millions of children go hungry in Africa, a vast continent whose agricultural abundance also makes it a net food exporter.

According to Lappé and Collins, the contradiction of poverty amid plenty stems from the policy of producing food for profits, not people. That is, corporations in rich nations collaborate with elites in poor countries to grow profitable crops for export. Thus, coffee is a main crop in much of Latin America, at the expense of crops like corn and beans, which are the staples for local consumption. Governments of poor societies often support the practice of growing for export rather than local consumption because

food profits help to repay massive foreign debt. The problem is complex, but its core, according to Lappé and Collins, is the global capitalist economic system.

Critical evaluation. The central contribution of dependency theory—that no society develops (or fails to develop) in isolation—points up how the system of global inequality shapes the destiny of all nations. Citing Latin America and other poor regions of the world, dependency theorists claim that development simply cannot proceed under the constraints presently imposed by rich countries. Addressing global poverty, they conclude, demands more than change within poor societies. Rather, these theorists call for radical reform of the entire world economy so that it operates in the interests of the majority of people.

Critics of the dependency approach identify some important weaknesses in the theory. First, they charge, dependency theory wrongly contends that the wealth of the most-developed nations resulted from stealing resources from poor societies. Farmers, small business owners, and industrialists can and do create new wealth through their imagination and drive. Put another way, wealth is not a zero-sum resource by which some gain only at the expense of others; the entire world's wealth expanded fivefold since 1950, largely due to technological advances and other innovations.

Second, critics reason, if dependency theory were correct in condemning rich nations for creating global poverty, then nations with the strongest ties to rich societies would be among the poorest. However, the least developed countries of the world (such as Ethiopia) have had relatively little contact with rich countries. Similarly, critics continue, a long history of trade with rich countries has dramatically improved the economies of nations including Singapore (a former British colony), South Korea, Japan, and Hong Kong (since 1842 a British colony that reverts to the People's Republic of China in 1997). More generally speaking, an increasing body of evidence indicates that foreign investment by rich nations fosters economic growth, as modernization theory claims, not economic decline, as dependency theorists assert (Vogel, 1991; Firebaugh, 1992).

Third, critics contend that dependency theory simplistically points the finger at a single factor—world capitalism—as the sole cause of global inequality (Worsley, 1990). By directing attention only to forces *outside* of poor societies, dependency theory casts poor societies as innocent victims, ignoring factors *inside* these countries that contribute to their economic plight. Sociologists have long recognized the vital role of culture in

NOTE: An example of what might be termed money wasting by dictators: in 1973, Alfredo Stroessner (Paraguay) and Juan Domingo Peron (Argentina) agreed to build a hydroelectric dam on the Parana River. To date, $4 billion has been spent; at least $3 billion more is needed to finish the job. According to *The Economist* (August 10–16, 1991:34), there is doubt that the dam is now even needed.
GLOBAL: *The Economist* (September 25, 1993:49) claims that the

GNP of the entire sub-Saharan African continent is less than that of Holland. This poor region of the world is the only sector of the world where absolute poverty is currently increasing.
GLOBAL: The World Bank claims that, during the 1990s, the population of poor countries will increase by about 2% annually versus 0.5% for rich nations; economic growth in poor countries, they predict, will be negative, against positive growth for the rich societies.

shaping human behavior. Cultural patterns vary greatly around the world; some societies embrace change readily while others staunchly resist economic development. As we noted earlier, for example, Iran's Islamic fundamentalism has deliberately discouraged economic ties with other countries. Capitalist societies, then, hardly need accept the blame for Iran's economic stagnation.

Nor can rich societies be saddled with responsibility for the reckless behavior of some foreign leaders. Members of poor societies have had to pick up the costs of far-reaching corruption and self-serving military campaigns that have marked the regimes of Ferdinand Marcos in the Philippines, François Duvalier in Haiti, Manuel Noriega in Panama, Mobutu Sese Seko in Zaire, and Saddam Hussein in Iraq. Governments may even use food supplies as a weapon in internal political struggles as occurred in Ethiopia, Sudan, and Somalia in Africa. Other regimes throughout Latin America, Africa, and Asia have failed to support programs to improve the status of women and control population growth.

Fourth, critics chide dependency theorists for downplaying the economic dependency fostered by the former Soviet Union. The Soviet army seized control of most of Eastern Europe during World War II and subsequently dominated its nations politically and economically. Critics of dependency theory see the uprisings between 1989 and 1991 against Soviet-installed leaders as well as the Soviet government itself, as clear evidence that the Soviet Union imposed a colonial system upon hundreds of millions of people. The Soviets forced Eastern Europeans to buy Soviet-manufactured goods and Soviet-produced energy and prevented them from trading more profitably on the world market. The Soviets did not broadly colonize other regions of the world but, until recently, supported regimes in Cuba and Angola that became highly dependent on this foreign aid.

A fifth criticism of dependency theory is that its adherents have remained vague about solutions to global poverty. Most dependency theorists suggest that poor societies end economic ties to rich countries, and some call for nationalizing foreign-owned industries. Generally, dependency theory implies that the path to ending global poverty begins with the overthrow of international capitalism. The bottom line, say the critics, is that dependency theory is a thinly disguised advocacy of some sort of world socialism. In light of the failure of government-run socialist societies to meet the needs of their own people, critics ask, should we really expect such a system to lift the entire world toward prosperity?

GLOBAL INEQUALITY: LOOKING AHEAD

People in the United States, sociologists included, are discovering ways in which global trends affect our lives at home. The U.S. economy is playing a pivotal role in the world as U.S. corporations invest abroad and business interests around the world gain control of properties here.

As Chapter 10 ("Social Class in the United States") explained, this process is reshaping inequality in this country. Profitable investments, many of them in poor nations, and lucrative sales of U.S. companies to foreign interests have brought greater affluence to those who already have substantial wealth. At the same time, increasing industrial production abroad has cut factory jobs in this country, exerting downward pressure on wages. The net result: gradual economic polarization in the United States.

As this chapter has noted, however, social inequality is far more striking in global context. The concentration of wealth among the most-developed countries, coupled with the grinding poverty typical of the least-developed countries, may well constitute the most important dilemma facing humanity in the twenty-first century. To some analysts, rich nations hold the keys to ending world hunger; to others, they are the cause of this tragic problem.

Faced with two radically different approaches to understanding global inequality, we might well wonder which one is "right." As with many controversies in sociology, each view has some merit as well as its own limitations. Table 11–2 summarizes important arguments made by advocates of each approach.

In searching for truth, we must consider empirical evidence. In some regions of the world, such as the "Pacific Rim" of eastern Asia, the market forces endorsed by modernization theory are raising living standards rapidly and substantially. Many Latin American nations, too, have recorded strong economic growth in recent years. At the same time, other poor societies, especially in Africa, are experiencing economic turmoil that frustrates hopes for market-based development.

The poor societies that have surged ahead economically have two factors in common. First, they are relatively small. Combined, the Asian nations of South Korea, Taiwan, Hong Kong, Singapore, and Japan equal only about one-fifth of the land area and population of India. The economic problems smaller countries face are more manageable; consequently, small

TABLE 11–2 Modernization Theory and Dependency Theory: A Summary

	Modernization Theory	Dependency Theory
Historical pattern	The entire world was poor just two centuries ago; the Industrial Revolution brought affluence to high-income countries; as industrialization gradually transforms poor societies, all societies are likely to become more equal and alike.	Global parity was disrupted by colonialism, which made some countries rich while simultaneously making other countries poor; barring change in the world capitalist system, rich nations will grow richer and poor nations will become poorer.
Primary causes of global poverty	Characteristics of poor societies cause their poverty, including lack of industrial technology, traditional cultural patterns that discourage innovation, and rapid population growth.	Global economic relations—historical colonialism and the operation of multinational corporations—have enriched high-income countries while placing low-income countries in a state of economic dependency.
Role of rich nations	Rich countries can and do assist poor nations through programs of population control, technology transfers that increase food production and stimulate industrial development, and investment capital in the form of foreign aid.	Rich countries have concentrated global resources, conferring advantages on themselves while producing massive foreign debt in low-income countries; rich nations represent a barrier to the economic development of poor nations.

societies more effectively administer programs of development. Second, these "best case" societies have cultural traits in common, especially traditions emphasizing individual achievement and economic success. In other areas of the world, where powerful group forces inhibit change and individualism, even smaller nations have failed to turn economic opportunities to their advantage.

The picture now emerging calls into question arguments put forward by both modernization and dependency theories. Theorists for both camps, for instance, are revising their views of the major "paths to development." On the one hand, few societies seeking economic growth now favor a market economy completely free of government control. This view challenges orthodox modernization theory, which endorses a free-market approach to development. On the other hand, recent upheavals in the former Soviet Union and Eastern Europe demonstrate that a global reevaluation of socialism is currently under way. These events, following decades of poor economic performance and political repression, make many poor societies reluctant to consider a government-mandated path to development. Because dependency theory has historically supported socialist economic systems, changes in world socialism will surely generate new thinking here as well.

In the immediate future, no plan for development is likely to effectively reduce the overwhelming problems of world hunger and rapid population growth. Moreover, as Chapter 22 ("The Natural Environment") explains, poverty is forcing members of poor societies to exploit the earth's resources in a way that cannot be sustained. A fair appraisal of the current world situation is, therefore, ominous.

Looking to the next century, however, there are reasons for hope. The approaches described in this chapter identify the two keys to combating global inequality. One factor, revealed by modernization theory, is that world hunger is partly a *problem of technology*. A higher standard of living for a surging world population depends on raising agricultural and industrial productivity. The second factor, derived from dependency theory, is that global inequality is also a *political issue*. Even with higher productivity, the human community must address crucial questions concerning how resources are distributed—both within societies and around the globe.

Debate over global inequality is sure to continue, not just because the paths to development remain contested but because development itself presents new problems. Imagine, for example, the added strain on the earth's natural environment if almost 1 billion people in India were to become "middle class," with automobiles gulping gasoline and spewing hydrocarbons into the atmosphere.

But, despite the challenges, the world is coming to recognize that the security of everyone depends on reducing the destabilizing extremes of contemporary global poverty. We can only hope that, with the end of the cold war, energy and resources will be redirected to the needs of humanity, many of whom are trapped in a desperate struggle for survival.

SUMMARY

1. Adopting a global perspective, we can discern a system of social stratification that involves all of humanity. About 15 percent of the world's people live in the most-developed countries, which are industrialized, rich nations such as the United States. Together, these advantaged countries receive 55 percent of the earth's total income. Another one-third of humanity live in less-developed countries with limited industrialization; they receive about 37 percent of all income. Half of the world's population lives in the least-developed countries that have yet to industrialize; they earn only 8 percent of global income.

2. In addition to relative poverty, poor societies contend with widespread, absolute poverty. The typical member of a low-income society struggles to survive on a fraction of the ample income enjoyed by the average member of our society.

3. Especially pronounced in the least-developed countries of the world, poverty places the lives of some 800 million people at risk. About 15 million people, many of them children, die of starvation every year.

4. Women are more likely than men to be poor nearly everywhere in the world. Gender bias against women is much greater in poor, agrarian societies than it is in industrial societies such as the United States.

5. The poverty found in much of the world is a complex problem reflecting limited industrial technology, rapid population growth, traditional cultural patterns, internal social stratification including male domination, and global power relationships that inhibit development.

6. Modernization theory maintains that development hinges on acquiring advanced productive technology. This approach views traditional cultural patterns as the key barrier to modernization.

7. Modernization theorist W. W. Rostow identifies four stages of development: traditional, take-off, drive to technological maturity, and high mass consumption.

8. Arguing that rich societies have the keys to creating wealth, modernization theory cites four ways rich nations can assist poor nations: by bolstering population control strategies, providing crop-enhancing technologies, encouraging industrial development, and providing investment capital and other foreign aid.

9. Critics of modernization theory maintain that this approach has produced limited economic development in the world, while ethnocentrically assuming that poor societies can follow the path to development taken by rich nations centuries ago.

10. Dependency theory claims global wealth and poverty are directly linked to the historical operation of the capitalist world economy.

11. The dependency of poor countries on rich ones is rooted in colonialism. Even though most poor countries have won political independence, dependency theorists argue, neocolonialism persists as a form of exploitation carried out by multinational corporations.

12. Immanuel Wallerstein views the high-income countries as the advantaged "core" of the capitalist world economy; poor societies form the global "periphery."

13. Three key factors—export-oriented economies, a lack of industrial capacity, and foreign debt—perpetuate poor countries' dependency on rich nations.

14. Critics of dependency theory argue that this approach overlooks the success of many nations in creating new wealth. Total global wealth, they point out, has increased fivefold since 1950. Furthermore, contrary to the implications of dependency theory, the world's poorest societies are not those with the strongest ties to rich countries.

15. Both modernization and dependency approaches offer useful insights into the development of global inequality. Some evidence supports each view. Less controversial is the urgent need to address the various problems caused by worldwide poverty.

KEY CONCEPTS

colonialism the process by which some nations enrich themselves through political and economic control of other countries

dependency theory a model of economic and social development that explains global inequality in terms of the historical exploitation of poor societies by rich societies

modernization theory a model of economic and social development that explains global inequality in terms of differing levels of technological development among societies

multinational corporation a large corporation that operates in many different countries

neocolonialism a new form of global power relationships that involves not direct political control but economic exploitation by multinational corporations

CRITICAL-THINKING QUESTIONS

1. In what basic sense is poverty in poor societies of the world a far more serious problem than poverty here in the United States?

2. What accounts for the more disadvantaged social standing of women in low-income countries relative to the United States?

3. State the basic tenets of modernization theory. What are several criticisms of this approach?

4. What key arguments constitute dependency theory? Identify several weaknesses of this model.

SUGGESTED READINGS

Classic Sources

W.W. Rostow. *The Stages of Economic Growth: A Non-Communist Manifesto.* Cambridge, U.K.: Cambridge University Press, 1960.
> Although this book draws on the thinking of several classic sociologists (including Emile Durkheim and Max Weber), it represents the first systematic statement of modernization theory.

Frantz Fanon. *The Wretched of the Earth.* New York: Grove Press, 1963.
> This classic analysis of global inequality, inspired by the thinking of Karl Marx, sets a radical agenda for change.

Contemporary Sources

United Nations Development Programme. *Human Development Report, 1993.* New York: Oxford University Press, 1993.

The World Bank. *World Development Report 1993: Investing in Health.* New York: Oxford University Press, 1993.
> These two annual publications provide a wide range of data regarding the comparative economic development of the world's nations.

Donald M. Snow. *Distant Thunder: Third-World Conflict and the New International Order.* New York: St. Martin's Press, 1992.
> In this analysis of global inequality and political developments, the author claims that poor societies are the major source of international instability and the primary danger to world peace.

Robert B. Reich. *The Work of Nations: Preparing Ourselves for 21st-Century Capitalism.* New York: Knopf, 1991.
> Appointed secretary of labor by President Bill Clinton, Robert Reich offers his insights about how global developments are affecting social stratification in the United States.

P. T. Bauer. *Equality, the Third World and Economic Delusion.* Cambridge, Mass.: Harvard University Press, 1981.
> This book offers a good overview of modernization theory and its policy implications.

Thomas Richard Shannon. *An Introduction to the World-System Perspective.* Boulder, Colo.: Westview Press, 1989.
> Here is a useful general reference that presents the essential arguments of dependency theory and describes the operation of the global economic system.

Global Sources

Nancy Scheper-Hughes. *Death Without Weeping: The Violence of Everyday Life in Brazil*. Berkeley: University of California Press, 1992.

Offering a moving portrait of suffering in the shantytowns of Brazil, this researcher identifies strongly with her subjects and makes an outspoken call for change.

Frances Moore Lappé and Joseph Collins. *World Hunger: Twelve Myths*. New York: Grove Press/Food First Books, 1986.

This book by two long-time hunger activists explains how most people in rich societies fail to grasp either the extent or the true causes of global suffering.

Peter Berger. *The Capitalist Revolution: Fifty Propositions about Prosperity, Equality, and Liberty*. New York: Basic Books, 1986.

A well-known contemporary sociologist assesses the consequences of the expansion of capitalism in the world. Berger argues that available evidence supports modernization theory and contradicts dependency theory.

Stewart R. Clegg and Gordon Redding, eds., assisted by Monica Cartner. *Capitalism in Contrasting Cultures*. Hawthorne, N.Y.: Aldine de Gruyter, 1990.

This collection of essays provides comparative analysis of capitalist economies, especially in the United States and East Asia.

Frederick C. Turner, ed. *Social Mobility and Political Attitudes: Comparative Perspectives*. New Brunswick, N.J.: Transaction, 1992.

Although making few direct comparisons, this collection of essays examines social hierarchy and mobility in a number of societies including Argentina, Norway, Japan, Nigeria, and India.

Ben Shahn, 1898–1969, *Einstein Among Other Immigrants.*

DATA FILE: An outline of this chapter, as well as lecture and discussion topics, is found in the *Data File*.

NOTE: The historical conflict in the former Yugoslavia has given us the word "Balkanization," meaning to divide into small, quarrelsome states.

Q: "After all, there is but one race—humanity." George Mead

Q: "How long does our family have to be here before we are called 'Americans' rather than 'Irish-Americans'?" Joseph Patrick Kennedy (father of President John Kennedy)

Q: "The problem of the twentieth century is the problem of the color-line." W. E. B. Du Bois

Race and Ethnicity

With his village in flames, twenty-four-year-old Hasan Mahmudagic fled for his life. The day had begun with rumors flying that Serbian soldiers were nearby; soon after, villagers were alarmed to discover that the telephone lines were dead. That was enough for most people in the Bosnian village to pack up what they could carry and leave. When the soldiers arrived, they marched quickly from door to door, warning those who dared to remain to vacate their homes immediately. Soldiers then splashed oil in doorways, on roofs, and down narrow alleyways, igniting the town and the worst fears of its people.

Mahmudagic, a Muslim, made his way to a nearby Muslim city hoping to find a safe haven. But, within days, Serbian soldiers confronted him once again, this time transporting him to a nearby detention camp. There he discovered almost eight thousand men of his own

kind. Discipline was harsh, and his captors demanded not only strict obedience but that he, like the other prisoners, sign away the right to his land and any remaining property. The bottom line was a simple choice: Promise to leave Bosnia forever, or never leave this camp alive. After more than a month, all the camp's inmates complied. Then they boarded trucks that carried them across the Croatian border, where they became refugees in a new country (Smolowe, 1992).

Since the latest outbreak of violent strife in the former Yugoslavia in 1991, the world has witnessed the bitter process of ethnic cleansing by which one category of people tries to rid the region of others who differ in some significant way. Although the term is new, such conflict is merely the latest outbreak in ongoing blood feuds that have boiled into violence again and again in the Balkans over the centuries.

Nor is ethnic or racial conflict limited to this one shuddering nation as it disintegrates. Across Eastern Europe, as the heavy hand of government control was lifted in the former Soviet empire, Ukrainians, Moldavians, Azerbaijanis, and a host of other ethnic peoples have struggled to recover their cultural identity after decades of subjugation. In the Middle East, efforts to end decades of conflict between Arabs and Jews continue. In South Africa, democratic government struggles to be born after centuries of racial separation. In India, Tibet, Malaysia, and other Asian nations, differences of color and culture frequently drive people into violent confrontation. In the United States, racial tensions ignited a civil war a century ago and all but destroyed the cultures of Native Americans. Today, the magnitude of strife is less, but race continues to spark conflict in countless communities.

In short, everywhere in the world human beings are set apart—and sometimes come together viciously—based on their culture or color. Surely one of the greatest ironies of the human condition is that those traits that are the roots of our greatest pride are also those that most often prompt us to war, and to degrade ourselves with hatred and violence.

This chapter examines the meaning of race and ethnicity, explains how these social constructs have shaped our history, and suggests why they continue to play such a central part—for better or worse—in the world today.

THE SOCIAL SIGNIFICANCE OF RACE AND ETHNICITY

People in the United States and elsewhere in the world frequently use the terms "race" and "ethnicity" imprecisely and interchangeably. For this reason, we begin with important definitions.

Race

A **race** is *a category composed of men and women who share biologically transmitted traits that members of a* society deem socially significant. People may classify each other into races based on physical characteristics such as skin color, hair texture, facial features, and body shape.

Racial traits have nothing to do with being human; all people on earth are members of a single biological species. The biological variations people describe as "racial characteristics" are the result of living for thousands of generations in different geographical regions of the world (Molnar, 1983). In regions of intense heat, for example, humans developed darker skin (from the natural pigment, melanin) that offers protection from the sun; in regions with moderate climates, people have lighter skin.

People the world over display a bewildering array of racial traits. This variety is the product of migration and intermarriage over the course of human history, so that many genetic characteristics once common to a single place are now spread throughout the world. The most striking racial variation is evident in regions—such as the Middle East (that is, western Asia)—that have long served as "crossroads" of human migration. Greater racial uniformity, by contrast, characterizes more isolated people such as the island-dwelling Japanese. But no society lacks genetic mixture, and increasing contact among the world's people will ensure that racial blending will accelerate in the future.

Nineteenth-century biologists responded to the world's racial diversity by developing a three-part scheme of racial classifications. They labeled people with relatively light skin and fine hair as *Caucasian*; they applied the name *Negroid* to those with darker skin and coarser, curlier hair; they termed *Mongoloid* people with yellow or brown skin and distinctive folds on the eyelids.

Sociologists consider such categories misleading, at best, since we now know that no society is composed of biologically pure individuals. In fact, the world traveler notices gradual and subtle racial variations from region to region around the globe. The people we might call "Caucasian" (or, more commonly, "white people") actually display skin color that ranges from very light (typical in Scandinavia) to very dark (widespread in southern India). We also find the same variation among so-called Negroids (commonly, "black people") and "Mongoloids" (that is, "Asians"). In fact, many "white people" of southern India actually have darker skin than many "black people," including the blond Negroid aborigines of Australia.

Although people in the United States readily distinguish "black" and "white" people, research confirms

RESOURCE: The role of race in the development of sociology is discussed by James R. Hayes, "Sociology and Racism: An Analysis of the First Era of American Sociology," *Phylon* 37, 4 (1973:330–41) and also Larry Reynolds, "Retrospective on 'Race': The Career of a Concept," *Sociological Focus* 25, 1 (1992:1–14).
NOTE: The faces shown below are from Taiwan, Ireland, Botswana, India, Peru, and Egypt.

DIVERSITY: Worth stressing is that race and ethnicity are categories that overlap with class and gender.
DIVERSITY: As Chapter 18 ("Religion") explores in detail, about 64% of U.S. adults identify themselves as Protestants, 22% as Catholics, 2% as Jews, and 9% claim no affiliation or preference. (GSS 1993, N = 1,598; *Codebook*, 1993:148)
NOTE: Is "American" an ethnic identity?

The range of biological variation in human beings is far greater than any system of racial classification allows. This fact is made obvious by trying to place all of the people pictured here into simple racial categories.

that our population is genetically mixed. Over many generations, the biological traits of Negroid Africans, Caucasian Europeans, and Mongoloid Native Americans (whose ancestors were Asian) spread widely throughout the Americas. Many "black" people, therefore, have a significant proportion of Caucasian genes, and many "white" people have some Negroid genes. In short, whatever people may think, race is no black-and-white issue.

Despite the reality of biological mixing, however, people in the United States and around the world racially classify each other and rank these categories in systems of social inequality. In some cases, they defend racial hierarchy with assertions that physical traits are signs of innate intelligence and other mental abilities, although no sound scientific research supports such beliefs. But, because so much is at stake, it is no wonder that societies strive to make racial labeling much more clear than facts permit. Earlier in this century, for example, many southern states legally defined as "colored" anyone who had as little as one thirty-second African ancestry (that is, one African-American great-great-great grandparent). Today, with

less of a caste distinction in the United States, the law enables parents to declare the race of a child (if they wish to do so at all).

Ethnicity

Ethnicity is *a shared cultural heritage*. Members of an *ethnic category* may have common ancestors, language, and religion that, together, confer a distinctive social identity. The forebears of Polish, Latino, and Chinese Americans, for example, lived in particular areas of the world. Millions of people in the United States speak Spanish, Italian, German, French, or other languages in their homes. The United States and Canada are predominantly Protestant societies, but most Americans and Canadians of Spanish, Italian, and Polish ancestry are Roman Catholic, while others of Greek, Ukrainian, and Russian ancestry are members of the Eastern Orthodox church. More than 6 million Jewish Americans (with ancestral ties to various nations) share a distinctive religious history. Similarly, several million women and men in the United States have a Muslim heritage.

Race and ethnicity, then, are quite different, since one is biological and the other is cultural. But the two sometimes go hand in hand. Japanese Americans, for example, have distinctive physical traits and—for those who maintain a traditional way of life—cultural attributes as well. But ethnic distinctiveness should not be viewed as racial. For example, Jews are sometimes described as a race although they are distinctive only in their religious beliefs as well as their history of persecution (Goldsby, 1977).

Finally, ethnicity involves even more variability and mixture than race does, for people can intentionally modify their ethnicity by adopting a different way of life. Polish immigrants to the United States who discard their cultural background over time simply cease to be so "Polish" and may gain other ethnic traits as they make friends, work, and marry within our multicultural society.

Minorities

A racial or ethnic **minority**[1] is *a category of people, distinguished by physical or cultural traits, who are socially disadvantaged*. Distinct from the dominant "majority," in other words, minorities are set apart and subordinated. The breadth of the term "minority" has expanded in recent years beyond people with particular racial and ethnic traits to include people with physical disabilities, and, as Chapter 13 ("Sex and Gender") explains, some analysts include all women as well.

Table 12–1 presents the broad sweep of racial and ethnic minorities in the United States as recorded by the 1990 census. White people of non-Hispanic background continue to predominate numerically in the United States—about 80 percent of the national population falls into this broad category. But the absolute numbers and share of population for virtually every minority category in the United States grew rapidly during the 1980s. As the box explains, some researchers even project that the historical *minorities*, taken together, will constitute a *majority* of people in the United States sometime during the coming century.

Minorities have two major characteristics. First, they share a *distinctive identity*. Because race is highly visible (and virtually impossible for a person to change), minority men and women—whether they are people of African descent in the United States or those of Chinese ancestry in South Africa—typically have a keen awareness of their physical distinctiveness. The significance of ethnicity (which people can change) is more variable. Throughout U.S. history, some people (many Reform Jews among them) have downplayed their historic ethnicity, while others (including many Orthodox Jews) have retained their

TABLE 12–1 Racial and Ethnic Categories in the United States, 1990

Racial or Ethnic Classification	Approximate U.S. Population	Percent of Total Population
African descent	29,986,060	12.1%
Hispanic descent	22,354,059	9.0
Mexican	13,495,938	5.4
Puerto Rican	2,727,754	1.1
Cuban	1,043,932	0.4
Other Hispanic	5,086,435	2.1
Native-American descent	1,959,234	0.8
American Indian	1,878,285	0.8
Eskimo	57,152	<
Aleut	23,797	<
Asian or Pacific Islander descent	7,273,662	2.9
Chinese	1,645,472	0.7
Filipino	1,406,770	0.6
Japanese	847,562	0.3
Asian Indian	815,447	0.3
Korean	798,849	0.3
Vietnamese	614,547	0.2
Hawaiian	211,014	<
Samoan	62,964	<
Guamanian	49,345	<
Other Asian or Pacific Islander	821,692	0.3
European descent	200,000,000	80.0
German	57,947,000	23.3
Irish	38,736,000	15.6
English	32,652,000	13.1
Italian	14,665,000	5.9
French	10,321,000	4.1
Polish	9,366,000	3.8
Dutch	6,227,000	2.5
Scotch-Irish	5,618,000	2.3
Scottish	5,314,000	2.1
Swedish	4,681,000	1.9
Norwegian	3,869,000	1.6
Russian	2,953,000	1.2
Welsh	2,034,000	0.8
Danish	1,635,000	0.6
Hungarian	1,582,000	0.6

People of Hispanic descent can be of any race. Many people also identify with more than one ethnic category. Thus figures total more than 100 percent. White people represent 80 percent of the U.S. population.

< Indicates less than 1/10 of one percent.

SOURCE: U.S. Bureau of the Census, 1993.

---

[1]We use the term "minority" rather than the commonly used "minority group" because, as explained in Chapter 7 ("Groups and Organizations"), minorities are categories, not groups.

Q: "'The American Dilemma' . . . is the ever-ranging conflict between, on the one hand, the valuations preserved on the general plane which we shall call the 'American Creed,' where the American thinks, talks, and acts under the influence of high national and Christian precepts, and, on the other hand, the valuations on specific planes of individual and group living, where personal and local interests; economic, social, and sexual jealousies; considerations of community prestige and conformity; group prejudice against particular persons or types of people; and all sorts of miscellaneous wants, impulses, and habits dominate his outlook." Gunnar Myrdal, *An American Dilemma*, 1944

DIVERSITY: About 7% of U.S. adults report being born outside of the United States; 15% claim at least one parent was born abroad. (GSS 1993, N = 1,598; *Codebook*, 1993:80)

SOCIAL DIVERSITY

The Coming Minority-Majority?

During the 1980s, Manhattan, the central borough of New York City, gained a *minority-majority*. This means that people of African, Asian, and Latino descent, together with other racial and ethnic minorities, became a majority of the population. As shown by National Map 12–1 on the next page, the same transformation has also taken place in 186 counties across the United States (some 6 percent of the total). In the final decades of the next century, according to some projections, minorities will be a majority in the United States as a whole.

Interest in the minority-majority was kindled by the results of the 1990 census. Between 1980 and 1990, the white, non-Hispanic population increased a modest 6 percent. The number of Asians or Pacific Islanders, however, more than doubled, soaring 108 percent.

The Hispanic population increased by more than half (53 percent), and the number of Native Americans, Eskimos, or Aleuts jumped by 37 percent. African Americans increased their numbers by 13 percent—twice the white rate. This population growth was highly concentrated, with more than half the increase taking place in just three states: California, Florida, and Texas.

Not everyone accepts the conclusion that this country will have a minority-majority in the foreseeable future. Stephan Thernstrom (1990) points out that such a projection rests on two questionable assumptions. First, he explains, the U.S. immigration rate would have to remain at its current high level. Government figures suggest, however, that immigration will fall during the 1990s. Beyond that, who

can be sure? Second, he adds, the high birth rates that characterize many immigrant minorities today would have to continue. But, he points out, past immigrants began to behave more like everyone else (their reproductive patterns included) as the years passed. To the extent that these two assumptions do not hold up, Thernstrom concludes, the coming of a minority-majority will be delayed.

But whatever the specific projections, few people doubt that a great change in the racial and ethnic profile of the United States is under way. It seems only a matter of time before people of European ancestry (other than Hispanics) will become minorities as a host of others—those often termed *people of color*—emerge as the majority in the United States.

cultural traditions and lived in distinctive ethnic neighborhoods.

A second characteristic of minorities is *subordination*. Chapter 10 ("Social Class in the United States") explained that U.S. minorities typically have lower incomes and occupational prestige and less schooling. Keep in mind, too, that class, race, and ethnicity, as well as gender, are not mutually exclusive issues but overlapping and reinforcing dimensions of social stratification.

But not all members of any such category are disadvantaged. Some Latinos, for example, are quite wealthy, certain Chinese Americans are celebrated business leaders, and African Americans are included among our nation's leading scholars. But even the most successful individuals rarely transcend their minority standing because it affects how others see

them (Benjamin, 1991). In other words, race or ethnicity often serves as a *master status* (described in Chapter 6, "Social Interaction in Everyday Life") that overshadows personal accomplishments.

The term "minority" suggests that these categories of people usually constitute a small proportion of a society's population. But there are exceptions. For example, black South Africans are a numerical majority in their society, although they are grossly deprived of economic and political power by whites. In the United States, women represent slightly more than half the population but are still struggling to obtain opportunities and privileges enjoyed by men.

As this chapter's opening vignette suggests, social conflict involving minorities and the majority is common around the world. Categories of people— African Americans in the United States, Kurds in Iraq,

Seeing Ourselves

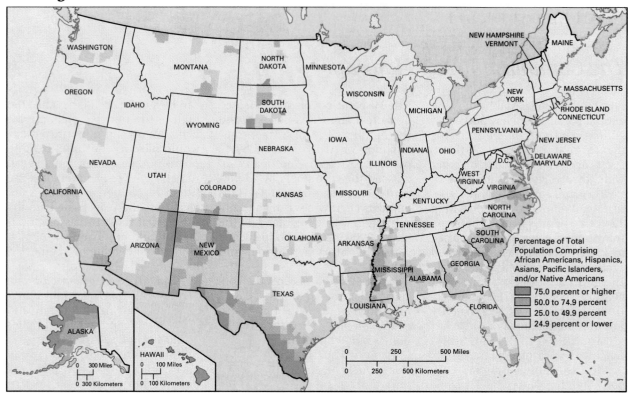

Percentage of Total Population Comprising African Americans, Hispanics, Asians, Pacific Islanders, and/or Native Americans

- 75.0 percent or higher
- 50.0 to 74.9 percent
- 25.0 to 49.9 percent
- 24.9 percent or lower

NATIONAL MAP 12–1 Where the Minority-Majority Already Exists

As recorded by the 1990 census, in 186 counties (out of about 3,000) minorities are already a majority. That is, the total number of African Americans, Asian Americans, Hispanics, and other minorities exceeds 50 percent of the population. The map also identifies some 40 counties in which minorities together exceed 75 percent of the population and more than 200 counties in which minority population surpasses the 25 percent mark. Why do you think most of these counties are in the South and Southwest?

From *Time*, July 12, 1993, p. 15. Copyright © 1993 Time Inc. Reprinted by permisson. Data from the 1990 decennial census.

Christians in Egypt, and Sikhs in India—are grappling to gain the rights guaranteed by law.

PREJUDICE

Prejudice is defined as *an attitude involving a rigid and irrational generalization about an entire category of people*. Prejudice is irrational insofar as people hold inflexible attitudes that are supported by little or no direct evidence. Prejudice can be directed against individuals of a particular social class, sex, sexual orientation, age, political affiliation, race, or ethnicity.

Prejudices are prejudgments that can be positive or negative, and most people hold some of each type. With positive prejudices, we tend to exaggerate the virtues of people like ourselves, while our negative prejudices condemn those who differ from us. Negative prejudice also runs along a continuum, ranging from mild aversion to outright hostility. Because attitudes are rooted in culture, everyone has at least some measure of prejudice.

Stereotypes

A common form of prejudice is the **stereotype** (*stereo* is derived from Greek meaning "hard" or "solid"), *a set*

DATA FILE: A discussion of how various political camps employ the term "racism" appears in the *Data File*.

Q: One of the earliest insights into how culture promotes prejudice was by French philosopher Michel de Montaigne (1580): "We call barbarous anything that is contrary to our own habits."

Q: "The United States was founded on the principle that it was a white man's country." Robert Blauner (1972:31)

DIVERSITY: Through most of human history, people identified and responded to one another in terms of social categories. The individualistic culture of industrial societies, however, has transformed such categorical responses into social problems. From a modern point of view, various "isms" (racism, ageism, sexism, classism, etc.) are all problematic because they deny people their individuality and value as distinct persons.

of prejudices concerning some category of people. Because stereotypes often involve emotions like love and loyalty (generally toward members of ingroups) or hate and fear (toward outgroups), they are hard to change even in the face of contradictory evidence. For example, some people have a stereotypical understanding of the poor as lazy and irresponsible freeloaders who would rather rely on welfare than support themselves (Waxman, 1983; NORC, 1993). As Chapter 10 ("Social Class in the United States") explained, this stereotype distorts reality: More than half of poor people in the United States are children, working adults, and elderly people.

Stereotypes have been devised for virtually every racial and ethnic minority, and such attitudes may become deeply rooted in a society's culture. As the opening to this chapter suggests, conflict among the various peoples in the war-torn Balkans is both cause and effect of long-standing stereotypes. In the United States, half of white people stereotype African Americans as lacking motivation to improve their own lives (NORC, 1993:294). Such attitudes assume social disadvantage is largely a matter of personal deficiency, which, in most cases, it is not. Moreover, stereotypes of this kind ignore the fact that most poor people in the United States are white and that most African Americans work as hard as anyone else and are *not* poor. In this case the bit of truth in the stereotype is that blacks are more likely than whites to be poor (and slightly more likely, if poor, to receive welfare assistance). But by building a rigid attitude out of a few selected facts, stereotypes grossly distort reality.

Racism

A powerful and destructive form of prejudice, **racism** refers to *the belief that one racial category is innately superior or inferior to another.* Racism has pervaded world history. Despite their considerable cultural achievements, the ancient Greeks, the peoples of India, and members of societies in Asia and Africa were quick to view anyone unlike themselves as in some way inferior. Racism has also been widespread in the United States; for centuries the enslavement of people of African descent was supported by notions of their innate inferiority. Today, overt racism in this country has been weakened by a more egalitarian culture that urges us to evaluate people, in Dr. Martin Luther King's words, "by the content of their character, not the color of their skin." Yet racism persists, though in less open and direct forms; research continues to document the injury and humiliation that racism causes to people of color (Feagin, 1991).

In a legal effort to improve the social standing of the lowest castes, India reserves half of all government jobs for members of particular castes deemed disadvantaged. Because the government is the largest employer, higher-caste students fear that this policy will keep them out of the labor force when they graduate from college. So intense are these concerns that recently eleven students killed themselves— five by fire—in public protest over this controversial policy.

Racism and Social Domination

Historically, the assertion that specific categories of people are *innately* inferior has been a powerful justification for subjecting others to *social* inferiority. By the end of the last century, European nations and the United States had forged empires throughout much of the world. Colonial exploitation was often ruthless and brutal, and colonizers justified their deeds by asserting the innate inferiority of subjugated people.

In this century, racism was central to the ideology of Nazi Germany. Nazi racial doctrine proclaimed a so-called Aryan superrace of blond-haired, blue-eyed Caucasians that was allegedly destined to rule the world. Such racist ideology encouraged the systematic slaughter of anyone deemed inferior, including some 6 million European Jews and millions of Poles, gypsies, homosexuals, and people with physical and mental disabilities.

More recently, racial conflict has intensified in Europe with the immigration of people from former colonies and from former Soviet-dominated nations and from Turkey seeking a higher standard of living. In Germany and elsewhere in Western Europe, growing

Q: "Racism is both overt and covert. It takes two, closely related forms: individual whites acting against individual blacks, and acts by the white community against the black community. We call these *individual racism* and *institutional racism*." Stokely Carmichael and Charles V. Hamilton, *Black Power* (Vintage, 1967:4)

DIVERSITY: Some researchers claim that evidence supports the conclusion that there exist genetic differences in brain size and

intelligence among racial categories, although social scientists have generally condemned such research as inherently racist. A review of some of this evidence and a discussion of research that has unacceptable political consequences is found in Joynson (1994).

NOTE: The term "scapegoat" is rooted in the practice of the ancient Hebrews of ritually placing everyone's sins on an animal that was then sacrificed (see Leviticus 16:15–22).

public intolerance of immigrants has fueled a resurgence of Nazi rhetoric and tactics. In the United States the recent decade has witnessed increasing racial tensions in cities and on college campuses. Racism—in thought and deed—remains a serious social problem everywhere.

Individual versus Institutional Racism

Stokely Carmichael and Charles Hamilton (1967) point out that we typically think of racism as the ideas or actions of specific individuals who are hateful or violent toward people they deem inferior. Such *individual racism* is commonplace, and such behavior—actions by white people, for example, to prevent a black family from moving into their neighborhood—are typically denounced by the public at large.

But, claim Carmichael and Hamilton, even greater harm results from *institutional racism*, which refers to racism that guides the operation of schools, hospitals, the police force, and the workplace. For example, the beating of Rodney King by police officers in Los Angeles (described at the beginning of Chapter 8, "Deviance"), was more than an isolated case of brutality to the extent that it symbolizes systematic police violence directed at that city's black community. According to Carmichael and Hamilton, the public is slow to condemn or even to recognize institutional racism, since it often involves "established and respected" public figures and officials, even though such powerful people sometimes seriously damage public well-being.

Theories of Prejudice

If prejudice does not represent a rational assessment of facts, what are its origins? Social scientists have provided various answers to this vexing question, citing the importance of frustration, personality, culture, and social conflict.

Scapegoat Theory of Prejudice

Scapegoat theory holds that prejudice springs from frustration. Such attitudes, therefore, are common among people who are themselves disadvantaged (Dollard, 1939). A white woman earning low wages in a textile factory, for example, might understandably be unhappy with her situation. But can she readily direct her hostility at the powerful people who operate the factory? Certainly not; she is more likely to find fault for her plight in powerless minority co-workers. Prejudice of this kind may not go far toward improving

the woman's situation in the factory, but it serves as a relatively safe way to vent anger, and it may give her the comforting feeling that at least she is superior to someone.

A **scapegoat**, then, is *a person or category of people, typically with little power, whom people unfairly blame for their own troubles*. Because they often are "safe targets," minorities are easily used as scapegoats. The Nazis painted the Jewish minority as responsible for all of Germany's ills fifty years ago. A less extreme example is the practice of some Germans (and other Europeans) today of attributing their nation's troubles to the presence of Turkish, Pakistani, or other immigrants.

Authoritarian Personality Theory

T. W. Adorno (1950) and his colleagues claim that extreme prejudice is a personality trait of certain individuals. They base this conclusion on research showing that people who display strong prejudice toward one minority are usually intolerant of all minorities. Such people exhibit *authoritarian personalities*, rigidly conforming to conventional cultural values, envisioning moral issues as clear-cut matters of right and wrong, and advocating strongly ethnocentric views. People with authoritarian personalities also look upon society as naturally competitive and hierarchical, with "better" people (like themselves) inevitably dominating those who are weaker.

By contrast, Adorno found, people tolerant toward one minority are likely to be accepting of all. They tend to be more flexible in their moral judgments and believe that, ideally, society should be relatively egalitarian. They feel uncomfortable in any situation in which some people exercise excessive and damaging power over others.

According to these researchers, authoritarian personalities tend to develop in people with little education and harsh and demanding parents. Raised by cold and insistent authority figures, they theorized, children may become angry and anxious people who seek out scapegoats whom they come to define as their social inferiors.

Cultural Theory of Prejudice

A third approach suggests that, while extreme prejudice may be characteristic of particular people, some prejudice is embedded in widespread cultural values. As noted in Chapter 3 ("Culture"), the social superiority of some categories of people is a core American value. Recent multicultural research echoes this idea,

DIVERSITY: Stereotypes are shaped by cultural values; U.S. stereotypes tend to personally discredit disadvantaged people. Thus, many people stereotype the homeless as mentally ill (although only about one-third are). Likewise, the poor are stereotyped as unworthy, even though 20% of poor heads of households are full-time "working poor."

Q: "Now as to the Negroes, I entirely agree with you that as a race and in the mass they are altogether inferior to the whites." Theodore Roosevelt

Q: "The ordinary English worker hates the Irish worker as a competitor who lowers his standard of life. . . . This antagonism is the secret of the impotence of the English working class . . . it is the secret by which the capitalist class maintains its power." Karl Marx

suggesting the need to broaden the traditionally Eurocentric attitudes of people in the United States to appreciate the culture and contributions of those of non-European backgrounds (Asante, 1987, 1988).

Emory Bogardus (1968) studied the effects of culturally rooted prejudices on interpersonal relationships for more than forty years. He devised the concept of *social distance* to assess how close or distant people feel in relation to members of various racial and ethnic categories. His research shows that people throughout the United States offer much the same evaluations; this commonality, in turn, suggests that such attitudes are culturally normative.

Bogardus concludes that members of our society hold the most positive views toward others of English, Canadian, and Scottish background, welcoming close relationships, including marriage, with them. Attitudes are somewhat less favorable toward the French, Germans, Swedes, and Dutch. At the other extreme, Bogardus discovered, the most negative prejudices target people of African and Asian descent.

If prejudice is so widespread, can we dismiss intolerance as merely a trait of a handful of abnormal people, as Adorno suggests? Rather, it seems that some bigotry is routinely expressed by people well adjusted to a "culture of prejudice."

Conflict Theory of Prejudice

A fourth approach views prejudice as the product of social conflict among various categories of people. According to this theory, powerful people employ prejudice as an ideology that justifies the oppression of minorities. To the extent that powerful people devalue illegal Latino immigrants in the Southwest, for example, rich landowners are able to pay these people low wages for hard work.

Conflict theories of prejudice take various forms. One argument, based on Marxist theory, is that elites foster prejudice to divide workers along racial and ethnic lines. This process serves the interests of capitalists insofar as such conflict decreases the chances

The efforts of these four women advanced the United States toward the goal of equal opportunity regardless of a person's color. Sojourner Truth (1797–1883) (right), born a slave, became an influential preacher and later employed her charisma in the abolitionist cause. Near the end of the Civil War, President Abraham Lincoln honored her at the White House. Harriet Tubman (1820–1913) (bottom left), after escaping from slavery herself, masterminded the flight from bondage of hundreds of African-American men and women. She was one of the most successful participants in what came to be known as the "Underground Railroad." Ida Wells-Barnett (1862–1931) (bottom middle), born to slave parents, was outspoken in pursuit of social equality in the antebellum era. After becoming a partner in a Memphis newspaper, she was a tireless crusader against the terror of lynching. Marion Anderson (1897–1993) (bottom right), had an exceptional voice, which stood out in her church choir when she was six years old. For years, Anderson's career was restrained by racial prejudice. Thus, when she sang in the White House (1936), and on the steps of the Lincoln Memorial to a crowd of almost 100,000 people (1939), she symbolically broke an important "color line."

SOCIAL SURVEY: "How important for getting ahead is being of the right race?" (*CHIP1 Social Survey Software*, OPRACE1, 2; GSS 1987, N = 1,444)

	"Very important"	"Less important"
Afri Amer	28.8%	71.2%
Hispanics	15.6%	84.4%
Whites	11.9%	88.1%

NOTE: Evidence suggesting institutional discrimination: The 1990 percentages of mortgage applications denied (based on Federal Reserve Board study of 6,400 loan applications at 9,300 lending institutions) were Asians, 12.9%; Whites, 14.4%; Hispanics, 21.4%; African Americans, 33.9%.

Q: "A sure way to lift oneself up is by helping to lift someone else." Booker T. Washington

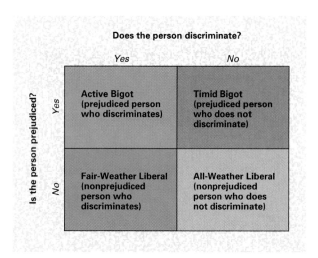

FIGURE 12–1 Patterns of Prejudice and Discrimination
(Merton, 1976)

that *all* workers will join together to advance their common interests (Geschwender, 1978; Olzak, 1989).

A different argument, recently advanced by Shelby Steele (1990), is that minorities themselves spark conflict as they encourage a climate of *race consciousness*, a political strategy to gain power and privileges for themselves. Race consciousness, Steele explains, amounts to the claim that minorities are victims and white people their victimizers. Moreover, being historically disadvantaged, minorities claim they are now entitled to special considerations based on their race. While this strategy may yield short-term gains for minorities, he cautions, such policies are likely to spark a backlash from white people or others who condemn "special treatment" for anyone on the basis of race or ethnicity as unfair.

Discrimination

Closely related to prejudice is the concept of **discrimination**, *an action that involves treating various categories of people unequally*. While prejudice refers to attitudes, discrimination is a matter of behavior. Like prejudice, discrimination can be either positive (providing special advantages) or negative (subjecting categories of people to obstacles). Discrimination also varies in intensity, ranging from subtle to blatant.

Prejudice and discrimination often—but not always—occur together. A personnel manager prejudiced against members of a particular minority may refuse to hire them. Robert Merton (1976) describes such a person as an *active bigot*, as shown in Figure 12-1.

Fearing legal action, however, a prejudiced personnel manager may not discriminate, thereby becoming a *timid bigot*. What Merton calls *fair-weather liberals* may be generally tolerant of minorities yet discriminate when it is expedient to do so, such as when a superior demands it. Finally, Merton's *all-weather liberal* is free of both prejudice and discrimination.

Not all kinds of discrimination are wrong. Individuals discriminate all the time, preferring the personalities, favoring the looks, or admiring the talents of particular people. Discriminating in this basic sense of *making distinctions* is necessary to everyday life and rarely causes problems.

Societies also consider some forms of discrimination to be normative, while condemning others. Colleges, for example, systematically favor applicants with greater abilities over those with less aptitude. This kind of discrimination is entirely consistent with our culture-based expectation that the greatest rewards go to people with more ability or those who work harder.

But what if a college were to favor one category of people (Christians) over another (Jews) regardless of individual talent? Unless the college had a religious mission (making a specific religion directly relevant to performance in a course), such a policy would discriminate in a manner that most of us (and the law) consider unfair.

Principles of fair play tend to change along with economic development. In less-developed societies, people routinely favor members of their families, clans, religious groups, and villages. Traditional people typically recognize a moral duty to "look after their own." In industrial societies, by contrast, cultural norms elevate the individual over the group, so that achievement rather than ascription guides our code of fairness. Many organizations, therefore, seek out the most qualified applicant while forbidding "nepotism" or "conflict of interest" by which employees would hire or favor a relative. More broadly, we condemn treating people categorically, although this practice has been commonplace throughout human history and continues in much of the world today.

Institutional Discrimination

Like prejudice, discrimination is a not just a matter of individual action but also involves the structure of society. **Institutional discrimination** refers to *discrimination that is a normative and routine part of the economy, the educational system, or some other social institution*. As minorities in the United States have learned through painful experience, traditional ideas of people's "place" can be deeply established in the

DIVERSITY: Appearing on all U.S. coins is the Latin phrase *E Pluribus Unum* ("one formed from many"). Whether our society should emphasize the "unum" (which often means, in practice, favoring a dominant cultural tradition) or the "pluribus" (which can also cause division) is part of the debate surrounding multiculturalism.

NOTE: A century ago, people assumed race (and biology, in general) directly affected human behavior; early anthropology and sociology were central in dispelling this view.

Q: "Once America was a microcosm of European nationalities; today, America is a microcosm of the world." Molefi Asante, Temple University

operation of the workplace, the courts, and the schools.

Until 1954, for example, the principle of "separate but equal" justified the practice of educating black and white children separately in different schools. While the education received by African-American children lagged far below that of white children, the law upheld what amounted to an educational caste system. This example of institutional discrimination was formally banned by the Supreme Court in the landmark decision *Brown* v. *Board of Education of Topeka.* Racial discrimination has proven difficult to end in the United States, however. Because black and white people generally live apart, forty years after the 1954 *Brown* ruling most young people still attend racially imbalanced schools.

Prejudice and Discrimination: The Vicious Cycle

Prejudice and discrimination frequently reinforce each other. W. I. Thomas offered a simple explanation of this fact, noted in Chapter 6 ("Social Interaction in Everyday Life"). The Thomas theorem states: *If situations are defined as real, they are real in their consequences* (1966:301; orig. 1931).

Thomas recognized that people socially construct reality. Thus stereotypes become real to those who believe them, sometimes even to those who are victimized by them. Power also plays a role here, since some categories of people have the ability to enforce their prejudices to the detriment of others.

Prejudice on the part of whites toward people of color, for example, does not produce *innate* inferiority but it can produce *social* inferiority, consigning minorities to poverty, low-prestige occupations, and poor housing in racially segregated neighborhoods. If white people interpret social disadvantage as evidence that minorities do not measure up to their standards, they unleash a new round of prejudice and discrimination, giving rise to a *vicious cycle* whereby each perpetuates the other, as illustrated in Figure 12–2, even from generation to generation.

MAJORITY AND MINORITY: PATTERNS OF INTERACTION

Social scientists describe patterns of interaction between minorities and more privileged members of a society in terms of four models: pluralism, assimilation, segregation, and genocide.

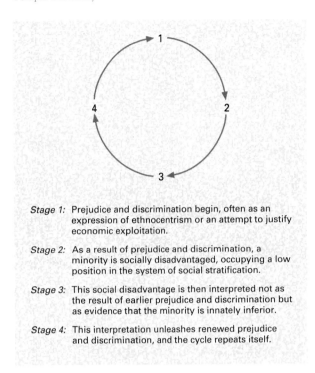

Stage 1: Prejudice and discrimination begin, often as an expression of ethnocentrism or an attempt to justify economic exploitation.

Stage 2: As a result of prejudice and discrimination, a minority is socially disadvantaged, occupying a low position in the system of social stratification.

Stage 3: This social disadvantage is then interpreted not as the result of earlier prejudice and discrimination but as evidence that the minority is innately inferior.

Stage 4: This interpretation unleashes renewed prejudice and discrimination, and the cycle repeats itself.

FIGURE 12–2 Prejudice and Discrimination: The Vicious Cycle

Prejudice and discrimination can form a vicious cycle, perpetuating themselves, as explained above.

Pluralism

Pluralism is *a state in which racial and ethnic minorities are distinct but have social parity.* Although categories of people are socially different, they share in basic social resources more or less equally.

The United States appears to be pluralistic in some respects. Large cities contain various "ethnic villages" where people proudly display the cultural traditions of their immigrant ancestors. In New York these include Spanish Harlem, Little Italy, and Chinatown; in Philadelphia, Italian "South Philly"; in Miami, "Little Havana"; in Chicago, "Little Saigon"; as well as Latino East Los Angeles.

Pluralism is also the goal of our society's recent trend toward multiculturalism. As described in Chapter 3 ("Culture"), this scholarly and political initiative seeks to promote respectful tolerance of and social parity for the many cultural traditions that make up our national life.

But the United States remains far from pluralistic for three reasons. First, while most people appreciate

	"Yes"	"No"	DK/NR
". . . mainly due to discrimination?"	41.1%	53.7%	5.2%
". . . because most blacks have less inborn ability to learn?"	12.5%	83.6%	3.9%
". . . because most blacks don't have the chance for education . . . ?"	52.5%	43.1%	4.4%
". . . because most blacks lack motivation and will power . . . ?"	48.8%	44.1%	7.1%

The ritual of Kwanza, devised in 1968, has gained popularity in recent decades as a celebration of African-American heritage. Observed soon after Chanukah and Christmas, Kwanza combines Christian and Jewish elements in a distinctly African ritual that builds the strength of families and communities.

Assimilation

Assimilation is *the process by which minorities gradually adopt patterns of the dominant culture*. Assimilation involves changing modes of dress, values, religion, language, or friends.

Many of us traditionally have viewed the United States as a "melting pot" in which various nationalities were fused into an entirely new way of life. This perception is beautifully expressed in this description by one European immigrant at the turn of the century:

> America is God's Crucible, the great melting-pot where all races of Europe are melting and reforming. Here you stand, good folks, think I, when I see them at Ellis Island [historical entry point for many immigrants in New York], here you stand with your fifty groups, with your fifty languages and histories, and your fifty blood-hatreds and rivalries. But you won't be long like that, brothers, for these are the fires of God . . . Germans and Frenchmen, Irishmen and Englishmen, Jews and Russians, into the Crucible with you all! God is making an American! (Zangwill, 1921:33; orig. 1909)

Although the melting pot remains an influential concept of how this country *ought* to operate, it is misleading as a statement of historical fact. The reality is less everyone "melting" into some new cultural pattern than minorities adopting the traits (the dress, accent, and sometimes even the names) of the dominant culture established by the earliest settlers.

Not surprisingly, elites tend to favor the assimilation model since it holds them up as the standard to which others should aspire. Many immigrants, too, have been quick to pursue assimilation in the hope that it will encourage upward social mobility and provide an escape from prejudice and discrimination directed against distinctive foreigners (Newman, 1973). But multiculturalists find fault with the assimilation model because it tends to paint minorities as "the problem" and define them (rather than elites) as the ones who need to do all the changing.

Certainly some assimilation has occurred over the course of our national history (witness the gradual "melting" of neighborhoods previously composed of European immigrants). But some categories of people (Germans and Irish contrasted to Italians, people of Japanese contrasted to Chinese ancestry, and, generally speaking, white people contrasted to black people) have "melted" much more than others. Moreover, as fast as some ethnic villages in our cities disappear, new ones appear, the product of a steady and substantial stream of immigrants. Almost 30 percent of New

their cultural heritage, only a small proportion of minorities want their race or ethnicity to set them apart to the point that they live only with their "own kind" (NORC, 1993). Second, in many cases, racial and ethnic identity is forced on people by others who shun them as in some way undesirable. For example, many communities in the Appalachian Mountains of the eastern United States remain culturally distinctive because their members are snubbed as "hillbillies" and subjected to discrimination that perpetuates their poverty. Third, especially in recent years, rising levels of immigration have stretched many people's tolerance for social diversity. One reaction has been a social movement seeking to establish English as the official language of the United States, hardly a strategy to encourage pluralism.

In global perspective, Switzerland presents a much sharper example of pluralism. In this European nation of almost 7 million people, German, French, and Italian cultural traditions run deep. The relative success of the Swiss in maintaining pluralism (albeit involving little difference in color) is evident in its official recognition of the languages of the three ethnicities. Just as important, the three categories have roughly the same economic standing (Simpson & Yinger, 1972).

Q: "The future of America can't be sustained if people keep only to their own ways and remain perpetual outsiders. The society has got to turn them into Americans." Allan Bloom

NOTE: The effects of assimilation are evident in name changing among U.S. celebrities; see the box, "What's In a Name? How Social Forces Affect Personal Choices," in Chapter 1.

SOCIAL SURVEY: "If you could find the housing that you would want and like, would you rather live in a neighborhood that is all black, mostly black, half black, half white, or mostly white?" (GSS 1982, N = 510; African-American respondents; *Codebook*, 1993:194)

"All black"	14.7%	"Mostly white"	5.1%
"Mostly black"	15.8%	DK/NR	10.4%
"Half black, half white"	54.0%		

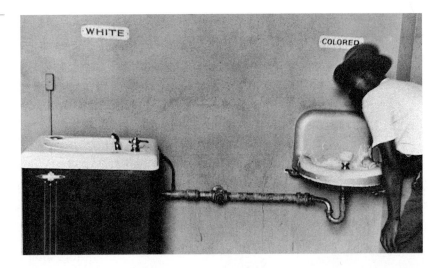

Even after the abolition of slavery in the United States, so-called "Jim Crow" laws continued to separate black and white people in hotels, restaurants, parks, buses, and even drinking fountains. The official policy of "separate but equal" was rarely that, as this scene suggests. During the 1950s and 1960s, courts struck down such laws.

Yorkers in 1990 were foreign born—the highest percentage in fifty years. Thus, some analysts argue that race and ethnicity endure as basic building blocks of our society (Glazer & Moynihan, 1970; Alba, 1985).

As a cultural process, assimilation involves changes in ethnicity but not in race. For example, many Americans of Japanese descent have discarded their traditional way of life but still have their racial identity. However, distinguishing racial traits do diminish over generations as the result of **miscegenation**, *the biological process of interbreeding among racial categories*. Although resistance to such biological mixing remains strong, miscegenation (often outside of marriage) has occurred throughout U.S. history.

Segregation

Segregation refers to *the physical and social separation of categories of people*. Some minorities, especially religious orders like the Amish, have voluntarily segregated themselves. Mostly, however, majorities segregate minorities involuntarily by excluding them. Various degrees of segregation characterize residential neighborhoods, schools, occupations, hospitals, and even cemeteries. While pluralism fosters distinctiveness without disadvantage, segregation enforces separation to the detriment of a minority.

South Africa's system of apartheid (described in Chapter 9, "Social Stratification") illustrates racial segregation that has been both rigid and pervasive. Apartheid was created by the European minority it served, and white South Africans historically have enforced this system through the use of brutal power (Fredrickson, 1981). Apartheid is currently breaking

down due to persistent and widespread opposition among black people and also a majority of white people. But the basic racial structure of South Africa has changed little as yet; this nation remains essentially two different societies that touch only when blacks provide services for whites.

In the United States, too, racial segregation also has a long history. Centuries of slavery gave way to racially separated lodging, schooling, and transportation. Decisions such as the 1954 *Brown* case have reduced overt and *de jure* (Latin meaning "by law") discrimination in the United States. However, *de facto* ("in fact") segregation continues.

In the 1960s, Karl and Alma Taeuber (1965) assessed the residential segregation of black people and white people in more than two hundred cities in the United States. On a numerical scale ranging from zero (a mixing of races in all neighborhoods) to 100 (mixing in no neighborhoods), they calculated an *average* segregation score of 86.2. Subsequent research has shown that segregation has decreased since then, but only a little; even African Americans with high incomes continue to find that their color closes off some opportunities for housing (Van Valey, Roof, & Wilcox, 1977; Hwang et al., 1985; Calmore, 1986; Saltman, 1991; Wilson, 1991; NORC, 1993).

We associate segregation with housing but, as Douglas Massey and Nancy Denton (1989) point out, racial separation involves a host of life experiences beyond neighborhood composition. Many African Americans living in inner cities, these researchers concluded, have little social contact of any kind with the outside world. Such *hypersegregation* affects about one-fifth of all African Americans but only a

In recent years, American Indians have taken advantage of the legal system to operate public gambling on reservation land in twenty-seven states. Some large casinos, such as this one in Ledyard, Connecticut, are extremely profitable. Gambling income reached $4 billion in 1993, making some American Indians quite rich.

few percent of comparably poor whites (Jagarowsky & Bane, 1990).

In short, segregation generally means second-class citizenship for a minority. For this reason, many minority men and women have struggled valiantly against such exclusiveness. Sometimes the action of even a single person can make a difference. On December 1, 1955, Rosa Parks boarded a bus in Montgomery, Alabama, and sat in a section designated by law for black people. When a crowd of white passengers boarded the bus, the driver asked Parks and three other blacks to give up their seats. Three did so, but Rosa Parks refused. The driver left the bus and returned with police, who arrested her for violating the racial segregation laws. A court later convicted Parks and fined her $14. Her stand (or sitting) for justice sparked the black community of Montgomery to boycott city buses, ultimately ending this form of segregation (King, 1969).

Genocide

Genocide is *the systematic annihilation of one category of people by another.* This racist and ethnocentric brutality violates nearly every recognized moral standard; nonetheless, it has occurred time and again in the human record.

Genocide has figured prominently in centuries of contact between Europeans and the original inhabitants of the Americas. From the sixteenth century on, the Spanish, Portuguese, English, French, and Dutch forcefully colonized vast empires. These efforts decimated the native populations of North and South America, allowing Europeans to gain control of the continents' wealth. Some native people fell victim to calculated killing sprees; most succumbed to diseases brought by Europeans and to which native peoples had no natural defenses (Cottrell, 1979; Butterworth & Chance, 1981; Matthiessen, 1984; Sale, 1990).

Genocide has also occurred in the twentieth century. Unimaginable horror befell the Jews of Europe during Adolf Hitler's reign of terror. Ultimately the Nazis exterminated more than 6 million Jewish men, women, and children in what has become known as the Holocaust. Between 1975 and 1980 the communist regime of Pol Pot in Cambodia slaughtered anyone thought to represent capitalist cultural influences. Condemned to death were men and women able to speak any Western language and even individuals who wore eyeglasses, viewed as a symbol of capitalist culture. In all, some 2 million people (one-fourth of the population) perished in the "killing fields" of Cambodia (Shawcross, 1979).

These four patterns of minority-majority interaction have all been played out in the United States. We proudly point to patterns of pluralism and assimilation; only reluctantly do we acknowledge the degree to which our society has been built on segregation (of African Americans) and genocide (of Native Americans). The remainder of this chapter examines how these four patterns have shaped the history and present social standing of major racial and ethnic categories in the United States.

RACE AND ETHNICITY IN THE UNITED STATES

Give me your tired, your poor,
Your huddled masses yearning to breathe free,
The wretched refuse of your teeming shore,
Send these, the homeless, tempest-tossed to me:
I lift my lamp beside the golden door.

These words by Emma Lazarus, inscribed on the Statue of Liberty, express cultural ideals of human

Q: "First they came for the Jews,
    but I did not speak out
    because I was not a Jew.
Then they came for the Communists,
    and I did not speak out
    because I was not a Communist.

Then they came for the trade unionists,
    and I did not speak out
    because I was not trade unionist.
Then they came for me,
    and no one was left
    to speak out for me."
Pastor Niemoeller, victim of the Nazis

dignity, personal freedom, and opportunity. But our nation's golden door has opened more widely for some than for others. Social inequality, entrenched in U.S. society since its beginnings, is readily evident in the history of this country's racial and ethnic minorities.

Native Americans

The term "Native Americans" refers to hundreds of distinct societies—including Aleuts, Eskimos, Cherokee, Zuni, Sioux, Mohawk, Aztec, and Inca—who first settled the Western Hemisphere. Some thirty thousand years before Christopher Columbus "discovered" the Americas, these people began migrating from Asia, crossing a land bridge where the Bering Strait off the coast of Alaska is today. Over the centuries they spread throughout the continents of North and South America (Dobyns, 1966).

What some Europeans called "taming the wilderness" actually amounted to the destruction of many ancient civilizations. Exposure to European diseases took a terrible toll among the native peoples, and tens of thousands died at the hands of Europeans seeking land and other wealth. From a population in the millions, the "vanishing Americans" numbered a mere 250,000 by the start of the twentieth century (Tyler, 1973).

It was Columbus who first referred to Native Americans as "Indians"; when he landed in the Bahama Islands in the Caribbean, he thought he had reached India. Columbus described these indigenous Americans as passive and peaceful (Matthiessen, 1984; Sale, 1990), different from Europeans, whose way of life was more competitive and aggressive. Even as Europeans seized the land of Native Americans, the invaders demeaned their victims as thieves and murderers to justify their actions (Unruh, 1979; Josephy, 1982).

After the Revolutionary War, the new United States government adopted a pluralist approach to Native-American societies and sought to gain more land through treaties. Payment for land was far from fair, however, and when Native Americans resisted surrender of their homelands, the U.S. government simply used superior military power to evict them. In perhaps the most regrettable incident of its kind, thousands of Cherokees died on a forced march—the Trail of Tears—from their homes in the southeastern United States to reservations in Indian Territory, later Oklahoma. By the early 1800s, few Native Americans remained east of the Mississippi River.

In 1871, the United States made Native Americans wards of the government and set out to resolve "the Indian problem" through forced assimilation.

TABLE 12–2 The Social Standing of Native Americans, 1990

	Native Americans	Entire United States
Median family income	$21,750	$35,225
Percent in poverty	30.9%	13.1%
Completion of four or more years of college (age 25 and over)	9.3%	20.3%

SOURCE: U.S. Bureau of the Census, 1993.

Native Americans continued to lose their land and were well on their way to losing their culture as well. Reservation schools taught English in place of ancestral languages and eroded traditional religion in favor of Christianity. Officials of the Bureau of Indian Affairs took many children from their parents and handed them over to boarding schools, where they were to be resocialized as "Americans." Authorities gave local control of reservation life to the few Native Americans who supported government policies and distributed reservation land—traditionally held collectively—as the private property of individual families (Tyler, 1973). Native Americans gradually were taught to be dependent on the government.

Not until 1924 were Native Americans entitled to U.S. citizenship. Since then, the government has recognized a host of problems associated with reservation life and encouraged migration into the larger society. Some Native Americans have responded by adopting more mainstream cultural patterns and marrying non-Native Americans; many large cities now contain sizable Native American populations. As is shown in Table 12–2, however, 1990 median family income for Native Americans was far below average in the United States, and Native Americans stand out as unlikely to earn a college degree.[2]

From in-depth interviews with Native Americans in a western city, Joan Albon (1971) concluded that this lower social standing reflects both cultural factors on the part of Native Americans themselves and racial hostility expressed by the larger society. Few Native Americans have aggressively pursued higher education,

---

[2]In making comparisons of the income and education of various categories of the U.S. population, keep in mind that the categories vary in average age. The 1991 median age for all people in the United States was 33.1 years. White people have a median age of 34.1 years; for Native Americans, the figure is 26.0 years. Because people's income and schooling rise through adulthood, this age difference accounts for some of the disparities shown here.

DIVERSITY: Traditional Native-American cultures tend to be more cooperative than European cultures. The languages of the Navajo and some other Native-American cultures contain no words for "free enterprise" or "market system."

NOTE: E. Digby Baltzell, who coined the term WASP, has suggested that, to many people in the United States, a true WASP is a person whose first name is a last name.

NOTE: The concept of private land ownership was foreign to virtually all American Indian societies.

Q: "I believe that the Negro race has tremendous gifts to bring to this country in the way of artistic accomplishment. I think things come by nature to many of them that we have to acquire, such as an appreciation of art and of music and of rhythm, which we really have to gain very often through education." Eleanor Roosevelt, 1934

and many have few marketable skills and speak less-than-perfect English. Albon adds that many Native Americans lack the individualism and competitiveness that contribute to success in the United States. This passivity stemmed from both cooperative traditional values and long dependence on government assistance. Further, their dark skin sometimes provokes prejudice and discrimination.

Like other racial and ethnic minorities in the United States, Native Americans have recently reasserted pride in their cultural heritage. As the 1990s began, Native-American organizations reported a surge of new membership applications, and many children are learning to speak native tongues better than their parents (Fost, 1991; Johnson, 1991). In lawsuits against the federal government, some Native Americans have pressed for return of lands forcibly taken in the past and sought democratic control of reservation lands by Native Americans themselves. In a few cases, confrontations with federal officials have erupted into violence. Few Native Americans support this means of addressing grievances, but the vast majority share a profound sense of the injustice endured at the hands of white people (Josephy, 1982; Matthiessen, 1983).

White Anglo-Saxon Protestants

White Anglo-Saxon Protestants (WASPs) were not the first people to inhabit the United States, but they came to dominate this nation once English colonization began. Not until the nineteenth century, in fact, did substantial migration of non-WASPs begin. Most WASPs are still of English ancestry, but the category also includes Scots and Welsh. With more than 50 million people of English ancestry, one in five members of our society claims some WASP background.

Historically, WASP immigrants were highly skilled. Just as important, what we now call the Protestant work ethic motivated them toward hard work and achievement. Also, because their numbers placed them in the majority, WASPs were not subject to the prejudice and discrimination experienced by other categories of immigrants. The historical dominance of WASPs has been so great that, as noted earlier, assimilation into U.S. society has led others to become more like the WASPs.

As social diversity increased during the nineteenth century, some WASPs bemoaned the presence of new arrivals they deemed "undesirable foreigners." Nativist political movements promoted laws to limit the rapidly growing immigration. Those who could afford to pursued a personal solution to the "problem"

by sheltering themselves in exclusive neighborhoods and restrictive clubs. Thus the 1880s—the decade in which the Statue of Liberty first welcomed immigrants to the United States—also saw the founding of the first country club with all WASP members. Soon afterward, WASPs began publishing the *Social Register* (1887), a listing of members of "society," and established various genealogical organizations such as the Daughters of the American Revolution (1890) and the Society of Mayflower Descendants (1894). These efforts served to further insulate wealthy WASPs from newly arrived immigrants (Baltzell, 1964).

By about 1930, the growing wealth of other categories of people and more egalitarian values undermined the WASPs' commanding privileges (Baltzell, 1964, 1976, 1988). Exemplifying this shift was the 1960 election of John Fitzgerald Kennedy as the first Irish Catholic president. Even so, WASPs continue to have great influence; with extensive schooling, they work in high-prestige occupations, enjoy above-average incomes, and still make up most of the upper-upper class (Greeley, 1974; Baltzell, 1979; Roof, 1981; Neidert & Farley, 1985).

Although now under fire by multicultural educational programs, the WASP cultural legacy persists. English remains the dominant language of the United States, and Protestantism is the majority religion. Our legal system, too, reflects its English origins. But the historical dominance of WASPs is most evident in the widespread use of the terms "race" and "ethnicity" to describe everyone but them.

African Americans

African Americans accompanied Spanish explorers to the New World in the fifteenth century. Most accounts, however, mark the beginning of black history in the United States as 1619, when a Dutch trading ship brought twenty Africans to Jamestown, Virginia. Whether these people arrived as slaves or indentured servants who paid their passage by performing labor for a specified period, being of African descent on these shores soon became virtually synonymous with being a slave. In 1661, Virginia enacted the first law recognizing slavery (Sowell, 1981).

Slavery was the foundation of the southern colonies' plantation system. Some white people prospered as plantation owners and, until it was outlawed in 1808, as slave traders. Traders forcibly brought some 10 million Africans to the Americas; about 400,000 entered the United States (Sowell, 1981). During the voyage, slaves were chained as human cargo. Filth and disease killed many and drove others

NOTE: John Hope Franklin has pointed out that, historically, racial problems were not limited to the South. In 1776, as the new nation was being formed, *all* states allowed slavery. By 1850, roughly equal numbers of free blacks (500,000) were found in both the South and the North. Also, segregation and various forms of discrimination were largely Northern in origin, because slavery in the South had spawned other forms of racial control. It was only after Abolition that the South adopted Northern forms of discrimination.

NOTE: The last nation in the Western Hemisphere to outlaw slavery was Brazil, in 1888. About half the people of color in Brazil (which is among the least-developed countries of the world) are descendants of slaves; blacks have roughly half the income of whites; and infant mortality is one-third higher.

At its foundation, agrarian slavery was an institution built on coercion and violence. As African-American painter Jacob Lawrence shows here, planters utilized the most brutal treatment in an effort to obtain compliance. The wide stance and clenched jaw convey the planter's determination to control the bound man at his feet. But despite the fear that such tactics generated, they also provoked periodic rebellion on the part of slaves.

to suicide. Overall, perhaps half died in route (Tannenbaum, 1946; Franklin, 1967).

Those fortunate enough to survive the journey faced a life of forced servitude. Although some worked in cities at a variety of trades, most slaves labored in the fields from daybreak until sunset, and for up to twenty hours a day during the harvest (Franklin, 1967). The law allowed owners to impose whatever disciplinary measures they deemed necessary to ensure that slaves labored continuously. Even the killing of a slave by an owner rarely prompted legal action. Owners also divided slave families at public auctions where human beings were bought and sold as pieces of property. Unschooled and dependent on their owners for all their basic needs, slaves had little control over their destinies (Sowell, 1981).

There were, however, free persons of color in both the North and the South: small-scale farmers, skilled workers, and small-business owners (Murray, 1978). But the lives of most African Americans stood in glaring contradiction to the principles of equality and freedom on which the United States was founded. The Declaration of Independence states:

> We hold these Truths to be self-evident, that all Men are created equal, that they are endowed by their Creator with certain unalienable Rights, that among these are Life, Liberty, and the Pursuit of Happiness.

Most white people, however, did not apply these ideals to black people. In the *Dred Scott* case in 1857, the U.S. Supreme Court addressed the question, "Are blacks citizens?" and answered, "We think they are not, and that they are not included, and were not intended to be included, under the word 'citizens' in the Constitution, and can therefore claim none of the rights and privileges which that instrument provides for and secures for citizens of the United States" (quoted in Blaustein & Zangrando, 1968:160). Thus arose what Swedish sociologist Gunnar Myrdal (1944) termed the *American dilemma*: a democratic society's denial of basic rights and freedoms to an entire category of people. To resolve this dilemma, many white people simply defined blacks as innately inferior.

In 1865, the Thirteenth Amendment to the Constitution outlawed slavery. Three years later, the Fourteenth Amendment reversed the *Dred Scott* ruling, conferring citizenship on all people born in the United States. The Fifteenth Amendment, ratified in 1870, stated that neither race nor previous condition of servitude should deprive anyone of the right to vote. However, so-called Jim Crow laws, which enshrined discrimination in the legal code, still divided U.S. society into two racial castes (Woodward, 1974). Especially in the South, white people beat and lynched black people (and some whites) who challenged the racial hierarchy.

The twentieth century has brought dramatic changes to African Americans. After World War I, tens of thousands of men, women, and children deserted the rural South for jobs in northern factories. Most did find more economic opportunity up North, but few escaped racial prejudice and discrimination, which set them apart from white immigrants who had arrived from Europe (Lieberson, 1980).

SOCIAL SURVEY: "Is the government obligated to help blacks, or should the government give no special treatment?" (*STUDENT CHIP Social Survey Software*, HELPBLK1; GSS 1983–91, N = 10,047)

	"Help"	"Undecided"	"No special"
Afri Amer	56.7%	30.9%	12.4%
Latinos	23.8%	35.2%	40.9%
Whites	14.4%	28.2%	57.4%

Q: "There is no Negro problem in the United States; there is only a white problem." Richard Wright

RESOURCE: An excerpt from William Julius Wilson's *The Truly Disadvantaged* on the ghetto underclass appears in the Macionis and Benokraitis reader, *Seeing Ourselves.*

SOCIAL POLICY

Affirmative Action: Problem or Solution?

After World War II, the government of the United States funded higher education for veterans of all races. At the time, the G.I. Bill held special promise for African Americans, and, by 1960, some 350,000 black men and women had gone to college with government funding. But these individuals were not finding the kinds of jobs for which they qualified. In short, *educational* opportunity was not producing the kind of *economic* opportunity the government hoped it would.

This was the context for devising a program that came to be known as "affirmative action." In the early 1960s, the Kennedy administration initiated affirmative action as a means of finding qualified minorities that the government knew were there—a process of throwing a broader "net of opportunity."

Affirmative action won many supporters by helping thousands of black women and men gain the kinds of jobs for which they were qualified. But this program also attracted criticism because, by the early 1970s, affirmative action had come to mean "group preferences" for minorities.

In practice, affirmative action means that employers and college admissions offices solicit applications from people of all races and ethnicities and carefully monitor hiring and promotion or admissions policies to eliminate discrimination—even if unintended—against minorities. Initially, the government's policy objective with the affirmative action program was to enable talented people to enter various occupations and educational programs without regard to their race.

Many people reasonably assumed that talent was spread throughout the population; therefore, they concluded, minorities should be present in jobs or universities in proportion to their numbers in the larger population. This line of argument has propelled some people to argue that affirmative action should take the form of a quota system that would guarantee a fixed number of minority members favorable treatment regardless of how they stack up against other applicants. In effect, under such a plan, an employer is required to find the best minority applicant, rather than the best worker, for the job. But rigid quota systems have been rejected by U.S. courts. Even so, the law does support preferences based on race and ethnicity as a means of increasing the proportion of minorities in settings that have historically excluded them.

Advocates applaud affirmative action as a fair and necessary corrective for historical discrimination. Everybody alive today, they argue, has been affected by privileges accorded or denied to their parents and grandparents. "Special treatment," from this point of view, is

In the 1950s and 1960s, black people and sympathetic white people mobilized in a broad attack on racism. The national civil rights movement led to landmark judicial decisions outlawing racially segregated schools and overt racial discrimination in employment and public accommodations. In addition, the "black power movement" gave African Americans a renewed sense of pride and purpose, which has more recently been reinforced through Afrocentric education, described in Chapter 3 ("Culture").

Gains notwithstanding, people of African descent continue to occupy a subordinate position in the United States, as shown in Table 12–3 on page 342. The median income of African-American families in 1992 ($21,161) was 54 percent of that earned by white families ($38,909)[3] and substantially below the average for all families across the United States ($36,812). Black households are also three times as likely as white households to be poor.

In 1992, about one in four African-American families was securely in the middle class with an annual

---

[3]Here again, a median age difference (white people, 34.1; black people, 28.1) accounts for some of the income and educational disparities shown here. Another part of this difference is due to a higher proportion of one-parent families among blacks than whites. If we were to compare only married-couple families, black families (earning $34,196 in 1992) received 80 percent as much as white families ($42,738).

Q: "We seldom study the condition of the Negro honestly and carefully. It is so much easier to assume that we know it all." W. E. B. Du Bois, *The Souls of Black Folk*

DIVERSITY: For a comparison of affluent black people and white people, see the box "Two Colors of Affluence: Do Black People and White People Differ?" in Chapter 10.

DIVERSITY: In 1965, among African Americans 25–29 years old who had begun college, the percentage of people who went on to complete four years or more was 90% that of whites; by the end of the 1980s, it had dropped to 60%. (Bunzel, 1991)

nothing new and is necessary for those denied opportunity through no fault of their own. Only in this way, advocates claim, can we break the vicious cycle of prejudice and discrimination.

Opponents of affirmative action agree that minorities have historically suffered from discrimination, but they see affirmative action as *reverse discrimination*. Why should whites today—many of whom are far from privileged—be penalized for past discrimination for which they were in no way responsible? Opponents also claim that minorities have largely overcome historical barriers to opportunity and that those who enjoy the most success are those who make the greatest efforts—which is as it should be. Giving entire categories of people special treatment inevitably compromises standards, opponents insist, while calling into question the real accomplishments of minorities and provoking a hostile backlash from white people. Moreover, critics point out, affirmative action typically helps minorities with more schooling (presumably those who least need help) while doing little for the persistently poor who need assistance the most.

When applied to African Americans, adults in the United States tend to oppose affirmative action policies, as the national survey responses described below indicate. Those polled were asked to respond to the following statement:

> Some people think that blacks have been discriminated against for so long that the government has a special obligation to help improve their living standards. Others believe that the government should not be giving special treatment to blacks.

The numbers 1 through 5 show the range of opinion in relation to the three responses.

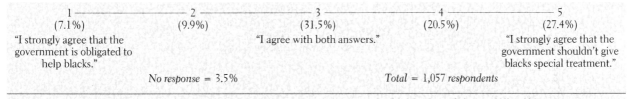

1 (7.1%)	2 (9.9%)	3 (31.5%)	4 (20.5%)	5 (27.4%)
"I strongly agree that the government is obligated to help blacks."		"I agree with both answers."		"I strongly agree that the government shouldn't give blacks special treatment."

No response = 3.5%   *Total* = 1,057 *respondents*

SOURCE: Survey data from *General Social Surveys, 1972–1993: Cumulative Codebook* (Chicago: National Opinion Research Center, 1993), p. 335.

income of at least $35,000—a 50 percent jump during the 1980s. Moreover, 15 percent of African-American families are affluent, with income exceeding $50,000. But during the 1980s, overall African-American earnings slipped a bit. This pattern reflects changes in the U.S. economy by which millions of factory jobs—vital to residents of inner cities—were lost to other countries where labor costs are lower. Thus black unemployment stands at more than twice the level of whites; among African-American teenagers in many cities, the figure exceeds 40 percent (Wilson, 1984; Jacob, 1986; Lichter, 1989; U.S. Bureau of the Census, 1993).

By 1992, the historical gap in schooling between the races had almost closed: The median figures were 12.3 years for African Americans and 12.8 years for whites. But a striking racial disparity remains at the college level. Table 12–3 shows that African Americans are still just half as likely as everyone else to complete four years of college. During the 1980s, the number of African Americans enrolling in college and graduate schools fell slightly, with one-fourth of high school graduates entering college compared to one-third a decade earlier (American Council on Education, 1987; *Black Issues in Higher Education*, 1987; U.S. Bureau of the Census, 1992).

The political clout of African Americans has increased along with the number of registered voters and elected officials. Black migration to cities, along

TABLE 12–3 The Social Standing of African Americans, 1992*

	African Americans	Entire United States
Median family income	$21,161	$36,812
Percent in poverty	33.3%	14.5%
Median education (years; age 25 and over)	12.3	12.7
Completion of four or more years of college (age 25 and over)	11.5%	21.4%

*For purposes of comparison with other tables in this chapter, 1990 data are as follows: median family income, $21,423; percent in poverty, 31.9%; median education, 12.4 years; completion of four or more years of college, 11.3%.

SOURCE: U.S. Bureau of the Census, 1993.

with white movement to the suburbs, has yielded black majorities in many large cities; by 1990 half of this country's ten largest cities had elected black mayors. At the national level, however, only 1 percent of elected leaders are African Americans. After the 1992 elections (which witnessed substantial gains for black national leadership), 39 black men and women (of 435) were in the House of Representatives and one black woman (of 100) sat in the Senate.

In sum, the struggle for social equality is the theme of more than 350 years of African-American history in the United States. Our nation can certainly take pride in notable accomplishments: Slavery was ended more than a century ago, and, more recently, this country has banned many forms of overt discrimination. More broadly, research supports the conclusion that our society is moving along a path of long-term decline in prejudice against black people (Firebaugh & Davis, 1988; J. Q. Wilson, 1992). During the 1970s, for example, about 60 percent of adults in the United States supported the right of a white person to refuse to sell a home to a nonwhite buyer; by 1993 that proportion had dropped below 30 percent (NORC, 1993:187).

Assessing the state of African Americans in 1913— fifty years after the abolition of slavery—W. E. B. Du Bois cited the achievements of people of color as grounds for optimism about the future. But Du Bois also cautioned that racial caste remained strong in the United States. Clearly, a color line still exists today. One response to continued bigotry is the government policy of affirmative action, or preferential treatment for categories of people historically subject to prejudice and discrimination. The box on pages 340–41 provides details.

Q: "Freedom is not enough. You do not wipe away the scars of centuries by saying: 'Now, you are free to go where you want, do as you desire, and choose the leaders you please.' You do not take a man who for years has been hobbled by chains, liberate him, bring him to the starting line of a race, saying, 'you are free to compete with all others,' and still justly believe that you have been completely fair." Lyndon Johnson, 1965

Asian Americans

Although Asian Americans share racial traits, enormous cultural diversity marks this category of people. The 1990 census placed their number at more than 7 million—approaching 3 percent of the population. As noted earlier (in the "Minority-Majority" box), the Asian and Pacific Islander population more than doubled during the 1980s.

The largest category of Asian Americans is people of Chinese ancestry (1.6 million), followed by those of Filipino (1.4 million), Japanese (848,000), Asian Indian (815,000), and Korean (800,000) background. Most Asian Americans live in the western United States; 40 percent live in California (U.S. Bureau of the Census, 1993).

Young Asian Americans have commanded respect as high achievers who are disproportionately represented at our country's best colleges and universities (Brand, 1987). Many of their elders have also made significant economic and social gains in recent years. Yet some people express attitudes ranging from aloofness to outright hostility in their relations with Asian Americans despite (and sometimes because of) this record of achievement.

But, as we shall see, the "model minority" image of Asian Americans obscures the poverty found among their ranks. We now focus on the history and current standing of Chinese Americans and Japanese Americans—the longest-established Asian American minorities—and conclude with comments on the most recent arrivals.

Chinese Americans

Chinese immigration to the United States began with the California Gold Rush of 1849. As new towns and businesses sprang up virtually overnight and the Central Pacific railroad pushed eastward, about 100,000 Chinese immigrants entered the country eager to offer their labor. Most were hard-working young men willing to take lower-status jobs shunned by whites (Ling, 1971). But the economy soured in the 1870s, and desperate whites were thrown into a fierce competition with the Chinese for jobs. Suddenly the industriousness of the Chinese and their willingness to work for low wages posed a threat. Illustrating a well-known pattern, economic hard times led to mounting prejudice and discrimination (Boswell, 1986).

Soon, whites acted to legally bar the Chinese from many occupations. Courts also withdrew legal protections, unleashing vicious campaigns against the so-called Yellow Peril (Sowell, 1981). Everyone seemed to

SOCIAL SURVEY: "Do you feel you can trust most white people, some white people, or no white people?" (GSS 1982, N = 354; African-American respondents only; *Codebook*, 1993:194)
  "Most white people"   6.2%   "No white people"   11.6%
  "Some white people"   80.2%   DK/NR   2.0%

DIVERSITY: The unassimilable character of Chinese is suggested by historic records such as this population count: "1,200 souls and two Chinamen." (Winnick, 1990)
NOTE: The U.S. government's extension of citizenship rights in 1943 to Chinese Americans born abroad was partly a reflection of China's position as a military ally in the war against Japan (Japanese Americans born abroad could not become U.S. citizens until 1952).

line up against the Chinese, and the saying that a person didn't have "a Chinaman's chance" gained currency (Sung, 1967:56).

In 1882, the U.S. government passed the first of several laws curtailing Chinese immigration. This action created great domestic hardship because, in the United States, Chinese men outnumbered women by almost twenty to one (Hsu, 1971; Lai, 1980). This sex imbalance limiting marriages sent the Chinese population plummeting to about 60,000 by 1920. Chinese women already in the United States, however, were so sought after that they soon became far less submissive to men (Sowell, 1981).

Responding to their plight, some Chinese moved eastward; many more sought the relative safety of urban Chinatowns (Wong, 1971). There Chinese traditions flourished, and kinship networks, called *clans*, provided financial assistance to individuals and represented the interests of all. At the same time, however, Chinatowns discouraged their residents from learning the English language and from taking jobs outside the local community.

A renewed need for labor during World War II prompted President Franklin Roosevelt to end the ban on Chinese immigration in 1943 and to extend the rights of citizenship to Chinese Americans born abroad. Many responded by moving out of Chinatowns and pursuing cultural assimilation. In turn-of-the-century Honolulu, for example, 70 percent of the Chinese people lived in Chinatown; by 1980, only 20 percent did (Lai, 1980).

By 1950, many Chinese Americans had experienced considerable upward social mobility. Today, people of Chinese ancestry are no longer restricted to self-employment in laundries and restaurants; many now work in a host of high-prestige occupations. Many Chinese Americans—including several Nobel prize winners—have excelled in science and technology (Sowell, 1981).

As shown in Table 12–4 on page 344, the median family income of Chinese Americans in 1990 ($41,316) stood above the national average ($35,225). The higher income of all Asian Americans reflects, on average, a larger number of family members in the labor force.[4] Chinese Americans also have an enviable record of educational achievement: a proportion of college graduates that is twice the national average.

---

[4]Median age for all Asian Americans is 29.6, somewhat below the median of 33.1 for the entire U.S. population and below the 34.1 years for whites.

Given the extent of global inequality, it is not surprising that tens of millions of people each year leave their homes in search of more opportunity. This ship, which recently sailed into San Francisco, contained some of the 100,000 Chinese immigrants who annually try to enter this country any way they can.

Despite this overall record of success, many Chinese Americans still grapple with subtle (and sometimes overt) prejudice and discrimination. Such hostility is one reason that poverty among Chinese Americans stands above the national average. Poverty is higher still among those who remain in the protective circle of Chinatowns. At the beginning of the 1980s, the poverty level of New York's Chinatown was twice as high as that of the city as a whole, with half of all Chinese men working in restaurants and three-fourths of Chinese women stuck in low-paying jobs in the garment industry (Sowell, 1981). This economic picture has sparked a debate over whether racial and ethnic enclaves exploit or economically assist their residents (Portes & Jensen, 1989; Zhou & Logan, 1989; Kinkead, 1992).

Japanese Americans

Japanese immigration to the United States began slowly in the 1860s, reaching only 3,000 by 1890. Owners of sugar plantations welcomed Japanese immigrants to the Hawaiian Islands (annexed by the United States in 1898 and made a state in 1959) as a source of cheap labor. Early in this century, however, the number of entrants to California rose along with demands for better pay; white people responded by

TABLE 12–4 The Social Standing of Asian Americans, 1990

	All Asian Americans	Chinese Americans	Japanese Americans	Korean Americans	Filipino Americans	Entire United States
Median family income	$42,240	$41,316	$51,550	$33,909	$46,698	$35,225
Percent in poverty	14.0%	14.0%	7.0%	13.7%	6.4%	13.1%
Median education (years; age 25 and over)	13.7	NA	NA	NA	NA	12.7
Completion of four or more years of college (age 25 and over)	37.7%	40.7%	34.5%	34.5%	39.3%	20.3%

SOURCE: U.S. Bureau of the Census, 1993.

seeking limits to immigration (Daniels, 1971). In 1907 the United States signed an agreement with Japan curbing the entry of men, who were deemed the greater economic threat, while allowing Japanese women to immigrate to ease the sex-ratio imbalance. By the 1920s, state laws in California and other states mandated segregation and banned interracial marriage. The net result was that Japanese immigration soon slowed to a trickle. Not until 1952 did the United States extend citizenship to foreign-born Japanese.

Japanese immigrants differed from the Chinese in three ways. First, the number of Japanese immigrants was smaller, so they escaped some of the hostility directed at the more numerous Chinese. Second, the Japanese arrived with more knowledge about the United States, so they were more skilled in easing racial conflict and encouraging assimilation (Sowell, 1981). Third, Japanese immigrants favored rural farming to clustering together in cities.

But many white people objected to Japanese ownership of farmland. California acted in 1913 to bar further purchases. Although principally motivated by economic considerations, such laws also reflected racial hostility, as suggested by this comment from the state's attorney general:

The fundamental basis of all legislation has been, and is, race undesirability. It seeks to limit [Japanese] presence by curtailing the privileges which they may enjoy here, for they will not come here in large numbers and abide with us if they may not acquire land. (quoted in Kitano, 1980:563)

Foreign-born Japanese (called the *Issei*) responded by placing farmland in the names of their U.S.-born children (*Nisei*), who were constitutionally entitled to citizenship. Others leased farmland with great success. Japanese Americans faced their greatest struggle after December 7, 1941, when a Japanese strike force destroyed much of the U.S. naval fleet at Hawaii's Pearl Harbor. Rage toward Japan was directed at the Japanese living in the United States. Some feared the Japanese here would commit acts of espionage and sabotage on behalf of Japan. Within a year, President Franklin Roosevelt signed Executive Order 9066, an unprecedented effort to protect the national security of the United States. This act designated areas of the West Coast as military zones from which anyone considered likely to be disloyal would be relocated inland to remote military reservations. Ninety percent of those with Japanese ancestry—110,000 people in all—found themselves forcibly interned in security camps.

While concern about national security always builds in times of war, this policy has been hotly criticized. First, it targeted an entire category of people, not one of whom was known to have committed any disloyal act. Second, roughly two-thirds of those imprisoned were *Nisei*, U.S. citizens by birth. Third, although the United States was also at war with Germany and Italy, no such action was taken against people of German or Italian ancestry.

Relocation meant selling homes, furnishings, and businesses on short notice for pennies on the dollar. As a result, almost the entire Japanese-American population was economically devastated. In military prison—camps surrounded by barbed wire and armed soldiers—families suffered greatly as they were crowded into single rooms, often in buildings that had previously been used for livestock (Fujimoto, 1971; Bloom, 1980). The internment ended in 1944, when the Supreme Court declared the policy unconstitutional. In 1988 Congress awarded $20,000 as token compensation to each victim of this policy.

After World War II, Japanese Americans staged a dramatic recovery. Having lost their traditional businesses, they pursued a wide range of new occupations. Because their culture places a high value on education and endorses hard work, Japanese Americans have enjoyed remarkable success. The 1990

DIVERSITY: Social standing profile of Vietnamese Americans:
Median family income (1990) $30,550
Percent in poverty   27.5%
Completion of four or more years
of college (age 25 and over)   17.4%

Q: "Injustice anywhere is a threat to justice everywhere." Rev.
Martin Luther King, Jr.
GLOBAL: According to some analysts, the world is experiencing
a resurgence of racial and ethnic enclaves with humanity clumping
together into four blocs—Latin America, Europe, Africa, and East
Asia—which are racially and ethnically distinct.

median income of a Japanese-American household
was almost 50 percent above the national average.
And the rate of poverty among Japanese Americans is
half that for the United States as a whole.

Upward social mobility has encouraged cultural
assimilation. The third and fourth generations of
Japanese Americans (the *Sansei* and *Yonsei*) rarely live
in residential enclaves, as many Chinese Americans still
do, and a majority now marry non-Japanese Americans.
In the process, many have abandoned their traditions,
including the ability to speak Japanese. A high proportion of Japanese Americans do participate in ethnic
associations as a way of maintaining some traditional
identity (Fugita & O'Brien, 1985). Still, some appear to
be caught between two worlds, belonging to neither. As
one Japanese-American man claims, "I never considered myself 100 percent American because of obvious
physical differences. Nor did I think of myself as
Japanese" (quoted in Okimoto, 1971:14).

Recent Asian Immigrants

More recent immigrants from Asia include Filipinos,
Indians, Koreans, Vietnamese, Samoans, and Gua-
manians. When added to the existing population of
Chinese and Japanese descent, Asian Americans are
this country's fastest-growing minority, accounting for
almost half of all immigration to the United States
(Winnick, 1990). A brief look at Koreans and Filipinos—both people from countries that have had special ties to the United States—reveals the social diversity of newly arriving people from Asia.

Koreans. The 1990 census recorded some 800,000
people of Korean descent in the United States; most
are recent arrivals. Immigration to the United States
was insignificant until the 1950s, after this country
played a major role in the Korean War. The presence
of U.S. troops in South Korea both gave members of
this society firsthand experience with Korean culture
(contact that, for some, led to marriage) and stimulated interest in immigration on the part of many
Koreans.

Generally speaking, the entrepreneurial spirit is
strong among Asian immigrants. Asians are slightly
more likely than whites, three times more likely than
Latinos, and four times more likely than African
Americans to own and operate small businesses (U.S.
Bureau of the Census, 1993). Among all Asian Americans, moreover, Koreans stand out as the most likely
to be entrepreneurs. Residents of New York City, for
example, know that the majority of grocery stores in
their city are Korean-owned; similarly, Los Angelinos

*Asian Americans are more likely than any other category of
people in the United States to be small-scale entrepreneurs.
Although families may earn above-average incomes operating
businesses such as this New York grocery store, they typically
rely on the labor of many people for long hours.*

recognize Koreans as operating a large share of local
liquor stores.

Many Koreans work long hours; nonetheless, the
income of Korean-American families falls slightly
below the national average, as shown in Table 12–4.
Moreover, Korean Americans have experienced limited social acceptance, even among other categories of
Asian Americans. Decades of social distance research
carried out by Emory Bogardus (1968) showed that
most people in the United States desired to avoid even
casual contact with Koreans. In short, the case of
Korean Americans shows that minorities struggle for
both economic success and social acceptance.

Filipinos. With a recorded population of 1.4 million in
1990, Filipinos are more numerous than most others of
Asian descent except for the Chinese. In part, this
large number is explained by the fact that the United
States controlled this south Asian island cluster
between 1898 (when Spain ceded it as partial settlement of the Spanish-American War) and 1946 (when
the Philippines became an independent republic).

Despite living under the U.S. government,
Filipinos did not enjoy rights of U.S. citizenship. But
as legal limits were placed on the immigration of other
Asian peoples, Filipinos came to the United States to
take low-paying agricultural work, especially in Hawaii
and California. Even more than others among Asian
immigrants, the vast majority of Filipino newcomers to

DIVERSITY: A gripping memoir of growing up in a Bronx neighborhood during the early decades of this century is Kate Simon's *Bronx Primitive: Portraits of a Childhood* (Harper & Row, 1982). This book vividly portrays the central role of ethnicity in the United States at that time.

DIVERSITY: Dade County, Florida, remains a national center of Hispanic culture. The composition of its population is 45% Hispanic (mostly Cuban), 37% Anglo, 18% African American, and 1% other categories.

Seeing Ourselves

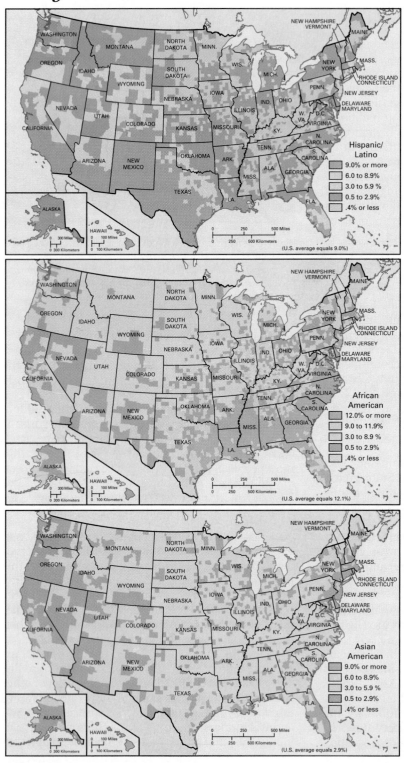

NATIONAL MAP 12–2
Percent Hispanic/Latino, African American, and Asian American, by County, 1990

In 1990, Hispanics represented 9 percent of the U.S. population, compared with 12 percent for African Americans and 3 percent for people of Asian descent. These three maps show the geographic distribution of these categories of people. Comparing them, we see that the southern half of the United States is home to far more minorities than the northern half. But are the three concentrated in the same specific areas? What patterns do the maps reveal?

From *American Demographics Desk Reference Series,* No. 1, June 1991, pp. 8, 14, 16. Reprinted with permission. © 1991, *American Demographics* magazine, Ithaca, New York. Data from 1990 decennial census.

RESOURCE: A resource for the study of racial and ethnic tensions in Europe is *Eurobarometer: Public Opinion in the European Community*, prepared by the Commission of the European Communities (November, 1989).
RESOURCE: William O'Hare's "The Rise of Hispanic Affluence" is one of the articles found in the Macionis and Benokraitis reader, *Seeing Ourselves*.

DIVERSITY: The 1990 census showed 28% of New York City residents to be foreign-born, the highest proportion in 50 years. New York has 2.1 million foreign-born residents, with 46% arriving between 1980 and 1990. New York still receives one-sixth of all immigration, especially immigrants from the Caribbean area (including the Dominican Republic, Jamaica, Guyana, and Haiti).

TABLE 12–5 The Social Standing of Hispanic Americans, 1990

	All Hispanics	Mexican Americans	Puerto Ricans	Cuban Americans	Entire United States
Median family income	$23,431	$23,240	$18,008	$31,439	$35,225
Percent in poverty	25.0%	25.0%	37.5%	13.8%	13.1%
Median education (years; age 25 and over)	12.0	10.8	12.0	12.4	12.7
Completion of four or more years of college (age 25 and over)	9.2%	6.2%	10.1%	18.5%	20.3%

SOURCE: U.S. Bureau of the Census, 1993.

the United States were men, which had the predictable effect of keeping the U.S. Filipino population small.

Generally speaking, Filipinos have fared better in this country than most other Asian Americans, as a glance back at Table 12–4 shows. A closer look reveals a mixed pattern by which some Filipinos stand out among successful professionals (especially in medicine), while others struggle in low-skill jobs just trying to get by (Parillo, 1994).

But the key to the relatively high income of Filipino-American families is gender. Almost three-fourths of Filipino-American women are in the labor force, compared to about half of Korean-American women. Moreoever, 42 percent of Filipino-American women have a four-year college degree, an achievement equaled by just 25 percent of Korean-American women. Thus, the typical Filipino-American family has relatively high income because both wives and husbands work, in many cases at high paying professional occupations.

In sum, the social history of Asians in this country is complex. The Japanese come closest to having achieved social acceptance; for the Koreans and other Asian Americans, even economic success has not toppled historical prejudice and discrimination. And, along with considerable prosperity, many Asian Americans continue to struggle with problems associated with poverty.

One thing seems clear: In light of their exceptionally high immigration rate, people of Asian ancestry are certain to play an even more central role in U.S. society in the century to come.

Hispanic Americans

In 1991, there were at least 23 million Hispanics, which is 9.3 percent of the U.S. population. Few people who fall into this category actually use the term "Hispanic" in everyday conversation to describe themselves. Like Asian Americans, Hispanics are really a cluster of smaller populations, each of which identifies with a particular country. "Hispanic" is thus a convenient shorthand term employed by the Census Bureau for collecting and organizing information about diverse peoples who share Spanish heritage perhaps mixed with African and Native-American ancestry (Marín & Marín, 1991). "Latino," an alternative to "Hispanic," finds favor primarily on the West Coast.

More than half of Latinos (at least 14 million) are Mexican Americans, commonly called "Chicanos." Puerto Ricans are next in population size (3 million), followed by Cuban Americans (1 million). Other societies of Latin America are represented in smaller numbers, totaling an additional 5 million. Because of a high birth rate and significant immigration, the Hispanic population is currently increasing by almost 1 million a year. Projections suggest that Hispanics will outnumber African Americans in the United States by 2010 (U.S. Bureau of the Census, 1993).

The U.S. Hispanic population resides primarily in the Southwest and especially in California, where one in four residents is Latino (in greater Los Angeles, the proportion is closer to one in two). National Map 12–2 locates counties across the United States favored by Hispanics and contrasts them with counties containing especially large African-American and Asian-American populations.

The social standing of Hispanics has improved in some respects. One researcher reports that, between 1984 and 1988, the number of Hispanic professionals jumped by half (Schwartz, 1989). Another calculation indicates that the number of affluent Hispanic households (with $50,000 or more in annual income) more than tripled between 1972 and 1988 (O'Hare, 1990). Nevertheless, family income for Hispanics—about $23,431 in 1990—represents only a slight increase in real purchasing power compared to 1980. Furthermore, as Table 12–5 indicates, this figure remains well below

Q: "A free man carries himself with dignity. He feels respect for others, and for himself. In a free society all are equals, and in a society of free men there exist no prejudices." Olaf Palme

Q: "When I first came to Washington, I saw myself as Puerto Rican. I quickly realized that the majority society saw me as a member of a larger group called Hispanic." Congressman Robert Garcia

This country's immigration policies have changed over time; today, as in the past, we have also seen fit to apply different standards to different categories of people. A recent case in point is Haitians who have fled their Caribbean nation because of poverty and political turbulence. The U.S. government has refused to allow most Haitians to enter this country, claiming that they are not true political refugees. Critics ask whether this policy would stand if the people in question were not both poor and dark skinned.

the national average.[5] As the following sections reveal, however, some categories of Hispanics have fared better than others.

Mexican Americans

For centuries, Mexican Americans have inhabited land once a part of Mexico and annexed by the United States after the Mexican American War (1846–48). Most, however, are recent immigrants. Between 1970 and 1990, more immigrants came to the United States from Mexico than from any other country. The official Mexican-American population is more than 13 million, but the actual total could be far higher since large numbers of people who have passed illegally from Mexico to the United States are not counted by the Census Bureau.

Like many other immigrants, many Mexican Americans have worked as low-wage farm laborers; many more hold other low-paying jobs. Table 12–5 shows that the 1990 median family income for Mexican Americans was $23,240, about 66 percent of the comparable national figure of $35,225. In 1990, the government classified one-fourth of Chicano families as poor—more than twice the national average but less than the proportion of African Americans living in poverty. Moreover, despite notable improvement, Mexican Americans receive significantly less education than U.S. adults as a whole and have a higher than average dropout rate.

Puerto Ricans

Puerto Rico (like the Philippines) became a possession of the United States in 1898 with the conclusion of the Spanish-American War. In 1917, islanders (but not Filipinos) became American citizens, so that Puerto Ricans can more freely move to and from the mainland (Fitzpatrick, 1980).

New York City is the center of Puerto Rican life in the continental United States. It was the start of regular airline service between New York City and San Juan, the capital of Puerto Rico, that sparked migration, and, by 1950, New York's Puerto Rican population stood at 187,000 (Glazer & Moynihan, 1970). Today New York is home to about 1 million Puerto Ricans.

Certainly many of these people have found in New York less than they wished. About one-third of that city's Puerto Rican population is now severely disadvantaged. Adjusting to cultural patterns on the mainland—including, for many, learning English—is a major challenge; Puerto Ricans with darker skin encounter especially strong prejudice and discrimination. As a result, about as many people return to Puerto Rico each year as arrive from the island.

This "revolving door" pattern has hampered cultural assimilation. Three-fourths of Puerto Rican families in the United States speak Spanish at home, compared with about half of Mexican-American

---

[5]The 1990 median age of the U.S. Hispanic population was 25.7 years, well below the national median of 33.1 years. This differential explains some of the disparity in income and education.

families (Sowell, 1981; Stevens & Swicegood, 1987). Speaking only Spanish may strengthen ethnic identity, but it also limits economic opportunity. Puerto Ricans also have a higher incidence of female-headed households than do other Hispanics, a pattern that places families at greater risk of poverty (Reimers, 1984). Table 12–5 shows that in 1990 median family income for Puerto Ricans was $18,008—51 percent of the national average. Throughout the 1980s, in short, Puerto Ricans were the most socially disadvantaged Hispanic minority.

Cuban Americans

Large numbers of Cubans came to the United States after the 1959 Marxist revolution led by Fidel Castro. By 1972, aided by special legislation, 400,000 Cubans had immigrated (Perez, 1980). Most settled in Miami, although the Cuban community in New York now numbers over 50,000. Those who fled Castro's Cuba were generally not the "huddled masses" described on the Statue of Liberty but highly educated business and professional people. They wasted little time building much the same success in the United States that they had enjoyed in their homeland (Fallows, 1983).

Table 12–5 shows that the median household income for Cuban Americans in 1990 was $31,439—consistent with the fact that these people are generally older and more successful than other categories of Hispanics (Krafft, 1993). But note that this income still lags below the national standard, just as poverty among Cuban Americans is higher than average.

Cuban Americans have managed a delicate balancing act—achieving success in the larger society while retaining much of their traditional culture. Of the categories of Hispanics we have considered, they are the most likely to speak Spanish in their homes; eight out of ten families do (Sowell, 1981). However, cultural distinctiveness and living in highly visible communities, like Miami's Little Havana district, provoke hostility from some white people.

The 1990 census placed the total number of Cuban Americans at more than 1 million. Substantial population growth during the 1980s followed the so-called Mariel boat lift, the influx of 125,000 refugees from Mariel Harbor in Cuba. Several thousand of these "boat people" had been released from Cuban prisons and mental hospitals, and they became the focus of mass media accounts fueling prejudice against Cuban Americans (Clark, Lasaga, & Regue, 1981; Portes, 1984).

About 90,000 of this second wave of Cuban immigrants settled in the Miami area while others—especially those with darker skin—entered cities in the Northeast (Perez, 1980). Typically poorer and less educated than those who had arrived a generation earlier, these recent immigrants clashed with the more conservative and established Cuban community in Miami (Fallows, 1983). But they, too, are quickly putting down roots. Soon after arriving, most applied for resident status so that relatives abroad could also be admitted to the United States.

White Ethnic Americans

The term *white ethnics* gained currency during the 1960s in recognition of the visible ethnic heritage—and social disadvantages—of many white Americans. This concept conveys a quasi-minority standing: members of the white majority who are not of privileged WASP ancestry. Thus white ethnics have some non-English European ancestry, perhaps tracing their heritage to Germany, Ireland, Poland, Italy, or other countries. Overall, more than half of the women and men in the United States fall into some white ethnic category, and, for many, it forms an important element of personal identity (Alba, 1990).

European immigration was pronounced during the nineteenth century. Initially, the Germans and Irish predominated. Italians, and Jews from many European countries, soon followed. Despite cultural differences, all shared the hope that the United States would offer greater political freedom and economic opportunity than they had known in their homelands. The belief that the streets of their new land were paved with gold contrasted sharply with the reality experienced by the vast majority of immigrants. Jobs were not always easy to find, and most demanded hard labor for low wages.

White ethnics also endured their share of prejudice and discrimination, which rose with the increasing tide of immigration. Nativist organizations opposed the entry of non-WASP Europeans to the United States. Newspaper ads seeking workers in the mid-nineteenth century often carried a warning to new arrivals: "None need apply but Americans" (Handlin, 1941:67).

Some of this prejudice and discrimination was based on class rather than ethnicity, since immigrants with little command of English were typically poor as well. But even distinguished achievers faced hostility. Fiorello La Guardia, the son of immigrants, half Italian and half Jewish, served as mayor of New York between 1933 and 1945 in spite of being rebuked by President Herbert Hoover in words that reveal unambiguous ethnic hatred:

NOTE: Figure 12–3 shows the *number* of immigrants over time; the *proportion* of immigrants was far higher (about 10% of the total population per year) until World War I. In recent years, this proportion has again been rising, although it still is below 3%.
Q: "What happens to a dream deferred?
    Does it dry up like a raisin in the sun?
    Or fester like a sore, and then run?

Does it stink like rotten meat?
Or crust and sugar over, like a syrupy sweet?
Maybe it just sags like a heavy load;
Or does it explode?"
Langston Hughes (*Harlem*, 1951)

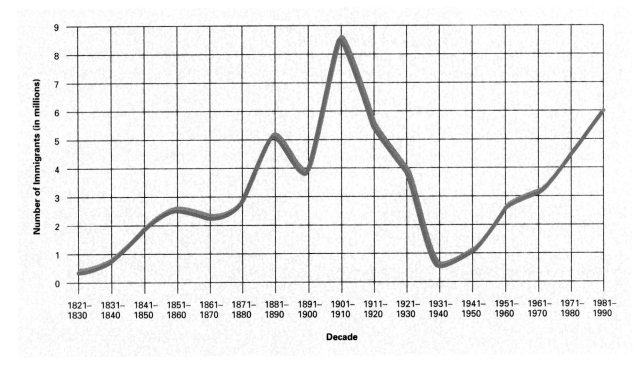

FIGURE 12–3 Immigration to the United States, by Decade

(U.S. Immigration and Naturalization Service)

You should go back where you belong and advise Mussolini how to make good honest citizens in Italy. The Italians are preponderantly our murderers and bootleggers. . . . Like a lot of other foreign spawn, you do not appreciate the country that supports and tolerates you. (Mann, 1959, cited in Baltzell, 1964:30)

Nativists were finally victorious. In 1921 the government enacted legislation that limited immigration by imposing a quota from each foreign country; this quota system remained until 1968. The most severe restrictions were placed on southern and eastern Europeans—people likely to have darker skin and to differ culturally from the dominant WASPs (Fallows, 1983).

In response to widespread bigotry, many white ethnics followed the old pattern of forming supportive residential enclaves. Some also gained footholds in specialized trades: The Italians entered the construction industry; the Irish worked in various building trades and took civil service jobs; Jews predominated in the garment industry; many Greeks (like the Chinese) worked in the retail food business (Newman, 1973).

White ethnics who prospered were likely to assimilate into the larger society. Many working-class "ethnics," however, still live in traditional neighborhoods. Despite continuing problems, white ethnics have achieved considerable success over the course of this century. Many descendants of immigrants who labored in sweatshops and lived in overcrowded tenements now earn high incomes and enjoy considerable social prestige. As a result, ethnic heritage now serves as a source of pride to many white men and women.

U.S. MINORITIES: LOOKING AHEAD

The United States has been—and will probably remain—a land of immigrants like no other. Immigration has generated striking cultural diversity, as well as tales of success, hope, and struggle, told in hundreds of tongues.

For most who came to this country in the first wave of immigration that peaked in 1910, the next two generations brought gradual economic gains and at

SOCIAL SURVEY: "Is there enough legislation on the books to improve conditions for blacks in this country, with further progress coming through private efforts? Or is more legislation needed?" (*Newsweek* poll, August, 1991)

	"Enough"	"More needed"	DK/NR
Afri Amer	24%	64%	12%
Whites	53%	35%	12%

"Can fairness in education and hiring and promotion be accomplished without quotas?"

	"Yes"	"No"	DK/NR
Afri Amer	26%	61%	13%
Whites	59%	29%	12%

least some cultural assimilation. The United States also granted basic freedoms where they earlier had been denied: Citizenship was extended to all African Americans (1868), Native Americans (1924), foreign-born Filipinos (1942), Chinese Americans (1943), and Japanese Americans (1952). In the 1950s, African Americans organized the civil rights movement that sparked further legal reforms.

As Figure 12–3 indicates, a second wave of immigration began after World War II and continued as immigration laws were relaxed during the 1960s. Since 1990, more than 1 million people have come to the United States each year, more than twice the number that entered annually during the "great immigration" a century ago (although newcomers now enter a country with five times as many people). Coupled with a weak economy, this elevated immigration has provoked opposition. Polls show that most people in the United States now think that the "golden door" has opened too wide (Church, 1993).

Controversy surrounding immigration is nothing new. What is different today are the names, faces, and cultural patterns of new arrivals. Most immigrants now come not from Europe but from Latin America and Asia, with Mexicans, Filipinos, and South Koreans arriving in the largest numbers. Rather than entering the large cities on the "European" side of the United States, most new immigrants are bringing profound cultural changes to cities in the South and West.

New arrivals face much the same prejudice and discrimination experienced by those who came before them. Also, like European immigrants of the past, many now struggle to enter U.S. society without entirely abandoning their traditional culture. Some have also built racial and ethnic enclaves: The Little Havana and Little Saigon of today stand alongside the Little Italy and Germantown of the past. New arrivals also share the hope that racial and ethnic diversity, while a dimension of difference, will not be a badge of inferiority.

SUMMARY

1. Race involves a cluster of biological traits. Although a century ago scientists identified three broad overarching categories—Caucasians, Mongoloids, and Negroids—there are no pure races. Ethnicity is not a matter of biology but of shared cultural heritage.

2. Minorities—including those of certain races and ethnicities—are categories of people who are socially distinctive and who have a subordinate social position.

3. A prejudice is an inflexible and distorted generalization about a category of people. Racism, a powerful type of prejudice, is any assertion that one race is innately superior or inferior to another.

4. Discrimination is a pattern of action by which a person treats various categories of people unequally.

5. Pluralism refers to a state in which racial and ethnic categories, although distinct, have equal social standing. Assimilation is a process by which minorities gradually adopt the patterns of the dominant culture. Segregation is the physical and

social separation of categories of people. Genocide is the extermination of a category of people.

6. Native Americans—the original inhabitants of the Americas—have endured genocide, segregation, and forced assimilation. Today the social standing of Native Americans is well below the national average.

7. WASPs, who predominated among the original European settlers of the United States, continue to enjoy high social position today.

8. African Americans lived for two centuries as slaves. Emancipation in 1865 gave way to rigid segregation prescribed by law. Despite legal equality today, African Americans remain relatively disadvantaged.

9. Chinese and Japanese Americans historically have suffered due to both racial and ethnic differences. Today, however, both categories have above-average income and education. More recent Asian immigration—especially of Koreans and Filipinos—has made this the fastest-growing racial category of the U.S. population.

10. Hispanics represent many ethnicities rooted in Spanish culture. Mexican Americans, the largest Hispanic minority, are concentrated in the Southwest. Puerto Ricans, most of whom live in New York, are poorer. Cubans, concentrated in Miami, are the most affluent category of Hispanics.

11. White ethnics include non-WASPs of European ancestry. While most families made gains during this century, many white ethnics still struggle for economic security.

12. Immigration has increased in recent years. No longer primarily from Europe, most immigrants now arrive from Latin America and Asia.

KEY CONCEPTS

assimilation the process by which minorities gradually adopt patterns of the dominant culture

discrimination an action that involves treating various categories of people unequally

ethnicity a shared cultural heritage

genocide the systematic annihilation of one category of people by another

institutional discrimination discrimination that is a normative and routine part of the economy, the educational system, or some other social institution

minority a category of people, distinguished by physical or cultural traits, who are socially disadvantaged

miscegenation the biological process of interbreeding among racial categories

pluralism a state in which racial and ethnic minorities are distinct but have social parity

prejudice an attitude involving a rigid and irrational generalization about an entire category of people

race a category composed of men and women who share biologically transmitted traits that members of a society deem socially significant

racism the belief that one racial category is innately superior or inferior to another

scapegoat a person or category of people, typically with little power, whom people unfairly blame for their own troubles

segregation the physical and social separation of categories of people

stereotype a set of prejudices concerning some category of people

CRITICAL-THINKING QUESTIONS

1. Clearly differentiate race and ethnicity. What is a minority?

2. In what ways are prejudice and discrimination mutually reinforcing?

3. Are *all* generalizations about minorities wrong? What distinguishes a fair generalization from an unfair stereotype?

4. Specify the relative social standing of the various minorities considered in this chapter. Can you assess how factors such as prejudice, discrimination, average age, family patterns, and cultural traits affect this hierarchy?

SUGGESTED READINGS

Classic Sources

W. E. Burghardt Du Bois. *The Souls of Black Folks*. New York: Penguin Books, 1982; orig. 1903.

This pioneering analysis of racial dynamics in the United States remains a source of insights decades after its publication.

Gunner Myrdal, with Richard Sterner and Arnold Rose. *An American Dilemma: The Negro Problem and Modern Democracy*. New York: Harper & Brothers, 1944.

This classic investigation of the United States by a noted Swedish social scientist highlighted the dilemma posed by a racial caste system in a society aspiring to be democratic.

Contemporary Sources

Peter I. Rose. *They and We: Racial and Ethnic Relations in the United States*. 5th ed. New York: McGraw Hill, 1994.

This text provides a more detailed discussion of this chapter's issues as well as a focus on the resurgence of racial and ethnic identity in the 1980s and 1990s.

Richard G. Majors and Jacob U. Gordon, eds. *The American Black Male: His Present Status and His Future*. Chicago: Nelson Hall, 1994.

This collection of twenty-one essays surveys a wide range of social problems experienced by African-American men.

Gwen Kinkead. *Chinatown: A Portrait of a Closed Society*. New York: HarperCollins, 1992.

This account of New York's Chinatown—the largest of its kind with 150,000 people, most of whom are recent immigrants—is valuable both for its striking analysis of race and ethnicity and its example of challenging fieldwork.

Maria P. P. Root, ed. *Racially Mixed People in America*. Newbury Park, Calif.: Sage, 1992.

This book offers a look at biracial children, whose numbers have risen steadily in the United States.

Kathleen M. Blee. *Women of the Klan: Racism and Gender in the 1920s*. Berkeley: University of California Press, 1991.

This study of the Indiana Ku Klux Klan demonstrates the important role of women in integrating klan themes in everyday life and giving the organization public legitimacy.

Cornel West. *Race Matters*. Boston: Beacon Press, 1993.

Stephen L. Carter. *Reflections of an Affirmative Action Baby*. New York: Basic Books, 1991.

The first of these books is one of the most widely discussed efforts in recent years to untangle the problems of race in the United States. The second book, also influential, examines racial issues from a more conservative point of view.

Herman Belz. *Equality Transformed: A Quarter-Century of Affirmative Action*. New Brunswick, N.J.: Transaction, 1991.

This history of racial preferences examines the complex consequences of affirmative action with regard to race relations.

George J. Borgas. *Friends or Strangers: The Impact of Immigrants on the U.S. Economy*. New York: Basic Books, 1990.

Are immigrants a source of innovation and economic vitality or a factor in raising unemployment? This book paints a portrait of newcomers to the United States and assesses the economic consequences of immigration.

Lewis H. Gann and Peter J. Duignan. *The Hispanics in the United States: A History*. Boulder, Colo.: Westview, 1986.

This book provides a general history of Hispanic cultures in the United States.

Global Sources

Philomenia Essed. *Understanding Racism: An Interdisciplinary Theory*. Newbury Park, Calif.: Sage, 1992.

Drawing on interviews with women of color, the author compares the experience of racism in the Netherlands and in the United States.

Eliezer Ben-Raphael and Stephen Sharot. *Ethnicity, Religion, and Class in Israeli Society*. Cambridge, U.K. Cambridge University Press, 1991.

This investigation of the resurgence of ethnicity in Israel also demonstrates its interaction with social class.

Walter P. Zenner. *Minorities in the Middle: A Cross-Cultural Analysis*. Albany, N.Y.: SUNY Press, 1991.

This global analysis highlights Jews, Scots, Chinese, and other ethnic categories that have marginal standing in various societies.

Lucy Nguyen-Hong-Nhiem and Joel Martin Halpern, eds. *The Far East Comes Near: Autobiographical Accounts of Southeast Asian Students in America*. Amherst, Mass.: University of Massachusetts Press, 1989.

These personal accounts chronicle the experiences of the more than 1 million Asian refugees that have come to the United States in recent decades.

Archibald J. Motley, Jr., *Cocktails,* c. 1926.

DATA FILE: An outline of this chapter, along with supplementary lecture material, is included in the *Data File*.
NOTE: The chapter-opening art is *Cocktails* by Archibald J. Motley, Jr.
RESOURCE: Naomi Wolf's "The Beauty Myth" is included in the Macionis and Benokraitis reader.

Q: "To be born a woman means to inhabit, from early infancy to the last day of life, a psychological world which differs from the world of man." Mirra Komarovsky
Q: ". . . we all live in single-sex worlds, and most of what we know—from history, the humanities, the social and behavioral sciences—deals with the male world." Jessie Bernard

Sex and Gender

*T*he Duchess of Windsor once quipped, "A woman cannot be too rich or too thin." Perhaps the first half of this observation might apply to men as well, but certainly not the second. Why is it that the $20-billion-a-year cosmetics industry aims almost exclusively at women? Why does the diet industry—which totals a whopping $40 billion each year—also target women?

According to Naomi Wolf (1990), the answer lies within the cultural patterns she terms the "beauty myth." The beauty myth means, first, that society teaches women to measure personal importance, accomplishment, and satisfaction in terms of physical appearance (Backman & Adams, 1991). Curiously, however, this myth also sets up unattainable standards of beauty for most women (such as the Playboy centerfold or the one-hundred-pound New York fashion model), making the pursuit of

satisfaction in this way ultimately self-defeating. It should not be surprising, argues Wolf, that the beauty myth surfaced in our culture during the 1890s, the 1920s, and the 1980s—all times of anxiety and heightened debate about the social standing of women.

A second meaning of the beauty myth is that society teaches women to value relationships with men, whom, presumably, they attract with their beauty. The relentless pursuit of beauty not only drives women toward being highly disciplined, but it also forces them to be highly attuned and responsive to men. Beauty-minded women, in short, try to please men and avoid challenging male power.

A third lesson found in the beauty myth is that society teaches men to possess women who embody beauty. In other words, a society's concept of beauty both reduces women to objects and motivates *men toward possessing them as if they were dolls rather than human beings.*

In short, Wolf asserts, beauty is really as much about *behavior as* appearance. *The myth, she sums up, is that beauty is the key to personal happiness for women (just as possessing a beautiful woman is vital to men). In fact, however, beauty amounts to an elaborate system—which this chapter explores—through which society teaches both women and men to embrace specific roles and attitudes that assume their positions in a social hierarchy.*

SEX AND GENDER

Many people think the fact that men seem concerned with getting rich while women appear preoccupied with remaining thin reflects some basic and innate difference between the sexes. But, as we shall see, the different social experiences of women and men are the creation of society far more than biology. To begin, we shall distinguish the key concepts of sex and gender.

Sex: A Biological Distinction

Sex refers to *the biological distinction between females and males.* Sex is closely related to reproduction, in which both females and males play a part. The female ovum and the male sperm, which join to form a fertilized embryo, each contain twenty-three pairs of chromosomes—biological codes that guide physical development. One of these chromosome pairs determines the child's sex. The mother always contributes an X chromosome; the father contributes either an X or a Y. A second X from the father produces a female (XX) embryo; a Y from the father yields a male (XY) embryo. A child's sex, then, is determined at conception.

Within weeks of conception, the sex of an embryo starts to guide its development. If the embryo is male, testicular tissues begin producing testosterone, a hormone that stimulates the development of the male genitals. Without testosterone, the embryo develops female genitals. In the United States, about 105 boys are born for every 100 girls, but a higher death rate among males renders females a slight majority by the time people reach their mid-thirties (U.S. National Center for Health Statistics, 1990).

Primary and Secondary Sex Characteristics

At birth, females and males are distinguished by **primary sex characteristics,** *the genitals, used to reproduce the human species.* Further sex differentiation occurs years later when children reach puberty and their reproductive systems become fully operational. At this point, humans exhibit **secondary sex characteristics,** *bodily development, apart from the genitals, that distinguishes biologically mature females and males.* To accommodate pregnancy, giving birth, and nurturing infants, adolescent females develop wider hips, breasts, and soft fatty tissue, thereby providing a reserve supply of nutrition for pregnancy and breastfeeding (Brownmiller, 1984). Usually slightly taller and heavier than females from birth, adolescent males typically develop more muscles in the upper body, more extensive body hair, and voices deeper in tone. These are general differences, since some males are smaller, have less body hair, and speak in a higher tone than some females.

Hermaphrodites

Sex is not always a clear-cut matter. In rare cases, a hormone imbalance before birth produces a **hermaphrodite** (a word derived from Hermaphroditus, the offspring of the mythological Greek gods Hermes and Aphrodite, who embodied both sexes), *a human being with some combination of female and male internal and external genitalia.* Because our culture is uneasy about sexual ambiguity, we often look upon hermaphrodites with confusion and even disgust. In contrast, the Pokot of eastern Africa are indifferent to what they define as a simple biological error, and the Navaho regard hermaphrodites with awe, viewing them as the embodiment of the full potential of both the female and the male (Geertz, 1975).

Transsexuals

Further complicating the story of human sexuality, some people deliberately choose to change their sex. Hermaphrodites may undergo genital surgery to gain the appearance (and occasionally the function) of a sexually normal female or male. Surgery is also commonly considered by **transsexuals,** *people who feel they are one sex though biologically they are the other.* Tens of thousands of transsexuals in the United States have medically altered their genitals to escape the sense of being "trapped in the wrong body" (Restak, 1979, cited in Offir, 1982:146).

SOCIAL SURVEY: "What about sexual relations between two adults of the same sex?" (GSS 1993, N = 1,075; *Codebook*, 1993:265)
"Always wrong"   62.4%   "Not wrong at all"   20.7%
"Almost always wrong"   4.1%   DK/NR   5.9%
"Wrong only sometimes"   6.9%

RESOURCE: J. M. Carrier's comparative look at homosexuality is among the cross-cultural selections in the Macionis and Benokraitis reader, *Seeing Ourselves*.
NOTE: *The New York Times* used the word "gay" for the first time in 1987. The paper adopted the term "Ms." in 1986.

Sexual Orientation

Sexual orientation is *the manner in which people experience sexual arousal and achieve sexual pleasure.* For most living things, sexuality is biologically programmed. In humans, however, sexual orientation is bound up in the complex web of cultural attitudes and rules. The norm in all industrial societies is *heterosexuality* (*hetero* is a Greek word meaning "the other of two"), by which a person is sexually attracted to someone of the opposite sex. However, *homosexuality* (*homo* is the Greek word for "the same"), by which a person is sexually attracted to people of the same sex, is not uncommon.

Although all cultures endorse heterosexuality, many tolerate—and some have even encouraged—homosexuality. Among the ancient Greeks, for instance, elite intellectual men celebrated homosexuality as the highest form of relationship, shunning women, whom they considered their intellectual inferiors. In this light, heterosexuality amounted to little more than a reproductive necessity and men who did not engage in homosexuality were defined as deviant. But because homosexual relations do not permit reproduction, no record exists of a society that has favored homosexuality to the exclusion of heterosexuality (Kluckhohn, 1948; Ford & Beach, 1951; Greenberg, 1988).

Homosexuality and the Pursuit of Gay Rights

By the 1960s, homosexuals became more outspoken in opposition to heterosexual norms, and they adopted the term *gay* to describe themselves. Gays intended this new terminology to express positive satisfaction with their sexual orientation, countering the traditionally negative view of gays measured against a heterosexual standard. Gays also began to organize in opposition to stereotypes—pointing out that the personalities of gay people vary as much as those of "straights"—and also against pervasive discrimination.

Tolerance of gay people is gradually increasing, especially in recent years as the gay rights movement has gained strength. But recent years have also brought an unprecedented challenge in the form of acquired immune deficiency syndrome, or AIDS. In the 1980s, when the disease largely targeted homosexual men, gays were subject to a renewed outburst of prejudice, discrimination, and outright violence. In the 1990s, although hostility persists, there has been a gradual softening of public attitudes. Although 70 percent of U.S. adults define homosexuality as morally wrong, the same majority thinks our society should allow gays and straights equal workplace opportunities (Salholz, 1990; NORC, 1991:257).

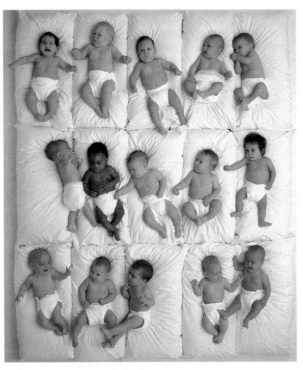

Sex is a biological distinction that develops prior to birth. Gender is the meaning that a society attaches to being female or male. That is, culture divides the range of human feelings, thoughts, and behavior into what people define as feminine or masculine. Moreover, gender differences are also a matter of power, as what is masculine typically has social priority over what is feminine. Gender differences are not evident among infants, of course, but the ways in which we think of boys and girls set in motion patterns that will continue for a lifetime.

Until our society becomes more accepting of homosexuality, some gay people will understandably choose to remain "in the closet," fearfully avoiding public disclosure of their sexual orientation. Heterosexuals can begin to understand what this secrecy means by imagining never speaking about their romances to parents, roommates, or colleagues (Offir, 1982).

For their part, many gay men and many gay women (commonly called *lesbians*) have adopted the term *homophobia* (with Greek roots meaning "fear of sameness") to place their opponents on the defensive. This word, first used in the late 1960s, designates an irrational fear of gay people (Weinberg, 1973). Instead of asking "What's wrong with gay people?" this label turns attention to society itself: "What's wrong with people who can't accept this sexual orientation?"

NOTE: Kinsey wrote not of "bisexual" but "ambisexual" behavior, suggesting sexual ambivalence rather than simply mixing two types of behavior.
Q: "This is first of all a report on what people do, which raises no questions of what they should do, or what kinds of people do it." Alfred Kinsey, 1948:7
NOTE: Twenty-two states still have laws on the books prohibiting sodomy; seven of these ban only homosexual sodomy; a recent Supreme Court decision upheld a Georgia ban on sodomy. At least three states (Massachusetts, Wisconsin, and Oregon) have passed antidiscrimination laws protecting homosexual rights.
Q: "Gender is what gender means. It has no basis in anything other than the social reality its hegemony constructs." Catharine MacKinnon

Determining the gay and straight share of the population is a vexing problem for researchers. For one thing, people are not always willing to describe their sexuality to strangers (or even family members); for another, sexual orientation is not a matter of neat, mutually exclusive categories. Pioneering research by Alfred Kinsey (1948, 1953) described sexual orientation as a continuum, from exclusively homosexual to equally homosexual and heterosexual, to exclusively heterosexual. Kinsey suggested that about 4 percent of males and 2 percent of females have an exclusively same-sex orientation, although he also estimated that at least one-third of men and one-eighth of women had a homosexual experience leading to orgasm.

In the wake of the Kinsey studies, most social scientists settled on a figure of 10 percent to describe the proportion of gays in the U.S. population. The gay rights movement, especially, has long maintained that 10 percent of our society's members are gay, which lends moral urgency to their pursuit of social acceptance and equal standing (Kirk & Madsen, 1989). In the last several years, a considerable number of studies, both in the United States and abroad, have challenged this assertion, suggesting that it is simply too high. A review of data from surveys conducted by the Centers for Disease Control, National Opinion Research Center (NORC), and social scientists in other countries points to the conclusion that while the share of men having some homosexual experience is probably at least 10 percent, those having an exclusively homosexual orientation is no more than 3 or 4 percent. In the case of women, the percentages are about half as large (Crispell, 1992; Cole & Gorman, 1993; Horowitz et al., 1993).

Bisexuality

Kinsey and his colleagues claimed that people who are more homosexual are, by definition, less heterosexual. But other researchers (Storms, 1980) take issue with this view, suggesting that sexual orientation is two-dimensional because some individuals experience little sexual attraction to people of either sex (an orientation termed *asexuality*), while others feel strong attraction to people of *both* sexes (known as *bisexuality*).

The importance of bisexuality lies in showing us that sexual orientation is not an "either/or" issue. Many bisexuals do not think of themselves as either gay or straight, and their behavior may not correspond to either gay or straight living; they experience their own particular joys and face their own distinctive problems.

The Origins of Sexual Orientation

How does a person develop a particular sexual orientation? The mounting evidence suggests that sexual orientation is rooted in biological factors present at birth and further reinforced by the hormone balance in the body as we grow (Gladue, Green, & Hellman, 1984; Weinrich, 1987; Isay, 1989; Puterbaugh, 1990; Angier, 1992; Gelman, 1992). Still other research points to the role of the social environment in encouraging sexual attitudes and behaviors (Troiden, 1988). The fact that most adults who describe themselves as homosexuals have had some heterosexual experience suggests how society can steer our thoughts, actions, and even feelings regardless of what biological forces are at work.

In short, both nature and nurture play a part in anyone's sexual orientation. To complicate matters further, there is no reason to think that sexual orientation is established in precisely the same way for everyone. At this point, while physical and social scientists have discovered a great deal about sexual orientation, we still have much more to learn.

Gender: A Cultural Distinction

Gender refers to *the significance a society attaches to biological categories of female and male.* Gender is evident throughout the social world, shaping how we think about ourselves, guiding our interaction with others, and influencing our work and family life. But gender involves much more than difference; it also involves disparities in virtually every social resource.

This inequality, which has historically favored males, is no simple matter of biological differences between the two sexes. Females and males do differ biologically, of course, but these variations are complex and inconsistent. Beyond the primary and secondary sex characteristics already noted, males around the world average 150 pounds, compared to about 120 pounds for females. In addition, males have more muscle in the arms and shoulders, so the average man can lift more weight than the average woman can. Furthermore, males can sustain greater strength, especially over short periods of time. Yet women can outperform men in some tests of long-term endurance because they can draw on the energy derived from greater body fat. Females also outperform males in life itself. According to the U.S. Bureau of the Census (1993), the average life expectancy for men is now 71.8 years, while women can expect to live 78.5 years.

Adolescent males exhibit greater mathematical ability, while adolescent females outperform males in

NOTE: As a counterpoint to Money and Ehrhardt's twin study, Dr. Milton Diamond states: "It is regrettable that so much of a theoretical and philosophical superstructure has been built on the supposed results of a single, uncontrolled and unconfirmed case." By puberty, the "female" twin felt ambivalent toward her gender, leading psychiatrists to conclude that future adjustment of this unhappy child (apparently unaware of her history) to being a woman was doubtful. (See "Sexual Identity: Monozygotic Twins Reared in Discordant Sex Roles and a BBC Follow-Up," *Archives of Sexual Behavior* 11, 2, April 1982:181–86.)

verbal skills, differences that reflect both biology and patterns of socialization (Maccoby & Jacklin, 1974; Baker et al., 1980; Lengermann & Wallace, 1985). But research supports the conclusion that there exist no overall differences in intelligence between males and females.

Biologically, then, the sexes are distinguished in limited ways with neither one naturally superior. Nevertheless, the deeply rooted *cultural* notion of male superiority may seem so natural that we assume it is the inevitable consequence of sex itself. But society, much more than biology, is at work here, as several kinds of research show.

An Unusual Case Study

In 1963 a physician was performing a routine penis circumcision on seven-month-old identical twins. While using electrocautery (surgery employing a heated needle), the physician accidentally burned off the penis of one boy. Understandably, the parents were horrified. After months of medical consultation, they decided to employ further surgery to change the boy's sex and to raise him as a girl.

The parents dressed the child as a girl, watched her hair grow long, and treated her according to cultural definitions of femininity. Meanwhile, the brother—born an exact biological copy—was raised as a boy.

Because of their different socialization, each child learned a distinctive **gender identity**, *traits that females and males, guided by their culture, incorporate into their personalities.* In this extraordinary case, one child learned to think of himself in terms that our culture defines as masculine, while the other child—despite beginning life as a male—soon began to think of herself as feminine. As the twins' mother observed:

> One thing that really amazes me is that [my daughter] is so feminine. I've never seen a little girl so neat and tidy. . . . She is very proud of herself, when she puts on a new dress, or I set her hair. She just loves to have her hair set; she could sit under the dryer all day long to have her hair set. She just loves it. . . . [My daughter] likes for me to wipe her face. She doesn't like to be dirty, and yet my son is quite different. I can't wash his face for anything. . . . She seems to be daintier. (quoted in Money & Ehrhardt, 1972:124)

The girl's development did not proceed smoothly, however, suggesting that some biological forces were coming into play. While feminine in many respects, the researchers reported that she also began to display some masculine traits, including a desire to gain dominance among her peers. Later, researchers following

In every society, people assume certain jobs, patterns of behavior, and ways of dressing are "naturally" feminine while others are just as obviously masculine. But, in global perspective, we see remarkable variety in such social definitions. These men, Wodaabe pastoral nomads who live in the African nation of Niger, are proud to engage in a display of beauty most people in our society would consider feminine.

the case reported that, by the time she was reaching adolescence, she was showing signs of resisting her feminine gender identity (Diamond, 1982). This complex case certainly shows how gender is the product of the social environment, although cultural conditioning does not proceed free from the influence of biology.

The Israeli Kibbutzim

To further investigate the roots of gender, researchers have focused on collective settlements in Israel called *kibbutzim*. The kibbutz (the singular form) is important for gender research because its members historically have embraced social equality, with men and women sharing in both work and decision making.

Both sexes in the kibbutzim typically perform all kinds of tasks, including child care, building maintenance, cooking, and cleaning. Boys and girls are raised in the same way, with children placed, from the first weeks of life, in dormitories under the care of specially trained personnel. Members of kibbutzim, then, regard sex as barely relevant to much of everyday life.

Margaret Mead

Q: "The [comparison of the three societies] suggests that we may say that many, if not all, of the personality traits which we have called masculine or feminine are as lightly linked to sex as are the clothing, the manners, and the form of head-dress that a society at a given period assigns to either sex . . . We are forced to conclude that human behavior is almost unbelievably malleable, responding accurately and contrastingly to contrasting cultural conditions."

Margaret Mead

RESOURCE: Margaret Mead's "Sex and Temperament in Three Primitive Societies" is in this text's companion reader.

Q: "Fifty-three percent of the world's population are women, they perform two-thirds of the world's work, receive one-tenth of its income, and own one-hundredth of its property." Patricia Schroeder, Representative from Colorado

But here, again, we find reason for caution about completely discounting any biological forces. Some observers note that women in the kibbutzim have resisted spending much of the day away from their own children; more generally, many of these collectives have returned to more traditional social roles over the years. Such a turnabout, say some researchers, suggests the persistent if subtle influence of biologically rooted differences in the sexes (Tiger & Shepher, 1975). But even if this is so—and this research has its critics—the kibbutzim certainly stand as evidence of wide cultural latitude in defining what is feminine and masculine. They also exemplify how, through conscious efforts, a society can pursue sexual equality just as it can encourage the domination of one sex by the other.

Global Comparisons

Another way to determine whether gender reflects culture or some inborn imperative is to take a global view of how the two sexes interact in many societies. To the extent that gender reflects the biological facts of sex, the human traits defined as feminine and masculine should be the same everywhere; to the extent that gender is cultural, these conceptions should vary.

The best-known research of this kind is a classic study of gender in three societies of New Guinea by anthropologist Margaret Mead (1963; orig. 1935). Trekking high into the mountains of New Guinea, Mead observed the Arapesh, whose men and women were remarkably similar in attitudes and behavior. Both sexes, she reported, were cooperative and sensitive to others—what our culture would label "feminine."

Moving south, Mead then studied the Mundugumor, whose culture of head-hunting and cannibalism stood in striking contrast to the gentle ways of the Arapesh. Here, Mead reported, females and males were again alike, although they were startlingly different from the Arapesh. Both Mundugumor females and males were typically selfish and aggressive, traits defined as more "masculine" in the United States.

Finally, traveling west to survey the Tchambuli, Mead discovered a culture that, like our own, defined females and males differently. Yet the Tchambuli reversed many of our notions of gender: Females tended to be dominant and rational, while males were submissive, emotional, and nurturing toward children.

Based on her observations, Mead concluded that what one culture defines as masculine may be considered as feminine by another. Further, she noted that societies can exaggerate or minimize social distinctions based on sex. Mead's research, therefore,

strongly supports the conclusion that gender is a variable creation of society.

A broader study of more than two hundred preindustrial societies by George Murdock (1937) revealed a few general patterns concerning gender. In most societies, Murdock found, hunting and warfare fall to males, while home-centered tasks such as cooking and child care are defined as female work. With only simple technology, preindustrial societies apparently adopt this strategy to benefit from men's greater size and short-term strength; because women bear children, their activities are likely to be more domestic.

But beyond these general patterns, Murdock found significant variation. About the same number of societies considered agriculture—the core of preindustrial production—to be feminine as to be masculine. In most societies, in fact, farming responsibilities were shouldered by both women and men. When it came to many other tasks—from building shelters to tattooing the body—Murdock observed that societies of the world were as likely to turn to one sex as the other.

In global perspective, then, societies define only a few specific activities consistently as feminine or masculine. And as societies industrialize, with a resulting decrease in the significance of muscle power, even those distinctions are minimized (Lenski, Lenski, & Nolan, 1991). Gender, in sum, is simply too variable across cultures to be considered a simple expression of the biological categories of sex. Instead, as with many other elements of culture, what it means to be female and male is mostly a creation of society.

The cultural variability of gender also means that, in any one part of the world, the lives of women and men are subject to transformation over time. Looking to the African nation of Botswana, the box points up how and why such change is often controversial.

Patriarchy and Sexism

Although conceptions of gender certainly vary, a universal pattern among world societies is some degree of **patriarchy** (literally, "the rule of fathers"), *a form of social organization in which males dominate females.* Despite mythical tales of societies dominated by female "Amazons," the pattern of **matriarchy**, *a form of social organization in which females dominate males*, is not at present part of the human record (Gough, 1971; Harris, 1977; Kipp, 1980; Lengermann & Wallace, 1985).

While some degree of patriarchy may be universal, there is significant variation in the relative power and privilege of females and males around the world. In Saudi Arabia, for example, the power of men over

Q: "To consider such traits as aggressiveness or passivity to be sex-linked is not possible in light of the facts." Margaret Mead

Q: "The male is by nature fitter for command than the female, just as the elder and full-grown is fitter than the younger and immature. . . . The courage of a man is shown in commanding, of a woman in obeying." Aristotle, *Politics*

Q: "Conventionality is not morality." Charlotte Brontë

Q: "The whole trend in the United States is away from every sort of biological limitation on human activity and achievement." Margaret Mead

Q: "There is in fact no true 'matriarchal,' as distinct from 'matrilineal,' society in existence or known from literature, and the chances are there never has been." Kathleen Gough

GLOBAL SOCIOLOGY

Patriarchy Under Fire: A Report from Botswana

As the judge handed down the decision, Unity Dow beamed a smile toward the friends sitting all around her; people in the courtroom joined together in hugs and handshakes. Dow, a thirty-two-year-old lawyer and citizen of the southern African nation of Botswana, had won the first round in her efforts to overturn the laws by which, she maintains, her country defines women as second-class citizens.

The law that sparked Unity Dow's recent suit against her government specifies the citizenship rights of children. Botswana is traditionally patrilineal, meaning that people trace family membership through males, so children are part of their father's—but not their mother's—family line. The nation models its citizenship law on this tradition, and this policy has special importance for anyone who marries a citizen of another country, as Unity Dow did.

Under the law, a child of a Botswanan man and a woman with another nationality would be a citizen of Botswana, since in that country legal standing passes through the father. But the child of a Botswanan woman and a man from another nation has no rights of citizenship. Because she married a man from the United States, Unity Dow's children had no citizen's rights in the country where they were born.

The Dow case attracted broad attention because its significance extends far beyond citizenship to the general legal standing of women and men. In rendering the decision in Dow's favor, High Court Judge Martin Horwitz declared, "The time that women were treated as chattels or were there to obey the whims and wishes of males is long past." In support of his decision, Horwitz pointed to the constitution of Botswana, which guarantees fundamental rights and freedoms to both women and men. Arguing for the government against Dow, Ian Kirby, a deputy attorney general, conceded that the constitution confers equal rights on the two sexes, but he claimed law can and should take account of sex where such patterns are deeply rooted in Botswanan male-dominated culture. To challenge such traditions in the name of Western feminism, he continued, amounts to cultural imperialism by

Around the world, patriarchy is most pronounced in less economically developed societies.

which some people seek to subvert an established way of life by advancing foreign notions that are popular elsewhere.

The fact that women from many African nations attended the Dow court case suggests that a growing push for social equality for the sexes is not as foreign to African cultures as some might think. Many analysts on both sides of the issue agreed that the victory for Unity Dow and her supporters probably signals the beginning of historic change.

To many people in the United States, the Dow case may seem strange, since the notion that men and women are entitled to equal rights and privileges is widely endorsed in our country. But, worth noting is the fact that it is the United States—not Botswana—that has no constitutional guarantee of equal standing under the law for women and men.

SOURCES: Author's personal communication with Unity Dow and Shapiro (1991).

NOTE: The phrase "the opposite sex" clearly conveys the idea that gender is a matter of opposition.

Q: "Differences between the male and female endocrine/central nervous system are such that—statistically speaking—males have a greater tendency to exhibit whatever behavior is necessary in any environment to attain dominance in hierarchies . . ." Steven Goldberg

RESOURCE: By and large, sociologists accept the view that biology plays no significant role in gender formation. Steven Goldberg's quote is therefore likely to elicit strong disapproval from most sociologists. Goldberg presents his evidence in "Reaffirming the Obvious" and "Utopian Yearning versus Scientific Curiosity," *Society*, Vol. 23, No. 6: (September/October 1986) 4–7; 29–39.

TABLE 13–1 Sexism: Echoes of Racial Stereotypes

	Women	African Americans
Link to highly visible biological distinctions	Secondary sex characteristics.	Skin color.
Assertion of innate inferiority	Women are mentally inferior. Women are irresponsible, unreliable, and emotional.	African Americans are mentally inferior. African Americans are irresponsible, unreliable, and pleasure seeking.
Notion of "proper place"	A woman's place is in the home. All women really enjoy being treated "like a woman."	African Americans should remain "in their place." African Americans are content living just as they do.
Notion of the need for protection	Men put women on a pedestal.	White people "take care of" African Americans.
Coping strategies on the part of victims	Behavior flattering to men; letting men think they are better even when they are not. Hiding one's real feelings. Attempting to outwit men.	Deferential behavior toward white people; letting white people think they are better even when they are not. Hiding one's real feelings. Attempting to outwit white people.
Barriers to opportunity	Women don't need an education. Women should be confined to "women's work." Women should stay out of politics.	African Americans don't need an education. African Americans should be confined to "black occupations." African Americans should stay out of politics.
Control strategies on the part of oppressors	Assertive women are "pushy." Ambitious women are trying to be "like men." Violence against women.	Assertive African Americans are "uppity." Ambitious African Americans are trying to be like white people. Violence against African Americans.

SOURCES: Adapted from Helen Mayer Hacker, "Women as a Minority Group," *Social Forces* 30 (October 1951): 60–69; and "Women as a Minority Group: Twenty Years Later," in Florence Denmark, ed., *Who Discriminates Against Women?* (Beverly Hills, Calif.: Sage, 1974), pp. 124–34.

women is as great as anywhere on earth; in the Nordic nation of Norway, by contrast, the two sexes approach equality in many respects.

Sexism, *the belief that one sex is innately superior to the other,* stands as an important ideological underpinning of patriarchy. Historically, patriarchy has been supported by a belief in the innate superiority of males who, therefore, legitimately dominate females. As Table 13–1 shows, sexism has much in common with racism, a key issue in Chapter 12 ("Race and Ethnicity"). Just as racism constitutes an ideology supporting white domination of people of color, so sexism is an ideology supporting male domination of females.

Also like racism, sexism is more than a matter of individual attitudes. The notion that one sex is superior to the other is also built into various institutions of our society. As we shall see presently, *institutionalized sexism* pervades the operation of the economy, with women highly concentrated in jobs that are less challenging and offer relatively low pay. Similarly, the legal system historically has winked at violence against

women, especially on the part of boyfriends, husbands, and fathers (Landers, 1990).

The Costs of Sexism

Sexism—especially when it is institutionalized—has clear costs to women, who lose opportunities, stand at increased risk of poverty, and endure sexual violence. But society as a whole also pays a high price for maintaining sexism. Limiting the opportunities available to women ensures that the full talents and abilities of half the population will never be developed.

Men, too, are hurt by sexism. Without denying that sexism confers on men a disproportionate share of wealth and power, this privilege comes at a high price. As Marilyn French (1985) argues, patriarchy compels men to relentlessly seek control—not only of women but of themselves and the entire world. The consequences include far higher rates of death from suicide, violence, accidents, stress, heart attacks, and other diseases related to lifestyle. The so-called Type

NOTE: In 1994, Barbie (full name, Barbie Millicent Roberts) turned 35. Over 500 million dolls have been sold, most recently wardrobed for a wider range of activities (for instance, as an astronaut). However, Barbie continues to symbolize the traditional feminine quality of passive physical beauty.
Q: "Why isn't 'man's best friend' woman?" Carol Tavris and Carole Offir

NOTE: E. Digby Baltzell points out that control of women's sexuality is not simply aimed at domination of women; it is society's means of ensuring endogamy, thus defending racial and class hegemony.
DIVERSITY: One indicator of the changing roles of U.S. women: They now represent 40% of business flyers on major airlines, up from 2% in 1970.

A personality—characterized by chronic impatience, driving ambition, competitiveness, and free-floating hostility—is closely linked to heart disease. This personality profile is precisely the behavior that our culture defines as masculine (Ehrenreich, 1983). Furthermore, insofar as men seek control over others, they lose the ability to experience intimacy and trust (French, 1985). One recent study concluded that although competition is supposed to separate "the men from the boys," in practice it separates men from men, and from everyone else (Raphael, 1988).

Overall, when human feelings, thoughts, and actions are rigidly scripted according to a culture's conceptions of gender, people cannot develop and freely express the full range of their humanity. Society pressures males to be assertive, competitive, and in control, a weighty burden for many to bear. Females are constrained to be submissive, dependent, and self-effacing, regardless of their individual talents and distinctive personalities.

Is Patriarchy Inevitable?

Patriarchy in technologically simple societies stems largely from lack of control by individuals over the natural differences of sex. Pregnancy and childbirth limit the scope of women's lives, while men's greater height and strength allow them to overpower women.

Technological advances, however, give members of industrial societies a wider range of choices in how the two sexes interact. Contraception has given women greater control over pregnancy, just as industrial machinery has diminished the primacy of muscle power in everyday life. Today, then, biological differences provide little justification for patriarchy.

Categorical social inequality—whether based on race, ethnicity, or sex—also comes under attack in the more egalitarian culture of industrial societies. In many industrial nations, laws mandate equal employment opportunities for women and men and equal pay for comparable efforts. Nonetheless, in all industrial societies, the two sexes continue to hold different jobs and receive unequal pay, as we will explain presently.

Does its persistent character mean that patriarchy is inevitable? Some sociologists claim that biological factors imprint on the sexes different behaviors and motivations—especially a greater level of aggressiveness on the part of males—that make the eradication of patriarchy difficult and perhaps even impossible (Goldberg, 1974, 1987; Rossi, 1985; Popenoe, 1993). Most sociologists, however, contend that gender is primarily a social construction subject to change. Simply because

TABLE 13–2 Traditional Notions of Gender Identity

Feminine Traits	Masculine Traits
Submissive	Dominant
Dependent	Independent
Unintelligent and incapable	Intelligent and competent
Emotional	Rational
Receptive	Assertive
Intuitive	Analytical
Weak	Strong
Timid	Brave
Content	Ambitious
Passive	Active
Cooperative	Competitive
Sensitive	Insensitive
Sex object	Sexually aggressive
Attractive because of physical appearance	Attractive because of achievement

no society has yet eliminated patriarchy, then, does not mean that we must remain prisoners of the past.

To understand the persistence of patriarchy, we now examine how gender is rooted and reproduced in society, a process that begins with the way we learn to think of ourselves as children, and continues through the work we perform as adults.

GENDER AND SOCIALIZATION

From birth until death, human feelings, thoughts, and actions reflect social definitions of the sexes. Children quickly learn that their society defines females and males as different kinds of human beings and, by about the age of three or four, they begin to apply gender standards to themselves (Kohlberg, 1966, cited in Lengermann & Wallace, 1985:37; Bem, 1981).

Gender is at work in our society's expectations for us as well as our aspirations for ourselves. We can see how different these visions are for the two sexes by noting that "becoming a woman" often involves bodily processes: starting to menstruate, losing virginity, or having a child. "Becoming a man," by contrast, is more likely to mean taking on significant responsibility (Wolf, 1992).

Table 13–2 sketches the traits that people in the United States traditionally have used to define females and males. Consider the overall pattern: Not only do we distinguish between the two sexes, we define them in *opposing* terms. Polarizing humanity in terms of gender is still widespread in this country, despite the fact that research suggests that most young people do

Q: "Most human beings live in single-sex worlds, women in a female world and men in a male world, and . . . the two are different from one another in a myriad of ways, both subjectively and objectively." Jessie Bernard (1981:3)

DIVERSITY: Without knowing the sex of the person involved, wouldn't people tend to evaluate the traits traditionally linked to females (Table 13–2) as negative?

Q: "Law may prescribe that the male nipple may be equal to the female one, but they will still not give milk." Allan Bloom

SOCIAL SURVEY: "If the husband in a family wants children, but the wife decides that she does not want any children, is it all right for the wife to refuse to have children?" (GSS 1972–82, N = 12,096; *Codebook*, 1993:289)

"Yes" 59.0%   "No" 30.8%   DK/NR 10.2%

PROFILE

Jessie Bernard: Carrying Gender into Sociology

For most of her ninety years, Jessie Bernard has made a remarkable contribution to the discipline of sociology, especially with regard to gender. Bernard notes that past sociologists—even those critical of the status quo—have historically paid little regard to women's lives. Karl Marx, for instance, all but ignored women in his writings.

A key reason for giving short shrift to women, Bernard suggests, is that sociology (like most other disciplines) developed largely under the control of men. One of Bernard's most important contributions lies in revealing how familiar sociological issues and concepts have a built-in male bias.

Consider the topic of social stratification. Sociological research on our class system has focused largely on men to the exclusion of women. We have assumed, in other words, that men earn their class position (an issue worthy of study), while women simply derive their social position from fathers and, subsequently, husbands. Further, in their study of prestige attached to work (see Table 10–1), sociologists have long ignored housework, which has long been primarily a responsibility of women. By defining occupational prestige so that it targets men almost exclusively, Bernard reasons, sociologists effectively ignore women in their research.

In sum, Bernard's example shows us the importance of ensuring that our work addresses the lives of both females and males. Anything less is the study of just half of society.

SOURCES: Based on Jessie Bernard (1981) and personal communication.

not develop consistently "feminine" or "masculine" personalities (L. Bernard, 1980).

Just as socialization incorporates gender into personal identity, so it teaches us to *act* in sex-linked ways. **Gender roles** (or sex roles) are *attitudes and activities that a culture links to each sex.* Gender roles are the active expression of gender identity. In other words, insofar as our culture defines males as ambitious and competitive, we expect them to engage in team sports and aspire to positions of leadership. To the extent that females are defined as deferential and emotional, we expect them to be good listeners and supportive observers.

Gender and the Family

The first question people usually ask about a newborn—"Is it a boy or a girl?"—looms so large because the answer involves far more than the infant's sex; it carries a great significance for the child's entire life.

Sociologist Jessie Bernard (1981), introduced in the box, suggests that the "pink world" of females contrasts sharply with the "blue world" of boys. In fact, the historical preference for boys among parents shows that gender is at work even before a child is born (Lengermann & Wallace, 1985).

In global perspective, the preference for boys is greater where patriarchy is more pronounced. Generally speaking, such societies are poor and face enormous population pressure. All too often patriarchy and poverty add up to **female infanticide**, *the practice of aborting female fetuses and neglecting, or even actively killing, infant girls by parents who would prefer to raise boys.* In North Africa and in most of Asia, life-threatening discrimination against females is commonplace. Researchers know that, assuming equal social treatment, a society should have about 106 females for every 100 males—a disparity that reflects the generally hardier physical condition of females. The People's Republic of China, however,

DIVERSITY: Ability in mathematics and gender continues to be a tangled issue; typically, males score 50 points higher on the math SAT than females do. Daniel Goleman claims that "psychometricians and test critics offer a mix of explanations, ranging from sex bias in the test items to social pressures that keep girls from excelling in math, to basic differences in brain function. The best answers, to date, seem to include all these factors, to a greater or lesser degree." ("Girls and Math: Is Biology Destiny?" *The New York Times Magazine*, August 2, 1987:42–44, 46)

Q: "Law may prescribe that the male nipple may be equal to the female one, but they will still not give milk." Allan Bloom

Q: "Throughout most of human history, the female population has not been a literate one, nor, worldwide, is it very literate today." Jessie Bernard (1981:203)

tallies only 94 females for every 100 males; roughly 12 percent of the females we would expect to find are not in the records. Some of this shortfall may be due to parents not reporting the birth of daughters. But much of the disparity surely results from sex-selective abortion or violence by families against daughters. Worldwide, researchers estimate, as many as 100 million females are "missing," and many presumably have fallen victim to deadly discrimination (United Nations Development Programme, 1991).

Children grow into the different expectations families have for daughters and sons. Research on parental attitudes suggests that parents want sons to be strong, aggressive achievers while they expect daughters to be sensitive and deferential (Witkin-Lanoil, 1984). Parents can convey these expectations unconsciously even in the way they handle their children. A researcher presented an infant dressed as either a boy or a girl to a number of women, noting that her subjects handled the "female" child tenderly, with frequent hugs and caresses, and the "male" child more aggressively, lifting him high in the air or bouncing him on the knee (Bonner, 1984). The message is clear: The female world revolves around passivity and emotion, while the male world involves action and independence.

Gender and the Peer Group

As they reach school age, children increasingly interact outside the family, especially with others their own age. Peer groups further socialize their members according to normative conceptions of gender. The box explains how play groups shaped one young boy's sense of himself as masculine.

Janet Lever (1978) spent a year observing fifth graders at play and concluded that female and male peer groups provide girls and boys with distinctive socialization. Boys, Lever reported, engage more in team sports—such as baseball and football—that involve many roles, complex rules, and clear objectives like scoring a run or making a touchdown. These games are nearly always competitive, separating winners from losers. Male peer activities reinforce masculine traits of aggression and maintaining control.

By contrast, girls in peer groups play hopscotch or jump rope, or simply talk, sing, or dance together. Spontaneous activities with few formal rules are commonplace, and this cooperative play rarely has "victory" as its ultimate goal. Instead of teaching girls to be competitive, Lever explains, female peer groups promote interpersonal skills of communication and cooperation—presumably the basis for family life.

Carol Gilligan (1982), whose work Chapter 5 ("Socialization") details, highlights gender differences in human development. Gilligan explains Lever's observations about play groups in terms of a gender-based theory of moral reasoning. Boys, Gilligan contends, reason according to abstract principles. For them, "rightness" consists largely of "playing by the rules." Girls, by contrast, consider morality more a matter of

SOCIOLOGY OF EVERYDAY LIFE

Masculinity as Contest

By the time I was ten, the central fact in my life was the demand that I become a man. By then, the most important relationships by which I was taught to define myself were those I had with other boys. I already knew that I must see every encounter with another boy as a contest in which I must win or at least hold my own. . . . The same lesson continued [in school], after school, even in Sunday School. My parents, relatives, teachers, the books I read, movies I saw, all taught me that my self-worth depended on my manliness, my willingness to stand up to the other boys. This usually didn't mean a physical fight, though the willingness to stand up and "fight like a man" always remained a final test. But the relationships between us usually had the character of an armed truce. Girls weren't part of this social world at all yet, just because they weren't part of this contest. They didn't have to be bluffed, no credit was gained by cowing them, so they were more or less ignored. Sometimes when there were no grownups around we would let each other know that we liked each other, but most of the time we did as we were taught.

SOURCE: Silverstein (1977).

DIVERSITY: Evidence that the sciences remain largely masculine: Of 2,700 members elected to the National Academy of Sciences since its founding in 1863, only 60 have been women. Vera Rubin (*Science*, July/August 1986:58–65)

GLOBAL: About 85% of U.S. parents desire that their children (regardless of sex) attend college. In Japan, 75% of parents want sons to go to college, but only 30% express this hope for daughters.

NOTE: Historically, few men were literate; even fewer women were. So that their works would be read, 19th-century women authors often used male pseudonyms. "George Eliot" was the pen name of Mary Ann Evans (author of *Silas Marner*). The Brontë sisters chose gender-neutral pseudonyms: Charlotte Brontë (*Jane Eyre*) used the name Currer Bell; Anne Brontë (*Agnes Grey*) used Acton Bell; Emily Brontë (*Wuthering Heights*) used Ellis Bell.

Some recent advertising reverses traditional gender definitions by portraying men as the submissive sex objects of successful women. Although the reversal is new, the use of gender stereotypes to sell consumer products is very old indeed.

responsibility to other people. We can observe these tendencies in female and male peer groups.

Gender and Schooling

Even before children enter school, their reading promotes gender distinctions. A generation ago, a survey of books for pre-elementary school children found that most focused on males rather than females (Weitzman et al., 1972). Researchers calculated the ratio of males to females in illustrations at about ten to one. When books did include females, they usually stayed home and were often preoccupied with pleasing males—who, for their part, were engaged in diverse and interesting activities.

More recently, growing awareness among authors, publishers, and teachers of the limiting effects of gender stereotypes of young people has led to changes. Researchers now document that most of today's books for children portray females and males in a balanced way (Purcell & Stewart, 1990).

In addition to the formal lessons of school, Raphaela Best (1983) explains that informal messages and experiences of school life encourage children to embrace appropriate gender patterns. By the time young people reach high school, topics of study reflect the different roles society expects of females and males as adults. Schools have long provided instruction to young women in home-centered skills such as nutrition, cooking, and sewing. Classes in woodworking and auto mechanics, conversely, contain mostly young men.

In college, this pattern continues, with men and women tending toward different majors. Men are disproportionately represented in natural sciences—including physics, chemistry, biology, and mathematics. Women cluster in the humanities (such as English), the fine arts (painting, music, dance, and drama), or the social sciences (including anthropology and sociology). New areas of study, as well, typically are gender linked. Computer science, for example, with its grounding in engineering, logic, and abstract mathematics, predominantly appeals to men (Klein, 1984); courses in gender studies, by contrast, tend to enroll women.

Extracurricular activities also segregate the two sexes. Athletics and other activities for men benefit from more attention and greater funding. Mass media coverage of men's athletics also far outstrips that devoted to women's sports. This male dominance signals to women that they should assume supportive roles as observers or cheerleaders rather than seeking to excel in their own right.

Gender and the Mass Media

Chapter 5 ("Socialization") explained that the mass media exert a powerful influence on the socialization process. Films, magazines, and especially television affect how we think and act.

Since television first captured the public imagination in the 1950s, this medium has placed the dominant segment of our population—white males—at center stage. Racial and ethnic minorities were all but absent from television until the early 1970s, and only in the last decade have a number of programs featured women in prominent roles.

Even when both sexes appear on camera, men generally play the brilliant detectives, fearless explorers, and skilled surgeons. Men take charge, give orders, and exude competence. Women, by contrast, generally rely

NOTE: In another literary pattern that reflects the power of gender, heroines are often orphans (from *Jane Eyre* to *The Unsinkable Molly Brown*). Only when freed from men (fathers or husbands) are such characters able to command the attention their central role demands.

RESOURCE: An excerpt from Deborah Tannen's *You Just Don't Understand* is included in the Macionis and Benokraitis reader, *Seeing Ourselves.*

NOTE: The "rational-emotional" distinction is inherently hierarchical. We would charge "control your emotions!" but never "control your intellect!" Rationality tends to be allied with dominance.

on men, are portrayed as less capable, and often become the targets of comedy (Busby, 1975). Women, traditionally valued for their sexual attractiveness, are spotlighted in shows that deal with romance. Such stereotypes have persisted into the 1990s, although more programming now involves interesting and responsible roles for women.

Change has come more slowly to advertising, which sells products by conforming to widely established cultural patterns. Historically, television and magazine advertising has presented women in the home, rather than in the workplace, to sell cleaning products, foods, clothing, and appliances. Men, on the other hand, predominate in ads for cars, travel, banking services, industrial companies, and alcoholic beverages. The authoritative "voiceover"—the faceless voice that promotes some product in television and radio advertising—is almost always male (Busby, 1975; Courtney & Whipple, 1983).

In a systematic study of magazine and newspaper ads, Erving Goffman (1979) found other, more subtle biases. Men, he concluded, are photographed to appear taller than women, implying male superiority. Women were more frequently presented lying down (on sofas and beds) or, like children, seated on the floor. The expressions and gestures of men exude competence and authority, whereas women are more likely to appear in childlike poses. While men focus on the products being advertised, women direct their interest to men, conveying their supportive and submissive role.

Advertising is also the key means of perpetuating Naomi Wolf's "beauty myth," described at the beginning of this chapter. The equation runs something like this: By embracing traditional notions of femininity and masculinity, we raise our prospects for personal and professional success. With that groundwork in place, advertising then dictates what we should consume. For example, the masculine man drives the "right" car, while the feminine woman is awash in beauty aids that will help her look younger and more attractive to men (Wolf, 1990).

Gender and Adult Socialization

Reinforced in so many ways by the surrounding culture, gender identity and gender roles come to feel natural long before we reach adulthood. As a result, the attitudes and behavior of adults commonly follow feminine and masculine patterns (Spender, 1980; Kramarae, 1981).

In Chapter 6 ("Social Interaction in Everyday Life"), we reviewed Deborah Tannen's (1990) account of why women and men see many routine situations so differently. Men, Tannen explains, hate to ask directions because, seeing any exchange as establishing a hierarchy, asking for help amounts to accepting subordination. But to women, who draw strength from establishing and maintaining connections with others, asking directions is both practical and sensible.

The two sexes, therefore, perceive different meaning in a wide range of everyday experiences. In light of this gender-based disparity, it is not surprising that husbands and wives often have considerable difficulty with one of the most basic human tasks—simply communicating with each other.

GENDER AND SOCIAL STRATIFICATION

Gender implies more than how people think and act. The concept of **gender stratification** refers to *a society's unequal distribution of wealth, power, and privilege between the two sexes.* In general, societies allocate fewer valued resources to women than to men. We see gender stratification, first, in the world of work.

Working Men and Women

In 1993, 66.2 percent of the U.S. population over the age of fifteen worked for income; the labor force included 75.2 percent of men and 57.9 percent of women (U.S. Bureau of Labor Statistics, 1994). In terms of working for pay, the profiles of women and men have been converging over the course of this century, a trend shown in Figure 13–1. In 1900, just one in five women was in the labor force; the proportion of working women has increased steadily since then. By the same token, the proportion of men in the labor force has slowly fallen, primarily due to earlier retirement. Today, 40 percent of all women aged sixteen or over and 50 percent of all comparable men are not only working but doing so full time. Thus, the traditional notion that earning an income is "man's work" no longer holds true.

What lies behind the changing character of the U.S. work force? A number of factors are involved, including the decline of rural farming, the growth of cities, the rising divorce rate, shrinking family size, and changing norms regarding appropriate roles for women. Most recently, economic stagnation has reduced the income of many families in the United States, which has driven the number of two-income couples steadily upward to 57.5 percent today.

GLOBAL: Proportion of adult women in the labor force: U.S., 58%; the Netherlands, 39%; West Germany, 50%; France, 53%; U.K., 54%; Denmark, 72%. Generally, rates are higher for northern and Western European nations, lower for southern and eastern European countries.

NOTE: In 1973 the new volunteer army had 1.9% females; in 1992 the figure was 11% (213,000). Chapter 16 ("Politics and Government") surveys the status of women in the various branches of the U.S. military.
Q: "We can no longer go to war without women." Lt. Gen. Colin Powell

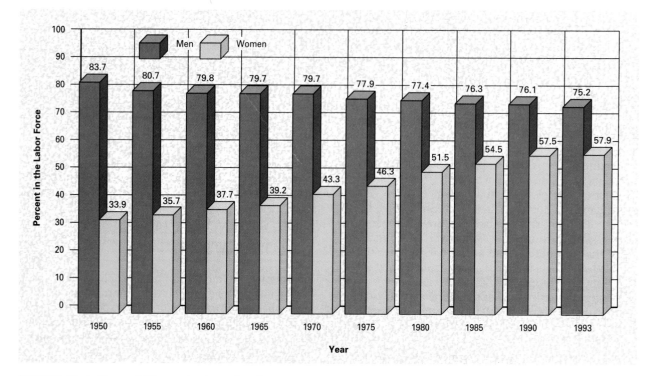

FIGURE 13–1 Men and Women in the U.S. Labor Force

(U.S. Bureau of Labor Statistics, 1994)

A common misconception (especially among middle-class people) holds that women in the labor force are single or, if married, without children. Of all married women, 59 percent work outside the home, as do 60 percent of married women with children under six. Among married women with children between six and seventeen years of age, 75 percent are employed. For divorced women with children, the comparable figures are 60 percent of women with younger children and 80 percent of women with older children (U.S. Bureau of the Census, 1993). A gradual increase in employer-sponsored child care programs (which are still quite rare) is giving more women and men the opportunity to combine the responsibilities of being workers and parents. This trend is especially important for divorced mothers.

Gender and Occupations

While the proportions of men and women in the labor force have been converging—especially since 1970—the work done by the two sexes remains distinct. According to the U.S. Bureau of Labor Statistics (1994), women engage in a narrow range of occupations, with half of working women holding just two types of jobs. Administrative support work, the first category, draws 26.8 percent of working women, most of whom serve as secretaries, typists, or stenographers. Of all such "pink-collar" jobholders, 79 percent are women.

The second broad category is service work, performed by 18 percent of employed women. These jobs include waitressing and other food service work as well health care positions. Both categories of jobs lie at the low end of the pay scale, offer limited opportunities for advancement, and are subject to supervision—most often by men.

Table 13–3, on page 370, identifies the ten occupations with the highest concentrations of women. The bottom line is that, despite increasing numbers of women working for pay, women remain highly segregated in the labor force because our society continues to perceive work through the lens of gender (Roos, 1983; Kemp & Coverman, 1989; U.S. Bureau of Labor Statistics, 1994).

Men predominate in most other job categories. Men overwhelmingly control the building trades: 98.1 percent of brickmasons, stonemasons, structural

Q: "The natural and proper timidity and delicacy which belongs to the female sex evidently unfits it for many of the occupations of civil life." Supreme Court Justice Joseph Bradley, responding in 1873 to Myra Bradwell's efforts to become a lawyer. (First U.S. woman lawyer: Arabella A. Mansfield, 1869)

NOTE: Several "firsts" for U.S. women: first woman physician, Elizabeth Blackwell, 1847; ordained minister, Antoinette Blackwell, 1853; surgeon, Mary Thompson, 1863; dentist (DDS), Lucy Hobbs, 1866; college president, Frances Williard, 1871.

NOTE: One way to generate gender parity within marriage: Virginia Woolf (*A Room of One's Own*) and Leonard Woolf pooled their income, paid their expenses, and equally divided whatever was left.

African-American artist Jacob Lawrence painted Ironers *(1943) to depict the daily lives of women in his working-class neighborhood in New York's Harlem. The painting suggests that the work women perform in the labor force often parallels the tasks women perform in the home.*

metalworkers, and heavy equipment mechanics are men. Men also hold the lion's share of positions that provide a great deal of income, prestige, and power. For example, 92.0 percent of engineers, 77.5 percent of lawyers and judges, 78.2 percent of physicians, 68.8 percent of corporate managers, and 70.1 percent of computer specialists are men. Only about 3 percent of the top executives of large corporations in the United States are women (U.S. Bureau of Labor Statistics, 1994).

An important exception to the pattern of men in decision-making positions is the fact that women own an increasing share—currently 30 percent—of all small businesses in the United States. The number of women-owned companies jumped by more than 50 percent during the 1980s. Although 90 percent of these businesses are sole proprietorships with a single employee, the success of tens of thousands of these entrepreneurs demonstrates that women have the power to create opportunities for themselves. Many women entrepreneurs find the rewards of self-employment to be far greater than those offered by larger, male-dominated companies (Ando, 1990; O'Hare & Larson, 1991; U.S. Bureau of the Census, 1993).

Overall, then, gender stratification permeates the workplace, where men typically fill the occupational positions that confer the most wealth and power. This gender-based hierarchy is often easy to spot in the job setting: Male physicians are assisted by female nurses, male executives have female secretaries, and male airline pilots work with female flight attendants.

In any occupation, moreover, the greater a job's income and prestige, the more likely that the position is held by a man. Among educators, for example, 98 percent of kindergarten teachers are women, as are 86 percent of elementary school teachers, 58 percent of secondary school teachers, 43 percent of college and university professors, and 12 percent of college and university presidents (American Council on Education, 1984; U.S. Bureau of Labor Statistics, 1994).

Housework: Women's "Second Shift"

One sound indicator of the global pattern of patriarchy is the extent to which housework—cleaning, cooking, and caring for children—is the province of women. Global Map 13–1, on page 371, shows that, in general, members of industrial societies divide housework more evenly than people in the poor societies of the world do. But in no society on earth is housework shared equally.

As Jessie Bernard (1981) points out, housework embodies a cultural contradiction: Although everyone agrees housework is essential, it carries little reward or prestige. Such low rewards help to explain why women's rapid entry into the labor force has prompted little change in who performs household chores. Over recent decades, in fact, the hours of housework performed by women declined only slightly while men's

SOCIAL SURVEY: "Do you approve or disapprove of a married woman earning money in business or industry if she has a husband capable of supporting her?" (GSS 1993, N = 1,024; *Codebook*, 1993:251)
"Approve" 78.6%   "Disapprove" 19.2%   DK/NR 2.2%
SOCIAL SURVEY: The same item appears on the *STUDENT CHIP Social Survey Software* (FEWORK; GSS 1972–91, N = 17,547).

	"Approve"	"Disapprove"
Women	75.7%	24.3%
Men	74.3%	25.7%
Afri Amer	72.7%	27.3%
Latino	65.5%	34.5%
White Anglo	75.8%	24.2%

TABLE 13–3 Jobs with the Highest Concentrations of Women, 1993

Occupation	Number of Women Employed	Percent in Occupation Who Are Women
1. Dental hygienist	75,468	99.3%
2. Child-care provider	298,980	99.0%
3. Secretary	3,546,554	98.9%
4. Dental assistant	117,018	97.8%
5. Prekindergarten and kindergarten teachers	489,477	97.7%
6. Receptionist	873,828	97.2%
7. Child-care worker/ private household	335,340	97.2%
8. Early childhood teacher's assistant	403,788	96.6%
9. Licensed practical nurse	402,050	94.6%
10. Typist	465,842	94.3%

SOURCE: U.S. Bureau of Labor Statistics, *Employment and Earnings*, vol. 41, no. 1, January 1994, pp. 205–10.

contribution hardly changed at all. The typical couple in the United States shares only the disciplining of children and management of finances. Home repairs and yard work (which most consider "weekend chores") are assumed by men; survey data suggest that this work demands some seven hours per week. Women, however, see to the daily tasks of shopping, cooking, and cleaning—tasks that consume twenty-six hours per week. Little wonder, then, that women commonly return from the workplace to face a "second shift" of unpaid work on the homefront (Schooler et al., 1984; Benokraitis & Feagin, 1986; Fuchs, 1986; Hochschild, 1989; Presser, 1993).

In short, men claim to support women's entry into the labor force, and many men depend on the income women earn. Young couples typically express their intentions to share housework and child care. In practice, however, men resist modifying their own behavior to help their partners establish successful careers and manageable home lives. Further, men are more likely to call special attention to housework they perform, while taking the contributions of women for granted (Komarovsky, 1973; Cowan, 1992; Robinson & Spitze, 1992).

Gender and Income

Another crucial dimension of gender stratification involves income and wealth. In 1992, the median earnings for women working full time were $22,167, while men working full time earned $31,012. Stated in terms of a work week, by lunchtime Thursday men earn as much as women do for working through the end of the day Friday. Or, most simply, for every dollar earned by men, women earned about 72 cents.

Among full-time workers, 58 percent of employed women earned less than $25,000 in 1992, compared to 36 percent of comparable men. At the upper end of the income scale, men were five times more likely than women (7.5 percent versus 1.5 percent) to collect more than $75,000 for their efforts (U.S. Bureau of the Census, 1993).

In global perspective, gender-based income disparity is less pronounced in the United States than in Japan but greater than it is in most other industrial nations, including Australia, Canada, Norway, and Sweden (Rosenfeld & Kalleberg, 1990; United Nations Development Programme, 1993). Over time, however, this disparity has gradually declined in the United States. In 1980, for example, working women earned only 60 percent as much as working men. This trend toward equal earnings is due, in part, to increasing economic opportunities for women and in part to a recent *decline* in the earnings of men.

Causes of Gender-Based Income Inequality

The most important reason for the lower earnings of working women is the clerical and service jobs they tend to hold. In effect, jobs and gender interact: Members of our society tend to perceive jobs with less clout as "women's work," just as people devalue work simply because it is performed by women (Parcel, Mueller, & Cuvelier, 1986; Blum, 1991; England, 1992).

During the 1980s, advocates of greater gender equality responded to this mind-set by proposing a policy of "comparable worth," by which women and men would be paid, not according to a historical double standard but according to the worth of what they actually do. Thus women should receive equal pay for work that has equal, or comparable, worth. Several nations, including Great Britain and Australia, have adopted such policies, which have found limited acceptance in the United States. Still, critics argue, women in this country are losing as much as $1 billion annually based on their sex.

A second cause of gender-based income disparity has to do with the family. Both men and women have children, of course, but our culture defines child care as more a woman's responsibility than a man's. Pregnancy, childbirth, and raising small children keep many younger women out of the labor force altogether at a time when men of the same age stand to

Q: "It looks as though men start in the middle and move to the top, and women start at the bottom and move to the middle." Heidi I. Hartmann (based on her study of promotion in an insurance firm, in Clair Brown and Joseph Pechman, eds., *Gender in the Workplace*, Washington, D.C.: Brookings, 1987)

DIVERSITY: The earnings disparity between men and women increases with age: 18–24, 92%; 25–34, 75%; 35–44, 65%; 45–54,

59%; 55–65, 54%. (U.S. Bureau of the Census)

SOCIAL SURVEY: Gallup poll, 1942: "If women replace men in industry, should they be paid the same wages as men?" "Yes," 78%; "No," 14%; undecided, 8%.

NOTE: Housework (unpaid work within the home) has as its complement volunteer work (unpaid work outside the home).

Window on the World

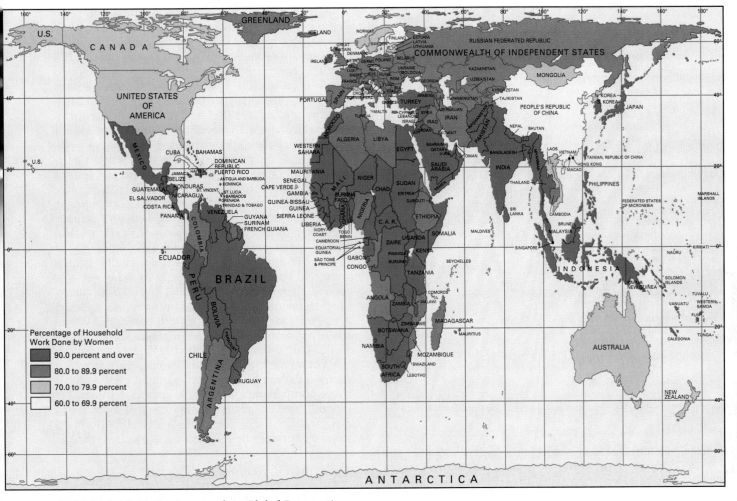

GLOBAL MAP 13–1 Housework in Global Perspective

To the extent that housework—made up of necessary, although tiring and repetitive, tasks—is carried out by only one sex, a society differentiates its members in terms of gender. In general, the greater the proportion of housework that women perform, the greater the social dominance of men. Housework is most rigidly assigned to women in poor societies, although in Japan and many European countries as well women do almost all these tasks. The United States is more egalitarian with regard to housework than most of the world. The People's Republic of China appears to divide housework most equally, the result of deliberate socialist policies and the need for both women and men to work in order to raise living standards.

From *Peters Atlas of the World* (1990). Updated by the author.

make significant occupational gains. As a result, women workers have less job seniority than their male counterparts (Fuchs, 1986).

Moreover, women who choose to have children may be reluctant or unable to maintain fast-paced jobs that tie up their evenings and weekends. Career women with children may resolve this classic case of role strain by favoring jobs that offer a shorter commuting distance, more flexible hours, and employer-sponsored child care services. The seriousness of the

GLOBAL: Sweden began a program to equalize the earnings of women and men in 1968; their income ratio today is about 85%.
NOTE: A study of the weekly schedules of physicians found that mothers chose to work about 12 fewer hours than childless women. Among men, having children had no appreciable effect on working hours. Comparing only physician parents, women worked 38 hours weekly, men 53 hours. (Grant et al., cited in Weiss & Lonnquist, 1994:171)
Q: "The cost of employing women in management is greater than the cost of employing men. This is a jarring statement, partly because it is true, but mostly because it is something people are reluctant to talk about . . . . We have become so sensitive to charges of sexism and so afraid of confrontation, even litigation, that we rarely say what we know to be true." Felice Schwartz (1989:65)

TABLE 13–4 Earnings of Full-Time U.S. Workers, by Sex, 1992*

Selected Occupational Categories	Median Income (dollars)		Women's Income as a Percentage of Men's
	Men	Women	
Executives, administrators, and managers	$42,509	$27,494	65%
Professional specialties	$44,015	$31,261	71%
Technical workers	$32,720	$24,767	76%
Sales	$31,346	$17,924	57%
Precision production, craft, and repair workers	$28,923	$19,045	66%
Clerical and other administrative support workers	$27,186	$20,321	75%
Transportation workers	$25,787	$20,131	78%
Machine operators and tenders	$23,884	$15,714	66%
Service workers	$20,606	$12,931	63%
Farming, forestry, and fishing workers	$14,897	$10,079	68%
All occupations listed above	$30,358	$21,440	71%

*Workers aged 15 and over.

SOURCE: U.S. Bureau of the Census, *Current Population Reports*, ser. P-60, no. 184 (Washington, D.C.: U.S. Government Printing Office, 1993).

dilemma faced by women pursuing both a career and a family is suggested by the fact that, among executive men who reach age forty, 90 percent have had a child; among executive women over age forty, only 35 percent have had a child. Women who do have children, in general, start to fall behind childless women in terms of earnings.

This situation, explains Felice Schwartz (1989), boils down to the fact that women risk their careers by having children. Rather than helping to meet the needs of a working mother, the typical corporation interprets a woman's choice to have a child as evidence that she intends to leave the company, taking with her a substantial investment in time and training. Schwartz sees an alternative, calling on corporations to develop "mommy tracks" that allow women to meet family responsibilities while continuing their careers, for a time, with less intensity. This proposal has won praise, but it has also provoked strong criticism. Opponents of the "mommy-track" concept fear that it

only plays into the hands of corporate men who have long stereotyped women as being less attached to careers in the first place. Further, critics add, since companies are unlikely to apply such a plan to men, it can only hurt rather than help the career aspirations of corporate women.

The two factors noted so far—type of work and family responsibilities—account for about two-thirds of the earnings disparity between women and men. Researchers assume that a third factor—discrimination against women—accounts for the remainder (Pear, 1987; Fuller & Schoenberger, 1991).

Because discrimination is illegal, it is often practiced in subtle ways, but it remains a major cause of economic disadvantage for working women. Corporate women often encounter the so-called *glass ceiling*, a barrier that, while formally denied by high company officials, effectively prevents women from rising above middle management. The traditional dominance of men at the highest corporate levels excludes women from "old-boy networks" that support many younger men on their way up. Then, too, some men are threatened by talented and ambitious women, just as some are uneasy about interacting with colleagues whom they find sexually attractive (Benokraitis & Feagin, 1986; Ward, Orazem, & Schmidt, 1992).

For all these reasons, then, women earn less than men—a pattern that we can document even within a single occupational category. As Table 13–4 shows, this disparity rises or falls according to type of work, but in only four of these selected job classifications do women earn more than 70 percent as much as men do.

Inequality of Wealth

Finally, because women typically outlive men, many people in the United States think that women end up owning most of the country's wealth. Government statistics, however, tell a different story: 57 percent of those individuals with $1 million or more in assets are men, although widows are highly represented. The distribution is the same (57 percent men, 43 percent women) among people with more modest wealth (between $250,000 and $1 million) (U.S. Bureau of the Census, 1993). And only about 20 percent of the individuals identified by the staffs of *Forbes* and *Fortune* as the richest people in the United States are women.

Gender and Education

Thinking advanced schooling to be unnecessary for homemakers, many of our forebears discouraged, and sometimes formally excluded, women from higher education. But times have changed. In 1990, 54 percent of all associate's and bachelor's degrees were earned by women, with the remaining 46 percent earned by men (National Center for Education Statistics, 1991).

Although the doors of colleges have opened to women, the two sexes still tend to pursue different courses of study, although to a decreasing degree. In 1970, for example, women earned just 17 percent of the bachelor's degrees in natural sciences, computer science, and engineering; by 1992, that proportion had doubled to one-third.

Today's women also enjoy greater opportunity for postgraduate education, often a springboard to high-prestige jobs. Counting all areas of study, women earn more master's degrees (51.1 percent of the total) than men do (48.9 percent). And, a growing number of women are pursuing programs that until recently were virtually all male. For example, in 1970 only a few hundred women received a master's of business administration (M.B.A.) degree; by 1990, the number exceeded twenty-three thousand (34 percent of all such degrees) (National Center for Education Statistics, 1991).

Most professional fields, however, remain predominately male. In 1990, men received two-thirds of doctorates (although women earned 52 percent of Ph.D.'s in sociology). Men also earned 60 percent of law degrees (LL.B. and J.D.), 66 percent of medical degrees (M.D.), and 74 percent of dental degrees (D.D.S. and D.M.D.) (National Center for Education Statistics, 1991). Our society still defines high-paying professions (and the drive and competitiveness needed to succeed in them) as masculine; conversely, *not* having a professional career is still normative for women. Thus, there is little surprise in the fact that, although women begin many professional programs of study in numbers equal to those of men, women are less likely to complete them (Fiorentine, 1987; Fiorentine & Cole, 1992). Nonetheless, the proportion of women in professional schools and the professions is steadily rising.

Gender and Politics

A century ago, virtually no women held elected office in the United States. In fact, women were legally barred from even casting a vote in national elections until the adoption of the Nineteenth Amendment to the Constitution in 1920. A few women, however, were candidates for political office even before they could vote. The Equal Rights party supported Victoria Woodhull for the American presidency in 1872; perhaps it

TABLE 13–5 Significant "Firsts" for Women in U.S. Politics

1869	Law allows women to vote in Wyoming territory; Utah follows suit in 1870.
1872	First woman to run for the presidency (Victoria Woodhull) represents the Equal Rights party.
1917	First woman elected to the House of Representatives (Jeannette Rankin of Montana).
1924	First woman elected state governors (Nellie Taylor Ross of Wyoming and Miriam ["Ma"] Ferguson of Texas); both followed their husbands into office. First woman to have her name placed in nomination for vice-presidency at the convention of a major political party (Lena Jones Springs).
1931	First woman to serve in the Senate (Hattie Caraway of Arkansas); completed the term of her husband upon his death and won reelection in 1932.
1932	First woman appointed to the presidential cabinet (Frances Perkins, secretary of labor).
1964	First woman to have her name placed in nomination for the presidency at the convention of a major political party (Margaret Chase Smith).
1972	First African-American woman to have her name placed in nomination for the presidency at the convention of a major political party (Shirley Chisholm).
1981	First woman appointed to the U.S. Supreme Court (Sandra Day O'Connor).
1984	First woman to be successfully nominated for the vice-presidency (Geraldine Ferraro).
1988	First woman chief executive to be elected to a consecutive third term (Madeleine Kunin, governor of Vermont).
1992	Political "Year of the Woman" yields record number of women in the Senate (six) and the House (forty-eight), as well as (1) first African-American woman to win election to U.S. Senate (Carol Moseley-Braun of Illinois); (2) first state (California) to be served by two women senators (Barbara Boxer and Dianne Feinstein); (3) first Puerto Rican woman elected to the House (Nydia Valasquez of New York).

SOURCE: Adapted from Sandra Salmans, "Women Ran for Office Before They Could Vote," New York Times, July 13, 1984, p. A11, and news reports.

was a sign of the times that she spent election day in a New York City jail. Table 13–5 cites subsequent milestones in women's gradual movement into political life.

Today, thousands of women serve as mayors of cities and towns across the United States, and tens of thousands more hold responsible administrative posts in the federal government (Mashek & Avery, 1983; Schreiner, 1984). At the state level, women constituted a mere 6 percent of legislators in 1970; by 1993, the proportion was approaching 25 percent. Less change has occurred at the highest levels of politics, although a majority of U.S. adults claim that they would support a qualified woman for any office, including the presidency. After the 1992 national elections, 3 of the

DIVERSITY: Historically, the labor force participation of women of color was higher than that of white women. In 1940, for example, 40% of African-American women worked for wages, compared to less than 30% of white women.

DIVERSITY: Of all families living below poverty level, 52.7% were headed by women in 1992. Of all poor African-American families, 75.4% were headed by women; for Hispanics, 43.3%, and for all whites, 42.7%. (U.S.Bureau of the Census, 1993)

DIVERSITY: Income figures for minority women may seem to indicate that economic disadvantages are due to race and gender alone. To make a more well-rounded assessment, however, one would have to factor in differences in education, work histories, age, and so on.

50 state governors were women (6 percent); in Congress, women held 48 of 435 seats in the House of Representatives (11 percent), and 6 of 100 senators (6 percent) were women.

Minority Women

Chapter 12 ("Race and Ethnicity") explained that minorities are socially disadvantaged; if so, are minority women doubly handicapped? Generally speaking, the answer is yes.

First, there is the disadvantage associated with race and ethnicity. For example, in 1992, median annual earnings for African-American women working full time were $20,299, 90.5 percent as much as the $22,423 earned by white women; Hispanic women earned $17,743, which was 79.1 percent as much as their white (non-Hispanic) counterparts.

Second, there is the obstacle associated with sex. Thus, African-American women earned 88.5 percent as much as African-American men, while Hispanic women earned about 87.4 percent as much as Hispanic men.

Combining these disadvantages, African-American women earned 64.0 percent as much as white men, and Hispanic women earned 55.9 percent as much (U.S. Bureau of the Census, 1993). These disparities reflect minority women's lower positions on the occupational and educational ladders in comparison to white women (Bonilla-Santiago, 1990). Further, whenever the economy sags, as it has in recent years, minority women are especially likely to experience declining income and unemployment.

Chapter 10 ("Social Class in the United States") noted that women are disproportionately represented among the nation's poor. The primary explanation for this fact is that more families are headed by women without husbands than by men without wives; furthermore, women who head families tend to have low-income jobs and some do not work at all. In 1992, 52.4 percent of poor families were headed by women, in contrast to 5.9 percent headed by men. The link between poverty and families headed by women is even more dramatic among African Americans: Families headed by women constituted 75.4 percent of all African-American families in poverty; the comparable figure for Hispanics was 43.3 percent, and for white families, 42.7 percent.

Scholars are now directing their attention to the heterogeneity of women in the United States. Being a woman entails disadvantage, but this experience is mediated by a host of other factors, including race, ethnicity, and class (Ginsburg & Tsing, 1990).

Are Women a Minority?

A minority, Chapter 12 explained, is a category of people both socially disadvantaged and physically or culturally distinctive. In a patriarchal society, women fit this definition (even as a slight majority of the population), since they contend with a number of social barriers due to their sex, as we have explained.

A counterpoint to this assertion is the fact that most white women do *not* think of themselves as members of a minority (Hacker, 1951; Lengermann & Wallace, 1985). This is partly because, unlike racial and ethnic minorities, white women are widely represented at all levels of the class structure, including the very top. But it remains true that, regardless of their class position, women typically have less income, wealth, and power than men do. In fact, patriarchy makes women dependent for their social standing on men—first their fathers and later their husbands (J. Bernard, 1981).

Another reason that all women may not consider themselves a minority is that they have been socialized to accept lesser economic achievement and a greater domestic role as natural. So we must conclude that only some women—especially those who are less privileged—think of themselves as part of a minority. Yet as a category of people in the United States, women have the distinctive identity and the social disadvantages that mark other minorities.

Violence Against Women

Perhaps the most wrenching kind of suffering that our society imposes on women is violence. As Chapter 8 ("Deviance") explained, official statistics reveal that criminal violence is overwhelmingly the actions of men. This fact is not surprising, since aggressiveness is a trait our culture defines as masculine. (What, for example, makes a man a "wimp," according to our norms and values? What, by contrast, makes him a "real man"?) Furthermore, a great deal of "manly" violence is directed at women, a circumstance we also might expect since a great deal of what is culturally defined as feminine is devalued and even despised.

Because violence is commonplace in our society, and closely linked to gender, it arises most often where men and women interact most. Richard Gelles (cited in Roesch, 1984) argues that, with the exception of the police and the military, the family is the most violent group in the United States. More violent attacks occur in the home, Gelles maintains, than anywhere else. Both sexes suffer from family violence, although, by and large, women sustain more serious injuries than men do (Straus & Gelles, 1986; Schwartz, 1987; Shupe,

Q: "[Men] think themselves superior to women, but they mingle that with the notion of equality between men and women. It's very odd." Jean-Paul Sartre

NOTE: The legal basis of sexual harassment is Section 703 of Title VII of the 1964 Civil Rights Act that outlaws workplace discrimination based on sex; also Title IX of the Education Amendments of 1972.

Q: "Sexual objectification is the primary process of the subjugation of women . . ." Catharine MacKinnon

Stacey, & Hazlewood, 1987; Gelles & Cornell, 1990). Chapter 17 ("Family") provides greater detail concerning the problem of family violence.

Violence against women also occurs in casual relationships. As Chapter 8 ("Deviance") explained, the notion that sexual violence involves strangers is a myth; most rapes, for instance, are perpetrated by men known (and sometimes even trusted) by women. A tendency toward sexual violence, in other words, is built into our way of life. Dianne F. Herman (1992) argues that all forms of violence against women—from the wolf whistles that intimidate women on city streets to a pinch in a crowded subway to physical assaults that occur at home—are expressions of a "rape culture." By this, Herman means that men resort to violence as a strategy to dominate women. Sexual violence, then, is fundamentally about *power* rather than sex, and that is why we include it as a dimension of gender stratification (Griffin, 1982).

Moreover, Herman continues, it is not primarily "weirdos" and misfits who engage in violence against women. Because our patriarchal way of life embraces the control of women as normative, men who use power in this way are actually well adjusted to their surroundings. No wonder, according to surveys, that women are several times more likely than men to feel fear even when walking in their own neighborhoods (NORC, 1993).

Sexual Harassment

The 1991 Senate confirmation hearings for Supreme Court Justice Clarence Thomas drew national attention to the concept of **sexual harassment**, defined as *comments, gestures, or physical contact of a sexual nature that are deliberate, repeated, and unwelcome.* Anita Hill, a law professor and former colleague, alleged that Thomas harassed her during the time that they worked together for the federal government. The Senate never clearly resolved the specific allegations made by Hill and vigorously denied by Thomas; however, people lined up on one side or the other as the episode touched off a national debate that has already significantly redefined the rules for workplace interaction between the sexes.

Both men and women can be victims of sexual harassment. For two reasons, however, it is easy to see why victims of harassment are typically women. First, our culture encourages men to be sexually assertive and to respond to women in sexual terms; thus, inappropriate sexuality easily finds its way into the workplace, the campus, and elsewhere. Second, most individuals in positions of power—including business

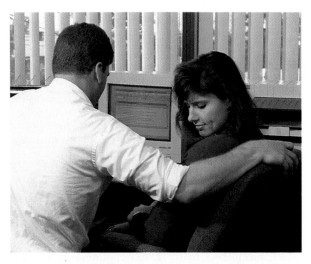

A debate over the concept of sexual harassment is now underway in the United States. No one doubts that supervisors who demand sexual favors from subordinates as a condition of employment or advancement are wrong to do so. But people do disagree as to precisely where to draw the line between friendly conversation and contact and unwarranted imposition of sexuality on another.

executives, physicians, bureau chiefs, assembly line supervisors, professors, and military officers—are men who oversee the work of women. Surveys carried out in widely different work settings confirm that women find unwelcome sexual overtures to be widespread; generally, more than half of respondents report receiving some form of recent, unwanted sexual attention (Loy & Stewart, 1984; Paul, 1991). In one study of colleges, one-third of women students reported uninvited sexual advances from their male teachers (Dziech & Weiner, 1984).

Sexual harassment is sometimes blatant and direct, as when a supervisor solicits sexual favors from a subordinate coupled with threat of reprisals if the advances are refused. Behavior of this kind—which not only undermines the dignity of an individual but prevents her from earning a living—is widely condemned. Courts have declared such *quid pro quo* sexual harassment (the Latin phrase means "one thing in return for another") to be an illegal violation of civil rights.

However, the problem of unwelcome sexual attention often involves subtle behavior—sexual teasing, off-color jokes, pinups displayed in the workplace—none of which any individual may *intend* to harass another person. But, using the *effect* standard favored by many feminists, such actions add up to another form of harassment: creating a *hostile environment*

SOCIAL SURVEY: "Women should take care of running their homes and leave running the country up to men." (GSS 1993, N = 1,080; *Codebook*, 1993:251)
"Agree" 14.3%   "Disagree" 82.2%   DK/NR 3.5%

NOTE: *Playboy* was founded in 1953, had a U.S. circulation of 110,000 in one year, and 1.4 million in ten years; peak circulation was 6 million in early 1970s; it has fallen to about half that now, although overseas circulation is up. (Joseph E. Scott and J. Cuvelier, "Violence in *Playboy* Magazine: A Longitudinal Analysis." *Archives of Sexual Behavior*, Vol. 16 (1987):279–88).

(Cohen, 1991; Paul, 1991). Incidents of this kind are far more complex because they involve very different perceptions of the same behavior. For example, a man may think that showing romantic interest in a co-worker is paying the woman a compliment; she, on the other hand, may deem his behavior offensive and a hindrance to her job performance.

Women's entry into the workplace does not in itself ensure that everyone is treated equally and with respect. Untangling precisely what constitutes a hostile working environment, however, demands clearer standards of conduct than exist at present. Creating such guidelines—and educating the public to embrace them—is likely to take some time (Cohen, 1991; Majka, 1991). In the end, courts (and, ultimately, the court of public opinion) will draw the line between what amounts to "reasonable friendliness" and behavior that is "unwarranted harassment."

Pornography

Pornography, too, underlies sexual violence. Defining pornography has long challenged scholars and lawmakers alike. Unable to set a single, specific standard to distinguish what is, and what is not, pornographic, the Supreme Court allows local cities and counties to decide for themselves what violates "community standards" of decency and lacks any redeeming social value.

But few doubt that pornography (loosely defined) is quite popular in the United States. X-rated videos, 900 telephone numbers providing sexual conversation, and a host of sexually explicit movies and magazines together constitute a $7-billion-a-year industry.

Traditionally, we have viewed pornography as a *moral* issue, involving how people should express their sexuality. National survey data support this view: 60 percent of U.S. adults endorse the assertion that "sexual materials lead to a breakdown of morals" (NORC, 1993:266).

A more recent view holds that pornography demeans women. From this point of view, pornography is framed as a *power* issue because it fosters the notion that men should control both sexuality and women. Catharine MacKinnon (1987) has branded pornography as one foundation of male dominance in the United States because it portrays women in dehumanizing fashion as the subservient playthings of men. Worth noting, in this context, is that the term pornography is derived from the Greek word *porne*, meaning a harlot who acts as a man's sexual slave.

A related charge is that pornography promotes violence against women. Certainly anyone who has viewed more recent "hard-core" videos finds this assertion plausible. Yet demonstrating a scientific cause-and-effect relationship between what people view and how they act is difficult. Research does support the contention, however, that pornography encourages men to think of women as objects rather than as people (Mallamuth & Donnerstein, 1984; Attorney General's Commission on Pornography, 1986). The public as a whole also shares a concern about the effects of pornography, with 55 percent of adults reporting the opinion that pornography encourages people to commit rape (NORC, 1993:266).

Like sexual harassment, the pornography issue raises complex and sometimes conflicting concerns. While everyone objects to material they find offensive, many also endorse rights of free speech and artistic expression. But pressure to restrict this kind of material is building through the efforts of an unlikely coalition of conservatives (who oppose pornography on moral grounds) and progressives (who condemn it for political reasons).

THEORETICAL ANALYSIS OF GENDER

Although they differ, the structural-functional and social-conflict paradigms each point up the importance of gender to social organization.

Structural-Functional Analysis

The structural-functional paradigm views society as a complex system of many separate but integrated parts. In this approach, every social structure contributes to the overall operation of society.

As Chapter 4 ("Society") explained, members of hunting and gathering societies had limited power over the forces of biology. Lacking effective birth control, women experienced frequent pregnancies, and the responsibilities of child care kept them close to home (Lengermann & Wallace, 1985). Likewise, to take advantage of their greater strength, norms guided men toward the pursuit of game and other tasks away from the home. Over many generations, this sexual division of labor became institutionalized and largely taken for granted.

Industrial technology opens up a vastly greater range of cultural possibilities. Human muscle power no longer serves as a vital source of energy, so the physical strength of men loses much of its earlier significance. At the same time, the ability to control reproduction gives women greater choice in shaping their lives. Modern societies come to see that traditional ideas

Q: "Presumably there is continuity from sub-human origins in one critical respect, namely the centering of the earliest child-care responsibilities on the mother. This fact, plus the disabilities of pregnancy and the fact that only recently has other than breast-feeding become widely feasible, lie at the basis of the differentiation of sex roles." Talcott Parsons (1951:155)

Q: "The one immutable, enduring difference between men and women is maternity. Maternity is not simply childbirth but a continuum that begins with an awareness of the ticking of the biological clock, proceeds to the anticipation of motherhood, includes pregnancy, childbirth, physical recuperation, psychological adjustment, and continues to nursing, bonding, and child rearing." Felice Schwartz (1989:66)

Given our notions about power being a masculine trait, it is little wonder that our popular culture typically portrays powerful women as decidedly unfeminine. This recent cartoon about Hillary Rodham Clinton depicts her in decidedly masculine terms.

about gender waste an enormous amount of human talent; yet change comes slowly, because gender-based assumptions about behavior are deeply embedded in social mores.

Talcott Parsons: Gender and Complementarity

In addition, as Talcott Parsons (1942, 1951, 1954) has explained, gender differences help to integrate society—at least in its traditional form. Gender, Parsons explained, forms a *complementary* set of roles that links men and women together into family units that carry out various functions vital to the operation of society. Women take charge of family life, assuming primary responsibility for managing the household and raising children. Men, by contrast, connect the family to the larger world, primarily by participating in the labor force.

Parsons further argued that distinctive socialization teaches the two sexes their appropriate gender identity and skills needed for adult life. Thus society teaches boys—presumably destined for the labor force—to be rational, self-assured, and competitive. This complex of traits Parsons termed *instrumental*. To prepare girls for child rearing, their socialization stresses what Parsons called *expressive* qualities, such as emotional responsiveness and sensitivity to others.

Finally, according to Parsons, society promotes gender-linked behavior through various schemes of social control. People incorporate cultural definitions about gender into their own identities, so that violations of gender norms produce guilt. Society further induces gender conformity by conveying subtle and not-so-subtle messages that straying too far from accepted standards courts rejection by members of the opposite sex. In simple terms, women learn to view nonmasculine men as sexually unattractive, while men learn to avoid unfeminine women.

Critical evaluation. Structural-functionalism advances a theory of complementarity by which gender integrates society both structurally (in terms of what people do) and morally (in terms of what they believe). This approach was very influential at mid-century; however, for several reasons it is rarely used today by researchers exploring the impact of gender.

First, critics charge, this analysis simply squares less and less with how people really live. Traditionally, for example, some women have worked outside the home due to economic necessity; today, the proportion doing so continues to rise steadily. A second problem, say the critics, is that Parsons's analysis minimizes personal strains and social costs produced by rigid, traditional gender roles (Giele, 1988). Third and finally, to critics whose goals include sexual equality, what Parsons describes as gender complementarity amounts to little more than male domination.

Social-Conflict Analysis

From a social-conflict point of view, gender involves not just differences in action but disparities in power.

Q: "Consider, I address you as a legislator, whether, when men contend for their freedom, and to be allowed to judge for themselves their own happiness, it be not inconsistent and unjust to subjugate women, even though you firmly believe that you are acting in the manner best calculated to promote their happiness? Who made man the exclusive judge, if woman partake with him of the gift of reason?" Mary Wollstonecraft, A *Vindication of the Rights of*

Women (1792)

Q: "Anyone who knows anything about history knows that great social changes are impossible without the feminine ferment." Marx

Q: "Differences of age and sex no longer have distinctive social validity for the working class. All are instruments of labor, more or less expensive to use, according to their age and sex." Karl Marx and Friedrich Engels

Conventional ideas about gender historically have benefited men while subjecting women to prejudice and discrimination, in a striking parallel to the treatment of racial and ethnic minorities (Hacker, 1951, 1974; Collins, 1971; Lengermann & Wallace, 1985). Thus gender promotes not cohesion but tension and conflict, as men seek to protect their privileges while women challenge the status quo.

A social-conflict analysis of gender also places sexism at center stage. A web of notions about female inferiority that justify depriving women of opportunities and subjecting them to manipulation and violence, sexism supports lower pay for women in the workplace, the exclusion of women from positions of power in national affairs, and the subordination of women in the home.

As earlier chapters noted, the social-conflict paradigm draws heavily on the ideas of Karl Marx. Yet Marx was a product of his time insofar as his writings focused almost exclusively on men. His friend and collaborator Friedrich Engels, however, did explore the link between gender and social classes (1902; orig. 1884).

Friedrich Engels: Gender and Class

Engels suggested that the activities of women and men in hunting and gathering societies—although different—had comparable importance. A successful hunt may have brought men great prestige, but the vegetation gathered by women constituted most of a society's food supply (Leacock, 1978). As technological advances led to a productive surplus, however, social equality and communal sharing gave way to private property and, ultimately, a class hierarchy. At this point, men gained pronounced power over women. With surplus wealth to pass on to heirs, upper-class men took a keen interest in their children. The desire to control property, then, prompted the creation of monogamous marriage and the family. That way, men could be certain of paternity—especially the lineage of their sons—and the law ensured that wealth passed to them. For their part, women were taught to remain virgins until marriage, to remain faithful to their husbands thereafter, and to build their lives around bearing and raising children.

Engels contended that capitalism intensified this male domination. First, capitalism created more wealth, which conferred greater power on men as the owners of property, the heirs of property, and the primary wage earners. Second, an expanding capitalist economy depended on defining people—especially women—as consumers and encouraging them to find fulfillment through the pursuit of personal beauty and consumer products. Third, to support men working in

factories, society assigned women the task of maintaining the home. The double exploitation of capitalism, then, lies in paying low wages for male labor and *no* wages for female work (Eisenstein, 1979; Barry, 1983; Jagger, 1983; Vogel, 1983).

Critical evaluation. Social-conflict analysis stresses how society places the two sexes in unequal positions of wealth, power, and privilege. As a result, the conflict approach is decidedly critical of conventional ideas about gender, claiming that society would be better off if we minimized or even eliminated this dimension of social structure.

But social-conflict analysis, too, has its critics. One problem, they suggest, is that this approach casts conventional families—defended by traditionalists as morally positive—as a social evil. Second, from a more practical point of view, social-conflict analysis minimizes the extent to which women and men live together cooperatively and often quite happily in families. A third problem with this approach, for some critics, is its assertion that capitalism stands at the root of gender stratification. Societies with socialist economic systems—including the People's Republic of China and the former Soviet Union—remain strongly patriarchal. Some researchers, in fact, argue that capitalism, with its emphasis on evaluating people on the basis of personal merit rather than categories, actually advances women's social standing more than socialism does (Moore, 1992).

FEMINISM

Feminism is *the advocacy of social equality for the sexes, in opposition to patriarchy and sexism.* The "first wave" of the feminist movement in the United States began in the 1840s as women opposed to slavery, including Elizabeth Cady Stanton and Lucretia Mott, drew parallels between the oppression of African Americans and the oppression of women (Randall, 1982). The primary objective of the early women's movement was securing the right to vote, which was achieved in 1920. But other disadvantages persisted and a "second wave" of feminism arose in the 1960s and continues today.

Basic Feminist Ideas

Feminism views the lives of women and men through the lens of gender. How we think of ourselves (gender identity), how we act (gender roles), and our sex's social standing (gender stratification) are all rooted in the operation of our society.

SOCIAL SURVEY: "Being born a man or a woman—how important is that for getting ahead in life?" (GSS 1987, N = 1,285; *Codebook*, 1993:586)

"Essential"	2.7%	"Not very important"	32.8%
"Very important"	11.4%	"Not important at all"	26.5%
"Fairly important"	22.7%	DK/NR	3.9%

SOCIAL SURVEY: "How important is the women's rights issue to you?" (GSS 1985, N = 804; *Codebook*, 1993:252)

"One of the most important"	9.6%	"Not important at all"	11.6%
"Important"	48.4%	DK/NR	1.7%
"Not very important"	28.7%		

Although people who consider themselves feminists disagree about many things, most support the following five ideas:

1. **The importance of change.** Feminism is critical of the status quo, advocating social equality for women and men. Thus feminism is not just sociological but decidedly political. Feminist thinking holds that "the personal is political," calling for individuals to examine how culture defines masculinity in terms of power over others while constructing femininity as a model of altruism.

2. **Expanding human choice.** Feminists argue that cultural conceptions of gender divide the full range of human qualities into two opposing and limited spheres: the female world of emotion and cooperation and the male world of rationality and competition. As an alternative, feminists pursue a "reintegration of humanity" by which each human being can develop *all* human traits (French, 1985).

3. **Eliminating gender stratification.** Feminism opposes laws and cultural norms that limit the education, income, and job opportunities of women. Supporters of the women's movement oppose the historical pattern by which the female half of the population has been subject to decisions made by the male half—whether in the privacy of the home or in the public world of national politics. For this reason, feminists have long advocated passage of the Equal Rights Amendment (ERA) to the U.S. Constitution, which states simply:

   Equality of rights under the law shall not be denied or abridged by the United States or any State on account of sex.

   The ERA, first proposed in Congress in 1923, has the support of two-thirds of U.S. adults (NORC, 1993:287). That it has not yet become law probably reflects the opposition of the men who dominate state legislatures around the country.

4. **Ending sexual violence.** A major objective of today's women's movement is eliminating sexual violence. Feminists argue that patriarchy distorts the relationships between women and men, encouraging violence against women in the form of rape, domestic abuse, sexual harassment, and pornography (Millet, 1970; J. Bernard, 1973; Dworkin, 1987). Thus feminism seeks to transform the power structure of society as a way to end violence against women.

5. **Promoting sexual autonomy.** Finally, feminism enhances women's control of their sexuality and

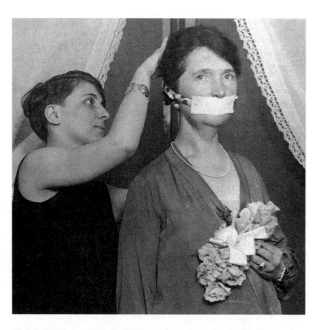

Margaret Higgins Sanger (1883–1966) was a pioneer activist in the crusade for women's reproductive rights, a cause that led her into frequent conflict with the laws of the time. Threatened with arrest if she spoke to a gathering in Boston in 1929, she made a powerful statement by appearing in public with tape over her mouth. Decades later, at the time of her death, some birth control devices (including condoms) still were not freely available in stores everywhere in the United States.

reproduction. Feminists advocate the free availability of birth control information, which, in some states, was illegal as recently as the 1960s. In addition, most feminists support a woman's right to choose whether to bear children or to terminate a pregnancy, rather than allowing men—as husbands, physicians, and legislators—to regulate sexuality. Many feminists also support gay peoples' efforts to overcome prejudice and discrimination in a predominantly heterosexual culture (Deckard, 1979; Barry, 1983; Jagger, 1983).

Variations Within Feminism

People pursue the goal of sexual equality in various ways, yielding three general types of feminism. Although the distinctions among them are far from clear-cut, each conceives of the problem of patriarchy in different terms and calls for correspondingly different changes in society (Barry, 1983; Jagger, 1983; Stacey, 1983; Vogel, 1983).

SOCIAL SURVEY: "Some people think that the best way for women to improve their position is through women's right groups (point 1). Other people think that the best way for women to improve their position is for each individual woman to become better trained and more qualified (point 7). Where would you place yourself on this scale?" (GSS 1983, N = 825; *Codebook*, 1993:395)

1 (Women's rights groups)	4.7%	5	13.7%
2	2.5%	6	14.1%
3	3.6%	7 (Better trained)	43.3%
4	16.5%	NR	2.5%

Liberal Feminism

Liberal feminism is rooted in classic liberal thinking that individuals should be free to develop their own abilities and pursue their own interests. Liberal feminists criticize our present society because women do not yet enjoy the same rights and opportunities as men. To that end, just as liberals endorse the civil rights movement in support of African Americans, liberal feminists endorse the Equal Rights Amendment and oppose prejudice and discrimination that have historically limited women's achievements.

One key to sexual equality is reproductive freedom for women. Only if women can choose whether to bear children, and only if parents share the responsibilities of child rearing, can women and men have equal opportunity in their working lives. For the same reason, liberal feminism advocates the right of women to maternity leave and child care. With Congressional passage of the Family Leave Act in 1992, the United States joined one hundred other nations that guarantee maternity leave for all working women. Moreover, while liberal feminists support the family as a social institution, they contend that families need to change to accommodate the ambitions of both women and men.

With their strong belief in the rights of individuals, liberal feminists do not think that all women need to march in lockstep toward any single political goal. Both women and men are capable of improving their lives if society simply ends legal and cultural constraints rooted in gender.

Socialist Feminism

Socialist feminism evolved from Marxist conflict theory, as a criticism of that approach's inattention to gender issues and also as a corrective for feminism's failure, up to that time, to challenge capitalism (Philipson & Hansen, 1992). As noted earlier, Engels claimed that patriarchy (like class oppression) has its roots in private property. Furthermore, explained Engels, although capitalism did not create patriarchy, it has intensified this form of domination by concentrating wealth and power in the hands of a small number of people, most of them men, while relegating women to lives of unpaid domestic labor.

As this approach has developed, socialist feminists have come to believe that a socialist revolution is necessary—but not in itself sufficient—to end women's oppression. This is because patriarchy and capitalism, as they see them, are distinct although interdependent systems of exploitation.

The family, an institution basically acceptable to liberal feminists, is targeted for transformation by socialist feminists. The "bourgeois family," fostered by capitalism, oppresses women by keeping them in the home where they work without wages and remain economically dependent on men. In addition, living in isolated families discourages women from political solidarity with other women and men. With little chance for cooperative solutions to their plight, women vainly try to derive personal satisfaction from the relentless pursuit of beauty and the consumption of products.

The solution to gender-based oppression, according to socialist feminists, begins with transforming the economy into a state-centered system that strives to meet the needs of all. But further change is needed, especially in the family system—dismissed by Engels as "domestic slavery"—in favor of a collective system for performing tasks like cooking and child care. Thus socialist feminists conclude that the reforms sought by liberal feminism are, by themselves, grossly insufficient to produce gender equality. Such a basic transformation of society requires that women and men pursue their personal liberation together, rather than individually, as liberal feminists maintain. (Further discussion of socialism is found elsewhere, especially in Chapter 15, "The Economy and Work.")

Radical Feminism

Radical feminism, too, finds the reforms of liberal feminism to be inadequate. Moreover, radical feminists argue that even a socialist revolution would not end patriarchy. According to this variant of feminism, the root of sexual oppression lies in the concept of gender itself.

As radical feminists see it, gender is based on the biological traits that constrain women to carry and bear children. The family, from this point of view, does not constitute merely an economic arrangement, as Engels claimed, but a system that institutionalizes heterosexual relations and confines women to the monotonous burdens of child care.

What is the alternative? Until recently, there were few options because the biological process of reproduction was beyond human control. But now advancing technology has made conventional heterosexual parenting—and thus the historical family—unnecessary. New reproductive technology (see Chapter 17, "Family"), which already allows conception outside of the body, promises to separate women's bodies from the process of childbearing. With the demise of motherhood, radical feminists reason, the entire family system could be left behind,

THE MAP: Generally, support for feminism is stronger on both coasts than in the Midwest and the South. The states won by the Democrats in the 1992 presidential election look more favorably on feminism than do those won by the Republicans (see National Map 16–1 on page 444).

NOTE: An Iowa study of married women found that 68% preferred the title Mrs.; 6% favored Ms.; 26% were unsure. (*Des Moines Register*)

Q: "It is very little for me to have the right to vote, to own property, et cetera, if I may not keep my body, and its uses, in my absolute right." Lucy Stone (1855)

Q: "All women are bunnies." Gloria Steinem

Seeing Ourselves

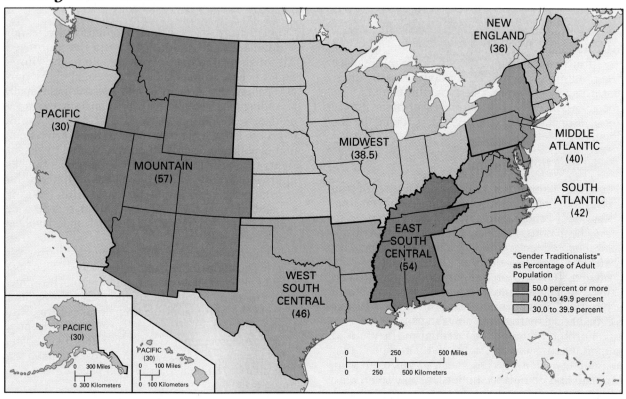

NATIONAL MAP 13–1 Attitudes Toward Feminism Across the United States

Nationally, only about 35 percent of all adults support a gender-based domestic system, claiming that men should be the achievers in the workplace while women take care of home and family. But, as the map shows, support for feminism varies significantly by region. In the Mountain states and the East South Central states, more than half of adults are "gender traditionalists." Across the remainder of the South and right up through the Middle Atlantic region, traditionalists constitute more than 40 percent, and in New England and the Midwest, they claim between 35 and 40 percent of all adults. The Pacific states are the least traditional with regard to gender, with 30 percent or less of adults endorsing different roles for men and women. How would you explain these regional differences? A key clue is that, generally speaking, support for feminism is greatest in regions where education is greatest and people are youngest.

Prepared by the author using data from *General Social Surveys, 1972–1991: Cumulative Codebook* (Chicago: National Opinion Research Center, 1991).

---

liberating women and men from the tyranny of gender and of sex itself. Radical feminism, in short, envisions a revolution much more far-reaching than that sought by Marx.

But, for the radical feminist vision to be realized, four other objectives must be achieved. First, similar to the argument made by socialist feminism, we must reorganize society to ensure freedom from basic need; only in this way will no one be economically dependent on anyone else. Second, responsibilities for raising children cannot fall on individuals; the tasks of parenthood must become the responsibility of society as a whole. Third, since no woman should have to bear children or conform to conventional definitions of motherhood (or men contend with fatherhood), children must also slip free of the historical dependencies and constraints of childhood. Thus radical feminism advocates a program of children's rights (Jagger, 1983).

Chapter 13 Sex and Gender   **381**

RESOURCE: Sally Helgesen argues that women have advantages as corporate leaders. See her article in the third edition of the Macionis and Benokraitis reader, *Seeing Ourselves*.

Q: "We hold these truths to be self-evident: that all men and women are created equal; that they are endowed by their Creator with certain inalienable rights . . ." Declaration of Sentiments, Seneca Falls, New York, 1848

GLOBAL: In 1990, 10% of the members of the Central Committee of the Communist Party in the People's Republic of China were women; none of 19 Politburo members was a woman.

Q: "My advice to the women of America is to raise more hell and fewer dahlias." William Allen White

Fourth, society must abandon conventional thinking about sexuality itself—including norms that favor heterosexuality over homosexuality or demand that sex take place only within certain relational forms like marriage (Dworkin, 1987).

If this radical feminist agenda were put in place, the resulting society would certainly be vastly different from any known to date. From this point of view, society would evolve toward the goal of eliminating all social distinctions based on sex, that is, toward the abolition of gender.

Resistance to Feminism

Feminism has provoked criticism and resistance from both men and women who embrace conventional ideas about gender. Some men oppose feminism for the same reasons that many white people have historically opposed social equality for people of color: They want to preserve their own privileges. Other men, including those who are neither rich nor powerful, distrust a social movement (especially its more radical expressions) that advocates socialism or seeks to abolish traditional marriage, family, and parenthood.

Further, for some men, feminism threatens an important basis of their status and self-respect: their masculinity. Men who have been socialized to value strength and dominance understandably feel uneasy about the feminist notion that they can also be gentle and warm (Doyle, 1983).

Some women, as well, shy away from feminism. For example, women who center their lives around their husbands and children may consider feminism as a threat to their most cherished values. From this point of view, feminism amounts to an effort to revise the law, the workplace, and the family—in short, to remake all of society—according to the radical political agenda of a few. Feminists, then, would dispose of the traditional values that have guided life and protected individual liberties in the United States for centuries. Additionally, some women worry that, in the process of recasting the conventional "feminine" spheres of life including the home and the family, women will lose rather than gain power and personal identity (Marshall, 1985).

Resistance to feminism also comes from within academic circles. Some sociologists are decidedly cool toward this approach because, as they see it, feminism ignores a growing body of evidence that men and women innately think and act in somewhat different ways. Furthermore, say critics, while feminism has directed considerable attention to enhancing women's presence in the workplace, it has all but ignored the fact that women make a crucial and unique contribution to the development of children—especially in the first years of life (Popenoe, 1993).

A final area of resistance to feminism involves *how* women's social standing should be improved. Although a large majority of people in the United States believe women should have equal rights, most also believe that women should advance individually, according to their abilities. In a national survey, 70 percent of respondents claimed that women should expect to get ahead on the basis of their own training and qualifications; only 10 percent thought women's rights groups or collective action represents the best approach (NORC, 1993:395). Thus it appears that resistance to feminism is primarily directed at its socialist and radical variants; by contrast, there is widespread support for the principles that underlie liberal feminism.

The embrace of traditional gender patterns is clearly declining in the United States. In 1977, 65 percent of all adults endorsed the statement, "It is much better for everyone involved if the man is the achiever outside the home and the woman takes care of the home and family." By 1993, support had dropped sharply, to 35 percent (NORC, 1993:286). Even so, the rate of change has been uneven across the nation, as indicated in National Map 13–1 on page 381.

GENDER: LOOKING AHEAD

Predictions about the future are, at best, informed speculation. Economists disagree about the inflation rate a year from now; surely we should not expect sociologists to predict the shape of society decades into the future. Based on analysis of our nation's past, however, we can venture some general observations about the likely future of gender.

To begin, change has been remarkable. The position of women in the United States two centuries ago was clear and striking subordination. Husbands controlled property in marriage, women were barred from most jobs, and no woman could vote. Although women remain socially disadvantaged, the movement toward equality has been dramatic.

Perhaps nowhere is this change toward the social parity of women and men more evident than in the workplace. A century ago, our society discouraged all but poor women from being wage earners; today's economy, by contrast, *depends* on the earnings of women (Hewlett, 1990). This economic trend will continue: Two-thirds of people entering the work force during the 1990s will be women.

Q: "The early socialists often argued that problems associated with gender stratification would simply disappear under socialism. The leadership in socialist countries still gives lip service to the ideal of gender equality and includes it among its long-term goals . . ." Charlotte G. O'Kelly and Larry S. Carney

Q: "Then, if either the class of men or that of women shows its excellence in some art or other practice, then we'll say that that art must be assigned to it. But if they look as though they differ in this alone, that the female bears and the male mounts, we'll assert that it has not thereby yet been proved that a woman differs from a man with respect to what we're talking about; rather, we'll still suppose that our [men and women] must practice the same things." Plato, *The Republic*

Many factors have contributed to this transformation. Perhaps most important, industrialization both broadened the range of human activity and shifted the nature of work from physically demanding tasks that favored male strength to jobs that require human thought and imagination, placing the talents of women and men on an even footing. Additionally, medical technology has afforded us control over reproduction, so women's lives are less circumscribed by unwanted pregnancies.

Many women and men have also made deliberate efforts in pursuit of social equality. Feminism objects to assigning activities and channeling self-expression simply on the basis of sex. As these efforts continue, and as more women enter positions of national power, the social changes in the twenty-first century may be even greater than those we have already witnessed.

In the midst of change, strong opposition to feminism persists. Gender still forms an important foundation of personal identity and of family life, and it is deeply woven into the moral fabric of our society. Therefore, attempts to change cultural ideas about the two sexes will continue to provoke opposition.

On balance, while dramatic and radical change in the way we understand gender may not occur in the short run, the movement toward a society in which women and men enjoy equal rights and opportunities seems certain to gain strength.

SUMMARY

1. Sex is a biological concept; a human fetus is female or male from the moment of conception. People with the rare condition of hermaphroditism combine the biological traits of both sexes. Transsexuals are people who deliberately choose to alter their sex surgically.

2. Heterosexuality is the dominant sexual orientation in virtually every society in the world, although people who have an exclusively homosexual orientation make up several percent of the population. Sexual orientation, however, is not always clear-cut, and a large share of our population has at least some homosexual experience or is bisexual.

3. Gender involves how cultures assign human traits and power to each sex. Gender varies historically and across cultures.

4. Some degree of patriarchy exists in every society of the world. The ideology of sexism defends male dominance, just as racism supports racial dominance.

5. The socialization process links gender to personality (gender identity) and human behavior (gender roles). The major agents of socialization—family, peer groups, schools, and the mass media—reinforce cultural definitions of what is masculine and feminine.

6. Gender stratification entails numerous social disadvantages for women. Although most women are now in the paid labor force, a majority of working women hold clerical or service jobs. Unpaid housework also remains predominantly a task for women.

7. On average, women earn 72 percent as much as men do. This disparity is due to differences in jobs and family patterns as well as to discrimination.

8. Historically excluded from higher education, women are now a slight majority of all college students and receive half of all master's degrees. Men still earn a majority of all doctorates and professional degrees.

9. The number of women in politics has increased sharply in recent decades. Still, the vast majority of elected officials nationwide are men.

10. Gender, in combination with class and race, affords striking social disadvantages to some women. Overall, minority women earn only half as much as white men, and almost half the households headed by women of color are poor.

11. On the basis of their distinctive identity and social disadvantages, all women represent a social minority, although many do not think of themselves in such terms.

12. Violence against women is a widespread problem in the United States. Our society is also grappling with the issues of sexual harassment and pornography.

13. Structural-functional analysis suggests that distinctive roles for males and females constitute a survival strategy in preindustrial societies. In industrial societies, extensive gender inequality becomes dysfunctional, yet long-established cultural norms related to gender change slowly. According to Talcott Parsons, complementary gender roles promote the social integration of the family and the larger society.

14. Social-conflict analysis views gender as a dimension of social inequality and conflict. Friedrich Engels tied gender stratification to the development of private property. He claimed that capitalism devalues women and housework.

15. Feminism supports the social equality of the sexes, greater choice for women and men, and women's control over their sexuality. It opposes patriarchy and sexism in the form of gender stratification and violence against women.

16. There are three variants of feminist thinking. Liberal feminism seeks equal opportunity for both sexes within current institutional arrangements; socialist feminism advocates abolishing private property as the means to social equality; radical feminism seeks to create a gender-free society.

17. Because gender distinctions stand at the core of our way of life, feminism has encountered strong resistance. Although two-thirds of adults in the United States support the Equal Rights Amendment, this legislation—first proposed in Congress in 1923—has yet to become part of the U.S. Constitution.

KEY CONCEPTS

female infanticide the practice of aborting female fetuses and neglecting, or even actively killing, infant girls by parents who would prefer to raise boys

feminism the advocacy of social equality for the sexes, in opposition to patriarchy and sexism

gender the significance a society attaches to biological categories of female and male

gender identity traits that females and males, guided by their culture, incorporate into their personalities

gender roles (sex roles) attitudes and activities that a culture links to each sex

gender stratification a society's unequal distribution of wealth, power, and privilege between the two sexes

hermaphrodite a human being with some combination of female and male internal and external genitalia

matriarchy a form of social organization in which females dominate males

patriarchy a form of social organization in which males dominate females

primary sex characteristics the genitals, used to reproduce the human species

secondary sex characteristics bodily development, apart from the genitals, that distinguishes biologically mature females and males

sex the biological distinction between females and males

sexism the belief that one sex is innately superior to the other

sexual harassment comments, gestures, or physical contact of a sexual nature that are deliberate, repeated, and unwelcome

sexual orientation the manner in which people experience sexual arousal and achieve sexual pleasure

transsexuals people who feel they are one sex though biologically they are the other

CRITICAL-THINKING QUESTIONS

1. Distinguish sex from gender. What connection do the biological forces of sex have in shaping cultural patterns of gender?

2. How do the family, peer groups, schools, and the mass media affect our thinking about gender?

3. Why is gender a dimension of social stratification? How does gender interact with other dimensions of inequality such as race and class?

4. What principles underlie feminism? Distinguish among liberal, socialist, and radical feminism.

SUGGESTED READINGS

Classic Sources

Alfred Kinsey et al. *Sexual Behavior in the Human Male*. Philadelphia: W. B. Saunders, 1948.

This pioneering study of sexuality explains that sexual orientation is not always a matter of rigid categories. The companion volume focusing on women was published in 1953.

Margaret Mead. *Sex and Temperament in Three Primitive Societies*. New York: William Morrow, 1963; orig. 1935.

This comparative study carried out in New Guinea was an early effort to advance the social equality of the sexes.

Jessie Bernard. *The Female World*. New York: The Free Press, 1981.

This more recent classic explores how females and males live within different, socially constructed worlds.

Contemporary Sources

Naomi Wolf. *The Beauty Myth: How Images of Beauty Are Used Against Women*. New York: William Morrow, 1990.

This book, highlighted at the beginning of this chapter, is a highly readable indictment of how cultural forces contribute to the oppression of women.

Deborah Tannen. *You Just Don't Understand: Women and Men in Conversation*. New York: Ballantine Books, 1990.

This delightfully engaging book explains how each sex has characteristic orientations to many everyday situations, producing miscommunication and conflict.

Michael S. Kimmel and Thomas E. Mosmiller. *Against the Tide: Profeminist Men in the United States, 1776–1990—A Documentary History*. Boston: Beacon Press, 1992.

As this book explains, support for the feminist movement in this nation's history has not come exclusively from women.

Karen V. Hansen and Ilene J. Philipson, eds. *Women, Class, and the Feminist Imagination: A Socialist-Feminist Reader*. Philadelphia: Temple University Press, 1992.

This collection of thirty essays is organized around the past, present, and future of socialist feminism and its agenda for change.

Marjorie L. Devault. *Feeding the Family: The Social Organization of Caring and Gendered Work*. Chicago: University of Chicago Press, 1991.

Based on interviews with women, this book examines the invisible task of housework and why it can become oppressive to women.

Paula England. *Comparable Worth: Theories and Evidence*. Hawthorne, N.Y.: Aldine de Gruyter, 1992.

This survey of the issue of comparable worth tackles problems of measuring occupational worth and enacting supportive legislation.

Peter M. Nardi, ed. *Men's Friendships*. Newbury Park, Calif.: Sage, 1992.

How have men's relationships with other men changed along with shifting ideas about masculinity?

Allan Bérubé. *Coming Out Under Fire: The History of Gay Men and Women in World War Two*. New York: The Free Press, 1990.

This interesting book provides the historical context for the recent debate about gays and the military.

David Gary Comstock. *Violence Against Lesbians and Gay Men*. New York: Columbia University Press, 1991.

This study explores violence directed against gays and lesbians, focusing on both victims and offenders.

Margaret T. Gordon and Stephanie Riger. *The Female Fear*. New York: The Free Press, 1988.

This book examines the causes and consequences of sexual violence in the United States.

Camille Paglia. *Sexual Personae: Art and Decadence from Nefertiti to Emily Dickinson*. New York: Vintage, 1991.

This widely discussed book claims that today's women's movement does not always serve the interests of women.

Global Sources

Gertrude Schaffner Goldberg and Eleanor Kremen, eds. *The Feminization of Poverty: Only in America?* New York: Praeger, 1990.

The authors of this book offer a comparison of this important trend in the United States, Canada, France, Sweden, Poland, Russia, and Japan.

Kathy Davis, Monique Leijenaar, and Jantine Oldersma, eds. *The Gender of Power*. Newbury Park, Calif.: Sage, 1991.

This analysis of gender and power offers essays on the women's movement in Chile, the Middle East, and Sri Lanka.

Cynthia Enloe. *Bananas, Beaches, and Bases: Making Feminist Sense of International Politics*. Berkeley: University of California Press, 1990.

This book pushes the issue of gender into the international arena, arguing that gender (along with race and class) are important dimensions of the global system.

Nirmala Banerjee, ed. *Indian Women in a Changing Industrial Scenario*. New Delhi: Sage, 1991.

Women's part in economic development is the focus of this collection of essays about change in India, which features authors from India as well as the United States.

David Hockney, *My Parents*, 1977.

DATA FILE: An outline of this chapter, along with supplementary lecture material and discussion topics, is found in the *Data File*.

Q: "We must wait until the evening to see how splendid the day has been." Sophocles

Q: "A demographic and social revolution is underway in the world today [which is] a byproduct of the reduction of the birth rate accompanied by an increased length of life . . ." Donald O. Cowgill

Q: "Life is one long process of getting tired." Robert Butler

Q: "Our society is getting older, but the old are getting younger. The 70-year-old of today is more like a person of 50 twenty years ago." Robert B. Maxwell, American Association of Retired Persons

Q: "If I had known I was going to live this long, I would have taken better care of myself." Hollywood producer Hal Roach, on his 100th birthday in 1992

Aging and the Elderly

The book Final Exit *shot to the top of the best-seller list in 1991. This is a book about dying—not about the death of a famous person, nor a philosophical treatise on death, but a "how to" manual explaining how to commit suicide.* Final Exit *gives specific instructions for killing yourself in a host of ways, from swallowing sleeping pills, to self-starvation, to suffocation with a plastic bag.*

The author of Final Exit, *Derek Humphrey, is a founder and executive director of the Hemlock Society. This organization, established in 1980, offers support and practical assistance to people who wish to die. Humphrey argues that the time has come for people in the United States to have straightforward information about how to end their own lives. The immediate and remarkable popularity of* Final Exit—*especially among the elderly—suggests that millions of people agree with him.*

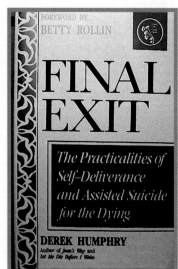

Not surprisingly, Final Exit *has sparked controversy. While supporters view the work as a humane effort to assist people who are painfully and terminally ill, critics claim that it encourages suicide by people who are experiencing only temporary depression (Angelo, 1991). A legal battle is also under way as laws are being tested that prohibit doctors—such as Michigan physician Jack Kevorkian—from assisting in the death of a patient.*

But the appearance of Final Exit *also raises broader questions that are no less disturbing and controversial. As this chapter explains, the ranks of the elderly are swelling rapidly as more and more men and women live longer and longer. As a result, younger people are uneasy about their responsibilities toward aging parents. Older people are, on the one hand, fearful of not being able to afford the medical care they may need and, on the other hand, alarmed at the prospect of losing control of their lives to a medical establishment that*

GLOBAL: In a ranking of the oldest countries (defined in terms of share of population aged 60 and over), the United States ranks 20th (16.9%). European nations and Japan are higher on the list. The top five: Sweden (22.8%), Norway (20.9%), Belgium and Italy (20.8%), United Kingdom (20.7%).

NOTE: Using the *STUDENT CHIP Social Survey Software* reveals that age corresponds to a relatively large difference in most atti-tudes: much more, typically, than one finds between the sexes.

DIVERSITY: In 1991, the median age for the U.S. population was 33.1 years. By race, median age was 34.1 for whites, 28.1 for African Americans, and 25.7 for Latinos. Among all categories of people median age is rising, although at different rates.

NOTE: Looking back to 1820, the median age of the U.S. population was 16.7, similar to that of many poor societies today.

often seeks to prolong life at any cost. And people of all ages worry whether the health care system can meet the escalating demands of seniors only by short-changing the young.

In the 1990s, issues relating to aging and the elderly will command the attention of policy makers as never before. In some respects, growing old in the United States is better than ever: People live longer, have better health care, and experience less poverty than they did a generation ago. But stubborn problems persist. Older people, for example, continue to grapple with prejudice and discrimination. And, as unprecedented numbers of women and men enter old age, new problems loom on the horizon.

THE GRAYING OF THE UNITED STATES

A quiet but powerful revolution is reshaping the United States: The number of elderly people—women and men aged sixty-five and over—is increasing more than twice as fast as the population as a whole. Put another way, the elderly population of the United States already outnumbers Canadians and is increasing faster than the overall population of India. The effects of this "graying" of the United States promise to be profound.

A few statistical comparisons bring this change into sharp focus. In 1900, half of the U.S. population was under twenty-three years of age and only one in twenty-five people had reached sixty-five. By 1990, as Figure 14–1 shows, the median age had climbed to almost thirty-three, with the elderly accounting for more than one-eighth of the population. By the year 2050—within the lifetimes of many readers of this book—the median age will be about forty years and one in five people will be over sixty-five. The graying of the United States also means that, between 1990 and 2020, our population *over* the age of fifty will soar upward by 75 percent, while the number of people *under* the age of fifty will increase by just 2 percent (Wolfe, 1991; U.S. Bureau of the Census, 1992, 1993).

What accounts for the aging of our society? Two factors stand out. The first is the baby boom that began in the late 1940s. With the end of World War II in 1945, men and women enthusiastically settled into family life and, by 1965, had some 75 million babies. This enormous cohort of baby-boomers first gained attention by forging the youth culture of the

1960s, and they are setting trends as middle-aged people in the 1990s. Their numbers alone ensure that they will continue to influence our society, causing an "elder-boom" by about 2025. The birth rate then took a sharp turn downward after 1965 (the so-called baby bust), making our population all the more "top-heavy."

The second cause of the aging of our society is increasing life expectancy. Females born in 1900 lived, on average, only about forty-eight years; males, only forty-six years. By contrast, females born in 1992 can expect to live 79.0 years; for men, life expectancy has stretched to 72.1 years (U.S. Bureau of the Census, 1993). This sharp and recent increase in the number of elderly people—here and around the world—supports the surprising fact that more than half of all elderly people who have ever lived are alive today.

This striking increase reflects medical advances that have virtually eliminated infectious diseases such as smallpox, diphtheria, and measles, which killed many infants and young people in the past. Just as important are more recent medical strides in combating cancer and heart disease, afflictions common to the elderly. In addition, a rising standard of living during this century has promoted the health of people of all ages.

The overall result is that the fastest-growing segment of the U.S. population is people over eighty-five, who are already more than twenty times more numerous that they were at the turn of the century. These men and women now number 3.1 million (about 1.2 percent of the total population). Projections place their number at 18 million (about 5 percent of the total) by the year 2050 (Kaufman, 1990; Harbert & Ginsberg, 1991; U.S. Bureau of the Census, 1992).

We can only begin to imagine the consequences of this transformation. As elderly people steadily retire from the labor force, the proportion of nonworking adults—already about ten times greater than in 1900—will generate ever-greater demands for social resources and programs. During this century, the share of federal spending supporting people over sixty-five has almost tripled, from 15 percent to more than 45 percent.

The elderly also draw heavily on the health care system, accounting for one-fourth of all medical expenditures. As Chapter 20 ("Health and Medicine") explains, the costs of medical care have skyrocketed in recent years. Unless steps are taken to meet the medical needs of tens of millions of additional older people—a problem that extends well beyond the current health care reforms—our society will face a monumental health care crisis in the next century.

Perhaps most important, in the coming decades interacting with elderly people will become commonplace. People in the United States are now accustomed

NOTE: As the ranks of the elderly swell, our society's share of people under eighteen will drop dramatically. From 36% in 1960, and 26% in 1990, young people will account for just over 20% of the U.S. population by 2030.

NOTE: Figure 21–2, an age-sex pyramid for the United States, illustrates the effect of the baby boom and the baby-bust.

NOTE: Elderly people with 1 year or less to live consume 30% of

Medicare funds; the average person in the U.S. receives more than one-third of all medical care in the last six months of life.

DIVERSITY: Currently, about 40,000 people in the U.S. are centenarians; the Census Bureau projects about 75,000 by the year 2000, and 1 million by the year 2050. Of today's oldest-of-the-old, 80 percent are women, and 82 percent are white. (African Americans are slightly overrepresented among centenarians.)

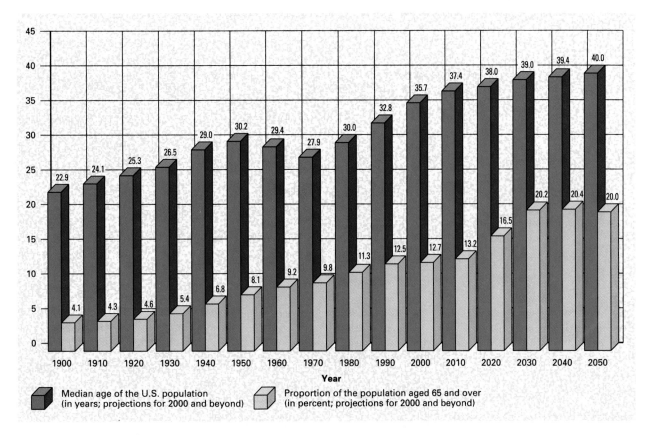

FIGURE 14–1 The Graying of U.S. Society

(U.S. Bureau of the Census, 1992)

to a considerable degree of age segregation. Young people rarely mingle in familiar settings with old people, so that most of the young know little about aging. In the twenty-first century, as the elderly population of the United States approaches twice its present size, those who are not elderly will have much more daily contact with people who are.

But, tomorrow as well as today, how frequently younger people interact with the elderly depends to some degree on where in the United States we live. National Map 14–1, on page 390, takes a look at residential patterns for people aged sixty-five and older.

Finally, the elderly represents an open category in which all of us, if we are lucky, end up. Thus elderly people in the United States are highly diverse, representing all cultures, classes, and races as well as both sexes. Even so, analysts sometimes draw a useful distinction between two cohorts of the elderly. The "younger elderly," who are between sixty-five and seventy-four years of age, typically enjoy good health,

are fairly comfortable financially, and are likely to be living as couples. The "older elderly" are at least seventy-five years of age and are more likely to have both health and money problems. Although women outnumber men in the elderly population (due to their greater longevity), this discrepancy increases with advancing age: Among the "older elderly," about two-thirds are women.

GROWING OLD: BIOLOGY AND CULTURE

Tracking the graying of the United States is the special focus of **gerontology** (derived from the Greek word *geron*, meaning "an old person"), *the study of aging and the elderly*. Gerontologists explore the biological processes of aging, ask if personalities change as we grow older, and investigate cultural assumptions about aging that vary around the world.

GLOBAL: In terms of size of the elderly population, P. R. China leads the world—due to its population size—with about 100 million elderly people (about 10% of its total population).

THE MAP: Young people migrate to regions of the country where jobs are plentiful; thus, counties with high proportions of elderly people are those that are contracting economically (especially rural counties in the middle of the country).

NOTE: Evidence of the graying of our society includes the rising proportion of college students over the age of 24: 41% in 1991 versus 33% in 1974. The rise is due to larger older cohorts more than a change in the rate of college attendance. (American Council on Education)

Q: "The older I grow, the more I distrust the common notion that age bring wisdom." H. L. Mencken

Seeing Ourselves

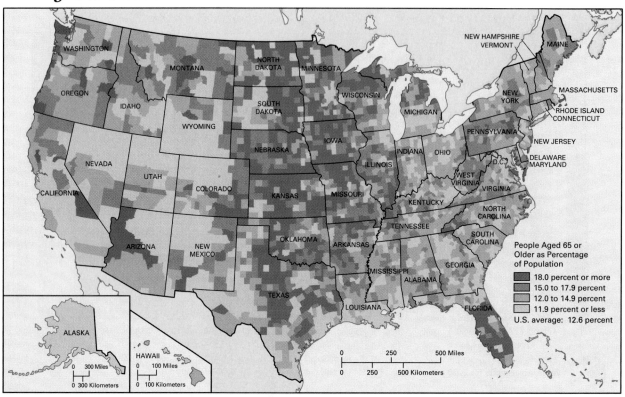

People Aged 65 or Older as Percentage of Population

- 18.0 percent or more
- 15.0 to 17.9 percent
- 12.0 to 14.9 percent
- 11.9 percent or less

U.S. average: 12.6 percent

NATIONAL MAP 14–1 The Elderly Population of the United States

Common sense suggests that elderly people live in the Sunbelt, enjoying the warmer climate of the South and Southwest. While it is true that Florida has a disproportionate share of people over the age of sixty-five, it turns out that counties with high percentages of older people predominate in the Midwest. What do you think accounts for this pattern? (Hint: Which regions of the United States do *younger* people leave in search of jobs?)

From *American Demographics* magazine, March 1993, p. 34. Reprinted with permission. ©1994, *American Demographics* magazine, Ithaca, New York. Data from the 1990 decennial census.

Biological Changes

As we age, the body undergoes a series of gradual, yet continual, changes. How we think about life's transitions—whether we cheer our maturity or bemoan our physical decline—depends largely on whether society as a whole labels such changes as positive or negative. The youth-oriented culture of the United States encourages us to view biological changes that occur early in life as positive. Growing children and adolescents approaching adulthood gain responsibility and look forward to additional legal rights.

At the same time, our culture looks on biological changes that unfold later in life with a negative eye. Few people are congratulated for getting old. We commiserate with those entering old age and make jokes about aging to avoid the harsh conclusion that the elderly are on a slope of physical and mental decline. We assume, in short, that at roughly the midpoint of the life course, people cease growing *up* and begin growing *down*.

It is true that physical problems eventually complicate old age. Gray hair, wrinkles, loss of height and weight, and an overall decline in strength and vitality

DATA FILE: Aging involves many myths; see Erdman Palmore's "aging quiz" in the *Data File* (originally published in *The Gerontologist*, Vol. 17, No. 4, August 1977:315–20).

Q: "The nation's rapidly aging white middle class will draw its retirement income from an increasingly black and Hispanic work force." Franklin A. Thomas

DATA FILE: Japanese society is graying faster than any other in the world. This is largely due to a falling birth rate: Japanese women of childbearing age now have a median 1.47 children contrasted to 4.54 in 1949. The *Data File* provides details.

GLOBAL: Auto rental agencies restrict renting automobiles to older people in many countries, although not in the United States. In most of Europe, the age limit is 70; in other regions of the world, the limit varies between 60 and 75.

all characterize the aging process that begins in middle age (Colloway & Dollevoet, 1977). After about the age of fifty, more brittle bones take longer to heal, and the odds of suffering from chronic illnesses (such as arthritis and diabetes) as well as life-threatening conditions (like heart disease and cancer) steadily rise. The sensory abilities—taste, sight, touch, smell, and especially hearing—also become less keen with age.

Without denying that health becomes more fragile with advancing age, the vast majority of older people are neither discouraged nor disabled by their physical condition. Only about one in ten reports trouble walking, and fewer than one in twenty requires intensive care in a hospital or nursing home. No more than 1 percent of the elderly are bedridden. Overall, about 70 percent of people over the age of sixty-five assess their health as "good" or "excellent," while 30 percent characterize their overall condition as "fair" or "poor" (U.S. National Center for Health Statistics, 1992).

Bear in mind, too, that patterns of well-being vary greatly within the elderly population. Generally speaking, health problems beset the "older elderly" past the age of seventy-five. Moreover, because women live longer, on average, than men do, women spend more of their lives suffering from chronic disabilities like arthritis. In addition, as Chapter 10 ("Social Class in the United States") explained, more well-to-do people are likely to live and work in a healthful and safe environment, which pays benefits well into old age. And, of course, richer people can afford much more preventive medical care. More than 80 percent of elderly people with incomes exceeding $35,000 assess their own health as "excellent" or "good," while only 60 percent of people with incomes under $10,000 do the same. Income disparity also explains why about three-fourths of elderly white people consider their health "good" or "excellent," in contrast to only half of older people of color (U.S. National Center for Health Statistics, 1992).

Psychological Changes

Just as we tend to overstate the physical problems of aging, so it is easy to exaggerate the psychological changes that accompany growing old. The conventional wisdom, in terms of intelligence over the life course, can be summed up in the simple rule: "What goes up must come down" (Baltes & Schaie, 1974).

In recent years, however, gerontologists have reassessed this pattern. They point out, first, that researchers can operationalize the concept of intelligence in various ways. If we look at sensorimotor coordination—including the ability to arrange objects to match a drawing—we find a steady decline after midlife. The facility to learn new material and to think quickly appears to subside among people over the age of seventy. But the ability to apply familiar ideas appears to remain steady with advancing age, and some studies actually show improvement in verbal and numerical skills (Baltes & Schaie, 1974; Schaie, 1980).

Most people wonder if they will think or feel differently when they are older. Gerontologists assure us, for better or worse, that the answer is usually no. Personality changes with advancing age are typically limited to becoming somewhat introverted—that is, more engaged with our own thoughts and emotions. Generally, however, two elderly people who were childhood friends would recognize in each other many of the same personality traits that distinguished them as youngsters (Neugarten, 1971, 1972, 1977).

Aging and Culture

A key sociological contribution to gerontology is that, whatever changes age brings to our minds and bodies, the *significance* of growing old is very much a matter of cultural definitions.

In global perspective, how well—and, more basically, how long—we live is closely linked to our society's technology and overall standard of living. Throughout most of human history, as English philosopher Thomas Hobbes (1588–1679) put it, people's lives were "nasty, brutish, and short" (although Hobbes himself survived to the ripe old age of ninety-one). In his day, most people married and had children while in their teens, became middle-aged in their twenties, and began to succumb to various illnesses in their thirties and forties. It took several more centuries for a rising standard of living and medical technology to curb infectious diseases that killed people of all ages. Living to, say, age fifty became commonplace only at the beginning of this century (Mahler, 1980; Cox, 1984). Since then, a rising standard of living coupled with medical advances have added another twenty years to people's longevity.

But living into what we call "old age" is not yet the rule in much of the world. Global Map 14–1 shows that, in the poorest nations of the world, the average life span is still just fifty years.

But aging is also a cultural issue, so that a society's longevity depends on *how* people live and the relative

NOTE: Life expectancy is affected by changes in infant mortality and tends to exaggerate the change in life span for those who reach old age. In 1900, Americans reaching age 65 typically lived to age 77; by 1990, they could expect to reach 83.

RESOURCE: Changes in the traditional care structures in Japan are examined in the film, *Aging in Japan: When Traditional Mecha-* *nisms Vanish*, available from Films for the Humanities and Sciences, Box 2053, Princeton, NJ 08543.

GLOBAL: Hoyt Alverson reports that, for the Tswana of southern Africa, the concept of aging is synonymous with the notion of "seeing with one's own eyes." For this traditional society, knowledge is "remembering things past" making the elderly the wisest of all. (*Mind in the Heart of Darkness*, Yale University Press, 1978:171)

Window on the World

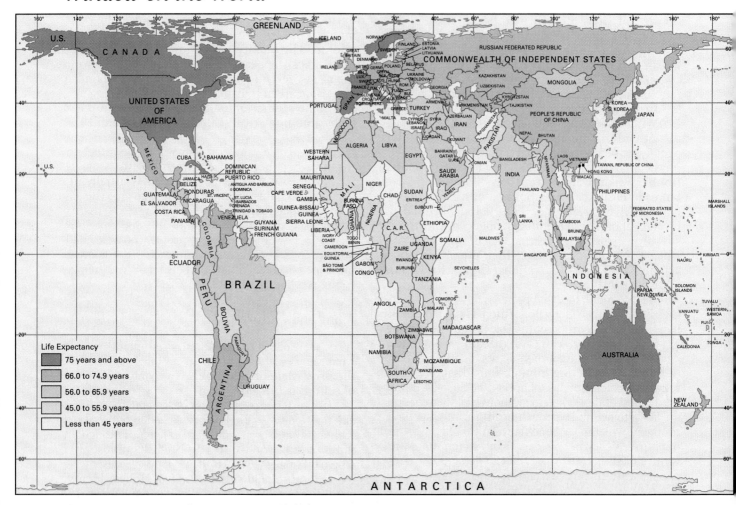

GLOBAL MAP 14–1 Life Expectancy in Global Perspective

Life expectancy has shot upward over the course of this century in industrial societies including Canada, the United States, the nations of Western Europe, Japan, and Australia. A newborn in the United States can expect to live about seventy-five years, and our life expectancy would be greater still were it not for the high risk of death among infants born into poverty. Since poverty is the rule in much of the world, lives are correspondingly shorter, especially in parts of Africa where life expectancy may be as low as forty years.

From *Peters Atlas of the World* (1990).

importance they attach to their senior members. Reports from Abkhasia, a republic of the former Soviet Union, suggest that if being an elder carries dignity and responsibility, people are motivated to live longer lives. The box on page 394 provides details.

Age Stratification: A Global Assessment

Like race, ethnicity, and gender, age is a basis for socially ranking individuals. **Age stratification**, then, is *the unequal distribution of wealth, power, and privileges*

Q: "The American core value . . . is self reliance. . . . A man in traditional China with no self-reliance as an ideal may not have been successful in his life. But suppose in his old age his sons are able to provide for him generously. Such a person not only will be happy and content about it, but is likely to also beat the drums before all and sundry to let the world know that he has good children who are supporting him. . . . On the other hand, an American parent who has not been successful in life may derive some benefit from the prosperity of his children, but he certainly will not want anybody to know about it." Francis Hsu (1961:216–19, as cited in Cowgill, 1986:48–49)

NOTE: The word "elderly" has the root *eld*, from Old English meaning "age" or "old age."

among people at different stages in the life course. As is true of other dimensions of social hierarchy, age stratification varies from one society to another.

Hunting and Gathering Societies

As Chapter 4 ("Society") explains, without the technology to produce a surplus of food, hunters and gatherers are nomadic. Thus they value the physical strength and stamina that contribute to their survival. As members of these societies age ("old" in this case meaning about thirty) and become less active, others consider them an economic burden (Sheehan, 1976).

Pastoral, Horticultural, and Agrarian Societies

With control over raising crops and animals, societies gain the capacity to produce a material surplus; consequently, individuals may accumulate considerable wealth over a lifetime. Older people in these societies generally become wealthier and more powerful, so that these societies tend toward **gerontocracy,** *a form of social organization in which the elderly have the most wealth, power, and privileges.* Old people, particularly men, are honored (and sometimes feared) by their families and, as in the case of the Abkhasians, they remain active leaders of society until they die. This veneration of the elderly also explains the widespread practice of ancestor worship in agrarian societies.

Industrial Societies

Industrialization generates rising living standards and advances in medical technology, which, in turn, increase life expectancy. But these forces simultaneously erode the power and prestige of the elderly. In part, this decline is due to a shift in the prime source of wealth from land (typically controlled by the oldest members of society) to factories and other goods (often owned or managed by younger people). The peak earning years among workers in the United States, for instance, are around age fifty.

The growth of cities also divides the generations physically and encourages children to depend less on their parents and more on their own earning power. Furthermore, because industrial, urban societies change rapidly, the skills, traditions, and life experiences that served the old have less relevance to the young. Finally, the tremendous productivity of industrial societies renders the labor of everyone unnecessary; as a result, most of the very old and the very young remain in nonproductive roles (Cohn, 1982).

The long-term effect of all these factors is transforming *elders* (a term with positive connotations) into the *elderly* (commanding far less prestige). In mature, industrial societies such as the United States and Canada, economic and political leaders are usually middle-aged people who combine seasoned experience and up-to-date skills. In rapidly changing sectors of the economy—especially high-tech fields—many key executives are much younger and sometimes not long out of college. Industrial societies often consign older people to marginal participation in the economy because they lack the knowledge and training demanded by a fast-changing marketplace.

Certainly some elderly men and women remain at the helm of businesses they own but, more commonly, older people predominate in traditional occupations (such as barbers, tailors, and seamstresses) and jobs that involve minimal activity (night security guards, for instance) (Kaufman & Spilerman, 1982).

Japan: An Exceptional Case

Japan represents an exceptional case: It has one of the largest proportions of elderly of any society (about 20 percent by the end of this decade) and also a traditional culture that still elevates the prestige of older people. Most aged people in Japan live with an adult son or daughter and continue to play a significant role in family life. Elderly men in Japan are also more likely than their counterparts in the United States to remain in the labor force, and in many Japanese corporations the oldest employees enjoy the greatest respect. But even Japan is steadily becoming more like other industrial societies, in which growing old means giving up a large measure of social importance (Harlan, 1968; Cowgill & Holmes, 1972; Treas, 1979; Palmore, 1982; Yates, 1986).

TRANSITIONS AND PROBLEMS OF AGING

Chapter 5 ("Socialization") explained that we confront change at each stage of the life course. People must unlearn self-concepts and social patterns that no longer apply to their lives and simultaneously learn to cope with new circumstances. Of all stages of the life course, however, old age presents the greatest personal challenges.

Although physical decline in old age is less serious than most younger people think, this change can cause emotional stress. Older people endure more

DATA FILE: A global look at the percentage of population over the ages of 60 and 75 for selected nations is found in the *Data File*.

RESOURCE: Another global perspective on aging is Donald Cowgill's comparative article in the Macionis and Benokraitis reader, *Seeing Ourselves*.

DIVERSITY: On average, a male in the United States can now look forward to 60 years of health; a female to 63.

GLOBAL: For the entire world, about 5% of females and 4% of males are over 60 years of age. In poor societies, the figures are lower (3.4% and 3.1%, respectively). For rich nations, they are much higher (9.6% and 6.2%).

GLOBAL SOCIOLOGY

Growing (Very) Old: A Report from Abkhasia

Anthropologist Sula Benet was sharing wine and conversation with a man in Tamish, a small village in the Republic of Abkhasia, once part of the Soviet Union. Judging the man to be about 70, she raised her glass and offered a toast to his long life. "May you live as long as Moses," she exclaimed. The gesture of goodwill fell flat: Moses lived to 120, but Benet's companion was already 119.

An outsider—especially an open-minded anthropologist who studies many of the world's mysteries—should be skeptical of the longevity claims made by some Abkhasians. In one village of twelve hundred visited by Benet, for example, two hundred people declared their age to be more than eighty. But government statistics do suggest that, even if some Abkhasians exaggerate their longevity, many outlive the average North American.

What accounts for this remarkable life span? The answer certainly is not the advanced medical technology in which people in the United States place so much faith; many Abkhasians have never seen a physician or a hospital.

The probable explanation is cultural, including diet and physical activity. Abkhasians eat little saturated fat (which is linked to heart disease), use no sugar, and drink no coffee or tea; few smoke or chew tobacco. They do consume large amounts of healthful fruits and vegetables and drink lots of buttermilk and low-alcohol wine. Additionally, Abkhasians maintain active lives built around regular physical work for people of all ages.

Moreover, Abkhasians live according to a well-defined and consistent set of traditional values, which confers on all a strong sense of belonging and clear sense of

purpose. Here the elderly remain active and valued members of the community, in marked contrast to our own practice of pushing old people to the margins of social life. As Benet explains: "The old [in the United States], when they do not simply vegetate, out of view and out of mind, keep themselves 'busy' with bingo and shuffleboard." For their part, the Abkhasians do not even have a word for old people and have no notion of retiring. Furthermore, younger people accord their senior members great prestige and respect since, in their minds, advanced age confers the greatest wisdom. Elders are indispensable guardians of culture and preside at important ceremonial occasions where they transmit their knowledge to the young. In Abkhasia, in short, people look to the old, rather than the young, for decisions and guidance in everyday life.

Given their positive approach to growing old, Abkhasians expect a long and useful life. They feel needed because, in their own minds and everyone else's, they are. Far from being a burden, elders stand at the center of society.

SOURCE: Based on Benet (1971).

pain, become resigned to limited activities, adjust to greater dependence on others, and see in the death of friends or relatives frequent reminders of their own mortality. Moreover, because our culture places such a high value on youth, aging may spark frustration, fear, and self-doubt (Hamel, 1990). As one retired psychologist recently said of his old age: "Don't let the current hype about the joys of retirement fool you. They are not the best of times. It's just that the alternative is even worse" (Rubenstein, 1991:13).

SOCIAL SURVEY: "As you know, many older people share a home with their grown children. Do you think this is generally a good idea or a bad idea?" (GSS 1993, N = 1,057; *Codebook*, 1993:232)

"A good idea"	43.0%	"Depends"	20.6%
"A bad idea"	34.9%	DK/NR	1.4%

SOCIAL SURVEY: Same question by age and race: (*STUDENT CHIP Social Survey Software*, AGED1, 2; GSS 1972–91, N = 13,000)

By age, "Good"/"Bad": 18–34, 58.0%/42.0%; 35–64, 47.0%/53.0%; 65 and up, 23.7%/72.7%. By race, "Good/Bad": Afri Amer, 60.1%/39.9%; Latino, 65.0%/35.0%; White Anglo, 45.3%/54.7%

Erik Erikson (1963, 1980) suggests that elderly people must resolve a tension of "integrity versus despair." No matter how much they still may be learning and achieving, older people recognize that their lives are nearing an end. Thus the elderly spend much time reflecting on their past accomplishments and disappointments. To shore up their personal integrity, Erikson explains, older women and men must accept past mistakes as well as savor their successes. Otherwise, this stage of life may turn into a time of despair—a dead end with little positive meaning.

Research suggests that most people cope fairly well with the challenges of growing old. In a study of people in their seventies, Bernice Neugarten (1971) acknowledged that a small number of people develop *disintegrated and disorganized personalities* because they find it nearly impossible to come to terms with old age. Despair is the common thread in the lives of these people, sometimes to the point of making them passive residents of hospitals or nursing homes.

Another segment of Neugarten's subjects, with *passive-dependent personalities*, were only slightly better off. They have little confidence in their abilities to cope with daily events, sometimes seeking help even if they do not actually need it. Always in danger of social withdrawal, their level of life satisfaction is relatively low.

A third category of people had *defended personalities*, living independently but fearful of advancing age. Such people try to shield themselves from the reality of old age by valiantly fighting to stay youthful and physically fit. While concerns about health are certainly positive, setting unrealistic standards for oneself can only breed stress and disappointment.

Most of Neugarten's subjects, however, fared far better, displaying what she termed *integrated personalities*. As she sees it, the key to successful aging lies in maintaining one's dignity, self-confidence, and optimism while accepting the inevitability of growing old.

There is little question that most younger adults in the United States imagine that the elderly are unhappy: One national survey found just 1 percent of people under age sixty-five thought that the best years of their lives awaited them in old age (Harris, 1976). But, research suggests, while personal adjustments are inevitable, the experience of growing old in the United States can also provide joy. In any case, a person's experience of aging reflects individual personality, family circumstances, and social class.

TABLE 14–1 Living Arrangements of the Elderly, 1992

	Men	Women
Living alone	16.3%	41.8%
Living with spouse	73.8%	39.8%
Living with other relatives	7.0%	16.4%
Living with nonrelatives	2.9%	2.0%
Living in nursing home	1.3%	1.7%

SOURCE: U.S. Bureau of the Census, 1992.

Social Isolation

Being alone can provoke anxiety among people of any age; this problem, however, is most common among elderly people. Retirement closes off one source of social interaction, physical problems may limit the ability to move about, and most older people in the United States prefer not to share a home with their adult children. Then, too, negative stereotypes depicting the elderly as "over the hill" may discourage younger people from close social contact with their elders.

The greatest cause of social isolation, however, is the inevitable death of significant others. Few human experiences affect people as profoundly as the death of a spouse. One study found that almost three-fourths of widows and widowers cited loneliness as their most serious problem (Lund, 1989). Widows and widowers must rebuild their lives in the glaring absence of people with whom, in many instances, they spent most of their adult lives. Some survivors choose not to live at all. One study of elderly men noted a sharp increase in mortality, sometimes by suicide, in the months following the death of their wives (Benjamin & Wallis, 1963).

The problem of social isolation falls most heavily on women, who typically outlive their husbands. Table 14–1 shows that three-fourths of men aged sixty-five and over live with spouses, while only four in ten elderly women do. Just over 40 percent of older women (especially the "older elderly") live alone, compared to 16 percent of older men. More pronounced isolation among elderly women in the United States may account for the research finding that their mental health is not as strong as that of elderly men (Chappell & Havens, 1980). Keep in mind, too, that living alone—which many older people see as a dimension of independence—presumes the financial means to do so (Mutchler, 1992).

For most older people, families provide the primary source of social support. Ethel Shanas (1979) found that more than half of older people lived less

SOCIAL SURVEY: "All employees should be required to retire at an age set by law" (GSS 1985; *Codebook*, 1987:379)

"Agree strongly,"	5.2%	"Disagree,"	42.7%
"Agree,"	12.6%	"Disagree strongly,"	21.6%
"Neither agree nor disagree,"	16.5%	NR,	1.4%

Q: "Among the countries that have adopted a stated normal retire-

ment age—and these are mostly modernized societies—it appears that the more modernized they are, the later the normal retirement age. Those developing countries that have specified normal retirement ages . . . appear prone to designate somewhat earlier ages, in the range of 55 to 60 rather than 60 to 70, as in the most developed countries. . . . In less developed societies, people are perceived to be old at younger ages." Donald Cowgill (1986:125)

The painting Willis Avenue Bridge *(1940) by U.S. artist Ben Shahn (1901–1969) conveys the social marginality that often accompanies growing older, especially for people of color in the cities of the United States.*

than ten minutes away from at least one adult child, and over three-fourths said they had seen one or more of their children during the preceding week. Only 10 percent reported that they had not visited with an adult child during the past month. Women (especially daughters and daughters-in-law) tend to be the primary care givers for aging people (Stone, Cafferata, & Sangl, 1987). Family members, then, emerge as the most important source of social activity among older people in this country.

Retirement

Work provides us not only with earnings; it also figures prominently in our personal identity. Retirement from paid work, therefore, generally entails some reduction in income, diminished social prestige, and loss of purpose in life (Chown, 1977).

Some organizations strive to ease this transition. Colleges and universities, for example, confer the title of "professor emeritus" (from Latin, meaning "fully earned") on retired faculty members, who are permitted to maintain their library, parking, and mail privileges.

For many older people, fresh activities and new interests minimize the personal disruption and loss of prestige brought on by retirement (Rose, 1968). Volunteer work can be personally rewarding, allowing individuals to apply their career skills to new challenges and opportunities. The American Association

of Retired People (AARP), with more than 15 million members over the age of fifty, supports a wide range of volunteer opportunities for experienced seniors.

Although the idea of retirement is familiar to us, it is actually a recent social creation, becoming widely adopted only in industrial societies during the last century with the establishment of private and public pension programs (Atchley, 1982). Advancing technology reduces the need for everyone to work as well as placing a premium on up-to-date skills. Retirement permits younger workers, who presumably have the most current knowledge and training, to predominate in the labor force. In poor societies, by contrast, labor is vital to survival, so most people work until they are incapacitated.

Around the world, there is little agreement as to when (or even if) a person should retire from paid work. In light of these different opinions, one might wonder if a society should formally designate any specific age for retirement. Vast differences in the interests and capacities of older people also render the notion of fixed retirement controversial. As a result, Congress began phasing out mandatory retirement policies in the 1970s and virtually ended the practice by 1987. Statistically, however, most workers in the United States still choose to retire by age sixty-five. In fact, the trend in recent decades has been toward "early" retirement.

In the United States, men more than women have faced the transition of retirement. Elderly women who spend their lives as homemakers do not retire per se, although the departure of the last child from home serves as a rough parallel. As the proportion of women in the labor force continues to rise, of course, both women and men will confront the changes brought on by retirement.

Aging and Poverty

For most people in the United States, retirement leads to a significant decline in income. For many, home mortgages and children's college expenses are paid; yet the expenses for medical care, household help, and home utilities typically rise. Many elderly people lack sufficient savings or pension benefits to be self-supporting; generally speaking, Social Security is the elderly person's greatest source of income. Because many will live with fixed incomes as they face rising costs, poverty rates rise somewhat as people enter old age, as shown in Figure 14–2. Children are the age category most at risk of poverty; thereafter the incidence of poverty declines until about age fifty-five.

DIVERSITY: Poverty rates for the elderly by race and ethnicity, 1990: Ages 65–74: all, 9.7%; white, 7.6%; African American, 29.6%; Hispanic, 20.6%; Ages 75 and over: all, 16.0%; white, 13.8%; African American, 40.6%; Hispanic, 26.2% (U.S. Bureau of the Census).
NOTE: Currently, a typical poor child in the U.S. receives less than $400 per month with no cost of living allowance; Social Security provides an average of more than $600 to older people with a COLA.

NOTE: Looking at a cross-section of the U.S. population, income is highest about age 50 and wealth is greatest about age 67.
DIVERSITY: The Age Discrimination in Employment Act, 1967, prohibits age discrimination against workers or job applicants aged 40 to 65. As amended in 1975, it outlaws discrimination in federally funded job programs; in 1986 an additional change banned mandatory retirement in almost all types of jobs.

comparable men earned $35,256. A quick calculation shows that this income disparity, by which these older full-time working women earn 61 percent as much as all comparable men, is greater than among workers taken as a whole (72 percent). This is because, among workers aged sixty-five and above, women have much less schooling than men and hold lower-paying jobs.

But most elderly people do not work full time. Broadening the picture to include the entire elderly population—nonworking as well as working—median income falls to $8,189 for women and $14,548 for men. In this case, we calculate a greater gender-based income disparity, with women receiving 56 percent as much as men.

In the United States, then, although the elderly are faring better than ever before, growing old still means a growing risk of poverty, especially among people of color and women. What is distinctive about the privation of the elderly, however, is that it is often hidden from view. Because of personal pride and a desire to maintain the dignity of independent living, many elderly people conceal financial problems even from their own families. It is often difficult for people who have supported their children for years to admit that they can no longer provide for themselves, even though it may be through no fault of their own.

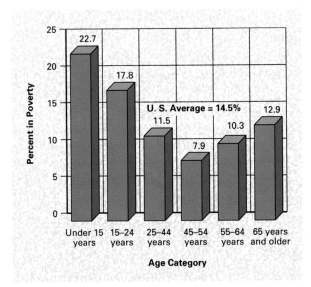

FIGURE 14–2 U.S. Poverty Rates, by Age, 1992

(U.S. Bureau of the Census, 1993)

Over time, the rate of poverty among the elderly has gone downward. From about 35 percent in 1960, the official poverty rate for elderly people in the United States stood at 12.9 percent in 1992 (U.S. Bureau of the Census, 1970, 1993). Early in the 1980s, an important turnaround took place as the poverty rate for the elderly actually fell below that for the nonelderly (Stone, 1986). As Figure 14–3 indicates, the 1980s were a boom decade for seniors, whose income jumped by more than 20 percent, while income of people under thirty-five actually fell.

Various factors contributed to this financial windfall: better health (allowing people to work more), more generous employer pension programs, and more couples with double incomes. But government policy played a key part, with programs targeting the elderly (including Social Security) swelling to almost half of all government spending. By contrast, during the 1980s, federal spending on children actually fell slightly.

But, the effects of race and ethnicity are not blunted by growing old. In 1992, the poverty rate among elderly Hispanics (22.0 percent) was twice the rate for their white, non-Hispanic counterparts (10.9 percent); elderly African Americans (33.3 percent) had three times the white risk of poverty.

Gender, too, continues to shape the lives of people as they age. Among full-time workers, women over sixty-five had median earnings of $21,548 in 1992;

FIGURE 14–3 Change in Median Household Income, 1980–1990, by Age

(U.S. Bureau of the Census, 1993)

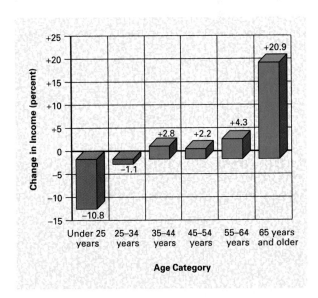

DATA FILE: The *Data File* includes information on daycare for the elderly.
NOTE: As noted in Chapter 8, crime rates drop with advancing age. But the elderly can be offenders as well as victims. In 1989, 82-year-old Jack Kelm was arrested for armed robbery, placing him among the oldest bank robbers on record.

NOTE: The cultural value of individualism encourages elderly people to fend for themselves in order to be self-reliant. This kind of social disengagement is vividly evident in the single-room occupancy (SRO) hotels inhabited by many poor, elderly men. (Cowgill, 1986:49)

Abuse of the Elderly

In the United States, we seem to awaken to social problems in stages: In the case of family violence, awareness of child abuse increased during the 1960s, spouse abuse was an issue of the 1970s, and abuse of the elderly was publicly acknowledged in the 1980s. Abuse of older people takes many forms, from passive neglect to active torment, and includes verbal, emotional, financial, and physical harm. Most elderly people suffer from none of these things; but research suggests that some 1 million elderly people (3 percent of the total) suffer serious maltreatment each year, and three times as many sustain abuse at some point. Like family violence against children or women, it is difficult to determine how widespread abuse of the elderly is because victims are understandably reluctant to talk about their plight. But as the proportion of elderly people rises, so does the incidence of abuse (Bruno, 1985; Clark, 1986; Pillemer, 1988).

What motivates people to abuse the elderly? Often the cause lies in the stress of caring—financially and emotionally—for aging parents. Today's middle-aged adults represent a "sandwich generation" who may well spend as much time caring for their aging parents as for their own children. This caregiving responsibility is especially pronounced among adult women who not only look after parents and children but hold down a job as well.

Even in Japan—where tradition demands that adult children care for aging parents at home—more and more people find themselves unable to cope with the problem. Abuse appears to be most common where the stresses are greatest: in families with a very old person suffering from serious health problems. Here, family life may be grossly distorted by demands and tensions that people simply cannot endure, even if their intentions are good (Douglass, 1983; Gelman, 1985; Yates, 1986).

In sum, growing old involves serious problems and transitions. Some are brought on by physical decline. But others—including social isolation, adjustment to retirement, risk of poverty, and abuse from family members—are social problems. In the next section, we bring to bear various theoretical perspectives on how society shapes the lives of the elderly.

THEORETICAL ANALYSIS OF AGING

Various theories developed from sociology's major theoretical paradigms shed light on the process of aging in the United States. We examine each in turn.

Structural-Functional Analysis: Aging and Disengagement

Based on the ideas of Talcott Parsons—an architect of the structural-functional paradigm—Elaine Cumming and William Henry (1961) point out that aging threatens society with disruption as physical decline and death take their toll. Society's response, they claim, is a gradual and orderly transfer of statuses and roles from the old to the young; this strategy ensures that tasks are performed with minimal interruption.

Continual turmoil would ensue if only incompetence or death brought about a changing of the guard. But a society heads off this outcome by disengaging the elderly from productive roles while they are still able to perform them. Such disengagement is also functional because, in a rapidly changing society, young workers typically have skills and training that are up-to-date. Formally, then, **disengagement theory** is *the proposition that society enhances its orderly operation by disengaging people, as they reach old age, from positions of responsibility.*

Disengagement may benefit elderly people as well as their society. Aging individuals with diminishing capacities presumably look forward to relinquishing some of the pressures of their jobs in favor of new pursuits of their own choosing (Palmore, 1979b). Society also grants older people greater freedom, so that unusual behavior on their part is construed as harmless eccentricity rather than dangerous deviance.

Critical evaluation. Disengagement theory—transferring responsibilities from older to younger people—amounts to a societal strategy for dealing with human decline. This approach also explains why, in rapidly changing industrial societies, people tend to define the elderly as marginal.

There are several limitations to this approach. First, many workers cannot readily disengage from paid work because they do not have sufficient financial security to fall back on. Second, many elderly people do not wish to disengage from their productive roles. Disengagement, after all, has high personal costs, including reduced income, loss of social prestige, and social isolation. Third, there is no compelling evidence that the benefits of disengagement outweigh its costs to society, which include the loss of human resources and the increased care of people who might otherwise be able to fend better for themselves. Then, too, any useful system of disengagement would have to take account of widely differing abilities of the elderly themselves.

Q: "Despite all the literature and all of the work of the American Association of Retired Persons, we still put too happy a face on growing old." Eli Rubinstein

NOTE: A limitation of activity theory is putting too much emphasis on physical activity. (Dale Lund)

DIVERSITY: The odds of living to age 65 for people born in the United States in 1990: Whites: females, 86.5%; males, 76.0%.

African Americans: females, 75.1%; males, 57.1%. (U.S. Bureau of the Census)

DIVERSITY: Edward Kain (1990) has calculated the odds of both spouses (married at age 25) surviving to a fortieth wedding anniversary (assuming they stay married) to be better than two-thirds for whites in the U.S. although less than half for people of color.

Symbolic-Interaction Analysis: Aging and Activity

One critical rebuttal to disengagement theory draws heavily on the symbolic-interaction paradigm. **Activity theory** is *the proposition that a high level of activity enhances personal satisfaction in old age.* Because individuals build their social identities from statuses and roles, this theory maintains, disengagement in old age undermines the satisfaction and meaning many elderly people find in their lives. What elderly people need, in short, are multiple roles—that is, various productive and recreational activities—in their retirement.

Activity theory proposes that, to the extent that elderly people do disengage, they substitute new roles and responsibilities for the ones they leave behind. After all, as members of a society that celebrates productivity, the elderly value active lives no less than younger people do. However, activity theory emphasizes, the elderly are no monolithic category. Older people have highly variable needs, interests, and physical abilities that guide their activities and attitudes about aging.

Research supports the general contention of this approach that elderly people who maintain high activity levels derive the most satisfaction from their lives. But advocates of activity theory stress that what activities people pursue, or how vigorously they pursue them, is always an individual matter (Havighurst, Neugarten, & Tobin, 1968; Neugarten, 1977; Palmore, 1979a; Moen, Dempster-McClain, & Williams, 1992).

Critical evaluation. Activity theory shifts the focus of analysis from the needs of society (as stated in disengagement theory) to the elderly themselves. This second approach also highlights social diversity among elderly people, an important consideration in formulating any government policy.

A limitation of this approach, from a structural-functionalist point of view, is a tendency to exaggerate the well-being and competence of the elderly. Proponents of this approach might ask if we really want elderly people actively serving as physicians or airline pilots, for example. From another perspective, activity theory falls short by overlooking the fact that many of the problems that beset older people have more to do with how well *society,* not any individual, operates. We turn now to that point of view, social-conflict theory.

Social-Conflict Analysis: Aging and Inequality

A social-conflict approach spotlights the fact that different age categories compete for scarce social

Through much of the century, social and geographic mobility eroded the importance of grandparents. But with more parents working today, a countertrend is now evident. And among categories of people with high rates of single parenting, grandmothers represent a vital resource.

resources. Various stages in the life course, therefore, form the basis of age stratification. By and large, middle-aged people in the United States enjoy the greatest social privileges, while the elderly (like children in some respects) contend with less power and prestige and face a higher risk of poverty. Employers often push elderly workers aside in favor of men and women who are younger because workers with less seniority typically command lower wages. The consequence, as conflict theorists see it, is that older people become second-class citizens (Atchley, 1982; Phillipson, 1982).

The roots of this age-based hierarchy reach into the operation of industrial-capitalist society. Following the ideas of Karl Marx, Steven Spitzer (1980) points out that, because our society has an overriding concern with profit, we devalue those categories of people who

NOTE: Robert Butler coined the term "ageism" in 1969.

NOTE: Robert Butler's statement "The Tragedy of Old Age in America," which challenges various myths about old age, is included among the classics in the Macionis and Benokraitis reader, *Seeing Ourselves.*

Q: "Aging is the neglected stepchild of the human life cycle." Robert Butler

NOTE: One example of age-bias: Women have the names April, May, or June, suggesting a positive attitude toward youth, but women are never named October, November, or December, which implies a negative view of old age. (Miriam Corcoran)

Q: "Let us recognize ourselves in this old man or in that old woman." Simone de Beauvoir

are economically unproductive. Thus, Spitzer reasons, most of the elderly have a mildly deviant status and are easily ignored. Old people are destined to be marginal members of a society consumed by material gain.

Social-conflict analysis also draws attention to social diversity in the elderly population. Differences of class, race, ethnicity, and gender splinter older people as they do everyone else. Thus the fortunate seniors in higher social classes have far more economic security, greater access to top-flight medical care, and more options for personal satisfaction in old age than others do. Likewise, elderly WASPs typically enjoy a host of advantages denied to older people of color. And women—who represent an increasing majority of the elderly population with advancing age—suffer the social and economic disadvantages of sexism.

Critical evaluation. Social-conflict theory adds further to our understanding of the aging process by underscoring age-based inequality and explaining how capitalism devalues elderly people who are less productive. The implication of this analysis is that the aged fare better in noncapitalist societies, a view that has some support in research (Treas, 1979).

One shortcoming of this approach goes right to the core contention: Rather than blaming *capitalism* for the lower social standing of elderly people, critics hold that *industrialization* is the true culprit; thus socialism might not work to lessen age stratification. Furthermore, the notion that capitalism dooms the elderly to economic distress is challenged by the recent rise in the income of elderly people in the United States.

AGEISM

In earlier chapters, we explained how ideology—including racism and sexism—seeks to justify the social disadvantages of minorities. Sociologists use the parallel term **ageism** to designate *prejudice and discrimination against the elderly.*

Like racism and sexism, ageism can be blatant (as when individuals deny elderly women or men a job simple due to their age) or subtle (as when people speak to the elderly with a condescending tone as if they were children) (Kalish, 1979). Also like racism and sexism, ageism builds physical traits into stereotypes; in the case of the elderly, people view graying hair, wrinkled skin, and stooped posture as signs of personal incompetence. Negative stereotypes picture the aged as helpless, confused, resistant to change, and generally unhappy (Butler, 1975). Even sentimental views of

sweet little old ladies and charmingly eccentric old gentlemen ignore the fact that all older people are complex individuals with distinct personalities and long years of experience and accomplishment.

Ageism, like other expressions of prejudice, may have some foundation in reality. Statistically speaking, old people are more likely than young people to be mentally and physically impaired. But we slip into ageism when we make unwarranted generalizations about an entire category of people, most of whom do not conform to the stereotypes.

Recently Betty Friedan, a pioneer of the contemporary feminist movement, has asserted that ageism is a central element of our culture. The box on page 401 takes a closer look.

The Elderly: A Minority?

The evidence is clear that, as a category of people in this country, the elderly do face social disadvantages. But sociologists differ as to whether the aged form a minority in the same way as, say, people of color or women.

On one side of the argument, Leonard Breen (1960) pronounces the elderly a minority, noting that older people have a clear social identity based on their age and are subject to prejudice and discrimination. But Gordon Streib (1968) responds that minority status is usually both permanent and exclusive. That is, a person is an African American or woman *for life* and cannot become part of the dominant category of white males. Being elderly, Streib continues, is an *open* status because, first, people are elderly for only part of their lives and, second, everyone who has the good fortune to live long enough grows old.

Streib makes a further point. The social disadvantages faced by the elderly are less substantial than those experienced by the minorities described in earlier chapters. For example, old people have never been deprived of the right to own property, to vote, or to hold office, as people of color and women have. Some elderly people, Streib concedes, do suffer economic disadvantages, but these do not stem primarily from old age. Instead, most of the aged poor fall into categories of people likely to be poor at any age. Streib concludes that "the poor grow old," *not* that "the old grow poor."

Thus, old people are not a minority in the same sense as other categories of people. Perhaps the best way to describe the elderly is simply as a distinctive segment of our population with characteristic pleasures and problems.

RESOURCE: An excerpt, "My Quest for the Fountain of Age," from Betty Friedan's new book, is included in the third edition of Macionis and Benokraitis reader, *Seeing Ourselves*.

NOTE: Evidence that people are retiring earlier includes the fact that, in 1956, 2% of Social Security beneficiaries received payments before 65; now more than two-thirds do.

NOTE: Today death is associated with old age; in contrast, a century ago death was common at any age. For instance, none of the Brontë sisters of literary fame lived to the age of 40; Anne (*Agnes Grey*) died at age 29, Elizabeth (*Wuthering Heights*) at 30, and Charlotte (*Jane Eyre*) at 39.

SOCIAL DIVERSITY

The Fountain of Aging

In 1963, Betty Friedan's book *The Feminine Mystique* asserted that our society defined women only in sexual relation to a man—as wife, mother, or, more commonly, as sex object. Thirty years later, Friedan is raising another call for change, this time in the way we view the elderly.

Surveying the mass media, Friedan concludes that elderly people are still conspicuous by their absence; only a small percentage of television shows, for example, contain central characters who are over sixty. In addition, when members of society do think about older people, it is in terms that are decidedly negative: The elderly *lack* jobs, have *lost* their vitality, and *look back* to their youth. In short, the "aging mystique" is that we define being old as a problem, as little more than decline and deterioration.

This culture-based ageism is as widespread as it is powerful. Why does our society still equate being old with living in a nursing home, when 95 percent of the elderly don't require any such institutionalization? Why do social service agencies seem focused on fostering dependency in older people rather than encouraging them to live— actively and independently—in society's mainstream?

Responding to this pervasive pessimism, Friedan claims that it is time we started seeking the "fountain of aging" by highlighting the potential and possibilities of this stage of life. All over the United States, there are women and men who are discovering they have far more to contribute than others give them credit for. Playing in orchestras, assisting small business owners, designing housing for the poor, teaching children to read—there are countless ways in which older people can enhance their own lives as they engage people around them. The bottom line, as Friedan adds it up, is that people do not stop living when they grow old; they grow old when they stop living.

SOURCE: Based on Friedan (1993).

DEATH AND DYING

To every thing there is a season,
And a time for every matter under heaven:
A time to be born and a time to die . . .

These well-known lines from the Book of Ecclesiastes in the Bible convey two basic truths about human existence: the fact of birth and the inevitability of death. Just as life varies in striking ways across history and around the world, so does death. We conclude this chapter with a brief look at the changing character of death—the final stage in the process of growing old.

Historical Patterns of Death

Throughout most of history, humans found death a familiar part of life. Until the modern era, no one assumed that a newborn child would live for long, and parents often delayed naming children until they reached several years of age (Herty, 1960). For those fortunate enough to survive infancy, illness brought on by poor nutrition, accidents, and natural catastrophes such as drought or famine combined to make life uncertain, at best. Sometimes death was deliberate, a strategy that even today emerges in societies that lack the resources to feed their people. Typically, societies sacrifice their least productive members so that others

Q: "It is possible that medicine's triumphant reconstruction of old age has also unwittingly created a demographic, economic, and medical avalanche, one that could ultimately (and perhaps already has) do great harm . . . ." Daniel Callahan

NOTE: Daniel Callahan's analysis raises important questions: Is getting older *good* for everyone? Is it even *possible* for everyone?

Q: "Death is a subject that is evaded, ignored, and denied by our youth-worshipping, progress-oriented society. It is almost as if we have taken on death as just another disease to be conquered." Joseph L. Braga and Laurie D. Braga, in Kübler-Ross, 1975:x

Q: "Do not go gentle into that good night; Rage, rage against the dying of the light." Dylan Thomas

SOCIAL POLICY

Setting Limits: How Much Old Age Can We Afford?

In almost any period of human history, the question, "Can people live *too long*?" would have seemed absurd. In recent decades in the United States, however, a surge in the elderly population, widespread support for using technology to prolong life, and a dizzying increase in funding for medical research directed toward diseases of old age have prompted people to confront this vexing question.

The graying of our society, Daniel Callahan warns, will eventually force us to limit the resources allocated to the needs of older people. To even raise this issue, he concedes, smacks of a lack of caring. But ignoring it poses a serious threat to the well-being of everyone.

Projections place the bill for the elderly's health care at $200 billion by the end of this decade—more than twice the cost in 1980. This dramatic boost reflects our current policy of directing more

and more medical resources toward studying and treating diseases and disabilities common to old age.

Callahan's call for limits is based, first, on the contention that to spend more on behalf of the elderly we must spend less on others. The growing problem of poverty among children, he points out, is placing more young people at risk.

Second, Callahan asserts that a *longer* life does not necessarily make for a *better* life. Costs aside, does stressful heart surgery that may prolong the life of an eighty-four-year-old woman a year or two truly improve the quality of her life? Costs considered, would those resources yield more "quality of life" if used, say, to transplant a kidney into a ten-year-old boy?

Third, Callahan urges us to reconsider our notion of death. Today many people rage against death as an enemy to be conquered at all costs. Yet, he suggests,

a sensible health care program in an aging society must acknowledge death as a natural end to the life course. If we cannot make peace with death for our own well-being, limited resources demand that we do so for the benefit of others.

In short, Callahan concludes, the aging of our society should provoke critical thinking about death, life, and old age, leading to:

> an understanding of the process of aging and death that looks to our obligations to the young and to the future, that sees old age as a source of knowledge and insight of value to other age groups, that recognizes the necessity of limits and the acceptance of decline and death, and that values the old for their age and not their continuing youthful vitality. (1987:223)

SOURCE: Callahan (1987).

can live. In some cases, societies resort to *infanticide*, the killing of newborn infants; in others, they engage in *geronticide*, the killing of the elderly.

If death was commonplace, it was also readily accepted. For medieval Europeans, for example, Christianity offered the consolation that death fit into the divine plan for human existence. To illustrate, historian Philippe Ariès describes how Sir Lancelot, one of King Arthur's fearless Knights of the Round Table, prepared for his own death when he believed himself mortally wounded:

> His gestures were fixed by old customs, ritual gestures which must be carried out when one is about to die. He removed his weapons and lay quietly upon the

ground. . . . He spread his arms out, his body forming a cross . . . in such a way that his head faced east toward Jerusalem. (1974:7–8)

As societies gradually gained control over many causes of death, attitudes began to change. Death became less of an everyday experience: Fewer children died at birth, and accidents and disease took a smaller toll among adults. Except in times of war or other catastrophes, people came to view dying as quite *extra*ordinary, except among the very old. In 1900, about one-third of all deaths in the United States occurred before the age of five, another third occurred before the age of fifty-five, and the remaining one-third of men and women died in what was then defined as old age. By

1990, 85 percent of our populations died *after* the age of fifty-five. Thus death and old age have become fused in our culture.

The Modern Separation of Life and Death

Less a part of everyday experience, we now regard death as something unnatural. Religious beliefs that place both life and death in a divine scheme have been eroded by medical technology's growing capacity to conquer disease and slow the physical deterioration that accompanies aging. If social conditions prepared our ancestors to accept their deaths, modern society has fostered a desire for immortality, or eternal youth. In this sense, death has become separated from life.

This denial of death, coupled with the rapid increase in the elderly population of the United States, has forced our society to confront difficult ethical questions. Should people extend life as long as technologically possible? Since half of an individual's expenditure on health care typically occurs during the final year of life, should our nation continue to commit an increasing share of medical resources to the task of prolonging life? Daniel Callahan answers these questions, arguing that society must place limits on longevity, as the box explains.

Death is also *physically* removed from the rest of life. The clearest evidence of this is that many of us have never seen a person die. While our ancestors typically died at home in the presence of family and friends, most deaths today occur in unfamiliar and impersonal settings such as hospitals and nursing homes (Ariès, 1974). Even hospitals commonly relegate dying patients to a special part of the building, and hospital morgues are located well out of sight of patients and visitors alike (Sudnow, 1967).

No doubt, our fear and anxiety about death have propelled the rapid increase in medical research aimed at prolonging life. However, we may be on the verge of forging a new norm relating to death and dying. As the opening to this chapter suggests, many aging people are less terrified of death than they are at the prospect of being kept alive at all costs. In other words, medical technology now threatens personal autonomy so that doctors rather than dying individuals are deciding a course of action. The surprising popularity of the book *Final Exit* demonstrates that people want control over their deaths no less than they seek control over their lives.

Consequently, patients and families are now taking the initiative, choosing not to make use of available medical technology to prolong life. After long deliberation, patients, families, and doctors may make a decision to forgo any "heroic measures" to resuscitate a person who is dying. Living wills—statements of what medical procedures an individual wants and does not want under specific conditions—are now widespread.

Certainly, there are dangers in this practice. Family members may exert subtle pressure on a failing parent to refuse medical care because others wish to be spared emotional stress or a financial burden. Patients and family members will face difficult decisions that are as much moral as they are medical; to assist them, hospitals now offer the services of biomedical ethics committees, composed of physicians, social service professionals, and members of the clergy. The trend seems clear: Decline and death may be inevitable, but people can demand choices about when and where and perhaps even how they will die.

Bereavement

In Chapter 5 ("Socialization"), we described stages by which people usually confront their own death. Elizabeth Kübler-Ross (1969) claims that individuals initially react with *denial*, then swell with *anger*, try to *negotiate* a divine intervention, gradually fall into *resignation* and, finally, reach *acceptance*. Those who will grieve the loss of a significant person must also adjust to the approaching death.

According to some researchers, bereavement parallels the stages of dying described by Kübler-Ross. Those close to a dying person, for instance, may initially deny the reality of impending death, reaching the point of acceptance only with time. Other investigators question any linear "stage theory," arguing that bereavement may not follow any rigid schedule (Lund, Caserta, & Dimond, 1986; Lund, 1989). But all the experts agree that how family and friends view a death influences the attitudes of the person who is dying. That is, acceptance by others of the approaching death helps the dying person do the same. Denial of death can also isolate the dying person, who is unable to share feelings and experiences with others.

One recent development intended to provide support to dying people is the *hospice*. Unlike a hospital that is designed to cure disease, a hospice helps people have a good death. These care centers for dying people work to minimize pain and suffering—either there or at home—and encourage family members to remain close by (Stoddard, 1978).

Even under the most favorable circumstances, bereavement may involve profound grief and social

NOTE: During the 1980s, the passage of catastrophic health insurance for elderly people revealed the financial dangers posed by illness. Subsequent repeal of the legislation, demanded by affluent elderly people who opposed the taxes, showed the increasing political clout of the elderly, now a well-organized, well-heeled, political alliance.

NOTE: In 1900, there were more men over sixty-five in the United States than there were women. The rate has changed from 100:98 in 1900 to 100:150 in 1990. Death rates (especially in childbirth) account for the change.

NOTE: Projections indicate that in the year 2000, the elderly will comprise 20% of the population of North America but 28% of drivers on North American roadways.

disorientation that persist for some time. Research shows us that bereavement is less intense among people who accept the death of a loved one and feel their relationship with the dying person has reached a satisfactory resolution. By taking the opportunity to bring an appropriate closure to their relationship with a dying person, in other words, family and friends are better able to comfort and support one another after the death has occurred (Atchley, 1983).

This chapter has explored the "graying" of the United States. As the ranks of the elderly swell, they will become a more visible and vocal part of everyday life. Gerontology, the study of the elderly, will also gain in stature paralleling an expansion of medical care directed toward old people. As part of this transformation, we can also expect changes in the way we view death, which will likely become less of a social taboo and more a natural part of the life course as it was in centuries past. Both young and old alike may benefit.

SUMMARY

1. From 4 percent of the population in 1900 and over 12 percent today, the elderly will represent 20 percent of the U.S. population by the middle of the next century.

2. Gerontology, the study of aging and the elderly, focuses on biological and psychological changes in old age, as well as cultural definitions of aging.

3. Growing old is accompanied by a rising incidence of disease and disability. Younger people, however, commonly exaggerate the extent of disability among the elderly.

4. Psychological research confirms that growing old results in neither overall loss of intelligence nor great change to individual personality.

5. The age at which people are defined as old has varied historically: Until several centuries ago, old age began as early as thirty. In poor societies today, in which life expectancy is substantially lower than in North America, people become old at fifty or even forty.

6. In global perspective, industrialization fosters a decline in the social standing of elderly people.

7. As people age, they commonly experience social isolation brought on by retirement, physical disability, and the death of friends or spouse. Even so, most elderly people find family members provide considerable social support.

8. Since 1960, poverty among the elderly has dropped sharply. The aged poor are categories of people—including single women and people of color—who are likely to be poor regardless of age.

9. Disengagement theory—based on structural-functional analysis—suggests that the elderly disengage from positions of social responsibility before the onset of disability or death. In this way, a society accomplishes the orderly transfer of statuses and roles from the older to the younger generation.

10. Activity theory, based on symbolic-interaction analysis—claims that a high level of activity affords people personal satisfaction in old age.

11. Age stratification is a focus of social-conflict analysis. The emphasis on economic output in capitalist societies leads to a devaluing of those who are less productive, including the elderly.

12. Ageism—prejudice and discrimination against old people—serves to justify age stratification.

13. Although many old people are socially disadvantaged, the elderly encompass people of both sexes and all races, ethnicities, and social classes. Thus older people do not qualify as a minority.

14. Modern society has set death apart from everyday life, prompting a cultural denial of human mortality. In part, this attitude is related to the fact that most people now die after reaching old age. Recent trends suggest that people are confronting death more directly and seeking control over the process of dying.

NOTE: We often assume that great figures of history were men and women of at least what we would call "middle age," but this is often not so. Joan of Arc, for example, was only 19 at the time of her martyrdom in 1431.

NOTE: Signs of the aging of U.S. society: Ringo Starr has an eight-year-old grandchild; Mickey Mouse is 66; Superman and Bugs Bunny are both past 55; Barbie is now thirty-something.

NOTE: Attitudes toward death are partly a matter of whether or not one believes in life after death. General Social Survey data indicates that 70% of U.S. adults claim they do.

Q: "I'm not afraid to die; I just don't want to be there when it happens." Woody Allen

Q: "Let us endeavor to live so that when we come to die even the undertaker will be sorry." Mark Twain

KEY CONCEPTS

activity theory the proposition that a high level of activity enhances personal satisfaction in old age

ageism prejudice and discrimination against the elderly

age stratification the unequal distribution of wealth, power, and privileges among people at different stages in the life course

disengagement theory the proposition that society enhances its orderly operation by disengaging people, as they reach old age, from positions of responsibility

gerontocracy a form of social organization in which the elderly have the most wealth, power, and privileges

gerontology the study of aging and the elderly

CRITICAL-THINKING QUESTIONS

1. What facts proclaim "the graying of the United States"? What are some of the likely consequences of this process?

2. Cite several findings by gerontologists that challenge common-sense ideas about growing old.

3. Why does industrialization erode the social standing of the elderly?

4. What important insight about growing old is offered by each of sociology's three major theoretical paradigms?

SUGGESTED READINGS

Classic Source

Robert N. Butler. *Why Survive? Being Old in America.* New York: Harper and Row, 1975.

This Pulitzer Prize–winning book launched a growing social movement critical of this country's approach to aging.

Contemporary Sources

Harold Cox. *Later Life: The Realities of Aging.* 3d ed. Englewood Cliffs, N.J.: Prentice Hall, 1993.

This text provides a detailed account of issues related to aging and the elderly.

James S. Jackson, Linda M. Chatters, and Robert Joseph Taylor. *Aging in Black America.* Newbury Park, Calif.: Sage, 1992.

This book is a broad survey of African-American elderly focusing on work, health, religion, and family life.

Timothy Diamond. *Making Gray Gold: Narratives of Nursing Home Care.* Chicago: University of Chicago Press, 1992.

Personal accounts by men and women form the basis of this description of living or working in nursing homes for the elderly.

Sara Arber and Jay Ginn. *Gender and Later Life.* Newbury Park, Calif.: Sage, 1992.

Through the lens of gender, this book explores poverty in later life, ageism, and abuse of the elderly.

P. L. Pearl Van Zandt. *The Invisible Woman: Women over Age 85 in Today's Society.* Hamden, Conn.: Garland, 1991.

Few researchers have targeted people over eighty-five, 80 percent of whom are women.

Herbert C. Covey. *Images of Older People in Western Art and Society.* Westport, Conn.: Greenwood, 1991.

This fascinating and richly illustrated analysis of aging highlights the treatment of the elderly in Western societies over the last one thousand years.

Andrew Cherlin and Frank Furstenburg, Jr. *The New American Grandparent: A Place in the Family; A Life Apart.* New York: Basic Books, 1986.

This book highlights how a common tension—between family ties and independence—affects today's seniors.

Michael C. Kearl. *Endings: A Sociology of Death and Dying.* New York: Oxford University Press, 1989.

This book examines all facets of death and dying, from the common death of pets to the uncommon death of children. There is also analysis of the health care profession, including the emerging hospice movement.

Global Source

Donald O. Cowgill. *Aging Around the World.* Belmont, Calif.: Wadsworth, 1986.

This global survey of the process of aging explains that many societies recognize in the elderly far more wisdom than ours does.

David Alfaro Siqueiros, Detail of workers from the *Sindicato de Electricitas*

DATA FILE: An outline of this chapter, supplementary mini-lectures, and suggested topics for discussion are found in the *Data File*.
Q: "The business of the United States is business." President Warren G. Harding
Q: "Banks are more dangerous than standing armies." Thomas Jefferson

SOCIAL SURVEY: "How much confidence do you have in the people running banks and financial institutions?" (GSS 1993, N = 1,057; *Codebook*, 1993:205)
  "A great deal"   15.0%   "Hardly any"   26.0%
  "Only some"   56.6%   DK/NR   2.5%
Q: "Economics is the study of money and why it is good." Woody Allen

The Economy and Work

"*A* merica First!" proclaimed the mayor of Greece, New York, an upstate community outside of Rochester. "We must do something to help the economy here at home," concluded the Greece town council. Amid bad economic news—a continuing recession, rising unemployment, and a deepening federal deficit—the town council voted to cancel their purchase of a $40,000 piece of excavating equipment from Japan's Komatsu corporation in favor of giving the business to U.S. manufacturer John Deere, despite the U.S. product's considerably higher price tag.

The action prompted applause from many corners of the land, reflecting the rising national anxiety that our country is slipping from its traditional place as the world's economic superpower. But the council's symbolic protest only ended up revealing how complicated

today's global economy really is. The Komatsu model, it turns out, is actually built in the United States, while the John Deere is powered by an engine manufactured—you guessed it—in Japan.

This chapter examines the economy, widely considered to be the most influential of all social institutions. (The other major social institutions are examined in subsequent chapters: Chapter 16, "Politics and Government"; Chapter 17, "Family"; Chapter 18, "Religion"; Chapter 19, "Education"; and Chapter 20, "Health and Medicine.") We explore the character of work in today's world, and explain some of the consequences of the emerging global marketplace for people in the United States. We will see—as did the Greece town council—that a good deal of the conventional wisdom about economic life no longer applies in the face of sweeping changes in the United States and around the world.

407

NOTE: The effects of technological advance are detailed in Chapter 4's opening section, which discusses "Society and Technology." Marvin Harris estimates the rising productive capacity linked to agrarian and industrial technology in terms of the ratio of calories expended to calories produced: hunting and gathering, 1:3; horticultural and pastoral, 1:5; agrarian, 1:50; industrial, 1:5,000.

Q: "[The preindustrial economy] was limited to what could be organized within a family, and within the lifetime of its head." Peter Laslett (1984)

NOTE: As Chapter 4 ("Society") explains, the Industrial Revolution was not merely a technological upheaval. For Marx, it was a capitalist revolution; for Weber, it marked the triumph of rationality; for Durkheim, it constituted a process of expanding specialization.

THE ECONOMY: HISTORICAL OVERVIEW

The **economy** is *the social institution that organizes the production, distribution, and consumption of goods and services.* To say that the economy is institutionalized implies that it operates in an established manner that is predictable, at least in its general outlines. *Goods* are commodities ranging from necessities (such as food, clothing, and shelter) to luxury items (such as automobiles, swimming pools, and yachts). *Services* refer to valued activities that benefit others (including the work of religious leaders, physicians, police officers, and telephone operators).

We value goods and services because they ensure survival or because they make life easier, more interesting, or more aesthetically pleasing. The things we produce and consume are also important to the formation of our self-concept and social identity. How goods and services are distributed, then, shapes the lives of everyone in basic ways.

The complex economies that mark modern industrial societies are themselves the product of centuries of technological innovation and social change. The following sections highlight three technological revolutions that reorganized the means of production and, in the process, brought changes to many other dimensions of social life.

The Agricultural Revolution

As Chapter 4 ("Society") explained, members of the earliest human societies relied on hunting and gathering to live off the land. In these technologically simple societies, there was no distinct economy; rather, production, distribution, and consumption of goods all were dimensions of family life.

The development of agriculture about five thousand years ago brought revolutionary change to these societies. Agriculture emerged as people harnessed animal power to plows, increasing the productive power of hunting and gathering more than tenfold. The resulting surplus meant that not everyone had to be engaged in food production. Some people began to adopt specialized economic roles, forging crafts, designing tools, raising animals, and constructing dwellings.

With the development of agriculture underway, towns emerged, soon to be linked by networks of traders dealing in food, animals, and other goods (Jacobs, 1970). These four factors—agricultural technology, productive specialization, permanent settlements, and trade—were the keys to a revolutionary expansion of the economy.

In agrarian societies, the world of work is characteristically distinct from family life, although production still occurs close to home. In medieval Europe, for instance, most people farmed nearby fields. Both country and city dwellers often labored in their homes—a pattern called *cottage industry*—producing goods sold in frequent outdoor "flea markets" (a term suggesting that not everything was of high quality).

The Industrial Revolution

By the mid-eighteenth century in England, a second technological revolution was in progress. This time, the development of industry was to transform social life even more than agriculture had done thousands of years before. Industrialization introduced five notable changes to the economies of Western societies.

1. **New forms of energy.** Throughout history, people had generated energy with their own muscles or by using those of animals. At the dawn of industrialization in 1765, the English inventor James Watt pioneered the application of steam power to machinery. Surpassing muscle power a hundred times over, steam engines soon made production far more efficient than ever before.

2. **The spread of factories.** Steam-powered machinery soon rendered cottage industries obsolete. Factories—centralized workplaces apart from the home—proliferated. Although a more productive system, factory work lacked the personal ties that had characterized family-based cottage industries.

3. **Manufacturing and mass production.** Before the Industrial Revolution, most work involved cultivating and gathering raw materials, such as crops, wood, and wool. The industrial economy shifted that focus to manufacturing raw materials into a wide range of salable products. For example, factories mass-produced lumber into furniture and transformed wool into clothing.

4. **Specialization.** Typically, a single skilled worker in a cottage industry fashioned a product from beginning to end. Factory work, by contrast, demands specialization so that a laborer repeats a single task over and over, making only a small contribution to the finished product. Thus as factories raised productivity, they also lowered the skill level of the average worker (Warner & Low, 1947).

5. **Wage labor.** Instead of laboring for themselves or joining together as households, industrial workers

NOTE: The term "spinster," referring to an older, unmarried woman, is derived from those women who spent much of their lives spinning in the early textile mills.

Q: "Women have always worked in factories. Indeed it was women's labor that was initially responsible for the very beginnings of the Industrial Revolution." Ellen Israel Rosen (1987:18)

NOTE: The steam engine was invented in England by Edward Somerset in 1628; the device was not applied to textile machinery for almost 150 years.

NOTE: Because of the low wages and strict control endured by women in early factories, people sometimes called wagons traveling across New England in search of workers "slavers," a comparison to the slave ships also well known to people of that time.

SOCIAL DIVERSITY

Women in the Mills of Lowell, Massachusetts

Few people paid much attention to the return from England of Francis Cabot Lowell, ancestor of two prominent Boston families, the Cabots and the Lowells, in 1822. But Lowell carried with him documents that would help change the course of the U.S. economy: plans, based on mills operating in England, for this country's first textile factory.

From the outset, 75 percent of Lowell mill workers were women. The factory owners preferred women because, earning $2 to $3 a week, these workers received half the wages men did. Many immigrant men were also willing to work for low wages, but prejudice was strong enough to disqualify "foreigners" from any job at all.

Recruiters, driving wagons from one small town to another throughout New England, urged parents to send their daughters to the mill where, they promised, the young women would learn skills and discipline. The offer appealed to many families who could barely provide for their children. Then, too, few occupations were open to women at that time, and those that were—including teaching and household service—paid even less than factory work.

Once at the Lowell factory, young women settled into dormitory-type housing, paying one-third of their wages for room and board. Employees were subject to a curfew and, as a condition of employment, regularly attended church. Any morally questionable conduct (such as bringing men to their rooms) brought firm disciplinary action.

The motives of the factory owners were not strictly moral, however; they also knew that closely supervised women were unable to organize among themselves. Working almost thirteen hours a day, six days a week, the Lowell employees had good reason to seek improvements in their working conditions. Yet any public criticism of the factory, or even possessing "radical" literature, could cost a worker her job.

SOURCE: Based on Eisler (1977).

became wage laborers. They sold their labor to strangers who often cared less for them than for the machines they operated. Supervision became routine and intense.

The impact of the Industrial Revolution gradually rippled outward from the factories to transform all of society. Greater productivity steadily raised the standard of living as countless new products and services filled an expanding marketplace. Especially at the outset, however, the benefits of industrial technology were shared very unequally. Some factory owners made vast fortunes, while the majority of industrial workers hovered perilously close to poverty. Children, too, worked in factories or deep in coal mines for pennies a day. Women factory workers, among the lowest paid, endured special problems, as the box explains.

The Postindustrial Society and the Information Revolution

Industrialization is by nature an ongoing process. In Europe and North America, workers gradually formed labor unions to represent their collective interests in negotiations with factory owners. During this century, governments outlawed child labor, forced wages upward, improved workplace safety, and extended schooling and political rights to a larger segment of the population.

By the middle of this century, the United States was becoming a **postindustrial economy**, *a productive*

NOTE: *GDP* is the value of goods and services produced within the borders of a country, regardless of who owns or operates them. *GNP* is the value of goods and services produced by all the facilities owned by people of a country, regardless of whether they are domestic or abroad. Therefore, GNP is derived by subtracting from GDP the profits of foreign-owned business in the country and adding to GDP the profits of businesses abroad owned by people of that country. Statisticians now use GDP because it allows more accurate national comparisons as the economy becomes more global.

DIVERSITY: The decline of farming is evident in the falling number of farms owned by African Americans: 926,000 in 1920 compared to 23,000 in 1990.

Window on the World

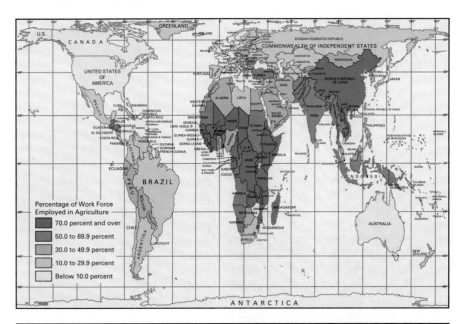

GLOBAL MAP 15–1
Agricultural Employment in Global Perspective

The primary sector of the economy predominates in societies that are least developed. Thus, in the poor countries of Africa and Asia, half, or even three-fourths, of all workers are farmers. This picture is altogether different among the world's most economically developed countries—including the United States, Canada, Great Britain, and Australia—which have less than 10 percent of their work force in agriculture.

From *Peters Atlas of the World* (1990).

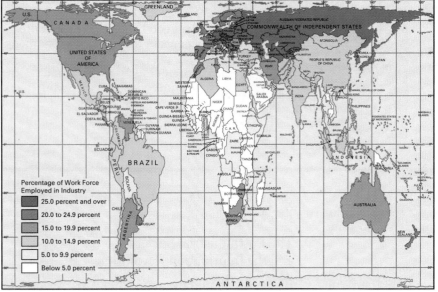

GLOBAL MAP 15–2
Industrial Employment in Global Perspective

The world's poor societies, by and large, have yet to industrialize. For this reason, in the countries of Latin America, Africa, and Asia, a small proportion of the labor force engages in industrial work. The nations of Eastern Europe, along with the Commonwealth of Independent States, have far more of their workers in industry. In the world's richest societies, we see a reversal of this trend, with more and more workers moving from industrial jobs to service work. Thus, the postindustrial economy of the United States now has about the same share of workers in industrial jobs as the much poorer nation of Argentina.

From *Peters Atlas of the World* (1990).

system based on service work and high technology. Automated machinery reduced the role of human labor in production, while bureaucracy simultaneously expanded the ranks of clerical workers and managers. Robert Heilbroner (1985) points out that, a century ago, managers accounted for only 7 percent of workers; now they represent one-third of all employees. Moreover, service industries—such as public relations, advertising, banking, and sales—employ the bulk of our country's present labor force. Distinguishing the postindustrial era, then, is a shift from industrial work to service jobs.

Q: "Among the purposes of a society should be to try to arrange for a continuous supply of work at all times and seasons." Pope Leo XIII

Q: "A fundamental characteristic of the world we have lost was the scene of labor, which was universally supposed to be the home." Peter Laslett (1984)

GLOBAL: About half of all consumer purchases in the United States are of products made outside of the United States.

GLOBAL: One indicator of relative economic productivity of capitalist and socialist economic systems is the rate (per 1,000 people) of passenger car ownership (world average, 78). Capitalist societies: U.S., 537; Australia, 500; West Germany (FRG), 438; Canada, 427; U.K., 292; Socialist societies: East Germany (GDR), 199; Czechoslovakia, 171; Bulgaria, 115; Poland, 98; Soviet Union, 40. Data for late 1980s. (The World in Figures, 1988)

Since 1950, a third technological transformation has been unleashed by the development of the computer. The *Information Revolution* in the United States and elsewhere is generating new kinds of information and new forms of communication, just as two centuries ago factories produced new tangible commodities. And, just as the Industrial Revolution did, the Information Revolution is now creating a host of new, specialized occupations. From a worker's point of view, in the same way that the acquisition of *technical* skills was in the past the key to success, today it is the enhancement of *literacy* skills that is valued in the marketplace. The economic reality is that people unable to speak, write, or otherwise communicate effectively face declining economic opportunity. To those able to rise to the challenge of the Information Age, however, the coming decades will bring new opportunities.

The Information Revolution is changing not just what people do but where they do it. The last economic revolution centralized the work force in factories, a pattern demanded by energy sources and the enormity of the new machinery. Today, however, consultants, salespeople, architects, writers, and other employees in "new cottage industries" can work virtually anywhere so long as they are equipped with computers, facsimile (fax) machines, electronic notebooks, and other new information devices that are increasingly lightweight and portable. Today's more educated and skilled workers also no longer require—and often do not tolerate—the close supervision that marked yesterday's factories.

Sectors of the Economy

The three revolutions just described reflect a shifting balance among the three sectors of a society's economy. The **primary sector** is *the part of the economy that generates raw materials directly from the natural environment*. The primary sector, which includes agriculture, animal husbandry, fishing, forestry, and mining, predominates in preindustrial societies. Global Map 15–1, on page 410, illustrates that the economies of developing nations of the world such as India and the People's Republic of China are still dominated by the primary sector.

The **secondary sector** is *the part of the economy that transforms raw materials into manufactured goods*. This sector grows quickly as societies industrialize, just as manufacturing grew rapidly in the United States during the first half of this century. Secondary sector production includes the refining of petroleum and the use of metals to manufacture tools and automobiles.

As Global Map 15–2 shows, societies that are still industrializing—such as the former Soviet Union and Greece—have a secondary economic sector that is roughly the same size as their primary sector. More broadly, the second global map is essentially a negative image of the first. The most-developed countries show large industrial employment (although this tends to decline as service work expands), with few workers remaining in primary sector jobs. In the world's least-developed countries, by contrast, most workers still engage in farming, while relatively few work in industrial positions.

The **tertiary sector** is *the part of the economy involved in services rather than goods*. Accounting for only a tiny share of work in preindustrial societies, the tertiary sector grows with industrialization, becoming dominant in the later, postindustrial era. Today, in the United States, 70 percent of the labor force is involved in some form of service work, including secretarial and clerical work and positions in food service, sales, law, advertising, and teaching.

The Global Economy

As technology draws people around the world closer together, another important economic transformation is under way. Recent decades have witnessed the emergence of a **global economy**, *interconnected economic activity throughout the world that pays little regard to national borders*.

The development of a global economy has three main consequences. First, an increasing number of products pass through the economies of more than one nation. For instance, workers in Taiwan may manufacture pairs of shoes, which a distributer in Hong Kong sends to Italy, where the shoes receive the stamp of an Italian designer; another distributer in Rome then forwards the shoes to New York, where they are sold in a department store owned by a firm having its headquarters in Tokyo.

A second consequence of the global economy is that national governments no longer can control the economic activity that takes place within their borders. In fact, governments cannot even control the value of their national currencies, since currencies are now traded around the clock in the financial centers of Tokyo, London, and New York. Global markets are one consequence of satellite communications that forge information links among the various cities of the world.

The third consequence of the global economy is that a small number of businesses, operating internationally, now control a vast share of the world's economic activity. One estimate concludes that the six

NOTE: The *Oxford English Dictionary* explains that the word "capitalism" entered the English language in the late 18th century. Peter Berger claims that Adam Smith never used the term. The etymology of the word reveals a Latin root, *caput*, meaning "of the head."

Q: "It is not from the benevolence of the butcher, the brewer, or the baker that we expect our dinner, but from their regard to their own interest." Adam Smith

Q: "The market delivers rough justice; the welfare state takes the roughness out of justice." Columnist George Will

NOTE: For Adam Smith, architect of capitalism, there is no explicit category of the social; social good springs from individual interests. By contrast, for Karl Marx, architect of socialism, there is no explicit category of the individual; individual satisfaction springs from collective activity.

hundred largest multinational companies account for fully half of the earth's entire total economic output (Kidron & Segal, 1991).

The world is still divided into roughly 190 politically distinct nations. But, in light of the proliferation of international economic activity, "nationhood" has lost much of its former significance.

COMPARATIVE ECONOMIC SYSTEMS

Analysts describe the economies of world societies in terms of two models—capitalism and socialism. No society has an economy that is either purely capitalist or purely socialist; these models represent two ends of a spectrum along which all actual economies can be located.

Capitalism

Capitalism refers to *an economic system in which natural resources and the means of producing goods and services are privately owned.* Ideally, a capitalist economy has three distinctive features.

1. **Private ownership of property.** A capitalist economy supports the right of individuals to own almost anything. The more capitalist an economy is, the more private ownership there is of wealth-producing property such as factories, real estate, and natural resources.

2. **Pursuit of personal profit.** A capitalist society encourages the accumulation of private property and defines a profit-minded orientation as natural and simply a matter of "doing business." Further, claimed the Scottish economist Adam Smith (1723–1790), the drive of individuals pursuing their own self-interest helps an entire society prosper (1937:508; orig. 1776).

3. **Free competition and consumer sovereignty.** A purely capitalist economy would operate with no government interference, sometimes called a *laissez-faire* (a French expression meaning "to leave alone") approach. Adam Smith contended that a freely competitive economy regulates itself by the "invisible hand" of the laws of supply and demand.

   The market system is dominated by consumers, Smith maintained, who select goods and services that provide the greatest value. Producers compete with one another by providing the highest-quality goods and services at the lowest possible price. Thus, while entrepreneurs are motivated by personal gain, everyone benefits from more efficient production and ever-increasing value. In Smith's time-honored phrase, from narrow self-interest comes the "greatest good for the greatest number of people." Government control of an economy would inevitably upset the complex market system, reducing producer motivation, diminishing the quantity and quality of goods produced, and shortchanging consumers.

The United States is the leading capitalist society, yet even here the guiding hand of government plays an extensive role in economic affairs. Through various regulatory agencies, government policies affect what companies produce, the quality and costs of merchandise, what businesses import and export, and how we consume or conserve natural resources.

The federal government also owns and operates a host of businesses, including the U.S. Postal Service, the Amtrak railroad system, the Tennessee Valley Authority (a large electrical utility company), and the Nuclear Regulatory Commission (which conducts atomic research and produces nuclear materials). The entire U.S. military is also government operated. Federal officials may step in to prevent the collapse of businesses, as in the recent "bailout" of the savings and loan industry. Further, government policies mandate minimum wage levels, enforce workplace safety standards, regulate corporate mergers, provide farm price supports, and funnel income in the form of Social Security, public assistance, student loans, and veterans' benefits to a majority of the people in the United States. Not surprisingly, local, state, and federal governments together represent this country's biggest employer, with 15 percent of the labor force on their payrolls (U.S. Department of Labor, 1992).

Socialism

Socialism is *an economic system in which natural resources and the means of producing goods and services are collectively owned.* In its ideal form, a socialist economy opposes each of the three characteristics of capitalism just described.

1. **Collective ownership of property.** An economy is socialist to the extent that it limits the right to private property, especially property used in producing goods and services. Laws prohibiting private ownership of property are designed to make housing and other goods available to all, not just to those with the most money.

Q: "Socialism, in addition to being a set of political programs and the source of social-scientific interpretations, is also one of the most powerful myths of the contemporary era; to the extent that socialism retains this mythic quality, it cannot be disconfirmed by empirical evidence in the minds of its adherents." Peter Berger (1986:204)

Q: "The function of socialism is to raise suffering to a higher level." Norman Mailer

SOCIAL SURVEY: "How do you feel about communism as a form of government?" (GSS 1991, N = 1,057; Codebook, 1993:144)

"It's the worst kind of all"	45.2%
"It's bad, but no worse than some others"	35.2%
"It's all right for some countries"	15.0%
"It's a good form of government"	1.2%
DK/NR	3.4%

The productivity of capitalist Hong Kong is evident in the fact that streets are choked with advertising and shoppers. Socialist Beijing, by contrast, is dominated by government buildings rather than a central business district. Here bicyclists glide past the Great Hall of the People.

Karl Marx asserted that private ownership of productive property spawns social classes as it generates an economic elite. Socialism, then, seeks to lessen economic inequality along with the goal of forging a classless society.

2. **Pursuit of collective goals.** The individualistic pursuit of profit also stands at odds with the collective orientation of socialism. Socialist values and norms condemn what capitalists celebrate as the entrepreneurial spirit. For this reason, private trading is branded as illegal "black market" activity.

3. **Government control of the economy.** Socialism rejects the idea that a free-market economy regulates itself. Instead of a laissez-faire approach, socialist governments oversee a *centrally controlled* or *command economy*.

Socialism also rejects the idea that it is consumers who guide capitalist production. From this point of view, consumers lack the information necessary to evaluate products and are manipulated by advertising to buy what is profitable for factory owners rather than what they, as consumers, genuinely need. Commercial advertising thus plays little role in socialist economies.

The People's Republic of China and a number of societies in Asia, Africa, and Latin America—some two dozen in all—model their economies on socialism, placing almost all wealth-generating property under state control (McColm et al., 1991). The extent of world socialism has declined in recent years, however, as societies in Eastern Europe and the former Soviet Union have been dramatically transformed. As change continues, these countries will eventually forge new economic systems from some combination of market forces and government regulation.

Socialism and Communism

Most people equate the terms *socialism* and *communism*. More precisely, as the ideal spirit of socialism, **communism** is *a hypothetical economic and political system in which all members of a society are socially equal.* Karl Marx viewed socialism as a transitory stage on the path toward the ideal of a communist society that had abolished all class divisions. In many socialist societies today, the dominant political party describes itself as communist, but nowhere has the communist goal been achieved.

Why? For one thing, social stratification involves differences of power as well as wealth. Socialist societies have generally succeeded in reducing disparities in wealth only through expanding government bureaucracies and subjecting the population to extensive regulation by political officials. In the process, government has not "withered away" as Karl Marx imagined. On the contrary, during this century political elites have gained enormous power and privilege in socialist societies.

Marx would have been the first to agree that such a society is a *utopia* (from Greek words meaning "not a place"). Yet Marx considered communism a

GLOBAL: The South Korean system of state capitalism has concentrated more than half of all GNP in just four major corporations, including Hyundai.

NOTE: Critics of socialism's lower productivity point to Marx's separation of reward from effort (implied in "from each according to ability; to each according to need") as a significant, practical flaw.

SOCIAL SURVEY: International data regarding whether or not the government should reduce income disparity. (*CHIP1 Social Survey Software*, REDISTR; ISSP 1985, N = 3,795)

	"Yes"	"No"
Australia	52.6%	47.4%
United Kingdom	71.5%	28.5%
Austria	77.4%	22.6%

Not all linkages between government and the private sector of the economy are constructive; some are even illegal. In recent years, Italy has been rocked by charges that high government officials have corrupt deals with business leaders. In this protest march, supporters of Umberto Bossi, a political leader in northern Italy who is contemptuous of the government in Rome, carry aloft a huge figure of their leader holding a saw symbolizing his desire to gain political independence for his region of the country.

worthy goal and probably would have disparaged reputedly "Marxist" societies such as North Korea, the former Soviet Union, the People's Republic of China, and Cuba for falling far short of his communist ideal.

Democratic Socialism and State Capitalism

A limited measure of socialism, however, does not necessarily stifle democracy. In fact, some of the nations of Western Europe—including Sweden and Italy—have merged socialist economic policies with a democratic political system. Analysts call this "third way" **democratic socialism,** *an economic and political system that combines significant government control of the economy with free elections.*

Under democratic socialism, the government owns some of the largest industries and services, such as transportation, the mass media, and health care. In Sweden and Italy, about 12 percent of economic production is state controlled or "nationalized." That leaves most industry in private hands, although subject to extensive government regulation. High taxation (aimed especially at the rich) funds various social welfare programs, transferring wealth to less-advantaged members of society.

Yet another blend of capitalism and socialism is **state capitalism,** *an economic and political system in*

which companies are privately owned although they cooperate closely with the government. Systems of state capitalism are common in the rapidly developing Asian countries along the Pacific Rim. Japan, South Korea, and Singapore, for example, are all capitalist nations, but their governments work closely with large companies, supplying financial assistance or controlling imports of foreign products to help businesses function as competitively as possible in world markets. Countries in East Asia and Western Europe illustrate that there are many ways in which governments and companies can work cooperatively.

Relative Advantages of Capitalism and Socialism

In practice, how do economic systems differ? Assessing economic models is difficult because nowhere do they exist in their pure states. Societies mix capitalism and socialism to varying degrees, and each has distinctive cultural attitudes toward work, different natural resources, unequal levels of technological development, and disparate patterns of trade, and some suffer the burdens of war more than others (Gregory & Stuart, 1985).

Despite such complicating factors, some crude comparisons are revealing. The following sections make comparisons between two categories of countries—those with predominantly capitalist economies and those with heavily socialist economies. The supporting data reflect economic patterns prior to recent changes in the former Soviet Union and Eastern Europe.

Economic Productivity

Perhaps the most important dimension of economic performance is productivity. A commonly used measure of economic output is gross domestic product (GDP), the total value of all goods and services produced annually by a nation's economy. "Per capita" (or per person) GDP allows us to compare societies of different population size.

While the economic output of predominantly capitalist countries at the end of the last decade varied somewhat, an average of the figures for the United States, Canada, and the nations of Western Europe yields a per capita GDP of about $13,500. The comparable average based on the output of the former Soviet Union and the nations of Eastern Europe was about $5,000. This means that the capitalist countries outproduced the socialist nations by a ratio of 2.7 to 1 (United Nations Development Programme, 1990).

SOCIAL SURVEY: Should the government in Washington reduce income differences between the rich and the poor? (1–7 Likert scale; GSS 1993, N = 1,057; *Codebook*, 1993:130)

(1) "Gov't should"	17.4%	(5)	12.3%
(2)	11.5%	(6)	7.7%
(3)	19.0%	(7) "Gov't should not"	12.3%
(4)	17.7%	DK/NR	2.1%

SOCIAL SURVEY: Same question, responses by SES (*STUDENT CHIP Social Survey Software*, EQWLTH; GSS 1978–91, N = 10,464)

SES	1, 2	3, 4, 5	6, 7
High	33.6%	19.0%	47.5%
Middle	48.8%	20.4%	30.8%
Low	60.8%	19.9%	19.3%

Economic Equality

How resources are distributed within the population is also important when comparing capitalist and socialist economies. A comparative study completed in the mid-1970s calculated income ratios by comparing the incomes of the richest 5 percent of the population and the poorest 5 percent (Wiles, 1977). This research found that societies with predominantly capitalist economies had an income ratio of about 10 to 1; the corresponding figure for socialist countries was 5 to 1.

This comparison of economic performance supports the conclusion that *capitalist economies support a higher overall standard of living but also generate greater income disparity.* Or, put otherwise, *socialist economies create less income disparity but offer a lower overall standard of living.*

Civil Liberties

As Chapter 16 ("Politics and Government") explains, a society's economic and political systems are closely linked. Capitalism depends on the freedom of producers and consumers to interact without extensive interference from the state. Thus economic capitalism fosters broad civil liberties and political freedom.

For their part, socialist governments strive to maximize economic equality. This goal requires considerable state intervention in the economy, limiting the personal liberty of citizens. Humanity has yet to devise a social system that will ensure political liberty while engendering economic equality. The implications of this tension are nowhere more evident than in many socialist societies that are now striving to forge a new balance between these two objectives.

Changes in Socialist Countries

During the last decade, a profound transformation has taken place in many socialist countries of the world. Beginning in the shipyards of Poland's port city of Gdansk in 1980, workers began organizing in opposition to their socialist government. Despite struggle and setback, the Solidarity movement eventually succeeded in dislodging the Soviet-backed party officials, electing its leader Lech Walesa as national president. Poland is now in the process of introducing market principles into the economy.

Other countries of Eastern Europe, all of which fell under the political control of the former Soviet Union at the end of World War II, also shook off socialist regimes during 1989 and 1990. These nations—including the German Democratic Republic, Czechoslovakia, Hungary, Romania, and Bulgaria—have

likewise introduced capitalist elements into what had for decades been centrally controlled economies. In 1992, the Soviet Union itself formally dissolved, a process that, along the way, liberated the Baltic states of Estonia, Latvia, and Lithuania and cast most of the remaining republics, except Georgia and Azerbaijan, into a new Commonwealth of Independent States.

The reasons for these sweeping changes are many and complex. In light of the preceding discussion, however, two factors stand out. First, these predominantly socialist economies grossly underproduced their capitalist counterparts. They were, as we have noted, successful in achieving remarkable economic equality; living standards for everyone, however, were low compared to those of Western European countries. Second, the brand of socialism that was imprinted on Eastern Europe by the former Soviet Union encouraged heavy-handed and unresponsive government that rigidly controlled the media as well as the ability of individuals to move about, even in their own countries.

In short, the socialist revolutions in these countries *did* do away with economic elites, as Karl Marx predicted. But, as Max Weber might have foreseen, they *expanded* the clout of political elites as party bureaucracies grew to gargantuan proportions.

At this stage, the market reforms are proceeding unevenly, with some nations faring better than others. Between 1990 and 1992, however, the closing of many inefficient, government-run industries plunged the already struggling economies of Eastern Europe into deeper decline. Within these countries, while some people (including those who have captured lucrative trading agreements with other nations) are thriving, most people are enduring harder times than ever. Although some analysts trumpet their contention that these economies have turned the corner and are now growing, many people remain uncertain about what lies ahead. In the long term, officials contend, the introduction of market forces should raise everyone's standard of living through greater productivity. Even so, to the extent that these countries gradually come to resemble their neighbors farther to the West, rising prosperity will be accompanied by increasing economic disparity.

WORK IN THE POSTINDUSTRIAL ECONOMY

Change is not restricted to the socialist world; the last century has also transformed the economy of the United States. As of 1993, 128 million people were in the labor force, representing two-thirds of those aged

NOTE: Chapter 13 ("Sex and Gender") presents additional analysis of the work of women and men. Note, too, that the government does not count housework as economic activity.

NOTE: Fueling the deindustrialization of the United States are the relatively low wage rates typical of poor societies: from about $1.25 per hour in Hong Kong to $.20 per hour in the People's Republic of China (see Figure 15–3, p. 426).

DIVERSITY: The percentage of workers who are actively seeking to change jobs is highest among teens (30%) and falls quickly with age to about 8% of men and women aged 35 to 44 and bottoms out at about 2% among workers over age 65. By age 30, says the Bureau of Labor Statistics, the average U.S. worker has held eight jobs.

TABLE 15–1 Participation in the Labor Force by Sex and Race, 1993

Category of the Population	In the Labor Force	
	Number (in millions)	Percentage
Men (aged 16 and over)	69.6	75.2%
White	60.2	76.1
Black	6.9	68.6
Women (aged 16 and over)	58.4	57.9
White	49.2	58.0
Black	7.0	57.4

SOURCE: U.S. Department of Labor, *Employment and Earnings*, vol. 41, no. 1 (January 1994), pp. 184–86.

sixteen and over. As shown in Table 15–1, a larger proportion of men (75.2 percent) than women (57.9 percent) hold income-producing jobs, although the gap between them has steadily diminished in recent decades. Among men, the proportion of people of African descent in the labor force (68.6 percent) is somewhat less than the proportion of white people (76.1 percent); among women, about the same share of African Americans (57.4 percent) and white people (58.0 percent) are employed.

Age also affects labor force participation. Typically, both women and men join the work force in their teens and early twenties. During their childbearing years, however, women's participation lags behind that of men. After about the age of forty-five, the working profiles of the two sexes again become similar, with a marked withdrawal from the labor force as people approach age sixty-five. After that point in life, only a small proportion of each sex continues steady, income-producing work.

National Map 15–1 shows labor force participation by county for the United States. Since work and income go hand in hand, regions of the country with above average labor force participation tend to be more affluent.

The Decline of Agricultural Work

In 1900, about 40 percent of the U.S. labor force engaged in farming. By 1993, this proportion had dropped below 3 percent. Figure 15–1, on page 418, graphically illustrates this rapid decline, which reflects the diminished role of the primary sector in the U.S. economy.

Still, because today's agriculture involves more machinery and fewer people, it is more productive than ever. A century ago, a typical farmer could feed five people; today, one farmer grows food for seventy-five. This dramatic rise in productivity also reflects new types of crops, pesticides that ensure higher yields, use of more sophisticated machinery, and other advances in farming techniques. The average U.S. farm has also doubled in size since 1950, to about 465 acres today.

This process signals the eclipse of "family farms," which are declining in number and produce a small part of our agricultural yield; more and more production today is carried out by *corporate agribusinesses*. But, more productive or not, this transformation has wrought painful adjustments for farming communities across the country, as a way of life is lost.

From Factory Work to Service Work

Industrialization swelled the ranks of blue-collar workers early in this century. As shown in Figure 15–1, in 1900 more than 40 percent of working people in the United States had blue-collar jobs—surpassing the share employed in agriculture. By 1950, however, a white-collar revolution had carried a majority of workers into service occupations. By 1994, about 70 percent of employed men and women held white-collar jobs, and blue-collar work had slipped to less than one-fourth of the labor force.

The growth of white-collar occupations is one reason for the widespread—although misleading—description of the United States as a middle-class society. As explained in Chapter 10 ("Social Class in the United States"), however, much so-called white-collar work is more accurately "service work," including sales positions, secretarial work, and jobs in fast-food restaurants. Such work yields little of the income and prestige of professional white-collar occupations and often provides fewer rewards than factory work. In short, more and more jobs in this postindustrial era provide a modest standard of living.

The Dual Labor Market

The change from factory work to service jobs represents a shifting balance between two categories of work (Edwards, 1979). The **primary labor market** includes *occupations that provide extensive benefits to workers.* This favored segment of the labor market contains the traditional white-collar professions and high management positions. These are jobs that people think of as *careers.* Work in the primary labor market provides high income and job security and is also personally challenging and intrinsically satisfying. Such occupations require a broad education rather than specialized training and offer solid opportunity for advancement.

THE MAP: Counties with low rates of labor force participation not only lack jobs but also are culturally conservative with high percentages of women who remain in the home.

RESOURCE: Karl Marx's analysis of "alienated labor" is one of the classic selections included in the Macionis and Benokraitis reader, *Seeing Ourselves*.

RESOURCE: Work in the secondary labor market is the focus of Mary Romero's article "Maid in the USA" in the *Seeing Ourselves* reader.

Seeing Ourselves

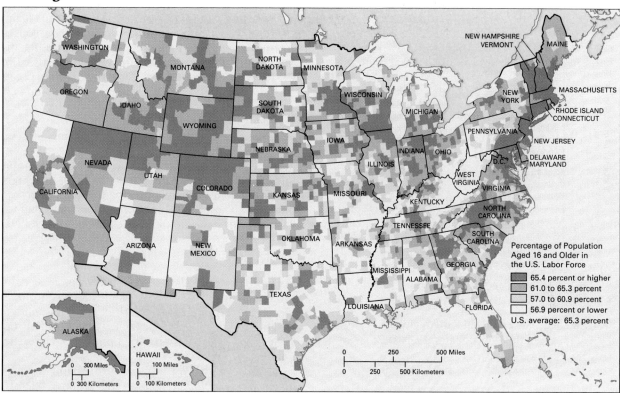

NATIONAL MAP 15–1 Labor Force Participation Across the United States

Counties that boast high levels of labor force participation can do so because they have within their borders steady sources of employment, including military bases, recreation areas, and large cities. By contrast, counties with low employment rates generally include a high proportion of elderly people (as well as students). Another important consideration revolves around gender: What do you think is the typical level of employment in regions of the country (stretching from the South up into coal-mining districts of Kentucky and West Virginia) in which traditional cultural norms encourage women to remain in the home?

From *American Demographics Desk Reference Series # 4*. Reprinted with permission. ©1992 *American Demographics* magazine, Ithaca, New York. Data from the 1990 decennial census.

But few of these advantages apply to work in the **secondary labor market**, *jobs providing minimal benefits to workers*. This segment of the labor force is employed in the low-skilled, blue-collar type of work found in routine assembly-line operations, and in low-level white-collar jobs including clerical positions. The secondary labor market offers workers much lower income, demands a longer work week, and affords less job security. Even if workers attain more schooling, they have little opportunity for advancement. In truth, many of these jobs are dead ends, and some even lack the benefits of a seniority system. Not surprisingly,

then, workers in the secondary labor market are most likely to experience alienation and dissatisfaction with their jobs. These problems most commonly beset women and other minorities, who are overly represented in this segment of the labor force (Mottaz, 1981; Kohn & Schooler, 1982; Kemp & Coverman, 1989; Hunnicutt, 1990).

Most new jobs in our postindustrial economy fall within the secondary labor market, and they involve the same kind of unchallenging tasks, low wages, and poor working conditions characteristic of jobs in factories a century ago (Gruenberg, 1980). Moreover, as

NOTE: In the U.S., only about 10% of service workers are unionized.
DATA FILE: A statistical analysis of multiple job-holding among U.S. workers is found in the *Data File*.

NOTE: The number of strikes has fallen steadily since the 1970s, paralleling the decline of unions but also the fading strength of U.S. industries that have been most unionized (such as the steel and auto industries).

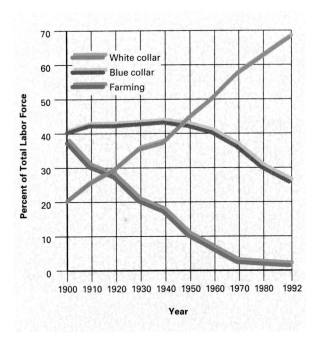

FIGURE 15–1 The Changing Pattern of Work in the United States, 1900–1992

(U.S. Department of Labor, 1994)

the box explains, our economy now shuttles an unprecedented share of workers from one temporary position to another.

Labor Unions

The changing economy has been accompanied by a declining role for **labor unions**, *organizations of workers seeking to improve wages and working conditions through various strategies, including negotiations and strikes.* Membership in labor unions increased rapidly in the United States after 1935, rising to more than one-third of the nonfarm labor force by 1950. Union membership peaked during the 1970s at almost 25 million people. Since then, it has steadily declined to about 16 percent of the nonfarm labor force, or about 16 million men and women.

In global perspective, unions now claim a far lower portion of workers in the United States than in other industrial societies. In the Scandinavian countries, at least 80 percent of workers belong to unions; in Europe as a whole, about half do. In Canada and Japan, the proportion is about one-third (Western, 1993).

This decline follows from other trends already noted. First, this country has lost tens of thousands of jobs in the highly unionized industrial sector as U.S. manufacturers "exported" jobs abroad to reduce their labor costs. At home, managers in many plants facing economic problems have succeeded in forcing concessions from workers, including, in some cases, the dissolution of labor unions. Moreover, most jobs being created today are service jobs, few of which are unionized. One notable consequence of the expanding use of temporary workers is that virtually none of these people belong to a labor union.

As some analysts see it, however, falling job security may well make union membership a higher priority for workers in the years to come. But to expand their membership, unions will also have to adapt to the new global economy. Instead of seeing foreign workers as a threat to their interests, in short, union leadership will have to forge new international alliances (Mabry, 1992).

Professions

All kinds of work today are described as professional—we hear of professional tennis players, even professional exterminators. As distinct from an *amateur* (from Latin meaning "lover," one who acts simply out of love for the activity itself), a professional pursues some task for a living.

More precisely, though, a **profession** is *a prestigious, white-collar occupation that requires extensive formal education.* The term suggests a "profession"—a public declaration—of faith or willingness to abide by certain principles. Traditional professions include the ministry, medicine, law, and academia (W. Goode, 1960). Today, workers describe their occupations as professions to the extent that they demonstrate the following four characteristics (Ritzer & Walczak, 1990).

1. **Theoretical knowledge.** Most jobs involve technical skills, but professions demand a theoretical understanding of some field, obtained through extensive schooling and regular interaction with others in the field. Anyone can master first-aid skills, for example, but physicians are set apart as having a theoretical understanding of human health and illness.

2. **Self-regulated training and practice.** While most work places people under direct supervision, people engaged in professions are generally self-employed. Professionals participate in associations that set standards for performing or "practicing," typically including a formal code of ethics.

3. **Authority over clients.** Many jobs—sales work, for example—require people to respond directly to the

SOCIAL SURVEY: How much confidence do you have in people running organized labor? (GSS 1993 N = 1,057; *Codebook*, 1993:206)

| "A great deal" | 8.2% | "Hardly any" | 32.2% |
| "Only some" | 52.3% | DK/NR | 7.3% |

SOCIAL SURVEY: "There will always be conflict between management and workers because they are really on opposite sides." (GSS 1989, N = 1,453; *Codebook*, 1993:628)

"Strongly agree"	8.2%	"Disagree"	29.3%
"Agree"	29.3%	"Strongly disagree"	5.7%
"Neither agree nor disagree"	22.7%	DK/NR	4.7%

SOCIOLOGY OF EVERYDAY LIFE

The Postindustrial Economy: The "Temping" of the United States

Three hundred years ago, Scottish landlords evicted thousands of farmers so that land could be put to a more profitable use: raising sheep to supply wool to the burgeoning textile factories. Almost overnight, the security of an established way of life vanished: The fortunate farmers emigrated to North America and started over; the least fortunate starved to death.

Today, the Information Revolution has signaled the rise of the postindustrial economy and, once again, economic change is undermining job security. A decade ago, workers confidently assumed that hard work and playing by the rules all but guaranteed that their jobs would be there until they were ready to retire. No longer. As one analyst puts it:

> The rise of the knowledge economy means a change, in less than twenty years, from an overbuilt system of large, slow-moving economic units to an array of small, widely dispersed economic centers, some as small as an individual boss. In the new economy, geography dissolves, the highways are electronic. Even Wall Street no longer has a reason to be on Wall Street. Companies become concepts . . . and jobs are almost as susceptible as electrons to vanishing into thin air. (Morrow, 1993:41)

In the short run, at least, the dislocation for U.S. workers is tremendous. Companies scrambling to "remain competitive" in the global economy are "downsizing" and embracing "flexibility." These trends mean not only cutting the number of people on the payroll but also replacing long-term employees with temporary workers. The advantages of doing so are significant. By hiring "temps," companies no longer have to worry about providing training programs, health insurance, paid vacations, or pensions. And, if next month workers are no longer needed, they can be

released without further cost or fear of lawsuits.

The "temping" of our society is one of the most important trends in the workplace today. The two largest suppliers of temporary workers—Manpower and Kelly Services—now boast 1.5 million employees. All varieties of "temps," from government contract workers to corporate part-timers, already number 35 million workers, accounting for 30 percent of the U.S. labor force, a share that may reach half by the end of this decade.

The easing of the Great Depression more than forty years ago ushered workers and employers into an era of relationships based on mutual loyalty. But recent trends are undoing workplace bonds with remarkable speed and at all levels of the labor force. Like workers at the dawn of the industrial era centuries ago, today's secretaries, engineers, bank officers, and even corporate executives are finding their job security vanishing before their eyes. For the foreseeable future, most analysts agree, there is probably no going back to the traditional notion of lifetime employment with one company.

SOURCE: Castro (1993) and Morrow (1993).

desires of customers. Professionals, by contrast, expect their clients to follow their direction and advice. Professionals claim this authority based on the possession of knowledge that lay people lack.

4. **Orientation to community rather than to self-interest.** The traditional "professing" of faith or

duty was a professional's declaration of intention to serve the needs of clients and the broader community rather than self-interest. Most business executives readily admit to working in pursuit of personal financial gain, and this pecuniary purpose is one reason that engaging in commerce was not

NOTE: The original meaning of the word "profession" was "a taking of a vow." A professor was thus a person who took a religious vow, revealing the origins of the European universities in the church. This helps to explain why ethics and public responsibility continue to figure in professional life.

Q: "A profession is a conspiracy against the layman." George Bernard Shaw

NOTE: Leslie Dunbar (1988) estimates that a 1% fall in unemployment saves the U.S. government $36 million in assistance payments.

During the Great Depression, a time of catastrophic unemployment in the United States, Isaac Soyer painted Employment Agency, *a powerful statement of the personal collapse and private despair that afflict men and women who are out of work.*

one of the traditional professions. Professionals such as priests or college professors, however, rarely admit to financial motives and prefer to think of their work as contributing to the well-being of others. Some professional associations, including the American Medical Association, even forbid their members from advertising their services. This aura of altruism also makes many professionals reluctant to discuss the fees that contribute to their high incomes.

Alongside the traditional professions, a number of other occupations stand as *new professions*. These occupations, which include architecture, psychiatry, social work, and accountancy, share most of the characteristics just presented.

Many new service occupations in the postindustrial economy have also sought to *professionalize* their work. This claim to professional standing often begins with a new name for the work that implies practitioners employ special, theoretical knowledge (and has the added benefit of distancing them from their previously less-distinguished reputation). Government bureaucrats, for example, become "public policy analysts," and dogcatchers are reborn as "animal control specialists."

Interested parties may also form a professional association that will formally attest to their specialized skills. This organization then begins to lobby for the legal right to license those who perform the work in question. It also develops a code of ethics, modeled on those

of traditional professions, which emphasizes the occupation's contribution to the community. In its effort to win public acceptance, a professional association may also establish schools or other training facilities and perhaps start a professional journal (Abbott, 1988).

Not every category of workers tries to claim full professional status. Some *paraprofessionals*, including paralegals and medical technicians, possess specialized skills but lack the extensive theoretical education required of full professionals.

Self-Employment

Self-employment—in effect, earning a living without working for a large organization—was once commonplace in the United States. Rural farms were owned and operated by families, and self-employed workers in the cities owned shops and other small businesses or sold their skills on the open market. C. Wright Mills (1951) estimated that in the early 1800s about 80 percent of the U.S. labor force was self-employed. With the onset of the Industrial Revolution, however, that proportion was to change, and self-employed workers now account for only 8 percent of the U.S. labor force (11 percent of men and 6 percent of women).

Lawyers, physicians, and some other professionals have been represented strongly among the ranks of the self-employed. But most self-employed workers are small-business owners, plumbers, carpenters, free-lance writers, editors, artists, house cleaners, child care

DATA FILE: The *Data File* includes an overview of African-American entrepreneurs.

GLOBAL: Unemployment rates (1991): Japan, 2.1%; Sweden, 2.6%; Germany, 4.4%; U.S., 6.7%; Netherlands, 7.0%; U.K., 8.8%; France, 9.6%; Canada, 10.3%. (U.S. Census Bureau)

Q: "Unemployment is a modern concept. It assumes the transmutation of work into employment; presupposes the reorganization of production into a collection of jobs that mediate the relation between market and subsistence; and requires the intervention of a market in which work becomes a prerogative contingent on the sale of labor." Michael B. Katz (1986:195)

FIGURE 15–2

Official U.S. Unemployment Rate Among Various Categories of Adults, 1993

(U.S. Department of Labor, 1994)

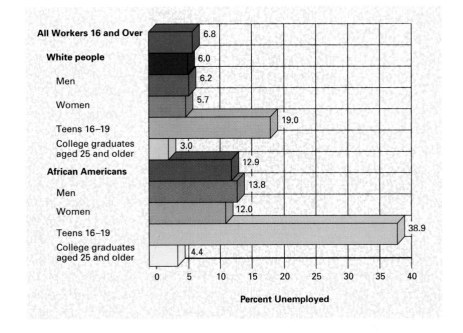

providers, and long-distance truck drivers. Overall, the self-employed are more likely to have blue-collar jobs than white-collar jobs.

Our society has always painted an appealing picture of working independently: no time clocks to punch and no one looking over your shoulder. For minorities who have long been excluded from some kinds of work, self-employment has been an effective strategy to broaden economic opportunity (Evans, 1989). Further, self-employment holds the potential—although it is rarely realized—of earning a great deal of money. But for all its advantages, self-employment is vulnerable to fluctuations in the economy, one reason that only one-fifth of small businesses survive for ten years. Another common problem is that the self-employed lack pension and health care benefits provided for employees by large organizations.

Finally, a notable trend is that the share of this nation's 14 million small businesses owned by women is up sharply, to about 30 percent. Many women find that going into business for themselves affords more opportunity, a more enjoyable working environment, and a more flexible schedule than laboring for large organizations.

Unemployment

Every society has some unemployment. Few young people entering the labor force find a job right away;

some workers temporarily leave the labor force while seeking a new job, to have children, or because of a labor strike; others suffer from long-term illnesses; and still others are illiterate or without the skills to perform useful work.

But unemployment is also caused by the economy itself. Jobs disappear as occupations become obsolete, as businesses close in the face of foreign competition, and as recessions force layoffs and bankruptcies. Since 1987, for example, the "downsizing" of businesses has eliminated at least 6 million jobs in the United States, including both blue-collar and white-collar positions.

In the United States, the unemployment rate rarely dips below 5 percent of the labor force. Public officials generally view this level of unemployment as natural and only begin to acknowledge an "unemployment problem" when the rate exceeds 7 or 8 percent (Albrecht, 1983).

In 1993, 8.7 million people over the age of sixteen were unemployed—about 7 percent of the civilian labor force. As a glance back at National Map 15–1 suggests, some regions of the country, including parts of West Virginia and New Mexico, contend with unemployment at twice the national rate.

Figure 15–2 shows the official unemployment rate for various categories of U.S. workers in 1993 (U.S. Department of Labor, 1994). Unemployment among African Americans stood more than twice as high (12.9 percent) as among white people (6.0 percent); this

SOCIAL SURVEY: "The government should provide a decent standard of living for the unemployed." (GSS 1985, N = 1,285; *Codebook*, 1993:598)

"Strongly agree"	6.2%	"Disagree"	29.2%
"Agree"	29.0%	"Strongly disagree"	5.7%
"Neither agree nor disagree"	25.8%	DK/NR	4.2%

One strategy used by law enforcement officials to discourage trafficking in illegal drugs—one of the largest segments of the underground economy—is the seizure of automobiles and boats used in drug transactions. This warehouse in southern Florida contains vehicles worth millions of dollars. Unfortunately, this policy seems to make at best a small dent in the illegal drug trade.

disparity is due mostly to the historical concentration of people of color in the secondary labor market (DiPrete, 1981). Younger people confront especially high levels of unemployment, and men now have an unemployment rate higher than that for women—a reversal of a historical pattern in the face of an economic recession that has hit male-dominated blue-collar industrial jobs particularly hard.

Government unemployment statistics, based on monthly national surveys, generally understate unemployment for two reasons. First, to be counted among the unemployed, a person must be actively seeking work; "discouraged workers," who have given up looking for a job, are omitted from the statistics. Second, many people unable to find jobs for which they are qualified settle, at least temporarily, for "lesser" employment: A former college professor, for example, may drive a taxi while seeking a new teaching position. Such people are included among the employed, although they might better be described as *underemployed*.

On the other hand, statistics also overlook the fact that many people officially out of work receive income from odd jobs or even from illegal activity. But, overall, the actual level of unemployment is probably several percentage points above the official figure.

The Underground Economy

Although our way of life celebrates individual initiative and free enterprise, the U.S. government requires

workers to maintain extensive records and to make regular reports of all economic activity. Any violation of this obligation places transactions within the **underground economy**, *economic activity involving income that one does not report to the government as required by law*.

On a small scale, most people participate in the underground economy on a regular basis: One family makes extra money by holding a garage sale; another allows its teenage children to babysit for the neighbors without reporting whatever income is received. Nevertheless, most of the underground economy is attributable to criminal activity such as the sale of illegal drugs, prostitution, bribery, theft, illegal gambling, and loan-sharking.

The single largest segment of the underground economy involves "honest" people who break the law by failing to report some or all of their legally obtained income. Self-employed persons such as carpenters, physicians, and owners of small businesses may understate their incomes on tax forms; waiters, waitresses, and other service workers may not report their entire earnings from tips. Even relatively small omissions and misrepresentations, when appearing on millions of individual income tax returns, add up to billions of dollars (Simon & Witte, 1982).

Social Diversity in the Workplace

Another major trend in the workplace involves change in the composition of the U.S. labor force. Traditionally, white men have been the mainstay of the U.S. labor force. As explained in Chapter 12 ("Race and Ethnicity"), however, our country's proportion of minorities is rapidly rising. During the 1980s, the increase in African Americans (13 percent) was twice as great as for white people (6 percent); even higher was the jump in the Hispanic population (more than 50 percent) and in the numbers of Asian Americans (topping 100 percent). If these trends continue, there will be a "minority-majority" in the United States toward the end of the next century. This change is having profound consequences already in businesses across the country. The box takes a closer look at how the increasing social diversity of our society is affecting the workplace during the 1990s.

Technology and Work

The central technology of the emerging postindustrial economy is the computer and related devices for processing information. The Information Revolution is changing the character of both the workplace and

GLOBAL: The Japanese are entitled to 15.1 paid holidays per year, on the average; they typically take 7.6. (Jared Lubarsky) With regard to the U.S., the average work week has increased by 15% since 1970 to about 46 hours.

RESOURCE: The lives of gay people in the corporate world are highlighted in the James Woods article, "The Corporate Closet," in the *Seeing Ourselves* reader.

SOCIAL DIVERSITY

The Work Force of the Twenty-First Century

In recent years, the significant rise in the U.S. minority population means a marked transformation of the labor force.

The figure shows that the number of white men in the U.S. labor force is projected to rise by a modest 8 percent during the 1990s. The rate of increase among African-American working men will be far greater, at 24 percent. Among Hispanic men, the rise will be a whopping 50 percent.

Among women, projected increases will be larger still. But, here again, the gains among minorities will be greatest: A 19 percent rise among white women will be surpassed by a 27 percent jump among African-American women and a 66 percent increase in Hispanic women.

Thus, non-Hispanic, white men—the traditional backbone of the U.S. labor force—will represent only 10 percent of new workers during the 1990s. By the end of this decade, they will amount to just 40 percent of all workers, a figure that will continue to drop. Companies that begin now to plan for growing social diversity will tap the largest talent pool and enjoy a competitive advantage in the twenty-first century.

Responding effectively to workplace diversity means more than maintaining affirmative action programs, which are aimed primarily at recruiting. The broader challenge—and greater opportunity—for companies in the next century lies in transforming the workplace environment to develop the potential of all workers. Employees, after all, are a company's most important resource, and utilizing this resource to greatest advantage will require change in several key areas.

First, companies must realize that the needs and concerns of women and people of color may not be the same as those of white men. For example, corporations will be pressed to provide workplace child care in the future.

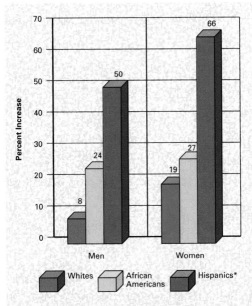

Projected Increase in the Numbers of People in the U.S. Labor Force, 1990–2000

*Hispanics can be of any race.

(U.S. Department of Labor, 1992)

Second, businesses will have to devise effective strategies for defusing the tensions that arise from social differences. They will have to work harder at treating all workers equally as well as respectfully. If it is to cultivate the full efforts of all workers, the emerging corporate culture cannot tolerate harassment related to gender and race.

Third, companies will have to rethink current promotion practices. At present, only 2 percent of Fortune 500 top executives are women, and just 1 percent are other minorities. In a broad survey of U.S. companies, the U.S. Equal Employment Opportunity Commission confirmed that white men (40 percent of adults aged twenty to sixty-four) hold 68 percent of management jobs; the comparable figures for white women are 41 and 23 percent; for African Americans, 12 and 5 percent; and, for Hispanics, 8 and 2 percent.

Any informal "glass ceiling" that prevents advancement by skilled workers clearly discourages achievement. In the emerging labor force of the next century, any such barriers will deprive companies of their largest source of talent—women and other minorities.

SOURCES: Bureau of National Affairs (1990) and Crispell (1990).

work itself. Shoshana Zuboff (1982) points to four ways in which computers already have altered the character of work.

1. **Computers are deskilling labor.** Just as industrial machinery "deskilled" the master crafts worker of an earlier era, so computers now threaten the skills of managers. More and more business decisions are based not on executive decision making but on computer modeling, in which a machine determines whether to buy or sell a product or to approve or reject a loan.

2. **Computers are making work more abstract.** Industrial workers typically have a "hands-on" relationship with their product. Postindustrial workers manipulate words or other symbols in pursuit of some sales goal or other abstract definition of business success.

3. **Computers limit workplace interaction.** The Information Revolution is directing employees to perform most of their work at computer terminals; this system isolates workers from one another.

4. **Computers enhance employers' control of workers.** Computers allow supervisors to monitor each worker's output precisely and continuously, whether employees are working at computer terminals or on an assembly line (Rule & Brantley, 1992).

Making a broader point, Zuboff contends that technology is not socially neutral; rather it shapes the way we work and enhances the power of employers over employees. Understandably, then, while workers may hail some dimensions of the Information Revolution, they are likely to oppose others.

CORPORATIONS

At the core of today's capitalist economy lies the **corporation**, *an organization with a legal existence, including rights and liabilities, apart from those of its members.* By incorporating, an organization becomes an entity unto itself, able to enter into contracts and own property. Of some 20 million businesses in the United States, 4 million are incorporated (*Statistics of Income Bulletin*, 1991).

The practice of legally incorporating accelerated with the rise of large businesses a century ago because it provides two benefits to company owners. First, incorporation shields them from the legal liabilities of their businesses, protecting personal wealth from lawsuits arising from business debts or harm to consumers. Second, under the tax laws of the United States, incorporation confers advantages that serve to increase the profits of owners.

The largest corporations are owned by millions of stockholders (including other corporations) rather than by single families. This dispersion of corporate ownership has spread wealth to some extent, making more people small-scale capitalists. Ralf Dahrendorf (1959) adds that the day-to-day operation of a corporation falls to white-collar executives who may or may not be major stockholders themselves. Typically, however, a great deal of corporate stock is owned by a small number of the corporation's top executives and directors (Useem, 1980).

Economic Concentration

About half of U.S. corporations are small, with assets worth less than $100,000. The largest corporations, however, dominate our country's economy. Throughout this century, the growth of corporations has resulted in an increasing concentration of national and international economic power. The productive assets of the two hundred largest manufacturing corporations in 1950 were surpassed by those of the biggest one hundred companies in 1970 (Fusfeld, 1982). Corporations on record in 1990 included 367 with assets exceeding $1 billion, representing 71 percent of all corporate assets and 73 percent of total corporate profits (U.S. Bureau of the Census, 1992).

Table 15–2 shows the twenty largest corporations in the United States in 1992, ranked by sales. At the top of the list, General Motors had more than $132 billion in sales and $190 billion in total assets. GM's sales during a single year roughly equaled the tax revenue of half the states combined. GM also employed more people than did the governments of all the states on the West Coast, including Alaska and Hawaii.

Conglomerates and Corporate Linkages

Economic concentration has spawned **conglomerates**, *giant corporations composed of many smaller corporations.* Conglomerates emerge as corporations enter new markets, spinning off new companies or carrying out takeovers of existing companies. Forging a conglomerate is also a strategy to diversify a company, so that new products can provide a hedge against declining profits in the original market. Faced with declining sales of tobacco products, for example, R. J. Reynolds merged with Nabisco foods, forming a conglomerate called RJR-Nabisco. Another

TABLE 15–2 The Twenty Largest Industrial Corporations in the United States, 1992

Corporation	Product	Sales ($ billions)	Assets ($ billions)	Number of Employees
General Motors	Motor vehicles	132.4	190.9	750,000
Exxon	Oil refining	103.2	85.0	98,000
Ford Motor	Motor vehicles	100.1	180.5	325,300
American Telephone & Telegraph (A T & T)	Telecommunications	64.9	57.2	314,900
International Business Machines (IBM)	Office equipment	64.5	86.7	357,300
General Electric	Electronics	57.1	192.9	276,000
Mobil	Oil refining	56.9	40.6	65,600
Wal-Mart Stores	Retail stores	55.5	20.6	398,000
Sears, Roebuck	Retail stores	52.3	83.5	403,000
Philip Morris Co.	Tobacco products	50.1	50.0	163,500
K-mart	Retail stores	38.0	18.9	353,500
Chevron	Oil refining	37.5	34.0	52,200
E.I. du Pont	Chemicals	37.2	38.9	129,000
Chrysler	Motor vehicles	36.9	40.7	126,000
Texaco	Oil refining	36.8	26.0	38,900
Citicorp	Banking	31.9	213.7	83,500
Procter & Gamble	Cleaning products	30.4	23.9	100,000
Boeing	Aerospace	30.2	18.1	148,600
American Express	Financial services	27.0	175.8	112,500
Amoco	Oil refining	25.3	28.5	50,600

SOURCE: "The Forbes 500s/Twenty-Fifth Annual Directory," *Forbes*, Vol. 151, no. 9 (April 26, 1993): Special issue.

example is Coca-Cola. Although Coke's soft drink market is still growing, the company now produces fruit drinks, coffee, bottled water, movies, and television programs. Beatrice Foods is another corporate "umbrella" containing more than fifty smaller corporations that manufacture well-known products including Reddi-Whip, Wesson cooking oils, Peter Pan peanut butter, Hunt's foods, Tropicana fruit juices, La Choy foods, Orville Redenbacher popcorn, Max Factor cosmetics, Playtex clothing, and Samsonite luggage (Beatrice, 1985).

Besides conglomerates, corporations are linked also through mutual ownership, since these giant organizations own each other's stock. In today's global economy, many U.S.-based companies have invested heavily in other corporations commonly regarded as their competitors. For instance, Ford owns a significant share of Mazda, General Motors is a major investor in Isuzu, and Chrysler is part owner of Mitsubishi.

One more type of linkage among corporations is the *interlocking directorate*, a social network of people serving simultaneously on the boards of directors of many corporations. These connections give corporations access to valuable information about each other's products and marketing strategies. Antitrust laws forbid linkages of this kind among corporations

that compete directly with one another. Yet beneficial linkages persist among noncompeting corporations with common interests—for example, a corporation building tractors may share directors with one that manufactures tires. Indirect linkages also occur when, for example, a member of General Motors' board of directors and a member of Ford's board of directors both sit on the board of Exxon (Herman, 1981; Scott & Griff, 1985).

Examining the membership of General Motors' board of directors, Beth Mintz and Michael Schwartz (1981) found directors who were shared with twenty-nine other major corporations. These companies, in turn, shared directors with seven hundred additional corporations, including major banks and insurance companies. Gwen Moore (1979) adds that corporate executives travel in many of the same social circles, allowing them to exchange valuable information informally.

Corporate linkages do not necessarily run counter to the public interest, but they certainly concentrate power and they may encourage illegal activity. Price fixing, for example, is legal in much of the world (the Organization of Petroleum Exporting Countries—OPEC—meets regularly to try to set oil prices), but not in the United States. By their nature, however,

NOTE: Oligopoly does not prevent economic challenges, even in old industries like automobiles; in new industries like software, Microsoft outdistanced IBM and other rivals to become a world standard and Microsoft founder Bill Gates became the U.S.'s richest person.

DATA FILE: Examples of capitalism in Cuba are highlighted in the *Data File*.

Q: "I have long dreamed of buying an island owned by no nation and of establishing the world headquarters of Dow Chemical Company on the truly neutral ground of such an island, beholden to no nation or society. . . . We could then really operate in the United States as U.S. citizens, in Japan as Japanese citizens, and in Brazil as Brazilians rather than being governed by the laws of the United States." Carl A. Gerstacker, chairman of Dow Chemical Company

Such legislation has eliminated total monopolies, but not **oligopoly**, *domination of a market by a few producers*. Oligopoly results from the vast investment needed to enter a new market such as the auto industry. Certainly the successful entry of foreign-owned corporations into the U.S. automobile market shows that new companies can challenge oligopolies. But all large businesses strive to avoid competition simply because it places profits at risk.

Although capitalism favors minimal government intervention in the economy, corporate power is now so great—and competition among corporations is sometimes so limited—that government regulation may be the only way to protect the public interest. Yet, the government is also the corporate world's single biggest customer. Washington also frequently intervenes to support struggling corporations, as in the Chrysler bailout during the 1980s. In short, corporations and government typically work together to make the entire economy more stable and profitable (Madsen, 1980).

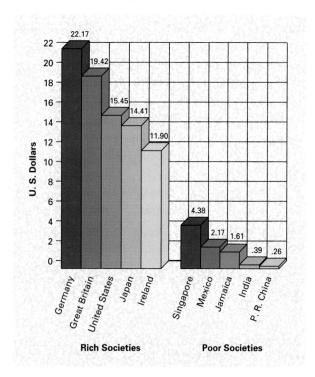

FIGURE 15–3 Hourly Wages for Workers in Manufacturing

(U.S. Bureau of Labor Statistics, 1992)

corporate linkages invite price fixing, especially when only a few corporations control an entire market.

Corporations and Competition

The capitalist model assumes businesses operate independently in a competitive market. However, the competitive sector of the U.S. economy is mostly limited to smaller businesses and self-employed people. The corporate core of the economy, meanwhile, is largely a *noncompetitive sector*. Large corporations are not truly competitive because, first, their extensive linkages mean that they do not operate independently. Second, a small number of corporations dominate many large markets.

No large company can engage legally in **monopoly**, *domination of a market by a single producer*, because such a company could simply dictate prices. A century ago, the federal government saw the public danger in monopolies and outlawed this strategy for cornering the market, beginning with the Sherman Antitrust Act of 1890.

Corporations and the Global Economy

Corporations have grown in size and power so fast that they are now responsible for most of the world's economic output. In the process, the largest corporations—centered in the United States, Japan, and Western Europe—have spilled across national borders and now view the entire world as one vast marketplace.

As discussed in Chapter 11 ("Global Inequality"), multinationals are large corporations that produce and market products in many different nations. Beatrice Foods, for example, operates factories in thirty countries and sells products in more than one hundred. General Motors, Ford, Exxon, and the other huge multinationals earn much—and in some cases most—of their profits outside the United States.

Corporations become multinational in order to make more money, since most of the planet's resources and three-fourths of the world's people are found in less-developed countries. Worldwide operations, then, offer access to plentiful materials and vast markets. In addition, as indicated in Figure 15–3, labor costs are far lower in poor countries of the world: A manufacturing worker in the People's Republic of China labors for three months to earn what a German worker earns in a single day.

The impact of multinationals on poor societies is controversial, as Chapter 11 ("Global Inequality") explains in detail. On one side of the argument,

GLOBAL: U.S. businesses invest about 3% of GNP into new plants, compared to 15% by Japanese businesses. This, in the view of some critics, has resulted in reduced U.S. competitiveness.

GLOBAL: In recent years, exports have accounted for most of the growth of the U.S. economy; and most of this is the output of multi-nationals.

NOTE: Arguments about development on the political right tend to focus on economic productivity; those on the left tend to highlight economic distribution. Global theories of economic development—modernization theory and dependency (world systems) theory—illustrate this pattern. See discussion of these approaches in Chapter 11, "Global Stratification."

The expansion of Western multinational corporations has altered patterns of consumption throughout the world, creating a homogeneous "corporate culture" that is—for better or worse—undermining countless traditional ways of life.

modernization theorists argue that multinationals unleash the great productivity of the capitalist economic system, which will drive economic development (Rostow, 1978; Madsen, 1980; Berger, 1986). Exxon corporation alone, for example, far outproduces any one of the least-productive nations in the world. Corporations offer poor societies tax revenues, capital investment, new jobs, and advanced technology—taken together, what modernization theorists call a certain recipe for economic growth.

On the other side of the argument, dependency theorists who favor a socialist economy claim that multinationals only intensify global inequality (Vaughan, 1978; Wallerstein, 1979; Delacroix & Ragin, 1981; Bergesen, 1983). Multinational investment, as they see it, may create a few jobs in poor countries but it also stifles the development of local industries which are a better source of employment. Further, critics charge, multinationals generally push developing countries to produce expensive consumer goods for export to rich societies rather than food and other necessities that would bolster the standard of living in local communities. From this standpoint, multinationals establish a system of neocolonialism, making poor societies poorer and increasingly reliant on rich, capitalist societies.

LOOKING AHEAD: THE ECONOMY OF THE TWENTY-FIRST CENTURY

Social institutions are organizational strategies by which societies attempt to meet basic human needs. But societies themselves change over time, so that the various institutions always seem somewhat at odds with the task we assume they are trying to accomplish.

One important transformation highlighted in this chapter revolves around the Information Revolution. New information technology is the main force behind the emergence of a postindustrial economy in the United States. The share of the U.S. labor force engaged in manufacturing is now just half of what it was in 1960, while service work has increased just as quickly. For workers who depend on their industrial skills to earn a living, then, this change has brought rising unemployment and declining wages. As a society, we also must recognize that millions of men and women lack the language and computer skills needed to participate in the postindustrial economy. To operate effectively, social institutions must be responsive to each other. Therefore, in the next century, families and schools must face up to the challenge of preparing young people to perform the kind of work their society makes available to them.

A second transformation that has held our atten-tion is the emergence of a global economy. In the earliest phase of our country's history, the ups and downs of a local economy depended on events or trends that took place within a single town. In time, local communities throughout the country became economically interconnected so that prosperity in one place typically depended on producing goods demanded by people in some other part of the coun-try. As we approach the next century, economic links are intensifying at the global level. It now makes far less sense to speak of a national economy; what people, say, in an Iowa farm town produce and con-sume may be affected more by what transpires in the wheat-growing region of Russia than by events in their own state capital. In short, U.S. workers are not only generating new products and services, but we are doing so in response to factors and forces that are dis-tant and unseen.

Finally, change is causing analysts around the world to rethink conventional economic models. The emerging global economic system revealed socialist economies to be far less productive than their capital-ist counterparts, one central cause of the recent col-lapse of socialist regimes in Eastern Europe and the former Soviet Union. Socialism, which at its peak organized the productive lives of about one-fourth of humanity, seems to be in decline around the world, although the People's Republic of China, Cuba, and other nations still hold steadfastly to government-based economies.

Capitalism, too, has seen marked changes and now operates with a significant degree of govern-ment regulation. The most significant change in the capitalist system is the emergence of multinational corporations. The global reach of today's giant busi-nesses means that U.S. corporations have expanded into more parts of the world, just as foreign-based corporations are increasing their investment in the United States.

Perhaps we are nearing the end of what some analysts call "the American century." Ours is still the most productive economy in the world. But a turning point occurred in 1990 when, for the first time, for-eign corporations owned more of the United States than U.S. corporations owned abroad. Foreign inves-tors now have title to half of the commercial property in downtown Los Angeles, 40 percent in Houston, 35 percent in Minneapolis, and 25 percent in Manhattan (Selimuddin, 1989).

What will be the long-term effects of all these changes? Two conclusions seem unescapable. First, the economic future of the United States and other nations will be played out around the world. The emergence of the postindustrial economy in the United States is, after all, inseparable from the increas-ing industrial production of other nations, especially in Asia's rapidly developing Pacific Rim. Second, everyone confronts the ever-pressing issue of global inequality. Whether the world economy ultimately reduces or deepens the disparity between rich and poor societies will likely be the factor that steers our planet toward peace or belligerence.

SUMMARY

1. The economy is the major social institution by which a society produces, distributes, and con-sumes goods and services.

2. In technologically simple societies, the economy is subsumed within the family. In agrarian soci-eties, most economic activity takes place apart from the home. Industrialization sparks signifi-cant economic expansion due to new energy sources, large factories, mass production, and worker specialization.

3. The postindustrial economy is characterized by the increasing production of services rather than goods. Just as the Industrial Revolution supplied the technology supporting the industrial economy of the past, the Information Revolution is now advancing the postindustrial economy.

4. The primary sector of the economy generates raw materials; the secondary sector manufac-tures various goods; the tertiary sector produces services. In preindustrial societies, the primary

sector predominates; the secondary sector is of greatest importance in industrial societies; the tertiary sector prevails in postindustrial societies.

5. Social scientists describe the economies of today's industrial societies in terms of two models. Capitalism is based on private ownership of productive property and the pursuit of personal profit in a competitive marketplace. Socialism is based on collective ownership of productive property and the pursuit of collective well-being through government control of the economy.

6. Although the U.S. economy is predominantly capitalist, government is broadly involved in economic life. Government plays an even greater role in the "democratic socialist" economies of some Western European nations and the "state capitalism" of Japan. The former Soviet Union has gradually introduced some market elements into its formerly centralized economy; the nations of Eastern Europe are making similar changes.

7. Capitalism is highly productive, providing a high overall standard of living. Socialism is less productive but generates greater economic equality. Capitalism is also more supportive of civil liberties than socialism is.

8. The emergence of a global economy means that nations no longer produce and consume products and services within national boundaries. Moreover, the six hundred largest corporations, operating internationally, now account for most of the earth's economic output.

9. In the United States, agricultural work has declined over the course of this century to just 2 percent of the labor force. The share of blue-collar jobs has also diminished, now accounting for one-fourth of the labor force. The share of white-collar service occupations, however, has been rising rapidly and now involves more than 70 percent of the labor force.

10. A profession is a special category of white-collar work based on theoretical knowledge, occupational autonomy, authority over clients, and a claim to serving the community.

11. Work in the primary labor market provides far more rewards than work in the secondary labor market. Most new jobs in the United States are service positions in the secondary labor market, and about one-third of today's workers hold jobs classified as temporary, with no promise of job security.

12. Today, 8 percent of U.S. workers are self-employed. Although many professionals fall into this category, most self-employed workers have blue-collar occupations.

13. Unemployment has many causes, including the operation of the economy itself; in the United States the unemployment rate is generally at least 5 percent.

14. The underground economy includes criminal as well as legal activity that generates income that goes unreported on income tax forms.

15. Corporations are the core of the U.S. economy. The largest corporations, which are conglomerates, account for most corporate assets and profits. Many large corporations operate as multinationals, producing and distributing products in most nations of the world.

KEY CONCEPTS

capitalism an economic system in which natural resources and the means of producing goods and services are privately owned

communism a hypothetical economic and political system in which all members of a society are socially equal

conglomerates giant corporations composed of many smaller corporations

corporation an organization with a legal existence, including rights and liabilities, apart from those of its members

democratic socialism an economic and political system that combines significant government control of the economy with free elections

economy the social institution that organizes the production, distribution, and consumption of goods and services

global economy interconnected economic activity throughout the world that pays little regard to national borders

labor unions organizations of workers seeking to improve wages and working conditions through various strategies, including negotiations and strikes

monopoly domination of a market by a single producer

oligopoly domination of a market by a few producers

postindustrial economy a productive system based on service work and high technology

primary labor market occupations that provide extensive benefits to workers

primary sector the part of the economy that generates raw materials directly from the natural environment

profession a prestigious white-collar occupation that requires extensive formal education

secondary labor market jobs that provide minimal benefits to workers

secondary sector the part of the economy that transforms raw materials into manufactured goods

socialism an economic system in which natural resources and the means of producing goods and services are collectively owned

state capitalism an economic and political system in which companies are privately owned although they cooperate closely with the government

tertiary sector the part of the economy involved in services rather than goods

underground economy economic activity generating income that one does not report to the government as required by law

CRITICAL-THINKING QUESTIONS

1. What is a social institution? Do all societies have an economy that operates as a distinct social institution apart from the family?

2. Identify several ways in which the Industrial Revolution reshaped the economy of the United States. How is the Information Revolution transforming the economy once again?

3. What key characteristics distinguish capitalism from socialism? Compare these two systems in terms of productivity, economic inequality, and support for civil liberties.

4. What are multinational corporations? What arguments favor their role in poor societies? What arguments criticize their operation?

SUGGESTED READINGS

Classic Sources

Thorstein Veblen. *The Theory of the Leisure Class*. New York: New American Library, 1953; orig. 1899.
    One of the earliest U.S. sociologists explains how patterns of consumption function to confer social status on people in an increasingly affluent and upwardly mobile society.

Daniel Bell. *The Coming of Post-Industrial Society: A Venture in Social Forecasting*. New York: Harper Colophon, 1976.
    Daniel Bell was among the first sociologists to recognize and analyze the emerging postindustrial society.

Contemporary Sources

Bette Woody. *Black Women in the Workplace: Impacts of Structural Change in the Economy*. Westport, Conn.: Greenwood, 1992.
    Economic changes have different effects on various segments of the labor force. This analysis highlights the consequences of the emerging postindustrial economy for women of color.

Stephen B. Knouse, Paul Rosenfeld, and Amy Culbertson, eds. *Hispanics in the Workplace*. Newbury Park, Calif.: Sage, 1992.
    This collection of essays is one of the first surveys of the problems and progress of Latinos in the U.S. labor force.

Peter L. Berger. *The Capitalist Revolution: Fifty Propositions about Prosperity, Equality, and Liberty*. New York: Basic Books, 1986.
    In this book, one of sociology's best contemporary thinkers examines the social consequences of capitalism.

James A. Yunker. *Socialism Revised and Modernized: The Case for Pragmatic Market Socialism*. New York: Praeger, 1992.
    This author envisions a fusion of capitalist and socialist models—involving public ownership of larger, profit-seeking corporations—as capturing the advantages of both economic systems.

Paula England. *Comparable Worth: Theories and Evidence.* Hawthorne, N.Y.: Aldine de Gruyter, 1992.

Gender is a powerful influence on the operation of the workplace, according to this data-filled study of feminine and masculine work.

Judith S. McIlwee and J. Gregg Robinson. *Women in Engineering: Gender, Power, and Workplace Culture.* Albany, N.Y.: SUNY Press, 1992.

These researchers use questionnaires and interviews to investigate the working lives of the 7 percent of U.S. engineers who are women.

George Ritzer and David Walczak. *Working: Conflict and Change,* 4th ed. Englewood Cliffs, N.J.: Prentice Hall, 1990.

This textbook focuses on work in the United States, with an emphasis on patterns of conflict within the workplace.

Michael Goldfield. *The Decline of Organized Labor in the United States.* Chicago: University of Chicago Press, 1987.

The 1980s were a decade of dwindling support for organized labor in the United States: This study assesses the present situation and future prospects of U.S. unions.

Frank A. Cowell. *Cheating the Government: The Economics of Evasion.* Cambridge, Mass.: MIT Press, 1990.

A major dimension of the underground economy is tax evasion. This treatise explains the economic reasons prompting people to violate tax laws.

Marilyn Loden and Judy B. Rosener. *Workforce America! Managing Employee Diversity as a Vital Resource.* Homewood, Ill.: Business One Irwin, 1991.

This book provides an overview of the increasing social diversity of the workplace in the United States and argues that opening opportunity to all categories of people can enhance the effectiveness of U.S. businesses.

Floyd Dickens, Jr., and Jacqueline B. Dickens. *The Black Manager: Making It in the Corporate World.* Rev. ed. New York: American Management Association, 1991.

According to these researchers, even well-educated and highly motivated people of color encounter racially based barriers in the corporate economy.

Global Sources

Merton J. Peck and Thomas J. Richardson, eds. *What Is to Be Done? Proposals for the Soviet Transition to the Market.* New Haven, Conn.: Yale University Press, 1992.

This collection of essays surveys strategies proposed by social scientists in both the former Soviet Union and Western countries for assisting that economically troubled country.

Eli Ginzberg. *A World Without Work: The Story of the Welsh Miners.* New Brunswick, N.J.: Transaction, 1990.

Written fifty years ago, this fieldwork study of a small British community in economic distress still offers fresh lessons about the human price of economic change.

Suzan Lewis, Dafna N. Izraeli, and Helen Hootsmans. *Dual-Earner Families: International Perspectives.* Newbury Park, Calif.: Sage, 1992.

This discussion highlights changing economic and family patterns in Hungary, Sweden, Singapore, Japan, India, and elsewhere.

Zhang Hongtu, Chairman Mao, Number 11, 1989.

DATA FILE: Consult the *Data File* for an outline of this chapter, supplementary lecture material, and discussion topics.
Q: "There is nothing wrong with the United States that a dose of smaller and less intrusive government will not cure." Milton and Rose Friedman
Q: "Society is produced by our wants, and government by our wickedness." Thomas Paine

Q: "Just be glad you're not getting all the government you're paying for." Will Rogers
Q: "Only the dead have seen the end of war." Plato
GLOBAL: The turbulence in Somalia suggests that even the evils of bad government are surpassed by the evils of no effective rule of law.

Politics and Government

*O*ne thousand years ago, halfway around the world, a man stood by the side of the road, surveying his homeland recently ravaged by war. As the cold wind pressed on his back, he could see that the soldiers had left, although graves of those who had fallen in battle seemed to be everywhere. An ox-drawn cart weighted down with crops ground slowly onward toward a distant city; in a few days, it would return, laden with different goods. A few peasants cautiously moved across the fields, scavenging for food. One woman passing by softly murmured that life was returning to normal. But as the man walked to his house, he knew that all was not the same. He sat by the road and wrote the following lines:

The war ended on the Huan border,

And the trading roads are open again;
Stray crows come and go,
Cawing in the wintry sky.
Alas for the white bones,
Heaped together in desolate graves;
All had sought military honors for their leader.

Chang Pin's "Lament for Ten Thousand Men's Graves" raises several timeless questions: How is power distributed in a society? Why do many people feel they have little control over their lives? Why do the many die in service to the few? His thoughts also draw us to the broader question of why nations fall into conflict. The sobering fact is that warfare has been present—at least somewhere in the world—virtually without end from long before Chang Pin's lifetime right down to our own.

This chapter investigates the dynamics of power in and between societies. A central concept of this inquiry is **politics,** or, more formally, "the polity," *the social institution that distributes power, sets a society's agenda, and makes decisions.* Since politics is about power, we begin by examining the role of power in societies around the world as well as in the United States. We conclude the chapter with a look at the military, asking why nations go to war and how they might, instead, pursue peace.

POWER AND AUTHORITY

Max Weber (1978; orig. 1921) declared **power** to be *the ability to achieve desired ends despite resistance from others.* History shows that *force*—physical might or psychological coercion—is the most basic form of power. But no society exists for long if power derives *only* from force, because people will break rules they do not respect at the first opportunity. Social organization, therefore, depends on generating some consensus about proper goals (cultural values) and the suitable means of attaining them (cultural norms).

The key to social stability is exercising power within a framework of justice, the concept of **authority,** which Weber defined as *power that people perceive as legitimate rather than coercive.* When parents, professors, or police perform their work in a normative way, their power is transformed into authority. The source of authority, Weber continued, differs according to a society's economy.

Traditional Authority

Preindustrial societies, Weber explained, rely on **traditional authority,** *power legitimized by respect for long-established cultural patterns.* Once woven into a traditional society's collective memory, normative use of power may seem almost sacred. The might of Chinese emperors in antiquity was legitimized by tradition, as was the rule of nobles in medieval Europe. In both cases, hereditary family rule supported by tradition imbued leaders with almost godlike authority.

Traditional authority declines as societies industrialize. Hannah Arendt (1963) explains that traditional authority is compelling only so long as everyone shares the same heritage and world view; this form of authority, then, is dissolved by the specialization demanded by industrial production and also by modern, scientific thinking and the cultural diversity that accompanies immigration. Thus, no president of the today's United States, for example, would claim to rule by grace of God. Even so, as E. Digby Baltzell (1964) points out, some well-established upper-class families—such as the Roosevelts, Rockefellers, and Kennedys—have occupied a privileged position for several generations and enter the political arena with some measure of traditional authority.

If traditional authority plays a smaller part in national politics, it persists in many dimensions of everyday life. Patriarchy, the traditional domination of women by men, is still widespread, although increasingly challenged, in the United States. Less controversial is the traditional authority parents exert over their young children. A familiar family experience also suggests that traditional authority is based on a person's status as parent rather than whatever wisdom the particular individual may display. To children who ask *why* they should obey, parents have long retorted, "Because I said so!" To debate the merits of such a command would, after all, place parent and child on the same level.

Rational-Legal Authority

Weber defined **rational-legal authority** (sometimes called *bureaucratic authority*) as *power legitimized by legally enacted rules and regulations.* Rational-legal authority is closely linked to **government,** *formal organizations that direct the political life of a society.*

As Chapter 7 ("Groups and Organizations") explains, Weber viewed bureaucracy as the organizational backbone of industrial societies. Bureaucracy is one expression of our modern, rational view of the world, an outlook that erodes traditional customs and practices. Rather than venerating the past, members of industrial societies typically build their lives around formal rules, and especially law.

Rationally enacted rules not only guide government in the United States; they also underlie much of our everyday life. The authority of classroom teachers, for example, rests primarily on their official status in bureaucratic colleges and universities. The police, too, are officers, within the governmental bureaucracy. Compared to traditional authority, then, rational-legal authority flows not from family background but from organizational position. Thus while a traditional monarch rules for life, a modern president accepts and relinquishes power according to law, with presidential authority remaining in the office.

Charismatic Authority

Max Weber described one additional type of authority that has surfaced throughout history. Charisma, a concept highlighted in Chapter 18 ("Religion"), designates

Q: ". . . the 'natural' leaders—in times of psychic, physical, economic, ethical, religious, and political distress—have been neither office holders nor incumbents of an 'occupation' . . . [They] have been holders of specific gifts of the body and spirit; and these gifts have been believed to be supernatural, not accessible to everybody." Max Weber

Q: "Prophets are followed by popes, revolutionaries by administrators." Peter Berger

Q: "Bureaucratic and patriarchal structures are antagonistic in many ways, yet they have in common a most important peculiarity: permanence. In this respect, they are both institutions of daily routine." Max Weber (1947:245)

exceptional personal qualities that people often take to be a sign of divine inspiration. Broadening this religious concept to take account of all kinds of leadership, Weber defined **charismatic authority** as *power legitimized through extraordinary personal abilities that inspire devotion and obedience.* But unlike tradition and rational law, charisma is less a quality of social organization and more a dimension of individual personality.

Members of every society regard some of their number as especially forceful, creative, and magnetic. Charisma enhances the stature of a leader, inside or outside of the established political system. By motivating an audience, charismatics often are able to make their own rules, as if drawing on a higher power. The extraordinary ability of charismatics to challenge the status quo is deeply engrained in global politics: Vladimir Lenin guided the overthrow of feudal monarchy in Russia in 1917, Mahatma Gandhi inspired the struggle to free India from British colonialism after World War II, and Martin Luther King, Jr., galvanized the civil rights movement in the United States.

Charisma may arise from personality, but it also reflects a society's expectations as to what kind of people emerge as leaders. Patriarchy encourages us to tap men as our national leaders, while steering charismatic women toward the arts, the family, and other social contexts traditionally defined as feminine. Yet, in recent years, charismatic women including Indira Gandhi of India, Benazir Bhutto of Pakistan, and Margaret Thatcher of the United Kingdom gained international political prominence.

Because charismatic authority emanates from a single individual, any charismatic regime faces a crisis of survival upon the death of its leader. The persistence of a charismatic movement is uncertain, Max Weber reasoned, depending on a process he termed the **routinization of charisma,** *the transformation of charismatic authority into some combination of traditional and bureaucratic authority.* Christianity, for example, began as a cult driven by the personal charisma of Jesus of Nazareth. After the death of Jesus, followers institutionalized his teachings in a church eventually centered in Rome and built on tradition and bureaucracy. As the Roman Catholic church it flourishes today, two thousand years later.

POLITICS IN GLOBAL PERSPECTIVE

Political systems display marked variety both throughout history and in today's world. Looking first back in time, technologically simple hunting and gathering societies had few specialized roles and minimal

A majority of the world's poor societies do not accord extensive rights and liberties to their citizens and many undergo continuous political turmoil. The people of Haiti, which is among the poorest countries in the Western hemisphere, elected Jean-Bertrand Aristide, a popular activist priest, as their president in 1990. Aristide soon found himself at odds with Haiti's business and military elites and, amid escalating tensions, was deposed less than one year after taking office. Haiti remains a long way from political stability.

material wealth, so that they operated like a large family. In general, members recognized as their leader a male with unusual strength, hunting skill, or personal charisma. But such leaders exercised little power over others, since they lacked the resources to reward supporters or punish challengers. In simple societies, then, leaders were barely discernible from everyone else, and government hardly existed as a distinct sphere of life (Lenski, Lenski, & Nolan, 1991).

Agrarian societies, which are larger and more complex, benefit from more specialized activity and generate material surplus. In these societies, hierarchy becomes pronounced, as a small elite gains control of much wealth and power. Intensifying inequality thrusts politics outside the family so that government becomes a social institution in its own right. Elites whose families have maintained their privileged position for generations may acquire traditional authority, sometimes claiming divine right to rule. These leaders may benefit further from Weber's rational-legal authority as they are served by a bureaucratic political administration and system of law.

As politics expands in this way, societal power eventually takes the form of a national government or *political state*. But the political state developed slowly in history because government power is limited by available technology. Only a few centuries ago, communication over even short distances was uncertain and the transportation of armies and supplies was slow and cumbersome. Thus governments could confidently control only very small areas. For this reason, early political empires—such as Mesopotamia in the Middle East about five thousand years ago—actually took the form of many, small *city-states* (Stavrianos, 1983).

More complex technology has helped the modern world develop the larger-scale system of *nation-states*. Currently, the world has roughly 190 independent nation-states, each of which operates a political system that is at least somewhat distinctive. Generally speaking, however, the world's political systems fall into four categories: monarchy, democracy, authoritarianism, and totalitarianism.

Monarchy

Monarchy (with Latin and Greek roots meaning "ruling alone") is *a type of political system that transfers power from generation to generation within a single family*. Monarchy dates back thousands of years to agrarian societies; the Bible, for example, tells of great kings such as David and Solomon. The British monarchy traces its lineage through centuries of nobility. In Weber's terms, monarchy is legitimized by tradition.

During the medieval era, *absolute monarchy*, in which hereditary rulers claimed a virtual monopoly of power based on divine right, flourished from England to China and in parts of the Americas. Monarchs in some nations—including Saudi Arabia—still exercise virtually absolute control over their people.

During this century, however, monarchs have gradually passed from the scene in favor of elected officials. Europe's remaining monarchs—in Great Britain, Spain, Norway, Sweden, Belgium, Denmark, and the Netherlands—now preside over *constitutional monarchies*. They are the symbolic heads of state, while actual governing is the responsibility of elected officials, led by a prime minister and guided by a constitution, a formal statement of political principles and governmental organization. In these nations, then, the nobility may formally reign, but elected officials actually rule (Roskin, 1982).

Democracy

The historical trend in the modern world has favored **democracy**, *a political system in which power is exercised by the people as a whole*. The members of democratic societies rarely participate directly in decision making; numbers alone make this an impossibility. Instead, a system of *representative democracy* places authority in the hands of elected leaders, who are accountable to the people.

Affluent, industrial societies tend to embrace democratic political systems. Economic development and democratic government go together because both depend on a literate populace who turn away from tradition. Additionally, in every industrial society, corporations and other formal organizations try to advance their interests within the political arena. Thus, in contrast to the high concentration of power in the absolute monarchies common to preindustrial societies, industrial societies have a more complex and diffuse political system.

The traditional legitimization of power in a monarchy gives way in democratic political systems to rational-legal authority. A rational election process places leaders in offices regulated by law. Thus democracy and rational-legal authority are linked just as monarchy and traditional authority are.

But democratic political systems are not just leaders and followers; they are built on extensive bureaucracy. Considerable formal organization is necessary to carry out the increasing range of government activities undertaken by democratic societies, and few doubt that government has grown well beyond what is needed to fulfill its duties. As it grows, government gradually takes on a life of its own, revealing an inherent antagonism between democracy and bureaucracy. The federal government of the United States, for example, employs more than 3 million people (excluding the armed forces), making it one of the largest bureaucracies in the world. Another 15 million people work in some eighty thousand local governments. The great majority of these bureaucrats were never elected and are unknown to the public they purport to serve. To elect them would seem impractical given their numbers and the need for highly specialized training. But, ironically, while the public focuses attention on a small number of elected leaders, most everyday decision making is carried out by career bureaucrats who are not directly accountable to the people (Scaff, 1981; Edwards, 1985; Etzioni-Halevy, 1985).

cept of "authority" has been of more interest to the right, while the left has critiqued the legitimizing character of "ideologies."
NOTE: Authoritarian regimes are concerned mostly with overt compliance, while totalitarian regimes seek to win "the hearts and minds" of their people.
GLOBAL: When the Berlin Wall fell in 1989, 38 of 45 nations in sub-Saharan Africa were led by one-party, often military, regimes.

Democracy and Freedom: Contrasting Approaches

Virtually all industrialized nations in the world have claimed to be democratic and politically free, despite a history of very different political systems. This curious fact suggests the need for a closer look at what societies mean by their people being "free."

The political life of the United States, Canada, and the nations of Europe is shaped by the free-market principles of capitalism. The operation of a market system demands that individuals have the personal freedom to pursue whatever they perceive as their self-interest. Thus, the capitalist approach to political freedom means personal *liberty*. Liberty is the freedom to vote for one's preferred leader or otherwise act with minimal interference from government.

On the down side, however, capitalist liberty translates into some people being far more "free" than others because of a striking inequality of wealth. Further, this inequality fuels charges by critics of capitalism that such a system is not really democratic insofar as the rich can manipulate the system to impose their will on others.

In socialist societies, by contrast, political officials closely regulate social life in order to provide every citizen with housing, schooling, a job, and medical care. The socialist approach to freedom thus emphasizes not freedom *to* do as one wishes, but freedom *from* basic want.

But the problem here, as recent uprisings in Eastern Europe and the former Soviet Union suggest, is that people may actually find government officials unresponsive to their needs and aspirations and heavy-handed in their suppression of any political opposition.

These contrasting views of freedom raise an important question: Are economic equality and political liberty compatible? To foster economic equality, socialism tends to infringe on individual initiative. Capitalism, on the other hand, provides broad political liberties, which, in practice, mean little to the poor.

The political transformation of much of the socialist world has led many analysts in our own society to trumpet the triumph of democracy. Global Map 16–1, on page 438, shows that, during the 1980s, what Western nations view as the cause of political freedom has made great strides in Latin America, Eastern Europe, and in other world regions.

By the beginning of this decade, according to Freedom House, a New York–based organization that tracks global political trends, more people in the world were "free" than "not free" for the first time in history.

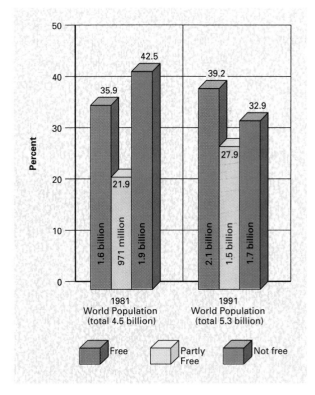

FIGURE 16–1 The Extent of Global Political Freedom, 1981 and 1991

Figure 16–1 provides details (Mathews, 1991; McColm et al., 1991).

Authoritarianism and Totalitarianism

Despite the trend toward democracy in many parts of the world, not all nations involve their people in politics. **Authoritarianism** refers to *a political system that denies popular participation in government.* As we have already noted, no society involves all its citizens in the daily activities of government, so each is, to some degree, authoritarian.

But truly authoritarian systems are indifferent to people's needs, lack the legal means to remove leaders from office, and provide people with little or no way to even voice their opinions. Polish sociologist Wlodzimierz Wesolowski (1990:435) sums up the matter, claiming that "the authoritarian philosophy argues for the supremacy of the state [over other] organized social activity."

The absolute monarchies that remain in Saudi Arabia and Kuwait are highly authoritarian. More

Window on the World

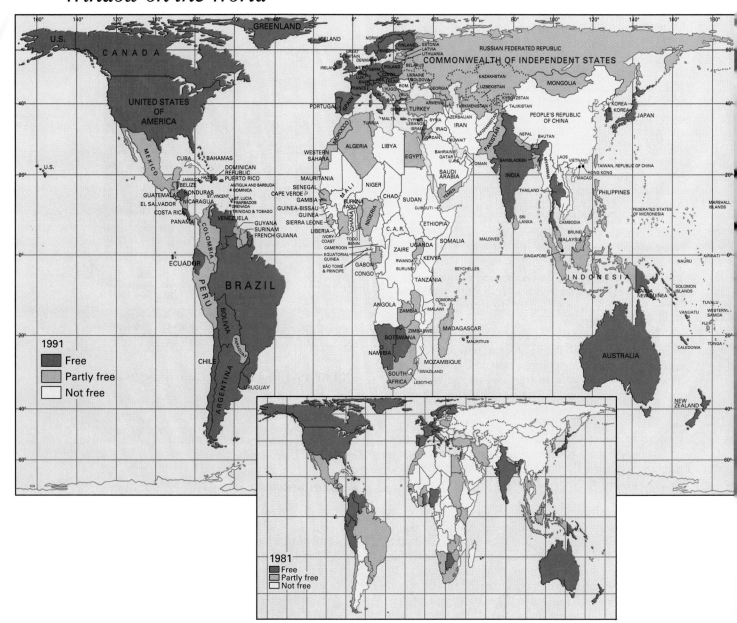

GLOBAL MAP 16–1 Political Freedom in Global Perspective

In 1991, seventy-five of the world's nations, containing almost 40 percent of all people, were politically "free"— that is, they offered their citizens extensive political rights and civil liberties. Another seventy-three nations that included almost 30 percent of the world's people were "partly free" with more limited rights and liberties. The remaining forty-two nations, with about one-third of humanity, remained "not free." In these countries government sharply restricts individual initiative. Comparing the two maps shows that, during the 1980s, democratic gains were made in Eastern Europe, the former Soviet Union, and South America. Political liberties are most extensive in the rich nations of the world and most restricted in the poorer countries of Africa and Asia.

Data from McColm et al. (1991).

common examples of authoritarian regimes are military juntas found today in Congo, Ethiopia, and Haiti. A recent and interesting development is a form of "soft authoritarianism" that, as the box on page 440 explains, now thrives in the small Asian nation of Singapore.

The most intensely controlled political form is **totalitarianism**, *a political system that extensively regulates people's lives*. Totalitarian governments emerged only during this century, with the development of technological means for rigid regulation of a populace. For decades, the government of the former Soviet Union broadly monitored the lives of all citizens, utilizing surveillance equipment and sophisticated computers to store vast amounts of information and thereby manipulate the entire population.

Although some totalitarian governments claim to represent the will of the people, most seek to bend people to the will of the government. Such governments are *total* concentrations of power, allowing no organized opposition. Denying the populace the right to assemble for political purposes and controlling access to information, these governments thrive in an environment of fear and social atomization. In the former Soviet Union, for example, most citizens were denied telephone directories, copying equipment, fax machines, and even accurate city maps.

Socialization in totalitarian societies puts political ideology at center stage, seeking not just outward compliance but inward commitment to the system. In North Korea, one of the most totalitarian states in the world, pictures of leaders and political messages over loudspeakers are familiar elements of public life that remind citizens that they owe total allegiance to the state. Schools and the mass media are government controlled and present only official versions of events.

Government indoctrination is especially intense whenever political opposition surfaces in a totalitarian society. In the aftermath of the prodemocracy movement in the People's Republic of China, for example, officials demanded that citizens report all "unpatriotic" people—even members of their own families. Further, Chinese leaders subjected all students at Beijing universities to political "refresher" courses (Arendt, 1958; Kornhauser, 1959; Friedrich & Brzezinski, 1965; Nisbet, 1966; Goldfarb, 1989).

Totalitarian governments span the political spectrum from the far right (including Nazi Germany) to the far left (including North Korea). Many people in the United States view socialist societies as totalitarian by definition, because they involve extensive governmental regulation of the economy. Yet socialist economic programs do not necessarily generate a totalitarian political climate. Limited economic socialism—as it exists in Sweden, for example—appears consistent with (and, as its supporters see it, even enhances) political democracy. Then, too, some societies with capitalist economies (Chile and South Africa among recent cases) have exercised totalitarian control over the lives of at least most of their citizens.

A Global Political System?

Chapter 15 ("The Economy and Work") pointed to the emergence of a global economy, meaning that more and more products and services routinely cross national boundaries. In part, the global economy reflects the expanding operations of multinational corporations; it also results from the Information Revolution that has drawn together the various regions of the world.

Is there a parallel development of a global political system? At one level, the answer is no. Although most of the world's economic activity now involves more than one nation, the planet remains divided into nation-states, just as it has been for centuries. The United Nations (founded in 1945) might seem a step toward global government, but it has played only a limited role in global politics up to this point.

At another level, however, politics has become a global process. In the minds of some analysts, multinational corporations represent a new political order, since they have enormous power to shape social life throughout the world. From this point of view, in short, politics is dissolving into business as corporations grow larger than governments. As one multinational leader asserted, "We are not without cunning. We shall not make Britain's mistake. Too wise to govern the world, we shall simply own it" (quoted in Vaughan 1978:20).

Then, too, the Information Revolution has pulled even national politics onto the world stage. Hours before the Chinese government sent troops to Tiananmen Square to crush the 1989 prodemocracy movement, officials "unplugged" the satellite transmitting systems of news agencies in an effort to keep the world from watching as events unfolded that day. Despite their efforts, news of the massacre was flashed around the world minutes after it began via the fax machines in universities and private homes. In short, just as no society can any longer control its own economy, so no national government can fully manage the political events that occur within its borders.

Q: "The essential problem of social order is the [legitimation] and not the elimination of social power." E. Digby Baltzell

NOTE: Ferdinand Toennies, too, described the social roots of authority: He linked authority to (1) advanced age, (2) force, and (3) wisdom or spirit.

Q: "It is evident that the state is a creation of nature, and man is by nature a political animal. . . . He who is unable to live in society, or who has no need because he is sufficient for himself, must be either a beast or a god: He is no part of a state." Aristotle, *Politics*

DATA FILE: The *Data File* surveys tax rates in various countries around the world.

GLOBAL SOCIOLOGY

"Soft Authoritarianism" or Planned Prosperity? A Report from Singapore

Singapore, a tiny nation on the tip of the Malay Peninsula with a population of just over 3 million people, seems to many to be an Asian paradise. Surrounded by poor societies that grapple with rapidly rising populations, squalid, sprawling cities, and rising crime rates, the cleanliness and tranquillity of Singapore make the North American visitor think more of a theme park than a country.

In fact, since its independence from Malaysia in 1965, Singapore has startled the world with its economic development; today, per capita income in this nation is among the highest in the world, rivaling that of the United States. But, unlike the United States, Singapore has never struggled with social problems such as crime, slums, unemployment, or children living in poverty. In fact, people in Singapore don't even fume about traffic jams, scowl at graffiti on subway cars, or dodge litter in the streets.

The key to Singapore's orderly environment is the ever-present hand of government, which regulates just about everything. The state owns and manages most of the country's housing and has a hand in many businesses. It provides tax incentives for proper family planning and completing additional years of schooling. To keep traffic under control, the government slaps hefty surcharges on cars, pushing the price of a basic sedan up around $40,000.

Singapore made headlines in the United States in 1994 after the government caned U.S. citizen Michael Fay for vandalism—a penalty illegal in this country. Singapore's laws also permit police to detain a person suspected of a crime without charge or trial. The government bans pornography outright. Even smoking in public brings a heavy fine, and drug offenders face death by hanging. To keep the city streets clean, the state forbids eating on a subway, imposes stiff fines for littering, and has even outlawed the sale of chewing gum.

In economic terms, Singapore defies familiar categories. As in socialist societies, the government retains control of scores of businesses, from television stations to

telephone service, from airlines to taxis. Yet, unlike socialist enterprises, these businesses are highly efficient and extremely profitable. Moreover, Singapore's capitalist culture celebrates the relentless pursuit of wealth, and this nation is home to hundreds of multinational corporations.

Singapore's political climate is as unusual as its economy. Members of this society feel the hand of government far more than their counterparts in the United States. Just as important, a single political organization—the People's Action party—has ruled Singapore without opposition since its independence thirty years ago.

Clearly, Singapore is not a democratic country in the conventional sense. But most people in this prospering nation seem content—even enthusiastic—about their lives. What Singapore's political system offers is a simple bargain: Government demands unflinching loyalty from the populace; in return, it provides security and prosperity. Critics charge that this system amounts to a "soft authoritarianism" that stifles dissent and gives government unwarranted control over people's lives. Most of the people of Singapore, however, know the struggles of living elsewhere and, for now at least, consider the trade-off a good one.

SOURCE: Adapted from Branegan (1993).

SOCIAL SURVEY: "How interested are you in politics and national affairs?" (GSS 1987, N = 1,466; *Codebook*, 1993:388)
  "Very interested"   22.9%   "Not interested"   8.4%
  "Somewhat interested"   42.4%   DK/NR   0.6%
  "Only slightly interested" 25.7%

Q: "The number employed in government must forever be very small [because] the indispensable wants of all are not to be obtained without the continual toil of ninety-nine in a hundred of mankind."
John Adams, 1789
DATA FILE: Discussion of term limits is found in the *Data File*.

The concept of political liberty burned brightly in the minds of many European thinkers during the eighteenth and nineteenth centuries; authoritarian regimes were often just as intent on stamping out dissent. In The Third of May, 1808, *the Spanish painter Francisco Goya (1746–1828) commemorated the death of Madrid citizens at the hands of the faceless soldiers. The martyrs shown here are dying not for religious salvation, as is depicted in so much Medieval art, but for the modern principle of political freedom.*

POLITICS IN THE UNITED STATES

Fighting a revolutionary war against Great Britain to gain political independence, the United States replaced the British monarchy with a democratic political system. Our nation's commitment to democratic principles has persisted through two centuries, shaped by a distinctive history, economy, and cultural heritage.

U.S. Culture and the Growth of Government

Our cultural emphasis on individualism is written into the Bill of Rights, the first ten amendments to the U.S. Constitution, which guarantees freedom from undue government interference. Many people in the United States, no doubt, support the sentiment of nineteenth-century philosopher and poet Ralph Waldo Emerson: "The government that governs best is the government that governs least."

Yet few of us would do away with government entirely because almost everyone thinks that it is necessary for some purposes, including maintaining national defense, a system of schools, and public law and order. In fact, as the United States has become larger, government has expanded even faster, from a federal budget of a mere $4.5 million in 1789 to about $1.5 trillion in 1993. During the first year of our nation's life, the federal government spent just $1.50 for every person in the country; today, per capita federal expenditure is almost $6,000. Government has become so extensive—and expensive—that even our leaders cannot comprehend its scope. The late senator Everett Dirksen once quipped to his colleagues in Congress that spending "a billion here and a billion there soon adds up to a lot of money."

In terms of officials, from one government employee serving every eighteen hundred citizens at the nation's founding, today we have one official for every thirteen citizens, counting government at all levels (U.S. Bureau of the Census, 1993). This amounts to almost 20 million workers, a number that recently surpassed the total employment in manufacturing. Government workers perform a host of jobs, from managing schools, monitoring civil rights, and setting safety standards for the workplace, to processing student loans and benefits for the elderly, poor people, and veterans. Just as important, a majority of U.S. adults now look to government for at least part of their income (Caplow et al., 1982; Devine, 1985).

The Political Spectrum

Political labels—including "conservative," "liberal," and "middle-of-the-roader"—are shorthand for an individual's place on the *political spectrum*. Table 16–1 shows how adults in the United States describe themselves in

DIVERSITY: Generally speaking, Republicans wish to use the power of government to regulate the moral environment, while Democrats enlist government in regulating the economic environment.

Q: "Politics makes strange bedfellows." Charles Dudley Warner

SOCIAL SURVEY: These items show how SES is related to economic issues and social issues. (*STUDENT CHIP Social Survey Software*, ABNOMOR1 (GSS 1972–91, N = 20,411) and EQWLTH1

(GSS 1978–91, N = 10,464). Undecided Rs omitted.

			Should gov't reduce income differences?	
	Pro-choice	Pro-life	"Yes"	"No"
High SES	58.5%	41.5%	41.4%	58.6%
Middle	44.5%	55.5%	61.3%	38.7%
Low SES	31.8%	68.2%	75.9%	24.1%

TABLE 16–1 The Political Spectrum: A National Survey, 1993

Question: "We hear a lot of talk these days about liberals and conservatives. I'm going to show you a seven-point scale on which the political views people might hold are arranged from extremely liberal—point 1—to extremely conservative—point 7. Where would you place yourself on this scale?"

1	2	3	4	5	6	7
Extremely liberal	Liberal	Slightly liberal	Middle of the road	Slightly conservative	Conservative	Extremely conservative
1.9 %	11.2 %	12.6 %	35.8 %	16.4 %	15.8 %	2.6 %

[*Don't know/no answer* 3.8 %]

SOURCE: *General Social Surveys, 1972–1993: Cumulative Codebook* (Chicago: National Opinion Research Center, 1993), p. 112.

terms of the political spectrum. Slightly more than one-fourth of the respondents fall on the liberal or "left" side, and more than one-third describe themselves as conservative to some degree, placing them on the "right." A substantial share (35.8 percent) claim to be moderates in the political "middle" (NORC, 1993:112).

One reason that many people describe themselves as moderates is that they hold conservative positions on some issues and liberal views on others (Barone & Ujifusa, 1981; McBroom & Reed, 1990). *Economic issues* focus on economic inequality and the opportunities available for all categories of people. *Social issues* refer to moral concerns about how people live.

Economic Issues

The industrialization of the United States after the Civil War generated enormous wealth, but much of it ended up in the pockets of a small elite. By the time the Great Depression began in 1929, mounting evidence suggested that, despite the undeniable productivity of our capitalist economy, many people had little financial security. The New Deal programs of President Franklin Delano Roosevelt responded to this dilemma by greatly expanding government efforts to promote social welfare. New programs regulated many aspects of the economy and provided everyone with pensions. Since then, the government has distributed financial benefits to more and more people.

Today, both the Democratic and Republican parties—the two major political organizations in the United States—support a large and active federal government, although they disagree about the kinds of activities that government should and should not undertake. Generally, the Democratic party supports extensive government involvement in the economy, while the Republican party favors allowing the economy to operate with minimal government regulation.

Thus, economic liberals (on the Democratic side of the fence) think that ensuring the health of the economy and an adequate supply of jobs are primary government responsibilities. Economic conservatives (likely to be Republicans) argue that government should interfere as little as possible with the operation of the economy since federal regulations tend to hamper economic productivity (Burnham, 1983).

Social Issues

Social issues are moral matters, ranging from abortion to the death penalty to gay rights and treatment of minorities. Broadly tolerant of social diversity, social liberals endorse equal rights and opportunities for all categories of people, view abortion as a matter of individual choice, and oppose the death penalty because, in their view, it does little to discourage crime and has been unfairly applied to minorities.

On the other side of the political spectrum, the "family values" agenda of social conservatives includes supporting traditional gender roles while opposing public acceptance of gay families and affirmative action and other "special programs" for minorities that, from this point of view, recognize group membership rather than rewarding individual initiative. Social conservatives condemn abortion and support the death penalty.

Overall, the Republican party is more conservative on both economic and social issues while the Democratic party is more liberal. In practice, then, Republicans celebrate traditional values and individual initiative while Democrats embrace government activism as a means of enhancing social well-being and reducing inequality. Yet each party has conservative and liberal wings so that the difference between a liberal Republican and a conservative Democrat may be insignificant. Further, Republicans as well as Democrats favor big government—as long as it advances their aims. The Republican Reagan administration greatly expanded this country's military strength in an effort to challenge the former

SOCIAL SURVEY: "How much influence do you think people like you have over local government decisions?" (GSS 1987, N = 1,466; *Codebook*, 1993:386)

"A lot"	14.0%	"None at all"	14.5%
"A moderate amount"	33.8%	DK/NR	2.1%
"A little"	35.7%		

Soviet Union; the Democratic Clinton administration more recently proposed a sweeping new system of national health care.

Mixed Positions

Pegging the political views of individuals is difficult because most people do not hold consistent positions on these two kinds of issues. Well-to-do men and women tend to be conservative on economic issues but liberal on social issues (due, in large part, to higher levels of education). Working-class people display the opposite pattern, combining economic liberalism with social conservatism. These women and men, in other words, seek more economic opportunity while taking pride in conforming to conventional cultural patterns (Nunn, Crocket, & Williams, 1978; Erikson, Luttbeg, & Tedin, 1980; Syzmanski, 1983; Humphries, 1984).

Race and ethnicity modify these patterns slightly. African Americans, with significantly less income than white people, are predictably more liberal on economic issues and, since the New Deal era of the 1930s, have overwhelmingly voted Democratic. On many social issues (including reproductive rights for women) disadvantaged African Americans resemble poor white people and lean in a conservative direction. But on racial issues (like busing schoolchildren or increasing government spending to assist minorities), people of African and Hispanic descent are much more liberal than white people and more liberal than their modest class position might suggest (NORC, 1993).

Party Identification

Because so many people hold mixed political attitudes—espousing liberal views on some issues and taking conservative stands on others—party identification is weak in the United States. In this way, our nation differs from European democracies, in which people usually adhere strongly to one political party (Wolfinger, Shapiro, & Greenstein, 1980). Table 16–2 shows the results of a national survey of party identification among U.S. adults (NORC, 1993). About 45 percent identified themselves—to some degree—as Democrats and about 40 percent favored the Republicans. Thirteen percent claimed to be independents, voicing no preference for either major party. Although a large majority have a party preference, most allegiances are weak. In 1992, for example, Democrat Bill Clinton won the support of millions of people who had voted for Republican George Bush four years earlier. National Map 16–1, on page 444, displays the outcome of the 1992 presidential election by county and state.

TABLE 16–2 Political Party Identification in the United States, 1993

Party Identification	Proportion of Respondents
Democrat	**45.9 %**
Strong Democrat	14.1
Not very strong Democrat	20.0
Independent, close to Democrat	11.8
Republican	**39.6**
Strong Republican	11.2
Not very strong Republican	18.6
Independent, close to Republican	9.8
Independent	**12.8**
Other party, no response	**1.6**

SOURCE: *General Social Surveys, 1972–1993: Cumulative Codebook* (Chicago: National Opinion Research Center, 1993), p. 104.

Special-Interest Groups

In 1993, President Bill Clinton repealed the luxury tax on expensive boats. The boating industry, which had charged that this regulation was choking their business, applauded loudly.

The boating industry, as well as associations of elderly people, women's organizations, and environmentalists, each exemplify a **special-interest group**, *a political alliance of people interested in some economic or social issue*. Special-interest groups flourish in societies where political parties are weak, and the United States encompasses a vast array of them. Special-interest groups employ *lobbyists* as their professional advocates in political circles.

An example of a special-interest group concerned with economic issues is the American Federation of Labor–Congress of Industrial Organizations (AFL-CIO), this nation's largest labor union. Special-interest groups that target social issues include the environmentalist Sierra Club, the American Civil Liberties Union, and the National Rifle Association.

Political action committees (PACs) are *organizations formed by a special-interest group, independent of political parties, to pursue political aims by raising and spending money*. Political action committees channel most of their funds directly to candidates likely to support their interests. Since the 1970s, as legal reforms have limited direct contributions to candidates, the number of PACs has grown rapidly to more than six thousand (Sabato, 1984; Jones & Miller, 1985; U.S. Bureau of the Census, 1993).

Because of the rising costs of campaigns, most candidates eagerly accept support from political action

Q: "The fact is that the political action committees movement is a *reform movement itself.*" Richard Lugar
THE MAP: Generally speaking, the South and the Mountain States are the most politically conservative regions of the country. In recent elections, this broad area has served as the Republican base.

NOTE: The Republican strategy for winning presidential elections has been to capture affluent people with conservative economic positions (no new taxes) while attracting lower-income people with a conservative social position (Willie Horton or Murphy Brown initiatives). Bill Clinton's strength was based on his "New Democrat" image as a moderate on social issues, regaining the so-called "Reagan Democrats."

Seeing Ourselves

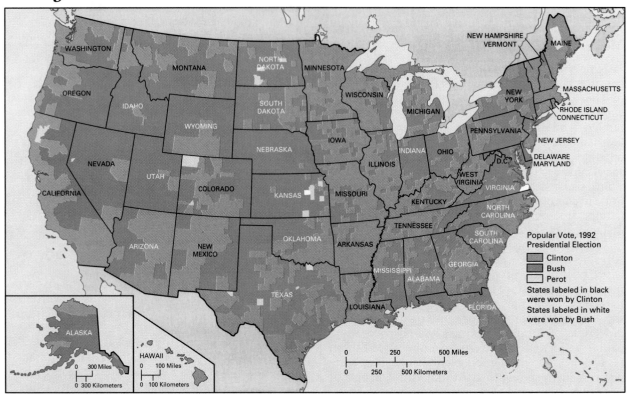

NATIONAL MAP 16–1 The Presidential Election, 1992: The Popular Vote

The map identifies the counties across the United States in which a majority of voters supported Bill Clinton, George Bush, and Ross Perot in the 1992 presidential election. When the returns were counted, Clinton had carried thirty-two states (with state names written in black), while Bush trailed with eighteen states (names in white), and Perot ended up with none at all. Looking at the map, in what regions of the country was Clinton's strength greatest? Where was Bush's support strongest? What might explain this pattern?

Prepared by the author using results of the 1992 presidential election.

committees. In the 1992 congressional election, 27 percent of all funding came from PACs; two-thirds of all Senators seeking reelection received more than $1 million each in PAC contributions. Supporters maintain that PACs represent interests of a vast array of businesses, unions, and church groups, thereby increasing political participation. Critics counter that organizations supplying cash to politicians expect to be treated favorably in return so that, in effect, PACs try to buy political influence (Sabato, 1984; Allen & Broyles, 1991; Cook, 1993).

Whether PACs are good or not, they have certainly enhanced the importance of money in our political

system. Rising campaign spending, in turn, favors incumbents, who have better access to PACs. In the 1992 congressional elections, 90 percent of PAC funds were channeled to incumbents, and 90 percent of these officials won reelection—even though 1992 was a year in which anti-incumbent sentiments ran high. The strength of incumbency seems to run counter to our democratic principles; indeed, members of Congress are almost as secure in their jobs as members of Britain's House of Lords—a post nobles hold until their death. This inconsistency is surely one reason that the electorates in many states have now endorsed *term limits* for their officials.

NOTE: The policies of the major U.S. parties shift over time. Republicans were the party of civil rights for decades; now Democrats claim to be so; Democrats supported large deficits, until the Reagan administration; Democrats supported foreign wars until 1950; now Republicans tend to. (Dennis Dedrick)

DATA FILE: Global data on voter turnout are presented in the *Data File*.

SOCIAL SURVEY: "Do you consider the amount of federal income tax which you have to pay as too high, about right, or too low?" (GSS 1993, N = 1,057; *Codebook*, 1993:132)

| "Too high" | 54.1% | "Too low" | 1.2% |
| "About right" | 40.6% | DK/NR | 4.1% |

Q: "True individual freedom cannot exist without economic security." Franklin Delano Roosevelt, 1944

Voter Apathy

In light of the courageous drive of people around the world to gain a greater voice in government—sometimes at the cost of their lives—a disturbing fact is that many people here in the United States seem indifferent to their political rights. A larger share of the U.S. population is eligible to vote today than in the nineteenth century—the Fifteenth Amendment, ratified in 1870, enfranchised African-American men; the Nineteenth Amendment extended voting rights to women in 1920. However, the share of eligible voters who actually go to the polls has dropped over the course of the last century. The problem of *voter apathy* is also greater in the United States than in most other industrialized democracies (Piven & Cloward, 1988). Even with a slight uptick in turnout, only 60 percent of adults aged eighteen or older claimed to have voted in the 1992 presidential election (U.S. Bureau of the Census, 1993).

Who is and is not likely to vote? Women and men are equally likely to cast a ballot. People over sixty-five, however, are twice as likely to vote as young adults. Voting is also more likely among white people (64 percent voted in 1992) than African Americans (59 percent), with Hispanics (32 percent) the least likely of all to vote. Generally speaking, older people and people with higher incomes, prestigious occupations, and extensive schooling are most likely to vote (Bennett, 1991; Hackey, 1992; U.S. Bureau of the Census, 1993).

What accounts for nonvoting? First, at any given time, millions of people are sick or disabled; millions more are away from home having made no arrangement to submit an absentee ballot. Second, many people forget to reregister after moving to a new neighborhood. Third, registration and voting depend on the ability to read and write, which discourages the tens of millions of U.S. adults who have limited literacy skills.

But the problem of voter apathy, as conservatives see it, is *indifference* to politics. Most people who do not vote, say conservatives, are probably content with life in the United States. Liberals, and especially political radicals, counter that most nonvoters are so deeply dissatisfied with society that they doubt elections will make any real difference. Thus, from this perspective, voter apathy signifies political *alienation*. Because we know that disadvantaged and powerless people are least likely to vote, the second explanation is probably closer to the truth. A final possibility is that apathy flows from our two parties having much in common. If parties represented a wider spectrum of political

opinion—as is the case in European countries—our population would have more reason to vote (Zipp & Smith, 1982; Zipp, 1985; Piven & Cloward, 1988).

THEORETICAL ANALYSIS OF POWER IN SOCIETY

Sociologists and political scientists have long debated how power is distributed in the United States. Power is among the most difficult topics of scientific research because decision making is complex and often occurs behind closed doors. Moreover, as Plato recognized more than two thousand years ago, theories about power are difficult to separate from the beliefs and interests of social thinkers themselves. From this mix of facts and values, two competing models of power in the United States have emerged.

The Pluralist Model

Formally, the **pluralist model** is *an analysis of politics that views power as dispersed among many competing interest groups*. This approach is closely tied to structural-functional theory.

Pluralists claim, first, that politics is an arena of negotiation. With limited resources, no organization can expect to realize all its goals. Organizations, therefore, operate as *veto groups*, realizing some success but mostly keeping opponents from achieving all of their ends. The political process, then, relies heavily on negotiating alliances and compromises that bridge differences among numerous interest groups and, in the process, produces policies that have wide support. In short, pluralists see power as widely dispersed throughout our society, and politics as the system for taking account of all constituencies.

A second pluralist assertion is that power has many sources—including wealth, political office, social prestige, personal charisma, and organizational clout. Only in exceptional cases do all these sources of power fall into the same hands. Here, again, the conclusion is that power is diffused across all of society (Dahl, 1961, 1982).

Research Results

Supporting the pluralist model, Nelson Polsby (1959) found that key decisions in New Haven, Connecticut, on various issues—including urban renewal, nominations of political candidates, and school policies—were made by different groups. Polsby also noted that few members of the New Haven upper

African-American artist Thomas Waterman Wood painted American Citizens (To the Polls) *in 1867 to acclaim the new right of black men to vote. We see an affluent Yankee, a working-class Irishman, a Dutch transportation worker, and an African American, whose clothing provides little clue as to his occupation or his social standing. Despite differences of class, ethnicity, and race, in other words, Wood was optimistic that our political system would forge a representative, democratic government.*

class—people listed in that city's *Social Register*—were also economic leaders. Thus, Polsby concluded, no one segment of society rules all the others.

Robert Dahl (1961) investigated New Haven's history, finding that politics had once been dominated by a small number of families, but, over the generations, power had increasingly become dispersed. Dahl echoed Polsby's judgments, concluding that "no one, and certainly no group of more than a few individuals, is entirely lacking in [power]" (1961:228).

The pluralist model implies that the United States is reasonably democratic, granting at least some power to everyone. Pluralists assert that not even the most influential people always get their way, and even the most disadvantaged are able to band together to ensure that some of their political interests are addressed.

The Power-Elite Model

The **power-elite model** is *an analysis of politics that views power as concentrated among the rich.* This second approach is closely allied with the social-conflict paradigm.

The term *power elite* is a lasting contribution of C. Wright Mills (1956), who argued that the upper class (described in Chapter 10, "Social Class in the United States") holds the bulk of society's wealth, prestige, and power. The power elite constitute this country's "superrich," families linked through business and marriage who are able to turn the national agenda toward their own interests.

The power elite, claimed Mills, historically has dominated the three major sectors of U.S. society—the economy, the government, and the military. Elites circulate from one sector to another, consolidating their power as they go. Alexander Haig, for example,

has held top positions in private business, was secretary of state under Ronald Reagan as well as a 1988 presidential candidate, and is a retired army general. Haig is far from the exception: A majority of national political leaders enter public life from powerful and highly paid positions—ten of thirteen members of the Clinton cabinet are reputed to be millionaires—and most return to the corporate world later on (Brownstein & Easton, 1983).

Power-elite theorists challenge claims that the United States is a political democracy; the concentration of wealth and power, they maintain, is simply too great for the average person's voice to be heard. Rejecting pluralist assertions that various centers of power serve as checks and balances on one another, the power-elite model suggests that those at the top encounter no real opposition.

Research Results

Supporting the power-elite position, Robert Lynd and Helen Lynd (1937) studied Muncie, Indiana (which they called "Middletown," to suggest that it was a typical city). They documented the fortune amassed by a single family—the Balls—from their business manufacturing glass canning jars, and showed how the Ball family dominated many dimensions of the city's life. If anyone doubted the Balls' prominence, the Lynds explained, there was no need to look further than the local bank, a university, a hospital, and a department store, which all bear the family name. In Muncie, according to the Lynds, the power elite more or less boiled down to a single family.

Floyd Hunter's (1963) study of Atlanta, Georgia, provided further support for the power-elite model. Atlanta, concluded Hunter, had no one dominant family; but there were no more than about forty people

SOCIAL SURVEY: "How much confidence do you have in Congress?" (GSS 1993, N = 1,057; *Codebook*, 1993:208)

    "A great deal"   6.9%   "Hardly any"   40.5%

    "Only some"   50.0%   DK/NR   2.7%

Q: "The executive of the modern state is but a committee for managing the common affairs of the whole bourgeoisie." Marx and Engels

Q: "Within American society, major national power now resides in the economic, the political, and the military domains." C. Wright Mills (1956:6)

RESOURCE: An excerpt from C. Wright Mills's *The Power Elite* is among the "classics" included in the Macionis and Benokraitis reader, *Seeing Ourselves*.

TABLE 16–3 The Pluralist and Power-Elite Models: A Comparison

	Pluralist Model	Power-Elite Model
How is power distributed in the United States?	Dispersed.	Concentrated.
How many centers of power are there?	Many, each with a limited scope.	Few, interconnected, with broad control over society.
How do centers of power relate to one another?	They represent different political interests and thus provide checks on one another.	They represent the same political interests and face little opposition.
What is the relationship between power and the system of social stratification?	Some people have more power than others, but even minority groups can organize to gain power. Wealth, social prestige, and political office rarely overlap.	Most people have little power, and the upper class dominates society. Wealth, social prestige, and political office commonly overlap.
What is the importance of voting?	Voting provides the public as a whole with a political voice.	Voting involves choosing between alternatives acceptable to elites.
What, then, is the most accurate description of the U.S. political system?	A pluralist democracy.	An oligarchy—rule by the wealthy few.

who held all the top positions in the city's businesses and controlled the city's politics.

Critical evaluation. While these two models of power, summarized in Table 16–3, paint quite different pictures of U.S. politics, some evidence supports each interpretation. Reviewing all the research on this issue, we find greater support for the power-elite model. Even Robert Dahl (1982)—one of the stalwart supporters of the concept of pluralism—concedes that the marked concentration of wealth, as well as the barriers to equal opportunity faced by minorities, constitute basic flaws in our nation's quest for a truly pluralist democracy.

Do these flaws mean that the pluralist model is entirely wrong? No, but they do suggest that our political system is not as democratic as most people think it is. The universal right to vote is a pluralist achievement, as is the right to form associations to pursue political ends. Even so, major political candidates usually support only those positions acceptable to the most powerful segments of society (Bachrach & Baratz, 1970).

POWER BEYOND THE RULES

Politics is always a matter of disagreement about goals and the means to achieve them. Yet a political system tries to resolve controversy within a system of rules. The foundation of the U.S. political system is the Constitution and its twenty-seven amendments. Countless other regulations guide each political official from the president to the county tax assessor. But political activity sometimes exceeds—or tries to do away with—established practices.

Revolution

Political revolution is *the overthrow of one political system in order to establish another.* In contrast to reform, which involves change *within* a system, revolution implies change *of the system itself.* The extreme case of reform is the overthrow of one leader by another—a *coup d'état* (in French, literally "stroke concerning the state"), which involves change only at the top. And while reform rarely escalates into violence, revolution often does. The revolutions throughout Eastern Europe beginning in 1989 successfully overthrew communist regimes without widespread violence except in Romania, where there were thousands of deaths.

No type of political system is immune to revolution; nor does revolution invariably produce any one kind of government. The American Revolution transformed colonial rule by the British monarchy into democratic government. French revolutionaries in 1789 also overthrew a monarch, only to set the stage for the return of monarchy in the person of Napoleon. In 1917, the Russian Revolution replaced monarchy with a socialist government built on the ideas of Karl

NOTE: The word "radical" is derived from the Latin meaning "of the root" (a radish is also a root). Thus, radical politics seeks not reform but a change in the system itself.

Q: "Since all political systems were created by [people], it follows that [people] can also change them." Peter Berger (1963:128)

Q: "Don't think people can't change the world; they're the only ones who ever have." Margaret Mead

NOTE: Stohl and Lopez (1984) differentiate among three related concepts. *Oppression* is denying some category of people social and economic rights and privileges. *Repression* is more pronounced, coercing some people, who are seen as opponents, in order to weaken them. *Terrorism* is more intense still, using violence to force compliance.

Because of highly publicized acts of violence against U.S. citizens by Middle Eastern people in recent years, some members of our society tend to link Islam with terrorism. More correctly, however, this religion (like Christianity) seeks harmony and justice. Officials in Egypt have countered a recent wave of terrorism by a few religious extremists by reminding citizens (and outsiders) of their religious responsibility to promote peace.

Marx. In 1992, the Soviet Union formally came to an end, as economic pressures propelled the new Commonwealth toward a market system and greater political democracy.

Despite their striking variety, claim analysts, revolutions share a number of traits (Tocqueville, 1955, orig. 1856; also Davies, 1962; Brinton, 1965; Skocpol, 1979; Lewis, 1984; Tilly, 1986).

1. **Rising expectations**. Although common sense suggests that revolution is more likely when people are grossly deprived, history shows that revolution generally occurs when people's lives are improving. Rising expectations, rather than bitter resignation, fuel revolutionary fervor.

2. **Unresponsive government**. Revolutionary zeal gains strength to the extent that a government is unwilling or unable to reform, especially when demands for change are made by large numbers of people or powerful segments of society.

3. **Radical leadership by intellectuals**. The English philosopher Thomas Hobbes (1588–1679) observed that political rebellion is often centered in the universities. During the 1960s in the United States, students were at the forefront of much of the political unrest that marked that tumultuous decade. Students also played a key role in China's recent prodemocracy movement, as they did in Eastern Europe.

4. **Establishing a new legitimacy**. The overthrow of a political system rarely comes easily, but more difficult still is ensuring a revolution's long-term success. Some revolutionary movements are unified merely by hatred of the past regime and fall victim to internal division once new leaders are installed. Revolutionaries must also guard against counter-revolutionary drives led by past leaders, often by disposing of these leaders with ruthlessness.

Scientific analysis cannot pronounce the effects of revolution as good or bad. The full consequences of such an upheaval depend on one's values and, in any case, become evident only after many years. For example, in the wake of recent revolution, the future of the former Soviet Union remains unsettled.

Terrorism

In 1993, police broke up a plot to blow up the United Nations building as well as New York City's major traffic tunnels, an effort to kill thousands of people and reduce this country's largest city to chaos (Church, 1993). Barely a year passes without such episodes, and many are successful and deadly. **Terrorism** is *violence or threat of violence employed by an individual or a group as a political strategy*. Like revolution, terrorism is a political act beyond the rules of established political systems. Paul Johnson (1981) offers four insights about terrorism.

First, explains Johnson, terrorists try to paint violence as a legitimate political tactic, despite the fact that virtually every society condemns such acts.

NOTE: The U.S. State Department's definition of terrorism: "Premeditated, politically motivated violence perpetuated against noncombatant targets by subnational groups or clandestine state agents, normally intended to influence an audience."
Q: "Terrorist? Who says that? George Washington was called a terrorist by the British." Yasir Arafat
Q: "Politics are almost as exciting as war, and even more dangerous.
In war, you can die once; but in politics, many times." Winston Churchill
GLOBAL: Ruth Sivard (1988) claims that 2 billion people live in poor societies in which governments make frequent use of torture and other forms of violence.
GLOBAL: Terrorist acts directed against citizens of the United States declined (as did terrorism in general) after 1988.

Terrorists also bypass (or are excluded from) established channels of political negotiation. Terror is thus a weak organization's strategy to harm a stronger foe. The people who held U.S. hostages in the Middle East until 1991 may have been morally wrong to do so, but they succeeded in directing the world's attention to that region of the globe.

Second, Johnson continues, terrorism is a tactic employed not just by groups but also by governments against their own people. **State terrorism** refers to *the use of violence, generally without support of law, against individuals or groups by a government or its agents.* While contrary to democratic political principles, state terrorism becomes an integral part of authoritarian and totalitarian societies, which survive by inciting fear and intimidation. The left-wing Stalinist regime in the Soviet Union and the right-wing Nazi regime in Germany each employed widespread terror. More recently, Saddam Hussein has maintained his rule of Iraq through the use of terror.

Third, although democratic societies reject terrorism in principle, democracies are especially vulnerable to terrorists because they afford extensive civil liberties to their people and have minimal police networks. This susceptibility helps to explain the tendency of democratic governments to suspend civil liberties if officials perceive themselves to be under attack. After the Japanese attack on Pearl Harbor at the outset of World War II, the U.S. government feared that Japanese Americans might engage in espionage or terrorism and responded by imprisoning one hundred thousand Japanese-American citizens for the duration of the war.

Generally speaking, citizens of the United States have been the targets of about one in four terrorist incidents worldwide (Jenkins, 1990). Hostage taking and outright killing provoke widespread anger, but devising an effective response to such acts poses several thorny problems. Because most terrorist groups are shadowy organizations with no formal connection to any established state, targeting reprisals may be impossible. Yet, terrorism expert Brian Jenkins warns, the failure to respond "encourages other terrorist groups, who begin to realize that this can be a pretty cheap way to wage war on the United States" (quoted in Whitaker, 1985:29). Then, too, a forcible military reaction to terrorism may broaden the scope of violence, increasing the risk of confrontation with other governments.

Fourth, and finally, terrorism is always a matter of definitions. Governments claim the right to maintain order, even by force, and may brand opponents who use violence as "terrorists." Similarly, political differences may explain why one person's "terrorist" is another's "freedom fighter."

WAR AND PEACE

Perhaps the most critical issue is **war**, *armed conflict among the people of various societies, directed by their governments.* As we suggested at the beginning of this chapter, war is as old as humanity. But if the presence of violent conflict remains the same, understanding it now takes on a new urgency. Because humans possess the technological capacity to destroy ourselves, war poses unprecedented danger to the entire planet. Most scholarly investigation of war has the aim of promoting **peace**, *a state of international relations devoid of violence*, which implies the absence of war although not necessarily the lack of all political conflict.

Many people think of war as extraordinary, yet it is peace that is actually rare, existing only for brief periods during this century. Our nation's short history includes participation in ten large-scale wars, identified in Figure 16–2, which together resulted in the deaths of more than 1.3 million U.S. men and women and caused injury to many times that number (Vinovskis, 1989). Thousands more died in "undeclared wars" and limited military actions, in countries from the Dominican Republic to Lebanon, Grenada, and Panama.

The Causes of War

The frequency of war in human affairs might imply that there is something natural about armed confrontation. Members of every culture embrace certain symbols and principles—such as patriotism and freedom—to the point that they are willing to fight to defend (or extend) them. But while many animals are naturally aggressive (Lorenz, 1966), research provides no basis for concluding that human beings inevitably go to war under any particular circumstances. As Ashley Montagu (1976) reminds us, governments around the world have to employ considerable coercion to enlist the support of their people for wars.

Like all forms of social behavior, warfare is a product of *society* that varies in purpose and intensity from culture to culture. The Semai of Malaysia, among the most peace-loving of the world's people, rarely resort to violence. In contrast, the Yąnomamö, described in Chapter 3 ("Culture"), are quick to wage war with others.

If society holds the key to war or peace, under what circumstances *do* humans engage in warfare? Quincy Wright (1987) identifies five factors that promote war.

RESOURCE: Jack Mendelsohn's article "Arms Control and the New World Order" is included in the Macionis and Benokraitis reader, *Seeing Ourselves*.

NOTE: As Figure 16-2 shows, in absolute terms the Civil War was the bloodiest of all for the United States; in proportion to population, it is even more so.

SOCIAL SURVEY: "How much confidence do you have in the U.S. military? (GSS 1993, N = 1,057; *Codebook*, 1993:208) (1991 data after Desert Storm in parentheses)

"A great deal"	41.7%	(47.1%)
"Only some"	45.1%	(19.8%)
"Hardly any"	11.0%	(31.1%)
DK/NR	2.2%	(2.1%)

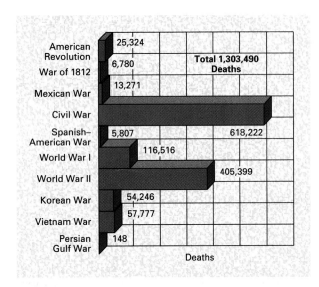

FIGURE 16–2 Deaths of Americans in Ten U.S. Wars

(Compiled from various sources by Maris A. Vinovskis, 1989, and the author)

1. **Perceived threats.** Societies mobilize in response to a perceived threat to their people, territory, or culture. The United States defined Iraq's invasion of Kuwait in 1990 as a threat to national security and eventually evicted Iraq using military force; our government has not defined the ethnic turmoil in the former Yugoslavia, however, as a national danger.

2. **Social problems.** Internal problems that generate widespread frustration may prompt a society's leaders to become aggressive toward others. In this way, societies "construct" enemies as a form of scapegoating. Sluggish economic development in the People's Republic of China, for example, periodically sparked that nation's hostility toward Vietnam, Tibet, and the former Soviet Union.

3. **Political objectives.** Leaders sometimes settle on war as a desirable political strategy. Poor societies, such as Vietnam, have fought wars to end foreign domination. For powerful societies such as the United States, a periodic "show of force" (such as sending troops to the Eastern African country of Somalia in 1993) may enhance global political stature.

4. **Moral objectives.** Rarely do nations claim to fight merely to increase their wealth and power. Leaders infuse military campaigns with moral urgency, rallying people around visions of "freedom" or the "fatherland." Although few doubted that the Persian Gulf War was largely about *oil*, U.S. strategists portrayed the mission as a drive to halt a Hitler-like Saddam Hussein.

5. **The absence of alternatives.** A fifth factor promoting war is the absence of alternatives. Article 1 of the United Nations charter defines that organization's task as "maintaining international peace." Despite some notable successes, however, its ability to resolve tensions among self-interested societies has been limited.

In short, war is rooted in the operation of society. Moreover, war is also a form of social organization subject to its own system of rules. The box takes a look at situations in which combatants act violently, contravening the norms of war—behavior termed *war crimes*.

Militarism and the Arms Race

The costs of armed conflicts extend far beyond battlefield casualties. Together, the world's nations spend some $5 billion annually for military purposes. While such expenditures, at least in part, may be justifiable, they divert resources from the desperate struggle for survival by millions of poor people throughout the world (see Chapter 11, "Global Stratification"). Assuming the will and the political wisdom of doing so, there is little doubt that resources currently spent for military purposes could be used to greatly reduce global poverty. A large proportion of the world's top scientists also direct their talents toward military research; this resource, too, is siphoned away from other work that might benefit humanity.

In recent years, defense has been the largest single expenditure by the U.S. government, accounting for 20 percent of all federal spending, or $289 billion in 1993. The reason for such high spending—amounting to about $1,162 for every man, woman, and child in the country—has been the *arms race*, a mutually reinforcing escalation of military might between the two military superpowers, the United States and the former Soviet Union.

The United States became a superpower as this nation emerged victorious from World War II with newly developed nuclear weapons. The atomic bomb was first used in war by U.S. forces to crush Japan in 1945. But the Soviet Union countered by exploding a nuclear bomb of its own in 1949, unleashing the "cold war," by which leaders of each superpower became

Q: "When we discuss national security, we tend too often to give it a military label. It is, in fact, much broader than military power and much more complex. There can be no security without social betterment." Hubert H. Humphrey

Q: "What most needs to be contained, as I see it, is not so much the Soviet Union as the weapons race itself." George Kennan

Q: "The problem with defense spending is to figure out how far you should go without destroying from within what you are trying to defend from without." Dwight D. Eisenhower

Q: "The arms race is not pre-ordained and part of some inevitable course of history. We can make history." Ronald Reagan

GLOBAL SOCIOLOGY

Violence Beyond the Rules: A Report from Yugoslavia

Former Yugoslavia

War is violent, but it also has rules. Many of the current rules of warfare emerged from the ashes of World War II, when the victorious Allies, including the United States, brought to trial German and Japanese military officials for war crimes. Subsequently, the United Nations added to the broad principles of fair play in war that have become known as the "Geneva Conventions" (which date back to 1864).

One of the most important principles of the rules of war is that, whatever violence soldiers inflict upon each other, they cannot imprison, torture, rape, or murder civilians; nor can they deliberately destroy civilian property or wantonly bomb or shell cities to foster widespread terror.

A growing body of evidence suggests that all these crimes have occurred as part of the protracted and bloody civil war in the former Yugoslavia. Serbs, Croats, and Muslims, according to the United

States, have committed war crimes, which have involved tens of thousands of deaths, rapes, and serious

Civil wars, such as the conflict in the former Yugoslavia, are among the most tragic forms of bloodshed because a large proportion of casualties are not soldiers but civilians who find themselves in harm's way. Dozens of people died on this street in Sarajevo as mortar rounds fired from the mountains surrounding the city rained down on men, women, and children who were going about their daily lives.

injuries and an incalculable loss of property. Late in 1993, therefore, a United Nations tribunal convened in the Netherlands to assess the evidence and consider possible responses.

After World War II, the Allies were able to successfully prosecute (and, in several cases, execute) German officers for their crimes against humanity based on evidence obtained from extensive Nazi records. This time around, however, the task of punishing offenders will be far more difficult. For one thing, there appear to be no written records of the Yugoslav conflict, so that many allegations stand with little or no proof and not one alleged war criminal is in United Nations custody.

The United Nations has decided not to try war criminals *in absentia*. Thus, the investigation will continue, but most observers suspect that no one will ever be convicted of war crimes in this tragic situation.

SOURCES: Adapted from Nelan (1993) and various news reports.

convinced that their counterparts were committed to military superiority. Ironically, for the next forty years, both sides pursued a policy of escalating military expenditures that neither nation wanted nor could afford.

To some analysts, the United States is dominated by a **military-industrial complex,** *the close association among the federal government, the military, and defense industries.* From this point of view, the U.S. economy has become so dependent on military

spending as a source of jobs and corporate profits that large cuts in the military budget are unlikely (Marullo, 1987). Primarily in response to the dissolution of the Soviet Union, the U.S. government has begun to make significant reductions in military spending. How far this reduction goes—given the continuing need to maintain national security and the economic pressure by some special-interest groups to keep military spending high—will remain a pressing issue for some time to come.

NOTE: Ruth Sivard (1988) notes that (1) fuel consumed by the Pentagon in a single year would maintain all U.S. mass transit for 22 years; (2) the global arms race has cost $15 trillion since 1960; (3) more wars were fought in 1987 than in any previous year; (4) 80% of war-related deaths in 1987 were of civilians; (5) budgeted AIDS research equaled only 10% of funds budgeted for the strategic defense initiative.

Q: "It will be a great day when our schools get all the money they need and the Air Force has to hold a bake sale to buy a bomber." Women's International League for Peace and Freedom

NOTE: Assessing the global "peace dividend": the world's military spending declined between 1987 ($1,016 billion) and 1989 ($950 billion), about a 6% decrease (U.N.'s *Human Development Report* 1991:80).

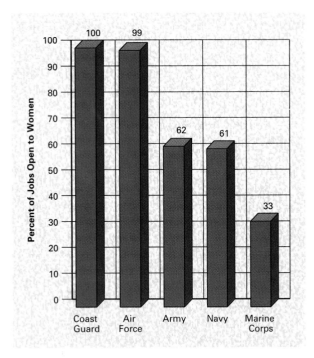

FIGURE 16–3 Proportion of Assignments Open to Women by Branch of Armed Forces

(U.S. Department of Defense, 1993)

Nuclear Weapons and War

The world still contains almost twenty-five thousand nuclear warheads perched on missiles or ready to be carried by aircraft. This number represents a destructive power equivalent to five tons of TNT for every person on the planet. Should even a small fraction of this arsenal be consumed in war, life as we know it might cease on much of the earth. Albert Einstein, whose genius contributed to the development of nuclear weapons, reflected: "The unleashed power of the atom has changed everything *save our modes of thinking*, and we thus drift toward unparalleled catastrophe." In short, nuclear weapons have rendered unrestrained war unthinkable in a world not yet capable of peace.

At present, although Great Britain, France, and the People's Republic of China have a substantial nuclear capability, the vast majority of nuclear weapons are held by the United States and Russia. The two superpowers have agreed to reduce their stockpiles of nuclear warheads to about one-fourth their present size by 2003. But even as the superpower rivalry is declining, the danger of catastrophic war is increasing along with **nuclear proliferation**, *the acquisition of*

nuclear-weapons technology by more and more nations. Most experts agree that Israel, India, Pakistan, and South Africa already possess some nuclear weapons, and other nations (including Argentina, Brazil, Iraq, Libya, and North Korea) are in the process of developing them. By the year 2000, as many as fifty nations could have the ability to fight a nuclear war. Because many of these countries have long-standing conflicts with their neighbors, nuclear proliferation places the entire world at risk (Spector, 1988).

Social Diversity and the Military

Debate about our country's military does not focus solely on halting nuclear proliferation or curbing the arms race. A current debate surrounds barriers that limit opportunity in the military for women and gay people.

Gender

Although women served in the armed forces even before this country's Revolutionary War, their representation began rising only recently. In 1940, during World War II, only 2 percent of armed forces personnel were women; by 1993, this figure had increased to 12 percent. In the 1991 Persian Gulf war, 35,000 women represented 6.5 percent of a total deployment of 540,000 U.S. troops. Five of the 148 military troops killed in the Gulf War were women.

Gender lies at the core of the historical low representation of women in the military. Figure 16–3 shows that the extent of gender-based exclusion varies by branch of the service: While all jobs in the Coast Guard are open to women, only 33 percent of positions in the Marine Corps are made available to women.

The most widespread gender-based prohibition involves women in combat roles. Defenders of this policy argue that, on average, women lack the physical strength of men. Critics respond that military women are better educated and score higher on intelligence tests than their male counterparts. The heart of the issue, however, turns on our society's deeply held view of women as *nurturers*—people who give life and help others—which clashes intolerably with the image of women as professional killers.

Still, based on the principle of equity, women are taking on more and more military assignments. In 1991, Congress acted to allow (but not require) women to operate combat aircraft in all branches of the armed forces. More broadly, the technology of war has undermined traditional distinctions between combat and noncombat personnel. A combat pilot often fires

GLOBAL: Status of gays in the military (1993): Banned in U.K., Egypt, Greece, New Zealand, Portugal, Saudi Arabia, South Korea, Turkey; accepted in Australia, Belgium, Canada, Denmark, France, Germany, Israel, Italy, Japan, Luxembourg, Netherlands, Norway, Spain.

Q: "Democracy presumes a dialogue between people and between nations." Olaf Palme

Q: "Except for revolution, nothing changes a country more than war." Charles Krauthammer

Q: "Sons bury their fathers in times of peace; in times of war, fathers bury their sons." Herodotus

NOTE: President Bush's budget for 1993 put Social Security ahead of the military as the single most expensive item in the budget—the first time that a nonmilitary item held that position.

missiles at a radar-screen target miles away; nonfighting medical evacuation teams often enter the immediate heat of battle (Moskos, 1985; Stiehm, 1989; May, 1991; McNeil, Jr., 1991; Segal & Hansen, 1992; Wilcox, 1992).

Sexual Orientation

Until 1993, all military services formally barred homosexual men and women. Nonetheless, tens of thousands of gay people have served their country, but, under past policy, admitting a homosexual orientation or engaging in any activity that raised suspicion of being homosexual was likely to result in dismissal. Roughly one thousand men and women were expelled annually from the armed forces on grounds of their sexual orientation.

The official reason for this historical policy is, first, that soldiers live in close quarters with minimal privacy. The presence of homosexuals, the argument goes, puts discipline at risk and may undercut the military's morale and effectiveness. Second, officials worry that soldiers exposed as gay might be blackmailed into compromising security. More recently, the danger of spreading the virus that causes AIDS has been added to the list.

As in the case of military women, this policy had a great deal to do with traditional stereotypes. Studies conducted by the military document that gay people have commendable performance records. Furthermore, gay people are eligible to hold civilian jobs that are far more sensitive than those of rank-and-file soldiers (Berube, 1990; Miller, 1991).

After his election in 1992, President Clinton moved to end the ban on homosexuals in the military. His effort was met with vigorous resistance from military leaders. The result of this confrontation is the "Don't ask, don't tell, don't pursue" compromise. According to the new policy, which is similar to the ones operating in many European nations, the military will not ask recruits about their sexual orientation, thus allowing gay people to join. At the same time, however, homosexual behavior (even holding hands in public) remains grounds for dismissal. In light of this new policy—and also the "Tailhook" scandal involving sexual harassment of women—the military is certain to generate new standards of sexual conduct during the next few years (Davis, 1993; Segal, Gade, & Johnson, 1993).

The Pursuit of Peace

How can the world reduce the dangers of war? Here are brief sketches of some recent approaches to promoting peace.

1. **Deterrence**. The logic of the arms race has linked security to a "balance of terror" between the superpowers. The principle of *mutually assured destruction* (MAD) demands that either side launching a first-strike nuclear attack against the other sustain massive retaliation. Such a system of deterrence has kept the peace for forty years. But it has three flaws. First, it has fueled an expensive arms race. Second, missiles are now capable of delivering their warheads more quickly, leaving computers with less time to react to an apparent attack. This has increased the risks of unintended war. Third, deterrence cannot control nuclear proliferation, which poses a growing threat to peace.

2. **High technology defense**. If technology created the weapons, perhaps it can deliver us from the threat of war. This is the idea behind the *strategic defense initiative* (SDI), proposed by the Reagan administration in 1981. SDI is a complex plan for satellites and ground installations to provide a protective shield or umbrella against enemy missiles. In principle, the system would detect enemy missiles soon after launch and destroy them with lasers and particle beams before they could reenter the atmosphere. If perfected, advocates argue, the "star wars" defense would render nuclear weapons obsolete.

   Critics maintain that, even after devoting many years and trillions of dollars to this plan, it would yield at best a leaky umbrella. The collapse of the Soviet Union also calls into question the need for such an extensive—and expensive—defense scheme.

3. **Diplomacy and disarmament**. Some analysts conclude that the best path to peace involves diplomacy rather than technology (Dedrick & Yinger, 1990). Diplomacy has the appeal of enhancing security through reducing rather than building weapons stockpiles.

   But disarmament, too, has limitations. No nation wishes to become vulnerable by reducing its defenses. Successful diplomacy, then, depends not on "soft" concession making, or "hard" demands, but on everyone involved sharing responsibility for a common problem (Fisher & Ury, 1988).

   The United States and the former Soviet Union have had recent success in negotiating arms reduction agreements. Given the rising costs of the arms race, the pressing domestic social problems of the two superpowers, and the easing

Attitudes in the United States toward gay people in the military are mixed. Public opinion polls show that a majority of people support the military's historic ban on gay recruits. At the same time, paradoxically, a majority of people also assert that gay people should have no special exemption from serving their country.

of the cold war in the 1990s, guarded optimism about large-scale disarmament seems reasonable.

4. **Resolving underlying conflict**. In the end, success in reducing the dangers of nuclear war may depend on resolving issues that have fueled the arms race. Even in the post–cold war era, basic differences between the United States and Russia remain. Moreover, militarism also springs from the nationalism, ethnic differences, and class inequality that have fired regional conflicts in Latin America, Africa, Asia, and the Middle East. If peace is rooted in solving international disputes, why do world nations currently spend three thousand times as much money on militarism as they do on peacekeeping (Sivard, 1988)?

LOOKING AHEAD: POLITICS IN THE TWENTY-FIRST CENTURY

Just as economic systems—the focus of the last chapter—are changing, so are political systems. As we look ahead to the next century, several important dilemmas and trends seem likely to command widespread attention.

One vexing problem in the United States is an inconsistency between our democratic ideals and low public participation in politics. Perhaps, as the power-elite model suggests, this nation's concentration of wealth simply constrains the political agenda to a relatively narrow range of options and policies acceptable to elites. The short-term trend, however, is toward higher turnouts at the polls. Perhaps this trend—should it continue—will widen the range of issues included in our national political debate.

A second transformation noted in this chapter is the expansion of a global political process. The Information Revolution is changing politics just as it is reformulating the economy (although political change seems to be somewhat slower). Communications technology now allows news and political analysis to flow instantly from one point in the world to another. This global flow of information should have the effect of empowering individuals, since governments can no longer seal their borders to new ideas. Today anyone with a television or short-wave radio (not to mention fax machines and other computer-based devices) has access to various sources of political information.

Third, a global reformulation of political thinking is currently underway. One effect of the cold war between the United States and the Soviet Union was to cast political debate in the form of two rigid political alternatives—the West's democratic capitalism and the East's state-centered socialism. Today, in the post–cold war era, the character of political systems is open to far greater discussion, with various ideas about how to integrate the operation of government and the economy. The system of "state capitalism" found in several Asian nations (notably Japan and South Korea) is but one case in point.

Fourth, and finally, the danger of war in the world remains great. Despite the decline of tensions between the two superpowers, vast stockpiles of weapons remain, and nuclear technology continues to proliferate. New superpowers are likely to arise in the century ahead (the People's Republic of China seems a likely candidate), just as surely as regional conflicts will continue to fester. One can only hope that humanity can enlist forces working for peace—including the United Nations, the expanding global economy, more widespread and rapid communication, and a developing sense of political justice—in the effort to devise a nonviolent solution to the age-old problems that provoke war.

Q: "How does it become a man to behave toward this American government today? I answered that he cannot without disgrace become associated with it." Henry David Thoreau

Q: "The good of man must be the end of the science of politics." Aristotle, *The Nicomachean Ethics*, I ii

Q: "No man ever went broke underestimating the intelligence of the American voter." H. L. Mencken

Q: "Si vis pacem, para bellum." ("If you seek peace, prepare for war.") Ancient Roman dictum; the intensity of war has increased with time; three-fourths of all deaths from war since Julius Caesar's time have occurred in this century. (Michael Renner, 1993)

Q: "I detest war; it spoils armies." Grand Duke Constantine of Russia

SUMMARY

1. Politics is the major social institution by which a society distributes power and organizes decision making. Max Weber explained that three social contexts transform coercive power into legitimate authority: tradition, rationally enacted rules and regulations, and the personal charisma of a leader.

2. Traditional authority is common to preindustrial societies; industrial societies legitimize power through bureaucratic organizations and law. Charismatic authority arises in every society; if charismatic leaders are to perpetuate their organizations, they must routinize charismatic authority into traditional or rational-legal authority.

3. Monarchy is based on traditional authority and is common in preindustrial societies. Although constitutional monarchies persist in some industrial nations, industrialization favors democracy based on rational-legal authority and extensive bureaucracy.

4. Authoritarian political regimes deny popular participation in government. Totalitarian political systems go even further, controlling people's everyday lives.

5. The world remains divided into roughly 190 politically independent nation-states; one dimension of an emerging global political system, however, is the growing wealth and power of multinational corporations. Additionally, new technology associated with the Information Revolution means that national governments can no longer control the flow of information across national boundaries.

6. The dramatic growth of the government of the United States during the past two centuries reflects more than population increase; it is tied in with wider government involvement in the economy and society.

7. Positions on economic and social issues distinguish liberals from conservatives. Liberals call for government regulation of the economy and action to ensure economic equality; conservatives believe the government should not interfere in these arenas. Conservatives do want, however, government regulation of moral issues, while liberals argue that government should not interfere in matters of conscience.

8. Special-interest groups advance the political aims of specific segments of the population. These groups employ lobbyists and political action committees in their efforts to influence the political process.

9. Many people in the United States do not readily describe themselves in political terms, nor do they strongly identify with either the Democratic or the Republican party. Furthermore, only 60 percent of those eligible to vote actually voted in the 1992 national elections.

10. The pluralist model holds that political power is widely dispersed in the United States; the power-elite model takes an opposing view, arguing that power is concentrated in a small, wealthy segment of the population.

11. Revolution radically transforms a political system. Terrorism, another unconventional political tactic, employs acts of violence in the pursuit of political goals. States as well as individuals engage in terrorism.

12. War is armed conflict directed by governments. The development of nuclear weapons, and their proliferation, has increased the threat of global catastrophe. Enhancing world peace ultimately depends on resolving the tensions and conflicts that fuel militarism.

KEY CONCEPTS

authoritarianism a political system that denies popular participation in government

authority power that people perceive as legitimate rather than coercive

charismatic authority power legitimized through extraordinary personal abilities that inspire devotion and obedience

democracy a type of political system that views power as exercised by the people as a whole

government formal organizations that direct the political life of a society

military-industrial complex the close association among the federal government, the military, and defense industries

monarchy a type of political system that transfers power from generation to generation within a single family

nuclear proliferation the acquisition of nuclear-weapons technology by more and more nations

peace a state of international relations devoid of violence

pluralist model an analysis of politics that views power as dispersed among many competing interest groups

political action committee (PAC) an organization formed by a special-interest group, independent of political parties, to pursue specific aims by raising and spending money

political revolution the overthrow of one political system in order to establish another

politics the social institution that distributes power, sets a society's agenda, and makes decisions

power the ability to achieve desired ends despite resistance from others

power-elite model an analysis of politics that views power as concentrated among the rich

rational-legal authority (also **bureaucratic authority**) power legitimized by legally enacted rules and regulations

routinization of charisma the transformation of charismatic authority into some combination of traditional and bureaucratic authority

special-interest group a political alliance of people interested in some economic or social issue

state terrorism the use of violence, generally without support of law, against individuals or groups by a government or its agents

terrorism violence or the threat of violence employed by an individual or group as a political strategy

totalitarianism a political system that extensively regulates people's lives

traditional authority power legitimized through respect for long-established cultural patterns

war armed conflict among the people of various societies, directed by their governments

CRITICAL-THINKING QUESTIONS

1. Distinguish authority from mere power. What forms of authority characterize preindustrial and industrial societies? Why does democracy gradually replace monarchy as societies industrialize?

2. How would you describe the attitudes of the U.S. population on the political spectrum? How is class position linked to political opinions?

3. Contrast the pluralist and power-elite models of societal power.

4. What sociological factors make war more likely or, contrarily, enhance prospects for peaceful relations among nations?

SUGGESTED READINGS

Classic Sources

Alexis de Tocqueville. *Democracy in America*. Garden City, N.Y.: Doubleday-Anchor Books, 1969; orig. 1834, 1840.

> This classic analysis of politics and society was written by a brilliant French aristocrat after a journey through the United States in the early 1830s. Many of Tocqueville's insights about this country's political system remain as fresh and valuable today as when he wrote them.

C. Wright Mills. *The Power Elite*. New York: Oxford University Press, 1956.

> This classic treatise has framed much of sociology's analysis of the structure of societal power.

Hannah Arendt. *The Origins of Totalitarianism*. Cleveland: Meridian Books, 1958.

> This classic description of totalitarianism and its rise in the modern world is written by a woman deeply influenced by her captivity in a Nazi death camp during World War II.

Contemporary Sources

Mary Ann Glendon. *Rights Talk: The Impoverishment of Political Discourse*. New York: The Free Press, 1991.

> This analysis of the political scene investigates recent trends and explores consequences of proliferating individual "rights."

Ralph C. Gomes and Linda Faye Williams, eds. *From Exclusion to Inclusion: The Long Struggle for African-American Political Power*. Westport, Conn.: Greenwood Press, 1992.

> This account traces the historical importance of race in shaping the political life of the United States.

Paul Stillwell, ed. *The Golden Thirteen: Recollections of the First Black Naval Officers*. Annapolis, Md.: Naval Institute Press, 1993.

> In 1943, the U.S. Navy initiated a significant change in personnel policy with the training of thirteen African-American men as naval officers.

Peggy Noonan. *What I Saw at the Revolution: A Political Life in the Reagan Era*. New York: Random House, 1990.

> One of this country's best political speechwriters (for Presidents Reagan and Bush) offers her reflections on the U.S. political system.

Edward D. Berkowitz. *American's Welfare State: From Roosevelt to Reagan*. Baltimore: Johns Hopkins Press, 1991.

> Political debate has long surrounded social welfare programs, seen by some as solutions to social problems and by others as the causes of national maladies. This book puts this tangled topic in historical perspective.

Theda Skocpol. *Protecting Soldiers and Mothers: The Political Origins of Social Policy in the United States*. Cambridge, Mass.: Belknap Press/Harvard University Press, 1992.

> In this work, a noted sociologist and political analyst provides a critical history of government involvement in U.S. social life.

Global Sources

Lawrence Howard. *Terrorism: Roots, Impact, Responses*. New York: Praeger, 1992.

> Eleven multidisciplinary essays span geographical regions (Mexico, the Middle East, and Europe) while providing a focus on the media's role in the reporting of terrorist attacks.

Stephen R. Graubard. *Exit from Communism*. New Brunswick, N.J.: Transaction, 1993.

> This collection of articles assesses the recent collapse of communism in Eastern Europe and the former Soviet Union, pointing out the difficulties encountered during this transition.

John G. Stroessinger. *Why Nations Go to War*. 6th ed. St. Martin's Press, 1992.

> This recent book examines seven twentieth-century conflicts, from World War I to the Persian Gulf War, and draws lessons about how wars arise.

Tony Saich and Benjamin Yang. *The Rise to Power of the Chinese Communist Party: Documents and Analysis*. Armonk, N.Y.: M. E. Sharpe, 1993.

> A collection of fundamental documents forms the basis of this exploration of the ascendance of the Communist party in the People's Republic of China.

Patrick J. Garrity and Steven A. Maaranen, eds. *Nuclear Weapons in the Changing World: Perspectives from Europe, Asia, and North America*. New York: Plenum, 1992.

> This collection of essays by experts examines nuclear weapons issues from the points of view of nations in various regions of the world.

Cynthia Enloe. *Bananas, Beaches, and Bases: Making Feminist Sense of International Politics*. Berkeley: University of California Press, 1990.

> This feminist analysis of the world political scene maintains that gender is at the center of global power structures.

Marisol, *Poor Family I*, 1986

DATA FILE: An outline of this chapter, suggested discussion topics, and supplementary lecture material highlighting cross-cultural family patterns are found in the *Data File*.

Q: "Home is the place where, when you have to go there, they have to take you in." Robert Frost

Q: "Happiness is having a large, loving, caring, close-knit family in another city." George Burns

Q: "As long as the term family is used to cover both the 'real' family and its antithesis—the single-parent version—the question of whether a society can do without families is hopelessly obfuscated. Moreover a challenging thesis is hidden: the thesis that it does not matter which social arrangements adults devise to bring up children." Amitai Etzioni

Family

17

Twelve-year-old Gregory walked to the witness stand in a Florida courtroom. He patiently explained to the judge and hundreds of riveted onlookers that all he wanted was "a place to be." In response to questions from his lawyer, Gregory disclosed that his childhood memories were few and mostly bad—the last years of his life were a blur of vicious fighting on the part of his mother and father and indifferent attention from foster parents. But his life had now changed, he continued, since he had found a woman who loved him and wanted to adopt him as her own. And that was the point of the legal proceedings: Gregory was asking the court to grant him a divorce from his biological mother so that he could become another woman's son. After careful deliberation and weighing of the evidence, the court found in Gregory's favor, ensuring

him a place in U.S. legal history (Wingert & Salholz, 1992).

Just imagining that other children across the country might line up to emulate Gregory's successful divorce suit gave added strength to a rising chorus of voices charging that families in the United States are fast becoming an endangered species. And the alarmists have some hard facts to back up their case. The divorce rate has doubled over the past thirty years so that, if the trend holds, almost half of today's marriages will end in divorce. Primarily as a result of divorce, one in four of today's newborns will live with a single parent at some time before age eighteen. And in an important parallel trend, even now, almost one in four children is born to an unmarried woman. Moreover, two-thirds of all mothers are now in the labor force along with three-fourths of all fathers, so that parents routinely find themselves torn between their obligations to provide emotional and financial support to their children. Finally,

459

Q: "Marriage is the beginning and the pinnacle of all culture. It makes the savage gentle . . . Marriage may sometimes be an uncomfortable state . . . as it should be. Are we not married to our conscience?" Johann Wolfgang von Goethe
Q: "I see the family as an institution in decline and believe that this should be a cause for alarm, especially as regard the consequences for children." David Popenoe

NOTE: The number of children living in multigenerational households jumped from 1.3 million in 1980 to 2.4 million in 1991; key reasons are the rising share of single mothers and the protracted economic recession.
Q: "Dependency, which is at the very heart of the extended family, appears as perhaps the ultimate weakness in American society." Richard Sennett and Jonathan Cobb

and most seriously, the proportion of U.S. children living in poverty has been rising steadily in recent years.

Together, these facts suggest a basic truth: Families in the United States are changing. Not long ago, the cultural ideal of the family consisted of a working husband, a homemaker wife, and their young children. Today, fewer people embrace such a singular vision of the family, and, at any given time, only about one in ten U.S. households fits that description.

This chapter examines family life in the United States and elsewhere in the world, explains how families are changing, and provides some clues as to why. Yet, as we shall also point out, changing family patterns are nothing new to this country. Families have always been evolving in one way or another. A century ago, for example, the Industrial Revolution drew men off the farm to work in factories. Then, as now, social critics warned that the new pattern of "absent fathers" was threatening to destroy the family. Today, critics also cite the pattern of "absent mothers" as further economic and cultural changes are reshaping the family.

THE FAMILY: BASIC CONCEPTS

The **family** is *a social institution, found in all societies, that unites individuals into cooperative groups that oversee the bearing and raising of children.* These social units are, in turn, built on **kinship**, *a social bond, based on blood, marriage, or adoption, that joins individuals into families.* Although people the world over recognize families, just who is included under the umbrella of kinship varies considerably from one society to another and with the passing of time.

Throughout this century, most members of our society have regarded a **family unit** as *a social group of two or more people, related by blood, marriage, or adoption, who usually live together.* Over the life course, the members of a family unit change. Individuals are born into a family composed of parents and siblings (sometimes termed the *family of orientation* since this group is central to socialization); in adulthood, people form a *family of procreation* in order to have or adopt children of their own.

Throughout the world, families form around **marriage**, *a legally sanctioned relationship, involving economic cooperation as well as normative sexual activity and childbearing, that people expect to be enduring.* Language offers an insight into our cultural belief that marriage alone is the appropriate context for procreation: Traditionally, people have attached the label of *illegitimacy* to children born out of wedlock; moreover,

matrimony, in Latin, means "the condition of motherhood." This link between childbearing and marriage has weakened, however, as the share of children born to single women (noted earlier to be approaching one in four) has increased.

Changing family patterns have commanded the attention of scholars and provoked intense public debate. Some people now object to defining as "families" only married couples and children because it implies that everyone should embrace a single standard of moral conduct. Moreover, many government programs designate benefits only for members of "families" as conventionally defined, so that committed partners—whether heterosexual or homosexual— are excluded. As a result, increasing numbers of people now think of kinship in terms of *families of affinity*, that is, people with or without legal or blood ties who feel they belong together and want to define themselves as a family.

What does or does not constitute a family, then, is a matter of personal morality and lies at the center of the contemporary "family values" debate (Dedrick, 1990). The Census Bureau also plays a role in this discussion; it defines family units as noted above, and sociologists who wish to use Census Bureau data describing "families" must, therefore, use this definition.[1] The trend in public opinion as well as in legal terms, however, favors a wider and more inclusive definition of the "family unit."

THE FAMILY IN GLOBAL PERSPECTIVE

All societies recognize families, although the precise shape and character of kinship arrangements varies (Murdock, 1945). One general pattern is that preindustrial societies attach great importance to the **extended family**, *a family unit including parents and children, but also other kin.* Extended families are also called *consanguine families*, meaning that they include everyone with "shared blood." The onset of industrialization, which sparks both geographic and social mobility (see Chapter 15, "The Economy and Work"), gives rise to the **nuclear family**, *a family unit composed of one or two parents and their children.* Because it is based on

---

[1]According to the Census Bureau, there were 95.7 million U.S. households in 1992, of which 67.2 million (70 percent) were family households. The remaining living units contained single people or unrelated people living together. In 1960, 85 percent of all households were families.

DIVERSITY: Statistically speaking, the typical U.S. family is a married couple, both of whom have graduated from high school and are in the labor force, with one child (mean) or no children (mode), living in a (mortgaged) home that they own. At any given point in time, about 25% of all households have a wife, husband, and one or more children, although more than half take this form at some point; at any given time, about one in ten households comprises a

working man, homemaker woman, and one or more children although, again, about 25% take this form at some point.

NOTE: Illustrating exogamy is the legal prohibition against homosexual marriages. Endogamy can be seen in the historical prohibition of interracial marriage.

marriage, the nuclear family is also known as the *conjugal family*. Although many members of our society live in extended families, the nuclear family has become the predominant form in the United States.

What about the future? Sweden is a progressive society that may point to some likely trends. Sociologist David Popenoe, who examined the state of the Swedish family, explains in the box on pages 462–63 that this Scandinavian nation may have the weakest families in the world.

Marriage Patterns

Cultural norms, and often laws, identify people as desirable or unsuitable marriage partners. Some of these norms promote **endogamy**, *marriage between people of the same social category*. Endogamy norms constrain marriage prospects to others of the same age, race, religion, or social class. Other norms encourage **exogamy**, *marriage between people of different social categories*. In rural India, for example, people expect a person to marry someone of the same caste (endogamy), but from a different village (exogamy). Throughout the world, societies pressure people to marry someone of the same social background but of the other sex. The logic of endogamy is that people of similar social position pass along their standing to offspring, thereby maintaining traditional social patterns. Exogamy, by contrast, helps to forge useful alliances and encourages cultural diffusion.

In every industrial society, laws prescribe **monogamy** (from Greek meaning "one union"), *a form of marriage involving two partners*. Because of the level of divorce and remarriage, however, *serial monogamy* more accurately describes this country's marital practice.

Global Map 17–1 , on page 464, shows that while monogamy is the rule throughout the Americas and in Europe, many preindustrial societies—especially in Africa and southern Asia—permit **polygamy** (from Greek meaning "many unions"), *a type of marriage uniting three or more people*. Polygamy takes two forms. By far the more common is **polygyny** (from the Greek, meaning "many women"), *a type of marriage uniting one male and two or more females*. Islamic societies in Africa and southern Asia, for example, permit men up to four wives. In these societies, however, most families are monogamous all the same because few men have the wealth needed to support several wives and even more children.

Polyandry (from the Greek, meaning "many men" or "many husbands") is *a type of marriage joining one female with two or more males*. This pattern appears

In modern industrial societies, the members of extended families pursue their careers independently and usually live apart from one another. However, various nuclear families may assemble periodically for rituals such as weddings, funerals, and family reunions.

only rarely; one example is among Tibetan Buddhists. In places where agriculture is difficult, polyandry discourages the division of land into parcels too small to support a family and divides the costs among many men. Polyandry also appears in societies that engage in female infanticide—the aborting of female fetuses or killing of female infants—so that the female population drops, forcing men to share women.

Globally and historically, the majority of world societies have permitted more than one marital pattern; even so, most marriages have been monogamous (Murdock, 1965). This cultural preference for monogamy reflects two key facts of life: The financial burden of supporting multiple spouses and children weighs heavily; and, second, the rough numerical parity of the sexes limits the possibility for polygamy.

Residential Patterns

Just as societies regulate mate selection, so they designate where a couple resides. In preindustrial societies, most newlyweds live with one set of parents, gaining economic assistance and security in the process. Most

GLOBAL SOCIOLOGY

The Weakest Families on Earth? A Report from Sweden

Sweden has a proud record of avoiding many of the social problems that plague the United States. Violent crime is rare in Swedish cities, and the nightmare of drug abuse hardly touches the lives of most Swedes. There is little of the grinding poverty that has blighted whole regions of our own cities. Sweden seems to fulfill the promise of the modern welfare state, with an extensive and professional government bureaucracy that sees to virtually all human needs.

But this is the reason, according to David Popenoe, that Sweden has the weakest families on earth. For one thing, Swedes are less likely to marry than members of any other industrialized society; Sweden also has the highest share of adults living alone (20 percent versus 12 in the United States). For another, a larger proportion of couples live

outside of marriage (25 percent versus 6 in the United States), and half of all Swedish children (compared to about one in four in the United States) are born to unmarried parents. Average household size is also the smallest in the world (2.2 persons versus 2.6 in the United States). Finally, Swedish couples (whether married or not) are more likely to break up than partners in any other country. Popenoe concludes that the family "has probably become weaker in Sweden than anywhere else—certainly among advanced Western nations. Individual family members are the most autonomous and least bound by the group, and the group as a whole is least cohesive" (1991:69).

The erosion of the Swedish family began in the 1960s, the product of trends also at work in the United States. Popenoe claims that a growing culture of individualism and self-fulfillment, coupled with the declining influence of religion,

set the stage for the weakening of Swedish families. Rising support for feminism also plays a part. Sweden has the lowest share of women who are housewives (10 percent versus about 25 in the United States) and the highest percentage of women in the labor force (77 percent versus 58 in the United States). But, most important, Popenoe contends, is the expansion of the welfare state.

Government programs to meet various human needs exist in every industrial society. Sweden, however, has embraced one of the most far-reaching schemes of its kind, entitling each citizen to a lifetime of services—and high taxes. Swedes can count on the government to give them jobs, sustain their income, deliver and educate their children, provide health care, and, when the time comes, pay for their funeral.

Many Swedes supported the creation of this welfare apparatus, Popenoe explains, thinking it would *strengthen* families. But with

such societies favor **patrilocality** (Greek for "place of the father"), *a residential pattern by which a married couple lives with or near the husband's family*. But some societies (such as the Iroquois in North America) endorse **matrilocality** (meaning "place of the mother"), *a residential pattern by which a married couple lives with or near the wife's family*.

A society's inclination toward one variant or the other often corresponds to military and economic patterns. Societies that engage in frequent local warfare tend toward patrilocality since families need their sons to stay close to home to offer protection. Societies that engage in distant warfare present a mixed picture,

favoring patrilocality or matrilocality depending on whether sons or daughters have greater economic importance (Ember & Ember, 1971, 1991).

Industrial societies show yet another pattern. When finances permit, at least, the preferred model is **neolocality** (from the Greek, meaning "new place"), *a residential pattern in which a married couple lives apart from the parents of both spouses*.

Patterns of Descent

Descent is a matter of defining relatives or, more formally, *the system by which members of a society trace*

NOTE: The personal significance of the family is suggested by the fact that four of the five most severe "social readjustment experiences" involve kinship: death of a spouse (100), divorce (73), marital separation (65), jail term (63), death of a close family member (63). (Holmes & Rahe, 1967)

Q: "Marriage has many pains, but celibacy has no pleasures." Samuel Johnson

DIVERSITY: Although the extended family is not favored in the United States partly because of the association of kin and dependency, the poor often establish fictional kin out of need (as in Carol Stack's *All Our Kin*). During economic recessions, families become more extended with, for example, more men and women in their twenties and thirties continuing to live with their parents.

the benefit of hindsight, he concludes, we can see that proliferating government programs actually have been *replacing* families. In other words, various programs encourage family members to look to government for economic support rather than looking out for their own.

The Swedish government operates public child care centers available to all. As officials see it, this system puts care in the hands of professionals, and makes this service equally accessible regardless of parents' income. At the same time, however, the government offers no subsidy for parents who desire to care for children in their own home. In effect, then, government policy has taken over many traditional family functions, leaving family units with uncertain importance.

During the last several generations, then, Swedes have relaxed their family ties as they have become more dependent on their government. But if this system has solved so many social problems, why should anyone care about the erosion of family life?

For two reasons, says Popenoe. First, government can do only at great cost what families used to do for themselves. Recently, Swedes voted to cut back on their burgeoning welfare system because of skyrocketing costs.

The second reason to protect what remains of the Swedish family centers on children and their need to be nurtured. Government programs have lifted from adults many of the personal and financial responsibilities of raising the young. But can government employees in large child care centers provide children with the security and love possible in a family setting? It may turn out that small, intimate groups can accomplish some human tasks much better than formal organizations can.

Popenoe thinks the Swedes have gone too far in delegating family responsibilities to government. But he cautions that we in the United States—where the welfare state is the least developed of all industrial societies—may not have gone far enough. Programs allowing new parents time off from the workplace is a case in point. A Swedish parent can apply for up to eighteen months' leave at 90 percent of salary; in the United States the Family and Medical Leave Act passed in 1993 allows workers up to ninety days without pay to care for newborns or sick family members. Should our society try to emulate Sweden? A reasonable goal of government is to assist working parents in caring for children. But does doing so strengthen or weaken families?

SOURCES: Popenoe (1991); also Herrstrom (1990).

kinship over generations. Most preindustrial societies trace kinship only through one side of the family—the father or the mother. The more prevalent pattern is **patrilineal descent**, *a system tracing kinship through males*. Practically speaking, patrilineal kinship directs fathers to pass on their property to their sons. Patrilineal descent is common to pastoral and agrarian societies, in which men produce the most valued resources.

Less common is **matrilineal descent**, *a system tracing kinship through females*. Here, people define only the mother's side as kin, and daughters inherit property from mothers. Matrilineal descent is often found in horticultural societies where women are the primary food producers (Haviland, 1985).

Industrial societies such as our own utilize **bilateral descent** ("two-sided descent"), *a system tracing kinship through both females and males*. In a bilateral society, children are linked by kinship to the families of both parents.

Patterns of Authority

The predominance of polygyny, patrilocality, and patrilineal descent in the world reflects the universal presence of patriarchy. Without denying that wives

	"Agree"	"Disagree"
Men	51.7%	48.3%
Women	44.9%	55.1%

	"Agree"	"Disagree"
High SES	34.7%	65.3%
Middle SES	47.3%	52.7%
Low SES	66.4%	33.6%
Afri Amer	49.2%	50.8%
Latino	48.2%	51.8%
White	47.9%	52.1%

Window on the World

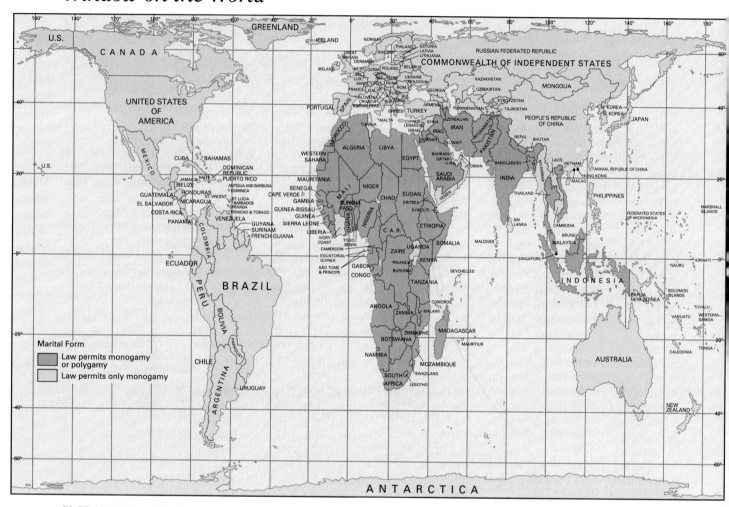

GLOBAL MAP 17–1 Marital Forms in Global Perspective

Monogamy is the legally prescribed form of marriage in all industrial societies and throughout the Western Hemisphere. In most African nations, as well as in southern Asia, however, polygamy is permitted by law. In the majority of cases, this practice reflects the historic influence of Islam, a religion that allows a man to have no more than four wives. Even so, most marriages in these traditional societies are monogamous, primarily for financial reasons.

From *Peters Atlas of the World* (1990).

and mothers exercise considerable influence in every society, as Chapter 13 ("Sex and Gender") explains, no truly matriarchal society is part of the human record. The universal pattern of patriarchy means that, to a greater or lesser extent, societies accord more wealth, power, and prestige to men than to women.

In industrial societies such as the United States, men usually head households, just as they dominate most areas of social life. More egalitarian family patterns are gradually evolving, especially as increasing numbers of women enter the labor force. However, the social power of wives remains lower than that of

Q: "Despite the profound changes in the nature of the family that have come with industrialization and urbanization in the past century, today's family remains the basic unit for the protection and rearing of young children, and the center of emotional life. Indeed, its role as the major source of psychological support for its members has, if anything, increased. The family is a 'haven in a heartless world,' an oasis of stable, diffuse and largely unquestioned love and

support." Lenore J. Weitzman (1982:2–3)

NOTE: The incest taboo limits kinship confusion. Rolling Stone Bill Wyman's (age 56) son, Stephen (age 30), recently announced his intention of marrying the mother of his father's ex-wife (age 22). That would make Stephen stepfather to his former stepmother, and Bill step-grandfather to his former wife. Bill would also be his son's son-in-law and the father of his father-in-law!

husbands. Parents in the United States also still prefer boys to girls and typically give children their father's last name.

THEORETICAL ANALYSIS OF THE FAMILY

As in earlier chapters, several theoretical approaches offer a range of insights about the family.

Functions of the Family: Structural-Functional Analysis

The structural-functional paradigm suggests that the family is vital to performing several of society's basic tasks. This view explains why we sometimes think of the family as "the backbone of society."

1. **Socialization.** As explained in Chapter 5 ("Socialization"), the family is the first and most influential setting for socialization. In ideal terms, parents help their children learn to be well-integrated and contributing members of society (Parsons & Bales, 1955). Of course, family socialization continues throughout the life cycle. Adults change within marriage, and, as any parent knows, mothers and fathers learn as much from raising their children as their children learn from them.

2. **Regulation of sexual activity.** Every culture regulates sexual activity in the interest of maintaining kinship organization and property rights. One universal regulation is the **incest taboo**, *a cultural norm forbidding sexual relations or marriage between certain kin.* Precisely which kin fall within the incest taboo varies from one culture to another. The matrilineal Navajo, for example, forbid marrying any relative of one's mother. Our bilateral society applies the incest taboo to both sides of the family but limits it to close relatives, including parents, grandparents, siblings, aunts, and uncles. But even brother-sister marriages found approval among the ancient Egyptian, Incan, and Hawaiian nobility (Murdock, 1965).

Reproduction between close relatives can adversely affect the mental and physical health of offspring. But this fact does not explain why, among all species of life, the incest taboo is observed only by human beings. The key reason to control incest, then, is social. Why? First, the incest taboo minimizes sexual competition within families by restricting legitimate sexuality to spouses. Second, it forces people to marry outside of their immediate families, forging useful alliances. Third, since kinship defines people's rights and obligations toward each other, forbidding reproduction among close relatives protects kinship from collapsing into chaos.

3. **Social placement.** Families are not biologically necessary for people to reproduce, but they do provide for the social placement of children. Social identity based on race, ethnicity, religion, and social class is ascribed at birth through the family. This fact explains the long-standing preference for so-called legitimate birth. Especially when parents are of similar social position, families clarify inheritance rights and allow for the stable transmission of social standing from parents to children.

4. **Material and emotional security.** People have long viewed the family as a "haven in a heartless world," looking to kin for physical protection, emotional support, and financial assistance. To a greater or lesser extent, most families do all these things, although not without periodic conflict. Not surprisingly, then, people living in families tend to be healthier than those living alone.

Critical evaluation. Structural-functional analysis identifies a number of the family's major functions. From this point of view, it is easy to see that society as we know it could not exist without families.

But this approach rests on a rather narrow conception of family and overlooks the great diversity of U.S. family life. Moreover, it pays little attention to how other social institutions (say, government) could meet at least some of the same human needs. Finally, it overlooks the problems of family life. Established family forms support patriarchy and incorporate a surprising amount of violence, with the dysfunctional effect of undermining individual self-confidence, health, and well-being, especially of women and children.

Inequality and the Family: Social-Conflict Analysis

Like the structural-functional approach, the social-conflict paradigm also sees the family as central to the operation of society. But rather than concentrating on ways that kinship benefits society, conflict theorists investigate how the family perpetuates social inequality. The role of families in the social reproduction of inequality takes several forms.

Q: "The bourgeoisie has torn away from the family its sentimental veil, and has reduced the family to a mere money relation." Karl Marx and Friedrich Engels, *The Communist Manifesto*

Q: "We do not protest the unequal advantage given . . . by virtue of genetic transmission of qualities of strength and acuity; why, then, should we protest the inheritance of cultural-material qualities . . . which are part of what we think of as family and ancestry?" Robert

A. Nisbet (1986:52)

Q: In *The Republic*, Plato advocates the abolition of the "private" family in the interests of justice: "All these women are to belong to all these men in common, and no woman is to live privately with any man. And the children, in their turn, will be in common, and neither will a parent know his own offspring, nor a child his parent." (Book V)

The family is a basic building block of society because it performs important functions such as conferring social position and regulating sexual activity. To most family members, however, the family (at least in ideal terms) is a "haven in a heartless world" in which individuals find a sense of belonging and emotional support, an idea conveyed in Marc Chagall's Scène Paysanne.

1. **Property and inheritance.** As noted in Chapter 13 ("Sex and Gender"), Friedrich Engels (1902; orig. 1884) traced the origin of the family to the need to identify heirs so that men (especially in the higher classes) could transmit property to their sons. Families thus support the concentration of wealth and reproduce the class structure in each succeeding generation (Mare, 1991).

2. **Patriarchy.** Engels also emphasized how the family promotes patriarchy. The only way men can know who their heirs are is to control the sexuality of women. Thus, Engels continued, families transform women into the sexual and economic property of men. A century ago in the United States, most wives' earnings belonged to their husbands. Although this practice is no longer lawful, other examples of men's power over women remain.

Despite moving rapidly into the paid work force, women still bear major responsibility for child rearing and housework (Haas, 1981; Schooler et al., 1984; Fuchs, 1986). Patriarchal families offer considerable benefits to men, but they also deprive men of the chance to share in the personal satisfaction and growth derived from close interaction with children.

3. **Race and ethnicity.** Racial and ethnic categories will persist over generations only to the degree that people marry others like themselves. Thus endogamous marriage also shores up the racial and ethnic hierarchy in our own society and elsewhere.

Later in this chapter, we will explore how the link between the traditional family and social inequality relates to a number of conflicts and changes, such as violence against women, divorce, and the trend of women choosing to raise their children outside of marriage.

Critical evaluation. Social-conflict analysis reveals another side of family life: its role in maintaining social inequality. During his era, Engels condemned the family as part and parcel of capitalism. Yet societies that have never developed or that have rejected the capitalist economy have families (and family problems) all the same. Kinship and social inequality are deeply intertwined, as Engels argued, but the family appears to carry out various societal functions that are not easily accomplished by other means.

Micro-Level Analysis

Both structural-functional and social-conflict analyses take a broad view of the family as a structural system with wide-ranging consequences for our lives. Micro-level approaches, by contrast, explore how individuals shape and experience family life.

Symbolic-Interaction Analysis

Seen from the inside, family life amounts to ongoing symbolic interaction. As they engage one another, individuals construct family life, building a reality that differs from case to case. Moreover, women and men, parents and children, boys and girls—all tend to see family life differently.

Family life also changes over time. A newlywed man and woman's initial expectations about their relationship will almost certainly change as they face the daily realities of life together. A new role for a spouse, such as a wife entering law school, alters the lives of

Q: "Our forefathers had conceived a strange opinion on the subject of marriage; as they had noticed that the small number of love-matches in their time almost always turned out badly, they resolutely inferred that it was dangerous to listen to the dictates of the heart on the subject. Accident appeared to them a better guide than choice." Alexis de Tocqueville

Q: "Since love is the most delicate and total act of a soul, it will reflect the state and nature of the soul. If the individual is not sensitive, how can his love be sentient? If he is not profound, how can his love be deep? As one is, so is his love." José Ortega y Gasset

Q: "Love: two minds without a single thought." Philip Barry

Q: "What's love got to do with it?" Tina Turner

all family members. Thus, from a symbolic-interaction point of view, marriage and the family are less rigid patterns than they are ongoing processes.

Social-Exchange Analysis

Social-exchange analysis is another micro-level approach that depicts courtship and marriage as forms of negotiation (Blau, 1964). In the case of courtship, dating allows each person the chance to assess the likely advantages and disadvantages of taking the other as a spouse, always keeping in mind the value of what one has to offer in return. In essence, exchange analysts suggest, individuals seek to make the best "deal" they can in selecting a partner.

Physical attractiveness is one critical dimension of exchange. In patriarchal societies around the world, beauty has long been a commodity offered by women on the marriage market. The high value assigned to beauty explains women's traditional concern with physical appearance and their sensitivity about revealing their age. For their part, men have traditionally been assessed according to the financial resources they command (Melville, 1983). Recently, however, because women are joining the labor force, they are less dependent on men to support them and their children. Thus, the terms of exchange have been converging for men and women.

Critical evaluation. Micro-level analysis offers a useful balance to structural-functional and social-conflict visions of the family as an institutional system. Adopting an interactional or exchange viewpoint, we gain a better sense of the individual's experience of family life and appreciate how people creatively shape this reality for themselves.

Using this approach, however, we run the risk of missing the bigger picture, namely, that family life is similar for people affected by any common set of economic and cultural forces. U.S. families vary in some predictable ways according to social class and ethnicity, and, as the next section explains, they typically evolve through stages linked to the life course.

STAGES OF FAMILY LIFE

The family is dynamic, with marked changes across the life course. Typically, family life begins with courtship, followed by settling into the realities of married life. Next, for most couples at least, is raising children, leading to the later years of marriage after children have left home to form families of their own. We will look briefly at each of these stages.

Courtship

Adults in preindustrial societies (who represent a majority of the world's people) generally consider courtship too important to be left to the young (Stone, 1977; Haviland, 1985). *Arranged marriages*, representing an alliance made by two extended families, usually involves a negotiation in terms of wealth, power, and prestige. Romantic love has little to do with it, and parents may make such arrangements when their children are quite young. A century ago in India, for example, half of all girls married before reaching the age of fifteen (Mayo, 1927; Mace & Mace, 1960).

Arranged marriages fit into Emile Durkheim's model of *mechanical solidarity* (see Chapter 4, "Society"). Because traditional societies are culturally homogeneous, almost any member of the opposite sex has been suitably socialized to perform the roles of spouse and parent. Thus parents can arrange marriages with little thought to whether or not the two individuals involved are *personally* compatible because they can be confident that virtually any couple will be *culturally* compatible.

Industrialization erodes the importance of extended families, weakens traditions, and enhances personal choice in courtship. Young people now expect to choose their own mates, and they delay doing so until gaining financial security and the experience they need to select a suitable marriage partner. Dating sharpens their skills and may serve as a period of sexual experimentation as well.

Our culture elevates *romantic love*—the experience of affection and sexual passion toward another person—as the basis for marriage. For us, marriage without love is difficult to imagine; popular culture—from remakes of traditional fairy tales like "Cinderella" to today's paperback romance novels—portrays love as the key to a successful marriage. Figure 17–1, on page 469, provides a comparative look at the importance of romantic love in several countries. While about half of today's college students in Pakistan and India claim they would marry partners they did not love, only a small percentage of students in industrial societies, including the United States, make the same assertion.

Our society's emphasis on romance has some useful consequences. Passionate love motivates individuals to "leave the nest" to form new families of their own, and it may also carry a new couple through difficult adjustments to the realities of living together (Goode, 1959). On the other hand, because feelings wax and wane, romantic love makes for a less stable foundation for marriage than do social and

RESOURCE: Among the classics included in the Macionis and Benokraitis reader, *Seeing Ourselves*, is Jessie Bernard's "'His' and 'Her' Marriage."

Q: "Shoring up marriages may require less infatuation and more responsibility." Amitai Etzioni

Q: "What does a woman do for herself and for her children by being fussy about her sexual partners? . . . if she focuses on male traits that are heritable, she sees to it that her kids start with a genetic edge. We aren't all created equal . . . [She also] makes it possible to pick males who will stick around and help raise the kids. A woman is not simply competing for quality sperm; she's competing for the man who goes with it." Heather Trexler Remoff (1984)

Although people in every society recognize the reality of physical attraction and romantic love, members of traditional societies often arrange marriages between people of the same social position with little consideration given to the partners' feelings for each other. In Japan, a society that has long been more traditional than our own, marriages guided by the head instead of the heart have been common. As the country has industrialized during this century, however, attitudes have changed so that most individuals, rather than their parents, now take primary responsibility for selecting a spouse.

economic considerations—an assertion supported by this country's high divorce rate compared to societies that afford people less choice about their partners.

But even in this age of choice, sociologists have long recognized that Cupid's arrow is aimed by society more than we like to think. Most people fall in love with others of the same race, of comparable age, and similar social class. All societies "arrange" marriages to the extent that they encourage **homogamy** (literally,

"like marrying like"), *marriage between people with the same social characteristics.*

In short, "falling in love" may be a strong personal feeling, but it is guided by a host of social forces. Perhaps we exaggerate the importance of romantic love to reassure ourselves that even in the midst of social controls we are capable of making personal choices.

Settling In: Ideal and Real Marriage

Our society presents marriage to the young in idealized, "happily-ever-after" terms. One consequence of such optimistic thinking is the danger of disappointment, especially for women—who, more than men, are taught to see in marriage the key to future happiness.

Then, too, romantic love involves a good deal of fantasy. We fall in love with others, not necessarily as they are, but as we want them to be (Berscheid & Hatfield, 1983). Only after marriage do many spouses regularly confront each other as they carry out the day-to-day routines of maintaining a household.

Sexuality is one source of disappointment. In the romantic haze of falling in love, people may anticipate marriage as an endless sexual honeymoon, only to face the sobering realization that sex becomes a less than all-consuming passion. While about two in three married people claim to be satisfied with the sexual dimension of their relationship, marital sex does decline over time, as Table 17–1, on page 470, shows.

Many experts agree that couples with the most fulfilling sexual relationships experience the greatest satisfaction in their marriages. This connection does not mean that sex is the key to marital bliss, but rather, that good sex and good relationships go together (Hunt, 1974; Tavris & Sadd, 1977; Blumstein & Schwartz, 1983).

Infidelity—sexual activity outside marriage—is another area in which the reality of marriage does not coincide with our cultural ideal. Traditional marriage vows "to forsake all others" appear to be strong, and in a recent survey, 90 percent of U.S. adults claimed that sex outside of marriage is "always wrong" or "almost always wrong." Even so, 21 percent of men and 13 percent of women indicated on a private, written questionnaire that they had—at least once—been sexually unfaithful to their partners (NORC, 1993:265, 715).

Child Rearing

Adults in the United States overwhelmingly identify raising children as one of life's greatest joys (NORC, 1993:616). This is so despite the undeniable fact that children make substantial demands on the time and

FIGURE 17–1

Percentage of College Students Who Express a Willingness to Marry Without Romantic Love

(Levine, 1993)

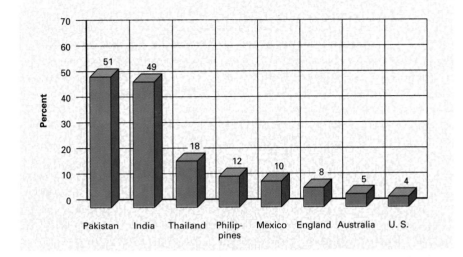

energy of parents, sometimes to the point of straining their marriage.

Not surprisingly, therefore, almost all adults in this society think that, ideally, a family should contain at least one child—as shown in Table 17–2, on page 470, —with two preferred by most.[2] Few people want more than four children, however, a marked change from two centuries ago, when *eight* children was the U.S. average (Newman & Matzke, 1984).

Families in preindustrial societies depend on children to perform labor, and people generally regard having children as a wife's duty. These assumptions, coupled with unreliable or nonexistent birth control technology, make childbearing a regular event. Finally, a high death rate in preindustrial societies prevents many children from reaching adulthood; as late as 1900, one-third of children born in the United States died by age ten (Wall, 1980).

Industrialization transforms children, economically speaking, from a vital asset to a burdensome liability. Today the expense of raising one child exceeds $100,000, a figure that doubles if the child attends college (U.S. Department of Agriculture, 1993). This expense helps to explain the steady drop in U.S. family size during the twentieth century to one child per family today.

Other industrial societies exhibit the same pattern of declining family size. But this trend contrasts sharply with poor societies in Latin America, Asia, and, especially, Africa, where many women have few alternatives to bearing and raising children. In such societies, four to six children is still the norm.

Parenting is not only expensive but is a lifetime commitment. As our society has afforded its members more choice about family life, more U.S. adults have opted to delay childbirth or to remain childless. In 1960, almost 90 percent of women between 25 and 29 who had ever married had at least one child; by 1990 this proportion had tumbled to 71 percent (U.S. Bureau of the Census, 1993). One recent survey indicates that about two-thirds of parents in the United States would like to devote far more of their time to child rearing (Snell, 1990). But unless we are willing to accept some decline in our material standard of living, economic realities demand that most parents pursue careers outside the home. Thus the child rearing patterns we have described reflect ways of coming to terms with economic change.

As explained in Chapter 13 ("Sex and Gender"), most women with young children are now working for income. In 1993, 58 percent of women over the age of fifteen were in the work force; the proportion of women with children under eighteen who work for income is now up to 68 percent (U.S. Bureau of the Census, 1993). But while women and men share the burden of earning income, women continue to bear the traditional responsibility for raising children and doing housework. Some men in our society are eager parents, yet most resist sharing responsibility for

---

[2]According to the U.S. Bureau of the Census, the median number of children per family was 0.96 in 1991; the median number of children among only married couples with children was about twice as great: 1.87 for whites, 1.90 for African Americans, and 2.18 for Hispanics (U.S. Bureau of the Census, 1993).

DIVERSITY: Later family life differs by sex: See Table 14-1 on page 395 for the different living arrangements of elderly women and men.
DIVERSITY: As people age, there are proportionately fewer males than females eligible for marriage. Regionally, this pattern is most pronounced in the Sunbelt; in San Diego, for example, there are three men aged 20 to 59 for every four women.

NOTE: Five of six U.S. women have at least one child during their lives.
GLOBAL: Ideal family size is higher in poor societies. One recent survey in Honduras placed the ideal figure as 3.2 children. In rural areas (containing 60% of the people) the actual family size is 6.9 children.

TABLE 17–1 Frequency of Sexual Activity Among Married Couples

Years Together	Sexual Intercourse (times per month)			
	1 or less	1–4	4–12	12 or more
0–2	6%	11%	38%	45%
2–10	6	21	46	27
10 or more	16	22	45	18

SOURCE: Adapted from Philip Blumstein and Pepper Schwartz, *American Couples* (New York: William Morrow, 1983), p. 196.

household tasks that our culture historically has defined as "women's work" (Radin, 1982).

As more women join men in the labor force, parents have less time for parenting. Currently, some 7 million young children—sometimes termed *latchkey kids*—are left by working parents to fend for themselves for some part of the day, and half of all nine-year-olds are unsupervised after school (U.S. Women's Bureau, 1989). Traditionalists such as Phyllis Schlafly (1984) condemn the trend toward more working mothers, claiming that families are simply neglecting their responsibilities to children. Progressives counter that such criticism targets women while assuming that men must work in order to support their families. But, they add, the same now holds for most working mothers (Keniston, 1985).

Congress took a step toward easing the conflict between family and job responsibilities by passing the Family and Medical Leave Act in 1993. This law allows up to ninety days of unpaid leave from work in order to care for a new child or because of a serious family emergency. But, for most adults in this country, there remains the problem of juggling parental and occupational responsibilities on a routine basis. This dilemma points to the heightened importance of child care facilities, as the box on page 471 explains.

The Family in Later Life

Increasing life expectancy in the United States means that, barring divorce, couples are likely to remain married for a long time. By about age fifty, most have completed the task of raising children. The remaining years of marriage—the "empty nest"—bring a return to living with only one's spouse.

Like the birth of children, their departure requires adjustments, although the marital relationship often becomes closer and more satisfying (Kalish, 1982). Years of living together may diminish a couple's sexual passion for each other, but mutual understanding and companionship are likely to increase.

Personal contact with children usually continues, since most older adults live a short distance from at least one of their children. Moreover, one-third of all U. S. adults (more than 50 million) are grandparents, and many of these men and women help their daughters and sons with child care and a host of other responsibilities. Among African Americans (who have a high rate of single parenting), many grandmothers assume a central position in family life (Shanas, 1979; Cherlin & Furstenberg, 1986; Crispell, 1993).

The other side of the coin, explained in Chapter 14 ("Aging and the Elderly"), is that more adults in midlife are facing the challenge of caring for their aging parents. The "empty nest" may not be filled by a parent coming to live in the home, but many adults find that parents living to eighty and beyond require practical, emotional, and financial care that can be more taxing than raising young children. The oldest of the "baby boomers"—now in their mid-forties—are being touted as the "sandwich generation" because they will spend as many years attending to their aging parents as they did caring for their own offspring.

Retirement, also discussed in Chapter 14 ("Aging and the Elderly"), brings further change to family life. If the wife has been a homemaker, the husband's retirement means that spouses will spend much more time together. Although the husband's presence is often a source of pleasure to both, it sometimes undermines wives' established routines to the point of intrusion. As one woman bluntly remarked: "I may have married him for better or worse, but not for lunch" (quoted in Kalish, 1982:96).

The final and surely the most difficult transition in married life comes with the death of a spouse. Wives typically outlive their husbands because of

TABLE 17–2 The Ideal Number of Children for U.S. Adults, 1990

Number of Children	Proportion of Respondents
0	1.1%
1	2.7
2	52.4
3	21.6
4	10.1
5	1.4
6 or more	0.7
As many as you want	6.0
No response	3.9

SOURCE: *General Social Surveys, 1972–1993: Cumulative Codebook* (Chicago: National Opinion Research Center, 1993), p. 260.

NOTE: According to the National Center for Health Statistics, 10% of U.S. births are unwanted, another 25% are "ill timed," meaning wanted but at a later date.
NOTE: The longest marriages in the U.S. today last about eighty years.

RESOURCE: Norval Glenn's article "Is Family Really Important?" is among the contemporary selections in the Macionis and Benokraitis reader, *Seeing Ourselves*.

SOCIAL POLICY

Who's Minding the Kids?

Traditionally, the task of providing daily care for young children fell to mothers. But with a majority of mothers and fathers now in the labor force, securing quality, affordable child care has become a high priority for parents.

The figure displays the source of care for U.S. children under five years of age whose mothers are working. The most common location of care—utilized in 36 percent of all cases—is the child's own home where the father or other relative usually provides supervision. An additional 31 percent of children receive care in another person's home, with either relatives or others (often neighbors or friends) looking after them. A small share of children accompany their mothers to work.

A day care facility or preschool is the setting for the remaining 23 percent of children with working mothers. The proportion in day care centers has doubled over the last decade because many parents have difficulty finding in-home care for their children.

Some day care centers handle dozens of children at one time, amounting to "tot lots" in which

children, "parked" by their parents for the day, receive little love and minimal attention. The impersonality of such settings, coupled with rapid turnover in staff, can undermine the warm and consistent nurturing that young children need in order to develop a sense of trust. Other child care centers, however, offer a secure and healthful environment. The balance of research suggests that *good* care centers are good for children; *bad* facilities are not.

Identifying high-quality child care facilities is not always easy. Parents must inspect centers carefully, inquiring about discipline policies, the ratio of children to care givers, and noting the cleanliness and safety of the surroundings. Such personal investigation is necessary since few states have comprehensive guidelines for operating child care centers, and some states have none at all.

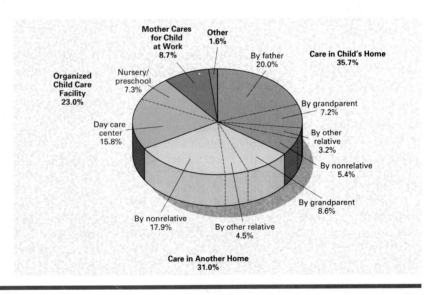

women's longer life expectancy and also because women usually marry men several years older to begin with. Wives can thus expect to spend a significant period of their lives as widows. The bereavement and loneliness accompanying the death of a spouse are always difficult. This experience may be even harder for widowers, who usually have fewer friends than widows do and may be unskilled at cooking and housework (Berardo, 1970).

U.S. FAMILIES: CLASS, RACE, AND GENDER

Dimensions of inequality—social class, ethnicity and race, and gender—are powerful forces that shape marriage and family life. Keep in mind that, while we will address each factor separately, they overlap in our lives.

Latinos traditionally have maintained strong kinship ties. Carmen Lomas Garza's 1988 painting, Tamalada ("Making Tamales"), *portrays the extended family that historically has undergirded Hispanic culture.*

Social Class

Social class molds a family's financial security and range of opportunities. Interviewing working-class women, Lillian Rubin (1976) found that wives deemed a good husband to be one who refrained from violence and excessive drinking and held a steady job. Rubin's middle-class informants, by contrast, never mentioned such things; these women simply *assumed* a husband would provide a safe and secure home. Their ideal husband was a man with whom they could communicate easily and share feelings and experiences.

Such differences reflect the fact that people with higher social standing have more schooling, and most have jobs that emphasize verbal skills. In addition, research points up that middle-class couples share a wider range of activities, while working-class life is more divided along gender lines. Conventionally masculine ideas of self-control, Rubin explains, can stifle emotional expressiveness on the part of working-class men, causing women to seek out members of their own sex as confidants.

Clearly, what women (and men) conclude that they can hope for in marriage—and what they end up with—is substantially linked to the social class that circumscribes their entire lives. Much the same holds for children in families; boys and girls lucky enough to be born into more affluent families enjoy better mental and physical health, develop higher self-confidence, and go on to greater achievement than poor children

do (Komarovsky, 1967; Bott, 1971; Rubin, 1976; Fitzpatrick, 1988; McLeod & Shanahan, 1993).

Ethnicity and Race

As Chapter 12 ("Race and Ethnicity") indicates, ethnicity and race are powerful social forces. The effects of both surface in family life.

Latino Families

Latinos in the United States are likely to enjoy the loyalty and support of extended families. Traditionally, too, Latino parents have exercised greater control over their children's courtship, defining marriage as an alliance of families rather than a union based simply on romantic love. A third trait of Latino family life is adherence to conventional gender roles. *Machismo*—masculine strength, daring, and sexual prowess—is pronounced among some Latinos, while women are both honored and closely supervised.

Assimilation into the larger society is gradually tempering these traditional patterns, however. Many Puerto Ricans who migrate to New York, for example, do not maintain the strong extended families they knew in Puerto Rico. Especially among affluent Hispanic families—whose number has tripled in the last twenty years—the traditional authority of men over women has diminished (Fitzpatrick, 1971; Ybarra, 1977; Staples & Mirande, 1980; Moore & Pachon, 1985; Nielsen, 1990; O'Hare, 1990).

Some Latinos have become quite prosperous; the overall social standing of this segment of the U.S. population, however, remains below average. The U.S. Census Bureau (1992) reports that, in 1990, the typical Hispanic family had an income of $23,901, about two-thirds that of the nation as a whole. Consequently, many Hispanic families contend with the stress of unemployment and other problems that accompany low income.

African-American Families

Analysis of African-American families must begin with the stark reality of economic disadvantage: As noted in earlier chapters, the typical African-American family earned $21,161 in 1992, not quite 60 percent of the national income standard. People of African ancestry are also three times as likely as whites to be poor, so that family patterns reflect unemployment, underemployment, and, in many cases, a physical environment replete with crime and drug abuse.

Q: "Each year more than a million American teenagers become pregnant. Four out of five of them are unmarried. Some 30,000 of those who become pregnant are under age thirteen. Both the pregnancy and birth rates for black teens are over four times higher than among white teens." Sharon P. Robinson (1987)

DIVERSITY: In 1990, there were some 720,000 so-called "mixed" marriages (some mix of African American/Asian/Native American/white), up from 450,000 in 1980. About 3% of U.S. births are racially mixed children. Annually, some 45,000 black/white children are born, along with 39,000 Asian/white children, 21,000 Native American/white children, and smaller numbers of other combinations.

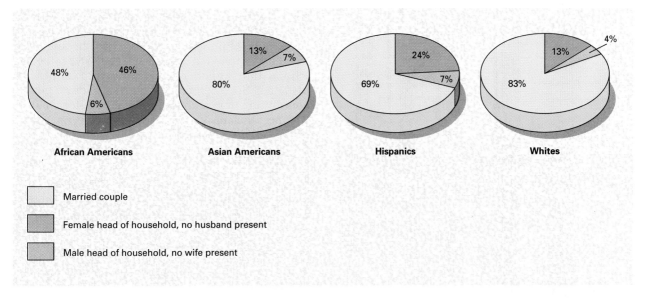

FIGURE 17–2 Family Form in the United States, 1992

(U.S. Bureau of the Census, 1993)

Under these circumstances, maintaining stable family ties is difficult. For example, 25 percent of African-American women now in their forties have never married, compared with about 10 percent of white women of the same age (Bennett, Bloom, & Craig, 1989). This means that women of color—often with children—are more likely to be single heads of households. As Figure 17–2 shows, women headed 46 percent of all African-American families in 1992, compared with 24 percent of Hispanic families, 13 percent of Asian or Pacific Islander families, and 13 percent of white families (U.S. Bureau of the Census, 1993).

Regardless of race, however, single-mother families are at high risk of poverty. About one-third of families headed by white women are poor, and the proportion is close to half among women of African or Hispanic ancestry. Note that African-American families with both wife and husband in the home—which represents half of the total—are not as economically vulnerable, earning 80 percent as much as comparable white families. But two-thirds of all African-American children are born to single women, and half of all African-American boys and girls are growing up poor, meaning that such families carry much of the burden of child poverty in the United States (Hogan & Kitagawa, 1985; U.S. Bureau of the Census, 1993).

A generation ago U.S. Senator Daniel Patrick Moynihan (1965) published a controversial report claiming the African-American family was in crisis because of the preponderance of single mothers and absent fathers. Such families, he argued, cannot provide the same level of supervision and care for children and, just as important, are likely to be poor. In Moynihan's view, a *cycle of poverty* had been unleashed in the black community that would pass disadvantage on to future generations.

Moynihan's analysis provoked strong criticism, largely because our society has no one model of ideal family life. African-American novelist and social critic Toni Morrison rebutted Moynihan's view stating, "I don't think a female running a house is a problem. It is perceived as one because of the notion that a 'head' is a man" (quoted in Angelo, 1989:120).

Critics also scolded Moynihan for implying that single-parent families were the *cause*—rather than the *consequence*—of poverty. According to William Ryan (1976), one way to blame poor people for their own poverty is to say they bring it on themselves because of how they choose to live. The reasons for the higher level of one-parent families among African Americans, Ryan maintains, lie in society: prejudice, discrimination, and lack of opportunity.

In support of Ryan's position, historical evidence indicates that the proportion of African-American families that are headed by women, although historically higher than among white people, increased after

SOCIAL SURVEY: "How much satisfaction do you get from your family life?" (GSS 1993, N = 1,057; *Codebook*, 1993:204)

"A very great deal"	40.9%	"Some"	2.9%
"A great deal"	34.2%	"A little"	2.5%
"Quite a bit"	9.4%	"None"	1.9%
"A fair amount"	7.4%	DK/NR	0.9%

GLOBAL: A consequence of traditional patriarchy and the introduction of a market system in the People's Republic of China is, according to the government, 18,692 investigations in 1990 of people allegedly selling women into slavery.

Q: "There are two marriages, then, in every marital union, his and hers. And his . . . is better than hers." Jessie Bernard

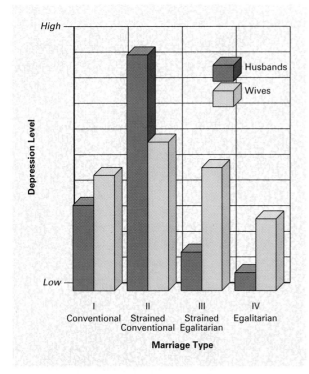

FIGURE 17–3 Depression in Four Types of Marriages

(Ross, Mirowsky, & Huber, 1983)

1940 when African Americans migrated in large numbers to cities. Many migrants came from rural areas with few industrial skills, and all were disadvantaged by racial prejudice and discrimination. The predictable result was that African Americans soon were caught up in a world of low-paying jobs that did not provide the financial security necessary to maintain a family (Gutman, 1976; Wilson, 1984).

More recently, the decline of manufacturing in the United States has hit African Americans hard. During the 1980s, the social standing of African Americans, on average, slipped slightly, and the black, urban underclass expanded (Updegrave, 1989). While Moynihan may have been wrong about the causes of this problem, his prediction thirty years ago has turned out to be tragically correct: A cycle of poverty has expanded among African-American women and their children (Ladner, 1986; Furstenberg, Brooks-Gunn, & Morgan, 1987).

At the same time, African Americans have devised distinctive strategies for coping with economic hardship. One source of strength is the extended family, which provides emotional and financial support. Grandparents play a special role: 11.6 percent of

African-American children live with a grandparent, compared to 6.0 percent of Hispanic children and 3.6 percent of white children. More broadly, men and women forge mutual dependence networks of people who assume kinlike roles (a substitute "aunt," for instance). Such resourcefulness has allowed people confronting tremendous barriers to care for children and meet their daily needs (Stack, 1975; Cherlin & Furstenberg, 1983; Leslie & Korman, 1989; Ruggles, 1994).

Gender

Among all races, Jessie Bernard (1982) asserts, every marriage is actually *two* different relationships: a woman's marriage and a man's marriage. Although the extent of patriarchy has diminished with time, even today few marriages are composed of two equal partners. College students of both sexes reported to Mirra Komarovsky (1973, 1976) that their ideal marriage had a dominant husband, evidence that this pattern is deeply embedded in our culture. No doubt, this fact explains why most of us expect men to be older as well as taller than their wives and to have more important careers (McRae, 1986).

What is curious, in light of patriarchy, is the persistent notion that marriage is more beneficial to women than to men (Bernard, 1982). The positive stereotype of the carefree bachelor contrasts sharply with the negative image of the lonely spinster. This idea is rooted in women's historic exclusion from the labor force, which made a woman's financial security dependent on having a husband.

But, Bernard claims, compared to single women, married women have poorer mental health and more passive attitudes toward life and report less personal happiness. Married men, by contrast, live longer than single men, have better mental health, and report being happier. These differences in marriage suggest why, after divorce, men are more eager than women to secure a new partner.

Bernard concludes that there is no better guarantor of long life, health, and happiness for a man than a woman well socialized to perform the "duties of a wife" by devoting her life to caring for him and providing the security of a well-ordered home. She is quick to add that marriage *could* be healthful for women if society would only end the practice of husbands' dominating wives and expecting them to perform all the housework.

A study of psychological depression among spouses in the United States helps to sort out the connections among gender, power, and mental health in marriage (Ross, Mirowsky, & Huber, 1983; Mirowsky &

Q: "... It is being relegated to the role of housewife rather than marriage itself that contributes heavily to the poor mental and emotional health of married women ..." Jessie Bernard

Q: "... [W]omen are always in some sense the 'second sex.'" Kathleen Gough

Q: "It is easier in these United States to walk away from a marriage than from a commitment to purchase a used car. Most contracts cannot be unilaterally abrogated; marriages in contemporary America can be terminated by practically anyone at any time, and without cause." Thomas Morgan

Ross, 1984). In what we might call "conventional" marriages (Type I in Figure 17–3, page 474), partners agree that only the husband will be employed and the wife will do all housework and child rearing. The researchers found that low to moderate levels of depression characterized spouses in conventional marriages, with men somewhat better off than women. This difference, according to the investigators, is due to husbands' benefiting from income and prestige derived from their jobs, while wives receive little prestige and no pay for their efforts.

In "strained conventional" marriages (Type II in the figure), the wife joins the husband in the labor force out of necessity, returning home to do all the housework and child rearing as well. This arrangement, as Figure 17–3 shows, is unfavorable for both partners: Depression is high for the wife (with two demanding jobs, one of which she does not want) but higher still for the husband (who thinks he should be able to support his wife but cannot). Note that this is the only marital pattern in which husbands have poorer mental health than wives.

In "strained egalitarian" marriages (Type III), both the husband and wife are happy that they both are working for income; yet, the wife is still responsible for almost all the housework and child care. Here, wives display somewhat lower levels of depression, and husbands benefit even more since they enjoy the benefits of greater family income.

"Egalitarian" marriages (Type IV) have both husband and wife happily working outside the home but also sharing most family responsibilities. This pattern is linked to the lowest depression levels for both husbands and wives in any of the four types of marriage. The researchers attribute this favorable pattern to the absence of tensions that arise when a working wife must also take responsibility for housework and children.

These findings support the conclusions by Jessie Bernard (1982) and others that more egalitarian marriages tend to be happier for husbands as well as wives. But such marriages are still relatively rare—probably involving no more than 10 percent of all couples—because conventional ideas about gender are deeply rooted in our way of life.

TRANSITION AND PROBLEMS IN FAMILY LIFE

Ann Landers (1984), a well-known observer of the U.S. scene, once remarked that "One marriage out of twenty is wonderful, four are good, ten are tolerable, and five are pure hell." Families can be a source of joy, but the reality of family life sometimes falls far short of this ideal.

Divorce

Our society strongly supports marriage, and nine out of ten people at some point "tie the knot." But many of today's marriages eventually unravel. Figure 17–4, on page 476, depicts the tenfold increase in the U.S. divorce rate over the last century. By 1990, according to government projections, about four in ten marriages were ending in divorce (for African Americans, about six in ten).

The high U.S. divorce rate is linked to a number of factors (Huber & Spitze, 1980; Kitson & Raschke, 1981; Thornton, 1985; Waite, Haggstrom, & Kanouse, 1985; Weitzman, 1985; Gerstel, 1987; Furstenberg & Cherlin, 1991):

1. **Individualism is on the rise.** Today, members of our society spend less time together than in the past. We have become more individualistic, seemingly more concerned with personal happiness and success than with the well-being of families.

2. **Romantic love often subsides.** Our culture emphasizes romantic love as a basis for marriage, rendering relationships vulnerable to collapse as sexual passion subsides. There is now widespread support for the notion that one may end a marriage in favor of a new relationship simply to renew excitement and romance.

3. **Women are now less dependent on men.** Their increasing participation in the labor force has reduced wives' financial dependency on husbands. As a practical matter, then, women find it easier to walk away from unhappy marriages.

4. **Many of today's marriages are stressful.** With both partners working outside the home in most cases, jobs consume time and energy that in the past were directed toward family life. Under such circumstances (and given the difficulty of securing high-quality, affordable child care), raising children is a particular burden. While children do stabilize some marriages, divorce is most common during the early years of marriage when many couples have young children.

5. **Divorce is more socially acceptable.** Divorce no longer carries the powerful, negative stigma it did a century ago. Couples considering divorce typically do not receive the discouragement from family and friends they once did.

SOCIAL SURVEY: "Should divorce in this country be easier or more difficult to obtain than it is now?" (GSS 1993, N = 1,080; *Codebook*, 1993:263)

| "Easier" | 25.9% | "More difficult" | 47.3% |
| "Same" | 19.5% | DK/NR | 7.2% |

SOCIAL SURVEY: Same question, by gender and race. (*STUDENT CHIP Social Survey Software*, DIVLAW1; GSS 1974–91, N = 14,655)

	"Easier"	"Same"	"Harder"
Afri Amer	51.2%	15.3%	33.5%
Latino	34.0%	19.1%	47.0%
Whites	24.2%	22.3%	53.5%
Women	25.0%	21.8%	53.3%
Men	30.1%	21.1%	48.8%

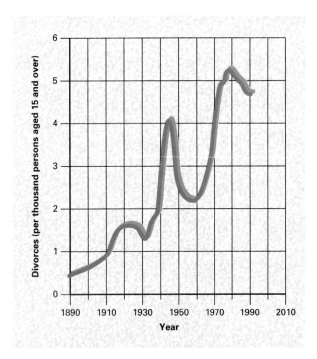

FIGURE 17–4 The Divorce Rate for the United States, 1890–1991

(U.S. Bureau of the Census, 1993)

6. **Divorce is legally easier to accomplish.** In the past, courts required divorcing couples to demonstrate that one or both were guilty of behavior such as adultery or physical abuse. Today most states allow divorce simply because a couple decides their marriage has failed. Almost half of all adults in the United States now think that a divorce is too easy to obtain (NORC, 1993:263).

The divorce rate has eased slightly downward over the last decade for two reasons. First, the large baby-boomer cohort that was born shortly after World War II is now reaching middle age, when divorce is less likely. Second, hard economic times discourage people from living alone, which, typically, is more expensive than living in families.

Although the trend may have turned for the moment, our society still has the highest divorce rate in the world: almost twice as high as Canada, four times as high as Japan, and ten times as high as Italy (U.S. Bureau of the Census, 1993). But Ed Kain (1990) reminds us that we commonly exaggerate the stability of marriage in the past when early death of a spouse ended as many marriages after a few years as divorce does now. But if marriages used to dissolve due to forces beyond people's control, they are now much more likely to end simply because people want to be single, or married to somebody else.

Who Divorces?

At greatest risk of divorce are young spouses, especially those who marry after a brief courtship, have few financial resources, and have yet to mature emotionally. People in lower social classes are also more likely to divorce due to financial strains. At all social levels, the risk of divorce rises if a couple marries in response to an unexpected pregnancy, or when one or both partners have alcohol- or other substance-abuse problems. People who are not religious have higher divorce rates than those who are.

Divorce also is more common among couples in which women have successful careers, partly due to the strains of a two-career marriage and, more important, because financially independent women are less inclined to remain in an unhappy marriage. Finally, men and women who divorce once are more likely to divorce again, presumably because problems follow them from one marriage to another (Booth & White, 1980; Yoder & Nichols, 1980; Glenn & Shelton, 1985).

Divorce is also more likely in some regions of the country than others. National Map 17–1 provides an overview of divorce rates across the United States.

Divorce as Process

Divorce is a form of *role exit*, as described in Chapter 6 ("Social Interaction in Everyday Life"). Paul Bohannan (1970) and others point to six distinct adjustments divorcing people make:

1. **Emotional divorce.** Distancing oneself from the former spouse usually begins before the formal break occurs. A deteriorating marriage can be fraught with disappointment and frustration, if not outright hostility.
2. **Legal divorce.** Since marriage is a legal contract, divorce involves a legal change of status. Often financial settlements are central to a divorce agreement.
3. **Psychic reorganization.** Many divorced people experience the ending of their marriage as personal failure. Loneliness, too, prompts ex-spouses to seek ways of restoring psychological health.
4. **Community reorganization.** Ending a marriage requires both partners to reorganize friendships

NOTE: Figure 17–4 illustrates the power of social forces in the individual decision to end a marriage: Besides climbing over the course of the century, divorce rates dropped during the Depression and rose rapidly at the end of World War II. Note, too, that the recent dip has a demographic component, since the baby boomers are now passing 40, when divorce becomes less likely.

NOTE: Among the U.S. population aged 18 or over, at any given time about 70% have been married; about 10% are currently divorced (and not remarried).

THE MAP: Correlates of higher divorce on the West Coast include a lower level of religiosity and a higher level of geographical mobility.

Seeing Ourselves

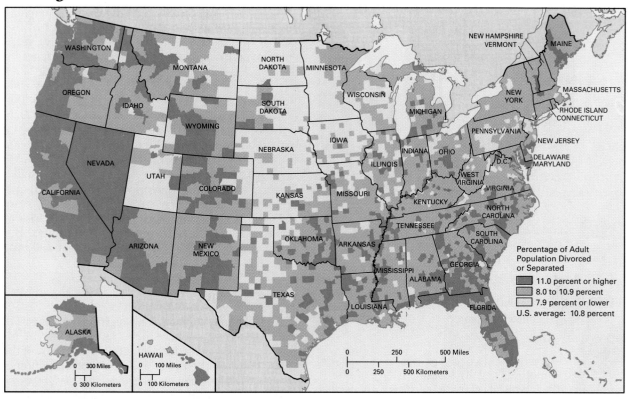

NATIONAL MAP 17–1 Divorce Rates Across the United States

Overall, about 11 percent of the U.S. population aged fifteen or over are divorced or separated. However, marriages are more vulnerable to breakup in the Pacific region of the country. Nevada has long been the U.S. divorce capital, due to its exceedingly liberal divorce laws. But divorce is also pronounced where religious values are weaker and where people are more likely to move often, thus distancing themselves from family and friends. How would you characterize the West Coast with regard to these factors?

From *American Demographics* magazine, October 1992, p. 5. Reprinted with permission. ©1992, *American Demographics* magazine, Ithaca, New York. Data from the 1990 decennial census.

and adjust relations with parents and other family members who are accustomed to seeing someone as part of a couple.

5. **Economic reorganization**. Recent no-fault divorce laws have reduced the amount of alimony and child support paid by men to their former wives. Further, divorce courts commonly require ex-spouses to sell homes and divide marital assets equally. While divorce raises the living standards of many men (who no longer support wives and children), it can mean financial calamity to women whose earnings are less than those of their husbands (Weitzman, 1985).

6. **Parental reorganization**. More than half of all divorcing couples must resolve the issue of child custody. Our society's conventional practice has been to award custody of children to mothers, based on the notion that women are better parents than men are. The recent trend, however, is toward joint custody, whereby children divide their time between the new homes of two parents. Joint custody is difficult if divorced parents live far apart or do not get along, but it has the advantage of keeping children in regular contact with both parents (Roman & Haddad, 1978; Cherlin & Furstenberg, 1983).

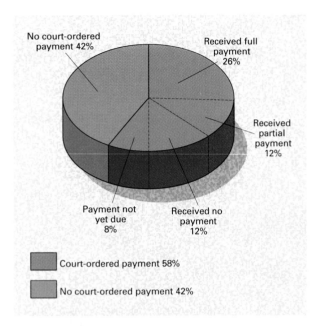

FIGURE 17–5 Payment of Child Support Following Divorce

(U.S. Bureau of the Census, 1993)

Because mothers usually secure custody of children but fathers typically earn more income, the well-being of children often depends on fathers making court-ordered child-support payments. As Figure 17–5 indicates, courts award child support in 58 percent of all divorces involving children. Yet, in any given year, nearly half of the children legally entitled to support receive partial payments or no payments at all. The failure of some 2.5 million "dead-beat dads" to support their youngsters prompted federal legislation mandating that employers withhold money from the earnings of parents who fail to pay up. Still, many fathers evade their responsibilities by moving or switching jobs (Weitzman, 1985; Waldman, 1992).

Conventional wisdom suggests that divorce is hardest on children. Divorce tears many young people from familiar surroundings, entangles them in bitter feuding, and frequently distances them from a parent they love. The tragedy of divorce is that, in their own minds, children often saddle themselves with blame for their parents' breakup. Some researchers contend that children who endure a parental divorce fare better than those who remain in a family torn by tension or violence. Ideally, of course, children thrive in the absence of both family conflict and divorce (Goetting, 1981; Zill, 1984; Wallerstein & Blakeslee, 1989).

Remarriage

Despite the rising divorce rate, marriage—and remarriage—remain as popular as ever. Four out of five people who divorce remarry, most within five years. Almost half of all marriages are now remarriages for at least one partner. Men, who derive greater benefits from wedlock, are more likely to remarry than women are.

Remarriage often creates *blended families*, composed of children and some combination of biological parents and stepparents. Members of blended families thus have to define precisely who is part of the child's nuclear family (Furstenberg, 1984). Blended families also require children to reorient themselves; an only child, for example, may suddenly find she has two older brothers. And, as already noted, the risk of divorce is high for partners in such families. But blended families also offer both young and old the opportunity to relax rigid family roles.

Family Violence

The ideal family serves as a haven from the dangers of the unfamiliar world. Since Cain's killing of his brother Abel as related in Genesis, the first book of the Bible, however, the disturbing reality of many homes has been **family violence**, *emotional, physical, or sexual abuse of one family member by another*. Sociologist Richard J. Gelles points to a chilling fact:

> The family is the most violent group in society with the exception of the police and the military. You are more likely to get killed, injured, or physically attacked in your home by someone you are related to than in any other social context. (quoted in Roesch, 1984:75)

Violence Against Women

Domestic violence against women exists in all social classes and among all races and ethnicities. Family brutality often goes unreported to police, but researchers estimate that about 9 million couples—or one in six—endure some form of violence each year. Between 1 and 2 million of these couples experience violence that results in serious physical injury. Researchers also note that men initiate most family violence and that women suffer most of the injuries (Straus & Gelles, 1986; Schwartz, 1987; Shupe, Stacey, and Hazlewood, 1987).

Government statistics show that almost 30 percent of women who are murdered—as opposed to 4 percent of men—are killed by partners or ex-partners.

Q: "'The family' is not 'here to stay.' Nor should we wish it were. On the contrary, I believe that all democratic people, whatever their kinship preferences, should work to hasten its demise. An ideological concept that imposes mythical homogeneity on the diverse means by which people organize their intimate relationships, 'the family' distorts and devalues the rich variety of kinship stories. And, along with class, racial, and heterosexual prejudices it promulgates this sentimental fictional plot authorizes gender hierarchy." Judith Stacey (1990:269–70)

DATA FILE: The Romanian policy of compulsory child rearing is described in the *Data File*.

NOTE: Primary groups are not immune to conflict, as suggested by the common sayings "You always hurt the one you love," and "Familiarity breeds contempt."

Nationwide, the death toll from family violence is four thousand women each year. Overall, women are more likely to be injured by a family member than to be mugged or raped by a stranger or hurt in an automobile accident.

Historically, the law declared wives the property of their husbands, so that no man could be charged with raping his wife. By 1990, however, forty states had passed *marital rape* laws although, in some cases, such a charge is permissible only under specific circumstances such as after legal separation (Russell, 1982; O'Reilly, 1983; Margolick, 1984; Goetting, 1989).

People who hear about a case of abuse often shake their heads and wonder, "Why didn't she just leave?" The answer is that most physically and emotionally abused women—especially those with children and without much money—have few options. Most wives are also committed to their marriages and believe (however unrealistically) that they can help abusive husbands to change. Some, unable to understand their husbands' violence, blame themselves. Others, raised in violent families, have learned to expect assault as part of family life.

In the past, the law regarded domestic violence as a private, family matter. Now, even without separation or divorce, a woman can obtain court protection from an abusive spouse. Since 1990, half the states have added "stalking laws" that prohibit an ex-partner from following or otherwise threatening a woman. Finally, communities across the United States have established shelters that provide counseling as well as temporary housing for women and children driven from their homes by domestic violence.

Violence Against Children

Family violence also victimizes children. Child abuse entails more than physical injury because abusive adults misuse power and trust to undermine a child's emotional well-being as well. Upwards of 2 million children—roughly 3 percent of all youngsters—suffer abuse each year, including several thousand who die as a result. Child abuse is most common among the youngest and most vulnerable children (Straus & Gelles, 1986; U.S. House of Representatives, 1987).

Many abused children suffer in silence, believing during their formative years that they are to blame for their own victimization. The initial abuse, compounded by years of guilt, can leave lasting emotional scars that prevent people abused as children from forming healthy relationships as adults.

About 90 percent of child abusers are men, but they conform to no simple stereotype. As one man

Nations, as well as parents, can abuse children. Prior to the fall of the Ceauçescu regime in 1989, the Romanian government denied women any form of birth control and banned abortion. Tens of thousands of unwanted children were the result, many of whom remain warehoused in orphanages like this one.

who entered a therapy group reported, "I kept waiting for all the guys with raincoats and greasy hair to show up. But everyone looked like regular middle-class people" (quoted in Lubenow, 1984). Most abusers, however, share one trait: having been abused themselves as children. Researchers have learned that violent behavior in close relationships is learned; in families, then, violence begets violence (Gwartney-Gibbs, Stockard, & Bohmer, 1987).

NOTE: Some of the changes in our thinking about family life involve a shift from family *form* to family *function*. Rather than defining the family as a single, traditional form, more people are saying, "If it works like a family, it *is* a family." The Latin root *familia* means simply "a household." Legally, the Lee Marvin palimony case advanced this idea, as have more recent laws in San Francisco and New York giving unmarried couples limited marital rights.

NOTE: In 1960, 5% of U.S. children were born to single mothers; the proportion has now risen above 20%. Of these mothers, about 40% are under age 20.

DIVERSITY: The share of African-American families with children headed by a married couple fell from 80% in 1890 to 39% in 1990.

ALTERNATIVE FAMILY FORMS

Most families in the United States are still composed of a married couple who raise children. But, in recent decades, our society has displayed greater diversity in family life.

One-Parent Families

About three in ten U.S. families with children under eighteen years of age have only one parent in the household—a proportion that doubled during the last generation. Put another way, more than half of all children now spend at least some time in a single-parent family before reaching eighteen years of age. *One-parent families*—four times as likely to include a mother than a father—may result from divorce, death, or the choice of an unmarried woman to have a child.

Entering the labor force has bolstered women's financial capacity to be single mothers, but single parenthood—especially when the parent is a woman—greatly increases the risks of poverty, as it limits the woman's ability to work and to further her education. At least one-third of women in the United States now become pregnant as unmarried teenagers, and many decide to raise their children. These young women with children—especially if they have the additional disadvantage of being minorities—form the core of the rising problem of child poverty in the United States (Kantrowitz, 1985; Wallis, 1985).

As shown earlier in Figure 17–2, 52 percent of African-American families are headed by a single parent. Single parenting is less common among Hispanics (31 percent), among Asian Americans (20 percent), and among non-Hispanic whites (17 percent). Among all categories of people, an increasing number of single-parent families are also multigenerational families. In practice, single parents (most of whom are mothers) commonly turn to their parents (again, typically, mothers) for support. Thus, more than 2.5 million U.S. children today are living in households with grandparents (U.S. Bureau of the Census, 1993).

Much contemporary research points to the conclusion that growing up in a one-parent family typically disadvantages children. Some studies suggest that a father and a mother each make a distinctive contribution to a child's social development, so it is unrealistic to expect one parent alone to do as good a job as two working together. But the most serious problem among families with one parent—especially if that parent is a woman—is poverty. On average, children growing up in a single-parent family start out with disadvantages and go on to lesser educational achievement, lower incomes, and greater chance of forming single-parent families themselves (Mueller & Cooper, 1984; McLanahan, 1985; Weisner & Eiduson, 1986; Wallerstein & Blakeslee, 1989; Astone & McLanahan, 1991; Li & Wojtkiewicz, 1992; Biblarz & Raftery, 1993; Popenoe, 1993).

Cohabitation

Cohabitation is *the sharing of a household by an unmarried couple*. A generation ago, widespread use of terms such as "shacking up" and "living in sin" indicated the common view of cohabitation as deviant. As our society has grown more accepting of premarital sex, the number of cohabiting couples in the United States has increased sharply, from about 500,000 in 1970 to 3.3 million by 1992, a figure that represents 6 percent of all couples (U.S. Bureau of the Census, 1993).

Certainly much cohabitation is the product of sexual passion; but, in today's uncertain economic climate, moving in together is also a practical way two people of the opposite sex can trim expenses. In any case, although most cohabitation occurs among the young, it usually does not lead to marriage. Rather, cohabiting is becoming a normative way to test the strength of a serious relationship (Gwartney-Gibbs, 1986).

In global perspective, cohabitation is common in Sweden and other Scandinavian societies as a long-term form of family life, with or without children. By contrast, this family form is rare in more traditional (and Roman Catholic) nations such as Italy. While cohabitation is gaining in popularity in the United States—perhaps 25 percent of our population does so at some point in their lives—such partnerships are still usually short-term, with perhaps 40 percent of couples marrying after several years, and the remainder splitting up (Blumstein & Schwartz, 1983; Macklin, 1983; Popenoe, 1988, 1991, 1992).

Gay and Lesbian Couples

In 1989, Denmark became the first country to formally recognize homosexual marriages, thereby extending to gay and lesbian couples legal advantages for inheritance, taxation, and joint property ownership, as well as social legitimacy. Danish law, however, stops short of allowing homosexual couples to adopt children. In the United States, while gay people cannot legally marry, some cities (including San Francisco

NOTE: In 1992, *The Star Tribune* in Minneapolis became the first newspaper to list gay "domestic partnerships" on the wedding page.

NOTE: Economic pressure and delaying marriage is encouraging single men and women to live with parents. In 1990, among single people 25–34, 32% of men and 20% of women were living with parents.

NOTE: The Census Bureau estimates the number of U.S. cohabiting couples at some 2.5 million, up 60% since 1970.

Q: "We have Model T laws catching up with space-age technology." Lori Andrews, American Bar Foundation, on legal and ethical issues arising out of new reproductive technologies

and New York) confer some of the legal benefits of marriage on such couples.

A decade ago, most gay couples in households including children were raising the offspring of previous, heterosexual unions. The 1980s witnessed a "gay-by boom," that is, a baby boom fueled by more adoptions by gay partners. Today, however, an increasing number of gay couples are having children of their own. A gay male couple can have a child by hiring a surrogate mother who agrees to allow doctors to impregnate her using the sperm of one of the men. Sperm banks provide the opportunity for one or both lesbian partners to become pregnant.

There are at least 1 million gay and lesbian couples in the United States who are now raising one or more children. While this pattern challenges many traditional notions about families in the United States, it also indicates that many gay and lesbian couples perceive the same rewards in child rearing that "straight" couples do (Bell, Weinberg, & Kiefer-Hammersmith, 1981; Gross, 1991; Pressley & Andrews, 1992).

Singlehood

Living alone in the United States is most common among young men (who have yet to marry) and elderly women (who are widows). The rate of singlehood, however, is now increasing among young and middle-aged people—especially women (Exner, 1992).

In 1950, only one household in ten consisted of a single person. By 1992, this proportion had risen to about one in four: a total of 23 million single adults. Most striking is the surging number of single young women. In 1960, 28 percent of women aged twenty to twenty-four were single; by 1992 the proportion had soared to two-thirds. Underlying this trend is women's greater participation in the labor force: Women who are economically secure view a husband as a matter of choice rather than a financial necessity.

By midlife, however, unmarried women sense a lack of available men. Because our culture frowns on women marrying partners much younger than they are (while encouraging a man to do so), middle-aged women who do wish to marry find the odds against them rising. In 1992, there were only four unmarried men aged forty to forty-four for every five unmarried women of the same age (U.S. Bureau of the Census, 1993). Because we expect women to "marry up," the older a woman is, the more education she has, and the better her job, the more difficulty she will have in finding a suitable husband (Leslie & Korman, 1989).

NEW REPRODUCTIVE TECHNOLOGY AND THE FAMILY

In 1991, Arlette Schweitzer, a forty-two-year-old librarian living in Aberdeen, South Dakota, became the first woman on record to bear her own grandchildren. Because her daughter was unable to carry a baby to term, Schweitzer agreed to have her daughter's fertilized embryos surgically implanted in her own womb. Nine months later, her efforts yielded a healthy boy and girl (Kolata, 1991).

Such a case illustrates how *new reproductive technology* has created new choices for families and sparked new controversies for society as a whole. The benefits of this rapidly developing technology are exciting; but its use raises daunting ethical questions about the creation and manipulation of life itself.

In Vitro Fertilization

In the twenty years since England's Louise Brown became the world's first "test-tube" baby, thousands of people have been conceived in this way. Early in the next century, 2 or 3 percent of the population of industrial societies may be the result of new birth technologies.

Technically speaking, test-tube babies result from *in vitro fertilization*, a procedure whereby the male sperm and the female ovum are united "in glass" rather than in a woman's body. In this complex medical procedure, doctors use drugs to stimulate the woman's ovaries to produce more than one egg during a reproductive cycle. Then they surgically "harvest" eggs from the ovaries and combine them with sperm in a laboratory dish. The successful fusion of eggs and sperm produces embryos, which surgeons then either implant in the womb of a woman who is to bear the child or, perhaps, freeze for use at a later time.

The immediate benefit of *in vitro* fertilization is to help couples who cannot conceive normally to have children. Looking further ahead, new birth technologies may help reduce the incidence of birth defects. By genetically screening sperm and eggs, medical specialists expect to increase the odds for the birth of a healthy baby (Vines, 1986; Ostling, 1987).

Ethical Issues

Ethical debate over these methods of manipulating life is a classic example of *cultural lag* (see Chapter 3, "Culture"), in which society has yet to catch up to the moral implications of a new technology.

SOCIAL SURVEY: "Should methods of birth control be available to teenagers between the ages of 14 and 16 if their parents do not approve?" (GSS 1993, N = 1,080; *Codebook*, 1993:262)
"Strongly agree"   25.8%   "Strongly disagree"   17.7%
"Agree"   30.1%   DK/NR   4.0%
"Disagree"   22.4%

Q: "Neither the pessimists who believe that the family is falling apart nor the unbridled optimists who claim that the family has never been in better shape provide an accurate picture of family life in the near future. But . . . what we have come to view as the 'traditional' family will no longer predominate." Andrew Cherlin and Frank F. Furstenberg, Jr.

LOOKING AHEAD: FAMILY IN THE TWENTY-FIRST CENTURY

Family life in the United States has changed in recent decades and will continue to do so. Transformation generates controversy, of course, with advocates of "traditional family values" locked in debate with supporters of new family forms and greater personal choice (Berger & Berger, 1983). Sociologists cannot predict the outcome of this debate but, more modestly, our discussions do suggest five directions of future change.

First, a high rate of divorce has dissolved the idea that marriage is a lifetime commitment. In fact, marital relationships are as durable today as they were a century ago, since back then many marriages were cut short by death (Kain, 1990). But more couples now *choose* to end their marriages. Although the divorce rate has stabilized recently, it is unlikely that marriage will regain the durability characteristic of the 1950s. One major reason is that increasing numbers of women are able to support themselves, and traditional marriages appeal to fewer of them. Men, as well, are seeking more satisfying relationships. We probably should view the recent trend toward higher divorce rates less as a threat to families than as a sign of change in family form. After all, most divorces still lead to remarriage, casting doubt on the notion that marriage is becoming obsolete.

Second, family life in the twenty-first century will be highly variable. We have noted an increasing number of cohabiting couples, one-parent families, gay and lesbian families, and blended families. Most families, of course, still are based on marriage, and most married couples still have children. But, taken together, the variety of family forms represents an emerging conception of family life as a matter of choice.

Third, in most families, men now play a limited role in child rearing. In the 1950s, a decade many people see as the "golden age" of families, men began the trend toward "hands-off" parenting (Snell, 1990; Stacey, 1990). A countertrend is now emerging as some fathers—older, on average, and more established in their careers—eagerly jump into parenting. But, on balance, the high U.S. divorce rate and a surge in single motherhood point to more children growing up with weaker ties to fathers than ever before. Not all researchers agree that the absence of fathers is directly and significantly detrimental to children; but there is little doubt that the absence of husbands and fathers from families contributes to rising levels of children living in poverty in the United States.

For better or worse, the family is certainly changing. But the fact that young people still find marriage so attractive—even amid the most severe adversity—suggests that families will continue to play a central role in society for centuries to come.

The high cost of *in vitro* fertilization (typically exceeding $10,000) places this procedure within reach of only a small number of people. In addition, as they decide when to employ or withhold this technique, medical experts are in a position to define what constitutes a proper "family." In most cases, doctors and hospitals have restricted *in vitro* fertilization to women under forty years of age who have male partners. Single women, older women, and lesbian couples are only gradually gaining access to this technology.

But all types of new reproductive technology— from laboratory fertilization to *surrogate motherhood*, in which one woman bears a child for another—force us to confront the inadequacy of conventional kinship terms (Arlette Schweitzer is, in one sense, mother and, in another way, grandmother, to the twins she bore). Then, too, we need to consider that, when it comes to manipulating life, what is technically possible may not always be morally desirable.

Fourth, economic changes are reforming marriage and the family. In many families, both household partners must work to ensure their financial security. As Arlie Hochschild (1988) points out, economic changes reshape society, but people *feel* these changes in family life. Marriage today is often the interaction of weary men and women; adults try their best to attend to children, yet worry that popular ideas like "quality time" amount to nothing more than justifications for minimal parenting (Dizard & Gadlin, 1990). Two-career couples may advance the goal of gender equality, but the long-term effects on families are likely to be mixed.

Fifth and finally, the importance of new reproductive technology will increase. While ethical concerns surely will slow these developments, new forms of reproduction will continue to alter the traditional meanings of parenthood.

Despite social changes that have buffeted the family in the United States, most people still report being happy as partners and parents (Cherlin & Furstenberg, 1983). Marriage and family life today may be more controversial than in the past, but both will likely remain the foundation of our society for some time to come.

SUMMARY

1. All societies are built on kinship, although family forms vary considerably across cultures and over time.

2. In industrial societies such as the United States, marriage is monogamous. Many preindustrial societies, however, permit polygamy, of which there are two types: polygyny and polyandry.

3. In global perspective, patrilocality is most common, while industrial societies favor neolocality and a few societies have matrilocal residence. Industrial societies utilize bilateral descent, while preindustrial societies tend to be either patrilineal or matrilineal.

4. Structural-functional analysis identifies major family functions: socializing the young, regulating sexual activity, transmitting social placement, and providing material and emotional support.

5. Social-conflict theories explore how the family perpetuates social inequality by strengthening divisions based on class, ethnicity, race, and gender.

6. Micro-level analysis highlights the variable nature of family life both over time and as experienced by various family members.

7. Families originate in the process of courtship. Unlike the United States, most societies limit the role of romantic love in the choice of a mate. But even among members of our society, romantic love tends to join people with similar social backgrounds.

8. The vast majority of married couples have children, although family size has decreased over time. The key reason for this decline is industrialization, which transforms children into economic liabilities, encourages women to join the labor force, and reduces infant mortality.

9. In later life, married life changes as children leave home to form families of their own. Many middle-aged couples, however, continue to care for aging parents and are active grandparents. The final stage of marriage begins with the death of one spouse, usually the husband.

10. Families differ according to class position, race, and ethnicity. Latino families, for example, are more likely than others to maintain extended kinship ties. African-American families are more likely than others to be headed by women. Among all categories of people, well-to-do families enjoy the most options and greatest financial security.

11. Gender affects family dynamics since husbands dominate the vast majority of families. Research suggests that marriage provides more benefits to men than to women.

12. The divorce rate today is ten times what it was a century ago; four in ten current marriages will end in divorce. Most people who divorce—especially men—remarry, often forming blended families that include children from previous marriages.

13. Family violence, victimizing both women and children, is far more common than official records indicate. Commonly, adults who abuse family members suffered abuse themselves as children.

14. Our society's family life is becoming more varied. One-parent families, cohabitation, gay and lesbian couples, and singlehood have proliferated in recent years. While the law does not recognize homosexual marriages, many gay men and lesbians form long-lasting relationships and, increasingly, are becoming parents.

15. Although ethically controversial, new reproductive technology is altering conventional notions of parenthood.

KEY CONCEPTS

bilateral descent a system tracing kinship through both females and males

cohabitation the sharing of a household by an unmarried couple

descent the system by which members of a society trace kinship over generations

endogamy marriage between people of the same social category

exogamy marriage between people of different social categories

extended family (consanguine family) a family unit including parents and children, but also other kin

family a social institution, found in all societies, that unites individuals into cooperative groups that oversee the bearing and raising of children

family unit a social group of two or more people, related by blood, marriage, or adoption, who usually live together

family violence emotional, physical, or sexual abuse of one family member by another

homogamy marriage between people with the same social characteristics

incest taboo a cultural norm forbidding sexual relations or marriage between certain kin

kinship a social bond, based on blood, marriage, or adoption, that joins individuals into families

marriage a legally sanctioned relationship, involving economic cooperation as well as normative sexual activity and childbearing, that people expect to be enduring

matrilineal descent a system tracing kinship through females

matrilocality a residential pattern in which a married couple lives with or near the wife's family

monogamy a form of marriage involving two partners

neolocality a residential pattern in which a married couple lives apart from the parents of both spouses

nuclear family (conjugal family) a family unit composed of one or two parents and their children

patrilineal descent a system tracing kinship through males

patrilocality a residential pattern in which a married couple lives with or near the husband's family

polyandry a form of marriage joining one female with two or more males

polygamy a form of marriage uniting three or more people

polygyny a form of marriage joining one male with two or more females

CRITICAL-THINKING QUESTIONS

1. What are several of the most significant trends affecting family life? What are the causes of family transformation?

2. Why do some analysts describe the family as the "backbone of society"? How do families perpetuate social inequality?

3. What are some typical changes that occur in an individual's participation in family life over the life course?

4. On balance, are families in the United States becoming weaker or not? What evidence supports your contention?

SUGGESTED READINGS

Classic Sources

Herbert G. Gutman. *The Black Family in Slavery and Freedom: 1750–1925.* New York: Pantheon Books, 1976.

This book is one of the most influential studies of the history of the African-American family in the United States.

Michael Young and Peter Willmott. *Family and Kinship in East London.* Berkeley: University of California Press, 1992 (orig. 1957).

One of the best studies of the working-class family, this account of the lives of "Eastenders" reveals the power of class to shape family life.

Contemporary Sources

Nijole V. Benokraitis. *Marriages and Families.* Englewood Cliffs, N.J.: Prentice Hall, 1993.

This comprehensive and authoritative textbook offers a detailed look at marriage and the family.

Lillian Rubin. *Families on the Fault Line: America's Working Class Speaks About the Family, the Economy, Race, and Ethnicity.* New York: HarperCollins, 1994.

Using interviews, Rubin conveys working-class families' sense of themselves and their society in hard economic times.

Stephanie Coontz. *The Way We Never Were: American Families and the Nostalgia Trap.* New York: Basic Books, 1992.

This historical study of families in the United States challenges the notion that families are in decline.

Corinne Azen Krause. *Grandmothers, Mothers, and Daughters: Oral Histories of Three Generations of Ethnic American Women.* Boston: Twayne Publishers/ G. K. Hall, 1991.

This account, rich in historical detail, explores changes in class, ethnicity, and family life over several generations.

Diana E. H. Russell. *Rape in Marriage.* Bloomington: Indiana University Press, 1990.

An updated edition of a widely read book that provides data on marital rape laws in each state.

Suzanne M. Retzinger. *Violent Emotions: Shame and Rage in Marital Quarrels.* Newbury Park, Calif.: Sage, 1991.

Despite the ideal of the family as a haven from trouble, troubled families are common in the United States.

Marcia Millman, *Warm Hearts and Cold Cash: The Intimate Dynamics of Families and Money.* New York: The Free Press, 1991.

Economics exerts a strong influence inside families. This book analyzes how making money, spending it, and giving it away affects relations among family members.

Kris Kissman and Jo Ann Allen. *Single Parent Families.* Newbury Park, Calif.: Sage, 1993.

This book offers practical help for social service workers seeking to understand the special needs of single-parent families.

Maria P. Root, ed. *Racially Mixed People in America.* Newbury Park, Calif.: Sage, 1992.

Although the number of racially mixed couples and their children is rising rapidly, sociologists have paid little attention to this distinctive type of family.

Global Sources

Marion J. Levy, Jr. *Maternal Influence: The Search for Social Universals.* New Brunswick, N.J.: Transaction, 1992.

This comparative look at motherhood examines global commonalities and asserts that social researchers tend to downplay the importance of mothering in child development.

Deborah Davis and Steven Harrell, eds. *Chinese Families in the Post-Mao Era.* Berkeley: University of California Press, 1992.

A dozen essays explore the state of family life in today's People's Republic of China.

Mark Mathabane. *African Women: Three Generations.* New York: HarperCollins, 1994.

A personal look at three women—grandmother, mother, and sister—by a South African details the struggles common to women under a system of racial oppression.

David Popenoe. *Disturbing the Nest: Family Change and Decline in Modern Societies.* New York: Aldine de Gruyter, 1988.

This comparative analysis of Sweden, Switzerland, New Zealand, and the United States explains the causes and consequences of what the author argues is a trend toward weaker families.

Jacob Lawrence, *Praying Ministers*, 1962

DATA FILE: An outline for this chapter, supplemental lecture material, and suggested discussion topics are provided in the *Data File*.
Q: "Religious insanity is very common in the United States." Alexis de Tocqueville

NOTE: The Latin root of the word "sacred" means both "devotion" and "holy"; the Latin *profan(us)* means "outside of the temple."
NOTE: A common Latin root join the words *faith* and *trust*.

Religion

*A*bout the time most people in the small town of Conyers, Georgia (population 7,380) are waking up, a long line of vehicles already clogs state highway 138. As state troopers wave cars, trucks, and tour buses into fields marked by "Pilgrim Parking" signs, a large crowd—including dozens of men and women in wheelchairs—swells over the thirty-acre farm of Nancy Fowler, a forty-three-year-old former nurse. The commotion began six years ago, when Fowler claims she started seeing visions in the sky of Jesus Christ and the Virgin Mary.

At noon, the crowd begins the Catholic ritual of chanting the Rosary. After almost an hour, Fowler whispers to a select group in her small, one-story home that Mary is descending, barely visible in the brilliant sunlight. The word spreads, and the crowd falls silent, video cameras whirring, as people intently

gaze upward at the sun. Suddenly some people shout that they see Mary, and the excitement ripples through the assembled faithful. After some time, an announcer intones, "The Virgin Mary will now bless us," and people thrust their arms upward, holding aloft beads, crosses, and pictures of Christ as their faces radiate a mix of wonder, excitement, and joy.

Divine sightings of this kind are reported regularly at several European sites—the best known are Lourdes in France and Fátima in Portugal—but most often in the United States. Although skeptical people dismiss such extraordinary experiences as little more than self-delusion and the Roman Catholic Church officially discourages reports of such miracles, the prospect of divine revelation draws hundreds of thousands of people each year to Conyers, Georgia, and elsewhere (Smolowe, 1993).

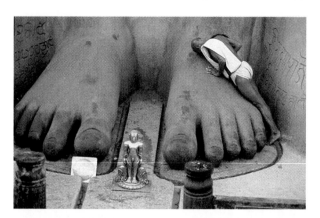

Religion is founded on the idea of the sacred, that which is set apart as extraordinary and which demands our submission. Bowing, kneeling, or prostrating oneself—each a common element of religious devotion—symbolizes this submissiveness.

The timeless human fascination with other-worldly truth lies at the heart of religion. This chapter explains what religion is, explores the changing face of religious belief throughout history and around the world, and examines the place of religion in today's modern, scientific culture. As we shall see, religion is a social institution that continues to address questions about the ultimate meaning of life in ways that no other dimension of society can.

RELIGION: BASIC CONCEPTS

French sociologist Emile Durkheim, whose ideas are discussed in detail in Chapter 4 ("Society"), claimed that the focus of religion is "things that surpass the limits of our knowledge" (1965:62; orig. 1915). As human beings, Durkheim explained, we organize our surroundings by defining most objects, events, or experiences as **profane** (from the Latin for "outside the temple"), *that which is an ordinary element of everyday life*. But we set some things apart, Durkheim continued, by designating them as **sacred**, *that which is defined as extraordinary, inspiring a sense of awe, reverence, and even fear*. Distinguishing the sacred from the profane is the essence of all religious belief. **Religion**, then, is *a social institution involving beliefs and practices based upon a conception of the sacred*.

A global perspective reveals that matters of faith vary greatly, with no one thing sacred to everyone on earth. Although people regard most books as profane, Jews view the Torah (the first five books of the Hebrew Bible or Old Testament) as sacred, in the same way that Christians revere the entire Bible and Muslims exalt the Quran (Koran).

However a community of believers draws religious lines, Durkheim (1965:62) claimed, people understand profane things in terms of their everyday usefulness: We sit down at a computer or turn the key of a car to accomplish various jobs. What is sacred, however, we reverently set apart from everyday life and denote as "forbidden." To make clear the boundary between the sacred and the profane, Muslims remove their shoes before entering a mosque to avoid defiling a sacred place of worship with soles that have touched the profane ground outside.

The sacred is the focus of **ritual**, which is *formal, ceremonial behavior*. Holy communion is the central ritual of Christianity; the wafer and wine consumed during communion symbolize the body and blood of Jesus Christ, and are never treated as food.

Religion and Sociology

Because religion deals with ideas that transcend everyday experience, neither common sense nor any scientific discipline can verify or disprove religious doctrine. Religion is a matter of **faith**, *belief anchored in conviction rather than scientific evidence*. For instance, the New Testament of the Bible defines faith as "the assurance of things hoped for, the conviction of things not seen" (Heb. 11:1) and exhorts Christians to "walk by faith, not by sight" (2 Cor. 5:7).

Throughout most of human history, human beings living in small societies attributed birth, death, and whatever happened in between to the operation of supernatural forces. Over the course of the last several hundred years, however, science has emerged as an alternative way of understanding the natural world, and scientific sociology offers various explanations of how and why societies operate the way they do.

Some people with strong faith may be disturbed by the thought of sociologists turning a scientific eye to what they hold as sacred. In truth, however, a sociological study of religion is no threat to anyone's faith. Sociologists recognize that religion is central to virtually every culture on earth, and they seek to understand how religious beliefs and practices guide human societies. They offer no comment on the meaning and purpose of human existence, nor can they pass judgment on any religion as right or wrong. Rather, scientific sociology delves into the consequences of religious activity for larger social life.

SOCIAL SURVEY: Illustrating religious social control, Carol Tavris and Susan Sadd (1977:38) found the following incidence of premarital sex:

"Strongly religious"   61%   "Slightly religious"   86%
"Fairly religious"   78%   "Not religious"   89%

THEORETICAL ANALYSIS OF RELIGION

Although, as individuals, sociologists may have any number of religious beliefs—or none at all—they all agree that religion has major importance for the operation of society. Each theoretical paradigm suggests ways in which religion affects social life.

Functions of Religion: Structural-Functional Analysis

Emile Durkheim (1965; orig. 1915) maintained that we confront the power of society every day. Society, he argued, has an existence and power of its own beyond the life of any individual. Thus, society itself is "god-like," surviving the ultimate deaths of its members whose lives it shapes. Durkheim contended that, in religious life, people celebrate the awesome power of their own society.

This insight explains the practice, in every society, of transforming certain everyday objects into sacred symbols of collective life. Members of technologically simple societies, Durkheim explained, do this with the **totem,** *an object in the natural world collectively defined as sacred.* The totem—perhaps an animal or an elaborate work of art—becomes the centerpiece of ritual, symbolizing the power of society to transform individuals into a powerful collectivity. In our society, the flag is a quasi-sacred totem. It is not to be used in a profane manner (say, as clothing) or allowed to touch the ground. In addition, placing the inscription "In God We Trust" on all currency (begun in the 1860s at the time of the Civil War) implies a national bond of religious belief. Local communities across the United States also gain a sense of unity through totemlike symbolism attached to sports teams: from the New England "Patriots," to the Ohio State University "Buckeyes," to the Los Angeles "Rams."

Durkheim pointed out three major functions of religion for the operation of society:

1. **Social cohesion.** Religion unites people through shared symbols, values, and norms. Religious doctrine and ritual establish rules of "fair play" that make organized social life possible. Religion also involves the vital human dimension of *love.* Thus, religious life also underscores both our moral and emotional ties to others (Wright & D'Antonio, 1980).

2. **Social control.** Every society uses religious imagery and rhetoric to promote conformity. Societies give many cultural norms—especially mores that deal with marriage and reproduction—religious justification. More broadly, religion confers legitimacy on the political system. In medieval Europe, in fact, monarchs claimed to rule by divine right. Few of today's political leaders invoke religion so explicitly, but many publicly ask for God's blessing, implying to audiences that their efforts are right and just.

3. **Providing meaning and purpose.** Religious beliefs offer the comforting sense that the vulnerable human condition serves some greater purpose. Strengthened by such convictions, people are less likely to collapse in despair when confronted by life's calamities. For this reason, major life-course transitions—including birth, marriage, and death—are usually marked by religious observances that enhance our spiritual awareness.

Critical evaluation. Durkheim's structural-functional analysis contends that religious symbolism, in essence, makes society possible. The major weakness of this approach, however, is its tendency to downplay religion's dysfunctions—especially the capacity of strongly held beliefs to generate social conflict. During the early Middle Ages, for example, religious faith was the driving force behind the Crusades, in which European Christians sought to wrest from Muslim control lands that both religions considered to be sacred. Conflict among Muslims, Jews, and Christians continues as a source of political instability in the Middle East today. Social divisions in Northern Ireland are also partly a matter of religious conflict between Protestants and Catholics; Dutch Calvinism historically supported apartheid in South Africa; and religious differences continue to fuel divisions in India, Sri Lanka, and elsewhere. In short, nations have long marched to war under the banner of their god; few analysts dispute the fact that differences in faith have provoked more violence in the world than have differences of social class.

The Social Construction of the Sacred

"Society," asserts Peter Berger (1967:3) "is a human product and nothing but a human product, that yet continuously acts back upon its producer." From a symbolic-interactionist point of view, religion (like all of society) is socially constructed (although perhaps

Q: "Science is meaningless because it gives no answer to our question, the only question important for us: 'What shall we do and how shall we live?'" Russian novelist Leo Tolstoy

Q: "The more of himself man attributes to God, the less he has left in himself." Karl Marx

Q: "In everyday life it is just as important that some things can be silently taken for granted as that some things are reaffirmed in so many words. Indeed, the most fundamental assumptions about the world . . . are so 'obvious' that there is no need to put them into words." Peter Berger

Religion has always held a special promise to the poor, reaffirming the dignity of people flogged by famine and holding out hope of a better life to come. Christian churches are currently thriving in the poorest regions of southern Africa. There, Christian ideals are expressed passionately in some of the world's most inspirational religious art.

with divine inspiration). This paradigm highlights how individuals—through various rituals from saying grace before daily meals to annual religious observances such as Easter or Passover—develop the distinction between the sacred and profane. Further, Berger explains, placing everyday events within a "cosmic frame of reference" confers on the fallible, transitory creations of human beings "the semblance of ultimate security and permanence" (1967:35–36).

Marriage is a good example. If we look on marriage as only a contract between two people, we assume we can end it whenever we want to. But if partners define their relationship as *holy matrimony*, this bond makes a far stronger claim on them. This fact is, no doubt, why the divorce rate is lower among people who are more religious.

Especially when humans confront uncertainty and life-threatening situations—such as illness, war, and natural disaster—we bring sacred symbols to the fore. By seeking out sacred meaning in any situation, in other words, we can lift ourselves above life's setbacks and even face the prospect of death with courage.

Critical evaluation. The symbolic-interaction approach views religion as a social construction, placing everyday life under a "sacred canopy" of meaning (Berger, 1967). Of course, Berger adds, the sacred's ability to legitimize and stabilize society depends on its constructed character going unrecognized. After all, we could derive little strength from sacred beliefs that we saw as mere devices for coping with tragedy. Then, too, this micro-level view pays little attention to religion's link with social inequality, to which we shall now turn.

Inequality and Religion: Social-Conflict Analysis

The social-conflict paradigm highlights religion's support for social hierarchy. Religion, claimed Karl Marx, serves ruling elites by legitimizing the status quo and diverting people's attention from social inequities.

The British monarchy, for example, is even today crowned by the head of the Church of England, illustrating the close alliance between religious and political elites. In practical terms, working for political change may mean opposing the church—and, by implication, God. Religion also encourages people to look hopefully to a "better world to come," minimizing the social problems of *this* world. In one of his best-known statements, Marx offered a stinging criticism of religion as "the sigh of the oppressed creature, the sentiment of a heartless world, and the soul of soulless conditions. It is the opium of the people" (1964:27; orig. 1848).

An additional link between religion and social inequality involves gender. Virtually all the world's major religions have reflected and encouraged male dominance of social life, as the box on pages 492–93 explains.

During Marx's lifetime, powerful Christian nations of Western Europe justified colonial exploitation of Africa, the Americas, and Asia, claiming that they were merely "converting heathens." In the United States, major churches in the South considered the enslavement of African Americans to be consistent with God's will, and churches throughout the country remain notably segregated to this day. In the words of

Q: "[Rationalization] means that principally there are no mysterious, incalculable forces that come into play, but rather that one can, in principle, master all things by calculation." Max Weber

RESOURCE: An excerpt from Max Weber's *The Protestant Ethic and the Spirit of Capitalism* is among the classics included in the Macionis and Benokraitis reader, *Seeing Ourselves.*

DIVERSITY: David Cone (Alabama State University) described

African-American novelist Maya Angelou, "Sunday at 11:30 A.M., America is more segregated than at any time of the week."

Critical evaluation. Social-conflict analysis shows that the power of religion can legitimize social inequality. Yet critics of religion's conservative face, Marx included, minimize ways in which religion has promoted change and also equality. Nineteenth-century religious groups in the United States, for example, were at the forefront of the movement to abolish slavery. During the 1950s and 1960s, religious organizations and their leaders (including the Reverend Martin Luther King, Jr.) were at the core of the civil rights movement. During the 1960s and 1970s, many clergy actively opposed the Vietnam War, and, as explained presently, some have supported revolutionary change in Latin America and elsewhere.

RELIGION AND SOCIAL CHANGE

Religion is not just the conservative force portrayed by Karl Marx. Historically, as Max Weber (1958; orig. 1904–5) explained, religion can promote dramatic social change.

Max Weber: Protestantism and Capitalism

Max Weber contended that new kinds of religious thought unleashed nothing less than the industrialization of Western Europe. Industrial capitalism, Weber observed, developed in the wake of Calvinism, a Christian movement within the Protestant Reformation.

As Chapter 4 ("Society") explains in detail, John Calvin (1509–1564) advanced the doctrine of *predestination.* Calvin held that an all-powerful and all-knowing God has predestined some people for salvation while condemning most to eternal damnation. With each individual's fate sealed even before birth and known only to God, the only certainty is what hangs in the balance: eternal glory or hellfire.

Driven by anxiety over their fate, Calvinists understandably sought signs of God's favor in *this* world and gradually settled on prosperity as a key symbol of divine favor. This conviction, coupled with their rigid devotion to duty, led Calvinists to become absorbed in the pursuit of prosperity. But riches were never to fuel self-indulgent spending; nor were Calvinists moved to share their wealth with the poor, whose plight they saw as a mark of God's rejection.

As agents of God's work on earth, Calvinists believed that their lifelong "calling" was best fulfilled by

the black church as itself a variant of liberation theology.

Q: ". . . Established religious institutions have generally had a stake in the status quo and hence have fostered conservatism . . . . On the other hand, as the source of both humanistic values and the strength that can come from believing one is carrying out God's will in political matters, religion has occasionally played a role in movements for radical social change." Gary T. Marx

Working among the poorest residents of Santo Domingo, capital city of the Dominican Republic in the Caribbean, Catholic priest Father Martin espouses the principles of liberation theology, displaying commitment to both his faith and to social change.

reinvesting profits and reaping ever-greater success in the process. All the while, they practiced personal thrift and eagerly embraced technological advances, thereby laying the groundwork for the rise of industrial capitalism. In time, the religious fervor that motivated early Calvinists was transformed into a profane Protestant "work ethic," leading Weber to describe industrial capitalism as a "disenchanted" religion. But his analysis leaves little doubt as to the power of religious thinking to alter the basic shape of society.

Liberation Theology

Christianity has a long-standing concern for the suffering of poor and oppressed people. Historically, the Christian response to poverty has been to strengthen the believer's faith in a better life to come. In recent decades, however, some church leaders and theologians have embraced **liberation theology,** *a fusion of Christian principles with political activism, often Marxist in character.*

This social movement started in the late 1960s in Latin America's Roman Catholic church. In addition to the church's efforts to free humanity from sin, Christian activists are helping people in the least-developed countries to liberate themselves from abysmal poverty. The message of liberation theology is simple: Social oppression runs counter to Christian morality and is also preventable. Therefore, as a matter of faith and social justice, Christians must promote greater social equality.

SOCIAL DIVERSITY

Religion and Patriarchy: Does God Favor Males?

Two-thirds of U.S. adults envision God in primarily or exclusively male terms (NORC, 1993:164). Because we link attributes such as wisdom and power to men, the fact that we tend to see God as masculine is not surprising.

By and large, organized religions also favor males, a fact that is evident in passages from many of the sacred writings of major world religions.

The Quran (Koran)—the sacred text of Islam—asserts that men are to have social dominance over women:

Men are in charge of women. . . . Hence good women are obedient . . . As for those whose rebelliousness you fear, admonish them, banish them from your bed, and scourge them (quoted in Kaufman, 1976:163).

Christianity—the dominant religion of the Western world—has also supported patriarchy. While many Christians revere Mary, the mother of Jesus, the New Testament also includes the following passages:

One way that religions support social inequality is by admitting to positions of leadership only certain categories of people. Historically, this has meant the dominance of white men; but this pattern has eroded in recent years. In 1989, for example, Barbara Harris became the first woman of color to be ordained as a bishop in the Episcopal Church.

A man . . . is the image and glory of God; but woman is the glory of man. For man was not made from woman, but woman from man. Neither was man created for woman, but woman for man. (1 Cor. 11:7–9)

As in all the churches of the saints, the women should keep silence in the churches. For they are not permitted to speak, but should be subordinate, as even the law says. If there is anything they desire to know, let them ask their husbands at home. For it is shameful for a woman to speak in church. (1 Cor. 14:33–35)

Wives, be subject to your husbands, as to the Lord. For the husband is the head of the wife as Christ is the head of the church. . . . As the church is subject to Christ, so let wives also be subject in everything to their husbands. (Eph. 5:22–24)

Let a woman learn in silence with all submissiveness. I permit no woman to teach or to have authority over men; she is to keep silent.

A growing number of Catholic men and women have allied themselves with the poor in the liberation theology movement. The costs of opposing the status quo, however, have been high. Church members—including Oscar Arnulfo Romero, the archbishop of San Salvador (the capital of El Salvador)—have been killed in the violence that engulfs much of that region.

Liberation theology has also polarized the Catholic community by provoking strong criticism. Pope John Paul II condemns this movement for distorting traditional church doctrine with left-wing politics. Despite the pontiff's objections, however, the liberation theology movement has become powerful in Latin America, fueled by the belief that Christian faith should drive people to improve the condition of the world's poor (Boff, 1984; Neuhouser, 1989).

TYPES OF RELIGIOUS ORGANIZATION

Sociologists have developed a broad scheme to categorize the hundreds of different religious organizations that exist in the United States. The most widely used model takes the form of a continuum with *churches* on one pole and *sects* on the other. We can describe any actual religious organization, then, in relation to these two ideal types by locating it on the church-sect continuum.

SOCIAL SURVEY: "Do you favor or oppose women as pastors, ministers, priests, or rabbis in your own faith or denomination?" (*STUDENT CHIP Social Survey Software*, FECLERGO; GSS 1986; N = 1,334)

	"Favor"	"Oppose"
Men	66.4%	33.6%
Women	57.6%	42.4%

13 + years school	69.6%	30.4%
12 years	57.1%	42.9%
0–11 years	54.5%	45.5%
18–34	69.4%	30.6%
35–64	58.4%	41.6%
65 and up	53.4%	46.6%

For Adam was formed first, then Eve; and Adam was not deceived, but the woman was deceived and became a transgressor. Yet woman will be saved through bearing children, if she continues in faith and love and holiness, with modesty. (1 Tm. 2:11–15)

Judaism, too, traditionally has supported patriarchy. Male Orthodox Jews include the following words in daily prayer:

Blessed art thou, O Lord our God, King of the Universe, that I was not born a gentile.
Blessed art thou, O Lord our God, King of the Universe, that I was not born a slave.
Blessed art thou, O Lord our God, King of the Universe, that I was not born a woman.

In another dimension of religious patriarchy, the major religions have long excluded women from the clergy, although this practice is now widely challenged. Islam continues to exclude women from such positions, as does the Roman Catholic church. A growing number of Protestant denominations—including the Church of England—have overturned historical policies and now ordain women. While Orthodox Judaism still upholds the traditional prohibition against women serving as rabbis, Reform Judaism has long elevated women to this role (and is the largest denomination to ordain gay and lesbian people). In 1985, the first woman became a rabbi in the Conservative denomination of Judaism. The proportion of women among students in seminary schools across the United States has never been higher (now roughly one-third), evidence that further change is only a matter of time.

Challenges to the patriarchal structure of organized religion—from the ordination of women to the introduction of gender-neutral language in hymnals and prayers— has sparked heated controversy, delighting progressives while outraging traditionalists. Propelling these developments is a lively feminism within most religious communities today. According to feminist Christians, for example, patriarchy in the church stands in stark contrast to the largely feminine image of Jesus Christ in the Scriptures as "nonaggressive, noncompetitive, meek and humble of heart, a nurturer of the weak and a friend of the outcast" (Sandra Schneiders, quoted in Woodward, 1989:61).

Most basically, feminists argue, unless traditional notions of gender are removed from our understanding of God, women will never have equality with men in the church. Theologian Mary Daly puts the matter bluntly: "If God is male, then male is God" (quoted in Woodward, 1989:58).

Church and Sect

Drawing on the ideas of his teacher Max Weber, Ernst Troeltsch (1931) defined a **church** as *a type of religious organization well integrated into the larger society.* Churchlike organizations usually persist for centuries and include generations of the same family. Churches have well-established rules and regulations and expect their leaders to undergo approved training before being formally ordained.

While concerned with the sacred, a church accepts the ways of the profane world, which gives it broad appeal. Church doctrine conceives of God in highly intellectualized terms (say, as a force for good), and favors abstract moral standards ("Do unto others as you would have them do unto you") over specific mandates for day-to-day living. By teaching morality in safely abstract terms, a church can avoid social controversy. For example, many churches that, in principle, celebrate the unity of all peoples, have, in practice, all-white memberships. Such duality minimizes conflict between a church and political life (Troeltsch, 1931; O'Dea & Aviad, 1983).

A church generally takes one of two forms. An **ecclesia** is *a church that is formally allied with the state.* Ecclesias have been common in history; for centuries the Catholic church was allied with the Roman Empire; Confucianism was the state religion in China

Q: "A permanent danger of an established church . . . is that a national church might become a nationalistic church." T. S. Eliot

Q: "No man has a body distinct from his soul." William Blake

NOTE: "Mainstream" denominations such as Episcopalian and Presbyterian have lost membership in recent years; in contrast, Southern Baptist, Seventh-Day Adventist, and Mormon denominations are gaining in popularity.

Q: "To be mistaken in believing that the Christian religion is true is no great loss to anyone; but how dreadful to be mistaken in believing it to be false!" Blaise Pascal (1623–1662)

NOTE: The Greek roots of the word "church" refer to what belongs to God, the greatest power. The word "sect" is derived from Latin, meaning "to cut." The word "cult" is derived from Latin roots meaning "to cultivate, refine, or worship."

Our national suspicion of unorthodox religious organizations is periodically reinforced by the kind of tragedy that occurred in 1993 in Waco, Texas. A confrontation between the Branch Davidians and federal authorities finally ended in a fiery conflagration resulting in the loss of one hundred lives.

until early in this century; the Anglican Church remains the official Church of England; and Islam is today the official religion of Pakistan and Iran. State churches typically define everyone in a society as a member; tolerance of religious difference, therefore, is sharply limited.

A **denomination**, by contrast, is *a church, independent of the state, that accepts religious pluralism.* Denominations thrive in societies that formally separate church and state. Ours is such a nation, with dozens of Christian denominations—including Catholics, Baptists, Methodists, and Lutherans—as well as various categories of Judaism and other traditions. While members of a denomination hold certain religious beliefs, they recognize the right of others to disagree.

A second general religious form is the **sect**, *a type of religious organization that stands apart from the larger society.* Sect members hold rigidly to their own religious convictions while discounting what others around them claim to be true. In extreme cases, members of a sect may withdraw completely from society in order to practice their religion without interference from outsiders. The Amish, described in Chapter 3 ("Culture"), are an example of a North American sect that has long isolated itself (Hostetler, 1980). Since our culture holds religious tolerance as a virtue, members

of sects are sometimes accused of being dogmatic in their insistence that they alone follow the true religion (Stark & Bainbridge, 1979).

In organizational terms, sects are less formal than churches. Thus, sect members often engage in highly spontaneous and emotional practices as they worship, while members of churches tend to be passively attentive to their leader. Sects also reject the intellectualized religion of churches, stressing instead the personal experience of divine power. Rodney Stark (1985:314) contrasts a church's vision of a distant God—"Our Father, who art in Heaven"—with a sect's more immediate God—"Lord, bless this poor sinner kneeling before you now."

A further distinction between church and sect turns on patterns of leadership. The more churchlike an organization, the more likely that its leaders are formally trained and ordained. Because more sectlike organizations celebrate the personal presence of God, members expect their leaders to exude divine inspiration in the form of **charisma** (from Greek meaning "divine favor"), *extraordinary personal qualities that can turn an audience into followers*, infusing them with the emotional experience that sects so value.

Sects generally form as breakaway groups from established churches or other religious organizations (Stark & Bainbridge, 1979). Their psychic intensity and informal structure render them less stable than churches, and many sects blossom only to disappear a short time later. The sects that do endure typically become more like churches, losing fervor as they become more bureaucratic and established.

To sustain their membership, many sects rely on active recruitment, or *proselytizing*, of new members. Sects place great value on the experience of **conversion**, *a personal transformation or rebirth resulting from adopting new religious beliefs*. Members of Jehovah's Witnesses, for example, share their faith with others in the hope of attracting new members.

Finally, churches and sects differ in their social composition. Because they are more closely tied to the world, well-established churches tend to include people of high social standing. Sects, by contrast, attract more disadvantaged people. A sect's openness to new members and promise of salvation and personal fulfillment may be especially appealing to people who perceive themselves as social outsiders. However, as we shall explain presently, many established churches in the United States have lost membership in recent decades. In the process, a number of sects now find themselves with more affluent members.

Q: "In societies under stress, there is a strong tendency for new cults to arise." Felicitas Goodman

NOTE: The charge that cults "brainwash" their members was investigated by Stuart Wright in a study of cult defectors: "Post-Involvement Attitudes of Voluntary Defectors from Controversial New Religious Movements," *Journal for the Scientific Study of Religion* 23, 2 (June 1984):172–82.

NOTE: Because animistic peoples perceive the entire world as "enchanted," it may be said that they do not distinguish between the sacred and the secular.

NOTE: By the 1950s, the Catholic Church claimed that science and religion were not incompatible. In the encyclical *Humani generis*, Pope Pius XII urged both scientists and theologians to study evolution.

Cult

A **cult** is *a religious organization that is substantially outside the cultural traditions of a society.* Whereas a sect emerges from within a conventional religious organization, a cult represents something else entirely. Cults typically form around a highly charismatic leader who offers a compelling message of a new way of life.

Because some cult principles or practices may seem unconventional, the popular view of cults pictures them as deviant or even evil. Negative publicity given to a few cults has raised suspicion about any unfamiliar religious group. The Branch Davidians, for example, a cult in Waco, Texas, led by David Koresh, held federal officers at bay for more than fifty days before almost one hundred cult members died in a shootout and subsequent fire in 1993. As a result of such aberrant behavior, some scholars assert that to call a religious community a "cult" amounts to declaring it unworthy (Richardson, 1990).

The connotations of the word "cult" are unfortunate because there is nothing intrinsically wrong with this kind of religious organization. Many long-standing religions—Christianity, Islam, and Judaism included—began as cults. Of course, not all or even most cults exist for very long. One reason is that cults are even more at odds with the larger society than sects. Many cults demand that members not only accept their doctrine but embrace a radically new lifestyle. Such significant changes suggest why people sometimes accuse cults of brainwashing new members, although research suggests that most people who join cults experience no psychological harm (Barker, 1981; Kilbourne, 1983).

RELIGION IN HISTORY

Religion shapes every society of the world. And, like other social institutions, religion shows considerable variation both historically and cross culturally.

Religion in Preindustrial Societies

Religion predates human history. Archaeological evidence suggests that our human ancestors routinely engaged in religious rituals some forty thousand years ago.

Early hunters and gatherers embraced **animism** (from Latin meaning "the breath of life"), *the belief that elements of the natural world are conscious life forms that affect humanity.* Animistic people view forests, oceans, mountains, even the wind as spiritual forces. Many Native-American societies are animistic, a characteristic that accounts for their historical reverence for the natural environment. Hunters and gatherers conduct their religious life entirely within the family. Members of such societies may look to a *shaman* or religious leader, but there are no full-time, specialized religious leaders.

Belief in a single divine power responsible for creating the world marked the rise of pastoral and horticultural societies. We can trace our society's conception of God as a "shepherd," directly involved in the world's well-being, to the roots of Christianity, Judaism, and Islam, of whose original followers were all pastoral peoples.

As societies develop more productive capacity, religious life expands beyond the family, and priests take their place among other specialized workers. In agrarian societies, the institution of religion gains in prominence, as evidenced by the centrality of the church in medieval Europe. Even the physical design of the city casts this dominance in stone, with the cathedral rising above all other structures.

Religion in Industrial Societies

The Industrial Revolution ushered in a growing emphasis on science. Increasingly, people looked to physicians and other practitioners of science for the comfort they had earlier sought from religious leaders.

Even so, religious thought persists simply because science is powerless to address issues of ultimate meaning in human life. In other words, learning *how* the world works is a matter for scientists; but *why* we and the rest of the universe exist is a question about which science has nothing to say. Whatever the benefits of science to our material lives, then, religion has a unique capacity to address the spiritual dimension of human existence.

Still, because they both offer powerful but distinct ways of viewing the universe, science and religion have often fallen into an uneasy relationship. Throughout this century, the question of human origins has provoked spirited debate, with scientific facts about human evolution appearing to stand at odds with religious "beliefs" commonly termed *creationism*. The box on pages 496–97 provides details.

WORLD RELIGIONS

Religion is found virtually everywhere on our planet, and, remarkably, the diversity of religious expression is almost as wide-ranging as culture itself. Many of the thousands of different religions are highly localized

NOTE: For any religion, literal interpretation of sacred texts has the effect of sharply limiting debate among adherents as to truth, thereby fostering consensus. But literal readings may still reveal inconsistencies; there are, for example, *two* creation stories in Genesis.

RESOURCE: To the basic philosophical question underlying creation—"How did *something* come from *nothing?*"—various cultures respond in surprisingly similar ways. See Raymond Van Over's *Sun Songs: Creation Myths from Around the World* (New American Library, 1980).

CRITICAL THINKING

The Creation Debate: Does Science Threaten Religion?

"In the beginning God created the heavens and the earth." A literal reading of this passage from the biblical Book of Genesis puts the origin of life on earth at the third day, when God created vegetation; on the fifth and sixth days, God created animal life, including human beings, fashioned in God's own image.

For centuries, this account of creation held sway in many Western societies. But, in 1859, the English scientist Charles Darwin published *On the Origin of Species*, a biological theory of human origins. Darwin's account of evolution states that, far from being present at the earth's creation, humans evolved from lower forms of life over a billion years.

Darwin's theory brought him fame and immediate notoriety. What some celebrated as a scientific breakthrough others condemned as an attack on sacred beliefs. On the surface, Darwin's science seems to contradict the Bible, setting the stage for the creation debate.

A major event in the course of this conflict occurred in 1925 in the town of Dayton, Tennessee. At that time, state law forbade teaching "any theory that denies the story of the Divine Creation of man as taught in the Bible" and especially any claim that "man descended from a lower order of animals." One afternoon in Doc Robinson's drugstore, John Thomas Scopes, a high school science teacher, conceded to a group of friends that he had, on occasion, taught evolution. To challenge the law, Scopes agreed to stand trial for his crime.

This photograph, from the courtroom of the 1925 Scopes trial, shows Clarence Darrow arguing on behalf of his client, with John Thomas Scopes sitting behind and to the right with arms folded on his chest.

with few followers. *World religions*, by contrast, are widely known and have millions of adherents. We shall briefly describe six world religions, which together claim the support of 3.8 billion people—almost three-fourths of humanity.

Christianity

Christianity is the most widespread religion, claiming 1.7 billion adherents, who constitute roughly one-third of humanity. Most Christians live in Europe or throughout the Americas; more than 85 percent of the people in the United States and Canada identify

with Christianity. Moreover, as shown in Global Map 18–1 on page 498, people who are at least nominally Christian represent a significant share of the population in many other world regions, with the notable exceptions of northern Africa and Asia. This diffusion is a consequence of the European colonization of much of the world during the last five hundred years. The dominance of Christianity in the West is evident in the practice of numbering years on the calendar beginning with the birth of Christ.

Christianity originated as a cult, incorporating elements of its much older predecessor Judaism. Like many cults, Christianity was propelled by the personal

NOTE: Although Judaism and Christianity are both monotheistic religions, there is evidence of polytheistic origins. In the original Hebrew, the accounts of creation in Genesis used plural pronouns ("Then God said, Let us make man in our image . . ." 1:26), leading scholars to speculate that the religion evolved from polytheistic roots.

SOCIAL SURVEY: "How close do you feel to God most of the time?" (GSS 1988–91, N = 3, 846; Codebook, 1993:160)

"Extremely close"	30.4%	"Not close at all"	5.3%
"Somewhat close"	49.8%	"Does not believe in God"	1.8%
"Not very close"	9.2%	DK/NR	3.5%

Public interest in the "Scopes Monkey Trial" was heightened by the presence of three-time presidential candidate William Jennings Bryan, a leading fundamentalist Christian who detested evolutionary science. Bryan enthusiastically prosecuted the case. Clarence Darrow, a renowned criminal lawyer, sat across the aisle to defend Thomas Scopes.

The trial proved to be one of Darrow's finest performances, while Bryan, aging, ill, and only days from death, did little to advance the creationist cause. Yet most people applauded when the court found Scopes guilty and fined him $100. His conviction was reversed on appeal (perhaps to prevent the case from reaching the U.S. Supreme Court), and Tennessee law continued to ban the teaching of evolution until 1967. A year later, the U.S. Supreme Court struck down all such laws as violating the Constitution's ban on government-supported religion.

But creationists were quick to regroup: If evolution was to be taught in schools, they maintained, creationism must be included to provide balance. Creationism, stripped of obvious religious qualities, emerged as *creation science.* Creationists won over some state legislatures that mandated the inclusion of creation science in school curricula. But again the Court stepped in, rejecting such teaching as violating the constitutional separation of church and state.

But this time, the Court went further, declaring that creation science was, in fact, not science at all. A science, the justices claimed, has a provisional character in that its theories are subject to change whenever new evidence appears. The theory of evolution has been altered by research, they concluded, but creation science has not; thus, creationism is religion, not science.

Members of our society remain divided over the validity of creationism. A third of U.S. adults claim that the Bible is the literal word of God; these people are, thus, creationists (NORC, 1993:176). But even many church leaders insist that, while biblical accounts of creation are inspired by God, they are not literal statements of truth. John S. Spong, the Episcopal bishop of Newark, New Jersey, argues that scientists and biblical scholars alike must accept the "enormous amount of evidence" that humanity did evolve over a billion years. But, he adds, science merely investigates *how* the natural world operates; only religion can address *why* we exist and God's role in this process. Human creation, then, must be understood from the perspective of both scientific fact and religious faith.

SOURCES: Based on Gould (1981), Numbers (1982), and Nelson & Jermain (1985). Professor J. Kenneth Smail of Kenyon College also contributed ideas to this section.

charisma of a leader, Jesus of Nazareth, who preached a message of personal salvation. Jesus did not directly challenge the political powers of his day, admonishing his followers to "Render therefore to Caesar things that are Caesar's" (Matt. 22:21). But his message was revolutionary, nonetheless, promising that faith and love would lead to triumph over sin and death.

Christianity is one example of **monotheism,** *belief in a single divine power.* This new religion broke with the Roman Empire's traditional **polytheism,** *belief in many gods.* Yet Christianity has a unique vision of the Supreme Being as a sacred Trinity: God the Creator; Jesus Christ, Son of God and Redeemer; and the Holy Spirit, a Christian's personal experience of God's presence.

The claim that Jesus was divine rests on accounts of his final days on earth. Tried and sentenced to death in Jerusalem on charges that he was a threat to established political leaders, Jesus endured a cruel execution by crucifixion, which transformed the cross into a sacred Christian symbol. According to Christian belief, Jesus was resurrected—that is, he rose from the dead—showing that he was the Son of God.

The apostles of Jesus spread Christianity widely throughout the Mediterranean region. Although the Roman Empire initially persecuted Christians, by the

SOCIAL SURVEY: "About how often do you pray?" (*STUDENT CHIP Social Survey*, PRAY1; GSS 1983–89, N = 8,997)

	Daily	Weekly	Less often/never				
Women	65.3%	20.2%	14.5%	Wh Anglo	52.5%	22.5%	24.9%
Men	42.8%	23.6%	33.6%	High SES	48.6%	25.4%	26.0%
Afri Amer	72.8%	16.0%	11.2%	Middle SES	55.4%	21.6%	23.0%
Latino	63.4%	21.0%	15.6%	Low SES	63.4%	17.4%	19.2%
				65 and older	74.6%	12.0%	13.3%
				35–64	56.5%	21.7%	21.8%
				18–34	43.8%	26.6%	29.6%

Window on the World

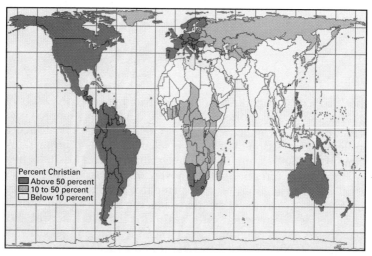

GLOBAL MAP 18–1 Christianity in Global Perspective

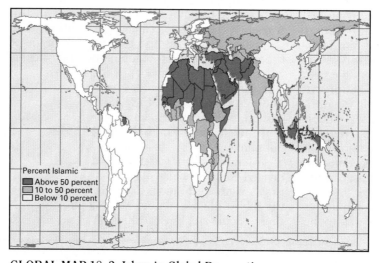

GLOBAL MAP 18–2 Islam in Global Perspective

fourth century Christianity became an ecclesia—the empire's official religion. What had begun as a cult four centuries before was by then an established church.

Christianity took various forms, including the Roman Catholic church and the Orthodox church, centered in Constantinople (now Istanbul, Turkey). Further division occurred toward the end of the Middle Ages, when the Protestant Reformation in Europe sparked the formation of numerous denominations.

More than a dozen denominations—the Baptists and Methodists are the two largest—now command sizable followings in the United States (Smart, 1969; Kaufman, 1976; Jacquet & Jones, 1991).

Islam

Islam has almost 1 billion followers (18 percent of humanity), called Muslims. A majority of people in

DIVERSITY: Muslims hold the Quran (Koran) to be the *literal* words of God. For this reason, even translation from Arabic into other languages raises fears of distortion.
RESOURCE: The article by Jane I. Smith, "Women and Islam," is among the cross-cultural selections found in the *Seeing Ourselves* reader.

NOTE: As members of many religions have done, the ancient Hebrews distinguished between the sacred and the secular through practices such as keeping the Sabbath, dietary restrictions, and maintaining holy places.

the Middle East are Muslims, which explains the tendency of people in the United States to associate Islam with Arabs in that region of the world. But most Muslims are *not* Arabs; Global Map 18–2 shows that a majority of people across northern Africa and western Asia are also Muslims. Moreover, significant concentrations of Muslims are found in Pakistan, India, Bangladesh, Indonesia, and the southern republics of the former Soviet Union. Although representing only a tiny share of the population, estimates place the number of North American Muslims at 5 million and rising (Roudi, 1988; Weeks, 1988).

Islam is the word of God as revealed to the prophet Muhammad, who was born in the city of Mecca (now in Saudi Arabia) about the year 570. To Muslims, Muhammad is a prophet, not a divine being as Christians define Jesus. The Quran (Koran), sacred to Muslims, is the word of God (in Arabic, "Allah") as transmitted through Muhammad, God's messenger. In Arabic, the word Islam means both "submission" and "peace," and the Quran urges submission to Allah as the path to inner peace. Muslims express this personal devotion in a daily ritual of five prayers.

Islam spread rapidly after the death of Muhammad, although divisions arose, as they did within Christianity. All Muslims, however, accept the Five Pillars of Islam: (1) recognizing Allah as the one, true God, and Muhammad as God's messenger; (2) ritual prayer; (3) giving alms to the poor; (4) fasting during the month of Ramadan; and (5) making a pilgrimage once to the Sacred House of Allah in Mecca (Weeks, 1988; El-Attar, 1991). Like Christianity, Islam holds people accountable to God for their deeds on earth. Those who live obediently will be rewarded in heaven, while unbelievers will suffer unending punishment.

Muslims are also obligated to defend their faith. Sometimes this tenet has justified holy wars against unbelievers (in roughly the same way that medieval Christians joined the Crusades to recapture the Holy Land from the Muslims). In recent decades, especially in Iran, Muslims have sought to rid their society of Western influences they regard as morally compromising (Martin, 1982; Arjomand, 1988).

Many Westerners view Muslim women as among the most socially oppressed people on earth. Muslim women do lack many of the personal freedoms enjoyed by Muslim men, yet patriarchy was well established in the Middle East at the time of Muhammad's birth. Some defenders argue that Islam actually improved the social position of women by demanding that husbands deal justly with their wives. Further, although Islam permits a man to have up to four

Followers of Islam reverently remove their shoes—which touch the profane ground—before entering this sacred mosque in the Southeast Asian nation of Brunei.

wives, it admonishes men to have only one wife if having more than one would encourage him to treat women unjustly (Quran, "The Women," v. 3).

Judaism

Speaking purely in numerical terms, Judaism, with only 17 million adherents worldwide, is less prominent as a world religion. Only in Israel is Judaism a majority religion. But Judaism has special significance to the United States because the largest concentration of Jews (7 million people) is found in North America.

Judaism has deep roots: Jews look to the past as a source of guidance in the present and for the future. Jewish history extends back some four thousand years before the birth of Christ to the ancient cultures of Mesopotamia. At this time, Jews were animistic; but this belief was to change after Jacob—grandson of Abraham, the earliest great ancestor—led his people to Egypt.

Under Egyptian rule, Jews endured centuries of slavery. In the thirteenth century B.C.E., a turning point came as Moses, the adopted son of an Egyptian princess, was called by God to lead the Jews from bondage. This exodus (this word's Latin and Greek roots mean "a marching out") from Egypt is commemorated by Jews today in the ritual of Passover. As a result of the Jews' liberation from bondage, Judaism became monotheistic, recognizing a single, all-powerful God.

Chanukah is an important Jewish ritual of commemoration that serves to teach young Jews their long and rich history.

A distinctive concept of Judaism is the *covenant*, a special relationship with God by which Jews became a "chosen people." The covenant also implies a duty to observe God's law, especially the Ten Commandments as revealed to Moses on Mount Sinai. Jews regard the Bible (or, in Christian terms, the Old Testament) as both a record of their history and a statement of the obligations of Jewish life. Of special importance are the first five books of the Bible (Genesis, Exodus, Leviticus, Numbers, and Deuteronomy), designated as the *Torah* (a word roughly meaning "teaching" and "law"). In contrast to Christianity's central concern with personal salvation, therefore, Judaism emphasizes moral behavior in this world.

Judaism is composed of three main denominations. Orthodox Jews (including more than 1 million people in the United States) strictly observe traditional beliefs and practices, maintaining historical forms of dress, segregating men and women at religious services, and consuming only kosher foods. Such traditional practices set off Orthodox Jews in the United States as the most sectlike. In the mid-nineteenth century, many Jews sought greater accommodation to the larger society, leading to the formation of more churchlike Reform Judaism (now including more than 1.3 million people in this country). More recently, a

third segment—Conservative Judaism (with about 2 million adherents)—has established a middle ground between the other two denominations.

All Jews, however, share a keen awareness of their cultural history, which has included battling considerable prejudice and discrimination. A collective memory of centuries of slavery in Egypt, conquest by Rome, and persecution in Europe have shaped Jewish awareness and identity. Interestingly, the urban ghetto (derived from the Italian word *borghetto*, meaning settlement outside of the city walls) was first home to Jews in Italy, and this form of residential segregation soon spread to other parts of Europe.

Jewish emigration to the United States began in the mid-1600s. Many early immigrants prospered, and many were also assimilated into largely Christian communities. But as larger numbers entered the country during the final decades of the nineteenth century, prejudice and discrimination against them—commonly termed *anti-Semitism*—increased. During World War II, anti-Semitism reached a vicious peak when Jews experienced the most horrific persecution in modern times as the Nazi regime in Germany systematically annihilated some 6 million Jews.

The history of Judaism is a grim reminder of a tragic dimension of the human record—the extent to which religious minorities have been the target of hatred and even slaughter (Bedell, Sandon, & Wellborn, 1975; Holm, 1977; Schmidt, 1980; Seltzer, 1980; B. Wilson, 1982; Eisen, 1983).

Hinduism

Hinduism is the oldest of all the world religions, originating in the Indus River Valley approximately forty-five hundred years ago. Hindus number some 700 million (13 percent of humanity). Global Map 18–3 shows that Hinduism remains an Eastern religion, the predominant creed of India and Pakistan today with a significant presence in a few societies of southern Africa as well as Indonesia.

Over the centuries, Hinduism and Indian culture have become intertwined, so that now one is not easily described apart from the other. This connection explains the fact that Hinduism, unlike Christianity, Islam, and Judaism, has not diffused widely to other nations. However, an estimated 1 million Hindus in the United States make this religion a significant part of the cultural diversity of our country.

Hinduism differs from most other religions by not being linked to the life of any single person. Hinduism also has no sacred writings comparable to the Bible or the Quran. Nor does Hinduism even envision God as

NOTE: One could say that, to the Hindu, nothing is sacred or everything is sacred.

NOTE: The diffusion of religious elements is generally selective. For instance, in the 1960s, many young people in the United States adopted the Hindu concepts of *dharma* (fate) and *karma* (spiritual progression of souls), while scorning the caste system historically associated with Hinduism.

Window on the World

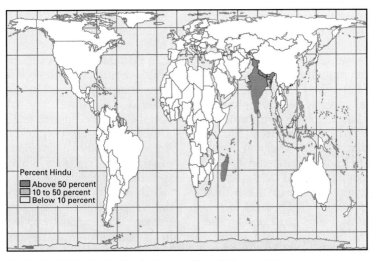

GLOBAL MAP 18–3 Hinduism in Global Perspective

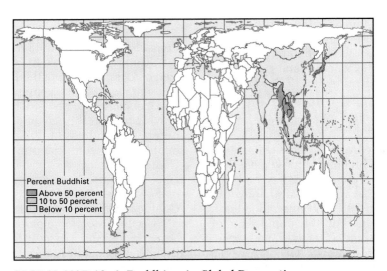

GLOBAL MAP 18–4 Buddhism in Global Perspective

a specific entity. For this reason, Hinduism—like other Eastern religions, as we shall see—is sometimes thought of as an "ethical religion." Hindu beliefs and practices vary widely, but all Hindus recognize a moral force in the universe that confronts everyone with responsibilities termed *dharma*. One traditional example of dharma is the need to act in concert with the traditional caste system, described in Chapter 9 ("Social Stratification").

A second Hindu principle, *karma*, refers to the belief in the spiritual progress of the human soul. To a Hindu, all actions have spiritual consequences, and proper living contributes to moral development. Karma works through *reincarnation*, a cycle of new birth following death, so that the individual is reborn into a spiritual state corresponding to the moral quality of a previous life. Unlike Christianity and Islam, Hinduism proclaims no ultimate justice at the hands

Chapter 18 Religion **501**

GLOBAL: In Japan, the emperor has traditionally been the head priest of the Shinto religion.

DIVERSITY: By 1990, chaplains in the U.S. Armed Forces represented 105 religious organizations, including one Buddhist chaplain (some 2,500 military personnel are adherents of this religion).

GLOBAL: Eastern religions—Buddhism, Hinduism, Confucianism, Shintoism—are sometimes termed "ethical religions" since they have no gods in the Western sense.

of a supreme god, although in the cycle of rebirth, each person reaps exactly what that individual has sown. The sublime state of *nirvana* represents spiritual perfection; when a soul reaches this rarefied existence, it is spared further rebirth.

Looking at Hinduism, we see also that not all religions can be neatly labeled monotheistic or polytheistic. Hinduism may be described as monotheistic because it envisions the universe as a single moral system; yet Hindus see evidence of this moral order in every element of nature. While central to a Hindu's life, rituals are performed in a variety of ways in countless Indian villages. Most Hindus practice private devotions, including, for example, ritual cleansing following contact with a person of lower caste position. Many also participate in public rituals, such as the *Kumbh Mela,* during which pilgrims flock to the sacred Ganges River to bathe in its purifying waters. This ritual, which occurs every twelve years, attracts 15 to 20 million people, making it the largest assembly of people on earth.

While elements of Hindu thought have characterized some cults in the United States over the years, Hinduism is still unfamiliar to most Westerners. But, like religions better known to us, Hinduism is a powerful force offering both explanation and guidance in life (Pitt, 1955; Sen, 1961; Embree, 1972; Kaufman, 1976; Schmidt, 1980).

Buddhism

Some twenty-five hundred years ago, the rich culture of India also gave rise to Buddhism. Today more than 300 million people (6 percent of humanity) embrace Buddhism, and almost all are Asians. As shown in Global Map 18–4, on page 501, adherents to Buddhism represent more than half of the population of Myanmar (Burma), Thailand, Cambodia, and Japan; Buddhism is also widespread in India and the People's Republic of China. Of the world religions considered so far, Buddhism most resembles Hinduism in doctrine, but, like Christianity, its inspiration stems from the life of one individual.

Siddhartha Gautama was born to a high-caste Indian family about 563 B.C.E. As a young man, he was preoccupied with spiritual matters. At the age of twenty-nine, he underwent a radical personal transformation, setting off for years of travel and meditation. His path ended when he achieved what Buddhists describe as *bodhi*, or enlightenment. Understanding the essence of life, Gautama became a Buddha.

Energized by the Buddha's personal charisma, followers spread his teachings—the *dhamma*—across

India. During the third century B.C.E., the ruler of India joined the ranks of Buddhists, subsequently sending missionaries throughout Asia and elevating Buddhism to the status of a world religion.

Central to Buddhist belief is the notion that human existence involves suffering. The pleasures of the world are real, of course, but Buddhists see such experiences as transitory. This doctrine is rooted in the Buddha's own travels throughout a society rife with poverty. But the Buddha rejected wealth as a solution to suffering; on the contrary, he warned that materialism inhibits spiritual development. Buddhism's answer to world problems is for individuals to pursue personal, spiritual transformation.

Buddhism closely parallels Hinduism in recognizing no god of judgment; rather, it finds spiritual consequences in each daily action. Another similarity lies in its belief in reincarnation. Here, again, only full enlightenment ends the cycle of death and rebirth, thereby finally liberating a person from the suffering of the world (Schumann, 1974; Thomas, 1975).

Confucianism

From about 200 B.C.E. until the beginning of this century, Confucianism was an ecclesia—the official religion of China. Following the 1949 Revolution, religion was suppressed by the communist government of the new People's Republic of China. Although officials provide little in the way of data to establish precise numbers, hundreds of millions of Chinese are still influenced by Confucianism. Almost all adherents to Confucianism live in China, although Chinese immigration has introduced this religion to other societies in Southeast Asia. Perhaps 100,000 followers of Confucius live in North America.

Confucius or, more properly, K'ung-Fu-tzu, lived between 551 and 479 B.C.E. Confucius shared with Buddha a deep concern for the problems and suffering of the world. The Buddha's response was a sectlike spiritual withdrawal from the world; Confucius, by contrast, instructed his followers to engage the world according to a strict code of moral conduct. Thus it was that Confucianism became fused with the traditional culture of China. Here we see a second example of what might be called a "national religion": As Hinduism has remained largely synonymous with Indian culture, Confucianism is enshrined in the Chinese way of life.

A central concept of Confucianism is *jen*, meaning humaneness. In practice, this means that we must always subordinate our self-interest to moral principle. In the family, the individual must display

SOCIAL SURVEY: "Where would you place your feelings about your faith?" (GSS 1988, N = 1,481; *Codebook*, 1993:415)
(1) "My faith is completely free of doubts"   27.1%
(2)   18.0%
(3)   15.5%
(4)   16.3%
(5)   9.3%
(6)   4.9%
(7) "My faith is mixed with doubts"   7.1%
DK/NR   1.8%
Q: "Faith is believing when you know it ain't so." Mark Twain
Q: "There is only one religion, although there are a hundred versions of it." George Bernard Shaw

loyalty and consideration for others. Likewise, families must remain mindful of their duties toward the larger community. In this way, layer upon layer of moral obligation integrates society as a whole.

Most of all, Confucianism stands out as lacking a clear sense of the sacred. We could view Confucianism, recalling Durkheim's analysis, as the celebration of society itself as sacred. Alternatively, we might argue that Confucianism is less a religion than a model of disciplined living. Certainly the historical dominance of Confucianism helps to explain why Chinese culture has long taken a skeptical attitude toward the supernatural. If we conclude that Confucianism is best thought of as a disciplined way of life, we must also recognize that it shares with religion a body of beliefs and practices that have as their goal goodness and the promotion of social unity (Kaufman, 1976; Schmidt, 1980; McGuire, 1987).

RELIGION IN THE UNITED STATES

The United States has experienced remarkable changes during its two-hundred-year history, with transformation in all its social institutions. Some wonder if the Industrial Revolution, the apparent erosion of the traditional family, and the advancing role of science and technology have undermined religion. Some scholars claim that religious beliefs remain central to our national life; others counter that religious faith is less a force than it once was. But scholars do agree that religion is considerably more influential in the United States than in other industrial societies (Collins, 1982; Greeley, 1989; Woodward, 1992; Hadaway, Marler, & Chaves, 1993).

Religious Affiliation

People in the United States claim to be surprisingly religious. National surveys reveal 90 percent of adults in the United States claim a religious preference (NORC, 1993:148). Table 18–1 reports results showing a Protestant preference among almost two-thirds of the population, Catholicism was favored by more than one-fifth of respondents, and 2 percent identified with Judaism. Just 9 percent claimed no religious preference. Two-thirds of adults note that, while growing up, they attended religious instruction classes more or less regularly, and 60 percent consider themselves to be a member of some religious organization (NORC, 1993:406–7). A look at survey data over the last fifty years reveals that religious affiliation has been relatively stable.

TABLE 18–1 Religious Identification in the United States, 1993

Religion	Proportion Indicating Preference
Protestant denominations	**64.1%**
Baptist	19.5
Methodist	10.6
Lutheran	7.3
Presbyterian	4.4
Episcopalian	2.1
All others or no denomination	20.2
Catholic	**22.0**
Jewish	**2.1**
Other or no answer	**2.7**
No religious preference	**9.1**

SOURCE: *General Social Surveys, 1972–1993: Cumulative Codebook* (Chicago: National Opinion Research Center, 1993), pp. 148–49.

National Map 18–1 shows the dominant religious affiliation of the United States by state and county, based on 1990 census data. It reveals a strong regional pattern in religious affiliation. New England and the Southwest are predominantly Catholic and the South is overwhelmingly Baptist, while Lutherans stand out in the northern Plains states. Members of the Church of the Latter Day Saints (Mormons) are heavily concentrated in and around Utah.

Religiosity

Religiosity designates *the importance of religion in a person's life*. North Americans are a comparatively religious people, more so, for example, than Europeans or the Japanese. Quantitative measures of religiosity in the United States, however, depend on precisely how this concept is operationalized.

Years ago, Charles Glock (1959, 1962) distinguished five distinct dimensions of religiosity. *Experiential* religiosity refers to the strength of a person's emotional ties to a religion. *Ritualistic* religiosity refers to frequency of ritual activity such as prayer and church attendance. *Ideological* religiosity concerns an individual's degree of belief in religious doctrine. *Consequential* religiosity has to do with how strongly religious beliefs figure in a person's daily behavior. Finally, *intellectual* religiosity refers to a person's knowledge of the history and doctrines of a particular religion. Anyone is likely to be more religious on some dimensions than on others; this inconsistency compounds the difficulty of measuring the concept of religiosity.

How religious, then, are members of our society? Almost everyone in the United States (95 percent)

SOCIAL SURVEY: "How important is following one's conscience even if it means going against what the churches or synagogues say and do?" (GSS 1988, N = 1,481; *Codebook*, 1993:414)

    (1) "Very important"   40.9%
    (2)   22.5%
    (3)   20.5%
    (4)   5.9%

(5) "Not very important"   7.4%
DK/NR   2.8%

THE MAP: Immigration (of Lutherans to the upper Midwest) and migration (of Mormons to Utah) shaped much of the religious diversity of the United States.

Seeing Ourselves

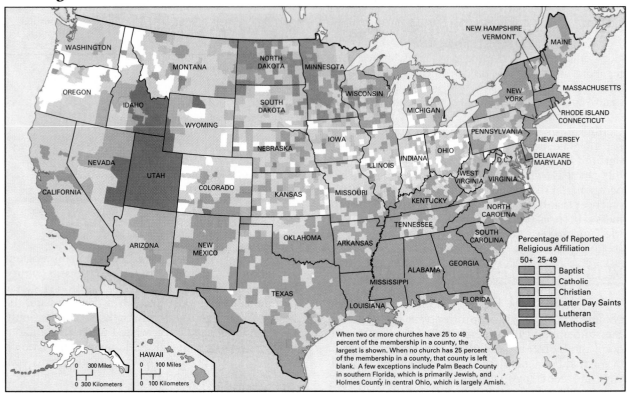

NATIONAL MAP 18–1 The Religious Diversity of the United States

In the vast majority of counties, at least 25 percent of people who report having a religious affiliation are members of the same organization. Thus, although the United States is religiously diverse at the national level, most people live in communities where one denomination is dominant. What historical facts might account for this pattern?

From the Glenmary Research Center, Atlanta, Georgia (1990).

claims to believe in a divine power of some kind, with 60 percent claiming they "know that God exists and have no doubts about it" (NORC, 1993:409). In terms of experiential religiosity, then, people in the United States would certainly seem to be notably religious.

But on other dimensions of religiosity, the pattern changes. In ideological terms, only about 70 percent, for example, report a belief in a life after death. On dimensions of ritualistic religiosity, the numbers drop even lower. For example, only half of adults claim to pray at least once a day, and just 40 percent say they attend religious services on a weekly or almost-weekly basis (NORC, 1993:144, 152, 158).

In short, the question "How religious are we?" yields no easy answers. Keep in mind, too, that being

religious is normative in our culture, so that people probably claim to be more religious than they really are. One team of researchers recently tallied actual church attendance of people living in Ashtabula County in northeast Ohio, concluding that twice as many people said they attended church on a given Sunday as really did so. Their estimate, in other words, is that no more than 20 percent of people attend church regularly (Hadaway, Marler, & Chaves, 1993). Our general conclusion, then, is that while most people in the United States claim to be at least somewhat religious, only about one-third are, in fact, strongly religious.

Religiosity also varies among denominations. Research suggests that, overall, Catholics are more

Q: "If God made us in his image, we have certainly returned the compliment." Voltaire
SOCIAL SURVEY: "Which of these statements comes closest to describing your feelings about the Bible?" (GSS 1993; N = 1,071; *Codebook*, 1993:176)

"The Bible is the actual word of God
and is to be taken literally"   33.2%

"The Bible is the inspired word of God
but not everything in it should be
taken literally, word for word"   48.9%
"The Bible is an ancient book of fables,
legends, history, and moral precepts
recorded by men"   15.2%
DK/NR   2.6%

religious than Protestants, and members of sects are the most religious of all (Stark & Glock, 1968; Hadaway, Marler, & Chaves, 1993).

Religion and Social Stratification

Sociologists study religion not only to comprehend how people address the sacred but because religious affiliation is related to a host of familiar social patterns.

Social Class

Religious preference is related to social class. Wade Roof (1979) found that Episcopalians, Presbyterians, and Jews had the highest overall social standing in the United States. In a middle position were other Protestant denominations, including Congregationalists and Methodists. Lower social standing was typical of Catholics, Lutherans, Baptists, and members of sects. All these categories, of course, display some internal variation.

By and large, Protestants with high social standing are people of northern European background whose families came to the United States at least a century ago. They encountered little prejudice and discrimination and have had the longest time to establish themselves socially. Roman Catholics, more recent immigrants to the United States, have contended with greater social barriers based on being a minority religion.

Jews command unexpectedly high social standing considering that many are fairly recent immigrants who confronted substantial anti-Semitism from the Christian majority. The reason is mostly cultural, since Jewish traditions place great value on both education and achievement. Although a large proportion of Jews began life in the United States in poverty, many—although certainly not all—improved their social position in subsequent generations.

Ethnicity and Race

Throughout the world, religion is tied to ethnicity. Many religions predominate in a specific geographical region or society. The Arab cultures of the Middle East, for example, are mostly Islamic, Hinduism is closely fused with the culture of India, as is Confucianism with the culture of China. Christianity and Judaism, however, diverge from this pattern; while these religions are predominantly Western, followers are found in numerous societies.

The link between religion and national identity is also evident in the United States. Our society, for example, encompasses *Anglo-Saxon* Protestants, *Irish* Catholics, *Russian* Jews, and *Greek* Orthodox. This linking of nation and creed results from the influx of immigrants to the United States from societies with a single major religion. Still, nearly every ethnic category displays at least some religious diversity. People of English ancestry, for instance, may be Protestants, Roman Catholics, Jews, or followers of other religions.

Historically, the church has been central to the spiritual—and also political—lives of African Americans. Transported to the Western Hemisphere in slave ships, most Africans were forced to become Christians—the dominant religion in the Americas—but they blended Christian belief and practice with elements of African religions. Guided by this religious mixture, many Christian people of color embraced ritual that was—by European standards—both spontaneous and emotional. These expressive qualities persist in many African-American religious organizations today (Frazier, 1965; Roberts, 1980).

As people of color migrated from the rural South to the industrial cities of the North, it was the church that played a major role in addressing problems of dislocation, poverty, and prejudice. Moreover, among people often cut off from the larger society, the church provided the opportunity for talented men and women to distinguish themselves as leaders. Ralph Abernathy, Martin Luther King, Jr., and Jesse Jackson each gained international recognition for leadership while serving as ministers in primarily African-American religious organizations.

RELIGION IN A CHANGING SOCIETY

All social institutions evolve with time. Just as the economy, politics, and family life have changed over the course of this century, so has our society's religious life.

Secularization

One of the most important patterns of social change is **secularization**, *the historical decline in the importance of the supernatural and the sacred.* For society as a whole, secularization points to a declining influence of religion in everyday life. For religious organizations, becoming more secular means that they direct attention less to otherworldly issues (such as life after death) and more to worldly affairs (such as sheltering the homeless and feeding the hungry).

Moreover, secularization also means that functions once performed by the church (such as charity) are now primarily the responsibility of government.

Secularization, with Latin roots meaning "the present age," is commonly associated with modern, technologically advanced societies (Cox, 1971; O'Dea & Aviad, 1983). Conventional wisdom holds that secularization is one result of the increasing importance of science in understanding human affairs. Evidence of contemporary secularization lies in the fact that, since mid-century, public schools have taught children little about religion. More broadly, people perceive birth, illness, and death less as the work of a divine power than as natural stages in the life course. Such events are now more likely to occur in the presence of physicians (whose knowledge is based on science) than religious leaders (whose knowledge is based on faith). The rise of science suggests that religion's sphere of influence has diminished. Theologian Harvey Cox elaborates:

> The world looks less and less to religious rules and rituals for its morality or its meanings. For some, religion provides a hobby, for others a mark of national or ethnic identification, for still others an aesthetic delight. For fewer and fewer does it provide an inclusive and commanding system of personal and cosmic values and explanations. (1971:3)

If Cox is correct, should we expect that religion will disappear completely some day? The consensus among sociologists is "no" (Hammond, 1985; McGuire, 1987). Recall that the vast majority of people in the United States continue to profess a belief in God, and as many people claim to pray each day as vote in national elections. Further, religious affiliation today is actually several times higher than it was in 1850 (Hout & Greeley, 1987).

Secularization does not, then, signal the impending death of religion. More correctly, a decline in some dimensions of religiosity (such as belief in life after death) are accompanied by an increase in others (such as religious affiliation). Moreover, in global perspective we see that while religion is declining in importance in some regions (the Scandinavian countries, for example), religious fervor is rising in others (such as Algeria) (Cox, 1990).

Our society is also of two minds as to whether secularization is good or bad. Conservative people tend to see the erosion of religion as a mark of moral decline. Progressives, however, see secularization as liberation from the all-encompassing beliefs of the past, affording people greater responsibility for what they choose to believe. Further, secularization has brought the practices of many religious organizations (for example, ordination of both men and women) in line with widespread social attitudes.

Civil Religion

One dimension of secularization is the rise of what Robert Bellah (1975) has called **civil religion**, *a quasi-religious loyalty binding individuals in a basically secular society*. In other words, even if some dimensions of religiosity are weakening, our patriotism and citizenship retain many religious qualities.

Certainly, most people in the United States consider our way of life to be moral and a force for good in the world. Many people differ as to what our society's moral purpose should be, but participants find religious qualities in political movements—liberal and conservative alike (Williams & Demerath, 1991).

Civil religion also involves a range of rituals, from rising to sing the National Anthem at sporting events to sitting down to watch public parades several times a year. And, like the Christian cross or the Jewish Star of David, the flag serves as a sacred symbol of our national identity that we expect people to treat with reverence.

Civil religion is not a specific doctrine. It does, however, incorporate many elements of traditional religion into the political system of a secular society.

Religious Revival

We have argued that overall religiosity in the United States has been stable in recent decades. But a great deal of change is going on inside the world of organized religion. Membership in established, "mainstream" churches like the Episcopalian and Presbyterian denominations has plummeted by almost 50 percent since 1960. During the same period, affiliation with other religious organizations (including the Mormons, Seventh-Day Adventists, and especially Christian sects) has risen just as dramatically.

Perhaps secularization is self-limiting so that, as churchlike organizations become more worldly in a religious "marketplace," many people abandon them in favor of more sectlike religious communities that better address their spiritual concerns (Stark & Bainbridge, 1981; Roof & McKinney, 1987; Jacquet & Jones, 1991; Warner, 1993).

Much the same pattern of change can be seen in other industrial societies. The box takes a look at the state of religious affiliation in Great Britain.

SOCIAL SURVEY: "Would you say that you have been 'born again,' or have had a 'born again' experience—that is, a turning point in your life when you committed yourself to Christ?" (GSS 1988, 1991, N = 2,840; *Codebook*, 1993:409)

    "Yes" 35.7%   "No" 62.2%   DK/NR 2.1%

GLOBAL: Proportion affirming "Religion is important in my life": U.S., 79%; Canada, 65%; Italy, 64%; W. Germany, 58%; Japan, 57%; Australia, 52%; U.K., 41%; France, 26%. (Survey Research Consultants International)

NOTE: Fundamentalism is, in part, a product of our frontier history in which circuit preachers employed dramatic presentations in the hopes of an immediate conversion by those attending. Fundamentalism is less pronounced in Europe because European churches are more "established," and usually linked to the state.

GLOBAL SOCIOLOGY

The Changing Face of Religion: A Report from Great Britain

Although the Church of England enjoys the status of being that nation's official religious organization, Anglicans number only one-fifth of regular worshipers in Great Britain today. As in the United States, Britain's established, "mainstream" churches have lost members. The figure demonstrates that the support for the Anglican, Roman Catholic, Presbyterian, and Baptist churches is down significantly in recent years.

Overall, however, religiosity in Great Britain is holding steady (although at a level below that of the United States). The reason for this persistence is that, as the established churches

lose members, newer religious organizations are showing surprising strength. Immigration is behind some of this religious revival; with

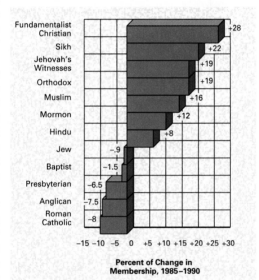

Percent of Change in Membership, 1985–1990

the number of Asians rising rapidly in Britain, the numbers of Muslims, as well as Sikhs and Hindus, are steadily increasing. Newly formed cults, too, contribute to religious resurgence; experts suggest that as many as six hundred cults exist at any one time.

But the most significant rise in British religious affiliation is among fundamentalist Christian organizations that embrace highly energetic and musical forms of worship, often under the direction of charismatic leaders. Like their counterparts in the United States, these religious communities typically express the experience of God's presence in a way that the more staid, "mainstream" churches do not.

SOURCES: Barker (1989) and *The Economist* (1993).

Religious Fundamentalism

A key dimension of this change is the growth of **fundamentalism,** *a conservative religious doctrine that opposes intellectualism and worldly accommodation in favor of restoring traditional, otherworldly spirituality.* In the United States, fundamentalism has made the greatest gains among Protestants. Southern Baptists, one such organization, form the largest religious community in the United States. But fundamentalist groups have also proliferated among Roman Catholics and Jews.

In response to what they see as the growing influence of science and the erosion of the conventional family, religious fundamentalists defend their version of traditional values. From this point of view, the liberal churches are simply too tolerant of religious pluralism and too open to change. Religious fundamentalism is

distinctive in five ways (Hunter, 1983, 1985, 1987, 1989; Willcox, 1989):

1. **Fundamentalists interpret the Scriptures literally.** Fundamentalists insist on a literal interpretation of the Scriptures as a means of countering what they see as excessive intellectualism among more liberal Christian organizations. Fundamentalists hold, for example, that God created the world precisely as described in Genesis.

2. **Fundamentalists do not accept religious pluralism.** Fundamentalists maintain that tolerance and relativism water down personal faith. They maintain, therefore, that their religious beliefs have validity while those of others do not.

3. **Fundamentalists pursue the personal experience of God's presence.** In contrast to the worldliness

DIVERSITY: Among Christians, *evangelism* (with Latin and Greek roots meaning "bring good news") refers to the movement to "spread the word" of the Gospels; most Christian fundamentalists are conservative evangelists. Some fundamentalists are Pentacostals, who stress the personal experience of the Holy Spirit.

RESOURCE: The *Seeing Ourselves* reader contains the "contemporary" selection, "Evangelicals in America," by Kenneth Briggs.

Q: "Believing in the Bible as I do, I would find it impossible to stop preaching the pure saving Gospel of Jesus Christ, and begin doing anything else—including fighting communism, or participating in civil rights reforms . . . Preachers are not called to be politicians but to be soul winners." Jerry Falwell, 1965

The painting Arts of the South, *by Thomas Hart Benton (1889–1975), suggests that religious fundamentalism is strongly integrated into the community life of rural people in the southern United States.*

and intellectualism of other religious organizations, fundamentalism seeks to propagate "good old-time religion" and spiritual revival. To fundamentalist Christians, being "born again" and establishing a personal relationship with Jesus Christ are expected to be clearly evident in a person's everyday life.

4. **Fundamentalism opposes "secular humanism."** Fundamentalists see accommodation to the changing world as undermining religious conviction. *Secular humanism* is a general term that refers to our society's tendency to look to scientific experts (including sociologists) rather than God for guidance about how to live.

5. **Many fundamentalists endorse conservative political goals.** Although fundamentalism tends to back away from worldly concerns, some fundamentalist leaders have entered the political arena in recent years to oppose what they see as the "liberal agenda" of feminism and gay rights. Fundamentalists oppose abortion as a matter of choice, seek to preserve the traditional two-parent family, want to return prayer to schools, and scold the mass media for coloring stories with liberal sentiments (Viguerie, 1981; Hunter, 1983; Speer, 1984; Ostling, 1985; Ellison & Sherkat, 1993; Green, 1993).

Taken together, these traits suggest why some people consider fundamentalism to be somewhat rigid and self-righteous. At the same time, this brief sketch also helps us to understand why others find in fundamentalism—with its greater religious certainty and emphasis on experiencing God's presence—an appealing alternative to the more intellectual, tolerant, and worldly "mainstream" denominations.

Which religions are "fundamentalist"? This term is most correctly applied to conservative Christian organizations in the evangelical tradition, including Pentecostals, Southern Baptists, Seventh-Day Adventists, and Assemblies of God. In national surveys, about 35 percent of U.S. adults describe their religious upbringing as "fundamentalist"; 38 percent claim a "moderate" religious tradition; and 24 percent call their religion "liberal" (NORC, 1993:169).

The Electronic Church

In contrast to small village congregations of years past, some religious organizations—especially fundamentalists—have become *electronic churches* dominated by "prime-time preachers" (Hadden & Swain, 1981). Electronic religion, a pattern known only in the United States, has propelled Oral Roberts, Pat Robertson, Robert Schuller, and others to greater prominence than all but a few clergy have enjoyed in the past. About 5 percent of the national television audience (about 10 million people) regularly view religious television, while perhaps 20 percent (about 40 million) watch some religious programming every week (Martin, 1981; Gallup, 1982; NORC, 1991).

During the 1980s, regular solicitation of contributions brought a financial windfall to some religious organizations. Broadcasting with thirty-two hundred stations in half the countries in the world, for example, Jimmy Swaggart received as much as $180 million annually in donations. But some media-based ministries were corrupted by the power of money. In 1989, Jim Bakker (who began his television career in 1965,

Q: "We have too many men of science, too few of God. We have grasped the mystery of the atom and rejected the Sermon on the Mount . . . . Ours is a world of nuclear giants and ethical infants. We know more about war than about peace, more about killing than about living." General Omar N. Bradley, 1948

NOTE: In a recent Time/CNN poll, 55% of U.S. adults thought religion would have a greater role in our society after the year 2000; 37% said it would play a lesser role.
Q: "If we do discover a complete theory [of physics] . . . it would be the ultimate triumph of human reason—for then we would truly know the mind of God." Stephen Hawking

with his wife Tammy, hosting a children's puppet show) was jailed following a conviction for defrauding contributors. Such cases, although few in number, attracted enormous national attention and undermined public support as people began to wonder whether television preachers were more interested in raising moral standards or cash.

LOOKING AHEAD: RELIGION IN THE TWENTY-FIRST CENTURY

The popularity of media ministries, the rapid growth of religious fundamentalism, and the persistent adherence of millions more people to the "mainstream" churches show that religion will remain a central element of modern society. Indeed, just as progressive political movements were launched from the pulpit in the 1950s and 1960s, the conservative politics of the 1980s was likewise religious in character (Stark & Bainbridge, 1981; Bateson & Ventis, 1982; Hunter, 1985; Warner, 1993). The world is becoming more complex, with rapid change almost outstripping our capacity to keep pace. But rather than undermining religion, these processes end up firing the religious imagination of people who seek a sense of religious community and ultimate meaning in life.

Science is simply unable to provide answers to the most central human needs and questions. Moreover, technological advances are confronting us with vexing moral dilemmas as never before—from new technologies for creating life to techniques for sustaining the lives of dying people. Against this backdrop of uncertainty, it is little wonder that many people continue to rely on their faith for assurance and hope. No doubt they will continue to do so for some time to come (Cox, 1977; Barker, 1981).

SUMMARY

1. Religion is a major social institution based on distinguishing the sacred from the profane. Religion is a matter of faith, not scientific evidence, which people express through various rituals.

2. Sociology analyzes the social consequences and correlates of religion but can make no claims as to the ultimate truth or falsity of any religious belief.

3. Emile Durkheim argued that, through religion, individuals experience the power of their society. His structural-functional analysis suggests that religion promotes social cohesion and conformity and confers meaning and purpose on life.

4. Using the symbolic-interaction paradigm, Peter Berger explains that religious beliefs are socially constructed as a means of responding to life's uncertainties and disruptions.

5. Using the social-conflict paradigm, Karl Marx charged that religion promotes social inequality. Historically, however, religious ideals have both supported hierarchy and motivated people to seek greater equality.

6. Max Weber's analysis of Calvinism's contribution to the rise of industrial capitalism demonstrates religion's power to promote social change.

7. Churches, which are religious organizations well integrated into their society, fall into two categories—ecclesias and denominations.

8. Sects, the result of religious division, are marked by suspicion of the larger society as well as charismatic leadership.

9. Cults are religious organizations that embrace new and unconventional beliefs and practices.

10. Technologically simple human societies were generally animistic, with religious life taking place within the family; in more complex societies, religion emerges as a distinct social institution.

11. Followers of six world religions—Christianity, Islam, Judaism, Hinduism, Buddhism, and Confucianism—represent three-fourths of all humanity.

12. Almost all adults in the United States identify with a religion; about 60 percent claim to have a religious affiliation, with the largest number belonging to various Protestant denominations.

13. How religious we conclude our nation is depends on how we operationalize the concept of religiosity. The vast majority of people say they believe in God, but probably only one-fifth of the U.S. population attends religious services regularly.

14. Secularization refers to the diminishing importance of the supernatural and the sacred. In the United States, while some indicators of religiosity (like membership in "mainstream" churches) have declined, others (such as membership in sects) are on the rise. Such complexity suggests secularization will not result in the demise of religion.

15. Civil religion is a quasi-religious belief by which people profess loyalty to their society, often in the form of patriotism.

16. Fundamentalism opposes religious accommodation to the world, favoring a more otherworldly focus. Fundamentalist Christianity also advocates literal interpretation of the Bible, rejects religious diversity, and pursues the personal experience of God's presence. Some fundamentalist Christian organizations actively support conservative political goals.

17. Some of the continuing appeal of religion lies in the inability of science (including sociology) to address timeless questions about the ultimate meaning of human existence.

KEY CONCEPTS

animism the belief that elements of the natural world are conscious forms of life that affect humanity

charisma extraordinary personal qualities that can turn an audience into followers

church a type of religious organization well integrated into the larger society

civil religion a quasi-religious loyalty binding individuals in a basically secular society

conversion a personal transformation or rebirth resulting from adopting new religious beliefs

cult a religious organization that is substantially outside the cultural traditions of a society

denomination a church, independent of the state, that accepts religious pluralism

ecclesia a church that is formally allied with the state

faith belief anchored in conviction rather than scientific evidence

fundamentalism a conservative religious doctrine that opposes intellectualism and worldly accommodation in favor of restoring a traditional, otherworldly spirituality

liberation theology a fusion of Christian principles with political activism, often Marxist in character

monotheism belief in a single divine power

polytheism belief in many gods

profane that which is defined as an ordinary element of everyday life

religion a social institution involving beliefs and practices based upon a conception of the sacred

religiosity the importance of religion in a person's life

ritual formal, ceremonial behavior

sacred that which is defined as extraordinary, inspiring a sense of awe, reverence, and even fear

sect a type of religious organization that stands apart from the larger society

secularization the historical decline in the importance of the supernatural and the sacred

totem an object in the natural world collectively defined as sacred

CRITICAL-THINKING QUESTIONS

1. Explain the basic distinction between the sacred and the profane that underlies all religious belief.

2. Explain Karl Marx's contention that religion tends to support the status quo. Develop a counterargument, based on Max Weber's analysis of Calvinism, that religion can be a major force for social change.

3. Distinguish between churches, sects, and cults. Is one type of religious organization inherently better than another?

4. What evidence suggests that religion is experiencing a decline in importance in the United States? In what ways does religion seem to be getting stronger?

SUGGESTED READINGS

Classic Sources

Max Weber. *The Protestant Ethic and the Spirit of Capitalism*. New York: Charles Scribner's Sons, 1958.

This is the classic account of the power of religion to effect sweeping social change.

Will Herberg. *Protestant-Catholic-Jew*. New York: Doubleday, 1955.

Herberg traces the historical development of three major religions in the United States, explaining how religion has lost and gained strength among immigrants and subsequent generations of their families.

Contemporary Sources

Meredith B. McGuire. *Religion: The Social Context*. 4th ed. Belmont, Calif.: Wadsworth, 1994.

This text provides a detailed analysis of the issues raised in this chapter.

Roger Finke and Rodney Stark. *The Churching of America, 1776–1990*. New Brunswick, N.J.: Rutgers University Press, 1992.

This historical account explains that, compared to other industrial societies, religion has had an exceptionally strong presence in the United States.

David E. Van Zandt. *Living in the Children of God*. Princeton, N.J.: Princeton University Press, 1991.

Participant observation allowed this researcher to gain considerable insight into one of today's Christian sects.

Anthony J. Blasi. *Making Charisma: The Social Construction of Paul's Public Image*. New Brunswick, N.J.: Transaction, 1991.

Focusing on the life of St. Paul, this book argues that charisma is not merely a personal trait but a collective phenomenon generated in response to a social need.

Robin Lorentzen. *Women in the Sanctuary Movement*. Philadelphia: Temple University Press, 1991.

This study of the sanctuary movement focuses on the women who participate in the morally motivated yet illegal effort to shelter political refugees.

Helen Rose Ebaugh. *Women in the Vanishing Cloister: Organizational Decline in Catholic Religious Orders in the United States*. New Brunswick, N.J.: Rutgers University Press, 1993.

This account, written by a nun-turned-sociologist, explores the drop in the number of women in Catholic religious orders since the 1960s.

Patrick H. McNamara. *Conscience First, Tradition Second: A Study of Young American Catholics*. Albany: State University of New York Press, 1992.

Based on interviews ten years apart, this book charts changes in the religious beliefs and identity of young Catholics in the United States.

Wade Clark Roof. *A Generation of Seekers: The Spiritual Journeys of the Baby Boom Generation*. New York: HarperCollins, 1992.

Mounting evidence points to a return to religion for many members of the generation of young people who came of age in the 1960s.

Freda Hussain, ed. *Muslim Women*. New York: St. Martin's Press, 1984.

Religion has long played a major part in the social relations between the sexes. This collection of ten essays examines both the ideal and the real social position of women in Islamic societies.

Wilson Jeremiah Moses. *Black Messiahs and Uncle Toms: Social and Literary Manipulations of a Religious Myth*. University Park, Pa.: Pennsylvania State University Press, 1986.

This book investigates the history of African-American religion, especially those promising "deliverance" to people suffering oppression.

Global Sources

David J. Hess. *Spirits and Scientists: Ideology, Spiritism, and Brazilian Culture*. University Park, Pa.: Pennsylvania State University Press, 1991.

This study of Brazilian religion highlights the continuing importance of spiritism, the belief in the lingering presence of the spirits of people who have departed this life.

James A. Beckford and Thomas Luckmann, eds. *The Changing Face of Religion*. Newbury Park, Calif.: Sage, 1989.

This collection of essays surveys religions around the world.

Christian Smith. *The Emergence of Liberation Theology: Radical Religion and Social Movement Theory*. Chicago: University of Chicago Press, 1991.

This account of the emergence of liberation theology among Catholics in Latin America in the 1960s points to the movement's successes and failures.

Martin E. Marty and R. Scott Appleby. *Fundamentalisms Observed*. Chicago: University of Chicago Press, 1991.

This collection of essays provides a global survey of the various forms of religious fundamentalism.

Diego Rivera, *Rural School Teacher*

DATA FILE: An outline for this chapter, supplementary lecture material, and discussion topics are found in the *Data File*.

Q: "A human being is not, in any proper sense, a human being until he is educated." Horace Mann

Q: "I am always ready to learn, although I do not always like being taught." Winston Churchill

GLOBAL: One key to Japanese educational achievement is powerful cultural discipline. While such cultural pressure generates collective distinction, it produces fewer highly innovative individuals. For instance, U.S. men and women have received proportionately far more Nobel prizes than have the Japanese.

Q: "An intellectual is a person who uses more words than necessary to tell you more than he knows." Dwight D. Eisenhower

Education

Thirteen-year-old Naoko Matsuo has just returned from school to her home in suburban Yokohama, Japan. Instead of dropping off her books and beginning an afternoon of fun, she settles in to do her homework. Several hours later, Naoko's mother reminds her that it is time to leave for the juku or "cram school" that she attends for three hours three evenings a week. Mother and daughter travel four stops on the subway to downtown Yokohama and climb to the second floor of an office building where Naoko joins dozens of other girls and boys for intensive training in Japanese, English, math, and science.

Tuition at the juku consumes several hundred dollars of the Matsuo family's monthly income. But they know well the realities of the Japanese educational system, and consider this investment in extra schooling a necessity. The extra hours in

the classroom will soon pay off when Naoko takes a national examination to determine her school placement. Three years later, she will face another hurdle with the high school placement exam; that, once again, will determine the quality of her education. Then will come the final test: earning admission to an exclusive national university, a prize awarded only to the one-third of Japanese students who perform best on this examination. Stumbling in the race that is Naoko's next five years will mean learning to settle for less. Like most other Japanese families, the Matsuos are convinced that one cannot work too hard or begin too early to prepare for university admission (Simons, 1989).

Why do the Japanese pay such attention to schooling? In this modern, industrial society, admission to an elite university all but ensures a high-paying, prestigious career.

513

Surveying the world as well as focusing on the United States, this chapter spotlights **education,** *the social institution guiding a society's transmission of knowledge—including basic facts, job skills, and also cultural norms and values—to its members.* In industrial societies, as we shall see, much education is a matter of **schooling,** *formal instruction under the direction of specially trained teachers.*

EDUCATION: A GLOBAL SURVEY

Like people in Japan, we in the United States expect children to spend much of their first eighteen years of life in school. During the last century, however, schooling in our society was a privilege restricted to a small elite. And so it is in poor societies today, where the vast majority of people receive only informal learning within the family.

Preindustrial Societies

Chapter 4 ("Society") explained that, throughout history, most humans have been hunters and gatherers. In such societies, the family was the central social institution; just as there were no governments or churches, so no formal system of education existed apart from the knowledge and skills adults taught to children (Lenski, Lenski, and Nolan, 1991).

In agrarian societies—in which most of the world's people live today—what schooling there is imparts practical knowledge needed to perform farming or other traditional tasks. By contrast, the opportunity to study literature, art, history, and science is a privilege generally available only to people freed by their wealth from the need to work. The English word "school," in fact, comes down to us from the Greek word for "leisure." In ancient Greece, renowned teachers such as Socrates, Plato, and Aristotle concentrated their efforts on aristocratic men to the exclusion of everyone else. Similarly, in ancient China, the famous philosopher Confucius shared his wisdom with only a select few (Rohlen, 1983). During the Middle Ages, European education took a step forward as the church established the first colleges and universities. But, here again, schooling remained a privilege of the ruling elites.

We find marked diversity in schooling throughout preindustrial societies today, in part, reflecting the influence of thousands of local cultural traditions. In Iran, for example, education and religion are closely linked, so Islam figures prominently in schooling there. In Bangladesh (Asia), Zimbabwe (Africa), and Nicaragua (Latin America) a distinctive cultural system has molded the process of schooling.

Schooling in poor societies also reflects Western colonialism by which various rich nations—including the United States—imposed their culture on others. But all poor societies have one trait in common: limited access to schooling. In the poorest nations (including several in Central Africa), only half of all elementary-aged children are in school; throughout the world, just half of children attend secondary school (Najafizadeh & Mennerick, 1992). As a consequence, illiteracy disadvantages one-third of Latin Americans, almost half of Asians, and two-thirds of Africans. Global Map 19–1 displays the extent of illiteracy around the world.

Industrial Societies

Industrial societies, by contrast, embrace the principle of schooling for everyone. Industrial production demands that workers gain at least basic skills in the so-called "three Rs"—reading, 'riting, and 'rithmetic. Our society has also looked to schooling as a means of forging a literate citizenry able to participate in democratic political life.

The United States was among the first countries to pursue the goal of mass education. By 1850 about half the young people between the ages of five and nineteen were enrolled in school. By 1918, every state had a *mandatory education law* that required children to attend school until at least the age of sixteen or completion of the eighth grade. These laws drew children from farms and factories to classrooms. Table 19–1 shows that a milestone was reached in the mid-1960s when a majority of adults had completed high school. In 1992, almost four out of five U.S.

TABLE 19–1 Educational Achievement in the United States, 1910–1992*

Year	High School Graduates	College Graduates	Median Years of Schooling
1910	13.5%	2.7%	8.1
1920	16.4	3.3	8.2
1930	19.1	3.9	8.4
1940	24.1	4.6	8.6
1950	33.4	6.0	9.3
1960	41.1	7.7	10.5
1970	55.2	11.0	12.2
1980	68.7	17.0	12.5
1992	79.5	21.4	12.7

*For persons twenty-five years of age and over.
SOURCE: U.S. Bureau of the Census (1993).

NOTE: U.S. college enrollment in 1890 (156,756) was 3% of 18–21-year-olds; in 1930 (1,100,737), 12%; in 1991 (7,010,000), 57%.

GLOBAL: A U.S. government study determined the following proficiency levels for 13-year-olds in mathematics: U.S., 474; Ireland, 504; United Kingdom, 510; Spain, 512; South Korea, 568.

GLOBAL: The high school dropout rate in Japan is about 10%, less than half of what it is in the United States. However, about 25% of U.S. young people are now gaining college degrees, twice the Japanese rate.

Window on the World

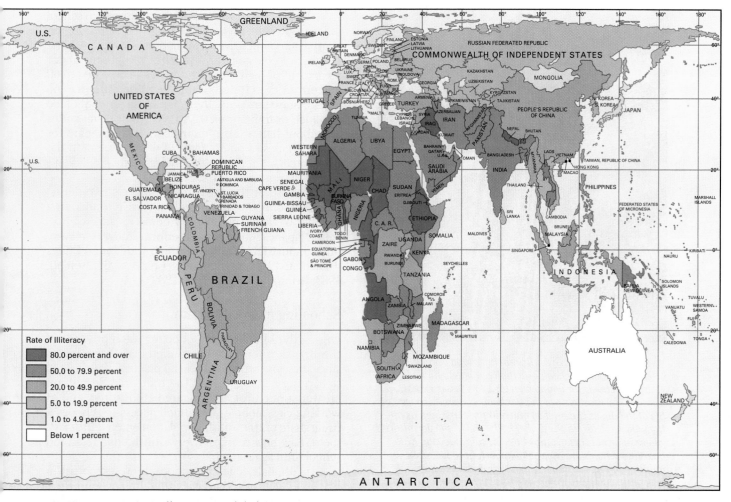

Rate of Illiteracy

- 80.0 percent and over
- 50.0 to 79.9 percent
- 20.0 to 49.9 percent
- 5.0 to 19.9 percent
- 1.0 to 4.9 percent
- Below 1 percent

GLOBAL MAP 19–1 Illiteracy in Global Perspective

Reading and writing skills are widespread in every industrial society, with illiteracy rates generally below 5 percent. Throughout Latin America, however, illiteracy is more commonplace—one consequence of limited economic development. In about a dozen nations of the world—many of them in Africa—illiteracy is the rule rather than the exception. In such societies, people rely on what sociologists call "the oral tradition" of face-to-face communication rather than communicating through the written word.

From *Peters Atlas of the World* (1990).

adults had a high school education, and more than one in five have completed four years of college. Today, officially at least, only a small proportion of people are illiterate in the United States as well as in Japan, Great Britain, and other industrial societies. As we shall now explain, however, each industrial society provides schooling in its own way.

Schooling in Japan

Before industrialization brought mandatory education to Japan in 1872, only a privileged few received schooling. Today's educational system in Japan is widely praised for generating some of the world's highest achievers.

Chapter 19 Education **515**

RESOURCE: John Wakeford points out that contemporary boarding schools replicate the historical pattern by which the adolescents of high social standing are "removed for a period from their parents' households to live in the company of their peers, and to participate in a specified kind of social life." *The Cloistered Elite: A Sociological Analysis of the English Public Boarding School* (New York: Praeger, 1969)

GLOBAL: Twice as many Japanese parents express the desire to send a son (73%) to college as a daughter (29%). Brinton (1988)
GLOBAL: The 976 British boarding schools (1992 average annual cost: $17,000) have been suffering declining enrollments in recent years primarily because parents are less willing to send youngsters (between 7 and 14) away to school.

scores, there is little even the richest families can do to place their children in a good university.

More men and women graduate from high school in Japan (90 percent) than in the United States (78 percent). But competitive examinations sharply curb the number of college-bound youths, so that only about 30 percent of high school graduates—compared to 60 percent in the United States—end up entering college. Understandably, then, Japanese students face entrance examinations with the utmost seriousness, and about half attend "cram schools" to prepare for them. Japanese women, most of whom are not in the labor force, often devote themselves to their children's success in school.

Because of the pressure it places on students, Japanese schooling produces impressive results. In a number of fields, notably mathematics and science, young Japanese students outperform students in every other industrial society, including the United States (Benedict, 1974; Hayneman & Loxley, 1983; Rohlen, 1983; Brinton, 1988; Simons, 1989).

Schooling in Great Britain

During the Middle Ages, schooling was a privilege of the British nobility, who studied classical subjects since they had little need for the practical skills related to earning a living. But as the Industrial Revolution created a need for an educated labor force, and as working-class people demanded access to schools, a rising share of the British population entered the classroom. Law now requires every British child to attend school until age sixteen.

Traditional social distinctions, however, persist in British education. Many wealthy families send their children to what the British call *public schools*, the equivalent of private boarding schools in the United States. Such elite schools not only teach academic subjects, they also convey to children from wealthy (especially *newly rich*) families the distinctive patterns of speech, mannerisms, and social graces of the British upper class. These schools are far too expensive for most students, however, who attend state-supported day schools.

To lessen the influence of social background on schooling, the British expanded their university system during the 1960s and 1970s and inaugurated a program of competitive examinations for admission. For those who score the highest, the government pays most of the costs of tuition and living expenses. Compared with those in Japan, however, British examinations are less crucial, since many well-to-do children

Wealth and power in Great Britain have long been linked to attending "public" schools—actually privately funded boarding schools for young men and, to a lesser extent, women. The most elite of these schools transmit the way of life of the upper class not so much in the classroom as on the playing fields, in the dining halls, and in the dormitories where informal socialization goes on continuously. Elite boarding schools are especially important to new-rich families; parents with modest backgrounds and big bank accounts send their children to these schools to mix with and learn from the offspring of "old-money" families.

The early grades concentrate on transmitting Japanese traditions, including obligation to family. By their early teens, as illustrated by the account of Naoko Matsuo at the beginning of this chapter, students encounter Japan's system of rigorous and competitive examinations. These written tests, which resemble the Scholastic Aptitude Tests (SATs) used for college admissions in the United States, all but determine a young Japanese student's future.

In Japan, schooling is more of a meritocracy than it is in the United States, where ability to pay for college is a major concern. In Japan, government support relieves families of much of the financial burden of higher education. But, without high examination

who do not score well still manage to attend Oxford and Cambridge, the most prestigious British universities on a par with Yale, Harvard, and Princeton in the United States. These "Oxbridge" graduates assume their place at the core of the British power elite: More than two-thirds of the top members of the British government have "Oxbridge" degrees (Sampson, 1982; Gamble, Ludlam, & Baker, 1993).

Schooling in the Former Soviet Union

Schooling has changed considerably in the former Soviet Union over the course of the last century. Before the socialist revolution of 1917, Russia was an agrarian society with schooling reserved primarily for nobles. By the 1930s, the Soviet Union had adopted mandatory education laws and embarked on a program to use schooling to reshape the new socialist society. By 1950, half of the young people in the Soviet Union were attending school and, by 1975, the Soviets began boasting of having achieved virtually universal schooling.

Soviet socialism generated an official policy of equal access to schooling for both women and men and for people of all ethnic backgrounds. In practice, however, Soviet women never reached educational parity with men and were overly represented in areas of study (such as teaching and medicine) with relatively low social prestige in that society. Men, by contrast, have long dominated higher-prestige fields like agriculture and engineering. Similarly, although considerable strides were made toward providing equal access to higher education for diverse ethnic groups, the Russian majority fares better than others.

Schooling in the former Soviet Union had important political purposes. Although changes are now under way as this society sheds its socialist past (see Chapters 15 and 16), the Soviet educational system employed a highly standardized curriculum to advance what the central government held to be proper patterns of socialist living. As in Japan and Great Britain, competitive examinations have long characterized the Commonwealth of Independent States, identifying the most academically able students who are admitted to higher education.

Further, as Chapter 9 ("Social Stratification") notes, disparity of wealth was less pronounced in the Soviet Union than in the United States, and the government paid most educational costs. This economic parity has gone a long way to creating a level playing field for young people in today's Commonwealth of Independent States—much more so than in our society. During the heyday of the Communist party,

however, being the daughter or son of an important official factored in significantly when it came to going to a select university (Avis, 1983; Matthews, 1983; Tomiak, 1983; Ballantine, 1989).

The overall theme of this brief comparison is that education is shaped by other institutions and social forces. Societies generally adopt mandatory education laws as a consequence of industrialization and growing political democracy. Also, schools show the influence of cultural patterns (such as the achievement orientation and intense competition of Japan), historical forces (seen in centuries of inequality in British schooling), and the political system (evident in decades of socialist education in the former Soviet Union).

Schooling in the United States

The educational system in the United States, too, has been shaped by our cultural traditions, which stress political participation. Thomas Jefferson thought the new nation could become democratic only if people can "read and understand what is going on in the world" (quoted in Honeywell, 1931:13). The United States now has a larger proportion of its people attending colleges and universities than any other society in the world—twice the share of Australia or Sweden, for example, and three times the proportion found in France or Ireland (U.S. Bureau of the Census, 1993).

Schooling in the United States also reflects the value of *equal opportunity*. National surveys show that most people think schooling is crucial to personal success (Gallup, 1982; NORC, 1993). We like to think that our society offers educational opportunity: 70 percent endorse the notion that people have the chance to get an education consistent with their abilities and talents (NORC, 1993). But this view better expresses our aspirations than our achievement. Until this century, women were all but excluded from higher education, and only among the wealthy do a majority of young people attend college even today.

Besides trying to make schooling more widely available, our educational system has also stressed the value of *practical* learning, that is, knowledge that has a direct bearing on people's work and interests. The educational philosopher John Dewey (1859–1952) maintained that children would readily learn those things they found useful, rather than a fixed body of knowledge passed from generation to generation. Thus Dewey (1968; orig. 1938) championed *progressive*

SOCIAL SURVEY: "How important for getting ahead in life is having a good education?" (GSS 1987, N = 1,285; *Codebook*, 1993:583).

"Essential"	34.7%	"Not very important"	1.3%
"Very important"	48.2%	"Not important at all"	0%
"Fairly important"	14.3%	DK/NR	1.5%

NOTE: Community colleges clearly express the U.S. cultural emphasis on widespread schooling with practical consequences. The most rapid growth in community colleges was between 1966 and 1976, when enrollments almost tripled. Community colleges now enroll some 5 million women and men—more than 40% of all college students.

SOCIOLOGY OF EVERYDAY LIFE

Following the Jobs: Trends in Bachelor's Degrees

College attendance in the United States has never been higher, with a striking increase in recent years in the number of bachelor's degrees earned by women. For both sexes, however, college education retains an emphasis on practicality: People pursue degrees in fields where they think jobs are plentiful.

Over the last decade, the figure shows that the greatest surge in bachelor's degrees was in computer science, a reflection of influence of the Information Revolution. The number of degrees in law and communications, both central to the postindustrial economy, also rose sharply. Business, management, and accounting—which have long been the most popular fields for students—also made gains. Engineering and the social

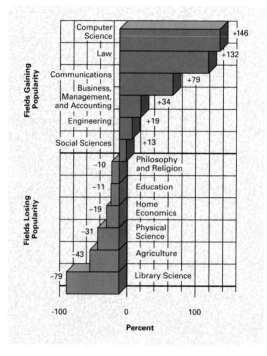

Percentage Changes in Bachelor's Degrees Earned, 1980–1990

SOURCE: U.S. Bureau of the Census (1993).

sciences—including sociology—are up as well.

By and large, students shied away from majors in areas where the demand for workers has slipped. Library science heads the list of fields posting reductions, followed by agriculture, the physical sciences, home economics, education, philosophy and religion.

---

education that addressed people's changing concerns and needs.

Reflecting this practical emphasis, today's college students select major areas of study with an eye toward future jobs. The box takes a closer look at the changing interests of college students.

THE FUNCTIONS OF SCHOOLING

Structural-functional analysis directs attention to ways in which formal education enhances the operation and stability of society. Central to the socialization process, schooling serves as a cultural lifeline linking the generations.

Socialization

Technologically simple societies transmit their ways of life informally from generation to generation through the family. As societies gain more complex technology, however, kin can no longer stay abreast of rapidly expanding information and skills; schooling gradually emerges as a distinctive social institution utilizing specially trained personnel to efficiently convey a wide range of knowledge.

At the primary school level, children learn basic language and mathematical skills. Secondary school builds on this foundation, and, for many, college allows further specialization. Because industrial societies change so quickly, schooling teaches students not only

NOTE: Consider the cultural values implicit in the classroom spelling bee (including competition, individual performance, universalistic standards of achievement).

DIVERSITY: Related to the social integration function of schooling is the multiculturalism debate, included in Chapter 3 ("Culture").

DIVERSITY: Racial segregation partly underlies the social placement function of schooling. According to a 1987 Congressional study, 33.2% of African-American children and 31.0% of Hispanic children were in "intensely segregated" schools.

NOTE: Richard Sennett and Jonathan Cobb (1973) claim that schooling provides "badges of personal ability" that largely reflect social privileges.

information (which may become obsolete) but also, at its best, empowers them to teach themselves so that they will be able to adapt to future changes.

Schools also transmit cultural values and norms. Civics classes, for example, provide students with explicit instruction in our ways of life. Sometimes important cultural lessons are learned in subtle ways, as students experience the operation of the classroom itself. Teachers give children in U.S. schools a great deal of individual responsibility; spelling bees and classroom drills also develop a keen sense of competitive individualism, enhance respect for authority, and establish norms of fair play. Likewise, rituals such as saluting the flag and singing "The Star-Spangled Banner" foster patriotism.

Cultural Innovation

Educational systems create as well as transmit culture. Schools stimulate intellectual inquiry and critical thinking, which spark the development of new ideas.

Today, for example, many college professors not only teach but engage in research that yields discoveries and innovations. Research in the humanities, the social sciences, and the natural sciences is changing attitudes and behavior throughout the United States and the larger world. Medical research, carried on mainly in major universities, has served to increase life expectancy, just as research by sociologists and psychologists helps us to take advantage of this longevity.

Social Integration

Schooling works to forge a mass of people into a unified whole. This function is especially important in nations with pronounced social diversity, where various cultures are indifferent or even hostile to one another. In the past, the Soviet Union and Yugoslavia relied on schools to tie their disparate peoples together—without ultimately succeeding—and similar cultural strains are evident in the United States.

Societies in the Americas, Africa, and Asia encompassing hundreds of ethnic categories all strive to foster social integration. Schools meet this challenge, first, by establishing a common language that encourages broad communication and forges a national identity. Of course, some ethnic minorities resist state-sponsored schooling for exactly this reason. In the former Soviet Union, for example, Lithuanians, Ukrainians, and Azerbaijanis long chafed at having to learn Russian, which they saw as a threat to their own traditions and emblematic of their domination by outsiders. Similarly, the Amish, a culturally distinctive people in the United

Proponents of Afrocentric schooling argue that teaching African languages and cultures will foster children's self-esteem and interest in learning. Critics respond that Afrocentrism promotes racial separation and diverts resources from the teaching of basic skills that children need to succeed in the larger society.

States, refuse to send their children to public schools.

Despite resistance to schooling on the part of some, the striking cultural diversity of the United States makes formal education a key path to social integration. A century ago, mandatory education laws coincided with the arrival of millions of immigrants. Even today, formal education plays a major role in integrating disparate cultures, as people from Latin America and Asia blend their traditions with the existing cultural mix. In recent years, racial and ethnic minorities have become a majority of the students in many of the largest school districts and, across the nation, a debate over multicultural education (highlighted in Chapter 3, "Culture") is under way.

Social Placement

Formal education helps young people assume culturally approved statuses and perform roles that contribute to the ongoing life of society. To accomplish this, schooling operates to identify and develop people's various aptitudes and abilities. Ideally, schools evaluate students' performance in terms of achievement while downplaying their social background.

In principle, teachers encourage the "best and the brightest" to pursue the most challenging and advanced studies, while guiding students of more ordinary abilities into educational programs suited to their talents. Schooling, in short, enhances meritocracy, linking social position to personal merit and fueling what our society holds to be desirable social mobility (Hurn, 1978).

Latent Functions of Schooling

Besides these purposeful, manifest functions of formal education, a number of latent functions are less widely recognized. One is child care. As the number of one-parent families and two-career couples rises, schools have become vital to relieving parents of some child care duties.

Among teenagers, too, schooling consumes much time and considerable energy, in many cases fostering conformity at a time of life when the likelihood of unlawful behavior is high. Because many students attend schools well into their twenties, education usefully engages thousands of young people for whom few jobs may be available.

Another latent function of schools is establishing relationships and networks. In the social circles of the high school, college, and university, many people meet their future spouses. Affiliation with a particular school also forms the basis of social ties that provide not only friendship but also valuable career opportunities later on in life.

Critical evaluation. Structural-functional analysis of formal education stresses the ways this social institution supports the operation of an industrial society by identifying both manifest and latent functions. The primary limitation of functionalism is overlooking how quality of schooling is far greater for some than for others. Indeed, critics of the U.S. educational system maintain that schooling actually operates to reproduce the class structure in each generation. In the next section, social-conflict analysis examines precisely these issues.

SCHOOLING AND SOCIAL INEQUALITY

Social-conflict analysis takes issue with the functionalist contention that schooling is a meritocratic strategy for developing people's talents and abilities. This view argues that, to the extent schools do take account of social background, they perpetuate social inequality based on sex, race, ethnicity, and social class.

Throughout the world, people traditionally have considered schooling more important for males than for females. Chapter 13 ("Sex and Gender") explained that the education gap between women and men has largely closed in recent decades, but many women still study conventionally feminine subjects such as literature, while men pursue mathematics and engineering. And by stressing the experiences of some types of people (say, military generals) while ignoring the lives of others (farm women) in the same society, schools reinforce the values and importance of dominant categories of people. As we shall see, too, affluent people have much more educational opportunity than their poorer counterparts.

Social Control

Social-conflict analysis suggests that schooling acts as a means of social control, reinforcing acceptance of the status quo with its inherent inequities. In various, sometimes subtle ways, schools serve to reproduce the status hierarchy.

Samuel Bowles and Herbert Gintis (1976) point out that the clamor for public education in the late nineteenth century arose at precisely the time that capitalists were seeking a docile, disciplined, and moderately educated work force. Mandatory education laws ensured that schools would teach immigrants with diverse cultural backgrounds the English language as well as cultural values supportive of capitalism. Compliance, punctuality, and discipline were—and still are—part of what conflict theorists call the **hidden curriculum**, *subtle presentations of political or cultural ideas in the classroom.*

Standardized Testing

Here is a question of the kind historically used to measure academic ability of school-age children in the United States:

Painter is to painting as _____ is to sonnet.

Answers: (a) driver   (c) priest
            (b) poet   (d) carpenter

The correct answer is (b) *poet*: A painter creates a painting as a poet creates a sonnet. This question purports to measure logical reasoning; but demonstrating this skill depends upon knowing what each term means. Unless students are familiar with sonnets as a Western European form of written verse, they are not likely to answer the question correctly.

Educational specialists claim that bias of this kind has been all but eliminated from standardized tests, since they carefully study response patterns and drop any question that appears to favor one racial or ethnic category over another. Critics, however, maintain that

From a functionalist point of view, schooling provides children with the information and skills they will need as adults. A conflict analysis adds that schooling differs according to the resources available to the local community. To the extent that some schools offer children much more than others do, education falls short of its goal of enhancing equality of opportunity.

some bias based on class, race, or ethnicity is inherent in any formal testing because questions inevitably reflect our society's dominant culture and, thereby, place people of color or other minorities at a disadvantage (Owen, 1985; Crouse & Trusheim, 1988; Putka, 1990).

School Tracking

Despite continuing controversy over standardized tests, most schools in the United States use them as the basis for **tracking,** *the assignment of students to different types of educational programs.* Tracking is also a common practice in many other industrial societies, including Great Britain, France, and Japan.

The educational justification for tracking is to give students the kind of schooling appropriate to their individual aptitude. For a variety of reasons, including innate ability and level of motivation, some students are capable of more challenging work than others are. Young people also differ in their interests, with some drawn to, say, the study of languages, while others seek training in art or science. Given this diversity of talent and focus, no single program for all students would serve any of them well.

According to critics, however, tracking actually works to perpetuate privilege rather than responding to individual needs. The basis of this argument is research indicating that social background has as much to do with tracking as personal traits do. Students from affluent families generally do well on standardized, "scientific" tests and so are placed in college-bound tracks, while tracking puts those from modest backgrounds

(including a disproportionate share of the poor) in programs that curb their aspirations and teach technical trades. Tracking, therefore, effectively segregates some students—academically and socially—from others.

Schools also tend to reserve their best teachers for students in favored tracks. Thus high-track boys and girls find that their teachers put more effort into classes, show more respect to students, and expect more from them. By contrast, teachers deal with low-track students by employing greater memorization, classroom drill, and other unstimulating techniques. Such classrooms also emphasize regimentation, punctuality, and respect for authority figures.

In light of these criticisms, schools across the United States are now cautious about making tracking assignments and allow more mobility between tracks. Some have even moved away from the practice entirely. Some tracking seems to be necessary to match instruction with student abilities. But rigid tracking has a powerful impact on students' learning and self-concept. Young people who spend years in higher tracks tend to see themselves as bright and able, whereas those in lower tracks develop lower ambition and self-esteem (Bowles & Gintis, 1976; Persell, 1977; Rosenbaum, 1980; Davis & Haller, 1981; Oakes, 1982, 1985; Hallinan & Williams, 1989; Kilgore, 1991; Gamoran, 1992).

Inequality Among Schools

Just as students are treated differently within schools, private schools as a whole differ in many ways from public schools, and public schools also vary from place to place.

SOCIAL SURVEY: "What about U.S. spending on improving the nation's education system?" (*STUDENT CHIP Social Survey Software*, NATEDUC1; GSS 1973–91, N = 16,374)

	"Too little"	"About right"	"Too much"
Afri Amer	72.1%	26.1%	1.8%
Hispanics	59.9%	36.4%	3.7%
Whites	55.7%	35.1%	9.1%

Public and Private Schools

In 1992 almost 90 percent of the 65 million school-aged children in the United States attended state-funded public schools. The remainder were in private schools.

A majority of private school students attend one of more than eight thousand *parochial schools* (from the Latin meaning "of the parish") operated by the Roman Catholic church. The Catholic school system grew rapidly a century ago as cities swelled with millions of Catholic immigrants and their children. These schools helped the new arrivals maintain their religious heritage in the midst of a predominantly Protestant society. Today, after decades of flight from the city by white people, many parochial schools enroll non-Catholics, including a growing number of young African Americans whose families eagerly seize this alternative to the neighborhood public school.

Protestants, too, have private schools or Christian academies, a more recent development among fundamentalist denominations. Both kinds of Christian schools are favored by parents who want their children to receive religious instruction or believe that parochial schools hold students to higher academic and disciplinary standards. Ironically, the Christian school can also represent a strategy by which parents maintain a racially homogeneous environment for their children in the face of school desegregation mandates (James, 1989).

Additionally, some fifteen hundred nonreligious private schools in the United States enroll students, mostly from well-to-do families. These prestigious and expensive preparatory schools are favored by those with established wealth, as well as "newly rich" parents eager for their daughters and sons to rub elbows with children of the "old rich." These institutions—many modeled on boarding schools in Great Britain—are academically outstanding and send a large share of their graduates to equally prestigious and expensive private universities. After learning the mannerisms, attitudes, and social graces of the socially prominent, "preppies" are likely to maintain lifelong school-based networks that provide numerous social advantages.

Are private schools better than public schools? Research indicates that, among children with similar backgrounds, private school students display higher rates of academic achievement than public school students. Private schools seem to generate greater interest in learning than do public schools, probably due to smaller class size and more student-teacher contact. Furthermore, private schools are more academically demanding and enforce stringent disciplinary policies, resulting in a safer, more orderly environment. By and

Total   57.6%   34.2%   8.2%

Q: "The [private] school—rather than the upper-class family—is the most important agency for transmitting the traditions of the upper classes, and regulating the admission of new wealth and talent.... It is by means of these schools more than by any other single agency that the older and the newer families . . . become members of a self-conscious upper class." C. Wright Mills (1959:64–65)

large, all other things equal, graduates of private schools are more likely than public school graduates to complete college and subsequently enter high-paying occupations (Coleman, Hoffer, & Kilgore, 1981; Coleman & Hoffer, 1987).

Inequality in Public Schooling

A general rule in U.S. education is that the more affluent the community, the better its schools. Winnetka, Illinois—one of the richest areas in the country—spends more than $8,000 annually per student, compared to less than $3,000 in a poor area like Socorro, Texas. Although cost-of-living differences may offset some of this disparity, it reflects the stark reality of unequal educational opportunities among the nation's fifteen thousand school districts (Carroll, 1990).

Most affluent, suburban school districts offer better schooling than less well funded systems in central cities. This disparity has an important racial dimension, since whites predominate in suburbia, while central cities are home to many African Americans and other minorities. To advance educational equality (often mandated by courts), some communities have initiated *busing*—transporting students to achieve a greater social mix. Although this policy currently affects only 5 percent of U.S. school children, it has generated heated controversy. Busing advocates claim that, given the extent of U.S. racial segregation, minority children in poor neighborhoods will have adequate funding for their schools only if white children from richer neighborhoods attend them. Critics respond that busing itself is expensive and transporting children undermines the concept of neighborhood schools. But both sides acknowledge that, given the racial imbalance of the larger urban area, any effective busing scheme would have to join central cities and suburbs—a plan that has almost never been politically feasible.

A report by a research team headed by James Coleman (1966) confirmed the handicap of attending predominantly minority schools: larger class size, insufficient libraries, and fewer science labs. But the Coleman report cautioned that money alone will not magically bolster academic quality. Even more important are the cooperative efforts and enthusiasm of teachers, parents, and students themselves. Supporting this conclusion, Christopher Jencks (1972) adds that even if school funding were exactly the same everywhere, the students whose families value and encourage education would still learn more than others.

The important conclusion, which remains valid today, is that we should not expect schools alone to

SOCIAL SURVEY: "How do you feel about opportunities for young people to go to college? Should opportunities be" (GSS 1983, N = 677; *Codebook*, 1993:526)

"Increased"   42.5%   "Reduced a little"   2.8%
"Increased a little"   25.6%   "Reduced a lot"   0.5%
"Kept the same as now"   25.6%   DK/NR   3.0%

Q: "In education, there should be no class distinction." Confucius

Q: "Education, then, beyond all other devices of human origin, is a great equalizer of conditions of men—the balance wheel of the social machinery." Horace Mann

THE MAP: Relatively affluent regions of the U.S. have a higher share of young people enrolled in college; in addition, high-enrollment counties are those where people are more supportive of greater opportunities for women (compare to National Map 13–1).

Seeing Ourselves

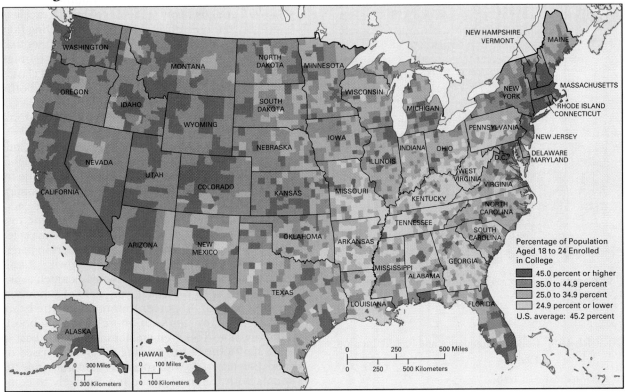

Percentage of Population Aged 18 to 24 Enrolled in College

- 45.0 percent or higher
- 35.0 to 44.9 percent
- 25.0 to 34.9 percent
- 24.9 percent or lower

U.S. average: 45.2 percent

NATIONAL MAP 19–1 College Attendance Across the United States

Generally speaking, college attendance is most common among adults along the Northeast and West coasts. By contrast, adults living in the Midwest and the South (especially the Appalachian region) are the least likely members of our society to attend college. How would you explain this pattern? (Income is one obvious consideration; would people's ideas about gender equality be another?)

From *American Demographics* magazine, April 1993, p. 60. Reprinted with permission. ©1993 *American Demographics* magazine, Ithaca, New York.

overcome marked social inequality in the United States. Yet our society can hardly afford to ignore the educational needs of poor minority children, who represent a steadily increasing proportion of the future work force (Cohen, 1989).

Access to Higher Education

Higher education is a path to occupational achievement; not surprisingly, the vast majority of parents would send their children to college if they could (Gallup, 1982). Yet, only 61 percent of high school graduates enroll in college the following fall (U.S. Bureau of the Census, 1993), and, among the U.S.

population aged twenty-five and older, just one-fifth are college graduates. National Map 19–1 shows where in the United States people are more or less likely to reach college.

In the United States, the most crucial factor affecting access to higher education is money. Unlike primary and secondary schooling, which is supported by public funds, people must purchase higher education. College is expensive, and the price is going up. Even at state-supported colleges and universities, annual tuition averages about $2,500, and the most expensive private colleges and universities top $20,000 a year. Add to these figures the costs of books, supplies, and travel to and from the campus.

Chapter 19 Education   **523**

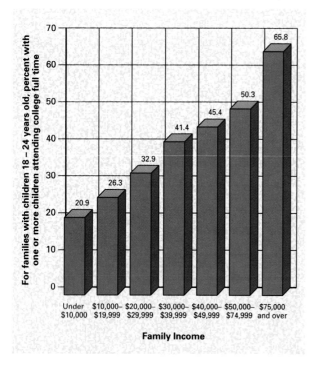

FIGURE 19–1 College Attendance and Family Income, 1992

(U.S. Bureau of the Census, 1994)

Given such expenses, family income is a good predictor of college attendance, as shown in Figure 19–1. Among families with children aged eighteen through twenty-four, only one in five with low incomes has a daughter or son in college. This share, however, rises to two-thirds among affluent families with $75,000 or more of annual earnings.

The financial burden of higher education dissuades many minorities, typically with below-average incomes, from attending college. Figure 19–2 shows that whites are more likely than African Americans and Hispanics to complete high school to begin with, and this disparity widens with each step up in the educational system. The long-term trend, however, may be toward greater equality. During the 1980s, the number of Hispanics attending college rose by about 70 percent and African-American enrollments increased by 20 percent; the non-Hispanic white rise was a modest 16 percent (U.S. Bureau of the Census, 1993).

But even among those privileged enough to commence higher education, not everyone receives the same type and quality of schooling. People of limited financial means typically attend less expensive community colleges and other government-supported schools. Certainly many students receive an excellent education in these public institutions, benefiting from faculty whose primary concern is teaching rather than research. But private schools, supported by high tuition and endowment earnings, allow smaller classes, expose students to renowned researchers, and offer higher prestige and admission to more networks of powerful people (Useem & Karabel, 1986; Monk-Turner, 1990).

For those who do attend college, rewards include not just intellectual and personal growth but higher income. Table 19–2 presents 1991 median income for full-time workers aged twenty-five and over according to their education. Women with an eighth-grade education typically earned about $13,000; income rose above $18,000 for high school graduates and averaged $28,000 for college graduates. The numbers in parentheses are ratios, showing that a woman with at least some graduate school earns 2.8 times as much as her counterpart with four or fewer years of schooling. Men earn about 40 percent more across the board than women do; moreover, more schooling boosts men's income at an even greater rate. Finally, bear in mind that some of the earning differential based on education has to do with social background, since the people with the most schooling are likely to come from relatively well-to-do families to begin with.

Credentialism

Sociologist Randall Collins (1979) has dubbed the United States a *credential society*, because people

TABLE 19–2 Median Income by Sex and Years of Schooling*

Schooling	Men	Women
Five or more years of college	$49,093 (3.2)	$33,771 (2.8)
Four years of college	39,115 (2.6)	28,042 (2.3)
1–3 years of college	31,566 (2.1)	22,227 (1.8)
Four years of high school	26,515 (1.8)	18,323 (1.5)
9–11 years of school	20,905 (1.4)	14,429 (1.2)
8 years of school	20,050 (1.3)	13,322 (1.1)
5–7 years of school	16,960 (1.1)	11,805 (1.0)
0–4 years of school	15,192 (1.0)	12,161 (1.0)

*Persons aged twenty-five years and over, working full-time, 1991. The earnings ratio, in parentheses, indicates how many times the lowest income level is earned by an individual with additional schooling.

SOURCE: U.S. Bureau of the Census (1992).

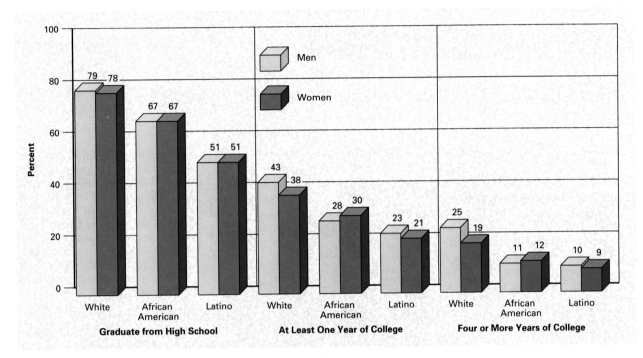

FIGURE 19–2 Educational Achievement for Various Categories of People, Aged 25 Years and Over

(U.S. Bureau of the Census, 1992)

view diplomas and degrees as evidence of ability to perform some specialized occupational role. As modern societies have become more technologically complex, culturally diverse, and socially mobile, a résumé now says "who you are" as much as family background.

Credentialism, then, is *evaluating a person on the basis of educational degrees.* Structural-functional analysis suggests that credentialism is simply the way our modern society goes about ensuring that important jobs are filled by well-trained people. But social-conflict analysis contends that credentials often bear little relation to the responsibilities of a specific job. Collins argues that advanced degrees serve as a short-hand way to sort out the people with the manners, attitudes, and even color desired by many employers. In short, credentialism amounts to a gate-keeping strategy that restricts important occupations to a small segment of the population.

Finally, this emphasis on credentials in the United States has encouraged *overeducation,* by which many workers have more formal education than they need to perform their jobs. Without denying the value of schooling, in other words, we need to recognize the inconsistency between more and more schooling for our population and the expansion of low-skill service jobs over the last few decades (described in Chapter 10, "Social Class in the United States").

Why are we intent on gaining more education if available jobs do not require it? Of course, most of us value education for its own sake. But Val Burris (1983) adds that if we define credentials as the key to getting a job, we will invest in schooling whether or not jobs demand it (Berg, 1970; Rumberger, 1981; Shockey, 1989).

Privilege and Personal Merit

A key theme of social-conflict analysis deserves to be highlighted: *Schooling transforms social privilege into personal merit.* Attending college, in effect, is a right of passage for men and women from well-to-do families.

But our cultural emphasis on individualism pushes us to see credentials as "badges of ability," as Richard Sennett and Jonathan Cobb (1973) put it, rather than as symbols of family affluence. When we congratulate the new graduate, we usually overlook the social resources that made this achievement possible. The

RESOURCE: A resource concerning private schools in the United States is Peter W. Cookson and Caroline Hodges Persell, *Preparing for Power: America's Elite Boarding Schools* (Basic Books, 1985).

NOTE: One study of the mathematical skills of 12th graders concluded that 48.2% knew the basics, 35.6% were below "basics" level, 13.6% were "proficient," and 2.6% were "advanced." (National Assessment of Educational Progress)

Q: "Discipline is the ultimate tenet of education. Discipline establishes the format, the environment for academic achievement to occur." Joe Clark, controversial former principal of Paterson, New Jersey's Eastside High School

SOCIAL DIVERSITY

"Cooling Out" the Poor: Transforming Disadvantage into Deficiency

Disadvantaged students are often labeled as "dumb" in school, and, over time, some even come to accept the notion that they are personally deficient. This process of "cooling out" their aspirations for themselves sets into motion a self-fulfilling prophecy by which they seem to deserve no more than what society handed them when they were born. Eleven-year-old Ollie Taylor describes his situation in these words:

> The only thing that matters in my life is school and there they think I'm dumb and always will be. I'm starting to think they're right. Hell, I know they put all the black kids

together in one group if they can, but that doesn't make any difference either. I'm still dumb. Even if

I look around and know that I'm the smartest in my group, all that means is that I'm the smartest of the dumbest, so I haven't got anywhere at all, have I? I'm right where I always was. Every word those teachers tell me, even the ones I like most, I can hear in their voice that what they're really saying is "All right you dumb kids. I'll make it as easy as I can, and if you don't get it then, you'll never get it. Ever." That's what I hear every day, man. From every one of them. Even the other kids talk that way to me too.

SOURCE: Cottle (1974): 22–24.

congratulations are much more appropriate for young people from families with fewer financial resources and little experience with the world of higher education who may have struggled far more to earn their college degree. At the same time, we transform social disadvantage into personal deficiency when we condemn the high school dropout with little thought to the social circumstances that surround that person's life. The box illustrates this process with the words of one bright but disillusioned boy.

Critical evaluation. Social-conflict analysis links formal education and social inequality, and shows how schooling transforms privilege into personal worthiness, and social disadvantage into personal deficiency. Critics claim that social-conflict analysis minimizes the extent to which schooling has met the intellectual and personal needs of students, helping many toward upward social mobility in the process. Further, especially in recent years, "politically correct" educational curricula—closely tied to conflict theory—are challenging the status quo on many fronts.

PROBLEMS IN THE SCHOOLS

An intense debate revolves about schooling in the United States. Perhaps because we expect our schools to do so much—equalize opportunity, instill discipline, fire the individual imagination—few people think that public schools are doing an excellent job. Table 19–3 shows that about half of all adults give our schools a grade of "C" or below (Elam, Rose, & Gallup, 1991). The most visible school problem is lack of discipline and outright violence. More generally, students display little interest in learning. And the record indicates that the trend in academic performance is downward.

School Discipline

While almost everyone agrees that schools should teach personal discipline, many suspect that the job is not being done (NORC, 1993:525). This suspicion is supported by some disturbing facts. The government estimates that several hundred thousand students and at least one thousand teachers are physically assaulted

NOTE: Of some 12,000 American Sociological Association members, only about 400 are specialists in the sociology of education.

Q: "There has come to be a recognition that many of the issues in education today are not in the domain of educational psychologists, but have to do with the social structure of the school and the world outside the school." James S. Coleman

Q: "Should we produce competent bureaucrats and narrowly trained technicians, or should we develop creative, reflective individuals who will help to transform the world into more democratic forms?" Harvey Holtz (1989:193)

NOTE: The blackboard, which may encourage passivity among college students, was first used at Bowdoin College in 1823.

on school grounds every year. About one-fourth of students attending school in central cities voice fear of being attacked in or around the school. And recent news reports suggest that thousands of young people now routinely arrive at school armed with guns and other deadly weapons (McGrath, 1984; U.S. Bureau of Justice Statistics, 1991).

Disorder spills into schools from the surrounding society. As Chapter 8 ("Deviance") explained, our nation is among the most violent in the world, and disorder is epidemic in poor communities. If schools do not create the problem of violence, however, they do have the power to effect change for the better.

Take the case of Malcolm X Elementary School in a poor neighborhood of Washington, D.C. known by residents simply as "the jungle" because, as one local police officer observes, "It's all about survival here." Engulfed by all the urban ills that plague this country, most students at Malcolm X live in poor, single-parent families and contend every day with prostitution, drugs, and seemingly endless waves of violence.

Yet crossing the threshold of this school brings an unexpected contrast: All the boys are dressed in school uniforms—white shirts and red ties—and all the girls wear plaid jumpers. By and large, the hallways are clean and quiet; classrooms are orderly. The extraordinary achievement of Malcolm X is that students are learning—not out of fear but because they want to.

The key to this remarkable school, as most of the staff sees it, is attitude. Skillful and committed teachers have ignited in students a sense of pride and a desire to achieve. Principal John Pannell, son of a West Virginia school-bus driver, states his simple philosophy: "If we don't have high expectations for these children, who will?" For their part, most students do feel that teachers really care about them. Beaming at her second-grade class, Avis Watts adds, "This is their lifeline really; they know that they'll be fed, loved, and everything else in this school" (Gup, 1992).

While schools like Malcolm X may be the exception, they demonstrate the power of education to bring constructive change to even the most disadvantaged students. The key to such success appears to lie in commitment to teaching, firm disciplinary policies, and the ability of school officials to garner support from parents and the larger community.

Student Passivity

If some schools are plagued by violence, many more are afflicted by passive, bored students. Some of the responsibility for failing to take advantage of educational opportunity can be placed on television (which

TABLE 19–3 Grading Public Schools in the United States, 1993

Rating*	Proportion of Respondents
A	10%
B	37
C	31
D	11
FAIL	4
Don't know	7

*These figures reflect the responses of a national sample of U.S. adults to the question: Students are often given the grades A, B, C, D, and FAIL to denote the quality of their work. Suppose the public schools themselves, in this community, were graded in the same way. What grade would you give the public schools here—A, B, C, D, or FAIL?

SOURCE: Prepublication data from Roper Center for Public Opinion Research, University of Connecticut.

now consumes more of young people's time than school does), on parents (who do not foster a desire to learn), and on students themselves. But schools, too, must share the blame, since our educational system has long generated student passivity (Coleman, Hoffer, & Kilgore, 1981).

Bureaucracy

A century ago, formal education in the United States took place in small, personal settings in countless local communities. Today, the one-room schoolhouse has been replaced by huge educational factories. A study of high schools across the United States led Theodore Sizer to identify five ways in which large, bureaucratic schools undermine education (1984:207–9).

1. **Rigid uniformity.** Bureaucratic schools are typically insensitive to the cultural character of local communities. Outsider "specialists" (such as state educational officials) operate schools with little understanding of the needs of particular students.

2. **Numerical ratings.** School officials define success in terms of numerical attendance rates, dropout rates, and achievement test scores. In doing so, they overlook dimensions of schooling difficult to quantify, such as the creativity of students and the energy and enthusiasm of teachers.

3. **Rigid expectations.** Officials expect fifteen-year-olds to be in the tenth grade, and eleventh-graders to score at a certain level on a standardized verbal achievement test. Rarely are exceptionally bright and motivated students permitted to graduate early. Likewise, the system pushes along students who have learned little so they can graduate with their class.

Q: "Instructors who want dialogue to return to the classroom must take it upon themselves to challenge students with a freer, more reflexive form of learning. Professors who rely solely on [lecture-oriented] teaching techniques—but then slouch on their podiums and lament that 'teaching is dead' when these techniques fail—are guilty of murder." Richard A. Wright, "Curing Doonesbury's Disease—A Prescription for Dialogue in the Classroom," *Quarterly*

Journal of Ideology 9, 4 (1985):3–8

Q: "By the time that students have finished high school, they have been imbued with the enormously strong belief that teachers are 'experts' who possess the 'truth'." David Karp and William Yoels

RESOURCE: The Karp and Yoels article, "Why Don't College Students Participate?" is included in the Macionis and Benokraitis reader, *Seeing Ourselves*.

In some cities of the United States, the level of violence has escalated to the point that students are in danger of harm not only while traveling to and from school but also in school itself. Estimates indicate that thousands of young people come to school each day carrying guns and other deadly weapons, forcing administrators to adopt desperate security measures.

Of course, some formal organization in schools is inevitable given the immense size of the task. The number of students in just the New York City public schools now exceeds the student population of the entire country a century ago. But, Sizer maintains, we need to "humanize" schools to make them more responsive to those they claim to serve. He recommends eliminating rigid class schedules, reducing class size, and training teachers more broadly to help them become more involved in the lives of their students. Perhaps his most radical suggestion is that graduation from high school should depend on what a student has learned rather than simply on the length of time spent in school.

College: The Silent Classroom

Here are the observations of a bright and highly motivated first-year student at a high-quality four-year college. Do they strike a familiar chord?

> I have been disappointed in my first year at college. Too many students do as little work as they can get away with, take courses that are recommended by other students as being "gut" classes, and never challenge themselves past what is absolutely necessary. It's almost like thinking that we don't watch professors but we watch television. (Forrest, 1984:10)

As this student observes, passivity is also common in colleges and universities. Martha E. Gimenez (1989) describes college as the "silent classroom." Sociologists tend not to conduct research on the college classroom—a curious fact considering how much time they spend there. A fascinating exception is a study at a coeducational university in which David Karp and William Yoels (1976) found that—even in small classes—just a handful of students said anything at all during the typical class period. In short, Karp and Yoels concluded, passivity is a classroom norm, and they observed that students themselves became irritated with one of their number who was especially talkative.

Gender also affects classroom dynamics. Karp and Yoels note that, in coeducational classes taught by a man, male students carried out most classroom discussion. With women as instructors, however, the two sexes were more equal in terms of participation. Why? Perhaps because women instructors directed questions to women students as frequently as to men, while male teachers favored their male students.

Students offered various explanations for classroom passivity, which are listed in Table 19–4. Note that they saw passivity as mostly their own fault,

4. **Specialization.** High school students learn Spanish from one teacher, receive guidance from another, and are coached in sports by still others. Although specialized officials may know more about their subjects, no school employee comes to know and appreciate the "complete" student. Students experience this division of labor as a continual shuffling among fifty-minute periods throughout the school day.

5. **Little individual responsibility**. Highly bureaucratic schools do not empower students to learn on their own. Similarly, teachers have little latitude in what and how they teach their classes; they dare not accelerate learning for fear of disrupting "the system."

NOTE: Dropout rates are very high in large, urban school systems: Boston, 46%; Chicago, 45%; Los Angeles, 45%; New York, 34%; St. Louis, 30%.
DIVERSITY: Dropping out of college is a growing problem among African Americans. Despite efforts to recruit more minorities, fewer black students complete school. In 1965, of all students beginning college, the proportion of African Americans completing four years

was 90% as high as for whites; it has now fallen to about 60%.
NOTE: Five years after the 1983 publication of *A Nation at Risk*, average teacher salaries had climbed from $19,000 to $28,000 and a number of states had initiated examinations for promotion and graduation, but the dropout rate had changed little, and achievement test scores had risen only slightly.

TABLE 19–4 Student Explanations of Classroom Passivity

	Men		Women	
	Percent	*Rank*	*Percent*	*Rank*
I had not done the reading assignment	80.9%	1	76.3%	2
The feeling that I didn't know enough about the subject matter	79.6	2	84.8	1
The large size of my class	70.4	3	68.9	4
The feeling that my ideas were not well enough formulated	69.8	4	71.1	3
The course simply isn't meaningful to me	67.3	5	65.1	5
The chance that I would appear unintelligent in the eyes of the teacher	43.2	6	41.4	7
The chance that I would appear unintelligent in the eyes of other students	42.9	7	45.4	6
The small size of the class	31.0	8	33.6	8
The possibility that my comments might negatively affect my grade	29.6	9	24.3	9
The possibility that other students might not respect my point of view	16.7	10	12.5	11
The possibility that the teacher might not respect my point of view	12.3	11	12.5	10

SOURCE: David A. Karp and William C. Yoels, "The College Classroom: Some Observations on the Meaning of Student Participation," *Sociology and Social Research*, vol. 60, no. 4 (July 1976):108.

which is, to some degree, a case of the victims of bureaucratic schooling blaming themselves. Long before reaching college, Karp and Yoels explain, students are taught to view instructors as "experts" who serve up "truth." Thus they find little value in classroom debate and perceive their proper role as quietly listening and respectfully taking notes. This perception explains the finding of Karp and Yoels that only 10 percent of class time is devoted to discussion.

Students also realize that instructors generally come to class ready to deliver a prepared lecture. Lecturing allows teachers to present a great deal of material in each class, but only to the extent that they avoid being sidetracked by student questions or comments (Boyer, 1987). Early in each course, the instructor and students alike recognize a few who are willing and able to provide the occasional, limited comments instructors desire. Taken together, these facts form a recipe for passivity on the part of the majority of college students.

Dropping Out

If many students are passive in class, others are not there at all. The problem of *dropping out*—quitting school before earning a high school diploma—leaves young people (many of whom are disadvantaged to begin with) ill equipped for the world of work and at high risk for poverty.

The dropout rate has eased slightly in recent decades; currently about 12 percent of people between the ages of fourteen and twenty-four have dropped out of school, a total of some 4 million young women and men. Dropping out is least pronounced among

non-Hispanic whites (9 percent), slightly greater among African Americans (14 percent), and the most serious among Hispanics (35 percent), many of whom have less facility with English than others do (Suro, 1990; U.S. Bureau of the Census, 1993).

The reasons for dropping out extend beyond problems with English to include pregnancy among young women and the need to work among those whose families are poor. The dropout rate among children growing up in the bottom 20 percent of households ranked by income (27 percent) is ten times higher than that for youngsters whose households fall in the top 20 percent by income (National Center for Education Statistics, 1992). These data point to the fact that many dropouts are young people whose parents also have little schooling and provide little encouragement to continue. Thus low educational achievement often takes the form of a multigenerational cycle of disadvantage.

For young people who drop out of school in a credential society, the risks of unemployment or becoming stuck in a low-paying job are easy to imagine. Faced with this reality, approximately one-third of those who leave school return to the classroom at a later time.

Academic Standards

Perhaps the most serious educational issue confronting our society involves the quality of schooling. *A Nation at Risk*, a comprehensive report on the quality of U.S. schools prepared in 1983 by the National Commission on Excellence in Education, began with an alarming statement:

Q: Asked to describe the most miserable state for humanity, Benjamin Franklin responded, "A lonely man on a rainy day who cannot read."

NOTE: Federal literacy programs involve several million adults each year, a small proportion of those who are functionally illiterate.

NOTE: Various surveys (see Alter & Denworth, 1990) suggest that a large share of U.S. high school students cannot identify major historical persons and events: the U.S. adversaries in World War II, 66% could name them; when FDR was president, 52% knew; who led the U.S.S.R. during World War II, 54% could say; 25% knew when Lincoln was president; 31% could identify the Magna Carta; and 40% knew who Dred Scott was.

SOCIAL POLICY

Functional Illiteracy: Must We Rethink Education?

Imagine being unable to read labels on cans of food, instructions for assembling a child's toy, the dosage on a medicine bottle, or even the information on your own paycheck. These are some of the debilitating experiences of *functional illiteracy*, reading and writing skills inadequate for carrying out everyday responsibilities.

As schooling became universal among our population, the U.S. government confidently concluded that illiteracy had been all but eliminated. The truth of the matter—now acknowledged by the government—is that some 25 million adults read and write at no more than a fourth-grade level, and another 25 million have only eighth-grade language skills. Together, then, one in four adults in the United States is functionally illiterate, and the proportion is higher among the elderly and minorities.

Functional illiteracy is a complex social problem. It is caused partly by an educational system that passes children from one grade to the next whether they learn or not. Another cause is community indifference to local schools that prevents parents and teachers from working together to improve children's learning. Still another cause is found in the home: Millions of children grow up with illiterate parents who offer little encouragement to learn language skills.

Functional illiteracy is estimated to cost our society more than $100 billion a year. This cost includes decreased productivity (by workers who perform their jobs improperly) and increased accidents (by people unable to understand written instructions). It also reflects the costs of supporting those unable to read and write well enough to find work who then end up on welfare or in prison.

Correcting this national problem requires one approach for the young and another for adults. To stop the functional illiteracy before it happens, the public must demand that schools not graduate children who have yet to learn basic language abilities. For adults who already suffer from this problem, the answer begins with diagnosis—a difficult issue since many women and men feel deep shame at their plight and avoid disclosing their need for help. Once such people are identified, however, communities must provide adult education programs.

Our society is one of the richest and most powerful nations on earth, yet at least a dozen other countries have a more literate population than we do. For those muddling through life with inadequate communication skills, functional illiteracy is a personal disaster; for all of us, it is an urgent national problem.

Paco learned to read last year. So did Dad.

Literacy Volunteers of America, Inc.

The problem of illiteracy in the United States is most serious among Latinos. In part this is due to a dropout rate among fourteen- to twenty-four-year-olds of almost 30 percent, which is three times the rate among whites or African Americans. The broader issue is that schools fail to teach many Spanish-speaking people to read and write any language very well.

SOURCES: Based on Kozol (1980, 1985a, 1985b).

Q: "The actual success of a teacher depends in large measure on the capacity to state the subject matter of instruction in terms of the experience of the [student]." George Herbert Mead

Q: "[The magnet school] is a blueprint for school desegregation in the future without relying on mandatory busing, which does not work in a very meaningful way." William Bradford Reynolds

Q: "We are doing better than in 1983. But we are certainly not doing well enough. . . . We are still at risk." Secretary of Education William Bennett, 1988

NOTE: The American Federation of Teachers (AFT) places the median U.S. public school teacher's salary at $35,104 in 1993; by state, Connecticut is highest ($48,918 median); lowest is South Dakota ($24,291).

If an unfriendly foreign power had attempted to impose on America the mediocre educational performance that exists today, we might well have viewed it as an act of war. As it stands, we have allowed this to happen to ourselves. (1983:5)

Supporting this conclusion, the report notes that "nearly 40 percent of seventeen-year-olds cannot draw inferences from written material; only one-fifth can write a persuasive essay; and only one-third can solve mathematical problems requiring several steps" (1983:9). Furthermore, scores on the Scholastic Aptitude Test (SAT) have declined since the early 1960s. Then, median scores for students were 500 on the mathematical test and 480 on the verbal test; by 1992, the averages had slipped to 476 and 423. Some of this decline may stem from the growing share of students taking the standardized test, not all of whom are well prepared (Owen, 1985). But few doubt that schooling has suffered a setback.

A *Nation at Risk* also noted with alarm the extent of **functional illiteracy**, *reading and writing skills insufficient for everyday living*. Roughly one in eight children in the United States completes secondary school without learning to read or write very well. For young people of color, the report continued, the proportion is more than one in three. The box on page 530 provides a closer look at this serious national problem.

A *Nation at Risk* recommends drastic reform. First, it calls for schools to require all students to complete several years of English, mathematics, social studies, general science, and computer science courses. Second, schools should cease pushing along failing students, keeping them in the classroom as long as necessary to teach basic skills. Third, teacher training must improve and teachers' salaries should rise to attract talent into the profession. A *Nation at Risk* concludes that educators must ensure that schools meet public expectations, and we citizens must be prepared to bear the costs of good schools.

A final concern is the low performance of U.S. students in global context. Students in the United States are not generally as motivated toward academic excellence as their counterparts in Japan, for example, nor do they do as much homework. Moreover, as Figure 19–3, on page 532, shows, Japanese young people spend sixty more days in school each year than students in this society do. Some educational experts think that we could remedy our schools' poor performance, at least in part, simply by requiring that students spend more time there.

RECENT ISSUES IN U.S. EDUCATION

Our society's schools continuously confront new challenges and technological innovation. This final section explores several recent and important educational issues.

School Choice

Some analysts claim that our schools do not teach very well because they have no competition. Thus, giving parents a range of options about where to school their children may force all schools to do a better job. This is the essence of the *school choice* proposal.

Proponents of school choice advocate creating a market for schooling, so that parents and students can shop for the best value. According to one proposal, the government would provide vouchers to all families with school-aged children, allowing them to spend the money at public, private, or parochial schools. Indianapolis, Minneapolis, and Milwaukee recently initiated parental choice plans in the hope that public schools would be forced to perform better in order to win the confidence of families.

But critics (including teachers' unions) charge that school choice amounts to abandoning our nation's commitment to public education. From their point of view, schools that already have bigger budgets will attract the best and brightest children while central city schools and will end up as "dumping grounds" for disadvantaged students and those with disciplinary problems. Such arguments led Californians to reject a statewide school choice plan in 1993.

A more modest form of school choice involves creating *magnet schools*, one thousand of which are now operating across the country. Magnet schools offer special facilities and programs to promote educational excellence in computer science, foreign languages, or science and mathematics. In school districts containing magnet schools, parents can choose the one best suited to a particular student's talents and interests.

Yet another recent development in the school choice movement is *schooling for profit*. According to advocates of this proposal, school systems can be operated by private profit-making companies more efficiently than by local governments. Of course, private schooling is nothing new; more than ten thousand schools are currently operated by private organizations and religious groups. What is new, however, is the assertion that private companies can carry out *mass* education in the United States. Chris Whittle, head of

NOTE: Overall, almost 30% of the U.S. population is attending some school at any given time.

Q: "In the first place, God made idiots. That was for practice. Then he made school boards." Mark Twain

GLOBAL: A major reason for Asian students outscoring U.S. children on mathematical tests involves parental attitudes. Asian parents demand much more from their children, while U.S. parents tend to accept less homework and effort.

DATA FILE: The *Data File* provides global data on school enrollments.

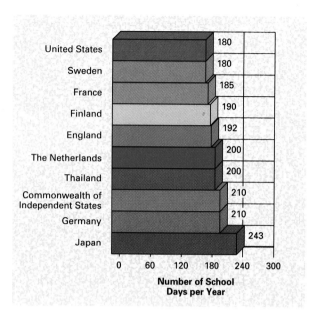

FIGURE 19–3 Length of the School Year, by Country

(Education Commission of the States)

a large media corporation that includes a commercial television channel for the classroom, has taken the lead in this area, with plans to open private schools-for-profit or to provide private management teams to operate existing public schools efficiently.

Research confirms that many public school systems suffer from bureaucratic bloat, spending far too much and teaching far too little. Further, it is not surprising that various "choice" proposals are gaining favor in a society that has long looked to competition as a strategy to improve quality. But whether education is consistent with commercialism and whether such plans will improve schools for everyone or only for some of our population are questions that remain, for now, unanswered (Putka, 1991; Toch, 1991).

Schooling People with Disabilities

Mandatory education embodies our society's commitment to provide everyone with a basic education. In 1992, more than 5 million children with a wide range of mental and physical disabilities were attending schools in the United States. Nevertheless, many of these boys and girls receive little effective schooling. A highly bureaucratized system of mass education simply does not readily meet the special needs of some children.

Schooling children with disabilities clearly poses a challenge. Many children with physical impairments have difficulty getting to and from school, and those who travel with crutches or wheelchairs cannot negotiate stairs and other obstacles inside school buildings. Children with developmental disabilities like mental retardation require extensive personal attention from specially trained teachers. As a result, many children with mental and physical disabilities have received a public education only because of persistent efforts by parents and other concerned citizens.

About one-fourth of children with disabilities are schooled in special facilities; the rest attend public schools, many participating in regular classes. This reflects the policy of **mainstreaming**, *integrating special students into the overall educational program.* An alternative to segregated "special education" classes, mainstreaming, also termed *inclusive education*, works best for physically impaired students who have no difficulty keeping up with the rest of the class. As an added advantage, children with disabilities learn how to interact with others just as other children benefit from interacting with them.

Mainstreaming is typically less effective for students who have serious mental or emotional impairments. These children may have difficulty matching the performance of other students, and they may simultaneously be deprived of appropriate special education. In any case, mainstreaming can be as expensive as special programs, requiring adaptive facilities and teachers capable of meeting the needs of special children.

Adult Education

Most schooling involves young people. However, the share of U.S. students aged twenty-five and older has risen steadily in recent years and now accounts for nearly one in five people in the classroom.

By 1993, more than 25 million U.S. adults were enrolled in some type of schooling. They range in age from the mid-twenties to well past sixty-five. Adult students are generally a fairly privileged slice of the population; most have above-average incomes.

What draws adults back to school? The reasons are as varied as the students, but usually the motivation is work related. Most return to study as a way to enhance their careers; this practical emphasis is reflected in high adult enrollments in business, health, and engineering courses. But others, who study everything from astronomy to Zen, return to school simply for the pleasure of learning.

GLOBAL: The government reports 366,000 foreign students in the United States. Their home regions: Africa, 7%; Asia, 63%; Europe, 12%; Latin America, 12%; North America, 5%; Oceania, 1%.

GLOBAL: Percent of population with a university degree: U.S., 23%; Canada, 15%; Japan, 13%; Sweden, 12%; Australia, Denmark, Finland, West Germany, 10%; Austria, 5%; Portugal, 4%.

DIVERSITY: Relatively few U.S. students learn a language other than English. The percent of high schoolers who take one or more years of: Spanish, 37%; French, 20%; German, 5%; Latin, 4%. (U.S. Department of Education)

LOOKING AHEAD: SCHOOLING IN THE TWENTY-FIRST CENTURY

Despite the fact that the United States leads the world in higher education, our public school system continues to struggle with serious problems. From what we have learned, it is clear that many of the problems of schools have their roots in the larger society. Thus we should not expect schools themselves to raise the quality of education as we approach the next century. At the same time, however, schools will only improve to the extent to which teachers, parents, and students themselves are committed to excellence and willing to embrace change. Furthermore, as important as issues of excellence are, there exists the parallel problem of educational inequality.

Another important trend now reshaping schools involves technology. Just as the Industrial Revolution had a major impact on schooling in the nineteenth century, computers and the Information Revolution are transforming formal education today. More than 95 percent of schools currently report having instructional computers and, across the country, one computer is available to every sixteen students (although, like other dimensions of education, computing is more accessible to affluent children than poor children) (U.S. Bureau of the Census, 1993).

The promise of new information technology goes beyond helping students learn basic skills to improving the overall quality of learning. Interacting with computers prompts students to be more active learners and has the added benefit of allowing them to progress at their own pace. For students with disabilities who cannot write using a pencil, computers permit easier self-expression. The introduction of computers into schools—in some cases, as early as kindergarten—appears to significantly increase learning speed and retention of information (Fantini, 1986).

The enthusiasm sparked by computers should not blind us to their limitations, however. Computers will never bring to the educational process the personal insight or imagination of a motivated human teacher. Nor can computers tap what one teacher calls the "springs of human identity and creativity" we discover through exploring literature and language rather than simply manipulating mathematical codes (Golden, 1982:56).

It is probably fair to say that, despite their rapidly increasing numbers, computers have yet to change teaching and learning in any fundamental sense or even to replace the traditional blackboard (Berger, 1991; Elmer-Dewitt, 1991). Thus as our society enters the twenty-first century, we should not look to technology to solve many of the problems—including violence and rigid bureaucracy—that plague our schools. What is needed is a broad plan for social change that refires this country's early ambition to embrace quality universal schooling—a goal that has so far eluded us.

SUMMARY

1. Education is the major social institution for transmitting knowledge and skills, as well as teaching cultural norms and values. In preindustrial societies, education occurs informally within the family; industrial societies develop formal systems of schooling.

2. The United States was among the first countries to institute compulsory mass education, reflecting both democratic political ideals and the needs of the industrial-capitalist economy.

3. Structural-functional analysis highlights major functions of schooling, including socialization, cultural innovation, social integration, and placing people in the social hierarchy. Latent functions of schooling involve child care and forging social networks.

4. Social-conflict analysis points out how class, race, and gender promote unequal opportunities for schooling. Formal education also serves as a means of generating conformity to produce compliant adult workers.

5. A debate surrounds the use of standardized achievement tests, which some see as a reasonably fair measure of academic aptitude and learning and others claim are culturally biased tools that unfairly define less privileged students as personally deficient.

6. Schools employ tracking to give students the kind of learning they desire and are capable of. Critics maintain that schools track students according to their social background, thereby providing privileged youngsters with a richer education.

7. The great majority of young people in the United States attend state-funded public schools. Private school students generally seek a religious education. A small proportion of students—usually well-to-do—attend elite, private preparatory schools.

8. One-fifth of U.S. adults over the age of twenty-five are now college graduates, marking the emergence of a "credential society." People with college degrees enjoy greatly increased lifetime earnings.

9. Most adults in the United States are critical of public schools. Violence permeates many schools, especially those in poor neighborhoods. The bureaucratic character of schools has also fostered high dropout rates and widespread student passivity.

10. Declining academic standards are reflected in today's lower average scores on achievement tests and the functional illiteracy of a significant proportion of high school graduates.

11. The school choice movement seeks to make educational systems more responsive to the public. Innovative options include magnet schools and schools-for-profit, both of which are topics of continuing policy debate.

12. Children with mental or physical disabilities historically have been schooled in special classes or not at all. Mainstreaming affords them broader opportunities.

13. Adults represent a growing proportion of students in the United States. Most older learners are engaged in job-related study.

14. The Information Revolution is changing schooling through the increasing use of computers. Although computers permit interactive, self-paced learning, they are not suitable for teaching every subject.

KEY CONCEPTS

credentialism evaluating a person on the basis of educational degrees

education the social institution guiding a society's transmission of knowledge—including basic facts, job skills, and also cultural norms and values—to its members

functional illiteracy reading and writing skills insufficient for everyday living

hidden curriculum subtle presentations of political or cultural ideas in the classroom

mainstreaming integrating special students into the overall educational program

schooling formal instruction under the direction of specially trained teachers

tracking the assignment of students to different types of educational programs

CRITICAL-THINKING QUESTIONS

1. Why is schooling a modern social institution, one that expanded after the onset of the Industrial Revolution?

2. Referring to various countries including the United States, describe ways in which schooling is shaped by economic, political, or cultural factors.

3. From a structural-functional perspective, why is schooling important to the operation of society?

From a social-conflict point of view, how does formal education operate to reproduce social inequality?

4. Do you agree with research findings presented in this chapter that, by and large, college students are passive in class? If so, what do you think colleges could do to ensure that classes involve everyone's active participation?

SUGGESTED READINGS

Classic Sources

John Dewey. *Experience and Education.* New York: Collier, 1963; orig. 1938.

    In this short book—originally presented as a series of lectures—Dewey sketches his vision of progressive education.

Caroline Hodges Persell. *Education and Inequality: The Roots and Results of Stratification in America's Schools.* New York: The Free Press, 1977.

    This is one of the earliest and most thoughtful investigations of the links between schooling and inequality by a long-time educational sociologist.

Contemporary Sources

Richard J. Altenbaugh, ed. *The Teacher's Voice: A Social History of Teaching in Twentieth-Century America.* Washington, D.C.: Falmer Press, 1992.

    This sociological look at U.S. education focuses not on administrators and educational policy but on the actual behavior of teachers in the classroom.

George H. Wood. *Schools That Work: America's Most Innovative Public Education Programs.* New York: Dutton, 1993.

    The good news about education in the United States is that a number of innovative programs are working quite well; this book details some of them.

Joan DelFattore. *What Johnny Shouldn't Read: Textbook Censorship in America.* New Haven, Conn.: Yale University Press, 1992.

    This book investigates how political and cultural battles have spilled into the textbook industry.

Howard Dickman, ed. *The Imperiled Academy.* New Brunswick, N.J.: Transaction, 1993.

    In this collection of essays, nine scholars offer assessments of the recent college trend widely described as "political correctness." A number of the articles ask whether multiculturalism is reducing or increasing racial conflict on the campus.

Elizabeth L. Ihle, ed. *Black Women in Higher Education: An Anthology of Essays, Studies, and Documents.* New York: Garland, 1990.

    This wide-ranging collection of materials traces the presence of African-American women in higher education in the United States.

Walter R. Allen, Edgar G. Epps, and Nasha Z. Haniff, eds. *College in Black and White: African American Students in Predominantly White and Historically Black Public Universities.* Albany, N.Y.: State University of New York Press, 1991.

    This collection of essays offers an empirical profile of African Americans and higher education based on four thousand responses from the National Study of Black College Students.

Steven Brint and Jerome Karabel. *The Diverted Dream: Community Colleges and the Promise of Educational Opportunity in America, 1900–1985.* New York: Oxford University Press, 1991.

    This historical account examines the significance of community colleges in the movement to expand higher education in the United States.

Dennis McGrath and Martin B. Spear. *The Academic Crisis of the Community College.* Albany, N.Y.: State University of New York Press, 1991.

    This book assesses the current state of U.S. community colleges, highlighting faculty vitality, describing curricular definition and direction, and evaluating student preparedness.

Chester Finn. *We Must Take Charge: Our Schools and Our Future.* New York: The Free Press, 1991.

    This account suggests that we cannot leave the problems of today's public schools to government.

David Tyack and Elisabeth Hansot. *Learning Together: A History of Coeducation in America.* New Haven, Conn.: Yale University Press, 1990.

    The practice of schooling boys and girls separately was common in Europe until recently. This book delves into how and why the United States developed the policy of coeducation.

Global Sources

David H. Kelly. *Women's Education in the Third World: An Annotated Bibliography.* New York: Garland, 1989.

    This useful resource identifies more than one thousand books and articles concerning the schooling of women in poor countries.

Nelly P. Stromquist, ed. *Women and Education in Latin America: Knowledge, Power, and Change.* Boulder, Colo.: Lynne Rienner, 1992.

    This book is a collection of thirteen essays that focus on the educational opportunities for women in this important world region.

Robert Arnove, Philip G. Altbach, and Gail P. Kelly, eds. *Emergent Issues in Education: Comparative Perspectives.* Albany, N.Y.: State University of New York Press, 1992.

    These essays survey educational trends around the world and make a case for the importance of comparative research on schooling.

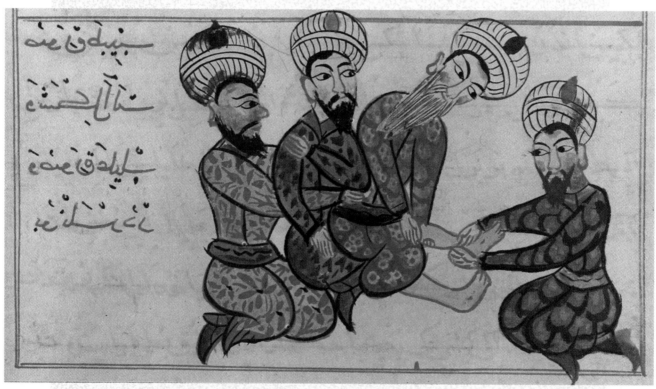

Reduction of a dislocated knee, Granger Collection

DATA FILE: An outline of this chapter, supplementary lecture material, and suggested discussion topics are included in the *Data File*.

NOTE: The chapter-opening art is a Turkish medical manuscript, "Reduction of a Dislocated Knee," circa 1465.

Q: "The ways in which the poor die reflect the conditions of their lives." Carol Stack (1975)

Q: "Differences in attitudes toward pain in Jewish, Italian, and 'Old American' families are closely related to the role and image of the father in the respective cultures in terms of his authority and masculinity." Mark Zborowski (1953)

Health and Medicine

*M*elody Barrett, a nineteen-year-old sophomore at an exclusive private college in Minnesota, squirms restlessly on her chair in the waiting room of her school's medical clinic. She feels annoyed and fearful; her roommate had pressured her to see the doctor, and she is afraid her parents will be angry if they find out that she is ill. There isn't anything wrong, *she keeps telling herself.* Her parents, both lawyers, live forty miles away in Minneapolis. They expect their daughter home for the weekend, but she is trying to think up an excuse for not going.

This young woman's problem is failing health due to starvation. Far from feeling that she is starving, however, she thinks of herself as fat. She knows that she weighs only eighty-seven pounds, and she expects the doctor to warn her that she weighs far too little for a woman five feet, three inches tall. But for over three years Melody has been

preoccupied—her roommate would say obsessed—with being thin.

Melody Barrett's problem, familiar to many college students, is anorexia nervosa, a disorder characterized by what specialists term "severe caloric restriction," or intense, often compulsive dieting. Like most diseases, anorexia nervosa has social as well as biological causes: About 95 percent of its victims are females, most of them white and from affluent families. Many women who contend with eating disorders are pressured by their parents to be high achievers. Although Melody Barrett's case is unusually severe, research suggests that up to half of college-aged women actively try to lose weight, although most of them are not, medically speaking, overweight. About one in seven diet to the point that their behavior falls within the clinical description of an eating disorder.

537

Q: "Health consists in having the same diseases as one's neighbors."
Quentin Crisp
NOTE: The terms "healthful" and "wholesome" are used to refer to what is both medically and morally desirable.

To better appreciate the social foundation of eating disorders[1], consider a comment once made by the duchess of Windsor: "A woman," she observed, "cannot be too rich or too thin." Women fall victim to eating disorders because our culture places such importance on women's physical appearance, with slenderness the ideal of femininity (Parrott, 1987). Some researchers suggest that our society socializes young women to believe that they are never "too thin to feel fat." Such an attitude pushes women toward a form of "mass starvation" that some critics claim "compares with foot-binding, lip-stretching, and other forms of woman mutilation" found in other cultures (Wooley, Wooley, & Dyrenforth, 1979; Levine, 1987; Robinson, 1987).

Health is obviously the concern of physicians and other medical professionals. But sociologists, too, study health because, as the case of Melody Barrett illustrates and this chapter explains, social forces greatly shape the well-being of the U.S. population and people throughout the world.

WHAT IS HEALTH?

The World Health Organization (1946:3) defines **health** as *a state of complete physical, mental, and social well-being.* This definition underscores the major theme of this chapter: *Health is as much a social as a biological issue.*

Health and Society

The health of any population is shaped by traits of the surrounding society.

1. **People judge their health relative to others.** Standards of health vary from society to society. René Dubos (1980; orig. 1965) points out that early in this century, yaws, a contagious skin disease, was so common in tropical Africa that societies there considered it normal. In truth, then, health is sometimes a matter of having the same diseases as one's neighbors (Quentin Crisp, cited in Kirk & Madsen, 1989).

2. **People pronounce as "healthy" what they hold to be morally good.** Members of our society (especially men) consider a competitive way of life to be "healthy" because it fits in with our cultural mores. (This is so despite the fact that stress is related to heart disease and many other illnesses.) Contrarily, some people who object to homosexuality on moral grounds claim that this sexual orientation is "sick" (even though it is quite natural from a medical point of view). In short, ideas about good health constitute a type of social control that encourages conformity to cultural norms.

3. **Cultural standards of health change over time.** Early in this century, some prominent physicians condemned women for enrolling in college, claiming that higher education placed an unhealthy strain on the female brain. Other specialists denounced masturbation as a threat to health. Today, however, such notions elicit little support from the medical community. Conversely, few physicians fifty years ago recognized the dangers of cigarette smoking, a practice that is now widely regarded as a threat to health.

4. **Health relates to a society's technology.** Members of poor societies routinely contend with malnutrition, poor or nonexistent sanitation, and all sorts of infectious diseases. As industrialization raised living standards, conceptions of health correspondingly rose. Industrial technology, on the other hand, creates new threats to health. As Chapter 22 ("The Natural Environment") explains, rich societies have the capacity to endanger health by overtaxing the world's resources as well as generating various forms of pollution.

5. **Health relates to social inequality.** Every society on earth unequally distributes the resources that promote personal well-being. The physical, mental, and social health of wealthier women and men in the United States is far better than that of poor people, as we shall explain presently. This pattern starts at birth, with infant mortality highest among the poor. Affluent people also live years longer than poor people do.

HEALTH: A GLOBAL SURVEY

Because health is an important dimension of social life, we find pronounced change in human well-being over the long course of history. Similarly, striking differences in health distinguish societies of the world today.

---

[1]This profile of victims of anorexia nervosa is based on Levine, 1987. Another eating disorder, *bulimia*, involves binge-eating coupled with induced vomiting to inhibit weight gain. The two diseases, which may be two expressions of the same intense involvement in dieting and weight control, have similar victim profiles. See also Striegel-Moore, Silberstein, & Rodin, 1986.

Health in Preindustrial Societies

Simple technology limited the ability of hunters and gatherers to sustain a healthful environment. As Gerhard and Jean Lenski (1991) suggest, food shortages sometimes forced mothers to abandon children. Children fortunate enough to survive infancy were still vulnerable to a host of injuries and illnesses for which there were few effective treatments, and half died before age twenty. Few lived to forty.

The agricultural revolution expanded the supply of food and other resources. Yet due to increasing social inequality, elites enjoyed better health while peasants and slaves faced hunger and endured crowded, unsanitary shelters. Especially in the growing cities of medieval Europe, human waste and other refuse fueled infectious diseases, including plagues that periodically wiped out entire towns (Mumford, 1961).

Health in Poor Societies Today

Striking poverty in much of the world (see Chapter 11, "Global Stratification") limits life expectancy to decades less than the seventy or more years typical of the most economically developed societies. A look back at Global Map 14–1 on page 392 shows that life expectancy among Africans is barely fifty, and in the poorest societies in the world, such as Ethiopia and Somalia, the figure drops to only forty.

According to the World Health Organization, 1 billion people around the world—one in five—suffer from serious illness due to poverty. Poor sanitation and malnutrition kill people of all ages, especially children. Health is undermined not just from having too little to eat, but also from consuming only one kind of food, as the box on page 540 explains.

In impoverished countries, sanitary drinking water may be as scarce as the chance for a balanced diet. Unsafe water is a major cause of the infectious diseases that imperil both adults and children. The leading causes of death in the United States a century ago, including influenza, pneumonia, and tuberculosis, are still widespread killers in poor societies.

To make matters worse, medical personnel are few and far between, so that the world's poorest people—many of whom live in central Africa—never consult a physician. Global Map 20–1 on page 541 illustrates the availability of doctors throughout the world.

Against this backdrop of overarching poverty and minimal medical care, it is no wonder that 10 percent of children in poor societies die in their first year of life; in some countries, half the children never reach

Medieval medical practice was heavily influenced by astrology, so that physicians and lay people alike attributed disease to astral influence; this is the root of our word "influenza." In this woodcut by Swiss artist Jost Amman (1580), as midwives attend a childbirth astrologers cast a horoscope for the newborn.

adulthood. Children in poor societies today die at the same rate as European children did in 1750 (George, 1977; Harrison, 1984).

Improving health in poor societies presents a monumental challenge. First, in a classic vicious cycle, poverty breeds disease, which, in turn, undermines people's ability to earn income. Second, when medical technology does control infectious disease, the populations of poor nations soar. Without resources to ensure the well-being of the people they have now, poor societies can ill afford population growth. Thus, efforts to reduce death rates will have little beneficial effect without programs to reduce birth rates as well.

Health in Industrial Societies

Industrialization dramatically changed patterns of human health in Europe, although, at first, not for the better. The Industrial Revolution had taken hold by 1800, and factories swelled the cities as people

NOTE: Until the end of the nineteenth century, Philadelphia drew water from one point on the Delaware River while discharging sewage at another. Such practices were common until discovery of the germ theory of disease led to programs to improve environmental quality.

Q: "Hunger may have been the human race's constant companion, and 'the poor may always be with us,' but in the twentieth century, one cannot take this fatalistic view of the destiny of millions of fellow creatures. Their condition is not inevitable but is caused by identifiable forces within the province of rational, human control." Susan George

GLOBAL SOCIOLOGY

Poverty: The Leading Cause of Death in Poor Societies

Recent famine in Africa brought home to people in the affluent United States the image of starving children. Some of the children portrayed by the mass media appeared bloated, while others seem to have shriveled to little more than skin drawn tightly over bones. Both of these deadly conditions, Susan George explains, are direct consequences of poverty.

Children with bloated bodies are suffering from protein deficiency. In West Africa this condition is known as *kwashiorkor,* which means literally "one-two." The term derives from the common practice among mothers of abruptly weaning a first child upon the birth of a second. Deprived of mother's milk, a baby may receive virtually no protein.

Children with shriveled bodies lack both protein and calories. This deficiency is the result of eating little food of any kind.

In either case, children usually do not die of starvation, strictly speaking. Their weakened condition makes them vulnerable to stomach ailments such as gastroenteritis or diseases like measles. The death rate from measles, for example, is a

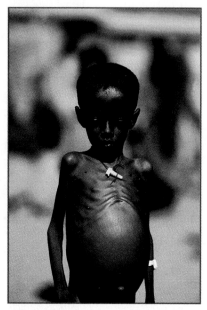

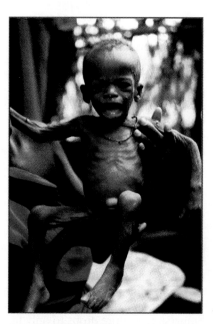

thousand times greater in parts of Africa than in North America.

Depending on a single food also undermines nutrition, causing a deficiency of protein, vitamins, and minerals. Millions of people in the least-developed societies of the world suffer from goiter, a debilitating, diet-related disease of the thyroid gland. Pellagra, a disease common to people who consume only corn, is equally serious,

frequently leading to insanity. Those who consume mostly processed rice are prone to beriberi.

We can understand health as a social issue simply by noting that a host of diseases virtually unknown to the members of rich societies are a common experience of life—and death—in poor countries.

SOURCE: Based, in part, on George (1977).

streamed from the countryside seeking economic opportunity. This great concentration of people spawned serious problems of sanitation and overcrowded housing. Moreover, factories continuously fouled the air with smoke, a health threat unrecognized until well into the twentieth century. Accidents in the workplace were common.

But as the nineteenth century progressed, health in Western Europe and North America began to improve. This change was mainly due to a rising standard of living that translated into better nutrition and safer housing for the majority of people. After 1850, medical advances promoted even better health, primarily by controlling infectious diseases in cities. To

DIVERSITY: Leading causes of death among 15- to 24-year-olds by sex and race (1991; Centers for Disease Control):
African-American females: homicide, accidents, cancer, heart disease, AIDS
African-American males: homicide, accidents, suicide, heart disease, AIDS

White females: accidents, homicide, suicide, cancer, heart disease
White males: accidents, suicide, homicide, cancer, heart disease
GLOBAL: Halfdan Mahler (1980) estimates that only one-third of the world's people have a safe water supply.

Window on the World

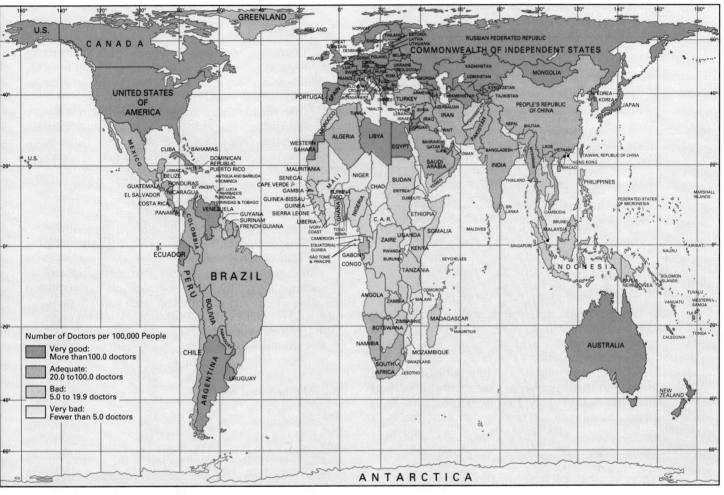

GLOBAL MAP 20–1 Medical Care in Global Perspective
Medical doctors, widely available to people in rich nations, are perilously scarce in poor societies. While traditional forms of healing do improve health, antibiotics and vaccines—vital for controlling infectious diseases—are often in short supply in poor societies. In these countries, therefore, death rates are high, especially among infants.

From *Peters Atlas of the World* (1990).

illustrate, in 1854 John Snow noted the street addresses of cholera victims in London and traced the source of this disease to contaminated drinking water (Mechanic, 1978). Soon after, scientists linked cholera to specific bacteria and developed a protective vaccine against the deadly disease. Armed with this knowledge, early environmentalists campaigned against age-old practices such as discharging raw

sewage into rivers used for drinking water. By the early twentieth century, death rates from infectious diseases had sharply fallen.

Over the long term, industrialization has had a dramatic, beneficial effect on human health. Leading killers in 1900—influenza and pneumonia—accounted for one-fourth of all deaths. Today these diseases cause fewer than 3 percent of deaths in the United States.

SOCIAL SURVEY: "Would you say your own health, in general, is . . ." (*STUDENT CHIP Social Survey Software*, HEALTH1; GSS 1972–91, N = 18,339)

	"Excellent"	"Good"	"Fair" or "Poor"
Men	34.4%	42.7%	22.9%
Women	31.1%	43.1%	25.8%
Afri Amer	22.3%	42.7%	35.0%
Latino	34.5%	42.6%	23.0%
Whites	33.9%	43.0%	23.1%

GLOBAL: The leading causes of death in the United States in 1900, as presented in Table 20–1, are the leading causes of death in poor societies today.

TABLE 20–1 The Leading Causes of Death in the United States, 1900 and 1992

1900	1992
1. Influenza and pneumonia	1. Heart disease
2. Tuberculosis	2. Cancer
3. Stomach/intestinal diseases	3. Cerebrovascular diseases
4. Heart disease	4. Lung disease (noncancerous)
5. Cerebral hemorrhage	5. Accidents
6. Kidney disease	6. Pneumonia and influenza
7. Accidents	7. Diabetes
8. Cancer	8. Suicide
9. Diseases in early infancy	9. HIV virus
10. Diphtheria	10. Homicide

SOURCES: Information for 1900 is from William C. Cockerham, *Medical Sociology*, 2d ed. (Englewood Cliffs, N.J.: Prentice-Hall, 1986), p. 24; information for 1992 is from U.S. Center for Health Statistics, *Monthly Vital Statistics Report* (Hyattsville, Md.: The Center, 1993), vol. 42, no. 2, (Aug. 31, 1993).

As Table 20–1 indicates, other infectious diseases that were once major causes of death no longer pose a threat to health.

As the prevalence of infectious diseases has declined, chronic illnesses including heart disease, cancer, and stroke are left to claim almost two-thirds of the population of the United States, generally in old age. In short, while nothing alters the reality of death, industrial societies manage to delay our demise for decades.

HEALTH IN THE UNITED STATES

Living in an affluent, industrial society, people in the United States have good health by world standards. Some categories of people, however, enjoy far more well-being than others. We survey how health is distributed throughout the U.S. population and then examine several issues that affect the health of everyone.

Social Epidemiology: The Distribution of Health

Social epidemiology is *the study of how health and disease are distributed throughout a society's population.* Just as early social epidemiologists examined the origin and spread of epidemic diseases, researchers today link health to physical and social environments.

Such analysis rests on comparing the health of different categories of people.

Age and Sex

Death is now rare among young people, with two notable exceptions: a rise in mortality resulting from accidents and, more recently, from acquired immune deficiency syndrome (AIDS).

Across the life course, women fare better in terms of health than men. Females have a slight biological advantage that renders them less likely than males to die before or immediately after birth. Then, as socialization takes over, males learn to be more aggressive and individualistic, and they have higher rates of accidents, violence, and suicide. Our cultural conception of masculinity also pressures adult men to be more competitive, to repress their emotions, and to engage in hazardous behaviors like smoking cigarettes and drinking alcohol to excess.

Doctors describe "coronary-prone behavior" (sometimes tagged the "Type-A personality") as a combination of chronic impatience, uncontrolled ambition, and frequent outbursts of hostility toward one's surroundings. A sociological perspective reveals that this syndrome is a fairly accurate description of how our culture defines masculinity.

Social Class and Race

Infant mortality—the death rate among newborns—is twice as high among disadvantaged children as it is among children born to privilege. While the health of the richest children in our society is the best in the world, our poorest children are as vulnerable as those in many poor countries, including Sudan and Lebanon.

Table 20–2 shows that almost 80 percent of adults in families with incomes over $35,000 evaluate their health as excellent or very good, while not quite half of those in families earning less than $10,000 make this claim. Conversely, while only about 4 percent of high-income people describe their health as fair or poor, almost one-fourth of low-income people respond this way.

Bear in mind that just as income shapes health, so does health affect income. Members of low-income families miss eight days of school or work each year due to illness, while higher-income people lose only five days for this reason (U.S. National Center for Health Statistics, 1992).

Because people of color are three times as likely as whites to be poor, they are more likely to die in infancy and to suffer the effects of violence and illness

NOTE: Chapter 17 ("Family") explains that, due to high mortality from infectious diseases, U.S. children were more likely to live in a one-parent family a century ago than they are today.

RESOURCE: The importance of the natural environment to health is now discussed in Chapter 22 ("The Natural Environment").

NOTE: The National Council on Alcoholism estimates that, by age 18, young people in the United States have viewed 100,000 beer ads in the various media.

Q: "Less access to the present health system would, contrary to popular rhetoric, *benefit* the poor." Ivan Illich

DIVERSITY: In Table 20-3, the "race gap" in life expectancy is 6.7 years (5.8 among women and 7.7 among men). The "gender gap" is 7.4 years (6.5 among whites and 8.4 among African Americans).

TABLE 20–2 Assessment of Personal Health by Income, 1991

Family Income	Excellent	Very Good	Good	Fair	Poor
$35,000 and over	48.7 %	30.2 %	17.0%	3.3%	0.8 %
$20,000–$34,999	38.9	29.7	23.7	5.7	1.9
$10,000–$19,999	28.7	26.9	28.8	11.1	4.5
Under $10,000	23.9	24.7	29.2	15.1	7.1

SOURCE: U.S. National Center for Health Statistics, *Current Estimates from the National Health Interview Survey United States, 1991*, series 10, no. 184 (Washington, D.C.: U.S. Government Printing Office, 1992).

as adults. Table 20–3 presents life expectancy for U.S. children born in 1991. Whites can expect to live more than seventy-six years; African Americans, about seventy years.

Sex is an even stronger predictor of health than race, since African-American females can expect to outlive males of either race. The table also indicates that 76 percent of white men—but only 58 percent of African-American men—will live to age sixty-five. The comparable chances for women are 86 percent for whites and 78 percent for African Americans.

Regardless of race, poverty condemns people to crowded, unsanitary dwellings that breed infectious diseases. Although tuberculosis is no longer a widespread threat to health in the United States, a higher risk of poverty means that African Americans are four times as likely as whites to die from this disease. Poor people of all races also suffer from nutritional deficiencies. Perhaps 20 percent of our population—up to 50 million people—can afford neither a healthful diet nor adequate medical care. As a result, wealthy people can expect to die in old age of chronic illnesses such as heart disease and cancer, while poor people are likely to die younger from infectious diseases linked to poor nutrition.

Poverty also breeds stress and violence. The leading cause of death among African-American men aged fifteen to twenty-four—who figure prominently in the urban underclass—is homicide. In 1992 about 5,164 African Americans were killed by others of their race—half the number of black soldiers killed in the entire Vietnam War.

Eating Disorders

An **eating disorder** is *an intense involvement in dieting or other forms of weight control in order to become very thin.* As the opening to this chapter suggests, eating disorders illustrate the power of culture to shape patterns of health.

The evidence that eating disorders have a significant cultural component begins with the fact that 95 percent of people who suffer from anorexia nervosa or bulimia are women, mostly from white, relatively affluent families. Why would women be preoccupied with thinness in this way? According to researcher Michael Levine (1987), our culture contains powerful messages that, for women, link being slender with being successful and attractive to men. Contrarily, Levine adds, notions that overweight people are "lazy," "ugly," "stupid," and "sloppy" are also widespread.

Studies show that most college-age women (1) widely accept the idea that "guys like thin girls," (2) think being thin is the most crucial dimension of physical attractiveness, and (3) believe that they are not as thin as men would like them to be. In fact, most college women want to be even thinner than college men say women should be. For their part, most men describe their actual body shape as just about what they want it to be; thus, men display little of the dissatisfaction over body shape expressed by women (Fallon & Rozin, 1985).

Chapter 13 ("Sex and Gender") explained that our culture embraces a "beauty myth" that teaches women to exaggerate the importance of physical attractiveness as well as to orient themselves toward pleasing men (Wolf, 1990). Such cultural patterns, Levine explains, teach women to see thinness as a form of perfection they should pursue at all costs. These messages about

TABLE 20–3 Life Expectancy for U.S. Children Born in 1991

	Females	Males	Both Sexes
Whites	79.7 (86%)	73.0 (76%)	76.4 (81%)
African Americans	74.3 (78%)	65.6 (58%)	70.0 (67%)
All races	79.1 (85%)	72.2 (74%)	75.7 (79%)

Figures in parentheses indicate the chances of living to age sixty-five.
SOURCE: U.S. Bureau of the Census (1993).

NOTE: The U.S. government banned cigarette advertising from radio and television in 1971.

NOTE: In 1988, former Surgeon General C. Everett Koop declared nicotine to be addictive, so that smoking is not simply a personal choice. This ruling is likely to have significance for health-related liability cases. More recently, the Food and Drug Administration (FDA) has sought to regulate tobacco products as addictive drugs.

DIVERSITY: Smoking is strongly linked to class. Blue-collar workers are twice as likely to smoke (50%) as white-collar workers are (25%).

GLOBAL: Singapore is likely to become the world's first smoke-free city. This so-called "socially engineered ministate" (see the box in Chapter 16) forbids public smoking and cigarette vending machines and prohibits tobacco companies from sponsoring public events.

thinness come from mothers and fathers—especially affluent parents—who pressure daughters to be "The Best Little Girl in the World." But television and other mass media also play a part in this process, almost exclusively employing actresses and models who are unnaturally thin and unrealistically beautiful.

The overall result of a "gendered" image of women's bodies is low self-image, since few women approach our culture's unrealistic standards of beauty. Those who do, moreover, are likely to engage compulsively in dieting behavior to the point of risking their health.

Cigarette Smoking

Many threats to health are matters of individual behavior, and cigarette smoking tops the list of preventable hazards. Smoking became popular in the United States after World War I. Despite growing evidence of its dangers, smoking remained fashionable even a generation ago. Today, smoking has been redefined as a mild form of social deviance.

Consumption of cigarettes has fallen since 1960, when almost 45 percent of U.S. adults smoked. By 1991, only 26 percent were smokers (U.S. Bureau of the Census, 1993). Quitting is difficult because cigarette smoke contains nicotine, which is physically addictive. People also smoke as a means of coping with stress. The link between cigarettes and stress probably explains why divorced and separated people are more likely to smoke, as are the unemployed and people in the military services.

Generally speaking, the less education people have, the greater their chances of smoking. In terms of gender, a larger proportion of men (28 percent) smoke than women (24 percent). But cigarettes—the only form of tobacco use to gain popularity among women—have taken a growing toll on women's health. In 1987, lung cancer surpassed breast cancer as a cause of death among women in the United States.

During the 1930s, medical researchers noted a sharp rise in smoking-related diseases such as lung cancer. Studies showed that roughly twenty years of smoking was required for lung cancer to develop. But not until the 1960s did the government act to discourage the use of tobacco, declaring that cigarettes—as well as cigar and pipe smoking—cause heart disease; cancer of the mouth, throat, and lungs; and lung diseases such as bronchitis and emphysema.

The number of men and women dying prematurely each year as a direct result of cigarette smoking approaches 450,000, more than the combined death toll from alcohol, cocaine, heroin, homicide, suicide, automobile accidents, and AIDS (Mosley & Cowley, 1991). Smokers also endure frequent minor illnesses such as flu, and pregnant women who smoke increase the likelihood of spontaneous abortion, prenatal death, and low birth-weight babies. Even nonsmokers exposed to cigarette smoke have a higher risk of smoking-related diseases.

Tobacco remains a $30 billion industry in the United States. The tobacco industry maintains that because the precise link between cigarettes and disease has not been specified, the health effects of smoking remain "an open question." But the tobacco industry is not breathing as easily today as it once did. Laws mandating a smoke-free environment are spreading rapidly. Furthermore, courts have increased the liability of cigarette manufacturers in lawsuits brought by people with smoking-related illnesses, or their survivors.

In response to these antismoking drives in the United States, the tobacco industry has been selling more products abroad, especially in poor societies where there is little legal regulation of tobacco sales and advertising. In the United States, however, more and more smokers are trying to break the habit, taking advantage of the fact that someone who has not smoked for ten years has about the same pattern of health as a lifelong nonsmoker (Shephard, 1982; Rudolf, 1985).

Sexually Transmitted Diseases

Sexual activity, while both pleasurable and vital to the continuation of our species, can transmit some fifty illnesses. Sometimes called *venereal diseases* (from Venus, the Roman goddess of love), these ailments date back to humanity's origins. Our culture has long linked sex to sin; therefore, some people regard venereal diseases not only as illness but also as a mark of immorality.

Sexually transmitted diseases (STDs) became a national issue during the "sexual revolution" of the 1960s. Before this time, perhaps two out of three men but only about one in ten women had premarital sexual intercourse; today, the figures are closer to three out of four men and two out of three women. With sexual activity typically occurring at an earlier age and with a greater number of partners, STDs have become a serious health problem—a notable exception to the general decline in infectious ailments during this century. In recent years, the growing danger of STDs—and especially AIDS—has prompted something of a sexual counterrevolution that has discouraged casual sex, not necessarily for

NOTE: Programs to combat STDs reveal characteristic political differences: Liberals accept the fact of casual sexual activity and urge availability of birth control devices and sex education; conservatives urge revival of an ethic of abstinence and greater marital fidelity.

NOTE: There are some 50 STDs overall; roughly 7,000 U.S. deaths annually are related to STDs other than AIDS.

GLOBAL: Japan is one of the few nations on earth to ban oral contraceptives (the "pill"), which are available only through a doctor's prescription for treatment of irregular menstrual cycles. The government's logic is that a ban on the pill will maintain the high level of condom use, which should discourage the transmission of HIV. As of mid-1991, Japan had 405 cases of AIDS and a total of 1,852 recorded infections with HIV.

moral reasons, but out of self-interest (Kain, 1987; Kain & Hart, 1987). The following section provides a brief overview of several common STDs.

Gonorrhea and Syphilis

Gonorrhea and syphilis, among the oldest diseases, are caused by a microscopic organism almost always transmitted by sexual contact. Untreated, gonorrhea can cause sterility; syphilis can damage major organs and result in blindness, mental disorders, and death.

Roughly 500,000 cases of gonorrhea and 110,000 cases of syphilis are reported each year, and the actual number may well be several times greater. Both diseases are more common among people of color than whites. Reporting suggests that 77 percent of infections involve African Americans, 12 percent affect whites, 4 percent afflict Latinos, and less than 1 percent affect Asian Americans and Native Americans (Masters, Johnson, & Kolodny, 1988; Moran et al., 1989; U.S. Centers for Disease Control, 1993).

Most cases of gonorrhea and syphilis are easily cured with penicillin, an antibiotic drug developed in the 1940s. Thus neither disease currently represents a major health problem in the United States.

Genital Herpes

An estimated 20 to 30 million adults in the United States (one in seven) are infected with the genital herpes virus. The infection rate among people of color, however, is about twice as high as among whites (Moran et al., 1989).

Although far less serious than gonorrhea and syphilis, herpes is incurable. It can be asymptomatic or it can exhibit periodic, painful blisters on the genitals accompanied by fever and headache. Although not fatal to adults, women with active genital herpes can transmit the disease to an infant during a vaginal delivery, to whom it can be deadly. Such women, therefore, usually give birth by cesarean section.

AIDS

The most serious of all sexually transmitted diseases is acquired immune deficiency syndrome, or AIDS. Identified in 1981, this disease is incurable and fatal. AIDS is caused by a human immunodeficiency virus (HIV). This virus attacks white blood cells, the core of the immune system, rendering a person vulnerable to a wide range of infectious diseases that eventually cause death.

Experts—and the public—disagree as to the best strategy for combating the spread of HIV. Liberals support the distribution of condoms to young people because condom use significantly reduces the chances for sexual transmission of the virus. Conservatives object to this policy, claiming it encourages casual sex, which, for them, is the heart of the problem: From this point of view, rethinking the notion that young people should be sexually active is a better approach.

Some 97,000 new cases of AIDS were reported in the United States during the twelve-month period ending September, 1993, raising the total number of people in the United States who have contracted this disease to 340,000. About 205,000 have already died (U.S.Centers for Disease Control and Prevention, 1993).

In global perspective, some 10 million people are infected with HIV, a figure that could increase three- or fourfold by the end of this decade. Global Map 20–2, on page 547, shows that the African continent (more specifically, countries south of the Sahara Desert) has the highest HIV infection rate and currently accounts for two-thirds of all world cases. In the cities of central African nations such as Burundi, Rwanda, Uganda, and Kenya, roughly one-fifth of all young adults are infected with HIV (Tofani, 1991). North Americans represent 15 percent of global HIV cases. In the United States, experts estimate the number of infected persons at 1 million.

People with HIV do not immediately contract AIDS. On the contrary, most initially display no symptoms whatever and are unaware of their infection. Symptoms of AIDS usually do not appear for a year or longer. Within about five years, one-third of infected

DATA FILE: Information about the global AIDS epidemic and AIDS as a women's issue is included in the *Data File*.

DATA FILE: Data from the Centers for Disease Control show that, among U.S. high school students, 61 percent of males and 54 percent of females have had sexual intercourse. The *Data File* provides further data on sexual activity and incidence of condom use.

NOTE: Estimates suggest that about 8 out of 1,000 college students are infected with HIV.

GLOBAL: Transmission of HIV is pronounced in poor societies partly because of the high incidence of genital lesions.

Q: "We don't say 'smoke carefully,' we say 'don't smoke'." Monsignor John Woolsey on discouraging sexual activity among young people

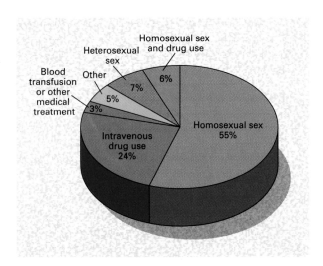

FIGURE 20–1 Type of Transmissions for Reported U.S. AIDS Cases, 1992

(U.S. Centers for Disease Control and Prevention, 1993)

people will develop AIDS; half display symptoms of AIDS within ten years, and medical experts expect that all but a few will do so eventually. With 340,000 active cases in the United States as of September 1993, the infection rate is still rising, although at a slowing rate of increase. As the death toll mounts, AIDS has turned out to be nothing less than catastrophic—potentially the most serious epidemic of modern times.

Transmission of HIV almost always occurs through blood, semen, or breast milk. This means that AIDS is not spread through casual contact—that is, by shaking hands, hugging, sharing towels or dishes, swimming together, or even by coughing and sneezing. The risk of transmitting AIDS through saliva (as in kissing) is extremely low. Oral and especially genital sex are dangerous, however, but the risk of transmitting the infection is reduced (but not eliminated) by the use of latex condoms. In the age of AIDS, abstinence or an exclusive relationship with an uninfected person is the only sure way to avoid contracting HIV.

Specific behaviors place people at high risk for HIV infection. The first is *anal sex*, which can cause rectal bleeding, allowing easy transmission of HIV from one person to another. This practice is extremely dangerous, and the greater the number of sexual partners, the greater the risk. Anal sex is commonly practiced by gay men, in some cases with multiple partners. As a result, homosexual and bisexual men represent about 55 percent of adolescents and adults with AIDS in the

United States. In response to the devastating effect of AIDS on gay communities across this country, gays (as well as nongays) have shunned sexual promiscuity in recent years (McKusick et al., 1985; Kain, 1987; Kain & Hart, 1987).

Sharing needles used to inject drugs is a second high-risk behavior. At present, intravenous drug users account for 24 percent of persons with AIDS. Sex with an intravenous drug user is also very risky. Because intravenous drug use is more common among poor people in the United States, AIDS is becoming a disease of the socially disadvantaged. Overall, 51 percent of AIDS patients are white people, with African Americans (12 percent of the population) accounting for 31 percent of people with AIDS (and half of all women with the disease). Latinos (7 percent of the population) represent 17 percent of AIDS cases (and 21 percent of women with AIDS). Asian Americans and Native Americans together account for less than 1 percent of people with AIDS (U.S. Centers for Disease Control and Prevention, 1993).

The rise of AIDS among young women of color stands out as a recent trend: For them, the disease is now the leading cause of death. Finally, 55 percent of young children with AIDS are African Americans (Huber & Schneider, 1992; U.S. Centers for Disease Control and Prevention, 1993).

Using any drug, including alcohol, also increases the risk of being infected with HIV to the extent that it impairs judgment. In other words, even people who understand what places them at risk of infection may act less responsibly once they are under the influence of alcohol, marijuana, or some other drug.

As Figure 20–1 shows, only 7 percent of people with AIDS in the United States became infected through heterosexual contact (although heterosexuals, infected in various ways, account for more than 30 percent of AIDS cases). So the likelihood of a runaway "breakout" of AIDS into the heterosexual population now seems less likely than it did several years ago. But heterosexual activity does transmit HIV, and the danger rises with the number of sexual partners, especially if they fall into high-risk categories. Worldwide, heterosexual relations are the primary means of HIV transmission, accounting for two-thirds of all infections (Eckholm & Tierney, 1990).

AIDS is throwing our health-care system into crisis. The cost of treating a single person with AIDS has already soared to hundreds of thousands of dollars, and this figure may rise as new therapies appear. At present, government health programs, private insurance, and personal savings rarely cover more than a fraction of the

GLOBAL: In global perspective, the use of condoms is highest in Japan ("the pill" is not widely available there); lowest use is in sub-Saharan Africa (where the AIDS epidemic is worst).
RESOURCE: Loretta Tofani's article, "The AIDS Epidemic in Africa," is included among the cross-cultural selections in the *Seeing Ourselves* reader, 3/e.

NOTE: The term "a negotiated death" has emerged to indicate the decision by family members, medical-legal-religious-ethical specialists, and sometimes patients themselves about how and when death should occur. A common outcome of such negotiation is to issue a "Do Not Resuscitate" order for a terminally ill patient.
NOTE: The first "wrongful life" suit against a hospital was brought in 1990 by a man who claims he was revived against his will.

Window on the World

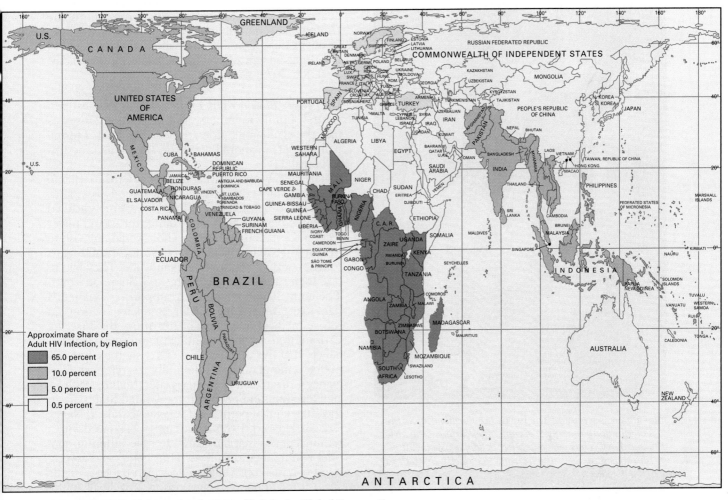

GLOBAL MAP 20–2 HIV Infection of Adults in Global Perspective

Approximately two-thirds of all global HIV cases are recorded in sub-Saharan Africa. This high infection rate reflects the prevalence of other venereal diseases and infrequent use of condoms, factors that promote heterosexual transmission of HIV. South and North America each represent another 10 percent of all cases. The incidence of infection is still low in Europe. Southeast Asia, where HIV is spreading most rapidly, accounts for another 10 percent of infections. Least affected by HIV are countries in North Africa and the Middle East, and the nations of Australia and New Zealand.

Prepared by the author using data from the *World Development Report* (World Bank, 1993). Map projection from *Peters Atlas of the World* (1990).

cost of treatment. In addition, there is the mounting cost of caring for the children orphaned by this disease; their numbers, some analysts predict, could rise to eighty thousand by the end of the 1990s. Overall, there is little doubt that AIDS represents both a medical and a social problem of monumental proportions.

Initially, the government responded slowly to the AIDS crisis, largely because gays and intravenous drug users are widely viewed as deviant. More recently, money allocated for AIDS research has increased rapidly (now totaling more than $4 billion annually), and researchers have identified some drugs, such as

Q: "I'm trying to knock the medical profession into accepting its responsibilities." Dr. Jack Kevorkian, creator of the "suicide machine"

DATA FILE: A summary of the controversial "suicide machine" case is included in the *Data File*.

GLOBAL: In the Netherlands, active euthanasia is common, although illegal. Some 10,000 cases occur each year.

Q: "There's a world of difference between ceasing treatment and acts of deliberate killing." Leon Kass, University of Chicago medical ethicist

Q: "Miracles can and do occur; I guess we've muddied the waters surrounding the question of a person's right to die." Jacqueline Cole

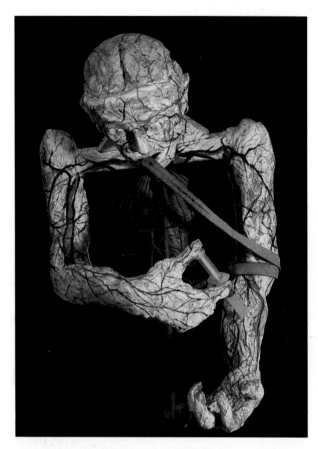

Paul Marcus's sculpture The Junkie *graphically depicts the loss of humanity that often accompanies serious drug abuse. The age of AIDS has added another deadly consequence of intravenous drug use—the transmission of HIV through the sharing of needles.*

AZT, that suppress the symptoms of the disease. But educational programs remain the most effective weapon against AIDS, since prevention is the only way to stop a disease that currently has no cure.

Ethical Issues: Confronting Death

Health issues always involve ethical issues. Moral questions are more pressing than ever now that technological advances have given human beings the power to prolong life and, therefore, to define life and death. We now grapple with how to use these new powers, or whether to use them at all.

When is a person dead? Common sense suggests that life ceases when breathing and heartbeat stop. But

the ability to revive or replace a heart and artificially sustain respiration have rendered such notions of death obsolete. Medical and legal experts in the United States now define death as an *irreversible* state involving no response to stimulation, no movement or breathing, no reflexes, and no indication of brain activity (Ladd, 1979; Wall, 1980).

Do people have a right to die? Today, medical personnel, family members, and patients themselves face the agonizing burden of deciding when a terminally ill person should die. Who should assume this responsibility?

In 1990, twenty-six-year-old Nancy Cruzan fell into an irreversible coma after an automobile accident. Physicians exhausted their efforts and solemnly assured Cruzan's parents that their daughter would never recover. Certain that their daughter would not wish to live in a permanent vegetative state, the Cruzans sought a legal decision to let Nancy die. They had to take their case all the way to the U.S. Supreme Court. The court issued a judgment supporting a patient's right to die by declaring that any competent person can refuse medical treatment or nutrition. Because the Cruzans were able to present "clear and convincing evidence" that this would be Nancy's wish, the court permitted removal of the feeding tube keeping her alive. Nancy Cruzan died twelve days later (Mauro, 1990).

Ten thousand people in the United States are in the same kind of permanent vegetative state as Nancy Cruzan (Howlett, 1990). Thousands more, faced with a terminal illness that may cause terrible suffering, consider ending their own lives. Thus courts and government commissions continue to weigh patients' rights against practitioners' obligations to provide all appropriate care to those in need. A 1983 presidential commission noted that the first responsibility of physicians and hospitals is to protect the patient's life. Doctors must explain every medical option available to patients or, when a patient is incapacitated, to family members. Even so, terminally ill patients can refuse treatment that may extend their lives but offer no hope of recovery. But the commission emphasized that a family decision such as that faced by the Cruzans must be made in the interest of the patient—no one else.

The commission also endorsed an individual's choice to create a *living will*, a statement of personal intention regarding treatment in the event of catastrophic illness. A 1991 federal law requires hospitals, nursing homes, and other medical facilities to explain to individuals that they may specify how medical decisions should be made if they are unable to speak for

Q: "Medicine, a synthesis of many disciplines, is essentially the practice of knowledge and skills and attitudes helpful in the care of the sick." Patricia L. Kendall and George G. Reader

Q: "One must ask whether the medical intellect functions only or even best solely on a foundation of natural science." John H. Knowles

themselves due to accident or illness. The law also recognizes people's right to appoint a representative to make their wishes known to doctors or others. The legal standing of a living will varies from state to state, as do the policies of particular hospitals. The national trend, however, is toward recognizing the right of people to accept or refuse treatment rather than allow medical officials alone to act on our behalf.

What about mercy killing? *Mercy killing* is the common term for **euthanasia,** *assisting in the death of a person suffering from an incurable disease.* Euthanasia (from the Greek, meaning "a good death") poses an ethical dilemma, being at once an act of kindness and a form of killing.

Support for a patient's right to die (that is, *passive* euthanasia) is growing in the United States. But assisting in the death of another person (*active* euthanasia) still provokes controversy and may violate the law. In 1992, for example, Jack Kevorkian, a physician who has helped people end their lives with his "suicide machine," was arrested in Michigan and charged with murder. No one thinks that Kevorkian's "clients"— people suffering from terminal illnesses—thought of him as their murderer. But our society is uneasy about legally empowering physicians to actively end a life in response to a patient's request.

The debate breaks down roughly as follows. Those who categorically view life—even with suffering—as preferable to death reject passive or active euthanasia. People who recognize circumstances under which death is preferable to life endorse passive or perhaps even active euthanasia, but they face the practical problem of determining just when life should be ended.

Family members also must confront the reality of medical costs, which skyrocket when extraordinary care is needed. A single attempt to revive a patient whose heart has stopped may cost $1,500. Monitoring the treatment of 146 critically ill patients over a three-year period, researchers at Duke Medical Center found that just over half could be revived at all, and fewer than ten ever improved enough to leave the hospital. The average costs of such heroic medical efforts, however, averaged $150,000 (reported in *Time,* March 29, 1993:19). Are such odds good enough to request extraordinary medical treatment? Should medical costs be considered in making this decision? Our society can no longer duck these questions, since a majority of hospital deaths in the United States now involve a decision by patients, family members, and physicians to withhold treatment (Flynn, 1991; Humphrey, 1991; Markson, 1992).

Finally, the ethical issues involved in health and medicine extend far beyond dealing with death. New medical technologies, such as genetic screening, promise to predict the onset of disease. But, vexing decisions remain about proper treatment, as the box on page 550 suggests.

THE MEDICAL ESTABLISHMENT

Medicine is *a social institution concerned with combating disease and improving health.* Medicine is a vital part of a broader concept of **health care,** which is *any activity intended to improve health.*

Through most of human history, health care was the responsibility of individuals and their families. Medicine emerges as a social institution only as societies become more productive, assigning their members formal, specialized roles. Members of preindustrial societies recognize medical specialists as knowing the healing properties of certain plants and offering insights into the emotional and spiritual needs of the ill. Members of industrial societies sometimes ethnocentrically dismiss traditional healers—from acupuncturists to herbalists—as "witch doctors," but these practitioners are helping to improve human health throughout much of the world (Ayensu, 1981).

As a society industrializes, health care becomes the responsibility of specially trained and legally licensed healers, from anesthesiologists to X-ray technicians. Today's medical establishment in the United States took form over the last 150 years.

The Rise of Scientific Medicine

In colonial times, herbalists, druggists, midwives, and ministers all engaged in various forms of healing arts. Unsanitary instruments, lack of anesthesia, and simple ignorance made surgery a terrible ordeal in which doctors probably killed as many patients as they saved.

Medical specialists gradually learned more about human anatomy, physiology, and biochemistry. By about 1850, doctors had established themselves as self-regulating professionals with medical school degrees. The American Medical Association (AMA), founded in 1847, symbolized the growing acceptance of the scientific model of medicine. The AMA widely publicized the successes of its members in identifying the cause of life-threatening diseases—bacteria and viruses—and in developing vaccines to combat disease.

Still, other approaches to health care, such as regulating nutrition, also had defenders. The AMA

NOTE: Technology has rapidly changed the character of modern medicine. The first heart transplant was done only 22 years ago; for several years thereafter, each effort was a major media event. Today, such transplants are commonplace (about 1,500 annually), and are covered (with special provisions) by Medicare.
NOTE: The first woman joined the American Medical Association board of directors in 1989.

Q: "Physicians have exceedingly high prestige in American society. ... Medicine thus attracts those who value status and income, who seek a challenging and interesting occupation, who enjoy exercising judgment, and who seek to do good." David Mechanic
NOTE: A 1991 New York Times poll found that 78% of U.S. adults are satisfied with the quality of health care available to them, but 62% are not satisfied with the cost of care.

SOCIAL POLICY

New Genetic Research: Ethical Dilemmas

For generations, the women in Anna Fischer's family have lived in the shadow of cancer. Her grandmother died of ovarian cancer fifty years ago; her mother survived one bout with breast cancer, only to die ten years later from the same disease; Fischer's maternal aunt and five cousins also contracted either ovarian or breast cancer.

Medical scientists have long recognized that such cancers "run in families." So Anna Fischer was distressed, but not entirely surprised, in 1990 when doctors diagnosed her own ovarian cancer. After surgery and chemotherapy, Fischer now seems to have made a full recovery.

What Fischer never expected came next. Given her family's history of cancer and her own recent illness, doctors declared that Fischer was still at high risk of breast cancer. They proposed that she should undergo a "prophylactic" double mastectomy to minimize the chance of later cancer and, in effect, save her life.

Anna Fischer was stunned by the idea of surgically removing her breasts just because she *might* become ill in the future. But she changed her mind after learning about research being carried out by California geneticist Mary-Claire King. Studying women who had contracted breast or ovarian cancer, King discovered that every woman in her study had an abnormal genetic pattern on the chromosome 17, one that is absent in cancer-free women. This "genetic marker," while not causing cancer, does indicate the presence of the genetic trait that does.

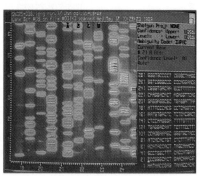

Scientists are steadily learning more about genetic factors that prompt some people to develop serious diseases. But the technological capacity to understand the workings of human genetics will likely outpace our ethical ability to determine how this information should be used.

According to King, 85 percent of the estimated one-half million U.S. women with the genetic trait will develop cancer before age sixty-five. With these odds, Anna Fischer decided to undergo surgery and she is now probably much more likely to live to old age.

Scientists already have similar genetic predictors for dozens of serious illnesses. Less clear, however, is how individuals—or others—should utilize such information. Can parents ethically use the results of genetic tests (as for Down's Syndrome) to decide if a fetus should develop to term? Should partners ask each other for a genetic screening (to assess, say, the risk of Huntington's Disease or Alzheimer's) before they decide to marry? Should employers or insurance companies require such testing before making a commitment to an individual? Our society already faces these questions; the ethical dilemmas will only mount as genetic research moves forward rapidly in the years to come.

SOURCES: Elmer-Dewitt (1994) and Thompson (1994).

responded boldly—some thought arrogantly—to these alternative ideas, trumpeting the superiority of its practitioners. By the early 1900s, state licensing boards agreed to certify only physicians trained in scientific programs approved by the AMA. With control of the certification process, the AMA effectively closed down schools teaching other healing skills, limiting the practice of medicine to those with an M.D. degree. In the process, both the prestige and income of physicians rose dramatically. Men and women with M.D. degrees have become among the highest-paid workers in the United States, with 1993 earnings, on average, of about $175,000.

Practitioners of some other approaches, such as osteopathic physicians, concluded that they had no choice but to fall in and follow AMA standards. Thus

SOCIAL SURVEY: "In general, some people think that it is the responsibility of the government in Washington to see to it that people have help in paying for doctors and hospital bills. Others think that these matters are not the responsibility of the federal government and that people should take care of these things themselves. Where do you place yourself on this scale?" (GSS 1993, N = 1,057; *Codebook*, 1993:334)

(1) "Government should help"	28.1%
(2)	22.1%
(3) "Agree with both views"	31.4%
(4)	9.3%
(5) "People should take care of themselves"	6.2%
DK/NR	2.9%

osteopaths (with D.O. degrees), originally concerned with manipulating the skeleton and muscles, today treat illness much as medical doctors (with M.D. degrees) do. Other practitioners—such as chiropractors, herbal healers, and midwives—held more to their traditional roles, but at the cost of being relegated to the fringe of the medical profession.

Scientific medicine, taught in expensive, urban medical schools, also changed the social profile of doctors. As the AMA gained power over the medical profession, they closed many rural medical colleges that had trained people of modest financial means, women, and people of color. As the number of medical schools in the United States steadily dropped to seventy-seven by 1950, the number of women and African Americans in medicine also reached a low point. Only in recent decades have women and people of color increased their representation among physicians, to 16 percent and 4 percent, respectively (Gordon, 1980; Starr, 1982; Huet-Cox, 1984; U.S. Bureau of the Census, 1993).

Today, people in some parts of the country have far more access to medical specialists than others do. National Map 20–1, on page 552, shows the distribution of physicians throughout the United States.

Holistic Medicine

The scientific model of medicine has recently been tempered by the more traditional notion of **holistic medicine,** *an approach to health care that emphasizes prevention of illness and takes account of the person's entire physical and social environment.*

Holistic practitioners also embrace the use of drugs, surgery, artificial organs, and high technology, but they caution that these developments risk transforming medicine into narrow specialties concerned with symptoms rather than people and with disease instead of health. The following are foundations of holistic health care (Duhl, 1980; Ferguson, 1980; Gordon, 1980):

1. **Patients are people.** Holistic practitioners are concerned not only with symptoms but with how each person's environment and lifestyle affect health. For example, the likelihood of illness increases under stress caused by poverty or intense competition at work. Holistic practitioners extend the bounds of conventional medicine, taking an active role in combating environmental pollution and other dangers to public health.

2. **Responsibility, not dependency**. The complexity of contemporary medicine fosters patients' dependence on physicians. Holistic medicine tries to shift some responsibility for health from physicians to people themselves by enhancing their abilities to engage in health-promoting behavior. Holistic medicine favors a more *active* approach to *health*, not a *reactive* approach to *illness.*

3. **Personal treatment.** Conventional medicine locates medical care in impersonal offices and hospitals, which are disease-centered settings. Holistic practitioners favor, as much as possible, a personal and relaxed environment such as the home. Holistic medicine seeks to reestablish the personal social ties that united healers and patients before the era of specialists. The AMA currently recognizes more than fifty specialized areas of medical practice, and a growing proportion of M.D.'s are entering these high-paying specialties rather than family practice. Thus there is a need for practitioners who are concerned with the patient in the holistic sense.

Clearly, holistic care does not oppose scientific medicine but shifts its emphasis away from narrowly treating disease toward the goal of achieving the highest possible level of well-being for everyone.

Paying for Health: A Global Survey

As medicine has come to rely on high technology, the costs of health care in industrial societies have skyrocketed. Countries employ various strategies to meet these costs.

Medicine in Socialist Societies

In societies with predominantly socialist economies, the government provides medical care directly to the people. It is an axiom of socialism that all citizens have the right to medical care on the same terms. To translate this ideal of equity into reality, people do not rely on their private financial resources to pay physicians and hospitals; rather, the government funnels public funds to pay medical costs. The state owns and operates medical facilities and pays salaries to practitioners, who are government employees.

People's Republic of China. The People's Republic of China, a poor, agrarian society that is only beginning to industrialize, faces the daunting task of attending to the health of more than a billion people. Traditional healing arts, including acupuncture and the use of medicinal herbs, are still widely practiced in China. In

Seeing Ourselves

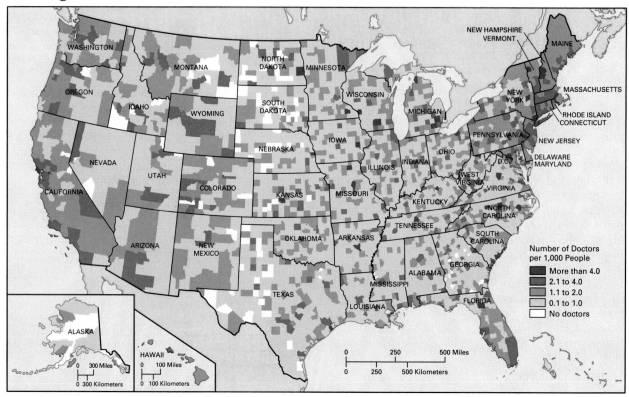

NATIONAL MAP 20–1 The Availability of Physicians Across the United States

There are about 630,000 doctors in the United States, but they are not evenly distributed throughout the population. This map shows the number of doctors for every 1,000 people in counties across the country. In general, people who live along the West Coast and much of the East Coast benefit from the greatest access to doctors. Why do you think doctors cluster in these areas? What consequences do you think this pattern has for public health?

From *Time*, June 14, 1993, p. 12. Copyright © 1993 Time Inc. Reprinted by permission.

addition, the holistic concern for the interplay of mind and body marks the Chinese approach to health (Sidel & Sidel, 1982b; Kaptchuk, 1985).

China recently experimented with private medical care, but by 1990 the government had reestablished control over this dimension of life. China's famed barefoot doctors, roughly comparable to U.S. paramedics, have brought some modern methods of medical care to millions of peasants in remote rural villages.

The former Soviet Union. The former Soviet Union is currently struggling to transform a state-dominated economy into more of a market system. For this reason, the scheme for providing medical care is in

transition. Nonetheless, the notion that everyone has a right to basic medical care is likely to remain strong.

Currently, the government provides medical care funded from taxes. As is the case in the People's Republic of China, people do not choose a physician but report to a local government health facility.

Physicians in the former Soviet Union have had lower prestige and income than their counterparts in the United States. They have received about the same salary as skilled industrial workers (compared to a roughly 5 to 1 ratio in this country). Worth noting, too, is that about 70 percent of physicians in the new Commonwealth of Independent States are women, compared with about 16 percent in the United States, and, as in our society, occupations dominated by women yield fewer financial rewards.

This system has trained enough physicians to meet the basic needs of a large population. However, rigid bureaucracy still results in highly standardized and impersonal care. As market reforms are adopted, rigid uniformity will likely diminish, but disparities in the quality of care among various segments of the population may well increase.

Medicine in Capitalist Societies

Members of societies with predominantly capitalist economies expect to provide for their own health care in accordance with their own resources and personal preferences. However, the economic inequality that marks capitalist societies means that adequate health care is beyond the means of a significant part of the population. Therefore every capitalist society provides some form of government assistance.

Sweden. In 1891 Sweden instituted a compulsory, comprehensive system of government medical care. Citizens of this Scandinavian country pay for this program with their taxes, which are among the highest in the world. Typically physicians receive salaries from the government rather than fees from patients, and most hospitals are government managed. Because this medical system resembles that of socialist societies, it is often described as **socialized medicine**, *a health care system in which the government owns and operates most medical facilities and employs most physicians.*

Great Britain. In 1948 Great Britain, too, instituted socialized medicine. The British did not do away with private care, however; today, there is a "dual system" of medical services. Thus all British citizens are entitled to medical care provided by the National Health Service, but those who can afford to may purchase more extensive care from doctors and hospitals that operate privately.

Canada. Canada represents the "single-payer" model of health care. Like a vast insurance company, the Canadian government pays doctors and hospitals, which operate privately. But the federal government, in consultation with provincial governments and medical associations, sets a schedule of fees for medical services. Thus Canada has government-funded and regulated medical care but, because practitioners operate privately, not true socialized medicine. Moreover, some physicians work entirely outside of the government-funded system, charging whatever fees they wish.

Canada's system can boast of providing care for everyone at a lower cost than the (nonuniversal) medical system in the United States. At the same time, however, the Canadian system makes less use of state-of-the-art technology and responds slowly to people's needs, often requiring those facing major surgery to wait months or even a year for attention (Grant, 1984; Vayda & Deber, 1984; Rosenthal, 1991).

Japan. Physicians in Japan operate privately, and a combination of private insurance and government programs pays medical costs. In general, employers provide comprehensive health coverage as an employee benefit. For those without such programs, government medical insurance covers most costs, and the elderly receive free care (Vogel, 1979).

Medicine in the United States

At the beginning of 1994, the United States stood alone among industrialized societies in having no government-sponsored medical system for every citizen. Europeans generally look to government to fund medical care from taxes, and about 75 percent of medical costs are paid in this way. In the United States, by contrast, the government pays just 40 percent of medical costs (Lohr, 1988). For the most part, medicine in the United States is handled as a private, profit-making industry. Called a **direct-fee system**, ours is *a medical care system in which patients pay directly for the services of physicians and hospitals.*

Affluent people in the United States can purchase the best medical care in the world; yet the poor fare worse than their counterparts in Europe. This is evident in relatively high death rates among both infants and adults in the United States compared to many European countries (United Nations, 1993).

Why does the United States have no national health care program? First, our society has historically favored limited government in the interest of greater personal liberty. Second, at least until recently, political support for a national medical program has not been strong, even among labor unions, which have concentrated on winning health care benefits from employers. Third, the AMA and the health insurance industry have strongly and consistently opposed any such program (Starr, 1982).

Figure 20–2 shows that expenditures for medical care increased dramatically between 1950 and 1991, from just $12 billion to more than $750 billion. Medical care absorbed about 5 percent of the gross national product in 1950, rising to 14 percent by 1991. This amounted to $2,868 per person, more than other

NOTE: The fact that 30% of U.S. children born today can expect to live to age 85 is one component of "The Graying of the United States," highlighted in Chapter 14 ("Aging and the Elderly").
GLOBAL: Between 1976 and 1991, U.S. scientists won 63 of 102 Nobel prizes in medicine, physics, and chemistry. (The U.K. and Germany were next with nine each.)

NOTE: There are some 600,000 physicians in the United States, about 84% of which are men (97% of all nurses are women). Men now receive 69% of medical degrees, so that their representation in the profession is declining.

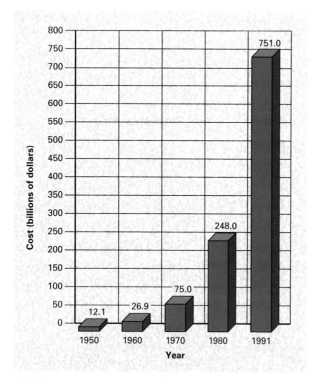

FIGURE 20–2 The Rising Cost of Medical Care in the United States

(U.S. Bureau of the Census, 1970, 1993)

industrial society spends for medical care, and double the figure in Germany and Japan (Whitney, 1991). Who pays the medical bills?

Private insurance programs. In 1990, 150 million people (61 percent) received some medical care benefits from a family member's employer or labor union. Another 35 million people (14 percent) purchased private coverage on their own. Private insurance (including Blue Cross and Blue Shield) rarely pays all medical costs, but three-fourths of our population has some private medical insurance (Health Insurance Association of America, 1991).

Public insurance programs. In 1965 Congress created Medicare and Medicaid. Medicare pays a portion of the medical costs of men and women over sixty-five; in 1991 it covered 35 million women and men, about 14 percent of the population. During the same year, Medicaid, a medical insurance program for the poor, provided benefits to nearly 27 million people, or about 11 percent of the population. An additional 25 million

veterans (10 percent) can obtain free care in government-operated hospitals. In all, 35 percent of this country's people enjoy some medical care benefits from the government, but most also participate in a private insurance program.

Health maintenance organizations. An increasing number of people in the United states belong to a **health maintenance organization** (HMO), *an organization that provides comprehensive medical care to subscribers for a fixed fee.* In 1992, some 550 HMOs in the United States enrolled 37 million individuals, about 15 percent of the population. HMOs vary in their costs and benefits, and none provides full coverage. But fixed costs give these organizations a financial interest in keeping their subscribers healthy; therefore, many have adopted a preventive approach to health (Ginsburg, 1983).

In all, 86 percent of the U.S. population has some medical care coverage, either private or public. Yet most plans pay only part of the cost of treating a serious illness, therefore threatening even middle-class people with financial ruin. And most programs also exclude many medical services, such as dental care and treatment for mental health problems. Most seriously, 34 million people (about 14 percent of the population) have no medical insurance at all. Many more people lose their medical coverage temporarily each year due to layoffs or job changes. While about one-sixth of those without coverage are young people (typically in their twenties) who simply take their good health for granted, most work part time or full time for small businesses that provide no health care benefits. Commonly, then, the people caught in a medical care bind are adults and children with limited incomes who can neither afford to become ill nor to purchase the medical care they need to remain healthy (Altman et al., 1989; Health Insurance Association of America, 1989; Hilts, 1991; Smith, 1993; Brookhiser, 1994).

The Clinton reforms. By 1994, there was strong public support for establishing some form of universal health care coverage in the United States. A number of plans are now under discussion ranging from a conservative Republican proposal to offer tax credits to people who purchase health insurance to a Canadian-type "single-payer" system sponsored by liberal Democrats.

President Bill Clinton currently proposes what is generally termed "managed competition." The "competition" element of such a program is that employees would join together to bargain with competing medical providers in order to receive the greatest

RESOURCE: A discussion of the sick role by Talcott Parsons is included among the "classics" in the Macionis and Benokraitis reader, *Seeing Ourselves*, 3/e.
GLOBAL: Physicians in most poor societies of the world do not share diagnostic information freely with patients.

Q: "We may say that illness is a state of disturbance in the 'normal' functioning of the total human individual, including both the state of the organism as a biological system and of his personal and social adjustments. It is thus partly biological and partly socially defined." Talcott Parsons (1951)

value. The "managed" dimension is that the government will ensure that everyone—regardless of income or present state of health—will have substantial medical coverage.

The president's proposal intends to reduce the health care costs of large employers (such as auto makers), who currently devote 19 percent of payroll to such benefits. But the government will require small employers, many of whom now provide no health care benefits to workers, to contribute toward their employees' coverage. Further, all benefits are to be "portable," so that no one can lose coverage due to a job change or layoff.

The Clinton reform intends to shift medical care away from the traditional, private fee-for-service system toward various types of health maintenance organizations (HMOs) and government-funded programs. In the process, supporters claim, costs will fall even as coverage becomes universal. Critics, however, counter with a "pro-choice" argument that patients should be able to choose their own doctor without government interference. Further, because it will create new government bureaucracies, critics fear, the Clinton plan will raise—not lower—the costs of health care; eventually, cost savings will have to be achieved through rationing care.

The debate over health care will hold center stage for some time to come. Most analysts agree, however, that some form of comprehensive health care plan is needed and will soon be in operation (Anders, 1993; Church, 1993; Goodgame, 1993).

THEORETICAL ANALYSIS OF HEALTH AND MEDICINE

Each of the major theoretical paradigms in sociology provides a means of organizing and interpreting the facts and issues presented in this chapter.

Structural-Functional Analysis

Talcott Parsons (1951) viewed medicine as a social system's way of keeping its members healthy. From this point of view, illness is dysfunctional, undermining the performance of social roles and, thus, the overall operation of society.

The Sick Role

The normative response to disease, according to Parsons, is for an individual to assume the **sick role**,

patterns of behavior defined as appropriate for people who are ill. As developed by Parsons, the sick role has four characteristics.

1. **Illness provides exemption from routine responsibilities.** Serious illness relaxes or suspends normal social responsibilities. To prevent abuse of this license, however, people do not simply declare themselves ill; they must enlist the support of others—especially a recognized medical expert—before assuming the sick role.

2. **A person's illness is not deliberate.** We assume that sick people are not responsible for their ailments; illness is something that happens to them. Therefore, the failure of ill people to fulfill routine responsibilities should carry no threat of punishment.

3. **A sick person must want to be well.** We also assume that no one wants to be sick. Thus people suspected of feigning illness to escape responsibility or to receive special attention have no legitimate claim to a sick role.

4. **An ailing person must seek competent help.** An additional obligation assumed by people who are ill is seeking competent assistance and cooperating with health care practitioners. By failing to seek medical help or to follow doctor's orders, a person gives up any claim on the sick role's exemption from routine responsibilities.

The Physician's Role

Physicians function to assess claims of sickness and to restore sick people to normal routines. The physician's power and responsibility in relation to the patient derive from specialized knowledge, Parsons explained. Physicians expect patients to follow "doctor's orders," and to provide whatever personal information may reasonably assist their efforts.

Although it is inevitably hierarchical, the doctor-patient relationship varies from society to society. In Japan, for example, tradition provides physicians with considerable authority. One manifestation of this elevated position is that Japanese physicians routinely withhold information about the seriousness of an illness on the grounds that such knowledge might undermine a patient's fighting spirit (Darnton & Hoshia, 1989).

Even three decades ago, physicians in the United States acted in much the same way. But the *patient rights movement* embodies the public demand that physicians readily share more and more medical information. A more egalitarian relationship between doctor

NOTE: Defining death is a good symbolic-interaction issue. Who participates in the definition of death? When does this definition become a negotiation among parties with various interests? What kinds of power are exercised by patients, family members, and physicians with scientific training?

RESOURCE: The power of religious activity to improve the health of the elderly is demonstrated in the *AJS* article by Idler &

Kasl (1992).

DIVERSITY: The infant mortality rate for the United States as a whole is 8.3. But poverty in many U.S. cities pushes this number up to the levels of the least-developed nations. New York, 13.4; Philadelphia, 16.8; Baltimore, 17.8; Newark, 19.8; Detroit, 20.9; Camden, N.J., 22.5. This is why the U.S. ranks only 19th among industrial societies in terms of infant mortality.

and patient is also developing in European societies and, gradually, in Japan as well.

Critical evaluation. Parsons's functionalist analysis links illness and medicine to the broader organization of society. The sick role—in essence, society's accommodation to illness—also has application to some non-illness situations, such as pregnancy (Myers & Grasmick, 1989).

One limitation of the sick-role idea is that it describes acute conditions (like the flu) better than chronic illness (like heart disease), which may not be reversible. Moreover, a sick person's ability to regain health depends on available resources. Many poor people can ill afford either medical care or time off from work.

Critics charge that Parsons's view of the physician's role suggests that doctors—rather than people themselves—should bear the primary responsibility for health. Treatment-oriented physicians respond to acute illness, of course; but a more prevention-oriented approach would cast physicians and patients as equal partners in the pursuit of health.

Symbolic-Interaction Analysis

Viewed according to the symbolic-interaction paradigm, society is less a grand system than a complex and changing reality. Both health and medical care are thus human constructions that people perceive subjectively.

The Social Construction of Illness

Since we socially construct both health and illness, members of a society where most people go hungry may view malnutrition as quite normal. Similarly, members of our own society defined smoking cigarettes as fashionable for decades, and we are complacent, even today, about the unhealthful effects of a rich diet.

How we respond to illness, too, is based on social definitions that may or may not square with medical knowledge. For instance, people with AIDS contend with fear and sometimes outright bigotry that has no basis in medical fact.

Even the "expert opinions" of medical professionals are influenced by nonmedical factors. David Mechanic (1978) notes that, in the former Soviet Union, physicians were more likely to diagnose illness when worker productivity was generally high and people could be spared for a day or two. In the same way, U.S. college students have been known to ignore signs of illness on the eve of a vacation, yet dutifully

march into the infirmary before a difficult examination. Health, in short, is not an objective commodity, but a negotiated outcome.

Constructed or not, how people define a medical situation often affects how they actually feel. Medical experts have long marveled at *psychosomatic* disorders (a fusion of Greek words for "mind" and "body"), in which state of mind guides physical sensations (Hamrick, Anspaugh, & Ezell, 1986). As sociologist W. I. Thomas (1931) pointed out, a situation defined as real becomes real in its consequences.

The Social Construction of Treatment

In Chapter 6 ("Social Interaction in Everyday Life"), we used the dramaturgical approach of Erving Goffman to explain how physicians craft their physical surroundings ("the office") and present themselves to others to foster specific impressions of competence and power.

Sociologist Joan Emerson (1970) further illustrates this process of reality construction by analyzing a situation familiar to women, a gynecological examination carried out by a male doctor. After observing seventy-five such examinations, she explains that this setting is especially precarious, because it is vulnerable to misinterpretation. The man's touching of a woman's genitals—conventionally viewed as a sexual act and possibly even an assault—must, in this case, be defined as impersonal and professional.

To ensure that people construct reality in this way, doctors and nurses remove sexual connotations as completely as possible. They furnish the examination room with nothing but medical equipment; all personnel wear medical uniforms. Staff members act as if such examinations are simply routine, although, from the patient's point of view, they may be quite unusual.

Further, rapport between physician and patient is established before the examination begins. Once under way, the doctor's performance is strictly professional, suggesting to the patient that inspecting the genitals is no different from surveying any other part of the body. A female nurse is usually present during the examination not only to assist the physician but to dispel any impression that a man and woman are "alone in a room."

The need to manage situational definitions has long been overlooked by medical schools. This omission is unfortunate because, as Emerson's analysis shows, understanding how reality is socially constructed in the examination room is just as crucial as mastering the medical skills required for effective treatment.

RESOURCE: A survey article "The Health of Black America" is included in the Macionis and Benokraitis reader, *Seeing Ourselves.*
Q: "Humana hospitals do not have the responsibility to provide care for the indigent except in emergencies or in those situations where reimbursement for indigent patients is provided." From Florida certificate-of-need application

Q: "Medicine and biology were of crucial importance, providing the basic concepts through which the class and sexual divisions of Victorian society were expressed and ultimately justified." Lesley Doyal (1981:141)

Fortunately, medical professionals are gradually recognizing the importance of sociological insights. At the Southwestern Medical School in Dallas, Texas, for example, Professor David Hemsell instructs his medical students to actually climb onto an examination table and place their feet in the metal stirrups with their legs apart, in order to gain an appreciation of the patient's point of view. Hemsell claims, "The only way to understand women's feelings is to be there." He adds, "You can see the impact of being in that position hit them in the face like a two-by-four."

Critical evaluation. One strength of the symbolic-interaction paradigm lies in revealing the relativity of sickness and health. What people view as normal or deviant, healthful or harmful, depends on a host of factors, many of which are not, strictly speaking, medical. This approach also shows that all medical procedures involve subtle interaction—a process of reality construction—between patient and physician.

By the same token, this approach seems to deny that there are any objective standards of well-being. Certain physical conditions do indeed cause specific negative changes in human capacities, whether we think so or not. People who lack sufficient nutrition and safe water, for example, suffer from their unhealthy environment however they define their surroundings.

Social-Conflict Analysis

Social-conflict analysis, following Karl Marx, ties health to the operation of capitalism. Researchers have focused on three main issues: access to medical care, the effects of the profit motive on treatment, and the politics of medicine.

The Access Issue

Personal health is the foundation of social life. Yet by making health a commodity, capitalist societies allow health to follow wealth. As already noted, this problem is more serious in the United States than in other industrialized societies because, as yet, our country has no universal health care system.

Most of the 34 million people who lack any health care coverage at present have low incomes. Conflict theorists claim that, while capitalism does provide excellent health care for the rich, it simply does not provide very well for the rest of the population.

The Profit Motive

For others, however, even a program of socialized medicine would not go far enough. More radical critics

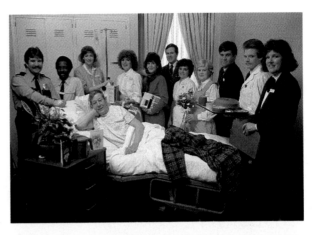

The cost of medical care in the United States has been rising at a dizzying rate. In part, this high rate of increase reflects the fact that hospitals are large, bureaucratic organizations that employ dozens of specialized workers in the treatment of any single patient. Here one man poses for a picture with just the medical staff who directly provide for him.

claim unequal access to health in capitalist countries is rooted in class conflict. These critics claim that the concentration of wealth makes equal medical care impossible, and that this inequality will persist even if Congress enacts a new health care program. Only a redistribution of economic resources, say the Marxists, would make medical care uniformly available (Bodenheimer, 1977; Navarro, 1977).

Moreover, beyond the access issue, radical critic John Ehrenreich (1978) argues, the profit motive turns physicians, hospitals, and the pharmaceutical industry into multibillion dollar corporate conglomerates. The quest for ever-increasing profits also encourages questionable medical practices, including administering needless tests, performing unnecessary surgery, and an overreliance on drugs (Kaplan et al., 1985).

For example, more than 2 million women in the United States have undergone breast implants under the assumption that the commonly used plastic packets of silicone were safe. Recently, however, it became clear that these implants are not safe enough, a fact apparently known to Dow Corning, their major manufacturer, for decades.

Of the 30 million surgical operations of all kinds performed annually in the United States, three-fourths are "elective," meaning that they were intended to promote a patient's long-term health rather then being prompted by a medical emergency. Critics charge that the decision to perform surgery often reflects the financial interests of surgeons and hospitals as well as the

Elizabeth Blackwell became the first woman in the United States to earn a medical doctor (M.D.) degree in 1847. For a century thereafter, medicine was the unchallenged preserve of men; even today, only 16 percent of U.S. physicians are women.

medical needs of patients (Illich, 1976). Perhaps 10 percent of this elective surgery could safely be refused or deferred, saving patients more than $1 billion each year. More important, since about one in two hundred patients dies from elective surgery (because surgery is itself dangerous), thousands of lives a year are needlessly lost (Sidel & Sidel, 1982a).

Finally, critics point out, the United States has been all too tolerant of physicians having a direct financial interest in the tests and procedures they order for their patients (Pear & Eckholm, 1991). In short, critics conclude, health care should be motivated by a concern for people, not profits.

Medicine as Politics

Although medicine declares itself to be politically neutral, scientific medicine frequently takes sides on significant social issues. For example, the medical establishment has long opposed government-operated health care programs. The history of medicine, critics contend, is replete with racial and sexual discrimination, defended by "scientific" facts (Leavitt, 1984).

Even today some critics see political mischief in scientific medicine. Scientists explain illness in terms of bacteria and viruses rather than as evidence of the effects of social inequality on health. From the scientific perspective, in other words, poor people become ill from a lack of sanitation and an unhealthy diet, even though poverty may be the underlying cause of these ills. In this way, critics charge, scientific medicine depoliticizes health in the United States by reducing political issues to simple biology.

Critical evaluation. Social-conflict analysis provides still another view of the relationships among health, medicine, and our society. In this case, social inequality is the reason some people have far better health than others; moreover, conflict theorists denounce the profit motive as inconsistent with the interests of patients.

The most common objection to the conflict approach is that it minimizes the improvement in U.S. health over the years and scientific medicine's contribution to our high standard of living today. Though there is plenty of room for improvement, health indicators for our population have risen steadily over the course of this century and compare fairly well with those of other industrial societies.

In sum, sociology's three major theoretical paradigms convincingly argue that health and medicine are social issues. The famous French scientist Louis Pasteur (1822–1895) spent much of his life studying how bacteria cause disease. Before his death, the record indicates, he remarked that health depends much less on bacteria than on the social environment in which bacteria operate (Gordon, 1980:7). Explaining Pasteur's insight is sociology's contribution to human health.

LOOKING AHEAD: HEALTH AND MEDICINE IN THE TWENTY-FIRST CENTURY

At the beginning of this century, deaths from infectious disease were widespread, and scientists had yet to develop basic antibiotics like penicillin. Thus, even common infections represented a deadly threat of health. Today, members of our society take for granted the good health and long life that was the exception, not the rule, a century ago. There is every reason to expect that the positive trend in U.S. health will continue into the next century.

Another encouraging trend is public recognition that, to a significant extent, we can take responsibility for our own health (Caplow et al., 1991). Every one of

NOTE: National Center for Health Statistics surveys show that 90 percent of U.S. nonsmokers claim they find cigarette smoke annoying.
NOTE: In 1987, lung cancer surpassed breast cancer as the leading cause of death among young U.S. women. "You've come a long way, baby"?

Q: "Tobacco is a filthy weed, That from the devil does proceed; It drains your purse and burns your clothes, And makes a chimney of your nose." Oliver Wendell Holmes
NOTE: The output of U.S. cigarette manufacturers is sufficient to provide 70 percent of U.S. adults with one pack a day.

us can live better and longer to the extent to which we avoid tobacco, eat sensibly and in moderation, and exercise regularly.

Yet, health problems will continue to plague U.S. society in the decades to come. For one thing, with no cure in sight, it seems likely that the AIDS epidemic will persist for some time. For the present, remaining out of danger of contracting HIV requires, above all, a personal decision to avoid any of the risky behaviors noted in this chapter.

But the changing social profile of people with AIDS—which increasingly afflicts the poor—reminds us that the United States has much to do to improve the health of marginalized members of our society. One important step, now taking shape, is establishing some system to provide at least basic medical care to all. Even those among us who do not easily embrace

the notion of serving as "our brother's keeper" should recognize the moral obligation that we as a people have to ensure that everyone has the security of medical care.

Finally, repeating a pattern seen in earlier chapters, we find that problems of health are far greater in the poor societies of the world than they are in the United States. The good news is that life expectancy for the world as a whole has been rising—from forty-eight years in 1950 to about sixty-five years today—and the biggest gains have been in poor countries (Mosley & Cowley, 1991). But in much of Latin America, Asia, and especially in Africa, hundreds of millions of adults and children lack adequate food, safe water, and medical attention. Improving health in the world's poorest societies remains a critical challenge as we enter the next century.

SUMMARY

1. Health is a social as well as a biological issue, and well-being depends on the extent and distribution of a society's resources. Culture shapes both definitions of health and patterns of health care.

2. Through most of human history, health has been poor by today's standards. Health improved dramatically in Western Europe and North America in the nineteenth century, first because industrialization raised living standards and later as medical advances controlled infectious diseases.

3. Infectious diseases were the major killers at the beginning of this century. Today most people in the United States die in old age of heart disease, cancer, or stroke.

4. Health in poor societies is undermined by inadequate sanitation and hunger. Average life expectancy is about twenty years less than in the United States; in the poorest nations, half of children do not survive to adulthood.

5. In the United States, more than three-fourths of children born today can expect to live to at least age sixty-five. Throughout the life course, however, people of high social position enjoy better health than the poor.

6. Cigarette smoking increased during this century to become the greatest preventable cause of death

in the United States. Now that the health hazards of smoking are known and social tolerance for tobacco use has declined, cigarette consumption is declining.

7. Sexually transmitted diseases are a health issue of growing concern. In the 1980s the spread of genital herpes discouraged casual sex. The spread of AIDS, a fatal and incurable disease, has reinforced this change.

8. Because of advancing medical technology, an increasing number of ethical issues surround death and the rights of the dying. Because of the capability to sustain life artificially, death now commonly results from a human decision.

9. Historically a family concern, health care is now the responsibility of trained specialists. The model of scientific medicine underlies the U.S. medical establishment.

10. The holistic approach to medicine balances science and technology with other procedures that promote health as well as treat disease. Highlighting the need for professional healers to gain personal knowledge of patients and their environment, holistic healers encourage people to assume greater responsibility for their own health and well-being.

11. Socialist societies define medical care as a right that governments offer equally to everyone. Capitalist societies view medical care as a commodity to be purchased, although most capitalist governments support medical care through socialized medicine or national health insurance.

12. The United States is the only industrialized society with no comprehensive medical care program. Within a direct-fee system, most people have private health insurance, government insurance, or membership in a health maintenance organization. One in five adults in the United States cannot afford to pay for medical care.

13. Structural-functional analysis links health and medicine to other social structures. A concept central to structural-functional analysis is the sick role, in which illness allows release from routine social responsibilities as long as patients seek to regain their health.

14. The symbolic-interaction paradigm investigates how health and medical treatments are largely matters of subjective perception and social definition.

15. Social-conflict analysis focuses on the unequal distribution of health and medical care. It criticizes the U.S. medical establishment for overly relying on drugs and surgery and for overemphasizing the biological rather than the social causes of illness.

KEY CONCEPTS

direct-fee system a medical care system in which patients pay directly for the services of physicians and hospitals

eating disorder an intense involvement in dieting or other forms of weight control in order to become very thin

euthanasia (mercy killing) assisting in the death of a person suffering from an incurable disease

health a state of complete physical, mental, and social well-being

health care any activity intended to improve health

health maintenance organization (HMO) an organization that provides comprehensive medical care to subscribers for a fixed fee

holistic medicine an approach to health care that emphasizes prevention of illness and takes account of a person's entire physical and social environment

medicine a social institution concerned with combating disease and improving health

sick role patterns of behavior defined as appropriate for those who are ill

social epidemiology the study of how health and disease are distributed throughout a society's population

socialized medicine a health care system in which the government owns and operates most medical facilities and employs most physicians

CRITICAL-THINKING QUESTIONS

1. Explain the assertion that health is as much a social as a biological issue.

2. In global context, which are the "diseases of poverty" that kill people in poor countries? Which are "diseases of affluence," the leading killers in rich nations?

3. In what sense are sexually transmitted diseases an exception to the historical decline in infectious illness?

4. Why is the cost of health care rising? How do other societies meet these costs?

SUGGESTED READINGS

Classic Sources

Elisabeth Kübler-Ross. *On Death and Dying.* New York: Macmillan, 1969.

    This study of the orderly process of dying illustrates the contribution of social research to assisting terminally ill patients.

Michel Foucault. *The Birth of the Clinic: An Archaeology of Medical Perception.* New York: Vintage Books, 1975.

    This history of medicine emphasizes not scientific developments but the cultural forces that gradually changed how people thought about illness and health care.

Contemporary Sources

Gregory L. Weiss and Lynne E. Lonnquist. *The Sociology of Health, Healing, and Illness.* Englewood Cliffs, N.J.: Prentice Hall, 1994.

    This book provides a detailed account of many of this chapter's issues.

Michael P. Levine. *How Schools Can Help Combat Student Eating Disorders: Anorexia Nervosa and Bulimia.* Washington, D.C.: National Education Association, 1987.

    This paperback is a highly readable analysis of eating disorders, emphasizing their social causes.

Ira Rosenwaike, ed. *Mortality of Hispanic Populations: Mexicans, Puerto Ricans, and Cubans in the United States.* New York: Greenwood Press, 1991.

    This book offers a look at how serious illness affects the most numerous Latino populations in the United States.

Don C. Locke. *Increasing Multicultural Understanding: A Comprehensive Model.* Newbury Park, Calif.: Sage, 1992.

    Here health professionals can find strategies for increasing their understanding of the effects of cultural differences on health care.

Susan Sherwin. *No Longer Patient: Feminist Ethics and Health Care.* Philadelphia: Temple University Press, 1992.

    This author argues that ethical issues in medicine should be resolved in a feminist context.

Ramona M. Asher. *Women with Alcoholic Husbands: Ambivalence and the Trap of Codependency.* Chapel Hill: University of North Carolina Press, 1992.

    The effects of illness often ripple through an entire family, straining and distorting relationships. Alcoholism is a case in point.

James Kinsella. *Covering the Plague: AIDS and the American Media.* New Brunswick, N.J.: Rutgers University Press, 1992.

    This book provides a critical assessment of the media portrayal of the AIDS crisis in the United States.

Robert Root-Bernstein. *Rethinking AIDS: The Tragic Cost of Premature Consensus.* New York: The Free Press, 1992.

    Investigating the political dimensions of how we confront disease, this analyst claims that policies to combat AIDS went wrong early in the last decade.

Wilbert M. Gesler and Thomas C. Ricketts. *Health in Rural North America: The Geography of Health Care Services and Delivery.* New Brunswick, N.J.: Rutgers University Press, 1992.

    Improving rural health care services presents one of the greatest challenges to North American societies, as demonstrated in this book.

David Mechanic. *Inescapable Decisions: The Imperatives of Health Reform.* New Brunswick, N.J.: Transaction, 1993.

    This book presents a critical analysis of the U.S. health care system that argues that we need to make basic changes in our national priorities.

Global Sources

Paul Farmer. *AIDS and Accusation: Haiti and the Geography of Blame.* Berkeley: University of California Press, 1992.

    The author provides a view of the AIDS crisis from the point of view of people in one of the Western hemisphere's poorest nations.

Barbara Jancar-Webster, ed. *Environmental Action in Eastern Europe: Response to Crisis.* Armonk, N.Y.: M.E. Sharpe, 1993.

    This book looks at the tragic environmental policies in Eastern Europe prior to the political changes there, and the prospects for the future.

Nicholas Dorn, Shiela Henderson, and Nigel South, eds. *AIDS: Women, Drugs, and Social Care.* London: Taylor & Francis, 1992.

    This volume documents the lives of British women with AIDS, focusing on their encounters with that nation's health care system.

Kenneth G. Zysk. *Religious Medicine: The History and Evolution of Indian Medicine.* New Brunswick, N.J.: Transaction, 1992.

    Folk medicine has both differences from and similarities to scientific medicine, as described in this account of the history of medical care in India.

Tony Bartnett and Piers Blaikie. *AIDS in Africa: Its Present and Future Impact.* New York: Guilford Press, 1992.

    This analysis of East Africa examines both the short- and long-term consequences of AIDS for this region of the world.

Red Grooms, *Taxi to the Terminal*, 1993

DATA FILE: An outline of this chapter, supplementary lecture material, and suggested discussion topics are found in the *Data File*.

Q: "In the course of my own lifetime, the earth's population has increased two and a half times, and most of this increase is now to be found in the exploding urban centers, especially in the slums and shantytowns of Africa, Asia, and Latin America." Isaac Asimov

Q: "The central problem of the sociologist of the city is to discover the forms of social action and organization that typically emerge in relatively permanent, compact settlements of large numbers of heterogeneous individuals." Louis Wirth (1938)

Q: "As a result of [the urbanite's] reserve, we frequently do not know by sight even those who have been our neighbors for years." George Simmel (1905)

Population and Urbanization

*I*n 1519 a band of Spanish conquistadors led by Hernando Cortés reached Tenochtitlán, the capital of the Aztec empire. They were stunned by the beautiful, lake-encircled city, teeming with some 300,000 people—more than lived in any European city at that time. Gazing down broad streets, exploring magnificent stone temples, and examining the golden treasures of the royal palace, Cortés and his soldiers wondered if they were dreaming.

Cortés soon woke up and set his mind to looting the city's many priceless treasures. Unable at first to overcome the superior military forces of Montezuma and the Aztecs, Cortés spent the next two years raising a vast army and finally returned to utterly destroy Tenochtitlán. On the rubble of this ancient urban center, he constructed a new city in the European fashion—Ciudad Imperial de México, *Mexico City.*

Today Mexico City is once more fighting for its life. Its soaring population will reach 28 million by the end of this decade—one hundred times the number that astonished Cortés. This huge population is grappling with a host of problems common to poor societies, including poverty and a deteriorating environment.

A triple burden of rising population, urban sprawl, and desperate poverty weighs on much of today's world. This chapter examines both population growth and urbanization—two powerful forces that have worked hand in hand to shape and reshape our planet for thousands of years. A steadily increasing population will be one of the most serious challenges facing the world in the coming century, and this compelling drama will be played out in cities of unprecedented size.

NOTE: *Life expectancy* is calculated at birth for people born in a given year. Because it is reduced by infant mortality, this term is distinguished from *longevity*, which refers to how long people can live. For example, when the United States was founded, life expectancy was about 35 years due to high death rates from infectious diseases, although living to 65 and beyond was not unknown. (George Washington died at age 67; Martha Washington at age 70.)

DIVERSITY: Life expectancy varies by race and sex: for African-American females, 74.3 years; African-American males, 68.1; white females, 79.7; white males, 73.0. Sex has a greater effect (6.9 years) than race (4.2 years) does.

NOTE: A dramatic illustration of mortality change is that a greater proportion of U.S. babies born today will reach age 65 than survived a single year in 1900.

DEMOGRAPHY: THE STUDY OF POPULATION

From the point at which the human species emerged about 200,000 B.C.E. until several centuries ago, the earth's population grew slowly to roughly 20 million—about the same number as the population of southern California today. Life for our ancestors was anything but certain; people were vulnerable to countless diseases and frequent natural disasters. For ten thousand generations, however, our species has managed to flourish. Ironically, perhaps, global population is now so large (5.8 billion in 1995), and growing so

rapidly (by about 100 million annually), that the future well-being of humanity is again in doubt.

The causes and consequences of this growth form the core of **demography**, *the study of human population.* Demography (from Greek meaning "description of people"), a close cousin of sociology, analyzes the size and composition of a population as well as how people move from place to place. Although much demographic research is a numbers game, the discipline also poses crucial questions about the effects of population growth and its control.

The following sections explain basic demographic concepts.

Fertility

The study of human population begins with how many people are born. **Fertility** is *the incidence of childbearing in a society's population.* During their childbearing years, from the onset of menstruation (typically in the early teens) to menopause (usually in the late forties), women are capable of bearing more than twenty children. But *fecundity*, or potential childbearing, is sharply reduced by cultural norms, finances, and personal choice.

Demographers measure fertility using the **crude birth rate**, *the number of live births in a given year for every thousand people in a population.* They calculate a crude birth rate by dividing the number of live births in a year by a society's total population and multiplying the result by 1,000. In the United States in 1993, there were 4.1 million live births in a population of 259 million (U.S. Bureau of the Census, 1993). According to this formula, then, the crude birth rate was 15.8.

This birth rate is "crude" because it is based on the entire population, not just women in their childbearing years. Comparing the crude birth rates of various countries can be misleading, then, if one society has a larger share of women of childbearing age than another. A crude birth rate also tells us nothing about how birth rates differ among people of various races, ethnicities, and religions. But this measure is an easy-to-calculate indicator of a society's overall fertility. Table 21–1 shows that the crude birth rate of the United States is low in world context.

MORTALITY

Population size is also affected by **mortality**, *the incidence of death in a society's population.* Corresponding to the crude birth rate, demographers use a **crude death rate**, *the number of deaths in a given year for every*

TABLE 21–1 Fertility and Mortality Rates in Global Perspective, 1993

	Crude Birth Rate	Crude Death Rate	Infant Mortality Rate
North America			
United States	16	9	8
Canada	15	7	7
Europe			
Belgium	12	10	7
Russia	13	11	28
Denmark	13	11	7
France	14	9	7
Spain	11	9	7
United Kingdom	14	11	7
Latin America			
Chile	21	6	16
Cuba	17	7	11
Haiti	41	19	110
Mexico	28	5	29
El Salvador	33	7	43
Puerto Rico	19	8	17
Africa			
Algeria	30	6	54
Cameroon	41	12	79
Egypt	32	9	78
Ethiopia	45	14	109
Nigeria	44	13	77
South Africa	34	8	48
Asia			
Afghanistan	44	19	159
Bangladesh	35	12	109
India	29	11	81
Saudi Arabia	39	6	55
Japan	10	7	4
Vietnam	28	8	46

SOURCE: U.S. Bureau of the Census, 1993.

African-American artist Jacob Lawrence completed a series of paintings that he titled The Migration of the Negro *(1940–41) to document a major population movement among people of color from the rural South to the urban centers of the Northeast and Midwest.*

thousand people in a population. This time, we take the number of deaths in a year, divide by the total population, and multiply the result by 1,000. In 1993 there were 2.3 million deaths in the U.S. population of 259 million, yielding a crude death rate of 8.9. As Table 21–1 shows, this rate is low by world standards.

A third widely used demographic measure is the **infant mortality rate**, *the number of deaths among infants under one year of age for each thousand live births in a given year.* We derive this rate by dividing the number of deaths of children under one year of age by the number of live births during the same year and multiplying the result by 1,000. In 1993 there were 33,900 infant deaths and about 4.1 million live births in the United States. Dividing the first number by the second and multiplying the result by 1,000 produces an infant mortality rate of 8.3.

Here again, bear in mind variation among different categories of people. For example, African Americans, with three times the burden of poverty as whites, have an infant mortality rate of about 19—the same as the people of Jamaica and more than twice the white rate of 8 (U.S. Bureau of the Census, 1993). But infant mortality offers a good general measure of overall quality of life. Table 21–1 shows that infant mortality in the United States, while low compared to poor countries, is slightly higher than it is in Canada, Denmark, and other nations that make medical care available to the entire population.

Low infant mortality greatly raises **life expectancy**, *the average life span of a society's population.* Males born

in 1992 can expect to live 72.3 years, while females can look toward 79.0 years. In poor societies with high infant mortality, however, life expectancy is about twenty years less (see Global Map 14–1 on page 392).

Migration

Population size is also affected by **migration**, *the movement of people into and out of a specified territory.* Migration is sometimes involuntary, such as the forcible transport of 10 million Africans to the Western Hemisphere as slaves (Sowell, 1981). Voluntary migration is usually motivated by complex "push-pull" factors. Dissatisfaction with life in a rural village may "push" people to move; a common "pull" factor is the greater opportunity found in a big city. As explained later in this chapter, precisely this situation is causing rapid urban growth in poor societies today.

People's movement into a territory—commonly termed *immigration*—is measured as an *in-migration rate*, calculated as the number of people entering an area for every thousand people in the population. Movement out of a territory—or *emigration*—is measured in terms of the *out-migration rate*, the number leaving for every thousand people. Both types of migration usually occur simultaneously; their difference is called the *net-migration rate.*

Population Growth

Fertility, mortality, and migration all affect a society's population. In general, rich societies (like the United

NOTE: One key predictor of fertility is women's income. As wages and salaries rise, fertility falls, and vice versa.

NOTE: Fertility in the United States has declined despite rising government tax deductions for children.

NOTE: According to the United Nations, four people are born each second; 300,000 each day. Two die every three seconds. The net result is a daily increase of about 250,000 people, almost 100 mil-

lion annually. About 90 percent of the *growth* in the world's population is taking place in the poorest countries of the world.

DIVERSITY: An imbalance in the sex ratio tends to give the less numerous category more relative power. Historically, men outnumbered women in the Western states. This may have contributed to the fact that many of the first women to gain state and national office were from the West.

Window on the World

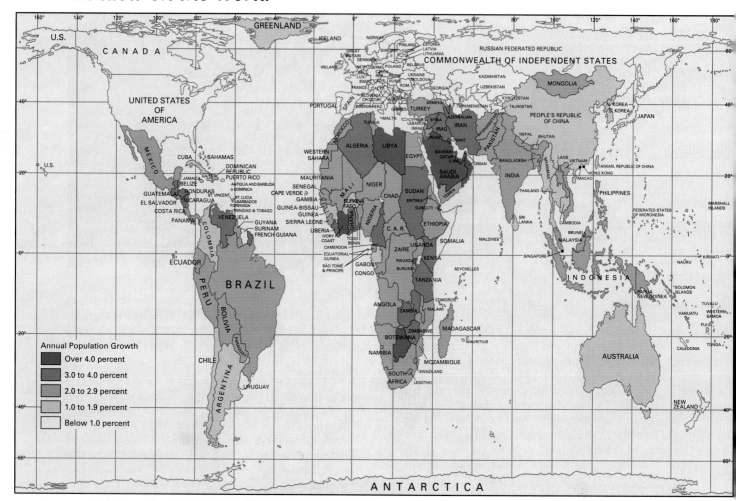

GLOBAL MAP 21–1 Population Growth in Global Perspective

The richest societies of the world—including the United States, Canada, and the nations of Europe—have growth rates below 1 percent. The nations of Latin America and Asia typically have growth rates of about 2 percent, which double a population in thirty-five years. The continent of Africa has an overall growth rate of 3.1 percent, which cuts the doubling time to less than twenty-four years. In global perspective, we see that a society's standard of living is closely related to its rate of population growth, meaning that population is rising fastest in the world regions that can least afford to support more people.

From *Peters Atlas of the World* (1990). Statistics updated by author.

States) grow as much from immigration as natural increase; less economically developed societies (like Mexico) grow almost entirely from natural increase.

To calculate a society's natural growth rate, demographers subtract the crude death rate from the crude birth rate. The natural growth rate of the U.S.

population in 1993 was 6.9 per thousand (the crude birth rate of 15.8 minus the crude death rate of 8.9), or about 0.7 percent annual growth.

Global Map 21–1 shows that population growth in the United States and other industrialized nations is well below the world average of 1.8 percent. In Europe,

GLOBAL: There are 110 million births annually in the world, 88% in less economically developed countries. Of 51 million annual global deaths, 77% are in poor countries. This yields global annual population increase of 90 million people, 94% in poor countries.
RESOURCE: David Berreby's analysis of "The Global Population Crisis" is included in the cross-cultural selections in the companion reader, *Seeing Ourselves*.

DATA FILE: Age-sex pyramids showing the life-course progression of the baby-boom generation are included in the *Data File*.
Q: "Although individual women [worldwide] are having fewer children, on average, than their mothers, there are simply more women having children, resulting in continuing increases in additions to world population." Population Reference Bureau

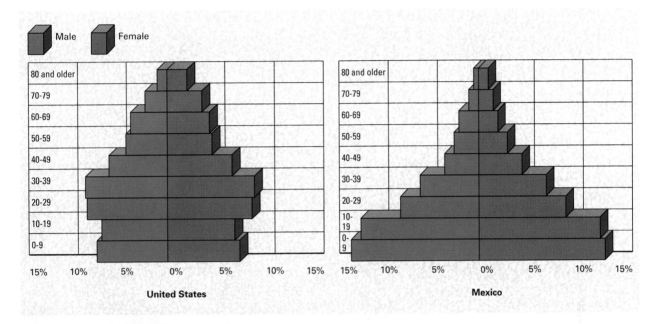

FIGURE 21–1 Age-Sex Population Pyramid for the United States and Mexico

(U.S. Bureau of the Census and Mexican Census data)

the current rate of growth is just 0.2 percent, and in Japan population is holding about steady. By contrast, high annual growth rates are at the global norm in Asia (currently about 1.6 percent) and Latin America (overall, about 1.8 percent). In Africa, a great population surge is occurring, with population growth averaging 3.1 percent.

A handy rule-of-thumb is that dividing a society's population growth rate into the number seventy yields the *doubling time* in years. Thus, an annual growth of 2 percent (as in Latin America) doubles a population in thirty-five years, and a 3 percent growth rate (as in Africa) pares the doubling time to twenty-four years. The rapid population growth of the poorest countries is deeply troubling because they can barely support the populations they have now.

Population Composition

Demographers also study the composition of a society's population at a given point in time. One simple variable is the **sex ratio**, *the number of males for every hundred females in a given population*. In 1992 the sex ratio in the United States was 95.2, or roughly 95 males for every 100 females. Sex ratios are usually below 100 because women typically outlive men. In India, however, the sex ratio is 108, because parents

value sons more than daughters. Thus women are more likely to abort a female fetus or, after birth, to provide less care to females than to males.

A more complex measure is the **age-sex pyramid**, *a graphic representation of the age and sex of a population*. Figure 21–1 presents two age-sex pyramids, showing the contrasting compositions of the population of the United States and Mexico. The rough pyramid shape of these figures results from higher mortality as people age. Looking at the U.S. pyramid, the bulge corresponding to ages twenty through forty-nine reflects high birth rates from the mid-1940s to the late 1960s, an era commonly termed the *baby boom*. The contraction just below—that is, males and females under twenty—represents the *baby bust* that followed as the birth rate dipped from 25.3 in 1957 to a low of 15.3 in 1986 (ending up at 15.8 by 1993).

Comparing the U.S. and Mexican pyramids, we see evidence of different demographic histories and likely futures. The age-sex pyramid for Mexico, like that of other less economically developed societies, is wide at the bottom (reflecting higher birth rates) and narrows quickly by what we would term middle age (due to higher mortality). Mexico, in short, is a much younger society with a median age of 20.4 compared to 32.8 in the United States. With a larger share of females still in their childbearing years, we

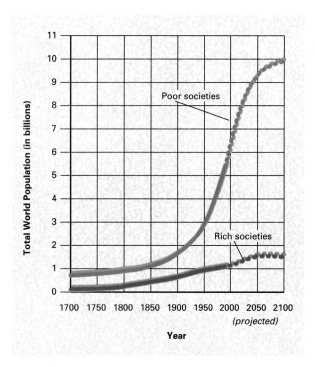

FIGURE 21–2 The Increase in World Population, 1700–2100

population increase, but the *rate* of growth accelerated. Population reached a third billion by 1962 (after just thirty-two years) and a fourth billion by 1974 (a scant twelve years later). The rate of world population increase has recently slowed, but our planet passed the 5 billion mark in 1987. In no previous century did the world's population even double. In the twentieth century, it has increased *fourfold*.

Currently, global population is increasing by 90 million people each year, with more than 90 percent of this growth in poor societies. At this rate, experts predict, global population will pass the 6 billion mark early in the next century, probably reaching 8 billion by 2025 and about 10 billion a century from now. Little wonder, then, that global population has become a matter of urgent concern (see also Chapter 22, "The Natural Environment").

Malthusian Theory

It was the sudden population growth two centuries ago that sparked the development of demography. Thomas Robert Malthus (1766–1834), an English clergyman and economist, devised a demographic theory that warned of impending social chaos. Malthus (1926; orig. 1798) began by claiming that population growth was the predictable result of timeless passion between the sexes.

Specifically, he predicted, population increase would approximate what mathematicians call a geometric progression, illustrated by the series of numbers 2, 4, 8, 16, 32, and so on. Noting the accelerating increase in these numbers, Malthus reached the sobering conclusion that world population would soon soar out of control.

Food production would also increase, Malthus reasoned, but only in arithmetic progression (as in the series 2, 3, 4, 5, 6) because, even with new agricultural technology, farmland is limited. Malthus's analysis yielded a troubling vision of the future: people reproducing beyond what the planet could feed, leading ultimately to catastrophic starvation.

What of limits to population growth? Malthus foresaw what he called *positive checks*, such as famine, disease, and war, and *preventive checks* like artificial birth control, sexual abstinence, and delayed marriages. He rejected birth control on religious grounds, and his common sense told him people would not abstain from sex or marry very much later. Famine stalked the future of humanity, in Malthus's scheme, a vision that earned him the title of "the dismal parson."

can understand why Mexico's crude birth rate (28) is considerably higher than our own (16), a fact that contributes to greater population growth.

HISTORY AND THEORY OF POPULATION GROWTH

Through most of human history, societies favored large families since human labor was the key to productivity. Additionally, until the development of rubber condoms 150 years ago, controlling birth was uncertain at best. But high death rates, resulting from widespread infectious diseases, served as a constant curb on population growth. World population at the dawn of civilization, about 6000 B.C.E., was about 20 million, increasing slowly across the millennia.

As shown in Figure 21-2, a demographic shift began as the earth's population turned upward, passing the 1 billion mark about 1800. This milestone (requiring some forty thousand years) was repeated by 1930 (barely a century later) when a second billion was added to the planet. In other words, not only did

FIGURE 21–3
Demographic Transition Theory

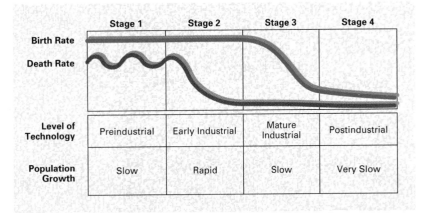

Critical evaluation. Fortunately, Malthus's prediction was flawed. First, by 1850 the birth rate in Europe began to drop, partly because children were becoming less of an economic asset and more of a liability, and partly because people began to use condoms as a means of birth control. Second, Malthus underestimated human ingenuity: Irrigation, fertilizers, and pesticides have increased farm production far more than he imagined, just as factories have generated a bounty of other products.

Critics also chided Malthus for ignoring the role of social inequality in world abundance and famine. Karl Marx (1967; orig. 1867) objected to viewing suffering as a "law of nature" rather than the mischief of capitalism.

Still, we should not entirely dismiss Malthus's distressing prediction. First, habitable land, clean water, and fresh air are certainly finite. And greater productivity has taken a toll on the natural environment. In addition, as medical advances have lowered death rates, world population has risen even faster. Population growth is especially rapid in poor societies, which are, in fact, experiencing much of the catastrophe Malthus envisioned.

In principle, finally, no level of population growth is sustainable over the long term. Thus, people everywhere must remain alert to the dangers of population increase.

Demographic Transition Theory

Malthus's rather crude analysis has been superseded by **demographic transition theory**, *a thesis linking population patterns to a society's level of technological development.*

Figure 21–3 shows the demographic consequences of four stages of technological development. Societies yet to industrialize—those at Stage 1—have high birth rates because of the economic value of children, the absence of effective birth control, and the high risk that children will not survive to adulthood. Death rates are also high, with periodic outbreaks of plague or other infectious disease, due to low living standards and the lack of medical technology. But deaths neutralize births, so population increase is modest, as it was for thousands of years before the Industrial Revolution in Europe.

Stage 2—the onset of industrialization—brings a demographic transition as population surges upward. Technology expands food supplies and combats disease. Death rates fall sharply although birth rates remain high, resulting in rapid population growth. It was in an era like this that Malthus formulated his ideas, and that goes a long way toward explaining his pessimism. Most of the world's least economically developed societies today are still in this high-growth stage.

In Stage 3—a mature industrial economy—the birth rates drop, finally coming into line with death rates, curbing population growth once again. Fertility falls, first, since most children born do survive to adulthood; moreover, rising living standards make raising children expensive. Affluence, in short, transforms offspring from economic assets into economic liabilities. Smaller families are also favored by women working outside the home and made possible by the widespread availability of birth control devices. As birth rates follow death rates downward, population growth slows further.

The most recent stage corresponds to a postindustrial economy. The birth rate in such societies continues to fall, in part because dual-income couples gradually become the norm and partly because the

Il paraît que je suis un phénomène socio-culturel.

LA FRANCE
A BESOIN
D'ENFANTS.

The birthrate in Europe has dropped so low that some analysts foresee an absolute drop in population in this world region. The French government, which sees children as a national resource, has turned to advertising to encourage people to have children. The ad implies children are becoming so rare that this baby can remark: "It appears that I am a sociocultural phenomenon." At the bottom right is added, "France needs children."

costs of raising children continue to rise. This trend, coupled to steady death rates, means that, at best, population grows only very slowly. In many European countries and Japan, for example, population is now virtually stable or slightly falling (van de Kaa, 1987).

Critical evaluation. Demographic transition theory suggests that technology holds the key to demographic patterns. Instead of the runaway population increase Malthus feared, this analysis foresees technology reining in population growth.

Demographic transition theory dovetails with modernization theory, one approach to global development discussed in Chapter 11 ("Global Stratification"). Modernization theorists are optimistic that industrialization will also solve the population problems that now exist in poor societies. But critics—notably dependency theorists—counter that current economic arrangements only ensure continued poverty in much of the world. Unless there is a significant redistribution of global resources, they maintain, our planet will become increasingly divided into industrialized "haves," enjoying low population growth, and

nonindustrialized "have-nots," struggling in vain to feed soaring populations.

Global Population: A Survey

What demographic patterns characterize today's world? Drawing on the discussion so far, we can highlight a number of key trends and reach several conclusions.

The Low-Growth North

When the Industrial Revolution began, population growth in Western Europe and North America peaked at 3 percent annually. But, in the centuries since, it steadily declined in countries of the Northern Hemisphere and, in 1970, dropped below 1 percent in the United States. As our postindustrial society enters Stage 4, the U.S. birth rate is approaching the replacement level of 2.1 children per woman, a point demographers term **zero population growth**, *the level of reproduction that maintains population at a steady state.*

Factors holding down population here and in other postindustrial societies include the high proportion of men and women in the labor force, the rising cost of raising children, trends toward later marriage and singlehood, and the use of contraceptives by about two-thirds of women of childbearing age. Voluntary sterilization has increased dramatically to become the most common form of birth control in the United States. Even U.S. Catholics, whose religious doctrine prohibits the use of artificial birth control, no longer differ from others in their contraceptive practices. Finally, abortion has been legal in the United States since 1973, and each year doctors terminate some 1.4 million pregnancies (Westoff & Jones, 1977; Moore & Pachon, 1985; U.S. Centers for Disease Control, 1993).

Poor families in the United States tend to be larger than average, contributing to the problem of child poverty. Overall, however, population growth here and in other industrial nations does not pose the great problem for these countries that it does in poor societies. Still, as Chapter 22 ("The Natural Environment") explains, an individual in our society uses many times the energy and other resources that people in poor countries do, placing greater stress on the global environment.

The High-Growth South

Population growth remains a serious problem in the poor societies of the Southern Hemisphere. Only a

GLOBAL: Immunization throughout poor societies has increased dramatically in recent decades. In 1975, 5% of infants were immunized against diseases such as measles, polio, tetanus, and diphtheria. By 1990, about half of all children were immunized against these diseases. One result: In Africa, not just infant mortality rates but the absolute number of infants dying has declined.

NOTE: Population "conservatives" tend to argue that rising populations reflect *success* in combating death rates; population "liberals" claim that rising population results from *failure* to control births.
GLOBAL: One way to solve the overpopulation of the People's Republic of China and the low population growth of Taiwan would be to allow people from PRC to migrate there.

few societies lack industrial technology altogether and are at demographic transition theory's Stage 1. Most countries in Latin America, Africa, and Asia have agrarian economies with some industry, placing them in Stage 2. Advanced medical technology supplied by rich societies has sharply reduced death rates, but birth rates remain high. A look back at Figure 21–2 shows that poor societies now account for two-thirds of the earth's people, a proportion that continues to rise.

In poor countries, birth rates remain high because children are still viewed as economic assets. Frequently children work eight- or ten-hour days for income; later, as adults, they care for aging parents. Throughout the less-developed world, families average four or five children; in rural areas, the number is commonly six or eight (The World Bank, 1991). But we must be careful about extending generalizations to more than one hundred societies. The box on page 572 contrasts the demographic profiles of the two Chinas—the People's Republic of China and Taiwan, Republic of China.

Any society's demographic profile has much to do with the options and opportunities available to women. Worldwide, we see that societies that define women's primary responsibilities as bearing children have high population growth. In Latin America, a combination of economic need, traditional patriarchy, and Roman Catholic doctrine discourages women from using birth control devices, with predictable effects on fertility. In much of Africa, many women in poor villages have no access at all to effective birth control (Salas, 1985). Asia is a study in contrasts: Many rural women are unable to acquire contraceptive devices, but some—as in the People's Republic of China—are the target of aggressive government campaigns to limit births.

In the long run, one key to population control is giving people more economic and educational opportunities. Simply put, women restricted to traditional child rearing roles have many children; similarly, men lacking jobs and schooling are likely to define their masculinity in terms of virility. One study involving Sudan (Africa) and Colombia (South America) concluded that women with seven years of schooling had half as many children as women with no education (Ross, 1985; Salas, 1985).

Taken together, various strategies to control fertility in poor societies have met with some success. But, in a majority of poor countries, birth rates are still too high to be sustainable. Just as important, most are now finding their death rates are falling, too.

Sex selection, the use of amniocentesis to determine the sex of a fetus, coupled with a decision to abort females, has become a popular practice in traditional, patriarchal societies of the world. This poster, by an organization in Bombay, India, reads "Once the woman becomes pregnant, after determination of the sex, everywhere there is murder of girls. Let's stop sex determination."

From "Sex Selection in India as a Bad Investment," an article by Les Levidow, in the premiere issue of *Science as Culture,* a quarterly published by Free Association Books in London. This poster was created by the Forum Against Sex Discrimination and Sex Pre-Selection Techniques in Bombay.

Although widely applauded, this trend exerts upward pressure on population.

In point of fact, population growth in poor societies of the world is due *primarily* to declining death rates. After about 1920, when Europe and North America began to export advances in scientific medicine, nutrition, and sanitation around the world, mortality tumbled. Since then, inoculations against infectious diseases and the use of antibiotics and insecticides have pushed down death rates with stunning effectiveness. For example, in Sri Lanka, malaria caused half of all deaths in the 1930s; a decade later, use of insecticide to kill malaria-carrying mosquitoes cut the malaria death toll in half. Although we hail such an achievement, this technological advance sent Sri Lanka's population soaring. Similarly, India's infant mortality rate slid from 130 in 1975 to 85 a generation later, a decline that helped boost that nation's population to more than 850 million.

In short, in much of the world, life expectancy is up and infant mortality is down. But birth control policies are now vital in poor countries where "death control" programs worked well several generations ago (Ehrlich, 1978; Piotrow, 1980).

GLOBAL: Currently, China (25%) and India (16%) together comprise more than 40% of humanity.

GLOBAL: In China, average number of births per woman is now steady at about 2.3, still double the U.S. figure.

GLOBAL: The single-child policy has given rise to what many Chinese describe as the "4-2-1 problem": four grandparents and two parents focusing their attention on one "little emperor."

GLOBAL: In 1990, there were more than 350 million Chinese under 14 years of age. Even with rigid regulation of birth, China will certainly have a serious population problem for decades to come. Even success in controlling population will produce strains: Rapidly dropping fertility would eventually result in more than half of China's population being over the age of 65, greatly taxing social resources.

GLOBAL SOCIOLOGY

Demographic Contrasts: A Report from the Two Chinas

P.R. China
Taiwan, R.O.C.

The People's Republic of China and Taiwan, Republic of China, contend with different population problems. The former—the world's most populous country with 1.3 billion people—is aggressively trying to limit population growth. The latter, by contrast, is endeavoring to raise the birthrate.

With fully one-fifth of humanity within its borders, it is no surprise that the People's Republic of China claims to "count mouths" rather than "heads," as we do. Ominously, a majority of the population is under thirty, raising the specter of a baby boom that could overwhelm the nation's food supply. As a result, since 1979, the government has pursued a tough "single-child" policy by which local officials encourage people to delay childbirth and, once one child is born, to submit to sterilization or abort subsequent pregnancies. In addition, one-baby couples enjoy income bonuses, and single children receive priority in school enrollment, health care, and, later, in employment and housing. This program has nudged annual population growth from 2.0 percent in the 1960s down to 1.8 percent today.

International criticism suggests that such efforts amount to forcing sterilization on people. Moreover, limited to one child, some parents choose to abort female fetuses or even kill female infants since, by tradition, Chinese parents look to sons to care for them in old age. Responding to these problems, the government has displayed some leniency in recent years. Yet unless fertility is curbed, China's population will double by 2025, undermining the country's struggle to raise its standard of living.

Taiwan faces a different problem, as its annual rate of population growth has fallen to 0.9 percent (almost as low as the 0.7 percent U.S. rate). The reason for the downward trend in fertility is that this nation (one of the four prospering "Little Dragons" along with South Korea, Hong Kong, and Singapore) is currently experiencing rapid economic development. Taiwanese women are leaving the home to enter the labor force, and the "two-income family" is becoming the norm as it already has in the United States. With affluence also comes independence; one result is that an increasing share of the adult population is remaining single.

Concerned that, if fertility continues to drop, soon there will be too many elderly people with too few younger workers to support them, the government has launched public relations campaigns to convince couples that "Two children is just right." Also, to counter the traditional prejudice against having girls, Taiwan has outlawed using medical procedures to find out the sex of a fetus.

Comparisons of this kind show how countries' concerns over demographic patterns can stem from very different reasons. They also reveal how misleading any single stereotype of poor societies can be.

SOURCES: World Bank (1984), Brophy (1989a, 1989b), Tien (1989), and *The Economist* (1993b).

FAMILY PLANNING—A BASIS NATIONAL POLICY OF CHINA

URBANIZATION: THE GROWTH OF CITIES

For most of human history, the small populations found around the world lived in nomadic groups, moving as they depleted vegetation or searched for migratory game. Small settlements marked the emergence of civilization in the Middle East some ten thousand years ago, but they held only a small fraction of the earth's people. Today the largest cities of the world, taken individually, contain as many people as the entire planet did then.

Urbanization is *the concentration of humanity into cities.* Urbanization both redistributes the population within a society and transforms many patterns of social life. We will trace these changes in terms of three urban revolutions—the emergence of cities five to ten thousand years ago, the development of industrial cities after 1750, and the explosive growth of cities in poor societies today.

The Evolution of Cities

Cities are a relatively new development in human history. Only about ten thousand years ago did our ancestors found a permanent settlement, setting the stage for the *first urban revolution.*

Preconditions of Cities

The founding of cities depended, first, on a *favorable ecology.* As glaciers drew back at the end of the last ice age, people congregated in warm regions with fertile soil. The second prerequisite was *changing technology.* At about the same time, humans discovered how to domesticate animals and cultivate crops. Whereas hunting and gathering demanded continual movement, raising food required people to remain in one place (Lenski, Lenski, & Nolan, 1991). Domesticating animals and plants also produced a material surplus, which freed some people from concentrating on food production and allowed them to build shelters, make tools, weave clothing, and take part in religious rituals. In this context, the founding of cities was truly revolutionary, enhancing specialization of labor and raising living standards as never before.

The First Cities

Historians identify Jericho as the first city. This settlement lies to the north of the Dead Sea in disputed land currently occupied by Israel. About 8000 B.C.E.,

Jericho contained about 600 people. By 4000 B.C.E., numerous cities were flourishing in the Fertile Crescent between the Tigris and Euphrates rivers in present-day Iraq and, soon afterward, along the Nile River in Egypt.

Some cities, with populations reaching fifty thousand, became centers of urban empires. Priest-kings wielded absolute power over lesser nobles, administrators, artisans, soldiers, and farmers. Slaves, captured in frequent military campaigns, labored to build monumental structures like the pyramids of Egypt (Kenyon, 1957; Hamblin, 1973; Stavrianos, 1983; Lenski, Lenski, & Nolan, 1991).

Humans independently developed cities in at least three other areas of the world. Several large, complex settlements bordered the Indus River in present-day Pakistan starting about 2500 B.C.E. Scholars date Chinese cities from 2000 B.C.E. And in Latin America, urban centers began about 1500 B.C.E. In North America, however, Native-American societies rarely formed settlements; significant urbanization did not begin until the arrival of European settlers in the seventeenth century (Lamberg-Karlovsky, 1973; Change, 1977; Coe & Diehl, 1980).

Preindustrial European Cities

European urbanization began about 1800 B.C.E. on the Mediterranean island of Crete. City-states, of which Athens is the most famous, soon grew up throughout Greece. During its Golden Age, lasting barely a century after 500 B.C.E., some three hundred thousand people living within a single square mile fashioned our Western way of life with their philosophy, arts, and political ideas. Despite such lasting achievements, Athenian society rested on the labor of slaves, perhaps one-third of the population. Their democratic principles notwithstanding, Athenian men also denied the rights of citizenship to women and foreigners (Mumford, 1961; Gouldner, 1965; Stavrianos, 1983).

As Greek civilization faded, the city of Rome grew to almost 1 million inhabitants and became the center of a vast empire. By the first century C.E., the militaristic Romans had subdued much of northern Africa, Europe, and the Middle East. In the process, Rome spread its language, arts, and technology. Four centuries later, the Roman Empire fell into disarray, a victim of its own gargantuan size, internal corruption, and militaristic appetite. Yet, between them, the Greeks and Romans had founded cities across Europe, including London, Paris, and Vienna.

The fall of the Roman Empire initiated an era of urban decline and stagnation lasting six hundred years.

The eruption of Mount Vesuvius in the year 79 C.E. buried the Italian city of Pompeii in lava, mud, and ash, killing the population before they knew what had happened. Now that archaeologists have excavated the region, visitors can see what life was like in this preindustrial city. Although modern conveniences such as electricity and indoor plumbing were absent, many of the residents of ancient Pompeii lived relatively comfortable lives.

Cities retreated within defensive walls; few encompassed more than twenty-five thousand people. Competing warlords battled for territory, inhibiting trade in the process. About the eleventh century, the "Dark Ages" came to an end as a semblance of peace allowed trade to invigorate cities once again.

Medieval cities slowly removed their walls as commerce expanded. The narrow and winding streets of London, Brussels, and Florence soon teemed with merchants, artisans, priests, peddlers, jugglers, and the occasional nobles tended by servants. Typically, occupational groups such as bakers, key makers, and carpenters clustered together in distinct sections or "quarters." In the medieval cities of Europe, cathedrals towered above all other buildings, signifying the preeminence of the Christian church.

By today's standards, medieval cities were surprisingly personal (Sjoberg, 1965). Family ties were strong, and people inside each "quarter" shared a trade and sometimes a religious and ethnic tradition. In some cases, this clustering was involuntary, as laws restricted minorities to certain districts. Jews were targets of extensive prejudice and discrimination in an era dominated by the Roman Catholic church. First in Venice and later in most of Europe, laws confined Jews to areas known as *ghettos* (from the Italian word *borghetto*, meaning "outside the city walls").

Industrial European Cities

Throughout the Middle Ages, steadily increasing commerce created an affluent urban middle class or *bourgeoisie* (French, meaning "of the town"). By the fifteenth century, the wealth-based power of the bourgeoisie rivaled the traditional authority of the hereditary nobility.

By about 1750 the Industrial Revolution was under way, triggering a *second urban revolution*, first in Europe and then in North America. Factories unleashed productive power as never before, causing cities to grow to unprecedented size, as Table 21–2 shows. During the nineteenth century the population of Paris soared from 500,000 to over 3 million, and London exploded from 800,000 to 6.5 million people (A. Weber, 1963, orig. 1899; Chandler & Fox, 1974). Most of this increase was due to migration from rural areas by people seeking a better standard of living.

Cities not only grew but changed as well. Because commerce (not religion) was dominant, the industrial-capitalist city evolved a new urban form. The old irregular streets were replaced by broad, straight boulevards that accommodated the increasing flow of commercial traffic. Steam and electric trolleys crisscrossed the expanding European cities, and, eventually, cars and trucks clogged the streets.

Lewis Mumford (1961) explains that developers divided the burgeoning industrial cities into regular-sized lots, transforming land into a commodity to be bought and sold. Finally, the cathedrals that had watched over the life of medieval cities were soon dwarfed by towering, brightly lit, and frantic central business districts made up of banks, retail stores, and office buildings.

Focused on business, cities became increasingly crowded and impersonal. People came to distance themselves from the waves of strangers all around them. Crime rates rose. Especially at the outset, a small number of industrialists lived in grand style, while for most men, women, and children, factory work proved exhausting and provided no more than bare subsistence.

Table 21–2 shows that European cities continued to grow during this century, although at a slower rate. Organized efforts by workers to improve their plight led to legal regulation of the workplace, better housing, and the right to vote. Public services such as water, sewage, and electricity further enhanced urban living. Today some urbanites still live in poverty, but a rising standard of living has partly fulfilled the city's historical promise of a better life.

Q: "American urban history began with the small town—five villages hacked out of the wilderness . . . each an "upstart" town with no past, an uncertain future, and a host of confounding and novel problems . . ." Alexander B. Callow, Jr.

Q: "In Europe, the modern European community emerged by gradual stages out of the simple town economy of the Middle Ages; by comparison, the American city leaped into being with breathtaking speed." Arthur M. Schlesinger, Jr.

Q: "I view great cities as pestilential to the morals, the health, and the liberties of man." Thomas Jefferson

The Growth of U.S. Cities

Inhabiting this continent for tens of thousands of years, Native Americans were migratory people, establishing few permanent settlements. Cities first sprang up, then, as a product of European colonization. The Spanish made an initial settlement at St. Augustine, Florida, in 1565, and the English founded Jamestown, Virginia, in 1607. New Amsterdam (later renamed New York) was settled in 1624 by the Dutch, and soon overshadowed these smaller settlements.

In 1990, the United States had 195 cities with more than 100,000 inhabitants. Three-fourths of our people live in urban places that cover a scant one-sixth of the country's land area. How we became an urban society is explained in the brief history that follows.

Colonial Settlement: 1624–1800

The metropolises of New York and Boston were, at their founding, tiny villages in a vast wilderness. Dutch New Amsterdam at the tip of Manhattan Island (1624) and English Boston (1630) each resembled medieval towns of Europe, with narrow, winding streets that still charm (and frustrate) visitors to lower Manhattan and downtown Boston. New Amsterdam was walled on the north, the site of today's Wall Street. In 1700, Boston was the largest U.S. city, with just 7,000 people.

The rational and expansive culture of capitalism soon transformed these quiet villages into thriving towns built with gridlike streets. Figure 21–4, on page 576, contrasts the medieval shape of New Amsterdam with the modern grid system of Philadelphia, founded after another half-century of economic development in 1680.

TABLE 21–2 Population Growth in Selected Industrial Cities of Europe (in thousands)

| City | Year | | | |
	1700	1800	1900	1992*
Amsterdam	172	201	510	713
Berlin	100	172	2,424	3,020
Lisbon	188	237	363	2,505
London	550	861	6,480	9,168
Madrid	110	169	539	4,577
Paris	530	547	3,330	8,589
Rome	149	153	487	3,028
Vienna	105	231	1,662	2,392

* for urban area

SOURCES: Based on data from Tertius Chandler and Gerald Fox, *3000 Years of Urban History* (New York: Academic Press, 1974), pp. 17–19; and U.S. Bureau of the Census, 1993.

TABLE 21–3 The Urban Population of the United States, 1790–1990

Year	Population (in millions)	Percent Urban
1790	3.9	5.1
1800	5.3	6.1
1820	9.6	7.3
1840	17.1	10.5
1860	31.4	19.7
1880	50.2	28.1
1900	76.0	39.7
1920	105.7	51.3
1940	131.7	56.5
1960	179.3	69.9
1980	226.5	73.7
1990	253.0	75.2

SOURCE: U.S. Bureau of the Census, 1993.

On the heels of independence from Great Britain, the United States was still an overwhelmingly rural society. In 1790 the government's first census tallied roughly 4 million people. As Table 21–3 shows, just 5 percent of them resided in cities.

Urban Expansion: 1800–1860

Early in the nineteenth century, towns began springing up along the transportation routes that opened the American West. In 1818 the National Road (now Route 40) funneled Easterners from Baltimore through the Appalachian Mountains to the Ohio Valley. A decade later the Baltimore and Ohio Railroad and the Erie Canal (1825) from New York touched off the development of cities along the Great Lakes, including Buffalo, Cleveland, and Detroit. The historical importance of water transportation for commerce accounts for the fact that virtually every one of the largest U.S. cities was founded on a waterway.

By 1860 about one-fifth of the U.S. population lived in cities. Underlying this urban expansion was the Industrial Revolution, which was transforming cities primarily in the northern states. In 1850, for example, New York City had a population ten times greater than that of Charleston, South Carolina. This division of the United States into the industrial-urban North and the agrarian-rural South was one key cause of the Civil War (Schlesinger, 1969).

The Metropolitan Era: 1860–1950

The Civil War gave an enormous boost to urbanization, as factories strained to produce the tools of combat. Now waves of people fled the countryside for cities in hopes of obtaining better jobs. Following the

NOTE: Cities grew upward, propelled by advances in building technology. In 1848, five-story iron frame buildings were big news; by 1884 a steel structure in Chicago reached 10 stories, and buildings began to utilize elevators (devised in the 1850s). By 1900 skylines reached 30 stories and, on the eve of World War I, New York had 61 buildings more than 20 stories tall. Today, Chicago's Sears Tower is the world tallest (110 stories and 1,454 feet). The technology exists to raise towers to a mile or more, restrained by high cost and people's reluctance to live that high above the ground.

Q: "In a space of time but little longer than Scarlett's seventeen years, Atlanta had grown from a single stake driven in the ground into a thriving small city of ten thousand that was the center of attention for the whole state." Margaret Mitchell, *Gone With the Wind*

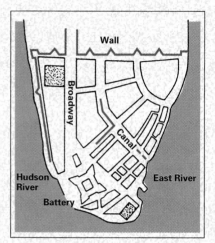
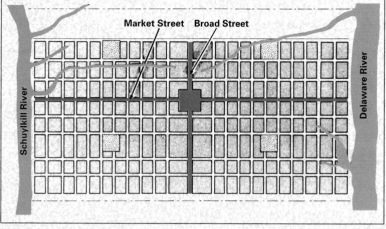

FIGURE 21–4 The Street Plans of Colonial New Amsterdam and Philadelphia
The plan of colonial New Amsterdam, shown at left, exemplifies the preindustrial urban pattern of walls enclosing a city of narrow, irregular streets. Colonial Philadelphia, founded fifty years later, reflects the industrial urban pattern of accessible cities with wide, regularly spaced, parallel and perpendicular streets to facilitate economic activity.

war tens of millions of immigrants—most from Europe—combined to form a culturally diverse urban mix. Table 21-4 shows the rapid growth of U.S. cities in the late nineteenth century.

In 1900 New York boasted 4 million residents, and Chicago—a city of scarcely 100,000 people in 1860—was closing in on 2 million. This growth marked the era of the **metropolis** (from Greek words meaning "mother city"), *a large city that socially and economically dominates an urban area.* Dozens of metropolises became the manufacturing, commercial, and residential centers of the United States.

Industrial technology changed not only the size but the physical shape of cities, pushing buildings well above the three or four stories common up to this point. By the 1880s, steel girders and mechanical elevators raised structures over ten stories high. In 1930, New York's Empire State Building became an urban wonder, a true "skyscraper" stretching 102 stories into the clouds. Railroads and highways helped cities expand outward so that, by 1920, the United States was a predominantly urban society.

Urban Decentralization: 1950–Present

The industrial metropolis reached its peak about 1950. Since then, something of a turnaround has occurred as people have deserted the downtowns in a process known as *urban decentralization* (Edmonston & Guterbock, 1984). As Table 21-4 shows, large cities of the Northeast and Midwest stopped growing—and some even lost population—in the decades after 1950. The 1990 census count found New York, for example, to have half a million fewer people than at mid-century.

But decentralization has not interrupted urbanization; cities are simply changing their form. Instead of densely packed central cities, the urban landscape now looks more and more like sprawling urban regions, a trend closely tied to the expansion of suburbs.

Suburbs and Central Cities

Just as central cities flourished a century ago, we have recently witnessed the expansion of **suburbs**, *urban areas beyond the political boundaries of a city.* Suburbs began to grow late in the nineteenth century as railroad and trolley lines enabled people to live beyond the commotion of the city and still commute "downtown" to work (Warner, 1962).

The first suburbanites were well-to-do people, imitating the pattern of the European nobility who shuttled between their country estates and town houses (Baltzell, 1979). But the growth of suburbs was also fueled by racial and ethnic prejudice. Rising immigration was adding to the social diversity of central cities, prompting many to flee to homogeneous, high-prestige

Q: "There's a green one and a pink one
   And a blue one and a yellow one,
   And they're all made out of ticky-tacky
   And they all look just the same."
   Malvina Reynolds, "Little Boxes"
DATA FILE: An analysis of urban renewal in the United States is included in the *Data File*.

NOTE: For a comparative look at urban planning, see *Urban Policies in Japan* (the Organization for Economic Cooperation and Development, 2001 L Street NW, Washington, DC 20036-4905).
RESOURCE: The Macionis and Benokraitis reader, *Seeing Ourselves*, includes two urban classics: Georg Simmel's "The Metropolis and Mental Life," and Louis Wirth's "Urbanism as a Way of Life."

TABLE 21–4 Population Growth in Selected U.S. Cities, 1870–1990

City	Population (in thousands)						
	1870	1890	1910	1930	1950	1970	1990
Baltimore	267	434	558	805	950	905	736
Boston	251	448	671	781	801	641	574
Chicago	299	1100	2,185	3,376	3,621	3,369	2,784
Dallas	7	38	92	260	434	844	1,007
Detroit	80	206	466	1,569	1,850	1,514	1,028
Los Angeles	6	50	319	1,238	1,970	2,812	3,485
Milwaukee	71	204	374	578	637	717	628
New Orleans	191	242	339	459	570	593	497
New York*	942	2,507	4,764	6,930	7,892	7,896	7,323
Philadelphia	674	1,047	1,549	1,951	2,072	1,949	1,586
St. Louis	311	452	687	822	857	622	397
San Francisco	149	299	417	634	775	716	724

*Population figures for New York in 1870 and 1890 reflect that city as presently constituted.

SOURCE: U.S. Bureau of the Census, 1993.

enclaves beyond the reach of the masses. In time, of course, less wealthy people also came to view a single-family house on its own piece of leafy suburban ground as part of the American Dream.

The postwar economic boom of the late 1940s, coupled with the mobility offered by increasingly affordable automobiles, placed suburbia within the grasp of the average household. After World War II, men and women eagerly returned to family life, igniting the baby boom described earlier in this chapter. Since central cities afforded little space for new housing construction, suburbs blossomed almost overnight. The government weighed in with guaranteed bank loans, and developers offered new, prefabricated homes at unheard-of low prices.

Levittown is the most famous of the low-cost suburbs. Built on potato fields on New York's Long Island in the late 1940s, Abraham Levitt's homes were dismissed by some as lookalike boxes, but buyers snatched up these homes as fast as Levitt could build them. By 1970, more of our population lived in the suburbs than in the central cities.

Not surprisingly, business, too, began eyeing the suburbs, and soon the suburban mall had largely replaced the downtown stores of the metropolitan era. Manufacturing companies also decentralized into industrial parks far from the high taxes, congested streets, and soaring crime rates of inner cities. The interstate highway system with its beltways encircling central cities made moving out to the suburbs almost irresistible for residents and business people alike (Rosenthal, 1974; Tobin, 1976; Geist, 1985).

Decentralization was not good news for everyone, however. Rapid suburban growth soon threw older

cities of the Northeast and Midwest into financial chaos. Population decline meant falling tax revenues. Further, as affluent people headed for the suburbs, cities were left with the burden of funding expensive social programs for the poor who stayed behind. The overall result was inner-city decay beginning about 1950. Some major cities, such as Cleveland and New York, actually plummeted to the brink of bankruptcy. Especially to white people, the deteriorating inner cities became synonymous with slum housing, crime, drugs, unemployment, the poor, and minorities. This perception fueled wave after wave of "white flight" and urban decline. Suburbs may have their share of poor housing, congestion, and crime, but they still appeal to many people because they remain largely white, unlike the inner cities, whose populations encompass a greater share of people of color (Clark, 1979; Gluck & Meister, 1979; Sternlieb & Hughes, 1983; Logan & Schneider, 1984; Stahura, 1986; Galster, 1991).

The official response to the plight of the central cities was **urban renewal**, *government programs intended to revitalize cities.* Federal and local funds have paid for the rebuilding of many inner cities. Yet critics of urban renewal charge that these programs have benefited business communities while doing little to meet the housing needs of low-income residents (Jacobs, 1961; Greer, 1965; Gans, 1982).

Postindustrial Sunbelt Cities

In the new postindustrial economy (see Chapter 15, "The Economy and Work"), people are not only moving beyond the boundaries of central cities; they are also migrating from the Snowbelt to the Sunbelt.

Q: ". . . cities, especially large cities, contribute more to the national budget than they get from it. On a per capita basis, the people living in a large urban area might get a little more than the people who live in the rest of the country, because the costs of providing some public services are often higher in densely populated areas; but the differences are never very large. On the other hand, on a per capita basis, the amount contributed to the budget by people living in a large urban area is substantially higher than the amount contributed by those who live in the rest of the country." Remy Prud'homme

Q: "The Northeastern seaboard of the United States is today the site of a remarkable development—an almost continuous stretch of urban and suburban areas from New Hampshire to northern Virginia and from the Atlantic shore to the Appalachian foothills." Jean Gottman (1961:3)

TABLE 21–5 The Ten Largest Cities in the United States, 1950 and 1990

1950

Rank	City	Population
1	New York	7,892,000
2	Chicago	3,621,000
3	Philadelphia	2,072,000
4	Los Angeles	1,970,000
5	Detroit	1,850,000
6	Baltimore	950,000
7	Cleveland	915,000
8	St. Louis	857,000
9	Boston	801,000
10	San Francisco	775,000

1990

Rank	City	Population
1	New York	7,323,000
2	Los Angeles	3,485,000
3	Chicago	2,784,000
4	Houston	1,631,000
5	Philadelphia	1,586,000
6	San Diego	1,111,000
7	Detroit	1,028,000
8	Dallas	1,007,000
9	Phoenix	983,000
10	San Antonio	936,000

SOURCE: U.S. Bureau of the Census, 1993.

The Snowbelt—the traditional industrial heartland of the United States—runs from the Northeast to the Midwest. In 1940, almost 60 percent of the U.S. population resided in the Snowbelt. By 1975, however, the Sunbelt—the South and the West—passed the Snowbelt in overall population and, by 1992, it was home to 56.2 percent of our people.

Table 21–5 shows this demographic shift by comparing the ten largest U.S. cities in 1950 and in 1990. In 1950, eight of the top ten were industrial cities of the Snowbelt, whereas, by 1990, six out of ten were postindustrial cities of the Sunbelt. The box provides a snapshot of how our nation's urban profile has changed in recent decades.

Why are Sunbelt cities faring so well? Unlike their counterparts in the Snowbelt, the postindustrial cities of the Sunbelt grew *after* urban decentralization began. Since Snowbelt cities have long been enclosed by a ring of politically independent suburbs, outward migration took place at the expense of the central city. Suburbs have played a much smaller role in the history of Sunbelt cities, which have simply expanded outward, annexing land and gaining population in the process. Chicago, for example, covers 228 square miles, whereas Houston now extends over 565.

The great sprawl of the typical Sunbelt city does have drawbacks, however. Traveling across town is time consuming, and automobile ownership is almost a necessity. Lacking a dense center, Sunbelt cities also generate far less of the excitement and intensity that draw people to New York or Chicago. Critics have long tagged Los Angeles, for example, as a vast cluster of suburbs in search of a center.

Megalopolis: Regional Cities

The decentralization of U.S. cities has produced vast urban areas that contain numerous municipalities. In 1993 the Bureau of the Census (1993) recognized 253 regional cities, which it calls *metropolitan statistical areas* (MSAs). Each MSA includes at least one city with 50,000 or more people plus densely populated surrounding counties. Almost all of the fifty fastest-growing MSAs are in the Sunbelt.

The biggest MSAs, containing more than 1 million people, are called *consolidated metropolitan statistical areas* (CMSAs). In 1991, there were nineteen CMSAs. Heading the list was New York and adjacent urban areas in Long Island, western Connecticut, and northern New Jersey, with a total population of 19 million. Next in size was the CMSA in southern California that includes Los Angeles, Riverside, and Anaheim, with a population of almost 15 million (U.S. Bureau of the Census, 1993).

Some regional cities have grown so large that they have collided with one another. The East Coast now contains a 400-mile supercity extending from New England all the way to Virginia. In the early 1960s, French geographer Jean Gottmann (1961) coined the term **megalopolis** to designate *a vast urban region containing a number of cities and their surrounding suburbs*. A megalopolis is composed of hundreds of politically independent cities and suburbs; from an airplane at night, however, one observes what appears to be a single continuous city. Other supercities of this kind are on the eastern coast of Florida and the land extending from Cleveland to Chicago. Future urban regions will undoubtedly emerge, especially in the fast-growing Sunbelt.

URBANISM AS A WAY OF LIFE

Various sociologists in Europe and the United States were among the first to contrast urban and rural life. We will briefly present their accounts of urbanism as a way of life.

Q: "Cities have been *delocalized . . .*" Jean Gottman

Q: "Urban life brings physical proximity but social distance among its inhabitants. In rural life, the people are physically far apart but socially together." L. G. Bonald

Q: "In *Gemeinschaft* [people] remain essentially united in spite of all separating factors, whereas in *Gesellschaft* they are essentially separated in spite of all uniting factors." Ferdinand Toennies

Q: "Empirically, pure *Gemeinschaft* is impossible, because all *Gemeinschaften* have rational aspects; likewise, pure *Gesellschaft* is impossible, because man's social conduct can never be entirely determined by intellect and reason." Rudolf Heberle

SOCIOLOGY OF EVERYDAY LIFE

Heading for the Sunbelt

Just as the twentieth century opened with tremendous urban growth in the North and Midwest, the twenty-first century will almost surely witness population increase and rapid urbanization in the South and West. The official tally from the 1990 census indicates that, taken as a whole, Snowbelt cities suffered a moderate drop in population, while Sunbelt population is soaring.

The figure in the box shows how the largest Snowbelt and Sunbelt cities fared during the 1980s. While two of the six most populous Snowbelt cities posted slight increases in population, four recorded substantial losses. Each of these six cities is now well below its 1950 size, when Snowbelt cities reached their peak population.

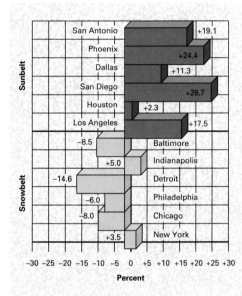

Percent Population Change, 1980–90

(U.S. Bureau of the Census, 1993)

The picture is very different if we turn to the cities of the Sunbelt, where population has grown rapidly since mid-century. All six of the largest Sunbelt cities registered population gains during the 1980s—even Houston and Dallas, which were hard hit by the economic downturn. The population growth in the other four Sunbelt cities is dramatic—similar to the explosive increases found in the Snowbelt a century ago.

Which cities—of any size—grew fastest of all during the 1980s? Across the United States, Mesa, Arizona, led the way with an 89 percent gain (to 288,000). Nine other cities had population increases of over 60 percent during the 1980s—every one in the Sunbelt.

Ferdinand Toennies: *Gemeinschaft* and *Gesellschaft*

In the late nineteenth century, the German sociologist Ferdinand Toennies (1855–1937) set out to chronicle the social traits emerging in the industrial metropolis. He contrasted rural and urban life using two concepts that have become a lasting part of sociology's terminology.

Toennies (1963; orig. 1887) used the German word ***Gemeinschaft*** (meaning roughly "community") to refer to *a type of social organization by which people are bound closely together by kinship and tradition.* Rural villagers, Toennies explained, are joined by kinship, neighborhood, and friendship. *Gemeinschaft*, then, describes any social setting in which people form what amounts to a single primary group.

By and large, argued Toennies, *Gemeinschaft* is not found in the modern city. On the contrary,

urbanization fosters ***Gesellschaft*** (a German word meaning roughly "association"), *a type of social organization by which people have weak social ties and considerable self-interest.* In the *Gesellschaft* scheme, women and men are motivated by their own needs and desires rather than a drive to enhance the well-being of everyone. City dwellers, Toennies suggested, have little sense of community or common identity and look to others mostly as a means of advancing their individual goals. Thus Toennies saw in urbanization the erosion of primary social relations in favor of the temporary, impersonal ties typical of business.

Emile Durkheim: Mechanical and Organic Solidarity

The French sociologist Emile Durkheim, whose ideas Chapter 4 ("Society") presents in detail, agreed with much of Toennies's thinking about cities. Yet

The painting Peasant Dance, *by Pieter Breughel the Elder (c. 1525/30–1569), conveys the essential unity of rural life forged by generations of kinship and neighborhood. By contrast, Fernand Léger's painting* The City *(1919) communicates the disparate images and discontinuity of experience that are commonplace in urban areas. Taken together, these two paintings capture Toennies's distinction between* Gemeinschaft *and* Gesellschaft.

Durkheim's analysis highlighted patterns of social solidarity—what binds people together. Traditional, rural life Durkheim conceptualized as *mechanical solidarity*, social bonds based on shared moral sentiments. Durkheim's concept of mechanical solidarity, with its emphasis on conformity to tradition, bears a striking similarity to Toennies's *Gemeinschaft.*

But if urbanization erodes mechanical solidarity, Durkheim explained, it also generates a new type of bonding, which he termed *organic solidarity*, social bonds based on specialization and interdependence. This concept, which parallels Toennies's *Gesellschaft*, reveals a key difference between the two thinkers. While each thought the expansion of industry and cities would undermine traditional social patterns, Durkheim was more optimistic about this historical transformation. Where societies had been built on *likeness*, in short, Durkheim now observed social organization based on *difference.*

Finally, as we noted in Chapter 4, Durkheim did not miss the fact that urban society typically offers more individual choice, moral tolerance, and personal privacy than people find in rural villages. In short, Durkheim concluded, something may be lost in the process of urbanization, but much is gained.

Georg Simmel: The Blasé Urbanite

We have already encountered the ideas of German sociologist Georg Simmel (1858–1918) in our discussion of how size affects the social dynamics of small groups (Chapter 7, "Groups and Organizations"). Simmel (1964; orig. 1905) also turned his characteristic micro-level focus to the question of how urban life shapes people's behavior and attitudes.

From the point of view of the individual, Simmel explained, the city is a crush of people, objects, and events. Understandably, the urbanite is easily overwhelmed with stimulation, he continued, and, as a coping strategy, develops a *blasé attitude*. In the city, in other words, people learn to respond selectively by tuning out much of what goes on around them. City dwellers are not without sensitivity and compassion for others, although they sometimes seem "cold and heartless." But urban detachment, as Simmel saw it, is better understood as a technique for social survival by which people stand aloof from most others so they can devote their time and energy to those who really matter.

The Chicago School: Robert Park and Louis Wirth

Sociologists in the United States soon joined their European colleagues in exploring the rapidly growing cities. The first major sociology program in the United States took root a century ago at the University of Chicago, then a major metropolis exploding with population and cultural diversity. The life of Chicago was the focus of generations of sociologists, and the research these men and women produced yielded a

SOCIAL SURVEY: "How much satisfaction do you get from the city or place you live in?" (*STUDENT CHIP Social Survey Software*, SATCITY1; GSS 1973–91, N = 19,648)

	High	Middle	Low
Hi SES	51.2%	44.7%	4.1%
Middle SES	47.2%	46.1%	6.7%
Low SES	45.9%	45.2%	8.9%

Afri Amer	37.5%	51.2%	11.3%
Latino	41.8%	49.9%	8.3%
Whites	49.4%	44.7%	6.0%

RESOURCE: A critical look at the physical and social development of U.S. cities is the article by Joe Feagin and Robert Parker, "The Urban Real Estate Game," included in the Macionis and Benokraitis reader, *Seeing Ourselves*.

rich understanding of many dimensions of urban life. While these early sociologists were inspired by European theorists like Toennies, Durkheim, and Simmel, their unique contribution was making the city a laboratory for actual research.

Perhaps the greatest urban sociologist of all was Robert Park, who for decades provided the leadership that established sociology in the United States. Park is introduced in the box on page 582.

A second major figure in the Chicago School of urban sociology was Louis Wirth (1897–1952). Wirth's (1938) best-known contribution is a brief essay in which he systematically blended the ideas of Toennies, Durkheim, Simmel, and Park into a comprehensive theory of urban life.

Wirth began by defining the city as a setting with a large, dense, and diverse population. These traits, he argued, combine to form an impersonal, superficial, and transitory way of life. Living among millions of others, urbanites come into contact with many more people than rural residents do. Thus, if city people pay any mind to others, they usually know them only in terms of *what they do*: as bus driver, florist, or grocery store clerk, for instance.

Urban relationships are not only specialized, Wirth explained, they are also founded on self-interest. For example, shoppers view grocers as the source ¡of goods, while grocers see shoppers as a source of income. These men and women may pleasantly exchange greetings, but friendship is not the reason for their interaction. Finally, limited social involvement coupled with great social diversity also make city dwellers more tolerant than rural villagers. Rural communities often jealously enforce their narrow traditions, but the heterogeneous population of a city rarely shares any single code of moral conduct (T. Wilson, 1985).

Critical evaluation. Both in Europe and in the United States, early sociologists focused on urban life. On balance, this research offers a mixed view of urban living. On the one hand, rapid urbanization troubled the sociological pioneers. Toennies and Wirth, especially, recognized that the personal ties and traditional morality of rural life are lost in the anonymous rush of the city. On the other hand, Durkheim and Park emphasized urbanism's positive face, including greater personal autonomy and a wider range of life choices.

And what of Wirth's specific claims about urbanism as a way of life? Decades of research have provided support for only some of his conclusions. Wirth correctly maintained that urban settings do sustain a weaker sense of community than do rural areas.

But one can easily forget that conflict is found in the countryside as well as the city. Furthermore, while urbanites treat most people impersonally, they typically welcome such privacy, and, of course, they do maintain close personal relationships with a select few (Keller, 1968; Cox, 1971; Macionis, 1978; Wellman, 1979; Lee et al., 1984).

Where the analysis of Wirth and others falls short, too, is in painting urbanism in broad strokes that overlook the effects of class, race, and gender. Herbert Gans (1968) explains that there are many types of urbanites—rich and poor, black and white, Anglo and Latino, women and men—all leading distinctive lives. In fact, cities often intensify these social differences. That is, we see the extent of social diversity most clearly in cities where different categories of people reside in the largest numbers (Spates & Macionis, 1987).

Urban Ecology

Sociologists (especially members of the Chicago School) also developed **urban ecology**, *the study of the link between the physical and social dimensions of cities.* Chapter 3 ("Culture") spotlighted cultural ecology, the study of how cultural patterns are related to the physical environment. Urban ecology is one application of this approach, revealing how the physical and social forms of cities are closely linked.

Consider, for example, why cities are located where they are. The first cities emerged in fertile regions where the ecology favored raising crops and, thus, settlement. Preindustrial societies, concerned with defense, built their cities on mountains (Athens was situated on an outcropping of rock) or surrounded by water (Paris and Mexico City were founded on islands). After the Industrial Revolution, the unparalleled importance of economics situated cities near rivers and natural harbors that facilitated trade.

Urban ecologists also study the physical design of cities. In 1925 Ernest W. Burgess, a student and colleague of Robert Park, described land use in Chicago in terms of *concentric zones* that look rather like a bull's-eye. City centers, Burgess observed, are business districts bordered by a ring of factories, followed by residential rings with housing that becomes more expensive the farther it stands from the noise and pollution of the city's center.

Homer Hoyt (1939) refined Burgess's observations by noting that distinctive districts sometimes form *wedge-shaped sectors*. For example, one fashionable area may develop along a major road next to another, or an industrial district may extend outward from a city's center along a railroad line.

PROFILE

Robert Ezra Park: Walking the City Streets

I suspect that I have actually covered more ground, tramping about in cities in different parts of the world, than any other living man. (1950:viii)

Robert Ezra Park (1864–1944) was a man with a single consuming passion—the city. Walking the streets of the world's great cities, he delighted in observing the full range of human turbulence and triumph. Through his thirty-year career at the University of Chicago, he led a group of dedicated sociologists in direct, systematic observation of urban life.

Park acknowledged his debt to European sociologists including Ferdinand Toennies and Georg Simmel (with whom Park studied in Germany). But Park established a new phase in urban sociology by advocating the *direct observation* of the city rather than what he thought amounted to armchair theorizing on the part of his European teachers. At Park's urging, generations of sociologists at the University of Chicago rummaged through practically every part of their city.

From this research, Park came to understand the city as a highly ordered mosaic of distinctive regions, including industrial districts, ethnic communities, and vice areas. These so-called natural areas all evolved in relation to one another, forming an urban ecology. To Park, the city was a living social organism: truly the human kaleidoscope. Urban variety, Park maintained, is the key to the timeless attraction of people to cities:

The attraction of the metropolis is due in part to the fact that in the long run every individual finds somewhere among the varied manifestations of city life the sort of environment in which he expands and feels at ease; he finds, in short, the moral climate in which his particular nature obtains the stimulations that bring his innate dispositions to full and free expression. It is, I suspect, motives of this kind . . . which drove many, if not most, of the young men and young women from the security of their homes in the country into the big, booming confusion and excitement of city life. (1967:41; orig. 1925)

Park was well aware that many people saw the city as disorganized and even dangerous. The urban sociologist recognized an element of truth in these assertions but, still, he found cities intoxicating. Walking the city streets, he became convinced that urban places offer a better way of life—the promise of greater human freedom and opportunity than we can find elsewhere.

SOURCES: Based on Park (1967; orig. 1925) and Park (1950).

Chauncy Harris and Edward Ullman (1945) added yet another insight: As cities decentralize, they lose their single-center form in favor of a *multicentered model*. As cities grow, residential areas, industrial parks, and shopping districts typically push away from one another. Few people wish to live close to industrial areas, for example, so the city becomes a mosaic of distinct districts.

Social area analysis adds another twist to urban ecology by investigating what people in specific neighborhoods have in common. Three factors seem to

explain most of the variation—family patterns, social class, and race and ethnicity (Shevky & Bell, 1955; Johnston, 1976). Families with children gravitate to areas offering large apartments or single-family homes and good schools. The rich generally seek high-prestige neighborhoods, often in the central city near many of the city's cultural attractions. People with a common social heritage tend to cluster together in distinctive communities.

Finally, Brian Berry and Philip Rees (1969) have managed to tie together many of these insights. They explain that distinct family types tend to settle in the concentric zones described by Ernest Burgess. Specifically, households with few children tend to cluster toward the city's center, while those with more children live farther away. Social class differences are primarily responsible for the sector-shaped districts described by Homer Hoyt as, for instance, the rich occupy one "side of the tracks" and the poor, the other. And racial and ethnic neighborhoods are found at various points throughout the city, consistent with Harris and Ullman's multicentered model.

Critical evaluation. After almost a century of research, urban ecologists have succeeded in linking the physical and social dimensions of urban life. But, as the researchers themselves concede, their conclusions paint an overly simplified picture of urban life. Critics chime in that urban ecology errs to the extent that it implies that cities take shape simply from the choices people make. More correctly, they assert, urban development responds more to powerful elites than to ordinary citizens (Molotch, 1976; Feagin, 1983).

A final criticism holds that urban ecologists have studied only U.S. cities and only during a single historical period. What we have learned about industrial cities may not apply to preindustrial towns; similarly, even among industrial cities, socialist settlements differ from their capitalist counterparts. In sum, there is good reason to doubt that any single ecological model will account for the full range of urban diversity.

The Historical Importance of Cities

While assessing the significance of urbanization, we need to step back and reflect on the central place of cities in the drama of human history. This importance is captured in the fact that the word "civilization" has the Latin root *civis*—meaning "city dweller." Like the ancient Romans, the early Greeks recognized this link; their word *polis*—meaning "city"—is the root of politics, the core of Greek life.

But our society has always been ambivalent about urban life. As he assumed the presidency in 1800, Thomas Jefferson repudiated the city as a "pestilence to the morals, the health and the liberties of man" (quoted in Glaab, 1963:52). Almost a century later, English author and Nobel prize winner Rudyard Kipling echoed those sentiments upon a visit to Chicago: "Having seen it, I urgently desire never to see it again. It is inhabited by savages" (quoted in Rokove, 1975:22). Others have disagreed, of course, siding with the ancient Greeks, who viewed the city as the only place where humanity can expect to find the "good life."

Why do cities provoke such spirited and divergent reactions? The answer lies in their ability to encapsulate and intensify human culture. Cities have been the setting for some of the greatest human virtues (the cultural developments of classical Athens) as well as the greatest human failings (the militarism and violence of classical Rome or Nazi Berlin).

For more than 350 years, the United States has steadily urbanized as people have sought a better way of life and, as National Map 21–1, on page 584, shows, baby boomers—the core of the U.S. labor force—are overrepresented in urban regions even today. But, despite greater economic opportunity, many social problems—poverty, crime, racial tensions, environmental pollution—are most serious in cities.

In short, the city is an intricate weave of noble accomplishments, attractive opportunities, and wretched shortcomings. As we shall see in the concluding sections of this chapter, the greatest test of the city to raise living standards is now underway in economically less-developed societies.

URBANIZATION IN POOR SOCIETIES

Twice in human history the world has experienced a revolutionary expansion of cities. The first urban revolution began about 8000 B.C.E. with the first urban settlements, and continued as permanent settlements later appeared on different continents. The second urban revolution began about 1750 and lasted for two centuries as the Industrial Revolution touched off rapid growth of cities in Europe and North America.

A third urban revolution was underway by 1950, but this time the change is taking place not in industrial societies where, as Global Map 21–2 shows, 75 percent of people are already city dwellers. Extraordinary urban growth is now occurring in the less-developed societies. In 1950, about 25 percent of the people living in poor societies inhabited cities; by 1990, the proportion had risen to 40 percent; by 2005, it will exceed 50 percent. Moreover, in 1950 only seven cities in the world had populations over 5 million, and just two of these were in poor societies. By 1990, thirty-three cities had passed this mark, and twenty-four of them were in less-developed countries (U.S. Bureau of the Census, 1993).

Table 21–6, on page 586, looks back to 1980 and ahead to 2000, comparing the size of the world's ten largest urban areas (cities and surrounding suburbs). In 1980, six of the top ten were in industrialized societies; three were in the United States. By the beginning of the next century, however, only four of the ten will be situated in industrialized nations: two in Japan, one in

NOTE: The Latin word *civis*—root of civilization—means a "city dweller."

THE MAP: Baby boomers have migrated to areas of the country where jobs are most plentiful. Not surprisingly, these counties are also those in which median incomes are relatively high.

GLOBAL: The population density of the United States (1990) is 69 people per square mile. The world total is 101. By region: Africa, 57; Latin America, 33; North America, 33; East Asia, 293; South Asia, 289; Europe, 266; Oceania, 8. (U.S. Bureau of the Census)

Seeing Ourselves

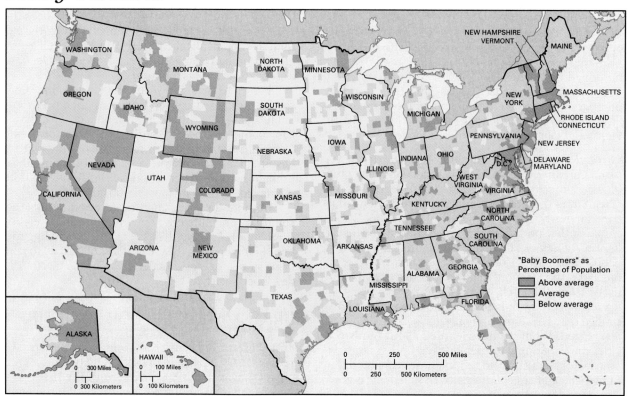

NATIONAL MAP 21–1 Baby Boomers: Residential Patterns Across the United States

About 30 percent of the U.S. population falls into the category of "baby boomers," the generation born between the end of World War II, in 1945, and 1970. The map identifies counties that have an above-average population of baby boomers. What can you say about the places that these men and women have chosen to live? Why do you think they have moved there?

Adapted from *American Demographics* magazine, Dec. 1992, p. 2. Reprinted with permission. ©1992, *American Demograhics* magazine, Ithaca, New York. Data from the 1990 decennial census.

South Korea, with just one in the United States. The majority will be in less economically developed societies.

These growing urban areas not only will be the world's largest; they will encompass unprecedented populations. Relatively rich societies such as Japan may have the resources to provide for cities with upwards of 30 million people, but for poor societies, such as Mexico and Brazil, such supercities will tax resources that are already severely strained.

To understand the third urban revolution, recall that many poor societies are now entering the high-growth stage of demographic transition. Falling death rates have fueled a population explosion in Latin America, Asia, and, especially, Africa. For urban areas, the rate of growth is *twice* as high because, in addition to natural increase, millions of migrants leave the countryside each year in search of jobs, health care, education, and conveniences like running water and electricity. Political events can also "push" migration as, for example, when elites seize land from peasants (London, 1987).

Cities do offer more opportunities than rural areas, but they provide no quick fix for the massive problems of escalating population and grinding poverty. Many burgeoning cities in less-developed societies—including Mexico City, described at the beginning of this chapter—are simply unable to meet the basic needs of much of their population. Thousands of rural people

GLOBAL: London was the first city to reach 2 million about 1840; by 1900, only four cities had this number of people (Berlin, Paris, and New York). In 1985, there were 85 cities with 2 million or more people; by 2000, projections place 170 cities over this mark.

Q: "Here where so late the appalling sound,
    Of savage yells, the woods resound,
    New smiling Ceres waves her sheaf,
    And cities rise in bold relief."
Unknown bard in early Cincinnati

Window on the World

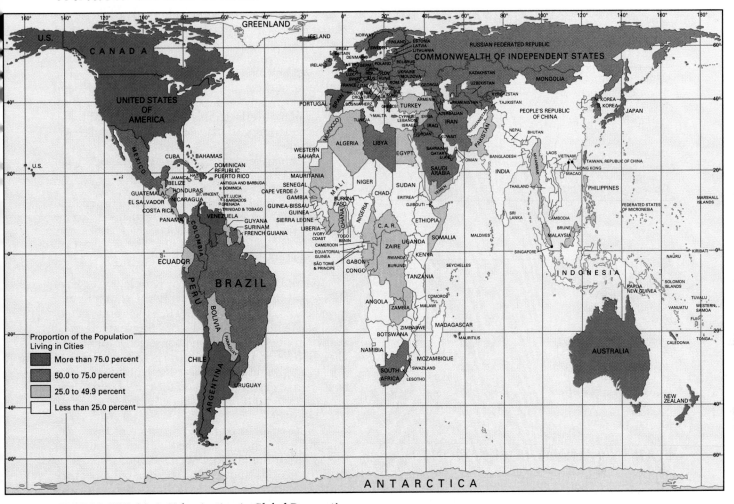

GLOBAL MAP 21–2 Urbanization in Global Perspective

Urbanization is closely linked to economic development. Thus rich nations—including the United States and Canada—have more than three-fourths of their populations in cities, while in the poorest countries of the world—found in Africa and Asia—fewer than one-fourth of the people live in urban centers. Urbanization is now extremely rapid in poor countries, however, with emerging "supercities" of unprecedented size.

From *Peters Atlas of the World* (1990).

stream into Mexico City every day, even though more than 10 percent of the *current* 25 million residents have no running water in their homes, 15 percent lack sewerage facilities, and the city can process only half the trash and garbage produced now. To make matters worse, exhaust from factories and cars chokes everyone, rich and poor alike (Friedrich, 1984; Gorman, 1991).

Like other major cities throughout Latin America, Africa, and Asia, Mexico City is surrounded by wretched shantytowns—settlements of makeshift homes built from discarded materials. As explained in Chapter 11 ("Global Stratification"), even city dumps are home to thousands of poor people, who pick through the waste hoping to find enough to ensure their survival for another day.

Chapter 21 Population and Urbanization **585**

Q: This late-medieval poem by Robert Crowley expressed the growing impersonality of city life:
"And this is a city,
In name but in deed
It is a pack of people
That seek after meed [profit]
For officers and all

Do seek their own gain
But for the wealth of the commons
No one taketh pain.
And hell without order
I may it well call
Where every man is for himself
And no man is for all."

TABLE 21–6 The World's Ten Largest Urban Areas, 1980 and 2000

1980

Urban Area	Population (in millions)
New York, U.S.A.	16.5
Tokyo-Yokohama, Japan	14.4
Mexico City, Mexico	14.0
Los Angeles-Long Beach, U.S.A.	10.6
Shanghai, China	10.0
Buenos Aires, Argentina	9.7
Paris, France	8.5
Moscow, U.S.S.R.	8.0
Beijing, China	8.0
Chicago, U.S.A.	7.7

2000 (projected)

Urban Area	Population (in millions)
Tokyo-Yokohama, Japan	30.0
Mexico City, Mexico	27.9
São Paulo, Brazil	25.4
Seoul, South Korea	22.0
Bombay, India	15.4
New York, U.S.A.	14.7
Osaka-Kobe-Kyoto, Japan	14.3
Tehran, Iran	14.3
Rio de Janeiro, Brazil	14.2
Calcutta, India	14.1

SOURCES: United Nations, 1993, and U.S. Bureau of the Census, 1993.

LOOKING AHEAD: POPULATION AND URBANIZATION IN THE TWENTY-FIRST CENTURY

The demographic analysis presented in this chapter points to some disturbing trends. We see, first of all, that the earth is gaining unprecedented population as death rates drop even as birth rates remain high in much of the world. The numbers lead us to the sobering conclusion that controlling global population in the next century will be a monumental task.

As we have seen, population growth is currently greatest in the least economically developed societies of the world, those that lack productive capacity to support their present populations, much less their

future ones. Most of the privileged inhabitants of rich societies are spared the trauma of poverty. But supporting about 90 million additional people on our planet each year—80 million of these added to poor societies—will require a global commitment to provide not only food but housing, schools, and employment—all of which are in tragically short supply. The well-being of the entire world may ultimately depend on resolving many of the economic and social problems of poor, overly populated countries and bridging the widening gulf between the "have" and "have-not" societies.

Describing recent population growth as "a great wave," one U.S. government official put it:

> I see the world population movement as the effort to construct a breakwater—a structure that will stop the wave and prevent it from engulfing and sweeping away centuries of human development and civilization. (quoted in Gupte, 1984:323)

As great concentrations of people, cities have always had the power to intensify the triumphs and tragedies of human existence. Thus the world's demographic, environmental, and social problems are most evident in cities, especially in poor societies. In Mexico City, São Paulo (Brazil), Kinshasa (Zaire), Bombay (India), and Manila (the Philippines), urban problems now seem to defy solution, and the end of remarkable urban growth in the poor societies of the world is nowhere in sight.

Earlier chapters point up two different answers to this problem. One view, linked with modernization theory, holds that as poor societies industrialize (as Western Europe and North America did a century ago), greater productivity will simultaneously raise living standards and this, in turn, will reduce population growth. A second view, associated with dependency theory, argues that such progress is unlikely as long as poor societies remain economically dependent on rich societies.

Throughout history, the city has improved people's living standards more than any other type of settlement. The question facing humanity now is whether cities in poor societies will be able to meet the needs of vastly larger populations in the coming century. The answer—which rests on issues of international relations, global economic ties, and simple justice—will affect us all.

SUMMARY

1. Fertility and mortality, measured as crude birth rates and crude death rates, are major components of population growth. In global terms, fertility, mortality, and population growth in North America are relatively low.

2. Migration, another key demographic concept, has special importance to the historical growth of cities.

3. Demographers employ age-sex pyramids to graphically represent the composition of a population and to project population trends. The sex ratio refers to a society's balance of females and males.

4. Historically, world population grew slowly because high birth rates were largely offset by high death rates. About 1750, a demographic transition began as world population rose sharply, mostly due to falling death rates.

5. Thomas Robert Malthus warned that population growth would outpace food production, resulting in social calamity. Contradicting Malthus's ominous predictions, demographic transition theory holds that technological advances gradually prompt a drop in birth rates. Although this leveling off has occurred in industrial societies, in poor societies declining death rates coupled with continued high birth rates are swelling population to unprecedented levels.

6. Research shows that lower birth rates and improved economic productivity in poor societies both result from improving the social position of women.

7. World population is expected to reach 8 billion by the year 2025. Such an increase will likely overwhelm many poor societies, where most of the increase will take place.

8. Closely related to population growth is urbanization. The first urban revolution began with the appearance of cities some 10,000 years ago; by the start of the common era, cities had emerged in most regions of the world except for North America.

9. Urbanization is associated with a dramatic increase in the division of labor, with people assuming a wide range of highly specialized, productive roles in society.

10. Preindustrial cities are characterized by small buildings and narrow, winding streets, personal social ties, and rigid social inequality.

11. A second urban revolution began about 1750 as the Industrial Revolution propelled rapid urban growth in Europe. The structure of cities changed, as planners created wide, regular streets to facilitate trade. Their emphasis on commercial life and the increasing size of urban areas rendered city life more anonymous.

12. Urbanism came to North America with European settlers. A string of colonial towns dotting the Atlantic coastline gave way by 1850 to hundreds of new cities from coast to coast.

13. By 1920, a majority of the U.S. population lived in urban settings, and several metropolises encompassed millions of inhabitants.

14. Since 1950, U.S. cities have decentralized. The growth of suburbs is one trait of the postindustrial society. Newer, rapidly growing Sunbelt cities are geographically larger than older, Snowbelt cities.

15. Rapid urbanization in Europe during the nineteenth century led early sociologists to contrast rural and urban life. Ferdinand Toennies built his analysis on the concepts of *Gemeinshaft* and *Gesellschaft*. Emile Durkheim's concepts of mechanical solidarity and organic solidarity closely parallel those of Toennies. Georg Simmel claimed that the overstimulation of city life produced a blasé attitude in urbanites.

16. At the University of Chicago, Robert Park hailed cities for permitting greater social freedom. Louis Wirth reasoned that large, dense, heterogeneous populations generated a way of life characterized by impersonality, self-interest, and tolerance of people's differences. Urban ecology studies the interplay of social and physical dimensions of the city.

17. A third urban revolution is now occurring in poor societies of the world, where most of the world's largest cities will soon be found.

KEY CONCEPTS

age-sex pyramid a graphic representation of the age and sex of a population

crude birth rate the number of live births in a given year for every thousand people in a population

crude death rate the number of deaths in a given year for every thousand people in a population

demographic transition theory a thesis linking population patterns to a society's level of technological development

demography the study of human population

fertility the incidence of childbearing in a society's population

Gemeinschaft a type of social organization by which people are bound closely together by kinship and tradition

Gesellschaft a type of social organization by which people have weak social ties and considerable self-interest

infant mortality rate the number of deaths among infants under one year of age for each thousand live births in a given year

life expectancy the average life span of a society's population

megalopolis a vast urban region containing a number of cities and their surrounding suburbs

metropolis a large city that socially and economically dominates an urban area

migration the movement of people into and out of a specified territory

mortality the incidence of death in a society's population

sex ratio the number of males for every hundred females in a given population

suburbs urban areas beyond the political boundaries of a city

urban ecology the study of the link between the physical and social dimensions of cities

urbanization the concentration of humanity into cities

urban renewal government programs intended to revitalize cities

zero population growth the level of reproduction that maintains population at a steady state

CRITICAL-THINKING QUESTIONS

1. Explain the significance of fertility and mortality. Change in which of these two variables has been of greater importance in increasing global population?

2. How does demographic transition theory link population patterns to technological development?

3. Sketch some of the changes wrought by the three urban revolutions in human history.

4. According to Ferdinand Toennies, Emile Durkheim, Georg Simmel, and Louis Wirth, what characterizes urbanism as a way of life? Note several differences in the ideas of these thinkers.

SUGGESTED READINGS

Classic Sources

Ehrlich, Paul R. *The Population Bomb*. New York: Ballantine Books, 1968.

This brief book, its reputation tarnished by some predictions that did not come to pass, nevertheless was crucial in igniting the contemporary debate over increasing global population.

Ferdinand Toennies. *Community and Society (Gemeinschaft und Gesellschaft)*. New York: Harper & Row, 1963; orig. 1887.

This classic comparison of rural and urban social organization—widely cited but rarely read—introduced many of the themes that shaped urban sociology ever since.

Robert E. Park and Ernest W. Burgess. *The City*. Chicago: University of Chicago Press, 1925.

Reading this collection of early essays by Park, Burgess, and their colleagues, one can trace the development of urban sociology in the United States.

Contemporary Sources

Steve H. Murdock and David R. Ellis. *Applied Demography: An Introduction to Basic Concepts, Methods, and Data*. Boulder, Colo.: Westview Press, 1991.

This book provides detail about demography, with an emphasis on applying its findings to policy formulation.

Rob Kling, Spencer Olin, and Mark Poster. *Postsuburban California: The Transformation of Orange County Since World War II*. Berkeley: University of California Press, 1991.

This historical case study of Orange County, which spreads south from Los Angeles and whose population has grown tenfold since 1945, explores the social changes that accompany a growth boom.

Stephanie Golden. *The Women Outside: Meaning and Myths of Homelessness*. Berkeley: University of California Press, 1992.

The author argues that our understanding of the urban problem of homelessness—especially when it involves women—is distorted by cultural mythology about the poor.

Ira Katznelson. *Marxism and the City*. New York: Oxford University Press, 1992.

This book describes the introduction of Marxist theory after the 1960s into an area of sociology previously dominated by the urban ecology approach.

Herbert J. Gans, *People, Plans, and Policies: Essays on Poverty, Racism, and Other National Urban Problems*. New York: Columbia University/Russell Sage Foundation, 1991.

A collection of essays by one of sociology's most engaging thinkers, this book links theory and social policy as it confronts a host of contemporary problems.

Min Zhou. *Chinatown: A Socioeconomic Portrait of an Urban Enclave*. Philadelphia: Temple University Press, 1992.

This account of economic life in New York's Chinatown argues that ethnic enclaves offer significant economic opportunity to many of their inhabitants.

Joe R. Feagin and Robert Parker. *Building American Cities: The Urban Real Estate Game*. 2d ed. Englewood Cliffs, N.J.: Prentice Hall, 1990.

The central role of wealth and power in the growth and decline of U.S. cities is the focus of this paperback.

Edmund P. Fowler. *Building Cities That Work*. Montreal: McGill-Queen's University Press, 1992.

This critique of urban development in the United States claims that the hundreds of billions of dollars spent on reshaping cities have little positive impact.

Ron Powers. *Far from Home: Life and Loss in Two American Towns*. New York: Random House, 1991.

This story of two communities—Cairo, Illinois, and Kent, Connecticut—explores the erosion of community ties in the United States.

Global Sources

Nezar Alsayyad. *Cities and Caliphs: On the Genesis of Arab Muslim Urbanism*. Westport, Conn.: Greenwood, 1991.

This examination of the historical emergence of the Muslim city in the seventh and eighth centuries explains that urbanization flourished in some parts of the world precisely as it waned in Europe.

Elise F. Jones, Jacquiline Darroch Forrest, Stanley K. Henshaw, Jane Silverman, and Aida Torres. *Pregnancy, Contraception, and Family Planning in Industrialized Countries*. New Haven, Conn.: Yale University Press, 1989.

This comparative analysis of twenty nations focuses on the availability of contraception and the effect of contraception policies on fertility.

Richard V. Knight and Gary Gappert, eds. *Cities in a Global Society*. Newbury Park, Calif.: Sage, 1989.

This collection of essays investigates the role of cities in an increasingly interconnected world.

Ed McGowin, *Grown Men Playing with the Planet Earth*

DATA FILE: The *Data File* provides an outline for this chapter, supplementary lecture topics, and discussion issues.

Q: "I am pessimistic about the human race because it is too ingenious for its own good. Our approach to nature is to beat it into submission. We would stand a better chance of survival if we accommodated ourselves to this planet and viewed it appreciatively instead of skeptically and dictatorially." E. B. White

Q: "The 'control of nature' is a phrase conceived in arrogance, born of the Neanderthal age of biology and philosophy, when it was supposed that nature exists for the convenience of man." Rachel Carson (1962:297)

RESOURCE: An excerpt from Rachel Carson's *Silent Spring* is among the classics included in the Macionis and Benokraitis reader, *Seeing Ourselves.*

The Natural Environment

*W*here can you go to enjoy truly "natural" surroundings? Surely not to the crowded and often litter-strewn beaches of New Jersey or to the boat-choked waters of the midwestern Great Lakes. Farther west, mining, development, and tourism have transformed many of the scenic peaks and valleys of the Rocky Mountains; and the great forests of the Pacific Northwest are falling under the march of commercial logging, road construction, and new housing projects.

Nor would we have an easier time finding "natural" surroundings elsewhere in the world. Industry in Latin America is rapidly expanding, leaving its mark on the land, the water, and the air. The population of African nations is rising faster than anywhere on earth, so that villages and cities continue to push farther and farther into the countryside. To the east, even Nepal—a remote Asian

kingdom high in the Himalaya Mountains—now swarms with visitors, and is awash with everything they leave behind.

Perhaps the single remaining "natural" region of the world is Antarctica, the frozen continent that spreads about the earth's South Pole. This expanse of ice and snow—covering five million square miles, making it larger than Europe—is essentially the same today as it was when British sea captain James Cook skirted it in 1773. What accounts for this remarkable stability? Simply put, Antarctica is the only continent on earth that is virtually uninhabited by human beings.

A steady-state environment may seem odd to members of our society. After all, over the last two hundred years, the United States and other industrial nations have engineered remarkable transformations of the land. According to one analyst, humanity's remaking of the earth during the last two

Q: "Man has lost the capacity to foresee and to forestall. He will end by destroying the earth." Albert Schweitzer

Q: "We cannot command nature except by obeying her." Francis Bacon

Q: "For the first time in the history of the world, every human being is now subjected to contact with dangerous chemicals from the moment of conception until death." Rachel Carson

NOTE: The sub-field of environmental sociology has emerged to focus on social dimensions of environmental issues; demographers and rural sociologists have also shared this concern.

NOTE: Environmentalists use the term "overshoot" to refer to exceeding the carrying capacity of an environment (intentionally or otherwise).

centuries has not only been greater than during the rest of our 250,000-year history, it actually exceeds changes to our planet from all causes over the course of the last billion years (Milbrath, 1989).

To be sure, many of these changes have been beneficial for humanity. As noted in past chapters, life expectancy in industrial societies has risen steadily to an unprecedented level. Moreover, as members of rich societies, we enjoy a level of material comfort that our ancestors scarcely could have imagined. However, as this chapter explains, we are also becoming aware that our achievements carry both costs and risks. Simply put, the way of life that has evolved in rich societies places such great strain on the earth's natural environment that it threatens the future of the planet and all life on it.

This disturbing fact also explains why environmental concerns fall within the scope of sociology. To state the matter explicitly: *Because humans have a profound effect on the world, the state of the natural environment depends primarily on how human beings organize social life.* In this chapter, we shall examine how and why environmental concerns have arisen wherever human societies have flourished—and especially where they have prospered the most.

ECOLOGY: THE STUDY OF THE NATURAL ENVIRONMENT

The focus of this chapter is **ecology**, *the study of the interaction of living organisms and the natural environment.* Ecology is by definition interdisciplinary, involving the work of sociologists, other social scientists, as well as natural scientists. The present discussion, however, is limited to those aspects of ecology that have a direct connection to other, now familiar sociological concepts and issues.

The concept **natural environment** refers to *the earth's surface and atmosphere, including various living organisms as well as the air, water, soil, and other resources necessary to sustain life.* Like every other living species, humans are dependent on the natural environment for everything from basic food, clothing, and shelter to the materials and advanced sources of energy needed to construct and operate our automobiles, airplanes, and all kinds of electronic devices. Yet humans stand apart from other species of life in our capacity for culture; we alone take deliberate action to remake the world according to our own interests and desires. Thus our species is unique in its capacity to transform the world, for better and worse.

There is now abundant evidence that, in the choices we have made in striving to build a life for ourselves, humanity has significantly threatened the natural environment. Ecologists describe this situation as an **environmental deficit**, *a situation in which the negative, long-term consequences of decisions about the natural environment outweigh whatever short-term benefits may accrue* (Bohrmann, 1990).

The concept of environmental deficit implies three important ideas. First, it reminds us again that the state of the environment is a *social issue*, because it reflects choices people make about how we should live. Second, this concept suggests that environmental damage—to the air, land, or water—is often *unintended*. By focusing on the short-term benefits of, say, cutting down forests or using easily disposable packaging, we fail to see (or choose to ignore) the long-term environmental effects of these choices. Third, in some but not all respects, the environmental deficit is *reversible*. In as much as societies have created environmental problems, in other words, societies can undo most of them.

The Global Dimension

Any study of the natural environment is necessarily global in scope. Regardless of humanity's political divisions, the planet constitutes a single **ecosystem**, defined as *the system composed of the interaction of all living organisms and their natural environment.*

The Greek meaning of *eco* is "house," consistent with the simple observation that our planet is our home. Even a brief look at the operation of the global ecosystem confirms that all living things and their natural environment are *interrelated*. Changes to any part of the natural environment ripple through the entire ecosystem, so that what happens in one part of the world inevitably has consequences in another.

To illustrate, consider the effects of our use of chlorofluorocarbons (CFCs, which are marketed under the brand name "Freon") as a propellant in aerosol spray cans and as a gas in refrigerators, freezers and air conditioners. There is little doubt that CFCs have improved our lives in various ways. But as CFCs are released into the air, they accumulate in the upper atmosphere, where, reacting with sunlight, they form chlorine atoms. These, in turn, destroy ozone. The ozone layer in the atmosphere serves to limit the amount of harmful ultraviolet radiation reaching the earth from the sun. Thus, recent evidence of a "hole" in the ozone layer (in the atmosphere over Antarctica) may signal a rise in human skin cancers and countless other effects to plants and animals (Clarke, 1984a).

GLOBAL: Even as Costa Rican beef production shot upward after 1960, the per capita consumption of beef in that country fell slightly. This is an example of the pattern of making products for export, which can ignore the needs of the local people.

GLOBAL: Over a lifetime, a child born in the United States will consume about five times the total resources that a child born in a poor society will.

Q: "Technology has not only failed to ease the conflict between man and nature, it has aggravated that conflict..." Mikhail Gorbachev

NOTE: The increase in productivity of industrial societies is not simply a matter of technology but also of greatly increased energy consumption.

GLOBAL SOCIOLOGY

The Hamburger Connection: The Global Consequences of What We Do at Home

The earth constitutes a single ecosystem, but not every region of the globe has the same power to shape the natural environment. Members of rich societies such as our own consume a disproportionate share of all the world's resources, so it stands to reason that even small decisions we make in our everyday lives can add up to large consequences for the planet as a whole.

Consider the commonplace practice of enjoying the all-American hamburger. McDonald's and dozens of other fast-food chains serve billions of hamburgers each year to eager customers across North America, Europe, and Japan. This appetite for beef creates a large market for cattle, which has greatly expanded cattle ranching in Latin America. As our consumption of hamburgers has grown (even as the price of beef has steadily gone up), ranchers in Brazil, Costa Rica, and other Latin American countries are devoting more and more land to cattle grazing.

Latin American cattle graze on grass (rather than being grain fed, as is the practice in this country). This diet produces the lean meat demanded by the fast-food corporations, but it also requires that a great deal of land be dedicated to grazing. Where is the land to come from? Ranchers in Latin America are solving their land problem by clearing forests at the rate of thousands of square miles each year. These tropical forests, as we shall explain presently, are vital to maintaining the

earth's atmosphere. Therefore, forest destruction threatens the well-being of everyone—even the people back in the United States who enjoy the hamburgers.

Notice that, despite the importance of this global environmental network, the people at each point in the process most likely are not aware of the long-term consequences of their actions. People in the United States simply want a quick hamburger. Fast-food companies want to make a profit by serving meals that people want. Ranchers want to make money by raising beef cattle. Taken together, these motives produce actions that have serious consequences for everyone. Thus, in a world of countless connections, we need to think critically about the effects of choices we make every day—like what's for lunch!

SOURCE: Based on Myers (1984a).

The use of CFCs illustrates the three principles we have already noted. Its problematic consequences result, first, from human decision making; second, these consequences are largely unintended; and, third, they are mostly reversible. In response to the dangers of ozone depletion, the United States and a number of other nations began in the early 1980s to restrict the use of CFCs.

But, in a world of countless environmental connections, many threats to the global environment remain unrecognized. The box explains that the popular,

although seemingly innocent, act of eating fast-food hamburgers has environmental effects in other parts of the world.

Technology

Why does humanity have such capacity to threaten the natural environment? Generally speaking, the answer lies in our capacity for culture, specifically for *technology*. Chapter 3 ("Culture") defined technology as knowledge that a society applies to the task of living

NOTE: One example of how consumption has expanded is the size of homes. In 1970, the average size of a newly constructed home was 1,385 square feet; in 1992, it was 1,920 square feet. Also, three-fourths of today's new homes have central air conditioning, compared to one-third in 1970.

GLOBAL: World population growth is currently almost 11,000 people per hour (more than 8,000 of whom live in poor societies).
GLOBAL: The world's ability to feed a growing population depends on greater agricultural efficiency. In part, this efficiency rests on developing new hybrids; however, it also depends on curbing topsoil erosion (perhaps 25 billion tons is lost annually) and maintaining an adequate supply of water.

in its natural surroundings. A basic principle is that the more complex a society's technology, the greater its capacity to affect the natural environment.

Societies with simple technology—the hunters and gatherers described in Chapter 4 ("Society")—have scarcely any ability to affect the environment. On the contrary, the members of such societies are immediately and directly dependent on nature, since their lives are defined by the migration of game and the rhythm of the seasons. They remain especially vulnerable to natural events, such as fires, floods, droughts, and storms.

Societies at intermediate stages of sociocultural evolution have a somewhat greater capacity to affect the environment. But the environmental impact of horticulture (small-scale farming), pastoralism (the herding of animals), and even agriculture (the use of animal-drawn plows) is limited by the reliance on muscle power for production of food and other goods.

The picture changes dramatically, however, with the introduction of industrial technology. Industry requires more than muscle power to operate large machinery. The burning of fossil fuels, first coal and then oil, was a key element in the Industrial Revolution, and this combustion both consumes natural resources and releases pollutants into the atmosphere. Furthermore, armed with industrial technology, humans become able to bend nature to their will far more than ever before, tunneling through mountains, damming rivers, irrigating deserts, and drilling for oil on the ocean floor.

Global Map 22–1 shows where in the world energy use is highest. The general pattern is clear: High energy consumption is linked to industrialization. In fact, the typical adult in the United States consumes up to one hundred times more energy each year than the average member of the world's poorest societies. Put another way, while the U.S. population accounts for less than 5 percent of the world's total, we consume roughly one-third of the world's energy. Taken together, the members of industrial societies represent 20 percent of humanity but utilize 80 percent of the world's energy (Connett, 1991; Miller, 1992).

But the environmental impact of industrial technology is not limited to energy consumption. Just as important is the fact that industrial societies produce one hundred times more goods than agrarian societies do. While these products raise the material standard of living, they also generate problems of solid waste (since people ultimately throw away much of what they produce) and pollution (since industrial production generates smoke and other toxic substances).

From the outset, people were eager to acquire many of the material benefits of industrial technology. But only a century after the dawn of industrial development did people begin to realize the long-term consequences of new technology for the natural environment. Indeed, one defining trait of postindustrial societies, detailed in Chapter 4 ("Society") and Chapter 15 ("The Economy and Work"), is a growing concern for environmental quality.

From today's vantage point, we draw an ironic and sobering conclusion: As we have reached our greatest technological power, we have placed the natural environment—including ourselves and all other living things—at greatest risk (Voight, cited in Bohrmann & Kellert, 1991:ix–x).

Population Growth

Paralleling the development of more powerful technology is a second underlying cause of environmental problems. As Chapter 21 ("Population and Urbanization") explained in detail, the last two centuries have witnessed an unprecedented population explosion.

At the time the ancient empires were taking form in Babylon and Egypt some five thousand years ago, the world's people numbered fewer than 50 million, about the population of the U.S. West Coast today. Furthermore, population growth was negligible, with gradual increases periodically offset by plague and other catastrophes.

But as the Industrial Revolution progressed in Western Europe, rising living standards and improving medical technology combined to send death rates plummeting. The predictable result was a sharp upturn in world population. By 1850 (the eve of the U.S. Civil War) global population had soared past the unprecedented level of 1 billion.

But that was just the beginning. In the decades that followed, global population accelerated further. The world's people numbered 2 billion by 1930, passed the 3 billion mark in 1962, reached 4 billion by 1974, and topped 5 billion in 1987. In 1994, the world's population stands at roughly 5.5 billion, and demographers predict that we will reach the 6 billion mark early in the next century. Although there are now signs that the world's rate of population increase is slowing, the numbers are going up, with the planet currently gaining an additional 250,000 people each day.

The danger of population growth is that it can quickly overwhelm available resources. An old illustration conveys how quickly runaway growth can wreak havoc on the natural environment (Milbrath, 1989:10):

NOTE: There are currently 112 nuclear power facilities in the United States; no new plants have been constructed since 1978. Plants were built to operate for 40 years; 50 of the plants are now at least 20 years old. Experts debate the degree to which reactor walls are weakened by continuous exposure to high-energy neutrons given off during the nuclear reaction.

GLOBAL: Poor nations are increasing their consumption of energy rapidly (use has almost tripled since 1970), while in rich nations the use has risen a more modest 20 percent over the same period. Some analysts see this as a (good) indication of modernization; others see it as evidence that high debt is forcing poor societies to quickly deplete resources.

Window on the World

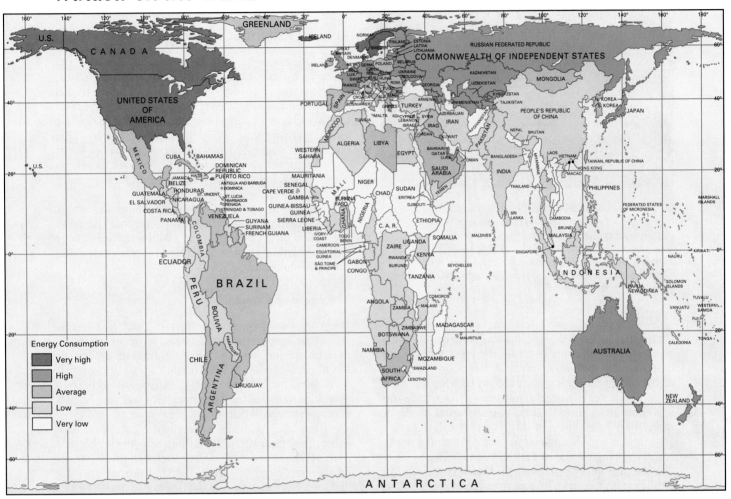

GLOBAL MAP 22–1 Energy Consumption in Global Perspective

The members of industrial societies consume far more energy than others on the planet. The typical U.S. resident uses the same amount of energy in a year as one hundred people in the Central African Republic. This means that the most economically productive societies are also those that place the greatest burden on the natural environment.

From *Peters Atlas of the World* (1990).

A pond has a single water lily growing on it. The lily doubles in size each day. In thirty days, it covers the entire pond. On which day did the lily cover half the pond?

The answer that comes readily to mind—the fifteenth day—is wrong because the lily was not increasing in size by the same amount every day. The correct answer is that the lily covered half the pond on the twenty-ninth day. The lesson of the riddle is that as the rate of growth increases, what begins as a very small lily soon overwhelms the entire pond (increasing from one-eighth of the surface to covering the entire pond in the final three days).

To apply the same logic to the earth, most experts now conclude that the world will have perhaps 10 billion people by the end of the next century. As

We blithely assume that eradicating the persistent poverty that paralyzes societies around the world is a desirable goal. But the environmental impact of global economic development might be devastating. What would happen, for example, if 850 million people in India became "middle class" and began operating that many automobiles, the way we in the United States do?

Chapters 11 ("Global Stratification") and 21 ("Population and Urbanization") explain, the most rapid population growth now is occurring in the poorest regions of the world. A glance back at Global Map 21-1 on page 566 reveals that the nations of Africa, taken together, are adding to their population at a rate of more than 3 percent annually. If sustained, this high growth rate will almost double that continent's population over the course of the next generation.

Rapid population growth and poverty go hand in hand. For one thing, a surging population quickly neutralizes any increase in living standards. If a society's population doubles, doubling its productivity amounts to no gain at all.

Poverty also places its own burden on efforts to protect the natural environment. The members of poor societies live on the edge of existence. Preoccupied with survival, they must consume whatever resources are at hand, without the luxury of being able to consider the long-term consequences of their actions.

And what would be the environmental consequences of industrialization for the billions of people in poor societies? Even at their current population levels, economic development would impose unprecedented stress on the natural environment. To offer just one example, the transformation of a poor society like India, with a population exceeding 850 million, into a middle-class society would put almost 1 billion

additional cars on the road. What would that mean for the world's oil reserves or for global air quality?

Cultural Patterns: Growth and Limits

In all fairness, we might hope that some day people living in the poor nations of Latin America, Africa, and Asia would enjoy the material prosperity that is widespread in the United States. But if people around the world lived as members of our society do, the global environment would soon be exhausted. This conclusion suggests that our planet suffers not just from the problem of economic *under*development in some regions but also from economic *over*development in others.

Looking at ourselves, we might well reflect about how we construct our cultural notion of "the good life." Such ways of thinking, in addition to technology and population growth, are a third factor underlying the environmental deficit.

The Logic of Growth

Why does our society designate specific areas as "parks" or "game reserves"? Doing so seems to imply that, except for these special areas, humans are free to intentionally utilize the earth and its resources for our own purposes (Myers, 1991). Such an aggressive approach to the natural environment has long been a central element of our way of life.

Chapter 3 ("Culture") described many of the core values that underlie cultural patterns in the United States (Williams, 1970). These included an emphasis on *material comfort*, the belief that money and the things it buys enrich our lives. We also embrace the idea of *progress*, thinking that the future will be better than the present. Moreover, we rely on *science*, looking to experts to apply technology to improving our lives. Taken together, such cultural values form the foundation for *the logic of growth*.

The logic of growth is an optimistic view of the world holding, first, that people have improved their lives through devising more productive technology and, second, that we shall continue to do so into the future. The logic of growth thus amounts to the arguments that "people are clever," "having things is good," and "life will improve." A powerful force throughout the history of the United States and other Western, industrial societies, the logic of growth has driven individuals to settle the wilderness, clear the land, build towns and roads, and pursue the goal of a materially affluent life.

NOTE: Despite concerns about burning of carbon fuels, the price of oil actually came down during the 1980s (controlling for inflation) from about $43 per barrel to between $20 and $30 per barrel a decade later. This drop is partly why the Clinton administration moved to raise taxes on gasoline.

NOTE: Given global connections, argues Lester Milbrath, a principle of environmentalism is that "We can never do just one thing."

RESOURCE: Lester Brown's essay, "The State of the World's Natural Environment," is one of the contemporary selections in the companion reader, Seeing Ourselves.

NOTE: The book The Limits to Growth largely set in motion the environmental movement; some 3 million copies of the book, published in 27 languages, have been sold.

But even optimistic people realize that what we often call "progress" creates unanticipated problems, environmental or otherwise. The logic of growth responds by arguing that people (and especially scientists and other technology experts) are inventive and will find a way out of any problems that growth places in our path. If, say, present resources should prove inadequate to our future needs, we should expect to find some new alternative resources that will do the job just as well.

To illustrate, most people in the United States would probably agree that automobiles have greatly improved our lives by providing swift and comfortable travel. Automobiles have also made us dependent on oil, but, says the logic of growth, by the time the growing number of cars in the world threatens to deplete the planet's oil reserves, scientists will have come up with electric, solar, or nuclear engines or some as-yet-unknown technology to free us from oil dependence.

The logic of growth remains an influential element of U.S. culture. But environmental scientists generally are critical of this line of reasoning. Lester Milbrath (1989) argues that the logic of growth is flawed by its assumption that natural resources on which we depend will always be found in ample supply. On the contrary, he warns, oil, clean air, fresh water, and the earth's topsoil are all *finite* resources that we can and will exhaust if we continue to pursue growth at any cost.

And what of our faith in human ingenuity and especially the ability of science to resolve problems of scarcity? Milbrath concedes that humans are quite clever at solving problems. But, he adds, just as there are limits to natural resources, there are limits to human resourcefulness. Do we dare to assume that we will be able to solve every problem that confronts us, especially those causing serious damage to the life-giving environment? Moreover, the more powerful and complex the technology (nuclear reactors, say, compared to gasoline engines), the greater the dangers posed by miscalculation and the more significant unintended consequences are likely to be. Thus, Milbrath reaches the troubling conclusion that our efforts to support increasing numbers of people using finite resources are almost certain to cause serious injury to the environment, and, ultimately, to ourselves.

The Limits to Growth

If we cannot "invent" our way out of the problems created by the logic of growth, perhaps an alternative

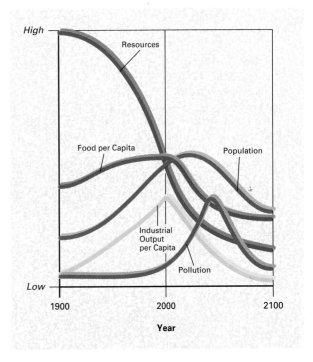

FIGURE 22–1 The Limits to Growth: Projections

(Based on Meadows et al., 1972)

way of thinking about the world is called for. Environmentalists tend to agree that the logic of growth has contributed to the deterioration of the natural environment, and they propose a counterargument—that growth must have limits (Meadows et al., 1972). The *limits to growth* thesis, stated simply, is that humanity must implement policies to control the growth of population, material production, and use of resources in order to avoid environmental collapse.

The Limits to Growth, a book that had a large hand in launching the environmental movement, presents projections from a computer model of the environment that calculates available resources, rates of population growth, amount of land available for cultivation, levels of industrial and food production, and amount of pollutants released into the atmosphere. The authors contend that the model is consistent with changes that have occurred since 1900, then projected forward to the end of the next century. Long-range predictions using such a complex model are always speculative, and some critics have challenged their validity (Simon, 1981). But the general conclusions of the study, shown in Figure 22–1, have remained influential ever since.

NOTE: The real dilemma of growth is that we need it to provide for the population we have now (much less what global numbers will be), but we can barely afford the environmental strain it will cause.

NOTE: One sign of increasing public concern with solid waste is that, between 1980 and 1990, the weight of discarded grocery packaging dropped by about 10% even as the U.S. population rose

10%. This was accomplished through lighter and more efficient packaging.

GLOBAL: Heavy reliance on landfills is typical of some industrial nations (U.S., U.K., Australia, Canada) but not others, where incineration is the favored means of disposal (Japan, Sweden, Switzerland, Luxembourg).

According to the limits to growth approach, humanity is quickly consuming the earth's finite resources. Supplies of oil, natural gas, and other sources of energy will fall sharply, a little faster or slower depending on policies in rich nations and the speed at which other nations industrialize. While food production per person should continue to rise into the next century, the authors calculate, hunger will continue to be widespread because existing food supplies are not equally distributed throughout the world. By mid-century, however, the model predicts a hunger crisis serious enough that rising mortality rates will first stabilize population and then draw it downward. Depletion of resources will eventually cripple industrial output as well. Only then will pollution rates fall.

The lesson of this study is grim: Current patterns of life are not sustainable for even another century. Either we make deliberate changes in how we live, or calamity will overtake us and force changes upon us.

Predictions of the kind found in *The Limits of Growth* bring to mind the warning of Thomas Robert Malthus (1766–1834), which was detailed in Chapter 21 ("Population and Urbanization"). Malthus suggested that, with population growth left unchecked, the world would experience shortages of food and ultimately catastrophic starvation. In retrospect, we now know that Malthus's dire predictions were exaggerated, since population growth in Europe slowed in the decades since his time, and agricultural productivity increased more than he imagined it would.

But consider that world population is now six times greater than it was in Malthus's day. Therefore, although the more recent limits of growth model does not trumpet our impending doom, it does remind us that *no* level of population increase can be sustained indefinitely. This model shares with the Malthusian thesis the idea that a "day of reckoning" is just a matter of time.

ENVIRONMENTAL ISSUES

We have reviewed how technological development, population growth, and cultural orientations have placed increasing demands on the natural environment. What, then, is the state of the natural environment today?

To begin, public opinion surveys in the United States and elsewhere reveal serious concern about the natural environment. Results of a study of twenty-two nations show that majorities in twenty of the countries judged their surrounding environments to be "fairly bad" or "very bad." Against this backdrop of general worries, however, the members of various societies give quite different assessments of their local environments (see Figure 22–2). In general, people in poor societies, who contend with the greatest problems of overpopulation and poverty, are most unhappy with their surroundings (Dunlap, Gallup, & Gallup, 1992).

People in the United States rate their local environment more favorably than people in poor societies do. But, compared to those living in other industrial societies, the U.S. population is more negative. And other studies suggest that members of our society are becoming more concerned about the natural environment. In one national poll, two-thirds of respondents reported that they thought the natural environment has "gotten worse" over the last twenty years, with 80 percent now claiming to consider themselves "environmentalists" (Gutfeld, 1991a).

Put another way, there are few problems that concern us as much as the state of the natural environment. Two-thirds of U.S. adults think that our society spends too little money on environmental problems. This places problems of the natural environment high up on the national agenda along with the need to improve schools, provide better health care, and control crime (NORC, 1991).

In sum, we certainly *perceive* the natural environment to be in danger. But what are the objective facts? In the following survey, we shall briefly examine various dimensions of the environmental problem with particular attention to the United States.

Solid Waste: The "Disposable Society"

As an interesting exercise, carry a trash bag over the course of a single day and collect all the materials you throw away. Most people would be surprised to find that the average person in the United States would almost fill the bag with several pounds of paper, metal, plastic, and other disposable materials. For the country as a whole, about 1 billion pounds of solid waste are generated *each and every day*.

It is easy to see why the United States has been dubbed a *disposable society*. Not only are we materially rich, but ours is a culture that values convenience. As a result, we consume more products than virtually any society in the world, and we purchase much of it with a great deal of packaging. The most commonly cited case is fast food, served with cardboard, plastic, and styrofoam containers that are thrown away within minutes. But countless other products—from film to fishhooks—are sold with excessive packaging for the

NOTE: Recycling is not a solution to the problem of solid waste since most of what is recycled eventually becomes refuse. The solution to the problem lies in producing and consuming less.

GLOBAL: In global perspective, we in the United States account for about one-fifth of all the world's trash. In general, the richer the nation, the more materials it consumes, and the more it ends up throwing away.

NOTE: In 1993, the space shuttle Endeavor had to change course quickly to avoid a large piece of "space junk" (an old USSR rocket). This near-collision raises the specter of future "space pollution." Currently, more than 1,000 pieces of space junk can be seen from Earth; the oldest being tracked is the remains of the 1958 Vanguard I satellite. The largest piece of space junk was Skylab, which rained debris into the Indian Ocean and Australia in 1979.

purpose of making the product more attractive to the customer (or harder to shoplift).

Consider, too, that manufacturers market soft drinks, beer, and fruit juices in aluminum cans, glass jars, or plastic containers, which not only consume finite resources but also generate solid waste. Then there are countless items intentionally designed to be disposable. A walk through any local supermarket reveals shelves filled with pens, razors, flashlights, batteries, and even cameras intended to be used once and dropped in the nearest trash can. Other products—from light bulbs to automobiles—are designed to have a limited useful life, and then become unwanted junk. As Paul H. Connett (1991:101) points out, even the words we use to describe what we throw away—*waste, litter, trash, refuse, garbage, rubbish*—reveal how little we value what we cannot immediately use and how we quickly try to push it out of sight and out of mind.

Living in a "disposable society" means that the average person in the United States consumes 50 times more steel, 170 times more newspaper, 250 times more gasoline, and 300 times more plastic each year than the typical individual in India (Miller, 1992). Just as this high level of consumption means that members of our society use a disproportionate share of the planet's natural resources, so it also means that we contribute the lion's share of the world's refuse.

We like to say that we "throw things away." But the 80 percent of our solid waste that is not burned or recycled does not "go away"; rather, it ends up in landfills. The practice of using landfills, originally intended to improve sanitation, is now associated with several threats to the natural environment.

First, the sheer volume of discarded material is literally filling landfills up all across the country. Especially in large cities like New York, there is simply little room left for disposing of trash. Second, material placed in landfills contributes to water pollution. Although, in most jurisdictions, law now regulates what can be placed in a landfill, the Environmental Protection Agency has identified thirty thousand dump sites across the United States containing hazardous materials that are polluting water both above and below the ground. Third, what goes into landfills all too often stays there—sometimes for centuries. Tens of millions of tires, diapers, and other items that we bury in landfills each year do not readily decompose and will become an unwelcome legacy for future generations.

Fifty years ago, it was common practice for manufacturing plants to dispose of all types of hazardous waste simply by dumping them in a woods or pouring

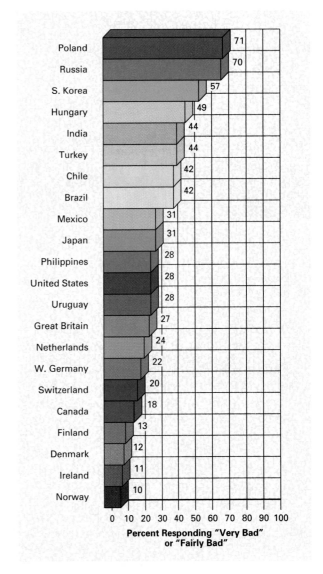

FIGURE 22–2 Rating the Local Environment: A Global Survey

Question: "When we say environment, we mean your surroundings—both the natural environment, namely, the air, water, land, plants, and animals—as well as buildings, streets, and the like. Overall, how would you rate the quality of the environment in your local community: very good, fairly good, fairly bad, or very bad?"

(Dunlap, Gallup, & Gallup, 1992)

them in a stream. Today, laws in most states provide stiff penalties for such actions, but enforcement has been lax. The problem of solid waste includes both the

People in the United States generate 1 billion pounds of solid waste each and every day. Most of this refuse ends up in dumping sites, but landfills—from New York to California—are filling up. This level of solid waste dumping is clearly not sustainable over the long term.

waste products of manufacturing and the solid waste each of us generates daily. To cope with its sheer volume, environmentalists argue that we must turn "waste" into a resource, one that will benefit, rather than burden, future generations. One such strategy that has caught on throughout the country is **recycling**, *programs to reuse resources we would otherwise discard as "waste."* But, as the box on page 601 explains, the United States is behind Japan and many other industrial societies in initiating recycling programs.

Finally, the oceans also have long served as a vast dumping ground for all kinds of waste; no one can calculate how much. Solid waste pollutes water, and polluted water kills fish or renders them dangerous to eat. Ocean dumping also spoils a source of great beauty and recreational pleasure. Perhaps most dramatically, in recent years the news media have reported large amounts of trash (including toxic materials and dangerous items like syringes) washing up on the shores of both coasts of the United States.

Preserving Clean Water

The oceans and other bodies of water are the lifeblood of the global ecosystem. Humans must have water to live, and they use it for drinking, bathing, cooling, cooking, agriculture, recreation, and a host of other activities.

The earth naturally recycles water and refreshes the land through what scientists call the *hydrological cycle.* The process begins as heat from the sun causes the earth's water—97 percent of which is in the

oceans—to evaporate and forms clouds. Next, water returns to earth as rain, which drains into streams and rivers and rushes toward the sea. The hydrological cycle not only renews the supply of water but cleans it as well. Because water evaporates at lower temperatures than most pollutants, the water vapor that rises from the seas is relatively pure and free of contaminants, which are left behind. Although the hydrological cycle generates clean water in the form of rain, it cannot destroy pollutants that steadily build up in the oceans.

Two key concerns, then, dominate discussions of water and the natural environment. The first is supply; the second is pollution.

Water Supply

The concern over an ample supply of water is hardly new. Water rights have been a major element of law since the ancient civilizations of China, Egypt, and Rome. Throughout Europe, aqueducts of brick, built by the ancient Romans, still stand as testimony to the importance of water to the growth of human settlements.

Today, some regions of the world—the tropics, for example—enjoy a plentiful supply of water, although most of the annual rainfall may occur over a relatively brief season. Other regions of Asia, North America, and Africa are more arid and depend for their water on the flow of rivers. Egypt, for instance, has long depended on the Nile River for most of its water. There, as population increases, the problem of water supply is fast reaching the critical stage. Egyptians today must make do with one-sixth as much water per person from the Nile as they did in 1900, and the supply will shrink by half again over the next twenty years (Myers, 1984c; Postel, 1993).

Much of the remainder of northern Africa and the Middle East faces an even more critical situation. Within thirty years, according to current predictions, 1 billion people in this region will lack necessary water. The world has recently witnessed the tragedy of hunger in the northeastern African nations of Ethiopia and Somalia. While the food shortage there is widely acknowledged, an even more serious problem for these societies is the lack of adequate water for irrigation and drinking.

Increasing population and complex technology in manufacturing and power-generating facilities have greatly increased the human appetite for water. The global consumption of water, estimated at about 5 billion cubic feet per year, has tripled since 1950 and is expanding faster than the world's population (Postel, 1993).

NOTE: A 1993 EPA survey of U.S. drinking water finds that systems serving 30 million people have too much lead.

NOTE: Water is a renewable resource, since the hydrological cycle helps clean it, but water is also a finite resource. Keep in mind, too, that water supplies must remain far larger than what we use in order for the oceans to be able to absorb pollutants.

GLOBAL: Israel stands as an example of a nation that has made remarkable strides towards curbing water use. This has been done largely through innovations in irrigation in which "micro-irrigation" systems bring water directly to a plant's roots rather than spraying the water over a wide area.

SOCIAL POLICY

The Second Time Around: Recycling in the United States

Walking around neighborhoods in Japanese cities, you will see large cans in which residents are required, by law, to place bottles, cans, and newspapers. Person for person, the Japanese consume only half as many of these things as we in the United States do. In addition, the Japanese recycle more than three times more of their disposable waste than we do.

While recycling is a common practice in Japan and in a number of other industrial societies, it is a relatively new idea in the United States. Here, just 10 percent of solid waste is recycled (compared to at least one-third in Japan), with another 10 percent being burned. Most solid waste ends up in landfills.

A growing number of communities, however, realize that this practice cannot continue. Landfills are filling up. As a consequence, many municipalities have initiated recycling programs. In 1990, thirty-eight states enacted at least one law regarding recycling (Gutfeld, 1991b). Some programs are voluntary, while others are mandatory, sometimes complete with "trash cops" who inspect roadside trash cans and issue tickets to those who fail to separate recyclable material from other refuse. All in all, the current trend is toward the Japanese approach, since

a broad program of recycling could prevent more than 100 billion pounds of solid waste from being consigned to landfills each year.

Most of what the typical household throws away can be recycled. As the figure shows, paper represents the largest share of household trash (estimated at 50 percent by volume). Glass, metals, and plastic (totaling an additional 24 percent) are also candidates for recycling. In the same spirit of conserving resources and lessening the load on landfills, households can donate old

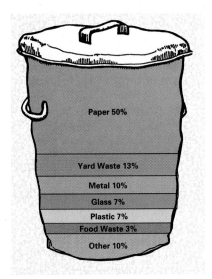

Paper 50%

Yard Waste 13%

Metal 10%

Glass 7%

Plastic 7%

Food Waste 3%

Other 10%

(Based on Franklin Associates, 1986, and Corley et al., 1993)

appliances, furniture, carpeting, and other unwanted items to technical schools or thrift shops for repair. Yard and food waste can also be recycled through composting. This process, which can be done at home by people with available space, involves placing organic materials (that is, what is or was living) in piles or containers to allow them to decompose naturally (and produces soil-enriching humus in the process).

An important consideration in assessing the prospects for widespread recycling in market-based societies like the United States is profitability. At present, the demand for some recycled materials (such as paper products) is not strong enough to support the recycling effort, so many recycling programs are operated by volunteers or municipal governments. It is likely, however, that as recycling processes improve, industries will see "waste" as a useful resource.

In any case, not all environmentalists think recycling should be left to market forces. Dedicating public funds to this purpose makes sense since local governments already operate landfills (rarely at a profit); moreover, any program to improve the natural environment is clearly in the public interest.

As a result, even in areas of the earth that receive significant rainfall, people are using groundwater faster than it can be naturally replenished. The Tamil Nadu region of southern India serves as an example. There, the rapidly growing population is pumping so much

groundwater that the local water table has fallen one hundred feet over the last several decades. In the United States, the pumping of water from the massive Ogallala aquifer, which lies below seven states from South Dakota down to Texas, is now so rapid that

GLOBAL: About 85% of the world's cropland is not artificially irrigated, receiving water only from rainfall. The 15% that is consumes a greatly disproportionate share of water reserves.

GLOBAL: Irrigation is not only the main source of water use, but a major source of energy consumption. In India, for example, some 8 million irrigation pumps consume one-fourth of that nation's power.

NOTE: Water use by industry in the United States has fallen by one-third since 1950 (as heavy industry has declined). This pattern is more or less true of other industrial societies.

NOTE: In 1988, Massachusetts became the first state to control toilet water flow, mandating a limit of 1.6 gallons on new units. Since then, fourteen other states have adopted similar controls.

The Aral Sea, which straddles Kazakhstan and Uzbekistan in the southwest region of the former Soviet Union, was once a plentiful source of water and fish. Today, due to policies that overly exploited this resource, the sea has all but vanished.

some experts fear it could be depleted several decades into the next century.

In light of such developments, we must face the reality that the amount of water we use cannot depend simply on our desires. Rather, we must treat water as a valuable, finite resource. Greater conservation of water by individuals in the home is part of the answer. But households around the world account for no more than 10 percent of water use. Of greater importance is industry, which currently draws 25 percent of global water. And, most important of all, the irrigation of croplands is responsible for two-thirds of humanity's consumption of water.

New irrigation technology may well reduce this demand in the future. But, here again, we are reminded of the importance of balancing plans for economic growth with an assessment of available resources and, of course, the urgency of establishing effective controls on population growth (Myers, 1984a; Goldfarb, 1991; Falkenmark & Widstrand, 1992; Postel, 1993).

Water Pollution

Still, in large cities—from Mexico City to Egypt's Cairo to China's Shanghai—many people have little choice but to drink water that is a known source of disease. In general, the poor suffer the most from the problem of unsafe water. As Chapter 20 ("Health and Medicine") noted, infectious diseases like typhoid, cholera, and dysentery, all caused by micro-organisms that contaminate water, run rampant in poor nations.

Water pollution is a major cause of death throughout less-developed regions of the world (Clarke, 1984b; Falkenmark & Widstrand, 1992).

The second environmental problem involving the world's water is pollution. No technologically sophisticated society has done a very good job of protecting the quality of its water. In most areas of the world, tap water is not safe for drinking.

Most members of our society, however, take for granted that tap water is free from harmful contaminants, and water quality in the United States is generally good by global standards. However, the problem of water pollution is steadily growing. According to the Sierra Club, an environmental activist organization, rivers and streams across the United States absorb some 500 million pounds of toxic waste each year. This pollution results not just from intentional dumping, but also from the runoff of agricultural fertilizers and lawn chemicals. Groundwater supplies, as we have already suggested, are also endangered as hazardous substances leech from thousands of landfills and dump sites across the country.

Despite the fact that even small amounts of pollutants can damage the aquatic ecosystem, only recently have water supplies had the protection of law. The federal government's Clean Water Act of 1972 was a first step toward cleaning this country's water. Before that time, many urban rivers were so polluted that the water was dangerous even for bathing, and deadly to fish and other aquatic life. It was a sign of the times that Cleveland's Cuyahoga River became so choked with oil and other toxic substances in the late 1960s that it actually caught fire.

Clearing the Air

Most people in the United States are more aware of air pollution than they are of contaminated water, in part, because air serves as our constant and immediate environment. Then, too, many of us are familiar with the smoke and fog (the origin of the word "smog") that hang over our urban centers.

One of the unanticipated consequences of the development of industrial technology—especially the factory and the motor vehicle—has been a deterioration of air quality. The thick, black smoke belched from factory smokestacks, often twenty-four hours a day, alarmed residents of early industrial cities a century ago. Writing in 1884, for instance, Williard Glazier was stunned by the nighttime view from the hills surrounding his city of Pittsburgh, ablaze with the fires of steel mills and swirling with factory smoke. It was as if someone had lifted the lid on hell itself, Glazier

NOTE: The military, say some analysts, is the most environmentally destructive institution, producing far more toxic waste than the five largest chemical corporations combined. An F-16 jet uses as much fuel in 30 minutes as the average U.S. motorist consumes in a year.

NOTE: Increasing global trade itself places greater stress on the environment due to more production, more energy consumption, and more disposal of waste. The energy needs to power just cargo ships in 1991 was roughly that consumed by all Brazilians and Turks during that year.
NOTE: Scientists estimate that three-fourths of Europe's remaining forests show damage from acid rain.

mused, and his fellow city dwellers were "tortured spirits writhing in agony" as they fought simply to breathe (cited in Glaab, 1963).

By the end of World War II, such scenes were commonplace in industrial cities of the Northeast and Midwest. By 1950, the automobile added another dimension to the problem of air pollution, shrouding cities like Los Angeles that had escaped the earlier rush of industrial development. There, on a clear day one could see across the city, but there were few clear days.

In London, factory discharge, automobile emissions, and smoke from coal fires used to heat households combined to create what was probably the worst urban air quality of the century. What some British jokingly called "pea soup" was, in reality, a deadly mix of pollution: Over just five days in 1952, an especially thick haze hanging over London killed four thousand people (Clarke, 1984a).

Fortunately, great strides have been made in combating air pollution caused by our industrial way of life. Laws now mandate the use of low-pollution heating fuels in most cities; the coal fires that choked London a half-century ago, for example, are now forbidden. In addition, scientists have effectively devised new technologies to reduce the noxious output of factory chimneys and, even more important, to lessen the pollution caused by the growing number of automobiles and trucks. The switch to unleaded gasoline initiated in the early 1970s, coupled with changes in engine design and exhaust systems, have moderated the automobile's environmental impact. Still, with almost 200 million vehicles in the United States alone, the challenge of cleaning the air remains enormous. National Map 22-1, on page 604, identifies the states that have the greatest problems with air pollution.

If people in the rich societies of the world can breathe a bit easier than they once did, people in poor societies find that air pollution is becoming more and more serious. In less economically developed countries people still rely on wood, coal, peat, or other "dirty" fuels for cooking fires and to heat their homes. Moreover, many nations are so eager to encourage short-term industrial development that they pay little heed to the longer-term dangers of air pollution. As a result, many cities in Latin America, Eastern Europe, and Asia have air pollution that rivals that found in London fifty years ago.

Acid Rain

Acid rain refers to *precipitation that is made acidic by air pollution and destroys plant and animal life.* The complex reaction that generates acid rain (or snow)

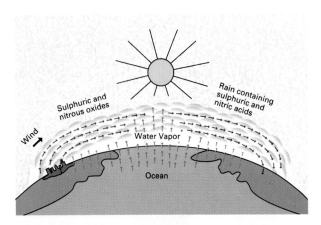

FIGURE 22-3 The Formation of Acid Rain

begins as power plants burning fossil fuels (oil and coal) to generate electricity release sulphur and nitrogen oxides into the air. Once the winds sweep these gases into the atmosphere, they react with the air to form sulfuric and nitric acid, which renders atmospheric moisture water acidic. Figure 22-3 illustrates the process that creates acid rain.

Studying this figure also shows that one type of pollution often causes another. In this case, air pollution (from smokestacks) ends up contaminating water (in lakes and streams that collect acid rain). Notice, too, that acid rain is a global phenomenon because the regions that suffer the effects of acid rain may be thousands of miles from the site of the original pollution. For instance, tall chimneys of British power plants have caused the acid rain that has devastated forests and fish in Norway and Sweden up to a thousand miles to the northeast. In the United States, much the same pattern appears as midwestern chimneys have poisoned the natural environment of New England (Clarke, 1984a).

The Rain Forests

Rain forests are *regions of dense forestation, most of which circles the globe close to the equator.* Global Map 22-2, on page 606, shows that the largest tropical rain forests are in South America (notably Brazil), but west central Africa and southeast Asia also have sizable rain forests. In all, the world's rain forests cover an area of some 2 billion acres, which accounts for 7 percent of the earth's total land surface.

Like the rest of the world's resources, the rain forests are falling victim to the needs and appetites of the surging human population. As noted earlier in this

Seeing Ourselves

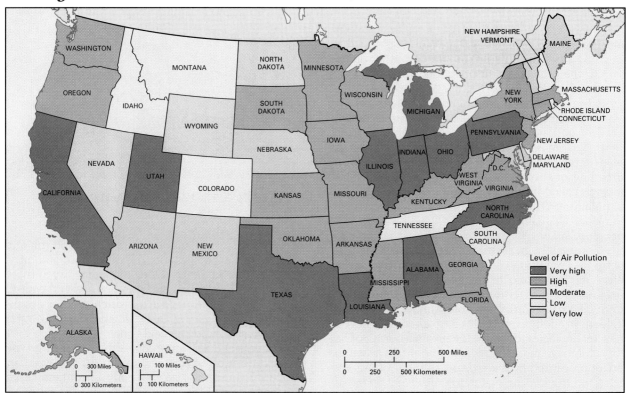

NATIONAL MAP 22–1 Air Pollution Across the United States

The Environmental Protection Agency (EPA) monitors the emission of 173 compounds into the atmosphere. In 1991, the five states that polluted the air the least were Hawaii, Nevada, Wyoming, North Dakota, and Vermont (although these states each emitted 500,000 pounds of toxics during that year). High-pollution states—including California, Texas, Illinois, Ohio, and Pennsylvania—each emitted one hundred times as much toxic material into the atmosphere. What traits distinguish high-pollution from low-pollution states?

Prepared by the author using data from the Environmental Protection Agency.

chapter, the demand for beef has prompted ranchers in Latin America to burn forested areas for grazing land. Just as important is the lucrative hardwood trade. High prices are paid for mahogany and other woods by people in rich societies who have, as environmentalist Norman Myers (1984b:88) puts it, "a penchant for parquet floors, fine furniture, fancy paneling, weekend yachts, and high-grade coffins." Under such pressure, the world's rain forests are now just half their original size, and they continue to shrink by about 1 percent annually, a loss of 65,000 square miles each year. If this rate of destruction remains unchecked, these forests will vanish before the end of the next century, and, with them, protections for the earth's

climate and biodiversity. We now examine each of these functions in turn.

Global Warming

Natural scientists explain that rain forests play an important part in removing carbon dioxide (CO_2) from the atmosphere. From the time of the Industrial Revolution, the amount of carbon dioxide humanity has produced (most generated by factories and automobiles) has risen tenfold. Much of this CO_2 is absorbed by the oceans. But plants, which take in carbon dioxide and expel oxygen, also play a major part in maintaining the chemical balance of the atmosphere.

The so-called mud men of the Asaro Valley of the Eastern Highlands province of Papua New Guinea are in increasing contact with outsiders (and, indeed, now perform their "mud men" ritual primarily for tourists). The way of life of these people, along with that of hundreds of other indigenous peoples around the world, is in danger of disappearing. Paralleling the loss of the planet's biodiversity, therefore, is the decline of humanity's cultural diversity.

The problem, then, is that production of carbon dioxide is rising while the amount of plant life on earth is shrinking. To make matters worse, the current loss of rain forests is accomplished mostly by burning, which releases even more carbon dioxide into the atmosphere. Experts estimate the atmospheric concentration of carbon dioxide is now 10–20 percent higher than it was 150 years ago.

High in the atmosphere, carbon dioxide behaves much like the glass roof of a greenhouse, letting heat from the sun pass through to the earth while preventing much of it from radiating back away from the planet. Thus ecologists are cautiously speculating about a possible **greenhouse effect**, *a rise in the earth's average temperature due to increasing concentration of carbon dioxide in the atmosphere.*

The reality of global warming is the topic of intense research and controversy. Some analysts warn that our planet is currently experiencing a rise in average temperature: From the current mean of 60 degrees Fahrenheit, they claim, the planet could warm by five to ten degrees by 2050. Such a rise would melt much of the polar ice caps, pushing the oceans up over low-lying land around the world, flooding Bangladesh, for example, and much of the coastal United States, including Washington, D.C., right up to the steps of the White House. On the other hand, the Midwest—currently one of the most productive agricultural regions in the world—would likely become arid.

Not all scientists share this vision of future global warming. Some point out that global temperature changes have been taking place throughout history, apparently with little or nothing to do with rain forests. Moreover, higher concentrations of carbon dioxide in the atmosphere might actually accelerate plant growth (since plants thrive on this gas), which would serve to correct this imbalance and nudge the earth's temperature downward once again (Silverberg, 1991).

Declining Biodiversity

Whatever the effects on this planet's climate, rain forest clearing has a second, more certain, result. The disappearance of rain forest is a major factor eroding the earth's *biodiversity* by causing many thousands of species of plant and animal life to disappear. While rain forests account for just 7 percent of the earth's surface, they are home to almost half of this planet's living species.

Scientists have only a vague idea of how many living species exist on earth; estimates of the total number of species of animals, bacteria, and plants range as high as 30 million. Researchers, in fact, have identified more than one thousand species of ants alone (Wilson, 1991). From the total biodiversity of the earth, dozens of unique species of plants and animals cease to exist each day.

Given the vast number of living species on the earth, why should we be concerned with a loss of biodiversity? Environmentalists point to three reasons. First, our planet's biodiversity provides a vast and varied source of foods. Agricultural technology currently "splices" familiar crops with more exotic plant life yielding crops that are more productive or resistant to insects and disease. Moreover, research by plant geneticists into the properties of unfamiliar plant and animal life shows considerable promise for helping the world generate the foods necessary to nourish our rapidly increasing population.

GLOBAL: The concentration of CO_2 has climbed almost 10% in the last 20 years.

GLOBAL: In the Western Hemisphere, cutting of rain forest accelerated with the proliferation of sugar cane plantations. By the 1700s, sugar had become a staple in the European diet, and a heavy and steady demand for sugar fueled this process.

NOTE: Most of the rain forest's nutrients are in the vegetation.

Thus cutting rain forests begins a process of turning the soil arid over a decade or so.

GLOBAL: With limited capital and technology, poor societies are financially pressed into exporting their raw materials, notably forest products and minerals. Such an emphasis, coupled with limited environmental regulations, places great stress on the environments of these nations.

Window on the World

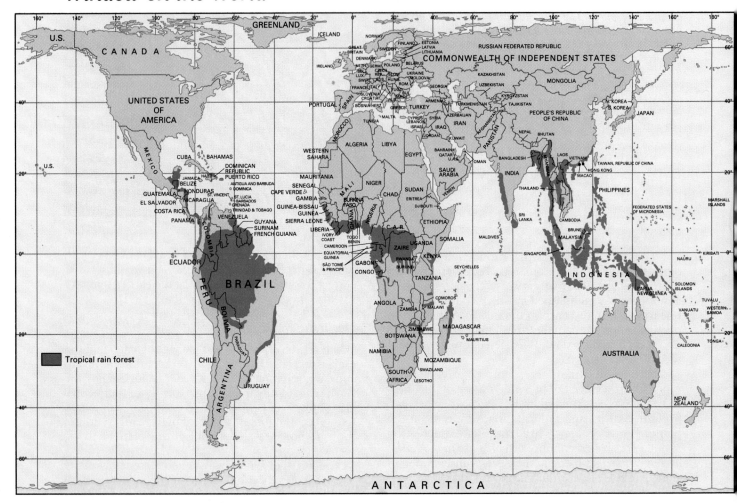

GLOBAL MAP 22–2 The Earth's Tropical Rain Forests

The earth's rain forests are situated along the equator in Latin America, Africa, and southeast Asia. The most massive rain forest is in the Amazon River region of South America, largely within the borders of Brazil. Although rain forests account for only 7 percent of the earth's land area, they are a vital element in the global ecosystem.

Prepared by the author. Map projection from *Peters Atlas of the World* (1990).

Second, the earth's biodiversity is a vital genetic resource. Medical and pharmaceutical industries depend on animal and plant biodiversity in their research to discover compounds that will cure disease and improve our lives. Children in the United States, for example, now have a good chance of surviving leukemia, a disease that was almost a sure killer two generations ago. What makes this possible? Credit goes to a compound derived from a pretty tropical flower called the rosy periwinkle. The oral birth control pill, used by tens of millions of women in this country, is another product of plant research, this time involving the Mexican forest yam. Scientists have tested tens of thousands of plants for their medical properties, and they have developed hundreds of new medicines each year based on this research.

GLOBAL: More than 90% of nuclear power facilities are in rich nations. The costs and complex technology that have made these systems controversial there also render them unsuitable for poor societies.
NOTE: California now generates enough solar and wind power to meet the needs of 2 million people.

NOTE: Farming in the U.S. utilizes 21 million tons of chemical fertilizer annually.
NOTE: Nuclear generating plants were being built by the dozens each year in the 1970s. The rate is now barely one per year. Still, this form of energy persists in the hope that problems of waste disposal and accidental contamination can be solved or avoided.

Third, with the loss of any species of life—whether it is one variety of ant, the spotted owl, the magnificent Asian tiger, or the famed Chinese panda—the beauty and complexity of our natural environment is diminished. And there are clear warning signs: Three-fourths of the world's nine thousand species of birds are currently declining in numbers.

Finally, keep in mind that, unlike pollution and other environmental problems, the extinction of species is irreversible and final. From an ethical standpoint, then, we should be probing whether those who live today should make decisions that will impoverish the world for those who live tomorrow (Myers, 1984b; Myers, 1991; Wilson, 1991; Brown, 1993).

SOCIETY AND THE ENVIRONMENT: THEORETICAL ANALYSIS

We have now introduced a number of key concepts and provided a host of data about problems of the natural environment. Sociological theory can help tie this material together to increase understanding of environmental issues.

Structural-Functional Analysis

The structural-functional paradigm offers three important insights about the natural environment. First, as earlier chapters have made clear, this approach highlights the fundamental importance of *values* and *beliefs* to the operation of a social system. Thus, in simple terms, the state of the environment depends largely on our attitude toward the natural world, for these values guide human actions.

Members of industrial societies generally see in nature resources to serve our needs; this point of view (described earlier as the "logic of growth") justifies imposing our human will on the planet. Motivated by this orientation, our forebears cleared forests for croplands, dammed rivers for irrigation and water power, and covered vast areas with concrete and erected buildings to make cities.

Moreover, Western cultures historically have embraced both materialism and acquisitiveness. That is, we have looked to *things* (more than, say, kinship or spirituality) as a source of comfort and happiness. At the same time, we tend to think that if owning *some* things is good, having *more* things is better. Our tendency toward "conspicuous consumption" leads us to purchase and display things as a way to indicate our social position to others. Such values, not surprisingly,

set the stage for the kinds of environmental stress this chapter has described.

Second, structural-functionalist theory highlights the interconnectedness of various dimensions of social life. Put otherwise, any investigation of the state of the natural environment requires a broad survey of how people organize their social life. Our ideas about efficient and private travel, for example, have much to do with the dizzying rate at which U.S. society has produced and consumed motor vehicles. Building and operating hundreds of millions of trucks and automobiles, in turn, has placed great stress on natural resources (like oil) and the environment (especially the air).

Third, structural-functional analysis provides some strategies for responding to environmental problems. In principle, given the many ways in which the operation of society interacts with the natural environment, environmental problems demand far-reaching and multifaceted solutions. There is little likelihood of controlling the rate at which humanity is consuming the earth's resources, for example, as long as almost 2 million people are added to the global population each week. Controlling population growth, in turn, depends on expanding the range of occupational and educational opportunities open to women to provide alternatives to remaining in the home and having more children.

However difficult the task may be, structural-functionalism provides grounds for optimism that societies can constructively respond to environmental dangers. Consider, once again, the case of air pollution. Air quality fell sharply with the onset of the Industrial Revolution. But gradually societies in Europe and North America recognized and responded to this problem, enacting new laws and employing new technology to improve air quality. Similarly, just as companies once fouled the natural environment in the process of making money, now new companies are profiting by cleaning up our physical surroundings. In short, given that a livable natural environment is essential to the operation of human society, we should expect determined efforts to cope with whatever environmental problems may arise.

Critical evaluation. Structural-functional analysis shows that the condition of the natural environment cannot be analyzed apart from the operation of society itself. To its credit, this approach reveals the extent to which the environment is a sociological concern.

Few people will take issue with the assertion that the organization of society and the state of the natural environment are closely tied together. But, as we have seen before, a limitation in this approach is

NOTE: The kinds of environmental policies societies adopt also are shaped by the interests of elites. Consider the relatively small amount of national support for solar power (a decentralized form of energy) compared to coal, gas, oil, or nuclear power (which remain under the control of corporate and technical elites).
NOTE: Researchers find that, although most adults in the United States claim to be environmentally concerned, people's behavior generally does not measure up to their principles.
Q: "If current predictions of population growth prove accurate and patterns of human activity on this planet remain unchanged, science and technology may not be able to prevent either irreversible degradation of the environment or continued poverty for much of the world." From a joint report by the U.S. National Academy of Arts and Sciences and the Royal Society of London

The poor of the world suffer most from environmental degradation. Tragically, poverty pushes people toward short-term strategies to survive (including cutting forests or hunting game to extinction) that have detrimental long-term consequences.

overlooking the issues of inequality and power. In other words, who benefits from various forms of environmental pollution, and who bears the consequences of a spoiled environment? As we shall see presently, the answer may turn out to be, respectively, the rich and the poor.

Furthermore, many environmentalists are skeptical of structural-functionalism's optimism about society's capacity to improve the natural world. On the one hand, many people have vested interests in continuing past ways, even if they threaten the well-being of the general public. Moreover, many of the environmental problems we face—especially the rapid growth of the population—are simply too far out of control at present to justify such optimism.

Social-Conflict Analysis

Social-conflict theory highlights the very issues that structural-functionalism tends to overlook: power and inequality. The basic insight here is that, far from being inevitable, problems of the natural environment result from social arrangements favored by elites. In other words, social-conflict theory indicts elites—especially capitalists—for directly or indirectly aggravating environmental problems as they pursue their self-interest. Extending this idea, social-conflict analysis also reminds us that the global disparity of wealth and power has important environmental consequences.

First, there is the issue of elites. As conflict theorists see it, in the hierarchical organization of our current society, a small proportion of a population has the power to control events. More specifically, what Chapter 16 ("Politics and Government") described as the "power elite" sets the national and global agenda by controlling the world's economy, law, and orientation to the natural environment.

Early capitalists shepherded the United States into the industrial age, hungrily tapping the earth's resources and frantically turning out manufactured goods in pursuit of profits with little regard for environmental consequences. By and large, it was they who reaped the benefits of the new industrial wealth, while workers toiled in dangerous factories and lived in nearby neighborhoods soiled with smoke and shaken by the vibrations of the big machines.

Just as important, our society has long winked at the most blatant instances of environmental destruction, even when elite perpetrators run afoul of environmental law. Corporate pollution, as Chapter 8 ("Deviance") explains, falls under the category of white-collar crime. Such offenses typically escape prosecution; when action is taken, it is usually in the form of fines levied on a company rather than criminal penalties imposed on individuals. Thus, corporate executives responsible for burning or dumping toxic waste have been subject to penalties no greater (and sometimes less) than ordinary citizens who throw litter from car windows.

Conflict theorists who embrace a Marxist view of society argue that capitalism itself poses a threat to the environment. The logic of capitalism is the pursuit of profit, and that pursuit demands continuous economic growth. As Marxists see it, what is personally profitable does not necessarily advance the public welfare, nor is it likely to be good for the natural environment. As noted earlier in this chapter, for example, capitalist industries have long ensured continuous profits by intentionally designing their products to be disposable or to have a limited useful life (the concept of "planned obsolescence"). Such policies may improve the "bottom line" in the near future, but they raise the long-term risk of depleting natural resources as well as generating solid waste.

A second issue raised by social-conflict theory is inequality. As shown earlier in Global Map 22–1, a small share of the earth's population currently consumes most of its energy. Generally, members of rich societies, including the United States, consume most of the earth's resources and, in the process, generate the most global pollution. We have achieved our affluent way of life, in short, by exploiting the earth and the poor of the less-developed countries and we have poisoned their air and water in the process. And now we scold them for overpopulation and overrapid industrialization that does not meet our environmental standards.

From this point of view, rich nations are actually *over*developed and consume too much. No one should expect that the majority of the earth's people, who live in poor societies, will be able to match the living standard in this country; nor, given the current environmental crisis, would that be desirable. What is needed is a more equitable distribution of resources among all people of the world. As conflict theorists see it, this is warranted both as a matter of social justice and as a strategy to preserve the natural environment.

Critical evaluation. The social-conflict paradigm complements other analyses by raising the important questions of who sets a society's agenda and who benefits (and suffers) most from decisions that are made. Environmental problems, from this point of view, are consequences of a society's class structure and the world's hierarchy of nations.

Like structural-functionalism, this approach is subject to criticism. While it may be true that elites have always dominated U.S. society, they have not been able to prevent a steady trend toward legal protection of the natural environment. These protections, in turn, have resulted in some significant improvements in our air and water quality.

And what of the charge that capitalism is particularly hostile to the natural world? There is little doubt that capitalism's logic of growth does place stress on the environment. At the same time, however, capitalist societies in North America and, especially, in Europe have made notable strides toward environmental protection. By contrast, the environmental record of socialist societies is far from exemplary. A look back to Figure 22–3 shows that citizens of Poland and Russia—two societies ruled for a half-century by socialist governments—are highly critical of environmental quality in their local communities (Dunlap, Gallup, & Gallup, 1992). This record reflects decades of policies

that pursued industrialization in utter neglect of environmental concerns, without challenge and with tragic consequences in terms of human health.

Finally, there is little doubt that rich societies currently place the greatest demands on the natural environment. However, this pattern is already beginning to shift as global population continues to build within poor countries. And environmental problems are also likely to grow worse to the extent that poor societies develop economically, using more resources and producing more waste and pollutants in the process.

In the long run, all nations of the world share a vital interest in protecting the natural environment. This general concern leads us to the final topic of this chapter, the concept of a sustainable environment.

LOOKING AHEAD: TOWARD A SUSTAINABLE SOCIETY AND WORLD

India's great leader Mahatma Gandhi once declared that societies must provide "enough for people's needs, but not for their greed." From an environmental point of view, this means that the earth will be able to provide for the basic needs of future generations only if humanity refrains from rapidly and thoughtlessly consuming finite resources such as oil, hardwoods, and even water. Nor can we persist in polluting the air, water, and ground at anything like the current levels. The loss of global forests—through cutting of trees and the destructive effects of acid rain—threatens to undermine the global climate. And we risk the future of the planet by adding people to the world at the rate of almost 2 million per week.

As explained at the beginning of this chapter, on every part of the earth inhabited by humanity, an environmental deficit is growing. In effect, our present way of life is borrowing against the well-being of our children and their children. And, looking to the global dimension of this process, members of rich societies who currently consume so much of the earth's resources are mortgaging the future security of the majority of people who live in the poor societies of the world.

In principle, the solution to the entire range of environmental problems described in this chapter is living in a way that is *sustainable* because it does not increase the environmental deficit. A **sustainable ecosystem** refers to *the human use of the natural environment to meet the needs of the present generation without threatening the prospects of future generations.*

Although the problem of topsoil erosion in the United States is serious primarily in California, desertification is also widespread in many countries of the world, including Nepal (Asia), Peru (Latin America), Turkey (bridging Europe and Asia), and Sudan and Lesotho (Africa). The causes of desertification are less climatic than human: The cutting of trees, burning of vegetation, and allowing cattle to overgraze land are the major causes of this problem. The overall effect is that, as the world's forests shrink in size, the planet's deserts are expanding.

Sustainable living that does not threaten the future of the planet will call for three basic strategies. The first is the conservation of finite resources. We must balance the desire to satisfy our present wants with our responsibility to preserve what will be needed by future generations. Conservation involves using resources more efficiently, seeking alternative resources, and, in some cases, learning to live with less.

Technology, no doubt, will provide the key to household devices (from light bulbs to furnaces) that are far more energy efficient than those available at present. Moreover, we should expand development of alternative energy sources, including harnessing the power of the sun, wind, and tides. But while relying on help from new technology, a sustainable way of life will require rethinking the proconsumption attitudes formed during decades of "cheap electricity" and "cheap oil."

The second basic strategy is reducing waste. Whenever possible, simply using less is the most effective way to reduce waste. In addition, societies around the world need to expand recycling programs. Success will depend both on educational efforts to enlist widespread support for recycling and on legislation requir-

ing the recycling of certain materials. Moreover, since most societies in the world favor market economies, the success of any recycling program is more likely to the extent that it becomes commercially viable.

The third key element in any plan for a sustainable ecosystem is bringing world population growth under control. As we have explained, the problems of supporting the current (1995) population of 5.5 billion are serious enough. Clearly, the higher world population climbs, the more difficult environmental problems will become. Global population is currently increasing at about 1.7 percent each year, a rate that will double the world's people in about forty years. Few analysts think that the earth can support a population of 10 billion or more; most argue that we must hold the line at about 7 billion. Controlling population growth will require urgent steps in poor regions of the world where growth rates are highest.

But no collection of environmental strategies, by themselves, will succeed without some fundamental changes in the ways in which we think about ourselves and our world. The basic problem is that we live according to our own immediate interests, and, in the process, we fail to perceive several important connections.

One link we overlook is, environmentally speaking, that the present is tied to the future. Simply put, today's actions shape tomorrow's world. Thus, we must learn to evaluate our short-term choices in terms of their long-range consequences for the natural environment.

A second connection is that we humans are linked in countless ways to all other species of life. Rather than viewing humans as "different" from other forms of life and assuming that we rightfully dominate the planet, we need to recognize that all forms of life are interdependent. To do otherwise not only harms other life forms, it will eventually undermine our own well-being. From this general realization of connectedness must follow specific programs that will protect the earth's biodiversity.

Third, and finally, achieving a sustainable ecosystem is a task that requires global cooperation. The planet's rich and poor nations are currently separated by their particular interests and by sharply different living standards. On the one hand, most societies in the northern half of the world are overdeveloped, using more resources than the earth can sustain over time. On the other hand, most societies in the southern half of the world are underdeveloped, currently unable to meet the basic needs of many of their people. There are no easy solutions to this imbalance. Still, the magnitude of the challenge cannot be allowed to justify the status quo. A sustainable ecosystem depends on bold and unprecedented programs of cooperation. The costs of change will certainly be high, but they pale before the eventual cost of not responding to the growing environmental deficit (Humphrey & Buttel, 1982; Burke, 1984; Kellert & Bohrmann, 1991; Brown, 1993).

Finally, realizing the goal of a sustainable society demands a critical reevaluation of the logic of growth that has dominated our way of life for several centuries. There is already evidence that the tide is turning on this issue: A recent Gallup poll found that majorities of people in twenty of twenty-two nations surveyed endorsed stronger action to protect the environment, even if doing so slowed economic growth (Dunlap, Gallup, & Gallup, 1992).

In closing, we might well consider that the great dinosaurs dominated this planet for some 160 million years and then perished forever. Humanity is far younger, having existed for a mere quarter of a million years. Compared to the rather dim-witted dinosaurs, our species has the gift of great intelligence. But how will we use this ability? What are the chances that our species will continue to flourish on the earth 160 million years—or even one thousand years—from now? As Tom Burke (1984) points out, it would be foolish to assume our present civilization is about to collapse. But it would be equally foolish to ignore the warning signs. One key insight stands out: The state of tomorrow's world will depend on choices we make today.

SUMMARY

1. The most important factor affecting the state of the natural environment is how human beings organize social life. Ecology, the study of how living organisms interact with their environment, is one important focus of sociology.

2. Societies harm the natural environment—in other words, increase the environmental deficit—by focusing on short-term benefits and ignoring the long-term consequences of policy and practice.

3. Studying the natural environment demands a global perspective. All parts of the ecosystem—including the air, soil, and water—are linked. Similarly, actions in one part of the globe affect the natural environment elsewhere.

4. Humanity's great influence on the natural environment springs from our capacity for culture. Human manipulation of the environment has expanded historically with the development of complex technology.

5. Population growth is also a major way in which humanity shapes the natural environment. The world population has soared upward over the course of the last two centuries and now threatens to overwhelm available resources.

6. The conventional *logic of growth* defends economic development and recognizes people's capacity to solve environmental problems that may arise. In opposition to this position, the *limits to growth* thesis states that societies have little choice but to curb development in order to avoid eventual environmental collapse.

7. Public opinion surveys suggest that most members of our society think the nation spends too little on programs to protect the natural environment. Over time, environmental concerns among members of our society have been increasing.

8. One problem of the natural environment is the burgeoning amount of solid waste. The United States is a "disposable society," generating 1 billion pounds of solid waste each day. Currently, our society burns 10 percent of solid waste, recycles another 10 percent, and disposes of the remaining 80 percent in landfills.

9. Water consumption is rapidly increasing throughout the world. Water supply in much of the world—notably Africa and the Middle East—is currently approaching a state of crisis.

10. The hydrological cycle purifies rainwater, but water pollution from dumping and chemical contamination still poses a serious threat to water quality in the United States. This problem is even more serious in the world's poor societies.

11. Air quality became steadily worse in Europe and North America after the Industrial Revolution. About 1950, however, a turnaround took place as these societies began making significant progress in curbing air pollution. In poor societies—

especially in cities—air quality remains poor due to burning of "dirty" fuels and little regulation of pollution.

12. Acid rain is created as pollutants in the atmosphere form acids that contaminate rain as it develops and falls, often thousands of miles away.

13. Tropical rain forests play a vital role in removing carbon dioxide from the atmosphere. Under pressure from commercial interests, global rain forests are now half their original size and are shrinking by about 1 percent annually.

14. Global warming refers to predictions that the average temperature of the earth is rising due to increasing levels of carbon dioxide in the atmosphere. Both carbon emissions from factories and automobiles and the shrinking global rain forests, which consume carbon dioxide, contribute to this problem.

15. The loss of rain forests is also reducing the planet's biodiversity, since these tropical regions are home to about half of all living species. Of a total number of species exceeding 30 million, dozens disappear each day. Biodiversity is important to agricultural and medical research and is also a source of great natural beauty.

16. Structural-functional theory points out that cultural values have much to do with a society's orientation to the natural environment, that many dimensions of social organization have consequences for the environment, and that societies can be expected to respond to environmental problems that endanger them.

17. Social-conflict analysis highlights the importance of inequality in understanding environmental issues. This perspective blames environmental decay on the self-interest of elites. It also places responsibility for the declining state of the world's natural environment primarily on rich societies, which consume the most resources.

18. A sustainable environment is one that does not threaten the well-being of future generations. Achieving this goal will require conservation of finite resources, reducing solid waste and pollution, and controlling the increase of world population.

KEY CONCEPTS

acid rain precipitation that is made acidic by air pollution and destroys plant and animal life

ecology the study of the interaction of living organisms and the natural environment

ecosystem the system composed of the interaction of all living organisms and their natural environment

environmental deficit the situation in which negative, long-term consequences of decisions about the natural environment outweigh whatever short-term benefits may accrue

greenhouse effect a rise in the earth's average temperature (global warming) due to increasing concentration of carbon dioxide in the atmosphere

natural environment the earth's surface and atmosphere including various living organisms and the air, water, soil, and other resources necessary to sustain life

rain forests regions of dense forestation, most of which circle the globe close to the equator

recycling programs to reuse resources that we would otherwise discard as "waste"

sustainable ecosystem the human use of the natural environment to meet the needs of the present generation without threatening the prospects of future generations

CRITICAL-THINKING QUESTIONS

1. What renders human beings capable of having such a great effect on the natural environment? How has this capacity changed over the course of human history?

2. Why are problems of the natural environment global in scope?

3. What is the current state of the natural environment with regard to solid waste? The quality of the air? The supply and quality of water?

4. Suggest ways in which life in your local community would change were we to establish an environmentally sustainable society.

SUGGESTED READINGS

Classic Sources

Rachel Carson. *Silent Spring*. Boston: Houghton Mifflin, 1962.
   This book about the dangers of chemical pollution helped launch the environmental movement in the United States and elsewhere.

Donella H. Meadows et al. *The Limits to Growth: A Report for the Club of Rome's Project on the Predicament of Mankind*. New York: Universe Books, 1972.
   This study utilizes computer modeling to predict future ecological trends. Its results support the "limits to growth" thesis.

Contemporary Sources

F. Kurt Cylke, Jr. *The Environment*. New York: Harper-Collins, 1993.
   This brief paperback offers a more detailed discussion of many of the environment-related issues raised in this chapter.

F. Herbert Bohrmann and Stephen R. Kellert, eds. *Ecology, Economics, and Ethics: The Broken Circle*. New Haven, Conn.: Yale University Press, 1991.
   This collection of thirteen essays dealing with environmental issues explains how the study of the natural environment is necessarily multidisciplinary.

Charles L. Harper. *Environment and Society: Social Perspectives on Environmental Issues and Problems*. Englewood Cliffs, N.J.: Prentice Hall, 1995.
   This new text applies various sociological approaches, including major theoretical paradigms, to the study of the environment.

Lester W. Milbrath. *Envisioning a Sustainable Society: Learning Our Way Out*. Albany: State University of New York Press, 1989.
   What is a "sustainable society"? What steps increase the chances to make it a reality? This book provides some answers.

Global Sources

Lester R. Brown et al. *State of the World: A Worldwatch Institute Report on Progress Toward a Sustainable Society*. New York: W. W. Norton, 1993.
   Published annually, this collection of essays provides a comprehensive look at the natural environment in global perspective.

Marius Jacobs. *The Tropical Rain Forest: A First Encounter*. Berlin: Springer-Verlag, 1988.
   This well-illustrated paperback details the environmental significance of the tropical rain forest and surveys the state of rain forests in various regions of the world.

David Attenborough, Philip Whitfield, Peter D. Moore, and Barry Cox. *The Atlas of the Living World*. Boston: Houghton Mifflin, 1989.
   This colorful and inviting book provides a good introduction to the earth as a natural and social system. Its focus ranges from the origin of our world to contemporary problems including acid rain and loss of biodiversity.

Riley E. Dunlap, George H. Gallup, Jr., and Alec M. Gallup. *The Health of the Planet Survey*. Princeton, N.J.: George H. Gallup International Institute, 1992.
   This report, based on surveys carried out in twenty-two nations, describes public attitudes concerning environmental problems and economic growth.

Malin Falkenmark and Carl Widstrand. "Population and Water Resources: A Delicate Balance." *Population Bulletin*, Vol. 47, no. 3 (November 1992).
   This issue of the *Population Bulletin*, published by the Population Reference Bureau in Washington, D.C., is devoted to the important question of maintaining adequate water resources in light of increasing global population growth.

William V. D'Antonio, Masamichi Sasaki, and Yoshio Yonebayashi, eds. *Ecology, World Resources and the Quality of Social Life*. New Brunswick, N.J.: Transaction, 1993.
   This collection of essays, reflecting the efforts of researchers from ten nations, probes the social implications of pressing environmental issues.

Umberto Boccioni, *Riot in the Gallery*, 1909.

DATA FILE: An outline of this chapter, suggested discussion topics, and supplemental lecture material on topics such as disaster research are found in the *Data File*.

Q: "For freedom and justice and so the troopers can't hit us anymore." An African-American school girl explaining why she was joining the Selma march, 1965

NOTE: The term collective behavior was coined by Robert E. Park; in fact, Park defined sociology as "the science of collective behavior," suggesting a focus on dynamic rather than stable social patterns. (See Ralph Turner's introduction to *Robert E. Park: On Social Control and Collective Behavior*, University of Chicago Press, 1967.)

Collective Behavior and Social Movements

*O*n a February morning in 1990, a reunion took place as four men walked into Woolworth's in Greensboro, North Carolina. Cameras clicked and whirred, as the four—feeling like celebrities—enjoyed a breakfast of eggs, grits, bacon, and coffee.

Why the commotion? Thirty years earlier to the day, the same four—then college students—had sat down at the same lunch counter and requested a meal from the same waitress. She refused to serve them because African Americans were not welcome in the segregated Greensboro Woolworth's. So the four young men just sat there nervously, amid a deafening silence broken only by a white police officer's rhythmic slap of his billy club into his hand.

After an hour, the four got up and peacefully left. Their courageous action called attention to the racial exclusion then commonplace in the South and sparked sit-ins at lunch counters throughout the

region. The sit-in was one tactic that defined the Civil Rights movement that aimed to end legal segregation in the United States.

More generally, **social movements** are *organized activity that encourages or discourages social change.* Social movements are perhaps the most important type of **collective behavior**, *activity involving a large number of people, often spontaneous, and typically in violation of established norms.* Other forms of collective behavior—each giving rise to controversy and some provoking change—are crowds, mobs and riots, rumor and gossip, public opinion, panics and mass hysteria, and fashions and fads.

This chapter surveys various topics that form the broad and internally diverse field of collective behavior. It then focuses on social movements, such as the Civil Rights movement and the women's movement in the United States and the democratic movements that recently swept Eastern Europe and the former Soviet Union.

615

NOTE: Turner and Killian (1987) report that Robert Park's dissertation (Heidelberg, 1903) was titled *Masse und Publikum* ("The Crowd and the Public").

Q: "Interest in the field [of collective behavior and social movements] has hardly been constant, tending instead to wax and wane partly in response to the level of movement activity in society." Doug McAdam, John D. McCarthy, and Mayer N. Zald

Q: "Collective behavior is not merely identical with the study of groups . . . Organizational behavior is the behavior of groups that are governed by established rules or procedures, which have the force of tradition behind them . . . Collectivities, or the groups within which collective behavior takes place, are not guided in a straightforward fashion by the culture of the society . . ." Ralph H. Turner and Lewis N. Killian (1987:4)

Sociologists distinguish between a group *and a* collectivity *on the basis of the extent of social interaction, clarity of social boundaries, and character of norms. These people lined up to vote in a recent election in El Salvador are a loose collectivity with little sense of being members of a well-defined group.*

COLLECTIVE BEHAVIOR

A half-century ago, sociologists paid little attention to collective behavior, preferring to focus on more established social patterns like the family and social stratification. Because collective behavior focused on actions generally deemed unusual or deviant, in other words, analysts thought this area of inquiry unworthy. The numerous social movements that burst on the scene during the tumultuous 1960s, however, ignited sociological interest in various types of collective behavior (Weller & Quarantelli, 1973; G. Marx & Wood, 1975; Aguirre & Quarantelli, 1983; Turner & Killian, 1987; McAdam, McCarthy, & Zald, 1988).

Studying Collective Behavior

Despite its importance, collective behavior is difficult for sociologists to study for the following three reasons.

1. **The concept of collective behavior is broad.** Collective behavior embraces a sometimes bewildering array of phenomena. The traits common to fads, rumors, and mob behavior, for example, are certainly not obvious.
2. **All collective behavior is complex.** A rumor seems to come out of nowhere and circulates in countless different settings. For no apparent reason, one new form of dress "catches on" while another does not. And, on the world scene, why would millions of people across Eastern Europe and the former Soviet Union patiently endure undemocratic rule for decades only to suddenly and decisively throw out their leaders?
3. **Much collective behavior is transitory.** Sociologists can readily study the family because it is an enduring element of social life. Fashions, rumors, and riots, by contrast, tend to arise and dissipate quickly, making them difficult to investigate systematically.

Some researchers point out that these problems apply not just to collective behavior but to *most* forms of human behavior (Aguirre & Quarantelli, 1983). Moreover, collective behavior is not always so elusive; no one is surprised by the crowds that form at sports events and music festivals, and sociologists can study these gatherings firsthand or by using videotapes or audio records. Researchers can even anticipate natural disasters in order to study the human response they provoke. We know, for example, that forty to eighty major tornadoes occur in particular regions of the United States each year; some sociologists interested in how disasters affect behavior stand prepared to initiate research on short notice (Miller, 1985). Researchers can also use historical documents to reconstruct the details of an unanticipated natural disaster or riot.

But sociologists have not resolved all the problems presented by this area of study. The most serious problem, according to Benigno Aguirre and E. L. Quarantelli (1983), is that sociologists have yet to devise theories that tie together all the diverse actions termed "collective behavior."

What we can say, at present, is that all collective behavior involves the action of some **collectivity**, *a large number of people whose minimal interaction occurs in the absence of well-defined and conventional norms.* Collectivities are of two kinds. *Localized collectivities* involve people in physical proximity to one another; this first type is illustrated by crowds and riots. *Dispersed collectivities* are composed of people who influence one another despite being spread over great distances; examples here include rumors, public opinion, and fashion (Turner & Killian, 1987).

Generally speaking, we can point to three ways in which collectivities differ from the already familiar concept of social groups (see Chapter 7, "Groups and Organizations"):

1. **Collectivities are based on limited social interaction**. Group members interact directly and frequently. Interaction in localized collectivities such as mobs is limited and temporary. People participating in dispersed collectivities like a fad typically do not interact at all.

2. **Collectivities have no clear social boundaries.** Greater interaction gives group members a sense of common identity usually missing among people engaged in collective behavior. Localized crowds may have a common object of attention (such as a despondent person on a ledge high above the street), but these people exhibit little sense of unity. Individuals involved in dispersed collectivities, such as "the public" that turns out to vote for a political candidate, have even less of an awareness of shared membership. People become more aware of "who their friends are" when a social movement gives rise to well-defined factions; even here, however, it is often difficult to discern who falls within the ranks of, say, the pro-life or pro-choice movement.

3. **Collectivities engender weak and unconventional norms**. Conventional cultural norms usually regulate the behavior of group members. Some collectivities, such as people traveling on an airplane, do operate according to social norms, but these rules usually amount to little more than respecting the privacy of people sitting in nearby seats. Other collectivities—such as emotional soccer fans who destroy property as they leave a stadium—spontaneously develop decidedly unconventional norms (Weller & Quarantelli, 1973; Turner & Killian, 1987).

Crowds

One important form of collective behavior is the **crowd**, *a temporary gathering of people who share a common focus of attention and whose members influence one another.* Historian Peter Laslett (1984) points out that crowds are a modern development; in medieval Europe, large numbers of people assembled in one place only when major armies faced off on the battlefield. Today, however, crowds reaching twenty-five thousand or even more are common at sporting events, rock concerts, and even the registration halls of large universities.

But all such crowds are not alike. Herbert Blumer (1969) identified four categories of crowds. A *casual crowd* is a loose collection of people who interact little, if at all. People who gather on the beach or collect at the scene of an automobile accident have only a passing awareness of one another. Few social patterns are typical of casual crowds beyond the momentary sharing of an interest.

A *conventional crowd* results from deliberate planning, as illustrated by a country auction, a college lecture, or a somber funeral. In each case, interaction typically conforms to norms deemed appropriate for the situation.

An *expressive crowd* forms around an event with emotional appeal, such as a religious revival, a wrestling match featuring Hulk Hogan, or the New Year's Eve celebration in New York's Times Square. Excitement is the main reason people join expressive crowds in the first place, which makes expressive crowds relatively spontaneous and exhilarating for those involved.

An *acting crowd* is a collectivity fueled by an intense, single-minded purpose, such as an audience rushing the doors of a concert hall or fleeing from a theater that is on fire. Acting crowds are ignited by emotions more powerful than those typical of expressive crowds, often reaching a feverish intensity that sometimes erupts into mob violence.

Any gathering of people can change from one type of crowd to another. In 1985, for example, a conventional crowd took form as sixty thousand fans assembled in a soccer stadium to watch the European Cup Finals between Italy and Great Britain. Once the game started, however, many British fans, already intoxicated, began taunting the Italians sitting in adjacent stands. At this point, an expressive crowd had formed. The two sides began to throw bottles at each other; then the British surged like a human wave toward the Italians. An estimated 400 million television viewers watched in horror as this acting crowd became a rampaging mob trampling hundreds of helpless spectators. In minutes, thirty-eight people were dead and another four hundred injured (Lacayo, 1985).

Deliberate action by a crowd is not the product simply of rising emotions. Participants in *protest crowds*—a fifth category we can add to Blumer's list—engage in a variety of actions, including strikes, boycotts, sit-ins, and marches, that have political goals (McPhail & Wohlstein, 1983). For example, students on college campuses who gather to express views about an issue are a protest crowd. These crowds vary in emotional energy, ranging from conventional to acting crowds. Sometimes a protest gathering begins peacefully, but individuals become aggressive when confronted with counter demonstrators, a process illustrated by recent clashes between pro-choice and pro-life activists.

DATA FILE: A brief account of lynching in U.S. history is found in the *Data File*.

NOTE: The term "mob" is derived from the Latin *mobile vulgus*, meaning "the movable or changeable common people." Note the historical association of mobs with common people.

NOTE: The word "riot" was used in medieval Europe to refer to a dispute or quarrel; its earlier Latin root is probably *rugire*, meaning "to roar."

DIVERSITY: Racial violence has a long history in the United States. By and large, it involved white attacks on black people, Asians, and Native Americans. The pattern of African Americans rioting against whites emerged later, in the 1960s.

The powers that be have often disparaged popular opposition as a "mob." Such an argument was used to justify police violence against strikers—including ten who died—in a bloody confrontation near Chicago's Republic Steel Mill in 1936. Philip Evergood commemorates the event in his painting American Tragedy, 1936.

Mobs and Riots

As an acting crowd turns violent, we may witness the birth of a **mob**, *a highly emotional crowd that pursues some violent or destructive goal*. Despite, or perhaps because of, their intense emotion, mobs tend to dissipate rather quickly. The duration of a mob incident also depends on whether its leadership tries to inflame or stabilize the crowd and on the mob's precise objectives.

Lynching is the most notorious example of mob behavior in the United States. This term is derived from Charles Lynch, a Virginia colonist who sought to maintain law and order in his own way before formal courts were established. The word soon became synonymous with terrorism and murder outside the legal system.

Lynching has always been colored by race. After the Civil War, whites' efforts to maintain their domination over emancipated African Americans fueled lynch mobs as a highly effective form of social control. African Americans who questioned white superiority or behaved in a nondifferential way risked hanging or being burned alive by vengeful whites. Black people and occasionally their white defenders became all-purpose scapegoats.

The activity of lynch mobs—typically composed of low-status whites most threatened by the emancipation of slaves—reached its peak between 1880 and 1930. About five thousand lynchings were recorded by police in that period; many more, no doubt, occurred. Most of these crimes were committed in the Deep South, where an agrarian economy still depended on a cheap and docile labor force, but lynchings took place in virtually every state and victimized every minority. On the western frontier, for example, lynch mobs frequently targeted people of Mexican and Asian descent. In about 25 percent of the cases, whites lynched other whites. The lynching of women, however, was rare; only about a hundred such instances are known, almost all involving women of color (White, 1969, orig. 1929; Grant, 1975).

A frenzied crowd without any particular purpose is a **riot**, *a social eruption that is highly emotional, violent, and undirected*. Unlike the action of a mob, then, a riot usually has no clear goal. Riots are generally fueled by long-standing anger, ignited by some minor incident, leading participants to indulge in seemingly random violence against property or persons (Smelser, 1962). Whereas a mob action usually ends when a specific violent goal has been achieved (or decisively prevented), a riot tends to disperse only as participants run out of steam or community leaders or police gradually bring them under control.

Throughout our nation's history, riots have been a collective expression of social injustice. Industrial workers, for example, have rioted to vent rage at their working conditions. In 1886 a bitter struggle by Chicago factory workers for an eight-hour workday led to the explosive Haymarket Riot, which left eleven dead and scores injured. Rioting born of anger and despair has also been commonplace within this country's penal system.

In addition, race riots have occurred with striking regularity. Early in this century, crowds of whites attacked African Americans in Chicago, Detroit, and other cities. In the 1960s, summers of violent riots rocked the minority ghettos of many cities as seemingly trivial events ignited anger at continuing prejudice and discrimination. In Los Angeles in 1992, an explosive riot was set off by the acquittal of police officers involved in the beating of Rodney King. The turmoil left more than fifty dead, caused thousands of injuries, and destroyed property worth hundreds of millions of dollars.

Riots are not always fired by hate. They can also result from positive feelings, such as the high spirits characteristic of young people who flock to resort areas during spring break from college. In March of 1986, for example, the exuberance of vacationing students in

Q: "What constituted a people, a unity, a whole, becomes in the end an agglomeration of individualities lacking cohesion." Gustave Le Bon
NOTE: Convergence theory reverses the causal link implied by contagion theory; the former suggests that motivation creates the crowd, the latter suggests that the crowd creates the motivation.

Q: "Perhaps there are situations such as a fire in a crowded theater in which people totally ignore others as they try to escape from danger. However, documented cases . . . are surprisingly rare in the literature." Norris Johnson
RESOURCE: Norris Johnson's account of "The Who Concert Panic" is included in the contemporary research found in the companion reader, *Seeing Ourselves*.

Palm Springs, California, erupted into a riot leading to a hundred arrests after crowds of young men began throwing rocks and bottles at passing cars and stripping clothing off terrified women (DeMott, 1986).

Contagion Theory

What makes the behavior of crowds unconventional? Social scientists have developed several different explanations over the last century. One of the first, by French sociologist Gustave Le Bon (1841–1931), is *contagion theory*.

The essence of Le Bon's (1960; orig. 1895) argument is that crowds exert a hypnotic influence on their members. In the anonymity of a crowd, he claimed, people evade personal responsibility and surrender to a collective mind. As a crowd assumes a life of its own, individual members slip free of social restraints and become irrational creatures driven by contagious emotion. As fear or hate resonates through the crowd, emotional intensity builds, driving individuals toward a violent outburst.

Critical evaluation. Some of Le Bon's assertions—that crowds foster anonymity and sometimes generate emotion—are surely true. Yet, as Clark McPhail (1991) points out, systematic research has shown that "the maddening crowd" does not take on a life of its own, apart from the thoughts and intentions of members. For example, Norris Johnson (1987), investigating the 1979 Who concert in Cincinnati, identified specific factors that sparked panic leading to the deaths of eleven people. These included an inadequate number of entrance doors, an open-seating policy, and little police supervision. Far from an episode of collective insanity, Johnson concluded, that crowd was composed of many small groups of people valiantly trying to help each another.

Convergence Theory

Convergence theory holds that motivations for collective action are not born in the crowd but are carried to the crowd by the individuals involved. From this point of view, crowds amount to a convergence of like-minded individuals. In 1985 a number of whites in southwest Philadelphia banded together to pressure an African-American couple to move from their neighborhood. Fearing violence, the couple fled; at this point, the crowd burned down the couple's house.

In such instances, convergence theorists contend, the crowd itself did not generate the hatred or the violence; more correctly, racial hostility had been simmering for some time among many local people. This crowd simply arose from a convergence of people sharing an attachment to their traditionally white neighborhood who opposed the presence of black residents and already had a propensity for violent action.

Critical evaluation. By linking crowds to broader social forces, convergence theory uncovers the roots of collective action. From this perspective, crowd behavior is not irrational, as Le Bon maintained, but a result of social structure and individual decision making (Berk, 1974).

It is probably true, however, that people do some things in a crowd that they would not have the courage to do alone. In addition, crowds can intensify a sentiment simply by creating a critical mass of like-minded people.

Emergent-Norm Theory

Ralph Turner and Lewis Killian (1987) have developed an *emergent-norm theory* of crowd dynamics. While these researchers maintain that social behavior is never entirely predictable, they quickly add that crowds are not the irrational settings described by Le Bon. And, while similar interests may draw people together, distinctive patterns of behavior do emerge within the crowd itself.

Turner and Killian explain that crowds begin as collectivities in which people have mixed interests and motives. Entering conventional or casual crowds, members understand what norms will guide their behavior. But the norms that steer less stable types of crowds—expressive, acting, and protest crowds—frequently surface only in particular settings. Usually leaders start the process of norm construction. For example, one member of the crowd at a rock concert holds up a lit cigarette lighter to signal praise for the performers, and others follow suit; or a few people in an angry street crowd throw bricks through store windows and others do the same, sparking a riot.

In the infamous New Bedford, Massachusetts, tavern rape in 1983, one man assaulted a twenty-one-year-old woman, raping her on the floor. Five other men then joined in, repeatedly raping the woman for an hour and a half. Still others in the bar cheered the rapists; apparently as some people sized up the situation, they concluded that this brutal action was somehow acceptable, while the rest were too intimidated to assist the woman or even call the police (*Time*, March 5, 1984).

Q: "Usually the judgment that someone has acted irrationally is made in hindsight or by someone who is not in the situation of the actor and thus has a different perspective." Ralph H. Turner and Lewis N. Killian

Q: "To regard gossip as 'idle chatter' is to underestimate its usefulness. . . . By making some people 'insiders,' gossip may serve the social needs of other-directed people." Jack Levin and Arnold Arluke (*Gossip: The Inside Scoop*, Plenum, 1987)

Critical evaluation. Emergent-norm theory represents a symbolic-interaction approach to crowd dynamics. Turner and Killian (1972:10) explain that crowd behavior is neither as irrational as contagion theory suggests, nor as purposeful as convergence theory implies. So while crowd behavior responds to participants' motives, it is guided by norms that emerge in a setting as the situation unfolds. This means that decision making plays a significant role in crowd behavior, even though it may not be evident to casual observers. For example, frightened people clogging the exits of a burning theater may appear to be victims of irrational panic but, from their point of view, fleeing a life-threatening situation is certainly a rational alternative to death. Experience and common sense play a part in precisely how people respond to any such event, of course; leaders on the scene also have a hand in guiding crowd response.

Further, people in a crowd may generate some pressure toward conformity, but emergent-norm theory points out that not every participant embraces emerging norms. Some assume leadership roles, others become lieutenants, rank-and-file followers, inactive bystanders, or opponents (Weller & Quarantelli, 1973; Zurcher & Snow, 1981).

Crowds, Politics, and Social Change

In March 1770 a crowd of Boston residents, angry over British domination, confronted an English soldier on the street. The soldier panicked and ran to summon reinforcements. The ensuing clash, which has become known as the Boston Massacre, left five people dead and galvanized support for independence from Britain. Three years later, another crowd of Bostonians gathered to angrily denounce the British taxation policy. Soon afterward, some of their number dressed as Native Americans and dumped tea from British commercial ships into Boston Harbor, an event dubbed the Boston Tea Party (Kelley, 1982). The British and their colonial supporters deplored these examples of "mob action," but to most colonists the participants were patriots opposing injustice and paving the way for independence.

Because crowds are linked to social change, they often provoke controversy. Defenders of the established social order have long feared and hated them. Gustave Le Bon's negative view of crowds as "only powerful for destruction" was common among members of the aristocracy (1960:18; orig. 1895). Oftentimes, collective action that privileged people condemn as destructive, the disadvantaged cheer as rightful protest against social wrongs.

But all crowds do not share a single political cast: Some call for change and some resist it. Throngs of Romans rallying to the Sermon on the Mount by Jesus of Nazareth, bands of traditional weavers destroying new industrial machinery that was making their skills obsolete, masses of marchers carrying banners and shouting slogans for or against abortion—these and countless other instances across the centuries show crowds to be an important means through which people challenge or support their society (Rudé, 1964; Canetti, 1978).

Rumor and Gossip

It is not just people in physical proximity who participate in collective behavior. Sociologists use the term **mass behavior** to refer to *collective behavior among people dispersed over a wide geographical area.*

A common example of mass behavior is **rumor**, *unsubstantiated information people spread informally, often by word of mouth.* Although people still spread rumors through face-to-face communication, modern technology—including telephones, electronic mail, and especially the mass media—allow rumors to spread more rapidly to a greater number of people than ever before.

Rumor has three essential characteristics.

1. **Rumor thrives in a climate of ambiguity.** Rumors arise among people who lack definitive information about a topic they care about. For example, workers fearing a massive layoff, and hearing little from management, will likely find themselves awash in rumors. In positive terms, rumor is an effort to define reality in the absence of substantiated facts (Shibutani, 1966; Rosnow & Fine, 1976).

2. **Rumor is unstable.** As people spread a rumor, they alter its content, usually to serve their own interests. Before long, many variations emerge. In a workplace beset by rumors, workers typically play up the shortcomings of management, while executives "spin" information in their own way.

3. **Rumor is difficult to stop.** The number of people aware of a rumor increases in geometric progression as each person spreads information to several others. Of course, some rumors dissipate with time, but, in general, only clear, widely dispersed, and substantiated information will put a rumor to rest.

Rumor can trigger the formation of crowds or other collective behavior. For this reason, authorities often establish rumor-control centers in times of crisis

NOTE: Levin and Arluke spread a rumor on their campus by widely distributing flyers announcing a fictitious wedding. The flyers were not circulated until a day before the supposed event. Still, the researchers found that, one week later, 52% of a campus sample had heard of the wedding, and 12% claimed to have actually attended it! (1987:14–15)

NOTE: Delbert Miller claimed that, in 1945, only a small number of people on his campus learned of the death of President Roosevelt directly from radio reports. Within 30 minutes, however, about 90% of the people had been informed by word of mouth (*American Sociological Review* 10:691–94). Obviously, today's more powerful mass media reduce the significance of word of mouth in spreading national rumor.

SOCIOLOGY OF EVERYDAY LIFE

The Rumor Mill: Paul Is Dead!

The Beatles—John Lennon, Paul McCartney, George Harrison, and Ringo Starr—led the music explosion of the 1960s as the world's celebrated rock band. Their unprecedented fame, perhaps with a little help from the Beatles themselves, spawned a rumor: the alleged death of Paul McCartney.

The rumor of McCartney's death probably began on October 12, 1969, when a young man telephoned a Detroit disk jockey and made two startling announcements:

1. At the end of the song "Strawberry Fields Forever" on the *Magical Mystery Tour* album, filtering out background noise allows the listener to hear a voice saying, "I buried Paul!"

2. The phrase "Number 9, Number 9, Number 9" from the song "Revolution 9" on the *White Album*, when played backward, seems to intone, "Turn me on, dead man!"

Two days later, the University of Michigan student newspaper ran a story titled "McCartney Is Dead: Further Clues Found." It sent millions of Beatles fans scurrying for their albums to confirm further "evidence."

3. A picture inside the *Magical Mystery Tour* album shows John, George, and Ringo wearing red carnations, while Paul is wearing a black flower.

4. The cover of the *Sergeant Pepper's Lonely Hearts Club Band* album presents a grave with yellow flowers arranged in the shape of Paul's bass guitar.

5. On the inside of that album, McCartney wears an armpatch with the letters "OPD." Is this the insignia of some police department, or confirmation that Paul had been "Officially Pronounced Dead"?

6. On the back cover of the same album, three Beatles are facing forward while McCartney has his back to the camera.

7. On the album cover of *Abbey Road*, John Lennon is clothed as a clergyman, Ringo Starr wears an undertaker's black tie, and George Harrison is clad in workman's attire as if ready to dig a grave. For his part, McCartney is barefoot—just as Tibetan burial rituals claim a corpse ready for interment should be. Further, a Volkswagen nearby displays the license plate "28 IF," correctly indicating that McCartney

would have been *28 if* he had not met his demise.

The report in the University of Michigan newspaper provided details of McCartney's alleged "death" in an automobile accident early in November 1966 and included a photograph allegedly of the musician's bloodied head. After the accident, the story continued, music company executives had secretly replaced Paul with a double.

Paul McCartney is, of course, very much alive and still jokes about the episode. Few doubt that the Beatles intentionally fabricated some of the clues to encourage the interest of their fans. But the incident has a serious side, showing how quickly rumors may arise and endure in a climate of distrust. During the late 1960s, many disaffected young people were quite ready to believe that the media and other powerful interests would conceal an event such as McCartney's death.

McCartney himself denied the rumor in a 1969 *Life* magazine interview. But thousands of suspicious readers also noticed that the back of the page containing McCartney's picture had an advertisement for an automobile: Holding this page up to the light, the car lay across McCartney's chest and blocked his head! Another clue!

SOURCES: Based on Rosnow & Fine (1976) and Kapferer (1992).

SOCIAL SURVEY: Scanning the General Social Survey data shows that a significant proportion of respondents have no opinion about many issues: Should authorities prevent parents from showing pornographic films to their 10-year-old child? (17% express no opinion); Does the average person influence government decisions? (8% express no opinion) Is the world getting better? (19% express no opinion) Is there a life after death? (8% express no opinion).

NOTE: The Greek root of the word "hysteria" is *hystero*, meaning "uterus." This reveals the historical association of irrational behavior and women. Moreover, most witches were women, often women who did not conform to conventional definitions of femininity.

as a form of information management and social control. Yet some rumors persist for years despite incontrovertible contrary evidence; the box on page 621 provides one notable example.

Closely related to rumor is **gossip**, *rumor about the personal affairs of others*. As Charles Horton Cooley (1962; orig. 1909) points out, while rumor involves issues or events of interest to a large segment of the public, gossip concerns a small circle of people who know a particular person. While rumors spread widely, then, gossip is typically localized.

Gossip can be an effective strategy for social control as its targets become aware that they are the subject of praise or scorn. People may also gossip about others to elevate their own standing as "insiders" in a social group. Those who gossip *too* often, however, may find themselves dismissed as disreputable. The need to control gossip suggests the power of this form of communication.

Public Opinion

One form of highly dispersed collective behavior is *public opinion*, which Chapter 5 ("Socialization") defined as widespread attitudes toward controversial issues. Although we frequently speak about "the public" in singular terms, there are really many publics since people have an interest in various issues and may belong simultaneously to many publics. Over the years in the United States, publics have waxed and waned over issues such as water fluoridation, air pollution, the social standing of women, handguns, and health care. As this listing suggests, public issues are important matters about which people disagree (Lang & Lang, 1961; Turner & Killian, 1987). At the same time, on any given issue, anywhere from 2 to 10 percent of people offer no opinion at all, due to indifference or ignorance. Moreover, over time, public interest in some issues rise or fall. For example, interest in the social position of women in the United States ran high during the decades of the women's suffrage movement but declined after 1920 when women won the right to vote. Since the 1960s, a second wave of feminism has again created a public with strong opinions about a host of gender-related issues.

On any issue, not everyone's opinion has the same clout. Some categories of people have more social influence than others because they are better educated, wealthier, or more powerful. As Chapter 16 ("Politics and Government") explained, many special interest groups shape public policy in the United States even though they represent only a small fraction of the population. For example, specialized training

and savvy political organizing—not to mention millions in donations to entrenched political figures—give physicians enormous influence over health care policy even though they represent just 2 percent of the U.S. population.

Political leaders, special interest groups, and businesses all attempt to influence public tastes and attitudes by using **propaganda**, *information presented with the intention of shaping public opinion*. Although the term has negative connotations, propaganda is not necessarily false. A thin line separates information from propaganda, and this difference is mostly a matter of the presenter's intention. People share information to enlighten others; by contrast, they utilize propaganda to sway an audience toward a particular viewpoint. Political speeches, commercial advertising, and even some college lectures disseminate propaganda not with the goal of helping people think for themselves but in an effort to steer people toward thinking or acting in some specific way.

Panic and Mass Hysteria

Panic and mass hysteria are closely related forms of collective behavior. A **panic** is *a form of localized collective behavior by which people react to a threat or other stimulus with irrational, frantic, and often self-destructive behavior*. The classic illustration of a panic is the scene of people streaming toward exits after someone yells "Fire!" in a crowded theater. As they flee in fear, however, they trample one another, blocking exits so that few actually escape.

Mass hysteria is *a form of dispersed collective behavior by which people respond to a real or imagined event with irrational, frantic, and often self-destructive behavior*. Whether the cause of the mass hysteria is real or not, a large number of people certainly take it very seriously. Parents' fears that their children may become infected from a schoolmate who has AIDS may cause as much hysteria in a community as the very real danger of an approaching hurricane. Moreover, actions of people in the grip of mass hysteria generally make the situation worse. At the extreme, mass hysteria leads to chaotic flight and sends crowds into panic. People who see others overcome by fear may become more afraid themselves, as hysteria feeds on itself.

During the evening before Halloween in 1938, CBS radio broadcast a dramatization of H. G. Wells's novel *War of the Worlds* (Cantril, Gaudet, & Herzog, 1947; Koch, 1970). From a New York studio, a small group of actors began by presenting what sounded like a program of dance music to a national audience of perhaps 10 million people. Suddenly, they interrupted

Q: "In many ways, witchcraft was brought into England on the same current of change that introduced the Protestant Reformation." Kai Erikson

NOTE: Several years ago, the people of Salem erected a memorial to the victims of the witchcraft hysteria (which continues to be a significant tourist attraction).

The most deadly episode of mass hysteria in U.S. history swept up the village of Salem, Massachusetts, in 1692. Fearing witches in their midst, villagers tried and executed 20 people within the year. Such cases of hysteria accompanied the declining strength of religion as the Middle Ages drew to a close.

the program with a "news report" of explosions on the surface of the planet Mars and, soon after, the crash landing of a mysterious cylinder near a farmhouse in New Jersey. The program then switched to an "on-the-scene reporter" who presented a graphic account of giant monsters equipped with death-ray weapons emerging from the spaceship. An "eminent astronomer," played by Orson Welles, somberly informed the audience that Martians had begun a full-scale invasion. At a time when most people relied on their radios for factual news and many were prepared to believe that intelligent life existed on Mars, this episode was chilling.

Even though three times during the program an announcer identified the broadcast as fiction, more than 1 million people concluded that the events were actually taking place as described. By the time the show was over, thousands were hysterical, gathering in the streets spreading news of the "invasion," while others flooded telephone switchboards with warnings to friends and relatives. Among those who jumped into their cars and fled were a college senior and his roommate:

> My roommate was crying and praying. He was even more excited than I was—or more noisy about it anyway; I guess I took it out in pushing the accelerator to the floor. . . . After it was all over, I started to think about that ride, I was more jittery than when it was happening. The speed was never under 70. I thought I was racing against time. . . . I didn't have any idea exactly what I was fleeing from, and that made me all the more afraid. (Cantril, Gaudet, & Herzog, 1947:52)

Fashions and Fads

Two additional types of collective behavior—fashions and fads—affect people dispersed over a large area. A **fashion** is *a social pattern favored for a time by a large number of people.* In contrast to more established norms, fashion is transitory, sometimes lasting for only months. Fashion characterizes the arts (including painting, music, drama, and literature), automobiles, language, architecture, and public opinion. The most widely recognized examples of fashion are clothing and other aspects of personal appearance.

Lyn Lofland (1973) suggests that, in preindustrial societies, clothing and personal adornment reflect traditional *style* that changes little over the years. Categories of people—women and men, and members of various classes and occupations—wear the distinctive clothes and hairstyles of their social and occupational position.

In industrial societies, however, style gives way to fashion for two reasons. First, modern people are less tied to tradition and often eagerly embrace new ways of living. Second, the high social mobility of industrial societies gives heightened significance to what people consume. German sociologist Georg Simmel (1971; orig. 1904) explained that people use fashion to craft their presentation of self in pursuit of approval and prestige. According to Simmel, affluent people are typically the trendsetters, since they have the money to spend on luxuries that bespeak privilege. In the lasting phrase of U.S. sociologist Thorstein Veblen (1953; orig. 1899), fashion involves *conspicuous consumption*, meaning

Chapter 23 Collective Behavior and Social Movements **623**

Q: "Fashion . . . is a product of class distinction." Georg Simmel
RESOURCE: Worth reading is Georg Simmel's essay, "Fashion." (1971; orig. 1904:294–323)

RESOURCE: Jo Freeman's article, "On the Origin of Social Movements," is among the classics included in the 3d edition of the Macionis and Benokraitis reader, *Seeing Ourselves*.

Because change in industrial societies is rapid and ongoing, differences in personal appearance—one important kind of fashion—are clearly evident over even a ten-year period. The five photographs above (beginning at the top, left) show hair styles commonly worn by men in the 1950s, 1960s, 1970s, 1980s, and 1990s.

that people buy expensive products (whether well made or not) simply to display their wealth to one another.

Less affluent people understandably aspire to own the trappings of wealth, so they snap up less expensive copies of what has become fashionable. In this way, a fashion ripples downward in society. But, as this happens, the fashion eventually loses its prestige, with the wealthy moving on to something new. Fashions, in short, are born at the top of the social hierarchy—on the Fifth Avenues and Rodeo Drives of the rich—rising to mass popularity in bargain stores across the country, and soon are all but forgotten by everyone.

A curious reversal of this pattern sometimes occurs among more egalitarian-minded people. In this case, a fashion that originates among people of lower social position is mimicked by the rich who wish to identify with the masses. A classic example is the "upward mobility" of blue jeans, or dungarees (from a Hindi word for a coarse and inferior fabric). First worn by manual laborers, jeans gained popularity among the affluent, especially those who supported the struggles of the socially disadvantaged. Jeans became the uniform of political activists in the civil rights and antiwar movements in the 1960s and, gradually, of college students across the country. Author Tom Wolfe (1970) coined the phrase "radical chic" to satirize the desire of the rich to look fashionably poor. By the 1980s, expensive designer jeans became the rage among people of every political persuasion.

A **fad** is *an unconventional social pattern that people embrace briefly but enthusiastically.* Fads, sometimes called *crazes*, are commonplace in affluent industrial societies in which people have the money to spend on amusing, if often frivolous, products. During the 1950s, two young entrepreneurs in California produced a brightly colored plastic version of a popular Australian toy, a three-foot-diameter hoop that one swung around the body by gyrating the hips. Dubbed the "hula hoop,"

Q: "Social movements and their goals represent, respectively, actual and potential social changes." C. Wendell King

DATA FILE: Supplementary lecture material on disaster research is included in the *Data File*.

Q: "All previous historical movements were movements of minorities, or in the interests of minorities. The proletarian movement is the self-conscious, independent movement of the immense majority, in the interest of the immense majority." Karl Marx and Friedrich Engels

these devices soon rose to the level of a national craze. Within a year, hula hoops disappeared from the scene almost as quickly as they emerged, but—decades later—they surfaced once again, this time in China.

Streaking—running naked in public—had an even briefer moment in the sun, lasting only for a few months in early 1974. Their fleeting duration suggests that fads happen almost at random. But research suggests that the popularity of any fad depends on its acceptance by high-prestige people. In addition, as we see in the case of streaking, fads fade from the scene if subjected to official repression by police or other authority figures (Aguirre, Quarantelli, & Mendoza, 1988).

Fads and fashions both involve dispersed collectivities and last only a short time. But they differ in several respects (Blumer, 1968; Turner & Killian, 1987). Fads are truly passing fancies—enthusiasms that capture the mass imagination but quickly burn out and disappear. Fashions, by contrast, reflect fundamental cultural values like individuality and sexual attractiveness and tend to evolve over time. In this way, a fashion but rarely a fad becomes incorporated into a society's culture. Streaking, for instance, came out of nowhere and soon vanished, while blue jeans originated in the rough mining camps of Gold Rush California more than a century ago and still influence clothing designs today. Such persistence explains the positive connotation of being called "fashionable" in contrast to the mildly insulting label "faddish."

SOCIAL MOVEMENTS

Crowds, rumors, fashions, and the other forms of collective behavior we have examined usually have little enduring significance for society as a whole. Social movements, by contrast, are deliberate and consequential forms of collective behavior.

As noted at the beginning of the chapter, a social movement involves organized activity that promotes or resists some dimension of change. Social movements stand apart from other types of collective behavior in three respects: They have a high degree of internal organization, they last longer, and their purpose is to reorganize or defend society in some respect.

Social movements are far more common today than in the past. Preindustrial societies are tightly integrated by tradition, making social movements extremely rare. Industrial societies, however, foster diversity in the form of subcultures and countercultures so that social movements develop around a wide range of public issues. In recent decades, for example, homosexual men and women—supported by

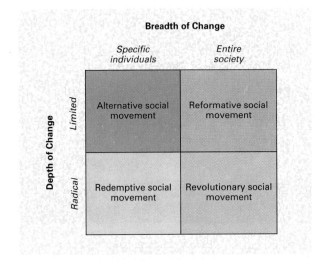

FIGURE 23–1 Four Types of Social Movements

(David F. Aberle, *The Peyote Religion Among the Navajo*, published by the University of Chicago Press, 1966. Reprinted by permission.)

heterosexuals sympathetic to their political aims—have organized to win economic and legal parity in our society. The gay rights movement has already succeeded in securing legislation in several major cities and states forbidding discrimination based on sexual preference. Like any social movement that challenges conventional practices, this one has sparked a countermovement as traditionalists try to block greater social acceptance of homosexuality. In today's society, almost every significant public issue gives rise to both a social movement favoring change and an opposing countermovement (Lo, 1982).

Types of Social Movements

Sociologists have classified social movements in various ways (Aberle, 1966; Cameron, 1966; Blumer, 1969). One variable is *breadth*, since some movements target selected people while others try to change everyone. A second variable is *depth*, with some movements attempting only superficial changes in how we live, while others pursue radical transformation. Combining these variables lets us identify four types of social movements, shown in Figure 23–1.

Alternative social movements are the least threatening to the established social order, seeking limited change only in some segment of the population. Planned Parenthood, one example of an alternative social movement, encourages individuals of childbearing age to take the consequences of sexual activity more seriously by practicing birth control.

RESOURCE: Joan Fitzgerald and Louise Simmons (1991) point out that operationalizing the success of any social movement cannot be limited to immediate effects; it must also assess the movement's contribution to future social change.

Q: "You cannot put a rope around the neck of an idea . . ." Sean O'Casey

Q: "As with every other revolutionary movement, the leadership, paradoxically, is likely to come from the least oppressed and marginal members of the population, or from people outside the group completely." Richard Farson

Q: "Psychological attributes of individuals, such as frustration and alienation, have minimal direct impact for explaining the occurrence of rebellion and revolution per se." Carol Mueller

Although women's absolute social standing has improved markedly in recent decades, many women continue to experience a sense of deprivation relative to their growing expectation of full social equality with men.

Redemptive social movements also have a selective focus, but they attempt radical change in those they engage. Examples include fundamentalist Christian organizations that reach out to new members through conversion. The resulting transformation is sometimes so great that converts describe their experience as being "born again."

Reformative social movements seek only limited social change but encompass the entire society. The multiculturalism movement, described in Chapter 3 ("Culture"), is an educational and political initiative that advocates working toward social parity for all racial and ethnic categories of people. Reformative social movements generally work inside the existing political system. They can be progressive (promoting a new social pattern) or reactionary (countermovements trying to preserve the status quo or to recover past social patterns). Just as multiculturalists are pushing for greater racial equality, for example, so do various white supremacist organizations persist in their efforts to maintain the historical dominance of one racial category.

Revolutionary social movements have the most severe consequences of all, striving for basic transformation of a society. Sometimes pursuing specific goals, sometimes spinning utopian dreams, followers of these social movements reject established social institutions as flawed while favoring radically new alternatives. Until recently, most people in the United States linked revolutionary social movements to left-wing politics, but such movements also emerge on the far right. In the United States, the John Birch Society

and other ultra-nationalist organizations decry the erosion of our political system by socialism and seek to radically alter our social institutions in defense of individual freedoms (Broyles, 1978).

Deprivation Theory

Because social movements are deliberately organized and often enduring, sociologists find this form of collective behavior somewhat easier to explain than fleeting incidents of mob behavior or mass hysteria. One approach, *deprivation theory*, holds that social movements arise among people who feel deprived of what they think they deserve. People who think they lack sufficient income, satisfactory working conditions, important political rights, or basic social dignity may engage in organized collective behavior to bring about a more just state of affairs (Morrison, 1978; Rose, 1982).

Following the Civil War, the rise of the Ku Klux Klan and the passage of so-called Jim Crow laws to enforce segregation throughout the South exemplify deprivation theory. Emancipation deprived white people, who had formerly owned African Americans as personal property, not only of their economic investment but also of the prosperity slave labor produced. Many whites responded to Emancipation, therefore, by trying to keep African Americans "in their place" (Dollard et al., 1939). The success of the Klan and segregation laws enabled whites to hold on to some relative advantages. For their part, African Americans had long experienced much greater deprivation, but they had relatively little opportunity to organize in the face of overwhelming white power. Not until well into this century did African Americans forge organizations that successfully pursued racial justice.

The deprivation approach also underlies Karl Marx's expectation that industrial workers would organize in opposition to capitalism. Labor unions and various political alliances of workers have addressed low wages and other economic problems, in efforts to eradicate the disadvantages experienced by many working-class men and women.

As Chapter 7 ("Groups and Organizations") explained, deprivation is a relative concept. Regardless of anyone's absolute amount of money and power, people feel either well off or deprived compared to some category of others. **Relative deprivation**, then, is *a perceived disadvantage arising from some specific comparison* (Stouffer et al., 1949; Merton, 1968).

More than a century ago Alexis de Tocqueville (1955; orig. 1856) studied the French Revolution. Why, he asked, did rebellion occur in progressive France rather than in more traditional Germany, where

NOTE: The conservative character of mass-society theory follows from the implication that it is the loss of traditional social ties (and not social inequality) that leads to social movements. Kornhauser follows Tocqueville rather than Marx in focusing on mass movements rather than on class movements. The distinction between

mass society and class society is developed in Chapter 24 ("Social Change and Modernity").

NOTE: The concept of "mass society" is explored in detail in the next chapter ("Social Change and Modernity").

peasants were, by any objective measure, worse off? Tocqueville's answer was that, as bad as their condition was, German peasants had known nothing but feudal servitude and thus had no basis for feeling deprived. French peasants, by contrast, had experienced various improvements in their lives that whetted their appetites for more. Thus the French—not the Germans—felt a keen sense of relative deprivation. In analyzing this apparent paradox, Tocqueville pinpointed one of the notable ironies of human history: Increasing prosperity, far from satisfying the population, is likely to promote a spirit of unrest (1955:175; orig. 1856).

Echoing Tocqueville's insight, James C. Davies (1962) suggests that as life gets better, people may take their rising fortunes for granted and come to expect even more. Relative deprivation can set in if the standard of living suddenly stops improving or, worse, begins to drop. As Figure 23–2, on page 628, illustrates, social movements aimed at changing society arise when an extended period of improvement in the standard of living is followed by a shorter period of decline.

Critical evaluation. Deprivation theory reveals the limits of common sense as a predictor of discontent. People do not organize in opposition to their situation simply because they are suffering in an absolute sense; social movements aimed at change are propelled by a perception of relative deprivation. We can discern the underlying truth of this insight by noting that it is found in the work of thinkers as diverse as Marx and Tocqueville.

But since most people experience some discontent all the time, we are left wondering why social movements emerge among some categories of people and not others. A second problem is that deprivation theory has a tendency toward circular reasoning: We assume that deprivation causes social movements, but often the only evidence of deprivation is the social movement itself (Jenkins & Perrow, 1977). A third limitation of this approach is that while it focuses on the setting in which a social movement develops, it tells us little about movements themselves (McAdam, McCarthy, & Zald, 1988). Fourth, some researchers have taken issue with this approach, claiming that relative deprivation has not turned out to be a very good predictor of social movements (Muller, 1979).

Mass-Society Theory

William Kornhauser's *mass-society theory* (1959) argues that social movements attract socially isolated people who feel personally insignificant. From this point of view, social movements are to be expected in large,

complex *mass* societies. Further, social movements are more *personal* than *political* in that they confer a sense of purpose and belonging on people otherwise adrift in society (Melucci, 1989).

This theory holds that categories of people with weak social ties are most readily mobilized into a social movement. People who experience strong social integration, by contrast, are unlikely to join the ranks of a movement.

Like Gustave Le Bon, discussed earlier, Kornhauser offers a conservative and critical view of social movements. He regards activists as psychologically motivated individuals prone to deviance who join groups in which leaders can easily manipulate them and subvert democratic principles. Thus extremist social movements on both ends of the political spectrum typically gain their most ardent support from people who belong to few social groups.

Critical evaluation. The strength of Kornhauser's theory lies in its explanation of social movements both in terms of the people who join them and the characteristics of the larger society. But one practical criticism is that, if we try to evaluate the notion that mass societies foster social movements, we run up against the problem of having no simple standard against which to measure the extent to which people form a "mass society."

A more political criticism holds that placing the roots of social movements in human psychology tends to minimize the importance of social justice. Put otherwise, this theory suggests that flawed people, rather than a flawed society, underlie the emergence of social movements.

Some research supports this approach; other evidence disputes its contentions. On the down side, some studies conclude that the Nazi movement in Germany recruited mostly people who were *not* socially isolated (Lipset, 1963; Oberschall, 1973). Similarly, urban rioters during the 1960s typically had strong ties to their communities (Sears & McConahay, 1973). Evidence also suggests that young people who join religious cults do not have particularly weak family ties (Wright & Piper, 1986). Finally, researchers who have examined the biographies of 1960s political activists find evidence of deep and continuing commitment to political goals rather than isolation from society or personal aberration (McAdam, 1988, 1989; Whalen & Flacks, 1989).

On the up side, research by Frances Piven and Richard Cloward (1977) shows that a breakdown of routine social patterns does contribute to social movements among poor people. Also, in a study of the New

NOTE: The Women's Movement illustrates the stages of Smelser's theory. (1) Historical pattern of patriarchy; women have the opportunity to organize in opposition. (2) Strain generated by contradiction between U.S. ideal of equality and reality of patriarchy. (3) Early feminist scholarship and organization. (4) First wave of feminism—passage of 13th, 14th, and 15th Amendments that extended rights to African-American men but ignored women of both races; second wave of feminism—African-American civil rights movement (which was predominantly led by men) and the increasing proportion of women in the labor force. (5) Organizations such as National Organization for Women (NOW); widespread publication of feminist ideas. (6) Passage of the 19th Amendment temporarily slowed the Women's Movement; ERA is unratified, but much legislation has advanced women's social and economic rights.

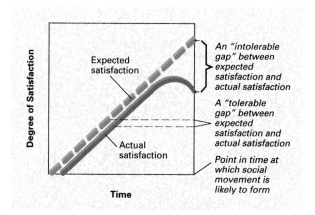

FIGURE 23–2 Relative Deprivation and Social Movements

In this diagram, the solid line represents a rising standard of living over time. The dotted line represents the expected standard of living, which is typically somewhat higher. Davies describes the difference between the two as "a tolerable gap between what people want and what they get." If the standard of living suddenly drops in the midst of rising expectations, however, this gap grows to an intolerable level. At this point, we can expect social movements to form.

(Davies, 1962)

Mexico State Penitentiary, Bert Useem (1985) found that suspending prison programs that promoted social ties among inmates was followed by an increase in chaotic and violent protest activity.

Structural-Strain Theory

One of the most influential approaches to understanding social movements is *structural-strain theory* developed by Neil Smelser (1962). This analysis identifies six factors that foster social movements. The more prevalent these conditions are, the greater the likelihood that a social movement will develop. Smelser's theory also offers insights into which situations spark unorganized mobs or riots and which create highly organized social movements. The prodemocracy movement that transformed Eastern Europe during the late 1980s serves to illustrate Smelser's six factors.

1. **Structural conduciveness.** The roots of social movements lie in significant problems that beset a society. The generally low standard of living in Eastern Europe in recent decades, coupled with the political repression of the socialist governments, created widespread dissatisfaction.

2. **Structural strain.** Relative deprivation and other kinds of strain flow from the inability of a society to meet the expectations of its people. The prodemocracy movement in Eastern Europe gained strength because people there could readily see that their quality of life was far lower than that of their counterparts in Western Europe or much lower than years of propaganda about prosperous socialism had led them to expect.

3. **Growth and spread of an explanation.** Any coherent social movement must formulate a clear statement of a problem, its causes, and likely solutions. To the extent that these are well articulated, people are likely to express their dissatisfaction in an organized way. If not, frustration may eventually explode in the form of unorganized rioting. Intellectuals propounded the notion that the plight of Eastern Europe was deep economic and political flaws, and at the same time movement leaders proposed strategies to increase democracy.

4. **Precipitating factors.** Discontent frequently festers for a long time, only to be transformed into collective action by a specific event. Such an event occurred in 1985 when Mikhail Gorbachev came to power in the Soviet Union and implemented his program of *perestroika* (restructuring). People in Eastern Europe seized this historic opportunity to reorganize political and economic life as Moscow relaxed its rigid control over their countries.

5. **Mobilization for action.** Widespread concern about a public issue sets the stage for collective action in the form of rallies, leafleting, building alliances with sympathetic organizations, and similar activities. The initial success of the Solidarity movement in Poland—covertly aided by the Reagan administration in the United States and by the Vatican—mobilized people throughout Eastern Europe to press for change. The rate of change accelerated as reform movements gained strength: What had taken a decade in Poland required only months in Hungary and only weeks in other countries.

6. **Lack of social control.** The responses of established authorities, such as political officials, police, and the military, largely determines the outcome of any social movement. Firm repression by the state can weaken or even destroy a social movement, as demonstrated by the crushing of prodemocracy forces in the People's Republic of China. By contrast, Gorbachev adopted a policy of nonintervention in Eastern Europe, thereby increasing the possibility for change there. Ironically, the

forces his program unleashed in these neighboring nations soon spread to the Soviet Union itself, ending the historic domination of the Communist party and producing a new political confederation in 1992. It also laid the groundwork for the three Baltic states—Estonia, Latvia, and Lithuania—to break away from the former Soviet Union and establish themselves as fully independent nations.

Critical evaluation. Smelser's approach—distinctly *social*, rather than psychological in focus—recognizes the complexity of social movements and suggests how various factors encourage or inhibit their development. Structural-strain theory also explains how social problems may give rise to either organized social movements or more spontaneous mob action or rioting.

Yet Smelser's theory contains some of the same circularity of argument found in Kornhauser's analysis. A social movement is caused by strain, he maintains, but the only evidence of this underlying strain appears to be the emerging social movement itself. Finally, this theory is incomplete, overlooking the important role of resources such as the mass media or international alliances in the success or failure of a social movement (Oberschall, 1973; Jenkins & Perrow, 1977; McCarthy & Zald, 1977; Olzak & West, 1991).

Resource-Mobilization Theory

Resource-mobilization theory adds an important consideration to our understanding of social movements. Drives for change are unlikely to succeed—or even get off the ground—without substantial resources, including money, human labor, office and communications facilities, contacts with the mass media, and a positive public image. In short, any social movement rises or falls on its capacity to attract resources and mobilize people. The collapse of socialism in Eastern Europe was largely the work of dissatisfied people in those countries. But assistance from outside, including fax machines, copiers, telecommunications gear, money, and moral support provided by other nations, was instrumental in allowing first the Poles and then other countries to oppose their leaders successfully.

As this example demonstrates, supplying resources makes outsiders as important as insiders to the outcome of a social movement. Socially disadvantaged people, by definition, lack the money, contacts, leadership skills, and organizational know-how that a successful movement requires, and it is here that sympathetic outsiders fill the resource gap. In our own country, well-to-do white people, including college students, performed a vital service to the black civil rights movement in the 1960s, and affluent men as well as women have taken a leading role in the current women's movement. Even a small core of powerful resource people can sometimes be enough to link a fledgling social movement to the larger sympathetic audience and practical resources it needs to be successful (McCarthy & Zald, 1977; Snow, Zurcher, & Ekland-Olson, 1980; Killian, 1984; Snow, Rochford, Jr., Worden, & Benford, 1986; Baron, Mittman, & Newman, 1991; Burstein, 1991).

On the other side of the coin, a lack of resources frustrates efforts toward intentional change. The history of the AIDS epidemic offers a case in point. Initially, the government made little response as the incidence of AIDS rose in the early 1980s. To a large extent, gay communities in cities like San Francisco and New York were left to shoulder the responsibility for treatment and educational programs on their own. Gradually, as the general public began to grasp the dimensions of the problem, public pressure prompted local, state, and federal governments to allocate more resources. Galvanizing the public, members of the entertainment industry lent their money, visibility, and prestige to the movement to combat this deadly disease. These extensive resources have transformed this fledgling social movement into a well-organized, global coalition of political leaders, educators, and medical specialists.

Critical evaluation. The strength of resource-mobilization theory lies in its recognition that resources as well as discontent are necessary to the success of a social movement. This theory also emphasizes the interplay between social movements and other groups and organizations that are capable of providing or withholding valuable resources. Continuing research in this area suggests that a movement's position in the power structure also affects the strategies it can employ; violence, for example, is a resource that can be used by people seeking entry into a political system (Grant & Wallace, 1991).

Critics of this approach maintain that even relatively powerless segments of a population can promote successful social movements if they are able to organize effectively and have strongly committed members. Research by Aldon Morris (1981) shows that people of color drew largely on their own skills and resources to fuel the civil rights movement of the 1950s and 1960s. A second problem with this theory is that it overstates the extent to which powerful people are willing to challenge the status quo. Some rich white people did provide valuable resources to the black civil

NOTE: A Marxist view of "new social movements" sees the state as entering more and more areas of private life in an effort to resolve the contradictions of late-capitalist economies. Social movements are thus collective efforts to regain control of areas previously defined as private.

DIVERSITY: Although some social movements that challenged the status quo have been dominated by men, not all have—the abolition movement, suffrage movement, child care movements, and anti–drunk driving movements are only a few examples.

rights movement, but, generally speaking, white elites remained unsympathetic (McAdam, 1982, 1983).

Overall, the success or failure of a social movement turns on the political struggle between challengers and supporters of intentional change. A strong and united establishment, perhaps aided by a countermovement, decreases the chances that any social movement will effect meaningful change. If, however, the established powers are divided, the movement's chances of success multiply.

New Social Movements Theory

During the 1980s one more theoretical approach emerged in response to the changing character of social movements. What is now called *new social movements theory* investigates the distinctive features of recent social movements in postindustrial societies of North America and Western Europe (Melucci, 1980; McAdam, McCarthy, & Zald, 1988; Kriesi, 1989).

Today's most notable social movements are concerned with global ecology, the social standing of women and gay people, reducing the risks of war, and animal rights, among others. One feature of these movements is their national and international scope. As Chapter 16 ("Politics and Government") explains, the power of the state continues to expand in the United States and other postindustrial societies. Not surprisingly, then, the critical response to state policies has also assumed national proportions. As global political connections multiply, moreover, social movements respond by becoming international in scope.

Second, while traditional social movements such as labor organizations are concerned primarily with economic issues, new social movements tend to focus on cultural change and the improvement of our social and physical surroundings. The international environmental movement, for example, opposes practices that aggravate global warming and other environmental dangers.

Third, whereas most social movements of the past were guided by economic interests and elicited strong support from working-class people, new social movements often have noneconomic agendas and usually draw disproportionate support from the middle class.

Critical evaluation. Because the new social movements theory is a recent development, sociologists are still assessing its utility. One clear strength of this analysis is its recognition that social movements are increasing in scale in response to the growing power of the state and the development of a global political system. This theory also spotlights the power of the

mass media to unite people around the world in pursuit of political goals.

This approach garners criticism, however, for exaggerating the differences between past and present social movements. The women's movement, for example, focuses on many of the same issues—workplace conditions and pay—that have consumed the energies of labor organizations for decades.

Each of the five theories we have presented offers some explanation for the emergence of social movements; no single theory can stand alone (Kowalewski & Porter, 1992). Table 23–1 summarizes the theories.

Gender and Movements

Gender is also at work in the operation of social movements. In keeping with traditional notions about gender in the United States, taking part in public life has been more characteristic of men than women.

Investigating "Freedom Summer," a 1964 voter registration project in Mississippi, Doug McAdam (1992) found that movement leaders were more likely to accept an offer of help from men than from women. At that time, most people viewed the potentially dangerous work of registering African-American voters in the midst of considerable opposition and even hostility from whites as "men's work" and unsuitable for women. Similarly, he discovered, project leaders were likely to assign women who did join to clerical and teaching assignments, leaving the actual field activities to men. Interestingly, McAdam notes that, by and large, women who participated in Freedom Summer were more qualified than their male counterparts in terms of years of activism and organizational affiliations. In all likelihood, only the more committed women were able to overcome the movement's gender barriers. In short, while women have played leading roles in many social movements (including the abolitionist and feminist movements in the United States), patriarchy has shaped the operation of many social movements—even those that otherwise opposed the status quo.

Stages in Social Movements

Despite the many differences that set one social movement off from others, all efforts at intentional change unfold in similar stages. Researchers have identified four phases in the life of the typical social movement (Blumer, 1969; Mauss, 1975; Tilly, 1978).

Stage 1: Emergence. Social movements are driven by the perception that all is not well. Some, such as the civil rights and women's movements, are born of

SOCIAL SURVEY: In 1993, the following proportion of adults responded that they have taken part in various kinds of protest actions: (GSS 1973, N = 1,504; *Codebook*, 1993:271)

"Picketing for a labor strike"   9.5%

"A civil rights demonstration"   4.3%
"An anti-war demonstration"   4.9%
"A pro-war demonstration"   0.4%
"A school-related demonstration"   5.3%

TABLE 23–1 Theories of Social Movements: A Summary

Deprivation Theory	People join as a result of experiencing relative deprivation. The social movement is a means of seeking change that brings participants greater benefits. Social movements are especially likely when rising expectations are frustrated.
Mass-Society Theory	People who lack established social ties are mobilized into social movements. Periods of social breakdown are likely to spawn social movements. The social movement is a way of gaining a sense of belonging and social participation.
Structural-Strain Theory	People join because of their shared concern about the inability of society to operate as they believe it should. The growth of a social movement reflects many factors, including a belief in its legitimacy and some precipitating event that provokes action.
Resource-Mobilization Theory	People may join for all the reasons noted above and also because of social ties to existing members. The success or failure of a social movement depends largely on the resources available to it. Also important is the extent of opposition to its goals within the larger society.
New Social Movements Theory	People who join are motivated by "quality of life" issues, not necessarily economic concerns. Mobilization is national or international in scope. New social movements arise in response to the expansion of the mass media and the growing power of the state in modern industrial societies to affect people's lives for good or ill.

widespread dissatisfaction. Others emerge only as a small vanguard group increases public awareness of some issue, as gay activists have done with respect to the threat posed by AIDS.

Stage 2: Coalescence. After emerging, a social movement must define itself and develop a strategy for "going public." Leaders must determine policies, select tactics, build morale, and recruit new members. At this stage, the movement may engage in collective action like rallies or demonstrations to attract media attention in hopes of capturing public notice. Additionally, the movement may form alliances with other organizations to gain necessary resources.

Stage 3: Bureaucratization. To become an established political force, a social movement must assume bureaucratic traits, as described in Chapter 7 ("Groups and Organizations"). As it becomes "routinized," a social movement depends less on the charisma and talents of a few leaders and relies more on a capable staff. Some social movements do not become established in this way, however. Many activist organizations on college campuses during the late 1960s were energized by a single charismatic leader and, consequently, did not endure for long. On the other hand, the well-established National Organization for Women (NOW), despite its changing leadership, offers a steady voice on behalf of feminists.

At the same time, bureaucratization can sometimes hinder a social movement. Frances Piven and Richard Cloward (1977), reviewing social movements

in U.S. history, noted that leaders can become so engrossed in building an organization that they neglect the need to sustain sentiments of insurgency among members. In such cases, the radical edge of protest is lost.

Stage 4: Decline. Social movements are inherently dynamic, so a decline is not necessarily a demise (Wright, 1987). Eventually, however, most social movements lose influence. Frederick Miller (1983) suggests four reasons that this may occur.

First, decline may simply signal success as members see nothing more to accomplish. For example, the women's suffrage movement disbanded after it won for women in the United States the right to vote. Such clear-cut successes are rare, however, since few social movements have one specific goal. More commonly, gaining one victory leads to new campaigns. Because issues related to gender extend far beyond voting, the women's movement has recast itself time and again.

Second, a social movement may flag due to organizational factors, such as poor leadership, loss of interest among members, exhaustion of resources, repression by authorities, or excessive bureaucratization. Some people attracted by the excitement of a new social movement lose interest when formal routines replace the excitement of early efforts at change. Fragmentation due to internal conflicts over goals and tactics is another common problem. Students for a Democratic Society (SDS), a student movement promoting participatory democracy and opposing the war

NOTE: Many social movements fall into one of two categories: equality movements seeking social equality for various categories of people (based on class, race, sexual orientation, etc.) and protest movements addressing specific dimensions of life (gun control, nuclear power, animal experimentation, etc.). (Caplow et al., 1991)

Q: "Do not make the mistake of thinking that a concerned group of people cannot change the world; it's the only thing that ever has." Margaret Mead

RESOURCE: One of the cross-cultural selections in the Macionis and Benokraitis reader, *Seeing Ourselves*, is Brian Russo's "Tiananmen Square: A Personal Chronicle from China."

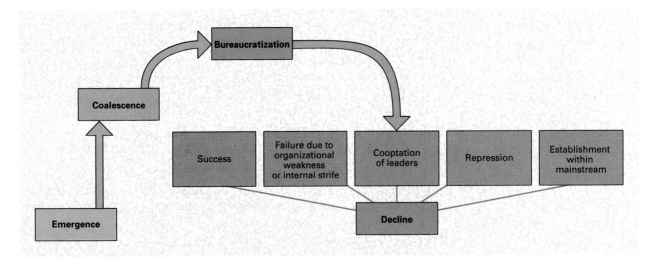

FIGURE 23–3 Stages in the Lives of Social Movements

in Vietnam, splintered into several small factions by the end of the 1960s, as members disagreed over strategies for social change.

Third, a social movement may degenerate if the established power structure, through offers of money, prestige, and other rewards, succeeds in diverting leaders from their goals. "Selling out" is one facet of the iron law of oligarchy, noted in Chapter 7 ("Groups and Organizations"), by which organizational leaders may use their positions to enrich themselves. Jerry Rubin, a political activist of the late 1960s, parlayed his celebrity status as a rebel into a career in the New York financial world. But this transformation can also work the other way: Some people leave lucrative, high-prestige occupations to become activists. Cat Stevens, a rock star of the 1970s, became a Muslim, changed his name to Yusuf Islam, and now promotes the spread of his religion.

Fourth and finally, the demise of a social movement may result from repression. Those in power may crush a movement for change by frightening away participants, discouraging new recruits, and even imprisoning leaders. The intensity of the state's reaction depends on officials' assessment of how revolutionary the social movement is. Until 1990, the government of South Africa, for example, banned the African National Congress (ANC), a political organization seeking to overthrow the state-supported system of apartheid, rendering even suspected members of the ANC subject to arrest. In 1990 Pretoria lifted the decades-old ban and released ANC leader Nelson Mandela after twenty-seven years of imprisonment.

Beyond the reasons noted by Miller, a fifth cause of decline is that a social movement may "go mainstream." Some movements become an accepted part of the system—typically after realizing at least some of their goals—to the point that they no longer challenge the status quo. The U.S. labor movement, for example, is now well established; its leaders control vast sums of money and, to some critics, at least, now resemble the business tycoons they opposed in the past.

Figure 23–3 provides a graphic summary of the various stages of social movements.

Social Movements and Social Change

Social movements exist to encourage—or to resist—social change. Whatever the intention, their success varies from case to case. Racial equality in the United States, although an unrealized goal, has certainly been advanced by the civil rights movement despite opposition from a handful of white supremacist countermovements like the Aryan Nation and the Ku Klux Klan.

Sometimes we overlook the success of past social movements and take for granted the changes that other people struggled so hard to win. Early workers' movements in the United States, for example, battled for decades to end child labor in factories, to limit working hours, to make the workplace safer, and to establish what we now consider the right to bargain collectively with employers. Legislation protecting the environment is also the product of successful social movements throughout this century. The women's movement in

SOCIAL SURVEY: "Should organizing protest marches and demonstrations against the government be allowed?" (GSS 1990, N = 1,217; *Codebook*, 1993:514)

"Definitely allowed"	35.3%	"Definitely not allowed"	10.8%
"Probably allowed"	31.0%	DK/NR	7.2%
"Probably not allowed"	15.8%		

SOCIAL SURVEY: "In general, would you say that people should obey the law without exception, or are there exceptional occasions on which people should follow their consciences even if it means breaking the law?" (GSS 1990, N = 1,217; *Codebook*, 1993:513)

"Obey the law"	39.1%
"Follow conscience"	52.1%
DK/NR	8.8%

the United States has yet to attain social equality for the sexes, but it has extended the legal rights and economic opportunities of women to the extent that many young people are surprised to learn that—earlier in this century—few women worked for income and, in most states, none was permitted to vote.

This broad view leads to one overarching conclusion: We can draw a direct link between social movements and change. In one direction, social transformations such as the Industrial Revolution and the rise of capitalism sparked the emergence of various social movements. Going the other way, the efforts of workers, women, racial and ethnic minorities, and gay people have sent ripples of change throughout our society. Thus social change is both the cause and the consequence of social movements.

LOOKING AHEAD: SOCIAL MOVEMENTS IN THE TWENTY-FIRST CENTURY

Since the turbulent decade of the 1960s—marked by widespread social protests and urban rioting—the United States has experienced a period of relative social calm (Caplow et al., 1991). Even so, the social explosion in Los Angeles in 1992, in response to the verdict in the first trial of police officers accused of beating Rodney King, signals that many of our society's most profound problems remain unresolved. In addition to debating the causes of racial tensions, we still argue about how to correctly respond to tens of millions of poor people in our midst. Moreover, new issues—such as preserving the environment and gay rights—have recently come on the scene.

Social movements have always been a part of U.S. society, although their focus, tactics, and intensity all change over time. Therefore, we can safely assume that social movements will continue to shape our way of life. However, for two reasons, the scope of social movements is likely to increase. First, the technology of the Information Revolution has drawn the world closer together than ever before. Today anyone with a satellite dish, personal computer, or fax machine can stay abreast of political events, often as they happen. Second, as a consequence of new technology as well as the emerging global economy, social movements are now joining people throughout the entire world. With the realization that many problems with the natural and social environments are global in the making, has come the understanding that they can be effectively addressed only on an international scale.

SUMMARY

1. A collectivity differs from a social group in its limited social interaction, its vague social boundaries, and its weak and often unconventional norms.

2. Crowds, an important type of collective behavior, take various forms: casual crowds, conventional crowds, expressive crowds, acting crowds, and protest crowds.

3. Crowds that become emotionally intense spawn violence in the form of mobs and riots. Mobs pursue a specific goal; rioting involves undirected destructiveness.

4. Contagion theory views crowds as anonymous, suggestible, and subject to escalating emotions. Convergence theory links crowd behavior to traits of participants. Emergent-norm theory suggests that crowds may develop their own behavioral norms.

5. Crowds have figured heavily in social change throughout history, although the value of their action depends on one's political outlook.

6. Rumor, which thrives in a climate of ambiguity, is concerned with public issues; gossip, a closely related concept, deals with personal issues of local interest.

7. Public opinion consists of people's positions on issues of widespread importance. Some people's attitudes carry more weight than others and, on any given issue, a small proportion of the population claims no opinion at all.

8. A panic (in a local area) or mass hysteria (across an entire society) are types of collective behavior by which people respond to a significant event, real or imagined, with irrational, frantic, and often self-destructive behavior.

9. In industrial societies, people adopt fashion as a source of social prestige. A fad is more unconventional than a fashion and is also of shorter duration, although people embrace fads with greater enthusiasm.

10. A social movement entails deliberate activity intended to promote or discourage change. Social movements vary in the range of people they seek to involve and the extent to which they seek to change society.

11. According to deprivation theory, social movements arise in response to relative deprivation more than the lack of well-being in an absolute sense.

12. Mass-society theory suggests that people join social movements to gain a sense of belonging and social significance.

13. Structural-strain theory explains the development of a social movement as a cumulative consequence of six factors. Well-formulated grievances and goals encourage the organization of social movements; undirected anger, by contrast, promotes rioting.

14. Resource-mobilization theory ties the success or failure of a social movement to the availability of resources such as money, human labor, and alliances with other organizations.

15. New social movements theory focuses on quality-of-life issues that are typically national or international in scope.

16. A typical social movement proceeds through consecutive stages: emergence (defining the public issue), coalescence (entering into public life), bureaucratization (becoming formally organized), and decline (due to failure or, sometimes, success).

17. The effects of social movements are evident in characteristics of society that people now take for granted. Just as movements produce change, so change itself sparks social movements.

KEY CONCEPTS

collective behavior activity involving a large number of people, often spontaneous, and typically in violation of established norms

collectivity a large number of people whose minimal interaction occurs in the absence of well-defined and conventional norms

crowd a temporary gathering of people who share a common focus of attention and whose members influence one another

fad an unconventional social pattern that people embrace briefly but enthusiastically

fashion a social pattern favored for a time by a large number of people

gossip rumor about the personal affairs of others

mass behavior collective behavior among people dispersed over a wide geographical area

mass hysteria a form of dispersed collective behavior by which people respond to a real or imagined event with irrational, frantic, and often self-destructive behavior

mob a highly emotional crowd that pursues some violent or destructive goal

panic a form of localized collective behavior by which people react to a threat or other stimulus with irrational, frantic, and often self-destructive behavior

propaganda information presented with the intention of shaping public opinion

relative deprivation a perceived disadvantage arising from a specific comparison

riot a social eruption that is highly emotional, violent, and undirected

rumor unsubstantiated information spread informally, often by word of mouth

social movement organized activity that encourages or discourages social change

CRITICAL-THINKING QUESTIONS

1. The concept of collective behavior encompasses a broad range of social patterns. What traits do they all have in common?

2. Imagine a beachside town during spring break in which the revelry of a throng of college students turns into a destructive rampage. What insights

into this event do contagion theory, convergence theory, and emergent-norm theory provide?

3. The 1960s were a decade of unprecedented affluence and widespread social protest. What sociological insights help to explain this apparent paradox?

4. In what respects do some recent social movements (those concerned with the environment, animal rights, and gun control) differ from older crusades (focusing on, say, civil rights and gender equality)?

SUGGESTED READINGS

Classic Sources

Gustave Le Bon. *The Crowd: A Study of the Popular Mind.* New York: Viking Press, 1960; orig. 1895.

One of the first studies of crowd behavior, this classic stimulated the investigation of collective behavior and sparked debates that persist even today.

Jo Freeman, ed. *Social Movements of the Sixties and Seventies.* New York: Longman, 1983.

This collection of essays, with a useful introductory essay by the editor, investigates social movements in terms of four processes: mobilization, organization, strategy, and decline.

Howard Koch. *The Panic Broadcast: Portrait of an Event.* Boston: Little, Brown, 1970.

A classic example of collective behavior is found in this story of the 1938 "War of the Worlds" broadcast.

Contemporary Sources

Ralph H. Turner and Lewis M. Killian. *Collective Behavior.* 4th ed. Englewood Cliffs, N.J.: Prentice Hall, 1993.

This book provides details on just about all the topics covered in this chapter.

Aldon D. Morris and Carol McClurg Mueller, eds. *Frontiers in Social Movement Theory.* New Haven, Conn.: Yale University Press, 1992.

This collection of essays assesses the current state of social movements theory.

Clark McPhail. *The Myth of the Maddening Crowd.* New York: Aldine De Gruyter, 1991.

Here is a historical account arguing that sociologists have misunderstood crowd behavior. This book is a useful counterpoint to the work of Le Bon, noted above.

Manning Marable. *Black American Politics: From the Washington Marches to Jesse Jackson.* London: Verso, 1985.

This broad investigation of African-American politics in the United States contrasts various political movements that span fifty years.

Steven M. Buechler. *Women's Movements in the United States: Woman Suffrage, Equal Rights and Beyond.* New Brunswick, N.J.: Rutgers University Press, 1990.

This book offers a sociological analysis of the women's movement from the early suffrage campaign to contemporary feminism.

James M. Jasper and Dorothy Nelkin. *The Animal Rights Crusade: The Growth of a Moral Protest.* New York: The Free Press, 1992.

Here is a survey of the organizations and politics that make up the animal protection crusade, one example of a new social movement.

Stewart Burns. *Social Movements of the 1960s: Searching for Democracy.* Boston: G.K. Hall/Twayne, 1990.

This book analyzes three important social movements that characterized a turbulent decade in U.S. history: the antiwar movement, the women's movement, and the civil rights movement.

Metta Spencer, ed. *Research in Social Movements, Conflicts and Change: A Research Annual.* Vol. 13. Greenwich, Conn.: JAI Press, 1991.

This collection of articles about North American peace efforts during the 1980s focuses on what defines and generates a social movement.

Global Sources

Jeffrey N. Wasserstrom. *Student Protests in Twentieth-Century China: The View from Shanghai.* Stanford, Calif.: Stanford University Press, 1991.

Gao Yuan. *Born Red: A Chronicle of the Cultural Revolution.* Stanford, Calif.: Stanford University Press, 1987.

The first of these books investigates episodes of student protest in the People's Republic of China from 1919 until 1989. The second is a personal account of a teenager's experiences during the Cultural Revolution in China between 1966 and 1969, which has been dubbed a mass movement out of control.

Russell J. Dalton and Manfred Kuechler, eds. *Challenging the Political Order: New Social and Political Movements in Western Democracies.* New York: Oxford University Press, 1990.

This collection of readings assesses the ability of various theories to explain the new social movements that have emerged in recent decades.

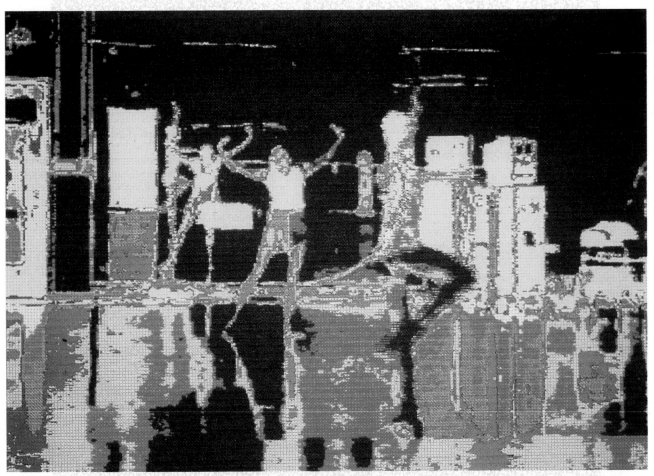

Glenn Rothman, *Purple Dance*

DATA FILE: An outline of this chapter, supplementary lecture material, and suggested discussion topics are included in the *Data File*.

Q: "The powerful play goes on, and you and I may contribute a verse." Walt Whitman

Q: "In 1967 two of our most respected futurists, Herman Kahn and Anthony Wiener, published a book titled *The Year 2000*, now a clas- sic in futurist literature. In that book there is no mention whatever of energy shortage, pollution, ecology, or women's rights—subjects that were to dominate our national debate the very next year after its publication." Richard Farson (1977)

RESOURCE: Marlise Simons describes the Kaiapo in more detail in a cross-cultural selection in the Macionis and Benokraitis reader, *Seeing Ourselves*.

Social Change: Traditional, Modern, and Postmodern Societies

*T*he firelight flickers in the gathering dark- ness as Chief Kanhonk sits, as he has done at the end of the day for many years, ready to begin an evening of animated talk and story- telling (Simons, 1989). This is the hour when the Kaiapo, a small society of Brazil's Amazon region, celebrate their heritage. Because the Kaiapo are a traditional people with no written language, the elders rely on evenings by the fire to teach their culture and instruct the grandchildren. In the past, evenings like this have been filled with tales of brave Kaiapo warriors fighting off Portuguese traders who came in pur- suit of slaves and gold.

But as the minutes pass, only a few villagers assemble for the evening ritual. "It is the Big Ghost," one man grumbles, ex- plaining the poor turnout. The "Big Ghost" has indeed descended upon them; its presence is evident in the bluish glow spilling from

windows of homes throughout the village. The Kaiapo children—and many adults as well—are watching television. The consequences of installing a satellite dish in the village three years ago have turned out to be greater than anyone imagined. In the end, what their enemies failed to do to the Kaiapo with guns they may well do to themselves with prime-time programming.

The Kaiapo are some of the 230,000 native peoples who inhabit the country we call Brazil. They stand out because of their striking body paint and ornate ceremonial dress. Recently, they have become rich as profits from gold mining and harvesting mahogany trees have flowed into the settlement. Now they must decide if their newfound fortune is a blessing or a curse. To some, affluence means the opportunity to learn about the outside world through travel and television. Others, like Chief

637

NOTE: The following quotations suggest the inevitably controversial character of social change. Whitehead's conservative sentiments are that "progressive" change inevitably undermines the foundations of morality. Marx takes an opposing view that the value of all intellectual endeavor is to bring about a more egalitarian social order.

Q: "The major advances in civilization are processes that all but wreck the societies in which they occur." Alfred North Whitehead
Q: "The philosophers have attempted to understand the world. The point, however, is to change it." Karl Marx
Q: "Only the wisest and the stupidest do not change." Confucius

Kanhonk, are not so sure. Sitting by the fire, he thinks aloud, "I have been saying that people must buy useful things like knives and fishing hooks. Television does not fill the stomach. It only shows our children and grandchildren white people's things." Bebtopup, the oldest priest, nods in agreement: "The night is the time the old people teach the young people. Television has stolen the night" (Simons, 1989:37).

The transformation of the Kaiapo raises profound questions about the causes of change and whether change—even toward a higher material standard of living—is always for the better. Moreover, the drama of the Kaiapo is being played out around the globe as more and more traditional cultures are drawn away from their past by the materialism and affluence of rich societies.

This chapter, then, examines social change as a process with both positive and negative consequences. Of particular interest to people in the United States is what sociologists call *modernity*, changes brought about by the Industrial Revolution, and *postmodernity*, more recent transformations sparked by the Information Revolution and the postindustrial economy. But we shall also consider how rich and powerful nations, such as the United States, are affecting the rest of the world.

WHAT IS SOCIAL CHANGE?

Earlier chapters have examined human societies in terms of both stability and change. The relatively *static* social patterns include status and roles, social stratification, and various social institutions. The *dynamic* forces that have recast humanity's consciousness, behavior, and needs range from innovations in technology to the growth of bureaucracy and the expansion of cities. Factors of this kind fuel **social change**, *the transformation of culture and social institutions over time.* The process of social change has four general characteristics.

1. **Social change happens everywhere, although the rate of change varies from place to place.** "Nothing is constant except death and taxes," goes the old saying. Yet social patterns related to death and taxes have changed dramatically as life expectancy in the United States has doubled since 1850. Taxes, meanwhile, unknown through most of human history, emerged only with complex social organization several thousand years ago. In short, one is hard-pressed to identify anything that is not subject to the twists and turns of change.

    Still, some societies change faster than others. As Chapter 4 ("Society") explained, hunting and gathering societies change quite slowly; members of technologically complex societies, on the other hand, can sense significant change even within a single lifetime.

    Moreover, even in a given society, some cultural elements change more quickly than others. William Ogburn's (1964) theory of *cultural lag* (see Chapter 3) recognizes that material culture (that is, things) usually change faster than nonmaterial culture (ideas and attitudes). For example, medical techniques that prolong the lives of seriously ill people have developed more rapidly than have ethical standards for deciding when and how to use them.

2. **Social change is sometimes intentional but often unplanned.** Industrial societies actively promote many kinds of change. For example, scientists seek more efficient forms of energy, and advertisers try to convince consumers that a new gadget is a "necessity." Yet even the experts rarely envision all the consequences of the changes they promote.

    Early automobile manufacturers certainly understood that cars would allow people to travel in a single day distances that had required weeks or months a century before. But no one foresaw how profoundly the mobility provided by automobiles would scatter family members, affect the environment, and reshape cities and suburbs. In addition, automotive pioneers could hardly have predicted the fifty thousand deaths each year in car accidents in the United States alone.

3. **Social change often generates controversy.** As the history of the automobile demonstrates, most social change yields both good and bad consequences. Capitalists welcomed the Industrial Revolution because advancing technology increased productivity and swelled profits. Many workers, however, fearing that machines would make their skills obsolete, strongly resisted "progress."

    In the United States, changing social patterns between people of color and whites, between

NOTE: Christopher Columbus's voyage across the Atlantic took 33 days; today, the journey can take as little as three hours via supersonic jet or about ten minutes on a spacecraft circling the earth. Commercial air travel was rare until after World War II; proliferation of "frequent flyer" programs suggests it is now commonplace in the United States.

NOTE: In light of how quickly today's information becomes obsolete, note that Euclidian mathematics texts remained up-to-date and more or less unchanged for 23 centuries.

SOCIAL SURVEY: "One trouble with science is that it makes our way of life change too fast." (GSS 1988, N = 1,481; *Codebook*, 1993:396)
    "Agree" 40.2%   "Disagree" 57.7%   DK/NR 2.1%

women and men, and between gays and heterosexuals give rise to misunderstandings, tensions, and, sometimes, hostility.

4. **Some changes matter more than others.** Some social changes have only passing significance, whereas other transformations resonate for generations. At one extreme, clothing fads among the young arise and dissipate quickly. At the other, members of our society (and people throughout the world) are still adjusting to powerful technological advances such as television half a century after its introduction. Looking ahead, who can predict with any certainty how computers will transform the entire world during the next century? Will the Information Revolution be as pivotal as the Industrial Revolution? Like the automobile and television, computers will have both positive and negative effects, providing new kinds of jobs while eliminating old ones, linking people in ever-expanding electronic networks while threatening personal privacy.

CAUSES OF SOCIAL CHANGE

Social change has many causes. And in a world linked by sophisticated communication and transportation technology, change in one place often begets change elsewhere.

Culture and Change

Culture is a dynamic system of symbols that continually gains new elements and loses others. Chapter 3 ("Culture") identified three important sources of cultural change. First, *invention* produces mechanical objects, ideas, and social patterns that reshape society to varying degrees. Rocket propulsion research, beginning in the 1940s, has produced increasingly sophisticated vehicles for space flight. Today we take such technology for granted; during the next century a significant number of people may well travel in space.

A second process, *discovery*, occurs when people first take note of existing elements of the world or learn to see them in a new way. Medical advances, for example, offer a growing understanding of how the human body operates. Beyond the direct effects for human health, medical discoveries have also stretched life expectancy, setting in motion what Chapter 14 ("Aging and the Elderly") terms the "graying of the United States."

Increasing technological sophistication is spreading cultural patterns more widely. In many parts of the world, Western cultural images are now common. Does this portend the emergence of a Western-based McCulture that will supplant thousands of historically distinctive ways of life? What are the advantages and drawbacks of the emergence of a global culture?

Third, *diffusion* creates change as trade, migration, and mass communication spread cultural elements from one society to another. Ralph Linton (1937) recognized that many familiar elements of our culture have come to us from other lands—for example, cloth (developed in Asia), clocks (invented in Europe), and coins (devised in Turkey). Generally, material things diffuse more readily than nonmaterial cultural traits. The Kaiapo, described at the beginning of this chapter, have been quick to adopt television but reluctant to embrace the materialism and individualism that sometimes seize those who spend hours watching Western commercial programming.

As a land of immigrants, the United States has steadily changed as a result of cultural diffusion. In recent decades, people from Latin America and Asia have been introducing new cultural patterns, clearly evident in the sights, smells, and sounds of cities across the country (Fallows, 1983; Muller & Espenshade, 1985). Conversely, the global power of the United States ensures that much of our culture—from the taste of hamburgers to the sounds of Harlem rap to the skills of Harvard M.B.A.s—are being diffused to other societies.

NOTE: Are "great people" or "average people" primarily responsible for social change? Historically, conservatives argued the former, since this individualistic position favored traditional hierarchy and elites. Liberals tended toward the more egalitarian, collectivist view. Tocqueville compared the United States and Britain in this regard and, with our nation's more democratic values in mind, suggested that wherever the English have a great person, the Americans have a committee. Marx suggested that average people bring about change under circumstances that promote understanding and action. Weber's argument linking world view to social change implies that average people are instrumental in social transformation; on the other hand, his theory of charisma spotlights the importance of extraordinary individuals to social change.

Conflict and Change

Tension and conflict within a society also produce change. Karl Marx heralded class conflict as the engine that drives societies from one historical era to another (see Chapter 4, "Society," and Chapter 9, "Social Stratification"). In industrial-capitalist societies, he maintained, struggle between capitalists and workers propels society toward a socialist system of production.

In the century since Marx's death, this model has proven simplistic. Yet, he correctly foresaw that social conflict arising from inequality (involving race and gender as well as social class) would reshape every society, including the United States.

Ideas and Change

Max Weber, too, contributed to our understanding of social change. While Weber acknowledged the importance of conflict based on material production, he traced the roots of social change to the world of ideas. He illustrated his argument by showing how people who display charisma (described in Chapter 16, "Politics and Government," and Chapter 18, "Religion") can convey a message that sometimes changes the world.

Weber also highlighted the importance of ideas by revealing how the world view of early Protestants drove them to embrace industrial capitalism (see Chapter 4, "Society"). By showing that industrial capitalism developed primarily in areas of Western Europe where the Protestant work ethic was strong, Weber (1958; orig. 1904–5) concluded that the disciplined rationality of Calvinist Protestants was instrumental in this change.

Ideas also fuel social movements. Chapter 23 ("Collective Behavior and Social Movements") explained that a social movement may emerge from the decision to modify society in some manner (say, to clean up the environment) or from a sense that existing social arrangements must be reformed. The international gay rights movement draws strength from the contention that lesbians and gay men should enjoy rights and opportunities equal to those of the heterosexual majority. Persistent opposition to the gay rights movement, moreover, reveals the power of ideas to inhibit as well as to advance social change.

The Natural Environment and Change

As Chapter 22 ("The Natural Environment") detailed, human societies are closely connected to their natural environment. For this reason, change in one tends to produce change in the other.

By and large, our culture casts nature as a force to be tamed and reshaped to human purposes. From the outset, European settlers systematically cut down forests to create fields for farming and acquire materials for building; they established towns, extended roads in every direction, and dammed rivers as a source of water and energy. Such human construction not only reflects our cultural determination to master the natural environment; it also points up the centrality of the idea of "growth" in our way of life.

But the consequences of such thinking have placed increasing stress on the natural environment. Our society contends with problems of solid waste and air and water pollution, all the while consuming the lion's share of global resources. A growing awareness that such patterns are not sustainable in the long term is forcing us to confront the need to change our way of life in some basic respects.

Demographic Change

Demographic factors (described in Chapter 21, "Population and Urbanization") also cause social change. Population increase places escalating demands on the natural environment, and, as the cultures of the Netherlands and Japan indicate, high-density living affects virtually every facet of life. For example, homes in Amsterdam are small and narrow compared to those in the United States, with extremely steep staircases to make efficient use of space. In Tokyo, commuters routinely endure subway crowding that would alarm most North Americans.

Such differences, of course, are due to the fact that our society has enjoyed a bounty of physical space. But, even so, urbanization has also changed our lives. About three-fourths of the U.S. population live in cities, which cover only a small percentage of U.S. land surface. The fast-paced and anonymous way of life that characterizes urban settings barely resembles the more tranquil rhythms that defined the rural villages and small towns of the past.

Profound change also results from the shifting composition of a population. Our population, collectively speaking, is growing older, as Chapter 14 ("Aging and the Elderly") explained. In 1992, 13 percent were over age sixty-five, triple the proportion in 1900. By the year 2030, seniors will account for one in five U.S. residents (U.S. Bureau of the Census, 1993). Medical research and health care services already focus on the elderly, and common stereotypes

NOTE: Leaving home—presumably for something better—has long been a measure of success in the United States. We have come to use the word "success" in a notably nonspecific manner. Its traditional meaning—to follow or replace another by descent—made sense in a relatively fixed social order with strong social ties. The term's contemporary meaning of achieving individual goals (whatever they may be) suggests a far more fluid social order.

NOTE: A fact related to the increasing pace of social change is that, while about 20 percent of all people who have ever lived are breathing today, about 90 percent of all scientists are now alive.

THE MAP: Florida is a prime retirement area with a large share of people over the age of fifty-five. Vermont is favored by young people—especially hip and somewhat countercultural individuals—who have conferred a specific character on that state.

Seeing Ourselves

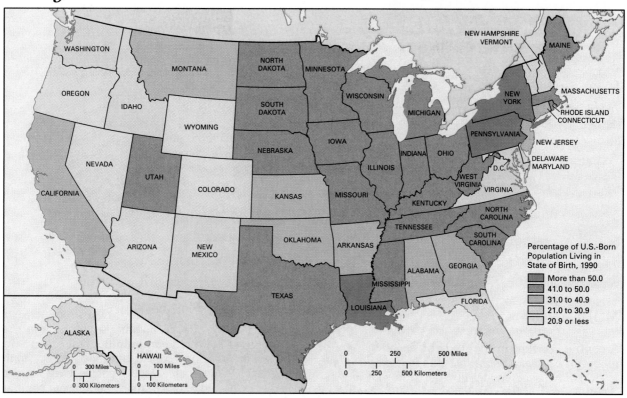

NATIONAL MAP 24–1 Moving On: Migration Across the United States

One in six households packs up and moves each year, making the United States one of the most geographically mobile societies on earth. The map indicates what percentage of each state's population is made up of migrants—people who were born somewhere else. Generally speaking, in the Snowbelt region (the Northeast and Midwest), migrants represent less than 30 percent of the people. By contrast, the western half of the United States contains the largest share of migrants, with "movers" making up absolute majorities in Oregon, Wyoming, Nevada, Colorado, and Arizona. Florida and Vermont are also home to a majority from elsewhere. Why, in each case, do you think this is so?

Prepared by the author using data from the 1990 decennial census.

about old people will be challenged as more men and women enter this stage of life. Life may change in countless additional ways as homes and household products are redesigned to meet the needs of growing ranks of older consumers.

Migration within and among societies is another demographic factor that often promotes dramatic social change. Between 1870 and 1930, tens of millions of immigrants swelled the industrial cities in the United States. Millions of rural people joined them.

As a result, farm communities declined, metropolises burgeoned, and the United States became for the first time a predominantly urban society. Similar changes are taking place today as people are moving from the Snowbelt to the Sunbelt, where they mingle with new immigrants from Latin America and Asia.

Demographic changes typically transform some parts of the country more than others. National Map 24–1 identifies the states whose population includes the greatest share of people born elsewhere.

Q: "A case can be made that the central question of sociology, from its inception in the rather fanciful philosophy of August Comte, has been the question about the nature of modernity." Peter Berger (1986:28)

NOTE: The term "lifestyle" emerged only in recent decades as one indication of the growing ability of individuals to shape their own lives (within the limits imposed by their resources, of course).

NOTE: Most of humanity still lives within powerful, ascriptive communities, thinking of themselves as embedded in kinship, locality, and tradition. From the point of view of such people throughout the world, we in the United States seem not only affluent but highly individualistic. From our point of view, behavior based on ascriptive solidarities (that is, reflecting categories rather than individual traits) seems wrongheaded and discriminatory.

In response to the accelerated pace of change in the late nineteenth century, Paul Gauguin (1848–1903) left his native France for the South Seas where he was captivated by a simpler and seemingly timeless way of life. He romanticized this environment in his 1894 painting Mahana no Atua (Day of the Gods).

MODERNITY

A central concept in the study of social change is **modernity**, *social patterns linked to industrialization.* In everyday usage, modernity (its Latin root means "lately") refers to the present in relation to the past. Sociologists include within this catchall concept the many social patterns set in motion by the Industrial Revolution beginning in Western Europe in the mid-eighteenth century. **Modernization**, then, is *the process of social change initiated by industrialization.*

Key Dimensions of Modernization

Peter Berger (1977) notes four general characteristics of modernization:

1. **The decline of small, traditional communities.** Modernity involves "the progressive weakening, if not destruction, of the concrete and relatively cohesive communities in which human beings have found solidarity and meaning throughout most of history" (Berger 1977:72). For thousands of years, in the camps of hunters and gatherers and in the rural villages of Europe and North America, people lived in small-scale settlements with family and neighbors. Such traditional worlds—based on sentiments and beliefs passed from generation to generation—afford each person a well-defined place. These primary groups limit people's range of experience while conferring a strong sense of identity, belonging, and purpose.

   Small, isolated communities still exist in the United States, of course, but they are now home to only a small percentage of people. Even for rural people, rapid transportation and efficient communication, including television, have brought individuals in touch with the pulse of the larger society and even the entire world. For everyone, too, the family is no longer the unrivaled center of everyday life. As Talcott Parsons (1966) noted, modern living is played out in distinct institutional settings, including schools, businesses, places of worship, and centers of recreation.

2. **The expansion of personal choice.** People in traditional, preindustrial societies view their lives as shaped by forces beyond human control—gods, spirits, or, simply, fate. Steeped in tradition, members of these societies grant one another a narrow range of personal choices.

   As the power of tradition erodes, however, a society's members come to see their lives as an unending series of options. Berger calls this process *individualization*. The United States, for instance, displays a variety of lifestyles, as the way of life that one person finds suitable may hold little appeal for another. Recognizing alternatives in everyday life, of course, parallels a willingness to embrace change. Modern people, then, easily imagine the world being different from the way it is now.

SOCIAL SURVEY: "Right and wrong are not usually a simple matter of black and white; there are many shades of gray." (GSS 1988, N = 1,481; *Codebook*, 1993:411)

"Agree strongly"   39.8%   "Disagree strongly" 6.9%
"Agree"   42.1%   DK/NR   3.4%
"Disagree somewhat" 7.8%

Q: "Our lives make sense in a thousand ways, most of which we are unaware of, because of traditions that are centuries, if not millennia, old." Robert N. Bellah et al. (1985:282).

Q: "As habit is essential to vice, it is essential to virtue as well." Ferdinand Toennies.

RESOURCE: The cold, utilitarian character of society presented in Toennies's analysis is wonderfully captured in Charles Dickens's novel *Hard Times*.

George Tooker's 1950 painting The Subway *depicts a common problem of modern life: Weakening social ties and eroding traditions create a generic humanity in which everyone is alike yet each person is an anxious stranger in the midst of others.*

3. **Increasing diversity in beliefs.** In preindustrial societies, strong family ties and powerful religious beliefs enforce conformity, frowning on diversity and change. Modernization promotes a more rational, scientific world view, in which traditional beliefs lose their force and morality becomes a matter of individual attitude. The growth of cities, expansion of impersonal organizations, and social mix of people from various places and backgrounds combine to foster a diversity of beliefs and behavior as well as a tolerant openness to people who differ from ourselves.

Chapter 18 ("Religion") spotlighted *secularization*, the historical decline of the importance of religion. The weakening of religious doctrine—especially the legal separation of church and state—helps expand the range of personal beliefs in modern societies.

4. **Future orientation and growing awareness of time.** People in modern societies share a distinctive appreciation of time. First, we tend to think more about the future, while preindustrial people focus more on the past. Modern people are not only forward looking but optimistic that discoveries and new inventions will enhance their lives.

Second, modern societies organize daily routines according to precise units of time. With the introduction of clocks in the late Middle Ages, and the growing importance of economic activity, Europeans began thinking not in terms of sunlight and seasons but in units of hours and minutes. Preoccupied with personal gain, modern people demand increasingly precise measurement of time and are likely to agree that "Time is money!" Berger suggests that one gauge of a society's degree of modernization is the proportion of people wearing wristwatches.

Finally, recall that modernization touched off the development of sociology itself. As Chapter 1 ("The Sociological Perspective") explained, the discipline originated in the wake of the Industrial Revolution in Western Europe, precisely where social change was proceeding most rapidly. Early European and U.S. sociologists tried to analyze and explain modernization and its consequences—both good and bad—for human beings.

Ferdinand Toennies: The Loss of Community

The German sociologist Ferdinand Toennies, whose brief biography appears in the box, produced the theory of *Gemeinschaft* and *Gesellschaft* (see Chapter 21, "Population and Urbanization"). Like Peter Berger, whose work he influenced, Toennies (1963; orig. 1887) viewed modernization as the progressive loss of *Gemeinschaft*, or human community. As Toennies saw it, the Industrial Revolution undermined the strong social fabric of family and tradition by introducing a businesslike emphasis on facts and efficiency. European and North American societies gradually turned rootless and impersonal as people came to associate mostly on the basis of self-interest—the condition Toennies termed *Gesellschaft*.

Early in this century, at least some areas of the United States approximated Toennies's concept of *Gemeinschaft*. Families that had lived for generations in rural towns and villages were tightly integrated into a hard-working, slow-moving way of life. Telephones (invented in 1876) were rare; the first coast-to-coast call was placed only in 1915. Before television (introduced in 1939, widespread after 1950), families entertained themselves, often gathering with friends in the evening—much like Brazil's Kaiapo—to share stories, sorrows, or song. Without rapid transportation (although

Q: "One of the most fundamental traits of modernization is a vast movement from fate to choice in human affairs." Peter Berger

NOTE: The term "individual," with a Latin root meaning "indivisible," only became widely used in early nineteenth-century Europe, at a time when traditional social ties were weakening.

RESOURCE: An excerpt from Robert Bellah's *Habits of the Heart* is included in the Macionis and Benokraitis reader, *Seeing Ourselves*.

NOTE: The 1920 census was the first to record a majority of the U.S population living in urban places.

PROFILE

Ferdinand Toennies: Is There Virtue in Modern Society?

Can traditional virtues such as selflessness and honor survive in the rapidly changing modern world? Pioneering sociologist Ferdinand Toennies (1855–1936) spent his life pursuing the answer to this important question. In the process, along with his colleagues Max Weber and Georg Simmel, Toennies helped to establish sociology as an academic discipline in Germany.

Born to a wealthy family in the German countryside, Toennies was raised in comfortable surroundings and received an extensive education. He also learned a great deal from observing the world about him—he was especially fascinated by how the Industrial Revolution was transforming Germany and other European countries.

But, to Toennies, change was not necessarily for the better. Toennies's work displays a deep distrust of the common-sense notion of "progress," which he feared amounted to the steady loss of traditional morality. His influential book *Gemeinschaft and Gesellschaft* (1887) is therefore both a chronicle of modernization and an indictment of an increasingly impersonal world.

Toennies's thesis is that traditional societies, built on kinship and neighborhood, nourish collective sentiments, virtue, and honor. Modernization washes across traditional

society like an acid, eroding human community and unleashing rampant individualism. Toennies stopped short of claiming that modern society was "worse" than societies of the past, and he made a point of praising the spread of rational, scientific thinking. Nevertheless, the growing individualism and selfishness characteristic of modern societies troubled him. Knowing that there could be no return to the past, he looked to the future, hoping that new forms of social organization would combine modern rationality with traditional collective responsibility.

SOURCE: Based on Cahnman & Heberle (1971).

Henry Ford's assembly line began in 1908, cars became commonplace only after World War II), many people perceived their town as their entire world.

Inevitable tensions and conflicts—sometimes based on race, ethnicity, and religion—characterized past communities. According to Toennies, however, the traditional ties of *Gemeinschaft* bound people of a community together, "essentially united in spite of all separating factors" (1963:65; orig. 1887).

Modernity turns societies inside out so that, as Toennies put it, people are "essentially separated in spite of uniting factors" (1963:65; orig. 1887). This is the world of *Gesellschaft* where, especially in large cities, most people live among strangers and ignore

those they pass on the street. Trust is hard to come by in a mobile and anonymous society in which, according to researchers, people tend to put their personal needs ahead of group loyalty and a majority of adults claim that "you can't be too careful" in dealing with people (NORC, 1993:203; Russell, 1993). No wonder, as one news report indicated, 15 million men and women attend weekly support groups (also made up of strangers) in which they establish temporary emotional ties and find someone who is willing simply to *listen* (Leerhsen, 1990).

Critical evaluation. Toennies's theory of *Gemeinschaft* and *Gesellschaft* is the most widely cited

NOTE: Durkheim's concept of "mechanical solidarity" implies that we can know an entire society by examining any one component of it, as we can understand a physical substance through analysis of a single molecule. This is not true of internally differentiated, organic bodies.
RESOURCE: Emile Durkheim's "Anomie and Modern Life" is one of the classics in the 3rd edition of Seeing Ourselves.

Q: ". . . frequently the world images [and] ideas have, like switchmen, determined the tracks along which action has been pushed . . ." Max Weber
RESOURCE: Max Weber's analysis of "The Disenchantment of Modern Life" is another of the classics in the companion reader, Seeing Ourselves.

model for describing modernization. The theory's strength lies in its synthesis of various dimensions of change—growing population, the rise of cities, increasing impersonality.

One problem with Toennies's theory is that modern life, while often impersonal, is not completely devoid of *Gemeinschaft*. Even in a world of strangers, friendships are often strong and lasting. Traditions are especially pronounced in many ethnic neighborhoods where residents maintain close community ties.

Another criticism is that Toennies's approach says little about which factors (industrialization, urbanization, weakening of families) are cause and which are effect. Some analysts have also asserted that Toennies favored—perhaps even romanticized—traditional societies.

Emile Durkheim: The Division of Labor

The French sociologist Emile Durkheim, whose work is discussed in Chapter 4 ("Society"), shared Toennies's interest in the profound social changes wrought by the Industrial Revolution. For Durkheim, modernization is marked by the increasing *division of labor,* or specialized economic activity (1964b; orig. 1893). Whereas every member of a traditional society performs more or less the same daily round of activities, modern societies function by having people perform highly distinctive roles.

Durkheim contended that preindustrial societies are held together by *mechanical solidarity*—social bonds resting on shared moral sentiments. Thus members of preindustrial societies have a sense that everyone is basically alike and belongs together. Mechanical solidarity, or what Toennies called *Gemeinschaft*, depends on a minimal division of labor, so that everyone's life follows much the same path. Durkheim's mechanical solidarity mirrors Toennies's *Gemeinschaft*.

Modernization takes place as the division of labor becomes more and more pronounced. Modern societies, then, are held together by *organic solidarity*, bonds of mutual dependency among people who engage in specialized work. Put simply, modern societies are bound together not by likeness but by difference, since we all find that we must depend on others to meet most of our needs. Organic solidarity corresponds to Toennies's concept of *Gesellschaft*.

Despite obvious similarities, Durkheim and Toennies interpreted modernity somewhat differently. To Toennies, modern *Gesellschaft* amounts to the loss of social solidarity—the inevitable result of the gradual erosion of "natural" and "organic" bonds of the rural past, leaving only the "artificial" and "mechanical" ties

of the present. Durkheim disagreed and even reversed Toennies's language to bring home the point. Durkheim labeled modern society as "organic," suggesting that today's world is no less natural than before, and he described traditional societies as "mechanical" because they are so regimented. Thus Durkheim viewed modernization not so much as a loss of community as a change in the basis of community—from bonds of likeness (kinship and neighborhood) to economic interdependence (the division of labor). Durkheim's view of modernity is both more complex and more positive than that of Toennies.

Critical evaluation. Durkheim's work stands alongside that of Toennies, which it closely resembles, as a highly influential analysis of modernity. Of the two, Durkheim is clearly the more optimistic; still, he feared that modern societies would become so internally diverse that they would collapse into *anomie*, a condition in which norms and values are so weak and inconsistent that society provides little moral guidance to individuals. In the midst of weak moral claims from society, modern people tend to be egocentric, placing their own needs above those of others.

Evidence supports Durkheim's contention that anomie plagues modern societies. Suicide rates, which Durkheim considered a prime index of anomie, have risen throughout this century. Moreover, surveys indicate that the vast majority of U.S. adults now see moral questions not in clear terms of right and wrong but as "shades of gray." Moreover, members of our society assert, as a matter of principle, that no single moral standard should be applicable to everyone (NORC, 1993:411).

On the other hand, shared norms and values are still strong enough to give most people at least some sense of meaning and purpose. Additionally, whatever the hazards of anomie and atomization, most people seem to value the privacy and personal autonomy that modern society affords.

Max Weber: Rationalization

Max Weber held that ideas and beliefs stand out as causes of social change; his thesis is detailed in Chapter 4 ("Society"). For Weber, modernity amounts to the progressive replacement of a traditional world view by a rational way of thinking.

In preindustrial societies, tradition acts as a constant brake on change. To traditional people, Weber explains, "truth" is roughly synonymous with "what has always been" (1978:36; orig. 1921). In modern societies, by contrast, people see truth as the product of

Max Weber maintained that the distinctive character of modern society was its rational world view. Virtually all of Weber's work on modernity centered on types of people he considered typical of their age: the scientist, the capitalist, and the bureaucrat. Each is rational to the core: The scientist is committed to the orderly discovery of truth, the capitalist to the orderly pursuit of profit, and the bureaucrat to orderly conformity to a rational system of rules.

deliberate calculation. Because efficiency is valued more than reverence for the past, individuals adopt whichever social patterns will allow them to achieve their goals. A rational view of the world, then, leads people to seek out and assess various options according to their specific consequences rather than according to any absolute standard of rightness.

Echoing the claim of Toennies and Durkheim that industrialization weakens tradition, Weber declared that modern society had become "disenchanted." What were once unquestioned truths have become subject to matter-of-fact calculations. Embracing rational, scientific thought, in short, modern society turns away from the gods.

Throughout his life, Weber explored various modern "types"—the capitalist, the scientist, and the bureaucrat. What these all have in common is the rational and detached world view Weber believed was coming to dominate humanity.

Critical evaluation. Compared with Toennies, and especially Durkheim, Weber was a profound critic of modern society. He recognized that science could produce technological and organizational wonders, yet he worried that it was carrying us away from more basic questions about the meaning and purpose of human existence. Weber feared that rationalization, especially in bureaucracies, would erode the human spirit with endless rules and regulations.

Finally, some of Weber's critics think that the alienation he attributed to bureaucracy is actually a product of social inequality. The root of this contention lies in the ideas of Karl Marx.

Karl Marx: Capitalism

While other analysts of modernity examined shifting patterns of social order, Marx focused on social conflict. For Marx, modern society was synonymous with capitalism; he saw the Industrial Revolution as being primarily a *capitalist revolution.* As Chapter 4 ("Society") explained, Marx traced the emergence of the bourgeoisie in medieval Europe as an effort to wrest control of society from the feudal nobility. The bourgeoisie were finally successful when the Industrial Revolution placed a powerful new productive system under their control.

Marx agreed that modernity weakened small-scale communities (as described by Toennies), sharpened the division of labor (as noted by Durkheim), and fostered a rational world view (as asserted by Weber). But he saw these factors simply as conditions necessary for capitalism to flourish. Capitalism, according to Marx, draws population from farms and small towns into an ever-expanding market system centered in the cities; specialization underlies efficient factories; and rationality is exemplified by the capitalist's relentless quest for profits.

NOTE: A characteristic of modernity is the rise of tolerance (from the Latin *tolerare*, meaning "to bear"). For most of us, the virtues of tolerance are easy to enumerate, if not always to act on. Contemporary people tend to embrace cultural relativism (especially as their schooling increases); traditional people (and those with less schooling) defend an ethnocentric, more absolutist world view.

SOCIAL SURVEY: "Morality is a personal matter and society should not force everyone to follow one standard." (GSS 1988, N = 1,481; *Codebook*, 1993:411)

"Agree strongly"	31.7%	"Disagree strongly"	7.6%
"Agree somewhat"	38.8%	DK/NR	4.4%
"Disagree somewhat"	17.5%		

TABLE 24–1 Traditional and Modern Societies: Dimensions of Difference

Elements of Society	Traditional Societies	Modern Societies
Cultural Patterns		
Values	Homogeneous; sacred character; few subcultures and countercultures	Heterogeneous; secular character; many subcultures and countercultures
Norms	High moral significance; little tolerance of diversity	Variable moral significance; high tolerance of diversity
Time orientation	Present linked to past	Present linked to future
Technology	Preindustrial; human and animal energy	Industrial; advanced energy sources
Social Structure		
Status and role	Few statuses, most ascribed; few specialized roles	Many statuses, some ascribed and some achieved; many specialized roles
Relationships	Typically primary; little anonymity and privacy	Typically secondary; considerably anonymity and privacy
Communication	Face to face	Face-to-face communication supplemented by mass media
Social control	Informal gossip	Formal police and legal system
Social stratification	Rigid patterns of social inequality; little mobility	Fluid patterns of social inequality; considerable mobility
Gender patterns	Pronounced patriarchy; women's lives centered on the home	Declining patriarchy; increasing number of women in the paid labor force
Economy	Based on agriculture; some manufacturing in the home; little white-collar work	Based on industrial mass production; factories become centers of production; increasing white-collar work
State	Small-scale government; little state intervention in society	Large-scale government, considerable state intervention in society
Family	Extended family as the primary means of socialization and economic production	Nuclear family retains some socialization functions but is more a unit of consumption than of production
Religion	Religion guides world view; little religious pluralism	Religion weakens with the rise of science; extensive religious pluralism
Education	Formal schooling limited to elites	Basic schooling becomes universal, with growing proportion receiving advanced education
Health	High birth and death rates; brief life expectancy because of low standard of living and simple medical technology	Low birth and death rates; longer life expectancy because of higher standard of living and sophisticated medical technology
Settlement patterns	Small scale; population typically small and widely dispersed in rural villages and small towns	Large scale; population typically large and concentrated in cities
Social Change	Slow; change evident over many generations	Rapid; change evident within a single generation

Earlier chapters have painted Marx as a spirited critic of capitalist society, but his vision of modernity also incorporates a considerable measure of optimism. Unlike Weber, who viewed modern society as an "iron cage" of bureaucracy, Marx believed that social conflict within capitalist social systems would sow seeds of revolutionary social change, ultimately producing an egalitarian socialism. Such a society, he claimed, would harness the wonders of industrial technology to enrich the lives of the many rather than the few—and thereby rid the world of the prime source of social conflict and dehumanization. While Marx's evaluation of modern capitalist society was highly negative, then, he anticipated a future with greater human freedom, blossoming human creativity, and renewed human community.

Critical evaluation. Marx's theory of modernization draws together many threads in a fabric dominated by capitalism. Yet Marx underestimated the significance of bureaucracy in shaping modern societies. As government apparatus expanded, the stifling effects of formal organization on humanity turned out to be as bad—or worse—in socialist societies than the dehumanizing impact of capitalism. The recent upheavals in Eastern Europe and the former Soviet Union reveal the depth of opposition to rigid state bureaucracies.

NOTE: Evidence of the increasing pace of our lives: In 1920, Emily Post advised widows to undergo three years of mourning; in the 1980s, Amy Vanderbilt suggested that a woman should get on with her life in about one week. (My own college gives employees three days of official leave, which officials apparently consider sufficient to conclude grieving.)

Q: "The people who are always hankering loudest for some golden yesteryear usually drive new cars." Russell Baker
NOTE: The conservative implication of mass-society theory is that social inequality still persists, but not as the severe problem that it was in the nineteenth century. Instead, the growing state is problematic.

THEORETICAL ANALYSIS OF MODERNITY

The rise of modernity is a complex process involving many dimensions of change, described in previous chapters and summarized in Table 24–1 on page 647. How is one to make sense of so many changes going on all at once? Sociologists have devised two broad explanations of modern society, one derived from the structural-functional paradigm and one based on the social-conflict approach.

Structural-Functional Theory: Modernity as Mass Society

One broad approach—drawing on ideas of Ferdinand Toennies, Emile Durkheim, and Max Weber—understands modernization as the emergence of *mass society* (Dahrendorf, 1959; Kornhauser, 1959; Nisbet, 1966, 1969; Baltzell, 1968; Stein, 1972; Berger, Berger, & Kellner, 1974; Pearson, 1993).

A **mass society** is *a society in which industry and bureaucracy have eroded traditional social ties.* A mass society is marked by weak kinship and impersonal neighborhoods so that individuals are socially atomized. In their isolation, members of mass societies typically experience feelings of moral uncertainty and personal powerlessness.

The Mass Scale of Modern Life

Mass-society theory argues, first, that the scale of modern life has increased momentously. Before the Industrial Revolution, Europe and North America were an intricate mosaic of countless rural villages and small towns. In these small communities, which inspired Toennies's concept of *Gemeinschaft*, people lived out their lives surrounded by kin and guided by a shared heritage. Gossip was an informal, yet highly effective, means of ensuring rigid conformity to community standards. Limited community size combined with strong moral values to stifle social diversity—the mechanical solidarity described by Durkheim.

For example, in England before 1690, both law and local custom demanded that all people regularly participate in the Christian ritual of Holy Communion (Laslett, 1984). Similarly, only Rhode Island among the New England colonies offered any support for the notion of religious dissent. Because social differences were repressed, subcultures and countercultures rarely flourished and change proceeded slowly. Individuals'

social positions were more or less set at birth, with little social mobility.

A surge in population, the growth of cities, and specialized economic activity driven by the Industrial Revolution gradually changed all this. People came to know one another by their functions (for example, as the "doctor" or the "bank clerk") rather than by their kinship group or hometown. The majority of people looked on others simply as a mass of strangers. The face-to-face communication of the village was eventually replaced by the mass media—newspapers, radio, television—as well as computer networks, furthering the process of social atomization. Large organizations steadily assumed more and more responsibility for daily needs that had once been fulfilled by family, friends, and neighbors; universal public education enlarged the scope of learning; police, lawyers, and formal courts supervised a criminal justice system. Even charity became the work of faceless bureaucrats working for various social welfare agencies.

Geographical mobility, mass communications, and exposure to diverse ways of life erode traditional values. Less certain about what is worth believing, people become more tolerant of social diversity, trumpeting individual rights and freedom of choice. Subcultures and countercultures multiply. Making categorical distinctions among people—that is, treating people differently based on their race, sex, or religion—has come to be defined as backward and unjust. In the process, minorities who have long lived at the margins of society have gained greater power and broader participation. Yet, mass-society theorists fear, transforming people of various backgrounds into a generic mass may end up draining meaning from our lives and dehumanizing everyone.

The Ever-Expanding State

In the small-scale, preindustrial societies of Europe, government amounted to little more than a local noble. A royal family formally reigned over an entire nation, but without efficient transportation or communication, the power of even absolute monarchs fell far short of that wielded by today's political leaders.

As technological innovation allowed government to expand, the centralized state grew in size and importance. At the time the United States gained independence from Great Britain, the federal government was a tiny organization whose prime function was national defense. Since then, government has entered more and more areas of social life—regulating wages and working conditions, establishing standards

GLOBAL: Tourism was all but unknown a century ago; today, the entire world copes with hundreds of millions of tourists. This change is one effect of technological advances.

NOTE: Many large charities ceased collecting at home and began soliciting in the workplace several decades ago, recognizing that people were more responsive to co-workers than to neighbors.

NOTE: In modern, rapidly changing societies, the origins of cultural elements are often forgotten. Lucky Strike cigarettes were named for a California gold strike; Baby Ruth candy bars were named for the birth of Grover Cleveland's daughter.

NOTE: For mass-society theorists, the essential problem of modernity is *anomie* (following Durkheim); for class-society theorists, it is *alienation* (following Marx). The *Data File* presents further differences between the two concepts.

Mass-society theory explains common feelings of isolation in the modern world as the result of rapid social change and the collapse of tradition. Edvard Munch captured this sense of impersonality and anonymity in the modern world in his painting (above) Evening on Karl Johan Street *(1892). Class-society theory, by contrast, ties the experience of powerlessness to the poverty of many amidst the privilege of the few, a situation depicted in this anonymous colored engraving (right) of winter in Manhattan,* The Hearth-Stone of the Poor *(1876).*

for products of all sorts, schooling the population, and providing financial assistance to the ill and the unemployed. Taxes have correspondingly soared, so that today's average worker labors for four months each year simply to pay for various government services.

In a mass society, power resides in large bureaucracies, leaving people in local communities little control over their lives. For example, state officials mandate that local schools must have a standardized educational program, local products must earn government certification, and every citizen must maintain extensive records for purposes of taxation. While such regulations may protect people and enhance uniformity of treatment, they force us to deal more and more with nameless officials in distant and often unresponsive bureaucracies, and they undermine the autonomy of families and neighborhoods.

Critical evaluation. The theory of mass society concedes that the transformation of small-scale communities has positive aspects, but it sees in historical change the loss of an irreplaceable heritage. Modern societies increase individual rights, magnify tolerance of social differences, and raise standards of living. But they seem prone to what Weber feared most—excessive bureaucracy—as well as Toennies's self-centeredness and

Durkheim's anomie. Their size, complexity, and tolerance of diversity all but doom traditional values and family patterns, leaving individuals isolated, anxious, and materialistic. As was noted in Chapter 16 ("Politics and Government"), voter apathy has become a serious problem in the United States. But should we be surprised that people in vast, impersonal societies tend to conclude that no one person can make a difference?

Critics of mass-society theory contend that it romanticizes the past. They remind us that many people in small towns were actually eager to set out for the excitement and higher standard of living found in cities. Critics also point out that this approach pays little attention to problems of social inequality. Mass-society analysis, critics conclude, attracts social and economic conservatives who defend conventional morality and often seem indifferent to the historical plight of women and other minorities.

Social-Conflict Theory: Modernity as Class Society

A second interpretation of modernity derives largely from the ideas of Karl Marx. From this point of view, modernity takes the form of a **class society**, *a capitalist*

Q: "The bourgeoisie . . . has pitilessly torn asunder the motley feudal ties that bound man to his 'natural superiors,' and has left remaining no other nexus between man and man than naked self-interest, than callous 'cash payment'." Marx and Engels

Q: "The need for a constantly expanding market for its products chases the bourgeoisie over the whole surface of the globe. It must nestle everywhere . . ." Karl Marx and Friedrich Engels

TABLE 24–2 Two Interpretations of Modernity: A Summary

	Key Process of Modernization	Key Effects of Modernization
Mass-society theory	Industrialization; growth of bureaucracy	Increasing scale of life; rise of the state and other formal organizations
Class-society theory	Rise of capitalism	Expansion of capitalist economy; persistence of social inequality

society with pronounced social stratification. According to this theory, social inequality is the cause of widespread feelings of powerlessness. This approach agrees that modern societies have enlarged to a mass scale but claims that the heart of modernization is an expanding capitalist economy. Capitalist societies still contain pronounced inequality and social conflict, even if the inequality is somewhat less severe than it was a century ago (Miliband, 1969; Habermas, 1970; Polenberg, 1980; Blumberg, 1981; Harrington, 1984).

Capitalism

Class-society theory follows Marx in claiming that the increasing scale of social life has resulted from the insatiable appetite of capitalism. Because a capitalist economy pursues ever-increasing profits, both production and consumption steadily expand.

According to Marx, capitalism emphasizes "naked self-interest" (1972:337; orig. 1848). This self-centeredness erodes the social ties that once cemented small-scale communities. Capitalism also fosters impersonality and anonymity by transforming people into commodities, both as a source of labor and a market for capitalist production. The net result is that capitalism reduces human beings to cogs in the machinery of material production.

Capitalism also embraces science, not just as the key to greater productivity but also as an ideology that justifies the status quo. In preindustrial Europe, nobles defended their rule with traditional notions of moral obligation and responsibility. In modern societies, capitalists legitimize their way of life by encouraging people to view their own well-being as a *technical* puzzle to be solved by engineers and other experts rather than through the pursuit of *social* justice (Habermas, 1970). A capitalist culture, for example, seeks to improve health through scientific medicine rather than

NOTE: A glance back to Figure 11–1 provides data on the distribution of economic resources around the world.

Richest	20%	70%
2nd	20%	20%
Middle	20%	5%
4th	20%	3%
Poorest	20%	2%

by eliminating poverty, which undermines many people's health in the first place.

Businesses also raise the banner of scientific logic when they claim that efficiency is achieved only through continual growth. As Chapter 15 ("The Economy and Work") explains, capitalist corporations have reached enormous size and control almost unimaginable wealth. They have done so by "going global," that is, by becoming multinationals that operate throughout the world. From the class-society point of view, then, the expanding scale of life is less a function of *Gesellschaft* than it is the inevitable and destructive consequence of capitalism.

Persistent Inequality

Modernity has gradually worn away some of the rigid categorical distinctions that divided preindustrial societies. Class-society theory maintains, however, that elites persist, albeit in a different form—as capitalist millionaires rather than as nobles who inherited their status. In the United States, we may have no hereditary monarchy, but the richest 5 percent of the population nevertheless controls half of all property.

What of the state, which mass-society theory suggests has an expanding role in combating social problems? Marx was skeptical that the state could accomplish more than minor reforms because, as he saw it, the state mostly defends the wealth and privileges of capitalists. Other class-society theorists add that, while working people and minorities enjoy greater political rights and a higher standard of living today, these changes are the fruits of political struggle, not expressions of government's benevolence. And, they add, despite our pretensions of democracy, power still rests primarily in the hands of those with wealth.

Critical evaluation. Table 24–2 spells out key differences between the interpretations of modernity offered by mass-society theory and class-society theory. While the former focuses on the increasing scale of life and the growth of government, the latter stresses the expansion of capitalism and the persistence of inequality.

Class-society theory also dismisses Durkheim's argument that people in modern societies suffer from anomie, claiming, instead, that they contend with alienation and powerlessness. Not surprisingly, then, the class-society interpretation of modernity enjoys widespread support among social and economic liberals and radicals who favor greater equality and call for extensive regulation (or abolition) of the capitalist marketplace.

A core criticism of class-society theory holds that this analysis overlooks the many ways in which modern societies have grown more egalitarian. After all, although discrimination based on race, ethnicity, and gender still exist, they are now illegal and widely regarded as social problems. Further, most people in the United States favor unequal rewards, at least insofar as they reflect differences in personal talent and effort.

Moreover, few observers think a centralized econ-omy would cure the ills of modernity in light of social-ism's failure to generate a high overall standard of living. Many other social problems found in the United States—from unemployment, homelessness, and industrial pollution, to unresponsive govern-ment—have also been commonplace in socialist nations such as the former Soviet Union.

Modernity and the Individual

Both mass- and class-society theories focus on broad patterns of change since the Industrial Revolution. From each macro-level approach we can also draw micro-level insights into how modernity shapes indi-vidual lives.

Mass Society: Problems of Identity

Modernity liberated individuals from small, tightly knit communities of the past. Most people in modern societies possess unprecedented privacy and freedom to express their individuality. Mass-society theory sug-gests, however, that extensive social diversity, atom-ization, and rapid social change make it difficult for many people to establish any coherent identity at all (Wheelis, 1958; Riesman, 1970; Berger, Berger, & Kellner, 1974).

Chapter 5 ("Socialization") explained that people forge distinctive personalities based on their social experience. The small, homogeneous, and slowly changing societies of the past provided a firm (if narrow) foundation for building meaningful identity. Even today, the Amish communities that flourish in the United States and Canada confer on members a strong sense of roots. There, young men and women learn the meaning of being Amish—that is, they know how they should think and behave—and most come to embrace this life as "natural" and right. Not everyone born into an Amish community can tolerate these demands for conformity, but most members establish a coherent and satisfying personal identity (Hostetler, 1980).

Mass societies, with their characteristic diversity and rapid change, provide only shifting sands on which to build a personal identity. Left to make their own life decisions, many of us—especially those with greater affluence—confront a bewildering array of options. Autonomy has little value without standards for making choices, and in a tolerant mass society, people may find one path no more compelling than the next. Not surprisingly, many people shuttle from one iden-tity to another, changing their lifestyle in search of an elusive "true self." They may fall in and out of relation-ships, experiment with various religions, or join one or another social movement in search of purpose and belonging. This difficulty in developing an identity is not psychological, although it is often treated as an individual problem. More accurately, such people are suffering from the widespread "relativism" of modern societies; without a moral compass, they have lost the security and certainty once provided by tradition.

David Riesman (1970; orig. 1950) has explained modernization as changes in **social character**, that is, *personality patterns common to members of a particu-lar society*. Preindustrial societies promote what Riesman terms **tradition-directedness**, *rigid confor-mity to time-honored ways of living*. Members of tradi-tional societies model their lives on what has gone before so that what is "good" is equivalent to "what has always been."

Tradition-directedness, then, carries to the level of individual experience Toennies's *Gemeinschaft* and Durkheim's mechanical solidarity. Culturally conserv-ative, tradition-directed people think and act alike. Unlike the conformity found in modern societies, this uniformity is not mimicry. Instead, it thrives because everyone draws on the same cultural foundation, defined as the one proper way to live. Amish women and men exemplify tradition-directedness; in the Amish culture, tradition ties everyone to ancestors and descendants in an unbroken chain of righteous living (Hostetler, 1980).

Many members of diverse and rapidly changing societies define a tradition-directed personality as deviant because it seems so rigid. Modern people, by and large, prize personal flexibility, the capacity to adapt, and sensitivity to others. Riesman describes this type of social character as **other-directedness**, *a recep-tiveness to the latest trends and fashions, often expressed in the practice of imitating others*. Because their social-ization occurs within societies that are continuously in flux, other-directed people develop fluid identities marked by superficiality, inconsistency, and change. They try on different "selves," almost like so many

NOTE: David Reisman used the term "social character" to mean "mode of conformity." Tradition-direction is conformity based on categorical memberships; inner-direction (not discussed in this chapter) is conformity to inwardly held values in the absence of strong tradition; other-direction is conformity to one's contemporaries.

NOTE: The saying "You can't argue with progress" suggests the inevitable and linear nature of change as our culture sees it.

NOTE: The "lonely crowd" thesis includes the argument that family had lost its socialization function to schools, various specialists, and mass media, prompting more "other direction" in children.

Q: "I never met a man I didn't like." Will Rogers, speaking as the typical other-directed American. A more recent study of other-direction is Woody Allen's *Zelig*, featuring a character whose personality is determined by his surroundings.

pieces of new clothing, seek out "role models," and engage in varied "performances" as they move from setting to setting (Goffman, 1959). In a traditional society, such "shiftiness" marks a person as untrustworthy, but in a changing, modern society, the chameleonlike ability to fit in virtually anywhere stands as a valued personal trait (Wheelis, 1958).

In societies that value the up-to-date rather than the traditional, people anxiously solicit the approval of others, looking to members of their own generation rather than to elders as significant role models. "Peer pressure" can sometimes be irresistible to people with no enduring standards to guide them. Our society urges individuals to be true to themselves. But when social surroundings change so rapidly, how can people determine to which self they should be true? This problem lies at the root of the identity crisis so widespread in industrial societies today. "Who am I?" is a nagging question that many of us struggle to answer. In sociological terms, this personal problem reflects the inherent instability of modern mass society.

Class Society: Problems of Powerlessness

Class-society theory paints a different picture of modernity's effects on individuals. This approach maintains that persistent social inequality undermines modern society's promise of individual freedom. For some, modernity delivers great privilege, but, for many, everyday life means coping with a gnawing sense of powerlessness.

For people of color, the problem of relative disadvantage looms even larger. Similarly, although women enjoy increasing participation in modern societies, they continue to run up against traditional barriers of sexism. In short, this approach rejects mass-society theory's claim that people suffer from too much freedom. Instead, class-society theory holds, our society still denies a majority of people full participation in social life.

On a global scale, as Chapter 11 ("Global Stratification") explained, the expanding scope of world capitalism has placed more of the earth's population under the influence of multinational corporations. As a result, about two-thirds of the world's income is concentrated in the richest societies, where only 15 percent of its people live. Is it any wonder, class-society theorists ask, that people in poor nations also seek greater power to shape their own lives?

Such problems led Herbert Marcuse (1964) to challenge Max Weber's contention that modern society is rational. Marcuse condemned modern society as irrational because, he maintained, it fails to meet the needs of so many people. While modern capitalist societies produce unparalleled wealth, poverty remains the daily plight of more than a billion people. Moreover, Marcuse argues, technological advances rarely empower people; instead, technology tends to reduce their control over their own lives. High technology generally means that specialists—not the majority of people—control events and dominate discussion, whether the issue is energy production for communities or health care for individuals. Specialists regard ordinary people as ill-equipped for decision making, urging the public to defer to elites. And elites, from this point of view, too often have little concern for the common interest. Countering the common view that technology *solves* the world's problems, then, Marcuse concludes that it may be more accurate to say science *causes* them. In sum, class-society theory asserts that people suffer because modern societies have concentrated both wealth and power in the hands of a privileged few.

Modernity and Progress

In modern societies, most people expect—and applaud—social change. We link modernity to the idea of *progress* (from Latin, meaning "a moving forward"), a state of continual improvement. By contrast, we denigrate stability as stagnation.

This chapter began by describing the Kaiapo of Brazil, for whom affluence has broadened opportunities but weakened traditional heritage. In examining the Kaiapo, we notice that social change, with all its beneficial and detrimental consequences, is too complex to be simply equated with progress.

More precisely, whether or not we see a given change as progress depends on our underlying values. A rising standard of living among the Kaiapo—or, historically, among the U.S. population—has helped make lives longer and more comfortable. But affluence has also fueled materialism at the expense of spiritual life, creating ambivalence toward change in the minds of many people. In a recent survey, most adults in the United States were divided on the consequences of scientific change; aware of its benefits, many nonetheless think that science "makes our way of life change too fast" (NORC, 1993:396).

Many people also celebrate modern society's recognition of basic human rights. The assertion that individuals have unalienable rights is a distinctly modern idea that can be found in the U.S. Declaration of Independence and the United Nations'

Q: "We know that we are in motion but do not know where we are going, and hence cannot predict the values of our children." Alan Wheelis (1958:23)

NOTE: Honor is a matter of specific status; dignity is generically human. One loses honor by violating normative roles; one loses dignity by giving up (or giving away) autonomy. Consider the differences between "dying with honor" and "dying with dignity."

GLOBAL: "Honor" in medieval Europe, "wa" in Japan, and "dharma" in India all express the power of the community to direct the thoughts and behavior of individuals. With modernization, all have tended to erode in favor of "dignity," "choice," and "individual rights."

NOTE: Another indication of the loss of traditional honor in modern societies is the decline of public civility.

SOCIOLOGY OF EVERYDAY LIFE

What's Happened to Honor?

Honor occupies about the same place in contemporary usage as chastity. An individual asserting it hardly invites admiration, and one who claims to have lost it is an object of amusement rather than sympathy. (1974:83)

Honor is a human virtue that seems distinctly out of place in modern society. This curious concept refers to acting according to traditional cultural norms. Since norms used to be quite different for various categories of people, men claimed honor by acting masculine as women did by being feminine. Honor, in short, is acting like the kind of person you are in a world of rigid social distinctions—between females and males, nobles and serfs, one's own family and outsiders.

Through observing the rules that apply to them, however, people of any social station can lay claim to honor. During the Middle Ages, European nobles were acting honorably when they performed their feudal obligations toward their social inferiors and displayed proper

respect for their peers. Similarly, commoners acted honorably to the extent that they fulfilled their duties to their superiors and everyone else. Honorable men assumed the cultural ideal of a fatherly, protective role toward women, while never "taking advantage" of them. For their part, women honorably observed proper morals and manners in the presence of men.

With modernization, cultural norms have become weaker and more variable, and categorical distinctions among people have been challenged by drives for social equality. Modern culture, then, holds that all people should treat others as equals. Therefore, although the concept of honor survives among some ethnic communities and traditional occupations like the military, it has less appeal to most members of modern societies.

Modernization enhances a concern for people as *individuals* that is expressed in the concept of *dignity*. Whereas various categories of people have distinctive codes of honor, dignity is a universal human trait,

resting on the inherent value of everyone. We recognize the dignity of others when we acknowledge our common humanity by overlooking social differences.

In the spirit of modern dignity, women may object to men's treating them as women rather than as individuals. The male practices of holding open a door for a woman and paying for a shared meal may be honorable by traditional standards, but now people may view such behavior as an affront to the dignity of women by underscoring gender differences.

As a result, honor is fading from industrial societies. The cultural diversity and rapid social change sweeping across the modern world render as suspect all traditional scripts for living. In contrast to codes of honor that guided people in the past, human beings now value individual self-worth and self-determination—the essence of dignity.

SOURCE: Based on Berger, Berger, & Kellner (1974).

Declaration of Human Rights. But, as Chapter 3 ("Culture") explained, we now have something of a "culture of rights" that emphasizes what others owe us more than what we owe to others. The box sharpens the distinction between rights and obligations by contrasting the modern concept of dignity and the traditional notion of honor.

In principle, almost everyone in our society supports the idea that individuals should have considerable autonomy in shaping their own lives. Thus, many people will applaud the demise of traditional concep-

tions of honor, viewing this trend as a sign of progress. Yet, as people exercise their freedom of choice, they inevitably challenge social patterns cherished by those who maintain a more traditional way of life. For example, people may choose not to marry, to live with someone without marrying, perhaps even to form a partnership with someone of their own sex. To those who support individual choice, such changes symbolize progress; to those who value traditional family patterns, however, these developments signal societal decay (Wallis, 1985).

NOTE: Postmodernism recognizes that, with the onset of the Information Revolution, *ideas* are gaining in importance as *things* decline in significance (New Age thinking as well as fundamentalist religious revival are examples). Such a change prompts us to look critically at the emphasis on material possessions that accompanied modern, industrial culture.

NOTE: In a recent Time/CNN poll, more people thought the world would be in better shape (41%) at the end of the next century than feared it would be worse (32%). "About the same" was the reply of 15%.

RESOURCE: Georg Simmel's classic about modernity, "The Metropolis and Mental Life," is included in the Macionis and Benokraitis reader, *Seeing Ourselves.*

As noted in earlier chapters, even new technology remains controversial. Rapid transportation and efficient communication may link us with the larger world, but by doing so they also erode traditional attachments to family and hometowns. Industrial technology has also unleashed an unprecedented threat to the natural environment. In short, social change gives rise to uncertainty, complexity, and controversy, making sweeping assertions about the effect of change risky at best.

POSTMODERNITY

If the concept of modernity encapsulates the social reality that owes its existence to the Industrial Revolution, does the Information Revolution and the development of a postindustrial society signal the beginning of yet another era? A number of scholars, answering affirmatively, now trumpet the arrival of *postmodernity.*

In its simplest formulation, **postmodernity** refers to *social patterns characteristic of postindustrial societies.* But precisely what postmodernism represents, for the present at least, is a matter of debate. This term—long used in literary, philosophical, and even architectural circles—has moved into sociology on a wave of social criticism that has been building since the explosion of left-leaning politics in the 1960s. Although there are many variants of postmodern thinking, the following five themes have emerged (Bernstein, 1992; Borgmann, 1992; Crook, 1992; Hall & Neitz, 1993):

1. **In important respects, modernity has failed.** The promise of modernity was a life free from want. As many postmodernist critics see it, however, the twentieth century was unsuccessful in eradicating social problems like poverty or even ensuring financial security for most people.

2. **The bright promise of "progress" is fading.** Modern people typically look to the future expecting that their lives will improve in significant ways. Members (even leaders) of a postmodern society, however, have less confidence about what the future holds. Furthermore, the buoyant optimism that carried society into the modern era more than a century ago has given way to stark pessimism on the part of most U.S. adults that life is getting worse (NORC, 1993:235).

3. **Science no longer holds the answers.** The defining trait of the modern era was a scientific outlook and a confident belief that technology would serve human purposes. But the postmodern critics contend that science has created more problems (such as degrading the environment) than it has solved.

More generally, postmodernist thinkers discredit the foundation of science—the assertion that there exists objective reality and truth. All reality amounts to so much social construction, they claim; moreover, "deconstructing" science shows that this system of ideas has been widely used for political purposes, especially by powerful segments of society.

4. **Cultural debates are intensifying.** As we have already explained, modernity ushered in an era of enhanced individuality and expanding tolerance. Critics claim, however, that the emerging postmodern society reveals the shortcomings of this process. Feminism is unmasking the extent to which patriarchy continues to shape society today just as multiculturalism seeks to empower minorities long pushed to the margins of social life.

5. **Social institutions are changing.** Industrialization brought sweeping transformation to social institutions; the rise of a postindustrial society is repeating this process. For example, just as the Industrial Revolution placed *material things* at the center of productive life, now the Information Revolution has elevated the importance of *ideas.* Similarly, the postmodern family no longer conforms to any singular formula; on the contrary, individuals are devising varied ways of relating to one another.

Critical evaluation. The contention by many analysts that the United States (and other rich societies) are entering a postmodern era amounts to an indictment of modernity for failing to meet human needs. But the debates sparked by these postmodernist critics also open them up to criticism. On the one hand, substantial evidence points to the conclusion that modernity has raised living standards during the course of this century; overall, in fact, members of our society live longer and enjoy greater affluence than ever before. On the other hand, even if we were to accept postmodernist criticism that science and traditional notions about progress are bankrupt, what are the alternatives?

Then, too, many voices offer very different understandings of recent social trends. The box provides one case in point.

SOCIAL SURVEY: "How important is each of the following in helping you to make decisions about your life?" (GSS 1988, N = 1,481; *Codebook*, 1993:412–13) (Percent saying "very important")

    "Your own personal judgment"   71.0%
    "Family and friends"   48.2%
    "The Bible"   34.1%

"The teachings of your church or synagogue"   28.6%

NOTE: We often describe changes in shorthand terms—for instance, "the go-go and greedy 1980s"—although this conceals complexities. The 1980s was a decade of fascination with wealth but it was also a period of increasing charity. Total giving in constant 1990 dollars rose in the United States from $80 billion in 1980 to $120 billion in 1990.

CRITICAL THINKING

The United States: A Nation in Decline?

Asked what was his greatest concern about the future of his country, the U.S. novelist Walker Percy responded:

> Probably the fear of seeing America, with all its great strength and beauty and freedom . . . gradually subside into decay and be defeated . . . from within by weariness, boredom, cynicism, greed and in the end helplessness before its great problems. . . .

Are we, in fact, a nation in decline? William Bennett, secretary of education in the Reagan administration from 1985 to 1988, points out that, by some measures, the United States is thriving. Between 1960 and 1990, for example, this nation's economic output tripled and median family income (controlled for inflation) was up by more than one-third. The official poverty rate dropped by half in that time span.

Nonetheless, Bennett maintains, a number of other indicators of well-being paint a very different—and disturbing—picture of U.S. life as we near the end of this century. Between 1960 and 1990, violent crime shot up 560 percent; the number of children born to single mothers rose more than 400 percent; the number of children supported by welfare increased just as fast; the divorce rate soared 300 percent; and teen suicide was up more than 200 percent. Since 1960, as television viewing has increased by 35 percent, the average student's college board scores have fallen by 75 points.

As Bennett sees it, our society cannot spend its way out of our current situation. Government expenditures (in constant 1990 dollars) rose fivefold between 1960 and 1990, while our population increased by just 41 percent. Clearly, then, a wide range of serious social problems continues to plague the United States despite determined efforts by government to address them. This fact leads Bennett to conclude that our nation's decline is primarily moral—a matter of weakening individual character:

> Our society now places less value than before on what we owe to others as a matter of moral obligation; less value on sacrifice as a moral good; less value on social conformity and respectability; and less value on correctness and restraint in matters of physical pleasure and sexuality.

Our current dilemma—that even as we make government bigger and more powerful, many social problems are getting worse—stems from the fact that government can do little to build individual character. Bennett continues:

> Our social institutions—families, churches, schools, neighborhoods, and civic associations—have traditionally taken on the responsibility of providing our children with love, order, and discipline—of teaching self-control, compassion, tolerance, civility, honesty, and respect for authority. . . . The social regression of the past thirty years is due in large part to the enfeebled state of our social institutions and their failure to carry out these critical and time-honored tasks.

From Bennett's point of view, the primary values of any society are set not by government but by people living in communities and, especially, by families raising their children. In effect, he concludes, we must not assume that affluence is the best—or even the only—measure of a society's well-being. Moreover, we cannot afford to ignore—nor can we hand over to the government—our basic responsibility to sustain civilization.

SOURCE: Based on Bennett (1993).

Postmodern culture lambasts the state of the world as we near the beginning of a new century. While the modern world was confident that orderly living would result in progress and prosperity, critics of the emerging postmodern world see little sense of meaning and security in comtemporary social arrangements. Postmodern art, such as William Haney's In Over Our Heads *captures this sense of confusion, anxiety, and uncertainty.*

LOOKING AHEAD: MODERNIZATION AND OUR GLOBAL FUTURE

This book opened by asking readers to imagine a village of one thousand people that represented all of humanity. About 175 residents of this "global village" live in the most economically developed countries, while about half of the people endure daily hunger. Most seriously, 200 people are so poor that they are at risk for their lives.

The tragic plight of the world's poor shows that some desperately needed change has not occurred at all. Chapter 11 ("Global Stratification") detailed two competing views of why 1 billion people the world over are poor. *Modernization theory* claims that in the past the entire world was poor and that technological change, especially the Industrial Revolution, enhanced human productivity and raised living standards. From this point of view, the solution to global poverty is to promote technological development in poor nations.

For reasons suggested earlier, however, global modernization may be difficult. Recall that David Riesman portrayed preindustrial people as *tradition-directed* and likely to resist change. So modernization theorists advocate that the world's rich societies offer assistance to poor countries to encourage productive innovation. Industrial nations can speed development by exporting technology to poor regions, welcoming students from abroad, and providing foreign aid to stimulate economic growth.

The review of modernization theory in Chapter 11 points to some limited success for these policies in Latin America and, especially, in the small Asian countries of Taiwan, South Korea, Singapore, and Hong Kong. But stimulating development in the poorest countries of the world poses the greatest challenges. Moreover, even where dramatic change has occurred, modernization entails a trade-off. Traditional people, such as Brazil's Kaiapo, may gain wealth through economic development, but only at the cost of losing their traditional identity and values as they are drawn into the "global village." In this way, they sacrifice their unique cultural heritage for some combination of Western materialism, pop music, trendy clothes, and fast food. Indeed, the "McDonaldization" of the United States, detailed in Chapter 7 ("Groups and Organizations"), is also proceeding on a world scale. This dilemma of development explains why some societies—including Algeria, Ethiopia, and Iran—have experienced limited modernization only to confront a powerful backlash from segments of the population (often religious) who seek to restore traditional culture.

A daunting problem, then, faces advocates of modernization theory: A higher material standard of living typically comes at the price of traditional culture. One Brazilian anthropologist expressed hope about the future of the Kaiapo: "At least they quickly understood

RESOURCE: An interesting discussion, spinning off mass-society theory, can be based on William Bennett's assertion that U.S. culture is in decline. See his article in the 3rd edition of the Macionis and Benokraitis reader, *Seeing Ourselves*.

Q: "Somewhere ages and ages hence: Two roads diverged in a wood, and I—I took the one less traveled by, And that has made all the difference." Robert Frost

Q: "Man will never fly. Not in a thousand years." Wilbur Wright

Q: "A man cannot get rich if he takes care of his family." Navajo saying

NOTE: The five U.S. presidents who recently assembled to dedicate the Ronald Reagan library had presided over startling change since 1968: eight armed conflicts, four recessions, $15 trillion in government spending (supported by only $12 trillion in taxes).

the consequences of watching television. . . . Now [they] can make a choice" (Simons, 1989:37).

But not everyone thinks that modernization is really an option. According to a second approach to global stratification, *dependency theory*, today's poor societies have little ability to modernize, even if they wanted to. From this point of view, the major barrier to economic development is not traditionalism but the global domination of rich, capitalist societies. Initially, as Chapter 11 explains, this system took the form of colonialism whereby European societies seized much of Latin America, Africa, and Asia. Trading relationships soon enriched England, Spain, and other colonial powers, and their colonies simultaneously became dependent and poor. Almost all societies subjected to this form of domination are now politically independent, but colonial-style ties continue in the form of multinational corporations operating throughout the world.

In effect, dependency theory asserts, rich societies achieved their modernization at the expense of poor nations, which provided valuable natural resources and human labor. Even today, the world's poorest countries remain locked in a disadvantageous economic relationship with rich nations, dependent on wealthy countries to buy their raw materials and in return provide them with whatever manufactured products they can afford. Continuing ties with rich societies, dependency theorist conclude, will only perpetuate current patterns of global inequality.

Dependency theory implies that social change occurs outside the control of individual societies. On the contrary, the fate and fortune of individual nations are tied to their position in the global economy. Thus, change to improve the plight of the world's poor demands corresponding changes in the lives of the world's rich.

Whichever approach one finds more convincing, we can no longer isolate the study of the United States from the rest of the world. At the beginning of the twentieth century, a majority of people in even the richest societies lived in relatively small settlements with limited awareness of the larger world. Now, at the threshold of the twenty-first century, people everywhere participate in a far larger human drama. The world seems smaller, and the lives of all people are increasingly linked. We now discuss the relationships among societies in the same way that people a century ago talked about the expanding ties among towns and cities.

The century now coming to a close has witnessed unprecedented human achievement. Yet solutions to many problems of human existence—including finding meaning in life, resolving conflicts among societies, and eradicating poverty—have eluded us. To this list of pressing matters new concerns have been added, such as controlling population growth and establishing a sustainable natural environment. As we approach the twenty-first century, we must be prepared to tackle such problems with imagination, compassion, and determination. The challenge is great, but our unprecedented understanding of human society gives us reason to look to the task ahead with optimism.

SUMMARY

1. Every society changes continuously, although with varying speed. Whether social change is intentional or unplanned, it often generates controversy.

2. Causes of social change include cultural processes (invention, discovery, and diffusion), social conflict, the ideas that dominate a society's understanding of the world, ways of confronting the natural environment, and demographic factors (including population growth and immigration).

3. Modernity refers to the social consequences of industrialization. According to Peter Berger, distinctive traits of modernity include the erosion of traditional communities, expanding personal choice, increasingly diverse beliefs, and a keen awareness of time, especially the future.

4. Ferdinand Toennies described modernization as the transition from *Gemeinschaft* to *Gesellschaft*. This process signifies the progressive loss of community amid growing individualism.

5. Emile Durkheim saw modernization as a function of a society's expanding division of labor. Mechanical solidarity, based on shared activities and beliefs, gradually gives way to organic solidarity, in which specialization makes people interdependent.

6. Max Weber explained modernization as the replacement of tradition by a rational world view. He feared the dehumanizing effects of rational organization.

7. In Karl Marx's view, modernity emerged in the triumph of capitalism over feudalism. Viewing capitalist societies as fraught with social conflict, Marx advocated revolutionary change to achieve a more egalitarian, socialist society.

8. According to mass-society theory, modernity increases the scale of life, enlarging the role of government and other formal organizations in carrying out tasks previously performed by family members and neighbors. Mass-society theory holds that cultural diversity and rapid social change prevent people in modern societies from developing stable identities and finding certainty and meaning in their lives.

9. Class-society theory states that capitalism is central to Western modernization. This approach charges that, by concentrating wealth, capitalism generates persistent social inequality and widespread feelings of powerlessness.

10. Although we sometimes equate modernity with social progress, social change is a complex process whose outcomes are rarely entirely good.

11. Postmodernity refers to cultural traits of postindustrial societies. Postmodern criticism of society centers on the failure of modernity, and specifically science, to fulfill its promise of progress and prosperity.

12. In a global context, modernization theory claims that global poverty is caused primarily by traditionalism. Therefore, some modernization theorists advocate intentional intervention by rich societies to stimulate the development of poor nations.

13. Dependency theory argues that a society's potential for development depends on its present position in the world economic system. Poor societies are unlikely to duplicate the modernization of rich societies, dependency theorists claim, because the power of multinational corporations ensures that they remain economically dependent on rich societies.

KEY CONCEPTS

class society a capitalist society with pronounced social stratification

mass society a society in which industry and bureaucracy have eroded traditional social ties

modernity social patterns linked to industrialization

modernization the process of social change initiated by industrialization

other-directedness a receptiveness to the latest trends and fashions, often expressed in the practice of imitating others

postmodernity social patterns characteristic of postindustrial societies

social change the transformation of culture and social institutions over time

social character personality patterns common to members of a particular society

tradition-directedness rigid conformity to time-honored ways of living

CRITICAL-THINKING QUESTIONS

1. Identify points of agreement among Toennies, Durkheim, Weber, and Marx regarding the character of modernity. What are several important differences?

2. What traits render the United States a "mass society"? What experiences are common among individuals living in such a society?

3. What is the difference between *anomie* (a trait of mass society) and *alienation* (a characteristic of class society)? Among which categories of the U.S. population would you expect each to be pronounced?

4. What developments lead some analysts to claim that the United States has become a postmodern society?

SUGGESTED READINGS

Classic Sources

Emile Durkheim. *The Division of Labor in Society*. New York: The Free Press, 1964; orig. 1895.

> This is the classic account of social change by one of the founders of sociology.

Derek Sayer. *Capitalism and Modernity: An Excursus on Marx and Weber*. New York: Routledge, 1991.

> This recent book examines the limits of modernity and assesses the prospects for postmodernity through a review of the ideas of two seminal sociologists.

Contemporary Sources

Daniel Chirot. *Social Change in the Modern Era*. New York: Harcourt Brace Jovanovich, 1986.

> This general resource provides further discussion of many of the topics found in this chapter.

Amitai Etzioni. *A Responsive Society: Collected Essays on Guiding Deliberate Social Change*. San Francisco: Jossey-Bass, 1991.

> While many sociologists have been content to study social change, this author suggests ways in which the discipline can promote desirable trends.

Rupert Wilkinson, ed. *American Social Character: Modern Interpretations*. New York: HarperCollins, 1992.

> This collection of essays about our society's favored cultural patterns features a number of well-known analysts including David Riesman and Margaret Mead.

Peter Berger, Brigitte Berger, and Hansfried Kellner. *The Homeless Mind: Modernization and Consciousness*. New York: Vintage Books, 1974.

Peter L. Berger. *Facing Up to Modernity: Excursions in Society, Politics, and Religion*. New York: Basic Books, 1977.

> Highly readable even for undergraduates, these books are filled with interesting insights about the modern world.

Anthony Giddens. *Modernity and Self-Identity: Self and Society in the Late Modern Era*. Stanford, Calif.: Stanford University Press, 1991.

Kenneth J. Gergen. *The Saturated Self: Dilemmas of Identity in Contemporary Life*. New York: Basic Books, 1991.

These books examine the consequences of new technology on society and the formation of individual identity.

Vytautas Kavolis. *Moralizing Cultures*. Lanham, Md.: University Press of America, 1993.

> In what ways do societies attempt to engender moral behavior in their members? This global survey of moralizing social processes pays particular attention to modernization.

Albert H. Teich, ed. *Technology and the Future*. 5th ed. New York: St. Martin's Press, 1990.

> This collection of articles by many well-known thinkers analyzes technological changes during this century and suggests likely future developments.

Christopher Lasch. *The True and Only Heaven: Progress and Its Critics*. New York: W.W. Norton, 1991.

> A well-known social critic provides a wide-ranging discussion of the state of politics, religion, and progress in today's world.

David C. Korten. *Getting to the 21st Century: Voluntary Action and the Global Agenda*. West Hartford, Conn.: Kumarian Press, 1990.

> This critical analysis of the 1980s stresses the need for grass-roots activism to reshape the world of the next century.

Global Sources

Mike Featherstone, ed. *Global Culture: Globalization, Nationalism and Modernity*. Newbury Park, Calif.: Sage, 1990.

> This collection of essays sheds light on how change in the United States is linked to transformation in other societies of the world.

Anthony D. King, ed. *Culture, Globalization, and the World-System: Contemporary Conditions for the Representation of Identity*. Binghamton, N.Y.: Department of Art and Art History, State University of New York at Binghamton, 1991.

> Does the globalization of culture mean that human identities are converging or becoming more diverse? This collection of essays explores the intersection of contemporary cultural forces.

Glossary

absolute poverty a deprivation of resources that is life threatening

achieved status a social position that someone assumes voluntarily and that reflects personal ability and effort

acid rain precipitation that is made acidic by air pollution and destroys plant and animal life

activity theory the proposition that a high level of activity enhances personal satisfaction in old age

Afrocentrism the dominance of African cultural patterns in people's lives

ageism prejudice and discrimination against the elderly

age-sex pyramid a graphic representation of the age and sex of a population

age stratification the unequal distribution of wealth, power, and privileges among people at different stages in the life course

agriculture the technology of large-scale farming using plows harnessed to animals or more powerful sources of energy

alienation the experience of isolation resulting from powerlessness

animism the belief that elements of the natural world are conscious forms of life that affect humanity

anomie Durkheim's designation of a condition of society in which individuals receive little moral guidance

anticipatory socialization the process of social learning directed toward gaining a desired position

ascribed status a social position that someone receives at birth or involuntarily assumes later in life

assimilation the process by which minorities gradually adopt patterns of the dominant culture

authoritarianism a political system that denies popular participation in government

authority power that people perceive as legitimate rather than coercive

beliefs specific statements that people who share culture hold to be true

bilateral descent a system tracing kinship through both females and males

blue-collar occupations lower-prestige work involving mostly manual labor

bureaucracy an organizational model rationally designed to perform complex tasks efficiently

bureaucratic inertia the tendency of bureaucratic organizations to perpetuate themselves

bureaucratic ritualism a preoccupation with organizational rules and regulations to the point of thwarting an organization's goals

capitalism an economic system in which natural resources and the means of producing goods and services are privately owned

capitalists people who own factories and other productive enterprises

caste system a system of social stratification based on ascription

cause and effect a relationship between two variables in which change in one (the independent variable) causes change in another (the dependent variable)

charisma extraordinary personal qualities that can turn an audience into followers

charismatic authority power legitimized through extraordinary personal abilities that inspire devotion and obedience

church a type of religious organization well integrated into the larger society

civil religion a quasi-religious loyalty binding individuals in a basically secular society

class conflict antagonism between entire classes over the distribution of wealth and power in society

class consciousness the recognition by workers of their unity as a social class in opposition to capitalists and to capitalism itself

class society a capitalist society with pronounced social stratification

class system a system of social stratification based on individual achievement

cohabitation the sharing of a household by an unmarried couple

cohort a category of people with a common characteristic, usually their age

collective behavior activity involving a large number of people, often spontaneous, and typically in violation of established norms

collectivity a large number of people whose minimal interaction occurs in the absence of well-defined and conventional norms

colonialism the process by which some nations enrich themselves through political and economic control of other countries

communism a hypothetical economic and political system in which all members of a society are socially equal

concept a mental construct that represents some part of the world, inevitably in a simplified form

concrete operational stage Piaget's term for the level of human development at which individuals first perceive causal connections in their surroundings

conglomerates giant corporations composed of many smaller corporations

control the ability to neutralize the effect of one or more variables in order to assess the relationships among other variables

conversion a personal transformation resulting from adopting new religious beliefs

corporation an organization with a legal existence, including rights and liabilities, apart from those of its members

correlation a relationship between two (or more) variables

counterculture cultural patterns that strongly oppose those widely accepted within a society

credentialism evaluating a person on the basis of educational degrees

crime the violation of norms a society formally enacts into criminal law

crimes against the person (violent crimes) crimes against people that involve violence or the threat of violence

crimes against property (property crimes) crimes that involve theft of property belonging to others

criminal justice system a formal response to alleged violations of the law on the part of police, courts, and prison officials

criminal recidivism subsequent offenses by people previously convicted of crimes

crowd a temporary gathering of people who share a common focus of attention and whose members influence one another

crude birth rate the number of live births in a given year for every thousand people in a population

crude death rate the number of deaths in a given year for every thousand people in a population

cult a religious organization that is substantially outside the cultural traditions of a society

cultural ecology a theoretical paradigm that explores the relationship between human culture and the physical environment

cultural integration the close relationship among various elements of a cultural system

cultural lag the fact that cultural elements change at different rates, which may disrupt a cultural system

cultural relativism the practice of judging a culture by its own standards

cultural transmission the process by which one generation passes culture to the next

cultural universals traits that are part of every known culture

culture the beliefs, values, behavior, and material objects that define a people's way of life

culture shock personal disorientation that accompanies exposure to an unfamiliar way of life

Davis-Moore thesis the assertion that social stratification is a universal pattern because it has beneficial consequences for the operation of a society

deductive logical thought reasoning that transforms general ideas into specific hypotheses suitable for scientific testing

democracy a type of political system that views power as exercised by the people as a whole

democratic socialism an economic and political system that combines significant government control of the economy with free elections

demographic transition theory a thesis linking population patterns to a society's level of technological development

demography the study of human population

denomination a church, independent of the state, that accepts religious pluralism

dependency theory a model of economic and social development that explains global inequality in terms of the historical exploitation of poor societies by rich societies

dependent variable a variable that is changed by another (independent) variable

descent the system by which members of a society trace kinship over generations

deterrence the attempt to discourage criminality through punishment

deviance the recognized violation of cultural norms

direct-fee system a medical care system in which patients pay directly for the services of physicians and hospitals

discrimination an action that involves treating various categories of people unequally

disengagement theory the proposition that society enhances its orderly operation by disengaging people from positions of responsibility as they reach old age

division of labor specialized economic activity

dramaturgical analysis Erving Goffman's term for the investigation of social interaction in terms of theatrical performance

dyad a social group with two members

eating disorder an intense focus on dieting or other forms of weight control in order to become very thin

ecclesia a church that is formally allied with the state

ecology the study of the interaction of living organisms and the natural environment

economy the social institution that organizes the production, distribution, and consumption of goods and services

ecosystem the system composed of the interaction of all living organisms and their natural environment

education the social institution guiding a society's transmission of knowledge—including basic facts, job skills, and also cultural norms and values—to its members

ego Freud's designation of a person's conscious attempt to balance pleasure-seeking drives and the demands of society

empirical evidence information we are able to verify with our senses

endogamy marriage between people of the same social category

environmental deficit the situation in which negative, long-term consequences of decisions about the natural environment outweigh whatever short-term benefits may accrue

ethnicity a shared cultural heritage

ethnocentrism the practice of judging another culture by the standards of one's own culture

ethnomethodology Harold Garfinkel's term for the study of the way people make sense of their everyday lives

Eurocentrism the dominance of European (especially English) cultural patterns

euthanasia (mercy killing) assisting in the death of a person suffering from an incurable disease

exogamy marriage between people of different social categories

experiment a research method for investigating cause and effect under highly controlled conditions

expressive leadership group leadership that emphasizes collective well-being

extended family (consanguine family) a family unit including parents and children, but also other kin

fad an unconventional social pattern that people embrace briefly but enthusiastically

faith belief anchored in conviction rather than scientific evidence

false consciousness Marx's term for explanations of social problems in terms of the shortcomings of individuals rather than flaws of society

family a social institution, found in all societies, that unites individuals into cooperative groups that oversee the bearing and rearing of children

family unit a social group of two or more people, related by blood, marriage, or adoption, who usually live together

family violence emotional, physical, or sexual abuse of one family member by another

fashion a social pattern favored for a time by a large number of people

female infanticide the practice of aborting female fetuses and neglecting, or even actively killing, infant girls by parents who would prefer to raise boys

feminism the advocacy of social equality for the sexes, in opposition to patriarchy and sexism

feminization of poverty the trend by which women represent an increasing proportion of the poor

fertility the incidence of childbearing in a society's population

folkways norms that have less moral significance than mores

formal operational stage Piaget's term for the level of human development at which individuals use highly abstract thought to imagine alternatives to reality

formal organization a large secondary group organized to achieve its goals efficiently

functional illiteracy reading and writing skills insufficient for everyday living

fundamentalism a conservative religious doctrine that opposes intellectualism and worldly accommodation in favor of restoring a traditional, otherworldly spirituality

Gemeinschaft a type of social organization by which people are bound closely together by kinship and tradition

gender the significance a society attaches to biological categories of female and male

gender identity traits that females and males, guided by their culture, incorporate into their personalities

gender roles (sex roles) attitudes and activities that a culture links to each sex

gender stratification a society's unequal distribution of wealth, power, and privilege between the two sexes

generalized other George Herbert Mead's term for widespread cultural norms and values we use as references in evaluating ourselves

genocide the systematic annihilation of one category of people by another

gerontocracy a form of social organization in which the elderly have the most wealth, power, and privileges

gerontology the study of aging and the elderly

Gesellschaft a type of social organization by which people have weak social ties and considerable self-interest

global economy interconnected economic activity throughout the world that pays little regard to national borders

global perspective the study of the larger world and our society's place in it

gossip rumor about the personal affairs of others

government formal organizations that direct the political life of a society

greenhouse effect a rise in the earth's average temperature (global warming) due to an increasing concentration of carbon dioxide in the atmosphere

groupthink the tendency of group members to conform by adopting a narrow view of some issue

hate crime a criminal act carried out against a person or personal property by an offender motivated by racial or other bias

Hawthorne effect a change in a subject's behavior caused by the awareness of being studied

health a state of complete physical, mental, and social well-being

health care any activity intended to improve health

health maintenance organization (HMO) an organization that provides comprehensive medical care to subscribers for a fixed fee

hermaphrodite a human being with some combination of female and male internal and external genitalia

hidden curriculum subtle presentations of political or cultural ideas in the classroom

high culture cultural patterns that distinguish a society's elite

holistic medicine an approach to health care that emphasizes prevention of illness and takes account of a person's entire physical and social environment

homogamy marriage between people with the same social characteristics

horticulture technology based on using hand tools to cultivate plants

humanizing bureaucracy fostering an organizational atmosphere that recognizes and encourages the contributions of everyone

hunting and gathering simple technology for hunting animals and gathering vegetation

hypothesis an unverified statement of a relationship between variables

id Freud's designation of the human being's basic drives

ideal culture as opposed to real culture, the social patterns mandated by cultural values and norms

ideal type an abstract statement of the essential characteristics of any social phenomenon

ideology cultural beliefs that, directly or indirectly, justify social stratification

incest taboo a cultural norm forbidding sexual relations or marriage between certain kin

income occupational wages or salaries and earnings from investments

independent variable a variable that causes change in another (dependent) variable

inductive logical thought reasoning that builds specific observations into general theory

industrialism technology that powers sophisticated machinery with advanced sources of energy

infant mortality rate the number of deaths among infants under one year of age for each thousand live births in a given year

ingroup a social group commanding a member's esteem and loyalty

institutional discrimination discrimination that is a normative and routine part of the economy, the educational system, or some other social institution

instrumental leadership group leadership that emphasizes the completion of tasks

intergenerational social mobility upward or downward social mobility of children in relation to their parents

interview a series of questions administered personally by a researcher to respondents

intragenerational social mobility a change in social position occurring during a person's lifetime

juvenile delinquency the violation of legal standards by the young

kinship a social bond, based on blood, marriage, or adoption, that joins individuals into families

labeling theory the assertion that deviance and conformity result, not so much from what people do, as from how others respond

labor unions organizations of workers seeking to improve wages and working conditions through various strategies, including negotiations and strikes

language a system of symbols that allows members of a society to communicate with one another

latent functions consequences of any social pattern that are unrecognized and unintended

least-developed countries societies with little industrialization in which severe poverty is the rule

less-developed countries societies characterized by limited industrialization and moderate-to-low personal income

liberation theology a fusion of Christian principles with political activism, often Marxist in character

life expectancy the average life span of a society's population

looking-glass self Cooley's assertion that the self is based on how others respond to us

macro-level orientation a focus on broad social structures that characterize society as a whole

mainstreaming integrating special students into the overall educational program

manifest functions the recognized and intended consequences of any social pattern

marriage a legally sanctioned relationship, involving economic cooperation as well as normative sexual activity and childbearing, that people expect to be enduring

mass behavior collective behavior among people dispersed over a wide geographical area

mass hysteria a form of dispersed collective behavior by which people respond to a real or imagined event with irrational, frantic, and often self-destructive behavior

mass media impersonal communications directed toward a vast audience

mass society a society in which industry and bureaucracy have eroded traditional social ties

master status a status that has exceptional importance for social identity, often shaping a person's entire life

material culture tangible products of human society, such as clothing and cities

matriarchy a form of social organization in which females dominate males

matrilineal descent a system tracing kinship through females

matrilocality a residential pattern in which a married couple lives with or near the wife's family

mean the arithmetic average of a series of numbers

measurement the process of determining the value of a variable in a specific case

mechanical solidarity Durkheim's term for social bonds, based on shared moral sentiments, that unite members of preindustrial societies

median the value that occurs midway in a series of numbers arranged in order of magnitude or, simply, the middle case

medicalization of deviance the transformation of moral and legal issues into medical matters

medicine a social institution concerned with combating disease and improving health

megalopolis a vast urban region containing a number of cities and their surrounding suburbs

meritocracy a system of social stratification based on personal merit

metropolis a large city that socially and economically dominates an urban area

micro-level orientation a focus on patterns of social interaction in specific situations

migration the movement of people into and out of a specified territory

military-industrial complex the close association among the federal government, the military, and defense industries

minority a category of people, distinguished by physical or cultural traits, who are socially disadvantaged

miscegenation the biological process of interbreeding among racial categories

mob a highly emotional crowd that pursues some violent or destructive goal

mode the value that occurs most often in a series of numbers

modernity social patterns linked to industrialization

modernization the process of social change initiated by industrialization

modernization theory a model of economic and social development that explains global inequality in terms of differing levels of technological development among societies

monarchy a type of political system that transfers power from generation to generation within a single family

monogamy a form of marriage involving two partners

monopoly domination of a market by a single producer

monotheism belief in a single divine power

mores norms that have great moral significance

mortality the incidence of death in a society's population

most-developed countries relatively rich, industrialized societies

multiculturalism an educational program recognizing past and present cultural diversity in U.S. society and promoting the equality of all cultural traditions

multinational corporation a large corporation that operates in many different countries

natural environment the earth's surface and atmosphere including various living organisms and the air, water, soil, and other resources necessary to sustain life

neocolonialism a new form of global power relationships that involves not direct political control but, rather, economic exploitation by multinational corporations

neolocality a residential pattern in which a married couple lives apart from the parents of both spouses

network a web of social ties that links people who may have little common identity and interaction

nonmaterial culture intangible creations of human society, such as values and norms

nonverbal communication communication using body movements, gestures, and facial expressions rather than speech

norms rules and expectations by which a society guides the behavior of its members

nuclear family (conjugal family) a family unit composed of one or two parents and their children

nuclear proliferation the acquisition of nuclear-weapons technology by more and more nations

objectivity a state of personal neutrality in conducting research

oligarchy the rule of the many by the few

oligopoly domination of a market by a few producers

operationalizing a variable specifying exactly what one is to measure in assigning a value to a variable

organic solidarity Durkheim's term for social bonds, based on specialization, that unite members of industrial societies

organizational environment a range of factors external to an organization that affects its operation

other-directedness a receptiveness to the latest trends and fashions, often expressed in the practice of imitating others

outgroup a social group toward which one feels competition or opposition

panic a form of localized collective behavior by which people react to a threat or other stimulus with irrational, frantic, and often self-destructive behavior

participant observation a research method in which researchers systematically observe people while joining in their routine activities

pastoralism technology that supports the domestication of animals

patriarchy a form of social organization in which males dominate females

patrilineal descent a system tracing kinship through males

patrilocality a residential pattern in which a married couple lives with or near the husband's family

peace a state of international relations devoid of violence

peer group a social group whose members have interests, social position, and age in common

personality a person's fairly consistent patterns of thinking, feeling, and acting

personal space the surrounding area to which an individual makes some claim to privacy

plea bargaining a legal negotiation in which the prosecution reduces a defendant's charge in exchange for a guilty plea

pluralism a state in which racial and ethnic minorities are distinct but have social parity

pluralist model an analysis of politics that views power as dispersed among many competing interest groups

political action committee (PAC) an organization formed by a special-interest group, independent of political parties, to pursue specific aims by raising and spending money

political revolution the overthrow of one political system in order to establish another

politics the social institution that distributes power, sets a society's agenda, and makes decisions

polyandry a form of marriage joining one female with two or more males

polygamy a form of marriage uniting three or more people

polygyny a form of marriage joining one male with two or more females

polytheism belief in many gods

popular culture cultural patterns that are widespread among a society's population

population the people who are the focus of research

positivism understanding the world based on science

postindustrial economy a productive system based on service work and high technology

postindustrialism technology that supports an information-based economy

postmodernity social patterns characteristic of postindustrial societies

power the ability to achieve desired ends despite resistance from others

power-elite model an analysis of politics that views power as concentrated among the rich

prejudice an attitude involving a rigid and irrational generalization about an entire category of people

preoperational stage Piaget's term for the level of human development in which individuals first use language and other symbols

presentation of self the effort of an individual to create specific impressions in the minds of others

primary group a small social group in which relationships are both personal and enduring

primary labor market occupations that provide extensive benefits to workers

primary sector the part of the economy that generates raw materials directly from the natural environment

primary sex characteristics the genitals, used to reproduce the human species

profane that which is defined as an ordinary element of everyday life

profession a prestigious white-collar occupation that requires extensive formal education

proletariat people who provide labor necessary for the operation of factories and other productive enterprises

propaganda information presented with the intention of shaping public opinion

qualitative research inquiry based on subjective impressions

quantitative research inquiry based on the analysis of numerical data

questionnaire a series of written questions a researcher prepares for subjects to answer

race a category composed of men and women who share biologically transmitted traits that members of a society deem socially significant

racism the belief that one racial category is innately superior or inferior to another

rain forests regions of dense forestation, most of which circle the globe close to the equator

rationality deliberate, matter-of-fact calculation of the most efficient means to accomplish a particular goal

rationalization of society Max Weber's term for the historical change from tradition to rationality as the dominant mode of human thought

rational-legal authority (also bureaucratic authority) power legitimized by legally enacted rules and regulations

real culture as opposed to ideal culture, the actual social patterns that only approximate cultural expectations

recycling programs to reuse resources that we would otherwise discard as "waste"

reference group a social group that serves as a point of reference in making evaluations or decisions

rehabilitation a program for reforming the offender to preclude subsequent offenses

relative deprivation a perceived disadvantage arising from a specific comparison

relative poverty the deprivation of some people in relation to those who have more

reliability the quality of consistent measurement

religion a social institution involving beliefs and practices based upon a conception of the sacred

religiosity the importance of religion in a person's life

replication repetition of research by others in order to assess its accuracy

research method a strategy for systematically conducting research

resocialization deliberate control of an environment intended to radically alter an inmate's personality

retribution an act of moral vengeance by which society subjects an offender to suffering comparable to that caused by the offense

retrospective labeling the interpretation of someone's past consistent with present deviance

riot a social eruption that is highly emotional, violent, and undirected

ritual formal, ceremonial behavior

role behavior expected of someone who holds a particular status

role conflict incompatibility among the roles corresponding to two or more different statuses

role set a number of roles attached to a single status

role strain incompatibility among roles corresponding to a single status

routinization of charisma the transformation of charismatic authority into some combination of traditional and bureaucratic authority

rumor unsubstantiated information spread informally, often by word of mouth

sacred that which is defined as extraordinary, inspiring a sense of awe, reverence, and even fear

sample a part of a population researchers select to represent the whole

Sapir-Whorf hypothesis a hypothesis stating that people perceive the world through the cultural lens of language

scapegoat a person or category of people, typically with little power, whom people unfairly blame for their own troubles

schooling formal instruction under the direction of specially trained teachers

science a logical system that bases knowledge on direct, systematic observation

secondary analysis a research method in which a researcher utilizes data collected by others

secondary group a large and impersonal social group devoted to some specific interest or activity

secondary labor market jobs that provide minimal benefits to workers

secondary sector the part of the economy that transforms raw materials into manufactured goods

secondary sex characteristics bodily development, apart from the genitals, that distinguishes biologically mature females and males

sect a type of religious organization that stands apart from the larger society

secularization the historical decline in the importance of the supernatural and the sacred

segregation the physical and social separation of categories of people

self George Herbert Mead's term for a dimension of personality composed of an individual's self-awareness and self-conception

sensorimotor stage Piaget's term for the level of human development in which individuals experience the world only through sensory contact

sex the biological distinction between females and males

sexism the belief that one sex is innately superior to the other

sex ratio the number of males for every hundred females in a given population

sexual harassment comments, gestures, or physical contact of a sexual nature that are deliberate, repeated, and unwelcome

sexual orientation the manner in which people experience sexual arousal and achieve sexual pleasure

sick role patterns of behavior defined as appropriate for those who are ill

social change the transformation of culture and social institutions over time

social character personality patterns common to members of a particular society

social conflict struggle between segments of society over valued resources

social-conflict paradigm a framework for building theory based on the assumption that society is characterized by inequality and conflict that generate change

social construction of reality the process by which people creatively shape reality through social interaction

social control various means by which members of a society encourage conformity to norms

social dysfunction the undesirable consequences of any social pattern for the operation of society

social epidemiology the study of how health and disease are distributed throughout a society's population

social fact any pattern that is rooted in society rather than the experiences of individuals

social function the consequences of any social pattern for the operation of society

social group two or more people who identify and interact with one another

social institution a major sphere of social life organized to meet a basic human need

social interaction the process by which people act and react in relation to others

socialism an economic system in which natural resources and the means of producing goods and services are collectively owned

socialization the lifelong social experience by which individuals develop human potential and learn patterns of their culture

socialized medicine a health care system in which the government owns and operates most medical facilities and employs most physicians

social marginality the state of being excluded from social activity as an "outsider"

social mobility change in people's position in a system of social stratification

social movement organized activity that encourages or discourages social change

social stratification a system by which society ranks categories of people in a hierarchy

social structure a relatively stable pattern of social behavior

societal protection a means by which society renders an offender incapable of further offenses temporarily through incarceration or permanently by execution

society people who interact in a defined territory and share culture

sociobiology a theoretical paradigm that explores ways in which biological forces affect human culture

sociocultural evolution the Lenskis' term for the process of change that results from a society's gaining new cultural information, particularly technology

socioeconomic status (SES) a composite ranking based on various dimensions of social inequality

sociology the scientific study of human society

special-interest group a political alliance of people interested in some economic or social issue

spurious correlation an apparent, although false, relationship between two (or more) variables caused by some other variable

state capitalism an economic and political system in which companies are privately owned although they cooperate closely with the government

state terrorism the use of violence, generally without support of law, against individuals or groups by a government or its agents

status a recognized social position that an individual occupies

status consistency the degree of consistency of a person's social standing across various dimensions of social inequality

status set all the statuses a person holds at a given time

stereotype a set of prejudices concerning some category of people

stigma a powerfully negative social label that radically changes a person's self-concept and social identity

structural-functional paradigm a framework for building theory based on the assumption that society is a complex system whose parts work together to promote stability

structural social mobility a shift in the social position of large numbers of people due more to changes in society itself than to individual efforts

subculture cultural patterns that distinguish some segment of a society's population

suburbs urban areas beyond the political boundaries of a city

superego Freud's designation of the presence of culture within the individual in the form of internalized values and norms

survey a research method in which subjects respond to a series of questions in a questionnaire or an interview

sustainable ecosystem the human use of the natural environment to meet the needs of the present generation without threatening the prospects of future generations

symbol anything that carries a particular meaning recognized by people who share culture

symbolic-interaction paradigm a theoretical framework based on the assumption that society is the product of the everyday interactions of individuals

technology knowledge that a society applies to the task of living in a physical environment

terrorism violence or the threat of violence employed by an individual or group as a political strategy

tertiary sector the part of the economy involved in services rather than goods

theoretical paradigm a set of assumptions that guides thinking and research

theory a statement of how and why specific facts are related

Thomas theorem W. I. Thomas's assertion that situations we define as real become real in their consequences

total institution a setting in which people are isolated from the rest of society and manipulated by an administrative staff

totalitarianism a political system that extensively regulates people's lives

totem an object in the natural world collectively defined as sacred

tracking the assignment of students to different types of educational programs

tradition sentiments and beliefs passed from generation to generation

traditional authority power legitimized through respect for long-established cultural patterns

tradition-directedness rigid conformity to time-honored ways of living

transsexuals people who feel they are one sex though biologically they are the other

triad a social group with three members

underground economy economic activity generating income that one does not report to the government as required by law

urban ecology the study of the link between the physical and social dimensions of cities

urbanization the concentration of humanity into cities

urban renewal government programs intended to revitalize cities

validity the quality of measuring precisely what one intends to measure

values culturally defined standards by which people judge desirability, goodness, and beauty, and which serve as broad guidelines for social living

variable a concept whose value changes from case to case

victimless crimes violations of law in which there are no readily apparent victims

war armed conflict among the people of various societies, directed by their governments

wealth the total amount of money and valuable goods that a person or family controls

white-collar crime crimes committed by people of high social position in the course of their occupations

white-collar occupations higher-prestige work involving mostly mental activity

zero population growth the level of reproduction that maintains population at a steady state

References

ABBOTT, ANDREW. *The System of Professions: An Essay on the Division of Expert Labor*. Chicago: University of Chicago Press, 1988.

ABERLE, DAVID F. *The Peyote Religion Among the Navaho*. Chicago: Aldine, 1966.

ADAMS, P. F., and V. BENSON. "Current Estimates from the National Health Interview Survey, 1989." U.S. National Center for Health Statistics. *Vital Health Statistics*, Vol. 10, No. 176. Washington, D.C.: U.S. Government Printing Office, 1990.

ADLER, JERRY. "When Harry Called Sally . . . " *Newsweek* (October 1, 1990):74.

ADORNO, T. W., et al. *The Authoritarian Personality*. New York: Harper & Brothers, 1950.

AGUIRRE, B. E., E. L. QUARANTELLI, and JORGE L. MENDOZA. "The Collective Behavior of Fads: Characteristics, Effects, and Career of Streaking." *American Sociological Review*. Vol. 53, No. 4 (August 1988):569–84.

AGUIRRE, BENIGNO E., and E. L. QUARANTELLI. "Methodological, Ideological, and Conceptual-Theoretical Criticisms of Collective Behavior: A Critical Evaluation and Implications for Future Study." *Sociological Focus*. Vol. 16, No. 3 (August 1983):195–216.

AKERS, RONALD L., MARVIN D. KROHN, LONN LANZA-KADUCE, and MARCIA RADOSEVICH. "Social Learning and Deviant Behavior." *American Sociological Review*. Vol. 44, No. 4 (August 1979):636–55.

ALAM, SULTANA. "Women and Poverty in Bangladesh." *Women's Studies International Forum*. Vol. 8, No. 4 (1985):361–71.

ALBA, RICHARD D. *Italian Americans: Into the Twilight of Ethnicity*. Englewood Cliffs, N.J.: Prentice Hall, 1985.

———. *Ethnic Identity: The Transformation of White America*. Chicago: University of Chicago Press, 1990.

ALBON, JOAN. "Retention of Cultural Values and Differential Urban Adaptation: Samoans and American Indians in a West Coast City." *Social Forces*. Vol. 49, No. 3 (March 1971):385–93.

ALBRECHT, WILLIAM P., JR. *Economics*. 3d ed. Englewood Cliffs, N.J.: Prentice Hall, 1983.

ALLAN, EMILIE ANDERSEN, and DARRELL J. STEFFENSMEIER. "Youth, Underemployment, and Property Crime: Differential Effects of Job Availability and Job Quality on Juvenile and Young Adult Arrest Rates." *American Sociological Review*. Vol. 54, No. 1 (February 1989):107–23.

ALLEN, MICHAEL PATRICK, and PHILIP BROYLES. "Campaign Finance Reforms and the Presidential Campaign Contributions of Wealthy Capitalist Families." *Social Science Quarterly*. Vol. 72, No. 4 (December 1991):738–50.

ALLSOP, KENNETH. *The Bootleggers*. London: Hutchinson and Company, 1961.

ALTMAN, DREW, ET AL. "Health Care for the Homeless." *Society*. Vol. 26, No. 4 (May–June 1989):4–5.

AMERICAN COUNCIL ON EDUCATION. "Senior Women Administrators in Higher Education: A Decade of Change, 1975–1983." Washington, D.C.: 1984.

AMERICAN COUNCIL ON EDUCATION, as reported in "Number of Black Students Still Falling, Study Finds." *The Chronicle of Higher Education*. Vol. XXXIV, No. 11 (November 11, 1987):2.

AMERICAN SOCIOLOGICAL ASSOCIATION. "Code of Ethics." Washington, D.C.: 1984.

ANDERS, GEORGE. "Doctors Lobby Patients in a Campaign to Shape Clinton Health-Care Package." *Wall Street Journal* (July 26, 1993): B1, B4

ANDERSON, JOHN WARD, and MOLLY MOORE. "World's Poorest Women Suffer in Common." *Columbus Dispatch* (April 11, 1993):4G.

ANDO, FAITH H. "Women in Business." In Sara E. Rix, ed., *The American Woman: A Status Report 1990–91*. New York: Norton, 1990:222–30.

ANG, IEN. *Watching Dallas: Soap Opera and the Melodramatic Imagination*. London: Methuen, 1985.

ANGELO, BONNIE. "The Pain of Being Black" (an interview with Toni Morrison). *Time*. Vol. 133, No. 21 (May 22, 1989):120–22.

———. "Assigning the Blame for a Young Man's Suicide." *Time*. Vol. 138, No. 2 (November 18, 1991):12–14.

ANGIER, NATALIE. "Scientists, Finding Second Idiosyncracy in Homosexuals' Brains, Suggest Orientation Is Physiological." *New York Times* (August 1, 1992):A7.

APA. *Violence and Youth: Psychology's Response*. Washington, D.C.: American Psychological Association, 1993.

ARCHER, DANE, and ROSEMARY GARTNER. *Violence and Crime in Cross-National Perspective*. New Haven, Conn.: Yale University Press, 1987.

ARENDT, HANNAH. *The Origins of Totalitarianism*. Cleveland, Ohio: Meridian Books, 1958.

———. *Between Past and Future: Six Exercises in Political Thought*. Cleveland, Ohio: Meridian Books, 1963.

ARIÈS, PHILIPPE. *Centuries of Childhood: A Social History of Family Life*. New York: Vintage Books, 1965.

———. *Western Attitudes Toward Death: From the Middle Ages to the Present*. Baltimore: The Johns Hopkins University Press, 1974.

ARJOMAND, SAID AMIR. *The Turban for the Crown: The Islamic Revolution in Iran*. New York: Oxford University Press, 1988.

ASANTE, MOLEFI KETE. *The Afrocentric Idea*. Philadelphia: Temple University Press, 1987.

———. *Afrocentricity*. Trenton, N.J.: Africa World Press, 1988.

ASCH, SOLOMON. *Social Psychology*. Englewood Cliffs, N.J.: Prentice Hall, 1952.

ASTONE, NAN MARIE, and SARA S. McLANAHAN. "Family Structure, Parental Practices and High School Completion." *American Sociological Review*. Vol. 56, No. 3 (June 1991):309–20.

ATCHLEY, ROBERT C. "Retirement as a Social Institution." *Annual Review of Sociology*. Vol. 8. Palo Alto, Calif.: Annual Reviews, 1982:263–87.

———. *Aging: Continuity and Change*. Belmont, Calif.: Wadsworth, 1983; 2d ed., 1987.

AVIS, GEORGE. "Access to Higher Education in the Soviet Union." In J. J. Tomiak, ed., *Soviet Education in the 1980s*. London: Croom Helm, 1983:199–239.

AXTELL, ROGER E. *Gestures: The DOs and TABOOs of Body Language Around the World*. New York: Wiley, 1991.

AYENSU, EDWARD S. "A Worldwide Role for the Healing Powers of Plants." *Smithsonian*. Vol. 12, No. 8 (November 1981):87–97.

BABBIE, EARL. *The Practice of Social Research*. 6th ed. Belmont, Calif.: Wadsworth, 1992.

BACHRACH, PETER, and MORTON S. BARATZ. *Power and Poverty*. New York: Oxford University Press, 1970.

BACKMAN, CARL B., and MURRAY C. ADAMS. "Self-Perceived Physical Attractiveness, Self-Esteem, Race, and Gender." *Sociological Focus*. Vol. 24, No. 4 (October 1991):283–90.

BAHL, VINAY. "Caste and Class in India." Paper presented to the Southern Sociological Society, Atlanta, April, 1991.

BAILEY, WILLIAM C. "Murder, Capital Punishment, and Television: Execution Publicity and Homicide Rates." *American Sociological Review*. Vol. 55, No. 5 (October 1990):628–33.

BAILEY, WILLIAM C., and RUTH D. PETERSON. "Murder and Capital Punishment: A Monthly Time-Series Analysis of Execution Publicity." *American Sociological Review.* Vol. 54, No. 5 (October 1989):722–43.

BAKER, MARY ANNE, CATHERINE WHITE BERHEIDE, FAY ROSS GRECKEL, LINDA CARSTARPHEN GUGIN, MARCIA J. LIPETZ, and MARCIA TEXLER SEGAL. *Women Today: A Multidisciplinary Approach to Women's Studies.* Monterey, Calif.: Brooks/Cole, 1980.

BALES ROBERT F. "The Equilibrium Problem in Small Groups." In Talcott Parsons et al., eds., *Working Papers in the Theory of Action.* New York: Free Press, 1953:111–15.

BALES, ROBERT F., and PHILIP E. SLATER. "Role Differentiation in Small Decision-Making Groups." In Talcott Parsons and Robert F. Bales, eds., *Family, Socialization and Interaction Process.* New York: Free Press, 1955:259–306.

BALLANTINE, JEANNE. *The Sociology of Education.* 2d ed. Englewood Cliffs, N.J.: Prentice Hall, 1989.

BALTES, PAUL B., and K. WARNER SCHAIE. "The Myth of the Twilight Years." *Psychology Today.* Vol. 7, No. 10 (March 1974):35–39.

BALTZELL, E. DIGBY. *The Protestant Establishment: Aristocracy and Caste in America.* New York: Vintage Books, 1964.

———. "Introduction to the 1967 Edition." In W. E. B. Du Bois, *The Philadelphia Negro: A Social Study.* New York: Schocken, 1967; orig. 1899.

———. ED. *The Search for Community in Modern America.* New York: Harper & Row, 1968.

———. "The Protestant Establishment Revisited." *The American Scholar.* Vol. 45, No. 4 (Autumn 1976):499–518.

———. *Philadelphia Gentlemen: The Making of A National Upper Class.* Philadelphia: University of Pennsylvania Press, 1979; orig. 1958.

———. *Puritan Boston and Quaker Philadelphia.* New York: Free Press, 1979.

———. "The WASP's Last Gasp." *Philadelphia Magazine.* Vol. 79 (September 1988):104–7, 184, 186, 188.

BANFIELD, EDWARD C. *The Unheavenly City Revisited.* Boston: Little, Brown, 1974.

BARASH, DAVID. *The Whispering Within.* New York: Penguin Books, 1981.

BARKER, EILEEN. *New Religious Movements: A Practical Introduction.* London: Her Majesty's Stationery Office, 1989.

———. "Who'd Be a Moonie? A Comparative Study of Those Who Join the Unification Church in Britain." In Bryan Wilson, ed., *The Social Impact of New Religious Movements.* New York: The Rose of Sharon Press, 1981:59–96.

———. *New Religious Movements: A Practical Introduction.* London: Her Majesty's Stationery Office, 1989.

BARON, JAMES N., BRIAN S. MITTMAN, and ANDREW E. NEWMAN. "Targets of Opportunity: Organizational and Environmental Determinants of Gender Integration within the California Civil Service, 1979–1985." *American Journal of Sociology.* Vol. 96, No. 6 (May 1991): 1362–1401.

BARONE, MICHAEL, and GRANT UJIFUSA. *The Almanac of American Politics.* Washington, D.C.: Barone and Co., 1981.

BARRY, KATHLEEN. "Feminist Theory: The Meaning of Women's Liberation." In Barbara Haber, ed., *The Women's Annual 1982–1983.* Boston: G. K. Hall, 1983:35–78.

BASSUK, ELLEN J. "The Homelessness Problem." *Scientific American.* Vol. 251, No. 1 (July 1984):40–45.

BATESON, C. DANIEL, and W. LARRY VENTIS. *The Religious Experience: A Social-Psychological Perspective.* New York: Oxford, 1982.

BAUER, P. T. *Equality, the Third World, and Economic Delusion.* Cambridge, Mass.: Harvard University Press, 1981.

BEATRICE COMPANY, INC. *Annual Report 1985.* Chicago: Beatrice, 1985.

BECKER, HOWARD S. *Outside: Studies in the Sociology of Deviance.* New York: Free Press, 1966.

BEDELL, GEORGE C., LEO SANDON, JR., and CHARLES T. WELLBORN. *Religion in America.* New York: Macmillan, 1975.

BEECHLEY, LEONARD. *The Structure of Social Stratification in the United States.* Needham Heights, Mass.: Allyn & Bacon, 1989.

BELL, ALAN P., MARTIN S. WEINBERG, and SUE KIEFER-HAMMERSMITH. *Sexual Preference: Its Development in Men and Women.* Bloomington: Indiana University Press, 1981.

BELLAH, ROBERT N. *The Broken Covenant.* New York: Seabury Press, 1975.

BELLAH, ROBERT N., RICHARD MADSEN, WILLIAM M. SULLIVAN, ANN SWIDLER, and STEVEN M. TIPTON. *Habits of the Heart: Individualism and Commitment in American Life.* New York: Harper & Row, 1985.

BELSKY, JAY, RICHARD M. LERNER, and GRAHAM B. SPANIER. *The Child in the Family.* Reading, Mass.: Addison-Wesley, 1984.

BEM, SANDRA LIPSITZ. "Gender Schema Theory: A Cognitive Account of Sex-Typing." *Psychological Review.* Vol. 88, No. 4 (July 1981):354–64.

BENEDICT, RUTH. "Continuities and Discontinuities in Cultural Conditioning." *Psychiatry.* Vol. 1 (May 1938):161–67.

———. *The Chrysanthemum and the Sword: Patterns of Japanese Culture.* New York: New American Library, 1974; orig. 1946.

BENET, SULA. "Why They Live to Be 100, or Even Older, in Abkhasia." *New York Times Magazine* (December 26, 1971):3, 28–29, 31–34.

BENJAMIN, BERNARD, and CHRIS WALLIS. "The Mortality of Widowers." *The Lancet.* Vol. 2 (August 1963):454–56.

BENJAMIN, LOIS. *The Black Elite: Facing the Color Line in the Twilight of the Twentieth Century.* Chicago: Nelson-Hall, 1991.

BENNETT, NEIL G., DAVID E. BLOOM, and PATRICIA H. CRAIG. "The Divergence of Black and White Marriage Patterns." *American Journal of Sociology.* Vol. 95, No. 3 (November 1989):692–722.

BENNETT, STEPHEN EARL. "Left Behind: Exploring Declining Turnout among Noncollege Young Whites, 1964–1988." *Social Science Quarterly.* Vol. 72, No. 2 (June 1991):314–33.

BENNETT, WILLIAM J. "Quantifying America's Decline." *Wall Street Journal* (March 15, 1993).

BENOKRAITIS, NIJOLE, and JOE FEAGIN. *Modern Sexism: Blatant, Subtle, and Overt Discrimination.* Englewood Cliffs, N.J.: Prentice Hall, 1986.

BERARDO, F. M. "Survivorship and Social Isolation: The Case of the Aged Widower." *The Family Coordinator.* Vol. 19 (January 1970):11–25.

BERG, IVAR. *Education and Jobs: The Great Training Robbery.* New York: Praeger, 1970.

BERGER, BRIGITTE, and PETER L. BERGER. *The War Over the Family: Capturing the Middle Ground.* Garden City, N.Y.: Anchor/Doubleday, 1983.

BERGER, PETER L. *Invitation to Sociology.* New York: Anchor Books, 1963.

———. *The Sacred Canopy: Elements of a Sociological Theory of Religion.* Garden City, N.Y.: Doubleday, 1967.

———. *Facing Up to Modernity: Excursions in Society, Politics, and Religion.* New York: Basic Books, 1977.

———. *The Capitalist Revolution: Fifty Propositions About Prosperity, Equality, and Liberty.* New York: Basic Books, 1986.

BERGER, PETER, BRIGITTE BERGER, and HANSFRIED KELLNER. *The Homeless Mind: Modernization and Consciousness.* New York: Vintage Books, 1974.

BERGER, PETER L., and HANSFRIED KELLNER. *Sociology Reinterpreted: An Essay on Method and Vocation.* Garden City, N.Y.: Anchor Books, 1981.

BERGER, PETER L., and THOMAS LUCKMANN. *The Social Construction of Reality: A Treatise in the Sociology of Knowledge.* Garden City, N.Y.: Anchor Books, 1967.

BERGESEN, ALBERT, ed. *Crises in the World-System.* Beverly Hills, Calif.: Sage, 1983.

BERK, RICHARD A. *Collective Behavior.* Dubuque, Iowa: Wm. C. Brown, 1974.

BERNARD, JESSIE. *The Female World.* New York: Free Press, 1981.

———. *The Future of Marriage.* New Haven, Conn.: Yale University Press, 1982; orig. 1973.

BERNARD, LARRY CRAIG. "Multivariate Analysis of New Sex Role Formulations and Personality." *Journal of Personality and Social Psychology.* Vol. 38, No. 2 (February 1980):323–36.

BERNSTEIN, RICHARD J. *The New Constellation: The Ethical-Political Horizons of Modernity/Postmodernity.* Cambridge, Mass.: MIT Press, 1992.

BERRILL, KEVIN T. "Anti-Gay Violence and Victimization in the United States: An Overview." In Gregory M. Herek and Kevin T. Berrill, *Hate Crimes: Confronting Violence Against Lesbians and Gay Men.* Newbury Park, Calif.: Sage, 1992:19–45.

BERRY, BRIAN L., and PHILIP H. REES. "The Factorial Ecology of Calcutta." *American Journal of Sociology.* Vol. 74, No. 5 (March 1969):445–91.

BERSCHEID, ELLEN, and ELAINE HATFIELD. *Interpersonal Attraction.* 2d ed. Reading, Mass.: Addison-Wesley, 1983.

BERUBE, ALLAN. *Coming Out Under Fire: The History of Gay Men and Women in World War Two.* New York: Free Press, 1990.

BEST, RAPHAELA. *We've All Got Scars: What Boys and Girls Learn in Elementary School.* Bloomington: Indiana University Press, 1983.

BIBLARZ, TIMOTHY J., and ADRIAN E. RAFTERY. "The Effects of Family Disruption on Social Mobility." *American Sociological Review.* Vol. 58, No. 1 (February 1993):97–109.

BINGHAM, AMY. "Division I Dilemma: Making the Classroom a Priority for Athletes." *The Kenyon Journal.* Vol. II, No. 3 (November 1987):2.

Black Issues in Higher Education. "Black Graduate Students Decline." Vol. 4, No. 8 (July 1, 1987):1–2.

BLAU, JUDITH R., and PETER M. BLAU. "The Cost of Inequality: Metropolitan Structure and Violent Crime." *American Sociological Review.* Vol. 47, No. 1 (February 1982):114–29.

BLAU, PETER M. *Exchange and Power in Social Life.* New York: Wiley, 1964.

——. *Inequality and Heterogeneity: A Primitive Theory of Social Structure.* New York: Free Press, 1977.

BLAU, PETER M., TERRY C. BLUM, and JOSEPH E. SCHWARTZ. "heterogeneity and intermarriage." *American Sociological Review.* Vol. 47, No. 1 (February 1982):45–62.

BLAU, PETER M., and OTIS DUDLEY DUNCAN. *The American Occupational Structure.* New York: Wiley, 1967.

BLAUSTEIN, ALBERT P., and ROBERT L. ZANGRANDO. *Civil Rights and the Black American.* New York: Washington Square Press, 1968.

BLOOM, LEONARD. "Familial Adjustments of Japanese-Americans to Relocation: First Phase." In Thomas F. Pettigrew, ed., *The Sociology of Race Relations.* New York: Free Press, 1980:163–67.

BLUM, LINDA M. *Between Feminism and Labor: The Significance of the Comparable Worth Movement.* Berkeley: University of California Press, 1991.

BLUMBERG, PAUL. *Inequality in an Age of Decline.* New York: Oxford University Press, 1981.

BLUMER, HERBERT G. "Fashion." In David L. Sills, ed., *International Encyclopedia of the Social Sciences.* Vol. 5. New York: Macmillan and Free Press, 1968:341–45.

——. "Collective Behavior." In Alfred McClung Lee, ed., *Principles of Sociology.* 3d ed. New York: Barnes & Noble Books, 1969:65–121.

BLUMSTEIN, PHILIP, and PEPPER SCHWARTZ. *American Couples.* New York: William Morrow, 1983.

BODENHEIMER, THOMAS S. "Health Care in the United States: Who Pays?" In Vicente Navarro, ed., *Health and Medical Care in the U.S.: A Critical Analysis.* Farmingdale, N.Y.: Baywood Publishing Co., 1977:61–68.

BOFF, LEONARD and CLODOVIS. *Salvation and Liberation: In Search of a Balance Between Faith and Politics.* Maryknoll, N.Y.: Orbis Books, 1984.

BOGARDUS, EMORY S. "Comparing Racial Distance in Ethiopia, South Africa, and the United States." *Sociology and Social Research.* Vol. 52, No. 2 (January 1968):149–56.

BOHANNAN, CECIL. "The Economic Correlates of Homelessness in Sixty Cities." *Social Science Quarterly.* Vol. 72, No. 4 (December 1991): 817–25.

BOHANNAN, PAUL. *Divorce and After.* Garden City, N.Y.: Doubleday, 1970.

BOHM, ROBERT M. "American Death Penalty Opinion, 1936–1986: A Critical Examination of the Gallup Polls." In Robert M. Bohm, ed., *The Death Penalty in America: Current Research.* Cincinnati: Anderson Publishing Co., 1991:113–45.

BOHRMANN, F. HERBERT. "The Global Environmental Deficit." *Bioscience.* Vol. 40 (1990):74.

BOHRMANN, F. HERBERT, and STEPHEN R. KELLERT. "The Global Environmental Deficit." In Herbert F. Bohrmann and Stephen R. Kellert, eds., *Ecology, Economics, and Ethics: The Broken Circle.* New Haven, Conn.: Yale University Press, 1991:ix–xviii.

BONILLA-SANTIAGO, GLORIA. "A Portrait of Hispanic Women in the United States." In Sara E. Rix, ed., *The American Woman 1990–91: A Status Report.* New York: Norton, 1990:249–57.

BONNER, JANE. Research presented in "The Two Brains." Public Broadcasting System telecast, 1984.

BOOTH, ALAN, and LYNN WHITE. "Thinking About Divorce." *Journal of Marriage and the Family.* Vol. 42, No. 3 (August 1980):605–16.

BORGMANN, ALBERT. *Crossing the Postmodern Divide.* Chicago: University of Chicago Press, 1992.

BOSWELL, TERRY E. "A Split Labor Market Analysis of Discrimination Against Chinese Immigrants, 1850–1882." *American Sociological Review.* Vol. 51, No. 3 (June 1986):352–71.

BOTT, ELIZABETH. *Family and Social Network.* New York: Free Press, 1971; orig. 1957.

BOULDING, ELISE. *The Underside of History.* Boulder, Colo.: Westview Press, 1976.

BOWLES, SAMUEL, and HERBERT GINTIS. *Schooling in Capitalist America: Educational Reform and the Contradictions of Economic Life.* New York: Basic Books, 1976.

BOYER, ERNEST L. *College: The Undergraduate Experience in America.* Prepared by The Carnegie Foundation for the Advancement of Teaching. New York: Harper & Row, 1987.

BRAITHWAITE, JOHN. "The Myth of Social Class and Criminality Reconsidered." *American Sociological Review.* Vol. 46, No. 1 (February 1981):36–57.

BRAND, DAVID. "The New Whiz Kids." *Time.* Vol. 130, No. 9 (August 31, 1987):42–46, 49, 51.

BRANEGAN, JAY. "Is Singapore a Model for the West?" *Time.* Vol. 141, No. 3 (January 18, 1993):36–37.

BREEN, LEONARD Z. "The Aging Individual." In Clark Tibbitts, ed., *Handbook of Social Gerontology.* Chicago: University of Chicago Press, 1960:145–62.

BRINTON, CRANE. *The Anatomy of Revolution.* New York: Vintage Books, 1965.

BRINTON, MARY C. "The Social-Institutional Bases of Gender Stratification: Japan as an Illustrative Case." *American Journal of Sociology.* Vol. 94, No. 2 (September 1988):300–334.

BROOKHISER, RICHARD. "Barefoot Doctors vs. Scroogecare." *Time.* Vol. 143, No. 2 (January 10, 1994):64.

BROPHY, GWENDA. "China, Part I." *Population Today.* Vol. 17, No. 3 (March 1989a):12.

——. "China: Part II." *Population Today.* Vol. 17. No. 4 (April 1989b):12.

BROWN, LESTER R., ET AL., EDS. *State of the World 1993: A Worldwatch Institute Report on Progress Toward a Sustainable Society.* New York: Norton, 1993.

BROWN, MARY ELLEN, ED. *Television and Women's Culture: The Politics of the Popular.* Newbury Park, Calif.: Sage, 1990.

BROWNMILLER, SUSAN. *Against Our Will: Men, Women and Rape.* New York: Simon & Schuster, 1975.

——. *Femininity.* New York: Linden Press/Simon & Schuster, 1984.

BROWNSTEIN, RONALD, and NINA EASTON. *Reagan's Ruling Class: Portraits of the President's Top One Hundred Officials.* New York: Pantheon Books, 1983.

BROYLES, J. ALLEN. "The John Birch Society: A Movement of Social Protest of the Radical Right." In Louis E. Genevie, ed., *Collective Behavior and Social Movements.* Itasca, Ill.: Peacock, 1978:338–45.

BRUNO, MARY. "Abusing the Elderly." *Newsweek* (September 23, 1985):75–76.

BURCH, ROBERT. Testimony to House of Representatives Hearing in "Review: The World Hunger Problem." October 25, 1983, Serial 98-38.

BUREAU OF NATIONAL AFFAIRS. "The Challenge of Diversity: Equal Employment and Managing Difference in the 1990s." Summary report. Washington, D.C.: The Bureau of National Affairs, 1990.

BURKE, TOM "The Future." In Sir Edmund Hillary, ed., *Ecology 2000: The Changing Face of the Earth.* New York: Beaufort Books, 1984:227–41.

BURNHAM, WALTER DEAN. *Democracy in the Making: American Government and Politics.* Englewood Cliffs, N.J.: Prentice Hall, 1983.

BURRIS, VAL. "The Social and Political Consequences of Overeducation." *American Sociological Review.* Vol. 48, No. 4 (August 1983):454–67.

BURSTEIN, PAUL. "Legal Mobilization as a Social Movement Tactic: The Struggle for Equal Employment Opportunity." *American Journal of Sociology.* Vol. 96, No. 5 (March 1991):1201–25.

References   **669**

BUSBY, LINDA J. "Sex Role Research on the Mass Media." *Journal of Communications.* Vol. 25 (Autumn 1975):107–13.

BUTLER, ROBERT N. *Why Survive? Being Old in America.* New York: Harper & Row, 1975.

BUTTERWORTH, DOUGLAS, and JOHN K. CHANCE. *Latin American Urbanization.* Cambridge: Cambridge University Press, 1981.

CAHNMAN, WERNER J., and RUDOLF HEBERLE. "Introduction." In *Ferdinand Toennies on Sociology: Pure, Applied, and Empirical.* Chicago: University of Chicago Press, 1971:vii–xxii.

CALLAHAN, DANIEL. *Setting Limits: Medical Goals in an Aging Society.* New York: Simon & Schuster, 1987.

CALMORE, JOHN O. "National Housing Policies and Black America: Trends, Issues, and Implications." In *The State of Black America 1986.* New York: National Urban League, 1986:115–49.

CAMERON, WILLIAM BRUCE. *Modern Social Movements: A Sociological Outline.* New York: Random House, 1966.

CANETTI, ELIAS. *Crowds and Power.* New York: Seabury Press, 1978.

CANTOR, MURIAL G., and SUZANNE PINGREE. *The Soap Opera.* Beverly Hills, Calif.: Sage, 1983.

CANTRIL, HADLEY, HAZEL GAUDET, and HERTA HERZOG. *Invasion from Mars: A Study in the Psychology of Panic.* Princeton, N.J.: Princeton University Press, 1947.

CAPLOW, THEODORE, ET AL. *Middletown Families.* Minneapolis: University of Minnesota Press, 1982.

CAPLOW, THEODORE, HOWARD M. BAHR, JOHN MODELL, and BRUCE A. CHADWICK. *Recent Social Trends in the United States, 1960–1990.* Montreal: McGill-Queen's University Press, 1991.

CARLEY, KATHLEEN. "A Theory of Group Stability." *American Sociological Review.* Vol. 56, No. 3 (June 1991):331–54.

CARLSON, NORMAN A. "Corrections in the United States Today: A Balance Has Been Struck." *The American Criminal Law Review.* Vol. 13, No. 4 (Spring 1976):615–47.

CARMICHAEL, STOKELY, and CHARLES V. HAMILTON. *Black Power: The Politics of Liberation in America.* New York: Vintage Books, 1967.

CARROLL, GINNY. "Who Foots the Bill?" *Newsweek.* Special Issue (Fall–Winter, 1990):81–85.

CASTRO, JANICE. "Disposable Workers." *Time.* Vol. 131, No. 14 (March 29, 1993):43–47.

CENTER FOR MEDIA and PUBLIC AFFAIRS. 1991 report by Robert Lichter, Linda Lichter, and Stanley Rothman.

CENTER FOR THE STUDY OF SPORT IN SOCIETY. *1991 Racial Report Card: A Study in the NBA, NFL, and Major League Baseball.* Boston: Northeastern University, 1993.

CHAGNON, NAPOLEON A. *Yanomamö* 3d ed. New York: Holt, Rinehart & Winston, 1983

———. *Yanomamö: The Fierce People.* 4th ed. New York: Holt, Rinehart & Winston, 1992.

CHANDLER, TERTIUS, and GERALD FOX. *3000 Years of Urban History.* New York: Academic Press, 1974.

CHANGE, KWANG-CHIH. *The Archaeology of Ancient China.* New Haven, Conn.: Yale University Press, 1977.

CHAPPELL, NEENA L., and BETTY HAVENS. "Old and Female: Testing the Double Jeopardy Hypothesis." *The Sociological Quarterly.* Vol. 21, No. 2 (Spring 1980):157–71.

CHERLIN, ANDREW. *Marriage, Divorce, Remarriage.* Rev. ed. Cambridge, Mass.: Harvard University Press, 1990.

CHERLIN, ANDREW, and FRANK F. FURSTENBERG, JR. "The American Family in the Year 2000." *The Futurist.* Vol. 17, No. 3 (June 1983):7–14.

CHILDREN'S DEFENSE FUND. *Child Poverty in America.* Washington, D.C.: 1991.

———. *The State of America's Children, 1992.* Washington, D.C.: 1992.

CHOWN, SHEILA M. "Morale, Careers and Personal Potentials." In James E. Birren and K. Warner Schaie, eds., *Handbook of the Psychology of Aging.* New York: Van Nostrand Reinhold, 1977:672–91.

CHURCH, GEORGE J. "Send Back Your Tired, Your Poor . . . " *Time.* Vol. 141, No. 25 (June 21, 1993):26–27.

———. "The Terror Within." *Time.* Vol. 142, No. 1 (July 5, 1993):22–27.

———. "Please Help Us." *Time.* Vol. 142, No. 19 (November 8, 1993):36–38.

CLARK, CURTIS B. "Geriatric Abuse: Out of the Closet." In *The Tragedy of Elder Abuse: The Problem and the Response.* Hearings before the Select Committee on Aging, House of Representatives, July 1, 1986:49–50.

CLARK, JUAN M., JOSE I. LASAGA, and ROSE S. REGUE. *The 1980 Mariel Exodus: An Assessment and Prospect: Special Report.* Washington, D.C.: Council for Inter-American Security, 1981.

CLARK, MARGARET S., ED. *Prosocial Behavior.* Newbury Park, Calif.: Sage, 1991.

CLARK, THOMAS A. *Blacks in Suburbs.* New Brunswick, N.J.: Rutgers University Center for Urban Policy Research, 1979.

CLARKE, ROBIN. "Atmospheric Pollution." In Sir Edmund Hillary, ed., *Ecology 2000: The Changing Face of the Earth.* New York: Beaufort Books, 1984a:130–48.

———. "What's Happening to Our Water?" In Sir Edmund Hillary, ed., *Ecology 2000: The Changing Face of the Earth.* New York: Beaufort Books, 1984b:108–29.

CLINARD, MARSHALL, and DANIEL ABBOTT. *Crime in Developing Countries.* New York: Wiley, 1973.

CLOWARD, RICHARD A., and LLOYD E. OHLIN. *Delinquency and Opportunity: A Theory of Delinquent Gangs.* New York: Free Press, 1966.

COAKLEY, JAY J. *Sport in Society: Issues and Controversies.* 3d ed. St. Louis, Mo.: Mosby, 1986; 4th ed., 1990.

COE, MICHAEL D., and RICHARD A. DIEHL. *In the Land of the Olmec.* Austin: University of Texas Press, 1980.

COHEN, ALBERT K. *Delinquent Boys: The Culture of the Gang.* New York: Free Press, 1971; orig. 1955.

COHEN, LLOYD R. "Sexual Harassment and the Law." *Society.* Vol. 28, No. 4 (May–June, 1991):8–13.

COHEN, MICHAEL. "Restructuring the System." *Transaction.* Vol. 26, No. 4 (May–June 1989):40–48.

COHN, RICHARD M. "Economic Development and Status Change of the Aged." *American Journal of Sociology.* Vol. 87, No. 2 (March 1982):1150–61.

COLEMAN, JAMES S., and THOMAS HOFFER. *Public and Private High Schools: The Impact of Communities.* New York: Basic Books, 1987.

COLEMAN, JAMES, THOMAS HOFFER, and SALLY KILGORE. *Public and Private Schools: An Analysis of Public Schools and Beyond.* Washington, D.C.: National Center for Education Statistics, 1981.

COLEMAN, RICHARD P., and BERNICE L. NEUGARTEN. *Social Status in the City.* San Francisco: Jossey-Bass, 1971.

COLEMAN, RICHARD P., and LEE RAINWATER. *Social Standing in America.* New York: Basic Books, 1978.

COLLINS, RANDALL. "A Conflict Theory of Sexual Stratification." *Social Problems.* Vol. 19, No. 1 (Summer 1971):3–21.

———. *The Credential Society: An Historical Sociology of Education and Stratification.* New York: Academic Press, 1979.

———. *Sociological Insight: An Introduction to Nonobvious Sociology.* New York: Oxford University Press, 1982.

———. *Weberian Sociological Theory.* Cambridge: Cambridge University Press, 1986.

COLLOWAY, N. O., and PAULA L. DOLLEVOET. "Selected Tabular Material on Aging." In Caleb Finch and Leonard Hayflick, eds., *Handbook of the Biology of Aging.* New York: Van Nostrand Reinhold, 1977:666–708.

COMTE, AUGUSTE. *Auguste Comte and Positivism: The Essential Writings.* Gertrud Lenzer, ed. New York: Harper Torchbooks, 1975.

CONGREGATION FOR THE DOCTRINE OF THE FAITH. *Instruction on Respect for Human Life in Its Origin and on the Dignity of Procreation: Replies to Certain Questions of the Day.* Vatican City, 1987.

CONNETT, PAUL H. "The Disposable Society." In Herbert F. Bohrmann and Stephen R. Kellert, eds., *Ecology, Economics, and Ethics: The Broken Circle.* New Haven, Conn.: Yale University Press, 1991:99–122.

CONRAD, PETER, and JOSEPH W. SCHNEIDER. *Deviance and Medicalization: From Badness to Sickness.* Columbus, Ohio: Merrill, 1980.

CONTRERAS, JOSEPH. "A New Day Dawns." *Newsweek* (March 30, 1992):40–41.

COOK, RHODES. "House Republicans Scored a Quiet Victory in '92." *Congressional Quarterly Weekly Report.* Vol. 51, No. 16 (April 17, 1993):965–68.

COOLEY, CHARLES HORTON. *Social Organization.* New York: Schocken Books, 1962; orig. 1909.

———. *Human Nature and the Social Order.* New York: Schocken Books, 1964; orig. 1902.

COSER, LEWIS A. *Masters of Sociological Thought: Ideas in Historical and Social Context.* 2d ed. New York: Harcourt Brace Jovanovich, 1977.

COTTLE, THOMAS J. "What Tracking Did to Ollie Taylor." *Social Policy.* Vol. 5, No. 2 (July–August 1974):22–24.

COTTRELL, JOHN, and THE EDITORS OF TIME-LIFE. *The Great Cities: Mexico City.* Amsterdam: 1979.

COUNCIL ON INTERNATIONAL EDUCATIONAL EXCHANGE. *Educating for Global Competence: The Report of the Advisory Committee for International Educational Exchange.* New York: The Council, 1988.

COUNTS, G. S. "The Social Status of Occupations: A Problem in Vocational Guidance." *School Review.* Vol. 33 (January 1925):16–27.

COURTNEY, ALICE E., and THOMAS W. WHIPPLE. *Sex Stereotyping in Advertising.* Lexington, Mass.: D.C. Heath, 1983.

COWAN, CAROLYN POPE. *When Partners Become Parents.* New York: Basic Books, 1992.

COWGILL, DONALD, and LOWELL HOLMES. *Aging and Modernization.* New York: Appleton-Century-Crofts, 1972.

COX, HAROLD. *Later Life: The Realities of Aging.* Englewood Cliffs, N.J.: Prentice Hall, 1984.

COX, HARVEY. *The Secular City.* Rev. ed. New York: Macmillan, 1971; orig. 1965.

———. *Turning East: The Promise and Peril of the New Orientalism.* New York: Simon & Schuster, 1977.

———. "Church and Believers: Always Strangers?" In Thomas Robbins and Dick Anthony. *In Gods We Trust: New Patterns of Religious Pluralism in America.* 2d ed. New Brunswick, N.J.: Transaction, 1990:449–62.

CRISPELL, DIANE. "Working in 2000." *American Demographics.* Vol. 12, No. 3 (March 1990):36–40.

———. "Grandparents Galore." *American Demographics.* Vol. 15, No. 10 (October 1993):63.

CROOK, STEPHAN, JAN PAKULSKI, and MALCOLM WATERS. *Postmodernity: Change in Advanced Society.* Newbury Park, Calif.: Sage, 1992.

CROUSE, JAMES, and DALE TRUSHEIM. *The Case Against the SAT.* Chicago: University of Chicago Press, 1988.

CRYSTAL, GRAEF S. "How Much CEOs Really Make." *Fortune* (June 17, 1991):72–80.

CUFF, E. C., and G. C. F. PAYNE, EDS. *Perspectives in Sociology.* London: Allen and Unwin, 1979.

CUMMING, ELAINE, and WILLIAM E. HENRY. *Growing Old: The Process of Disengagement.* New York: Basic Books, 1961.

CURRIE, ELLIOTT. *Confronting Crime: An American Challenge.* New York: Pantheon Books, 1985.

CURTIS, JAMES E., EDWARD G. GRABB, and DOUGLAS BAER. "Voluntary Association Membership in Fifteen Countries: A Comparative Analysis." *American Sociological Review.* Vol. 57, No. 2 (April 1992):139–52.

CURTISS, SUSAN. *Genie: A Psycholinguistic Study of a Modern-Day "Wild Child."* New York: Academic Press, 1977.

CUTRIGHT, PHILLIP. "Occupational Inheritance: A Cross-National Analysis." *American Journal of Sociology.* Vol. 73, No. 4 (January 1968):400–416.

DAHL, ROBERT A. *Who Governs?* New Haven, Conn.: Yale University Press, 1961.

———. *Dilemmas of Pluralist Democracy: Autonomy vs. Control.* New Haven, Conn.: Yale University Press, 1982.

DAHRENDORF, RALF. *Class and Class Conflict in Industrial Society.* Stanford, Calif.: Stanford University Press, 1959.

DALY, MARTIN, and MARGO WILSON. *Homicide.* New York: Aldine, 1988.

DAMON, WILLIAM. *Social and Personality Development.* New York: Norton, 1983.

DANIELS, ROGER. "The Issei Generation." In Amy Tachiki et al., eds., *Roots: An Asian American Reader.* Los Angeles: UCLA Asian American Studies Center, 1971:138–49.

DANNEFER, DALE. "Adult Development and Social Theory: A Reappraisal." *American Sociological Review.* Vol. 49, No. 1 (February 1984):100–116.

DARNTON, NINA, and YURIKO HOSHIA. "Whose Life Is It, Anyway?" *Newsweek.* Vol. 113, No. 4 (January 13, 1989):61.

DAVIES, CHRISTIE. *Ethnic Humor Around the World: A Comparative Analysis.* Bloomington: Indiana University Press, 1990.

DAVIES, JAMES C. "Toward a Theory of Revolution." *American Sociological Review.* Vol. 27, No. 1 (February 1962):5–19.

DAVIES, MARK, and DENISE B. KANDEL. "Parental and Peer Influences on Adolescents' Educational Plans: Some Further Evidence." *American Journal of Sociology.* Vol. 87, No. 2 (September 1981):363–87.

DAVIS, CHARLES L. "Lifting the Gay Ban." *Society.* Vol. 31, No. 1 (November–December 1993):24–36.

DAVIS, KINGSLEY. "Extreme Social Isolation of a Child." *American Journal of Sociology.* Vol. 45, No. 4 (January 1940):554–65.

———. "Final Note on a Case of Extreme Isolation." *American Journal of Sociology.* Vol. 52, No. 5 (March 1947):432–37.

DAVIS, KINGSLEY, and WILBERT MOORE. "Some Principles of Stratification." *American Sociological Review.* Vol. 10, No. 2 (April 1945):242–49.

DAVIS, SHARON A., and EMIL J. HALLER. "Tracking, Ability, and SES: Further Evidence on the 'Revisionist-Meritocratic Debate.'" *American Journal of Education.* Vol. 89 (May 1981):283–304.

DECKARD, BARBARA SINCLAIR. *The Women's Movement: Political, Socioeconomic, and Psychological Issues.* 2d ed. New York: Harper & Row, 1979.

DEDRICK, DENNIS K. Personal communication, 1990.

DEDRICK, DENNIS K., and RICHARD E. YINGER. "MAD, SDI, and the Nuclear Arms Race." Manuscript in development. Georgetown, Ky.: Georgetown College, 1990.

DELACROIX, JACQUES, and CHARLES C. RAGIN. "Structural Blockage: A Crossnational Study of Economic Dependency, State Efficacy, and Underdevelopment." *American Journal of Sociology.* Vol. 86, No. 6 (May 1981):1311–47.

DEMOTT, JOHN S. "Wreaking Havoc on Spring Break." *Time.* Vol. 127, No. 14 (April 7, 1986):29.

DEPARLE, JASON. "Painted by Numbers: 1980s are Rosy to G.O.P., While Democrats See Red." *New York Times* (September 26, 1991a):B10.

———. "Poverty Rate Rose Sharply Last Year as Incomes Slipped." *New York Times* (September 27, 1991b):A1, A11.

Der Spiegel. "Third World Metropolises Are Becoming Monsters; Rural Poverty Drives Millions to the Slums." *World Press Review* (October 1989).

DEVINE, JOEL A. "State and State Expenditure: Determinants of Social Investment and Social Consumption Spending in the Postwar United States." *American Sociological Review.* Vol. 50, No. 2 (April 1985):150–65.

DEWEY, JOHN. *Experience and Education.* New York: Collier Books, 1968; orig. 1938.

DIAMOND, MILTON. "Sexual Identity, Monozygotic Twins Reared in Discordant Sex Roles and a BBC Follow-Up." *Archives of Sexual Behavior.* Vol. 11, No. 2 (April 1982):181–86.

DICKENS, CHARLES. *The Adventures of Oliver Twist.* Boston: Estes and Lauriat, 1886; orig. 1837–39.

DIPRETE, THOMAS A. "Unemployment over the Life Cycle: Racial Differences and the Effect of Changing Economic Conditions." *American Journal of Sociology.* Vol. 87, No. 2 (September 1981):286–307.

DIZARD, JAN E., and HOWARD GADLIN. *The Minimal Family.* Amherst: The University of Massachusetts Press, 1990.

DOBSON, RICHARD B. "Mobility and Stratification in the Soviet Union." *Annual Review of Sociology.* Vol. 3. Palo Alto, Calif.: Annual Reviews, 1977:297–329.

DOBYNS, HENRY F. "An Appraisal of Techniques with a New Hemispheric Estimate." *Current Anthropology.* Vol. 7, No. 4 (October 1966):395–446.

DOLLARD, JOHN, ET AL. *Frustration and Aggression.* New Haven, Conn.: Yale University Press, 1939.

DOMHOFF, G. WILLIAM. *Who Rules America Now? A View of the '80s.* Englewood Cliffs, N.J.: Prentice Hall, 1983.

DONOVAN, VIRGINIA K., and RONNIE LITTENBERG. "Psychology of Women: Feminist Therapy." In Barbara Haber, ed., *The Women's Annual 1981: The Year in Review.* Boston: G. K. Hall, 1982:211–35.

DOUGLASS, RICHARD L. "Domestic Neglect and Abuse of the Elderly: Implications for Research and Service." *Family Relations.* Vol. 32 (July 1983):395–402.

DOW, UNITY. Personal communication, 1990.

DOYAL, LESLEY, with IMOGEN PENNELL. *The Political Economy of Health.* London: Pluto Press, 1981.

DOYLE, JAMES A. *The Male Experience*. Dubuque, Iowa: Wm. C. Brown, 1983.

DU BOIS, W. E. B. *The Philadelphia Negro: A Social Study*. New York: Schocken Books, 1967; orig. 1899.

DUBOS, RENÉ. *Man Adapting*. New Haven, Conn.: Yale University Press, 1980; orig. 1965.

DUHL, LEONARD J. "The Social Context of Health." In Arthur C. Hastings et al., eds., *Health for the Whole Person: The Complete Guide to Holistic Medicine*. Boulder, Colo.: Westview Press, 1980:39–48.

DUNLAP, RILEY E., GEORGE H. GALLUP, JR., and ALEC M. GALLUP. *The Health of the Planet Survey*. Princeton, N.J.: The George H. Gallup International Institute, 1992.

DUNN, JOHN. "Peddling Big Brother." *Time*. Vol. 137, No. 25 (June 24, 1991):62.

DURKHEIM, EMILE. *The Division of Labor in Society*. New York: Free Press, 1964a; orig. 1895.

———. *The Rules of Sociological Method*. New York: Free Press, 1964b; orig. 1893.

———. *The Elementary Forms of Religious Life*. New York: Free Press, 1965; orig. 1915.

———. *Suicide*. New York: Free Press, 1966; orig. 1897.

———. *Selected Writings*. Anthony Giddens, ed. Cambridge: Cambridge University Press, 1972.

———. *Sociology and Philosophy*. New York: Free Press, 1974; orig. 1924.

DURNING, ALAN THEIN. "Supporting Indigenous Peoples." In Lester R. Brown et al., eds., *State of the World 1993: A Worldwatch Institute Report on Progress Toward a Sustainable Society*. New York: Norton, 1993:80–100.

DWORKIN, ANDREA. *Intercourse*. New York: Free Press, 1987.

DZIECH, BILLIE WRIGHT, and LINDA WEINER. *The Lecherous Professor: Sexual Harassment on Campus*. Boston: Beacon Press, 1984.

EBAUGH, HELEN ROSE FUCHS. *Becoming an EX: The Process of Role Exit*. Chicago: University of Chicago Press, 1988.

ECKHOLM, ERIK. "Malnutrition in Elderly: Widespread Health Threat." *New York Times* (August 13, 1985):19–20.

ECKHOLM, ERIK, and JOHN TIERNEY. "AIDS in Africa: A Killer Rages On." *New York Times* (September 16, 1990):A1, 14.

THE ECONOMIST. "Worship Moves in Mysterious Ways." Vol. 326, No. 7802 (March 13, 1993a–.):65, 70.

———. "Taiwan's Little Problem." Vol. 327, No. 7814 (June 5, 1993b):41.

EDMONSTON, BARRY, and THOMAS M. GUTERBOCK. "Is Suburbanization Slowing Down? Recent Trends in Population Deconcentration in U.S. Metropolitan Areas." *Social Forces*. Vol. 62, No. 4 (June 1984):905–25.

EDWARDS, DAVID V. *The American Political Experience*. 3d ed. Englewood Cliffs, N.J.: Prentice Hall, 1985.

EDWARDS, RICHARD. *Contested Terrain: The Transformation of the Workplace in the Twentieth Century*. New York: Basic Books, 1979.

EHRENREICH, BARBARA. *The Hearts of Men: American Dreams and the Flight from Commitment*. Garden City, N.Y.: Anchor Books, 1983.

EHRENREICH, JOHN. "Introduction." In John Ehrenreich, ed., *The Cultural Crisis of Modern Medicine*. New York: Monthly Review Press, 1978:1–35.

EHRLICH, PAUL R. *The Population Bomb*. New York: Ballantine Books, 1978.

EICHLER, MARGRIT. *Nonsexist Research Methods: A Practical Guide*. Winchester, Mass.: Unwin Hyman, 1988.

EISEN, ARNOLD M. *The Chosen People in America: A Study of Jewish Religious Ideology*. Bloomington: Indiana University Press, 1983.

EISENSTEIN, ZILLAH R., ed. *Capitalist Patriarchy and the Case for Socialist Feminism*. New York: Monthly Review Press, 1979.

EISLER, BENITA. *The Lowell Offering: Writings by New England Mill Women 1840–1845*. Philadelphia and New York: J. B. Lippincott, 1977.

EKMAN, PAUL. "Biological and Cultural Contributions to Body and Facial Movements in the Expression of Emotions." In A. Rorty, ed., *Explaining Emotions*. Berkeley: University of California Press, 1980a:73–101.

———. *Face of Man: Universal Expression in a New Guinea Village*. New York: Garland Press, 1980b.

———. *Telling Lies: Clues to Deceit in the Marketplace, Politics, and Marriage*. New York: Norton, 1985.

EKMAN, PAUL, WALLACE V. FRIESEN, and JOHN BEAR. "The International Language of Gestures." *Psychology Today* (May 1984):64–69.

ELAM, STANLEY M., LOWELL C. ROSE, and ALEC M. GALLUP. "The 23rd Annual Gallup Poll of the Public's Attitudes Toward Public Schools." *Phi Delta Kappan*, Vol. 73 (September 1991):41–56.

EL-ATTAR, MOHAMED. Personal communication, 1991.

ELIAS, ROBERT. *The Politics of Victimization: Victims, Victimology and Human Rights*. New York: Oxford University Press, 1986.

ELKIN, FREDERICK, and GERALD HANDEL. *The Child and Society: The Process of Socialization*. 4th ed. New York: Random House, 1984.

ELKIND, DAVID. *The Hurried Child: Growing Up Too Fast Too Soon*. Reading, Mass.: Addison-Wesley, 1981.

ELLIOT, DELBERT S., and SUZANNE S. AGETON. "Reconciling Race and Class Differences in Self-Reported and Official Estimates of Delinquency." *American Sociological Review*. Vol. 45, No. 1 (February 1980):95–110.

ELLISON, CHRISTOPHER G., and DARREN E. SHERKAT. "Conservative Protestantism and Support for Corporal Punishment." *American Sociological Review*. Vol. 58, No. 1 (February 1993):131–44.

ELMER-DEWITT, PHILIP. "The Revolution that Fizzled." *Time*. Vol. 137, No. 20 (May 20, 1991):48–49.

———. "Catching a Bad Gene in the Tiniest of Embryos." *Time*. Vol. 140, No. 14 (October 5, 1992):81–82.

———. "The Genetic Revolution." *Time*. Vol. 143, No. 3 (January 17, 1994):46–53.

EMBER, MELVIN, and CAROL R. EMBER. "The Conditions Favoring Matrilocal versus Patrilocal Residence." *American Anthropologist*. Vol. 73, No. 3 (June 1971):571–94.

EMBER, MELVIN M., and CAROL R. EMBER. *Anthropology*. 6th ed. Englewood Cliffs, N.J.: Prentice Hall, 1991.

EMBREE, AINSLIE T. *The Hindu Tradition*. New York: Vintage Books, 1972.

EMERSON, JOAN P. "Behavior in Private Places: Sustaining Definitions of Reality in Gynecological Examinations." In H. P. Dreitzel, ed., *Recent Sociology*. Vol. 2. New York: Collier, 1970:74–97.

ENDICOTT, KAREN. "Fathering in an Egalitarian Society." In Barry S. Hewlett, ed., *Father-Child Relations: Cultural and Bio-Social Contexts*. New York: Aldine, 1992:281–96.

ENGELS, FRIEDRICH. *The Origin of the Family*. Chicago: Charles H. Kerr & Company, 1902; orig. 1884.

ENGLAND, PAULA. *Comparable Worth: Theories and Evidence*. Hawthorne, N.Y.: Aldine, 1992.

ERIKSON, ERIK H. *Childhood and Society*. New York: Norton, 1963; orig. 1950.

———. *Identity and the Life Cycle*. New York: Norton, 1980.

ERIKSON, KAI T. *Wayward Puritans: A Study in the Sociology of Deviance*. New York: Wiley, 1966.

ERIKSON, ROBERT, and JOHN H. GOLDTHORPE. *The Constant Flux: A Study of Class Mobility in Industrial Societies*. Oxford: Clarendon Press, 1992.

ERIKSON, ROBERT S., NORMAN R. LUTTBEG, and KENT L. TEDIN. *American Public Opinion: Its Origins, Content, and Impact*. 2d ed. New York: Wiley, 1980.

ETZIONI, AMITAI. *A Comparative Analysis of Complex Organization: On Power, Involvement, and Their Correlates*. Rev. and enlarged ed. New York: Free Press, 1975.

———. "Too Many Rights, Too Few Responsibilities." *Society*. Vol. 28, No. 2 (January–February 1991):41–48.

ETZIONI-HALEVY, EVA. *Bureaucracy and Democracy: A Political Dilemma*. Rev. ed. Boston: Routledge & Kegan Paul, 1985.

EVANS, M. D. R. "Immigrant Entrepreneurship: Effects of Ethnic Market Size and Isolated Labor Pool." *American Sociological Review*. Vol. 54, No. 6 (December 1989):950–62.

EXTER, THOMAS G. "The Costs of Growing Up." *American Demographics*. Vol. 13, No. 8 (August 1991):59.

———. "Home Alone in 2000." *American Demographics*. Vol. 14, No. 9 (September 1992):67.

FALK, GERHARD. Personal communication, 1987.

FALKENMARK, MALIN, and CARL WIDSTRAND. "Population and Water Resources: A Delicate Balance." *Population Bulletin*. Vol. 47, No. 3 (November 1992). Washington, D.C.: Population Reference Bureau.

FALLON, A. E., and P. ROZIN. "Sex Differences in Perception of Desirable Body Shape." *Journal of Abnormal Psychology.* Vol. 94, No. 1 (1985):100–105.

FALLOWS, JAMES. "Immigration: How It's Affecting Us." *The Atlantic Monthly.* Vol. 252 (November 1983):45–52, 55–62, 66–68, 85–90, 94, 96, 99–106.

FANTINI, MARIO D. *Regaining Excellence in Education.* Columbus, Ohio: Merrill, 1986.

FARRELL, MICHAEL P., and STANLEY D. ROSENBERG. *Men at Midlife.* Boston: Auburn House, 1981.

FEAGIN, JOE. *The Urban Real Estate Game.* Englewood Cliffs, N.J.: Prentice Hall, 1983.

FEAGIN, JOE R. "The Continuing Significance of Race: Antiblack Discrimination in Public Places." *American Sociological Review.* Vol. 56, No. 1 (February 1991):101–16.

FEATHERMAN, DAVID L., and ROBERT M. HAUSER. *Opportunity and Change.* New York: Academic Press, 1978.

FEATHERSTONE, MIKE, ED. *Global Culture: Nationalism, Globalization, and Modernity.* London: Sage, 1990.

FEDARKO, KEVIN. "Who Could Live Here?" *Time.* Vol. 139, No. 3 (January 20, 1992):20–23.

FENNELL, MARY C. "The Effects of Environmental Characteristics on the Structure of Hospital Clusters." *Administrative Science Quarterly.* Vol. 29, No. 3 (September 1980):489–510.

FERGUSON, TOM. "Medical Self-Care: Self Responsibility for Health." In Arthur C. Hastings et al., eds., *Health for the Whole Person: The Complete Guide to Holistic Medicine.* Boulder, Colo.: Westview Press, 1980:87–109.

FERGUSSON, D. M., L. J. HORWOOD, and F. T. SHANNON. "A Proportional Hazards Model of Family Breakdown." *Journal of Marriage and the Family.* Vol. 46, No. 3 (August 1984):539–49.

FINKELSTEIN, NEAL W., and RON HASKINS. "Kindergarten Children Prefer Same-Color Peers." *Child Development.* Vol. 54, No. 2 (April 1983):502–8.

FIORENTINE, ROBERT. "Men, Women, and the Premed Persistence Gap: A Normative Alternatives Approach." *American Journal of Sociology.* Vol. 92, No. 5 (March 1987):1118–39.

FIORENTINE, ROBERT, and STEPHEN COLE. "Why Fewer Women Become Physicians: Explaining the Premed Persistence Gap." *Sociological Forum.* Vol. 7, No. 3 (September 1992):469–96.

FIREBAUGH, GLENN. "Growth Effects of Foreign and Domestic Investment." *American Journal of Sociology.* Vol. 98, No. 1 (July 1992):105–30.

FIREBAUGH, GLENN, and KENNETH E. DAVIS. "Trends in Antiblack Prejudice, 1972–1984: Region and Cohort Effects." *American Journal of Sociology.* Vol. 94, No. 2 (September 1988):251–72.

FISCHER, CLAUDE S., ET AL. *Networks and Places: Social Relations in the Urban Setting.* New York: Free Press, 1977.

FISCHER, CLAUDE W. *The Urban Experience.* 2d ed. New York: Harcourt Brace Jovanovich, 1984.

FISHER, ELIZABETH. *Woman's Creation: Sexual Evolution and the Shaping of Society.* Garden City, N.Y.: Anchor/Doubleday, 1979.

FISHER, ROGER, and WILLIAM URY. "Getting to YES." In William M. Evan and Stephen Hilgartner, eds., *The Arms Race and Nuclear War.* Englewood Cliffs, N.J.: Prentice Hall, 1988:261–68.

FISKE, ALAN PAIGE. "The Cultural Relativity of Selfish Individualism: Anthropological Evidence that Humans Are Inherently Sociable." In Margaret S. Clark, ed., *Prosocial Behavior.* Newbury Park, Calif.: Sage, 176–214.

FITZPATRICK, JOSEPH P. *Puerto Rican Americans: The Meaning of Migration to the Mainland.* Englewood Cliffs, N.J.: Prentice Hall, 1971.

———. "Puerto Ricans." In *Harvard Encyclopedia of American Ethnic Groups.* Cambridge, Mass.: Harvard University Press, 1980:858–67.

FITZPATRICK, MARY ANNE. *Between Husbands and Wives: Communication in Marriage.* Newbury Park, Calif.: Sage, 1988.

FLAHERTY, MICHAEL G. "A Formal Approach to the Study of Amusement in Social Interaction." *Studies in Symbolic Interaction.* Vol. 5. New York: JAI Press, 1984:71–82.

———. "Two Conceptions of the Social Situation: Some Implications of Humor." *The Sociological Quarterly.* Vol. 31, No. 1 (Spring 1990).

FLORIDA, RICHARD, and MARTIN KENNEY. "Transplanted Organizations: The Transfer of Japanese Industrial Organization to the U.S." *American Sociological Review.* Vol. 56, No. 3 (June 1991):381–98.

FLYNN, PATRICIA. "The Disciplinary Emergence of Bioethics and Bioethics Committees: Moral Ordering and its Legitimation." *Sociological Focus.* Vol. 24, No. 2 (May 1991):145–56.

FORD, CLELLAN S., and FRANK A. BEACH. *Patterns of Sexual Behavior.* New York: Harper & Row, 1951.

FORREST, HUGH. "They Are Completely Inactive . . ." *The Gambier Journal.* Vol. 3, No. 4 (February 1984):10–11.

FOST, DAN. "American Indians in the 1990s." *American Demographics.* Vol. 13, No. 12 (December 1991):26–34.

FOWLER, FLOYD J., JR., and THOMAS W. MANGIONE. *Standardized Survey Interviewing: Minimizing Interviewer-Related Error.* Newbury Park, Calif.: Sage, 1989.

FRANK, ANDRÉ GUNDER. *On Capitalist Underdevelopment.* Bombay: Oxford University Press, 1975.

———. *Crisis: In the World Economy.* New York: Holmes & Meier, 1980.

———. *Reflections on the World Economic Crisis.* New York: Monthly Review Press, 1981.

FRANKLIN, JOHN HOPE. *From Slavery to Freedom: A History of Negro Americans.* 3d ed. New York: Vintage Books, 1967.

FRAZIER, E. FRANKLIN. *Black Bourgeoisie: The Rise of a New Middle Class.* New York: Free Press, 1965.

FREDRICKSON, GEORGE M. *White Supremacy: A Comparative Study in American and South African History.* New York: Oxford University Press, 1981.

FREE, MARVIN D. "Religious Affiliation, Religiosity, and Impulsive and Intentional Deviance." *Sociological Focus.* Vol. 25, No. 1 (February 1992):77–91.

FREEMAN, DEREK. *Margaret Mead and Samoa: The Making and Unmaking of an Anthropological Myth.* Cambridge, Mass.: Harvard University Press, 1983.

FRENCH, MARILYN. *Beyond Power: On Women, Men, and Morals.* New York: Summit Books, 1985.

FRIEDAN, BETTY. *The Fountain of Age.* New York: Simon & Schuster, 1993.

FRIEDRICH, CARL J., and ZBIGNIEW BRZEZINSKI. *Totalitarian Dictatorship and Autocracy.* 2d ed. Cambridge, Mass.: Harvard University Press, 1965.

FRIEDRICH, OTTO. "A Proud Capital's Distress." *Time.* Vol. 124, No. 6 (August 6, 1984):26–30, 33–35.

———. "United No More." *Time.* Vol. 129, No. 18 (May 4, 1987):28–37.

FRUM, DAVID, and FRANK WOLFE. "If You Gotta Get Sued, Get Sued in Utah." *Forbes.* Vol. 153, No. 2 (January 1994):70–73.

FUCHS, VICTOR R. "Sex Differences in Economic Well-Being." *Science.* Vol. 232 (April 25, 1986):459–64.

FUGITA, STEPHEN S., and DAVID J. O'BRIEN. "Structural Assimilation, Ethnic Group Membership, and Political Participation among Japanese Americans: A Research Note." *Social Forces.* Vol. 63, No. 4 (June 1985):986–95.

FUJIMOTO, ISAO. "The Failure of Democracy in a Time of Crisis." In Amy Tachiki et al., eds., *Roots: An Asian American Reader.* Los Angeles: UCLA Asian American Studies Center, 1971:207–14.

FULLER, REX, and RICHARD SCHOENBERGER. "The Gender Salary Gap: Do Academic Achievement, Intern Experience, and College Major Make a Difference?" *Social Science Quarterly.* Vol. 72, No. 4 (December 1991):715–26.

FURSTENBERG, FRANK F., JR., J. BROOKS-GUNN, and S. PHILIP MORGAN. *Adolescent Mothers in Later Life.* New York: Cambridge University Press, 1987.

FUSFELD, DANIEL R. *Economics: Principles of Political Economy.* Glenview, Ill.: Scott, Foresman, 1982.

GAGLIANI, GIORGIO. "How Many Working Classes?" *American Journal of Sociology.* Vol. 87, No. 2 (September 1981):259–85.

GALLUP, GEORGE, JR. *Religion in America.* Princeton, N.J.: Princeton Religion Research Center, 1982.

GALSTER, GEORGE. "Black Suburbanization: Has It Changed the Relative Location of Races?" *Urban Affairs Quarterly.* Vol. 26, No. 4 (June 1991):621–28.

GAMBLE, ANDREW, STEVE LUDLAM, and DAVID BAKER. "Britain's Ruling Class." *The Economist*. Vol. 326, No. 7795 (January 23, 1993):10.

GAMORAN, ADAM. "The Variable Effects of High-School Tracking." *American Sociological Review*. Vol. 57, No. 6 (December 1992):812–28.

GANS, HERBERT J. *People and Plans: Essays on Urban Problems and Solutions*. New York: Basic Books, 1968.

———. *Popular Culture and High Culture*. New York: Basic Books, 1974.

———. *Deciding What's News: A Study of CBS Evening News, NBC Nightly News, Newsweek and Time*. New York: Vintage Books, 1980.

———. *The Urban Villagers: Group and Class in the Life of Italian-Americans*. New York: Free Press, 1982; orig. 1962.

GARFINKEL, HAROLD. "Conditions of Successful Degradation Ceremonies." *American Journal of Sociology*. Vol. 61, No. 2 (March 1956):420–24.

———. *Studies in Ethnomethodology*. Cambridge: Polity Press, 1967.

GEERTZ, CLIFFORD. "Common Sense as a Cultural System." *The Antioch Review*. Vol. 33, No. 1 (Spring 1975):5–26.

GEIST, WILLIAM. *Toward a Safe and Sane Halloween and Other Tales of Suburbia*. New York: Times Books, 1985.

GELLES, RICHARD J., and CLAIRE PEDRICK CORNELL. *Intimate Violence in Families*. 2d ed. Newbury Park, Calif.: Sage, 1990.

GELMAN, DAVID. "Who's Taking Care of Our Parents?" *Newsweek* (May 6, 1985):61–64, 67–68.

———. "Born or Bred?" *Newsweek* (February 24, 1992):46–53.

GEORGE, SUSAN. *How the Other Half Dies: The Real Reasons for World Hunger*. Totowa, N.J.: Rowman & Allanheld, 1977.

GERSTEL, NAOMI. "Divorce and Stigma." *Social Problems*. Vol. 43, No. 2 (April 1987):172–86.

GERTH, H. H., and C. WRIGHT MILLS, EDS. *From Max Weber: Essays in Sociology*. New York: Oxford University Press, 1946.

GESCHWENDER, JAMES A. *Racial Stratification in America*. Dubuque, Iowa: Wm. C. Brown, 1978.

GIBBONS, DON C., and MARVIN D. KROHN. *Delinquent Behavior*. 4th ed. Englewood Cliffs, N.J.: Prentice Hall, 1986.

GIBBS, NANCY. "When Is It Rape?" *Time*. Vol. 137, No. 22 (June 3, 1991a):48–54.

———. "The Clamor on Campus." *Time*. Vol. 137, No. 22 (June 3, 1991b):54–55.

———. "How Much Should We Teach Our Children About Sex?" *Time*. Vol. 141, No. 21 (May 24, 1993):60–66.

GIDDENS, ANTHONY. *Sociology: A Brief but Critical Introduction*. New York: Harcourt Brace Jovanovich, 1982.

GIELE, JANET Z. "Gender and Sex Roles." In Neil J. Smelser, ed., *Handbook of Sociology*. Newbury Park, Calif.: Sage, 1988:291–323.

GILBERT, DENNIS, and JOSEPH A. KAHL. *The American Class Structure: A New Synthesis*. 4th ed. Belmont, Calif: Wadsworth, 1993.

GILBERT, NEIL. "Realities and Mythologies of Rape." *Society*. Vol. 29, No. 4 (May–June 1992):4–10.

GILLIGAN, CAROL. *In a Different Voice: Psychological Theory and Women's Development*. Cambridge, Mass.: Harvard University Press, 1982.

GILLIGAN, CAROL, ET AL. *Making Connections: The Relational Worlds of Adolescent Girls at Emma Willard School*. Cambridge, Mass.: Harvard University Press, 1990.

GIMENEZ, MARTHA E. "Silence in the Classroom: Some Thoughts about Teaching in the 1980s." *Teaching Sociology*. Vol. 17, No. 2 (April 1989):184–91.

GINSBURG, FAYE, and ANNA LOWENHAUPT TSING, EDS. *Uncertain Terms: Negotiating Gender in American Culture*. Boston: Beacon Press, 1990.

GINSBURG, PAUL B. "Market-Oriented Options in Medicare and Medicaid." In Jack B. Meyer, ed., *Market Reforms in Health Care: Current Issues, New Directions, Strategic Decisions*. Washington, D.C.: American Enterprise Institute for Public Policy Research, 1983:103–18.

GIOVANNINI, MAUREEN. "Female Anthropologist and Male Informant: Gender Conflict in a Sicilian Town." In John J. Macionis and Nijole V. Benokraitis, eds., *Seeing Ourselves: Classic, Contemporary, and Cross-Cultural Readings in Sociology*. 2d ed. Englewood Cliffs, N.J.: Prentice Hall, 1992:27–32.

GLAAB, CHARLES N. *The American City: A Documentary History*. Homewood, Ill.: Dorsey Press, 1963.

GLADUE, BRIAN A., RICHARD GREEN, and RONALD E. HELLMAN. "Neuroendocrine Response to Estrogen and Sexual Orientation." *Science*. Vol. 225, No. 4669 (September 28, 1984):1496–99.

GLASS, DAVID V., ED. *Social Mobility in Britain*. London: Routledge & Kegan Paul, 1954.

GLAZER, NATHAN, and DANIEL P. MOYNIHAN. *Beyond the Melting Pot*. 2d ed. Cambridge, Mass.: MIT Press, 1970.

GLENN, NORVAL D., and BETH ANN SHELTON. "Regional Differences in Divorce in the United States." *Journal of Marriage and the Family*. Vol. 47, No. 3 (August 1985):641–52.

GLOCK, CHARLES Y. "The Religious Revival in America." In Jane Zahn, ed., *Religion and the Face of America*. Berkeley: University of California Press, 1959:25–42.

———. "On the Study of Religious Commitment." *Religious Education*. Vol. 62, No. 4 (1962):98–110.

GLUCK, PETER R., and RICHARD J. MEISTER. *Cities in Transition*. New York: New Viewpoints, 1979.

GLUECK, SHELDON, and ELEANOR GLUECK. *Unraveling Juvenile Delinquency*. New York: Commonwealth Fund, 1950.

GOETTING, ANN. "Divorce Outcome Research." *Journal of Family Issues*. Vol. 2, No. 3 (September 1981):350–78.

———. Personal communication, 1989.

GOFFMAN, ERVING. *The Presentation of Self in Everyday Life*. Garden City, N.Y.: Anchor Books, 1959.

———. *Asylums: Essays on the Social Situation of Mental Patients and Other Inmates*. Garden City, N.Y.: Anchor Books, 1961.

———. *Stigma: Notes on the Management of Spoiled Identity*. Englewood Cliffs, N.J.: Prentice Hall, 1963.

———. *Interactional Ritual: Essays on Face to Face Behavior*. Garden City, N.Y.: Anchor Books, 1967.

———. *Gender Advertisements*. New York: Harper Colophon, 1979.

GOLD, ALLAN R. "Increasingly, Prison Term Is the Price for Polluters." *New York Times* (February 15, 1991):B6.

GOLDBERG, STEVEN. *The Inevitability of Patriarchy*. New York: William Morrow, 1974.

———. Personal communication, 1987.

GOLDEN, FREDERIC. "Here Come the Microkids." *Time*. Vol. 119, No. 18 (May 3, 1982):50–56.

GOLDFARB, JEFFREY C. *Beyond Glasnost: The Post-Totalitarian Mind*. Chicago: University of Chicago Press, 1989.

GOLDFARB, WILLIAM. "Groundwater: The Buried Life." In Herbert F. Bohrmann and Stephen R. Kellert, eds., *Ecology, Economics, and Ethics: The Broken Circle*. New Haven, Conn.: Yale University Press, 1991:123–35.

GOLDSBY, RICHARD A. *Race and Races*. 2d ed. New York: Macmillan, 1977.

GOLDSMITH, H. H. "Genetic Influences on Personality from Infancy." *Child Development*. Vol. 54, No. 2 (April 1983):331–35.

GOODE, WILLIAM J. "The Theoretical Importance of Love." *American Sociological Review*. Vol. 24, No. 1 (February 1959):38–47.

———. "Encroachment, Charlatanism, and the Emerging Profession: Psychology, Sociology and Medicine." *American Sociological Review*. Vol. 25, No. 6 (December 1960):902–14.

GOODGAME, DAN. "Ready to Operate." *Time*. Vol. 142, No. 12 (September 20, 1993):54–58.

GORDON, JAMES S. "The Paradigm of Holistic Medicine." In Arthur C. Hastings et al., eds., *Health for the Whole Person: The Complete Guide to Holistic Medicine*. Boulder, Colo.: Westview Press, 1980:3–27.

GORING, CHARLES BUCKMAN. *The English Convict: A Statistical Study*. Montclair, N.J.: Patterson Smith, 1972; orig. 1913.

GORMAN, CHRISTINE. "Mexico City's Menacing Air." *Time*. Vol. 137, No. 13 (April 1, 1991):61.

GORTMAKER, STEVEN L. "Poverty and Infant Mortality in the United States." *American Journal of Sociology*. Vol. 44, No. 2 (April 1979):280–97.

GOTTMANN, JEAN. *Megalopolis*. New York: Twentieth Century Fund, 1961.

GOUGH, KATHLEEN. "The Origin of the Family." *Journal of Marriage and the Family*. Vol. 33, No. 4 (November 1971):760–71.

GOULD, STEPHEN J. "Evolution as Fact and Theory." *Discover* (May 1981):35–37.

GOULDNER, ALVIN. *Enter Plato.* New York: Free Press, 1965.

———. "The Sociologist as Partisan: Sociology and the Welfare State." In Larry T. Reynolds and Janice M. Reynolds, eds., *The Sociology of Sociology.* New York: David McKay, 1970a:218–55.

———. *The Coming Crisis of Western Sociology.* New York: Avon Books, 1970b.

GRANOVETTER, MARK. "The Strength of Weak Ties." *American Journal of Sociology.* Vol. 78, No. 6 (May 1973):1360–80.

GRANT, DON SHERMAN II, and MICHAEL WALLACE. "Why Do Strikes Turn Violent?" *American Journal of Sociology.* Vol. 96, No. 5 (March 1991):1117–50.

GRANT, DONALD L. *The Anti-Lynching Movement.* San Francisco: R and E Research Associates, 1975.

GRANT, KAREN R. "The Inverse Care Law in the Context of Universal Free Health Insurance in Canada: Toward Meeting Health Needs Through Public Policy." *Sociological Focus.* Vol. 17, No. 2 (April 1984):137–55.

GRAY, PAUL. "Whose America?" *Time.* Vol. 137, No. 27 (July 8, 1991):12–17.

GREELEY, ANDREW M. *Ethnicity in the United States: A Preliminary Reconnaissance.* New York: Wiley, 1974.

———. *Religious Change in America.* Cambridge, Mass.: Harvard University Press, 1989.

GREEN, JOHN C. "Pat Robertson and the Latest Crusade: Resources and the 1988 Presidential Campaign." *Social Sciences Quarterly.* Vol. 74, No. 1 (March 1993):156–68.

GREENBERG, DAVID F. *The Construction of Homosexuality.* Chicago: University of Chicago Press, 1988.

GREENHOUSE, LINDA. "Justices Uphold Stiffer Sentences for Hate Crimes." *New York Times* (June 12, 1993):1, 8.

GREER, SCOTT. *Urban Renewal and American Cities.* Indianapolis, Ind.: Bobbs-Merrill, 1965.

GREGORY, PAUL R., and ROBERT C. STUART. *Comparative Economic Systems.* 2d ed. Boston: Houghton Mifflin, 1985.

GREGORY, SOPHFRONIA SCOTT. "The Knife in the Book Bag." *Time.* Vol. 141, No. 6 (February 8, 1993):37.

GRISWOLD, WENDY. "The Fabrication of Meaning: Literary Interpretation in the United States, Great Britain, and the West Indies." *American Journal of Sociology.* Vol. 92, No. 5 (March 1987):1077–117.

GROSS, JANE. "New Challenge of Youth: Growing Up in a Gay Home." *New York Times* (February 11, 1991):A1, B7.

GRUENBERG, BARRY. "The Happy Worker: An Analysis of Educational and Occupational Differences in Determinants of Job Satisfaction." *American Journal of Sociology.* Vol. 86, No. 2 (September 1980):247–71.

GUP, TED. "What Makes This School Work?" *Time.* Vol. 140, No. 25. (December 21, 1992):63–65.

GUPTE, PRANAY. *The Crowded Earth: People and the Politics of Population.* New York: Norton, 1984.

GUTFELD, ROSE. "Enforcing Recycling Laws Is a Dirty Job." *Wall Street Journal* (July 29, 1991b):B1.

———. "Eight of Ten Americans are Environmentalists." *Wall Street Journal* (August 2, 1991a):A1.

GUTMAN, HERBERT G. *The Black Family in Slavery and Freedom, 1750–1925.* New York: Pantheon Books, 1976.

GWARTNEY-GIBBS, PATRICIA A. "The Institutionalization of Premarital Cohabitation: Estimates from Marriage License Applications, 1970 and 1980." *Journal of Marriage and the Family.* Vol. 48, No. 2 (May 1986):423–34.

GWARTNEY-GIBBS, PATRICIA A., JEAN STOCKARD, and SUSANNE BOHMER. "Learning Courtship Aggression: The Influence of Parents, Peers, and Personal Experiences." *Family Relations.* Vol. 36, No. 3 (July 1987):276–82.

HAAS, LINDA. "Domestic Role Sharing in Sweden." *Journal of Marriage and the Family.* Vol. 43, No. 4 (November 1981):957–67.

HABERMAS, JÜRGEN. *Toward a Rational Society: Student Protest, Science, and Politics.* Jeremy J. Shapiro, trans. Boston: Beacon Press, 1970.

HACKER, HELEN MAYER. "Women as a Minority Group." *Social Forces.* Vol. 30 (October 1951):60–69.

———. "Women as a Minority Group: 20 Years Later." In Florence Denmark, ed., *Who Discriminates Against Women?* Beverly Hills, Calif.: Sage, 1974:124–34.

HACKEY, ROBERT B. "Competing Explanations of Voter Turnout Among American Blacks." *Social Science Quarterly.* Vol. 73, No. 1 (March 1992):71–89.

HADAWAY, C. KIRK, PENNY LONG MARLER, and MARK CHAVES. "What the Polls Don't Show: A Closer Look at U.S. Church Attendance." *American Sociological Review.* Vol. 58, No. 6 (December 1993):741–52.

HADDEN, JEFFREY K., and CHARLES E. SWAIN. *Prime Time Preachers: The Rising Power of Televangelism.* Reading, Mass.: Addison-Wesley, 1981.

HAGAN, JOHN, and PATRICIA PARKER. "White-Collar Crime and Punishment: The Class Structure and Legal Sanctioning of Securities Violations." *American Sociological Review.* Vol. 50, No. 3 (June 1985):302–16.

HAIG, ROBIN ANDREW. *The Anatomy of Humor: Biopsychosocial and Therapeutic Perspectives.* Springfield, Ill.: Charles C. Thomas, 1988.

HALBERSTAM, DAVID. *The Reckoning.* New York: Avon Books, 1986.

HALL, EDWARD T. *The Hidden Dimension.* Garden City, N.Y.: Doubleday, 1966.

HALL, JOHN R., and MARY JO NEITZ. *Culture: Sociological Perspectives.* Englewood Cliffs, N.J.: Prentice Hall, 1993.

HALLINAN, MAUREEN T., and RICHARD A. WILLIAMS. "Interracial Friendship Choices in Secondary Schools." *American Sociological Review.* Vol. 54, No. 1 (February 1989):67–78.

HAMBLIN, DORA JANE. *The First Cities.* New York: Time-Life Books, 1973.

HAMEL, RUTH. "Raging Against Aging." *American Demographics.* Vol. 12, No. 3 (March 1990):42–45.

HAMMOND, PHILIP E. "Introduction." In Philip E. Hammond, ed., *The Sacred in a Secular Age: Toward Revision in the Scientific Study of Religion.* Berkeley: University of California Press, 1985:1–6.

HAMRICK, MICHAEL H., DAVID J. ANSPAUGH, and GENE EZELL. *Health.* Columbus, Ohio: Merrill, 1986.

HANDLER, JOEL F., and YEHESKEL HASENFELD. *The Moral Construction of Poverty: Welfare Reform in America.* Newbury Park, Calif.: Sage, 1991.

HANDLIN, OSCAR. *Boston's Immigrants 1790–1865: A Study in Acculturation.* Cambridge, Mass.: Harvard University Press, 1941.

HANEY, CRAIG, CURTIS BANKS, and PHILIP ZIMBARDO. "Interpersonal Dynamics in a Simulated Prison." *International Journal of Criminology and Penology.* Vol. 1 (1973):69–97.

HARBERT, ANITA A., and LEON H. GINSBERG. *Human Services for Older Adults.* Columbia: University of South Carolina Press, 1991.

HAREVEN, TAMARA K. "The Life Course and Aging in Historical Perspective." In Tamara K. Hareven and Kathleen J. Adams, eds., *Aging and Life Course Transitions: An Interdisciplinary Perspective.* New York: Guilford Press, 1982:1–26.

HARLAN, WILLIAM H. "Social Status of the Aged in Three Indian Villages." In Bernice L. Neugarten, ed., *Middle Age and Aging: A Reader in Social Psychology.* Chicago: University of Chicago Press, 1968:469–75.

HARLOW, CAROLINE WOLF. *Female Victims of Violent Crime.* Bureau of Justice Statistics report. Washington, D.C.: U.S. Government Printing Office, 1991.

HARLOW, HARRY F., and MARGARET KUENNE HARLOW. "Social Deprivation in Monkeys." *Scientific American.* Vol. 207 (November 1962):137–46.

HARRIES, KEITH D. *Serious Violence: Patterns of Homicide and Assault in America.* Springfield, Ill.: Charles C. Thomas, 1990.

HARRINGTON, MICHAEL. *The New American Poverty.* New York: Penguin Books, 1984.

HARRIS, CHAUNCEY D., and EDWARD L. ULLMAN. "The Nature of Cities." *The Annals.* Vol. 242 (November 1945):7–17.

HARRIS, LOUIS, and ASSOCIATES. *The Myth and Reality of Aging in America.* Washington, D.C.: National Council on Aging, 1976.

HARRIS, MARVIN. *Cows, Pigs, Wars and Witches: The Riddles of Culture.* New York: Vintage Books, 1975.

———. "Why Men Dominate Women." *New York Times Magazine* (November 13, 1977):46, 115–23.

———. *Good to Eat: Riddle of Food and Culture.* New York: Simon & Schuster, 1985.

———. *Cultural Anthropology.* 2d ed. New York: Harper & Row, 1987.

HARRISON, PAUL. *Inside the Third World: The Anatomy of Poverty.* 2d ed. New York: Penguin Books, 1984.

HARTMANN, BETSY, and JAMES BOYCE. *Needless Hunger: Voices from a Bangladesh Village.* San Francisco: Institute for Food and Development Policy, 1982.

HAVIGHURST, ROBERT J., BERNICE L. NEUGARTEN, and SHELDON S. TOBIN. "Disengagement and Patterns of Aging." In Bernice L. Neugarten, ed., *Middle Age and Aging: A Reader in Social Psychology.* Chicago: University of Chicago Press, 1968:161–72.

HAVILAND, WILLIAM A. *Anthropology.* 4th ed. New York: Holt, Rinehart & Winston, 1985.

HAYNEMAN, STEPHEN P., and WILLIAM A. LOXLEY. "The Effect of Primary-School Quality on Academic Achievement Across Twenty-nine High- and Low-Income Countries." *American Journal of Sociology.* Vol. 88, No. 6 (May 1983):1162–94.

HEALTH INSURANCE ASSOCIATION OF AMERICA. *Sourcebook of Health Insurance Data.* Washington, D.C.: The Association, 1989.

———. *Source Book of Health Insurance Data.* Washington, D.C.: The Association, 1991.

HEILBRONER, ROBERT L. *The Making of Economic Society.* 7th ed. Englewood Cliffs, N.J.: Prentice Hall, 1985.

HELGESEN, SALLY. *The Female Advantage: Women's Ways of Leadership.* New York: Doubleday, 1990.

HELIN, DAVID W. "When Slogans Go Wrong." *American Demographics.* Vol. 14, No. 2 (February 1992):14.

HELMUTH, JOHN W. "World Hunger Amidst Plenty." *USA Today.* Vol. 117, No. 2526 (March 1989):48–50.

HENLEY, NANCY, MYKOL HAMILTON, and BARRIE THORNE. "Womanspeak and Manspeak: Sex Differences in Communication, Verbal and Nonverbal." In John J. Macionis and Nijole V. Benokraitis, eds., *Seeing Ourselves: Classic, Contemporary, and Cross-Cultural Readings in Sociology,* 2d ed. Englewood Cliffs, N.J.: Prentice Hall, 1992:10–15.

HERITAGE, JOHN. *Garfinkel and Ethnomethodology.* Cambridge: Polity Press, 1984.

HERMAN, DIANNE F. "The Rape Culture." In John J. Macionis and Nijole V. Benokraitis, eds., *Seeing Ourselves: Classic, Contemporary, and Cross-Cultural Readings in Sociology.* 2d ed. Englewood Cliffs, N.J.: Prentice Hall, 1992.

HERMAN, EDWARD S. *Corporate Control, Corporate Power: A Twentieth Century Fund Study.* New York: Cambridge University Press, 1981.

HERRNSTEIN, RICHARD J. *IQ and the Meritocracy.* Boston: Little, Brown, 1973.

HERRSTROM, STAFFAN. "Sweden: Pro-Choice on Child Care." *New Perspectives Quarterly.* Vol. 7, No. 1 (Winter 1990):27–28.

HERTY, ROBERT. "The Collective Representation of Death." In *Death and the Right Hand.* Aberdeen: Cohen and West, 1960:84–86.

HESS, STEPHEN. "Reporters who Cover Congress." *Society.* Vol. 28, No. 2 (January–February 1991):60–65.

HEWLETT, BARRY S. "Husband-Wife Reciprocity and the Father-Infant Relationship Among Aka Pygmies." In Barry S. Hewlett, ed., *Father-Child Relations: Cultural and Bio-Social Contexts.* New York: Aldine, 1992:153–76.

HEWLETT, SYLVIA ANN. "The Feminization of the Work Force." *New Perspectives Quarterly.* Vol. 7, No. 1 (Winter 1990):13–15.

HILTS, PHILIP J. "Demands to Fix U.S. Health Care Reach a Crescendo." *New York Times* (June 9, 1991):1, 5.

HIROSHI, MANNARI. *The Japanese Business Leaders.* Tokyo: University of Tokyo Press, 1974.

HIRSCHI, TRAVIS. *Causes of Delinquency.* Berkeley: University of California Press, 1969.

HOCHSCHILD, ARLIE, with ANNE MACHUNG. *The Second Shift: Working Parents and the Revolution at Home.* New York: Viking Books, 1989.

HODGE, ROBERT W., DONALD J. TREIMAN, and PETER H. ROSSI. "A Comparative Study of Occupational Prestige." In Reinhard Bendix and Seymour Martin Lipset, eds., *Class, Status, and Power: Social Stratification in Comparative Perspective.* 2d ed. New York: Free Press, 1966:309–21.

HOERR, JOHN. "The Payoff from Teamwork." *Business Week.* No. 3114 (July 10, 1989):56–62.

HOGAN, DENNIS P., and EVELYN M. KITAGAWA. "The Impact of Social Status and Neighborhood on the Fertility of Black Adolescents." *American Journal of Sociology.* Vol. 90, No. 4 (January 1985):825–55.

HOLLAND, DOROTHY C., and MARGARET A. EISENHART. *Educated in Romance: Women, Achievement, and College Culture.* Chicago: University of Chicago Press, 1990.

HOLM, JEAN. *The Study of Religions.* New York: Seabury Press, 1977.

HOLMES, LOWELL. "A Tale of Two Studies." *American Anthropologist.* Vol. 85, No. 4 (December 1983):929–35.

HONEYWELL, ROY J. *The Educational Work of Thomas Jefferson.* Cambridge, Mass.: Harvard University Press, 1931.

HOROWITZ, IRVING LOUIS, ET AL. "Realities and Fallacies of Homosexuality." *Society.* Vol. 30, No. 5 (July–August 1993):2–3.

HOSTETLER, JOHN A. *Amish Society.* 3d ed. Baltimore: The Johns Hopkins University Press, 1980.

HOUT, MICHAEL, and ANDREW M. GREELEY. "The Center Doesn't Hold: Church Attendance in the United States, 1940–1984." *American Sociological Review.* Vol. 52, No. 3 (June 1987):325–45.

HOWE, NEIL, and WILLIAM STRAUSS. "America's 13th Generation." *New York Times* (April 16, 1991).

HOWLETT, DEBBIE. "Cruzan's Struggle Left Imprint: 10,000 Others in Similar State." *USA Today* (December 27, 1990):3A.

HOYT, HOMER. *The Structure and Growth of Residential Neighborhoods in American Cities.* Washington, D.C.: Federal Housing Administration, 1939.

HSU, FRANCIS L. K. *The Challenge of the American Dream: The Chinese in the United States.* Belmont, Calif.: Wadsworth, 1971.

HUBER, JOAN, and GLENNA SPITZE. "Considering Divorce: An Expansion of Becker's Theory of Marital Instability." *American Journal of Sociology.* Vol. 86, No. 1 (July 1980):75–89.

HUET-COX, ROCIO. "Medical Education: New Wine in Old Wine Skins." In Victor W. Sidel and Ruth Sidel, eds., *Reforming Medicine: Lessons of the Last Quarter Century.* New York: Pantheon Books, 1984:129–49.

HULS, GLENNA. Personal communication, 1987.

HUMPHREY, CRAIG R., and FREDERICK R. BUTTEL. *Environment, Energy, and Society.* Belmont, Calif.: Wadsworth, 1982.

HUMPHREY, DEREK. *Final Exit: The Practicalities of Self-Deliverance and Assisted Suicide for the Dying.* Eugene, Oreg.: The Hemlock Society, 1991.

HUMPHRIES, HARRY LEROY. *The Structure and Politics of Intermediary Class Positions: An Empirical Examination of Recent Theories of Class.* Unpublished Ph.D. dissertation. Eugene: University of Oregon, 1984.

HUNNICUT, BENJAMIN K. "Are We All Working Too Hard? No Time for God or Family." *Wall Street Journal* (January 4, 1990).

HUNT, MORTON. *Sexual Behavior in the 1970s.* Chicago: Playboy Press, 1974.

HUNTER, FLOYD. *Community Power Structure.* Garden City, N.Y.: Doubleday, 1963; orig. 1953.

HUNTER, JAMES DAVISON. *American Evangelicalism: Conservative Religion and the Quandary of Modernity.* New Brunswick, N.J.: Rutgers University Press, 1983.

———. "Conservative Protestantism." In Philip E. Hammond, ed., *The Sacred in a Secular Age.* Berkeley: University of California Press, 1985:50–66.

———. *Evangelicalism: The Coming Generation.* Chicago: University of Chicago Press, 1987.

HURN, CHRISTOPHER. *The Limits and Possibilities of Schooling.* Needham Heights, Mass.: Allyn & Bacon, 1978.

HWANG, SEAN-SHONG, STEVEN H. MURDOCK, BANOO PARPIA, and RITA R. HAMM. "The Effects of Race and Socioeconomic Status on Residential Segregation in Texas, 1970–1980." *Social Forces.* Vol. 63, No. 3 (March 1985):732–47.

HYMAN, HERBERT H., and CHARLES R. WRIGHT. "Trends in Voluntary Association Memberships of American Adults: Replication Based on Secondary Analysis of National Sample Survey." *American Sociological Review.* Vol. 36, No. 2 (April 1971):191–206.

ILLICH, IVAN. *Medical Nemesis: The Expropriation of Health.* New York: Pantheon Books, 1976.

IRWIN, JOHN. *Prison in Turmoil*. Boston: Little, Brown, 1980.

ISAY, RICHARD A. *Being Homosexual: Gay Men and Their Development*. New York: Farrar, Straus, & Giroux, 1989.

JACOB, JOHN E. "An Overview of Black America in 1985." In James D. Williams, ed., *The State of Black America 1986*. New York: National Urban League, 1986:i–xi.

JACOBS, DAVID. "Inequality and Police Strength." *American Sociological Review*. Vol. 44, No. 6 (December 1979):913–25.

JACOBS, JANE. *The Death and Life of Great American Cities*. New York: Random House, 1961.

——. *The Economy of Cities*. New York: Vintage Books, 1970.

JACOBSON, JODI L. "Closing the Gender Gap in Development." In Lester R. Brown et al., eds., *State of the World 1993: A Worldwatch Institute Report on Progress Toward a Sustainable Society*. New York: Norton, 1993:61–79.

JACQUET, CONSTANT H., and ALICE M. JONES. *Yearbook of American and Canadian Churches 1991*. Nashville, Tenn.: Abingdon Press, 1991.

JAGAROWSKY, PAUL A., and MARY JO BANE. *Neighborhood Poverty: Basic Questions*. Discussion paper series H-90-3. John F. Kennedy School of Government. Cambridge, Mass.: Harvard University Press, 1990.

JAGGER, ALISON. "Political Philosophies of Women's Liberation." In Laurel Richardson and Verta Taylor, eds., *Feminist Frontiers: Rethinking Sex, Gender, and Society*. Reading, Mass.: Addison-Wesley, 1983.

JAMES, DAVID R. "City Limits on Racial Equality: The Effects of City-Suburb Boundaries on Public-School Desegregation, 1968–1976." *American Sociological Review*. Vol. 54, No. 6 (December 1989):963–85.

JANIS, IRVING. *Victims of Groupthink*. Boston: Houghton Mifflin, 1972.

——. *Crucial Decisions: Leadership in Policymaking and Crisis Management*. New York: Free Press, 1989.

JEFFERSON, THOMAS. Letter to James Madison, October 28, 1785. In Julian P. Boyd, ed., *The Papers of Thomas Jefferson*. Princeton, N.J.: Princeton University Press, 1953:681–83.

JENCKS, CHRISTOPHER. "Genes and Crime." *The New York Review* (February 12, 1987):33–41.

JENCKS, CHRISTOPHER, ET AL. *Inequality: A Reassessment of the Effect of Family and Schooling in America*. New York: Basic Books, 1972.

JENKINS, BRIAN M. "Terrorism Remains a Threat." Syndicated column, *The Columbus Dispatch* (January 14, 1990):D1.

JENKINS, HOLMAN, JR. "The 'Poverty' Lobby's Inflated Numbers." *Wall Street Journal* (December 14, 1992):A10.

JENKINS, J. CRAIG, and CHARLES PERROW. "Insurgency of the Powerless: Farm Worker Movements (1946–1972)." *American Sociological Review*. Vol. 42, No. 2 (April 1977):249–68.

JOHNSON, DIRK. "Census Finds Many Claiming New Identity: Indian." *New York Times* (March 5, 1991):A1, A16.

JOHNSON, NORRIS R. "Panic at 'The Who Concert Stampede': An Empirical Assessment." *Social Problems*. Vol. 34, No. 4 (October 1987):362–73.

JOHNSON, PAUL. "The Seven Deadly Sins of Terrorism." In Benjamin Netanyahu, ed., *International Terrorism*. New Brunswick, N.J.: Transaction Books, 1981:12–22.

JOHNSTON, R. J. "Residential Area Characteristics." In D. T. Herbert and R. J. Johnston, eds., *Social Areas in Cities. Vol. 1: Spatial Processes and Form*. New York: Wiley, 1976:193–235.

JOINT ECONOMIC COMMITTEE. *The Concentration of Wealth in the United States: Trends in the Distribution of Wealth Among American Families*. Washington, D.C.: United States Congress, 1986.

JONES, DAVID A. *History of Criminology: A Philosophical Perspective*. Westport, Conn.: Greenwood Press, 1986.

JONES, RUTH, and WARREN E. MILLER. "Financing Campaigns: Macro Level Innovation and Micro Level Response." *The Western Political Quarterly*. Vol. 38, No. 2 (June 1985):187–210.

JOSEPHY, ALVIN M., JR. *Now That the Buffalo's Gone: A Study of Today's American Indians*. New York: Alfred A. Knopf, 1982.

KAELBLE, HARTMUT. *Social Mobility in the 19th and 20th Centuries: Europe and America in Comparative Perspective*. New York: St. Martin's Press, 1986.

KAIN, EDWARD L. "A Note on the Integration of AIDS Into the Sociology of Human Sexuality." *Teaching Sociology*. Vol. 15, No. 4 (July 1987):320–23.

——. *The Myth of Family Decline: Understanding Families in a World of Rapid Social Change*. Lexington, Mass.: Lexington Books, 1990.

KAIN, EDWARD L., and SHANNON HART. "AIDS and the Family: A Content Analysis of Media Coverage." Presented to National Council on Family Relations, Atlanta, 1987.

KALISH, RICHARD A. "The New Ageism and the Failure Models: A Polemic." *The Gerontologist*. Vol. 19, No. 4 (August 1979):398–402.

——. *Late Adulthood: Perspectives on Human Development*. 2d ed. Monterey, Calif.: Brooks/Cole, 1982.

KAMINER, WENDY. "Volunteers: Who Knows What's in It for Them." *Ms.* (December 1984):93–94, 96, 126–28.

KANTER, ROSABETH MOSS. *Men and Women of the Corporation*. New York: Basic Books, 1977.

——. *The Change Masters: Innovation and Entrepreneurship in the American Corporation*. New York: Simon & Schuster, 1983.

——. "All That Is Entrepreneurial Is Not Gold." *Wall Street Journal* (July 22, 1985):18.

——. *When Giants Learn to Dance: Mastering the Challenges of Strategy, Management, and Careers in the 1990s*. New York: Simon & Schuster, 1989.

KANTER, ROSABETH MOSS, and BARRY A. STEIN. "The Gender Pioneers: Women in an Industrial Sales Force." In R. M. Kanter and B. A. Stein, eds., *Life in Organizations*. New York: Basic Books, 1979: 134–60.

KANTER, ROSABETH MOSS, and BARRY STEIN. *A Tale of "O": On Being Different in an Organization*. New York: Harper & Row, 1980.

KANTROWITZ, BARBARA. "Mothers on Their Own." *Newsweek* (December 23, 1985):66–67.

KAPFERER, JEAN-NÖEL. "How Rumors Are Born." *Society*. Vol. 29, No. 5 (July–August 1992):53–60.

KAPLAN, ERIC B., ET AL. "The Usefulness of Preoperative Laboratory Screening." *Journal of the American Medical Association*. Vol. 253, No. 24 (June 28, 1985):3576–81.

KAPTCHUK, TED. "The Holistic Logic of Chinese Medicine." In Shepard Bliss et al., eds., *The New Holistic Health Handbook*. Lexington, Mass.: The Steven Greene Press/Penguin Books, 1985:41.

KARP, DAVID A., and WILLIAM C. YOELS. "The College Classroom: Some Observations on the Meaning of Student Participation." *Sociology and Social Research*. Vol. 60, No. 4 (July 1976):421–39.

KAUFMAN, MARC. "Becoming 'Old Old.'" *Philadelphia Inquirer* (October 28, 1990):1-A, 10-A.

KAUFMAN, ROBERT L., and SEYMOUR SPILERMAN. "The Age Structures of Occupations and Jobs." *American Journal of Sociology*. Vol. 87, No. 4 (January 1982):827–51.

KAUFMAN, WALTER. *Religions in Four Dimensions: Existential, Aesthetic, Historical and Comparative*. New York: Reader's Digest Press, 1976.

KELLER, HELEN. *The Story of My Life*. New York: Doubleday, Page, 1903.

KELLER, SUZANNE. *The Urban Neighborhood*. New York: Random House, 1968.

KELLERT, STEPHEN R., and HERBERT F. BOHRMANN. "Closing the Circle: Weaving Strands Among Ecology, Economics, and Ethics." In Herbert F. Bohrmann and Stephen R. Kellert, eds., *Ecology, Economics, and Ethics: The Broken Circle*. New Haven, Conn.: Yale University Press, 1991:205–10.

KELLEY, ROBERT. *The Shaping of the American Past. Vol. 2: 1865 to the Present*. 3d ed. Englewood Cliffs, N.J.: Prentice Hall, 1982.

KEMP, ALICE ABEL, and SHELLEY COVERMAN. "Marginal Jobs or Marginal Workers: Identifying Sex Differences in Low-Skill Occupations." *Sociological Focus*. Vol. 22, No. 1 (February 1989):19–37.

KENISTON, KENNETH. "Working Mothers." In James M. Henslin, ed., *Marriage and Family in a Changing Society*. 2d ed. New York: Free Press, 1985:319–21.

KENNICKELL, ARTHUR, and JANICE SHACK-MARQUEZ. "Changes in Family Finances from 1983 to 1989: Evidence from the Survey of Consumer Finances." *Federal Reserve Bulletin*. (January 1992):1–18.

KENYON, KATHLEEN. *Digging Up Jericho*. London: Ernest Benn, 1957.

KERCKHOFF, ALAN C., RICHARD T. CAMPBELL, and IDEE WINFIELD-LAIRD. "Social Mobility in Great Britain and the United States." *American Journal of Sociology*. Vol. 91, No. 2 (September 1985):281–308.

KIDRON, MICHAEL, and RONALD SEGAL. *The New State of the World Atlas.* New York: Simon & Schuster, 1991.

KILBOURNE, BROCK K. "The Conway and Siegelman Claims Against Religious Cults: An Assessment of Their Data." *Journal for the Scientific Study of Religion.* Vol. 22, No. 4 (December 1983):380–85.

KILGORE, SALLY B. "The Organizational Context of Tracking in Schools." *American Sociological Review.* Vol. 56, No. 2 (April 1991):189–203.

KILLIAN, LEWIS M. "Organization, Rationality and Spontaneity in the Civil Rights Movement." *American Sociological Review.* Vol. 49, No. 6 (December 1984):770–83.

KING, KATHLEEN PIKER, and DENNIS E. CLAYSON. "The Differential Perceptions of Male and Female Deviants." *Sociological Focus.* Vol. 21, No. 2 (April 1988):153–64.

KING, MARTIN LUTHER, JR. "The Montgomery Bus Boycott." In Walt Anderson, ed., *The Age of Protest.* Pacific Palisades, Calif.: Goodyear, 1969:81–91.

KINKEAD, GWEN. *Chinatown: A Portrait of a Closed Society.* New York: HarperCollins, 1992.

KINSEY, ALFRED, ET AL. *Sexual Behavior in the Human Male.* Philadelphia: Saunders, 1948.

———. *Sexual Behavior in the Human Female.* Philadelphia: Saunders, 1953.

KIPP, RITA SMITH. "Have Women Always Been Unequal?" In Beth Reed, ed., *Towards a Feminist Transformation of the Academy: Proceedings of the Fifth Annual Women's Studies Conference.* Ann Arbor, Mich.: Great Lakes Colleges Association, 1980:12–18.

KIRK, MARSHALL, and PETER MADSEN. *After the Ball: How America Will Conquer its Fear and Hatred of Gays in the '90s.* New York: Doubleday, 1989.

KITANO, HARRY H. L. "Japanese." In *Harvard Encyclopedia of American Ethnic Groups.* Cambridge, Mass.: Harvard University Press, 1980: 561–71.

KITSON, GAY C., and HELEN J. RASCHKE. "Divorce Research: What We Know, What We Need to Know." *Journal of Divorce.* Vol. 4, No. 3 (Spring 1981):1–37.

KITTRIE, NICHOLAS N. *The Right to Be Different: Deviance and Enforced Therapy.* Baltimore: The Johns Hopkins University Press, 1971.

KLEIMAN, DENA. "Changing Way of Death: Some Agonizing Choices." *New York Times* (January 14, 1985):1, 11.

KLEIN, SUSAN SHURBERG. "Education." In Sarah M. Pritchard, ed., *The Women's Annual, Number 4, 1983–1984.* Boston: G. K. Hall, 1984:9–30.

KLUCKHOHN, CLYDE. "As An Anthropologist Views It." In Albert Deuth, ed., *Sex Habits of American Men.* New York: Prentice Hall, 1948.

KOCH, HOWARD. *The Panic Broadcast: Portrait of an Event.* Boston: Little, Brown, 1970.

KOHLBERG, LAWRENCE. *The Psychology of Moral Development: The Nature and Validity of Moral Stages.* New York: Harper & Row, 1981.

KOHLBERG, LAWRENCE, and CAROL GILLIGAN. "The Adolescent as Philosopher: The Discovery of Self in a Postconventional World." *Daedalus.* Vol. 100 (Fall 1971):1051–86.

KOHN, MELVIN L. *Class and Conformity: A Study in Values.* 2d ed. Homewood, Ill.: Dorsey Press, 1977.

KOHN, MELVIN L., and CARMI SCHOOLER. "Job Conditions and Personality: A Longitudinal Assessment of Their Reciprocal Effects." *American Journal of Sociology.* Vol. 87, No. 6 (May 1982):1257–83.

KOLATA, GINA. "When Grandmother Is the Mother, Until Birth." *New York Times* (August 5, 1991):1, 11.

KOMAROVSKY, MIRRA. *Blue Collar Marriage.* New York: Vintage Books, 1967.

———. "Cultural Contradictions and Sex Roles: The Masculine Case." *American Journal of Sociology.* Vol. 78, No. 4 (January 1973):873–84.

———. *Dilemmas of Masculinity: A Study of College Youth.* New York: Norton, 1976.

KOMINSKI, ROBERT, and ANDREA ADAMS. *School Enrollment—Social and Economic Characteristics of Students: October 1991.* Current Population Reports, Series P-20, No. 469. Washington, D.C.: U.S. Government Printing Office, 1993.

KORNHAUSER, WILLIAM. *The Politics of Mass Society.* New York: Free Press, 1959.

KOWALEWSKI, DAVID, and KAREN L. PORTER. "Ecoprotest: Alienation, Deprivation, or Resources." *Social Sciences Quarterly.* Vol 73, No. 3 (September 1992):523–34.

KOZOL, JONATHAN, *Prisoners of Silence: Breaking the Bonds of Adult Illiteracy in the United States.* New York: Continuum, 1980.

———. "A Nation's Wealth." *Publisher's Weekly* (May 24, 1985a):28–30.

———. *Illiterate America.* Garden City, N.Y.: Doubleday, 1985b.

———. *Rachel and Her Children: Homeless Families in America.* New York: Crown Publishers, 1988.

———. *Savage Inequalities: Children in America's Schools.* New York: Crown, 1991.

KRAFFT, SUSAN. "¿Quién es Numero Uno?" *American Demographics.* Vol. 15, No. 7 (July 1993):16–17.

KRAMARAE, CHERIS. *Women and Men Speaking.* Rowley, Mass.: Newbury House, 1981.

KRIESI, HANSPETER. "New Social Movements and the New Class in the Netherlands." *American Journal of Sociology.* Vol. 94, No. 5 (March 1989):1078–1116.

KÜBLER-ROSS, ELISABETH. *On Death and Dying.* New York: Macmillan, 1969.

KUHN, THOMAS. *The Structure of Scientific Revolutions.* 2d ed. Chicago: University of Chicago Press, 1970.

KUZNETS, SIMON. "Economic Growth and Income Inequality." *The American Economic Review.* Vol. XLV, No. 1 (March 1955):1–28.

———. *Modern Economic Growth: Rate, Structure, and Spread.* New Haven, Conn.: Yale University Press, 1966.

LACAYO, RICHARD. "Blood in the Stands." *Time.* Vol. 125, No. 23 (June 10, 1985):38–39, 41.

———. "Law and Disorder." *Time.* Vol. 137, No. 13 (April 1, 1991):18–21.

LADD, JOHN. "The Definition of Death and the Right to Die." In John Ladd, ed., *Ethical Issues Relating to Life and Death.* New York: Oxford University Press, 1979:118–45.

LADNER, JOYCE A. "Teenage Pregnancy: The Implications for Black Americans." In James D. Williams, ed., *The State of Black America 1986.* New York: National Urban League, 1986:65–84.

LAI, H. M. "Chinese." In *Harvard Encyclopedia of American Ethnic Groups.* Cambridge, Mass.: Harvard University Press, 1980:217–33.

LAMAR, JACOB V., JR. "Redefining the American Dilemma." *Time.* Vol. 126, No. 19 (November 11, 1985):33, 36.

LAMBERG-KARLOVSKY, C. C., and MARTHA LAMBERG-KARLOVSKY. "An Early City in Iran." In *Cities: Their Origin, Growth, and Human Impact.* San Francisco: Freeman, 1973:28–37.

LANDERS, ANN. Syndicated column: *Dallas Morning News* (July 8, 1984):4F.

LANDERS, RENE M. "Gender, Race, and the State Courts." *Radcliffe Quarterly.* Vol. 76, No. 4 (December 1990):6–9.

LANE, DAVID. "Social Stratification and Class." In Erik P. Hoffman and Robbin F. Laird, eds., *The Soviet Polity in the Modern Era.* New York: Aldine, 1984:563–605.

LANG, KURT, and GLADYS ENGEL LANG. *Collective Dynamics.* New York: Thomas Y. Crowell, 1961.

LAPPÉ, FRANCES MOORE, and JOSEPH COLLINS. *World Hunger: Twelve Myths.* New York: Grove Press/Food First Books, 1986.

LAPPÉ, FRANCES MOORE, JOSEPH COLLINS, and DAVID KINLEY. *Aid as Obstacle: Twenty Questions about Our Foreign Policy and the Hungry.* San Francisco: Institute for Food and Development Policy, 1981.

LARMER, BROOK. "Dead End Kids." *Newsweek* (May 25, 1992):38–40.

LASLETT, PETER. *The World We Have Lost: England Before the Industrial Age.* 3d ed. New York: Charles Scribner's Sons, 1984.

LEACOCK, ELEANOR. "Women's Status in Egalitarian Societies: Implications for Social Evolution." *Current Anthropology.* Vol. 19, No. 2 (June 1978):247–75.

LEAVITT, JUDITH WALZER. "Women and Health in America: An Overview." In Judith Walzer Leavitt, ed., *Women and Health in America.* Madison: University of Wisconsin Press, 1984:3–7.

LE BON, GUSTAVE. *The Crowd: A Study of the Popular Mind.* New York: Viking Press, 1960; orig. 1895.

LEE, BARRETT A., R. S. OROPESA, BARBARA J. METCH, and AVERY M. GUEST. "Testing the Decline of Community Thesis: Neighborhood Organization in Seattle, 1929 and 1979." *American Journal of Sociology*. Vol. 89, No. 5 (March 1984):1161–88.

LEERHSEN, CHARLES. "Unite and Conquer." *Newsweek* (February 5, 1990):50–55.

LEIFER, ERIC M. "Inequality Among Equals: Embedding Market and Authority in League Sports." *American Journal of Sociology*. Vol. 96, No. 3 (November 1990):655–83.

LEMERT, EDWIN M. *Social Pathology*. New York: McGraw-Hill, 1951.

———. *Human Deviance, Social Problems, and Social Control*. 2d ed. Englewood Cliffs, N.J.: Prentice Hall, 1972.

LENGERMANN, PATRICIA MADOO, and RUTH A. WALLACE. *Gender in America: Social Control and Social Change*. Englewood Cliffs, N.J.: Prentice Hall, 1985.

LENSKI, GERHARD. *Power and Privilege: A Theory of Social Stratification*. New York: McGraw-Hill, 1966.

LENSKI, GERHARD, and JEAN LENSKI. *Human Societies: An Introduction to Macrosociology*. 4th ed. New York: McGraw-Hill, 1982.

LENSKI, GERHARD, JEAN LENSKI, and PATRICK NOLAN. *Human Societies: An Introduction to Macrosociology*. 6th ed. New York: McGraw-Hill, 1991.

LEONARD, EILEEN B. *Women, Crime, and Society: A Critique of Theoretical Criminology*. New York: Longman, 1982.

LESLIE, GERALD R., and SHEILA K. KORMAN. *The Family in Social Context*. 7th ed. New York: Oxford University Press, 1989.

LESTER, DAVID. *The Death Penalty: Issues and Answers*. Springfield, Ill.: Charles C. Thomas, 1987.

LEVER, JANET. "Sex Differences in the Complexity of Children's Play and Games." *American Sociological Review*. Vol. 43, No. 4 (August 1978):471–83.

LEVINE, MICHAEL P. *Student Eating Disorders: Anorexia Nervosa and Bulimia*. Washington, D.C.: National Educational Association, 1987.

LEVINE, ROBERT V. "Is Love a Luxury?" *American Demographics*. Vol. 15, No. 2 (February 1993):27–28.

LEVINSON, DANIEL J., with CHARLOTTE N. DARROW, EDWARD B. KLEIN, MARIA H. LEVINSON, and BRAXTON MCKEE. *The Seasons of a Man's Life*. New York: Alfred A. Knopf, 1978.

LEVITAN, SARA, and ISAAC SHAPIRO. *Working but Poor: America's Contradiction*. Baltimore: The Johns Hopkins University Press, 1987.

LEVY, FRANK. *Dollars and Dreams: The Changing American Income Distribution*. New York: Russell Sage Foundation, 1987.

LEWIS, FLORA. "The Roots of Revolution." *New York Times Magazine* (November 11, 1984):70–71, 74, 77–78, 82, 84, 86.

LEWIS, OSCAR. *The Children of Sanchez*. New York: Random House, 1961.

LI, JIANG HONG, and ROGER A. WOJTKIEWICZ. "A New Look at the Effects of Family Structure on Status Attainment." *Social Science Quarterly*. Vol. 73, No. 3 (September 1992):581–95.

LIAZOS, ALEXANDER. "The Poverty of the Sociology of Deviance: Nuts, Sluts and Preverts." *Social Problems*. Vol. 20, No. 1 (Summer 1972):103–20.

LICHTER, DANIEL R. "Race, Employment Hardship, and Inequality in the American Nonmetropolitan South." *American Sociological Review*. Vol. 54, No. 3 (June 1989):436–46.

LIEBERSON, STANLEY. *A Piece of the Pie: Black and White Immigrants Since 1880*. Berkeley: University of California Press, 1980.

LIEBOW, ELLIOT. *Tally's Corner*. Boston: Little, Brown, 1967.

LIN, NAN, WALTER M. ENSEL, and JOHN C. VAUGHN. "Social Resources and Strength of Ties: Structural Factors in Occupational Status Attainment." *American Sociological Review*. Vol. 46, No. 4 (August 1981):393–405.

LIN, NAN, and WEN XIE. "Occupational Prestige in Urban China." *American Journal of Sociology*. Vol. 93, No. 4 (January 1988):793–832.

LINDEN, EUGENE. "Can Animals Think?" *Time*. Vol. 141, No. 12 (March 22, 1993):54–61.

LING, PYAU. "Causes of Chinese Emigration." In Amy Tachiki et al., eds., *Roots: An Asian American Reader*. Los Angeles: UCLA Asian American Studies Center, 1971:134–38.

LINK, BRUCE G., BRUCE P. DOHRENWEND, and ANDREW E. SKODOL. "Socio-Economic Status and Schizophrenia: Noisome Occupational Characteristics As a Risk Factor." *American Sociological Review*. Vol. 51, No. 2 (April 1986):242–58.

LINTON, RALPH. "One Hundred Percent American." *The American Mercury*. Vol. 40, No. 160 (April 1937):427–29.

———. *The Study of Man*. New York: D. Appleton-Century, 1937.

LIPSET, SEYMOUR MARTIN. *Political Man: The Social Bases of Politics*. Garden City, N.Y.: Anchor/Doubleday, 1963.

LIPSET, SEYMOUR MARTIN, and REINHARD BENDIX. *Social Mobility in Industrial Society*. Berkeley: University of California Press, 1967.

LISKA, ALLEN E. *Perspectives on Deviance*. 3d ed. Englewood Cliffs, N.J.: Prentice Hall, 1991.

LISKA, ALLEN E., and MARK TAUSIG. "Theoretical Interpretations of Social Class and Racial Differentials in Legal Decision Making for Juveniles." *Sociological Quarterly*. Vol. 20, No. 2 (Spring 1979):197–207.

LISKA, ALLEN E., and BARBARA D. WARNER. "Functions of Crime: A Paradoxical Process." *American Journal of Sociology*. Vol. 96, No. 6 (May 1991):1441–63.

LITTMAN, MARK S. "Poverty in the 1980s: Are the Poor Getting Poorer?" *Monthly Labor Review*. Vol. 112, No. 6 (June 1989):13–18.

LO, CLARENCE Y. H. "Countermovements and Conservative Movements in the Contemporary U.S." *Annual Review of Sociology*. Vol. 8. Palo Alto, Calif.: Annual Reviews, 1982:107–34.

LOFLAND, LYN. *A World of Strangers*. New York: Basic Books, 1973.

LOGAN, JOHN R., and MARK SCHNEIDER. "Racial Segregation and Racial Change in American Suburbs, 1970–1980." *American Journal of Sociology*. Vol. 89, No. 4 (January 1984):874–88.

LOHR, STEVE. "British Health Service Faces a Crisis in Funds and Delays." *New York Times* (August 7, 1988):1, 12.

LONDON, BRUCE. "Structural Determinants of Third World Urban Change: An Ecological and Political Economic Analysis." *American Sociological Review*. Vol. 52, No. 1 (February 1987):28–43.

LONG, EDWARD V. *The Intruders: The Invasion of Privacy by Government and Industry*. New York: Praeger, 1967.

LORENZ, KONRAD. *On Aggression*. New York: Harcourt, Brace & World, 1966.

LOY, PAMELA HEWITT, and LEA P. STEWART. "The Extent and Effects of Sexual Harassment of Working Women." *Sociological Focus*. Vol. 17, No. 1 (January 1984):31–43.

LUBENOW, GERALD C. "A Troubling Family Affair." *Newsweek* (May 14, 1984):34.

LUND, DALE A. "Conclusions about Bereavement in Later Life and Implications for Interventions and Future Research." In Dale A. Lund, ed., *Older Bereaved Spouses: Research With Practical Applications*. Taylor-Francis-Hemisphere, 1989:217–31.

LUND, DALE A., MICHAEL S. CASERTA, and MARGARET F. DIMOND. "Gender Differences Through Two Years of Bereavement Among the Elderly." *The Gerontologist*. Vol. 26, No. 3 (1986):314–20.

LUTZ, CATHERINE A. *Unnatural Emotions: Everyday Sentiments on a Micronesia Atoll and Their Challenge to Western Theory*. Chicago: University of Chicago Press, 1988.

LUTZ, CATHERINE, and GEOFFREY M. WHITE. "The Anthropology of Emotions." In Bernard J. Siegel, Alan R. Beals, and Stephen A. Tyler, eds., *Annual Review of Anthropology*, Vol. 15 (1986):405–36. Palo Alto, Calif.: Annual Reviews.

LYND, ROBERT S. *Knowledge for What? The Place of Social Science in American Culture*. Princeton, N.J.: Princeton University Press, 1967.

LYND, ROBERT S., and HELEN MERRELL LYND. *Middletown in Transition*. New York: Harcourt, Brace & World, 1937.

MA, LI-CHEN. Personal communication, 1987.

MABRY, MARCUS. "New Hope for Old Unions?" *Newsweek* (February 24, 1992):39.

MCADAM, DOUG. *Political Process and the Development of Black Insurgency, 1930–1970*. Chicago: University of Chicago Press, 1982.

———. "Tactical Innovation and the Pace of Insurgency." *American Sociological Review*. Vol. 48, No. 6 (December 1983):735–54.

———. *Freedom Summer*. New York: Oxford University Press, 1988.

———. "The Biographical Consequences of Activism." *American Sociological Review.* Vol. 54, No. 5 (October 1989):744–60.

———. "Gender as a Mediator of the Activist Experience: The Case of Freedom Summer." *American Journal of Sociology.* Vol. 97, No. 5 (March 1992):1211–40.

McAdam, Doug, John D. McCarthy, and Mayer N. Zald. "Social Movements." In Neil J. Smelser, ed., *Handbook of Sociology.* Newbury Park, Calif.: Sage, 1988:695–737.

McBroom, William H., and Fred W. Reed. "Recent Trends in Conservatism: Evidence of Non-Unitary Patterns." *Sociological Focus.* Vol. 23, No. 4 (October 1990):355–65.

McCarthy, John D., and Mayer N. Zald. "Resource Mobilization and Social Movements: A Partial Theory." *American Journal of Sociology.* Vol. 82, No. 6 (May 1977):1212–41.

Maccoby, Eleanor Emmons, and Carol Nagy Jacklin. *The Psychology of Sex Differences.* Palo Alto, Calif.: Stanford University Press, 1974.

McColm, R. Bruce, James Finn, Douglas W. Payne, Joseph E. Ryan, Leonard R. Sussman, and George Zarycky. *Freedom in the World: Political Rights & Civil Liberties, 1990–1991.* New York: Freedom House, 1991.

Mace, David, and Vera Mace. *Marriage East and West.* Garden City, N.Y.: Doubleday (Dolphin), 1960.

McGrath, Ellie. "Preparing to Wield the Rod." *Time.* Vol. 121, No. 4 (January 23, 1984):57.

McGuire, Meredith B. *Religion: The Social Context.* 2d ed. Belmont, Calif.: Wadsworth, 1987.

McHenry, Susan. "Rosabeth Moss Kanter." In *Ms.* Vol. 13 (January 1985):62–63, 107–8.

Macionis, John J. "Intimacy: Structure and Process in Interpersonal Relationships." *Alternative Lifestyles.* Vol. 1, No. 1 (February 1978):113–30.

———. "The Search for Community in Modern Society: An Interpretation." *Qualitative Sociology.* Vol. 1, No. 2 (September 1978):130–43.

———. "A Sociological Analysis of Humor." Presentation to the Texas Junior College Teachers Association, Houston, 1987.

———. "Making Society (and, Increasingly, the World) Visible." In Earl Babbie, ed., *The Spirit of Sociology.* Belmont, Calif.: Wadsworth, 1993:221–24.

MacKay, Donald G. "Prescriptive Grammar and the Pronoun Problem." In Barrie Thorne, Cheris Kramarae, and Nancy Henley, eds., *Language, Gender and Society.* Rowley, Mass.: Newbury House, 1983:38–53.

MacKinnon, Catharine A. *Feminism Unmodified: Discourses on Life and Law.* Cambridge, Mass.: Harvard University Press, 1987.

Macklin, Eleanor D. "Nonmarital Heterosexual Cohabitation: An Overview." In Eleanor D. Macklin and Roger H. Rubin, eds., *Contemporary Families and Alternative Lifestyles: Handbook on Research and Theory.* Beverly Hills, Calif.: Sage, 1983:49–74.

McKusick, Leon, et al. "Reported Changes in the Sexual Behavior of Men at Risk for AIDS, San Francisco, 1982–84—The AIDS Behavioral Research Project." *Public Health Reports.* Vol. 100, No. 6 (November–December 1985):622–29.

McLanahan, Sara. "Family Structure and the Reproduction of Poverty." *American Journal of Sociology.* Vol. 90, No. 4 (January 1985):873–901.

McLeod, Jane D., and Michael J. Shanahan. "Poverty, Parenting, and Children's Mental Health." *American Sociological Review.* Vol. 58, No. 3 (June 1993):351–66.

McNeil, Donald G., Jr. "Should Women Be Sent Into Combat?" *New York Times* (July 21, 1991):E3.

McPhail, Clark. *The Myth of the Maddening Crowd.* New York: Aldine, 1991.

McPhail, Clark, and Ronald T. Wohlstein. "Individual and Collective Behaviors Within Gatherings, Demonstrations, and Riots." *Annual Review of Sociology.* Vol. 9. Palo Alto, Calif.: Annual Reviews, 1983:579–600.

McRae, Susan. *Cross-Class Families: A Study of Wives' Occupational Superiority.* New York: Oxford University Press, 1986.

McRoberts, Hugh A., and Kevin Selbee. "Trends in Occupational Mobility in Canada and the United States: A Comparison." *American Sociological Review.* Vol. 46, No. 4 (August 1981):406–21.

Madsen, Axel. *Private Power: Multinational Corporations for the Survival of Our Planet.* New York: William Morrow, 1980.

Mahler, Halfdan. "People." *Scientific American.* Vol. 243, No. 3 (September 1980):67–77.

Majka, Linda C. "Sexual Harassment in the Church." *Society.* Vol. 28. No. 4 (May–June, 1991):14–21.

Malthus, Thomas Robert. *First Essay on Population 1798.* London: Macmillan, 1926; orig. 1798.

Mangan, J. A., and Roberta J. Park. *From Fair Sex to Feminism: Sport and the Socialization of Women.* London: Frank Cass, 1987.

Marcuse, Herbert. *One-Dimensional Man.* Boston: Beacon Press, 1964.

Mare, Robert D. "Five Decades of Educational Assortative Mating." *American Sociological Review.* Vol. 56, No. 1 (February 1991):15–32.

Margolick, David. "Rape in Marriage Is No Longer Within the Law." *New York Times* (December 13, 1984):6E.

Marín, Gerardo, and Barbara Vanoss Marín. *Research With Hispanic Populations.* Newbury Park, Calif.: Sage, 1991.

Markoff, John. "Remember Big Brother? Now He's a Company Man." *New York Times* (March 31, 1991):7.

Markson, Elizabeth W. "Moral Dilemmas." *Society.* Vol. 29, No. 5 (July–August 1992):4–6.

Marriott, Michael. "Fathers Find that Child Support Means Owing More than Money." *New York Times* (July 20, 1992):A1, A13.

Marsden, Peter. "Core Discussion Networks of Americans." *American Sociological Review.* Vol. 52, No. 1 (February 1987):122–31.

Marshall, Susan E. "Ladies Against Women: Mobilization Dilemmas of Antifeminist Movements." *Social Problems.* Vol. 32, No. 4 (April 1985):348–62.

Martin, John M., and Anne T. Romano. *Multinational Crime: Terrorism, Espionage, Drug and Arms Trafficking.* Newbury Park, Calif.: Sage, 1992.

Martin, Richard C. *Islam: A Cultural Perspective.* Englewood Cliffs, N.J.: Prentice Hall, 1982.

Martin, William. "The Birth of a Media Myth." *The Atlantic.* Vol. 247, No. 6 (June 1981):7, 10, 11, 16.

Marullo, Sam. "The Functions and Dysfunctions of Preparations for Fighting Nuclear War." *Sociological Focus.* Vol. 20, No. 2 (April 1987):135–53.

Marx, Gary T., and James L. Wood. "Strands of Theory and Research in Collective Behavior." In Alex Inkeles et al., eds., *Annual Review of Sociology.* Vol. 1. Palo Alto, Calif.: Annual Reviews, 1975:363–428.

Marx, Karl. Excerpt from "A Contribution to the Critique of Political Economy." In Karl Marx and Friedrich Engels, *Marx and Engels: Basic Writings on Politics and Philosophy.* Lewis S. Feurer, ed. Garden City, N.Y.: Anchor Books, 1959:42–46.

———. *Karl Marx: Early Writings.* T. B. Bottomore, ed. New York: McGraw-Hill, 1964a.

———. *Karl Marx: Selected Writings in Sociology and Social Philosophy.* T. B. Bottomore, trans. New York: McGraw-Hill, 1964.

———. *Capital.* Friedrich Engels, ed. New York: International Publishers, 1967; orig. 1867.

———. "Theses on Feuer." In Robert C. Tucker, ed., *The Marx-Engels Reader.* New York: Norton, 1972:107–9; orig. 1845.

Marx, Karl, and Friedrich Engels. "Manifesto of the Communist Party." In Robert C. Tucker, ed., *The Marx-Engels Reader.* New York: Norton, 1972:331–62; orig. 1848.

———. *The Marx-Engels Reader.* Robert C. Tucker, ed. New York: Norton, 1977.

Mashek, John W., and Patricia Avery. "Women Politicians Take Off the White Gloves." *U.S. News and World Report* (August 15, 1983):41–42.

Massey, Douglas S., and Nancy A. Denton. "Hypersegregation in U.S. Metropolitan Areas: Black and Hispanic Segregation Along Five Dimensions." *Demography.* Vol. 26, No. 3 (August 1989):373–91.

Masters, William H., Virginia E. Johnson, and Robert C. Kolodny. *Human Sexuality.* 3d ed. Glenview, Ill.: Scott, Foresman/Little, Brown, 1988.

Matthews, Mervyn. "Long Term Trends in Soviet Education." In J. J. Tomiak, ed., *Soviet Education in the 1980s.* London: Croom Helm, 1983:1–23.

MATTHIESSEN, PETER. *In the Spirit of Crazy Horse.* New York: Viking Press, 1983.

———. *Indian Country.* New York: Viking Press, 1984.

MAURO, TONY. "Cruzan's Struggle Left Imprint: Private Case Triggered Public Debate." *USA Today* (December 27, 1990):3A.

MAUSS, ARMAND L. *Social Problems of Social Movements.* Philadelphia: Lippincott, 1975.

MAY, ELAINE TYLER. "Women in the Wild Blue Yonder." *New York Times* (August 7, 1991):21.

MAYO, KATHERINE. *Mother India.* New York: Harcourt, Brace, 1927.

MEAD, GEORGE HERBERT. *Mind, Self, and Society.* Charles W. Morris, ed. Chicago: University of Chicago Press, 1962; orig. 1934.

MEAD, MARGARET. *Coming of Age in Samoa.* New York: Dell, 1961; orig. 1928.

———. *Sex and Temperament in Three Primitive Societies.* New York: William Morrow, 1963; orig. 1935.

MEADOWS, DONELLA H., DENNIS L. MEADOWS, JORGAN RANDERS, and WILLIAM W. BEHRENS III. *The Limits to Growth: A Report on the Club of Rome's Project on the Predicament of Mankind.* New York: Universe, 1972.

MECHANIC, DAVID. *Medical Sociology.* 2d ed. New York: Free Press, 1978.

MELTZER, BERNARD N. "Mead's Social Psychology." In Jerome G. Manis and Bernard N. Meltzer, eds., *Symbolic Interaction: A Reader in Social Psychology.* 3d ed. Needham Heights, Mass.: Allyn & Bacon, 1978.

MELUCCI, ALBERTO. "The New Social Movements: A Theoretical Approach." *Social Science Information.* Vol. 19, No. 2 (May 1980):199–226.

———. *Nomads of the Present: Social Movements and Individual Needs in Contemporary Society.* Philadelphia: Temple University Press, 1989.

MELVILLE, KEITH. *Marriage and Family Today.* 3d ed. New York: Random House, 1983.

MERTON, ROBERT K. "Social Structure and Anomie." *American Sociological Review.* Vol. 3, No. 6 (October 1938):672–82.

———. *Social Theory and Social Structure.* New York: Free Press, 1968.

———. "Discrimination and the American Creed." In *Sociological Ambivalence and Other Essays.* New York: Free Press, 1976:189–216.

MICHELS, ROBERT. *Political Parties.* Glencoe, Ill.: Free Press, 1949; orig. 1911.

MILBRATH, LESTER W. *Envisioning a Sustainable Society: Learning Our Way Out.* Albany: State University of New York Press, 1989.

MILGRAM, STANLEY. "Behavioral Study of Obedience." *Journal of Abnormal and Social Psychology.* Vol. 67, No. 4 (1963):371–78.

———. "Group Pressure and Action Against a Person." *Journal of Abnormal and Social Psychology.* Vol. 69, No. 2 (August 1964):137–43.

———. "Some Conditions of Obedience and Disobedience to Authority." *Human Relations.* Vol. 18 (February 1965):57–76.

MILIBAND, RALPH. *The State in Capitalist Society.* London: Weidenfield and Nicolson, 1969.

MILLER, ARTHUR G. *The Obedience Experiments: A Case of Controversy in Social Science.* New York: Praeger, 1986.

MILLER, DAVID L. *Introduction to Collective Behavior.* Belmont, Calif.: Wadsworth, 1985.

MILLER, FREDERICK D. "The End of SDS and the Emergence of Weatherman: Demise Through Success." In Jo Freeman, ed., *Social Movements of the Sixties and Seventies.* New York: Longman, 1983:279–97.

MILLER, G. TYLER, JR. *Living in the Environment: An Introduction to Environmental Science.* Belmont, Calif.: Wadsworth, 1992.

MILLER, MARK. "Under Cover, In the Closet." *Newsweek* (January 14, 1991):25.

MILLER, MICHAEL. "Lawmakers Begin to Heed Calls to Protect Privacy." *Wall Street Journal* (April 11, 1991):A16.

MILLER, WALTER B. "Lower Class Culture as a Generating Milieu of Gang Delinquency." In Marvin E. Wolfgang, Leonard Savitz, and Norman Johnston, eds., *The Sociology of Crime and Delinquency.* 2d ed. New York: Wiley, 1970:351–63; orig. 1958.

MILLET, KATE. *Sexual Politics.* Garden City, N.Y.: Doubleday, 1970.

MILLMAN, JOEL, NINA MUNK, MICHAEL SCHUMAN, and NEIL WEINBERG. "The World's Wealthiest People." *Forbes.* Vol. 152, No. 1 (July 5, 1993):66–69.

MILLS, C. WRIGHT. *White Collar: The American Middle Classes.* New York: Oxford University Press, 1951.

———. *The Power Elite.* New York: Oxford University Press, 1956.

———. *The Sociological Imagination.* New York: Oxford University Press, 1959.

MINK, BARBARA. "How Modernization Affects Women." *Cornell Alumni News.* Vol. III, No. 3 (April 1989):10–11.

MINTZ, BETH, and MICHAEL SCHWARTZ. "Interlocking Directorates and Interest Group Formation." *American Sociological Review.* Vol. 46, No. 6 (December 1981):851–69.

MIROWSKY, JOHN. "The Psycho-Economics of Feeling Underpaid: Distributive Justice and the Earnings of Husbands and Wives." *American Journal of Sociology.* Vol. 92, No. 6 (May 1987):1404–34.

MIROWSKY, JOHN, and CATHERINE ROSS. "Working Wives and Mental Health." Presentation to the American Association for the Advancement of Science. New York, 1984.

———. *The Social Causes of Psychological Distress.* Hawthorne, N.Y.: Aldine, 1989.

MOLNAR, STEPHEN. *Human Variation: Races, Types, and Ethnic Groups.* 2d ed. Englewood Cliffs, N.J.: Prentice Hall, 1983.

MOLOTCH, HARVEY. "The City as a Growth Machine." *American Journal of Sociology.* Vol. 82, No. 2 (September 1976):309–33.

MOLOTCH, HARVEY L., and DEIRDRE BODEN. "Talking Social Structure: Discourse, Domination, and the Watergate Hearings." *American Sociological Review.* Vol. 50, No. 3 (June 1985):273–88.

MONEY, JOHN, and ANKE A. EHRHARDT. *Man and Woman, Boy and Girl.* New York: New American Library, 1972.

MONK-TURNER, ELIZABETH. "The Occupational Achievement of Community and Four-Year College Graduates." *American Sociological Review.* Vol. 55, No. 5 (October 1990):719–25.

MONTAGU, ASHLEY. *The Nature of Human Aggression.* New York: Oxford University Press, 1976.

MOORE, DAHLIA. "Economic Development, Socio-Political Ideology, and Women's Employment: The Case of Israel." *International Sociology.* Vol. 7, No. 4 (December 1992):413–31.

MOORE, GWEN. "The Structure of a National Elite Network." *American Sociological Review.* Vol. 44, No. 5 (October 1979):673–92.

———. "Structural Determinants of Men's and Women's Personal Networks." *American Sociological Review.* Vol. 55, No. 5 (October 1991):726–35.

———. "Gender and Informal Networks in State Government." *Social Science Quarterly.* Vol. 73, No. 1 (March 1992):46–61.

MOORE, JOAN, and HARRY PACHON. *Hispanics in the United States.* Englewood Cliffs, N.J.: Prentice Hall, 1985.

MOORE, WILBERT E. "Modernization as Rationalization: Processes and Restraints." In Manning Nash, ed., *Essays on Economic Development and Cultural Change in Honor of Bert F. Hoselitz.* Chicago: University of Chicago Press, 1977:29–42.

———. *World Modernization: The Limits of Convergence.* New York: Elsevier, 1979.

MORAN, JOHN S., S. O. ARAL, W. C. JENKINS, T. A. PETERMAN, and E. R. ALEXANDER. "The Impact of Sexually Transmitted Diseases on Minority Populations." *Public Health Reports.* Vol. 104, No. 6 (November–December 1989):560–65.

MORRIS, ALDON. "Black Southern Sit-in Movement: An Analysis of Internal Organization." *American Sociological Review.* Vol. 46, No. 6 (December 1981):744–67.

MORRISON, DENTON E. "Some Notes Toward Theory on Relative Deprivation, Social Movements, and Social Change." In Louis E. Genevie, ed., *Collective Behavior and Social Movements.* Itasca, Ill.: Peacock, 1978:202–9.

MORROW, LANCE. "Rough Justice." *Time.* Vol. 137, No. 13 (April 1, 1991):16–17.

———. "The Temping of America." *Time.* Vol. 131, No. 14 (March 29, 1993):40–41.

MOSKOS, CHARLES C. "Female GIs in the Field." *Society.* Vol. 22, No. 6 (September–October 1985):28–33.

MOSLEY, W. HENRY, and PETER COWLEY. "The Challenge of World Health." *Population Bulletin.* Vol. 46, No. 4 (December 1991). Washington, D.C.: Population Reference Bureau.

MOTTAZ, CLIFFORD J. "Some Determinants of Work Alienation." *The Sociological Quarterly*. Vol. 22, No. 4 (Autumn 1981):515–29.

MUELLER, DANIEL P., and PHILIP W. COOPER. "Children of Single Parent Families: How Do They Fare as Young Adults?" Presentation to the American Sociological Association, San Antonio, Texas, 1984.

MULLER, EDWARD N. *Aggressive Political Participation*. Princeton, N.J.: Princeton University Press, 1979.

MULLER, THOMAS, and THOMAS J. ESPENSHADE. *The Fourth Wave: California's Newest Immigrants*. Washington, D.C.: The Urban Institute Press, 1985.

MUMFORD, LEWIS. *The City in History: Its Origins, Its Transformations, and Its Prospects*. New York: Harcourt, Brace & World, 1961.

MURDOCK, GEORGE P. "Comparative Data on the Division of Labor by Sex." *Social Forces*. Vol. 15, No. 4 (May 1937):551–53.

———. "The Common Denominator of Cultures." In Ralph Linton, ed., *The Science of Man in World Crisis*. New York: Columbia University Press, 1945:123–42.

MURDOCK, GEORGE PETER. *Social Structure*. New York: Free Press, 1965; orig. 1949.

MURRAY, MEGAN BALDRIDGE. "Innovation Without Geniuses." In *Yale Alumni Magazine and Journal*. Vol. XLVII, No. 6 (April 1984):40–43.

MURRAY, PAULI. *Proud Shoes: The History of an American Family*. New York: Harper & Row, 1978.

MYERS, NORMAN. "Disappearing Cultures." In Sir Edmund Hillary, ed., *Ecology 2000: The Changing Face of the Earth*. New York: Beaufort Books, 1984c:162–69.

———. "Humanity's Growth." In Sir Edmund Hillary, ed., *Ecology 2000: The Changing Face of the Earth*. New York: Beaufort Books, 1984a:16–35.

———. "The Mega-Extinction of Animals and Plants." In Sir Edmund Hillary, ed., *Ecology 2000: The Changing Face of the Earth*. New York: Beaufort Books, 1984b:82–107.

———. "Biological Diversity and Global Security." In Herbert F. Bohrmann and Stephen R. Kellert, eds., *Ecology, Economics, and Ethics: The Broken Circle*. New Haven, Conn.: Yale University Press, 1991:11–25.

MYERS, SHEILA, and HAROLD G. GRASMICK. "The Social Rights and Responsibilities of Pregnant Women: An Application of Parsons' Sick Role Model." Paper presented to Southwestern Sociological Association, Little Rock, Arkansas, March 1989.

MYRDAL, GUNNAR. *An American Dilemma: The Negro Problem and Modern Democracy*. New York: Harper & Brothers, 1944.

NAJAFIZADEH, MEHRANGIZ, and LEWIS A. MENNERICK. "Sociology of Education or Sociology of Ethnocentrism: The Portrayal of Education in Introductory Sociology Textbooks." *Teaching Sociology*. Vol. 20, No. 3 (July 1992):215–21.

NATIONAL CENTER FOR EDUCATION STATISTICS. *Digest of Education Statistics: 1990*. Washington, D.C.: U.S. Government Printing Office, 1991:244.

NATIONAL COMMISSION ON EXCELLENCE IN EDUCATION. *A Nation at Risk*. Washington, D.C.: U.S. Government Printing Office, 1983.

NAVARRO, VICENTE. "The Industrialization of Fetishism or the Fetishism of Industrialization: A Critique of Ivan Illich." In Vicente Navarro, ed., *Health and Medical Care in the U.S.: A Critical Analysis*. Farmingdale, N.Y.: Baywood Publishing Co., 1977:38–58.

NEIDERT, LISA J., and REYNOLDS FARLEY. "Assimilation in the United States: An Analysis of Ethnic and Generation Differences in Status and Achievement." *American Sociological Review*. Vol. 50, No. 6 (December 1985):840–50.

NELAN, BRUCE W. "Crimes Without Punishment." *Time*. Vol. 141, No. 2 (January 11, 1993):21.

NELSON, HARRY, and ROBERT JERMAIN. *Introduction to Physical Anthropology*. 3d ed. St. Paul, Minn.: West, 1985:22–24.

NEUGARTEN, BERNICE L. "Grow Old with Me. The Best Is Yet to Be." *Psychology Today*. Vol. 5 (December 1971):45–48, 79, 81.

———. "Personality and the Aging Process." *The Gerontologist*. Vol. 12, No. 1 (Spring 1972):9–15.

———. "Personality and Aging." In James E. Birren and K. Warner Schaie, eds., *Handbook of the Psychology of Aging*. New York: Van Nostrand Reinhold, 1977:626–49.

NEUHOUSER, KEVIN. "The Radicalization of the Brazilian Catholic Church in Comparative Perspective." *American Sociological Review*. Vol. 54, No. 2 (April 1989):233–44.

NEW HAVEN JOURNAL COURIER. "English Social Structure Changing." November 27, 1986.

NEWMAN, JAMES L., and GORDON E. MATZKE. *Population: Patterns, Dynamics, and Prospects*. Englewood Cliffs, N.J.: Prentice Hall, 1984.

NEWMAN, WILLIAM M. *American Pluralism: A Study of Minority Groups and Social Theory*. New York: Harper & Row, 1973.

NIELSEN, JOYCE MCCARL, ED. *Feminist Research Methods: Exemplary Readings in the Social Sciences*. Boulder, Colo.: Westview, 1990.

1991 Green Book. U.S. House of Representatives. Washington, D.C.: U.S. Government Printing Office, 1991.

NISBET, ROBERT. "Sociology as an Art Form." In *Tradition and Revolt: Historical and Sociological Essays*. New York: Vintage Books, 1970.

NISBET, ROBERT A. *The Sociological Tradition*. New York: Basic Books, 1966.

———. *The Quest for Community*. New York: Oxford University Press, 1969.

NORBECK, EDWARD. "Class Structure." In *Kodansha Encyclopedia of Japan*. Tokyo: Kodansha, 1983:322–25.

NORC. *General Social Surveys, 1972–1991: Cumulative Codebook*. Chicago: National Opinion Research Center, 1991.

———. *General Social Surveys, 1972–1993: Cumulative Codebook*. University of Chicago: National Opinion Research Center, 1993.

NUMBERS, RONALD L. "Creationism in 20th-Century America." *Science*. Vol. 218, No. 5 (November 1982):538–44.

NUNN, CLYDE Z., HARRY J. CROCKETT, JR., and J. ALLEN WILLIAMS, JR. *Tolerance for Nonconformity*. San Francisco: Jossey-Bass, 1978.

OAKES, JEANNIE. "Classroom Social Relationships: Exploring the Bowles and Gintis Hypothesis." *Sociology of Education*. Vol. 55, No. 4 (October 1982):197–212.

———. *Keeping Track: How High Schools Structure Inequality*. New Haven, Conn.: Yale University Press, 1985.

OBERSCHALL, ANTHONY. *Social Conflict and Social Movements*. Englewood Cliffs, N.J.: Prentice Hall, 1973.

O'DEA, THOMAS F., and JANET O'DEA AVIAD. *The Sociology of Religion*. 2d ed. Englewood Cliffs, N.J.: Prentice Hall, 1983.

OFFIR, CAROLE WADE. *Human Sexuality*. New York: Harcourt Brace Jovanovich, 1982.

OGBURN, WILLIAM F. *On Culture and Social Change*. Chicago: University of Chicago Press, 1964.

O'HARE, WILLIAM. "In the Black." *American Demographics*. Vol. 11, No. 11 (November 1989):25–29.

———. "The Rise of Hispanic Affluence." *American Demographics*. Vol. 12, No. 8 (August 1990):40–43.

O'HARE, WILLIAM, and JAN LARSON. "Women in Business: Where, What, and Why." *American Demographics*. Vol. 13, No. 7 (July 1991):34–38.

OKIMOTO, DANIEL. "The Intolerance of Success." In Amy Tachiki et al., eds., *Roots: An Asian American Reader*. Los Angeles: UCLA Asian American Studies Center, 1971:14–19.

OLZAK, SUSAN. "Labor Unrest, Immigration, and Ethnic Conflict in Urban America, 1880–1914." *American Journal of Sociology*. Vol. 94, No. 6 (May 1989):1303–33.

OLZAK, SUSAN, and ELIZABETH WEST. "Ethnic Conflict and the Rise and Fall of Ethnic Newspapers." *American Sociological Review*. Vol. 56, No. 4 (August 1991):458–74.

O'REILLY, JANE. "Wife Beating: The Silent Crime." *Time*. Vol. 122, No. 10 (September 5, 1983):23–24, 26.

ORLANSKY, MICHAEL D., and WILLIAM L. HEWARD. *Voices: Interviews with Handicapped People*. Columbus, Ohio: Merrill, 1981:85, 92, 133–34, 172.

ORSHANSKY, MOLLIE. "How Poverty Is Measured." *Monthly Labor Review*. Vol. 92, No. 2 (February 1969):37–41.

OSTLING, RICHARD N. "Jerry Falwell's Crusade." *Time*. Vol. 126, No. 9 (September 2, 1985):48–52, 55, 57.

———. "Technology and the Womb." *Time*. Vol. 129, No. 12 (March 23, 1987):58–59.

OSTRANDER, SUSAN A. "Upper Class Women: The Feminine Side of Privilege." *Qualitative Sociology*. Vol. 3, No. 1 (Spring 1980):23–44.

———. *Women of the Upper Class.* Philadelphia: Temple University Press, 1984.

OUCHI, WILLIAM. *Theory Z: How American Business Can Meet the Japanese Challenge.* Reading, Mass.: Addison-Wesley, 1981.

OWEN, DAVID. *None of the Above: Behind the Myth of Scholastic Aptitude.* Boston: Houghton Mifflin, 1985.

PALMORE, ERDMAN. "Predictors of Successful Aging." *The Gerontologist.* Vol. 19, No. 5 (October 1979a):427–31.

———. "Advantages of Aging." *The Gerontologist.* Vol. 19, No. 2 (April 1979b):220–23.

———. "What Can the USA Learn from Japan About Aging?" In Steven H. Zarit, ed., *Readings in Aging and Death: Contemporary Perspectives.* New York: Harper & Row, 1982:166–69.

PAMPEL, FRED C., KENNETH C. LAND, and MARCUS FELSON. "A Social Indicator Model of Changes in the Occupational Structure of the United States: 1947–1974." *American Sociological Review.* Vol. 42, No. 6 (December 1977):951–64.

PARCEL, TOBY L., CHARLES W. MUELLER, and STEVEN CUVELIER. "Comparable Worth and Occupational Labor Market: Explanations of Occupational Earnings Differentials." Paper presented to the American Sociological Association, New York, 1986.

PARENTI, MICHAEL. *Inventing Reality: The Politics of the Mass Media.* New York: St. Martin's Press, 1986.

PARILLO, VINCENT N. *Strangers to These Shores.* 4th ed. New York: Macmillan, 1994.

PARK, ROBERT E. *Race and Culture.* Glencoe, Ill.: Free Press, 1950.

———. "The City: Suggestions for the Investigation of Human Behavior in the Human Environment." In Robert E. Park and Ernest W. Burgess, *The City.* Chicago: University of Chicago Press, 1967; orig. 1925:1–46.

PARKINSON, C. NORTHCOTE. *Parkinson's Law and Other Studies in Administration.* New York: Ballantine Books, 1957.

PARROTT, JULIE. "The Effects of Culture on Eating Disorders." Paper presented to Southwestern Social Science Association, Dallas, Texas, March 1987.

PARSONS, TALCOTT. "Age and Sex in the Social Structure of the United States." *American Sociological Review.* Vol. 7, No. 4 (August 1942):604–16.

———. *Essays in Sociological Theory.* New York: Free Press, 1954.

———. *The Social System.* New York: Free Press, 1964; orig. 1951.

———. *Societies: Evolutionary and Comparative Perspectives.* Englewood Cliffs, N.J.: Prentice Hall, 1966.

PARSONS, TALCOTT, and ROBERT F. BALES, EDS. *Family, Socialization and Interaction Process.* New York: Free Press, 1955.

PAUL, ELLEN FRANKEL. "Bared Buttocks and Federal Cases." *Society.* Vol. 28. No. 4 (May–June, 1991):4–7.

PEAR, ROBERT. "Women Reduce Lag in Earnings, But Disparities With Men Remain." *New York Times* (September 4, 1987):1, 7.

PEAR, ROBERT, with ERIK ECKHOLM. "When Healers Are Entrepreneurs: A Debate Over Costs and Ethics." *New York Times* (June 2, 1991):1, 17.

PEARSON, DAVID E. "Post-Mass Culture." *Society.* Vol. 30, No. 5 (July–August 1993):17–22.

PENNINGS, JOHANNES M. "Organizational Birth Frequencies: An Empirical Investigation." *Administrative Science Quarterly.* Vol. 27, No. 1 (March 1982):120–44.

PEREZ, LISANDRO. "Cubans." In *Harvard Encyclopedia of American Ethnic Groups.* Cambridge, Mass.: Harvard University Press, 1980:256–60.

PERSELL, CAROLINE HODGES. *Education and Inequality: A Theoretical and Empirical Synthesis.* New York: Free Press, 1977.

PESSEN, EDWARD. *Riches, Class, and Power: America Before the Civil War.* New Brunswick, N.J.: Transaction, 1990.

PETER, LAURENCE J., and RAYMOND HULL. *The Peter Principle: Why Things Always Go Wrong.* New York: William Morrow, 1969.

Peters Atlas of the World. New York: Harper & Row, 1990.

PETERS, THOMAS J., and ROBERT H. WATERMAN, JR. *In Search of Excellence: Lessons From America's Best-Run Companies.* New York: Warner Books, 1982.

PHILIPSON, ILENE J., and KAREN V. HANSEN. "Women, Class, and the Feminist Imagination." In Karen V. Hansen and Ilene J. Philipson, eds.,

Women, Class, and the Feminist Imagination: A Socialist-Feminist Reader. Philadelphia: Temple University Press, 1992:3–40.

PHILLIPSON, CHRIS. *Capitalism and the Construction of Old Age.* London: Macmillan, 1982.

PHYSICIANS' TASK FORCE ON HUNGER IN AMERICA. "Hunger Reaches Blue-Collar America." Report issued 1987.

PILLEMER, KARL. "Maltreatment of the Elderly at Home and in Institutions: Extent, Risk Factors, and Policy Recommendations." In U.S. Congress. House, Select Committee on Aging and Senate, Special Committee on Aging. *Legislative Agenda for an Aging Society: 1988 and Beyond.* Washington, D.C.: U.S. Government Printing Office, 1988.

PINES, MAYA. "The Civilization of Genie." *Psychology Today.* Vol. 15 (September 1981):28–34.

PIOTROW, PHYLLIS T. *World Population: The Present and Future Crisis.* Headline Series 251 (October 1980). New York: Foreign Policy Association.

PIRANDELLO, LUIGI. "The Pleasure of Honesty." In *To Clothe the Naked and Two Other Plays.* New York: Dutton, 1962:143–98.

PITT, MALCOLM. *Introducing Hinduism.* New York: Friendship Press, 1955.

PIVEN, FRANCES FOX, and RICHARD A. CLOWARD. *Poor People's Movements: Why They Succeed, How They Fail.* New York: Pantheon Books, 1977.

———. *Why Americans Don't Vote.* New York: Pantheon Books, 1988.

PLOMIN, ROBERT, and TERRYL T. FOCH. "A Twin Study of Objectively Assessed Personality in Childhood." *Journal of Personality and Sociology Psychology.* Vol. 39, No. 4 (October 1980):680–88.

POLENBERG, RICHARD. *One Nation Divisible: Class, Race, and Ethnicity in the United States Since 1938.* New York: Pelican Books, 1980.

POLSBY, NELSON W. "Three Problems in the Analysis of Community Power." *American Sociological Review.* Vol. 24, No. 6 (December 1959):796–803.

POMER, MARSHALL I. "Labor Market Structure, Intragenerational Mobility, and Discrimination: Black Male Advancement Out of Low-Paying Occupations, 1962–1973." *American Sociological Review.* Vol. 51, No. 5 (October 1986):650–59.

POPENOE, DAVID. *Disturbing the Nest: Family Change and Decline in Modern Societies.* New York: Aldine, 1988.

———. "Family Decline in the Swedish Welfare State." *The Public Interest.* No. 102 (Winter 1991):65–77.

———. "The Controversial Truth: Two-Parent Families are Better." *New York Times* (December 26, 1992):21.

———. "Parental Androgyny." *Society.* Vol. 30, No. 6 (September–October 1993):5–11.

POPKIN, SUSAN J. "Welfare: Views from the Bottom." *Social Problems.* Vol. 17, No. 1 (February 1990):64–79.

PORTES, ALEJANDRO. "The Rise of Ethnicity: Determinants of Ethnic Perceptions Among Cuban Exiles in Miami." *American Sociological Review.* Vol. 49, No. 3 (June 1984):383–97.

PORTES, ALEJANDRO, and LEIF JENSEN. "The Enclave and the Entrants: Patterns of Ethnic Enterprise in Miami Before and After Mariel." *American Sociological Review.* Vol. 54, No. 6 (December 1989):929–49.

POSTEL, SANDRA. "Facing Water Scarcity." In Lester R. Brown et al., eds., *State of the World 1993: A Worldwatch Institute Report on Progress Toward a Sustainable Society.* New York: Norton, 1993:22–41.

POWELL, CHRIS, and GEORGE E. C. PATON, EDS. *Humour in Society: Resistance and Control.* New York: St. Martin's Press, 1988.

PRESSER, HARRIET B. "The Housework Gender Gap." *Population Today.* Vol. 21, No. 7/8 (July–August 1993):5.

PRESSLEY, SUE ANNE, and NANCY ANDREWS. "For Gay Couples, the Nursery Becomes the New Frontier." *Washington Post* (December 20, 1992):A1, A22–23.

PRIMEGGIA, SALVATORE, and JOSEPH A. VARACALLI. "Southern Italian Comedy: Old to New World." In Joseph V. Scelsa, Salvatore J. LaGumina, and Lydio Tomasi, eds., *Italian Americans in Transition.* New York: The American Italian Historical Association, 1990:241–52.

PURCELL, PIPER, and LARA STEWART. "Dick and Jane in 1989." *Sex Roles.* Vol. 22, Nos. 3–4 (1990):177–85.

PUTERBAUGH, GEOFF, ED. *Twins and Homosexuality: A Casebook.* New York: Garland, 1990.

PUTKA, GARY. "SAT to Become a Better Gauge." *Wall Street Journal* (November 1, 1990):B1.

——. "Whittle Develops Plan to Operate Schools for Profit." *Wall Street Journal* (May 15, 1991):B1.

QUEENAN, JOE. "The Many Paths to Riches." *Forbes.* Vol. 144, No. 9 (October 23, 1989):149.

QUINNEY, RICHARD. *Class, State and Crime: On the Theory and Practice of Criminal Justice.* New York: David McKay, 1977.

RADEMAEKERS, WILLIAM, and RHEA SCHOENTHAL. "Iceman." *Time.* Vol. 140, No. 17 (October 26, 1992):62–66.

RADIN, NORMA. "Primary Caregiving and Role-Sharing Fathers." In Michael E. Lamb, ed., *Nontraditional Families: Parenting and Child Development.* Hillsdale, N.J.: Lawrence Erlbaum, 1982:173–204.

RANDALL, VICKI. *Women and Politics.* London: Macmillan Press, 1982.

RAPHAEL, RAY. *The Men from the Boys: Rites of Passage in Male America.* Lincoln and London: University of Nebraska Press, 1988.

RECKLESS, WALTER C., and SIMON DINITZ. "Pioneering with Self-Concept as a Vulnerability Factor in Delinquency." *Journal of Criminal Law, Criminology, and Police Science.* Vol. 58, No. 4 (December 1967):515–23.

REICH, ROBERT B. "As the World Turns." *The New Republic* (May 1, 1989):23, 26–28.

——. *The Work of Nations: Preparing Ourselves for 21st-Century Capitalism.* New York: Alfred A. Knopf, 1991.

REID, SUE TITUS. *Crime and Criminology.* 6th ed. Fort Worth, Tex.: Holt, Rinehart & Winston, 1991.

REIMERS, CORDELIA W. "Sources of the Family Income Differentials Among Hispanics, Blacks, and White Non-Hispanics." *American Journal of Sociology.* Vol. 89, No. 4 (January 1984):889–903.

REINHARZ, SHULAMIT. *Feminist Methods in Social Research.* New York: Oxford University Press, 1992.

REMOFF, HEATHER TREXLER. *Sexual Choice: A Woman's Decision.* New York: Dutton/Lewis, 1984.

RICHARDSON, JAMES T. "Definitions of Cult: From Sociological-Technical to Popular Negative." Paper presented to the American Psychological Association, Boston, August, 1990.

RIDGEWAY, CECILIA L. *The Dynamics of Small Groups.* New York: St. Martin's Press, 1983.

RIEFF, PHILIP. "Introduction." In Charles Horton Cooley, *Social Organization.* New York: Schocken Books, 1962.

RIESMAN, DAVID. *The Lonely Crowd: A Study of the Changing American Character.* New Haven, Conn.: Yale University Press, 1970; orig. 1950.

RILEY, MATILDA WHITE, ANNE FONER, and JOAN WARING. "Sociology of Age." In Neil J. Smelser, ed., *Handbook of Sociology.* Newbury Park, Calif.: Sage, 1988:243–90.

RITZER, GEORGE. *Sociological Theory.* New York: Alfred A. Knopf, 1983:63–66.

——. *The McDonaldization of Society: An Investigation Into the Changing Character of Contemporary Social Life.* Thousand Oaks, Calif.: Pine Forge Press, 1993.

RITZER, GEORGE, and DAVID WALCZAK. *Working: Conflict and Change.* 4th ed. Englewood Cliffs, N.J.: Prentice Hall, 1990.

ROBERTS, J. DEOTIS. *Roots of a Black Future: Family and Church.* Philadelphia: The Westminster Press, 1980.

ROBINSON, DAWN. "Toward a Synthesis of Sociological and Psychological Theories of Eating Disorders." Paper presented to Southwestern Social Science Association, Dallas, Texas, March 1987.

ROBINSON, JOYCE, and GLENNA SPITZE. "Whistle While You Work? The Effect of Household Task Performance on Women's and Men's Well-Being." *Social Science Quarterly.* Vol. 73, No. 4 (December 1992):844–61.

ROBINSON, VERA M. "Humor and Health." In Paul E. McGhee and Jeffrey H. Goldstein, eds., *Handbook of Humor Research, Vol. II, Applied Studies.* New York: Springer-Verlag, 1983:109–28.

ROESCH, ROBERTA. "Violent Families." *Parents.* Vol. 59, No. 9 (September 1984):74–76, 150–52.

ROETHLISBERGER, F. J., and WILLIAM J. DICKSON. *Management and the Worker.* Cambridge, Mass.: Harvard University Press, 1939.

ROGERS, ALISON. "The World's 101 Richest People." *Fortune.* Vol. 127, No. 13 (June 28, 1993):36–66.

ROHLEN, THOMAS P. *Japan's High Schools.* Berkeley: University of California Press, 1983.

ROKOVE, MILTON L. *Don't Make No Waves, Don't Back No Losers.* Bloomington: Indiana University Press, 1975.

ROMAN, MEL, and WILLIAM HADDAD. *The Disposable Parent: The Case for Joint Custody.* New York: Holt, Rinehart & Winston, 1978.

ROOF, WADE CLARK. "Socioeconomic Differentials Among White Socioreligious Groups in the United States." *Social Forces.* Vol. 58, No. 1 (September 1979):280–89.

——. "Unresolved Issues in the Study of Religion and the National Elite: Response to Greeley." *Social Forces.* Vol. 59, No. 3 (March 1981):831–36.

ROOF, WADE CLARK, and WILLIAM MCKINNEY. *American Mainline Religion: Its Changing Shape and Future.* New Brunswick, N.J.: Rutgers University Press, 1987.

ROOS, PATRICIA. "Marriage and Women's Occupational Attainment in Cross-Cultural Perspective." *American Sociological Review.* Vol. 48, No. 6 (December 1983):852–64.

ROSE, ARNOLD M. "The Subculture of the Aging: A Topic for Sociological Research." In Bernice L. Neugarten, ed., *Middle Age and Aging: A Reader in Social Psychology.* Chicago: University of Chicago Press, 1968:29–34.

ROSE, JERRY D. *Outbreaks.* New York: Free Press, 1982.

ROSEN, ELLEN ISRAEL. *Bitter Choices: Blue-Collar Women In and Out of Work.* Chicago: University of Chicago Press, 1987.

ROSENFELD, RACHEL A., and ARNE L. KALLEBERG. "A Cross-National Comparison of the Gender Gap in Income." *American Journal of Sociology.* Vol. 96, No. 1 (July 1990):69–106.

ROSENTHAL, ELIZABETH. "Canada's National Health Plan Gives Care to All, With Limits." *New York Times* (April 30, 1991):A1, A16.

ROSENTHAL, JACK. "The Rapid Growth of Suburban Employment." In Lois H. Masotti and Jeffrey K. Hadden, eds., *Suburbia in Transition.* New York: New York Times Books, 1974:95–100.

ROSKIN, MICHAEL G. *Countries and Concepts: An Introduction to Comparative Politics.* Englewood Cliffs, N.J.: Prentice Hall, 1982.

ROSNOW, RALPH L., and GARY ALAN FINE. *Rumor and Gossip: The Social Psychology of Hearsay.* New York: Elsevier, 1976.

ROSS, CATHERINE E., JOHN MIROWSKY, and JOAN HUBER. "Dividing Work, Sharing Work, and In-Between: Marriage Patterns and Depression." *American Sociological Review.* Vol. 48, No. 6 (December 1983):809–23.

ROSS, SUSAN. "Education: A Step Ladder to Mobility." *Popline.* Vol. 7, No. 7 (July 1985):1–2.

ROSSI, ALICE S. "Gender and Parenthood." In Alice S. Rossi, ed., *Gender and the Life Course.* New York: Aldine, 1985:161–91.

ROSSIDES, DANIEL W. *Social Stratification: The American Class System in Comparative Perspective.* Englewood Cliffs, N.J.: Prentice Hall, 1990.

ROSTOW, W. W. *The Stages of Economic Growth: A Non-Communist Manifesto.* Cambridge: Cambridge University Press, 1960.

ROSTOW, WALT W. *The World Economy: History and Prospect.* Austin: University of Texas Press, 1978.

ROTHMAN, STANLEY, STEPHEN POWERS, and DAVID ROTHMAN. "Feminism in Films." *Society.* Vol. 30, No. 3 (March–April 1993):66–72.

ROUDI, NAZY. "The Demography of Islam." *Population Today.* Vol. 16, No. 3 (March 1988):6–9.

ROWE, DAVID C. "Biometrical Genetic Models of Self-Reported Delinquent Behavior: A Twin Study." *Behavior Genetics.* Vol. 13, No. 5 (1983):473–89.

ROWE, DAVID C., and D. WAYNE OSGOOD. "Heredity and Sociological Theories of Delinquency: A Reconsideration." *American Sociological Review.* Vol. 49, No. 4 (August 1984):526–40.

RUBENSTEIN, ELI A. "The Not So Golden Years." *Newsweek* (October 7, 1991):13.

RUBIN, BETH A. "Class Struggle American Style: Unions, Strikes and Wages." *American Sociological Review.* Vol. 51, No. 5 (October 1986):618–31.

RUBIN, LILLIAN BRESLOW. *Worlds of Pain: Life in the Working-Class Family.* New York: Basic Books, 1976.

RUDÉ, GEORGE. *The Crowd in History: A Study of Popular Disturbances in France and England, 1730–1848.* New York: Wiley, 1964.

684   References

RUDOLPH, BARBARA. "Tobacco Takes a New Road." *Time*. Vol. 126, No. 20 (November 18, 1985):70–71.

RUGGLES, STEVEN. "The Origins of African-American Family Structure." *American Sociological Review*. Vol. 59, No. 1 (February 1994):136–51.

RULE, JAMES, and PETER BRANTLEY. "Computerized Surveillance in the Workplace: Forms and Delusions." *Sociological Forum*. Vol. 7, No. 3 (September 1992):405–23.

RUMBERGER, RUSSELL. *Overeducation in the U.S. Labor Market*. New York: Praeger, 1981.

RUSSELL, CHERYL. "The Master Trend." *American Demographics*. Vol. 15, No. 10 (October 1993):28–37.

RUSSELL, DIANA E. H. *Rape in Marriage*. New York: Macmillan, 1982.

RYAN, WILLIAM. *Blaming the Victim*. Rev. ed. New York: Vintage Books, 1976.

RYTINA, JOAN HUBER, WILLIAM H. FORM, and JOHN PEASE. "Income and Stratification Ideology: Beliefs About the American Opportunity Structure." *American Journal of Sociology*. Vol. 75, No. 4 (January 1970):703–16.

SABATO, LARRY J. *PAC Power: Inside the World of Political Action Committees*. New York: Norton, 1984.

SAGAN, CARL. *The Dragons of Eden*. New York: Ballantine, 1977.

SALAS, RAFAEL M. "The State of World Population 1985: Population and Women." *Popline*. Vol. 7, No. 7 (July 1985):4–5.

SALE, KIRKPATRICK. *The Conquest of Paradise: Christopher Columbus and the Columbian Legacy*. New York: Alfred A. Knopf, 1990.

SALHOLZ, ELOISE. "The Future of Gay America." *Newsweek* (March 12, 1990):20–25.

SALTMAN, JULIET. "Maintaining Racially Diverse Neighborhoods." *Urban Affairs Quarterly*. Vol. 26, No. 3 (March 1991):416–41.

SAMPSON, ANTHONY. *The Changing Anatomy of Britain*. New York: Random House, 1982.

SAMPSON, ROBERT J. "Urban Black Violence: The Effects of Male Joblessness and Family Disruption." *American Journal of Sociology*. Vol. 93, No. 2 (September 1987):348–82.

SAMPSON, ROBERT J., and JOHN H. LAUB. "Crime and Deviance Over the Life Course: The Salience of Adult Social Bonds." *American Sociological Review*. Vol. 55, No. 5 (October 1990):609–27.

SAPIR, EDWARD. "The Status of Linguistics as a Science." *Language*. Vol. 5 (1929):207–14.

——— . *Selected Writings of Edward Sapir in Language, Culture, and Personality*. David G. Mandelbaum, ed. Berkeley: University of California Press, 1949.

SCAFF, LAWRENCE A. "Max Weber and Robert Michels." *American Journal of Sociology*. Vol. 86, No. 6 (May 1981):1269–86.

SCHAIE, I. WARNER. "Intelligence and Problem Solving." In James E. Birren and R. Bruce Sloane, eds., *Handbook of Mental Health and Aging*. Englewood Cliffs, N.J.: Prentice Hall, 1980:262–84.

SCHEFF, THOMAS J. *Being Mentally Ill: A Sociological Theory*. 2d ed. New York: Aldine, 1984.

SCHELLENBERG, JAMES A. *Masters of Social Psychology*. New York: Oxford University Press, 1978:38–62.

SCHLAFLY, PHYLLIS. "Mothers, Stay Home; Your Kids Need You." *USA Today* (May 30, 1984):10A.

SCHLESINGER, ARTHUR. "The City in American Civilization." In A. B. Callow, Jr., ed., *American Urban History*. New York: Oxford University Press, 1969:25–41.

SCHLESINGER, ARTHUR, JR. "The Cult of Ethnicity: Good and Bad." *Time*. Vol. 137, No. 27 (July 8, 1991):21.

SCHMIDT, ROGER. *Exploring Religion*. Belmont, Calif.: Wadsworth, 1980.

SCHOOLER, CARMI, JOANNE MILLER, KAREN A. MILLER, and CAROL N. RICHTAND. "Work for the Household: Its Nature and Consequences for Husbands and Wives." *American Journal of Sociology*. Vol. 90, No. 1 (July 1984):97–124.

SCHREINER, TIM. "Your Cost to Bring Up Baby: $142,700." *USA Today* (October 19, 1984):1D.

SCHUMANN, HANS WOLFGANG. *Buddhism: An Outline of Its Teachings and Schools*. Wheaton, Ill.: The Theosophical Publishing House/Quest Books, 1974.

SCHUTT, RUSSELL K. "Objectivity versus Outrage." *Society*. Vol. 26, No. 4 (May/June 1989):14–16.

SCHWARTZ, FELICE N. "Management, Women, and the New Facts of Life." *Harvard Business Review*. Vol. 89, No. 1 (January–February 1989):65–76.

SCHWARTZ, JOE. "Rising Status." *American Demographics*. Vol. 11, No. 1 (January 1989):10.

SCHWARTZ, JOHN E., and THOMAS J. VOLGY. *The Forgotten Americans: Thirty Million Working Poor in the Land of Opportunity*. New York: Norton, 1992.

SCHWARTZ, MARTIN D. "Gender and Injury in Spousal Assault." *Sociological Focus*. Vol. 20, No. 1 (January 1987):61–75.

SCHWARTZ-NOBEL, LORETTA. *Starving in the Shadow of Plenty*. New York: McGraw-Hill, 1981.

SCOTT, JOHN, and CATHERINE GRIFF. *Directors of Industry: The British Corporate Network, 1904–1976*. New York: Blackwell, 1985.

SCOTT, W. RICHARD. *Organizations: Rational, Natural, and Open Systems*. Englewood Cliffs, N.J.: Prentice Hall, 1981.

SEARS, DAVID O., and JOHN B. MCCONAHAY. *The Politics of Violence: The New Urban Blacks and the Watts Riot*. Boston: Houghton Mifflin, 1973.

SEGAL, DAVID R., PAUL A. GADE, and EDGAR M. JOHNSON. "Homosexuals in Western Armed Forces." *Society*. Vol. 31, No. 1 (November–December 1993):37–42.

SEGAL, MADY WECHSLER, and AMANDA FAITH HANSEN. "Value Rationales in Policy Debates on Women in the Military: A Content Analysis of Congressional Testimony, 1941–1985." *Social Science Quarterly*. Vol. 73, No. 2 (June 1992):296–309.

SELIMUDDIN, ABU K. "The Selling of America." *USA Today*. Vol. 117, No. 2525 (March 1989):12–14.

SELLIN, THORSTEN. *The Penalty of Death*. Beverly Hills, Calif.: Sage, 1980.

SELTZER, ROBERT M. *Jewish People, Jewish Thought: The Jewish Experience in History*. New York: Macmillan, 1980.

SEN, K. M. *Hinduism*. Baltimore: Penguin Books, 1961.

SENNETT, RICHARD, and JONATHAN COBB. *The Hidden Injuries of Class*. New York: Vintage Books, 1973.

SEWELL, WILLIAM H., ARCHIBALD O. HALLER, and GEORGE W. OHLENDORF. "The Educational and Early Occupational Status Attainment Process: Replication and Revision." *American Sociological Review*. Vol. 35, No. 6 (December 1970):1014–27.

SHANAS, ETHEL. "Social Myth as Hypothesis: The Case of the Family Relations of Old People." *The Gerontologist*. Vol. 19, No. 1 (February 1979):3–9.

SHAPIRO, NINA. "Botswana Test Case." *Chicago Tribune* (September 15, 1991):1.

SHAWCROSS, WILLIAM. *Sideshow: Kissinger, Nixon and the Destruction of Cambodia*. New York: Pocket Books, 1979.

SHEEHAN, TOM. "Senior Esteem as a Factor in Socioeconomic Complexity." *The Gerontologist*. Vol. 16, No. 5 (October 1976):433–40.

SHEEHY, GAIL. *Passages: Predictable Crises of Adult Life*. New York: Dutton, 1976.

SHELDON, WILLIAM H., EMIL M. HARTL, and EUGENE MCDERMOTT. *Varieties of Delinquent Youth*. New York: Harper, 1949.

SHEPHARD, ROY J. *The Risks of Passive Smoking*. London: Croom Helm, 1982.

SHERMAN, LAWRENCE W., and DOUGLAS A. SMITH. "Crime, Punishment, and Stake in Conformity: Legal and Informal Control of Domestic Violence." *American Sociological Review*. Vol. 57, No. 5 (October 1992):680–90.

SHERRID, PAMELA. "Hot Times in the City of London." *U.S. News & World Report* (October 27, 1986):45–46.

SHEVKY, ESHREF, and WENDELL BELL. *Social Area Analysis*. Stanford, Calif.: Stanford University Press, 1955.

SHIBUTANI, TAMOTSU. *Improvised News: A Sociological Study of Rumor*. Indianapolis, Ind.: Bobbs-Merrill, 1966.

SHIPLER, DAVID K. *Russia: Broken Idols, Solemn Dreams*. New York: Penguin Books, 1984.

SHIPLEY, JOSEPH T. *Dictionary of Word Origins*. Totowa, N.J.: Roman & Allanheld, 1985.

SHIVELY, JOELLEN. "Cowboys and Indians: Perceptions of Western Films Among American Indians and Anglos." *American Sociological Review.* Vol. 57, No. 6 (December 1992):725–34.

SHOCKEY, JAMES W. "Overeducation and Earnings: A Structural Approach to Differential Attainment in the U.S. Labor Force (1970–1982)." *American Sociological Review.* Vol. 54, No. 5 (October 1981):856–64.

SHUPE, ANSON, WILLIAM A. STACEY, and LONNIE R. HAZLEWOOD. *Violent Men, Violent Couples: The Dynamics of Domestic Violence.* Lexington, Mass.: Lexington Books, 1987.

SIDEL, RUTH, and VICTOR W. SIDEL. *The Health Care of China.* Boston: Beacon Press, 1982b.

———. *A Healthy State: An International Perspective on the Crisis in United States Medical Care.* Rev. ed. New York: Pantheon Books, 1982a.

SILLS, DAVID L. "The Succession of Goals." In Amitai Etzioni, ed., *A Sociological Reader on Complex Organizations.* 2d ed. New York: Holt, Rinehart & Winston, 1969:175–87.

SILVERBERG, ROBERT. "The Greenhouse Effect: Apocalypse Now or Chicken Little?" *Omni* (July 1991):50–54.

SILVERSTEIN, MICHAEL. In Jon Snodgrass, ed., *A Book of Readings for Men Against Sexism.* Albion, Calif.: Times Change Press, 1977:178–79.

SIMMEL, GEORG. *The Sociology of Georg Simmel.* Kurt Wolff, ed. New York: Free Press, 1950:118–69.

———. "The Mental Life of the Metropolis." In Kurt Wolff, ed., *The Sociology of Georg Simmel.* New York: Free Press, 1964:409–24; orig. 1905.

———. "Fashion." In Donald N. Levine, ed., *Georg Simmel: On Individuality and Social Forms.* Chicago: University of Chicago Press, 1971; orig. 1904.

SIMON, CARL P., and ANN D. WITTE. *Beating the System: The Underground Economy.* Boston: Auburn House, 1982.

SIMON, JULIAN. *The Ultimate Resource.* Princeton, N.J.: Princeton University Press, 1981.

SIMONS, CAROL. "Japan's *Kyoiku* Mamas." In John J. Macionis and Nijole V. Benokraitis, eds., *Seeing Ourselves: Classic, Contemporary, and Cross-Cultural Readings in Sociology.* Englewood Cliffs, N.J.: Prentice Hall, 1989:281–86.

SIMONS, MARLISE. "The Amazon's Savvy Indians." *New York Times Magazine* (February 26, 1990):36–37, 48–52.

SIMPSON, GEORGE EATON, and J. MILTON YINGER. *Racial and Cultural Minorities: An Analysis of Prejudice and Discrimination.* 4th ed. New York: Harper & Row, 1972.

SIMPSON, JANICE C. "Buying Black." *Time.* Vol. 140, No. 9 (August 31, 1992):52–53.

SINGER, JEROME L., and DOROTHY G. SINGER. "Psychologists Look at Television: Cognitive, Developmental, Personality, and Social Policy Implications." *American Psychologist.* Vol. 38, No. 7 (July 1983):826–34.

SIVARD, RUTH LEGER. *World Military and Social Expenditures, 1987–88.* 12th ed. Washington, D.C.: World Priorities, 1988.

SIZER, THEODORE R. *Horace's Compromise: The Dilemma of the American High School.* Boston: Houghton Mifflin, 1984.

SJOBERG, GIDEON. *The Preindustrial City.* New York: Free Press, 1965.

SKOCPOL, THEDA. *States and Social Revolutions: A Comparative Analysis of France, Russia, and China.* Cambridge: Cambridge University Press, 1979.

SKOLNICK, ARLENE. *The Psychology of Human Development.* New York: Harcourt Brace Jovanovich, 1986.

SLATER, PHILIP. *The Pursuit of Loneliness.* Boston: Beacon Press, 1976.

SLATER, PHILIP E. "Contrasting Correlates of Group Size." *Sociometry.* Vol. 21, No. 2 (June 1958):129–39.

SMART, NINIAN. *The Religious Experience of Mankind.* New York: Charles Scribner's Sons, 1969.

SMELSER, NEIL J. *Theory of Collective Behavior.* New York: Free Press, 1962.

SMILGAS, MARTHA. "The Big Chill: Fear of AIDS." *Time.* Vol. 129, No. 7 (February 16, 1987):50–53.

SMITH, ADAM. *An Inquiry into the Nature and Causes of the Wealth of Nations.* New York: The Modern Library, 1937; orig. 1776.

SMITH, DOUGLAS A. "Police Response to Interpersonal Violence: Defining the Parameters of Legal Control." *Social Forces.* Vol. 65, No. 3 (March 1987):767–82.

SMITH, DOUGLAS A., and PATRICK R. GARTIN. "Specifying Specific Deterrence: The Influence of Arrest on Future Criminal Activity." *American Sociological Review.* Vol. 54, No. 1 (February 1989):94–105.

SMITH, DOUGLAS A., and CHRISTY A. VISHER. "Street-Level Justice: Situational Determinants of Police Arrest Decisions." *Social Problems.* Vol. 29, No. 2 (December 1981):167–77.

SMITH, ROBERT B. "Health Care Reform Now." *Society.* Vol. 30, No. 3 (March–April 1993):56–65.

SMITH, ROBERT ELLIS. *Privacy: How to Protect What's Left of It.* Garden City, N.Y.: Anchor/Doubleday, 1979.

SMITH-LOVIN, LYNN, and CHARLES BRODY. "Interruptions in Group Discussions: The Effects of Gender and Group Composition." *American Journal of Sociology.* Vol. 54, No. 3 (June 1989):424–35.

SMOLOWE, JILL. "Land of Slaughter." *Time.* Vol. 139, No. 23 (June 8, 1992):32–36.

———. "A Heavenly Host in Georgia." *Time.* Vol. 141, No. 3 (January 18, 1993):55.

SNELL, MARILYN BERLIN. "The Purge of Nurture." *New Perspectives Quarterly.* Vol. 7, No. 1 (Winter 1990):1–2.

SNOW, DAVID A., E. BURKE ROCHFORD, JR., STEVEN K. WORDEN, and ROBERT D. BENFORD. "Frame Alignment Processes, Micromobilization, and Movement Participation." *American Sociological Review.* Vol. 51, No. 4 (August 1986):464–81.

SNOW, DAVID A., LOUIS A. ZURCHER, JR., and SHELDON EKLAND-OLSON. "Social Networks and Social Movements: A Macrostructural Approach to Differential Recruitment." *American Sociological Review.* Vol. 45, No. 5 (October 1980):787–801.

SNOWMAN, DANIEL. *Britain and America: An Interpretation of Their Culture 1945–1975.* New York: Harper Torchbooks, 1977.

SOUTH, SCOTT J., and STEVEN F. MESSNER. "Structural Determinants of Intergroup Association: Interracial Marriage and Crime." *American Journal of Sociology.* Vol. 91, No. 6 (May 1986):1409–30.

SOWELL, THOMAS. *Ethnic America.* New York: Basic Books, 1981.

SOYINKA, WOLE. "Africa's Culture Producers." *Society.* Vol. 28, No. 2 (January–February 1991):32–40.

SPATES, JAMES L. "Sociological Overview." In Alan Milberg, ed., *Street Games.* New York: McGraw-Hill, 1976a:286–90.

———. "Counterculture and Dominant Culture Values: A Cross-National Analysis of the Underground Press and Dominant Culture Magazines." *American Sociological Review.* Vol. 41, No. 5 (October 1976b):868–83.

———. "The Sociology of Values." In Ralph Turner, ed., *Annual Review of Sociology.* Vol. 9. Palo Alto, Calif.: Annual Reviews, 1983:27–49.

SPATES, JAMES L., and JOHN J. MACIONIS. *The Sociology of Cities.* 2d ed. Belmont, Calif.: Wadsworth, 1987.

SPATES, JAMES L., and H. WESLEY PERKINS. "American and English Student Values." *Comparative Social Research.* Vol. 5. Greenwich, Conn.: Jai Press, 1982:245–68.

SPECTOR, LEONARD S. "Nuclear Proliferation Today." In William M. Evan and Stephen Hilgartner, eds., *The Arms Race and Nuclear War.* Englewood Cliffs, N.J.: Prentice Hall, 1988:25–29.

SPEER, JAMES A. "The New Christian Right and Its Parent Company: A Study in Political Contrasts." In David G. Bromley and Anson Shupe, eds., *New Christian Politics.* Macon, Ga.: Mercer University Press, 1984:19–40.

SPENDER, DALE. *Man Made Language.* London: Routledge & Kegan Paul, 1980.

SPITZER, STEVEN. "Toward a Marxian Theory of Deviance." In Delos H. Kelly, ed., *Criminal Behavior: Readings in Criminology.* New York: St. Martin's Press, 1980:175–91.

STACEY, JUDITH. *Patriarchy and Socialist Revolution in China.* Berkeley: University of California Press, 1983.

———. *Brave New Families: Stories of Domestic Upheaval in Late Twentieth-Century America.* New York: Basic Books, 1990.

STACK, CAROL B. *All Our Kin: Strategies for Survival in a Black Community.* New York: Harper & Row, 1975.

STAHURA, JOHN M. "Suburban Development, Black Suburbanization and the Black Civil Rights Movement Since World War II." *American Sociological Review.* Vol. 51, No. 1 (February 1986):131–44.

STANLEY, LIZ, ED. *Feminist Praxis: Research, Theory, and Epistemology in Feminist Sociology*. London: Routledge & Kegan Paul, 1990.

STANLEY, LIZ, and SUE WISE. *Breaking Out: Feminist Consciousness and Feminist Research*. London: Routledge & Kegan Paul, 1983.

STAPLES, ROBERT, and ALFREDO MIRANDE. "Racial and Cultural Variations Among American Families: A Decennial Review of the Literature on Minority Families." *Journal of Marriage and the Family*. Vol. 42, No. 4 (August 1980):157–72.

STARK, RODNEY. *Sociology*. Belmont, Calif.: Wadsworth, 1985.

STARK, RODNEY, and WILLIAM SIMS BAINBRIDGE. "Of Churches, Sects, and Cults: Preliminary Concepts for a Theory of Religious Movements." *Journal for the Scientific Study of Religion*. Vol. 18, No. 2 (June 1979):117–31.

———. "Secularization and Cult Formation in the Jazz Age." *Journal for the Scientific Study of Religion*. Vol. 20, No. 4 (December 1981):360–73.

STARK, RODNEY, and CHARLES Y. GLOCK. *American Piety: The Nature of Religious Commitment*. Berkeley: University of California Press, 1968.

STARR, PAUL. *The Social Transformation of American Medicine*. New York: Basic Books, 1982.

The Statesman's Yearbook 1993–1994. New York: St. Martin's Press, 1993.

Statistics of Income Bulletin. Vol. 11, No. 3 (Winter 1991–92).

STAVRIANOS, L. S. *A Global History: The Human Heritage*. 3d ed. Englewood Cliffs, N.J.: Prentice Hall, 1983.

STEELE, SHELBY. *The Content of Our Character: A New Vision of Race in America*. New York: St. Martin's Press, 1990.

STEIN, MARUICE R. *The Eclipse of Community: An Interpretation of American Studies*. Princeton, N.J.: Princeton University Press, 1972.

STEPHENS, JOHN D. *The Transition from Capitalism to Socialism*. Urbana: University of Illinois Press, 1986.

STERNLIEB, GEORGE, and JAMES W. HUGHES. "The Uncertain Future of the Central City." *Urban Affairs Quarterly*. Vol. 18, No. 4 (June 1983):455–72.

STEVENS, GILLIAN, and GRAY SWICEGOOD. "The Linguistic Context of Ethnic Endogamy." *American Sociological Review*. Vol. 52, No. 1 (February 1987):73–82.

STEVENS, ROSEMARY. *American Medicine and the Public Interest*. New Haven, Conn.: Yale University Press, 1971.

STIEHM, JUDITH HICKS. *Arms and the Enlisted Woman*. Philadelphia: Temple University Press, 1989.

STODDARD, SANDOL. *The Hospice Movement: A Better Way to Care for the Dying*. Briarcliff Manor, N.Y.: Stein and Day, 1978.

STONE, LAWRENCE. *The Family, Sex and Marriage in England 1500–1800*. New York: Harper & Row, 1977.

STONE, ROBYN. *The Feminization of Poverty and Older Women*. Washington, D.C.: U.S. Department of Health and Human Services, 1986.

STONE, ROBYN, GAIL LEE CAFFERATA, and JUDITH SANGL. *Caregivers of the Frail Elderly: A National Profile*. Washington, D.C.: U.S. Department of Health and Human Services, 1987.

STOUFFER, SAMUEL A., ET AL. *The American Soldier: Adjustment During Army Life*. Princeton, N.J.: Princeton University Press, 1949.

STRAUS, MURRAY A., and RICHARD J. GELLES. "Societal Change and Change in Family Violence from 1975 to 1985 as Revealed by Two National Surveys." *Journal of Marriage and the Family*. Vol. 48, No. 4 (August 1986):465–79.

STREIB, GORDON F. "Are the Aged a Minority Group?" In Bernice L. Neugarten, ed., *Middle Age and Aging: A Reader in Social Psychology*. Chicago: University of Chicago Press, 1968:35–46.

STRIEGEL-MOORE, RUTH, LISA R. SILBERSTEIN, and JUDITH RODIN. "Toward an Understanding of Risk Factors for Bulimia." *American Psychologist*. Vol. 41, No. 3 (March 1986):246–63.

SUDNOW, DAVID N. *Passing On: The Social Organization of Dying*. Englewood Cliffs, N.J.: Prentice Hall, 1967.

SUMNER, WILLIAM GRAHAM. *Folkways*. New York: Dover, 1959; orig. 1906.

SUNG, BETTY LEE. *Mountains of Gold: The Story of the Chinese in America*. New York: Macmillan, 1967.

SURO, ROBERTO. "Hispanics in Despair." *New York Times: Education Life* (November 4, 1990):section 4a, page 25.

SUTHERLAND, EDWIN H. "White Collar Criminality." *American Sociological Review*. Vol. 5, No. 1 (February 1940):1–12.

SUTHERLAND, EDWIN H., and DONALD R. CRESSEY. *Criminology*. 10th ed. Philadelphia: J. B. Lippincott, 1978.

SWARTZ, STEVE. "Why Michael Milken Stands to Qualify for Guinness Book." *Wall Street Journal*. Vol. LXX, No. 117 (March 31, 1989):1, 4.

SYZMANSKI, ALBERT. *Class Structure: A Critical Perspective*. New York: Praeger, 1983.

SZASZ, THOMAS S. *The Manufacturer of Madness: A Comparative Study of the Inquisition and the Mental Health Movement*. New York: Dell, 1961.

———. *The Myth of Mental Illness: Foundations of a Theory of Personal Conduct*. New York: Harper & Row, 1970; orig. 1961.

TAEUBER, KARL, and ALMA TAEUBER. *Negroes in Cities*. Chicago: Aldine, 1965.

TAJFEL, HENRI. "Social Psychology of Intergroup Relations." *Annual Review of Psychology*. Palo Alto, Calif.: Annual Reviews, 1982:1–39.

TANNEN, DEBORAH. *You Just Don't Understand Me: Women and Men in Conversation*. New York: William Morrow, 1990.

TANNENBAUM, FRANK. *Slave and Citizen: The Negro in the Americas*. New York: Vintage Books, 1946.

TAVRIS, CAROL, and SUSAN SADD. *The Redbook Report on Female Sexuality*. New York: Delacorte Press, 1977.

TAYLOR, JOHN. "Don't Blame Me: The New Culture of Victimization." *New York Magazine* (June 3, 1991):26–34.

TERKEL, STUDS. *Working*. New York: Pantheon Books, 1974:1–2, 57–59, 65, 66, 69, 221–22. Copyright © 1974 by Pantheon Books, a division of Random House, Inc.

TERRY, DON. "In Crackdown on Bias, A New Tool." *New York Times* (June 12, 1993):8.

THEEN, ROLF H. W. "Party and Bureaucracy." In Erik P. Hoffmann and Robbin F. Laird, eds., *The Soviet Polity in the Modern Era*. New York: Aldine, 1984:131–65.

THEODORSON, GEORGE A., and ACHILLES G. THEODORSON. *A Modern Dictionary of Sociology*. New York: Barnes and Noble Books, 1969.

THERNSTROM, STEPHAN. "The Minority Majority Will Never Come." *Wall Street Journal*. (July 26, 1990):A16.

THOITS, PEGGY A. "Self-labeling Processes in Mental Illness: The Role of Emotional Deviance." *American Journal of Sociology*. Vol. 91, No. 2 (September 1985):221–49.

THOMAS, EDWARD J. *The Life of Buddha as Legend and History*. London: Routledge & Kegan Paul, 1975.

THOMAS, PIRI. *Down These Mean Streets*. New York: Signet, 1967.

THOMAS, W. I. "The Relation of Research to the Social Process." In Morris Janowitz, ed., *W. I. Thomas on Social Organization and Social Personality*. Chicago: University of Chicago Press, 1966:289–305; orig. 1931.

THOMPSON, LARRY. "The Breast Cancer Gene: A Woman's Dilemma." *Time*. Vol. 143, No. 3 (January 17, 1994):52.

THORNBERRY, TERRANCE, and MARGARET FARNSWORTH. "Social Correlates of Criminal Involvement: Further Evidence on the Relationship Between Social Status and Criminal Behavior." *American Sociological Review*. Vol. 47, No. 4 (August 1982):505–18.

THORNE, BARRIE, CHERIS KRAMARAE, and NANCY HENLEY, EDS. *Language, Gender and Society*. Rowley, Mass.: Newbury House, 1983.

THORNTON, ARLAND. "Changing Attitudes Toward Separation and Divorce: Causes and Consequences." *American Journal of Sociology*. Vol. 90, No. 4 (January 1985):856–72.

THUROW, LESTER C. "A Surge in Inequality." *Scientific American*. Vol. 256, No. 5 (May 1987):30–37.

TIEN, H. YUAN. "Second Thoughts on the Second Child." *Population Today*. Vol. 17, No. 4 (April 1989):6–9.

TIGER, LIONEL, and JOSEPH SHEPHER. *Women in the Kibbutz*. New York: Harcourt Brace Jovanovich, 1975.

TILLY, CHARLES. *From Mobilization to Revolution*. Reading, Mass.: Addison-Wesley, 1978.

———. "Does Modernization Breed Revolution?" In Jack A. Goldstone, ed., *Revolutions: Theoretical, Comparative, and Historical Studies*. New York: Harcourt Brace Jovanovich, 1986:47–57.

Time. "The Crime That Tarnished a Town." Vol. 123, No. 10 (March 5, 1984):19.

TITTLE, CHARLES R., and WAYNE J. VILLEMEZ. "Social Class and Criminality." *Social Forces*. Vol. 56, No. 22 (December 1977):474–502.

TITTLE, CHARLES R., WAYNE J. VILLEMEZ, and DOUGLAS A. SMITH. "The Myth of Social Class and Criminality: An Empirical Assessment of the Empirical Evidence." *American Sociological Review.* Vol. 43, No. 5 (October 1978):643-56.

TOBIN, GARY. "Suburbanization and the Development of Motor Transportation: Transportation Technology and the Suburbanization Process." In Barry Schwartz, ed., *The Changing Face of the Suburbs.* Chicago: University of Chicago Press, 1976.

TOCH, THOMAS. "The Exodus." *U.S. News and World Report.* Vol. 111, No. 24 (December 9, 1991):68-77.

TOCQUEVILLE, ALEXIS DE. *The Old Regime and the French Revolution.* Stuart Gilbert, trans. Garden City, N.Y.: Anchor/Doubleday Books, 1955; orig. 1856.

TOENNIES, FERDINAND. *Community and Society (Gemeinschaft und Gesellschaft).* New York: Harper & Row, 1963; orig. 1887.

TOFANI, LORETTA. "AIDS Ravages a Continent, and Sweeps a Family." *Philadelphia Inquirer* (March 24, 1991):1, 15-A.

TOMIAK, JANUSZ. "Introduction." In J. J. Tomiak, ed., *Soviet Education in the 1980s.* London: Croom Helm, 1983:vii-x.

TOOMEY, BEVERLY, RICHARD FIRST, and JOHN RIFE. Research described in "Number of Rural Homeless Greater than Expected." Ohio State *Quest* (Autumn 1990):2.

TREAS, JUDITH. "Socialist Organization and Economic Development in China: Latent Consequences for the Aged." *The Gerontologist.* Vol. 19, No. 1 (February 1979):34-43.

TREIMAN, DONALD J. "Industrialization and Social Stratification." In Edward O. Laumann, ed., *Social Stratification: Research and Theory for the 1970s.* Indianapolis, Ind.: Bobbs-Merrill, 1970.

TROELTSCH, ERNST. *The Social Teaching of the Christian Churches.* New York: Macmillan, 1931.

TROIDEN, RICHARD R. *Gay and Lesbian Identity: A Sociological Analysis.* Dix Hills, N.Y.: General Hall, 1988.

TUMIN, MELVIN M. "Some Principles of Stratification: A Critical Analysis." *American Sociological Review.* Vol. 18, No. 4 (August 1953):387-94.

———. *Social Stratification: The Forms and Functions of Inequality.* 2d ed. Englewood Cliffs, N.J.: Prentice Hall, 1985.

TURNER, RALPH H., and LEWIS M. KILLIAN. *Collective Behavior.* 2d ed. Englewood Cliffs, N.J.: Prentice Hall, 1972; 3d ed., 1987.

TYGIEL, JULES. *Baseball's Great Experiment: Jackie Robinson and His Legacy.* New York: Oxford University Press, 1983.

TYLER, S. LYMAN. *A History of Indian Policy.* Washington, D.C.: U.S. Department of the Interior, Bureau of Indian Affairs, 1973.

TYREE, ANDREA, MOSHE SEMYONOV, and ROBERT W. HODGE. "Gaps and Glissandos: Inequality, Economic Development, and Social Mobility in 24 Countries." *American Sociological Review.* Vol. 44, No. 3 (June 1979):410-24.

UCHITELLE, LOUIS. "But Just Who Is That Fairy Godmother?" *New York Times* (September 29, 1991):section 4, page 1.

UNITED NATIONS DEVELOPMENT PROGRAMME. *Human Development Report 1990.* New York: Oxford University Press, 1990.

———. *Human Development Report 1991.* New York: Oxford University Press, 1991.

———. *Human Development Report 1993.* New York: Oxford University Press, 1993.

UNNEVER, JAMES D., CHARLES E. FRAZIER, and JOHN C. HENRETTA. "Race Differences in Criminal Sentencing." *The Sociological Quarterly.* Vol. 21, No. 2 (Spring 1980):197-205.

UNRUH, JOHN D., JR. *The Plains Across.* Urbana: University of Illinois Press, 1979.

U.S. BUREAU OF THE CENSUS. *Statistical Abstract of the United States 1970.* 91st ed. Washington, D.C.: U.S. Government Printing Office, 1970.

———. Press release on homeless count (CB91-117). Washington, D.C.: U.S. Government Printing Office, 1991.

———. *Statistical Abstract of the United States: 1991.* 111th ed. Washington, DC: U.S. Government Printing Office, 1991.

———. *Educational Attainment in the United States: March 1991 and 1990.* Current Population Reports, Series P-20, No. 462. Washington, D.C.: U.S. Government Printing Office, 1992.

———. *Marital Status and Living Arrangements: March 1992.* Current Population Reports, Series P-20, No. 468. Washington, D.C.: U.S. Government Printing Office, 1992.

———. *Marriage, Divorce, and Remarriage in the 1990s.* Current Population Reports, Series P-23, No. 180. Washington, D.C.: U.S. Government Printing Office, 1992.

———. *1987 Survey of Minority-Owned Business Enterprises—Summary.* Washington, D.C.: U.S. Government Printing Office, 1992.

———. *Population Projections of the United States by Age, Sex, Race, and Hispanic Origin: 1992 to 2050.* Current Population Reports, Series P-25, No. 1092. Washington, D.C.: U.S. Government Printing Office, 1992.

———. *Statistical Abstract of the United States: 1992.* 112th ed. Washington, D.C.: U.S. Government Printing Office, 1992.

———. *Money Income of Households, Families, and Persons in the United States: 1992.* Current Population Reports, Series P-60, No. 184. Washington, D.C.: U.S. Government Printing Office, 1993.

———. "New Definitions for Metropolitan Areas." *Monthly Product Announcement* (February 1993).

———. *Poverty in the United States: 1992.* Current Population Reports, Series P-60, No. 185. Washington, D.C.: U.S. Government Printing Office, 1993.

———. *Statistical Abstract of the United States: 1993.* 112th ed. Washington, D.C.: U.S. Government Printing Office, 1993.

———. *We the American . . . Asians.* Washington, D.C.: U.S. Government Printing Office, 1993.

———. *We the . . . First Americans.* Washington, D.C.: U.S. Government Printing Office, 1993.

———. *School Enrollment—Social and Economic Characteristics of Students: October 1992.* Current Population Reports, Series P-20, No. 474. Washington, D.C.: U.S. Government Printing Office, 1994.

U.S. BUREAU OF JUSTICE STATISTICS. *Sourcebook of Criminal Justice Statistics 1990.* Timothy J. Flanagan and Kathleen Maguire, eds. Washington, D.C.: U.S. Government Printing Office, 1991.

———. *Compendium of Federal Justice Statistics, 1989.* Washington D.C.: U.S. Government Printing Office, 1992.

———. *Survey of State Prison Inmates, 1991.* Washington, D.C.: U.S. Government Printing Office, 1993.

U.S. BUREAU OF LABOR STATISTICS. *Employment and Earnings.* Vol. 39, No. 1 (January). Washington, D.C.: U.S. Government Printing Office, 1992.

———. *Employment and Earnings.* Vol. 44, No. 1 (January 1994). Washington, D.C.: U.S. Government Printing Office.

U.S. CENTERS FOR DISEASE CONTROL and PREVENTION. *HIV/AIDS Surveillance Report.* Vol. 5, No. 3 (October 1993). Washington, D.C.: U.S. Department of Human Services, National Center for Prevention Services, 1993.

———. *STD Surveillance 1992.* Washington, D.C.: U.S. Department of Human Services, National Center for Prevention Services, 1993.

U.S. CONGRESS. House Select Subcommittee On Children, Youth, and Families. *U.S. Children and Their Families: Current Conditions and Recent Trends, 1989.* Washington, D.C.: U.S. Government Printing Office, 1989.

U.S. DEPARTMENT OF AGRICULTURE. Agricultural Research Service. Family Economics Research Group. *Expenditures on a Child by Families, 1992.* Hyattsville, Md.: The Group, 1993.

U.S. DEPARTMENT OF DEFENSE. Office of Personnel and Readiness: 1993.

U.S. DEPARTMENT OF HEALTH and HUMAN SERVICES. National Center for Health Statistics. *Monthly Vital Statistics Report.* Vol. 42, No. 2. (August 31, 1993):44.

———. Public Health Service. *Health United States 1992 and Healthy People 2000 Review.* Hyattsville, Md.: The Department, 1993.

U.S. DEPARTMENT OF LABOR. Bureau of Labor Statistics. *Employment and Earnings.* Vol. 39, No. 1 (January). Washington, D.C.: U.S. Government Printing Office, 1992.

———. Bureau of Labor Statistics. *Employment and Earnings.* Vol. 41, No. 1 (January). Washington, D.C.: U.S. Government Printing Office, 1994.

USEEM, BERT. "Disorganization and the New Mexico Prison Riot of 1980." *American Sociological Review*. Vol. 50, No. 5 (October 1985):677–88.

USEEM, MICHAEL, and JEROME KARABEL. "Pathways to Corporate Management." *American Sociological Review*. Vol. 51, No. 2 (April 1986):184–200.

U.S. FEDERAL BUREAU OF INVESTIGATION. *Crime in the United States 1990*. Washington, D.C.: U.S. Government Printing Office, 1991.

———. *Uniform Crime Reports for the United States 1992*. Washington, D.C.: U.S. Government Printing Office, 1993.

U.S. HOUSE OF REPRESENTATIVES. "Street Children: A Global Disgrace." Hearing on November 7, 1991. Washington, D.C.: U.S. Government Printing Office, 1992.

U.S. HOUSE OF REPRESENTATIVES, SELECT COMMITTEE ON CHILDREN, YOUTH, and FAMILIES. *Abused Children in America: Victims of Neglect*. Washington, D.C.: U.S. Government Printing Office, 1987.

U.S. IMMIGRATION and NATURALIZATION SERVICE. *Statistical Yearbook*. Washington, D.C.: U.S. Government Printing Office, 1991.

U.S. NATIONAL CENTER FOR HEALTH STATISTICS. *Current Estimates from the National Health Survey, 1989*. Washington, D.C.: U.S. Government Printing Office, 1990.

———. *Vital Statistics of the United States, 1988, Vol. 1, Natality*. Washington, D.C.: U.S. Government Printing Office, 1990.

———. *Current Estimates from the National Health Interview Survey, 1991*. Hyattsville, Md.: The Center, 1992.

———. *Life Tables*. Hyattsville, Md.: The Center, 1992.

———. *Health United States 1992 and Healthy People 2000 Review*. Hyattsville, Md.: The Center, 1993.

———. *Monthly Vital Statistics Report*. Vol. 42, No. 2 (August 31, 1993). Hyattsville, Md.: The Center, 1993.

U.S. WOMEN'S BUREAU. *Employers and Child Care: Benefiting Work and Family*. Washington, D.C.: U.S. Government Printing Office, 1989.

VAN DE KAA, DIRK J. "Europe's Second Demographic Transition." *Population Bulletin*. Vol. 42, No. 1 (March 1987). Washington, D.C.: Population Reference Bureau.

VAN DEN HAAG, ERNEST, and JOHN P. CONRAD. *The Death Penalty: A Debate*. New York: Plenum Press, 1983.

VAN VALEY, T. L., W. C. ROOF, and J. E. WILCOX. "Trends in Residential Segregation." *American Journal of Sociology*. Vol. 82, No. 4 (January 1977):826–44.

VATZ, RICHARD E., and LEE S. WEINBERG. *Thomas Szasz: Primary Values and Major Contentions*. Buffalo, N.Y.: Prometheus Books, 1983.

VAUGHAN, MARY KAY. "Multinational Corporations: The World as a Company Town." In Ahamed Idris-Soven et al., eds., *The World as a Company Town: Multinational Corporations and Social Change*. The Hague: Mouton Publishers, 1978:15–35.

VAYDA, EUGENE, and RAISA B. DEBER. "The Canadian Health Care System: An Overview." *Social Science and Medicine*. Vol. 18, No. 3 (1984):191–97.

VEBLEN, THORSTEIN. *The Theory of the Leisure Class*. New York: The New American Library, 1953; orig. 1899.

VEUM, JONATHAN R. "Accounting for Income Mobility Changes in the United States." *Social Science Quarterly*. Vol. 73, No. 4 (December 1992):773–85.

VIGUERIE, RICHARD A. *The New Right: We're Ready to Lead*. Falls Church, Va.: The Viguerie Company, 1981.

VINES, GAIL. "Whose Baby Is It Anyway?" *New Scientist*. No. 1515 (July 3, 1986):26–27.

VINOVSKIS, MARIS A. "Have Social Historians Lost the Civil War? Some Preliminary Demographic Speculations." *Journal of American History*. Vol. 76, No. 1 (June 1989):34–58.

VOGEL, EZRA F. *Japan as Number One: Lessons for America*. Cambridge, Mass.: Harvard University Press, 1979.

———. *The Four Little Dragons: The Spread of Industrialization in East Asia*. Cambridge, Mass.: Harvard University Press, 1991.

VOGEL, LISE. *Marxism and the Oppression of Women: Toward a Unitary Theory*. New Brunswick, N.J.: Rutgers University Press, 1983.

VOLD, GEORGE B., and THOMAS J. BERNARD. *Theoretical Criminology*. 3d ed. New York: Oxford University Press, 1986.

VON HIRSH, ANDREW. *Past or Future Crimes: Deservedness and Dangerousness in the Sentencing of Criminals*. New Brunswick, N.J.: Rutgers University Press, 1986.

VONNEGUT, KURT, JR. "Harrison Bergeron." In *Welcome to the Monkey House*. New York: Delacorte Press/Seymour Lawrence, 1968:7–13; orig. 1961.

WAITE, LINDA J., GUS W. HAGGSTROM, and DAVID I. KANOUSE. "The Consequences of Parenthood for the Marital Stability of Young Adults." *American Sociological Review*. Vol. 50, No. 6 (December 1985):850–57.

WALDMAN, STEVEN. "Deadbeat Dads." *Newsweek* (May 4, 1992):46–52.

WALL, THOMAS F. *Medical Ethics: Basic Moral Issues*. Washington, D.C.: University Press of America, 1980.

WALLERSTEIN, IMMANUEL. *The Modern World-System: Capitalist Agriculture and the Origins of the European World-Economy in the Sixteenth Century*. New York: Academic Press, 1974.

———. *The Capitalist World-Economy*. New York: Cambridge University Press, 1979.

———. "Crises: The World Economy, the Movements, and the Ideologies." In Albert Bergesen, ed., *Crises in the World-System*. Beverly Hills, Calif.: Sage, 1983:21–36.

———. *The Politics of the World Economy: The States, the Movements, and the Civilizations*. Cambridge: Cambridge University Press, 1984.

WALLERSTEIN, JUDITH S., and SANDRA BLAKESLEE. *Second Chances: Men, Women, and Children a Decade after Divorce*. New York: Ticknor & Fields, 1989.

WALLIS, CLAUDIA. "Children Having Children." *Time*. Vol. 126, No. 23 (December 9, 1985):78–82, 84, 87, 89–90.

WALTON, JOHN, and CHARLES RAGIN. "Global and National Sources of Political Protest: Third World Responses to the Debt Crisis." *American Sociological Review*. Vol. 55, No. 6 (December 1990):876–90.

WARD, PATRICIA A., PETER F. ORAZEM, and STEFFEN W. SCHMIDT. "Women in Elite Pools and Elite Positions." *Social Science Quarterly*. Vol. 73, No. 1 (March 1992):31–45.

WARNER, R. STEPHEN. "Work in Progress Toward a New Paradigm for the Sociological Study of Religion in the United States." *American Journal of Sociology*. Vol. 98, No. 5 (March 1993):1044–93.

WARNER, SAM BASS, JR. *Streetcar Suburbs*. Cambridge, Mass.: Harvard University and MIT Presses, 1962.

WARNER, W. LLOYD, and J. O. LOW. *The Social System of the Modern Factory*. Yankee City Series, Vol. 4. New Haven, Conn.: Yale University Press, 1947.

WARNER, W. LLOYD, and PAUL S. LUNT. *The Social Life of a Modern Community*. New Haven, Conn.: Yale University Press, 1941.

WATSON, JOHN B. *Behaviorism*. Rev. ED. New York: Norton, 1930.

WAXMAN, CHAIM I. *The Stigma of Poverty: A Critique of Poverty Theories and Policies*. 2d ed. New York: Pergamon Press, 1983.

WEBER, ADNA FERRIN. *The Growth of Cities*. New York: Columbia University Press, 1963; orig. 1899.

WEBER, MAX. *The Protestant Ethic and the Spirit of Capitalism*. New York: Charles Scribner's Sons, 1958; orig. 1904–5.

———. "Science as a Vocation." In H. H. Gerth and C. Wright Mills, *From Max Weber: Essays in Sociology*. New York: Oxford University Press, 1958:129–56; orig. 1918.

———. *General Economic History*. Frank H. Knight, trans. New York: Collier Books, 1961; orig. 1919–20.

———. *Economy and Society*. G. Roth and C. Wittich, eds. Berkeley: University of California Press, 1978.

WEEKS, JOHN R. "The Demography of Islamic Nations." *Population Bulletin*. Vol. 43, No. 4 (December 1988).

WEINBERG, GEORGE. *Society and the Healthy Homosexual*. Garden City, N.Y.: Anchor Books, 1973.

WEINER, ANNETTE B. "Ethnographic Determinism: Samoa and the Margaret Mead Controversy." *American Anthropologist*. Vol. 85, No. 4 (December 1983):909–19.

WEINRICH, JAMES D. *Sexual Landscapes: Why We Are What We Are, Why We Love Whom We Love*. New York: Charles Scribner's Sons, 1987.

WEISBURD, DAVID, STANTON WHEELER, ELIN WARING, and NANCY BODE. *Crimes of the Middle Class: White Collar Defenders in the Courts*. New Haven, Conn.: Yale University Press, 1991.

WEISNER, THOMAS S., and BERNICE T. EIDUSON. "The Children of the '60s as Parents." *Psychology Today* (January 1986):60–66.

WEITZMAN, LENORE J. *The Divorce Revolution: The Unexpected Social and Economic Consequences for Women and Children in America.* New York: Free Press, 1985.

WEITZMAN, LENORE J., DEBORAH EIFLER, ELIZABETH HODAKA, and CATHERINE ROSS. "Sex-Role Socialization in Picture Books for Preschool Children." *American Journal of Sociology.* Vol. 77, No. 6 (May 1972):1125–50.

WELLER, JACK M., and E. L. QUARANTELLI. "Neglected Characteristics of Collective Behavior." *American Journal of Sociology.* Vol. 79, No. 3 (November 1973):665–85.

WELLFORD, CHARLES. "Labeling Theory and Criminology: An Assessment." In Delos H. Kelly, ed., *Criminal Behavior: Readings in Criminology.* New York: St. Martin's Press, 1980:234–47.

WELLMAN, BARRY. "The Community Question: Intimate Networks of East Yorkers." *American Journal of Sociology.* Vol. 84, No. 5 (March 1979):1201–31.

WENKE, ROBERT J. *Patterns of Prehistory.* New York: Oxford University Press, 1980.

WERMAN, JILL. "Who Makes What?" *Working Woman* (January 1989):72–76, 80.

WESOLOWSKI, WLODZIMIERZ. "Transition from Authoritarianism to Democracy." *Social Research.* Vol. 57, No. 2 (Summer 1990):435–61.

WESTERMAN, MARTY. "Death of the Frito Bandito." *American Demographics.* Vol. 11, No. 3 (March 1989):28–32.

WESTERN, BRUCE. "Postwar Unionization in Eighteen Advanced Capitalist Countries." *American Sociological Review.* Vol. 58, No. 2 (April 1993):266–82.

WESTOFF, CHARLES F., and ELISE F. JONES. "The Secularization of U.S. Catholic Birth Control Practices." *Family Planning Perspective.* Vol. X, No. 5 (September–October 1977):203–7.

WHALEN, JACK, and RICHARD FLACKS. *Beyond the Barricades: The Sixties Generation Grows Up.* Philadelphia: Temple University Press, 1989.

WHEELIS, ALLEN. *The Quest for Identity.* New York: Norton, 1958.

WHITAKER, MARK. "Ten Ways to Fight Terrorism." *Newsweek* (July 1, 1985):26–29.

WHITE, RALPH, and RONALD LIPPITT. "Leader Behavior and Member Reaction in Three 'Social Climates.'" In Dorwin Cartwright and Alvin Zander, eds., *Group Dynamics.* Evanston, Ill.: Row, Peterson, 1953:586–611.

WHITE, WALTER. *Rope and Faggot.* New York: Arno Press and *New York Times,* 1969; orig. 1929.

WHITMAN, DAVID. "Shattering Myths about the Homeless." *U.S. News & World Report* (March 20, 1989):26, 28.

WHITNEY, CRAIG R. "British Health Service, Much Beloved but Inadequate, Is Facing Changes." *New York Times* (June 9, 1991):11.

WHORF, BENJAMIN LEE. "The Relation of Habitual Thought and Behavior to Language." In *Language, Thought, and Reality.* Cambridge, Mass.: The Technology Press of MIT/New York: Wiley, 1956:134–59; orig. 1941.

WHYTE, WILLIAM FOOTE. *Street Corner Society.* 3d ed. Chicago: University of Chicago Press, 1981; orig. 1943.

WHYTE, WILLIAM H., JR. *The Organization Man.* Garden City, N.Y.: Anchor Books, 1957.

WIARDA, HOWARD J. "Ethnocentrism and Third World Development." *Society.* Vol. 24, No. 6 (September–October 1987):55–64.

WIATROWSKI, MICHAEL A., DAVID B. GRISWOLD, and MARY K. ROBERTS. "Social Control Theory and Delinquency." *American Sociological Review.* Vol. 46, No. 5 (October 1981):525–41.

WILCOX, CLYDE. "Race, Gender, and Support for Women in the Military." *Social Science Quarterly.* Vol. 73, No. 2 (June 1992):310–23.

WILES, P. J. D. *Economic Institutions Compared.* New York: Halsted Press, 1977.

WILLIAMS, RHYS H., and N. J. DEMERATH III. "Religion and Political Process in an American City." *American Sociological Review.* Vol. 56, No. 4 (August 1991):417–31.

WILLIAMS, ROBIN M., JR. *American Society: A Sociological Interpretation.* 3d ed. New York: Alfred A. Knopf, 1970.

WILLIAMSON, JEFFREY G., and PETER H. LINDERT. *American Inequality: A Macroeconomic History.* New York: Academic Press, 1980.

WILSON, ALAN B. "Residential Segregation of Social Classes and Aspirations of High School Boys." *American Sociological Review.* Vol. 24, No. 6 (December 1959):836–45.

WILSON, BRYAN. *Religion in Sociological Perspective.* New York: Oxford University Press, 1982.

WILSON, CLINT C., II, and FELIX GUTIERREZ. *Minorities and Media: Diversity and the End of Mass Communication.* Beverly Hills, Calif.: Sage, 1985.

WILSON, EDWARD O. *Sociobiology: The New Synthesis.* Cambridge, Mass.: Belknap Press of the Harvard University Press, 1975.

———. *On Human Nature.* New York: Bantam Books, 1978.

———. "Biodiversity, Prosperity, and Value." In Herbert F. Bohrmann and Stephen R. Kellert, eds., *Ecology, Economics, and Ethics: The Broken Circle.* New Haven, Conn.: Yale University Press, 1991:3–10.

WILSON, JAMES Q. *Bureaucracy: What Government Agencies Do and Why They Do It.* New York: Basic Books, 1991.

———. "Crime, Race, and Values." *Society.* Vol. 30, No. 1 (November–December 1992):90–93.

WILSON, JAMES Q., and RICHARD J. HERRNSTEIN. *Crime and Human Nature.* New York: Simon & Schuster, 1985.

WILSON, LOGAN. *American Academics Then and Now.* New York: Oxford University Press, 1979.

WILSON, THOMAS C. "Urbanism and Tolerance: A Test of Some Hypotheses Drawn from Wirth and Stouffer." *American Sociological Review.* Vol. 50, No. 1 (February 1985):117–23.

WILSON, WILLIAM JULIUS. *The Declining Significance of Race.* Chicago: University of Chicago Press, 1978.

———. "The Black Underclass." *The Wilson Quarterly.* Vol. 8 (Spring 1984):88–99.

———. "Studying Inner-City Social Dislocations: The Challenge of Public Agenda Research." *American Sociological Review.* Vol. 56, No. 1 (February 1991):1–14.

WINKLER, KAREN J. "Scholar Whose Ideas of Female Psychology Stir Debate Modifies Theories, Extends Studies to Young Girls." *Chronicle of Higher Education.* Vol. XXXVI, No. 36 (May 23, 1990):A6-A8.

WINN, MARIE. *Children Without Childhood.* New York: Pantheon Books, 1983.

WINNICK, LOUIS. "America's 'Model Minority'." *Commentary.* Vol. 90, No. 2 (August 1990):22–29.

WIRTH, LOUIS. "Urbanism As a Way of Life." *American Journal of Sociology.* Vol. 44, No. 1 (July 1938):1–24.

WITKIN-LANOIL, GEORGIA. *The Female Stress Syndrome: How to Recognize and Live with It.* New York: Newmarket Press, 1984.

WOLF, NAOMI. *The Beauty Myth: How Images of Beauty Are Used Against Women.* New York: William Morrow, 1990.

———. Commencement address, Scripps College, Claremont, Calif.:1992.

WOLFE, DAVID B. "Killing the Messenger." *American Demographics.* Vol. 13, No. 7 (July 1991):40–43.

WOLFE, TOM. *Radical Chic.* New York: Bantam, 1970.

WOLFGANG, MARVIN E., ROBERT M. FIGLIO, and THORSTEN SELLIN. *Delinquency in a Birth Cohort.* Chicago: University of Chicago Press, 1972.

WOLFGANG, MARVIN E., TERRENCE P. THORNBERRY, and ROBERT M. FIGLIO. *From Boy to Man, From Delinquency to Crime.* Chicago: University of Chicago Press, 1987.

WOLFINGER, RAYMOND E., and STEVEN J. ROSENSTONE. *Who Votes?* New Haven, Conn.: Yale University Press, 1980.

WOLFINGER, RAYMOND E., MARTIN SHAPIRO, and FRED J. GREENSTEIN. *Dynamics of American Politics.* 2d ed. Englewood Cliffs, N.J.: Prentice Hall, 1980.

WONG, BUCK. "Need for Awareness: An Essay on Chinatown, San Francisco." In Amy Tachiki et al., eds., *Roots: An Asian American Reader.* Los Angeles: UCLA Asian American Studies Center, 1971:265–73.

WOODWARD, C. VANN. *The Strange Career of Jim Crow.* 3d rev. ed. New York: Oxford University Press, 1974.

WOODWARD, KENNETH L. "Rules for Making Love and Babies." *Newsweek.* Vol. 109, No. 12 (March 23, 1987):42–43.

———. "Feminism and the Churches." *Newsweek*. Vol. 13, No. 7 (February 13, 1989):58–61.

———. "Talking to God." *Newsweek*. Vol. 119, No. 1 (January 6, 1992):38–44.

———. "The Elite, and How to Avoid It." *Newsweek* (July 20, 1992):55.

WOOLEY, ORLAND W., SUSAN C. WOOLEY, AND SUE R. DYRENFORTH. "Obesity and Women—II: A Neglected Feminist Topic." *Women's Studies International Quarterly*. Vol. 2 (1979):81–92.

THE WORLD BANK. *World Development Report 1984*. New York: Oxford University Press, 1984.

———. *World Development Report 1991: The Challenge of Development*. New York: Oxford University Press, 1991.

———. *World Development Report 1993*. New York: Oxford University Press, 1993.

WORLD HEALTH ORGANIZATION. *Constitution of the World Health Organization*. New York: World Health Organization Interim Commission, 1946.

WORSLEY, PETER. "Models of the World System." In Mike Featherstone, ed., *Global Culture: Nationalism, Globalization, and Modernity*. Newbury Park, Calif.: Sage, 1990:83–95.

WREN, CHRISTOPHER S. "In Soweto-by-the-Sea, Misery Lives On as Apartheid Fades." *New York Times* (June 9, 1991):1, 7.

WRIGHT, ERIK OLIN. *Classes*. London: Verso, 1985.

WRIGHT, ERIK OLIN, ANDREW LEVINE, and ELLIOTT SOBER. *Reconstructing Marxism: Essays on Explanation and the Theory of History*. London: Verso, 1992.

WRIGHT, ERIK OLIN, and BILL MARTIN. "The Transformation of the American Class Structure, 1960–1980." *American Journal of Sociology*. Vol. 93, No. 1 (July 1987):1–29.

WRIGHT, JAMES D. "Address Unknown: Homelessness in Contemporary America." *Society*. Vol. 26, No. 6 (September–October 1989):45–53.

WRIGHT, STUART A. "Social Movement Decline and Transformation: Cults in the 1980s." Paper presented to the Southwestern Social Science Association, Dallas, Texas, March 1987.

WRIGHT, STUART A., and WILLIAM V. D'ANTONIO. "The Substructure of Religion: A Further Study." *Journal for the Scientific Study of Religion*. Vol. 19, No. 3 (September 1980):292–98.

WRIGHT, STUART A., and ELIZABETH S. PIPER. "Families and Cults: Familial Factors Related to Youth Leaving or Remaining in Deviant Religious Groups." *Journal of Marriage and the Family*. Vol. 48, No. 1 (February 1986):15–25.

WRONG, DENNIS H. "The Oversocialized Conception of Man in Modern Sociology." *American Sociological Review*. Vol. 26, No. 2 (April 1961):183–93.

YATES, RONALD E. "Growing Old in Japan; They Ask Gods for a Way Out." *Philadelphia Inquirer* (August 14, 1986):3A.

YBARRA, LEA. *Conjugal Role Relationships in the Chicano Family*. Unpublished doctoral dissertation, University of California, 1977 (cited in Nielsen, 1990).

YODER, JAN D., and ROBERT C. NICHOLS. "A Life Perspective: Comparison of Married and Divorced Persons." *Journal of Marriage and the Family*. Vol. 42, No. 2 (May 1980):413–19.

ZANGWILL, ISRAEL. *The Melting Pot*. New York: Macmillan, 1921; orig. 1909.

ZASLAVSKY, VICTOR. *The Neo-Stalinist State: Class, Ethnicity, and Consensus in Soviet Society*. Armonk, N.Y.: M. E. Sharpe, 1982.

ZEITLIN, IRVING M. *The Social Condition of Humanity*. New York: Oxford University Press, 1981.

ZHOU, MIN, and JOHN R. LOGAN. "Returns of Human Capital in Ethnic Enclaves: New York City's Chinatown." *American Sociological Review*. Vol. 54, No. 5 (October 1989):809–20.

ZILL, NICHOLAS. National Survey conducted by Child Trands, Inc., Washington, D.C., 1984. Reported by Marilyn Adams. "Kids Aren't Broken by the Breakup." *USA Today* (December 20, 1984):5D.

ZIMBARDO, PHILIP G. "Pathology of Imprisonment." *Society*. Vol. 9 (April 1972):4–8.

ZIPP, JOHN F. "Perceived Representativeness and Voting: An Assessment of the Impact of `Choices' vs. `Echoes.'" *The American Political Science Review*. Vol. 79, No. 1 (March 1985):50–61.

ZIPP, JOHN F., and JOEL SMITH. "A Structural Analysis of Class Voting." *Social Forces*. Vol. 60, No. 3 (March 1982):738–59.

ZUBOFF, SHOSHANA. "New Worlds of Computer-Mediated Work." *Harvard Business Review*. Vol. 60, No. 5 (September–October 1982):142–52.

ZURCHER, LOUIS A., and DAVID A. SNOW. "Collective Behavior and Social Movements." In Morris Rosenberg and Ralph Turner, eds., *Social Psychology: Sociological Perspectives*. New York: Basic Books, 1981:447–82.

Photo Credits

Chapter 1: Jacob Lawrence, *Nigerian Series: Street to Mbari*, 1964. Gouache on paper, 22 1/4 x 30 3/8 inches. Courtesy of Terry Dintenfass Gallery, New York, xxviii; Y. Arthus-B/Peter Arnold, 1; Paul Liebhardt, 3; Eastcott/Monatiuk/The Image Works, 4; Alexandra Avakian/Contact Press Images, 8; Brown Brothers, 10; New York Public Library, 12; Bettmann, 13; © The Pierpont Morgan Library, 1992, NY. m.399, f.5v., 14 (left); Archive Photos, 14 (right); Marc Chagall, *I and the Village*, 1911. Oil on canvas, 6'3 5/8 x 59 5/8 inches. The Museum of Modern Art, New York. Mrs. Simon Guggenheim Fund, 17; New York Public Library Picture Collection, 18; Joseph Decker, *Our Gang*. Private Collection, 19; Brown Brothers, 20; Martineau: Mrs. Harriet, 1802-1876. Author of *Society in America*, 1837. Retrospect of Western Travel, 1837, 21 (left); Brown Brothers, 21 (right); Irene Klar, Hat Dance, 1991. Watercolor, 25 x 41 inches. Courtesy of the artist, 22; Jacob Lawrence, *Strike*, 1949. Tempera on masonite, 20 x 24 inches. The Howard University Gallery of Art (Permanent Collection), Washington, D.C., 24.

Chapter 2: Jack Levine, *On The Block*, 1986-92. Oil on Canvas, 72 x 63 inches. Midtown Payson Galleries, New York, 28; David Lissy/Picture Cube, 29; Roxanne Swentzell, The Emergence of the Clowns, 1988. Coiled and scraped clay: 48 x 48 x 23 inches. The Collection of The Heard Museum, Phoenix, Arizona, 31; Ian O'Leary/Tony Stone Images, 34; No Credit, 36; Herscovici/Art Resource, NY, R. Magritte, *L' Appel des Cimes*, 1942, 66 x 56cm., 38; Jeffrey Mark Dunn/Stock Boston, 40; Nubar Alexanian/Woodfin Camp & Associates, 42; Mike Greenbar/The Image Works, 44; Billy E. Barnes/Jeroboam, 45; Reuben Burrell/Courtesy Lois Benjamin, 47; Sloan, John (1871-1951). Oil on Canvas. 30 1/2 x 36 1/8 inches. Signed (lower left): John Sloan. Painted in 1928. The Metropolitan Museum of Art, Gift of Friends of John Sloan, 1928. (28.18), 50; Jasper Johns, Target with Four Faces, 1955. Assemblage: encaustic and collage on canvas with objects, 26 x 26", surmounted by four tinted plaster faces in wood box with hinged front. Box, closed, 3 3/4 x 26 x 3 1/2". Overall dimensions with box open, 33 5/8 x 26 x 3". The Museum of Modern Art, NY. Gift of Mr. & Mrs. Robert C. Scull, 56.

Chapter 3: James Ensor, *L'Intrique*, 1890. Museum of Art, Antwerp. Giraudon/Art Resource (Consignment: S0025393), 60; G. Humer/Gamma-Liaison, 61; Paul Liebhardt, 63 (top, left; top, center; top, right; middle, left; middle, right; bottom, left); David Austen/Stock Boston, 63 (middle, center); Jack Fields/Photo Researchers, 63 (bottom, right). Jeff Greenberg/Picture Cube, 66 (left); Alex Webb/ Magnum Photos, 66 (center); Pedrick/The Image Works, 66 (right); Sabina Dowell, 67 (left); CLEO Photo/Jeroboam, 67 (center); David Young-Wolff/Photoedit, 67 (right); Paul Liebhardt, 69; Sally Swain/*Great Housewives of Art*, 71; Karen Hofer/Actuality, 72; M. Courtney-Clarke, 75; Grandma Moses, Joy Ride, 1953. Copyright 1991, Grandma Moses Properties Co., NY, 76; Keith Dannemiller/SABA, 80; Gerald Ludwig/Collins Publishers, 83; Jesse Levine, Laguna Sales, Palo Alto, 84; Paul Kuroda/The Orange County Register, 86; Paul Liebhardt, 87; John Moss/Tony Stone Images, 89 (top, left); Pete Turner/The Image Bank, 89 (top, center); Brun/Photo Researchers, 89 (top, right); George Holton/Photo Researchers, 89 (bottom, left); Elliot Erwitt/Magnum Photos, 89 (bottom, center); Bruno Hadjih/Gamma-Liaison, 89 (bottom, right).

Chapter 4: Jerry Jacka Photography, 94; Hinterleiner/Gamma-Liaison, 95; Will Owens/Courtesy of the Lenskis, 97; Patrick Borden/Photo Researchers, 98; Victor Englebert/Photo Researchers, 99; Robert Frerck/Woodfin Camp & Associates, 100; J. Barry O'Rourke/Stock Market, 103; Brown Brothers, 106; Robert E. Murowchick/Photo Researchers, 108; Sir Luke Fildes (1844-1927), *Awaiting Admission to the Casual Ward*. Royal Holloway and Bedford New College, Surrey. (Bridgeman/Art Resource, New York) (Consignment: S0025411),
109; Gamma-Liaison, 111; New York Public Library Picture Collection, 112; George Tooker, *Landscape with Figures*, 1963. Egg tempera on gesso panel, 26 x 30 inches. Private collection, 116; Bettmann, 117; Paul Liebhardt, 119.

Chapter 5: Hale Woodruff, *Girls Skipping*, 1949. Oil on canvas, 24 x 32 inches. Courtesy of Michael Rosenfeld Gallery, New York, 124; Blair Seitz/Photo Researchers, 125; Ted Horowitz/Stock Market, 127 (left); Henley & Savage/Stock Market, 127 (center); Tom Pollak/Monkmeyer Press, 127 (right); Alon Reininger/Woodfin Camp & Associates, 128; Mary Evans/Sigmund Freud Copyrights, Courtesy of W. E. Freud, 129; Elizabeth Crews, 131; Keith Carter, 133; Courtesy of the University of Chicago Archives, 134; Fateh Al-Moudarres (Syrian), *Les Refugies*. Institut du Monde Arabe, Paris. Photo © *Philippe Maillard*, 135; *Henry Ossawa Tanner*, *The Banjo Lesson*, 1893. Oil on Canvas. Hampton University Museum, Hampton, Virginia, 137; Brown Brothers, 140; Laura Dwight/Peter Arnold, 144; The Stanley Burns, M. D. Collection, 146; Danny Lyon/Magnum Photos, 147.

Chapter 6: Pierre Auguste Renoir, Le Moulin de la Galette, 1876. Musee d' Orsay, Paris. Giraudon Art Resource, New York, 152; John J. Macionis, 153; Paul Liebhardt, 155; Ian Berry/Magnum Photos, 156; John Focht, 158; Paul Liebhardt, 160; Jacob Lawrence, Theatre Series, No. 8: *Vaudeville*, 1951. Tempera on fiberboard, 29 7/8 x 19 15/16 inches. Hirshhorn Museum and Sculpture Garden, Smithsonian Institution, Gift of Joseph H. Hirshhorn, 1966, 163; David Cooper/Gamma-Liaison, 165 (top, left); Alan Weiner/Gamma-Liaison, 165 (top, center); Lynn McLaren/Picture Cube, 165 (top, right); Ellis Herwig/Picture Cube, 165 (bottom, left); Richard Pan/The Image Bank, 165 (bottom, center); Erik Leigh Simmone/The Image Works, 165 (bottom, right); Paul Liebhardt, 168; Tony Freeman/Photoedit, 171; Emile Ardolino/Sygma, 172.

Chapter 7: Paul Gauguin, *The Market*, 1892. Kunstmuseum, Basle, 176; Tony Freeman/Photoedit, 177; Frank Siteman/Picture Cube, 178; Douglas Kirkland/The Image Bank, 184; Bob Daemmrich/Stock Boston, 185; Ann States/SABA, 187; Bibliothêque Nationale, Paris. From "The Horizon History of China," by the editors of *Horizon* Magazine, American Heritage Publishing Co., Inc., 551 5th Avenue, New York, NY 10017 © 1969, 189; Paul Liebhardt, 192; George Tooker, *Government Bureau*, 1956. Egg tempera on gesso panel, 19 5/8 x 29 5/8 inches. The Metropolitan Museum of Art, George A. Hearn Fund, 1956 (56.78), 193; Peter Charlesworth/JB Pictures, 195; Julie Houck, 196; AP/Wide World Photos, 199; Karen Kasmauski/Woodfin Camp & Associates, 201.

Chapter 8: Leon Golub, *Mercenaries V*, 1984. Acrylic on linen, 120 x 172 inches. Courtesy Josh Baer Gallery, New York, 206; Andrew Lichtenstein/Impact Visuals, 207; Sipa Press, 209; Jacques Chenet/Woodfin Camp & Associates, 211; Stephen Shames/Matrix International, Inc., 212; Springer/Bettmann, 214; Gerry Gropp/Sipa Press, 215; Edward Gargan/*New York Times* Pictures, 216; Frank Romero, *The Closing of Whittier Boulevard*, 1984. Oil on canvas. 6 x 10 feet, 219; Lara Jo Regan/SABA, 220; Sipa Press, 222; Schoenrock/Action Press/SABA, 225; Courtesy of Bennetton, 228; Najlah Feanny/SABA, 229; Vincent Van Gogh, 1853-1890. *Prisoners Round*. Dutch. Pushkin State Museum, Moscow. Superstock, 233.

Chapter 9: Diego Rivera. *The Dinner of the Capitalist*. Secretaria de Educacion Publica, Mexico City, 238; Ken Marshall/Collection of Joseph M. Ryan, 239; Sebastiao Salgado/Magnum Photos, 241; Paula Bronstein/Impact Visuals, 242; Reuters/Bettmann, 244; Sygma, 246; Katie Arkell/Gamma-Liaison, 247; Limbourg Brothers, *Le Duc de Berry à Table*, *Tres Riches Heures du Duc de Berry*, January, folio iv. Chantilly, Musée Conde, 249; Reuters/Bettmann, 252; John George Brown/Art Resource, 254 (left); Jacob A. Riis/Museum of the City of New York, 254 (right); Granger Collection, 255.

Index

Name Index

Abbott, Andrew, 420
Abbott, Daniel, 228, 230
Abbott, Sandra, 222, 223
Aberle, David F., 625
Abernathy, Ralph, 505
Adams, Andrea, 4
Adams, Murray C., 355
Addams, Jane, 21
Adler, Freda, 237
Adler, Jerry, 171
Adorno, T. W., 330
Aguirre, Benigno, 616, 625
Akers, Ronald L., 218
Alam, Sultana, 311
Alba, Richard D., 335, 349
Albon, Joan, 337, 338
Albrecht, William P., Jr., 421
Alfaro, David, 406
Allen, Jo Ann, 485
Allen, Michael Patrick, 444
Allen, Walter R., 535
Allsop, Kenneth, 214
Alsayyad, Nezar, 589
Altbach, Philip, 535
Altenbaugh, Richard J., 535
Amman, Jost, 539
Anders, George, 555
Andersen, Hans Christian, 168
Anderson, Elijah, 59
Anderson, John Ward, 307
Anderson, Leon, 293
Anderson, Marian, 331
Ando, Faith H., 369
Andrews, Nancy, 481
Ang, Ien, 140
Angelo, Bonnie, 387, 473
Angelou, Maya, 491
Angier, Natalie, 358
Anspaugh, David J., 556
Appleby, R. Scott, 511
Aquinas, St. Thomas, 11
Arber, Sara, 405
Archer, Dane, 234
Ardener, Shirley, 123
Arendt, Hannah, 434, 439, 457
Ariès, Philippe, 151, 402, 403
Aristide, Jean-Bertrand, 435
Aristotle, 11, 249
Arjomand, Said Amir, 499
Arnove, Robert, 535
Asante, Molefi Kete, 79, 93
Asch, Solomon, 182, 183
Ash, Adrian, 175
Asher, Ramona A., 561
Astin, Alexander W., 82
Astor, John Jacob, 254
Atchley, Robert C., 396, 399, 404

Atkins, Sharon, 110
Aurelius, Marcus, 11
Avery, Patricia, 373
Aviad, Janet O'Dea, 493, 506
Avis, George, 517
Axtell, Roger E., 67, 93
Ayensu, Edward S., 549

Babbie, Earl, 45
Bachrach, Peter, 447
Backman, Carl B., 355
Baer, Douglas, 188
Bahl, Vinay, 243
Bailey, William C., 234
Bainbridge, William Sims, 494, 506, 509
Baker, David, 517
Baker, Mary Anne, 359
Bales, Robert F., 181, 182, 205, 465
Ballantine, Jeanne, 137, 517
Baltes, Paul B., 391, 434, 576
Baltzell, E. Digby, 20, 52–55, 214, 254, 271, 272, 277, 338, 350, 648
Bane, Mary Jo, 336
Banerjee, Nirmala, 385
Banfield, Edward, 287, 288, 292
Banks, Curtis, 43
Bannister, Robert C., 27
Barash, David, 89
Baratz, Morton S., 447
Barber, Bernard, 123
Baritz, Loren, 293
Barker, Eileen, 507, 509
Barker, Ellen, 495
Baron, James N., 629
Barone, Michael, 442
Barry, Kathleen, 90, 305, 378, 379
Bartnett, Tony, 561
Bassuk, Ellen J., 290
Bateson, C. Daniel, 509
Bauer, P. T., 307, 312, 320
Beach, Frank A., 357
Becker, Howard S., 59, 208, 215
Beckford, James A., 511
Bedell, George C., 500
Beeghley, Leonard, 259
Bell, Alan P., 481
Bell, Daniel, 103, 430
Bell, Wendell, 582
Bellah, Robert N., 71, 90, 93, 506
Belsky, Jay, 136
Belz, Herman, 353
Bem, Sandra Lipsitz, 363
Bendix, Reinhard, 244, 280
Benedict, Ruth, 142, 516

Benet, Sula, 394
Benford, Robert D., 629
Benjamin, Bernard, 395
Benjamin, Lois, 29, 30, 36, 46–49, 293, 327
Bennett, Neil G., 473
Bennett, Stephen Earl, 445
Bennett, William, 655
Benoit, Joan, 23
Benokraitis, Nijole V., 27, 173, 370, 372, 485
Berado, F. M., 471
Berg, Ivar, 525
Berger, Brigitte, 482, 648, 651, 653, 659
Berger, Peter L., 2, 27, 39, 148, 159, 259n, 307, 312, 321, 427, 430, 482, 489, 490, 509, 533, 642, 643, 648, 651, 653, 657, 659
Bergesen, Albert, 314, 427
Berk, Richard A., 619
Berkowitz, Edward D., 457
Bernard, Jessie, 270, 364, 369, 374, 379, 385, 474
Bernard, Larry Craig, 364
Bernard, Thomas J., 218, 220
Bernstein, Richard J., 654
Berrill, Kevin T., 237
Berry, Brian, 582
Berscheid, Ellen, 468
Bérubé, Allan, 385, 453
Best, Raphaela, 138, 366
Bhutto, Benazir, 435
Bias, Len, 22
Biblarz, Timothy J., 480
Biggart, Nicole Woolsey, 205
Bingham, Amy, 22
Blackwell, Barbara, 558
Blaikie, Piers, 561
Blakeslee, Sandra, 478, 480
Blasi, Anthony J., 511
Blau, Judith, 228
Blau, Peter M., 21, 39, 186, 203, 228, 244, 279, 467
Blaustein, Albert P., 339
Blee, Kathleen M., 353
Bloom, David E., 473
Bloom, Leonard, 344
Blum, Linda M., 370
Blumberg, Paul, 280, 282, 650
Blumer, Herbert G., 617, 625, 630
Blumstein, Philip, 468, 480
Boas, Franz, 37
Boden, Deidre, 159
Bodenheimer, Thomas S., 557
Boff, Leonard, 492

Bogardus, Emory, 331, 345
Bohannan, Paul, 476
Bohannon, Cecil, 290
Bohm, Robert M., 234
Bohmer, Susanne, 479
Bohrmann, F. Herbert, 592, 594
Bonilla-Santiago, Gloria, 374
Bonner, Jane, 365
Booth, Alan, 207, 476
Borgas, George J., 353
Borgatta, Edgar F., 205
Borgmann, Albert, 654
Bormann, Herbert F., 611
Boswell, Terry E., 342
Bott, Elizabeth, 278, 472
Boulding, Elise, 100, 101
Bowles, Samuel, 19, 520, 521
Boxer, Barbara, 373
Boyce, James, 305
Boyer, Ernest L., 528
Braithwaite, John, 228
Brand, David, 342
Branegan, Jay, 440
Brantley, Peter, 423
Braun, Carol Mosely, 373
Braungart, Margaret M., 82
Braungart, Richard G., 82
Breen, Leonard, 400
Breugel, Pieter the Elder, 580
Brint, Steven, 535
Brinton, Crane, 448
Brinton, Mary C., 516
Brissett, Dennis, 175
Brodie, John, 201
Brody, Charles, 166
Brookhiser, Richard, 554
Brooks-Gunn, J., 474
Brophy, Gwenda, 572
Brown, John George, 254
Brown, Lester R., 607, 611
Brown, Mary Ellen, 140, 151, 175
Brownmiller, Susan, 223, 356
Brownstein, Ronald, 446
Broyles, J. Allen, 626
Broyles, Philip, 444
Bruno, Mary, 398
Bryan, William Jennings, 497
Brzezinski, Zbigniew, 439
Buddha, 502
Buechler, Steven, 635
Burch, Robert, 304
Burgess, Ernest W., 581, 583, 589
Burnham, Walter Dean, 442
Burns, Stewart, 635
Burris, Val, 525
Burstein, Paul, 629
Busby, Linda J., 367

Fergusson, D. M., 278
Ferraro, Geraldine, 373
Ferree, G. Donald, Jr., 263
Figlio, Robert M., 228, 234
Fildes, Sir Luke, 109
Fine, Gary Alan, 620, 621
Fine, Michele, 175
Finke, Roger, 511
Finkelstein, Neal W., 137
Finn, Chester, 535
Fiorentine, Robert, 373
Firebaugh, Glenn, 316, 342
Fischer, Claude S., 187
Fischer, Claude W., 35
Fisher, Elizabeth, 99–101
Fisher, Roger, 453
Fiske, Marjorie, 59, 255
Fitzpatrick, Ellen, 27
Fitzpatrick, Joseph P., 348, 472
Fitzpatrick, Mary Anne, 472
Flacks, Richard, 627
Flaherty, Michael, 173
Florida, Richard, 201
Flynn, Patricia, 549
Foch, Terryl T., 127
Foner, Anne, 136, 146
Ford, Clellan S., 357
Ford, Henry, 644
Form, William H., 290
Forrest, Hugh, 528
Forrest, Jacquiline Darroch, 589
Fost, Dan, 338
Foucault, Michel, 561
Fowler, Edmund P., 589
Fowler, Floyd J., Jr., 46, 59
Fox, Gerald, 14, 574, 575
Frank, André Gunder, 313, 314
Frankfort-Nachmias, Chava, 59
Franklin, Benjamin, 116
Franklin, John Hope, 339
Frazier, Charles E., 228
Frazier, E. Franklin, 292, 505
Fredrickson, George M., 243, 335
Free, Marvin D., 215
Freeman, Derek, 37, 149, 210, 511
Freeman, Jo, 635
French, Marilyn, 362, 363, 379
Freud, Anna, 129
Freud, Sigmund, 129–31, 133, 135, 136, 148
Friedan, Betty, 400, 401
Friedrich, Carl J., 439
Friedrich, Otto, 251, 585
Frum, David, 181
Fuchs, Victor R., 370, 371, 466
Fugita, Stephen S., 345
Fujimoto, Isao, 344
Fuller, Rex, 372
Furstenberg, Frank F., Jr., 405, 470, 474, 475, 477, 478, 483
Fusfeld, Daniel R., 423
Fussell, Paul, 293

Gade, Paul A., 453
Gadlin, Howard, 483
Gagliani, Giorgio, 256
Gaines, Donna, 237
Galileo, 12
Gallup, Alec M., 526, 598, 599, 609, 611
Gallup, George, Jr., 45, 271, 508, 522, 598, 599, 609, 611
Galster, George, 577

Gamble, Andrew, 517
Gamoran, Adam, 521
Gandhi, Indira, 435
Gandhi, Mahatma, 435, 609
Gann, Lewis H., 353
Gans, Herbert J., 77, 140, 577, 581, 589
Gappert, Gary, 589
Garcia, Carmen Lomas, 472
Garfinkel, Harold, 160, 216
Garrity, Patrick J., 457
Gartin, Patrick A., 218
Gartner, Rosemary, 234
Gaudet, Hazel, 622, 623
Gauguin, Paul, 176, 642
Gautama, Siddhartha, 502
Geertz, Clifford, 356
Geist, William, 577
Gelles, Richard J., 374, 375, 478, 479
Gelman, David, 358, 398
Gendin, Sidney, 59
George, Susan, 539, 540
Gergen, Kenneth J., 659
Gerhardt, Uta, 123
Gerstel, Naomi, 475
Gerth, H. H., 114
Geschwender, James A., 332
Gesler, Wilbert M., 561
Gibbons, Don C., 210
Gibbs, Nancy, 142, 222, 223
Giddens, Anthony, 256, 659
Giele, Janet Z., 377
Gilbert, Dennis, 272, 293
Gilbert, Neil, 223
Gilder, George, 151
Gilligan, Carol, 130, 132, 133, 135, 149, 151, 365
Gimenez, Martha E., 528
Ginn, Jay, 405
Ginsberg, Leon H., 388
Ginsburg, Faye, 93, 374
Ginsburg, Paul B, 554
Gintis, Herbert, 19, 520, 521
Ginzberg, Eli, 431
Giovanni, Maureen, 40
Glaab, Charles N., 583, 603
Gladue, Brian A., 358
Glass, David V., 244
Glazer, Nathan, 335, 348
Glazier, William, 602
Glendon, Mary Ann, 457
Glenn, Norval D., 476
Glock, Charles Y., 503, 505
Gluck, Peter R., 577
Glueck, Eleanor, 209
Glueck, Robert B., 445
Glueck, Sheldon, 209
Goethe, Johann Wolfgang von, 250
Goetting, Ann, 478, 479
Goffman, Erving, 21, 147, 148, 162, 163, 166–68, 170n, 188, 216, 217, 367, 556, 652
Gold, Allan R., 220
Goldberg, Gertrude Schaffner, 385
Goldberg, Steven, 363
Golden, Frederic, 533
Golden, Stephanie, 293, 589
Goldfarb, Jeffrey C., 439
Goldfarb, William, 602
Goldfield, Michael, 431
Goldsby, Richard A., 326
Goldthorpe, John H., 280, 293
Golub, Leon, 206
Gomes, Ralph C., 457

Goode, William J., 418, 467
Goodgame, Dan, 555
Goodwin, Joseph P., 151
Gorbachev, Mikhail, 248, 628
Gordon, Jacob U., 353
Gordon, James S., 551, 558
Gordon, Margaret T., 385
Gore, Susan, 151
Goring, Charles Buckman, 209
Gorman, Christine, 358, 585
Gortmaker, Steven L., 276
Gottman, Jean, 578
Gough, Kathleen, 360
Gould, Stephen J., 497
Gouldner, Alvin, 39, 59, 573
Goya, Francisco, 441
Grabb, Edward G., 188
Granovetter, Mark, 187
Grant, Donald L., 618
Grant, Don Sherman, II, 629
Grant, Karen R., 553
Grasmick, Harold G., 556
Graubard, Stephen R., 457
Gray, Paul, 78, 313
Greeley, Andrew M., 338, 503, 506
Green, John C., 508
Green, Richard, 358
Greenberg, David F., 357
Greenhouse, Linda, 225
Greenstein, Fred J., 443
Greer, Scott, 577
Gregory, Paul R., 414
Gregory, Sophronia Scott, 182
Griff, Catherine, 425
Griswold, David B., 215
Griswold, Wendy, 161
Grooms, Red, 562
Gross, Jane, 481
Gruenberg, Barry, 417
Grusky, David B., 263
Gup, Ted, 527
Gupte, Pranay, 586
Guterbock, Thomas M., 576
Gutfield, Rose, 598, 601
Gutiérrez, Felix, 141
Gutman, Herbert G., 474, 485
Gwartney-Gibbs, Patricia A., 479, 480
Gwathmey, Robert, 264

Haas, Linda, 466
Habermas, Jurgen, 650
Hacker, Helen Mayer, 362, 374, 378
Hackey, Robert B., 445
Hadaway, C. Kirk, 503–5
Haddad, William, 477
Hadden, Jeffrey K., 508
Hagan, John, 220
Haggstrom, Gus W., 475
Haig, Alexander, 446
Haig, Robin Andrew, 172
Halberstam, David, 191
Hall, Edward T., 83
Hall, John R., 76, 77, 86, 654
Hall, Richard H., 205
Haller, Archibald O., 39
Haller, Emil J., 521
Hallinan, Maureen T., 521
Halpern, Joel Martin, 353
Hamblin, Dora Jane, 64, 573
Hamel, Ruth, 394
Hamilton, Charles, 330
Hamilton, Mykol, 166, 167, 169

Hammond, Philip E., 506
Hamrick, Michael H., 556
Handel, Gerald, 126
Handler, Joel F., 291
Handlin, Oscar, 349
Haney, Craig, 43
Haniff, Nasha Z., 535
Hansen, Karen V., 380, 385, 453
Hansot, Elisabeth, 535
Harbert, Anita A., 388
Hare, A. Paul, 205
Hareven, Tamara K., 145
Harlan, William H., 393
Harlow, Caroline Wolf, 226
Harlow, Harry, 127–28
Harlow, Margaret, 127–28
Harrell, Steven, 485
Harrington, Michael, 650
Harris, Barbara, 492
Harris, Chauncy, 582, 583
Harris, Judith Rich, 151
Harris, Louis, 395
Harris, Marvin, 64, 82, 88, 93, 97, 102, 360
Harrison, Paul, 539
Hart, Shannon, 545, 546
Hartmann, Betsy, 305
Harvey, Philip L., 293
Hasenfeld, Yeheskel, 291
Haskins, Ron, 137
Hatfield, Elaine, 468
Hauser, Robert M., 279
Havens, Betty, 395
Havighurst, Robert J., 399
Haviland, William A., 463, 467
Hayneman, Steven P., 516
Hazlewood, Lonnie R., 375, 478
Heberle, Rudolf, 644
Heilans, Hans-Gunther, 237
Heilbroner, Robert, 410
Helgesen, Sally, 198, 205
Helin, David W., 85
Hellman, Ronald E., 358
Helmuth, John W., 303
Hemsell, David, 557
Henderson, Sheila, 561
Henley, Nancy, 166, 167, 169
Henretta, John C., 228
Henry, William, 398
Henshaw, Stanley K., 589
Herberg, Will, 511
Herek, Gregory M., 237
Heritage, John, 160
Herman, Dianne F., 375
Herman, Edward S., 425
Herrnstein, Richard J., 127, 209
Herrstrom, Staffan, 463
Herty, Robert, 401
Herzog, Herta, 622, 623
Hess, David J., 511
Hess, Stephen, 141
Heward, William L., 156
Hewlett, Barry S., 98
Hewlett, Sylvia Ann, 382
Hill, Anita, 375
Hill, George H., 151
Hilts, Philip J., 554
Hiroshi, Mannari, 247
Hirschi, Travis, 213, 215
Hobbes, Thomas, 12, 14, 391, 448
Hochschild, Arlie, 144, 370, 483
Hockney, David, 386
Hodge, Robert W., 39, 244, 268
Hoerr, John, 201

Winn, Marie, 142
Winnick, Louis, 345
Wirth, Louis, 181, 581, 587
Wise, Sue, 40
Witkin-Lanoil, Georgia, 126, 365
Witte, Ann D., 422
Wohlstein, Ronald T., 617
Wojtkiewicz, Roger A., 480
Wolf, Naomi, 355, 356, 363, 367, 385, 543
Wolfe, David B., 388
Wolfe, Frank, 181
Wolfe, Tom, 624
Wolfgang, Marvin E,, 228, 234
Wolfinger, Raymond E., 277, 443
Wong, Buck, 343
Wood, George S., 535

Wood, James L., 616
Wood, Thomas Waterman, 446
Woodruff, Hale, 124
Woodward, C. Vann, 339
Woodward, Kenneth L., 141, 493, 503
Woody, Betty, 430
Wooley, Orland W., 538
Wooley, Susan C., 538
Worden, Steven K., 629
Worsley, Peter, 316
Wren, Christopher S., 243
Wright, Charles R., 277
Wright, Erik Olin, 255, 256, 263
Wright, James D., 289
Wright, Quincy, 449

Wright, Stuart A., 489, 631
Wrong, Dennis, 148

Xie, Wen, 268

Yang, Benjamin, 457
Yates, Ronald E., 393, 398
Ybarra, Lee, 472
Yeltsin, Boris, 248
Yinger, J. Milton, 334
Yinger, Richard E., 453
Yoder, Jan D., 476
Yoels, William C., 175, 528, 529
Young, Michael, 293, 485
Yuan, Gao, 635

Yunker, James A., 430

Zald, Mayer N., 616, 627, 629, 630
Zangrando, Robert L., 339
Zangwill, Israel, 334
Zaslavsky, Victor, 248
Zeitlin, Irving M., 108
Zenner, Walter P., 353
Zhou, Min, 343, 589
Zill, Nicholas, 478
Zimbardo, Philip, 43, 44, 54
Zuboff, Shoshana, 424
Zurcher, Louis A., Jr., 620, 629
Zysk, Kenneth G., 561

Subject Index

Abkhasia, 2, 392, 394
Aborigines, 98
Abortion, 379, 570, 572
  sex-selective, 306–7, 365
Absolute monarchy, 426, 437
Absolute poverty, 283, 300, 302, 303
Academic standards, 529, 531
Achieved status, 155
Achievement, as value, 70, 72–73, 266
Acid rain, 603
Acquired immune deficiency syndrome (AIDS), 74, 215, 306, 307, 357, 453, 542, 545–46, 559, 629
  HIV infection, global map, 547
Acting crowds, 617
Activity, value of, 70
Activity theory, 399
Addictions, 72
Adolescence, 142–44
Adult education, 532
Adulthood, 144–45
Advertising, 140, 366, 367, 420
Affirmative action, 340–42
Affluence (see Income)
AFL-CIO (see American Federation of Labor-Congress of Industrial Organizations)
Africa, 299–301, 303, 305, 306, 314, 316, 364, 547, 571, 591, 596, (see also specific countries)
African Americans, 9
  and advertising, 140
  and affirmative action, 340–42
  and aging, 397
  and art, 24, 163, 339, 369, 446, 486, 563, 565
  and civil rights movement, 9, 158, 336, 340, 351, 491, 615, 629–30
  and crime, 228
  and education, 4, 80, 270, 341, 523, 529
  and family, 270, 472–74, 480
  geographic distribution of, 346
  great women, 331
  and health, 542–43, 545, 546
  and income, 270, 271, 340–41, 374, 472

  and infant mortality, 565
  and life expectancy, 276, 543
  and lynching, 339, 618
  and mass media, 140–41
  and politics, 71–72, 341–42, 443
  population, national, map, 346
  population growth, 327
  and poverty, 284, 285, 374
  and racism, 29–30, 46–48
  and religion, 505
  residential patterns of affluent, 53
  and segregation, 335–36
  and slavery, 313–14, 335, 338–39
  and social mobility, 279–80
  and social stratification, 270
  and sports, 23–25
  and stereotypes, 329
  and suicide, 5, 6
  and unemployment, 341
  and workplace, 422, 423
African National Congress (ANC), 632
Afrocentrism, 80
Ageism, 400
Age segregation, 389
Age-sex pyramid, 567
Age stratification, 392–93, 399
Aggregate, 178
Aging, 9, 32, 145, 156, 387–405
  and ageism, 400–401
  and biology, 389–91
  and culture, 391–92, 394
  and death, 146, 395, 401–4
  elderly abuse, 398
  and family, 470–71
  graying of U.S., 382–90
  and health, 388, 402
  and income, 391, 396, 397
  life expectancy, global map, 392
  and poverty, 284, 396–97
  problems of, 393–98
  and psychological changes, 391
  retirement, 395, 396
  and social change, 640–41
  social-conflict analysis of, 399–400
  structural-functional analysis of, 398–99

symbolic-interaction analysis of, 399
  and work, 416
Agrarian societies, 100–101, 104–5, 108
  aging in, 393
  agricultural employment, global map, 410
  economy of, 408
  education in, 514
  politics in, 435–36
  religion in, 100–101
  social stratification in, 258, 259, 305
AIDS (see Acquired immune deficiency syndrome)
Air pollution, 602–4, 607
Aka, 97
Albania, 299
Alcohol use, 218
Aleuts, 327
Algeria, 299, 656
Alienation, 650
  bureaucratic, 192
  political, 445
  and rationality, 116–17
  worker, 110–11
Alternative social movements, 625
Amazons, 360
American Civil Liberties Union (ACLU), 443
American dilemma, 339
American Federation of Labor-Congress of Industrial Organizations (AFL-CIO), 443
American Medical Association (AMA), 549–51, 553
American Revolution, 447
American Sociological Association (ASA), 41
Amish, 76, 86–87, 335, 494, 651
Amniocentesis, 571
ANC (see African National Congress)
Androcentricity, 39
Anglican Church, 494
Animism, 495
Anomie, 118, 645, 650
Anorexia nervosa, 537–38, 543
Antarctica, 591

Anticipatory socialization, 138, 184
Anti-Semitism, 500
Antiwar movement, 9
Apartheid, 242–43, 251, 335
Apathy, voter, 445, 649
Aral Sea, 602
Arapesh of New Guinea, 360
Argentina, 299, 451
Arms race, 450–51
Arranged marriage, 467
Artifacts, 75
Ascribed status, 155
Asia, 300, 301, 303, 306, 317, 364, 571, (see also specific countries)
Asian Americans, 80, 229, 342–47
  geographic distribution of, 346
  and health, 546
  and income, 343, 345
  population, national map, 346
  population growth, 327
  and poverty, 284, 285
  and workplace, 422
Assimilation, 334–37, 343
Australia, 6, 297
Authoritarianism, 437, 439–40
Authoritarian leadership, 182, 191
Authority, 463–64
  charismatic, 434–35
  rational-legal, 434, 436
  traditional, 434
Azerbaijan, 324, 415
AZT, 546

Baby boom, 388, 470, 567, 577
Baby bust, 567
Bangladesh, 298–300, 305, 311
Barbados, 299
Barter, 100
Batek of Malaysia, 98
Beauty myth, 355–56, 367
Behaviorism, 126
Beliefs, 31, 70, 643–47, 651–52
Bereavement, 403–4
Bilateral descent, 463
Biodiversity, declining, 605–7
Biology, 36–37, 126, 127, 129
  and aging, 389–91

and deviance, 208–10
and gender, 356–58
and race, 324–25
Birth control, 310, 363, 379, 568, 570, 571
Birth rates, 564, 569, 570
Bisexuality, 217, 358
Black Americans (*see* African Americans)
Black power movement, 340
Blasé urban attitude, 580
Blended families, 478
Blue-collar occupations, 255, 268–70, 417
Blue jeans, 624
Body language, 163, 166
Bosnia, 324
Botswana, 299, 361
Bourgeoisie, 108, 254, 574
Branch Davidians, 495
Brazil, 230, 299, 304, 451, 586, 603, 637–38, 656–57
Breast implants, 220, 557
Brown v. *Board of Education of Topeka* (1954), 335
Buddhism, 461, 502
  global map, 501
Bulgaria, 299, 415
Bulimia, 538n, 543
Burakumin, 246, 247
Bureaucracy, 434
  characteristics of, 189–91
  and democracy, 436
  and education, 527–28
  global map, 188
  humanizing, 197–98
  informality of, 191–92
  in mass society, 649
  origins of, 188
  privacy and, 193–94
  problems of, 192–97
  and rationality, 116
  and social movements, 631
Bureaucratic authority, 434, 436
Bureaucratic ritualism, 192–93
Bushmen, 98

Calvinism, 112, 114–15, 489, 491
Cambodia, 336
Camden, New Jersey, 265–66, 275
Canada, 6, 297, 553
Capitalism, 107, 378, 454
  and aging, 400
  and alienation, 111
  and bureaucracy, 116
  and Calvinism, 114–15
  characteristics of, 412
  and class conflict, 109–10
  and democracy, 437
  and deviance, 218–19
  and gender stratification, 380
  Marxist analysis of, 254–56
  and modernity, 646–47, 650
  and rationality, 113–14
  versus socialism, 414–15
Capitalist world economy, 314–15
Capital punishment, 232, 233
Caste system, 241–44
Casual crowds, 617
Category, 178
Catholic Church, 5, 115, 116, 325, 489, 491–92, 493, 498, 503–5, 507, 521, 570, 571, 574

Caucasian, 324
Cause and effect, 34
Central America, 299, 305
Charisma, 494
Charismatic authority, 434
Cherokee Indians, 337
Chicago School, 580–81
Chicanos, 347
Child abuse, 398, 479
Child care, 288, 370, 380, 470, 471
Child custody, 477–78
Child labor, 142
  global map, 143
Child rearing, 278, 468–70
Children, (*see also* Family)
  child labor, global map, 143
  and cognitive development, 130–32
  and development of self, 135
  and divorce, 477–78
  hurried child, 142
  and moral development, 132
  and poverty, 284, 285, 304, 460
  and socialization, 128–30, 142
Chile, 439
Chinese Americans, 342–43, 351
Chinese language, 67, 68
Chlorofluorocarbons (CFCs), 592, 593
Christianity, 488, 492, 495–98, 505
  global map, 498
Churches, 492–94
Cigarette smoking, 544
Cities, (*see also* Urbanization)
  evolution of, 13–14, 573–74
  historical importance of, 583
City-states, 436, 573
Civil law, 220
Civil liberties, 415
Civil religion, 506
Civil rights movement, 9, 158, 336, 340, 351, 491, 615, 629–30
Class conflict, 109–10
Class consciousness, 110
Class (*see* Social class; Social stratification)
Class-society theory, 649–52
Class system, and caste system, 244–47
Closed-ended format, 46
CMSAs (*see* Consolidated metropolitan statistical areas)
Coercive organizations, 188
Cognitive development, 130–32
Cohabitation, 480
Cohort, 146
Collective behavior, 615–25, (*see also* Social movements)
Collective conscience, 119
Collectivities, 616–17
College, 269–70
  and African Americans, 341
  attendance, national map, 523
  degrees, 373
  majors, and gender, 366
  student passivity, 528
  trends in bachelor's degrees, 518
Colombia, 230, 571
Colonialism, 306, 313–14, 329, 490, 657
Commonwealth of Independent States, 248, 298, 415, (*see also* Soviet Union)
Communications, 8, 85, 101, 191, 192

Communism, 108, 256, 413–14
Complementarity, theory of, 377
Computers (*see* Information Revolution)
Concentric zone urban model, 581, 583
Concept, 32
Concrete operational stage (Piaget), 131
Conflict, (*see also* Social conflict)
  role, 157–58
  value, 71–72
Conflict theory of prejudice, 331–32
Conformity, 182–84, 213, 215
Confucianism, 493, 502–3
Conglomerates, 424–25
Congo, 439
Conjugal family, 461
Conservative politics, 441–43, 508
Consolidated metropolitan statistical areas (CMSAs), 578
Conspicuous consumption, 277, 607, 623–24
Constitutional monarchy, 426
Contagion theory of collective behavior, 619
Contraception (*see* Birth control)
Control, scientific, 35
Control theory (Hirschi), 213, 215
Conventional crowds, 617
Conventional level of moral development, 132
Convergence theory of collective behavior, 619
Conversion, religious, 494
Corporations:
  agribusinesses, 416
  and competition, 426
  conglomerates, 424–25
  and global economy, 426–27
  multinational, 306, 314–15, 412, 426–28, 439
  women in, 423
Correlation, of variables, 34–35
Cottage industry, 408
Counterculture, 81, 102
Coup d'état, 447
Courts, 231–32
Courtship, 467–68
Creationism, 495–97
Credentialism, 524–25, 529
Credit, 194
Crime, (*see also* Violence)
  components of, 225–26
  and gender, 227–28
  hate, 222–25
  hate crime legislation, national map, 224
  punishment, 232–34
  and race, 228–29
  statistics, 226, 227
  and social class, 228
  types of, 226
  white-collar, 219–21
Criminal justice system, 208, 230–34
Criminal law versus civil law, 220
Criminal recidivism, 233–34
Crowds, 178, 617–18
Crude birth rate, 564
Crude death rate, 564–65
Crusades, 489
Cuban Americans, 347, 349
Cults, 495, 627
Cultural change, 81–82

Cultural diversity, 5, 9, 11, 64, 65, 77–86, 126, (*see also* Ethnicity; Race)
  counterculture, 81
  and cultural change, 81–82
  cultural relativism, 5, 83
  and deviance, 221–24
  ethnocentrism, 83
  multiculturalism, 78–81
  subculture, 78
  in workplace, 422
Cultural ecology, 88, 97
Cultural integration, 82
Cultural lag, 82, 103–4, 481, 638
Cultural relativism, 83, 85
Cultural theory of prejudice, 330–31
Cultural transmission, 69
Cultural universals, 87
Culture, 32, 60–93
  and aging, 391–92, 394
  as constraint, 90
  defined, 62, 64
  diversity (*see* Cultural diversity)
  as freedom, 90
  and gender distinctions, 358–59
  global, 85–86
  and global inequality, 309
  high and popular, 76–77
  and human intelligence, 64
  ideal and real, 75
  language, 65–70
  norms, 73–74
  and social change, 639
  social-conflict analysis of, 87–88
  and sociobiology, 88–90
  structural-functional analysis of, 86–87
  symbols, 65
  and technology, 75–76
  values and beliefs, 70–73
  of victimization, 71–73
Culture shock, 62
Czechoslovakia, 415

Date rape, 221–23
Dating, 467–68
Davis-Moore thesis, 251–53, 255, 261
Day care centers, 471
Death, 145–46
  and bereavement, 403–4
  denial of, 403
  ethics and, 547–48
  historical patterns of, 401–3
  median age at, global map, 303
  poverty as cause of, 540
  of spouse, 470–71
Death instinct, 129
Death rate, 564–65, 569, 570, 571, 594
Declaration of Independence, 14, 339, 652
Deductive logical thought, 54, 55
De facto segregation, 335
Degradation ceremony, 216
Dehumanization, 200
Deindustrialization, 283
Deinstitutionalization, 289
De jure segregation, 335
Demeanor, 166
Democracy, 71, 436–37, 454
  political freedom, global map, 438
Democratic leadership, 182, 191
Democratic socialism, 414
Demographic transition theory, 569–70

To my daughter Trisha, her husband Stephen and son, Seth Shrider

About the Author

For more than a quarter of a century, Michael R. Tyran has initiated and developed advanced computerized accounting and financial planning techniques and systems. He supervised their implementation and provided financial user orientation. The techniques involved the various aspects concerned with the accounting/planning functional environment as it pertained to the acquisition of relevant financial data, its analysis, interpretation, and reporting to meet the varying needs of the responsible user and management.

Michael R. Tyran has held key positions with General Dynamics, Pomona Division as Assistant to the Controller and Chief of Computerized Financial Planning. His background includes such positions as Manager of Management Budgets and Forecasts as well as Manager of Computerized Financial Systems at Lockheed Missile and Space Division. Mr. Tyran has held positions as Corporate Management Budget Director at Collins Radio Company and Budget Administrator and Computerized Financial Project Designer at Ramo-Woolridge (now a part of TRW).

He is the author of numerous financial accounting articles for the National Association of Accountants, which were published in their *Management Accounting* periodical, and he was awarded two Lybrand Gold Medals and six Certificates of Merit for outstanding contribution to accounting literature. Other articles were published by the Planning Executive Institute (PEI) and Management Services.

He is an Emeritus Life Associate (ELA) member of NAA and a FELLOW in PEI. He has made several presentations at accounting and planning seminars. His education includes a B.S. degree from Rider College and an M.B.A. from the University of Southern California with a major in industrial management.

Michael R. Tyran is the author of six books, which include *Computerized Accounting Methods and Controls,* second edition, *Computerized Financial Forecasting and Performance Reporting, Product Cost Estimating and Pricing: A Computerized Approach,* all published by Prentice-Hall, Inc.